Contemporary Literary Criticism

Guide to Gale Literary Criticism Series

For criticism on	**Consult these Gale series**
Authors now living or who died after December 31, 1959	*CONTEMPORARY LITERARY CRITICISM (CLC)*
Authors who died between 1900 and 1959	*TWENTIETH-CENTURY LITERARY CRITICISM (TCLC)*
Authors who died between 1800 and 1899	*NINETEENTH-CENTURY LITERATURE CRITICISM (NCLC)*
Authors who died between 1400 and 1799	*LITERATURE CRITICISM FROM 1400 TO 1800 (LC)* *SHAKESPEAREAN CRITICISM (SC)*
Authors who died before 1400	*CLASSICAL AND MEDIEVAL LITERATURE CRITICISM (CMLC)*
Authors of books for children and young adults	*CHILDREN'S LITERATURE REVIEW (CLR)*
Black writers of the past two hundred years	*BLACK LITERATURE CRITICISM (BLC)*
Short story writers	*SHORT STORY CRITICISM (SSC)*
Poets	*POETRY CRITICISM (PC)*
Dramatists	*DRAMA CRITICISM (DC)*
Major authors from the Renaissance to the present	*WORLD LITERATURE CRITICISM, 1500 TO THE PRESENT (WLC)*

For criticism on visual artists since 1850, see

MODERN ARTS CRITICISM (MAC)

ISSN 0091-3421

Volume 80

Contemporary Literary Criticism

Excerpts from Criticism of the Works of Today's Novelists, Poets, Playwrights, Short Story Writers, Scriptwriters, and Other Creative Writers

James P. Draper
EDITOR

Jennifer Brostrom
Jeffery Chapman
Jennifer Gariepy
Christopher Giroux
Margaret Haerens
Drew Kalasky
Marie Lazzari
Thomas Ligotti
Brigham Narins
Sean René Pollock
David Segal
Janet Witalec
ASSOCIATE EDITORS

Gale Research Inc. • DETROIT • WASHINGTON, D.C. • LONDON

STAFF

James P. Draper, *Editor*

Jennifer Brostrom, Jeffery Chapman, Jennifer Gariepy, Christopher Giroux, Drew Kalasky, Marie Lazzari, Thomas Ligotti, Brigham Narins, Sean René Pollock, David Segal, Janet Witalec, *Associate Editors*

Joseph Cislo, Nancy Dziedzic, Ian A. Goodhall, Margaret Haerens, Michael Magoulias, Matt McDonough, Lynn M. Spampinato, *Assistant Editors*

Jeanne A. Gough, *Permissions & Production Manager*
Linda M. Pugliese, *Production Supervisor*
Donna Craft, Paul Lewon, Maureen A. Puhl, Camille P. Robinson, Sheila Walencewicz, *Editorial Associates*
Jill H. Johnson, *Editorial Assistant*

Sandra C. Davis, *Permissions Supervisor (Text)*
Maria L. Franklin, Josephine M. Keene, Michele Lonoconus, Shalice Shah, Kimberly F. Smilay, *Permissions Associates*
Jennifer A. Arnold, Paula M. Labbe, Brandy C. Merritt, *Permissions Assistants*

Margaret A. Chamberlain, *Permissions Supervisor (Pictures)*
Pamela A. Hayes, Arlene Johnson, Keith Reed, *Permissions Associates*
Susan Brohman, Barbara A. Wallace, *Permissions Assistants*

Victoria B. Cariappa, *Research Manager*
Maureen Richards, *Research Supervisor*
Robert S. Lazich, Mary Beth McElmeel, Donna Melnychenko, Tamara C. Nott, Jaema Paradowski, *Editorial Associates*
Karen Farrelly, Kelly Hill, Julie A. Kriebel, Stefanie Scarlett, *Editorial Assistants*

Mary Beth Trimper, *Production Director*
Shanna Heilveil, *Production Assistant*

Cynthia Baldwin, *Art Director*
Barbara J. Yarrow, *Graphic Services Supervisor*
C. J. Jonik, *Desktop Publisher*
Willie F. Mathis, *Camera Operator*

Library of Congress Catalog Card Number 76-46132
ISBN 0-8103-4984-1
ISSN 0091-3421

Printed in the United States of America
Published simultaneously in the United Kingdom
by Gale Research International Limited
(An affiliated company of Gale Research Inc.)
10 9 8 7 6 5 4 3 2 1

Contents

Preface

A Comprehensive Information Source on Contemporary Literature

Named "one of the twenty-five most distinguished reference titles published during the past twenty-five years" by *Reference Quarterly*, the *Contemporary Literary Criticism (CLC)* series provides readers with critical commentary and general information on more than 2,000 authors now living or who died after December 31, 1959. Previous to the publication of the first volume of *CLC* in 1973, there was no ongoing digest monitoring scholarly and popular sources of critical opinion and explication of modern literature. *CLC*, therefore, has fulfilled an essential need, particularly since the complexity and variety of contemporary literature makes the function of criticism especially important to today's reader.

Scope of the Series

CLC presents significant passages from published criticism of works by creative writers. Since many of the authors covered by *CLC* inspire continual critical commentary, writers are often represented in more than one volume. There is, of course, no duplication of reprinted criticism.

Authors are selected for inclusion for a variety of reasons, among them the publication or dramatic production of a critically acclaimed new work, the reception of a major literary award, revival of interest in past writings, or the adaptation of a literary work to film or television.

Attention is also given to several other groups of writers—authors of considerable public interest—about whose work criticism is often difficult to locate. These include mystery and science fiction writers, literary and social critics, foreign writers, and authors who represent particular ethnic groups within the United States.

Format of the Book

Each *CLC* volume contains about 500 individual excerpts taken from hundreds of book review periodicals, general magazines, scholarly journals, monographs, and books. Entries include critical evaluations spanning from the beginning of an author's career to the most current commentary. Interviews, feature articles, and other published writings that offer insight into the author's works are also presented. Students, teachers, librarians, and researchers will find that the generous excerpts and supplementary material in *CLC* provide them with vital information required to write a term paper, analyze a poem, or lead a book discussion group. In addition, complete bibliographical citations note the original source and all of the information necessary for a term paper footnote or bibliography.

Features

A *CLC* author entry consists of the following elements:

- The **Author Heading** cites the author's name in the form under which the author has most commonly published, followed by birth date, and death date when applicable. Uncertainty as to a birth or death date is indicated by a question mark.

- A **Portrait** of the author is included when available.

- A brief **Biographical and Critical Introduction** to the author and his or her work precedes the excerpted criticism. The first line of the introduction provides the author's full name, pseudonyms (if applicable), nationality, and a listing of genres in which the author has written. Previous volumes of *CLC* in which the author has been featured are also listed in the introduction.

- A list of **Principal Works** notes the most important works by the author.

- The **Excerpted Criticism** represents various kinds of critical writing, ranging in form from the brief review to the scholarly exegesis. Essays are selected by the editors to reflect the spectrum of opinion about a specific work or about an author's literary career in general. The excerpts are presented chronologically, adding a useful perspective to the entry. All titles by the author featured in the entry are printed in boldface type, which enables the reader to easily identify the works being discussed. Publication information (such as publisher names and book prices) and parenthetical numerical references (such as footnotes or page and line references to specific editions of a work) have been deleted at the editor's discretion to provide smoother reading of the text.

- Critical essays are prefaced by **Explanatory Notes** as an additional aid to readers. These notes may provide several types of valuable information, including: the reputation of the critic, the importance of the work of criticism, the commentator's approach to the author's work, the purpose of the criticism, and changes in critical trends regarding the author.

- A complete **Bibliographical Citation** designed to help the user find the original essay or book follows each excerpt.

- A concise **Further Reading** section appears at the end of entries on authors for whom a significant amount of criticism exists in addition to the pieces reprinted in *CLC.* Cross-references to other useful sources published by Gale Research in which the author has appeared are also included: *Children's Literature Review, Contemporary Authors, Something about the Author, Dictionary of Literary Biography, Drama Criticism, Poetry Criticism, Short Story Criticism, Contemporary Authors Autobiography Series,* and *Something about the Author Autobiography Series.*

Other Features

CLC also includes the following features:

- An **Acknowledgments** section lists the copyright holders who have granted permission to reprint material in this volume of *CLC.* It does not, however, list every book or periodical reprinted or consulted during the preparation of the volume.

- A **Cumulative Author Index** lists all the authors who have appeared in the various literary criticism series published by Gale Research, with cross-references to Gale's biographical and autobiographical series. A full listing of the series referenced there appears on the first page of the indexes of this volume. Readers will welcome this cumulated author index as a useful tool for locating an author within the various series. The index, which lists birth and death dates when available, will be particularly valuable for those authors who are identified with a certain period but whose death dates cause them to be placed in another, or for those authors whose careers span two periods. For example, Ernest Hemingway is found in *CLC,* yet a writer often associated with him, F. Scott Fitzgerald, is found in *Twentieth-Century Literary Criticism.*

- A **Cumulative Nationality Index** alphabetically lists all authors featured in *CLC* by nationality, followed by numbers corresponding to the volumes in which the authors appear.

- A **Title Index** alphabetically lists all titles reviewed in the current volume of *CLC.* Listings are followed by the author's name and the corresponding page numbers where the titles are discussed. English translations of foreign titles and variations of titles are cross-referenced to the title under which a work was originally published. Titles of novels, novellas, dramas, films, record albums, and poetry, short story, and essay collections are printed in italics, while all individual poems, short stories, essays, and songs are printed in roman type within quotation marks; when published separately (e.g., T. S. Eliot's poem *The Waste Land*), the titles of long poems are printed in italics.

- In response to numerous suggestions from librarians, Gale has also produced a **Special Paperbound Edition** of the *CLC* title index. This annual cumulation, which alphabetically lists all titles reviewed in the series, is available to all customers and is published with the first volume of *CLC* issued in each calendar year. Additional copies of the index are available upon request. Librarians and patrons will welcome this separate index: it saves shelf space, is easy to use, and is recyclable upon receipt of the following year's cumulation.

Citing *Contemporary Literary Criticism*

When writing papers, students who quote directly from any volume in the Literary Criticism Series may use the following general forms to footnote reprinted criticism. The first example pertains to material drawn from periodicals, the second to material reprinted in books:

[1]Anne Tyler, "Manic Monologue," *The New Republic* 200 (April 17, 1989), 44-6; excerpted and reprinted in *Contemporary Literary Criticism,* Vol. 58, ed. Roger Matuz (Detroit: Gale Research Inc., 1990), p. 325.

[2]Patrick Reilly, *The Literature of Guilt: From 'Gulliver' to Golding* (University of Iowa Press, 1988); excerpted and reprinted in *Contemporary Literary Criticism,* Vol. 58, ed. Roger Matuz (Detroit: Gale Research Inc., 1990), pp. 206-12.

Suggestions Are Welcome

The editor hopes that readers will find *CLC* a useful reference tool and welcomes comments about the work. Send comments and suggestions to: Editor, *Contemporary Literary Criticism,* Gale Research Inc., Penobscot Building, Detroit, MI 48226-4094.

Acknowledgments

The editors wish to thank the copyright holders of the excerpted criticism included in this volume, the permissions managers of many book and magazine publishing companies for assisting us in securing reprint rights, and Anthony Bogucki for assistance with copyright research. We are also grateful to the staffs of the Detroit Public Library, the Library of Congress, the University of Detroit Library, Wayne State University Purdy/Kresge Library Complex, and the University of Michigan Libraries for making their resources available to us. Following is a list of the copyright holders who have granted us permission to reprint material in this volume of ***CLC.*** Every effort has been made to trace copyright, but if omissions have been made, please let us know.

COPYRIGHTED EXCERPTS IN *CLC,* VOLUME 80, WERE REPRINTED FROM THE FOLLOWING PERIODICALS:

America, v. 152, April 27, 1985; v. 154, May 10, 1986. © 1985, 1986. All rights reserved. Both reprinted with permission of America Press, Inc., 106 West 56th, New York, NY 10019.—***The American Scholar,*** v. 46, Spring, 1977. Copyright © 1977 by Martin Mayer. Reprinted by permission of the publisher.—***The Americas Review,*** v. XVII, Summer, 1989; v. XIX, Spring, 1991. Copyright © 1989, 1991 *The Americas Review.* Both reprinted by permission of the publisher.—***Approach,*** n. 59, Spring, 1966. Copyright 1966 by *Approach.* Reprinted from the Approach Collection, by permission of George Arents Research Library for Special Collections at Syracuse University.—***Ariel: A Review of International English Literature,*** v. 16, July, 1985 for "Victims in the Writing of Athol Fugard" by Robert M. Post. Copyright © 1985 The Board of Governors, The University of Calgary. Reprinted by permission of the publisher and the author.—***Best Sellers,*** v. 42, November, 1982. Copyright © 1982 Helen Dwight Reid Educational Foundation. Reprinted by permission of the publisher.—***The Bloomsbury Review,*** v. 7, January-February, 1987 for "Small but Telling Moments" by Alicia Fields. Copyright © by Owaissa Communications Company, Inc. 1987. Reprinted by permission of the author.—***Book World-The Washington Post,*** November 29, 1981. © 1981, *The Washington Post.* Reprinted by permission of the publisher.—***Books Aboard,*** v. 39, Autumn, 1965; v. 43, Winter, 1969. Copyright 1965, 1969 by the University of Oklahoma Press. Both reprinted by permission of the publisher.—***Cahiers Roumains D'Etudes Litteraires,*** n. 2, 1988. Both reprinted by permission of the publisher.—***The Christian Century,*** v. XCIV, April 6, 1977. Copyright 1977 Christian Century Foundation. Reprinted by permission from *The Christian Century.*—***Christianity Today,*** v. 36, October 5, 1992. © 1992 by Christianity Today, Inc. Reprinted by permission of the publisher.—***Commonweal,*** v. CXII, September 6, 1985. Copyright © 1985 Commonweal Foundation. Reprinted by permission of Commonweal Foundation.—***The Commonweal,*** v. XXXVIII, October 8, 1943. Copyright 1943, renewed 1971 Commonweal Publishing Co., Inc. Reprinted by permission of Commonweal Foundation.—***Contemporary Literature,*** v. XIV, Spring, 1973. © 1973 by the Regents of the University of Wisconsin; v. 31, Winter, 1990. © 1990 by the Board of Regents of the University of Wisconsin System. Both reprinted by permission of The University of Wisconsin Press.—***The Critic,*** Chicago, v. 36, Spring, 1978. © *The Critic* 1978. Reprinted with the permission of the Thomas More Association, Chicago, IL.—***Discurso Literario,*** v. 5, Autumn, 1987. Copyright by Discurso © Literario. Reprinted by permission of the publisher.—***The Economist,*** v. 265, October 1, 1977. © 1977 The Economist Newspaper Group Inc. Reprinted with permission. Further reproduction prohibited.—***Encounter,*** v. LIV, March, 1980. © 1980 by Michael Ashley.—***Film Quarterly,*** v. XXXV, Summer, 1982; v. XL, Spring, 1987. © 1982, 1987 by The Regents of the University of California. Both reprinted by permission of the Regents.—***French Literature Series,*** v. XVI, 1989. Copyright © 1989 University of South Carolina. Reprinted by permission of the publisher.—***The French Review,*** v. LXIV, December, 1990. Copyright 1990 by the American Association of Teachers of French. Reprinted by permission of the publisher.—***The Georgia Review,*** v. XXVII, Spring, 1973. Copyright, 1973, by the University of Georgia. Reprinted by permission of the publisher.—***The Hemingway Review,*** v. X, Fall, 1990 for "Pilar's Tale: The Myth and the Message" by Robert E. Gajdusek; v. XI, Fall, 1991 for "The Other War in 'For Whom the Bell Tolls': Maria and Miltonic Gender-Role Battles" by Wolfgang E. H. Rudat. Copyright 1990, 1991 by the Ernest Hemingway Foundation. Both reprinted by permission of the publisher and the respective authors.—***Hispanic***

Review, v. 40, Autumn, 1972. Reprinted by permission of the publisher.—***The Hudson Review,*** v. XXV, Spring, 1972; v. XXXI, Spring, 1978; v. XXXVIII, Summer, 1985. Copyright © 1972, 1978, 1985 by The Hudson Review, Inc. All reprinted by permission of the publisher.—***Latin American Literary Review,*** v. XVIII, January-June, 1990. Reprinted by permission of the publisher.—**Library Journal,** v. III, July, 1986 for a review of "Unveiling Claudia: A True Story of Serial Murder" by Gregor A. Preston. Copyright © 1986 by Reed Publishing, USA, Division of Reed Holdings, Inc. Reprinted from *Library Journal,* published by R.R. Bowker, Co., Division of Reed Publishing, USA, by permission of the publisher and the author./v. 116, May 1, 1991. Copyright © 1991 by Reed Publishing, USA, Division of Reed Holdings, Inc. Reprinted from *Library Journal,* published by R.R. Bowker, Co., Division of Reed Publishing, USA, by permission of the publisher.—***Los Angeles Times Book Review,*** January 27, 1985; August 5, 1990. Copyright, 1985, 1990, *Los Angeles Times.* Both reprinted by permission of the publisher.—***Maclean's Magazine,*** v. 102, March 13, 1989. © 1989 by Maclean's Magazine. Reprinted by permission of the publisher.—***MELUS,*** v. 9, Winter, 1982; v. 11, Fall, 1984. Copyright, *MELUS,* The Society for the Study of Multi-Ethnic Literature of the United States, 1982, 1984. Both reprinted by permission of the publisher.—***Modern Drama,*** v. XXXIII, March, 1990. Copyright 1990 *Modern Drama,* University of Toronto. Reprinted by permission of the publisher.—***The New Republic,*** v. 157, September 9, 1969; v. 195, September 8, 1986. © 1969, 1986 The New Republic, Inc. Both reprinted by permission of *The New Republic.*/v. 103, October 28, 1940. Copyright 1940 The New Republic, Inc. Renewed 1968 by Edmund Wilson. Reprinted by permission of *The New Republic.*—***New Statesman & Society,*** v. 5, August 7, 1992. © Statesman & Nation Publishing Company Limited. Reprinted by permission of the publisher.—***New Theatre Quarterly,*** v. VI, February, 1990 for " 'Between Me and My Country': Fugard's 'My Children! My Africa!' at the Market Theatre, Johannesburg," by Stephen Gray. © 1990 Cambridge University Press. Reprinted by permission of the publisher and the author.—***New York,*** v. 18, June 10, 1985. Copyright © 1993 K-III Magazine Corporation. All rights reserved. Reprinted with permission of *New York* Magazine.—***The New York Review of Books,*** v. XXXI, October 25, 1984. Copyright © 1984 Nyrev, Inc. Reprinted with permission from *The New York Review of Books.*—***The New York Times,*** March 7, 1966. Copyright © 1966 by The New York Times Company. Reprinted by permission of the publisher.—***The New York Times Book Review,*** October 2, 1977; May 20, 1979; November 15, 1981; November 25, 1984; March 22, 1987; May 20, 1990; November 18, 1990. Copyright © 1977, 1979, 1981, 1984, 1987, 1990 by The New York Times Company. All reprinted by permission of the publisher./February 11, 1940; September 26, 1943. Copyright 1940, renewed 1968; 1943, renewed 1971 by The New York Times Company. Both reprinted by permission of the publisher.—***The New Yorker,*** v. XV, February 10, 1940 for "Thirties-Welsh Bards and English Reviewers" by Clifton Fadiman. Copyright 1940, renewed 1967 by The New Yorker Magazine, Inc. Reprinted by permission of the author.—***The Paris Review,*** v. 31, Summer, 1989. © 1989 The Paris Review, Inc. Reprinted by permission of the publisher.—***Parnassus: Poetry in Review,*** v. 5, 1977. Copyright © 1977 Poetry in Review Foundation, NY. Reprinted by permission of the publisher.—***Persistence of Vision,*** n. 7, 1989. Copyright © 1989 by The City University of New York on behalf of the Film Faculty of The City University of New York. Both reprinted by permission of the publisher.—***Perspectives on Contemporary Literature,*** v. 7, 1981. Copyright © 1981 by The University Press of Kentucky. Reprinted by permission of the publisher.—***Philosophy and Literature,*** v. 2, Fall, 1978. Copyright © 1978 by the University of Michigan—Dearborn. Reprinted by permission of the publisher.—***Poetry,*** v. CVIII, July, 1966 for "What We Are, and Are Not" by Bruce Cutler; v. CXX, August, 1972 for "Pursuits and Followings" by Richard Howard; v. CXXXV, March, 1980 for "In a Middle Style" by Alan Williamson; v. CXLVI, June, 1985 for a review of "Black Hair" by David Wojahn; v. CLI, January, 1988 for "Main Things" by Alice Fulton. © 1966, 1972, 1980, 1985, 1988, by the Modern Poetry Association. All reprinted by permission of the Editor of *Poetry* and the respective authors./v. XCIX, November, 1961 for "Revelations and Homilies" by William Dickey. © 1961, renewed 1989 by the Modern Poetry Association. Reprinted by permission of the Editor of *Poetry* and the author.—***Prairie Schooner,*** v. XXXVIII, Fall, 1964. © 1964, renewed 1992 by University of Nebraska Press. Reprinted from *Prairie Schooner* by permission of the University of Nebraska Press.—***Publishers Weekly,*** v. 194, August 12, 1968. Copyright © 1968 by R.R. Bowker Company; v. 218, July 25, 1980. Copyright © 1980 by Xerox Corporation. Both reprinted from *Publishers Weekly,* published by R.R. Bowker Company, a Xerox company, by permission.—***Revista Chicano-Riqueña,*** v. XI, Summer, 1982 for an interview with Gary Soto by Ernesto Trejo. Copyright © 1982 *Revista Chicano-Riqueña.* Reprinted by permission of Gary Soto.—***The Saturday Review of Literature,*** v. XXI, February 10, 1940. Copyright 1940, renewed 1967

Saturday Review magazine.—***Shenandoah,*** v. XVII, Winter, 1966 for "Weights and Measures" by Dabney Stuart. Copyright 1966 by Washington and Lee University. Reprinted from *Shenandoah* with the permission of the Editor and the author.—***Shakespeare Quarterly,*** v. 36, Winter, 1985. © The Folger Shakespeare Library 1985. Reprinted by permission of the publisher.—***Sight and Sound,*** v. 35, Autumn, 1966. Copyright © 1966 by The British Film Institute. Reprinted by permission of the publisher.—***Southerly,*** v. 45, September, 1985 for "Character and Ideology in Christina Stead's 'House of All Nations' " by Bruce Holmes. Copyright 1985 by the author. Reprinted by permission of the publisher and the author.—***Southwest Review,*** v. 78, Summer, 1993 for an interview with Athol Fugard by Lynn Freed. © 1993 by Lynn Freed. Reprinted by permission of the Wallace Literary Agency, Inc.—***Stand Magazine,*** v. 23, 1982 for "Inheriting the Future: 'For Love Alone' " by Lorna Sage; v. 23, 1982 for "The Virtue of the Story: 'The Salzburg Tales' " by Lorna Tracy; v. 23, 1982 for "Christina Stead—A Tribute" by Rebecca West. Copyright © 1982 by the respective authors. All reprinted by permission of the publisher.—***Studies in Comparative Religion,*** v. 10, Spring, 1976 for "Small is Beautiful" by J.C. Cooper. Reprinted by permission of the author.—***Studies in Twentieth Century Literature,*** v. 11, Spring, 1987. Copyright © 1987 by Studies in Twentieth Century Literature. Reprinted by permission of the publisher.—***The Times Literary Supplement,*** n. 3360, July 21, 1966; n. 3734, September 28, 1973; n. 4005, December 21, 1979; n. 4139, July 30, 1982; n. 4515, October 13, 1989. © The Times Supplements Limited 1966, 1973, 1979, 1982, 1989. All reproduced from *The Times Literary Supplement* by permission.—***TriQuarterly,*** n. 7, Fall, 1966 for "Carolyn Kizer" by Richard Howard. © 1966 by *TriQuarterly,* Northwestern University. Reprinted by permission of the author.—***University Review,*** v. XXX, Summer, 1964 for "Theme and Character in Hemingway: 'For Whom the Bell Tolls' " by Jack Adler. Copyright 1964, renewed 1992 The Curators of the University of Missouri. Reprinted by permission of the publisher and the author.—***The Village Voice,*** v. XXXII, August 4, 1987 for "Motor City Breakdown" by Michael Covino. Copyright © 1987 News Group Publications, Inc., 1987. Reprinted by permission of *The Village Voice* and the author.—***The Virginia Quarterly Review,*** v. 67, Winter, 1991. Copyright, 1991, by *The Virginia Quarterly Review,* The University of Virginia. Reprinted by permission of the publisher.—***Western American Literature,*** v. XXII, February, 1988; v. XXIV, May, 1989; v. XXVII, August, 1992. Copyright, 1988, 1989, 1992 by the Western Literature Association. All reprinted by permission of the publisher.—***The Women's Review of Books,*** v. IV, September, 1987 for "Poets of Our Time" by Diane Wakoski. Copyright © 1987. All rights reserved. Reprinted by permission of the author.—***World Literature Written in English,*** v. 23, Winter, 1984 for "Christina Stead and the 'Bildungsroman' " by Rudolf Bader. © copyright 1984 *WLWE-World Literature Written in English.* Reprinted by permission of the publisher and the author.

COPYRIGHTED EXCERPTS IN *CLC,* VOLUME 80, WERE REPRINTED FROM THE FOLLOWING BOOKS:

Baker, Carlos. From ***Hemingway: The Writer as Artist.*** Fourth edition. Princeton University Press, 1972. Copyright © 1952, 1956, 1963, 1972, by Carlos Baker. All rights reserved. Reprinted by permission of the publisher.—Benson, Jackson, J. From ***Hemingway: The Writer's Art of Self-Defense.*** University of Minnesota Press, 1969. © copyright 1969 by the University of Minnesota. All rights reserved. Reprinted by permission of the publisher.—Brée, Germaine. From "Experimental Novels? Yes, But Perhaps "Otherwise" Nathalie Sarraute, Monique Wittig,"in ***Breaking the Sequence: Women's Experimental Fiction.*** Edited by Ellen G. Friedman and Miriam Fuchs. Princeton University Press, 1989. Copyright © 1989 by Princeton University Press. All rights reserved. Reprinted by permission of the publisher.—Brotherston, Gordon. From ***The Emergence of the Latin American Novel.*** Cambridge University Press, 1977. © Cambridge University Press 1977. Reprinted with the permission of the publisher and the author.—Buache, Freddy. From ***The Cinema of Luis Buñuel.*** Translated by Peter Graham. A.S. Barnes & Co., 1973. English translation copyright © 1973 by The Tantivy Press.—Carringer, Robert L. From ***The Making of "Citizen Kane."*** University of California Press, 1985. © 1985 by The Regents of the University of California. Reprinted by permission of the publisher.—Clancy, Laurie. From "The Economy of Love: Christina Stead's Women," in ***Who Is She?*** Edited by Shirley Walker. St. Martin's Press, 1983. © University of Queensland Press 1983. All rights reserved. Reprinted with permission of the publisher.—Durgnat, Raymond. From ***Luis Bunuel.*** University of California Press, 1977. © 1977 by Raymond Durgnat. Reprinted by permission of the publisher.—Estève, Michel. From " 'The Exterminating Angel': No Exit from the Human Condition," translated by Sallie Iannotti, in ***The World of Luis Buñuel: Essays in Criticism.*** Edited by Joan Mellen. Oxford University Press, Inc., 1978. Copyright © 1978 by Joan Mellen. Reprinted by permission of Oxford University Press, Inc.—France, Richard. From ***The Theatre of Orson Welles.*** Bucknell University Press, 1977. © 1977 by Associated University Presses, Inc. Reprinted by permission of Associated University Presses.—Goba, Bonganjalo. From "A Theological Tribute to Archbishop Tutu," in ***Hammering Swords into Ploughshares: Essays in Honor of Archbishop Mpilo Desmond Tutu.*** Edited by Buti Tlhagale and Itumeleng Mosala. Skotaville Publishers, 1986. Copyright © 1986 The Desmond Tutu Theology Series Committee. All rights reserved. Reprinted by permission of the publisher.—Hassan, Ihab. From ***The Dismemberment of Orpheus: Toward a Postmodern Literature.*** Oxford University Press, 1971. Copyright © 1971, 1982 Ihab Hassan. All rights reserved. Reprinted by permission of the author.—Keyes, Daniel. From ***Flowers for Algernon.*** Harcourt Brace Jovanovich, 1966. Copyright © 1959, 1966 by Daniel Keyes.—Kizer, Carolyn. From ***Mermaids in the Basement: Poems for Women.*** Copper Canyon Press, 1984. Copyright © 1984 by Carolyn Kizer. All rights reserved.—Kizer, Carolyn. From ***The Nearness of You: Poems.*** Copper Canyon Press, 1986. Copyright © 1986 by Carolyn Kizer. All rights reserved.—Langford, Walter M. From ***The Mexican Novel Comes of Age.*** University of Notre Dame Press, 1971. Copyright © 1971 by University of Notre Dame Press; Notre Dame, IN 46556. Reprinted by permission of the publisher.—Lewis, Robert W., Jr. From ***Hemingway on Love.*** University of Texas Press, 1965. Copyright © 1965 by Robert W. Lewis, Jr. Reprinted by permission of the publisher and the author.—Micu, Dumitru. From ***Tudor Arghezi.*** Translated by H.A. Richard and Michael Impey. Meridiane Publishing House, 1965. All rights reserved.—McBride, Joseph. From ***Orson Welles: Actor and Director.*** Jove, 1977. Copyright © 1977 by Jove Publications, Inc. All rights reserved. Reprinted by permission of the publisher.—Naremore, James. From ***The Magic World of Orson Welles.*** Oxford University Press, 1978. Copyright © 1978 by Oxford University Press, Inc. Copyright © 1989 by James Naremore. All rights reserved. Reprinted by permission of the publisher.—Rulfo, Juan, and Fernando Benitez. From a conversation in ***Inframundo: The Mexico of Juan Rulfo.*** Translated by Frank Janney. Ediciones del Norte, 1983. Copyright © 1983, Ediciones del Norte. Reprinted by permission of the publisher.—Rybczynski, Witold. From ***Paper Heroes: A Review of Appropriate Technology.*** Anchor Press, 1980. Copyright © 1980 by Witold Rybczynski. All rights reserved. Reprinted by permission of Brandt & Brandt Literary Agents, Inc.—Schade, George D. From an introduction to ***The Burning Plain and Other Stories.*** By Juan Rulfo, translated by George D. Schade. University of Texas Press, 1967. Copyright © 1967 Fonde de Cultura Económica. All rights reserved. Reprinted by permission of the publisher and the author.—Scholes, Robert. From ***Structural Fabulation: An Essay on Fiction of the Future.*** University of Notre Dame Press, 1975. Copyright © 1975 by University of Notre Dame Press; Notre Dame, IN 46556. Reprinted by permission of the publisher.—Sheridan, Susan. From ***Christina Stead.*** Harvester Wheatsheaf, 1988. © 1988, Susan Sheridan. All rights reserved. Reprinted by permission of the publisher. In North America by Indiana University Press.—Sommers, Joseph. From ***After the Storm: Landmarks of the Modern Mexican Novel.*** University of New Mexico Press, 1968. © The University of New Mexico Press, 1968. All rights reserved. Reprinted by permission of the publisher.—Sontag, Susan. From ***Against Interpretation, and Other Essays.*** Farrar, Straus and Giroux, 1966. Copyright © 1961, 1962, 1963, 1964, 1965, 1966 by Susan Sontag. All rights reserved. Reprinted by permission of Farrar, Straus and Giroux, Inc. In the British Commonwealth by Random Century Group Ltd.—Stead, Christina. From ***The Man Who Loved Children.*** Holt, Rinehart and Winston, 1940.—Stone, Eddie. From ***Donald Writes No More: A Biography of Donald Goines.*** Holloway House Publishing Co., 1988. Copyright © 1974, 1988 by Eddie Stone. All rights reserved. Reprinted by permission of the publisher.—Sturm, Terry. From "Christina Stead's New Realism: The Man Who Loved Children and Cotters' England," in ***Cunning Exiles: Studies of Modern Prose Writers.*** Edited by Don Anderson and Stephen Knight. Angus and Robertson Publishers, 1974. © Don Anderson and Stephen Knight 1974. Reprinted by permission of Stephen Knight.—Vidal, Gore. From ***Homage to Daniel Shays: Collected Essays 1952-1972.*** Random House, 1972. Copyright © 1969, 1970, 1971, 1972 by Gore Vidal. Reprinted by permission of Random House, Inc.—Walder, Dennis. From ***Athol Fugard.*** Macmillan Publishers Ltd., 1984. © Dennis Walder 1984. All rights reserved. Reprinted by permission of Macmillan, London and Basingstoke.—Waldhorn, Arthur. From ***A Reader's Guide to Ernest Hemingway.*** Farrar, Straus and Giroux, 1972. Copyright © 1972 by Arthur Waldhorn. All rights reserved. Reprinted by permission of the author.—Welles, Orson, and Peter Bogdanovich. From ***This Is Orson Welles.*** Edited by Jonathan Rosenbaum. HarperCollins, 1992. Copyright © 1992 by Oja Kodar, Jonathan Rosenbaum, and Peter Bogdanovich. All rights reserved. Reprinted by permission of HarperCollins Publishers, Inc.

PHOTOGRAPHS AND ILLUSTRATIONS APPEARING IN *CLC*, VOLUME 80, WERE RECEIVED FROM THE FOLLOWING SOURCES:

UPI/Bettmann: **p. 59;** AP/Wide World Photos: **pp. 66, 170, 260, 360;** Cover of ***White Man's Justice: Black Man's Grief***, by Donald Goines. Holloway House, 1973. Reproduced by permission of Holloway House Publishing Co., Los Angeles, CA: **p. 93;** Hans Malmberg/Black Star: **p. 100;** Herbert Matthews: **pp. 115, 137;** Lloyd Arnold: **p. 147;** Photograph by Aurea, courtesy of Daniel Keyes: **p. 161;** Photograph by Mark Gerson: **pp. 187, 304;** Cover of ***None But the Lonely Heart***, by Richard Llewellyn (Michael Joseph, 1943) Copyright © Michael Joseph Ltd., 1943. Reproduced by permission of Michael Joseph Ltd.: **p. 193;** Drawing by Oswaldo Guayasamín: **p. 213;** Photograph by Jaques Robert: **p. 226;** Editions de Minuit: **p. 232;** Illustration by Barry Root: **p. 297;** Cover of ***Living Up the Street***, by Gary Soto. Dell Publishing, 1992. Copyright © 1985 by Gary Soto. Cover art by Carmen Lomas Garza. Used by permission of Dell Books, a division of Bantam Doubleday Dell Publishing Group, Inc.: **p. 299;** Photograph by Peter van Niekerk (PTY) Ltd.: **p. 355;** The Museum of Modern Art/Film Stills Archive: **p. 369;** Charles Higham Collection: **pp. 376, 391, 397;** Courtesy of RKO General Pictures: **p. 418.**

Tudor Arghezi

1880-1967

(Pseudonym of Ion N. Theodorescu; also wrote under the name Ion Theo) Rumanian poet, novelist, journalist, essayist, and author of children's books.

The following entry provides an overview of Arghezi's career.

INTRODUCTION

Regarded as one of Rumania's foremost modern poets, Arghezi emphasized the individual's search for stability and selfhood in the twentieth century in his writings. Credited with bringing the language of the peasantry into Rumanian poetry, Arghezi experimented with traditional poetic patterns and incorporated personal experience in his verse. George Ivaşcu has written that Arghezi's poetry "reflects, as a whole, the essential problems of our century . . . and thus to a large extent also the questions, the often acute uncertainties faced by modern man in a time when man's destiny is itself in doubt."

Born in Bucharest, Arghezi left home at eleven years of age to avoid joining the Roman Catholic priesthood as his parents wished. He studied at the Liceul Sf. Sava, and began publishing poetry when he was sixteen. In 1899 he became a monk in the Orthodox Church, but left the order in 1904 because of what he perceived as attempts to convert him to Roman Catholicism. Arghezi spent the next six years traveling through Switzerland and France, performing odd jobs to support himself. He returned to Rumania in 1910 and founded the journal *Cronica* with former classmate Gala Galaction. During World War I Arghezi's conspicuous support of the Germans and his work on a pro-German newspaper led to his trial and conviction on charges of treason by the Rumanian government. He was again imprisoned during World War II for writing pamphlets that condemned church and state. In 1947, disillusioned with communist rule and the prevalence of socialist realism in Rumanian literature, Arghezi initiated a seven-year artistic hiatus. Many critics assert that Arghezi's post-1954 writing lacks the emotional intensity and lyricism of his earlier work, yet it was during this period that he gained recognition and critical acclaim from the Rumanian government. Arghezi was eventually elected to the Rumanian Academy and was named poet laureate. He died in 1967.

Cuvinte potrivite, which was both acclaimed and repudiated for its experimentation with language and verse form, was influenced by Rumanian folk mythologies and French Symbolism. Filled with images of tormented longing, *Cuvinte potrivite* emphasizes Arghezi's search for spiritual tranquility in a chaotic world. In *Flori de mucigai* Arghezi focused on the perverse beauty of decay, which is reflected in the title's translation—"flowers of mold." After *Flori de mucigai,* which incorporates violent and sexually graphic imagery, Arghezi began writing lighter poetry infused with pagan spirituality and childlike curiosity. These new concerns are most notably exhibited in *Cărticică de seară* and *Ce-ai cu mine, vîntule?* Although critics generally note a decline in the artistic quality of Arghezi's later poetry, Thomas Amherst Perry has observed that Arghezi's best poems voice "the universal cry for meaning, the warmth and joy of childhood, the Rumanian's sense of his timeless past, and a sympathy for the underdog." In his novels Arghezi often drew upon personal history and his journalism background. The plot and themes of *Poarta neagră,* for instance, derive in part from his prison experiences, while *Icoane de lemn* satirizes the hypocrisy and immorality Arghezi associated with monastic life. Both novels piece together journalistic vignettes in what Monica Spiridon has called "mosaics of press notices combined at random with a sovereign disregard of norms."

PRINCIPAL WORKS

Cuvinte potrivite (poetry) 1927
Icoane de lemn (novel) 1929
Poarta neagră (novel) 1930
Cartea cu jucării (juvenilia) 1931
Flori de mucigai (poetry) 1931
Tablete din ţara de Kuty (novel) 1933
Ochii Maicii Domnului (novel) 1934
Cărticică de seară (poetry) 1935
Cimitirul Buna-Vestire (novel) 1936
Ce-ai cu mine, vîntule? (prose poetry) 1937
Hore (poetry) 1939
Lina (novel) 1942
Manual de morală practică (essays) 1946
Una sută poeme (poetry) 1947
1907 (poetry) 1955
Stihuri noi (poetry) 1955
Stihuri pestriţe (poetry) 1957
Lume veche, lume nouă (essays) 1959
Tablete de cronicar (essays) 1960
Frunze (poetry) 1962
Poeme noi (poetry) 1963
Cadenţe (poetry) 1964
Silabe (poetry) 1965
Răzleţe (poetry) 1966
Ritmuri (poetry) 1966
Noaptea (poetry) 1967
XC (poetry) 1970

Selected Poems of Tudor Arghezi [translated by Michael Impey and Brian Swann] (poetry) 1976

CRITICISM

Dumitru Micu (essay date 1965)

[*In the following excerpt from his book* Tudor Arghezi, *Micu discusses Arghezi's exploration of religious and existential crises in his poetry.*]

How should life be lived? That is the question Arghezi took, while still in his youth, as the starting point in his search for the supreme ideal of existence. His personality took shape in a period dominated by fierce ideological conflicts, conflicts that occurred not only in Rumania, but all over Europe, with the emergence of innumerable political currents and theories. The confusion and contradictions that arose in men with searching minds, who lacked any definite guide as to a possible solution, was heightened by the tendency of the reactionary classes to introduce diversionary measures, so as to keep the intellectuals away from the path of revolution.

What then were the obstacles that prevented the poet from realizing his aspirations? In the first place, his own inner structure. In **"Nehotărîre"** the poet expresses the fear of having to bear the "burden of two lives." The burden was, however, inevitable, for its source lay in his own conscience. The poet was fated—as he admits in **"Triumf "**—to grow "twined and twisted." Conflicting calls that rend him asunder fill numerous pages of his work. Perfection appears constantly as a state of exaltation, achieved by the sublimation of earthly passions [cf. **"Graiul noptii" ("The Voice of Night")**, **"Muntele Măslinilor" ("The Mount of Olives")**, and the poem in prose **"Robul" ("The Thrall")**, etc.].

The call of the imaginary heights is contrasted with another call—imperiously present in his poetic conscience—that of the call of the earth, of real life, also voiced in his **"Nehotărîre."** Rebelling against the interdictions sounded by the "bell of the Holy Ghost," the poet searches for pleasures belonging to this world, the fleeting joys of earthly life:

> I hunger after sand and clay
> I thirst for springs whence I have never drunk . . .
>
> **("PSALM")**

A battle rages in the poet's heart, a struggle between these two aspirations that is constantly being resumed, with temporary victories and defeats on either side, but never with a decisive result. The human being naturally rebels against an abstract and imaginary perfection, that is essentially inimical to his humaneness. But when he descends from the blue realms down to the "clay" of earthly life, the poet finds no rest here either. "The ice-cold skies" and the "mould and rot" are equally alien and unbearable to him. The poet is torn "between two nights." Even as he embraces worldly existence he is stricken with remorse for having betrayed a sacred mission, for having killed what was best in himself, for repressing one of his egos: his true self, "crushing in seven days what had been forged in seven" **("Triumf ")**.

Several of his poems brought out after the First World War contain a sombre atmosphere, a feeling of despondency. Everywhere the poet records the debasement of spiritual values. As a sign of this deeply-rooted moral decadence that foreshadows social upheaval, the poet feels that those called to shed light in this world have betrayed their mission and bartered their heavenly grace:

> Apollo teaches the mandoline
> And Pan holds foreign language classes

Hercules is a "typist in an oil firm," Joe "a druggist," Paul the Apostle "a poor money-lender," Chrysostomus "a shop assistant,"

> While locked in a cage, the Holy Spirit, frail
> Has turned into a young, minute and tender quail
>
> **("EVOLUTIONS")**

In such a world, a man searching for perfection and unconscious of the political battle being waged to overthrow a corrupt and essentially inhuman society and to recover spiritual values from the wreckage could naturally feel forlorn and despondent, "a sick cherubin." To him everything appears distorted and barren.

Raised to the pitch of terror, his restlessness and dread assume in **"Duhovnicească" ("Confession")** forms of delirium.

> What a thick night, a heavy night!
> Hark, there's someone knocking from the bottom of the world.

A knock that echoes in the poet's mind, terrified at the thought of having betrayed his mission, of having "fled from the cross." Left alone, in his despair, his mind is haunted by visions. His inner senses communicate to him the light steps of a ghost in the garden, "an errant soul." Roused for a moment, he is deluded into believing that the wandering phantom may be his mother. The image of his mother is the symbol of all his yearnings. The images that evoke the feeling of desolation, of paralyzing fear left by his mother's death are extraordinarily forceful and expressive:

"All have gone, since you left / All have gone to sleep as you have done, / All have turned in for the night / all have died, / Even Grivei spun round his muzzle and dropped dead. / The corn is stricken with blight / The sweet basil and mulberry-tree have withered away. / From the eaves of the world / The martins and swallows have fled. / The beehives are barren. / The poplars are tainted with brick / The walls have crumpled and caved in / And the garden has rotted away."

What increases still more the grimness of this picture of desolation is the death of commonplace objects:

> Dead too are the numbers on the gates,

The bell, the key, the bolt.

We are on the brink of the end of life. Nothing really exists any longer; anything may take on any shape. In the apparition of his mother: "there may be who knows who . . . / He who has never been and who is still to come / and who is peering through the dark at me / And reading all my thoughts." It may be the Crucified One, a symbol in Arghezi's vision of the sacrifice made for an exalted "calling," or it could also be the severe, but just and supreme arbiter. In this image, which fades imperceptibly at times into that of his mother, the poet seems finally to recognize his own self. His own conscience, his own spirit "scattered among thorns and boulders" follows him closely, from out of the thick night, with the invisible eyes of the "black-clad" who "forlorn and weary at the door",

. . . scrapes the walls with his flesh
His finger pointed like a nail
Digging deep into my very wounds.

The circumstances command flight. Flight from his own self, from the torment of his restless soul:

. . . open neighbour
Here are stains of blood
And glory, and manna and poison.
I have fled from the cross
Hold me in your arms and hide me from all eyes.

Mercilessly, the indictment of his conscience is not left unanswered. And as always the reply is shattering. In practice, absolute renunciation of the world, the search for perfection outside an earthly life can only lead to entering a monastery. Arghezi in fact took vows and led the life of a monk for a number of years. But what did this experience reveal? It revealed a world of mountebanks, traitors, simoniacs and sodomites—the world of ***Icoane de Lemn*** **(*Wooden Icons*)**. Far from finding a world of godliness within the walls of the monastery into which he had stepped, he discovered the abode of the Devil. Very logically he concluded that the road to heaven is not through the gates of the cloister. For the soul to enter into communion with God, the mediation of the Church is superfluous, it is even undesirable. This idea emerges clearly both from some of his earlier pamphlets printed in *Facla* and from several articles published in his ***Bilete de Papagal.***

The Church in its everyday affairs presented the spectacle of the trivialization of an idea, of betraying and deluding the tenderest feelings cherished by the "crippled and wretched" human soul in its ignorance or in mistaken belief. The scourge of society, a hotbed of moral infection, an agency of Hades on earth, a tool of "the powers of darkness," a "vestige of the shallowest past," "a shameful blot on the country". In Arghezi's opinion, constantly reiterated, the Church ought to be abolished. Thus, in his lampoon **"Maimuţoii judecători" ("The Ape Judges")**, published in 1911, the writer pleaded "the social necessity of officially abolishing an institution that had become a symbol of corruption and a denial of intelligence". The same plea is voiced in **"Cuvinte duhovniceşti" ("A Confessor's Words")** where he maintains that the only service that could be rendered to our Church is to destroy it—discredited as it has been for so long. Similarly, in a polemical reply to the daily *Neamul Românesc* (*The Rumanian Nation*), he asserts that the clergy is threatened with the prospect of "being cast aside" or "ridden over". The **"Epistle to Sabin Drăgoi" ("Epistolă lui Sabin Drăgoi")** is a genuinely anti-orthodox and anti-clerical diatribe. Contrary to those authors who tended to assimilate "orthodoxy" with the notion of being "Rumanian", Arghezi discloses the basic realities that rule out such an identification. "During the many centuries of Christianity in their country, the Rumanians," he states, "never contributed anything of value to the growth of the Orthodox Church. They gave the Church nothing, for they got nothing back from the Church. The Orthodox Church is not Rumanian and the Rumanians are not orthodox."

"Not only are they not orthodox"—the pamphlet goes on—"but they are not even Christians; they are utterly lacking in religious feelings" . . . "Not once has there ever been any initiative prompted by orthodox feeling. Everything was copied from the Greeks, word by word, form by form, and to this Greek treasure, the Rumanians have added nothing, neither acts of faith, nor saints."

Can Arghezi then, a writer who, in scores of pamphlets, attacked the Church, Orthodoxy, Christianity, be called an unbeliever? Decidedly not, for the writer believed in God. In a God of his own. None the less he was a schismatic, a pagan even.

Tudor Arghezi is above all the exponent of a Rumanian sensitivity and of a specifically Rumanian vision of the world. The naturalism and organicism of his conception, the bucolic inclinations, evident in his lyrical imagery, are features fundamentally characteristic of both Rumanian folklore and Arghezian writings. In many respects these features remind one of the form and spirit of the Old Testament, which mirrors, in many of its books, the life of a population of shepherds and agricultural workers, not so very different from that led for centuries by the Rumanian people. But what has that in common with Orthodoxy? As Sadoveanu too pointed out: the spiritual nature of the common man is that of a pious pagan.

If we were to search Arghezi's works for elements reflecting a sociological conception, a kinship with Eminescu, Sadoveanu and the "Poporanist" movement could be established in certain points of detail. Thus, Arghezi too pictures an ideal society, a Commonwealth of Nature, formed of productive categories engaged in manual work and enlightened by the addition of a "cultured stratum." The Church too is called to fulfil an active role in this work of enlightenment, of raising man to a position of human dignity. It is only the carrying out of this mission of social utility, unimpaired by any interest in the saving of souls for another life, that can justify, in Arghezi's view, the existence of the priesthood.

In denying the Church—diverted by the clergy from its true mission—the role of the comforter of the soul, Arghezi implicitly rejects the Church's right to represent divine authority on earth. God as envisaged by the Church is consistently denied and mocked by the writer. Their God is denied for the very reason that He embodies the negation of an ideal, the search for which constitutes the reason for man's existence. To satisfy man's thirst for knowledge, the soaring aspiration of the human spirit:

> That my mind—unbowed to nature
> May grasp the secret sense of things

The Church can only offer the image of a bearded, sullen God, a fierce tyrant, holding up a staff threateningly, a sharp-tempered old man, taking pleasure only in scolding and reproving his creatures:

> You've shown yourself to human eyes
> As ever clothed in kingly gowns,
> Always in anger and in frowns
> From you even the vulture shies
> **("PSALM")**

As spiritual nourishment for man's fervour and lofty aspirations, ecclesiastical bureaucracy offers: dogma, ossified scripture, destitute of content and spirit, a dead letter, a corpse. The nations, in their thousands, "submissive and gentle," bent on their path in search of God "in heaven, dream or earth," realize bitterly when they strip these icon-words down to the core, the hollowness of the fetishes to which they had lowered their knees in prayer.

In his search for godliness, the poet does not seek a master, an object to adore, but something entirely different. The God Arghezi dreams of is a beautiful abstraction, an idea:

> You're like a thought, you are and yet you're not
> Something between a vision and a memory
> **("PSALM")**

Partly consciously, partly lulled by an illusion, the poet with heart-rending eagerness assigns divine attributes to a dream he cherishes, building up a naïve, childish portrayal of bliss. All the good things he had been deprived of in his childhood (as we learn from his autobiographical confessions), his unsatiable yearning for tenderness, pure affection, motherly and fatherly devotion, all this he fancies raised, floating, like Orlando's heart, somewhere in the world of stars. When he prays, the psalmist beseeches his "Heavenly Father" to grant him, as he grants to "trees with savoury fruit"

> . . . tiny scraps of tenderness
> Little songs of sparrows and of martins . . .

He yearns after

> . . . a twittering bird
> Who should break its flight
> And in my branches should alight.
> And sing in me and fly away
> And through my hazy shadow wing its way

His desolation is due to the fact that "The Lord, Everlasting and Righteous," talks "too seldom to his humble servants" and no longer sends them his guardian angels—those who, in biblical times, "cared for child and man and wife."

There is, no doubt, a form of mysticism in this manner of envisaging ideal perfection and happiness. And yet, it is not the mysticism of the Church. From the Holy Scriptures, the poet drew in abundance, images, words, stylistic patterns, into which he poured a spiritual content, unique, profoundly personal, assigning them functions vitally different from those they fulfil in books of prayer and sermons. What draws him to the universe of biblical representations is "the beauty of the symbols." Arghezi appeals to the Old or New Testament just as other poets—and he himself, at times—appeal to pagan mythology or folklore. He is, if the term may be used, a paganiser of the Bible. To ask why he resorts to the Bible and not to Egyptian mythology, for instance, or, for that matter to the Indian or Nordic mythology explored by Eminescu, would be irrelevant. Following on from a literature mainly of homilies, psalms, and prayers, modern Rumanian literature has made substantial use of the expressive values contained in religious books. Arghezi thus continues and develops a tradition of long standing. His readings during his monastic life, which undoubtedly also included sacred books, as well as the influence of Russian *émigrés,* who, as the writer recalls—would discuss "at any hour of the day or night, the most widely differing problems, the most fundamental one of which being: is there a God or not,", must have inevitably played a significant part in fashioning his way of thinking. Like the Russian "God-builders," to a certain extent, for whom the notion of divinity meant a complex of ideas, elaborated by the tribe, nation and mankind, which rouse and shape man's social sense, binding the individual to society, and putting a curb on "animal individualism," Arghezi signifies by the term "God" an almost undefinable concept of his own, an ideal of humaneness, goodness, and perfection.

As far as the invocation of divinity represents a conception, a *Weltanschauung,* a philosophy, this feature of his literary work is the author's tribute to mystical idealism and spiritualism. Art never remains ideologically barren. In all great creations—as is the case in Arghezi's lyrical work—the crust of erroneous vision is shattered by the eruption of ebullient images, epitomizing either minute and piercing observations on objective reality or tumultuous spiritual experiments. Where life is embodied in a work of art, all ideas inconsistent with its precepts are either ruthlessly cut out or so altered that the reader or spectator is often led to conclusions quite different from those intended by the artist in his philosophical shortsightedness. When, however, the artist's conception of life coincides with the reality of life itself—such as is the case, for instance, in **"Cîntare Omului" ("Ode to Man")**, the outcome is the birth of a grandiose work, in which all the elements join together in perfect harmony to convey the soul-stirring and ennobling message.

An artistically original interpretation of the grim struggle for knowledge, Arghezi's early philosophic poetry is neither a fideistic manifesto nor contemplative literature. The poet constantly condemned scholastic speculation, as well as booklore, based on abstract deductions, divorced from life. Of the mystery of the Trinity, for example, Arghezi repeatedly spoke disparagingly. The announcement of a lecture that took place in 1911, "to demonstrate, in the Athenaeum in Bucharest, the existence of God," the writer considered a ludicrous presumption. For their sterility and fastidiousness all theological disputes exasperated him beyond measure.

It is not theological preoccupations, but the ethicognosiological torment of man that produced the substance of Arghezi's ***Psalms.*** The poet's spirit was stirred, to its utmost depths, by the very same issues that throughout the course of history all thinkers had tried to solve. It has only been however in the years of socialism in [Rumania] that Tudor Arghezi has been able to benefit from the findings of advanced scientific thought. Until he reached a truly progressive philosophical understanding of the phenomena of existence, the poet did battle with the apparently impenetrable "mysteries" of the world, with a fierceness that recalls the night of the legendary fight of Jacob with God himself. And just as the biblical patriarch was left, at the clash, with a hip wound that crippled him for life, so Arghezi's work, born out of his battle with a chimera that refused to reveal its secret was left scarred with wounds and stained with blood. In his hope to discover the deep-rooted causality, the inner law that governs human existence and which would ensure the spiritual peace of self-understanding, the poet strives to explore the nature of the supposed Supreme Being, in order to understand the relationship between Him and man, and His bonds with creation as a whole. The poet's search for divinity is not—as some critics observed—an ingrained, organic mystical thirst. Rather it is the outcome of an extremely lucid urge, intensely coloured by affection, an endeavour to understand and to give precise and accurate representations of everything existing in the world. Like all creators of myths, Arghezi assumes that the projection into the absolute of his own confused aspirations to attain a state of Eden-like beatitude has a transcendental reality, identifiable with God. Therefore, he proclaims his desire to see his dream, "the most beautiful of all," descend from the ideal spheres to be embodied, as in Christian mythology, in Logos. It is from this attitude that the drama of his haunting quest springs and takes shape in the sensitive interpretation of his ***Psalms*** and other poems that bear witness to a power of lyrical expression unprecedented in Rumanian literature, equal in intensity but different in nature to the pathos of Victor Hugo's vitalistic poems and to the chained tempest of Baudelaire's obsessions. There never has been a lover to call to his sweetheart in more heartrending tones than the poet's appeal to God in his ***Psalms.*** There could be no worshipper more anguished in his doubts than this seeker of divinity, whose conscience is shaken by such ferocious storms of uncertainty. It is only the stag in the ancient psalm or the "wild bull" in Arghezi's imagery that seeks spring water with the same burning thirst as that with which the creator of these Rumanian psalms pursues his "grim and futile search" to "confirm his faith or to deny it." The existence of this Being, whom he dimly senses, remains a riddle for ever.

Unwilling to resign himself to worshipping a remote abstraction, the poet, like Doubting Thomas, demands proof of the divine presence:

> I want to touch and hold you tight
> and cry out: He is!

A strange love story emerges from Arghezi's verses, a story of deep longings, illusory successes and forced estrangements from the object of his hopes, of violent conflicts and reconciliations, recalling the place of cherished trysts one moment shyly, with a hardly perceptible trembling, and the next more aggressively, with a hostile gritting of the teeth. The poet raises entreaties, reproaches, and even threats to the Heaven that refuses to open its gates to him.

Inclined to interpret mystically the spiritual needs inherent in human nature—seeking joys lying beyond the mere gratification of daily needs—the poet likens his thirst for what he calls "God" to the longing of a "blind-born baby, who has never seen his mother, but has once felt her existence with the tip of his fingers." Thus, this tiny child too feels "the touch of his soul filled with thee, oh Lord" and "the tips of his fingers" imbued with the "forgotten odour of milk" sucked in a previous existence, **"Psalmistul singuratic" ("The Lonely Psalmist")**.

On a journey of discovery, in which he comes up against an unending succession of pitfalls, the psalmist rings the changes on all the tones ranging from entreaty to revolt, in a vain attempt to get God the Invisible to reveal himself. Thus, one moment he piously prays: "I want you to talk to your humble servant more often," another moment he cries to him in despair: "Oh Lord, who art my fountain and my songs! / My only hope and thing worth striving for!", or lustily stalks him "like wild game" and, like another Lucifer, boldly bends his bow at his Heavenly Father. To unbolt the barred "gate of his great dream" the poet calls out to whoever is able to come to his aid. But in vain, for such a miracle never takes place. Neither is the knock at the gate of the unknown of any avail, nor the wanderings "over plains, across mountains or waters" to rescue the hopeless pilgrim from his "drifting course."

His urge to see and finger God produces a fundamental contradiction. Since God for Arghezi is, ultimately, the absolute, the unfathomable, how can He reveal himself as a being, perceptible to the human senses? If for this purpose He should ever assume a relative, finite shape, He would implicitly cease to be infinite.

Proceeding from the *a priori* acceptance of the existence of a personified absolute, which is essentially a nonsense, the **"Lonely Psalmist"**'s quest could naturally never be crowned with success. This individual failure merely repeats the vain endeavours of mankind, which has wasted millenniums in its unavailing efforts to solve some of the fundamental problems of existence. The Odyssey of the futile searchings of an errant soul is outlined in many of his writings. Worth noting, above all, is a prose-poem, published long after it was written—**"Gura vetrei" ("The Hearth")**, printed in *Adevărul literar şi artistic* on 29th of January 1933, which has never been reproduced in any of his volumes.

"My search for God"—the poet remarks bitterly—"in the skies brought no answer; nor in the soil did I get a reply; nor did any response come from the mountain rocks or the rippling springs. His voice may be heard in the echoes of the world, lingering in forests, fading into the grey expanse of the wide plain, but one can never catch the complete being."

This atmosphere of desolation, this fear of eerie solitude, this feeling of suspense in the void is condensed with supreme artistry in **"Între două nopţi" ("Between Two Nights")** to an expression of extreme laconism.

> I've dug my sharp spade in my chamber
> The wind outside is soughing. The rain is falling fast,
> I've scooped my chamber deep under the earth's amber.
> Outside the rain is pouring. Outside the wind will blast.

The futility of the effort of inching one's way towards "the great mysteries," the failure of reason to grasp the absolute is masterly suggested by the picture of the earth dug out of the pit, the only fruit of the strenuous exploration. In other words, the poet views any attempt to probe the essence of things as leading to confusion rather than enlightenment in the explorer's mind:

> I threw the dug-up earth out of my window.
> The earth was black: its curtain though was blue.
> The earth piled up at my window rose to soaring heights.
> The peak was high as mountains and on its top wept Christ.

By sacrificing candour, innocence, spiritual purity, even in the final analysis the destiny of life itself—embodied here in the image of Christ—to the vain ambition of attaining rational understanding, the spirit in the end sees itself stripped of all its weapons.

The searcher for God feels his mind disintegrate when he attempts to gauge the primary principle and measure his strength to God's:

> In digging my spade broke. I could labour no farther.
> Who broke it? With his bones of stone, no other than the Father.

His despair has reached its climax, his spirit can sink no lower. If in **"Duhovnicească"** mystic awe produced convulsions and frantic cries ("Take me in your arms and hide me from all eyes"), in **"Între două nopţi"** he accepts with resignation his fall into the blackness of hell. As in his poem **"Gura Vetrei,"** in his longing for peace the poet returns wearily to his original starting-point. (pp. 42-55)

Dumitru Micu, in his Tudor Arghezi, *translated by H. A. Richard and Michael Impey, Meridiane Publishing House, 1965, 163 p.*

George Ivaşcu (essay date Winter 1969)

[In the essay below, Ivaşcu provides an overview of Arghezi's work.]

It could be said that the poetic *œuvre* of Tudor Arghezi (1880-1967), covering more than seven decades, reflects, as a whole, the essential problems of our century, this "spiritual adventure of the twentieth century" (to use the formula and title of a well-known work of R. M. Albérès), and thus to a large extent also the questions, the often acute uncertainties faced by modern man in a time when man's destiny is itself in doubt.

The spiritual trajectory of Arghezi's artistic development displays, in its biographic facts—some of them rather unusual—and, especially, in the content and evolution of his work, a number of significant manifestations and perspectives. In the following, we will simply sketch the profile of this writer who shares with Sadoveanu pride of place in twentieth-century Romanian literature, flanked by Enescu in music and Brancusi in sculpture.

Arghezi was discovered and enthusiastically praised by Macedonski, mentor of poetic innovation at the turn of the century. After becoming well known, Arghezi collaborated with the *Revista moderna* and *Vieaţa nouă,* publications embracing the spirit of symbolism as the innovative force of the time. He also worked as an apprentice stone mason, secretary of an art exhibit, and chemist in a sugar factory. At eighteen, he joined a religious order and became a monk—but not as a result of a mystical crisis: "I passed from the ordinary world to another, completely unknown one, without the aid of any romantic appurtenances. Neither angels nor whispers issuing from the blue Ocean nor winged steeds carrying me on their backs." He confesses later, in the autobiographical novel ***Ochii Maicii Domnului* (*The Eyes of the Madonna*)** that this was the decision of a tormented soul, "obsessed by finality," anxious to know "a new order, undecided between a philosophy of conciliation and a concept of revolt," yet feeling himself as a poet "equally seduced" by both. Here, as in certain passages from ***Icoane de lemn* (*Wooden Icons*)**, we discover the germ of the later dialectics in ***Psalmi.*** His first collection of verse, ***Cuvinte potrivite*** (1927), was greeted with immediate admiration as well as with violent repudiation.

The volumes of poetry, the prose, and even the pamphlets that were to follow at short intervals, all display the same complex process of gestation, an effervescent fermenting and settling of meaning and poetic expression. ***Icoane de lemn*** (1930), ***Poarta neagră*** (1930), ***Tablete din tara de Kuty* (*Tablets from the Land of Kuty,*** 1933), ***Ochii Maicii Domnului*** (1934), ***Cimitirul Buna-Vestire* (*The Cemetery of Annunciations,*** 1936), ***Lina*** (1942), with novels and pamphlets, round out the literary profile of the poet who produced during this period collections of poetry and poems in prose, fundamental to his aesthetics, and which echoed profoundly in the consciousness of writers and readers of his time: ***Flori de mucigai* (*Flowers of Mildew*)** and ***Cartea cu jucării* (*Book of Toys*)**, both 1931, ***Cărticica de seară* (*Little Book of Evening,*** 1935), ***Ce-ai cu mine, vîntule?* (*Wind, What Do You Want of Me?,*** 1937), ***Hore* (*Rounds,*** 1939). After World War II came the well-known poems ***Cîntare omului*** and ***1907*** (both 1955), followed by ***Frunze, Cîntece noi* (*New Songs*), *Silabe, Cadenţe, Ritmuri, Noaptea.***

Because of the novelty of his style, Arghezi has been classified by many literary historians as a modernist, yet he rejects these rigid lines. In the private crucible of his sensibility, he has assimilated and recast the influences, giving first place to originality in the construction of poetic images.

Cuvinte potrivite represents not only a remarkable debut but marks a date, now historic, in the evolution of contemporary Romanian literature. This first collection of one hundred poems established Arghezi as an artist of striking novelty, creator of a highly original universe of thought and sensibility, and a daring craftsman in language.

The critic E. Lovinescu rightly claimed credit for having noted already in his study of 1923 in *Poezia nouă* (*Critice* IX), the "characteristic complexity of Arghezian psychology: a Faustian soul, harboring not only two souls, but a battlefield of the contradictory principles of modern man," arriving at the natural conclusion: "Arghezian poetry is part of the great tradition of lyric poetry, bringing to it a new aesthetic, a new poetic language, and marking the beginning of a literary century."

As with Eminescu, as with all great creative spirits, the poetry of Arghezi is, regardless of its century and origin, a revealing synthesis of man's attitude toward the world and, by the same token, a painful self-examination. His thirst to know, the Faustian ferment of his mind in search of certainty, will be concretized in ***Psalmi.*** After a long oscillation between "denial and faith," he tries to define the relation of man—modern man—to divinity, to the force that he believes he is recapturing, not in mystic molds, but in universal germination, in the primary and eternal force of beginnings. The poet erases the boundary between real and transcendental; saints descend peaceably among the beasts and the furrows; paradise has its gardens and its flowers. This is a pantheistic cosmogony, not a religious one: the poet does not exact of the divine force a revelation but rather a demonstration of its existence through signs, as in Biblical legends:

When the magi set out, following a star,
You spoke to them—this was possible.
When Joseph, too, set forth,
His name was inscribed in the books,
And you sent an angel to guide him—
And the angel stayed beside him.
From this time on, your angels watched
Over the newborn, over the man, over his wife.
(***Psalmi***)

In his restless loneliness, he would wish at least the movement of angels' wings—which does not come. Expectations beyond the limits of certitudes cannot satisfy the Promethean experience of life, only more sublime for being rough, evading "facile and benign temptations," keeping only "the poisonous and acrid taste":

I bathe in ice and sleep on rock,
Where shadows penetrate, I make sparks fly,
Where silence reigns, I shake my irons,
And with my chains break down the door.
When I reach the summit,
I seek out danger and incite it,
I choose to jump the narrow path,
Carrying on my shoulders the whole mountain.
(***Psalmi***)

This Luciferian daring admits defeat openly, without humility:

My real sin
Is much more grave and unpardonable.
With my bow I had tried
To topple you, God!

Always present—directly or implicitly—is the aspiration toward an integral cognition. The poet is no longer content to decipher divinity in traditional symbols; religious texts are not enough. Thus he exclaims, "Break the words—the words are empty." The supreme achievement is certainty, in terrestrial dimensions:

Alone, at present, in the long course of history,
We must measure ourselves one against the other,
Without my wishing to be victorious.
I wish to touch you and shout: "He exists!"
(***Psalmi***)

Arghezi's ideology is an integral part of his poetic universe; there are many instances of the process, even of cognition of the poet's situation in a world of insipid and lame responses. Always present is the dualism of a spirit torn between heaven and earth, thirsting for the absolute, defeated, yet raising himself again as a Prometheus or a Demiurge. In these powerful tensions the contemporary character of his poetry is revealed, its slice of life, its aura of authentic humanism.

The problems he poses himself are unique and original, and the contingency with Biblical images implies no more than a common frame of reference. His originality consists in the way the problems are *not* solved. The equally ideological balance between the *possible* and the *impossible,* between *daring* and *defeat,* transmits a heat of combustion conferring vibrations of authenticity.

A charged atmosphere of thought repeatedly tried and tormented by frustration permeates most of the poems in ***Cuvinte potrivite.*** **"Tîrziu de toamnă" ("Tardy Autumn")** is one of these sonatas of sadness at a closed horizon, a spirit petrified by defeat and transforming even nature into a vast hospital. Nature constitutes nevertheless the richest reservoir of metaphors and of suggestions for the transfiguration and expression of deep and elusive spiritual processes. His ***Psalmi*** reflect a time of dramatic dilemmas and violent upheavals in the landscape of both the thought and the feeling of this traumatized seeker after certitudes.

At the antipode of the aspiration toward the ideal in ***Psalmi, Flori de mucigai*** (1931) explores with the same artistic acuity the degrading zone of matter, of hideous clay. The title symbolizes the unique beauty that lights up misery and promiscuity, the essence of impure matter in spiritual splendor. The poems of this cycle compound confusion, with their mixture of lyric, epic, and dramatic elements, slipping at times to the level of the anecdote. Yet they reveal once again the virtuosity of the great artist. The atmosphere and personae recall the somber scenes of the prose volume ***Poarta neagră:*** a bandit rots in a dungeon, gnawed by rats (**"Ion Ion"**); another screams out his masculine hungers (**"Streche"—"Madness"**); prisoners march to their evening meal in a grotesque file (**"Cina"—"Dinner"**). The poet discloses the beauty of a world devoid of moral sense but also of perversity. The human portraits are above all disturbing. In uncovering the strange, depraved beauty of these beings outside the law, Arghezi defies the social order of his time, and he does so with skepticism and irony.

The collection ***Càrticica de searà*** is imbued in part by the despair of the poet, who, faced by the ever deepening waves of night, feels within himself "the soul of all the defeated armies":

> Thought, arriving late in its blaze of rain,
> Grows pale and sinks like a wax taper.
> The window is plunged in mourning by a beech
> On which the whole night hangs like a half-staff flag.
>
> **("Ploaie"—"Rain")**

But this poetic universe derives its special vibrations from the disturbing feeling of intimate correspondence between the minuscule world and macrocosmic, universal existence. On a reduced scale, Arghezi's tiny beings commune with the stars: the spider, "minuscule architect," constructs "labyrinths of raw silk" by the same laws that underlie the construction of the universe.

The same sense of communion is felt in ***Hore.*** The image of the poet-gardener, in pure enchantment with the fertile mysteries of the earth, expresses a separation from daily torment in order to live in the noncontingent miracle of creation. There is in ***Hore*** the jovial and exuberant tone of a facetious wag who amuses himself gravely, combining the wisdom of age with the candor of childhood.

In developing one of the great themes of world literature, Arghezi gives it new splendor by reconstructing its original elements in the perspective of dialectical materialism with regard to man and the world. ***Cîntare omului,*** the great poem of 1955, becomes the supreme Arghezian incantation, a synthesis of syntheses, focusing the whole history of mankind in its central point in time and space, its subject and object—Man. The poet shows us modern Man, so far advanced along the spiral of cognition as to become master of his own nature and, consequently, more and more master also of Nature. Having created his own destiny precisely by deciphering the mysteries he had formerly affronted in his well-known ***Psalmi,*** the poet has achieved victory in the conflict between cognizance and noncognizance. The ideas and philosophic projection of his verse assure it a place among the best of modern poetry.

The first act of self-cognition of primitive Man in the reality surrounding him was his dialogue with his shadow, in which he made his inner life an outer event and thus took his place in the universe. In this upsetting separation of Man from his shadow, the poet, with an intense projection of philosophic thought back through millennia, reveals Man's first step in the conquest of Nature. Thus also Man's impetuous gesture of lifting himself on a vertical axis symbolizes a qualitative jump toward his spiritual elevation. By the light of the Promethean torch, Arghezian Man clears the threshold of a new civilization—the metalworking era—becoming *homo faber* and inventor. The poet, seeing the whole universe transformed into an immense workshop, eulogizes the technical progress of mankind.

Arghezi's idea of work is of a moving force in progress, part of the human essence, a fundamental principle of knowledge of the world and self.

Arrived at a new crucial moment, Man will identify himself with the succession of great social events. This is evoked in somber colors, marking in tears and blood the dramatic contortions of a subject humanity. Arghezi's vision of history revolutionized by accumulated suffering and the dialectical law of social explosion is now extended significantly in his thinking. The poet's talent now consists of his capacity to be the synthesizing chronicler of modern complexity as a culmination of evolution, where humanity in its upward march has reached the spiral of final liberation. This is the last, grandiosely important hypostasis of Arghezian Man: **"Cel ce gîndeste singur" ("The One Who Thinks Alone")**. To him, master of human fate, the poet dedicates the final apotheosis of his symphonic chant, a veritable "Ode to Joy." The ascension of Man the Demiurge from his animal beginnings to our time is now projected into cosmic dimensions:

> Man, a weakling, lifts himself on wings to higher regions,
> And brings back new evidence and new laws.

Among those who place human thought on the highest pinnacle of its history, Arghezi in his ***Cîntare omului*** stands out with his praise of contemporary humanism.

The collections of this seventh decade, ***Frunze, Poeme noi, Cadențe, Silabe, Ritmuri, Naoptea,*** add to Arghezi's lyric poetry a new and marvelously fresh tone. The poet's attitude toward the universe is calm, of an almost Olympian perfection, dissolving into a sense of balance the restless groping of the past. At an age when writers usually rest or live on memories, Arghezi continued to probe his soul keenly, discovering—in ineffable zones—the invigorating air of great heights.

Instead of psalms addressed to the divinity of an ideal world, he lifts up a pagan prayer to Nature, invoking in turn the sun, the dew, the rain, the pine, the butterfly, the earth. The presentiment of death—sometimes as sadness, sometimes melancholy or hidden restlessness—touches lightly as a mist the "fragility of the serene chords" of Arghezi's new lyricism.

In the last volumes of Tudor Arghezi, and especially in ***Poeme noi*** (1963), the old motif of a debate between ideal and reality which formed the substance of ***Psalmi*** and ***Cuvinte potrivite*** returns once more. But the anguish does not have the former intensity: one feels at its center a lucid mind about which it is no longer possible to delude oneself. Life "beyond the stars" is an illusion, a nothingness, as in the words of the Bible.

Taking up once more the old theme of battle between Man and his destiny, the poem **"Cale frîntă" ("Tortuous Road")** in the collection ***Silabe*** (1965), presents the image of Man trying to confront his fate with his puny force. Frail creature made of smoke, Arghezian Man follows a desolate road strewn with rocks and ravines, and finally overcomes "the chimera with his fists and shoulders."

Another time, probing the deepest strata of his soul, the poet finds there the desert, complete desolation (**"Sufletească"—"Spiritual"**). The image is that of an empty town, irrevocably dead, in a landscape of dried brambles. The clocks in the belltowers are also dead, and with them time itself. Penetrating deeper into this strange world, he feels its nothingness to be accentuated still more: a classroom with empty benches, a blackboard on which one can hardly make out the mathematical sign for infinity next to the sign for absolute zero. The only movement in this petrified world is the gentle settling of dust.

However, presentiment of death does not always appear in Arghezi's poetry in conjunction with the fear of nothingness and disintegration. From the perspective of a loftier conception of life, the poet imagines a bold gesture that stops time and destiny.

> And in the book you are leafing, the chapter is
> interrupted,
> You wait for the last page to turn.
> No! Put a stone on the book, for it may keep
> The page from turning unconcernedly by itself.
> **("Adiere"—"Breeze")**

The same as at the beginning, in the inner structure of his genius, yet always different in the spiral of his artistic achievement, Arghezi incarnates the *vates,* the inspired prophet who has put his seal of permanence on contemporary Romanian poetry, erecting, as did Brancusi, an "infinite column" of the human spirit. Springing from the landscape of Romanian spirituality. (pp. 32-6)

George Ivaşcu, "Tudor Arghezi: Poet for Contemporary Man," translated by Astric Ivask, in Books Abroad, *Vol. 43, No. 1, Winter, 1969, pp. 32-6.*

Stavros Deligiorgis (review date 1977)

[Deligiorgis is a Rumanian-born American writer, educator, and translator. In the following review, he offers praise for Selected Poems of Tudor Arghezi.]

Ion N. Theodorescu (1880-1967) takes up a Greek historian's name for a Romanian river as a pen name, but somehow cannot help being conscious of its Italian resonance. Arghezi, true to the name's double coup, will be the poet of the arresting undertones. He translates Baudelaire (as early as 1904), Rimbaud, Villon, Dostoievsky, Molière, and Brecht. He survives penury, two world wars, two long imprisonments (once in 1943 for offending the German ambassador to Bucharest), and poor health. At one time or another he is a stone-cutter; chemist; editor; monk; traveler; journalist; revolted theology student at the Catholic University in Fribourg; deacon of the Eastern Orthodox Church; and an apprentice to a watchmaker. He writes incessantly, however, which alone ought to show what [translators Michael] Impey and [Brian] Swann had to match [in ***Selected Poems of Tudor Arghezi***]. They have certainly put together a book that does justice to Arghezi's work, but also to their own work as poets and translators. The selections from four books by Arghezi in addition to the poems in the Epilogue illustrate the range of the originals and confirm the Introduction which stresses the importance of these poems within the framework of Romanian Literature. Which is almost like explaining why Arghezi had to be translated. To most of us for whom Romania between the world wars is synonymous with innovation and modernism (Tristan Tzara; Brancusi; Eugene Ionescu!) the presence of Arghezi is of immediate interest. He overlapped with the avant-garde, even contributed to it, yet he was not of it; in many ways he anticipates all modern poetry that chose not to be of the avant-garde, and all poets who avoid making their positions more interesting than their work. Lastly, Arghezi chose to join his writing and writhing life to native folk wisdom than to the abstractions of high obliterature.

The first collection in the volume suggests an activity in writing that may be placed within the tradition of expressing matter and desire. ***Fitting Words,*** as the collection is called, lays out all the difficult ways which make writing a social language like speech, error, and faith. **"Flowers of Mildew,"** the title poem of the second collection, makes the same concept even more clear and necessary. We hear, toward the end, of writing that cannot go on as it always did. The angelic nail of the right hand has been eroded by the prison wall—the wall obviously doing its own kind of writing on the hand—the left, obviously, continuing by default, but leaving us with the penultimate state of the right explicitly described as a claw in pain, a claw that cannot close. In **"Morning,"** from the same second collection, death reveals the point of human organs in life about as obscenely as the functionary's pen checking off the body of a dead woman. **"John John"** is inscribed, in his death, by lice arranged in herds. **"Rada"** 's transitive dancing of willows, water, and water lilies, in spite of its sensuous attraction ("and as she leaped . . . revealed her maidenhood. You'd think a jeweler's box of blood opened and closed. You'd put your mouth to it and suck hard. . . . ") is merely dance if she will not dance lying down and groan. The conclusions are about re-definition, re-naming, perhaps about the process of un-writing in the heart of any poem. There may be no better illustration for what Arghezi is doing than the beautiful second-century painted sarcophagus found in Odessa showing on its sides the painter at work in his studio painting a large triptych on an easel, not sarcophagi.

Arghezi seems to be saying not merely that poems are in one way or another statements on poetry, or statements on the production of poetry as *écriture* and the countless ways in which poetry is scripted, but all, regardless of the classification that a motif-index would introduce, about the loss of the original point and the assumption of a new one that was not entirely to be predicted from the old. He might as well have been talking about translation, or, as semioticians would call it, transcoding. A catalogue of gypsy cures sweeps the ridiculous over the profane and both over the occult only to end with a popular recipe for magical success that could have come from Hermes Trismegistus' *Lithica.*

> A potion
> For fever,
> Spirits of ammonia
> For those with a chill.
> Eyes weeping pus
> Are rubbed with garlic.
> When they pop out
> Smear them with shit.
> Piss is fine
> For a violent attack;

. . . .

An ace turns up at cards,
Shields you from death.
And when you want
To snatch someone's soul
For the devil
You use the whole zodiac.
So there you are, that's what gives you class:
An emerald and two rubies.

The title Arghezi gives to this is **"Work."** The "workers" of the cures satisfy, naturally, the program of the stupefying ***Flowers of Mildew,*** the collection to which they belong. But the half logic of humanity trying to answer its needs is matched by the other half that keeps humanity a perpetual loser scribing the same kind of dateless chronicle everywhere: bodies in their material fortune in runic conformations, or bodies run through because they stood for something. The knifings disposing of bodies as victims also descry them as knife-like minims spelling out the primitive as few of us would. But there is also the objectless Arghezi, the Arghezi who wonders with Buddha whether there is such a thing as a self. Especially a self wondering:

My blood isn't my own.
I'm afraid to say "I" and "me."
By what right
Should I expand my breast-beams
And over the horizon
Stretch my entire back?

Who would I ask
To tell me
If I am at least alive?

("I Gaze")

This is the first in the section of translations from Arghezi's ***Evening Verses.*** **"Grace"** continues on the obverse of the "gaze":

From all the crumbs
They become pregnant like cats
With swollen dugs.
Do you hear?
The potatoes were but lately confined.
Listen, grace seized them, godlike,
Virginal, innocent spinsters.
The power that deigns
To probe its holy instruments
Deep as the tubers
And cast spells on potatoes' warm warts
As though they were diamonds. . . .

The Japanese poet who tells us in a flat voice that there are mountains and rivers "inside of one potato" [Shinkichi Takahashi, translated by Harold P. Wright; in the *Seventies,* 1971, p. 21] only restates the point that the eastern and the western tradition are not to be contrasted, except in classes of creative writing. Arghezi is not alien to the long European line that acknowledges the problematic structure of all verse, beginning, most likely, with the reputation of the Homeric Hymns known already in antiquity as *prooimia* (overtures!), and continuing with the *spermatikoi logoi* (seedling/seeded? words) as the perfect equivalent of the sutras and the Koans. The subject persists in Arghezi's ***One Hundred and One Poems*** which compress the workings of the proverbial One Thousand Nights and One Night into one febrile vigil alternating oracles and seduction, despair and topology in the well-ordered corners of a very dark cosmos.

Did you see the
Mad moon?
It slyly entered
Rush and reed.
In one fell sweep scything
Snakes frogs and sedge.

. . . .

Poison comes with blood. Mill-rush.
Don't drink the filthy slime.

("Hot Ashes")

Images that terrify in their clarity and seeming indifference to the human sensibilities around their edges. The razors in Arghezi's good send whole villages adrift, rain on the innocent, and shred the inside of the sick and the lovelorn. Still, it is not terribilist stuff for as long as we do not lose sight of the poet telling us all. Impey and Swann help us see how good Arghezi is at holding our attention:

You believe the tale that is done and gone
And yet is hardly begun.

. . . .

Patching together tale after tale,
Don't worry about running dry.

. . . .

. . . I turned the tales back to front
Only to show once again
That from frozen sparks and chips
You can create a starred sky.
The mirror broke and I blew up the fire;
Mirrors were made on the spot.

(pp. 186-90)

Stavros Deligiorgis, "On the Subdominant," in Parnassus: Poetry in Review, *Vol. 5, No. 2, 1977, pp. 186-90.*

Monica Spiridon (essay date 1988)

[*In the following essay, Spiridon examines Arghezi's integration of poetry and journalism in his work.*]

In the history of Romanian literature, Tudor Arghezi, an industrious publicist, illustrates an original symbiosis of poetry and journalism.

Arghezi and Eminescu are the two outstanding Romanian writers whose poetic output was paralleled by journalism of the same scope and eminence. By this I mean that their journalism forced the *journalistic discourse* of the time into a refurbishing of its foundations and of its functions, just as their poetic work compelled their contemporaries to abandon the current norms of the *poetic discourse.*

In journalism, as well as in poetry and prose, Arghezi took advantage of the word's *opacity,* not of its *transparency.* This is true of all his journalistic periods and sections. At the time of his début as a poet (***Cuvinte potrivite*** [***Words Made to Measure***], 1927), Arghezi had already established a reputation as a well-known and fierce journalist who, in Eugen Lovinescu's words, used foul language in most delightful ways. Starting with 1910—the year of his return from abroad—, Arghezi became as assiduous contributor to several periodicals—*Linia dreaptă, Natiunea, Viața socială, Facla* and *Cugetul românesc,* of which he was the director engaged in polemics and advanced numberless "poetic manifestoes," prior to establishing his reputation as a poet. Two remarks have to be made concerning this rich and controversial journalistic output, to be disavowed subsequently by the poet himself when at the acme of his fame. On the one hand, it is the kind of rhetorical and discursive journalism, of which the hot immediacy is born of personal animus and unchecked emotions. *On the surface* it leaves the *impression* that it originates in contingencies only to meet contingent ends. On the other hand, however, Arghezi's pamphleteering went hand in hand with programmatic statements which throw light on the way the journalist perceived the meaning and the ends of his "art." The red-hot journalism to which we referred earlier was not to Arghezi what it had been to Eminescu or to the generation of 1848, namely, a means of circulating and imposing ideas. The kind of inflamed, bellicose journalism Arghezi practiced before the publication of ***Cuvinte potrivite*** was by no means a prose of ideas, but rather a sort of verbal magic, evolving free of contingent pretexts. The pamphlet, so Arghezi would have it, should be able to astound the reader by *ingenium* and, in so doing, should cast a spell over its very victim. By shifting the emphasis from the idea onto the word, the writer effected a *functional conversion* turning the pamphlet from a persuasive genre to one of linguistic virtuosity.

While the journalistic output prior to 1927 can be said to have smoothed the way for the poetry that was coming—especially relevant in this respect is the way in which things were enhanced and ennobled by the linguistic treatment—the poetry which came out in volumes after 1927 had a distinct impact on the journalistic writings which thus acquired the unique and unmistakable flavour they have in the history of Romanian literature. For this second "age" of Arghezi's journalism, subject matter is of little consequence; he never looked down on any subject, as a thing of little value in itself. What really mattered was the twist he gave to what he wrote, or, to put it more accurately, the way he *handled* whatever topic he came across. As a contributor to several periodicals, Arghezi tackled a vast number of subjects. In his columns—**"Tableta de cronicar" ("Chronicler's Notice"), "Biletul" ("The Note"), "Subiectul" ("The Topic"), "Noţiunile" ("Some Notions")**—Arghezi schooled himself in the art of concise and alert writing, seizing whatever chance topics were offered him, concocting his "homeophatic pills" out of the most unusual materials. His volumes in prose—from ***Icoane de lemn*** **(*Icons on Wood*)** and ***Poarta neagră*** **(*The Black Gate*)** to ***Cartea cu jucării*** **(*A Book of Toys*)**, from ***Tablete din Ţara de Kuty*** **(*Sketches from the Land of Kuty*)** to ***Ce-ai cu mine, vîntule?*** **(*Why Are You Cross with Me, oh, Wind*)** or to ***Pravila de morală practică*** **(*Laws of Practical Morality*)**—are mosaics of press notices combined at random with a sovereign disregard of norms. However, in spite of the self-indulgent ease with which Arghezi will clutch at any "subject" and of his nonchalant permutations of the sketches from one prose volume to another, of his unbridled combinatorial fantasy, there is ultimately a *cause of all causes.* The writer will feel no contempt for any subject whatever; this is so because his *creative technique is based on functional shifts and on the conversion of the materials used.*

Arghezi would cast his prose writings into forms already run in press, and in this he is very close to Caragiale, in spite of the significant dissimilarities in other respects. Both Arghezi and Caragiale favoured a kind of prose writing which was short, concise and alert, one which had its formal origins in the "brief notes," fake reportages, everyday facts, "insignificant nothings," "fantasy chronicles" and stories published in the periodicals of the time under the general heading "Mofturi" ("Trifles"). There was a strict economy of the editorial space which fostered habits of concise writing, a situation which could not fail to influence both writers' aesthetic beliefs. Both practiced what might be termed a *process of conversion of the journalistic discourse into canonical prose* (a process underlying, according to the Russian formalists, the history of forms in literature). Caragiale's *moft* (trifle) is ultimately an equivalent of the sketch and both genres made their début as canonical prose following a process of *formal manipulation* which is worth considering in parallel, the more so as the two writers expounded it in arresting aesthetic commentaries.

Caragiale saw in the journalistic discourse writing habits which made the word *yield to circumstances and individual characters,* subordinating it to functionality as it were; conversely, literature is, according to Caragiale, dominated by uncommendable conventions which make the word a mere *ornament.* In a well-known text (*Cîteva păreri* "A Few Opinions"), Caragiale anathematized all stylistic devices, that is, the kind of creative habits of which Arghezi's rhetoric was the ultimate expression. Caragiale used his journalistic texts to turn his prose writings into a "musée imaginaire" of styles and stylistic timbres. The ideal playground of "stylistic variations," the journalistic genres are exemplary exercises serving the cause of *diversity.* Turning to good account the idiom of the press, Caragiale responded to the seduction of the word's *flexibility,* of its capacity *to be cast in life's moulds.* One of the basic axioms of his aesthetics states the necessity for the writer to pick up a fact of life—the "living" material offered by the press—and turn it into genuine literature; on the same principle he would discard fastidious and academic literature of the kind which relies on the word as ornament for its effects. This act of "canonization" of the humbler genres was, in Caragiale's case, a manifesto for the *word's transparency.*

Arghezi saw things in the exactly opposite way. For him, processing the language amounted to levelling it out. While Caragiale will uncover the word's functionality, Arghezi will do his best to *pervert* it. Caragiale's voice would be heard *from the outside* as it were, it would hover above his texts and reveal the way language works and the way it moulds (or should mould) real life. Arghezi is heard *from within,* he will sit at the epicentre of his text and this will in turn bear his unmistakable stylistic "mark." While the catchword of Caragiale's poetics was ADEQUACY, Arghezi was looking for a rhetoric of ADDITION:

> Heaven knows that I was never so bold as to pretend that I was making literature; I only looked for the words that jump and the sentences that move of their own accord. Who knows, I am inclined to believe that I never hit upon them or that they may never come my way. Upon finding out, however, that jumping words are scarce, *I have added to their deficient nature,* and gave them springs to jump with. (Tudor Arghezi, **"Ars poetica. Scrisori unei fetiţe,"** *Adevărul literar şi artistic,* 1927)

Arghezi's poetics was based on the axiom of the word's quintessential coarseness and opacity, of its irreductibility to life. The "tropes" which Caragiale so loathed and which Arghezi used in such profusion have a major part to play in the "divorce" of literature from life, of the word from the world. This is the reason why for Arghezi—and this sets him apart from Caragiale—language processing was a *levelling* affair. There is stylistic identity between genres tackled by Arghezi, whether fiction, poetry, anecdote or reportage. His verbal alchemy proceeds from the *Multiple* to the *One.*

Arghezi's prodigious journalistic career proceeded from his belief that art is able to represent a territory "of addition," one that stands apart from life, a rival to life.

Let us now examine the ways in which the creative mechanisms actualize themselves in Arghezi's prose writings.

The corpus of "precepts" included in ***Manual de morală practică—A Handbook of Practical Morality*** ("sketches" scattered by Arghezi in sundry periodicals, but mostly in *Adevărul literar şi artistic*) is made up of inquiries into the "humours," pamphlets, anecdotes in dialogue form, fragments of prose poems, allegories and Aesopian fables, *faits divers*—frequently "case-for-trial" stories—a.o. The biographies of real people (Gala Galaction or George Metaxa) are used for their *exemplary* value. Arghezi's preaching will come out as almost Biblical "homilies," where extensive use is made of allegories, apologues, parables and animal fables—all devices less familiar to journalism. The journalistic discourse runs the whole stylistic gamut from the exquisite poem in prose to didactic lecturing, the kind of edifying discourse dealing with *contingent themes,* such as family life, manners, social institutions, education, perfect breeding, culture, success and happiness, women's liberation, urban civilization, politics, private life, professions, etc. The starting point lies in the humble everyday facts, in the commonplace anecdote. Not one of the stories told by Arghezi—the case studies he attempts from all possible sources, the tales about Oriental nabobs, Mexican dictators and American oil tycoons—is interesting in itself, they all serve as "launching pads" into other worlds. In such cases, Arghezi's mode will be based on a "trope" of the *pars pro toto* kind, extensively used in *parabolic discourse,* starting with the Gospels. The writer will sometimes forget to dismantle the scaffolding, and let us follow his ascension, step by step, from the "case-for-trial" story to the *genus proximum*—mankind—thus emerging from the empirical into the symbolic. As is well known, Hegel included the parable among those forms of art which make use of a *deliberate symbolism.* To put it in less pretentious terms, the parable is an epic *mode,* a dimension of the epic obvious in those double-structure stories which simultaneouly offer an *anecdote* and point to a "lesson" beyond it which always has MAN as its subject-matter. The parable will point to anthropological, humanistic and, not least, to ethic truths, and this was made clear from the very beginning by the Biblical stories, which obviously established the paradigm. The collection of sketches in the ***Manual de morală practică*** perfectly illustrates this.

Here is, for instance, a quite harmless real-life story, one which apparently cannot point to anything beyond it. It begins thus: "The most feared dog on my estates is now full of scabies. He will no longer bark, nor will thieves and honest men alike beware of his rage." The story then lingers for a time in poem-like episodes where the world of things is shattered into meaninglessness by the burden of the linguistic superstructure it is made to sustain: "The bad dog's scabies started on the hips, like a bishop's tonsure with clearings of raw skin in the network of thick hair." The fable with the sick dog—with its poetic interpolations—is only a pretext for a sudden inroad into social manners and customs. "The sick dog taught me that if my enemy—or any ordinary citizen for that matter—is to be happy, he must be given something to do, some private pursuit, an onset of scabies. . . . " There is a *paradigmatic extension* in Arghezi's anecdote, from the sick dog to the human individual caught within the intricacies of the social mechanism. It is only a matter of surface structure that Arghezi's ***Handbook*** deals with a *he,* a *she,* a *somebody* or a *such-and-such person.* His are actually stories about *everyman,* about *Man.* These are unlimited temporal and spatial horizons which the writer ends up by opening behind inconsequential newspaper sketches, and they can only be measured against the evolution of the species. "Beware of the stupidity of princes enthroned by virtue of the authority of family statuary and oil portraits. History has seen dumb morons halting the lives and evolution of millions of people for ten or twenty years, which, multiplied by that number, will yield uncomputable millennia. . . . " Elsewhere, speaking about flattery, Arghezi would predictably jump from the *here and now* to the *always and everywhere,* concluding that things were in 1929 the same as they had been "seventy-seven centuries earlier." The text **"Un singuratic" ("A Loner"),** published in 1929 in *Adevărul literar şi artistic,* starts as a mere reportage relating a visit to an eccentric man's house in the countryside: "I have just been a guest in the house of a most learned man, the rich owner of a large household. For a whole day I was entertained under his tall roof, designed after the most exquisite early examples of peasant architecture. . . . " Thus, taking his time as he always did, Arghezi would carefully and minutely erect his scaffolding of words, meant to lead us unerringly to the generalizing contentions, to the teachings of a native Confucius addressing his disciples: "Thus, behold, if you can, my dear boy, the advantage which severe solitude has over the tragedy of a multiple life, over its bitter sweetness and hot suffering, and see on which side your being as a human individual will reach its fuller richness. . . . "

There is a universal creative recipe underlying the edifying sketches published in the press, the same in the most diverse of the series of "subject matters," "notions" and "note-book jottings," namely, the deflection of the most varied literary genres and material, their processing and conversion meant to build up a carefully prepared effect. A stylistically autonomous group in Arghezi's journalism includes poetic texts, afterwards collected in mosaic-volumes, such as ***Ce-ai cu mine, vîntule? (Povestirile boabei şi ale fărîmei—Tales of the Grain and the Crumb), Pe o palmă de ţărînă (A Strip of Land***) or ***Carlea cu jucării.*** A piece like **"O intîlnire de necrezut", ("Unbelievable Encounter")** apparently starts quite innocently from a narrative pretext: an encounter in the woods. It soon becomes obvious that it actually puts into words the process which turns any identity or determination (the elements making for the narrative's specificity) into the latency-laden indeterminacy of poetry. The story's *He* gradually becomes "The-One-Whose-Face-Is-Ever-Unseen" or "The Unknown One." *The grammatical personae undergo a symbolical projection while the deictic system is neutralized,* which is exactly what happens in poetry.

Elsewhere the starting point for verbal alchemy is no longer provided by a narrative, but by *landscape,* which will ultimately depend for its reality on an impasto description. While about to put the finishing touches to the story **"Apa mare" ("In Deep Waters")**, Arghezi is amused to undo the verbal wrappings before his audience's supposedly spell-bound eyes in order to uncover the triteness of the captive "landscape." The actual world disentangles itself from the word-world, shamefacedly peeping from behind the word curtain. Literary processing is a glove turned inside out. The following is an almost comical example of disproportionality between the real-life basis and the majestic word architecture: "A tortoise with her twenty little ones has advanced in the sands towards the edge of the sea: it is the sanatorium with its surrounding tabernacles. A monster with a unique red eye is noisily emerging from the Sea landwards, clattering and chattering, shaking heaven and earth, like a string of millstones: the ten a.m. express-train."

For his effects to come out as planned, Arghezi would set into motion the very accessories of rhetoric Caragiale used to defile so vehemently: the tropes. The word acquired a life of its own in Arghezi's hands, he would teach it to stand up against life in fierce revolt: "When the time came for me to weave for myself a flying carpet out the cobweb of words, I grew increasingly impatient with the kind of literature that was being written at the time: it did not express anything, it was inert with mouldy outgrowths. I felt the urge, heaven knows why, to give weight to the words, to load them with leaden small shot, to make them spin round like celluloid figurines." Creation is, to Arghezi, irreducible to life's norms and, as such, it has to be "admired in its own parallel world of meanings." Hence, Arghezi's opposition to Rebreanu who took real life to be the test case for invention.

In a two-step approach, Arghezi would elevate the humblest subjects to literature's higher dignity. The first step was *to make a sharp distinction between creation and life* by means of the aforementioned functional shift. The second was *to distinguish uncompromisingly between orality—however refined—and the written form.* His ambition was to purge the journalistic idiom itself of colloquial contaminations and annex it to *the scriptorial style.* "Journalism with its encyclopaedic character," Arghezi said,

> has two ways of betraying the craft of literary writing: it will deprive literature of the gifted pens which could otherwise aspire to consummate craftsmanship and second, it will force the young people who took refuge in the press for lack of other hospitable islands, into second best creation, into second-best personalities and second-best intellectual attitudes. Books of fiction *are not built, they are not told, stories are not narrated: they are written.* To write a book is to write a page; to write a page is to write a line, the line which gets the page started. . . . *Writing means to write, nothing more or less, propelled by the motivations that are proper to the craft.* (**"Tablete, Despre cîteva lucruri ştiute,"** *Adevărul literar şi artistic,* 1932)

Arghezi was persuaded that there existed an unbridgeable gap between the written and the spoken word. In the history of Romanian journalism, Arghezi represents the scriptorial style at its best, just as Eminescu before him had typified the perfect overlapping of the written and the oral styles. Eminescu had been a brilliant public speaker, an orator. Arghezi's journalistic output was entirely the outcome of *writing-desk labour.* Between these two extremes, Romanian journalism took all the possible liberties and assumed all the possible nuances.

There is a scholarly and scriptorial paradigm to everything that Arghezi wrote as poetry, prose fiction or journalism.

Writers as diverse as Rebreanu and Creangă were accused by Arghezi of being allegedly incapable of handling the written word. His professed preference for the *tranparent* word placed Rebreanu on the side of those writers who made fiction "adhere" to real-life shapes, thus violating the iron rule of creative freedom. Creangă, however, is—no less than Arghezi himself—an artisan writer, one who can hardly be taken for a realistic chronicler of events. Arghezi was simply annoyed with the *orality* of Creangă's *Amintiri din copilărie* (*Memories of My Boyhood*), which *left him with a false impression of rudeness, of untransposed and untransfigured idiom.* While practicing, just like Arghezi, an *art of addition,* Creangă would, however, violate the essential opposition underlying Arghezi's literature: *the written word vs. the spoken word:* "He," Arghezi wrote in a confession included in the volume ***Dintr-un foişor (From a Watch Tower)***,

> wrote about his boyhood and was unable to transfigure it in the way that, in the Japanese prints, an ordinary hen will be transfigured. It is the jumping-over-hedges sort of boyhood and, as written by him, not different from any other boyhood. A fact of life is not worth writing about unless an artistic equivalence is thrust upon an urchin's pranks. He is clever at jotting things down by ear as it were, but is hardly able to make transpositions or to fictionalize a living thing; his WRITTEN boyhood is thus not different from any other UNWRITTEN boyhood,

> since his pen cannot place the accents in the requisite places.

Seen in a historical perspective, the creative habits illustrated by Arghezi's journalistic texts can be easily subsumed to the modernistic view. A belief in the force of the word, in the latter's status as something superimposed on life, the "mechanistic" metaphors the writer sometimes used to uncover the fabrication ("The device is actually easy to make; you place the word so as to be squeezed between a spring and a lid, so that, when you wish the word to jump, you take the lid away and when you want it to contract in strained expectancy, you put the lid on and shut it tight"), all bespeak the affinities with the modernist age. Several other characteristics of Arghezi's writing foster similar conclusions: the kaleidoscopic fragmentary quality—of which a classicist such as Caracostea did not approve—the skill in functionally shifting any kind of discourse so as to blur all frontiers existing between genres and styles. The way Arghezi regarded journalism as based on the same aesthetic principles which govern poetry writing is likewise one of the tenets of modernism according to which there is a latent poetic quality underlying any kind of discourse.

If, however, we are to consider Arghezi from perspectives other than those pertaining to *poïetics*—where his modernistic cast of mind is striking—the writer's choice of themes and ideology seems to belong to a more traditionalistic line, one which had evolved earlier in Romanian literature. Should one ignore the noble contempt in which the writer held his starting points—his subject matter seen as a mere pretext—one could more readily regard his moralism, his conservative or downright patriarchal ideology, his apparently outdated didactic biases, as so many traditionalistic assets apt to counterbalance his alleged, bellicose modernism. One should keep in mind that Lovinescu revised his view of Arghezi and, from initially labelling him modernist, he later came to reassess his achievement as a synthesis of tradition and modernity. Like all genuine literature, Arghezi's journalistic writings lend themselves to a plurality of readings: the "contingent" reading is unmistakably there, but then it is there in Eminescu's poetry as well, meant to enchant the ear of a less educated audience who will be deaf to its deeper meanings.

Taken in isolation, however, and seen against the directions in which literature was moving at the time, Arghezi's journalistic prose writings were definitely "swimming against the tide." They illustrated an "earlier" modernist period, if one may say so. A "belletristic" kind of prose writing appeared at a time of "anti-belletristic" beliefs when ornate writing had been discarded. Hence, the accusations of the young advocates of "authenticity"—Mircea Eliade among them—against the "artificial character of Arghezi's art as a writer." Arghezi's achievement of a lifetime is only apparently outdated. Seen in a historical perspective, this delay will emerge as a paradoxically upturned anachronism. The obsolete Arghezi is, in many respects, a forerunner. (pp. 35-42)

Monica Spiridon, "Tudor Arghezi, the Journalist-Poet," in Cahiers Roumains D'Etudes Litteraires, *No. 2, 1988, pp. 35-42.*

Ion Bogdan Lefter (essay date 1988)

[In the essay below, Lefter examines elements of Rumanian Modernism in Arghezi's poetry and discusses critical reception of his work.]

Whether we like it or not, we have to agree that the history of the reception of Arghezi's work has so far taken the sprightly form of series of paradoxes: disputed and declared a genius before having published any volume; editorial débutant (in 1927) only at the age of forty-seven; vehemently negated while he was publishing his most important books (between—let us say—1927 and 1936, the year of the "definitive edition" of ***Verse*** printed by the Royal Foundation); then, "eliminated" from literature (in 1948) exactly when the praises were becoming uniform and indicated the "classicization" of the author; surrounded afterwards only by a too well-balanced success of esteem when he had returned to the "surface" and was accepted as a "sacred monster" of the Romanian literature of our century; commented upon more and more seldom during the period when, after his death (1967), he had irreversibly and irrevocably won access among the great reference points of the national culture; and finally arrived to being again "selected" (in Ibrăileanu's terms) during the 80's in a central position of the current horizon of expectations, due to the reorientation of the national literary contexts, but in a moment of contradictorial exegetic timidity which is not at all easy to explain, but remains however perceptible, even in the circumstances of a review issue dedicated to the poet.

At this last "paradox" I shall stop in what follows. Examining it might prove relevant in several ways. First of all—of course—as concerns Arghezi's image in the "receiving conscience" of the day. Then, as a "study of case" which reflects the mentalities of several successive cultural moments. And in the third place, because it might introduce the preceding "paradoxes" into a coherent equation, bringing them to the common denominator of a historical "normality" less visible at first glance. But before sketching (with these declared intentions) my hypothesis on the present-day understanding of Arghezi, I shall say a few words—the minimum necessary—about the yesterday's and today's exegesis of the poet's work. These things are known enough on their "factological" side, thanks to the praiseworthy so-called "instruments of work" which we have at our disposal: two anthologies of critical commentaries (both of them in the Critical Library collection of the Eminescu Publishing House, under the same title, *Tudor Arghezi:* the former, shorter, probably drawn up by the editorial staff, in 1971, no mention on it about the person who worked it out; and the latter larger, belonging to Alex. Ştefănescu, in 1981), bibliographical contributions (Sevastiţa Bălăşescu, "Bibliografie critică Tudor Arghezi [1920–1944]," *Limbă şi literatură,* XXII, 1969, plus other lists of critical references in the different monographs about the poet and in the latter anthology mentioned above), as well as a meticulous registering of the whole process of reception of the work (Dorina Grăsoiu, *"Bătălia" Arghezi,* Dacia Publishing House, 1984).

Without entering into details, I confine myself to reminding its stages, in an approximate delimitation. The first echoes of Arghezi's verse (a sort of Arghezi *avant* Arghezi, as the poet was not yet using the pseudonym under which he remained in literature and was signing with a name close to his real one: Ion Theo—from Ion Teodorescu) indicate—in the immediate post-Junimea moment around 1900—a "symbolist" coming from the school of Macedonski. After 1900 and up to 1930, the author was listed under several labels corresponding to different literary tendencies: he was taken one after the other as a "modernist," an "avant-gardist," a "traditionalist" and so on, always considered to be in the first lines of the respective movements and rejected (when rejected) in the same "extreme" quality. After the analysis devoted to him by E. Lovinescu in his volume abour *Evoluţia poeziei lirice* (*The Evolution of Lyrical Poetry*) belonging to *Istoria literaturii române contemporane* (*The History of Romanian Contemporary Literature* [1927]) Arghezi was more and more often placed in the hypothetical point of confluence (of "synthesis") between "modernism" and "traditionalism," in a moment when the first important monographs dedicated to his work (G. Călinescu, *Tudor Arghezi,* The Literary Journal collection, 1939, Pompiliu Constantinescu, *Tudor Arghezi,* Royal Foundation for Literature and Art, 1940, and Şerban Cicculescu, *Introducere în poezia lui Tudor Arghezi,* the same publishing house, 1946) were marking the beginnings of the author's classicization. But he will be discovered all of a sudden as "decadent" in 1948, and it will take almost a decade for him to become "progressive" again! So that the monographs printed between 1960 and 1965 (Ov. S. Crohmălniceanu, *Tudor Arghezi,* State Publishing House for Literature Art, 1960, Mihai Petroveanu, *Tudor Arghezi, Poetul,* Publishing House for Literature, 1961, Tudor Vianu, *Arghezi, poet al omului,* the same publishing house, 1964, and Dumitru Micu, *Opera lui Tudor Arghezi,* the same publishing house, 1965) carry out the function of reinstalling the author on the upper level of the national literary values. The next stage corresponded to the recognition of the so-called generation of the 60s and extended up toward 1980, a period of quasi-general influence of Blaga's poetry on the literature of the day, so that Arghezi came to a marginal interest from the point of view—essential—of the productivity of the model proposed by this work. The fact was registered—among others—by Eugen Simion: "The effective literary influence decreases, the young writers of 1960 discover other models for a poetry that tends to purify the verse and give it an emblematical character. The new waves of poets address to the initiatic lyricism of Blaga or to the conceptual poetry of Ion Barbu. . . . For the generation of 1960 Arghezi is . . . "an exemplary poet, of course, but not a starting point" (*Scriitori români de azi* [Bucharest: Cartea Românească Publishing House, 1976]; an explanatory analysis of this situation—going up to 1979—was done by Dorina Grăsoiu in "Bătălia", *Arghezi.* It is only after the festive—but meagre in real exegetic novelty—wave of the commemoration of the author's centenary (in 1980) that the Arghezi work was offered the chance of rebecoming an active model, while the Blaga one ended its period of full fashion. In the proscenium of Romanian literature there came a new poetry of everyday prosaisms and of linguistic verve, preferring again the colour and language brutalities (I noted for the first time this phenomenon in the article "Arghezi şi poeţii," *Amfiteatru,* 18, No. 7 [July 1984]).

This being the general, simplified table of the reception of Arghezi's work, let us see what the causes of the paradoxical stagnation of its exegesis could be. They surpass—I think—the particular case of the author and raise the global problem of the Romanian cultural epochs of the 20th century, especially as concerns the conceptual systems attached to them. Trying to adopt such a perspective, I come to the level of the theoretical models of our literature, searching for the advantages of the equidistance from—on the one hand—effective "factology," too closely tied to the concreteness of "everyday" cultural existence, and—on the other—the pure phenomenological, isolating analysis, separated from the above-mentioned concreteness, too ignorant as for the influence suffered by texts from the part of their historical contexts. In a way, these two extreme variants were symbolically represented by the two most recent Arghezi monographs, one that methodically registered the history of its reception (the quoted *"Bătălia" Arghezi*) and the other concerned with a semiotic investigation (Emilia Parpală, *Poetica lui Tudor Arghezi: modele semiotice şi tipuri de text* [Bucharest: Minerva Publishing House, 1984]). Of course, I do not ignore some objective difficulties of a (let us call it so:) practical order, which one confronts if trying to reestablish and reinterpret Arghezi's work: for instance, its vastness indefatigably growing (unknown poems continue to come to light in a perfect disorder, without the necessary explanatory notes and without the compulsory guarantees of paternal authenticity); or the absence of a rigorous edition, of a critical type, as the one of ***Scrieri* (*Writings*)** inaugurated by the author himself in 1962 (and reaching today the 37th volume) is only a first partial excavation of the work following criteria difficult to control; or—generally speaking—the methodological crisis of the model of monographical investigation, illustrated by the small number of such books that have appeared as memorable during the last decades.

But the dilemma of the correct establishment and understanding of Arghezi arises from farther away. If I make no mistake, the present-day paradox of his reception is no more than the expression of older conceptual confusions that got propagated by inertia, concerning the whole Romanian literature of the first half of the 20th century. The terminological imprecision inherited from them is responsible for the categorial difficulty that the critics nowadays meet in front of Arghezi, beyond the complexity of his work. Considered sometimes a "modernist," sometimes a "traditionalist," the poet had—in fact—been disputed in the field of a false opposition that dominated the disputes of cultural ideology in the epoch. He probably inferred its limits, as he periodically disowned the labels attached to him. When claimed by the "traditionalism" of the review *Gândirea,* he negated ironically, exactly as he had done when he had been praised out of excessive breadth of criteria as a remarkable representative of the "integralist" avant-gardist movement.

The false opposition I am referring to, which concentrated the theoretical thinking of the epoch, is—as already understood—that between "modernism" and "traditionalism." I did discuss it on a previous occasion (see "Secvenţe despre scrîerea unui "roman de idei," *Caiete critice,* Nos. 1-2 [1986]). This is not the place for a debate on the establishment of the two terms, which need a historical sociological analysis, going back to the mechanisms of Romania's development toward the modern age after 1900 (willing to clarify them at this time, Lovinescu came to write the three volumes of *Istoria civilizaţiei române moderne* ["The History of Romanian Modern Civilization"]). Fact is that "modernism" had become after the first world war a banner of the renewal of literature, of the "progress" in poetry and prose while "traditionalism" was proclaimed heir of the past values and of the national spirit. The former wanted to be emancipated and "cosmopolite," the latter, pious and "nationalist." This scission, justified (I have to repeat) by the historical context of the beginning of the century, after the period dominated by the movements of *sămănătorism* and *poporanism,* disturbed for a long period the unitary understanding of the Romanian modernist epoch, as the prestige of the terminology used in those times has contributed up to now to the maintenance of an image built on polarities. The truth is that "modernism" and "traditionalism" defined themselves on practically different levels: the former was seen especially from the angle of the innovating structure of the literary language, thus on a formal level, while the latter described its conservatism on prevalent criteria of essence. The "two" paradigms made—in fact—one alone, as the so-called "traditionalism" was also using the modernist language of the epoch, attached to other thematic fields. However, the strategical reasons of the terms have lost their traces and left behind the false opposition, due to which the Romanian critical-theoretical thinking continues to feel difficulties in noticing the structural unity of the modernist literary trend in our culture! It is at *this* level, among the great *literary trends,* close to classicism and romanticism, that we must understand modernism, and not as a tendency among others of a given cultural moment.

This is also the main explanation of the exegetic timidity about which I spoke in the beginning. No matter how "promoted" Arghezi would be as a result of the current evolution of Romanian poetry and—generally speaking—literature, the reinterpretation of this work cannot be fulfilled before an attentive preparation of the conceptual instruments that are necessary for the description of his epoch, before elucidating the structural paradigm it is included in. The great modern(ist) writer Arghezi still awaits the regulation of our historical classifications. A new understanding of this creation, from a global, profound perspective, demands first a trial of the real Romanian modernism, that is the work at a (I paraphrase the title of Hugo Friedrich's well-known book) *Structure of Romanian Modern Lyricism.* (pp. 109-13)

Ion Bogdan Lefter, "Arghezi and Romanian Modernism: Notes on a Paradox of Reception," in Cahiers Roumains D'Etudes Literaires, *No. 2, 1988, pp. 109-13.*

FURTHER READING

Micu, Dumitru. *Tudor Arghezi.* Translated by H. A. Richard and Michael Impey. Bucharest: Meridiane Publishing House, 1965.

Chronological overview of Arghezi's artistic development.

Additional coverage of Arghezi's life and career is contained in the following source published by Gale Research: *Contemporary Authors,* Vol. 116 [obituary].

Luis Buñuel

1900-1983

Spanish screenwriter, filmmaker, and autobiographer.

The following entry presents an overview of Buñuel's career. For further information on Buñuel's life and works, see *CLC,* Volume 16.

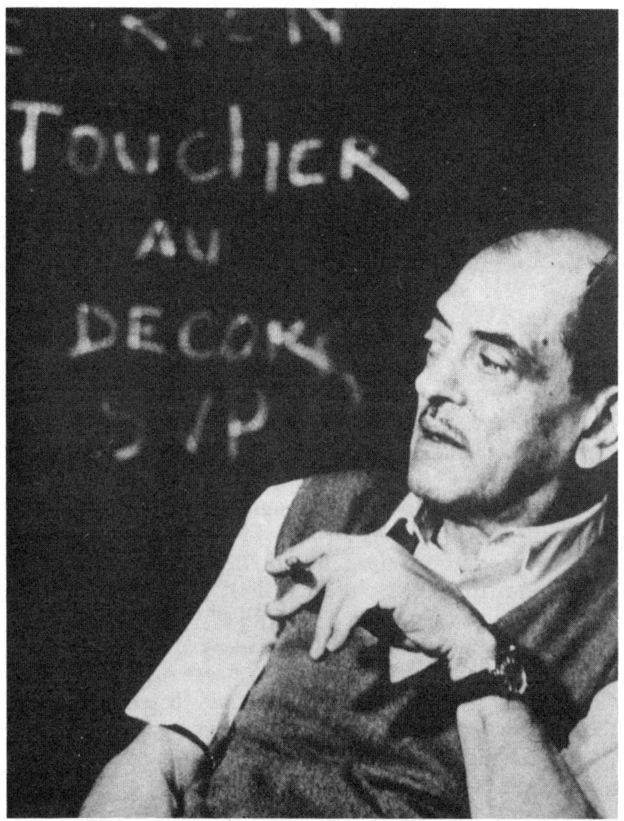

INTRODUCTION

The hallucinatory and imaginative qualities of Buñuel's films have earned him the reputation as Spain's greatest filmmaker and as one of the most significant director-writers in the history of the cinema. Although he acquired enduring fame as a result of his early Surrealistic works, many of his most critically acclaimed films are traditionally narrative in structure and contain graphic depictions of the ways in which the individual's impulses and desires are thwarted by social conventions.

Buñuel was born into a middle-class family in the Spanish region of Aragón. During the years 1906 to 1915 he was educated at Jesuit schools in Zaragoza, where the prevailing atmosphere of repressiveness instilled in him a lifelong penchant for anticlericalism and blasphemy. At the University of Madrid in the early 1920s, Buñuel studied engineering and entomology and became interested in the arts through personal contact with such figures as José Ortega y Gasset, Federico García Lorca, and Salvador Dalí. On graduation he went to Paris, where he studied at the Academie du Cinéma and worked as an assistant director for the filmmaker Jean Epstein. At this time he frequently discussed aesthetic issues with members of the avant-garde artistic community, including André Breton, Pablo Picasso, Max Ernst, Giorgio de Chirico, and Joan Miró. In 1928 Buñuel collaborated with Dalí to produce his first film, *Un chien andalou.* Owing to the film's disturbing assemblage of images, specifically intended to offend the bourgeoisie, Bunuel expected a negative reaction from the audience; however, the film was enthusiastically received. Buñuel's next film, *L'age d'or,* contained a more overt denunciation of bourgeois values, with the result that its second showing prompted a fight in the audience and the crowd's destruction of paintings by Dalí, Ernst, and Miró in the theater's lobby.

After *L'age d'or,* Buñuel studied American film techniques in Hollywood. He returned to Spain to film *Las hurdes—tierra sin pan* (*Land without Bread*), an eerie documentary exposing the poverty of rural Spain. Following the Spanish Civil War, Buñuel returned to America, where he worked on several film projects that were eventually abandoned. In 1947 he moved to Mexico, where he made commercial films and melodramas, as well as one of his most highly regarded works, *Los olvidados.* Many of Buñuel's Mexican films, including *El* and *Ensayo de un crimen* (*The Criminal Life of Archibaldo de la Cruz*), featured distinctive black humor and eroticism that helped to earn him an international reputation.

In the late 1950s and 1960s, Buñuel worked in both France and Spain. Many of his films from this period, especially *Viridiana* and *El ángel exterminador* (*The Exterminating Angel*), display pessimism, social protest, and anti-Catholicism, and were occasionally censored in Catholic countries. *Viridiana,* for example, was banned in France and Spain although the film won the Golden Palm Award at the 1961 Cannes Film Festival. In the late 1960s, Buñuel settled in France and embarked on a period of collaboration with producer Serge Silberman and screenwriter Jean-Claude Carrière. His last films, culminating in the critically acclaimed *Le fantôme de la liberté* (*The Phantom of Liberty*), reveal the same iconoclastic stance toward social conventions that characterizes his entire body of work. In 1982 he completed his memoirs, *Mon dernier soupir* (*My Last Sigh*). Two years later he died in Mexico City.

Buñuel's first two films created in collaboration with artist Salvador Dalí have often been viewed as cinematic representations of Surrealist ideas. In accordance with the tenets of Surrealism, Buñuel believed that the desire for continuity and coherence reflects humanity's attempt to civilize irrationality by imposing an arbitrary organization on nature. *Un chien andalou* condemns this effort by presenting a series of fragmented and startling images, including a man slitting a woman's eyeball and a pair of breasts transforming into buttocks. The cumulative effect is one of dreamlike irreality that mirrors Buñuel's belief that sleep is the mind's most natural state. *L'age d'or* differs from *Un chien andalou* in eschewing random imagery in favor of a more straightforward narrative. The story concerns the struggle of two lovers to remain together despite efforts to separate them. The film ends with the lovers reunited and a sequence of fantastic images, including Christ leading a band of celebrants from an orgy at the Marquis de Sade's castle. After a hostile initial reception, *L'age d'or* was virtually ignored until the 1960s. It is now considered a masterpiece, and Carlos Fuentes has described it as "the greatest of the Surrealist films and one of the most personal and original works in the history of the cinema."

Buñuel's early Surrealist films explore subjects which became central to his later works. Paramount among these are the themes of social injustice and hypocrisy. *Land without Bread,* for example, documents the primitive living conditions of villagers who have inbred for generations and lack the resources to improve their lot. The film's narrator notes that "the only luxurious buildings we came across were the churches." A similarly intense depiction of poverty is presented in *Los olvidados,* a film portraying the lives of young criminals in the slums of Mexico City. Critics have noted that Buñuel refuses to sentimentalize the slum boys, while nevertheless offering implicit criticism of the social agencies which make only token gestures at ameliorating their condition.

The antibourgeois sentiment in Buñuel's films is complemented by attacks against the institutions and doctrines of Christianity. Considered one of his broadest treatments of religion, *Nazarin* focuses on a defrocked priest's struggle to emulate the life of Christ. In seeking to better the lives of his fellow men, he unwittingly causes catastrophe at every turn. At the film's conclusion, the priest is offered a pineapple by a kind stranger and thereby replaces his faith in Christ with faith in humanity. *Viridiana* presents the story of a young woman intent on becoming a nun, who inherits a country estate that she converts into a refuge for local beggars. The latter abuse Viridiana's charity by engaging in bacchic revelry, filmed by Buñuel in one of his most celebrated sequences as a grotesque parody of Leonardo da Vinci's *Last Supper.* The film ends with Viridiana playing cards with her friends while her religious possessions—including a cross, nails, and a crown of thorns—are consumed in a bonfire.

Many of Buñuel's films also depict sexual repression resulting from bourgeois values and religiosity. *The Criminal Life of Archibaldo de la Cruz* features a protagonist who possesses a magic box that can cause the death of whoever its owner wishes and which is used to destroy the subjects of his sexual fantasies. *Belle de jour* narrates the story of Séverine, a woman whose Catholic beliefs regarding the sinful nature of sensuality are so deeply ingrained that she is incapable of consummating her marriage. Instead, she resorts to erotic daydreams and eventually attempts to overcome her guilt and fears by working during the day as a prostitute.

During his long career, Buñuel modified his theory of the cinema. In 1960 he declared that "the screen is a dangerous and wonderful instrument, if a free spirit uses it." In 1974, however, with the release of *The Phantom of Liberty,* he acknowledged that "it is no longer possible to scandalize people as we did in 1930." His critics nevertheless maintain that by revealing the emptiness of so many entrenched mores and by proclaiming the revolutionary freedom inherent in the imagination, Buñuel substantially realized his vision for the cinema as "a quest for pleasure and inquiry which isn't followed by the pounding hooves of guilt."

PRINCIPAL WORKS

Un chien andalou [with Salvador Dalí] (screenplay) 1928
L'age d'or [with Salvador Dalí] (screenplay) 1930
Las hurdes—tierra sin pan (screenplay) 1932
*[*Land without Bread*]
Los olvidados [with Luis Alcoriza] (screenplay) 1950
Las aventuras de Robinson Crusoe [with Hugo Butler] (screenplay) 1952
*[*The Adventures of Robinson Crusoe*]
El (screenplay) 1952
Ensayo de un crimen [with Eduardo Ugarte] (screenplay) 1955
*[*The Criminal Life of Archibaldo de la Cruz*]
La mort en ce jardin [with Luis Alcoriza and Raymond Queneau] (screenplay) 1956
Nazarin [with Julio Alejandro] (screenplay) 1958
La fièvre monte à El Pao [with Luis Alcoriza, Louis Sapin, and Charles Dorat] (screenplay) 1960
Viridiana [with Julio Alejandro] (screenplay) 1961
El ángel exterminador [with Julio Alejandro] (screenplay) 1962
*[*The Exterminating Angel*]
Le journal d'une femme de chambre [with Jean-Claude Carrière] (screenplay) 1963
*[*Diary of a Chambermaid*]
Simon del desierto (screenplay) 1965
*[*Simon of the Desert*]
Belle de jour [with Jean-Claude Carrière] (screenplay) 1966
La voie lactée [with Jean-Claude Carrière] (screenplay) 1969
*[*The Milky Way*]
Tristana [with Julio Alejandro] (screenplay) 1970
Le charme discret de la bourgeoisie [with Jean-Claude Carrière] (screenplay) 1972
*[*The Discreet Charm of the Bourgeoisie*]
Le fantôme de la liberté [with Jean-Claude Carrière] (screenplay) 1974

*[*The Phantom of Liberty*]
Cet obscur object du désir [with Jean-Claude Carrière] (screenplay) 1977
*[*That Obscure Object of Desire*]
Mon dernier soupir (autobiography) 1982
[*My Last Sigh,* 1983]

*The translated titles are those under which the films were released in the United States.

CRITICISM

Octavio Paz (essay date 1951)

[*An author of works on literature, art, anthropology, culture, and politics, Paz is primarily recognized as one of the greatest modern Spanish-American poets. In the following essay, originally written on the occasion of the 1951 Cannes Film Festival, he offers an analysis of* Los olvidados.]

Un Chien Andalou (1928) and ***L'Age d'Or*** (1931) marked poetry's first aggressively deliberate invasion of the art of the cinema. The union of film image and poetic image might seem shocking, even subversive. Indeed, it was. The subversive nature of Buñuel's early films consisted entirely in this: the conventional phantoms—social, moral, and artistic—of which our "reality" is composed were no sooner lightly brushed by the hand of poetry than they fell into dust. Over these ruins a new reality arose, the reality of man and of men's desires. Buñuel demonstrated that a chained man need only shut his eyes to make the world explode. His films, then, are more than a fierce attack on so-called "reality." They are the revelation of another reality that is enslaved by modern civilization. The man of ***L'Age d'Or*** slumbers in every one of us and is only waiting for a sign—the sign of love—to awaken. As André Breton has said, this film is one of the rare attempts in modern art to bare the terrible face of a love that is free.

Shortly afterward, Buñuel filmed ***Las Hurdes,*** a documentary which is also in its way a masterpiece. In ***Las Hurdes*** the poet hides and is silent, so that reality may speak out alone and in its own language. If the theme of Buñuel's surrealist films is man's struggle against a reality that mutilates and smothers him, the theme of ***Las Hurdes*** is the brutalizing triumph of that same reality. Thus this great documentary comes as a necessary complement to his earlier works. It explains and justifies them. Here, by different paths Buñuel pursues his unremitting war with—or more exactly, against—reality. His own realism is allied, in the highest Spanish tradition, to that of Goya, Quevedo, the picaresque novels, Valle-Inclán, Picasso. The battle is waged in a hand-to-hand combat that gives no quarter. Reality emerges from this encounter stripped to the bone. His art is in no way related to the sentimental or aesthetic description that customarily passes as being realistic. Quite the contrary. All Buñuel's work provokes in us a liberating eruption of something secret and precious, something dreadful and pure, something that our concept of reality ordinarily shrouds from our sight.

Whether he uses the device of dream or poetry or cinematic narrative, Buñuel the poet penetrates man's profoundest being and reaches the most unexpressed, deep-lying areas of his inner self. His hell. And his heaven . . .

If, on one hand, ***Los Olvidados*** represents a high point of artistic maturity, on the other it testifies to a more complete and total despair. The threshold of the dream seems eternally barred, and only that of the blood stands open. The film is a synthesis of the best of Buñuel's previous work and at the same time is a new point of departure. He does not deny any part of the great experience of his youth, but he has been made more aware of changes wrought by the passing of time—changes that have only made the reality prefigured in his first films even more dense—and he has constructed a work whose action unfolds, as precise as a machine, as hallucinatory as a dream, as implacable as the silent downward flow of lava. ***Los Olvidados*** has a social theme: juvenile delinquency. The initial situation in the scenario was taken from police records. The characters are alive, or could be. They are our contemporaries. They are the age of our own children. But ***Los Olvidados*** is more than a realistic film. Dream, desire, horror, delirium, chance, the night portion of life, all find in it their due place. The weight of the "reality" of which Buñuel makes us aware is so atrocious that we are tempted to believe it impossible to endure. And so it is. Reality is not to be endured. That is why man kills and dies, loves and creates, in turn.

The physical and human limits within which the drama takes place could not be more circumscribed: the life and death of some children, caught within the four walls of their solitude, and thrown like so much fodder to their fate. The city, with all that it implies of human solidarity, turns its back on their little hovels. The modern city does turn its back, morally and physically, on its children. What we call civilization is for them a wall, a huge NO for them to stumble against. These are Mexican children, but they could be of any country, living in the outskirts of any large city. In one sense they no more live in Mexico than anywhere else. They are *los olvidados*—the forgotten ones—inhabitants of those great wastelands that the modern city breeds around it. Theirs is a world closed in upon itself, a world where all action is circular, and where every step they take forces them toward the point they started from. No one is able to escape the presence of others, no one is able to get outside himself except via the blind alley of death. Other worlds do exist in which chance opens doors. Here it closes them.

The continual presence of chance invests ***Los Olvidados*** with a special meaning that prevents our confusing it with fate. The chance that governs the actions of the heroes of the story is presented as an absolute necessity, and yet one that "could have been avoided." (Why not call it, as in tragedy, by its right name—destiny?) Stripped of its supernatural attributes, the ancient fatality marches on. Today ours is a psychological and social fatality, or, to use the current catchword, our new intellectual fetish—a histori-

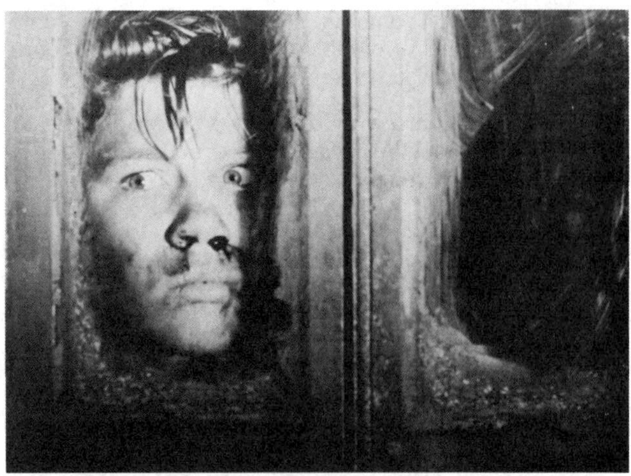

A juvenile delinquent in Los olvidados.

cal necessity. But it is not enough that society or history or circumstance be hostile to the heroes of the story for catastrophe to fall upon them; its determinants must coincide with the will of those who are involved. Pedro fights against chance and the bad luck that Jaibo represents for him. When finally he faces these forces squarely and submits to them, he transforms chance into destiny. He dies, but he has made his death his own. The tragedy derives from the impact between human awareness and external fatality. Buñuel has rediscovered a fundamental ambiguity: without human complicity destiny cannot be fully achieved and tragedy is impossible. Fatality dons the mask of liberty, and liberty that of destiny.

Los Olvidados is not a documentary. Still less is it a film with a thesis, or a propaganda or a moralizing film. But if no preachments tarnish its admirable objectivity, it would be libelous to suggest, on the other hand, that it is a film in which only artistic values (always suspect, in any case) are important.

The film of Buñuel and Figueroa is as remote from realism, whether social, psychological, or uplifting, as it is from aestheticism. It takes its place in the tradition of a passional and fierce art, a contained and delirious art reminiscent of Goya and of the Mexican engraver Posada, who of all plastic artists have unquestionably pushed the grotesque to its furthest extremes. Cold lava, volcanic frost . . .

The moral value of ***Los Olvidados*** has nothing to do with propaganda. When art is free it does bear witness; it is conscience. Buñuel and Figueroa's work is proof of what the creative talent and conscience of two artists can accomplish when nothing but their own freedom constrains or enslaves them. (pp. 186-89)

Octavio Paz, "The Tradition of a Fierce and Passional Art," in Luis Buñuel: An Introduction *by Ado Kyrou, translated by Adrienne Foulke, Simon and Schuster, 1963, pp. 186-89.*

Emilio Garcia Riera (essay date Summer 1960)

[In the following essay, Riera provides a critical appraisal of Buñuel's career from Un chien andalou *to* Nazarin.*]*

It is well known that the Mexican cinematography is undergoing a very serious period. Commercial interests have destroyed almost all the hope stirred by the first phase of the Mexican cinema. Today, it is painful to note that artistically Mexico is at a much lower level than during the years 1940-50. The career of Emilio Fernandez, el Indio, (creator of *Maria Candelaria, La Perla,* and *Pueblerina*) ended abruptly. Those who could have been authentic film creators—Julio Bracho, Chano Urueta, Roberto Gavaldon, and others—have been forced to follow an exclusively commercial route. Our Mexican cinema produces at present about eighty features per year among which it is rather difficult to find anything of real value. Even the "entertaining" pictures are completely devoid of the least spirit of invention, the most minimum originality.

Within this framework, the emergence of the producer Manuel Barbachano Ponce appears noteworthy. This man, surrounded by a good team, has given to the Mexican film three of its most important works during the past six years: *Raices, Torero,* and ***Nazarin.*** But, above all, the presence of Luis Buñuel, director of ***Nazarin,*** is truly exceptional.

The collaboration of these two personalities produced a great film. It could be said that Barbachano's only merit is to have given to Buñuel the necessary elements for the production of ***Nazarin*** without interfering in the least with the direction. Yet, can any well-intentioned producer aspire to a greater distinction than to give creative talent a free hand? There is no doubt this question can be answered very quickly if we remember the fashion in which Mexican films are made, where the producer is usually an almighty dictator. Buñuel, then, enjoyed complete freedom to direct ***Nazarín.*** The result has been most rewarding. The controversial director has been almost unanimously praised, even by those who doubted his talent. ***Nazarín*** is being universally acclaimed as a masterful work and the recognition of the International Jury given at Cannes in 1959, confirms it.

This would seem to be an appropriate time to do a critical appraisal of the work of Luis Buñuel. Let us start from his first work and go on to this latest film, ***Nazarín,*** which is, in many aspects, the most completely and fully realized of all his films.

Luis Buñuel was born in 1900, in Calanda, a small town of Aragon, Spain. In 1928, in collaboration with Salvador Dalí in Paris, he made his first film: ***Un chien andalou.*** Very much has been written and said about this famous film. However, it is not superflous to remember here some of its ideological characteristics, as well as those of the following film, ***L'age d'or*** (1930), also produced with the collaboration of Dali, because the influence of the surrealistic period is evident in the subsequent work of this film maker.

As we know, the production techniques of the two surrealistic films previously mentioned are based upon "the paradoxical and inconsistent montage of shapes and words as dictated by chance and the subconscious" [Georges Sadoul in *Histoire de l'art du cinema*]. The film makers desired to express an important idea to Buñuel: "Since the mechanical production of cinematographic images is, because of its mode of operation, of all human expressions the one which most resembles the behaviour of the human mind in its sleeping state" . . . the film "seems to have been invented to express the subconscious life, that life which, with its roots, so deeply penetrates poetry."

The surrealistic period advanced a non-conformist and revolutionary attitude which, through the exaggeration of the irrational, attacked all the moral, juridical, religious, and political values established by human reason. (A typical attitude in an age when the precarious state of all such values had been so thoroughly exposed.) In reference to this surrealistic period, it is easy to speak today of ingenuousness . . . of useless nihilism. The sad path followed by some surrealists like Salvador Dalí could make us think the worst about that esthetic effort to destroy the most solid foundations of apparent reality. But in the case of Buñuel and some other surrealists, the attitude, the rebellion, has been maintained as a firm moral attitude. Thirty years have gone by since ***Un chien andalou*** but Buñuel has remained the same in many important aspects. I would say that the one thing he has learned is to give his eternal rebellion a more complete and comprehensive, and therefore more powerful, artistic expression. But let's not get ahead of ourselves.

After the completion of his first two films, Buñuel signed a contract with Metro Goldwyn Mayer and moved to Hollywood in 1930. This contract called for a six-month stay but he only remained four months. Back in Spain, in 1932, he made his only film to date produced in his own country, ***Tierra sin pan.*** This documentary film takes place in a very poor region of Spain, Las Hurdes. Buñuel exhibited the horrible misery of its inhabitants. He neglected all the picturesque details. For example, officials of the Spanish Republic reproached him for his refusal to record the colorful native costumes. Instead of doing this, Buñuel took advantage of a local wedding to photograph a savage and truly "irrational" ritual! The wedding guests, on horseback and at full gallop, pulled off with their bare hands the heads of roosters suspended along their way. Buñuel depicted a hard reality. He took, at the same time, "irrational" and "incomprehensible" elements to shock the foundations of the spectator's ideas about good taste, morality, and established decency—everything Buñuel associates with conformism.

In ***Tierra sin pan*** Buñuel finds the irrational within reality itself. He does not create it by means of "paradoxical and inconsistent montage." This is the major difference between ***Tierra sin pan*** and the earlier films. This latter film marks an important step in the career of Buñuel insofar as it proves the possibility of expression without the need to reject objective reality. And, we must say, that it was through the representation of this objective reality that the film maker found a way to communicate effectively with the audience, thus freeing himself from the snobbish and limited audiences which were amused rather than horrified by his surrealistic films. It is not a mere coincidence that ***Tierra sin pan*** was the first film made by Buñuel without the cooperation of Salvadore Dalí. The rightist government of Spain in power at the time, prohibited the exhibition of ***Tierra sin pan.*** Buñuel did not make another film until 1946.

In 1939 Buñuel left again for the U.S.A. This time he came as Technical Advisor on motion pictures concerning the Spanish Civil War. In New York he worked with Kenneth McGowan for the Museum of Modern Art, headed, at that time, by Nelson Rockefeller. His work was merely a bureaucratic task: The production of foreign language versions of war propaganda films. From here he went on to Warner Brothers as producer of foreign versions. The three months with Warner Brothers were dedicated exclusively to the "dubbing" of films. At the end of the war he went to Mexico.

In Mexico Buñuel was to produce his most important works. The beginning, however, was far from promising. In 1946 he directed a typical commercial film, ***Gran casino,*** to the glory of its two very popular stars, Jorge Negrete and Libertad Lamarque. Buñuel had to survive and he made himself available for any film work as long as it did not transgress his own morality. ***Gran casino*** is considered by its director as a simple and inoffensive tournament between Negrete and Lamarque to see who could sing more tangos during the 90-minute length of the film. A clean film, nothing more. On the other hand, Buñuel has always avoided sentimental expressions. Kisses are extremely rare in his films. In ***Gran casino*** he avoided them by using his camera to search for narrative elements which would, as substitutes, symbolize them sarcastically. Buñuel considers the merely sentimental as immoral.

Three years passed before Buñuel worked in films again. In 1949, at long last he directed ***El gran calavera.*** The plot of this film is based on a comedy by the Spanish writer Adolfo Torrado.

During all the time Buñuel spent unoccupied with films, he travelled up and down the city of Mexico. The poverty of many of its inhabitants impressed him deeply, as would be natural in the case of a man who, in search of the "irrational," could never find it reasonable that while a hypocrite society speaks emphatically of good order and good habits it is possible to see in Mexico (as well as in other great cities) situations like the ones depicted in ***Los olvidados.***

Buñuel, having decided to make his film on the life of abandoned children, patiently consulted—with utmost diligence—the files of a local reformatory. The story of ***Los olvidados*** is based on actual cases. ***Los olvidados,*** produced in 1950, is perhaps the first important Mexican film to be made in Mexico City. (The best films of Emilio Fernandez take place in rural localities). In ***Los olvidados*** (as in ***Tierra sin pan***) Buñuel shows the sad condition of the poor without embellishing them, because if there is one thing Buñuel hates it is that artificial sweetness imparted to all the poor which we so frequently see in the traditional film. If, as usually happens in motion pictures, the moral

A scene from Un chien andalou.

principles approved by conventional society are carefully observed by members of the poorest classes (the girl who keeps her honor, the drunkard with the golden heart, etc.) then these principles have some universal validity. However, Buñuel is concerned with exposing the opposite. The adult characters of ***Los olvidados*** are not only materially poor but morally so as well; the debased mother who gives herself to her son's friend, the cruel and merciless blind man, the peasant who abandons his young son. In an environment like the one depicted in ***Los olvidados*** moral principles do not retain their values. Nevertheless, Buñuel fills his films with tenderness for children. As Claude Mauriac has pointed out, there is in Buñuel a feeling of indignation similar to that of Ivan Karamazov, the Dostoyevsky character, who felt that nothing whatsoever justified the suffering of a child. This gives to ***Los olvidados*** real poetical strength—a poetical strength that exists not only because of the film's surrealistic scenes. These scenes, which represent the strictly subjective vision of the dreamer and which are of a dramatic composition we already know objectively, are not among the best achieved by Buñuel and, more than anything else, they merely appear to provide esthetic relief.

Los olvidados was premiered in Mexico City and the public received it with great indifference. In 1951 it was awarded the Cannes Festival prize. Re-premiered in Mexico City, in another theatre and after the Cannes recognition, it was given a better reception. Buñuel had taken his first firm step. Today he is still proud of ***Los olvidados,*** the film he prepared so carefully and for such a long time; however, he is ashamed of some "sentimental" concessions, i.e., the scene in which the director of the reformatory proclaims dramatically: "Wish to God we could close the doors to poverty!" And, really, the whole reformatory sequence does not conform with the general characteristics of the film.

Buñuel began to receive work in abundance. In that same year (1950) he collaborated with Luis Alcoriza in the script of an insignificant film directed by Julian Soler, ***Si usted no puede, yo sí.*** Buñuel does not even remember the plot of this film. He also directed a melodramatic film, ***Susana, carne y demonio,*** which, according to Buñuel, would not have been so bad if it had had a less forced and conventional finale. The Mexican dramatist Rodolfo Usigli wrote the script for this latter film. It was the first collaboration between Usigli and Buñuel. Later we shall see how these two personalities clashed on ***Ensayo de un crimen.***

In 1951 Buñuel made three films. Of the first two, ***La hija del engaño*** and ***Una mujer sin amor,*** very little can be said. These are bread-winners, that is, films which are good only to feed their makers. The third one, however, is the famous ***Subida al cielo.*** This film, also entered at Cannes in 1952, is, at first sight, a comedy of manners, based on popular characters of the Southwest of Mexico. The film is graceful and attractive, no doubt. In a way, however, it indicated a retrogression in Buñuel's career. In this instance, the film-maker seems to disdain the possibility of expression through objective reality which he had realized in ***Tierra sin pan.*** The key scene, violent and erotic, is based upon the "paradoxical and inconsistent montage. . . . ." characteristic of the surrealistic period but, in this case, there is no justification for the oneiromantic. The film remains, nevertheless, agreeable and suggestive. But, although we praised the film we are afraid that Buñuel's path had veered toward estheticism and purist art. We are wrong but the film gave us a bad moment. ***Subida al cielo*** had been produced with the capital of a distinguished Spanish poet, Manuel Altolaguirre, co-author with Juan de la Cabada of the film script. The fortune of this man, unfortunately, used to take unexpected turns, and Buñuel and the film were the victims of one of these turns. Hence, ***Subida al cielo*** was finished in a hasty manner, that is it remained unfinished.

From an artistic point of view, 1952 was a good year for Buñuel. During this year he made ***Robinson Crusoe*** and ***El.*** Before these two films he directed ***El bruto,*** a somber story based on a character of interest to Buñuel, a slaughterhouse worker. This main role was given an erratic performance by Pedro Armendariz. In fact, the artistic failure of this film was caused, to a large extent, by the actors. There is in ***El bruto*** a great difference between what Buñuel desired and what was produced.

But in ***Robinson Crusoe*** Buñuel achieved a great triumph. This film was made, in part, with private American capital. It appears to measure up to the desires of the film maker. Buñuel found that the well-known story of Daniel Defoe lent itself for the production of an experimental work. The exceptional circumstances of the life of Robinson offer a unique base for the exploration of his interior life, in his irrational and subconscious motivations. In this solitary man the instincts and the remains of those first childhood impressions so important to psychoanalysts, are expressed without limitations. For example, in the moving scene where the protagonist, feverish and in delirium, sees some running water he cannot reach and the image of his father appears as a result of the guilt complex which Robinson has toward his father who had advised him against travelling. Also, as soon as Friday dons some colorful garments, Robinson's sexual instinct is aroused. In this there is no allusion to homosexuality, even though we are left with the feeling of having touched a point where homosexuality can be explained by the irrationality of the subconscious. One could say, based on many reasons, that the character of Robinson has been created especially for Buñuel. For, as we shall see again when we comment on ***El,*** it is precisely through exceptional characters, alienated by circumstance from the elemental norms of common sense and customary morality, that Buñuel often penetrates into the mysterious, and therefore poetical, regions of the human being. To Buñuel, this poetry and this mystery, are equal to that which "completes and amplifies tangent reality" and "increases the knowledge of things and beings. . . . opening the marvellous world of the unknown." But, naturally, "tangent reality" is not excluded.

El is the story of a paranoiac. The story of a paranoiac who sees reality, of course, in his own way, disfigured in respect to the reality everybody else sees. (It concerns a case which has reached the extremes of subjective vision, different from those others which Buñuel supposes in every person.) The paranoiac of ***El*** suffers constant obsessions with which he torments his wife. But the interest-point about this character is that being the madman he is, he passes as a perfect gentleman, completely and impeccably adapted to the most accepted and traditional moral and religious norms. In reality, the paranoiac and the well-meaning, well-intentioned citizen are two facets of a perfectly defined social type, the parasite. There is between the two facets a mutual determination and upon this determination lies the value of the film as social criticism. That is, Buñuel ultimately attacks the hypocritical morality of parasitic burgeoisie when he exposes the irrational impulses of a paranoiac who is, at the same time, a representative of the burgeoisie and who also, in spite of himself, cannot avoid being "a poet."

I like this interpretation of the film, even though Buñuel does not seem to have intended to say as much. But Buñuel is neither surprised nor annoyed when, because of the nature of his art which is in great part intuitive, varied and different interpretations are given to his films. These interpretations are legitimate and fully justified even when they have not been foreseen by the film maker. In this manner, the above interpretation of ***El*** resembles in some aspects, according to Buñuel himself, the interpretations of two critics highly respected by Buñuel, George Sadoul and Ado Kyrou. But Buñuel, nevertheless, speaks favorably of this film because it is a well-documented record of a pathological and incurable case. The finale of the film is admirable: The protagonist, confined to a monastery, humbly promises to one of the monks, to behave well and to dedicate himself to the reading of pious books. But when he walks away, his zigzagging steps give him away because these same steps are a symptom of the paranoia which possesses him and will never abandon him. This complete, detailed and fully documented exposition of a psychopathic process appeared unbelievable to the general public. The showings of the film were frequently received with great laughter. This confirmed, to Buñuel, the fact that the traditional, everyday film has cultivated in the general public a great attachment for the conventional, the common sense, the superficial, and the false. From ***El*** its director would gladly suppress what he calls the "melodramatic part." That is, what precedes the marriage of the protagonist; which is nothing more than a romantic intrigue concerning the future bride of the paranoiac, the current boyfriend of this girl, and the paranoiac himself. Even though we might agree with Buñuel on this point, ***El*** remains, as it is, one of his most suggestive films. Personally, ***El*** with ***Los olvidados, Ensayo de un crimen*** and ***Nazarin*** compose the great work of Buñuel.

In 1953 Buñuel had the opportunity to realize one of his most cherished illusions. That is, to make a cinematographic version of Emily Bronte's famous novel *Wuthering Heights.* Buñuel's film was titled, in the Mexican version, ***Abismos de Pasion*** and it was a resounding failure, possibly the failure most deeply felt by Buñuel. Here once more, the cast (of heterogenous temperaments) failed to respond to the director. Moreover, Raul Lavista's background music offered Wagnerian motives at the most inopportune moments. It must be stated that failures like those of ***El bruto*** and ***Abismos de Pasion*** can be explained (without reducing the blame the director might have properly deserved) by the organization of the Mexican film which reduces the director to just another hand in the production of the film. As a matter of fact, the director neither casts nor edits his film. As far as the sets are concerned, models are not used in Mexico and consequently the director must use whatever the designers have prepared without his prior consultation. This system imposes a serious handicap on film makers like Buñuel, who evolve in their own mind, in complete detail, the equivalent in images of the plot they are to realize. Buñuel, having to work with actors whose faces did not correspond to those he had imagined for the characters of Emily Bronte and faced with the insistence of these actors to outshine each other even at the cost of giving the film a cheap and common melodramatic tone, had to give in, and what could have been a great film was not. In spite of all this, Buñuel believes that this film reflects more of the spirit of Emily Bronte's work than the 1939 William Wyler production starring Laurence Olivier and Merle Oberon.

In 1953, Buñuel also made ***La ilusion viaja en tranvia,*** a gray film in which many of us seemed to notice a neo-realistic influence. In effect, the theme of this film was very similar to that of *Muchos suenos por la calle* (*Many dreams in the streets*) an Italian film by Mario Camerini which many consider (not too strictly, however) neo-realistic.

Camerini's film evolves around the theft of an automobile. Buñuel's film takes place in Mexico City and a streetcar is stolen in very similar circumstances to those of the Italian film. Buñuel, let us clear the record, had never seen the Italian film. He has always opposed, ideologically, the neo-realistic movement, saying: "Neo-realism has introduced to the cinematographic expression several changes which enrich its language and nothing more. Neo-realistic reality is incomplete, official, above all reasonable, but poetry, mystery . . . are completely non-existent in its productions. Neo-realism confuses ironic fantasy with the fantastic and with black humor." In this last phrase Buñuel seems to refer to De Sica's *Miracle in Milan.* Buñuel is against theories which are reflected as such in films because these theories, for the sake of proving what they pretend, have a tendency to limit the expression of reality and to destroy the substance of reality. The truth is that ***La illusion viaja en tranvia,*** neo-realistic or not, was shot almost in its entirety in the street and, to an amazing degree, it lacks color. It is precisely this lack of color, this lack of spirit of invention, that mars so many neo-realistic films.

In 1954 Buñuel continued to work with rather bad luck. ***El rio y la muerte*** was a film with educational pretensions which repelled the director. Some of us felt that after so many failures the career of Buñuel had begun to decline. But just a year later Buñuel made ***Ensayo de un crimen.*** This latter film was based on Rodolfo Usigli's story about Archibaldo de la Cruz, a man whom Buñuel called a typical example of social parasitism.

The story begins when Archibaldo as a small child receives from his mother, as a present, a music box with such marvellous powers that the protagonist need only to touch the box to effect anybody's death he desires. Thus, Archibaldo "kills" indirectly, his wet nurse. This lady is hit by a stray bullet fired by a revolutionary and when she falls her legs are seen uncovered. This is the first indication of the unity between the erotic element and death which will be evident throughout the film. Archibaldo grows up and, already a mature man, he comes across the music box once more. With the help of the music box he provokes, "indirectly," a series of deaths which are always related to his erotic life and of which he feels sincerely guilty. Archibaldo delivers himself to the authorities who naturally acquit him (since he has not directly committed the crimes of which he accuses himself). Archibaldo then marries the only girl who has not been his "victim." This girl has endured the "death test" because when the assassin decided to act directly for once, a chance happening saved her. Archibaldo symbolically burns a doll which reproduces the girl who came close to being his "victim." A difficult and complex film ***Ensayo de un crimen,*** lends itself to the most varied symbolic interpretations. The one point which makes it outstanding is the portrait of the central figure Buñuel offers us. This central character is really an assassin who wishes and enjoys the death of his fellow beings and who, nevertheless, is quite innocent before the eyes of society; innocent to such a point that when the film ends, he is moving toward the enjoyment of a happy and peaceful future. This is a case of monstrous impunity. If, at the end of the film (as it usually happens in a certain type of film), justice would eventually impose itself, even beyond human justice, through any one of the typical cinematic or technical devices used in similar cases, Buñuel would have committed the most serious treason to his principles. It is not very difficult to arrive at the conclusion that society only punishes minor crimes, those less premeditated, because society rules itself by a series of principles which take into consideration only the most superficial characteristics of the human being. It is curious, and instructive, to learn that Rodolfo Usigli objected to the significance that Buñuel had given to his original story. Usigli sympathized with his character, Archibaldo, who possessed—according to him—a series of virtues very dear to a certain type of burgeoisie decadence. To Usigli Archibaldo's crimes are justified "esthetically." The argument of Usigli and his followers was nothing more than a repetition of the hollow and conformist words we have heard before . . . "Crime considered as one of the fine arts. . . . etc. . . ." The one certain point, above all, is that whenever ***Ensayo de un crimen*** may be mentioned, the name of Buñuel and not Usigli will come to mind. The film is excellent. This time the film maker was able to give his work a complete unity, a complete unity without any concessions. The development of the film was brilliant and one of the critics was right when he said "the film evolves toward the marvelous every time the path seems to be already defined. . . . . the marvellous blends with the real and it extracts from the real a force which moves us" [Philippe Demonsamblon, *Cahiers du cinema,* 1957].

In the same year of 1955, Luis Buñuel moved to France to direct ***Cela s'appelle l' aurore,*** one of the films he has found most satisfactory. Unfortunately, this film has not been shown in Mexico and I will have to limit myself to a quote from one of Buñuel's favorite critics, Georges Sadoul (who was also a surrealist at the time of ***Un chien andalou***). Sadoul, in his description of the film states: "A man, slave of his daily routine life and his own prejudices, comes to understand—through the drama of his own life—that he must move closer toward true liberty, love, and the people, not because he feels it is his duty but because his own honesty and character demand it." Sadoul speaks of the film as a model of purity and counterpoise. Buñuel also said in reference to the novel by Emmanuel Robles on which he based his film: "It is a story so perfectly pure."

In the following year (1956), Buñuel made a Franco-Mexican film, ***La mort en ce jardin.*** This film has not been shown in Mexico, in spite of the fact that it was shot in this country. I do not have, then, the elements necessary to judge it.

And, in 1958, Buñuel creates ***Nazarín.***

Nazarín is based on a novel by one of the most famous Spanish writers: Benito Perez Galdós (1843-1920). This man is considered by many as the greatest novelist Spain has had since Cervantes. His books take a prominent place in Buñuel's library as well as in the libraries of countless Spaniards. A liberal man of clear, healthy and profound ideas, Galdós is the author of a copious work which includes his famous "National Episodes." These "National Episodes" comment thoroughly on the history of Spain of the XIX century. His biographers estimate that Galdós created 8000 perfectly defined characters. It is only natural that this gallery would attract Buñuel, and, among them, the protagonist of the novel ***Nazarín*** possesses particular characteristics which explain the special attraction the film maker felt toward him.

The development of the film takes place in Mexico and not in Spain as does the novel upon which it is based. In spite of this, Buñuel has remained extremely true to the intention of the author insofar as the nature of the characters are concerned. Nazarin is, in the film, a humble and kindly young priest who lives in a sordid inn of the Mexico of 1900. It is the era of Porfirio Díaz, whose oligarchic powers Buñuel suggests through the deliberately somber atmosphere of the film. Nazarín, who survives on alms, finds himself forced to give refuge in his room to a poor prostitute called Andara. The police are searching for Andara who is accused of having knifed another woman. Nazarin, in turn, is interested in a hysterical servant, Beatriz, who has been abandoned by a man whom she loves and despises at the same time. Finding himself chased by the two women, Nazarín is forced to abandon the inn and to travel, like don Quixote, trying to be kind and good to the whole world. But everything turns out bad. He tries to find work in a railway unit and causes a conflict among the workers; he attends a sick girl and provokes the relatives of the girl, ignorant and superstitious women, to worship him hysterically as if he were a magician capable of producing miracles; in a town devastated by the plague he is not successful in helping anyone because his "spiritual" help does not mean anything to the inhabitants who are very desirous, above all, of remaining alive.

At the end, he is taken into jail where he comes in contact with a fellow inmate, a sacrilegious thief, who says to him: "We are not useful in any manner whatsoever, neither you who try to do good nor I who do evil." Nazarín is possessed by his first doubt. Under the strain of this doubt and accompanied by a guard he walks along the highway. Beatriz passes alongside him in her carriage and in the company of her despotic lover. A humble woman offers him a fruit and only this disinterested act seems to revive his faith. At first sight, what has happened to Nazarín could simply be said to be a transformation of his faith in the divine to faith in the human. This could be so in its broadest meaning but never within the temporal limits of the story in the film. Within these limits, Nazarín believes he has effectively recuperated his former faith, his faith in the divine, when he received the assistance of the woman whose fruit he accepted after a moment of hesitation. But that moment of hesitation is sufficiently expressive to understand that Buñuel, enemy of all dogmas, is indicating that the first doubt will be inevitably followed by many more. In effect what Nazarín feels when he hears the words of the sacrilegious is only the beginning of a long and contradictory psychic process which will result in the complete and total loss of Nazarín's faith.

The double beat on the drums during the last scene of the film symbolizes the Calvary ahead of Nazarín, Calvary which awaits not those who have faith but those who rebel against it—those who acquire that new type of faith represented by rebellion.

In the beginning, Nazarin, like all dogmatic men, has simplified to the maximum his scale of values. Good and evil are, for him, perfectly defined. Buñuel takes this man and confronts him with reality—reality as he, the director sees it, full of contradiction and mysteries. Nazarín feels how the meanings of things abandon him. Meaning which Buñuel himself does not try to explain. One of the important effects of the film lies in the contrast developed between the protagonist and the world around him; a world where a hump-back dwarf is capable of the most emotive platonic love; a world where a woman falls desperately in love with the man who harms her; a world inhabited by obsessive images transfigured by the subjective vision. How can we explain "reasonably" for example, the fact that a little girl, crying and dragging a white sheet suggests to us all the desolation and havoc of a town attacked by the plague?

Nazarín is a key film insofar as it gives up a good understanding of the thinking of its director, never so clearly expressed in his previous films. It is interesting to note, that in this instance Buñuel has expressed himself in a clear and perfectly understandable form. This form is completely free of the "paradoxical and inconsistent" montage of ***Un chien andalou.*** This indicates that very often an avant-garde form may cloak a lack of ability to express oneself properly. (This latter idea, by the way, is not always valid. We may apply it to Buñuel but not to Picasso, for example. The ways to art are made with constant negations). As I said before, it is quite possible that the Buñuel of ***Un chien andalou*** is the same Buñuel, basically, of ***Nazarín.*** But what Buñuel could only indicate in 1928 he says quite clearly thirty years later.

At this time it is almost redundant to say that Buñuel is an authentic "Author" of films. But we cannot consider him so merely because he has written as well as directed some of his best films. We are not concerned with that point. Buñuel is an authentic "Author" because he knows how to use the cinematographic image to express his most profound "Self." A long practice has been necessary to make possible the communication between Buñuel's "Self" and that of others through the means of his art.

The career of Buñuel is full of hesitations and obstacles precisely because of his determination to express himself completely. Buñuel has always resisted that "reasonable" path of shaping objective reality to one's adopted theories, to more or less identifying oneself with it and then to expose it "esthetically" with the ornaments of one's own style. The style of Buñuel is born without premeditation, as a consequence of the need to give form to what he wants to say. The film maker never resorts to any formal point merely to give exterior beauty to his work. Buñuel, then, is in no way a formalist. This is precisely why his famous "cruelty" is never superfluous. Buñuel does not resort to images in order to give himself a "personality," a way, a superficial style. Buñuel is "cruel" when his "Self," when expressed, must be so. And, in that same manner, he knows how to be tender.

Buñuel has given the freedom of expression to the most inner regions of his own self. He has let his instinct speak and he has given form to those associations of ideas, often inconsistent and absurd (our interior madnesses), which appear in the mind of every man. All this has been, it must be said, because of the desire of a true artist to know himself. Buñuel, non-conformist and rebel, searches in the subjective, as we have already seen, for elements which will prove the falsity of those moral, juridical, religious and political norms which try to reduce human reality to prescribed limits. The elements he searches for, however, must also give a more complete understanding to that same human reality.

But when Buñuel has searched in the subconscious of the paranoiac of ***El, Robinson Crusoe, Archibaldo de la Cruz,*** or ***Nazarín,*** placing his own self in the being of his characters, he has kept in mind that man must be studied "not isolated, as an individual case, but in relations with his fellow beings." That is, the deep penetration of the subjective does not exclude, but, on the contrary, presupposes the need to take into consideration the social nature of the human being. Because of this, in the work of Buñuel there is an analysis of the characters considered not as unique entities, isolated, but in the function of their representative social value. (We cannot say that Buñuel is always conscious of this point when he creates a character but, since he delineates him veridically, he cannot prevent the evidence of the social nature of the character. This is what happened, for example, in ***El***).

We have spoken previously of association of ideas. In Buñuel these do not have a symbolic value "a priori." This would deny the substance of the free exposition of subjective feelings. Buñuel's associations of ideas, the origin of violent contrasts, are not preconceived by any symbolic intention but arise from an intuitive and spontaneous process. This does not, however, prevent their having a symbolic explanation "a posteriori." The spectator must find it. And no two spectators will find the same explanation. Any object is viewed by each one of us in different form, "Each person charges with affectivity what he sees and nobody sees the object as it really is, but as his own desires and feelings wish to see it." Thus, Buñuel's film aspires to provoke among the spectators the most different feelings, always with a desire to disturb us, to stimulate our capacity for doubt and to create in us a constant dissatisfaction with our own ideas of reality—this in accordance with the mission given to the artist by Engels in a phrase Buñuel likes to quote: "The novelist (film maker) will have discharged his duty honestly when, through a faithful description of the authentic social relations, he will destroy the conventional ideas on the nature of these relations, will weaken the optimism of the burgeoisie world, and will force the reader (spectator) to doubt the perennity of the existing order, even though he may not indicate directly a conclusion or even take sides sensibly."

The paths of art are many and it cannot be said that the path followed by Buñuel is the most "advisable" to the majority of artists. It is a dangerous path, full of risks, and in this path, everything, absolutely everything, is entrusted to the moral strength of the artist. In the case of Buñuel it was necessary for him to possess rather uncommon moral virtues in order to prevent his subjectivism of method from degenerating into a subjectivism of content, in an aristocratic and puristic position. After his surrealistic attempts, and now that Buñuel has succeeded in expressing himself clearly, we have found a man who is extraordinarily conscious of his duties as an artist before society.

But we must see that Buñuel's is a social conscience determined by a powerful inner need, a social conscience which is expressed (inclusively) intuitively. There is in it a background of authentic sincerity difficult to find in some other types of film; i.e. the neo-realist where the overt purpose of reflecting and denouncing a social situation seems to include some enjoyment of the photogenic aspects of misery—adopting, also, the attitude of a devout donor of spiritual alms.

In our time there is a certain convenience in maintaining a "Standard" social conscience, whereby it is easy to feel in possession of a "complete" vision of reality. The admirable in Buñuel, that which makes him oppose all dogmas and isms, is a message of rebellion and his power to suggest to us an unlimited universe. And the universe is, truly, unlimited. (pp. 42-58)

Emilio Garcia Riera, "The Eternal Rebellion of Luis Bunuel," translated by Jack Bolanos, in Film Culture, *No. 21, Summer, 1960, pp. 42-60.*

Ado Kyrou (essay date 1962)

[*In the following excerpt, originally published in French in 1962, Kyrou examines Buñuel's film* Viridiana.]

You may remember Theda Bara and the fact that her name was an anagram of "Arab death." The famous man-eater—or her press agent—had cast about for a lurid label and found one.

With Buñuel it is a very different matter; his choice of the title [***Viridiana***] is, rather, one more triumph of instinct. The essence of the film is condensed in this admirable combination of "virus" and "Diana."

Let us indulge in a little wild speculation. (Isn't Buñuel himself, no matter what he is doing, always in something of a delirium?) The woman who could have been the huntress is attacked by a virus that makes her the quarry instead. The virus is Buñuel; the fabulous woman, who is prepared to explode anything and everything in her path, is that perennial victim of many faces who, from film to film, from ***Susana*** to ***El,*** attracts the virus by her femininity—and also by her strength, for victims are often stronger than their tormentors.

The title is happily chosen, then. It is a woman's name, and a woman who bears such a name already exists: she is beautiful, intense, and passionate, but these qualities are smothered by forces as powerful as they are futile. Such is the intelligence of a society that is able to channel mighty currents into seas that are calm and sometimes, in their stagnation, harmful.

As to theme, is there one? Do any of Buñuel's films have a theme? In any event, there is no conventional plot—which is one more way in which Buñuel is a poet.

Nevertheless, the public, snob or not, that frequents the movie houses requires some semblance of a story; ***Viridiana's*** is as simple as it is scandalous—scandalous not because it strives to be so, but because it is simple and obvious. At the age of sixty-one, Buñuel had achieved great serenity and lost the desire to shock; he had become a splendid wild creature spreading a salutary fear. ***Viridiana*** is a film that frightens those who have reason to be afraid.

L'Age d'Or was deliberately scandalous. The ***Viridiana*** scandal is unintentional and intrinsic. Buñuel himself is an object of scandal. He reveals himself in this film, pours all the wealth of his being into it until it bursts into flames. The fire is brilliant, but it is not for everyone.

Viridiana came about in this way. A Mexican producer, commissioning a film, said to Buñuel, "Do whatever you like. I won't interfere." Strangely, incredibly, the producer kept his word. Buñuel wrote his scenario, which he did not even show to the producer, and was preparing to film it in Mexico; the other man, meanwhile, was making financial arrangements for it to be produced in Spain. A co-producer was readily found. Franco and his secret police could hardly keep from tooting a triumphant horn. Think of it! The uncompromising Buñuel, a man who never concealed his—shall we say, unfriendly?—feelings for all dictatorships, but especially for the one that was ravaging his native country, was relenting, returning to the fold. Mere pecadilloes, those youthful excesses; once their rebellious stage is behind them, are not all Spaniards the natural sons of Franco and of that Most Holy and Apostolic Roman Catholic Church? Miró, Picasso, Cassals, Buñuel—and why boggle?—even those who died from the bullets of Fascism belong to us—even Lorca. Such is the boundless magnanimity of dictatorships and religion! All the while, the jails are jammed, and poverty lays waste to a magnificent country. In order to survive, men are obliged to become policemen, priests, or pederasts. This is no exaggeration, nor am I straying from my subject. (Do we ever stray from the subject, whatever it may be, if we shout aloud our hatred of dictatorship?)

For years, following a very astute policy, the Franco regime had been trying to recapture Buñuel. In fact, in 1951, when he was in Cannes in connection with the showing of ***Los Olvidados,*** he had already been officially approached. Fascism knows that it paralyzes all creative expression, and that first it must accept its enemies the better to muzzle them, then appropriate them, and by tarnishing their prestige, destroy them.

To talk to a Spaniard about his homeland is tantamount to winning him over, and Buñuel, who genuinely worships his family, and his mother in particular, had dreamed since 1936 of returning to Spain. And return he did, almost clandestinely, avoiding all publicity. When the producer informed him that ***Viridiana*** would be filmed in Spain, he agreed. To be once more among friends and brothers, to see and to smell the Spanish earth was, for a man fashioned of longings and dreams and instincts, a rare joy.

He definitely did not want his film to be sugar-coated, however—nor did he *want* to create a scandal. The Spanish censor read the material and found only a few details to be altered. (All censorship offices are staffed on principle with oblivious drones.) The dissatisfaction centered on the film's ending. Buñuel changed it, and in the process transformed it from the mediocre to the sublime. (Presently we will compare the two endings.) So even censorship helped Buñuel. And the bomb burst.

Viridiana is the freest of Buñuel's films that followed ***L'Age d'Or.*** What I have always loved above all else in him is the naïveté, even the unawareness, with which he injects his personal world into all that he does. Nothing is held back. He is unafraid; he pours forth his image with no qualms about the *déjà vu* or socalled bad taste. ***Viridiana*** is a film composed (as are ***L'Age d'Or*** and, to a lesser extent, ***El*** and ***Ensayo de un Crimen***) uniquely of Buñuel's obsessions and manias. ***Viridiana*** is the second pillar—the other being ***L'Age d'Or***—that supports the admirable Buñuelian edifice.

At one extreme, the shock of ***L'Age d'Or,*** a deliberate blow struck against prohibitions of any kind; at the other, ***Viridiana,*** created in perfect serenity and perhaps for that reason even more shocking. Buñuel's evolution lies between these poles. As he said to me, "Once upon a time, when I was offered the consecrated wafer I would spit on it; now I simply say, 'I couldn't care less.' " Once upon a time, anticlericalism and blasphemy; today, atheism, total tenderness, lightninglike sympathy for men and things. I have not reached Buñuel's age, but I think that the second attitude—which, for that matter, does not contravene the first but simply goes beyond it—is the more revolutionary. This would be true, obviously, only in the case of a personality like Buñuel's, containing within it all the forces of moral and social health, which he is able to project on the screen with the complete unselfconsciousness of the truly great.

In ***Viridiana*** Buñuel is no longer trying to convince the public of anything at all; he is no longer interested in generalizations; he simply offers images, his own photographic images, and thereby comes full circle, joining ***Viridiana*** to ***Un Chien Andalou.*** But if the earlier film remains pure visual shock, ***Viridiana*** goes further; it is a supremely profound moral and perceptual shock, for the simple images of Buñuel are at once tender and abusive, grand and strident, sublime and gross—they are like the draperies that hang in romantic rooms where anything can happen.

For all that he is no longer trying to make a point with his public, Buñuel, despite himself, launches into a vast dialogue with those who are prepared to be enriched by the nature of the man who is addressing them.

He used to say to me that it is not his intention to photograph the "impious," and that if there were a "pious" image that seemed to him interesting or sympathetic, he would certainly put it in a film. "But," he added, with a little smile, "no pious images come to mind." There is not a trace of affectation or trickery, much less any calculation, in Buñuel. His eyes are filled with extraordinary images, and we must be grateful to him for showing them to us, for they are the supreme expression of man's total liberation. Buñuel is a free man and believes that others should be as free as he—which is why he sometimes balks at explaining himself. ***Viridiana,*** however, is so personal a film that no further statement from him is necessary.

Viridiana is a novice in a convent. She is about to take her vows. Her only relative is a somewhat elderly uncle, Don Jaime, of whom she is not very fond because he has never concerned himself with her. Her Mother Superior insists, however, that she go to see her uncle, who has sent for her, before she takes the veil. Viridiana is most reluctant to make the trip. This beautiful young woman is absorbed in her devotion to her God and her convent, and she has a presentiment that "outside" everything is dangerous; like all people in the grip of false ideals, she fears experiences that threaten to unseal her eyes.

Already in this first sequence we have several Buñuelian themes. Wishing to be "kind," the Mother Superior unconsciously pushes Viridiana toward catastrophe. The curé of ***La Mort en Ce Jardin*** had this same kindness. "Kindness" (remember ***Nazarín,*** too) is a monstrosity, and "noble" motives can lead to results exactly the opposite of those anticipated.

In the Buñuelian world—of all worlds the most realistic because the most unexpected—everything is possible, even the consequence most at variance with human intentions.

So, in obedience to her Mother Superior, Viridiana arrives at her uncle's estate. He lives alone, neglecting his properties, and is cared for by a servant, Ramona, whom he took in some years earlier together with her little daughter.

As Don Jaime receives Viridiana, he says to her, "You will live here as you do in the convent." Then, wishing to show that he is as kind as the nuns, he saves a bee that is drowning in a tub of water.

All the uneasiness that already grips the novice is echoed in the phrase "as you do in the convent." That is to say, what does go on in the convent? Perhaps some day Buñuel will answer that question with another film—but does not Monk Lewis' *The Monk* already provide an answer?

In the uncle's gesture, we see again the fascination that insects have for Buñuel. His heroes destroy them in hate (***L'Age d'Or, Abismos de Pasión***), helplessly endure them (***Un Chien Andalou, L'Age d'Or, Las Hurdes***), egg them on to kill each other (***Robinson Crusoe***), or, ironically, refuse to kill them (***Ensayo de un Crimen***). All Buñuel's work belongs under the sign in the prologue of ***L'Age d'Or,*** does it not? The insect is a cold and terrible thing, the monster par excellence that may tomorrow become master of the world. Buñuel is closely related to Lautréamont.

One insect suffices to create atmosphere: unease enters and pervades the scene. One simple detail seemingly in no way connected with what is conventionally called the "action" enriches the film first by its visual impact, which reinforces realism to the point of surrealism, and secondly by its disturbing appearance, which announces the manifold surprises to follow.

A subjective note: the attraction of insects is introduced instinctively, in an almost irrational way, and as a result the film advances to a higher level of meaning; it goes beyond the merely anecdotal and becomes the reflection of a complex, irradiant world.

To return to Don Jaime, whom we are beginning to know better. This still hale old man has a great secret. He had passionately loved his wife, who died of a heart attack on their wedding night before they had had time to make love. Like the hero of ***El,*** Don Jaime respected the marriage laws, and in consequence developed a pronounced neurosis. He has, it is true, one illegitimate son, whose existence he tries to ignore because he was born of a union unsanctified by the Church, but his one love experience has been disastrous. Ramona, his servant, is patently willing to sleep with him, but the old man cannot even conceive of such a liaison. He is reduced to eying the legs of her daughter as the little girl jumps rope, and to becoming aroused by trying on his dead wife's wedding gown. Voyeurism and masturbation, accordingly, are the elements of

Don Jaime's sexuality, for all that he is a "noble," "believing," and "worthy" man.

Voyeurs are quite frequent in Buñuel's work; the hotel sequence in ***El*** is a minute analysis of the sickly dread of the voyeur. Don Jaime is more subtle. His motivation is no doubt unconscious when he presents the little girl with a new jumping rope that has one revealing characteristic: it has wooden handles, very phallic handles that the child must grip tightly as she jumps and twists and turns in a series of complicated maneuvers that make her socks slip down. The rope is a kind of Ariadne's thread that guides us through the entire film; we will meet it several times again.

Masturbation is present in ***L'Age d'Or*** (repetition of gesture, feathers, etc.) and is also one of the themes in ***El*** and ***Robinson Crusoe.*** In ***Viridiana,*** as, for that matter, also in ***Robinson Crusoe*** and in the first sequence of ***Ensayo*** it is complicated by transvestitism and, as in ***El, Ensayo,*** and ***Robinson Crusoe,*** by a foot fetish.

Every evening Don Jaime opens a large trunk and takes out his wife's wedding gown and the other clothing that she was wearing when she died. To recapture her beloved image, he tries these garments on himself. He first puts on her high-heeled shoes, then her corset. Lacing the corset tightly, he goes to the mirror and looks at himself for a long time. Thus the boy in ***Ensayo*** puts on his mother's corset as a joke, before he discovers the erotic pleasure it gives him to look at his teacher's corpse. Thus Friday dresses up as a woman, which disturbs the prudish Robinson.

The legs and feet of women, and, by extension, their shoes, are a curious constant in Buñuel's films. The hero of ***El*** falls in love with a woman's feet; in ***Ensayo,*** a coquette puts her stocking on a gaming table; in ***Susana*** "respectable" people eye the feet of a "fallen" girl. In ***Viridiana,*** the foot becomes even more obsessive than in ***El.*** Don Jaime plays the organ, and his feet, which we see in a close-up, are monstrous, for they are the same feet that he tries to slip into a woman's shoes.

The moment Viridiana arrives, her uncle notices her feet. His plans begin to take shape: the feet of the novice can wear the dead woman's shoes. For Don Jaime finds a strange resemblance between his niece and his dead wife. His niece must be, then, the wife who for him has never died.

The first day Viridiana spends on the estate is only outwardly calm. The novice has brought along all her religious paraphernalia—a heavy cross, a stone, a hammer, nails, and a crown of thorns. These assorted instruments of torture are among the surrealist elements to be found in several Buñuel films. Automatism and irrational enumeration are disturbing, especially when associated with a young and pretty woman. Is there a spectator who will not ask himself what the purpose of such objects may be? Are they customary in the convent? But, as I said earlier, let us await the film in which Buñuel will reveal convent life to us.

Viridiana arranges these instruments of piety and torture in her room. During the meal that follows, she indulges in the little game of peeling an apple with a single circular motion. Previously, in the dream in ***Subida,*** the sustained peeling motion united variously the lovers and the son and the mother, thus becoming the umbilical cord.

I have no intention of explaining every detail in the film. On the contrary, in an instance such as the fruit peeling I am astonished by the irrational element that governs the sequence. I asked Buñuel about it, but he had forgotten even the existence of the peeling scene in ***Subida*** and had no idea why he used this detail at this particular point. This, then, is freedom in action; this is the constant intervention of imagination freed of all logical restraints in a work that never seeks to explain itself any more than we attempt to explain our own dreams while we are dreaming.

The second day the uneasiness mounts. The uncle wants to keep the girl with him. Finally he confesses his strange love, but only after he has asked the maid for help and she, devoted to him body and soul (Don Jaime feels no compunction in letting her understand that she is virtually his slave), is prepared to serve her master in everything.

So the servant is an accomplice; what is worse is that the old gentleman, finding himself in a dilemma, must demean himself by asking help from a person he despises. You will remember the hero of ***El,*** weeping before his valet, and the indifference of the guests in ***L'Age d'Or*** when confronted by the dramas that were taking place in the kitchen quarters.

While a spider's web is being spun around Viridiana, she is tasting for the first time the "wholesome joys of the country" and beginning to understand that everything on this earth will, in spite of herself, remind her that she is a woman. A farm hand is milking a cow, and suddenly she longs for a drink of milk. What more innocent desire? Yet the farm hand, no less innocent, urges her, "Try your hand at milking her!" "But—I don't know how!" "Try!" She kneels and reaches timidly for the teat. Now, a teat has a very definite form, and the hand of the novice does not dare, does not want to touch it.

The girl is a sleepwalker. She gets out of bed and, carrying a basket with knitting needles and wool, enters the room where Don Jaime listens endlessly to the Mozart Requiem. She throws needles and wool into the fireplace and then scatters the ashes on her uncle's bed beside the dead wife's bridal wreath, which he has not had time to hide. This brief scene, resembling surrealist collages (a young girl in her nightgown enters an old man's bedroom and throws ashes on his bed), illustrates once again the working of Buñuel's mind, which is more than ever profoundly surrealist. Also, following on the scene with the teat, this erotic scene carries us still further into the unexpected.

Viridiana, who has previously indulged in a highly obscene strip tease (a nun's strip tease, after all!) when she discovers that under her supremely unfeminine garments—heavy stockings, coarse underwear—she is very beautiful, is not at all upset to learn on awakening that she has suffered a sleepwalking attack. "It happens to me at the convent, too." However, things are not so simple as they seem. She wants to leave and regain the safety of the convent in whose familiar waters she can move about without creating problems for herself. The uncle cannot prevent it, so he begs her to do him one last favor—to wear her aunt's gown. Viridiana is shocked, but she gives in to an old man's "harmless" caprice. He, in the presence of Ramona, pays fervent court to this dual woman. He finally confesses his deepest desire and asks her to marry him—or, rather, Ramona acts as intermediary and puts the question for him. Viridiana refuses, obviously. She starts to leave the room, the uncle calms her, asks her forgiveness, and Ramona pours the coffee that we know has been drugged. Viridiana falls asleep. Don Jaime picks up her inert body, dismisses Ramona (who goes looking for her daughter), and carries Viridiana to the bed.

Ramona's little daughter is upset. She has seen "the big black bull come in through the ceiling." In a film in which all the characters are poetic, this girl is the most poetic of all. She, more than any of the others, represents Buñuel. Like him, she is afraid of animals who become mythical creatures: the giraffe (***L'Age d'Or***), the mangy dog (***Subida, Los Olvidados***), the cocks (***Los Olvidados, El Bruto***), the pigeon (***Los Olivadados, Viridiana***), the tortoise (***Cela S'Appelle l'Aurore***), not to mention all the animals of ***Las Hurdes, Nazarín, La Mort en Ce Jardin,*** etc. They comprise a disturbing bestiary. They are portents, harbingers of trouble and catastrophe. The black bull of the girl's imagination hovers over the house of Don Jaime. Ramona's daughter, more curious than her mother, wants to see the bull and to find out what he has brought with him. So she climbs a tree and through the window watches Don Jaime worshiping the unconscious body of Viridiana.

The kiss he gives the young woman in the wedding gown recalls the orchestra leader's kissing Lya Lys (***L'Age d'Or***) and the kissing of the dead woman in ***Abismos de Pasión.***

The uncle's eyes devour his niece. First the feet, of course; then he opens her bodice and looks at her breasts; finally he falls upon her but at the last moment restrains himself from rape. Did he renounce making love to his wife in the same way, when he saw that she was dead?

The next day, however, he believes he has an unanswerable argument that will keep Viridiana on the estate. He lies to her, pretending that he has raped her. The young woman feels the earth rock under her feet. She is no longer pure, she can no longer enter the convent. She runs blindly away, not caring where she goes.

She is about to board a bus when the authorities intercept her and take her back to the estate. "There's been an accident." Her uncle has killed himself. He has hung himself with the little girl's jumping rope—which the child quickly recovers despite the injunction that "a hangman's rope brings bad luck."

With this, the first part—or, rather, the prologue—of the film ends.

Viridiana cannot return to the convent. Convinced that she has been raped and believing herself (rightly, for that matter) the cause of her uncle's suicide, she feels corrupted. Her faith, however, is strong; like Nazarín, she wants, even outside the Church, to continue to be a Christian. She is now beyond the boundaries of what one could call clericalism and has little or nothing to do with "the true Christian vocation."

As he moves her out of an official religious context, Buñuel unconsciously casts about for a difficulty. Everyone (even the fiercest champions of the Roman Church) attacks external aspects of religion—erring curés, erring flocks, even errant rites—but this is done in order the better to defend the essence of religion.

Christianity—in this, like any well-established religion—is a vast enterprise of coercion, the purpose of which is the defense of the established social and moral order. Channeling the people's need for the miraculous, it contributes brilliantly to the maintenance of that order at whatever cost.

Since this is an inadmissable objective, since the Pope cannot say, "Pray so that you will forget about going out on strike," religion hides its bloodstained hands (witness the wars of religion, the Inquisition, etc.) in gloves of immaculate whiteness. These gloves bear high-sounding names—pity, charity, Christian love, renunciation.

"Pure" spirits see only the gloves, never imagining that inside them are murderous fingers, and they serve the gloves, not knowing that they are thus fortifying the hands. Still purer spirits want blindly to carry out all the orders given by the gloves, eliminating, knowingly or not, the hands that animate them. But gloves without hands are lifeless casings, and any directions they give are lifeless, too.

The hands of religion drive Viridiana out, as Nazarín was driven out, and she thereupon seizes upon the gloves as if they were invested with a life of their own. As a result, while the novice renounces her vows, she does not give up being a Christian. She installs herself in one of the detached buildings on the estate, and when the worried Mother Superior comes to find out what has happened to her, she refuses to tell her real reasons for isolating herself and giving up the monastic life forever. The exasperated Mother Superior insists: "You must tell me everything. I order you to tell me." To no effect. The hand is withdrawn, the glove remains. The separation is complete.

Hypocrites aside, no one dares defend the bloody hand of religion. Let us now see how the immaculate glove can defend itself alone. (I was right to say that Buñuel is looking for a difficulty.)

Like Lizardi, Nazarín, and the naïve curé in ***El,*** Viridiana is moved by all the great Christian precepts that weave the fabric of the gloves, and she wants to do good. In a nearby village she gathers up beggars, tramps, cripples, various old people, a blind man, and a leper, and she installs them in a part of her uncle's house, where she now lives, hoping to "save" them.

Jorge, the illegitimate son of Don Jaime, also arrives, accompanied by a rather ordinary young woman who is his current mistress. He is the sole heir, and so comes as master of the estate.

Jorge is an architect. It seems that for Buñuel this profession represents a kind of security, a mental well-being, a way of thinking that is stripped of poetry, a materialism not far removed from rationalism. Jorge resembles the young man who is so concerned about time toward the end of ***Un Chien Andalou,*** and especially the architect Raoul, in ***El.*** In other circumstances, he would also resemble the anarchist, Marchal, in ***La Mort en Ce Jardin.*** Jorge is never in doubt about anything. For that matter, he does not think much; he possesses the common sense that is so contrary to the "no-sense" of the monsters. He differs from the neurotics and exalted poets who are Buñuel's real heroes. Jorge is also "healthy" and therefore "good," but not to excess, just as he is "bad," but, again, not to excess. He is normal. He is a man who loves to be alive, to eat, to drink, to make love, but he is incapable of great passion.

The new master is amused by Viridiana's "whims." He is also very much attracted by her but is quickly discouraged. Making advances to a slightly touched mystic is a waste of time, the more so since he must busy himself about the estate. He launches various projects to clear the land and restore the big house. Being a practical man, he wants to make this capital that has fallen into his lap turn a profit for him.

To Viridiana he comes as a great surprise. There are, then, such coarse spirits who boast of their lack of faith, who admit that they offend against moral laws. Still, she accepts him, almost forgives him, for is she not a Christian? And, in any case, she must busy herself with her derelicts.

They are all monsters—not only the dwarf and the blind man, and not only in a physical sense. They are monsters because, like Nazarín's prison companions, they represent "evil."

Note that when in a Buñuel film we meet "good" (Viridiana, for example) or "evil" (her protégés) this does not mean what it means in the films of other people because for Buñuel absolute good and absolute evil are beguiling, impassioning monstrosities. Buñuel loves Viridiana the pure as well as her impure wards. Were the world composed only of Jorges, it would not be viable, for in this child of nature the two elements of good and evil do not coexist; indeed, they are lacking altogether. Dr. Jekyll is a remarkable person, as Mr. Hyde is, also, and doubtless their coexistence would have produced a genius, a dual monstrosity—perhaps perfection.

We come here, I think, to the essential in all Buñuel's work. With a miraculous serenity, this extraordinary man, who is so drawn by the unusual and the rare, achieves a major synthesis, uniting in his hatred all that is mediocre and uniting in his love all that is exceptional and shocking, all that threatens to rock the foundations of our everlastingly tedious way of thinking, our shoddy way of living. He loves all these monsters, never forgetting that some monstrosities are more necessary than others. Thus he has the poor priest Lizardi killed by a mystical madman. He saves Nazarín by infecting his mind with doubt. He will save Viridiana by hurling her into the midst of life.

Again let us not forget that Buñuel is a Spaniard, like Zurbarán, Goya, Lazarillo, like the dynamiters of the Civil War. He loves monsters; they are his children, even if because of their nature he prefers some to others, and even if he seeks to channel their monstrosity.

For Buñuel the true monsters, the ones whom he despises, are the men and women who are incapable of loving excessively, of being wrong and of revolting, always to excess; the men and women who are not really alive; the zombies we meet daily in the street, on the subway, everywhere, whom dutifully learned precepts and habits corrupt.

Buñuel is a humane man, with a genuine capacity for love, who is devoted to de Sade because de Sade was the same sort of man, also capable of love and prepared to pay in his own person for his great rebellions. De Sade stands at the opposite pole from petty Nazi torturers or the bloody killer-heroes of cheap fiction, from small-time murderers or the promoters of genocide and the atomic bomb droppers. De Sade was a liberator and he knew how to hate precisely because he was capable of love.

"I love all men, but I do not love the society that some of them have created!" Buñuel says, obviously meaning by "society" the whole contemporary moral and social order. He loves all his characters who do not represent that order, all the outsiders. With one exception: the blind. Buñuel once told a journalist that the only antipathetic character in ***Viridiana*** is the blind beggar. The beggar is hypocritical, evil, repugnant from every point of view; it is he, furthermore, who stands for Christ in a scene from the film that will be discussed presently.

In ***L'Age d'Or,*** Modot vengefully kicks a blind man; the blind man in ***Los Olvidados*** is an old lecher dreaming of revenge and denouncing the boys he exploits, like his confrere in *Lazarillo de Tormes.*

Except for the blind men, then, the troupe that Viridiana wants to save is made up of men and women no worse than you or I. They are "evil" because that's the way they have turned out, because heredity and education drove them in that direction. Until they meet the young missionary, they have lived from hand to mouth, begging by the church door, maybe stealing here and there a bit of bread or a few pennies. They belong to the *Lumpenproletariat,* which is no longer capable of rebellion; they accept their situation and at the most grouse about it. They are the necessary reverse side of the gilded coin: the poor must exist so that the rich, as they come from Mass, can give them alms.

One of these beggars, however, sees that he will become a slave to Viridiana's complexes about kindness, and he does rebel. He wants to be free. After announcing his decision to his would-be benefactress, he has the further effrontery to ask her for a handout. This is the kind of sublime character one finds only in Buñuel. Here in a film of great violence is one simple detail invested with all the dignity and pride in the world. Here is someone who, choosing to be free, dares mock his "benefactress" by forcing her to perform the ritual gesture of charity in behalf of someone who has just spat upon it.

Two servants on the estate presently display a similar dignity. They refuse to have anything to do with this strange asylum and go off, leaving Viridiana alone with her flock, while Jorge and his workmen labor nearby.

Viridiana's little "ideal society" gets itself organized, the tramps taking over the kitchen while the beggars work at whatever they have some aptitude for. The whole charming community works in the fields as well, for the queen of their kingdom believes that if she is giving them food and lodging, and especially if she is saving their souls, they should toil. Is this not how the Bible justifies man's exploitation of man?

Viridiana's protégés play along with consummate hypocrisy. Are they not all believers? "With all the troubles I've got, if I didn't have faith . . . !" one of them says. Only the leper finds it hard to be accepted as one of the group; being a Christian does not help anyone not to fear leprosy.

The leper deserves special attention. He has tried to cure himself with holy water. Results: negative. He feels alone. The others make him drag an old iron box behind him so that people can hear him approach. He chases some pigeons and catches one, which he hides inside his shirt. Without question, he is the most solitary figure in all Buñuel's work, not excepting Robinson Crusoe—and we know how powerfully obsessed by solitude Buñuel is. In ***L'Age d'Or,*** Modot throws white feathers out the window, and, in the same way, during the orgy that presently ensues, the solitary leper scatters the feathers of the pigeon he has undoubtedly already eaten. According to Freud's interpretation, feathers are a clear symbol of masturbation. You will remember that as a solitary Puritan Robinson rejects masturbation and, upon the arrival of Friday, also homosexuality. So solitude is one further form of the monstrous.

Viridiana, at last, is happy and full of smiles. "Her children" provide her with the opportunity to be a saint. She is the very incarnation of charity, and great is her reward when at evening in the fields, her chorus of tramps intone a ringing Angelus.

Here the cinemagraphic genius of Buñuel is again evident. Utilizing a parallel montage, he alternates the Angelus scenes with shots of the men working on the estate. Every time the tramps pronounce the name of God, the Virgin, or Christ, we pass without transition to shots of timber falling with a sinister crash, mortar being thrown on bricks, cement being mixed. The visual shock is extraordinary and, if one wishes, all possible revolutionary symbols can be seen in the contrast, but I think that the heavy accent on the holy names is sufficient.

Jorge, the rationalist, the unbeliever, is the hero of a fable that parallels the charitable efforts of Viridiana and that perfectly expresses Buñuel's intention. This is the fable of the dog and the cart.

At a certain point, a cart comes down the road. A mongrel dog is tied to the cart, which is rattling along apace, its good Christian owner being in a hurry to sell his merchandise. The exhausted dog is dragging its feet and seems on the verge of collapse, perhaps even of death. The upstanding young architect sees this scene, pities the dog, and speaks to the driver.

"You could put that poor dog in your wagon.
He'll die if he has to go on like that."
"A dog doesn't belong in a wagon."
"Then unleash him, at least."
"No, he has to be leashed."
"Sell him to me!"
"I won't say no to that."

The transaction is quickly concluded, and Jorge goes off happily with his dog, who looks back at his old master with a certain regret. Jorge, very proud of himself for having saved one dog, does not see another wagon, identical to the first, coming from the opposite direction and dragging with it a dog even more spent than the first.

As a fable, this is far more instructive than all the foolishness of La Fontaine.

Jorge does not hesitate to tell Viridiana his opinion of her project. What he cannot understand is why she has chosen the ugliest of all the beggars. He does not realize that the uglier the beggar, the more deserving of charity he is.

Soon Jorge's mistress becomes jealous of Viridiana and she leaves her lover, who promptly finds consolation by going to bed with the maid, Ramona. Jorge bears no resemblance to his father; he is one to take advantage of every opportunity that comes his way, he lives by exploiting everything. As I have said before, he is an atrociously normal man.

But the drama is not slow to explode. The fine Christian order Viridiana has established collapses.

I use the word "drama" ironically, since before going further I must emphasize the fact that ***Viridiana*** is a comedy or, in any case, a comic film. Buñuel's humor—macabre, obviously—is present in every shot. It has never been more searing than at the end of ***Viridiana.***

Ramona's little daughter has to have a tooth pulled in the village, and her mother goes with her. Jorge must go with Viridiana to a notary to sign some papers. The beggars find themselves sole masters of the estate.

The tramps begin by inspecting rooms that until then had been closed to them, and quite soon they are rifling the drawers for luxurious table linens. A lamb is slaughtered, and the company assembles, "like the masters," around the large dining table for a feast. Only the leper sits apart.

Soon, with the help of wine, this splendid banquet turns into an orgy. There is much storytelling and rolling under the table, until one of the women has an amusing inspiration. She will immortalize the scene by taking a photograph with, she specifies, an old camera that her parents had given her, which still works.

In grouping themselves, they reproduce as if by chance da Vinci's *Last Supper.* The blind man, the one evil man in the film, is none other than Christ; the cripples, the dwarfs, and the leper are the apostles.

No sooner have they struck this pose than we hear the stentorian crowing of a cock (again a cock, and here all the more disturbing because he also crows in the Bible). The woman who is to take the photograph moves in front of the table and, in an utterly obscene gesture, lifts her skirts.

Not since the ending of ***L'Age d'Or*** has Buñuel achieved so free a sequence. Everything about it is great, incredible, marvelously simple.

There are incorrigibles, I know, who insist that blasphemy is the token of great piety, that one must believe in order to want to destroy what one believes, and such nonsense. But let us be serious. Let us suppose that we were to say that every man, every Christian who does not blaspheme, is depriving himself of that pleasure because in his heart of hearts he does not believe. The great atheists, in this case, would be Claudel, Mauriac, the Pope. . . . How easy it is to reverse specious arguments! Or to put it another way: Would an old-line Communist who had been tortured under the czars have no right to curse the memory of his torturers without being accused of being secretly pro-czarist?

Furthermore, I must repeat that Buñuel is no longer trying to be blasphemous. He very serenely and simply offers us violent, hilarious images. As any psychoanalyst can explain, everyone's freely associated images are conditioned by the individual's childhood and education, especially if one has fought, rejected, conquered, and gone beyond those early experiences.

On the other hand, the almost pornographic eroticism in blasphemy is characteristic of the Spanish spirit. Let us not forget that the richest, most splendid oaths are Spanish.

The tramps' orgy is made up of little Goya-like tableaux. The violence of these scenes seems to me unique in the history of the cinema. Misshapen bodies copulate behind a handsome divan. "You have to do a lot of sinning to be able to do a good job of repenting," one of the beggars says. They empty Don Jaime's trunk, dance to the Mozart Requiem, which someone has put on the gramophone. The female dwarf, the cripples, and the leper dress up in the bridal gown and veils of Don Jaime's dead wife. Others, too drunk to stand up, sit and admire: "You would call it *Ecce Homo.*"

An informer tells the blind man that the beggar woman he occasionally sleeps with is making love at that very moment with another man, and the jealous blind man wrecks everything in reach with his cane. The vast room, through which the Requiem still sounds, is now a sordid shambles.

At this point, Viridiana, Jorge, Ramona, and the little girl arrive home. The latter two run back to the village for help, while the cousins enter the house in time to see the heroes of this memorable dinner stagger away as fast as they can. The blind man gets entangled in the bride's veil.

The leper and one other man remain alone in the bedroom of the late Don Jaime to receive Jorge and Viridiana. Their reception is rather special, for while the leper attacks and binds Jorge, the other man, who is wearing the little girl's jumping rope as a belt, tries to rape Viridiana.

This second near-rape is much more than just an attempt, for even if the beggar does not achieve his purpose, Viridiana, who is wide awake this time, finally learns the nature of the carnal act. Buñuel underlines this very precisely: in her struggle, the young woman seizes the handles of her attacker's improvised belt with both hands. And so the circle is complete: the uncle gives the jumping rope to the little girl so that he can watch her dance, he hangs himself

Parody of Leonardo da Vinci's Last Supper *in* Viridiana.

with it when his erotic dreams become unattainable, and through the same rope Viridiana encounters sex.

Jorge regains consciousness and, to save Viridiana from her attacker, bribes the leper, who is standing by, waiting his turn: "Perhaps when he's finished he'll pass her on to me." The lust for money is even stronger than sexuality; the leper kills his friend with a fireplace shovel and frees Viridiana.

Only then do the police arrive.

Once order has been restored, there remains the epilogue. It is made up of two sequences, both high points in Buñuel's achievement.

Having seen the consequences of her charity and having, to a degree, known a man, Viridiana feels lost. Who was she? Who is she? Her religious paraphernalia, like her dress, have become meaningless.

One evening, we find the little girl sitting before a wood fire. She is playing with Viridiana's crown of thorns. The object intrigues and amuses her, but one of the thorns pricks her finger and she throws the crown into the fire.

Is there any sight more beautiful than a burning crown of thorns? The child is wonderstruck; she takes a stick and pulls the crown from the fire, the better to watch it burn.

Here again Buñuel's immense tenderness breaks through. The little girl is beauty itself; she is all purity, all poetry. She has not yet been destroyed by middle-class morals and prohibitions; she is still capable of appreciating the sublime image of the burning crown. If there is a symbol beyond this image, so much the better, but I am sure that for Buñuel it is merely the power of the image, the rest being instinct. The great revolutionary poems are like that—for example, those of Lautréamont and Rimbaud.

The second part of the epilogue offers some hints about Viridiana's future.

The original ending of the film had shocked the Spanish censor, who insisted that Buñuel find an alternative. The first version had Jorge and Ramona playing *belote*, and it is clear that they have just made love. Viridiana arrives, bewildered and haggard. Not knowing what to do or where to turn, she comes to see the man who can offer her the many marvelous things that she is only now beginning to glimpse. Delighted with this windfall, Jorge dismisses Ramona and closes the door behind her. The maid spies through the keyhole.

Spanish censorship winced. This was impossible; the public would perfectly well understand that Jorge and Viridiana were making love. Never! This must be changed. So Buñuel changed it, with the result that a felicitous but fairly tame ending became sublime.

Nothing is altered up to the point where Viridiana arrives, but then Jorge does not send Ramona away. He invites Viridiana to sit down, and the three of them, good companions all, play a hand of *belote*. Jorge has the last line in the film: "I knew very well that one day we would all play a little game together."

All this takes place to the accompaniment of a crude rock 'n' roll record that Jorge has put on the phonograph. So, a film that opened musically with Handel's Hallelujah Chorus, which is played during the credits, ends with rock 'n' roll. The whole evolution of Viridiana follows the sound track. The Mozart Requiem serves as the sound background for the erotic follies of the uncle and the Hallelujah Chorus for the beggars' orgy, but for the "little game" *à trois*, we have rock 'n' roll.

Viridiana has discarded the trappings of holiness to move out into life, beginning with something that could not be flatter or more humdrum, a little game of cards.

Such is the destiny of saints who recognize how inane is their sanctity. Perhaps Viridiana will be saved—and on this point the film ends, for Viridiana no longer interests Buñuel unless, rescued from religion, she someday becomes a monster of another sort—a sublime monster, perhaps, and no longer a ridiculous or merely moving one. Maybe she will become a great lover or a revolutionary. For the moment, our heroine has moved into the prevailing order; she learns to play *belote*, and she plays with the man who will certainly go to bed with her.

Other Buñuel characters have completed their cinematic (but not their human) destiny in the same fashion, for creating points of suspension is one of Buñuel's great strengths—for instance, Francisco in the monastery (***El***), or, even earlier, Modot throwing the feathers of solitude out the window (***L'Age d'Or***). And is not the calm that is re-established after the arrest in ***Susana*** similar, and the cure in ***Ensayo de un Crimen*** equally ambiguous?

In ***Viridiana*** Buñuel has given us his most fully realized work in that it is the most freely personal. The government officials were not wrong when they banned the film in Spain, even forbade any mention of it in the press, and fired the censorship employee responsible for allowing this affront to religion to pass. And let us not speak of the articles in the Catholic press, and the *mea culpas* of the simpletons who dared claim that ***Nazarín*** was a Christian film. (pp. 77-99)

Ado Kyrou, in his Luis Buñuel: An Introduction, *translated by Adrienne Foulke, Simon and Schuster, 1963, 208 p.*

Michel Estève (essay date 1963)

[*In the following essay, originally written in French in 1963, Estève analyzes the themes and imagery of Buñuel's film* The Exterminating Angel, *comparing this film to Jean-Paul Sartre's play* Huis clos *(1945).*]

Free, at last, of financial worries, and sufficiently known and appreciated to impose his own views upon his productions, Luis Buñuel has become the grand master of the cinema he could never have been in the era of silent films. In releasing three fine pictures one after another, ***Nazarin, Viridiana,*** and ***The Exterminating Angel,*** he has shown himself indisputable an artist of the first rank.

The Exterminating Angel (the name, if I remember rightly, given Green's protagonist in Moïra who was obsessed by a false purity, and the title of the unpublished play by

José Bergamin) is not Buñuel's most satisfactory film. But the richness of its inspiration makes it a key film which throws his other works into a profound relief.

Luis Buñuel is by nature, almost by instinct, a visionary, a poet of the screen. Like a novelist, who uses an association of images, both real and imaginary, to create a flow of action and to breathe life into his characters, the author of ***Un Chien Andalou*** bases his films on the unfolding of an image, or the memory of a landscape. Of ***Viridiana*** Buñuel himself once said: "I thought of the story for the film in Mexico; it came from an image. This is the way I proceed every time, and the whole work gushes forth like a fountain. . . ." According to Buñuel's son, Juan, the idea for ***The Exterminating Angel*** originated in the famous painting by Géricault, *The Raft of Medusa.*

The reader may well ask what possible connection can be established between the two tattered creatures, prisoners of the sea tormented by hunger and thirst, and Nobile's elegant guests, gathered together in a luxurious manor house after an evening at the opera. Indeed, the connection is at first surprising, but it is completely justified, as a close examination of the progression of sequences will show. For these elite aristocrats—nobles, generals, magistrates of the court—find themselves, once dinner is over, quite unable to leave the salon. No apparent reason is given; in fact, the doors remain wide open, yet not one of them can bring himself to cross the room and step over the threshold. Cutaways wilt, ball gowns rumple, paint and coiffure little by little shift and fade, until the elegance of dress and manner has given way entirely to a vulgarity of mien and attitude. Hunger and thirst become progressively more insistent. So, by the end of the first evening, the midnight guests and Géricault's castaways have become recognizable companions in distress.

The Exterminating Angel, however, is not simply a cinematic transposition of Géricault's canvas. Nobile's salon, a latter-day raft of Medusa, is also the Second Empire drawing room of *No Exit;* indeed, Buñuel's film suggests Sartre's hell much more forcefully than Jacqueline Audrey's mediocre production.

The connections between *No Exit* and ***The Exterminating Angel*** are numerous and significant. In both, the basic story is quite simple, the setting and the action equally symbolic. In Sartre and in Buñuel, we are given a parable that points an accusing finger at the basic state of human life. In the opening scenes of the film, the ponderous gates swinging shut upon Nobile's posh estate, 1109 Providence Street (an ironic twist typical of Buñuel), hint to the spectator of the sequestering that awaits the characters. With the exception of the very last sequence, the action takes place in a single setting: Nobile's modern Mexican salon of 1962, which corresponds to the 1860 salon in *No Exit.* Both artists choose details for their overt symbolism. The bronze on the mantel obviously represents the "pure" object, the "self" as Sartre conceived it, deprived of consciousness. The presence of a letter opener and the absence of books implies a dissolution of cultural values. In ***The Exterminating Angel,*** art itself is reduced to nothingness, when the pianist can extract from her instrument nothing more than plaintive monotones, and again when the elegant company breaks up the cellos to build a fire. In Sartre's drawing room, with the door bolted on the outside and the bell broken, help from without is inconceivable. In Buñuel, the characters, as if held in by an invisible force, cannot leave in spite of the open doors, and the curious bystanders who wait outside cannot be of any service whatsoever. In both Sartre and Buñuel, the one room becomes a closed universe, with no passage to the exterior world.

Several years ago, Buñuel made this statement: "On the screen time and space become flexible; they expand and contract at will. Chronological order and the relative value of duration no longer correspond to reality." Seen in this light, Buñuel's use of cinematic space and time is quite remarkable. It is fascinating that in a single setting, a bounded, limited space, the characters can be inexorably hounded and entrenched. And as this room is imperceptibly transformed into a "prison," so Nobile's reception becomes progressively an "abominable eternity," where the orderly fluctuation of time has been abolished.

It goes without saying that the business of a director is to produce a filmic space, a specific duration, playing upon the double chords of psychological time (the subjective unfolding of time perceived through the consciousness of the hero) and imaginary time (dreams and hallucinations). But it seems that in this film Buñuel is even more concerned with the representation of time than in most of his other films.

For the prisoners of Providence Street, lived time is oppressive. The rhythm of the film, a calculated languor (and a careful study of the editing reveals how extraordinarily long the sequences are) traces the subjective perception of time: if space is collapsed, time is lengthened. In *No Exit,* Sartre projected an imaginary future, eternity, into the present, in order to give us an insight into reality, conceived as a hell. In ***The Exterminating Angel,*** Buñuel goes even further; without recourse to the hypothesis of an imaginary eternity, even an atheist one, he projects, not in the future, but in our present daily lives the reality of our human fate. And though, at the end of the film, the characters have a fleeting illusion of having escaped their horrible destiny by effacing time (the guests take up the initial conversation and the places they occupied at the beginning of the party, hoping by some miracle to escape from the salon), they very quickly find themselves captive once more, this time forever, in the Cathedral. The circle has opened only to snap shut again, more firmly, inexorably, upon their mediocrity.

Through this use of space and time, Buñuel displays many of his characteristic themes of reflection and mirror imagery. For Inez, Estelle, and Garcin, who think they are dead, the absence of mirrors symbolizes the impossibility of contemplating the superficial "self," the impossibility of retrieving a flattering image of themselves. With death, according to Sartre, comes the end of "bad faith."

The characters in ***The Exterminating Angel*** live on in our world, but they live under the sentence of death, with greater or lesser reprieve. In Nobile's salon, acts of bad faith can be given only so much free rein. As the hours pass, and day follows night in a rigorous, implacable monotony, the masks fall, one by one, reduced to ashes in the fire of truth. And this, man's truth, as it is presented by Buñuel, reveals, little by little, its fundamental ferocity. By a violence as subtle as it is insistent, ***The Exterminating Angel*** underscores the conflict between the essence of the individual and his mask. Abandoning their coats, shedding their gowns, the guests—prisoners now in their own hell—cast off their facades. Seen in this perspective, Buñuel's film is the antithesis to his ***Robinson Crusoe.*** As opposed to the sound man "in a state of nature," the "social" man, elegant, sophisticated, distinguished in diplomatic or military circles, becomes, in the face of peril, "a wolf of a man."

Three major aspects of Sartrean existentialism can be traced through this film: the theme of the absurd, the failure of communication, and the conception of the Other as executioner. Absurdity appears in situations (Nobile returns home with a dozen guests and finds all his servants, except for the butler, have gone); in events (the succulent main dish is spilt on the floor the very moment the hostess announces it); and in the characters themselves, thrashing about in their foolishness.

Communication breaks down within the group of characters; this is first suggested by a ridiculous series of introductions, a misfiring, if you will, of a basic ritual (one character, responding to an introduction, replies: "It's all Greek to me."). Communications break down between one class and another (the guests are addressed, in vain, by the crowd of spectators, among them several of Nobile's servants who have gathered at the doors). And finally, there is the failure between the individual and the authorities (the officers who come to the manor cannot make contact with the people within).

In this film, as in *No Exit,* the Other is conceived as executioner. He is a shackle, a hindrance to the individual's desires by the very fact of his existence. He is, by definition, "excess baggage" (for example, the lovers have to wait for nightfall so that they can make love in the closet). In relationships with one another, each of us is in the position of the "misunderstood," and quarrels are inevitable. In the process of our lives, the Other becomes our judge. Here, the majority of the guests end by condemning Nobile to death, simply because his sumptuous home has become their prison.

Faced with the Other and his power as executioner, each character reveals his hideous afflictions: egoism, cowardice, cruelty. In ***The Exterminating Angel,*** acts of brutality are legion: a piano, slammed shut on the player's fingers, a comb deliberately broken to humiliate a woman still concerned with her appearance, as if beauty might survive the destruction of the mask, as if beauty might resist the test of truth. Characters slap one another. The colonel knocks a woman to the floor. Someone tosses a sick man's pills out of the room. It is impossible not to recall Sartre's words: "This, then, is hell. I would never have believed it. You know how it goes: the sulphur, the stake, the rack. . . . Oh what a joke! We don't need a rack. Hell is other people."

The undeniable presence of these three themes, however, is not enough to make us define ***The Exterminating Angel*** as a totally existential work. While Buñuel meets Sartre on a number of points, he diverges profoundly on others. To understand the purpose of the artist, it is necessary to examine two other perspectives, political and social satire, and, of course, surrealism.

Explicit or covert, satire is present in most of Buñuel's films. We see it in certain details: the salon in ***L'Age d'Or,*** which opens onto a kitchen where a serving girl is on fire; the choice of protagonist in ***El;*** the choice of all the protagonists in ***Archibaldo de la Cruz;*** criticism of dictatorship in ***La Fièvre Monte á El Pao.*** Absent from *No Exit,* satire is very much present in ***The Exterminating Angel.*** In the guise of an evening's gala, from which the servants have taken the precaution to flee (the butler who stays is, in the final analysis, nothing more than a papier-maché figure), Buñuel castigates the aristocracy. He makes these nobles—aristocrats in name, wealth, or power—prisoners of their own habits and rules, and the taboos of their society. The guests leave the salon at last, but they can only understand the Te Deum as a new call to the old social structure, and they quickly don their masks of respectability and go on as before. (Their self-complacency is picked up in a long, lateral tracking shot.) The church becomes their definitive prison, and in the concentric circles of light, the cloistering goes on, and is extended in the course of the final shots, to include all members of that social class.

Here ***The Exterminating Angel*** resembles ***Land Without Bread.*** The tone changes at the end, and is applied to a new domain. Yet nothing has really changed at all; the same general plan persists. Buñuel has a passion for clinical examinations, which he uses to evoke a feeling of "distance." Several of his films open with a documentary: the treatise on scorpions in ***L'Age d'Or;*** the sugar cane in ***Subida al Cielo;*** the meager resources of the poor in ***La Fièvre Monte á El Pao.*** This documentary form is present in ***The Exterminating Angel,*** when the rites and customs of a particular class are forced through the sieve of satire.

The Exterminating Angel, like ***Land Without Bread,*** focuses upon a micro-society, whose foundations the artist undermines by denunciation. The micro-society in ***Land Without Bread*** is that of the poor, the disinherited victims of the world. In ***The Exterminating Angel,*** it is that of the powerful, the rich, the opulent. In the one, the tone is rightly pathetic, in spite of the rigor and aridity of the commentary. In ***The Exterminating Angel,*** it is full of bite and humor; in both, the micro-societies are examined without self-righteousness, in their own terms, and in their internal conflicts. For in both films, Buñuel is denouncing a single crime.

That crime is the human condition itself, in which poor and rich alike are fragmented and alienated. The major difference between Sartre and Buñuel lies in this point. For in Sartre man is a prisoner in the sight of others only when he refuses to assume responsibility for his own destiny. And for Buñuel, man is kept captive by society, no matter whether he controls power in that society or is a helpless victim of it. *No Exit* suggests a metaphysical alienation; ***The Exterminating Angel*** is about the alienation imposed

Doomed society figures in The Exterminating Angel.

by a specific social order. In this film, Buñuel makes a powerful statement, which also appeared in ***L'Age d'Or,*** that man is split apart and crippled by everything that diverts him from himself—that is to say, by all forms of esoteric doctrine and rule (in this film, freemasonry, for example), of religious creed (Catholicism), and primitive, instinctive belief (magic).

This is the point of view of the surrealist, for whom liberty itself is only a hypothesis, and difficult if not impossible to acquire in reality. And here is a second point of Buñuel's divergence from Sartre's thought, for the author of *No Exit* and *The Flies* identifies himself with his freedom. "I am my freedom," says Orestes, and this liberty makes him the peer of the gods. So Sartre's character is condemned to be free by assuming responsibility for his actions; Buñuel's hero knows how to approach this ambivalent liberty only by attacking it, by attacking the ideological structures of society.

In 1954, in an interview [in *Cahiers du Cinéma* 36, 1954] with André Bazin and J. Doniol-Valcrose, Buñuel said:

> Surrealism has taught me that life has a moral significance that man cannot afford to ignore. Through surrealism I also discovered for the first time that man is not free. I used to believe our freedom was unlimited, but I have found in surrealism, a discipline that must be followed. This has been one of the great lessons in my life, a marvelous and poetic step.

In the final analysis, ***The Exterminating Angel*** cannot be fully understood outside the perspective of surrealism. To deliberately ignore it would be to rob the content and form of the film of their full significance. In his *First Manifesto,* André Breton wrote: "the marvelous is always beautiful; it doesn't matter what specific marvel is beautiful; it is enough that it is marvelous for it to be beautiful."

The plot of ***The Exterminating Angel*** testifies to the presence of the marvelous, or of "mystery," to use Buñuel's word. Recently he said, "It is mystery that interests me. Mystery is the essential element in any work of art." The obscure and dream-like sequences in ***The Exterminating Angel*** can, of course, be explained as the effects of prolonged confinement. But they are, more than that, elements necessary to the very form of surrealism. This is true in most of Buñuel's films. The same interpretation can be applied to the presence of the menagerie, which also functions on more than one level. For if the bear, for example, affirms, in the words of Philippe Durand, "a lost paradise for a corrupt class, or a rising force parallel yet incomprehensible to that class," it also functions as a symbol of the animal world itself, as the quintessential nonconformist by the very fact that it has never lived in a society.

The real content of ***The Exterminating Angel*** is not ordered politically, but metaphysically. "I want an integral vision of reality," Buñuel has said. This vision implies, surely, the negation of all social conformities; but the surrealist revolt always takes place on the moral plane, not the political one. Beginning with ***Un Chien Andalou,*** Luis Buñuel has never ceased to incite us to revolt. This call to revolution, however, is not in the Marxist vein, because the director of ***Viridiana*** believes that reformation of social and political structures can neither remove nor change the facts of life. Nor can it transform the human heart. Buñuel's revolution is a surrealist one, and the surrealist spirit rises up once more in ***The Exterminating Angel,*** in the "absolute nonconformity" which Breton spoke of, in the taste for blasphemy (for example, the dream sequence in which the Pope stands trial), and in the quest of man to go beyond the face of despair.

In this film, seemingly so despairing, mankind is nonetheless passionately cherished. One social class goes to its doom, envying the servants who have escaped. But I am not so sure Buñuel saves the domestics entirely because they belong to an oppressed class. He saves them because they are simple men, sane and healthy, close to their feelings and instincts. The beggars in ***Viridiana*** were much more repulsive than Don Jaime or Jorge or the young novice, and ordinarily Buñuel shows man alienated by society no matter what his social status may be. Among the captives in the salon in ***The Exterminating Angel,*** Nobile possesses an undeniable nobility, for he is willing to sacrifice himself in an attempt to deliver his guests. And in the suicides of the lovers, there is possibly a tinge of hope that true love, separated from the conditions of human life, can be realized. Actually, ***The Exterminating Angel*** suggests a nostalgia not so much for "impassioned love" (which was the theme of ***Un Chien Andalou*** and ***L'Age d'Or***) but for that "passion for immortality" invoked by Breton in his comments on Monk Lewis's *The Monk.*

Realism is always present in Buñuel's aesthetics. In ***The Exterminating Angel,*** man's ghastly wounds are not those of the flesh, as they were for the poor creatures in ***Land Without Bread,*** the blind and legless beggars in ***Los Olvidados,*** the dwarf in ***Nazarin,*** and the beggars in ***Viridiana.*** They are wounds which show in behavior and actions; horror, filth and misery give way to a leprosy of the soul. The brutal reality is the same. This is in the Spanish tradition, of course, and in his choice of details Buñuel can be thought of as a modern Goya. But the brunt of realism in Buñuel is carried not so much by his aesthetics as by his metaphysics. Over the ugliness, cruelty, and horror, a voice may be heard which bears witness to love among men, and repudiates the evil which is a natural part of life. The will to denounce despair soars above the despair itself. In the violence of his protestation, Buñuel achieves a caustic blasphemy, and yet there is evidence, too, of a sacred devotion. Because the sacred is ambivalent, linked to the quest of the atheist as well as to the passion of the faithful, it affirms in both, according to the poet Jean-Claude Renard, "something inviolable in man, a point of purity, a center of life that neither degradation nor despair and constraint can ever totally consume." (pp. 244-54)

Michel Estève, " 'The Exterminating Angel': No Exit from the Human Condition," translated by Sallie Iannotti, in The World of Luis Buñuel: Essays in Criticism, *edited by Joan Mellen, Oxford University Press, Inc., 1978, pp. 244-54.*

Freddy Buache (essay date 1970)

[In the following excerpt, originally published in French in 1970, Buache examines antireligious themes in Buñuel's films, including La mort en ce jardin, Nazarin, *and* La fièvre monte à El Pao.]

The whole of ***La Mort en ce jardin*** is a veiled attack on Christianity, the church and its clergy. In it, Buñuel places the believer in such a predicament that under the pressure of his most vital, daily necessities his belief reveals itself to be an imposture. A religion that is based on the blackmail of divine grace is subjected to one of Buñuel's favourite disquisitive methods. Just as once you have removed an object's utilitarian relationship with its environment its latent reality emerges, so if you abolish social conventions and strip away the masks that are imposed on us by the comedy of human relations the characters suddenly reveal their genuine mentality. Crusoe on his island, the group of people in ***Le Mort en ce jardin*** who have to hack their way through virgin forest, and the bourgeois in ***The Exterminating Angel*** who are trapped in their drawing-room have all been forced to come face to face with themselves. They have had to drop their intellectual and moral disguises and reveal themselves nakedly for what they are. This method results, of course, in a direct attack on the very *raison d'être* of our civilisation's masquerades, and especially that of the biggest sham of all: God.

If the beginning of the story told in ***La Mort en ce jardin*** drags a little it is because Buñuel wants us to be perfectly acquainted with the men and women whose terrible trek through the jungle he then goes on to describe. One might very well suppose that the whole thing begins when a white cat pushes open a door and has a book flung at it by Chark. But in fact nothing either begins or ends in this film. Everything is transitory. Good is but a transitory aspect of evil, and evil a fleeting guise of good, and it is no good referring to the tenets of classical morality. What may seem to be a crime can turn out to be a good deed, and vice versa. It is a film about ambiguity.

It falls into three parts. First we are shown the lives of the people in a diamond-prospecting village—their pleasures, their hopes and their chicanery, as well as their revolt when they receive an expulsion order from the military governor of the province. Two people in particular stand out in this not very savoury context: Chark, an athletic, courageous and down-to-earth adventurer, and Maria, a gentle deaf and dumb girl. The others—the missionary, Maria's aged father, the prostitute, the trader, the soldiers, the officers—are all, in their various ways, models of selfishness, pride, vanity and cowardice. It should be noted that the missionary proves no exception to the rule. Father Lizzardi, who goes around in a white civilian suit, gives himself the airs of an *avant-garde* priest in order to be able to inculcate, almost without seeming to do so, the message of Christ that calls for submissiveness in the oppressed: "Take care, the rebellion will result in repression . . . I'm talking to you as a friend and not as a priest . . . For all they that take the sword shall perish with the sword . . ." He wears a superb wristwatch ("It also tells you the date"), which was given to him as well as to all the other priests at the mission by the directors of a colonialist company ("It was a present from Northern Refineries"). Castin, the old church-going father, wants to marry Djin, the tart, and open a bistro with her in Marseille, so he can finish his days in peace and make Maria happy. He wears close to his heart a little leather purse full of the rough diamonds which will enable him to succeed in his project and keep Djin for himself alone. Chark is arrested by some soldiers. They accuse him of theft, and frogmarch him off to prison through the church in the middle of a service that is being conducted by Father Lizzardi (whose lay brother is the devout and circumspect Castin). As they pass the altar, each soldier genuflects, but Chark, whose hands are tied behind his back, does not budge. One of the soldiers forces him down on to his knees by hitting his legs with a rifle butt.

After the service, Father Lizzardi goes to see Chark in his prison cell which he is sharing, and finds a man whose gunshot wounds have not been treated by the police. "Remember your soul," says the priest to the dying wretch.

In heartfelt tones, Chark tells Lizzardi that he wants to make a confession and to send a letter to his mother. He asks for something to write with. Hardly has one of the jailers given him pen and ink when he leaps on him, viciously stabs him in the eye with the pen, throws the ink-pot in the other jailer's face, shuts them in his cell and escapes. He then blows up the army's munitions dump, which sets off rioting everywhere. Martial law is declared, the army fires on the population, takes hostages and shoots them. A price is set on the heads of Chark and Castin who are believed (wrongly) to be behind the riots. Father Lizzardi is completely overwhelmed by events.

The second part of the film begins with five very different people, who might almost have been chosen for their capacity to hate or to love each other (Chark, Castin, Lizzardi, Maria and Djin), hastily leaving a province that is being put to fire and sword. They are helped in their escape by Chenko, the trader, who takes them away in his yacht. But when the police take chase, Chenko betrays them and is killed by Chark; and the five refugees find themselves in the depths of a dangerous terrain that seethes with snakes, strident birds, thorns and insects. Their contact with physical suffering very quickly engenders a feeling of helplessness, which reduces them to the condition of an ordinary group of human beings whose only concern is survival. Their whole system of values is upset by the pressures of loneliness, hunger, rain, cold, darkness and fear. They come near to delirium. The priest mumbles prayers, or tells the story of what happened to the boiled eggs when he was at the seminary. Castin keeps on saying: "We are all guilty." Djin gives way to despondency. Maria seems to be somewhere else. Only Chark has any spunk left in him. He hacks his way through the jungle, determined to get the better of the situation by acting vigorously. Lizzardi follows his example, and veers imperceptibly from contemplation and resignation to action. He digs up roots to feed himself and his companions, gives them water to drink in his holy chalice (this time to quench their thirst and not to give them Holy Communion), and after much heart-searching decides to tear out the pages of his Bible in order to light a fire.

In so doing, Lizzardi shows that he has realised the fallacy of traditional Christian attitudes; he demonstrates that for him the struggle for the survival of those with him is much more important than praying for the salvation of their souls.

The third part of the film opens with Chark going on reconnaissance and finding the wreck of a crashed aeroplane. There are no survivors. Their luggage contains food, clothes, and jewellery. "God has saved us," cries Castin. "And fifty people had to die for him to be able to do so," retorts Chark. In a flash, the situation changes. Our five characters forget that adversity had made them friends, and revert to what they were "before" (c.f. Crusoe's and Man Friday's arrival in England). As though back in a society based on profit and a hypocritical morality, Castin's sanity gives way; one by one, he throws the diamonds into a pond as though they were pebbles, and kills first Djin, then Father Lizzardi who tries to bring him to his senses. In the end, Chark shoots him. The film finishes with Chark, the positive hero, and Maria, the innocent girl, managing to escape the forest by going down river on an inflatable dinghy. But will they survive? And for how long?

This very simply narrated story is interspersed with strikingly unusual images that lend poetry and tragedy to what seems to be no more than an adventure story. One thinks, for instance, of Maria with her hair caught in some thorns, of the snake being devoured by ants (a reminder of the bees that kill the donkey in ***Las Hurdes***), the postcard on which the bustle and clamour of the Champs-Elysées suddenly comes to life, Djin in evening dress in the middle of a clearing, or the priest caught in the prostitute's bedroom and laid open to the ribald jests of those who find him there without being able to explain himself. ("Don't judge me from appearances," he says. "Difficult, isn't it?" remarks Djin, "to have people judge you when you're not guilty.")

La Mort en ce jardin is a film that makes the most thorough use of ambiguity because it is an accurate reflection of the way people hesitate, recoil from, and decide against certain acts, and then change their mind. But its fundamental meaning could not be clearer. Buñuel is once again pointing to the total pointlessness of Christian faith in adversity. Man can count only on himself in such situations; God, who is generally a cosy alibi, proves to be a useless hypothesis. Father Lizzardi is obviously the character who most interests Buñuel in ***La Mort en ce jardin.*** The director does not hate him because he is a priest, or because he has more or less been bribed by the financial powers that be. He simply watches him act, from the same humanist viewpoint he adopts in every film. Unlike Fellini, Bresson and Rossellini, he does not feel that it is worth wasting his time on theology; nor is he torn, like the intellectually exhibitionistic Pasolini, between Marx and Christ, or between Freud and Jakobson. On the other hand, he would be thoroughly at home making a film based on the diary of a country priest who was having difficulty in staying on the straight and narrow path of virtue, so long as his outpourings were sincere. For Buñuel, it is an incontrovertible fact that priests are men, and that in certain rare circumstances the man wearing the dog collar can act in a way which almost challenges the very vocation of a priest, such as the Carmelites (enclosed nuns) who in a famous incident left their cloister to run to the help of the wounded, such as the worker-priests, or those who wish to get married, or those who take to the hills and fight alongside the guerrilleros. And Lizzardi does precisely this sort of thing: he needs to drink in order to quench his thirst, and the chalice is a suitable vessel; he needs to make a fire in order to warm himself, and the pages of the Bible are made of paper. I do not think that Buñuel had any blasphemous intentions here. He simply wanted to illustrate the vital demands of practical morality when they contrast with those of a mystifying morality. This constructively critical approach, which sees things in humanist rather than theological perspective, becomes even subtler in ***Nazarin.*** Nazarin takes over where Lizzardi left off. He knows everything there is to know about starvation and poverty, both his own and other people's. As a result, he sides resolutely with the oppressed and refuses to compromise with the Pharisees, even if they are his superiors. And yet his goodness, his love and his charity keep on bobbing to the surface; and all his attempts to achieve a fraternal victory are hounded almost diabolically by failure. Like worker-priests, or all priests who are out fighting on a social or even political front, his role remains basically that of a missionary. All things considered, he is no different from someone like Billy Graham; he uses a less shockingly brash kind of approach, but is nevertheless an equal hindrance to the cause of man's freedom. His aim is proselytism, and not the definitive deliverance of the individual from the superstitions and countless spiritual obligations that are imposed on him by the Church. Nazarin, because of his faith, is blind to the fact that by siding with the victims rather than first taking up arms against their oppressors he is prolonging and reinforcing his own illusions. Nazarin's sincerity has feet of clay, and can only result in a combination of resignation and trickery. This comes home to him when he accepts the pineapple, as will be seen from the plot.

Nazarin is adapted from a novel by Benito Pérez Galdós (1843–1920), a Spanish writer who also wrote ***Tristana*** (which Buñuel also made into a film), and who has often been compared to Tolstoy, Balzac, Zola, and, perhaps most accurately, to Dickens minus the sentimentality. ***Nazarin*** was written in 1895, and belongs to Galdós's "mystical" or "evangelical" phase, which began in 1892 and was his final creative period. The novelist describes a priest, Don Nazario Zaharin, who towards the end of the Nineteenth century tries to live in as faithful a manner as possible to the Gospel. Andara, a prostitute, follows him; then they are joined by the beautiful Beatriz. He teaches them resignation, asceticism, love of their neighbour and forgiveness. As poor as the people around them, they travel from village to village in the best tradition of the picaresque novel, and answer the malice of those they meet, both the governed and the governors, with meekness and kindness. When he is struck on the right cheek, our quixotic Franciscan proffers his left cheek. They are abused, scorned, beaten up, and accused of charlatanism. When they are escorted into town, the similarity between Nazarin's Calvary and the Passion of Christ becomes increasingly striking. Nazarin is struck down with typhus; during his delirium in hospital he sees himself walking up towards Golgotha, hoping that he will be nailed to the cross; then, as he conducts Mass he meets Jesus, who speaks to him. They are the last words of the book: "You are still alive, my son. You are in my holy hospital, suffering for me. The two unfortunate women and the thief who followed your teaching are in prison. You cannot conduct Mass, I cannot be with you in flesh and blood, and this Mass is but a hallucination of your sick mind. Take some rest, you deserve it. You have done something for me. Be satisfied; I know that you will do much more."

Buñuel transfers the action from Spain to Mexico at the turn of the century, at the time when Porfirio Diaz's dictatorship was in power with the support of big landowners. His film may at first sight seem to be a faithful adaptation of Galdós's novel; but in fact, through certain changes of emphasis and the addition of a scene here and there that bear his own particular stamp, Buñuel completely changes the overall meaning and integrates the film into his personal universe. Even when he seems simply to be illustrating certain of Galdós's scenes, he always enriches them with a little touch, a detail, or a gesture that completely changes their centre of gravity. What is so striking about the poor, resourceless Nazarin is no longer his exemplary humility, his devotion to Christ, or his practical experience of faith, hope and charity, nor even his redeeming taste of suffering, but his uselessness, his masochism, and the harmful effects of his activity. The final sequence, which is open to any number of interpretations, is both the most intensely disturbing and at the same time the most revealing if one takes the trouble to see it in the context of the director's overall poetic terms of reference. Buñuel deliberately veers away from Galdós's original before Nazarin's typhus attack. He has his hero separated from his followers, imagining, most plausibly, that the Church establishment is embarrassed by the scandal he has caused and does not want to draw too much attention to him. A clergyman says to him: "By order of the diocese, which has arranged everything with the civil authorities, you will no longer be accompanied by your followers. You will be escorted separately by a man in civilian clothes. That is all they managed to obtain, but even so it'll be less humiliating. Aren't you interested in knowing how your case is progressing? You'll at least have to admit your rash and foolish acts. They are right to say that you are an anticonformist, a rebellious character. It's going to be difficult to make you see reason and realise that your habitual behaviour is not only most unpriest-like but highly offensive to the Church that you claim to love and obey . . ."

So Nazarin walks along in the heat of the sun with his guardian. An unknown woman comes up to him and offers him a pineapple. At first he refuses it; but when he remembers that this is not a gift to a priest, as the woman cannot possibly know that he is one, he accepts it. Meanwhile, in the background, we can hear the deafening roll of the drums of Calanda.

During the twenty-four hours of Good Friday, from midday to the following midday, all the inhabitants of the Spanish town of Calanda come out into the streets and madly beat drums of all sizes until they are exhausted and their hands are bloody. While still a very small boy, Buñuel was deeply struck by this obsessive din that accompanies the agony of Christ. In 1964, he thought of making a medium-length film about this event and about the celebration of Holy Week in his native village. But he gave up the project. In 1966, his son, Juan-Luis Buñuel made a short film in Calanda which concentrated on the people who, alone or in groups, persist in drumming all through the night as though exorcising demons. His film won the Grand Prix at the Tours Festival in 1967.

The drums of Calanda can be heard in ***L'Age d'Or,*** where they emphasise certain sequences, and in particular those where Modot gives free rein to his bottled-up desires; their use in ***Nazarin*** has a similar purpose.

Nazarin, which Buñuel made in Mexico in 1958 immediately after two French productions (***La Mort en ce jardin*** and ***Cela s'appelle l'aurore***), and just before ***La Fièvre monte à El Pao,*** was widely underestimated and misunderstood. At the time, for those who were unable to draw the vital parallels with ***L'Age d'Or,*** its deeper significance seemed difficult to decipher. Its thematic ambiguity even resulted in contradictory interpretations: the representatives of the Office Catholique International du Cinéma were thinking of awarding their prize to it at the 1959 Cannes Film Festival, while militant atheists described the film as a masterpiece of blasphemy.

This temporary atmosphere of ambiguity vanished when people saw what Buñuel went on to make (in particular ***Viridiana, Simon of the Desert*** and ***La Voie lactée,*** all of which develop the themes of ***Nazarin*** with a verve reminiscent of the stark, explosive violence of ***L'Age d'Or***).

Nazarin is an extraordinary rich and complex film. It moves forward by continually turning situations upside down. It is thought-provoking not because it works out a thesis but because it uses poetry to pose fundamental questions about our condition. Buñuel condemns all metaphysical hypocrisy and demands that man be recognised by man. This recognition can only genuinely occur when all types of hypothetical recourse to a transcendental order have been ruled out. The parable contained in ***Nazarin*** combines the passion of a man who is tempted by saintliness with variations on the theme of the misfortunes of virtue. The allusion to Sade is quite explicit in the superb scene where the plague-stricken woman refuses the priest's help and calls for her lover:

DON NAZARIO. Remember that this life is but a highway. Bear with your suffering and prepare your soul for the joy of seeing yourself in God's presence.

LUCIA. I just want to see Juan.

DON NAZARIO. Forget the passions of this world, my daughter. The Lord is giving you time to examine your conscience. Think of the heaven that awaits you.

LUCIA. Juan!

DON NAZARIO. I'm speaking to you as a priest and I assure you that you can still save yourself. You only need repent your sins.

LUCIA. Juan!

This priest of the poor is utterly devoted to his ministry, and sincerely wants to live out the lessons of Christ. But at the same time he has trouble in coping with the demands of practical morality and those of a religious code of conduct. On one side, the Church frowns on his activity, and on the other he feels cut off from society. Although his actions spring from the noblest and most genuine motives, they always result in disaster for him and for others. He prays for the life of a sick child, and the child recovers. So he is taken to be a miracle-worker and is asked to continue his performance, thus fanning the flames of superstition. He accepts the presence of Beatriz and Andara because he wants them to live in communion with God. But he soon realises that they have followed him not because they want to get closer to God, but because, subconsciously, they want to obtain the love of a flesh-and-blood human being rather than the ethereal kindness of one of God's messengers. He lives off alms, and asks a grasping head-foreman if he can have a piece of bread in return for working; in so doing, he replaces workers who are on strike and becomes, in effect, a blackleg. Most of the scenes demonstrate how failure inevitably attends all behaviour based on the principles of Christianity, an ethos that destroys man in order better to be able to save him, and saves him temporarily in order better to destroy him again, here on earth, and save him even more thoroughly in paradise. It is an ethos that humbles man and exalts him according to the whim of circumstance, that hoodwinks and lauds him by constantly ramming the image of Christ down his throat. This Christ is a Protean figure, alternately elusive and close, imperceptible and intrusive, fraternal and distant, tyrannical and obliging, accusing and defending—all because of his double nature, a quality enlarged upon with great relish by Monsieur Richard, the distinguished-looking head waiter of the posh Tours restaurant in ***La Voie lactée.*** Nazarin is in the thrall of the New Testament just as Don Quixote is totally guided by the canons of chivalry; he is unable to reconcile within himself his aspirations as a man and his Christ-like exaltation. He is torn between the human and the divine.

At the end of the story of Nazarin, we realise that Buñuel has been developing his criticism on two levels: first, he completely debunks the contradictions of the common attitude of arrogant humility by demonstrating that Christian charity is ineffectual; secondly, he uses the example of the ingenuous Nazarin to expose the repugnant Pharisaism of a complacent Christian establishment that gives all the help it can to landlords, judges and colonels. When the story ends (and there has been no musical accompaniment up to then), the rolling drums that can be heard as Nazarin receives the pineapple bring home to us the utter collapse of all his illusions: suddenly, he seems to spring back to real life as he discovers his primordial loneliness—and his freedom. The whole film's narrative and poetic strands converge towards this limpidly beautiful image. One feels that from this moment on Nazarin's unsheathed conscience is going to draw from within him the strength he needs for his salvation, rather than begging it from On High.

The critics, who always start quibbling about the form of Buñuel's films when the content proves too much for them, often dismiss his moral message as simplistic, limited and crude. They condescendingly slate his films in the name of the admiration they feel towards the director of ***L'Age d'Or*** (while pretending to forget they hate ***L'Age d'Or*** as well).

Buñuel's message may be limited; but I fail to see why it should be any broader or more complicated. It is brutally succinct, calling a spade a spade, and dividing our society into two categories—the baddies and those who are not baddies. Action and passivity are the result of a choice that totally commits a man and has less to do with morals than with politics. In other words, there is the Right and there is the Left. This simplification must necessarily seem frightfully vulgar to those well brought-up people who would never dream of kicking a blind man, give money to good causes, raise their hats to passing hearses, and listen, with concern written all over their faces, to a poor man's hard luck story while keeping an attentive eye on his

Catherine Deneuve in Tristana.

niece's breasts. These are the same people who feel shocked at the accounts they read in their newspapers of massacres or of apartheid, and who are moved when they hear military music or see a dignitary of the Church blessing some weapons. One probably has to be left-wing in order to understand the blazing truth of this necessary simplification. The French philosopher, Alain, said in 1930 that anyone who tells you that the words "left-wing" and "right-wing" are meaningless is bound not to be a man of the Left. When faced with Buñuel's films, the conscious or unconscious champions of the Right comfort themselves by putting on a rather disgusted air and talking of his "obsessions."

Buñuel is a left-wing film-maker. A quarter of a century after the end of the Second World War, the Left of the western world is weary, disillusioned, divided, megalomaniac, and tortured, and has become bourgeoisified and bureaucratic. It could, I think, learn a lot from Buñuel's attitudes, his hatred for authority and its attendant priests, policemen and soldiers, his rehabilitation of *amour fou,* and his advocacy of a return to revolutionary fervour.

All Buñuel's works contain, by implication, the warning against the Utopia of reformism that is to be found in ***La Fièvre monte à El Pao.***

"It's like many other films I've made," is Buñuel's comment on the film (which was Gérard Philipe's last appearance on the screen). What Buñuel was implying by that understated remark was that it was made under a commercial set-up and that he probably did not have quite as free as hand as he would have liked. The film does indeed have serious faults. After a short introductory sequence whose documentary virulence is reminiscent of ***Las Hurdes,*** there is a flurry of purely anecdotal twists and turns. When Inès, a widow with a black veil over her face, comes to see Governor Gual, he pounces on her and rips open her bodice—a vintage piece of Buñuel. But it is only one of many such isolated good moments in a narrative that often drags terribly.

There is no sinew in the construction of the film, and inspiration more than once seems to be lacking. The characters are always signing documents or picking up the telephone for no apparent reason; one would like to see them involved in a nexus of more visually conceived contradictions. This overall flaw becomes particularly irritating towards the end: the whole meaning of the film is put across by one sentence of the commentary which has obviously been tacked on in the last resort to make up for the ambiguity of the narrative itself.

It would however be a great mistake to suppose that ***La Fièvre monte à El Pao*** is just a standard adventure film concocted from a mixture of exoticism and conventional psychology. Yet again Buñuel shows an absolutely uncompromising attitude when it comes down to basic essentials, and one realises that a minor film by Buñuel is always worth more than a so-called major work by Bresson or Pasolini. ***La Fièvre monte à El Pao*** is an unquestionably honest political film about Fascism and its accomplices.

It is set in an imaginary South American country, with a dictatorship of wealthy landowners over a *Lumpenproletariat.* The Church is right behind the State. Union leaders and other opponents of the regime (the intellectuals, in particular) are behind bars. Opposite the governor's luxurious villa looms a sinister-looking prison. The "political" prisoners are treated like common criminals and work in irons.

We then see the governor in a fit of jealousy, slapping his wife who has just been unfaithful to him, then putting his white uniform back in place and striding out of his drawing-room on to a terrace where he makes a patriotic speech to the crowds in honour of the country's national holiday. Behind him, seated on a dais, an impressive selection of Church and army dignitaries listen to him, then pompously applaud him. His high-flown speech is particularly unconvincing because we have just seen him behaving in such a childishly petulant way with his wife.

During the speech, a rebel who has been hiding in a barn shoots the governor. The patriotic festivities, which have begun in an atmosphere of enthusiasm thanks to a well-timed distribution of free meat, end in chaos. And the days that follow are marked by intrigues in the palace and the parliament for the appointment of an interim successor, arbitrary arrests, summary judgements, wrangling and blackmail. The police, who are stupid and unreasoning by definition, carry out the orders of the civil servants with all the efficiency of the SS. The man who holds the reins of power during this troubled period is Ramon Vasquez, an ambitious, idealistic under-secretary. He seizes this opportunity to reinforce one or two clauses of a forgotten law and tries to improve the prisoners' lot. He insists that they no longer be deprived of their statutory rest period, and has the irons taken off the political prisoners. But he is not any the less ambitious for being idealistic. He seduces the governor's widow in order to satisfy a thirst for power that is hardly, if at all, tempered by his sense of justice. He revels in his own happiness. He has managed to "humanise" the repression.

But a permanent new governor is appointed. He honours the prison with an official visit and brings Ramon back to reality with a bump. "What are these men doing?" he asks, pointing at the convicts. "They're resting," Ramon answers. "I want them to get back to work immediately," retorts the governor, "because when they rest they start thinking, and that's dangerous."

Ramon is perfectly aware of the double game he is forced to play by his position in a system that he has agreed to serve. He realises that both politically and socially the *régime* is detestable. But he tries to improve it rather than fight it, in the very best tradition of Christians and sentimental socialists. He wants to be a just man, in Camus's sense of the word. Like Nazarin, he prefers an absolute purity of attitude and of emotions to the ambivalence of a fully conscious act which, in the case of the wandering priest for instance, would consist of staying on the building site, taking part in the class struggle and standing up to the foreman rather than going off and plucking a twig through lack of interest in a reality that does not fit in with his saintly designs. Ramon refuses to get his hands dirty by answering conservative violence with a violence that liberates. He persists in flying in the face of the evidence and thinking that the origins of oppression lie in an inevitable flaw in the institutions (which are imperfect because they are human, as Christ would have said), whereas in fact they result from an inhuman concentration of means of production. If he dared rip away the deceptive labels ("evil," "injustice," "egoism," "the Devil"), he would find that they concealed more concrete scourges, such as banks, stock exchanges, barracks, United Fruit, Union Minière, Raffineries du Nord, or wealthy traders (like a certain Praxédès Mateo who offers Simon of the Desert a new, and higher, column).

Ramon Vasquez is a kind of lay saint, who believes passionately in lenient and charitable behaviour, but who fails to see that his position is untenable: it is impossible to be a just man in a world where the most everyday gesture and the most trifling thought are perverted by a system based on the profit motive. Ramon Vasquez sees as a disgrace what is simply a rigged interplay of capital appreciation and constitutional liberties. He indulges in a bit of breast-beating: "The rest of our lives will not suffice for us to get ourselves pardoned!" This fallacious sense of guilt instils an even fiercer desire in him to defend his ideal; but not for a moment does he think of putting his ideal to the test with a few facts, which would enable him to realise that he was using it as an alibi. His upright attitude, his wishy-washy accusations, his hinted condemnations and his silent way of seeing that as little damage as possible is done are simply unconscious grist to the government's mill: they adore his abortive courage, his abstract sense of rebellion, and his attachment to the mirage of an inner life—all things which make the obscenities of dividends and of police and military legislation look morally respectable. The president of the Republic sings the praises of the young man. Ramon is decorated and becomes the pride of the country—a kind of Dr. Schweitzer. He is well on the road towards a Nobel Peace Prize.

At the end Ramon realises how blind he has been; he sees himself as a traitor. He tears up a decree that is going to destroy people's liberty—an act that is bound to result in his being removed from office and sentenced to death. The commentary concludes: "This categorical refusal is the harbinger of his own death and the sign that he is a free man. Ramon Vasquez has fulfilled his destiny." This last-minute salvation obviously does not convince either the spectator or for that matter the character. Inès has previously hinted that pulling this sort of rabbit out of a hat is not enough: "One second of courage is not enough to redeem years of cowardice." This is Buñuel's lucidly political answer to all those who (to the delight of those in power) talk cleverly about the relationship between collaborationism and the metaphysics of redemption. It has a remarkable power to ungild the pill that film-makers like Bresson and Rossellini would have us swallow. And more specifically it unmasks, by implication, the abject way in which a film like *Il Generale della Rovere* dishonestly glosses over and justifies the conduct of its hero.

Reflecting as it did the state of affairs in several South American, Middle Eastern and African countries, the imaginary dictatorship under which Ramon Vasquez lives was extraordinarily topical in 1960; it still is today. The police methods of El Pao are exactly those which were enforced by Gaullist France in Algeria. A rebel is captured and coolly murdered (like the gamekeeper's son in ***L'Age d'Or***) by the two soldiers who are bringing him back to the town in a jeep and who tell him to get out and stretch his legs; later they talk of an attempted escape. This was the device that in Algeria became notorious under the name of "*corvée de bois*" (woodgathering party). This sort of thing has been continuing ever since the film was made, and not just in Vietnam; and political prisoners still fill prisons, detention centres and psychiatric hospitals. And the Ramon Vasquez of this world are still concerned about them and still sign petitions demanding their freedom.

But above all Buñuel is painting a picture of Franco's Spain. His parable shows that it is not possible to reform a dictatorial *régime* from within, and purely through intellectual force of argument; one has to have the courage to overthrow it by force first by organising rebellious action (from union militancy to the constitution of a revolutionary militia), to sow the seeds of defeatism in the army, and encourage desertion, or else to leave the country and undertake a campaign from outside aimed at undermining its authority and its good name. From his exile in Mexico, Buñuel was giving us his thoughts on the whole problem of ends and means. ***La Fièvre monte à El Pao*** is a great Spanish film of considerable international relevance that most critics dismissed just a little too hastily. *Cahiers du Cinéma* (No. 104, February 1960), for instance, said of it: "Buñuel has been too respectful towards the intentions of his second-rate subject—a prisoners' uprising on a South American island and the attitudes of various governments towards it—and has forgotten to direct his actors." The writer of the same article nevertheless described Buñuel not only as a genius but as a great technician, which is a naïve or sly way of casting aspersions of his genius: "Figueroa's photography is dreadfully amateurish. But we should not forget that in ***Nazarin*** Buñuel showed that he had become a technician, and also one of the greatest technicians of all time." Few and far between were the perspicacious critics who devoted to ***La Fièvre monte à El Pao*** the sympathetic attention it deserved. One of these was Raymond Borde in particular, who managed to point to an aspect of it which, I think, escaped all other critics: "***La Fièvre monte à El Pao*** has a farcical side to it that contains some excellent political sacrilege. The serious-looking tyrants are always trying to get the better of each other. Gual has a go at Vasquez, and just as he is about to get rid of him he is himself executed. Vasquez steps straight into his boots, but gets involved in a government plot. The president eases out his own brother, and so on. The only constants in this merry-go-round are two symbolic policemen, who imperturbably obey whoever happens to be in power. And everything happens as though some grotesque collection of puppets were playing at being governors, presidents and ministers. The mechanics of the system are stripped open to the light of day, and as a result nothing can withstand the winds of satire. What can there be behind the haughtiness of officials, behind the demagogy ("I was myself a simple worker," simpers President Barreiro), or behind the uniforms? Nothing but a startling political vacuum and a load of nasty ham actors who end up by believing in their own characters." (pp. 81-102)

Freddy Buache, in his The Cinema of Luis Buñuel, *translated by Peter Graham, A. S. Barnes & Co., 1973, 207 p.*

Raymond Durgnat (essay date 1977)

[*In the following excerpt, Durgnat provides an assessment of Buñuel's films* Diary of a Chambermaid *and* Simon of the Desert.]

Buñuel's version of Octave Mirbeau's *Journal d'une Femme de Chambre* follows the spirit, rather than the letter, of its original which was previously filmed by Jean Renoir in 1945, with Paulette Goddard.

Célestine (Jeanne Moreau) quits the Paris of 1928 to take up the post of chambermaid in a country town. Her aged, fastidious employer requires her to read Huysmans to him, but she can't read sensitively enough, so he has her walk round his study in items from his choice collection of ladies' boots, remarking: 'I want to see them live . . .' His married daughter's obsession for tidiness extends to inner cleanliness. She spends much time in her bathroom with an enigmatic apparatus which seems to be designed for mixing a vaginal moistener. She certainly complains to the local curé about the painful demands made on her by her husband (Michel Piccoli), a shamefaced, sullen philanderer who, when rebuffed by Célestine, consoles himself with the older, plainer maid. Her sudden burst of tears at this nasty parody of the warm love that she has never had is one of Buñuel's tensely, scathingly tragic vignettes. This family, upstanding royalists all, are at loggerheads with their neighbour, a retired Army officer who gratifies his staunch Republicanism by hurling his garbage into their grounds.

Célestine becomes preoccupied with her employers' gamekeeper, Joseph, an extreme right-winger dedicated to the moral rebirth of France. She suspects him of having raped and murdered a little girl whom she took to her heart. She sets out to seduce him, so that she can betray him to the police. Despite his suspicions, he loves her. But he also has his moral principles; he only sleeps with her on the firm understanding that she will become his wife, and by her charm attract sailors to the café for which he is saving. She finds her evidence, inculpates Joseph and is sacked. But he clears himself, and we next see him standing at the door of his café, his arms round another rather blowsy girl, watching the Fascists march by and taking up their shout of 'Vive Chiappe'. The name just happens to be that of the Prefect of Police who, a few years after the film's action, was to take the side of the right-wing Fascists against ***L'Age d'Or.***

Meanwhile, the gallant Captain next door, taken with Célestine, drops his old servant, cook and mistress as if she were a dishcloth and proposes to Célestine instead. She accepts, and after a month or two of marriage she is treating this irresponsible baby as if he were her servant.

The film has certain parallels with Losey's *The Servant.* Indeed, Buñuel's dramatic structures sometimes resemble Losey's: Célestine and Joseph are locked in something like a pact of mutual destruction like Gual and Ines, like Losey's Eve and Tyvian, like the Gypsy and the Gentleman. But Buñuel's tone is characteristically quieter. In its feeling for the morose mediocrity of a French country-town, Buñuel's film touches on an ingrained gloom celebrated more lyrically by Bresson's *Journal d'un Curé de Campagne* (especially the château scenes) and by Franju's faithful, yet agnostic version of Mauriac's *Thérèse Desqueyroux,* in which the provincial bourgeoisie are denounced from a Catholic viewpoint.

The film's special eeriness lies in its intimate inhumanities—the old man stiff as a clockwork toy, with his olde worlde manners and his sudden prickly stare, treating the maid as if she were a tea-trolley, or rather a shoe-tree; his daughter's 'sincere' innocence of his perversity, and his rigid shyness about it; the curé's sudden jump from sexual topics to the neglected state of his churchbells. The bourgeoisie of ***Viridiana*** are romantics compared with the denizens of this Cartesian household, who stare blankly past one another's transparent masks. The film's lyrical 'brittleness' registers their tinny hearts. Only the boots are still alive.

Célestine is the film's central character, but she's not a heroine in the idealistic-romantic sense, still less is she an exemplary character. This may seem an obvious point, but Tom Milne in *Sight and Sound* criticizes the film on the astonishing grounds that there are 'contradictions' in Célestine's character. Yet such contradictions are surely traditional in psychological analysis, and Jeanne Moreau, thoroughly Buñuelised, catches the nuances of a complex character with a mesmerising precision. Célestine's behaviour to her employers is a mixture of deference and insolence. She has a nose for where the real power lies, for whom she can insult and whom she can't. At the same time, she has a certain consistency and dignity, so her insolence is quiet and her deference is suave. She befriends and avenges the little girl in whose innocence and reserve she rightly sees something of herself, all that is not yet corrupt; and she loses. Her relationship with Joseph is the focus of her ambivalence, and obsesses her. He insists (as Gual to Ines) that they're two of a kind, that she is his female counterpart. In a sense, that is true, for both are servile and ambitious, yet in another sense, it is false, for he is a killer, his innocence is pathological. In terms of strength, he's her real mate, and her resentment of his strength is a factor in goading her to destroy him. So she loses him, and finishes as a lady of the house herself, rich, bored and almost dead. Like Viridiana and Laetitia, she is something of a Valkyrie, and in the little girl she sees, among other things, her own innocence, lost so long ago. But whereas Laetitia found a (brief) awakening with Nobile, Célestine meets only Joseph, the anti-Chark. The most virile character in the film, he is also, society being what it is, the most bestial, innocent only in his bestiality. Instead of awakening her, he murders the child whose innocence is most human and authentic.

Surely, after Freud, we can appreciate that character is formed out of ambivalence; it is a dialectic of contrary urges (impulse and control), and cannot be understood until its contradictions are shown. For Buñuel as for Freud, a character-trait is an expression of the relative strengths of desire and inhibition, love and frustration, egocentricity and generosity, integrity and impressionability. Virtues may be harnessed by vices, as vices by virtues. Purification and degradation are always incomplete, so much so that, in a sense, they are only the heads and tails of each other. Hence, one cannot understand a man by psychological analysis of the rationalist kind (which looks for consistency), but by following the dialectic between impulse, consciousness, social interjections, social pressures, and the vectors imparted to its syntheses by culture. A conformist is just a special sort of fetishist and a man's actions are as relevant to his real character as the nuances and reservations in his consciousness: the former commit one, and cost more; the latter are too often the alibis of those who go with the system but want a clear conscience, or the fantasy of being 'really' free.

Because Buñuel's view of character is fundamentally dialectical, we feel no contrivance, no schematism, when he (following Mirbeau) makes Joseph not only a Fascist but also a sex murderer. Buñuel isn't saying that all Fascists are quite likely to murder children. Quite arguably, rape, as spiritual impulse, is no more callous than the Fascist vision of what society ought to be. Buñuel is simply noting a possible, unsuspected affinity between physical aggression and political aggression. The potential criticism here, is, surely, that of excessive consistency, rather than of excessive contradiction.

Jeanne Moreau and Jean Ozenne in Diary of a Chambermaid.

Yet the sex murder is contradictory in its very quietness, in being the result of an afterthought of Joseph's (one recalls the *whimsicality* of Archibaldo). It springs not from an outflow of libido, but from contempt: 'why shouldn't I?' The girl is carrying a jar of snails in one hand, and is pushing strawberries into her mouth with the other. The censor excised a shot of the dead girl lying in the undergrowth with the snails crawling over her naked thighs. That's all she was to Joseph—flesh, sweetness and slime—so why not? Through Joseph's every gesture, Buñuel catches that strange combination of brutality and inertness which makes sense and which underlies the ambition, the Fascism, the murder. It underlies also Joseph's puritanical restraint with Célestine. The moral scruples of this immoralist are only his rationalisation for his inhibitions, not in the sexual act, but in sexual emotion. For him, sexuality is just sweet slime, it's meaningless without marriage, i.e. absolute possession unto death, another form of murder. His diffidence is matched by the idealistic Nazarin's. Nazarin and he are Christ and Blangis, two impotents, who, on a deeper level, are one.

Because they maintain the Buñuel sense of contradictions, of a dialectic, his characters can be in the orthodox sense 'types', and yet retain their qualities of inner life, of unpredictability. In stressing that action is commitment, that vices may overpower virtues (or the reverse), that injustice frequently justifies revolutionary or merely retaliatory violence, Buñuel may seem to subscribe to Manichean divisions. But these divisions, once established, are promptly undermined by contradictions that are made clear by the sardonic placidity of Buñuel's style. He rejects, notably, anarchist and liberal clichés to the effect that man is basically good or kind. His life-force is ambivalent, and its brutality is authentic, not a result of alienation or frustration. A fully decent humanity is possible only when a coincidence of free amorality and lucid generosity enables egoism to be satisfied through sympathy and reciprocation. This decency is a precarious balance. It implies stoic renunciations. It is never won once and for all. It needs help from outside, but its concomitants are a sustaining fraternity with the freedom of lucidity, and the right to be, in the words Buñuel used of Crusoe and Friday, *'fiers comme des hommes'.*

A forty-two minute feature, ***Simón del Desierto*** was awarded a Special Jury Prize at the 1965 Venice Film Festival. At the time of writing it still awaits a suitable companionpiece to make its showing commercially more viable. (pp. 130-36)

Buñuel 'shot the film in fifteen days on location, and ten days in the studio shooting and editing. After the film was shot, he already had the edited version in his head, so that all of the shots coincided with the number of scenes in the final film. He has always used this method.'

It is a study of the temptations of St Simon Stylites, the desert anchorite who spent thirty-seven years atop a sixty-foot column near Aleppo, preaching to flocks of pilgrims from all over Christendom, before dying in 459 A.D.

Buñuel uses the historical Simon as ground-bass only to a little *capriccio* of his favourite motifs. Simon (Claudio Brook), a man as aloof and kind as Nazarin, has ascended his pillar in order to evade the world's temptations and approach heaven. As the film begins, fellow-monks and admiring citizens invite him to move over to the higher, grander column built for him by a rich local merchant, in gratitude for the prayer-power which had surely brought him prosperity. Thus, despite himself, the holy hermit is not merely a cog, but a kingpin, in the socio-economic whirl.

A poor man prevails on him miraculously to restore his hands. 'Yes, not bad,' the spectators concede, only ordinarily impressed by the extraordinary become ordinary. His example goads a fellow-monk into a condition of demonic possession. He can see that a young novice is too clean in his habits ever to make a good monk. In fact, among post-mediaeval saints as well as among the anchorites, cleanliness was not next to godliness, which correlated rather with self-mortification by self-neglect and filth. In Simon's solitude, his mind wanders. Looking around for something to bless, he absently picks a scrap of food from between his teeth, and automatically makes the sign of the cross over it. He resists the devil's various onslaughts, which include an appearance as a little girl in a 1900 sailor suit. At length, though, the devil whisks him off on a long journey—right into the twentieth century, and leaves him in a discothèque crammed with youngsters frienziedly dancing the 'Radioactive Flesh'. It's the latest dance, in fact, the devil adds, 'it's the last dance'.

The saint's various misadventures are treated in the tone of a *divertissement,* at once festive and saturnine. Festive, because Buñuel has used his new freedom to the hilt, to present attitudes and events so grotesque that any attempt to manoeuvre the spectator into a suspension of disbelief, let alone a passionate involvement with any of the characters, was bound to fail. With an unprecedented and revivifying baldness, therefore Buñuel introduces such surprises as a self-propelled coffin snaking along over the desert sands, like a cross between a lizard and a torpedo, or the devil's appearance in the form of a beautiful young lady (Silvia Pinal), unconvincingly garnished with a beard and a lamb to persuade the semi-delirious saint that she's his Saviour. And the tone is saturnine, not only because so many non-believers still respect Christianity so much that any but a very respectful, almost elegiac, criticism of any of its forms seems to them 'black', but because, quite apart from that, it is a jovially pessimistic film. We are finally lost *with* Simon, watching a mad, mad world doing a masochistic dance.

The film is malicious but not malevolent, compassionate but not complacent, all the more tragic in that Simon is not an inconsiderable man. There is real nobility, real beauty in his motives, in his gestures, in his countenance. If Buñuel, in his most Swiftian film, reveals his prowess as being derisory in its results, his attitude to the man is friendlier and kinder than Swift's.

Simon, in a sense, is Robinson Crusoe on a pillar. Or he is trying to be Robinson, though the world is too much with him; when it isn't, his imagination obsessively conjures up that worst of all possible Man Fridays, the eternal adversary of his ideal, garbed in femininity. Trying for heaven, the Saint has given himself up to a delirious existence: he is lost in the wild blue yonder, high on the pillar of delirium. He is the first astronaut, alone on a Space Platform.

From another angle, Simon, the prophet, the inspirer, the pillar of society, the miraculous healer, has achieved all that Christianity could promise and hope for: in particular, real moral authority without temporal responsibility, attained through authentic inner purity. Simon's prophetic pillar is still an island, in a desert of worldliness. His mother obstinately camps at the column's base. The dwarf, who as in ***Nazarin,*** seems to represent a kind of life-force—stunted, perhaps, but engagingly scurrilous—asks for Simon's blessing on his goats, and then on himself, 'but not the same blessing as on my animals!' Simon himself is sustained by an umbilical cord between his splendid isolation and Mother Earth—the rope hauling up the food-bag and wineskins, forms which, during a diabolical intervention, acquire a disturbing overtone, reminiscent of the udders in ***Viridiana.***

If every image and idea in the film plunges its roots into familiar Buñuel territory, the effect is not in the least that of *déjà vu.* Any familiarity is welcome in this disorientating world. And this time the motifs are not half-smothered by a familiar dramatic world—permeated by them, certainly, but also permeating them. This time, they exist in a world of naive piety, of naive craziness open to heaven as to demons, an innocently pre-rationalistic world in which irrational fetishes have free space because this world is composed out of them.

But suddenly we are plunged into modern New York. Now called skyscrapers, the columns cluster close and black over us, cutting out the sky. Simon's solitary perch is replaced by structures which are half-prison, half ants'-nest. The discothèque is a darkness within darkness. Here, the epoch's heart still beats, feverishly, resignedly. The pounding music evokes that of the last scene in ***Viridiana.*** New York's forest of columns could be the spawn of Simon's monument to individualist asceticism. No doubt it is an anti-Christian argument that the devil is more at home here than he. Simon wanders, lost, in the discothèque which, being dark, claustrophobic, crowded, Godless and sensual, is the negation of his column; he blindly resolves to grope his way, somehow, back to the fifth century. While the saintly champion of a now anachronistic morality was resisting the wiles of a charming female demon, a Mother of Lies, of course we took the devil's part against his. Now it is he who represents some sort of life-force, not the bright young things, doped as they are with flesh so titillated that only radioactivity can go further. From mortification to titillation is a case of *plus ça change,* for their minds are, if anything, more schizophrenic than his. The uprooted saint is a lost soul now, but this lost soul is the last soul left.

Apparently a succession of Buñuelian whims, the film's structure is almost obsessively orderly. The future appears as a little girl (sailor-suited, in the desert!) with her hoop, symbol of eternity. Later, the attractive woman suddenly becomes an ugly old hag (taking up the temporal argument justifying so much Christian hatred of the erotic: 'the body decays . . .'). Subsequently, the future appears as a coffin—Simon's own death—before he himself is whisked off, like Faust, to posthumous epochs. The envious monk has the face of the blind man in ***Los Olvidados,*** of the blind beggar in ***Viridiana,*** the face of Buñuel. (pp. 130-38)

Raymond Durgnat, in his Luis Bunuel, *University of California Press, 1977, 176 p.*

Elliot Rubinstein (essay date Fall 1978)

[*In the following excerpt, Rubinstein explores the pessimism of Buñuel's worldview.*]

The world of any Buñuel film is first of all, in William S. Pechter's phrase, the worst of all possible [*Twenty-four Times a Second: Films and Film-makers,* 1971]. But the phrase misleads, implying that better worlds are imaginable, let alone photographable, let alone otherwise available. Neither sexual fascination ***(L'Âge d'or, Él*** **[*This Strange Passion*],** ***Ensayo de un crimen*** **[*The Criminal Life of Archibaldo de la Cruz*],** ***Abismos de pasión*** **[*Wuthering Heights*],** ***Diary of a Chambermaid, Belle de Jour)*** nor faith ***(Nazarín, Robinson Crusoe, Viridiana, The Milky Way),*** nor any other agency of spiritual transcendence delivers us to a world fit for human habitation. Trailing clouds, but not of glory, do we come, and beneath these clouds we proceed to make fools and martyrs and killers of one another, of ourselves.

Unhappily, such views, seized upon as novelties, leave Buñuel at the mercy of some of the most sophomoric adulators ever to hound a major artist. Happily, Buñuel's vision justifies his views; happily, his career transcends his vision. His particular achievement is the sheer variety of worlds he has discovered or reanimated, none quite like another except in the *way* it is seen—and each the worst of all possible.

The world of ***Nazarín*** appears, on the relentlessly gray surface of its film stock, the most conventional in any of Buñuel's works. (I am not thinking of, for one must try to think as little as possible of, some of the potboilers Buñuel had to produce during his Mexican captivity of the late 1940s and 1950s.) Its story of a persecuted priest is left to progress without worrisome spatial or temporal discontinuities. The myth on which its story feeds, explicit in the title, is the most familiar of all, and the inescapable implications of the Quixote and of Dostoyevsky's tale of the Grand Inquisitor further cater to our certainty of the correctness of our responses. The sole plainly Surreal moment occurs when the picture of Jesus on the priest's wall explodes into a wicked Bosch-like grin, but the image is subjective, "psychological," reflecting the delirium of a wounded prostitute whom the priest is sequestering, and seen only by her. Emotional valences are respected: there is nothing perplexing about the characters' reactions and interplayings. And things are in their place.

Such an account of ***Nazarín*** recalls Robbe-Grillet's account of Balzacian fiction [in *For a New Novel,* 1965]:

> All the technical elements of narrative—systematic use of the past tense and the third

> person, unconditional adoption of chronological development, linear plots, regular trajectory of the passions, impulses of each episode toward a conclusion, etc.—everything tended to impose the image of a stable, coherent, continuous, unequivocal, decipherable universe. Since the intelligibility of the world was not even questioned, to tell a story did not raise a problem. The style of the novel could be innocent.

I trust there is no reason to belabor the frailness (I mean with respect to any reading of Balzac) of an argument that pushes to *that* last sentence. Still, the point is plain enough, and, in its way, and, in its limits, true enough. Because ***Nazarín*** (based, by the way, on a novel of Galdós) tells a story in an age when "To tell a story has become strictly impossible" it cannot lay claim to a place in the realm of New Narrative.

But there is more to ***Nazarín*** than its action and its actors. In the belief that all of Buñuel's work is at least in some sense consanguineous with New Narrative I turn to the film, to its last sequence, and to its exegetes.

Nazarín tells of a priest who consecrates his life to a scrupulous *imitatio Christi,* and so succeeds, episode by episode, in rendering himself increasingly unendurable to both state and church. At the end we watch as he is led off to prison. A peasant woman vending fruit (unaware that this convict is also a self-defrocked priest) offers him a pineapple. He first refuses but then, plainly very troubled by the gift, accepts, telling the woman, "May God reward you." Accompanied by a guard, the priest begins his march. The only sound now is slow, cadenced drumming, louder and louder. The priest passes into close range of the camera. We are given full sight of his torment. Then, the pineapple finally crooked in his right arm, he disappears from our sight. The camera holds on an empty vista, and the film is over.

Because it images the climax of the priest's spiritual adventure, the final shot must be crucial to any reading of ***Nazarín.*** Commentators tell us that the priest's tears reflect his loss of faith, or else his loss of faith in the church, or else his agonized recognition that his kind of otherworldliness is absurd and that his kind of holiness is anyone's undoing, or else his excruciating yet passionately joyful submission to a new secular humanism. The drums announce his imminent execution, or else, less dramatically, just the failure of his dreams, or else the ancient annual ceremonies of self-flagellation in Buñuel's native Calanda. The pineapple, that vexed pineapple, symbolizes humane charity as opposed to required almsgiving and so expresses—you have your choice—(1) Don Nazario's terror or (2) Don Nazario's sense of emancipation.

In the spirit of sheer perversity, probably the only spirit in which to respond to Buñuel, let me suggest still another interpretation, one arrived at most quickly by reference to an earlier shot in the film.

Driven from the city as the result of his passion for charity and his powerfully willed innocence of church politics, Don Nazario has embarked on a pilgrimage across the land. In a village he meets two women from his former quarter who have also fled to the country; persuaded of his sainthood, they ask him to heal a dying child. Soon a group of village women have surrounded him, begging that the exercise miraculous powers of which he himself denies the possession. Here Buñuel cuts to a low-angle shot of a young Indian woman. She points to the priest's feet and says, "He came barefoot, like our Lord Jesus Christ."

The woman's unexpected domination of the frame renders her suddenly formidable, while the equally unexpected camera angle that lifts her above us bestows on her gesture the force of a moral condemnation. She is, I submit, publishing the crime of the priest's existence: through her, Buñuel is saying that the priest's impersonation of Jesus constitutes the most outrageous possible assertion of pride. From the onset, Don Nazario has been guilty of resisting his own humanity and of reacting with dismay and impatience to the humanity of others. His bare feet (he has given his shoes to a peasant), like his numberless other gestures of self-abnegation—the gestures that define his public self—reveal his intolerable self-possession. Now, refusing to attempt to cure the child, asking, "How can I succeed where science has failed?," he dares deny God the power of miracles; he appears unchastened even by the fact that the child recovers promptly once he has consented to pray.

By the end Don Nazario must survey the failure of his proud mission. The prison toward which he marches will be the real thing, not the exquisite torture chamber he furnished for himself; cruel jailers and crueler comrades will continue his instruction in the natural ways of mankind. The character identified as the Parricide Thief who tormented him in an earlier prison sequence brought him to hatred; the peasant woman in the final sequence brings him to love. The suffering imposed by his discoveries finally justifies his Christlike trappings. Christian at long last, he submits to the pressure of tears.

Nazarín is thus a perfectly orthodox, exquisitely subtle tale of Christian discovery and conversion. Its landscape is that of the Gospels: Saint Mark would have been at home among its whores and beggars and cripples. (Despite the specific historical placement in the Mexico of Porfirio Díaz, the film gives a dramatic sense of timelessness. The uniforms—of whores and priests, colonels and peons—withstand chronology. Similarly, the arid reaches, so irrelevant to human space, that Don Nazario will never finish crossing, are not merely those of Mexico, or of Spain, or of Palestine.) Buñuel acknowledges, and honors, the pain and the glory of the Christian experience. The ironies of the title are pointed not at the beautiful priest but at those in the audience who would believe that atheism exerts a more irresistible force over Buñuel's cinema than any other religious persuasion.

As he leaves the frame at the end, Don Nazario is headed not for any civil jail, but for more terrible bondage—for the adjoining soundstage, where they're shooting a Bresson film.

This Christian reading of the film is naturally false. But how much less false is any reading that seeks to restrict or codify Buñuel's meanings? And a Christian reading is in truth much closer to the experience of the film, ignores much less of its iconographical and emotional testimony, than readings that reduce it to a self-satisfied exercise in iconoclasm. A Christian reading does, however, repudiate its own share of textual evidence. If Buñuel's sympathy for the priest is passionate, so is his belief, as inescapable in ***Nazarín*** as in ***Las Hurdes*** or ***Viridiana,*** that it is folly to suppose that we are *not* all past redemption. The other thief of the prison sequence, the one known as Sacrilegist, speaks more explicitly for Buñuel than any other character (in this or in any Buñuel film) when he reveals that he, no less contemptuous than Don Nazario or Buñuel himself of the bourgeois world, of bourgeois worldliness, is as of little use as either Buñuel or Don Nazario (or Jesus) in undermining it. Of course good men are crucified—of course, and there's the end to it.

And so back to the pineapple; back, after what I apologize for as a shamelessly protracted exercise in willful misreading, to *chosisme* and to Robbe-Grillet:

> In this future universe of the novel, gestures and objects will be *there* before being *something;* and they will still be there afterwards, hard, unalterable, eternally present, mocking their own "meaning," that meaning which vainly tries to reduce them to the role of precarious tools, of a temporary and shameful fabric woven exclusively—and deliberately—by the superior human truth expressed in it, only to cast out this awkward auxiliary into immediate oblivion and darkness.
>
> Henceforth, on the contrary, objects will gradually lose their instability and their secrets, will renounce their pseudo-mystery, that suspect interiority which Roland Barthes has called "the romantic heart of things." No longer will objects be merely the vague reflection of the hero's vague soul, the image of his torments, the shadow of his desires. Or rather, if objects still afford a momentary prop to human passions, they will do so only provisionally, and will accept the tyranny of significations only in appearance—derisively, one might say—the better to show how alien they remain to man.

Don Nazario's pineapple puts all in doubt. If it signifies, it signifies its own impotence to signify. Yes, it stands for, or stands in for, a certain secular pity, but what spiritual secrets does it yield? The pineapple is what there is, all there is, but still not enough. It is useless to the priest because he has no knife; useless because, even if he might eat it, it would be neither the blood nor the body of his Lord which alone might sustain him.

In its perverse attentions to food, ***Nazarín*** stands second only to ***The Discreet Charm*** in the Buñuel canon. In the latter film, the incessant failure of the pack of *grands bourgeois* to eat together is the failure of community. (Isn't Buñuel, so often pictured a kind of antichrist, more nearly a kind of antirenoir?) In ***Nazarín,*** failures of eating are failures of Communion. Food and drink are bitterly secular; though he begs, and consumes, his landlady's tortillas, we believe Don Nazario when he tells us he knows how to go hungry. (In the strikingly directed sequence in which the old priest Don Ángel explains to Don Nazario that he has so outraged the church as to endanger his priesthood, the two are at table: the camera, denying the subjectivity of Don Nazario's response to the cup of chocolate and pitcher of hot milk and plate of biscuits before him, pursues, its own courses, independent of the priest's regards, in its contemplation of the food.) The world of ***Nazarín*** is one in which things remain stubbornly things, "alien" to those who most require the spirituality of things. Don Nazario may find in the pineapple "a momentary prop" to his "human passions," but not the salvaging of his spirit.

Early in the film the whore Ándara, wounded and delirious, is desperate for water. She drinks the bloody liquid from the bowl in which her wounds were washed. For her, blood is enough—her own blood, not God's—to slake a bodily thirst.

"In Godard's films," Susan Sontag observes [in *Styles of Radical Will,* 1969] "things display a wholly alienated character. Characteristically, they are used with indifference, neither skillfully nor clumsily; they are simply there. 'Objects exist,' Godard has written, 'and if one pays more attention to them than to people, it is precisely because they exist more than these people. Dead objects are still alive. Living people are often already dead'." Buñuel pushes Godard's point still further: the camera can, and Buñuel's camera does, make more emphatic than the naked human eye the essential unimportance of pursuing points of difference between things and people, or among people merely dead and people merely frozen in a frame, and other varieties of things. Buñuel (unlike Godard, at least much of the time) is not republishing that tiresome lament about the dehumanizing powers of modern life: it is not *modern* life, it is this world, and it is not dehumanization, it is the fact that, animal or vegetable or mineral, alive or not quite alive or medically dead, things we are and shall remain, passing items in the world's inventory.

Buñuel's Archibaldo de la Cruz, in the most lunatic of all farces, is possessed by the belief that he has brought about the deaths of several women and by the wish to bring about the deaths of several more. When he becomes acquainted with a beautiful model, he acquires from a dress salon a dummy mannequin made in the woman's exact image, seats the mannequin in his parlor, and invites the model to visit; the camera begins almost at once to stress the identity of live mannequin and inert mannequin. Archibaldo is now ready to embark on his plan to incinerate the woman in his large potter's kiln; but when she is called away, Archibaldo, enraged, settles for second best and drags the dummy toward the kiln. One of her legs becomes disengaged and lies isolated on the floor. Finally Archibaldo reaches the oven and inches his victim inside. Buñuel's camera records with its usual imperturbable gaze the immolation of the dummy. As the victim writhes and splutters and melts, Buñuel cuts to, of all things, the worst thing—a close-up of the dummy's face—but it is not the dummy's face at all: it is a freeze frame of the face of the living woman.

People, like things, will come apart. The hideous disengaged leg on Archibaldo's floor—it reminds us to be grateful that we know how to laugh—adumbrates the leg amputated from Catherine Deneuve in the bleakest of all Buñuel's films, ***Tristana.*** And throughout Buñuel's work, the camera reduces a "character" to a hand or a head or a garment or—*passim*—a foot, much in the manner of Eliot's early Imagist verse. The disintegration of the self—in ***L'Âge d'or, Él, Archibaldo, Nazarín, Viridiana, Belle de Jour***—is irresistibly imaged in the dismantling of the body.

"If," according to Pechter, in the "ubiquitous fetishism" of Buñuel's world, "some can see only the indication of Buñuel's own idiosyncrasies, they must disregard the fact that the fetish is a perfect physical manifestation of the principle of functionless or dislocated energy around which that world revolves and of the harvest of frustration in which that principle has its issue." The vocabulary of *chosisme* allows for an alternative definition. Buñuel's fetishes are things. Things, in a world whose desperate souls share no community, can at best furnish certain specific meanings to certain desperate souls. Fetishes are failed metaphors, or ruined metaphors, functioning for Buñuel as the natural parody of metaphor.

The ferocity of his assault on metaphor animates all Buñuel's work. Viridiana, fresh from her convent, lines up the heinous metaphors of her self-preservation: "Close-up of a crucifix of rough wood, surrounded by replicas of the instruments of the crucifixion: the crown of thorns, the hammer, the nails, the sponge. These are all placed on a cushion on the ground. Viridiana, clad in a nightgown, is crouched in front of these things praying." In a world of a dead Christianity (of random half-dead half-Christians) these "things" to which one prays make a madness of prayer itself. As well pray to shoes—as Don Jaime, Viridiana's uncle, faithfully does. As well weep for pineapples.

The image of Viridiana before her things recalls one of the most terrible images even Buñuel has granted us: needle, thread, antiseptic, and the rest—all neatly placed before mad Don Francisco in ***Él***—the instruments with which to sew up his wife's orifices. Metaphors drawn from the Marquis de Sade are as hilariously fertile, as sadly barren in this world, as metaphors drawn from the Gospels.

In "Time and Description," Robbe-Grillet accounts for the cinema's seduction of the New Novelists: "It is not the camera's objectivity which interests them, but its possibilities in the realm of the subjective, of the imaginary." He stresses expressive potentials of the soundtrack, "the possibility of acting on two senses at once," and concludes that "the possibility [exists] of presenting with all the appearance of incontestable objectivity what is, also, only dream or memory—in a word, what is only imagination." Thus far the argument holds good; good enough, at least, for Buñuel as for Robbe-Grillet himself. But the next sentence is not without its problems: "There is in the sound the spectator hears, in the image he sees, a primary quality: it is *there,* it is present." The formula calls for qualification. The sights and sounds of the film are indeed present to us, but the time of the film is irretrievably past. Buster Keaton succeeded in defying the temporal difference between audience and film when, in *Sherlock, Jr.,* he walked into the screen. He came to grief.

Stanley Cavell [in *The World Viewed: Reflections on the Ontology of Film,* 1971], among others, has considered such problems at such length and with such care that I should gratefully have let the subject lie were it not for the remark to which Robbe-Grillet's sense of cinema inevitably leads: "The cinema knows only one grammatical mode: the present tense of the indicative." Had Robbe-Grillet thought otherwise, we could not have had *Last Year at Marienbad,* as he goes on to demonstrate: "The universe in which the entire film occurs is, characteristically, that of a perpetual present which makes all recourse to memory impossible." Resnais and Robbe-Grillet subvert the conventions by means of which a sense of anteriority had always been communicated, but these conventions, most particularly the flashback in all its modes, managed to survive our witness of *Marienbad.* To be sure, any flashback sequence in any film may look the same as any sequence in the primary narrative tense: there exist no verb endings to *keep* reminding us. But an introductory dissolve, to take only the least innovative device, is all we need to translate the scene pastward and keep it there. *Marienbad* assaults the very grammar of cinema. The campaign succeeds, but the war will not be won.

Still, it is less the "present" than the "indicative" that seems to me to deny the range of cinema, to misrepresent Buñuel and especially to misrepresent the triumph of Buñuel's later career, ***Belle de Jour.*** Robbe-Grillet speaks of the camera's "possibilities in the realm of the subjective;" ***Belle de Jour*** speaks of the camera's possibilities in the realm of the subjunctive. My desk dictionary (*Webster's Seventh New Collegiate*) announces ***Belle de Jour*** in defining subjunctivity: "Of, relating to, or constituting a verb form or set of forms that represents a denoted act or state not as fact but as contingent or possible or viewed emotionally (as with doubt or desire)."

The "Introductory Note" to the published script of ***Belle de Jour*** runs as follows:

> In this film we have attempted to bring out the masochistic nature of Séverine's impulses. To achieve this, her story is interrupted a number of times by sequences which are either childhood memories or, more often, daydreams, in which certain typical obsessions appear and reappear.
>
> Although these sequences are intended to be imaginary, no distinction, either in the picture or in the sound, is made between them and the other sequences of the film, which seem to describe objectively the relationships between the principal characters and the development of these relationships.

Buñuel's second paragraph—if these indeed are Buñuel's words—comes close to negating the first: the sly "intended to," the "seem to," and the "objectively" are Buñuelian weapons. (Would that the perpetrators of the English-subtitled version of the film had paid attention. Notoriously, they discriminate by means of italicization between what they would have us take to be "objective" and what they would have us take to be "imaginary." One is certain that, if they had had their way, they would also have included a helpful voice-over commentary, explaining why blondes have more fun, but only in brothels.) Even so, these paragraphs oversimplify: trust the film, not the script (be it as accurate, and as scrupulous in description, as that of ***Belle de Jour*** as edited for publication by Robert Adkinson). I turn to five sequences at the center of the film, each separated from the next (as the shots within each are separated) by scalpel strokes.

(1) The first opens with "Long shot of the Bois de Boulogne, as seen from the terrace of an open-air café." A landau arrives: it is the same vehicle we saw in the opening sequence. But then, what did we see in the opening sequence? We saw Séverine/Belle de Jour and her adoring surgeon husband landauing through the Bois. He forces her out of the carriage to be beaten and molested by Coachman and Footman. As in Preston Sturges's *Sullivan's Travels,* which opens with an unannounced film-within-a-film that we cannot know is *not* part of the primary narrative until "The End" appears on the screen, in ***Belle de Jour*** we cannot recognize the supposed primary narrative until Buñuel cuts to Séverine and her husband in their flat. But can we know even then? Our response to either sequence is governed by the ontological nature of the screen itself: which, the sadistic doings on film or the sapped bourgeois domesticity on film, is to be credited? Naturally enough, the Surrealists of the twenties clutched at film as if for their very lives.

In the cafe, Séverine accepts an invitation from a Duke that leads to the queerest necrophiliac ritual you ever saw—but is it any queerer than the finely detailed masochistic ritual exacted by a gynecologist observed by Séverine in the brothel to which she has escaped (all this presumably in the indicative mood) in order to calm her own masochistic urges? (And who should be seated at a table in the Bois café, observing the Duke's overtures, but Don Luis? After the manner of Hitchcock, Buñuel certifies the bizarre happenings by presencing himself as *the* logical attendant.)

(2) Séverine and her husband, in their flat, are preparing to retire for the night. Unable to make love, she assures him that she loves him more every day.

(3) We return to Séverine's flat. M. Husson, the man she fears and hates and perhaps desires more than any other (because he knows better than any other how to humiliate her), the man who provided her with the precise address of the brothel, arrives to pay a visit. He is denied.

(4) "Suddenly the interior of the bar at the winter sports resort, which we have already seen, reappears." This is the kind of place in which Séverine and her husband are, or act, at home among their own kind. This, then, is presumably a sequence in the indicative. Séverine and husband, Husson and his friend Renée, are seated at table. Husson and Séverine "disappear under the table." Renée sneaks a peek and tells Séverine's husband that Husson is "taking out a little envelope . . . a little packet of lily seeds." Séverine's and Husson's descent echoes the Duke's disappearance under the catafalque in the necrophiliac episode; the lily seeds resume the asphodels we saw in abundance in that same sequence.

(5) The script reads:

> Long shot of the Champs-Elysées in the daytime. A young NEWSPAPER-SELLER walks along the pavement towards the camera, shouting: PAPER-SELLER: *"Herald Tribune!—New York Herald Tribune!"*

No moviegoer of the sixties should have suffered confusion over this establishing shot, for what it establishes is, specifically, the world of *Breathless,* and more generally the world of American criminality translated to the streets of Paris, the world recast by Jean-Pierre Melville. Gangsters will, inevitably, now penetrate this scene (a robbery-murder will follow within seconds), and one of the gangsters will, inevitably, become the lover of Séverine and assassin *manqué* of her husband—all this, presumably, within the "objective" world of the "principal characters." But if the world of movies is not the world of our "daydreams," none will ever be. Séverine's gangster-lover is born of film itself.

All of the last third of ***Belle de Jour,*** that section of the film in which Séverine's world of prostitution and humiliation collides with her world of *seizième* complacencies, proves as fantastic as anything that precedes. There can be no line of discrimination: though both are clearly denoted, the abrupt advent of gold-toothed gangster lovers in Séverine's world is neither more nor less subjunctive than her husband's stunning recovery from paraplegia and blindness at the end.

The opening title of ***Las Hurdes*** proclaims that most appalling of documentaries "a filmed essay in human geography." Francisco Aranda speaks of Buñuel's essayistic (but never, I find, livresque) tendencies in his analysis of ***The Milky Way.*** But it is the "human geography" that calls up not only ***Las Hurdes*** but all the best of Buñuel's work. In the manner of a geographer who refuses to restrict his field of study, Buñuel with passionate curiosity examines human beings in their longitudes and latitudes, their climates—their spaces. (pp. 237-47)

Elliot Rubinstein, "Buñuel's World, or the World and Buñuel," in Philosophy and Literature, *Vol. 2, No. 2, Fall, 1978, pp. 237-48.*

John Flasher and Douglas Radcliff-Umstead (essay date 1981)

[*In the following essay, Flasher and Radcliff-Umstead analyze Buñuel's satiric vision as expressed in the film* That Obscure Object of Desire.]

As a filmmaker the Spanish director Luis Buñuel (b. 1900) requires motion pictures to serve as mocking witnesses to a deforming reality which reduces human beings to grotesque creatures of impotent resentment. Since the surrealistic experiment of Buñuel's first film ***Un Chien Andalou*** of 1928, his screen works have represented a world of spiritually and physically warped victims struggling in vain against a fate that ridicules their futile efforts: the diseased beggar in ***Viridiana*** hoping to contaminate an affluent society that considers him an outcast; the Black fugitive and the White game-warden of ***The Young One*** who discover their common identity as outlaws; the unloved adolescents of ***Los Olvidados*** who transcend their aloneness through acts of brutality; the frigid wife in ***Belle de Jour*** who seeks in prostitution the erotic fulfillment absent in marriage; the idealistic prison reformer of ***La Fièvre monte à El Pao*** who becomes the puppet of an authoritarian regime. Opposed to bourgeois morality, Buñuel has sought in his films to satirize society's unjust institutions of family, religion, and nationalism. With derisive humor this director attacks the hypocrisy of the powerful individuals who abuse their advantages of wealth and position to compel others to submit to their pleasure. This filmmaker presents an ambivalent reality where oppressor and victim alike appear under Buñuel's sardonic scrutiny as he exposes their self-calculating motivations. This ambivalence of satiric vision especially characterizes the recent motion picture ***Cet Obscur Objet du Désir*** (1977) whose derisive humor will be the subject of our essay. In that film the director focuses upon the laughable decadence of society in which rich and poor alike treat each other as instruments for the satisfaction of the lust for power or libidinous desire. Humor for Buñuel is a trenchant irony that undermines and demolishes the bourgeois world that the filmmaker finds to be ultimately destructive of human potential. In ***Cet Obscur Object du Désir*** the director creates a situational satire for the savage aggressions, manipulation, exploitation, and humiliating compromises of contemporary social life. Often employing surrealist techniques, Buñuel holds a humoristic distortion mirror up to oppressive reality to capture debasing images of the victims of his punitive satire. A motion picture like ***Cet Obscur Object*** uses satire to assault the structures of modern-day society whose false values the cinematic artist rejects for being totally corrupt. In this essay we intend to explore the literary source for ***Cet Obscur Object du Désir*** and to demonstrate Buñuel's satiric humor.

Collaborating with Jean-Claude Carrière, the Spanish director derived his script from Pierre Louÿs' novel *La Femme et le Pantin* of 1898. No fewer than five films have been based on that novel. Geraldine Farrar appeared in the earliest version of 1920. Nine years later Jacques De Baroncelli featured Conchita Montenegro in an ill-fated venture that was never commercially screened. In 1935 Josef von Sternberg used a script by John Dos Passos for *The Devil Is a Woman* with Marlene Dietrich in the title role. Julien Duvivier took up the same subject in 1958 with Brigitte Bardot in *A Woman like Satan.* What distinguishes all the preceding movie versions from Buñuel's is a common acceptance of Louÿs' characterization of the diabolically cruel enchantress who degrades her impassioned lover while forever frustrating his erotic desire. Buñuel's artistry remains too profoundly ambivalent for him to reproduce the schematic opposition of the *femme fatale* and her enamored victim as represented in the French novel. Louÿs took his inspiration from a Goya painting in Madrid's Prado Museum which is described in the novel as showing four women dressed in Spanish skirts merrily laughing on a lawn while they toss a man-sized puppet up in the air. Woman is thus portrayed as the pitiless puppeteer, the exploiter who pulls the strings of her marionette lover according to her caprices. Louÿs builds his narrative upon the mistress/slave relationship with the female's ability to dominate the male. Buñuel instead shows the predatory mentality of the bourgeois man who equates eros with a commercial exchange of cash for sexual services. Through the woman's resistance and her success at extracting ever larger sums of money from her well-to-do pursuer without succumbing to his advances, the Spanish filmmaker demonstrates the symbiotic rapport that binds the couple together in reciprocal need. Therefore Buñuel realizes a dimension of inquiry into the humorous interdependence of a man and a woman such as no previous motion picture director ever developed from Louÿs' novel.

Buñuel draws the title of his movie from a declaration by the novel's protagonist Don Mateo Diaz: " . . . je n'avais jamais eu de maîtresse blonde. J'aurai toujours ignoré ces pâles objets du désir." For the elusively obscure object of male desire in the film version the director originally selected the darkly androgynous Maria Schneider. Upon that actress's withdrawal from the cast the filmmaker decided by a stroke of inspiration to execute a major visual jest by splitting the role of the temptress between two women: the rather refined but somewhat morose Carole Bouquet; and the sultry Angela Molina with her long black eyelashes. Instead of representing opposing qualities of the enchantress's personality, the two actresses merge into one another often within a brief sequence of shots. The deliberate blurring of reality is further reinforced by the dubbing of a single voice, that of Florence Jordetti, for the two different actresses. Buñuel forever remains a surrealist laughing at the conventional view of the real world and compelling his spectators to question the fast-moving images before their very eyes. This splitting of the female lead for the movie results in a cinematic *Doppelgänger* whose unpredictable appearance from moment to moment continually teases not only the viewers but also the picture's main actor as portrayed by Fernando Rey. Just as the director distanced the public from the leading female role, he similarly had Rey's Spanish-accented French replaced with dubbing by the native French actor Michel Piccoli. These filmic jokes with the two main characters contribute toward a continual undercutting of the orderly and logically structured world of wealthy gentlemen and the servant-girls who become the object of seduction. This distortion of the two lead parts acts as one of the forms of violence to occur to the satiric victims of Buñuel's motion picture.

In its opening sequences ***Cet Obscur Objet du Désir*** unfolds with the ease of the automatic flow of the unconscious. The director's choice of color film over black and white not only heightens the intensity of experience but also participates in the work's prevailing irony. Certain colors, like the flaming red of roses or of a raging fire following an explosion, come to be associated with the drama of suppression and evasion taking place across the screen. Buñuel abandons the *fin de siècle* time period of the French novel to situate his picture in the mounting social turbulence of the nineteen-seventies. To create the movie's protagonist the director blends facets from two characters in Louÿs' narrative: the impassioned Spaniard Don Mateo and his apprentice in the art of amorous pursuit the young Frenchman André Stévenol, who both become the film's Gallic lover Mathieu. The world to which Mathieu has always been accustomed is one of elegance and deluxe comfort, but as the director jokingly illustrates, that world is literally blowing apart. At the movie's start Mathieu is chauffeured to a travel agency where he buys a first-class ticket for himself on the Seville-Madrid-Paris train, and a second-class ticket for the valet who will always accompany him on his journeys. As Mathieu returns to his limousine, the camera cuts to a banker (played, with typical Buñuelian mirth, by the movie's actual producer Serge Silberman) walking toward his own car. No sooner does the banker's chauffeur turn the ignition key than a bomb explodes covering the screen with engulfing red flames. This act of violence occurs so suddenly and unexpectedly on a busy street basking in the glare of the summer sun in Seville that it produces a quick jolt and nervous laugh on the part of filmgoers. But by ironical contrast Mathieu remains only slightly perturbed as he remarks to his driver: "We are going to be late, turn around . . ." On hearing that terrorists are at work everywhere, this well-dressed gentleman mentally shuts off the unwanted information. The banker's death is much less of a concern to Mathieu than a fly in his martini as he refuses to recognize the terrorists' threat to his class and his privileged way of life. Throughout the course of the film numerous acts of terrorist violence will occur—shots ringing out on the street at night to mark an assassination, passenger airliners being bombed in flight—to undermine everyday existence. But Mathieu and the feminine object of his desire attempt to pretend that they can insulate themselves from the almost daily atrocities. In Louÿs' novel events are taking place in the last years of the nineteenth century during the period of the Cuban struggle for independence from Spain, and as an ardent Royalist Don Mateo laments the loss of the Spanish Empire. But the political dimension of the French work never involves the militant effort to destroy bourgeois society that occupies the motion picture from its initial sequences.

To relate the background of Mathieu's enslavement to the imperious Conchita Pérez, the film director has the protagonist describe his misadventures to some strangers on the train to Paris. In the comfort of a first-class compartment the traveling occupants seem a microcosm of the bourgeoisie: a strict law-and-order judge who advocates fighting terrorists with the most severe decrees of the courts; a "prim and proper" mother who grows so enthralled with the risqué details of Mathieu's story that she sends her young daughter into the corridor; and a dwarf who is a criminologist with a degree in psychology from the Sorbonne. Buñuel frequently introduces dwarfs in his films, as in the Mexican-produced ***Nazarin*** of 1958, as a grotesque commentary on life's cruelty. In ***Cet Obscur Objet*** the dwarf criminologist reveals the freakish distortions of present-day psychological theory by providing instant analyses for the incidents in Mathieu's tale of amorous obsession without ever once shedding light on the lover's true motivations. Mathieu recounts his story as an explanation to his traveling companions for having startled them by dumping a bucket of water on an apparently harmless young woman who was attempting to board the train. Framing devices like this story *en route* on a train are a nineteenth-century narrative technique that was widely employed by writers such as Maupassant. The major portion of Louÿs' novel is Don Mateo's recounting to Stévenol the long history of the Spaniard's degrading relationship with Conchita. These narrative framing devices of a story within a story as related by a member of the social elite at some gathering aroused Jean Paul Sartre's disapproval in *Situations II* for the apparent solidification of experience that the technique makes possible. But Buñuel uses the frame to expose the emptiness of experience. None of the travelers succeeds in recognizing the parallel between Conchita's erotic terrorism and the political violence. Instead of placing the actors of the frame into a situation of social superiority as belonging to the supposedly real world, the director focuses upon the falseness of their values and institutions. Buñuel handles his frame to satirize the short-sighted self-satisfaction of the social hierarchy represented by the companions of the first-class compartment.

For the flashbacks to recapture the agonized past, the camera switches to Mathieu's elegantly furnished Parisian apartment where a medium shot shows Carole Bouquet as Conchita in a maid's uniform carrying to the dinner table a vase of red roses. This servant, whose full first name is Concepción in ironical reference to the Immaculate Conception of the Virgin Mary, immediately fired Mathieu's passionate interest. As an employer Mathieu had become accustomed to winning the cooperation of his dependents to further his sexual intrigues. Conchita's eventual resistance will gain for her the characterization for being "the worst of women." Mathieu fails to see just what the director permits the viewers to behold: that he is an urbane satyr who takes advantage of wealth, position, and government contacts. The seduction scene which follows dinner ends in an evasion that Mathieu had never experienced before. Although the master enjoyed the connivance of his valet, who sent the maid to the drawing room with an aphrodisiac beverage for Mathieu, the employer's suave tactics achieved nothing for him except a clumsily executed kiss and caress. Angela Molina as Conchita smilingly rejected her would-be seducer's reassurances that in his house she was his equal. Having lost her father, the girl must work to support herself and her mother, whose sole occupation was going to church. Despite her severe economic need Conchita would not yield to her employer's sexual harassment, and on the following morning the valet greeted Mathieu with the dismal news that the maid had left without collecting her pay. That act of evasion marked the beginning of the girl's hold over her former employer, for she set a value upon herself that he would struggle to match. Buñuel has portrayed the bourgeois household as a corrupt center of exploitation. The director mocks the vitiated values of middle-class society where Mathieu's frustration over not obtaining with money an object of his desire causes him to find that object increasingly desirable. All of the sensuality and jubilant sexuality of the bourgeois male aim at the elusive lower-class woman.

A certain malicious destiny seems to bring Mathieu and Conchita together in a series of coincidental encounters. Taking a holiday in Switzerland, Mathieu becomes the victim of a gang of young thugs wielding a butcher knife who take his wallet away. The use of camera long-shots here serves to relate the actors to the physical environment: an idyllic moment in a neatly trimmed Swiss park where a fashionably attired gentleman nearly meets his death. Along with presenting the contrast between the deceptive pastoral peacefulness of the scene and the violent disorder threatened by the toughs, this sequence reunites Mathieu with the young woman. For by an extension of logic it turns out that Conchita is a friend of the thieving gang, whom she apologetically represents to her previous employer as students down on their luck in need of traveling funds. For Mathieu the theft has brought him back into contact with the unattainable One. This man has gained no insight whatsoever from the violence that the knife's blade almost visited upon him. Unlike the privileged characters in Buñuel's film ***Le Charme Discret de la Bourgeoisie*** (1972), the protagonist here fails to arrive at a moment of consciousness from the fear of violence. So great does Mathieu's erotic obsession remain, that the mugging cannot rouse him from spiritual torpor. Everything stays extraneous to the pursuit of the inaccessible Conchita.

After Mathieu and the girl resume their relationship in Paris, the film closely follows the novel except that the director inserts in serio-comical fashion anarchic scenes illustrating the chaotic conditions disrupting society in the 1970s. On visiting Conchita's shabby apartment, Mathieu meets her pious mother who never questions the older man's interest in her daughter. The sequences in the cluttered lower-class apartment possess a surrealistic quality of self-reflexion with grainy shots of mirror images where Mathieu assiduously courts the young woman who appears now as Carole Bouquet and then as Angela Molina. Forever claiming that she is still "*mocita*" (a virgin), Conchita further enflames the man's desires and raises her price in his estimation. One day Mathieu comes across Conchita at a restaurant-cocktail lounge where she has taken a job as hat-check girl. The red carnation as a boutonniere for the restaurant's tyrannical manager becomes the sequence's outstanding color image as Mathieu offers to take Conchita away from the drudgery of the job and set her up in her own apartment. In order to placate the mother, Mathieu invites the woman to his flat where the camera zooms in to catch the Frenchman stuffing an envelope with banknotes as he successfully purchases collaboration in his erotic strategy. This sequence is typical Buñuelian satire of religious hypocrisy. For although the señora Incarnación Pérez devoutly clutches a Bible and a rosary in one hand, with the other she greedily grasps the envelope. While this exchange is taking place, the film maker plays an auditory and visual joke as an off-screen sound of a springing trap is heard and then the valet finds a rat caught in a trap on the living-room floor of the luxurious apartment. Just as Conchita's mother represents avarice, betrayal of maternal duty through complicity in immoral acts, and religious hypocrisy, the rat symbolizes the turpitude and decadence of the bourgeoisie. Buñuel's obvious delight in making religion his satirical target also shows itself in the crucifixes that hang respectively over Conchita's bed in her apartment and in the bedroom of the country house where Mathieu will attempt once again to seduce Conchita. In this director's films religion is ridiculed as a force that rarely upholds moral purity but contributes to corruption.

This motion picture reaches its supreme moment of black humor in the bedroom sequence where Mathieu at last hopes to consummate his passion. To the satyr's utter amazement he discovers that underneath Conchita's flimsy slip she is wearing athletic pants of whipcord and leather lacings to frustrate his feverish lunges. His inability to strip away the chastity pants seems to drain away his very lifeblood. Supposedly to appease her exasperated lover but apparently to goad his lust still further, Conchita fondles him tenderly as she snuggles alongside him in bed. While playing the role of amorous virgin, the girl explains that her temporary refusal is motivated only by the fear that if she did submit to Mathieu's desire he would afterward reject her. Conchita's insight is correct because the act of erotic submission would result in her immediate decline in Mathieu's esteem. The young woman also understands that her control over her lover depends on his never losing hope of one day consummating his desire. Buñuel maintains a teasing sense of ambiguity about Conchita. Is she a virgin or a shameless exploiter of Mathieu's emotions? Has she always told the truth, or has she mastered the art of mendacious calculation? Mathieu's chief error in regard to the girl is his belief that with money he can overcome her elusiveness through eros. His is the mistake of the bourgeois who constantly objectify other persons in order to manipulate them. Buñuel's humor arises in Conchita's being a thinking subject who rebels by tantalizing the man who attempts to possess her. In the same way that the director visually teases viewers with two actresses as Conchita and sometimes fools the public into believing they are watching one and the same person, the elusive young woman evades definition.

Since Buñuel wishes to explore beyond a woman's manipulation of her puppet-lover, the filmmaker presents the violent vindictiveness with which Mathieu tries to reassert his role as social superior. Even though Conchita reassures her older lover that she detests younger men as idiots and prefers mature men, Mathieu's nagging fear seems to find confirmation one evening when he discovers that the girl has hidden in one of the spare rooms of his spacious apartment a Spanish youth called "El Morenito." Conchita explains that after the young man, the brother of a girl friend of hers, was evicted from his hotel, she allowed him to share the bed she would use whenever she stayed at Mathieu's apartment. Trembling with consternation and believing Conchita to have played him for a fool, Mathieu drives the two out onto the street. Once again the girl's claim to being a virgin comes into question. Pierced to the quick by her actions, Mathieu responds with a ferocity equal to that of any terrorist. Buñuel's portrayal of the severity in this bourgeois citizen brings to mind this observation by Gogol: ". . . seeing how much . . . savage brutality lies hidden under refined cultured politeness, . . . even in a man whom the world accepts as a gentleman and a man of honor." Partly to punish the girl and partly to put himself away from temptation, Mathieu has his cousin the district attorney evict Conchita and her mother from their apartment by police order and then deport them to Spain as undesirable aliens. This act of cruelty against impoverished, defenseless creatures allows the bourgeois to demonstrate his ultimate mastery through the legal means at his disposal. The filmmaker, however, reveals through a sardonic remark of the dwarf-psychologist that Mathieu's savage attempt at revenge fails to liberate him from thralldom to the elusive girl.

Because repressive measures do not secure release, Mathieu undertakes a journey to Spain to locate Conchita. To represent the radically disruptive effect that the young woman has worked on the older man's life, the director employs surrealistic sequences where Mathieu's obsessed mentality beholds a strangely altered world. The magic illuminations of surrealism, as in ***Un Chien Andalou,*** disclose the perverse moral directions that the contemporary ruling class has followed. One day in Seville as Mathieu strolls through a square, two women accost him asking for alms. A close-up shot shows the younger of the women carrying a pink-skinned pig, lovingly wrapped like a baby in a blanket. As Mathieu graciously hands the younger woman some money, the pig grunts with satisfaction. This gentleman smiles approvingly, caresses the pig, and appears to admire the beggars' original idea of using the animal instead of a famished infant for their mendicant trade. In Buñuel's movies animals embody distinctly human traits, such as a pig's insatiable appetite as a metaphor for lust and greed. Mathieu contemplates with amusement his own porcine bestiality.

In both the novel and the film the protagonist eventually finds Conchita working as a flamenco dancer at a Seville cabaret. Don Mateo and his cinematic counterpart display an equal naïveté in accepting the girl's story that she is allowed certain rest periods between the strenuous dance numbers. After a short period the truth comes out that Conchita gives private performances in the nude to small groups of freely spending foreigners. With Buñuel's droll awareness of present-day tourism in Europe the novel's "*Inglès*" (foreigners in general) are transformed for the movie into goggling Japanese travelers whose strong currency could well afford them the voluptuous spectacle of Conchita's (Angela Molina's) frenzied execution of the "jota" dance. The girl succeeds in placating her lover's furious outburst of jealousy by appealing to his knowledge of her economic insecurity. Once again the film director, closely following the novel's plot, exposes the acquisitive mentality of the bourgeoisie with their businesslike transactions. There can never be a genuine communication between the lovers, not just on account of Conchita's spiritual and physical impenetrability but also in the movie because of Mathieu's insistence in believing he can buy her like anything else he desires. When Conchita promises to abandon dancing and accept him as her lover if Mathieu would provide her with a small house in Seville and a dowry, he readily agrees since he regards the affair as a high-risk venture that requires constant outlays of cash to insure success. But even after the girl receives the deed and key to a house, her newly won financial independence will permit her to rebel against the desirous representative of the master class.

A scene of supreme humiliation occurs in the novel and film when Conchita bars her frustrated lover outside the iron-grill gate leading to her patio. All the contempt that she has managed to mask is revealed as the disdainful young woman tells the older man of her horror and disgust toward him. To degrade Mathieu still further, Conchita calls Morenito out and engages in an act of intimacy in the patio while her former patron looks on like a powerless convict behind prison bars. While the novel suggests that Morenito is a resolutely virile type, Buñuel intensifies Mathieu's humiliation by showing the youth as one of the effete androgynes that have appeared in his movies ever since ***Un Chien Andalou.*** That a well-to-do gentleman long-accustomed to conquest must suffer defeat by an effeminate student becomes a crushing indignity. After this sequence of emotional terrorism the movie director plunges his protagonist into a scene of urban terrorism when a gang of thugs who might be criminals or political activists stop Mathieu on the way to his Seville residence and steal his car. Buñuel's derisive art forever works to undermine the self-confidence and well-being of the bourgeois who constantly find themselves under attack in their intimate relationships and public life.

Divergence between the novel and the motion picture takes place during the aftermath of the humiliation. In both works Conchita visits her would-be lover's villa to say that he does not understand women, only to receive a violent beating, but in the novel the girl succumbs at last to Don Mateo's desire and becomes for a period his mistress, while in the film Mathieu leaves for France with Conchita in vengeful pursuit. Louÿs represents the reversal of the master-slave relation between the lovers who live together bound by Mateo's physical abuse and Conchita's sadistic tantalization of his jealousy. After Mateo flees his tormentor by escaping to Tangier, Conchita marries a wealthy man who later moves to Bolivia and leaves her to a life of amorous dalliance in Seville. The novel's central irony arises in the development that no one profits from Don Mateo's frame story of his sentimental enslavement. For Stévenol immediately strikes up a liaison with Conchita and plans to take her to Paris at the very moment when she receives a letter from Mateo pleading that he cannot live without her. Louÿs explored how sensual triumph did not result in satisfaction but produced a feeling of emptiness that had to be filled with mutually destructive exchanges of outraged passions. Mateo always remains the puppet awaiting a mistress to pull the strings of desire.

Buñuel's finale achieves a heightened suspense as the quest after that obscure object continues because Conchita appears to stay a virgin until the end. A fatal bond of mutual dependence compels Mathieu and the girl to avoid a definitive separation. Conchita revenges herself on her attacker by bursting into the train compartment to dump a bucket of water over the impeccably dressed gentleman. Reunited, the couple appear in the film's last sequence walking through an enclosed shopping mall. In a display window a woman is seated sewing a hole in a lace bridal gown marked by blood stains that recall Conchita's bloodied pillow, panties and shoes from an early sequence in the film after Mathieu punished her for the humiliating charade in the patio with Morenito. Even though Mathieu wanted to believe the girl's story that Morenito was a homosexual, his wounded pride forced him to beat her ferociously until in ecstasy she acknowledged that he truly loved her. The torn, blood-streaked gown stands for their violent relationship that has resembled a sterile marriage. Perhaps the needle and thread symbolize virginity, just as in Buñuel's movie ***El*** (1952) where a jealous husband sews his wife's vagina together. The gown may have come from a burlap sack in a corner of the window. This sack is one of the director's visual gags. At one moment in the motion picture Mathieu's valet answered his employer's request for an opinion about women by quoting an amorous friend who called females "a sack of excrement." In another sequence Mathieu and Conchita were walking along the Seine as he was carrying for no apparent reason a burlap sack. Then one evening at a Seville nightclub Mathieu absent-mindedly left a sack behind upon leaving until a waiter called him back to retrieve the mysterious bag. Are all these sacks one and the same? Does the sack stand for all the decadent desires that the bourgeoisie and their victims must bear as their burden? That sack's destructive potential becomes evident as the movie enters its last moments. As the camera follows Mathieu and Conchita advancing along in the shopping district, a radio loudspeaker conveys a police report about the murder of the bishop of Siena by an alliance of extremist groups known as the P.O.P., the PRIQUE, the GRIP, and the RUT in a campaign of violence under the direction of the R.A.I.J. (Revolutionary Army of the Infant Jesus). Buñuel combines terrorism and institutional religion to criticize them both, juxtaposing erotic acronyms and religious movements to poke fun at them while suggesting a common repressiveness. The filmmaker may have also been trying to show that the terrorists' violence expressed their own frenetic pursuit of some "obscure object of desire." Just after the radio announcement the movie ends explosively with a blast that covers the screen with black smoke and fiery reds. This explosion could be interpreted as an hallucination on Mathieu's part to anticipate the flaming apocalypse toward which his bourgeois-controlled world is headed. Perhaps the burlap sack which Mathieu carried around Paris and Seville was actually loaded with dynamite. Then the bombing might mark a fatal resolution reached by Mathieu to avenge himself for being denied the only object he desired in this chaotic and irrational world that had nothing else to offer to his decadent, self-indulgent spirit. The director intentionally closes the film with an enigma as he ridicules both the respresentatives of social order and their terroristic opponents for their destructive violence.

In ***Cet Obscur Objet du Désir*** Buñuel's vision appears as humorous in nature but not ultimately comic because no new society will emerge from the ashes of the cataclysmic explosion. Pierre Louÿs in his novel wished to reveal time as an endless round of comically obsessed lovers carrying on their intimate affairs. In the film the director does not redeem society but condemns it. Both Mathieu and Conchita vanish in the bombing without having ever experienced an epiphanic moment of insight into the obsessions that joined their destinies. For Buñuel the world of those two frustrated lovers does not deserve reinforcement or futurity. His satiric art employs all the negative powers of film as a dangerous weapon to annihilate a ridiculous bourgeois society. The derisive distortions to which unfulfilled erotic desires drive the main characters must lead to the obliteration of the cinematic world. In final analysis, we the viewers of the film are the victims of Buñuel's satiric assault as the director's humor aims at the laughable absurdities of our own fragile world. (pp. 7-17)

John Flasher and Douglas Radcliff-Umstead, "The Derisive Humor of Luis Buñuel," in Perspectives on Contemporary Literature, *Vol. 7, 1981, pp. 7-17.*

Jonathan Romney (essay date 7 August 1992)

[In the following excerpt, Romney discusses Buñuel's last seven films, maintaining that while their use of humor occasionally seems dated, they nevertheless retain the power to unsettle the viewer.]

There is a moment early in Luis Buñuel's ***The Discreet Charm of the Bourgeoisie*** that is more unsettling for me than anything else in the film. It is not one of its famous tilts at bourgeois mores (the many aborted feasts, the appearance of a platoon of dope-smoking militia), or even one of its uncanny returns of the repressed (a ghostly Bloody Sergeant, a torturer's piano disgorging a flood of cockroaches). Instead, it is when, in the middle of one of Buñuel's staid group shots. Bulle Ogier suddenly walks straight up to the camera and starts looking around the room, as if absent-mindedly surveying the parameters of the cinema screen—as if asking "What the hell are we doing in this film anyway?"

This is one of the rare moments when Buñuel seems to be interested in film as film, rather than as a manifestation of his own peculiar dream language. It probably appeals for entirely subjective reasons, because of my own academic fetish about self-reflexive cinema, but at least it stands out for me as a more derisive gesture towards the complacent viewer than any of the film's obvious satirical barbs.

This throwaway scene, in which the character seems to acknowledge the stuffy classicism of Buñuel's style and attempts for a second to puncture it, is simply one of the film's better jokes. And as a joke, I *get* it. Conversely, I *understand* some of its more elaborate gags, but I don't *get* them. They just don't strike a chord.

This wholly personal reaction to Buñuel is in the nature of his cinema. ***The Discreet Charm*** does have a vestigial plot, about a group of rich friends repeatedly failing to get fed, but it is more like a dream than a conventional narrative, and we know what Freud tells us about dreams and jokes.

Just as some dreams leave us in a sweat on waking and others don't, only some of Buñuel's images touch a nerve, and the same goes for his jokes. Even when he seems to have a message to impart, Buñuel is more interested in the ways that messages can get scrambled. When his films make sense, they also unmake it. They leave a lot to the viewer's subjectivity, acknowledging that in the final analysis, meaning is always up for grabs.

This appeal to the potential randomness of response makes it still possible to call Buñuel "Surrealist", long after the term has ceased to refer to anything other than a failed art movement of the 1920s and 1930s. His own early films—***Un Chien Andalou*** and ***L'Age d'Or***—made the Surrealist image concrete and visible. They thereby helped bring about a climate in which Surrealism could be seen less as an ethic of mobilising the unconscious against social stabilities, and more as a clever technique for stringing together imagistic puns.

Surrealism became a tic very quickly, and we're still seeing the worst of it today, when it means nothing more than the latest Silk Cut ad or the insouciantly wacky name of some indie band. The Suburban Surreal, a somewhat complacent mindset in which the mid-American imagination at once parodies and distances itself from its own excesses, currently dominates the mainstream in films like *Edward Scissorhands* and *Meet the Applegates,* and in TV's brand leader *Twin Peaks.* (pp. 31-2)

According to many critics, adapting himself to the style of French bourgeois comedy was the most subversive thing Buñuel ever did. In this light, the final films look innocuous (flat lighting, overwrought realist decor, stiff theatrical composition) all the better to deliver their shocks. But for much of the time, there is a claustrophobic dullness to their look, and a rather too measured pace, as if we're constantly being told to settle down and wait patiently for the next shock.

These films are disappointing if we're after undiluted delirium—if, to paraphrase André Breton on beauty, we expect Buñuel to be "convulsive or not at all". Their formal sobriety, especially in ***Belle de Jour*** and the visually oppressive ***Tristana,*** makes them far more staid than that. And when they do turn out to be jack-in-the-box bundles of oneirism like ***The Phantom of Liberty,*** they still disappoint, because the craziness is so often placed at the service of social or religious observations that today seem redundant or pedantic (unless you happen to be a French cleric or aristocrat, or an ex-Surrealist for that matter).

We're bound to feel short-changed, in fact, if we believe in the received image of Buñuel as a reckless provocateur, a purveyor of irreducibly crazed dream imagery, an anarchic baiter of clericalism and the state. But this image presumes that Buñuel had an ideology before he had a cinema, whereas the films actually give rise to the ideology *and* at the same time blithely militate against it. . . .

[Buñuel's last seven] films fall into two categories: moral narratives with twists, adapted from arcane, dusty texts by authors like Perez Galdós and Pierre Louys, and labyrinthine constructions like ***The Phantom of Liberty,*** which, even when it was first released here in 1974, had its sting dulled by the fact that *Monty Python* had got there first.

Two films stand out, if only because they are less celebrated as classics. ***The Diary of a Chambermaid,*** the only black-and-white film of the seven, is the most stylistically rich, despite its strictly classical visuals that recall Jean Renoir (who made his own version of Octave Mirbeau's novel in 1946).

Jeanne Moreau, whose reserved sassiness knocks Catherine Deneuve's much-vaunted "glacial" quality in ***Belle de Jour*** right back into the icebox, is the chambermaid who defiantly cuts a swathe through a household of repressive fetishists and fascists. It seems quite a classical narrative of *fin-de-siècle* social conquest, but just when we seem to reach the moral payoff, Buñuel pulls the rug from under our feet with a bewildering succession of jump cuts and an in-joke about the police chief who banned ***L'Age d'Or.***

The other wild card is ***The Milky Way,*** the first of Buñuel's Cerberus-headed shaggy-dog stories. Two tramps *en route* for Santiago de Compostella encounter assorted divine and demonic manifestations, while Buñuel intersperses anecdotes from the life of Christ and a series of episodes illustrating famous heresies. The pettifogging minutiae of theological debate are actually more mesmerising than the commonsensical anti-clerical jabs in the other films, as if Buñuel dares us to take seriously something beyond normal comprehension and clearly absurd in its claim to all-importance. The film is not really about theology at all, but about the possibility of spinning narrative gags out of theological premises. It's a kind of dare, a Ripley's Believe-It-Or-Not of film construction.

Even when you can't really like these films, you have to admire their ability to leave you stranded. They seem to make obvious points, but wander increasingly away from them until Buñuel pulls his trick endings, and suddenly there seems to be no point at all. The jump-cuts in ***Diary,*** or the mystifying footage tacked onto ***Tristana*** like an anti-trailer of previous attractions, suddenly unravel the carpet we've just walked across and make us start again. We must try to figure out the pattern from scratch.

A character in ***The Milky Way*** muses: "God's designs are impenetrable." By that, he presumably means Buñuel's. If these films are dreams, all the more reason that they should be impenetrable—open to interpretation, but indifferent to it. That's a point worth remembering when Buñuel takes his shots at sitting targets. The obvious jokes may not be that funny, but the suspicion is that there are always other jokes we aren't getting, and which are therefore at our expense. In the things we don't get, but which unsettle us anyway, we find the films' last residue of unadulterated Surrealism. (p. 32)

Jonathan Romney, "Delirium Diluted," in New Statesman & Society, *Vol. 5, No. 214, August 7, 1992, pp. 31-2.*

FURTHER READING

Conrad, Randall. " 'I Am Not a Producer!'—Working with Buñuel." *Film Quarterly* XXXIII, No. 1 (Fall 1979): 2-11.

Interview with film producer Serge Silberman, who worked with Buñuel on such films as *That Obscure Object of Desire* and *The Phantom of Liberty.*

Harcourt, Peter. "Luis Buñuel: Spaniard and Surrealist." *Film Quarterly* XX, No. 3 (Spring 1967): 2-19.

Assesses the importance of Surrealism and Spanish Catholicism to an understanding of Buñuel's films.

Kuenzli, Rudolf E., ed. *Dada and Surrealist Film.* New York: Willis Locker & Owens, 1987, 255 p.

Includes essays on Surrealist elements in Buñuel's films.

Lyon, Elizabeth H. "Luis Buñuel: The Process of Dissociation in Three Films." *Cinema Journal* XIII, No. 1 (Fall 1973): 45-8.

Discusses the Surrealist principle of displacement with reference to *Un chien andalou, L'age d'Or,* and *Land without Bread.*

Taylor, John Russell. "Luis Buñuel." In his *Cinema Eye, Cinema Ear: Some Key Film-Makers of the Sixties,* pp. 82-114. New York: Hill and Wang, 1964.

Overview of Buñuel's career, maintaining that "Buñuel's total *oeuvre* is greater than the sum of its parts."

Wall, James M. "Luis Buñuel and the Death of God." In his *Three European Directors,* pp. 111-212. Grand Rapids, Mich.: William B. Eerdmans, 1973.

Analyzes Buñuel's demythologizing of Christianity.

Additional coverage of Buñuel's life and career is contained in the following sources published by Gale Research: *Contemporary Authors,* Vols. 101, 110 (obituary); *Contemporary Authors New Revision Series,* Vol. 32; *Contemporary Literary Criticism,* Vol. 16; and *Hispanic Writers.*

Athol Fugard

1932-

(Full name Harold Athol Lannigan Fugard) South African playwright, novelist, screenwriter, stage director, and actor.

The following entry provides an overview of Fugard's career. For further information on his life and works, see *CLC,* Volumes 5, 9, 14, 25, and 40.

INTRODUCTION

South Africa's foremost dramatist, Fugard addresses humanitarian concerns and explores the processes of victimization that beset all levels of South African society in his plays. Because he often focuses on the injustices perpetuated by the nation's apartheid system of government, which denies basic human rights to nonwhite residents, South African officials have deemed many of Fugard's works subversive and have periodically attempted to prevent the publication or production of his plays. Fugard feels, however, that his purpose is to "bear witness" to the inequities of his society, and he argues—somewhat controversially in the South African context—that "all human beings are in some sense victims."

Fugard was born in Cape Province and raised in Port Elizabeth, which has served as the setting for many of his plays. His father was English and his mother was an Afrikaner, a white South African descended from Dutch settlers. Fugard credits his father with instilling in him the love of storytelling, but describes him as a man "full of pointless, unthought-out prejudices." His mother, on the other hand, felt "outrage and anger over the injustice of [South African] society." In 1950 Fugard received a scholarship to study philosophy at the liberal University of Cape Town. However, he dropped out just before graduation and instead toured the world while working aboard a merchant ship. During this period he attempted to write a first novel but, disappointed with his efforts, destroyed the manuscript. A few years later, around the time of his marriage, in 1956, to South African actress Sheila Meiring, Fugard developed an interest in writing for the theater. He later dismissed early plays such as *The Cell* and *Klaas and the Devil* as "imitative exercises," insisting that his first authentic plays grew out of his experience in Johannesburg in the late 1950s. While befriending and collaborating with a group of black writers and actors in Sophiatown, one of the ghetto townships of Johannesburg, Fugard worked briefly as a clerk in the Native Commissioner's Court, which tried cases against nonwhites who had been arrested for failing to carry identification. "I knew that the system was evil," Fugard recalls, "but until then I had no idea of just how systematically evil it was. That was my revelation." Out of these experiences came *No-Good Friday* and *Nongogo,* his first two full-length plays, both of which were initially performed by Fugard and black amateur actors for small private audiences.

After a brief move to England in 1959, where his work was overshadowed by the early plays of John Osborne, Harold Pinter, and Arnold Wesker, Fugard returned to South Africa and completed a novel, *Tsotsi.* Although he attempted to destroy the manuscript, a copy survived and was published two decades later. Fugard's first major theatrical success was *The Blood Knot,* a story about the oscillating sense of conflict and harmony between two nonwhite half-brothers. The play was first presented in 1961 to a private audience and featured Fugard as the light-skinned brother, Morris, and actor Zakes Mokae—who became a close friend and long-time collaborator—as the dark-skinned brother, Zach. In the early 1960s Fugard also helped found the Serpent Players, an all-black theater group composed of residents of New Brighton, the black township of Port Elizabeth. Despite frequent harassment from the police, the Serpent Players performed works by Niccolò Machiavelli, Bertolt Brecht, Georg Büchner, and Wole Soyinka. Fugard's involvement with the group did much to establish black South African theater, and his plays gained increasing critical acclaim and popular support around the world. Fugard worked with black South African actors John Kani and Winston Ntshona, members of the Serpent Players, to create three highly acclaimed improvisational plays with political themes: *The Island, Sizwe Bansi Is Dead,* and *Statements after an Arrest under the Immorality Act.* In the late 1970s Fugard wrote and acted in a number of films, including *The Guest at Steenkampskraal* and *Marigolds in August.* Critics note that around this time his writings became more personal and autobiographical than his earlier works. The most famous of Fugard's later dramas is *"Master Harold". . . and the Boys.* Based on his boyhood relationship with Sam Semela, a family servant who was like a second father to Fugard, the play became his longest-running Broadway production and was officially banned in South Africa.

The major concerns of Fugard's dramas of the sixties include hopelessness, the effect of the past on the present, and the individual's search for identity in a country which denies essential freedoms. In *The Blood Knot,* for instance, Fugard dramatizes the ambivalence and racial hatred that infect many South African relationships, perverting the "blood knot," or common bond of humanity. Commenting on the play's 1985 revival, Jack Kroll called it "one of the wisest, sweetest, even noblest plays about the balked brotherhood of racism ever written." In *Hello and Goodbye* and *People Are Living There,* Fugard compassionately examines characters with thwarted aspirations and impoverished emotional lives. *Boesman and Lena* explores the relationship of a homeless, mixed-race couple whom Fugard has termed "archetypal South Africans." Although Boesman expresses his hatred of the South African political system in the form of violence toward Lena, who suffers Boesman's misplaced rage with dignity, both are ultimately revealed to be victims of the human condition. Reminiscent of Samuel Beckett's *En attendant Godot* (1953; *Waiting for Godot*) in its stark staging and unflinching analysis of human existence, *Boesman and Lena* secured Fugard's reputation as a major dramatist.

After experiencing an intense period of writer's block after *Boesman and Lena,* Fugard experimented with collaborative theater. Influenced by the works of Jerzy Grotowski, R. D. Laing, and Peter Brook, *Orestes* juxtaposes the Greek tragedy of Orestes with a contemporary incident of violent protest in South Africa. The play was created in the rehearsal room by Fugard and the actors, and with only three hundred words of dialogue it all but defied transcription into a formal text. In what Fugard has described as "a series of strange dream images," *Orestes* depicted "a metaphor of innocence [meeting] a metaphor of evil." Despite its limited number of performances, *Orestes* is considered a significant work which profoundly affected his ensuing plays. *Statements after an Arrest under the Immorality Act* concerns the discovery by government authorities of a biracial couple's love affair. This was Fugard's first play created in collaboration with John Kani and Winston Ntshona, and his work with these actors spurred further exploration of the relationship between actor and playwright. *Sizwe Bansi Is Dead* and *The Island,* both one-act plays, were developed by asking actors to improvise within a broadly sketched scenario. The first play portrays the degrading experiences of a man who, through no fault of his own, has been denied official papers that would allow him to work and earn a living to support his family. In the second drama, which is based on an actual incident, two men serving sentences in a political prison perform a version of Sophocles' play *Antigone* as a means of expressing solidarity and resistance. Initially performed together in repertory in New York, both works received overwhelmingly positive reviews.

Although Fugard's plays remain preoccupied with ambivalence, despair, and the struggle for freedom, the characters and situations of his works written since the mid-1970s differ markedly from those of his early dramas. For example, white characters in *A Lesson from Aloes* debate whether they should flee their homeland or remain true to their political beliefs by facing their country's growing racial tension. *"Master Harold". . . and the Boys,* widely considered one of Fugard's best and most autobiographical plays, revolves around the relationship of two black waiters, Sam and Willy, to Hally ("Master Harold"), a white youth embittered by the neglect of his alcoholic, racist father. In the end, the boy vents his anger—just as Fugard had done in a similar situation—by spitting in Sam's face, thereby rejecting his substitute father and lifelong friend. *The Road to Mecca* depicts several days in the life of an eccentric and rebellious elderly woman who seeks self-discovery through artistic expression after the death of her husband. *A Place with the Pigs,* described by Fugard as a personal parable, departs from his preceding works in its affirmative ending and its avoidance of dramatic realism. Set "somewhere in the author's imagination," the play concerns a Soviet soldier named Pavel who abandons his post and avoids punishment by hiding in a pigsty for forty years. Despite the absurd bleakness of the situation, the drama contains elements of Chaplinesque slapstick and concludes with Pavel pulling himself out of the sty and reentering the world. In *My Children! My Africa!* Fugard returns to the realism of his earlier works with the story of an elderly black schoolteacher who places his faith in the power of education as a tool for social progress. Reflecting Fugard's own frustration over his inability to effect significant change in South Africa, the play provocatively depicts the teacher's confrontation with and ultimate betrayal of a black militant student.

Although faulted by some critics for his failure to denounce the injustices of apartheid in a more confrontational manner, Fugard commands respect for his unfailing opposition to the racial policies of the South African government and for his sophisticated explorations of their subtly destructive effects. Critics note that by powerfully and skillfully describing the impact of apartheid on a personal level, Fugard has persuasively argued against its continuation.

PRINCIPAL WORKS

No-Good Friday (drama) 1956
Nongogo (drama) 1957
**The Blood Knot* (drama) 1961

**Hello and Goodbye* (drama) 1965
**Boesman and Lena* (drama) 1969
People Are Living There (drama) 1969
The Coat (drama) 1971
Orestes (drama) 1971
†*The Island* [with John Kani and Winston Ntshona] (drama) 1972
†*Sizwe Bansi Is Dead* [with John Kani and Winston Ntshona] (drama) 1972
†*Statements after an Arrest under the Immorality Act* [with John Kani and Winston Ntshona] (drama) 1972
Dimetos (drama) 1975
The Guest: An Episode in the Life of Eugene Marais [with Ross Devenish] (drama) 1977
The Guest at Steenkampskraal (screenplay) 1977
‡*A Lesson from Aloes* (drama) 1978
The Drummer (drama) 1980
Marigolds in August (screenplay) 1980
Tsotsi (novel) 1980
‡*"Master Harold". . . and the Boys* (drama) 1982
Notebooks, 1960-1977 (notebooks) 1983
‡*The Road to Mecca* (drama) 1984
A Place with the Pigs (drama) 1987
My Children! My Africa! (drama) 1990
Playland (drama) 1992

*These works are collectively known as *The Family Trilogy.*

†These plays are frequently referred to as *The Statements Trilogy* or *The Political Trilogy.*

‡These works comprise what is commonly known as *The Afrikaner Trilogy.*

CRITICISM

Dennis Walder (essay date 1984)

[*Walder is a South African educator and critic who wrote the first book-length analysis of the playwright,* Athol Fugard, *in 1984. In the following excerpt from that work, Walder details Fugard's career, describing his work as "extreme [theater]. . . in response to an extreme situation."*]

Sunday is not generally a day when anything happens in South Africa. But on Sunday, 3 September 1961, in a cramped, unventilated room on the third floor of an abandoned factory in Eloff Street, Johannesburg, something did happen. A new South African play was performed in which, for the first time, a white man and a black man appeared together on stage. And for nearly four hours the two held their invited, multiracial audience spellbound. Traffic noises drifted up from the front of the building, drumming and chanting from an African miners' hostel at the back penetrated the empty egg-boxes pinned to the windows. But the journalists, theatre people and assorted friends who packed the new 'Rehearsal Room' of the African Music and Drama Association in Dorkay House were gripped as never before by a passionate duet which probed and revealed the feelings associated with that perennial South African subject—race.

The play was ***The Blood Knot,*** by Athol Fugard; the actors, 'Arrie Potgieter' (Fugard himself, using his maternal grandfather's name) and Zakes Mokae. Fugard also directed, using Barney Simon as a 'third eye'. When the performers awoke the next morning, the event was all over the newspapers. Oliver Walker devoted his entire 'Arts and Entertainment' column in the *Star* (usually dominated by fulsome accounts of productions such as *The Amorous Prawn*) to praise for the new work. On 8 November, cut to two-and-a-half hours, the play reopened under professional management at the Intimate Theatre, Johannesburg. Approval was unanimous, and a tour practically sold out before it began. From the barely known author of two 'township' plays—***No-Good Friday*** (1958) and ***Nongogo*** (1959)—Athol Fugard had become a national figure, virtually overnight. Successful production and publication in London and New York followed in due course and, slowly but surely, an international reputation. With twelve plays (including joint ventures such as ***Sizwe Bansi Is Dead,*** 1973) currently in print, and his latest—***'Master Harold'. . . and the boys*** (1982)—a phenomenal success both at home and abroad, Fugard may be said to have become a major modern playwright. His plays now command an audience whenever and wherever they are performed. He has transformed the limitations of his South African background into theatre of great power and lasting implication.

Fugard's theatre is radical, even extreme; but this is in response to an extreme situation. He lives in a society familiar the world over for its unique system of racial oppression. Brutality and degradation are, of course, to be found elsewhere than in South Africa. But there is a level and quality of humiliation, suffering and despair present in the lives of millions of ordinary South Africans—mostly, but not exclusively black—which demands recognition. Fugard's plays help obtain that recognition. His plays make us aware not only of the South African dimension of man's inhumanity to man, but also of the secret pain we all inflict upon each other in the private recesses of our closest relationships. His works all focus upon two or three people inextricably entangled by the ties of blood, love or friendship. He shows them struggling to survive in an arbitrary, bleak and almost meaningless world. This does not mean his plays lack feeling: on the contrary, they are filled with anger and compassion. It is his great strength to move us deeply by showing the plight of ordinary people caught up in the meshes of social, political, racial and even religious forces which they are unable to understand or control. It is his weakness that he cannot reflect upon or analyse these forces himself. He is like the actor in Brecht's *Messingkauf Dialogues* who provokes 'all sorts of passions, but a passion for argument—oh no'. For Fugard, the message is too urgent. This does not mean that he is simply a propagandist—although propaganda has its place. What it does mean is that there is a characteristic intensity of effect gained by his work, an effect of painful, shared awareness, which it is perhaps uniquely possible to create in the theatre. And Fugard is, above all, in the clichéd phrase, a man of the theatre. As actor, director and playwright, he is obsessed with the idea that what he has to say can only be said indirectly, as an *image,* embodied in the 'living moment' on stage.

He began by going back to the so-called 'Method' school, according to which actors authenticate their roles by finding in them some relation to their own experience. In the—mainly American—development of this approach, the tendency has been to rely on naturalistic performances of pre-existing texts, constructed according to the familiar hierarchy of writer, director, producer and actor. But, although naturalism remains an important thread in Fugard's work, he has moved away from it, towards a more characteristically modern, symbolic realm. Surface reality, or the 'facts' of everyday experience, are never entirely ignored; but the suggestive 'sub-text' is often more important. He is fundamentally opposed to the parochial consumer art with which most Western playgoers are, alas, all too familiar: that mode of drama which pushes the performers into a well-lit picture frame behind a proscenium arch, where they converse with one another according to a given script, while the audience looks on passively. Like such influential and innovative directors as Peter Brook and Jerzy Grotowski, whose work and ideas (especially Grotowski's) have been important for him, Fugard is inspired and sustained by the actuality of performance, by live actors before a live audience, 'flesh and blood, sweat, the human voice, real pain, real time'. For him, as for that great progenitor of 'living theatre' in our day, Antonin Artaud (1896-1948), the trappings of the institutionalised, illusionistic theatre—buildings, props, costumes, lighting and so on—only interest in so far as they aid the primary function of drama: to find the 'truth' of the 'living moment'.

The living moment in a Fugard play tends to emerge as the climax of a shifting pattern of emotions of gradually increasing strength, a moment of revelation, expressed as an image. Words are only a part of what he defines—in terms borrowed from Ezra Pound—as the 'image': 'the presentation of a psychological and emotional complex in an instant of time'. Any script which has not stood the test of production is 'provisional' and 'rough'; and, whatever else may change during workshops, rehearsals or production, he does not concede 'any alteration with the central image—once that happens you have a new play'. Most of Fugard's plays begin life as, and finally focus on, one central image or cluster of images. The climax of ***Hello and Goodbye*** (1965), for instance, occurs when Johnnie, unable to leave home and face life, takes up his father's crutches: 'Why not? It solves problems. Let's face it, a man on his own two legs is a shaky proposition.' A chilling and disturbing moment: the crippling inadequacies of family life are exposed simultaneously with—on the deeper, sub-textual level—the failure of the 'poor white' Afrikaner to come to terms with his past. And, when, in ***Sizwe Bansi Is Dead,*** the central character sits frozen in a grotesquely comic pose, a 'studio' cigarette balanced nonchalantly in one hand, his own pipe gripped firmly in the other, the photographer's studio backdrop of city skyscrapers behind him, while a beatific smile spreads slowly across his features . . . the image sums up the truth of his life: Robert/Sizwe is a naïve dreamer, a simple man who wishes to survive with dignity, but it is a wish as far out of reach as those skyscrapers, for a black man in his situation.

The dramatic impact of the living moments in Fugard's plays represent a stage on a journey, when the 'external story' he has found in the lives and circumstances of those around him coincides with his own 'inner dynamic'. He is engaged in a 'slow trek through the detours of art', as it was put by a writer he resembles as well as admires, Albert Camus (1913-60)—a trek to rediscover 'those two or three great and simple images in whose presence his heart first opened'. Without the coincidence of 'external' and 'internal' in an image, Fugard's plays could not be written. For all the 'external', even documentary detail of his work, it always demonstrates a deeply personal concern for the fate of the 'ordinary', anonymous, *little* people with whom he most closely identifies. The opening entry of Camus's notebooks reads, 'I must bear witness. When I see things clearly, I have only one thing to say. It is in this life of poverty, among these vain or humble people, that I have most certainly touched what I feel is the true meaning of life.' Similarly for Fugard: his 'true meaning', he says in *his* notebooks, his 'life's work', is 'just to witness' as 'truthfully' as he can 'the nameless and destitute' of his 'one little corner of the world'. For Camus, that 'corner' lay in North Africa, among the white *colons* and their despised local helotry; for Fugard it is the Eastern Cape region of South Africa, among the 'poor whites', the 'Coloureds' (mixed race) and, occasionally, members of the subject African majority. Like Camus, Fugard belongs by birth and upbringing to the relatively underprivileged sector of the white group which rules his country, a lower middle-class, verging on 'poor white', group, which tends to provide the strongest anti-black feelings and which therefore considers him a 'traitor' for turning against their own apparent interests. Camus was led to exile; Fugard insists on staying, believing that only while living where he is can he testify to the lives of those around him, the disinherited and the lost—whether it is Morris and Zach, the two 'Coloured' brothers of ***The Blood Knot,*** or Sizwe Bansi, or Johnnie, or Milly (***People Are Living There,*** 1968) or ***Boesman and Lena*** (1969)—or even, in her way, which is the way of insanity, Gladys Bezuidenhout, the busdriver's wife in ***A Lesson from Aloes*** (1978). When Fugard leaves these 'small' people, as in ***Dimetos*** (1975), and attempts to create and study a character who is heroic, even mythical, he loses his way, becoming abstract and unsympathetic.

Yet, like other modern artists (including Camus, whose notebooks provided the story of Dimetos), Fugard frequently returns to the mythical—or, at least, to the early myths of the classical Greek era, the bloody family feuds dramatised by Aeschylus, Sophocles and Euripides. Hence the little-known work entitled ***Orestes*** (1971); hence the use of *Antigone* in ***The Island*** (1973). He feels he is touching on the basic drives which motivate us all, and so is naturally drawn to the most powerful and lasting embodiment of them, in the Greek drama. Is there then no closer tradition which might have provided him with a source of inspiration? Where is the South African tradition?

There is no systematic or comprehensive account of drama in South Africa—much less of South African literature as a whole, incorporating (as it should) the various strands, oral and written, in African as well as European languages, going back to the earliest times. The only half-decent book on the subject, Stephen Gray's *Southern African Literature* (1979) begins by confessing the impossibility of his task: he refers to the fact that by the late 1960s at least half South Africa's English-speaking writers of all colours had been expelled from the country into 'an international diaspora' with the result that South African literature in English had split so 'irremediably and bitterly into two' that it only makes sense to talk of 'two distinct literatures at present'. And this is while focusing only on South African writing *in English.* Gray goes on to identify what he calls an 'archipelago' of literatures, somehow associated merely by being where they are. He omits not only the writers to whom he cannot have access as a scholar working in South Africa, but also the larger framework which might make sense of his material: that is, *history.* But, as Dan Jacobson once remarked [in his introduction to *Olive Schreiner's Story of an African Farm*], a colonial culture is precisely one in which the sense of history is 'deficient'. This deficiency means that the enmities engendered by the conditions which first brought the colony into existence tend to be regarded 'as so many given, unalterable facts of life, phenomena of nature, as little open to human change or question as the growth of leaves in spring'. Typically, the members of such a culture delude themselves into believing that things have always been the way they are, and always will be. South Africa is a good example: it is a fragmented ex-colonial culture; and it is a culture in which the potential for unity and integration has not only been resisted by the dominant white minority, but has been corrupted according to an ideology which emphasises and exploits difference, so as to manipulate and control the vast majority. Even apart from the specific effects of apartheid laws—of censorship, of bannings, imprisonment and exile—there is a history of division and isolation which has made it difficult, if not impossible, for people to know what is going on in their own country. For writers and artists, this leads to the common feeling that they are operating in a vacuum.

When Fugard was asked what dramatists he had met during the early years of his career in the 1950s, he replied, 'There were none around.' In fact there was taking place at the time a so-called 'renaissance' of English drama, including plays by Alan Paton, James Ambrose Brown and Lewis Sowden—the last of whom wrote a play, *Kimberley Train* (1958), which anticipates the subject of ***The Blood Knot.*** But in terms of quality and relevance Fugard may seem right to have presumed 'There were none around.' On the other hand, there was also a less well documented or known 'renaissance' in the urban black 'townships', an upsurge of popular theatre, of song and dance, of satire and jazz, which white entrepreneurs in Johannesburg at least were aware of, and which became more familiar with the emergence in 1959 of the jazz opera *King Kong. King Kong* was essentially urban, and should not be confused with such dubious successors as *uMabatha* (1970) or *Ipi Tombi* (1973), all-black musical productions designed by their white managements to present the impression of black South Africans as a crowd of smiling, dancing, bare-breasted rural illiterates. The last decade has, in fact, seen a flood of 'township' drama, ranging from the sensational accounts of everyday urban life purveyed by Gibson Kente and Sam Mhangwani (the latter's unpublished *Unfaithful Wife* remains a hit after twenty years) to the more serious, politically committed work of writers such as Maishe Maponya (*The Hungry Earth,* 1979) and Matsemela Manaka (*Egoli,* 1980)—to name only a few from Soweto alone.

Fugard has acknowledged his debt to black *performers:* those first befriended in Sophiatown, the multiracial Johannesburg ghetto, in the late fifties, and whose talents and experiences were embodied in his first full-length plays, ***No-Good Friday*** and ***Nongogo;*** as well as those who came to him from New Brighton, Port Elizabeth, in 1963 to form the Serpent Players, a remarkable group whose collaborative work led to (amongst other plays) ***Sizwe Bansi Is Dead*** and ***The Island.*** Fugard's own influence upon 'township' theatre is recognised and is continuing. Playwrights in the townships have had to learn a tough lesson in survival, a lesson they articulate in a variety of forms, using whatever means they can—including the aid of those few, such as Fugard and writer-director Barney Simon, willing and able to 'cross over' from the white side to offer the knowledge and experience to which they have privileged access. But such contact barely deflects the pressures of the situation. Dramatists still feel they must start from scratch, unable to draw on the fragmented, unknown or unacknowledged traditions of their own country.

So it is not altogether surprising that Fugard's acknowledged mentors should not be South African. One of the few playwrights to whom he admits he owes anything is Samuel Beckett—an allegiance confirmed by his small casts, sparse sets, flat, seemingly pointless dialogue and inconsequential plots. But, even if some such influence can be traced, Fugard's plays are all ultimately derived 'from life and from encounters with real people', as he put it in the Introduction to his published notebooks. These notebooks reveal the secret, slow and painful germination of his plays over many years, culminating in ***'Master Harold' . . . and the boys***—which, based upon an incident in his adolescence, has had the longest incubation of them all, no doubt because it is the most personal, and has been the most difficult to expose. Evidently, ***'Master Harold'*** was a cathartic experience for him; and so it is for his audiences, too. There is nothing 'literary' about this: it is primarily a matter of transferring emotions, of arousing in us a powerful and deep emotional awareness, which burns into our consciousness the imagery of a group of individual human beings caught within the conflicting tensions of their specific situation. The nature of their relationships suggests the profound forces at work in their society; the characters in his plays are revealed struggling to survive with some shred of dignity the almost intolerable burden of suffering imposed upon them by an apparently irresistible fate. If this seems to suggest an endorsement of suffering, of passivity in the face of oppression, that seems to be true; but it is not the whole truth. Fugard's work also contains a potential for subversion, a potential which, I would suggest, is the hallmark of great art, and which qualifies his best work to be called great.

Art is often called revolutionary if it represents a radical quality in style or technique; but there is a more important sense in which it can be revolutionary—or, as I would prefer to put it, subversive. This lies in its potential to undermine the status quo, a potential revealed in its tendency to make us realise that things need not be the way they have been, or the way they are. If racialism and exploitation seem natural as 'the growth of leaves in spring', then it is in the capacity of art to show us that this is not so. As Brecht said, to make the ordinary extraordinary. Before a word was uttered in that first performance of ***The Blood Knot*** in September 1961, the audience was presented with a curious sight: a pale-skinned man, shabbily dressed (Morris, played by Fugard), coming in and setting about preparing a footbath, timing his actions (which are evidently routine) by means of an old alarmclock; an equally shabby man, of African appearance (Zach, played by Mokae) but wearing a greatcoat and obviously returning from a hard day's work, then enters, and makes a great show of being surprised at the footbath, testing the water with one toe, and so on, before finally and luxuriously resting his calloused feet in it. In that 'living moment', that 'image', a relationship was suggested which thrilled the audience with disturbing implications: revealing a white man behaving like a housekeeper, a servant, to a black. The relationship at the centre of the structure of South African society was being subverted before their eyes. ***The Blood Knot*** went on to reveal that the two were mixed-race brothers, outcasts tormented by the fact that one of them was more 'European' in appearance than the other; and the alternating pattern of dominance and dependence between them which this generated in a racialist society. But it is the lasting, subversive resonance of that initial image and the variations upon it which follow that provide the play with the possibility of its continuing power and relevance.

All Fugard's plays approximate to the same basic model, established by ***The Blood Knot:*** a small cast of 'marginal' characters is presented in a passionately close relationship embodying the tensions current in their society, the whole first performed by actors directly involved in its creation, in a makeshift, 'fringe' or 'unofficial' venue. This is 'poor theatre', although less as a matter of theory (Grotowski's *Towards a Poor Theatre* only came to Fugard in 1970) than as a matter of preferred practice. With few resources and impelled to operate under rough, workshop conditions, relying on actors to impart their own experiences, Fugard has always worked outside the conventional, mainstream theatre, implicitly challenging by his conditions of production the prevailing assumptions about theatre—i.e. that it is a form of packaged entertainment which confirms the status quo. Despite the subsequent, inevitable assimilation of his most well-known works into that mainstream theatre, as far as he is concerned all that the theatre, *his* theatre needs is (as he put it at the time of ***The Blood Knot,*** and has repeated ever since)

> the actor and the stage, the actor *on* the stage. Around him is space, to be filled and defined by movement and gesture; around him is also silence to be filled with meaning, using words and sounds, and at moments when all else fails him, including the words, the silence itself.

This helps explain his reliance upon his chosen actors, as well as his determination always to have a controlling hand in the production of all his plays; the end product is not so much a written text, which may only be a record of a performance, but an existential moment, in a particular place at a particular time. What his plays mean is determined less by their written words than by the total conditions of performance. This became especially important to him when, under the impact of the ideas of Grotowski and the workshop practice developed with the Serpent Players, he attempted his most 'extreme excursion' into radical communication by means of image and gesture, rather than pre-established text: ***Orestes,*** which defies translation into a script, and the separate performances of which are 'scored' in three large drawing-books, a pale shadow of the eighty minutes of strange, somnambulistic action which took place at the time. Here Fugard attempted an apparently total reliance upon the 'creative' as opposed to merely 'illustrative' abilities of his cast, two women and a man. Yet the 'truth' discovered was the result of the performers responding to the director—scribe's challenges, expressed as a complex of images Fugard derived from ancient and modern sources; the playwright himself remained in charge. This 'new' type of theatre focused on an event very close to South Africans—and, especially, white liberals: the explosion of a bomb as an act of protest on Johannesburg station, which killed an elderly white woman and led to the execution of its perpetrator, a white schoolteacher. If ***Orestes*** represents an extreme, even a limit, to what Fugard has been able to do in the theatre, this may have more to do with its subject, than with what ideas about the theatre released in him. The play explored the effect of violence upon those who carry it out: the central image was created by the slow, deliberate and silent destruction in each performance of a unique, irreplaceable and innocent object—a chair—by the actress, who sank down eventually into the debris, exhausted and terrified by what she had done. In a context in which violence is breeding more violence, this image is important; but, if Fugard persistently condemns violence, he is also careful to show its inevitability in a society which has adopted violent means to stifle opposition and prevent change. (pp. 1-13)

The South African experience which emerges in his plays is bitter and painful to contemplate; but, at the same time, there is a deep faith in the potential for survival of the individual human being. He wants to 'bear witness' to what is happening in his time. This is another way of saying that, as he puts it,

> as a South African I want to talk to other South Africans about what is happening here and now. Now, being a South African means that I have got to acknowledge the fact that my whole style of living, everything, comes down to . . . how many decisions have I got that are not related to my white skin? I can only acknowledge that

> these exist, that they are facts. . . . Thorn trees don't protest the endless drought of the Karroo. . . . They just go on trying to grow. Just a basic survival informs the final, mutilated, stunted protest. . . .

Fugard's plays are all, on some level, more or less explicitly, a protest about the quality of life in South Africa. To ignore this would be to render them meaningless. Many critics (especially in South Africa) prefer to stress their 'universitality'; and so help maintain the status quo. He himself prefers not to be called a 'political playwright'; nor am I suggesting that he is; but, in embodying what he sees as the 'truth' of his place in his work, in his textures and imagery, he cannot help but also embody its politics. Failure to recognise or admit this involves a failure to respond to his kind of theatre, as well as to what he is saying. (pp. 17-18)

Dennis Walder, in his Athol Fugard, *Macmillan Publishers Ltd., 1984, 142 p.*

Robert M. Post (essay date July 1985)

[In the following essay, Post surveys Fugard's writings, examining the playwright's depictions of victimization under the system of apartheid.]

Although Athol Fugard, South Africa's leading playwright, eschews "the label of political writer," most of his writings make strong political statements. In ["Athol Fugard in London," *African Literature Today* 8 (1976), which reviews three of his plays]—***Sizwe Bansi Is Dead, The Island,*** and ***Statements After an Arrest Under the Immorality Act***—Julian Mitchell finds that "the truth being told is so saturated in politics that politics never have to be mentioned." [In an interview in *Theater* 14 (1982)] Zakes Mokae, the South African actor who recently originated the role of Sam in ***"Master Harold" . . . and the boys,*** believes "anything coming out of South Africa is automatically political." Margaret Munro feels [in her "The Fertility of Despair: Fugard's Bitter Aloes," *Meanjin* 40 (1981)] that, in a sense, "South African literature could be said to be a metaphor for the larger betrayal embodied in *apartheid.*" In most of his plays and in his one novel characters who are victims of the system of apartheid insisted upon by the minority white government embody Fugard's political statements. The victims come from all three major races inhabiting South Africa—black, coloured, and white. Out of forty-six characters in twelve plays, twenty-four are black, six are coloured, and sixteen are white; most of the characters in ***Tsotsi,*** Fugard's novel, are black.

The brothers, Morris and Zachariah, in ***The Blood Knot*** are typical victims of the system of apartheid and bigotry pictured by Fugard. The brothers personify the racial conflict of South Africa; Morris is light coloured, so light coloured that he has passed for white, while Zach's skin is darker. The darker brother, in spite of himself, admires Morris's whiteness: " . . . you're pretty . . . a pretty white," and enjoys the idea that the white woman he has accidentally acquired as a pen-pal believes he is white also, but he realizes he can never even meet her: "The whole, rotten, stinking lot is all because I'm black!" Morris believes the government considers it a crime for a coloured man even to think of a white woman, and that "All they need for evidence is a man's dreams." When Morris asks Zach what he would do if he did meet Ethel and her white relatives subsequently attacked him physically, Zach replies that he would call for the police, and Morrie counters this response with the belief that the police are on the side of the whites, not the coloureds. When they believe the pen-pal is actually coming for a visit, they begin to prepare for Morris, who sees himself as a Judas betraying his brother, to meet her as a white Zachariah. In addition to wearing "white" clothes, Morris must act and sound like a white man. The most difficult pretense has to do with the eyes because "They [white people] look at things differently," meaning that a white person's eyes project courage instead of the fear reflected in the eyes of coloured people. In an ugly parody of the relationship between white and coloured, Morris and Zach pretend that Morris is a white man who is visiting the park where Zach stands in the sun at the gate to keep black children away. As Morris gets into his role, he castigates his brother by calling him names, such as *Swartgat* ["black arse"]. The name-calling is especially cruel since we have previously been made aware of Zach's sensitivity at being called names. The future for Morrie and Zach is bleak; they have only each other and their racist "game." [In his "Athol Fugard's *Hello and Goodbye,*" *Modern Drama* 13 (September 1970)] Robert J. Green has called the characters' confrontation in ***The Blood Knot*** "a microcosm of South Africa's explosive racial situation."

Morris is not really correct when he tells Zach that the police are on the side of the white members of South African society. He would have been more accurate in saying the police are on the side of those obeying the laws of the apartheid government. In ***Statements After an Arrest Under the Immorality Act,*** a title which summarizes the action of the play, the white librarian Frieda Joubert and the coloured location school principal Errol Philander, who have been lovers for about a year, are arrested after they are reported to the police. Fear is a common emotion experienced by the victims of Fugard's world, and Frieda and Errol are no exceptions; Frieda is afraid the entire time she spends with her coloured friend, and Errol, who has had to suppress his pride by coming to her back door after dark, is justifiably terrified when the policeman discovers the lovers together. Mitchell has pointed out that "even before the lovers are discovered, their affair is ruined by the fear in which it is conducted." The contemporary action of ***Statements,*** like that of ***The Island,*** parallels the ancient conflict between individual rights and the laws of government. Under the law Frieda Joubert and Errol Philander are forbidden to love each other. Government has interjected itself into the most private aspect of their lives, but in South Africa Frieda is bound to her white skin just as the coloured man is bound to his neighbourhood in Bontrug. Philander reacts with amazement to the fact that "Life . . . is three billion years old"; the inclusion of this fact reminds us how little progress humankind has made since the beginning of life. It also shows just how insignificant the relationship of the lovers is when measured against three billion years of life. The final irony expressed

Fugard with actor Azkes Mokae in a scene from a 1985 production of Blood Knot *staged in New York City.*

by the coloured man is that although he is nothing (in historical terms and to the present government), he is arrested. As long as he does not break the law, the government treats him as nothing, but when he does break the law, he suddenly becomes some*thing* (not necessarily some*body*). Derek Cohen [in his "Drama and the Police State: Athol Fugard's South Africa," *Canadian Drama/L'Art Dramatique* 9 (Spring 1980)] sees this play as "a total image of the flinty cruelty of South Africa's institutionalized racialism," and Mshengu feels [in "Political Theatre in South Africa and the Work of Athol Fugard," *Theatre Research International* 7 (Autumn 1982)] that "By showing the human effects of such [racial] legislation he [Fugard] has effectively demonstrated its inhuman nature" in most of his plays.

The Island, devised by Fugard in collaboration with John Kani and Winston Ntshona for whom the characters are named, shares the basic conflict of the individual versus the government with ***Statements*** and the concept of brotherhood with ***The Blood Knot.*** John and Winston, who are in prison, are not blood brothers, but they are political brothers, belonging to an organization whose motto is "*Nyana we Sizwe*" ["*Brother of the Land*"]. In ***The Island*** the tension in Sophocles's *Antigone* is juxtaposed against the situation in modern-day South Africa. The conflict between individual conscience and individual rights (symbolized by Antigone, whom the prisoners see as innocent although she pleads guilty) and governmental decrees (symbolized by Creon) corresponds to the conflict between the individual conscience and rights of black prisoners and white government. John and Winston perform the roles of Creon and Antigone in a concert for their fellow prisoners, and, while Winston is not pleased to be playing Antigone with a wig and breasts because he knows the audience will laugh, John convinces him the message the play conveys is worth it: "But who cares . . . as long as they laugh in the beginning and listen at the end."

The Coat, which "*was evolved during a series of improvisations,*" shows the effect imprisonment of black men have on their families. The play is based on an actual happening in which a man sentenced to prison on Robben Island sends his coat home to his wife. The Serpent Players of New Brighton imagined a few scenes in which the coat functions as a symbol of her husband to the woman. Only when faced with eviction from her home would she sell the coat.

Prisoners are not the only persons in Fugard's world who leave their families. There is also the man from the country who journeys to the city in search of a job so he can support the family left behind. These victims include the title character in ***Sizwe Bansi Is Dead*** (like ***The Island*** devised by Fugard with Kani and Ntshona), Gumboot Dhlamini in ***Tsotsi,*** and Tobias and Moses in ***No-Good Friday.*** Obligatory passbooks compound the problems of these and many other South Africans. Sizwe Bansi, for instance, gives up his name, emblematic of his manhood, so he can "die" because a stamp, indicating that he has only three days to leave Port Elizabeth, is placed in his passbook. Bunti, who had trouble getting the proper stamps even though he was born in the area, tells Bansi how "simple" the solution to his problem would be if he knew a white man who could offer him work:

> You talk to the white man, you see, and ask him to write a letter saying he's got a job for you. You take that letter from the white man and go back to King William's Town, where you show it to the Native Commissioner there. The Native Commissioner in King William's Town reads that letter from the white man in Port Elizabeth who is ready to give you the job. He then writes a letter back to the Native Commissioner in Port Elizabeth. So you come back here with the two letters. Then the Native Commissioner in Port Elizabeth reads the letter from the Native Commissioner in King William's Town together with the first letter from the white man who is prepared to give you a job, and he says when he reads the letters: Ah yes, this man Sizwe Bansi can get a job. So the Native Commissioner in Port Elizabeth then writes a letter which you take with the letters from the Native Commissioner in King William's Town and the white man in Port Elizabeth, to the Senior Officer at the Labour Bureau, who reads all the letters. Then he will put the right stamp in your book and give you another letter from himself which together with the letters from the white man and the two Native Affairs Commissioners, you take to the Administration Office here in New Brighton and make an application for Residence Permit, so that you don't fall victim of raids again. Simple.

Bansi does not know any white men, so the solution to his problem is not "simple." Instead he takes the passbook and the identity of a dead man; Sizwe Bansi dies and is reborn Robert Zwelinzima so that he may continue to live in the city and work.

Hope of returning home from the city is thwarted in Fugard's portrait of this world. In ***Tsotsi,*** Dhlamini commutes to and from work because, as is common, he was not permitted to live in the city where he worked. He is brutally murdered—"Butcher worked the [bicycle] spoke up and into his heart"—by a street gang on the train, ironically only one week before he planned to return home. The usually careful Dhlamini, cheerful at the prospect of seeing his family again, makes three mistakes which cause him to stand out from the crowd at the railway station: he smiles, he wears a brilliant red tie, and he opens his pay packet to get his fare. The black street gangs, victims themselves of the South African system of government, in turn victimize other blacks. The same kind of victimization is found in ***No-Good Friday*** when the characters pay money to a black bully and his fellow thugs to protect them from the kind of attack that was made on Dhlamini. As Fugard has written, these people are doubly threatened by "white laws and black gangsters." In ***No-Good Friday*** Moses, like Sizwe Bansi and Gumboot Dhlamini, writes his family letters full of hope. He has been writing these letters for ten years and is seemingly no nearer his dream than he was in the beginning, while Tobias has just arrived from the Eastern Transvaal and is killed by the "protecting" gangsters because he fails to comprehend their demand for money. Tobias's dream is destroyed before it has barely had a chance to live. As Sizwe Bansi says, "A black man stay out of trouble? Impossible, Buntu. Our skin is trouble." Patrick goes so far in ***Nongogo*** as to declare that "they should make it that we blacks can't have babies."

The leader of the four hoodlums who attack Dhlamini in ***Tsotsi*** is the title character or David, which is his real name. He is the protagonist in the novel, and the government is the antagonist. David's early years were pleasant, symbolized by the novelist in images of light. When we first see him, however, he is deep in darkness; he has no memory of his childhood, and the innocence and salvation of those early years are lost. His fall from grace at the age of ten was caused by the trauma of having his mother taken from him by the police in a raid. He never saw her again. The disappearance of his mother and his father's subsequent hysterical anger left David so wounded that for many years the events were erased from his mind. Only certain images—including a yellow dog, a spider, and damp newspapers—flash through his mind as relics of his past life. David's loss of his mother is paralleled in the novel by Miriam Ngidi's loss of her husband, who " 'went to work and didn't come back.' "

Unlike most of Fugard's victims, Tsotsi transcends his situation by emerging a hero. Before the narrative ends, he has experienced a kind of conversion or restoration of at least a partial state of grace. The steps toward his return to the light from the darkness begin with his fellow-hoodlum Boston's telling Tsotsi that he must have a soul because everybody has one. The turning point comes when a woman thrusts a baby upon him. The baby becomes a new talisman—his knife was the old one—in which he senses his past self. The baby represents the David Tsotsi once was; in fact, he gives the baby his own name. The climactic step in Tsotsi's salvation comes after he, an emotional cripple, has pursued the physically crippled Morris Tshabalala in order to rob and murder him. When he catches his victim, Tsotsi suddenly realizes that he has a choice: he *may* or *may not* kill. The fact that there is an alternative to killing the man is a revelation for Tsotsi because a black person in South Africa has few choices. Cohen explains [in "A South African Drama: Athol Fugard's *The Blood Knot,*" *Modern Language Studies* 7 (Spring 1977)]: "The black man has his role chosen for him, and for the whole of his life he is a victim of that choice in whose making he had no part." The crippled beggar arouses Tsotsi's hidden sympathy, which is an extension of his feelings for the baby, and the sympathy is the key which unlocks his memory. With the restoration of his full memory the former Tsotsi starts on a mystical quest for God—something or someone he does not understand. David dies when he tries to save the baby from the bulldozers in the slum clearance at the end of the novel.

He has grown from the Tsotsi who took lives to the man who spared a life and tries to save another; the child who "died" when his mother was abruptly taken from him is reborn.

In an attempted act of communion David offers Boston sourmilk and bread, but Boston refuses to participate in the "sacrament." However, David does succeed in participating in a symbolic communion when he accepts Isaiah's tin cup of tea. There is also a kind of salvation for Lena in ***Boesman and Lena.*** There is a faint glimmer of hope for this woman who demands, "I want my life. Where's it?" She finds some meaning in life in her relationship with Outa, the old black man. Both Lena and Boesman are prejudiced against him because he is black and not brown or coloured like them. Although she calls him names, just as white people no doubt calls her names, she does show compassion and feels a kinship with him. Her partial salvation is celebrated in a symbolic communion—called "Lena's Mass" by the playwright—in which she and Outa share her tea and bread: "*Hotnot* and a *Kaffer* got no time for apartheid on a night like this." Lena has prepared us for her religious experience through an earlier reference to Christ, "Somewhere else a donkey looked at it [pain]."

Lena's salvation may be slight, but there is no salvation at all for Boesman. Fugard tells us that what Boesman "really hates is himself," and he hates himself because he is kept from becoming a complete man by apartheid. Persecuted by the white race, Boesman, like other of Fugard's characters, makes scapegoats out of others, in this case Outa and Lena, especially Lena; as Willie says in ***No-Good Friday,*** "Everybody wants a backside to kick in this country." Boesman is cruel to the old black man possibly because he is jealous that Lena seems to find some comfort and companionship with him. Robert L. Berner believes Boesman and Lena are "taking out on each other the rage and frustration which they cannot express against the world" ["Athol Fugard and the Theatre of Improvisation," *Books Abroad* 50 (Winter 1976)]. Like practically all of Fugard's characters, Boesman and Lena are "victims of a common, a shared predicament, and of each other."

The setting of ***Boesman and Lena*** reflects the characters' suffering. Like Fugard's other coloured and black characters, Boesman and Lena live in squalor. The couple make their way from one shantytown (Korsten, where ***The Blood Knot*** is set, is one of them) to another after the whites have demolished their latest shack with a bulldozer similar to the one that brought the wall down on David at the end of ***Tsotsi.*** During the play Boesman builds their temporary shelter for the night out of odds and ends, including pieces of wood, corrugated iron, and an old car door. Their odyssey from squalid town and miserable shack to squalid town and miserable shack is emblematic of the numb condition of their lives. As Frank Levy concludes [in his "Fugard's *Boesman and Lena:* Physical and Metaphysical Exhaustion," *Yale/Theater* 4 (Winter 1973)], "time and habit have dulled the poignancy of their awareness, their consciousness of justification or cause." They do not remember which town followed which; the towns become blurs just as their lives are blurred.

In ***Nongogo*** Queeny does not wander from place to place but lives in her shebeen which is expensively furnished according to the standards of its location, yet it is characterized by "*a suggestion of slovenliness.*" While considerably preferable to the settings of other plays—such as ***Boesman and Lena, The Blood Knot,*** and ***No-Good Friday***—the setting of ***Nongogo*** is, nevertheless, depressing, in part because it is an illegal drinking establishment. It is the symbol that Queeny has worked her way up the hierarchy of unsavoury professions, from prostitute to proprietor of a shebeen.

Queeny has never been released from the guilt she feels as a result of abandoning her young brothers and sisters after their mother died and for becoming a prostitute to make the money to finance the shebeen. She also feels guilty about serving people like Patrick, a man with a large family, but running a shebeen is good business because these natives are "always thirsty." Drinking is obviously a way of temporarily escaping the reality of their unhappy lives. Queeny is happy for the first time after she meets Johnny because he treats her like the decent woman she wants to be. For once she can hope for a respectable future with a man and a home, but this is not to be because Johnny is also a victim of South African society who, too, was forced into a kind of prostitution when at the age of seventeen he worked in the mines and lived in the compound where there were no women, and the stronger men took advantage of him sexually. This has traumatized him to the extent that he cannot associate with the "unclean" Queeny after he learns of her past. Both Johnny and Queeny hate themselves for what they have had to do to survive in their world, and Johnny cannot forgive.

Willie in ***No-Good Friday*** wonders if he and the other members of his race, such as Johnny and Queeny, have not helped make their world what it is:

> The world I live in is the way it is not in spite of me but because of me. You think we're just poor suffering come-to-Jesus-at-the-end-of-it-all black men and that the world's all wrong and against us so what the hell. Well I'm not so sure of that any more. I'm not so sure because I think we helped to make it, the way it is.

Willie, a bright, thoughtful young man who has despaired of life and who has seen his illusions and dreams fade, is angered by the deference of his black people to the white minority. He is aware that his heroic acts of attending Tobias's funeral and reporting the murder to the authorities will go only a very small way toward alleviating suffering in his country, but his shame for not trying to help Tobias forces him to act. He, like David in ***Tsotsi,*** will die as a result of his good deeds. In Fugard's world the heroic is victim along with the not-so-heroic.

As was seen in ***Statements After an Arrest Under the Immorality Act,*** it is not only black and coloured characters who become victims under the system of apartheid, but white characters suffer also. Suffering of members of all three races is explored in Fugard's latest plays—***A Lesson from Aloes*** and ***"Master Harold" . . . and the boys.*** Fugard has been quoted as saying that " 'At one level . . . [***A Lesson from Aloes***] is about survival. Survival in South

Africa, and choosing to stay here or choosing to go. And if you choose to go, do you choose to go physically or do you choose to go mad?' " In this three-character play the Afrikaner Piet chooses to stay (like the author himself), the coloured Steve chooses to go to England, and the white Gladys goes mad. Steve along with Piet, like the two men in ***The Island,*** rebelled against the government, and an informer—incorrectly identified by many as Piet—leads the officials to Steve, and he is banned and jailed. Although he is a qualified mason and bricklayer, he will never again be able to practice his trade in South Africa. Realizing he will never be free in his native country, he leaves. It is a painful decision for him, especially painful because once he leaves he is forbidden ever to return. Relocation is a common occurrence in the land of apartheid. Steve's family had been moved out of his childhood home because the community was "declared white," and Steve's father lost his home, his money, and the sea where he loved to fish, events which led the old man to the conclusion that "Ons geslag is verkeerd" ["Our generation . . . our race is a mistake"]. Although the authorities have laughed away Steve's manhood and he has lost his country, he has maintained his sanity and has his wife and children with him.

Gladys, who did not share Steve and Piet's interest in "the cause," loses everything of importance, her sanity and the relationship with her husband, after a raid by the authorities on their home. In an act of violation or a kind of rape, they confiscate her diaries, which she considered so personal that they were an extension of her very self. Munro sees the aloes of the title "as grotesque thorny phallic symbols opposed to female secretiveness in this context." Gladys summarizes her own suffering for Steven:

> I accept Steven that I am just a white face on the outskirts of your terrible life, but I'm in the middle of mine and yours is just a brown face on the outskirts of that. Do you understand what I'm saying? I've got my own story. I don't need yours. I've discovered hell for myself. It might be hard for you to accept Steven, but you are not the only one who has been hurt. Politics and blackskins don't make the only victims in this country.

Piet is also a victim, but he survives, in a sense, the loss of a best friend and a wife. He is left with both his native country and his sanity. Like the symbolic title aloe, a succulent plant capable of enduring drought, Piet has paid a price, but he has endured the drought of emotion and understanding. He and his aloes remain, while Steven leaves for England and Gladys leaves for the mental institution.

Zakes Mokae has summarized ***"Master Harold". . . and the boys*** as being, in part,

> about a young cat dealing with two servants, underline, capital letters on servants. Sam and Willie are older, but they have to put up with Hally's treatment of them as boys. It's like they're not justified in being angry, like anger belongs to certain people. So Hally can be angry about his personal problems. But Sam just has to deal.

This play demonstrates just how invidious and permeating bigotry can be. The two black servants, "the boys" of the title, are victims of the dominating white society, but Hally or "Master Harold," a white seventeen-year-old boy, is also a victim, especially of his parents' bigotry. We soon learn that Hally has a warmer relationship with Sam and Willie than with his own father; in fact, Sam is a substitute father to the boy. Hally is an intelligent person who has good rapport with the black men. He appears to be considerate of them, mentioning, for example, how he and Sam used to let Willie win at chess so he would continue to play with them. Hally does order the men around, but they are, after all, employees, and he is the *"Baas."* Hally has shared his education with Sam, who possesses a very good memory, while Sam, realizing the boy's crippled, alcoholic father is no model, tries to guide Hally toward manhood. Hally both loves and hates his father. The boy obviously feels a great sense of guilt over preferring the black Sam to his own white father, and this guilt, fed by the racial prejudice of his father, causes him to turn against Sam. Hally's attempts to humiliate Sam result only in self-humiliation. He first humiliates himself by demanding that Sam call him "Master Harold" instead of "Hally," and follows this command with the ultimate humiliation: he spits in Sam's face. Blood ties, skin colour in particular, cause Hally to reject Sam, the man who took the boy kite flying because "I wanted you to look up, be proud of something, of yourself." The events of the afternoon leave their marks on Hally, who now has more guilt to expiate. The play, autobiographical to a large degree, is an attempt on the part of the playwright to expiate, partially at least, his own guilt over spitting in the face of the real Sam Semela.

Characters suffer in the few plays by Fugard in which all of the dramatis personae are white, but their suffering is only indirectly, if at all, related to the system of apartheid and racism. The title character of ***Dimetos,*** the only Fugard play which is not explicitly set in Southern Africa, is a victim of his passion for his niece. ***People Are Living There,*** which the playwright has called "an aberrant work," focuses on white characters who spell "Life with a capital F," and mention other races occasionally in a demeaning way: Zulus are tough, "some old Coolie shop," "Here we have Natives to do the dirty work. You're saved by your white skin." ***Hello and Goodbye,*** a play about a crippled father who emotionally cripples his children, parallels the relationship of Hally and his father in ***"Master Harold"*** without the overt racial conflict.

The victims in Fugard's writing cope with their situations in various ways. We have seen how Willie in ***No-Good Friday,*** David in ***Tsotsi,*** and, to some degree, Lena in ***Boesman and Lena*** elevate themselves by caring for others. Brotherhood is a source of survival for some. The relationship of Morris and Zach in ***The Blood Knot*** is the only thing rendering their situation bearable. The concept, "brother," has led Morris, who has pretended to be white, back to his darker-skinned brother and keeps him there. Standing up for the brotherhood of their race led John and Winston to prison in ***The Island,*** and it is in the spirit of brotherhood that Buntu, "whose name means 'human kindness' " [according to Mshengu], helps Sizwe change his identity in ***Sizwe Banzi Is Dead.*** Boesman and Lena find sad comfort in their companionship.

Characters cope by dreaming and imagining. A major dream, that of the country man of finding a city job and returning home with money to provide for his family, has already been mentioned. The brothers in ***The Blood Knot,*** imitating George and Lennie in John Steinbeck's *Of Mice and Men,* save money to buy their dream farm. Morris and Zachariah recapture their youth by imagining they are riding in a car through a blizzard of butterflies, while Winston and John pretend to make telephone calls to friends outside the prison in ***The Island.*** Errol dreams of beginning life anew in ***Statements,*** and, in encouraging a little boy to expand the two-room house to five rooms in the drawing he was making in the sand, he instructs the child in dreaming.

Flying birds and dancing are two symbols of escape used by Fugard. In ***The Blood Knot*** birds—*white* birds—represent release for Morris: "But the mystery of my life, man, is the birds. Why, they come and settle here and fly around so white and beautiful on the water and never get dirty from it too!" Birds stand for freedom for Lena, too, in ***Boesman and Lena,*** but she is passionately jealous of them: "Tomorrow they'll hang up there in the wind and laugh. We'll be in the mud. I hate them." In ***Tsotsi*** David dreams that his father is a bird carrying him and his mother "away to better times," but the father does not stay aloft long. Dancing is the major symbol in ***"Master Harold"***: "it's beautiful because that is what we want life to be like."

Not all of the escapes are pleasant for these victims. In ***A Lesson from Aloes,*** for example, Gladys's escape from reality is into madness. Finally, some Fugard characters, like those of other modern playwrights such as August Strindberg and Edward Albee, suggest that the only escape is death. In ***Sizwe Bansi Is Dead*** Buntu says, "The only time we'll find peace is when they dig a hole for us and press our face into the earth," and Lena comments that Outa's "troubles are over" after he dies.

Fugard copies his characters and their situations directly from the life he knows in South Africa; he has said that his mission " 'is to witness as truthfully as I can the nameless and destitute of one little corner of the world.' " According to his writings, there is very little happiness in that "one little corner," and what happiness is there becomes overshadowed by suffering and fear. There are no truly happy endings in any of this writer's works. Perhaps, he will write happier endings when the life he imitates in his writing is happier. Fugard's plays and novel are political statements in which characters are presented as victims of the theory and practice of apartheid. The implied major solution to these characters' problems is, of course, reforming the attitude upon which apartheid is based. (pp. 3-16)

Robert M. Post, "Victims in the Writing of Athol Fugard," in Ariel: A Review of International English Literature, *Vol. 16, No. 3, July, 1985, pp. 3-17.*

Dennis Walder on Fugard, South African politics, and South African drama:

As South Africa lurches from crisis to crisis in the trauma and confusion of transition to a non-racial democratic state, the playwright Athol Fugard finds himself 'a lot more hopeful', though 'aware of how precarious the moves towards a new dispensation are'. His new hopefulness applies to the theatre in South Africa, too—a theatre unique because 'In no other country is there as direct and electrifying a relationship between an event on the stage and the social and political reality on the streets.' According to Fugard, this relationship will continue to be important since, although the country appears at last to be moving towards real democracy, its characteristic moral tensions and challenges will long continue to exert creative pressure upon its playwrights.

Dennis Walder, in his "Resituating Fugard: South African Drama as Witness," in New Theatre Quarterly, *November 1992.*

Athol Fugard with Lloyd Richards (interview date 13 October 1985)

[*Richards was Dean of the Yale School of Drama and Artistic Director of the Yale Repertory Theater at the time of this interview, which was occasioned by the twenty-fifth anniversary revival of Fugard's* The Blood Knot. *In the following discussion, published in 1989, Fugard addresses his reasons for becoming a writer, the artist's role in society, and his methods of writing, rehearsing, and directing.*]

[*Richards*]: *When did you realize that you wanted to become a writer? Was there some precipitating event, or did it grow naturally out of a commitment to literature?*

[Fugard]: There was no one moment, but you could see it growing. You can see it in ***"Master Harold" . . . and the boys***—that gauche young schoolboy playing around with words. Young Hallie talking about what would be a good title for a novel, thinking about writing a short story. From early on there were two things that filled my life—music and storytelling, both of them provoked by my father. He was a jazz pianist and also a very good storyteller, an avid reader. He passed both those interests on to me. Thoughts about being a concert pianist or a composer started to fall away from about the age of fifteen. By eighteen, by the time I went to university, I knew that somehow my life was going to be about putting words on paper. Originally I thought I was going to write the great South African novel, then poetry, and only when I was twenty-four or five did the thought of theater come into my head. That obviously relates to my meeting my wife Sheila, who, when I met her, was an out-of-work actress.

What is your reason for writing?

Well, it's a convergence of two things. I can't think of a single one of my plays that does not represent a coincidence between an external and an internal event. Something outside of me, outside even my own life, something

I read in a newspaper or witness on the street, something I see or hear, fascinates me. I see it for its dramatic potential. That external event affords me the opportunity to deal with what has been building up inside me. For example, the writing of ***The Bloodknot.*** I remember the genesis of that, even though it happened twenty-five years ago. I am singularly prone to that most human of all diseases—guilt. I've had my fair measure of it. But the image that generated ***The Bloodknot*** had absolutely nothing to do with the racial situation in South Africa. The seminal moment was my returning home late one night and going into the room where my brother was sleeping. My brother is a white man like myself. I looked down at him, and saw in that sleeping body and face, all his pain. Life had been very hard on him, and it was just written on his flesh. It was a scalding moment for me. I was absolutely overcome by my sense of what time had done to what I remembered as a proud and powerful body. I saw the pain: that is the seminal image in ***The Bloodknot.***

And that translated into the injection of race and whiteness?

I was trying to examine a guilt more profound than racial guilt—the existential guilt that I feel when another person suffers, is victimized, and I can do nothing about it. South Africa afforded me the most perfect device for examining this guilt without going into the area of the absurd as Ionesco did by giving a man a rhinoceros's horn.

Can you describe the conjunction of external and internal events in **A Lesson from Aloes?**

The external provocation is very simple: I got to know an Afrikaner in Port Elizabeth who had been committed to the struggle for decency and dignity and human rights, but who was suddenly suspected of being a police informer. His name was Piet. Piet's story gave me a chance to deal with the fact that you cannot simply dispose of the Afrikaner as the villain in the South African situation. If that's the only sense you have of the Afrikaner in South Africa at this moment, your thinking is too naive, and you are never really going to understand what is happening in that country. You'll never understand how we landed in the present situation or what's going to come out of it. The terrible and challenging thing about the Afrikaner is his complexity: he is not just bad; there's good as well. The case of Piet Bezuidenhout occurred at a time when I was ready to put an Afrikaner—not a hero, but a survivor—up on the stage. That was my internal provocation.

Why do you use the symbol of aloes? I have an image of the aloe as tangled in the roots of South Africa. It can either be strangled, or survive to produce a flower. . . .

Yes, I think the aloe is one of South Africa's most powerful, beautiful and celebratory symbols. It survives out there in the wild when everything else is dried. At the end of one of our terrible recurrent droughts, the aloe is still there.

You once told a story about being in England for a while and saying you had to go back to South Africa because you could not look at the people on the street and identify where they had come from. . . .

That is true. That one little corner of South Africa, Port Elizabeth and its immediate surroundings, is a region which I know like the back of the hand which holds my pen as I write about it. I can stand on a street corner in Port Elizabeth, look at anybody and put together some sort of biography. I know where they come from, where they're going. I have a feel of the textures of their life. If I stand on a street corner in New Haven, which is a place I've gotten to know as well as any place outside of South Africa, I am still at a total loss to identify the people passing me on that street.

Do you identify with Piet's inability to leave South Africa?

I don't think I could. Of course I'm saying this on American soil. I'm facing a few more months of work in this city, but at the end of it, I will be returning to South Africa. I would like to believe that if for some reason the situation deteriorated to the point where I was told, "If you leave South Africa, you can never come back," I'd stay there. There were periods in my life when I could have been seduced away. I am incredibly fortunate that the government took away my passport at the point when I was most open to seduction. With my passport gone, I could have left on a one-way ticket. But the issue was so starkly highlighted that I had no problem in saying, "No."

Why was your passport taken away?

I don't know. I think they identified me as a liberal. And in the late sixties a liberal was a dangerous animal. Liberals aren't dangerous animals anymore, so they don't hassle me too much. I know they open my mail, I know my telephone is tapped—but I have a passport, a perfectly normal passport. The likes of myself aren't seen as a threat to the establishment anymore. Now they have to deal with men and women who make bombs and set them off. Of course this could change—the government doesn't seem to pursue any sort of consistent policy. Their attitude toward me depends on how they feel when they wake up in the morning. Nadine Gordimer, J. M. Coetzee, Andre Brink are as baffled by how and why the government does things as I am. There just doesn't seem to be any logic to it.

What about the government and censorship?

I have never had trouble publishing my work in South Africa. Although there've been a couple of occasions when school authorities threw my books out of their libraries.

That seems pretty serious to me. Don't you have any reservations about going back to a country where that sort of thing goes on?

No. Nobody can take what I love away from me. I would like to believe that love is the only energy I've ever used as a writer. I've never written out of anger, although anger has informed love. When I return, that love will still be there, even if the South Africa I go back to in five months' time is radically different from the one I left. I would like to believe that my absence from South Africa won't affect my relationship to that country, which has been the source of my inspiration, the soul of my writing.

Is pain a part of that?

Yes. One wishes that pain weren't the potent achemical element that it is.

You tend, in your plays, to take a few crucial people, put them into a space and let them thrash out their lives. Is that a part of your own way of functioning?

Yes. How one human being deals with another remains the most critical fact in history. You can kill a man, or you can bless him. We all know about our potential to kill; we have dangerously lost sight of the fact that each of us can also bless.

At the end of the last performance of **The Bloodknot** *at the Yale Repertory Theatre, you and Zakes Mokae stood at the front of the stage, with the audience standing and applauding. You held hands and raised them. There was something about the event that was more than just the applause of an audience for a performance.*

In my country there's an Athol Fugard trying to kill a Zakes Mokae at this very moment, and there's a Zakes Mokae who wants to kill an Athol Fugard. But Zakes and I were together on that stage.

Does hope still exist today? Where does it reside?

My faith in human nature, in the capacity to change, grows with every year. My faith in the essential goodness of life increases. Yet my faith in politics has withered.

If you ever lost that sense of hope, would that be the moment at which writing became impossible? Could you write out of despair?

That would be a moment at which a lot of things would become impossible. I don't know what I would do with my life if I lost faith in human nature.

What was the conjunction between the external event and the internal impetus with **"Master Harold" . . . and the boys?**

For fifteen years I kept thinking to myself, when am I going to get around to writing about those two extraordinary men, Sam and Willie, who were literally my closest and virtually my only friends for a period of my childhood. Suddenly one day I put a white boy, Hallie, in with them. There it was. I had it. I was locked in to the tensions, the polarity, the dynamic. I had the chance and the courage to deal with something that I had never dealt with in my life. The particular moment was the spitting event—Hallie spits in the black man's face. Before that I was convinced I'd created the necessary dynamic simply by putting Hallie in there with Sam and Willie, and that I could write the play without resorting to anything like the vulgarity of spitting on stage. I thought I could deal with all my problems, my guilts, and wash my dirty linen in a place of public entertainment without having to resort to that. But I just couldn't avoid it. The moment came: I wrote, "Hallie spits in Willie's face."

How did you feel after that?

Well, there's a vulgar aspect to the craft. Even when you're dealing with the most private, intensely personal moment of pain, if you do it well enough, if you handle it correctly, you immediately pat yourself on the back. . . . I might as well be honest about it.

Did the writing of the play absolve any feeling of guilt?

No, but it was necessary for me to deal with it, I've realized your life can be stained so deeply that you can never get rid of it. It's soaked into the fabric.

What was the background of **The Road to Mecca?** *Was it guilt?*

No, quite different. An extraordinary sculptress, Helen Martins, lived in the little village in the Karroo where my house is. For twenty-two years of her life, starting at the age of fifty, she handed herself over to an incredible creative energy. She sculpted away, single-mindedly, with a total obsession. Then, mysteriously, her creativity dried up and she committed suicide. From time to time I'd say to myself, "Come on, deal with it. You're a writer; this is extraordinary." But I kept pushing her aside. Then her story became such an urgent reality inside me, I needed to examine it. ***The Road to Mecca*** focuses on the possibility that creative energy can exhaust itself, probably the most frightening reality an artist can face. Every artist lives in total fear of that—I know I do. I kept wondering whether, with an act of terrible prescience, in describing the end of Helen Martins's creative energy, I was in fact writing my own epitaph.

Is **The Road to Mecca** *your favorite play?*

I think every writer has a special relationship with his most recent work. In my case that would be ***The Road to Mecca.*** Firstly, the process of writing it, creating it, the traumas or difficulties that you live through in order to get it written—those are close to you still. Also the most recent play says something about where you are in your life. It still needs a certain protection; it is very young. Its life has just been started, and you feel very paternal about it. ***The Bloodknot*** is also a very recent experience in my life, but I see it primarily as the work which launched my career in theater, the work in which I found my own voice for the first time. ***A Lesson from Aloes*** has a very special meaning for me because it was the first play I wrote after two or three agonizing years of writer's block, when I just couldn't get anything down on paper.

How does a play come from you as a craftsman? How do you write?

I write by dealing with what I lovingly describe as the inquisition of blank paper—lovingly despite the terror that it's had for me in the past, and no doubt will continue to have in the future. My most important tool is my notebook. I've been a bit careless these past two or three weeks, but even while producing ***The Bloodknot*** at Yale, I spent a few minutes with it every day. I jot down random images, thoughts, ideas, speculations, and a little bit of personal misery. It's a five-finger exercise. Every one of my plays started off a long time before the actual writing took place as an image in those notebooks. There comes a point when one of these images from the past, such as Sam or Piet or Helen Martins, presents itself again. If it is the right moment, and if, as I tried to describe earlier, there is a coincidence between the external and the internal, the things start happening. First I just free associate. It's almost as if the seminal image has a certain magnetic power of its own which helps me focus on the things of daily living that relate to it. This is the first step. It usually results in an accumulation of ideas, scraps of dialogue, rough structures for scenes and a mass of paper. I can lift up that paper and feel its weight metaphorically and think, "Yeah, there's enough here now." Next it's got to be ordered and organized. I never actually start to write a play—by that I mean put "1" up at the top of a blank sheet of paper and open a bracket for my first stage direction—until I have completely structured the play. I have never started to write a play without knowing with total certainty what my final image is. Other writers work differently, I know. They say, "Oh, the material did this to me, I got surprised, it sent me off in a different direction." That has never happened to me. While it may be a flaw, I am absolutely brutal about my disciplining of the material before I write the words "page one" and get to work.

When you begin to write, does the dialogue flow in your head as you write it down?

It's a very slow and painful process. I'm very conscious of how faltering the first few steps are, how much stalling and drowning in the blankness of paper there is. Nothing flows in my head. There have been occasions when I've found my head working away quite energetically with my hand a foot behind, watching in amazement. But there have never been sustained outpourings. If I've got three full pages done, longhand, that's a good day. That's a damn good day in fact. Sometimes there is nothing, or what I have written goes into the wastepaper basket. I tear up and throw away furiously when I write. I don't accumulate a lot of paper. For something to stay on paper longer than two days it has to pass some very critical tests. I usually work through three drafts, longhand, in the course of writing a play; it takes about nine months.

Are your plays ever revised during rehearsal? Do you know how good a line or a scene is before you hear it spoken, or is your ear so developed that there's no need to revise?

I've had varying experiences. Some plays have gone through rehearsal and ended up on the stage without even so much as the punctuation having changed. Others have benefited substantially from the rehearsal process. Sometimes the actors have made me aware, in the course of the rehearsal process, of moments that needed fleshing out and points that hadn't been made strongly enough.

I come from a country which is so highly politicized that there is no act, even the most private you can think of, which does not resonate politically.

—Athol Fugard

What, do you feel, is the relationship of a playwright to politics?

I think it varies. There are as many answers to that as there are playwrights. It is a facile, glib thing to say—but I think I am fortunate in that my relationship to politics is resolved very simply: I come from a country which is so highly politicized that there is no act, even the most private you can think of, which does not resonate politically. Obviously when it comes to the question of telling stories about other people's lives in a situation as political as South Africa, you get to be political. So political commitment isn't really something I've had to look for; it was an automatic by-product of my being a storyteller—one who is going to try to tell stories truthfully and through them bear witness to the South African situation. Talking with young students at Yale recently, I was asked whether I agreed with a fellow South African writer—I am going to be cowardly and not name that writer—who said that all writers in that country had an obligation to make a political stand. I got angry about this because I don't think any writer should presume to give orders to another. The place from which you take your orders is probably the most secret place you have. If you have a word like "God" in your vocabulary, then that is an area in which you and God deal with each other. So, no writer must ever presume to tell another writer what his or her political responsibilities are. It is a poet's right in South Africa to write a poem which seemingly has no political resonance.

Is the duty of a playwright in South Africa to his society different than the duty of an American to his?

I don't think so. This is really just a way of asking about the relationship of the artist to his society. Some writers do nothing but talk about the objective moral obligations that artists must live up to. If you're Brecht, you're going to write as Brecht writes; you're going to be as committed as Brecht. There may be pale imitations, but there will only be one Brecht. Every artist does as he needs to. There is a desperate tendency to try to legislate artists, to try to lay down rules for their obligations to society. Just leave artists alone. If you are a true artist, you will have a very finely tuned moral mechanism. If you're a Georgia O'Keeffe, a Bertolt Brecht or a Harold Pinter, you'll do it your way.

You have chosen not to leave your country, for various reasons. Do you consider yourself, even there, in exile to any extent? How does exile fit into your art, or does it?

Exile is a phenomenon I have watched with morbid curiosity over the years because it is a fate that has befallen a lot of my friends. It is something I have watched but not experienced. I do not consider myself to be in exile. I could play around with words and say that I consider myself an exile from the society that I believe South Africa should be, but that's just being clever. No, I don't really know what exile means.

You said your faith in politics has withered. How did this happen?

My faith in politics and politicians has withered, but as I was saying my faith in human nature grows stronger. But politicians screw up so often now—when did we last have a decent statesman? Let's not even talk about South Africa; let's look at America, England. Where's the statesmanship? The mess is global. My skepticism is something that has come with experience, a certain world-weariness as I have looked at the past decades. The world wasn't getting better. I don't think the moral tone of the Western world has significantly improved in the fifty-odd years that I've been alive. Technologically it has, but morally it damn sure hasn't.

How do you feel the role of art in bringing about social change compares to that of politics and persuasion?

Art has a role. Art is at work in South Africa. But art works subterraneanly. It's never the striking, superficial cause and effect people would like to see. Art goes underground into people's dreams and surfaces months later in strange, unexpected actions. People bring a sort of instant-coffee expectation to art; they'd like the results to be immediate. It doesn't work that way. I like that image of art dropping down through the various layers of the individual's psyche, into dreams, stirring around there and then surfacing later in action.

In a recent article you spoke about the role of alcohol in your life, and its subsequent absence. Does alcohol open up new channels of access to the muse? How was your work affected when you quit drinking?

Oh God, I'm only too prepared to talk about that. For a long time I thought that drinking had a great influence on my imagination. Not that I've used alcohol at any of the few desks where I've done my writing; I've always sat down at my desk very sober, but alcohol was there as a part of my life. Especially at night, after a day working, I used to enjoy my whiskeys, my wines, my beer. And then with the last carafe at night I brainstormed, putting down ideas for the next day. It was a critical aspect of my writing cycle and it led me to believe that if I decided to give up drinking I would end up not writing any longer. I won't go into the circumstances that led me to give up drinking, except that obviously one of the reasons was the recognition that I would become an alcoholic. Another was its effect on relationships that were very important to me. Anyway, one day three-and-a-half years ago I decided to stop. In the course of that time I have written ***The Road to Mecca*** and directed it in South Africa, America and London. I also returned to the anniversary production of ***The Bloodknot*** with Zakes Mokae, which started at Yale and ended up on Broadway. The three-and-a-half years prove I can get on with a creative life even though I don't drink. I must confess that I had moments of unbelievable terror, fear and panic, with the devil inside me trying to persuade me that the reason that I hadn't done any writing that day was that I hadn't been able to get any drinking in; that the real reason the rehearsal had gone so badly and I hadn't gotten any sleep and had a headache was because I wasn't drinking; that I had made a mess of a number of critical moments in the past several years while honoring my resolve to stay sober. Fortunately, I was able to resist those low moments. Starting three-and-a-half years ago, life has become a most extraordinary adventure. I didn't ever believe I would have such a sense of rebirth, of rediscovery.

Would you share with us what your family means to you as a writer, and how your relationship with your family either facilitates, implements or impedes your work? I ask this knowing that your wife Sheila was in the theater before you were.

Yes, and now Sheila is a novelist. Theater didn't turn out to be what she wanted to do. Prose and poetry have become her life. We have lived together as two writers. The marriage has survived on the basis of one absolute rule: total privacy. It came about quite unconsciously, without any fuss; we never addressed ourselves to the issue. I think two writers living together can be dangerous. I never know what Sheila is writing, what her novel is about, until the first copy comes from the publisher. And she, by and large, knows nothing about the play that I'm working on until she sits down in a preview or a first-night audience. We exchange sighs of relief or groans of despair at the end of the day, but it's as general as that. They are noises, like two draft animals stabled together, blowing and groaning away. That makes the work possible. Obviously, there is incredible mutual respect and support. And Lisa, my daughter, is very inspirational. I think that she's a major reason for a lot of what I do.

You have been at once both the playwright and the director. Is the relationship between these two roles an easy one?

It started out of economic necessity. The blunt and simple reality was that twenty-five years ago, when I wrote ***The Bloodknot,*** nobody in South Africa wanted to touch it. If I hadn't got hold of Zakes, whom I had already known from some previous work we had done in the theater, and said, "Let's do it," and then tried to sort out the traffic on the stage—in addition to taking on the role of Morris—the play wouldn't have got done. It was the same with ***Hello and Goodbye, People are Living There, Boesman and Lena, Sizwe Bansi is Dead, The Island*** and ***Statements after an Arrest under the Immorality Act.*** I only started enjoying the luxuries so taken for granted in the American theater when I came to Yale. I had never had designers in my life. I had never had dramaturges—I'm still trying to discover what to do with that animal; what do you *do* with a dramaturge? I think they are asking themselves that question as well. God knows I have no conceits as a director. Someone has to organize the traffic. That's what I do: I see that people don't bump into each other on the stage. I look after the six-foot rule.

Forgive me, what is the six-foot rule?

The six-foot rule is that no two actors must come nearer to each other than six feet unless there is a crisis. Get closer than six feet and you've got a crisis in the action. So I organize the traffic. I also understand the text, because I wrote it. With those two contributions to the event, I have discharged my responsibilities as a director.

Would you lose a certain amount of the autonomy you feel as a writer if you turned a play over to another director?

I've no experience with that. I make very certain that I handle the first productions of the play in South Africa, in London and in New York. When those three events are behind me, I cut the umbilical cord, and the play looks after itself. Once or twice I've dropped in on other productions of my work and had varying experiences—some good, some bad, quite a few indifferent. I've no working relationship with other directors and I think it will probably stay that way.

What about the experience of acting in your own plays? When you're writing do you have it in mind that certain words will be for you to speak?

I'm glad I'm an actor. I'm glad I've had acting experience, because I think it has sharpened my craft as a playwright. Acting has made the writer realize what actors need up there on stage to make a moment work. I feel that's the reason actors have such a good time with my plays—they often tell me they do. I often think of my plays as being written with three characters sitting at the desk: the writer himself, and then behind his left shoulder is the actor, watching as he writes and nudging his arm, and behind the other shoulder is the director who's eventually going to be responsible for the staging of it. There's a triple psychology that functions when I write a play. I don't want to become too conscious of this aspect of my writing in case it interferes with its progress, but it seems there is a three-pronged attack on the blank paper when I sit down to write a play.

You said earlier that you gather your material before you set out to write. Could you talk a little about the plays that were worked on improvisationally?

My work with the actors during one stage of the rehearsals is for both rehearsing and improvising. With ***The Island,*** when I got together with John Kani and Winston Ntshona, I always came prepared with questions, ideas, provocations. This would set them up; they are both consummate personal storytellers who love acting out their lives. I fed them a constant stream of provocations relating to the central idea on which we had decided.

How were John and Winston involved in the genesis of **Sizwe Bansi is Dead?**

Yes, very simple, easy to talk about that. I had been working with John and Winston in an amateur context, a black drama group from New Brighton, the black ghetto of Port Elizabeth. They approached me one day and said that they wanted to turn professional. I listened to them with disbelief. At that point in South Africa's theater history, twelve years ago, the notion that a black man could earn a living being an actor in South Africa was just the height of conceit. But they were insistent, and so we looked around for a play for them to do. We couldn't find anything that really excited us, anything that I wanted to direct them in. Then John said, "Couldn't we *make* a play?" We tried various ideas, all of which petered out, and then I remembered something: it was a photograph I'd once seen in the display window of a pokey little backstreet photographer in Port Elizabeth, an extraordinary photograph of a man wearing what was obviously a new suit, seated on a chair, smiling broadly, a hat on his head. I think there was even an umbrella across his knees. In one hand he had a pipe and in the other a cigarette. It was an extraordinary photograph, a great celebratory moment captured by that backstreet photographer. I finally put this down as a mandate; I said to these chaps, "Come on now, for that chap to be smiling like that, he's got to have a reason. Maybe that's the story we're looking for. Maybe that's where our play lies." I asked them why he was smiling. Again it was John who said, "One reason why a black man smiles as broadly as you've suggested is if his reference book, his much-hated passbook, is in order, or if he's just managed to get some problem in connection with it sorted out." That was the start of it, that stupid question. In fact, the passbook does lie at the core of ***Sizwe Bansi is Dead.*** That question, and a whole series of others—all concerning the man in the blue suit with the umbrella, smiling at the camera, with the cigarette in one hand and a pipe in the other—was the start of ***Sizwe Bansi.*** He was our seminal image, I fed John and Winston constant provocations from what I knew about them and their lives. It was my job to take home whatever had happened in the rehearsal room and start shaping it. I used my craft to structure and define and dramatically shape what they had provided by way of raw improvisation. That was my process. I am a great believer in architecture, in structuring. It's my discipline.

Can you talk about the original production of that play in Johannesburg? Was there censorship involved?

We felt that the play was far too dangerous for us to go public with it; there was the problem of mixed audiences. So we launched the play by underground performances to which people had to have a specific invitation—a legal loophole in the censorship structure in South Africa, and one we continued to exploit for many years. During our underground period, we had a lot of police interference. They rolled up once or twice and threatened to close us down, arrest us—the usual bully tactics of security police anywhere in the world. We just persisted, carried on and survived it. We eventually did go public with ***Sizwe Bansi,*** many years later, but only after it had played in London and New York. After that, we felt that the play's reputation protected us.

What are some of the limits you perceive in the American theater? You spoke recently about the difficulties of producing an off-Broadway show.

Well, I could talk endlessly about the limits of Broadway theater. Broadway, oh God, what a pain! It is going through a long process of dying—it should just get on with the business and do it. Broadway's become one hell of a mess, but then Broadway isn't American theater. If Broadway wants to die, and if legitimate theater, straight theater, hasn't got a place on Broadway, well then good. Theater's flourishing out in the regions. I look around and all sorts of very exciting things are happening.

Did you seek out a relationship with the New York theater world and the Yale Rep?

Not any more than any writer or playwright who tries to get his work done. When it gets done, you earn a living, you earn royalties, you can pay the rent. Fortunately American audiences and American actors go for the same sort of theater that I try to write. I don't think it's an accident that I earn eighty or ninety per cent of my living as a playwright in America. In England it's only about ten or fifteen per cent. The English don't tune in to my plays as strongly as American audiences and critics. This relationship between New York, American theater and myself is one which I'm very happy with and hope to continue.

How has your relationship with Zakes changed through all

this? What was it like working with a very unprofessional actor twenty-five years ago as opposed to the experienced actor he is now?

Oh, I've got a lovely answer to that question: I was as unprofessional as Zakes then. We both thought we were as good then as we think we are now. Zakes had seen five plays twenty-five years ago; I had seen six.

So the ego does not change.

The ego does not change. Now we've seen a dozen each. (pp. 131-51)

Athol Fugard and Lloyd Richards, in an interview in The Paris Review, *Vol. 31, No. 111, Summer, 1989, pp. 128-51.*

Stephen Gray (essay date February 1990)

[*Gray is a South African critic and editor. In the following excerpt, he favorably reviews the Johannesburg production of Fugard's* My Children! My Africa!, *discussing its place in Fugard's body of work and analyzing the ways in which it exemplifies a new approach to representing strife in South African society.*]

At the time of writing, September 1989, Athol Fugard's new play, ***My Children! My Africa!*** is coming to the end of its long and successful premiere run at the Market Theatre, Johannesburg. About the production Fugard has been quoted as saying: 'This one is between me and my country'. That was in *Time* magazine, on 10 July 1989, and again on 7 August, 1989: and the *Time* coverage of this domestic affair is evidence of just how internationally consumable Fugard's theatre has become. *Time* insists on calling him 'the greatest active playwright in English', no less—and we may be sure a little private transaction with his home audience will not stop here.

Nevertheless, Fugard the man of provocative stances meant it: South African audiences should have this play first . . . and for sound, practical reasons. Apart from the fact that ***My Children! My Africa!*** will not play quite the same way out of here, Fugard knows there is a hard, tough core in the South African skull that loves a hefty moral pummelling, and that night after night guilt-ridden, unrepentant masses will stream in to their community cockpit for something they're not getting in the world outside. And like any good Calvinist preacher, Fugard knows just how to dole out the punishment accurately. He also knows that South Africans are no longer impressed by *their* plays appearing at the National or on Broadway first.

In July 1987, only two years earlier, on the same main stage of the Market Theatre complex, Fugard spectacularly failed to bring in the crowds with his cumbersome two-hander, ***A Place with the Pigs.*** After three decades in theatre in Johannesburg—let us say as the single most potent force to drive the performing arts into what they are today, or can rise to being—Fugard found all but his most faithful supporters judging ***Pigs*** as gruellingly self-indulgent.

That parabolic script did not yield its meaning easily. One could only admire Fugard's manic devotion, as night after night he grovelled in pig-shit, dousing himself in bucketfuls of water on bare boards in zero-degree temperatures. Atonement for years of addiction to booze, to be sure, but the larger references to South Africans wilfully clinging to their own versions of filth somehow never came home. The play was too devious for the needling to strike flesh.

But one factor that has indubitably grown with Fugard here over the years is the grittiness of his audience: ***Pigs*** was met with an outcry alike from intellectuals (as not relevant to the cause of social engagement and transformation) and fans (as a literary game evading the process of achieving liberty). Fiercely sensitive to such rebukes (and to rows of empty seats), Fugard was obviously pressured to swing back into a more literal mode.

In the pre-publicity for ***My Children! My Africa!*** he virtually said so: *this* one you *will* like. It was both promise and threat: recognize it this time. Tired of the ambiguous pussyfooting of much western stage fare, yet disillusioned by the witless and facile agit-prop of much South African committed theatre, audiences were now very ready for a mammoth work that steered between the two, using the strengths of both, leaving nothing out.

It is faith in the power of theatre artistry to reflect division, but to triumph over it—to portray the politics of betrayal and treachery, but practise alternatives to it—that makes much South African contemporary theatre so assertively positive.

—Stephen Gray

The subject of ***My Children! My Africa!*** is situated differently, too. Instead of middle-aged artistic angst, which Fugard may have a right to, but which during a vicious, day-after-day state of emergency seems to have marginal importance, this time his subject is squarely in the arena of the main action in the South Africa of the recent past: the schoolroom. No one can fail to recognize that blackboard and chalk, the school-bell, the desk, and register—the only props used.

Two of the three characters in ***My Children! My Africa!*** are indeed 'children'—at least, the right-less youths of South Africa. There they are in their pre-matriculation uniforms that subtly over the years have come not to mean promise and fulfilment, but oppression and regimentation: bitter obedience to an untenable moral order and its deforming brainwash.

Just as the country chafes for freedom, so do Thami and Isabel: their aching, battling decencies struggle, practically throttle, on the indecencies of a system so dishonest and death-dispensing that we root for them and their future from the start. By the end—for this is the story of their bleeding, devastating friendship and how it is all but destroyed—one can only gaspingly applaud their endurance. May the rising generation be just as resilient. May the future be *theirs.*

Fugard's previous 'school' play, ***'Master Harold'. . . and the Boys*** was also one of his most popular and accessible. But the very ellipsis of the title indicated the distribution of power in its triangle: white Master Harold (the young Fugard) alone on one side of the old segregated divide, stacked against the two adult 'black boys' of the deep South African south. For local audiences the insult of the play that stuck in the memory was John Kani as Sam lowering his pants and pointing his butt at the audience.

Tracing the roots of apartheid's human affronts back to the 1950s of his youth, Fugard wrote that play in terms of privilege and class alliance. The theatrical game was only too recognizable: masters and servants defined by their skin-differences and the insult thereof. Although it stirred notes of deep guilt in the colonial-born, ***Master Harold*** was actually about as disruptive of the prevailing social order and as titillating as, say, Genet; when all was said and done, Harold still wore the uniform of education, and Sam and Willie were left to safer and less ambitious exercises—specifically, ballroom dancing.

That was in 1982. The system was not cracking then, and only one of the trio was socially upwardly mobile. In 1982, one should also mention, few blacks left the popular ballrooms to go to the Market Theatre. ***Master Harold*** feels like a museum piece today.

Now, in 1989, one should also mention that most of the seats in the Market Theatre are not occupied by whites. Black theatregoers outnumber them, just as Isabel in ***My Children! My Africa!*** is outnumbered on stage. Isabel now faces Thami and his teacher, Anela Myalatya (the magnificent John Kani again, whose association with Fugard goes back to the Serpent Players in their hometown of Port Elizabeth in the 1960s).

During the course of the play, Fugard works this triangle every possible way, to be sure, but the alignment is not finally one of black-versus-white. Surprisingly, the two young ones (mixed team) turn out the winners; the old-stager teacher loses out—not for his colour, but for his outmoded, no longer tenable beliefs. Fugard points out that that is where the divide has shifted in contemporary South Africa: from the old statutory colour-line to the explosive new generation gap. Isabel and Thami lose their every cherished hope during the course of the play, but the unyielding Anela Myalatya loses his life.

The staging of this contest in ***My Children! My Africa!*** derives very much from Fugard's 'theatre of poverty' days, when, in ***Sizwe Bansi is Dead*** (1973), for example, two actors impersonating multitudes could travel light with a table, a chair, a few home-made posters, and a camera on a tripod. Here, the bare schoolroom setting occupies the inner stage, the blackboard serving to announce the text of the lesson to come. The audience is situated within the classroom: we are fiercely targetted for the full force of a didactic wrangle.

For more intimate scenes, one or another of the performers cuts off the inner stage with a long curtain on which are scrawled the shadows of chaotic hieroglyphics—a neat reminder that in dark South Africa protest avidly emerges on bare wall-space as graffiti, literally the writing on the walls. At one point the teacher recounts how he tries to stop the 'erupting township riot' (to describe the event in South African media terms) of his schoolkids: 'Little Sipho Fondini from Standard Six was there, writing on a wall: "Liberation First, then Education." He saw me and called out: "Is the spelling right, Mr M?" ' Slogans like these, topical of the time of the action in 1984, are the subtext of the play. (pp. 25-8)

The statement within which the play is enclosed is overwhelmingly this: no matter how divided they are in society outside, inside the Market Theatre by their art they are united. It is this simple reassertion of faith in the power of theatre artistry to reflect division, but to triumph over it—to portray the politics of betrayal and treachery, but practise alternatives to it—that makes much South African contemporary theatre so assertively positive. So shrunken are the channels of debate, so inaccessible the dialectics of power, that often such theatre is the *only* public channel open to the country's citizens for discussion of crucial issues.

The opening scene is an *exemplum,* instructing the audience how the rest of the action is to be assessed. Isabel is set up versus Thami—the best girl of the Camdeboo High School (white) versus the best boy of Zolile High School (black). They are two able rhetoricians, summarizing their highly committed cases: Isabel's for women's lib before black liberation, Thami's the reverse.

Thami speaks with all the zeal of the call for black power:

> The opposition has spoken about sexual exploitation and the need for women's liberation. Brothers and sisters, these are foreign ideas. Do not listen to them. They come from a culture, the so-called Western Civilisation, that has meant only misery to Africa and its people . . .

Isabel's reply is shaky but confident:

> The argument against equality for women, based on alleged 'differences' between the two sexes, is an argument that can very easily be used against any other 'different' group.

Votes are taken. The audience is forced to take sides, too, for Fugard uses the Market Theatre ushers—strapping youths in shorts too short and striped ties stopping at the sternum—as unruly hecklers, Thami's classmates. Their interjections from all corners heat up the battle to violent pitch.

What is this but every South African's nightmare? Being caught in the crossfire of your own most basic choices. Wonderfully, in the eyes of the all-male black schoolroom, Isabel just wins this debate.

The contest, the winning and losing: this is the resultant paradigm of the action, and the protocol of debate and of the school sports-field duly becomes the regulation of human issues. Then the rules become suspended . . . and the only possible outcome, sacrifice and bare survival, is also the logical outcome. In what follows Fugard scarily declares his own 'state of emergency' in dramatic terms, suspending the rules of theatrical law and order, as it were, just as in the outside world this occurs in the history we live.

Only in two further scenes will the three protagonists meet again. Mostly we are in for duologues—Isabel and Thami getting to know one another; Mr. M. (as the teacher is known to parent and pupil alike) coercing Isabel into joining Thami in a combined literary quiz team; the two of them drilling themselves through the chestnuts of Eng. Lit.; and then, when the boycott and strike action divide them, the failure of the team—not now, one day.

In the second half it is Thami versus Mr. M.—Mr. M. who has been ringing his schoolbell in vain for Thami, his best pupil, to resume his desk, and Thami come as a comrade to persuade Mr. M. to choose the Cause of the People rather than the policy of Bantu education. Mr. M. chooses rather the chance to teach a last class—and as he walks out to give it he is felled, necklaced and burnt.

Thami goes into exile, torn from Isabel—one day, maybe tomorrow: 'Sahle kakuhle, Isabel. That's the Xhosa goodbye.' 'I know. Sis Phumla taught me how to say it. Hamba kakuhle, Thami,' she replies—and it is Isabel who is left to give the epilogue: 'We are all your children, Mr. M.'

Interspersing the duologues are monologues given to each of the three on a rotating basis: we hear Isabel's own story in great detail, we hear Mr. M's, we hear Thami's. Each is given the same access to the audience: equal space (the forestage and a bench) and equal time (fifteen to twenty minutes), as it is no less clear that they are not given equal access in real life.

Isabel tells us what we know already; some of Mr. M. we know; Thami is new. The monologues serve of course to deepen and advance the action, to make the confrontations between words and actions, people and political destiny that are to come all the more heartrending and, as Fugard insists, explicable.

But the monologues have another function: they are delivered straight, eyeball to eyeball, to the particular audience of each night. These are not the old-style soliloquies of European theatre, but rather related to the new popular art form so prevalent in (usually illegal) gatherings: the public speech as testimony. At trade union rallies, mass funerals, religious commemorations it is this individual, oral expressiveness which is practised, and now Fugard has taken it into the theatre as a dramatic convention.

Possibly this is why he insisted on South Africans seeing the play first; restlessly he wanted to test a new direction in his theatrical vocabulary where it would be most familiar and telling. For the rally, the mob-trial, the flag-waving insurrectionism, and the media images made of such mass mobilization, Fugard sees, are all ineffably theatrical. The stoning to death of a Mr. M. in the outside world is as much a dramatic event as anything enacted inside the theatre. Law may be suspended in South Africa (as are the media), but performance codes as old as the Greeks have taken their place.

On stage in ***My Children! My Africa!*** Mr. M. is killed as follows: having betrayed his colleagues, friends, and pupils to the police, for his own good reasons—he chooses words above stones—he gives Thami the rock hurled through the school-window.

Fugard's original stage direction was: 'Breaking away from Thami, ringing his bell furiously, he goes outside and confronts the mob. They kill him.' But in rehearsal the following was decided on: Kani as Mr. M. calmly advances on the audience, *Concise Oxford English Dictionary* in hand. There is the only sound effect of the production—a rising march with dogs barking, coming to a rumbling stop before the school. [Mr. M] tears the fly-leaf with his name on it from the dictionary, crumples it, lays it on top. He pulls out a matchbox, lights the page. We watch it flare up, reduce to ash. The actor walks with dignity into the dark.

Possibly this is a specific reference to Winnie Mandela's notorious statement that 'we will take the country with our matchboxes'. Certainly, within the context of the play the matchbox is the tinder of cleansing fire, the medium of apocalypse. Only then can Thami take the journey north, to prepare to return as a liberator, and Isabel 'go to the mountain' for her last, bitter lesson, that hope *must* be kept alight.

The play ends there: Thami and Isabel separated again, not by the old divide between 'white town' and 'black location', but by one being trapped in the final laager or redoubt, the other armed and knocking at its gate. That takes us to the end of 1984, and the open point at which the play finishes, concluded but unresolved. Fugard promises a sequel, in which Thami and Isabel are to meet up again closer to us in time—or possibly even in the future.

A final comment about the impact of ***My Children! My Africa!*** on contemporary South Africa must be reserved for some of the daring and daredevilry, the sheer cheek, that has gone into the whole enterprise. Fugard, we know by now, has made a career out of taking theatrical risks. Although an extremely successful playwright commercially, he has never 'sold out' to easy interests, and with ***My Children! My Africa!*** seems less likely to than ever. (pp. 28-30)

Stephen Gray, " 'Between Me and My Country': Fugard's 'My Children! My Africa!' at the Market Theatre, Johannesburg," in New Theatre Quarterly, *Vol. VI, No. 21, February, 1990, pp. 25-30.*

Jeanne Colleran (essay date March 1990)

[*In the essay below, Colleran discusses* A Place with the Pigs *and examines the work's place in Fugard's œuvre and contemporary South African theater.*]

In a span of three years, Athol Fugard directed the world premières of his two most recent dramas at the Yale Repertory Theatre: in 1984 he staged ***The Road to Mecca,*** and in 1987 he produced and acted in ***A Place with the Pigs. Mecca*** has been extraordinarily well received; after being performed at Yale, it played at Britain's National Theatre in 1985, at the Charleston, South Carolina Spoleto Festival in 1987, and on Broadway in 1988. As the fourth major New York production of the decade, the success of ***Mecca*** confirmed, in the words of [William A. Henry III], Fugard's "standing as the greatest active playwright in the English-speaking world" ["Enemy of the People," *Time* (18 April 1988)].

A Place with the Pigs, conversely, has been considerably less successful; the Yale production received rather mediocre reviews, and the play has since garnered no critical attention. While there are a number of reasons for the drama's failure to attract favorable notice, the most obvious cause is that this play, a "personal parable" set "somewhere in the author's imagination" and concerning the forty years spent in a pigsty by Pavel Ivanovich Navrotsky, a Red Army deserter, simply does not conform to the audience's expectations of what a work by Athol Fugard should be like. As one of the foremost internationally-recognized spokesmen against apartheid, Fugard has been called, among other things, a "South African visionary" [Samuel G. Freeman, "Master Athol," *Vanity Fair* (April 1987)]. ***Pigs,*** however, seems to have little in common with either the angry indictments made in early works, such as ***The Blood Knot*** or ***Sizwe Bansi is Dead,*** or the agonized confessions of later dramas, such as ***Master Harold . . . and the Boys.*** Despite the fact that ***A Place with the Pigs,*** as both Allan Wallach [in "Fugard's Latest: In a Different Place," *Newsday* (30 March 1987)] and Frank Rich [in "Stage: Fugard's *Place with the Pigs,*" *New York Times* (3 April 1987)] have pointed out, has obvious connections to the South African situation, Fugard's parable, like many other works of art that are purposefully indirect, has been more dismissed than deciphered. Thus, for many theatre-goers, Rich's remark that ***Pigs*** is an anomalous work that may play better in the classroom than it does on stage is an apt one.

Such a dismissal is, in my estimation, most unfortunate. Certainly, Rich is correct in claiming that the play is flawed; both he and Wallach have focused accurately on the too-small part played by Praskovya, Pavel's wife and the play's only other character. Similarly, both have recognized that the drama's primary images—flies and butterflies—bear too great a symbolic weight. Despite its problems, however, ***Pigs*** is an important play for at least three reasons: from an historical perspective, it speaks to the altered position of the white liberal in South Africa; as part of contemporary South African literature, it fits into what Nadine Gordimer has called the "cryptic" mode; and within Fugard's own canon, it represents a new kind of dramatic enterprise. For these reasons, as well as for the play's own considerable merits, it is vital that the play not be reduced to some kind of twentieth-century closet drama.

Perhaps the most striking way of realizing the changes that have taken place in recent South African theatre and, consequently, Fugard's place in it, is to compare Fugard's recent plays with two other South African exports: the 1980 production of *Woza Albert!* and the dramas that comprised the *Woza Afrika!* theatre festival performed at Lincoln Center in September 1986. *Woza Albert!,* written by Percy Mtwa, Mbongeni Ngema, and Barney Simon, introduced a "new kind of theater" to South African audiences, new because it moved beyond the two dramatic models previously available to South African playwrights. Until recently, South African theatre was dominated by two very different writers, Gibson Kente and Athol Fugard. To the makers of revolutionary theatre, neither model was acceptable: Kente's energetic musicals overemphasized spectacle at the expense of political commentary, and Fugard's eloquent, dilemma-ridden dramas, though more explicitly political, seemed to focus too narrowly on the situation of white South Africans. The authors of *Woza Afrika!,* strongly influenced by the Black Consciousness Movement of the seventies, chose instead to forge a "new theatre" which continues to draw heavily upon the traditions of oral performance and makes use of music and movement but which infuses these with direct, forceful, political commentary. The focus of many of these contemporary dramas, the desperation and fury of township life, is, moreover, a subject which these black playwrights believe to be beyond the scope of the white writer, a point made by Amiri Baraka in his preface to the *Woza Afrika!* anthology: "The lives that *Bopha!* or *Gangsters* or *Woza Albert!* speak to cannot really be stated directly by the well-meaning white South African authors. The fact that theirs has been heretofore the only voice out of South Africa points to the deep continuity of western chauvinism, even while ostensibly fighting racial chauvinism!" Rejecting the political passivity of Kente's popular theatre as well as the hopelessness typical of dramas by white South Africans, the new dramatists have created [according to Pico Iyer in "Cries of the Silenced," *Time* (22 September 1986)] a kind of "guerilla drama" or "revolutionary theatre" which sounds the rallying call to political action.

For Athol Fugard, the implications of the growth of the Black Consciousness Movement and the rise of the "new theatre" have been profound. Despite his early collaborative work with John Kani and Winston Ntshona and his involvement with the Serpent players, there is no longer an unequivocal acceptance of Fugard's dramas within his own homeland. Two examples will suffice to indicate how Fugard, once lionized at home and abroad, has had the nature of his theatrical activity challenged by those who feel compelled to reject completely "white expertise and white values as potentially corruptive."

The first instance is an account of the criticism directed at one of Fugard's most personal plays, ***Master Harold. . . and the Boys.*** To some black critics, the character of Sam is a grotesquerie. His forbearance and forgiveness, far from being virtues, are embodiments of the worst kind of Uncle Tom-ism. That these criticisms have affected Fugard is evident in the remarks he made in a 1984 speech to the Anson Phelps Stokes Institute's Africa Roundtable:

> I am not a spokesman for Black political consciousness. ***Master Harold . . . and the Boys,*** for example, has come in for some very strong criticism from both exiled South Africans and Black Americans, as being a disservice to the cause by virtue of its portrayal of Sam as a man capable of infinite, almost saintly patience, a

> man with a capacity for forgiveness. I want to say very clearly in writing that play I never set out to serve a cause. I addressed myself in the first instance to telling a story. . . . The question of being a spokesman for Black politics is something I've never claimed for myself.

The second example of the kind of criticism leveled at Fugard and his dramas is best represented by that of Robert Kavanaugh ("Mshengu"). In his 1985 book, *Theatre and Cultural Struggle in South Africa,* Kavanaugh undertook an extensive analysis of one of Fugard's early collaborative works, ***No-Good Friday,*** and concluded that "Fugard and the others assisted the process of domination in South Africa." In other essays, Kavanaugh has called upon Fugard to "turn his attention away from London, Paris, and New York" and return to majority theatre in South Africa. He also has exhorted him to write in the languages of the black majority, for when he does so, his work will "be of greater value to the people in their struggle for a non-exploitative South Africa."

My point in citing these examples is to recognize that their cumulative effect has been to back Fugard gradually into a corner. His position as a defector to the Afrikaner cause, as a "traitor in the laager," has been a long-standing one; now, however, Fugard cannot write of Johannesburg or of township suffering without incurring the wrath of Black South Africans who regard him as a self-appointed and presumptuous spokesman; nor can he claim value for the position previously held by white liberals without being assailed by the more powerful and vociferous radical left. Thus, ironically, in a nation with draconian censorship laws meant to silence subversive opinion, Fugard has been forced to practise a kind of self-censorship by those whose cause he shares. Backed into a corner, Fugard has responded by making his "little room an everywhere." Refusing to give in to what he has called the "ignominy of silence," he has found a new direction for his plays by writing about what is unarguably his: the corner of his birthplace.

Turning his attention almost exclusively to the Eastern Cape region is one of the ways in which Fugard has continued to pursue what has become an increasingly solitary vision. Beginning with ***A Lesson from Aloes,*** all of Fugard's plays, with the exception of a short piece he wrote for the Actors Theatre of Louisville, have been set in or near Port Elizabeth. Like ***Aloes,*** each of the plays also has at least one character who is of Afrikaner descent—Piet in ***Aloes*** itself, Hallie in ***Master Harold,*** and Marius Byleveld and Miss Helen in ***The Road to Mecca***—and who must work out some measure of self-acceptance in a world to which such characters feel bound and by which they feel betrayed. The short piece written for the Actors Theatre, ***The Drummer,*** is a significant deviation from this practice, however, because in form and tone it foreshadows the fuller statement made in ***A Place with the Pigs.*** Further, all of Fugard's plays from ***Aloes*** on, though with considerable surface differences, are linked thematically to the concerns expressed in both ***Drummer*** and ***Pigs.***

The Drummer is a mime about a tramp who discovers a pair of drumsticks in a pile of rubbish and then proceeds joyously through the crowded streets of New York practising his newly-found art. For Fugard, the five-minute play is a radical departure from the resignation of ***The Blood Knot*** or the anguish of ***The Island.*** Of it, Fugard has remarked, "I think that actually from now on all I'm interested in is what I can celebrate. I've dealt with my pain. I've dealt with the misery of my county [*sic*] as much as I can." ***A Place with the Pigs*** is similarly affirmative and also employs a consciously indirect manner of presentation. Like the mime, Fugard's use of the parable is a wily choice, as it invites but does not confirm a variety of speculations about its sub-text. Through its indirection, Fugard may make the kind of pronouncements prohibited him—by their unpopularity and by his own disdain for propagandizing—and take refuge under the wings of an aesthetic form meant both to provoke and to protect.

Fugard's use of indirect presentation in ***Pigs*** is in keeping with an identifiable strain of contemporary South African literature termed the "cryptic mode." This designation, originally made by Nadine Gordimer to describe the poetry being written by Black South Africans in the early seventies, was extended by Rowland Smith to describe the narrative style of white writers who choose not to employ the method of historical realism. The most established writer in this tradition is J. M. Coetzee, whose postmodern novels deal obliquely with South African issues. But Fugard may have been influenced by a source closer to home: his wife, novelist Sheila Fugard, used the cryptic mode in *The Castaways,* and her novel has the oracular quality Fugard may have been seeking for his own work. By locating his protagonist in a remote setting, Fugard gained the distance needed to raise issues which, given the ideological rigidity of the various opposing factions in South Africa, might otherwise be reduced and dismissed. By adding that the setting is also "somewhere in the author's imagination," Fugard diminishes the very distance he establishes and thereby reclaims the relevance of the story he is about to tell.

The story is a very simple one: enervated by hunger, cold and homesickness, Pavel Ivanovich Navrotsky, a soldier in the Soviet army during World War II, abandons his post for what he intends to be a single night of comfort at home. By the time he reaches his wife, Praskovya, however, he is incoherent; clutching a pair of embroidered slippers his mother has sewn, he staggers into the pigsty and collapses. As Scene One begins, Pavel has already been hidden in the sty for over ten years. In the course of the next three scenes, he will remain confined for thirty more, first from his fear of being shot as a deserter but ultimately from his inability to summon the courage needed to extricate himself from this "dank, unwholesome place."

In depicting Pavel's incarceration and despair, Fugard is re-exploring the psychopathology of victimization he had examined previously in works like ***The Blood Knot*** and ***Master Harold. . . and the Boys.*** But unlike his interests in these earlier plays, Fugard's focus is not on the oppression of an identifiable group—the black South African—by an identifiable evil—apartheid. In a less polemical manner, Fugard's parable investigates the dynamics of victimization and self-victimization without reference to particular historical circumstances. In the course of the presentation, however, it is impossible to ignore the voice of one who, having anguished over an inherited guilt, now pleads for some bit of forgiveness and acceptance. Just as Fugard's plays of the fifties, sixties, and seventies demanded that some understanding be given to the oppression experienced by black and coloured South Africans, his dramas of the eighties ask that this same understanding be extended to the Afrikaner.

Seeking forgiveness for the Afrikaner is surely a position bound to be misunderstood given the "manichean" tendency in South African politics to establish polarities, react reductively, and foreclose dialogue. But as the play following what Fugard has acknowledged to be an Afrikaner trilogy—***Aloes, Harold,*** and ***Mecca***—***Pigs*** presents central issues which are extensions of those already raised: the nature of guilt and responsibility, the pain of social exclusion, the role of self-forgiveness, the need for courage, the unbreakable bonds of home. And in ***Pigs*** Fugard goes even further than he did in ***Mecca*** to advocate what is certainly an unpopular political stance: the right of the white African tribe to remain in its homeland.

Pavel Navrotsky is possessed of the eloquence of a Dostoevskian peasant. As the play opens, he is rehearsing the speech he will give at the village's memorial service for the fifty gallant dead—himself included—who perished at the Russian front. He plans to surrender himself as a "deeply repentant man" who "acknowledges in full his guilt" but pleads that his punishment be tempered with mercy. For he has suffered enough already, Pavel intends to argue; for "ten years he has been imprisoned by his own conscience in circumstances which would make the most hardened among you wince." Pavel's shaky courage falters completely, however, when he learns that his army uniform, used for rags and nibbled on by mice, is unfit to wear. Unable to summon even enough bravado to steady his resolve, Pavel reverses his former faith in humanity and convinces himself that the townspeople will never forgive him, for doing so may entail some recognition of a similar weakness. Cowardice wins out, and he dispatches Praskovya to play the part of the widow. She returns to report, in what is surely one of the drama's funniest, most adept speeches, that it was best that Pavel did not appear after all, since the villagers, enjoying their elevated thoughts and patriotic grief, surely would have resented his resurrection.

The first scene lays the beginnings of what becomes a complex psychological portrait of self-imprisonment. Through Pavel, Fugard suggests that unresolved corporate guilt is suppressed through a certain self-protecting blindness. More than this, even when one musters the courage to acknowledge the truth, as Pavel does, he can expect little sympathy from a society engaged in a kind of communally-sanctioned amnesia. Pavel, in his weakness, has committed an act of cowardice to which every villager is prone; their intolerance signifies both a deep-rooted refusal to acknowledge blame and anger that a tacit agreement to maintain silence has been broken.

Given a situation where man's baser tendency to rationalize or exculpate his offenses is not only allowed but is in fact encouraged, how is it possible to find a way out of the squalor of self-deceit? For Pavel, the issue is not only escaping the filth of the pigsty; it is also escaping the filth of self-loathing. In grandiloquent speeches and grandiose gesture, Pavel relates the horror of the two "existential realities" which dominate his life: pigshit and time. He meditates, histrionically, on ways "profitably" to spend his time in the sty; he might set to evangelizing the pigs, foremost among the great unwashed, or better still, he might inspire them to revolution, instill in them a political consciousness. Pavel's ruminations, comically overstated though they are, actually describe the situation of writers in South Africa whose works must reflect a prescribed political agenda or be deemed irrelevant.

The first scene also establishes the important role of Praskovya who, though she sleeps in a bed rather than a stall, is as much a victim of Pavel's cowardice as Pavel himself. More importantly, it is the stolid Praskovya who, litany-like, utters what is to become an important motif in the play. When re-constructing any personal crisis, Pavel habitually embellishes the actual event, cosmically inflating its significance. Earth-bound Praskovya reins him back: three times in the first scene, she begins a sentence with the proviso, "if you're interested in the truth, Pavel," and then offers some nugget of hard information. Though Pavel protests that there must be "a simple solution" to his problem, it is Praskovya who recognizes that "life goes on." In the course of the play, she deals with nothing more exalted than peeling potatoes or scrubbing floors, and though her husband doesn't realize it, she models what it will take Pavel years to learn: the ability to walk away from a situation beyond her control or remedy. The first scene ends in this way: unwilling to listen to Pavel's ranting, Praskovya warns him, "I'm going to walk away from you." "Just like that?" asks the incredulous Pavel. "Just like that," she responds.

By the second scene, Pavel has lapsed into mindless apathy; his sole diversion is swatting flies. The cramped space, the tallies of dead flies across the stalls, the cherished slipper now employed as a fly swatter, all combine to indicate what Pavel's cloistral existence has made him: he is either utterly dispirited or maniacally violent. The petty tyrant of an empire of pig-shit and flies, Pavel is momentarily transported by the chance appearance of a butterfly. When a pig swallows it, he loses all control, seizes a knife and kills the beast. Praskovya, alarmed by the noise, rushes in to find Pavel covered with blood and sobbing. Forced to reveal that it is pig's blood that he is smeared with, Pavel sobs loudly that he "bleeds" too: "My soul Praskovya . . . it's my soul that bleeds." Praskovya, ever the realist, sponges her husband clean and listens once again to his exaggerated ramblings. He had feared that his confinement would make him lose his mind, Pavel informs her, but the reality is that he is losing his soul and will be no more than a brute himself. He is tempted to suicide since "A life with nothing sacred left in it is a soulless existence." Impatient, Praskovya interrupts him: does this mean she shouldn't make dinner?

Of the play's four scenes, the second is weakest. The butterfly's sudden appearance and Pavel's ecstasy border on the melodramatic and only are saved from being so by the black comedy of the pig-killing scene that follows. The scene also closes weakly, especially in contrast to the first and third scenes surrounding it, where Praskovya's exiting lines have greater force and relevance. Clumsy as these sections of the second scene are, however, they are necessary for establishing Pavel's continued degradation. And though the butterfly chase is invested with a too obvious symbolism, the pig-beating, an activity which recurs in the final act, becomes a kind of motif for the brutality of the man enraged by his own captivity and helplessness. It serves, too, as a reminder of man's infinite capacity for finding a being lesser than himself to tyrannize. Perhaps the most significant statement made in the second scene is Pavel's remark that "the days of my one and *only* life on this earth are passing while I sit in mindless imbecility at that table swatting flies." At this point, however, Pavel's observation is but a partial realization; he must descend even further from ennui to desperation before the pitch of his pain becomes intense enough to incite him to act.

The third scene, in which Pavel, nearly suffocated by the stench of the sty, convinces Praskovya to take him for a midnight stroll, is the finest in the play, and, in fact, ranks in Fugard's canon as one of his most effectively drawn comic scenes. Pavel, wearing a babushka that does little to hide his coarse whiskers, fusses about the fit of the dress he has donned and sends Praskovya off to hunt for some brooch or pin to finish off his outfit. Ever fretful and ridiculously literal, Praskovya worries that hooligans will "take advantage of two helpless women" out for a walk.

Once outside, Pavel is intoxicated by freedom and the "star-studded rose-scented magnificence" of the dark, but he feels he has no moral right to such beauty since his sins have made him an "outcast" on earth. Stimulated by the night air, Pavel feels his soul returned to him. He even—to Praskovya's dismay—feels aroused by "strange and powerful urges." Unable to face going back to the pigsty, he begs Praskovya to run away with him. She refuses to abandon their home, however, and leaves Pavel to escape alone. Again, as in the first scene, Pavel's courage wanes, and he hurries back to Praskovya with the excuse that a dog came snarling at him out of the darkness. When he realizes that he must again resume living among the pigs, Pavel abandons the last vestiges of his humanity. He strips off his clothes and dives into one of the pens. Praskovya can endure no more: she seizes a stout stick and begins pummelling Pavel until he crawls out of the pens and stands erect. "You're on your two legs again, Pavel, and talking," she says as she leaves, "That's as much as I can do for you. Now help yourself."

The third scene is especially significant in this Afrikaner parable, for it encapsulates the warring tensions of two opposed emotions: the love of homeland and the desire for exile. It affirms the deep-rooted attachment to country that the butterfly symbolism of the second scene had partially intimated. The scene also suggests, however, that despite this profound love for his homeland, thoughts of escape and exile are tempting for the white South African who at his worst feels himself to be a kind of moral pariah, and at his most realistic anticipates no place for himself after the inevitable power change in South Africa.

Exile, as Pavel's actions ultimately indicate, is no real solution to his problem. Not only does it necessitate a despicable kind of leaving—in the cloak of darkness and the disguise of a woman's dress—but it also offers only physical relief from the dirt of the sty. Escape will do nothing to lessen Pavel's self-hatred. Even more importantly, exile will not satisfy Pavel's basic homesickness, his longing not only for bed and hearth but for the company of other men. "A man's scenery is other men," Fugard has written in one of his notebooks, and the largest portion of Pavel's pain is his isolation. This pain is so enormous that Pavel ultimately considers the company of a firing squad preferable to his "long loneliness." Nadine Gordimer has popularized a statement made by Antonio Gramsci by affixing it as an epigraph to her novel, *July's People.* Gramsci's observation that "the old is dying and the new cannot be born; in the interregnum there arises a great diversity of morbid symptoms" also sums up the world of ***Pigs.*** As a prisoner of conscience as well as of cowardice, Pavel's own morality as well as his sense of guilt keep him cut off from other men. The "morbid symptom" of Pavel's life is a loneliness born equally of fault and virtue.

In the fourth scene, hours rather than years have passed, and Pavel, though he is still naked, dirty, and exhausted, longs for sleep but refuses to spend another night in one of the pens. With the constant sound of grunts and squeals in the background, Pavel, almost trance-like, talks himself awake, in an imaginary conversation with the Commissar. As though he is on trial, Pavel responds to accusations of craven desertion, of being a "traitor to your motherland." Afraid that he will fall asleep "and that will be the end of it," Pavel desperately seeks a solution to his dilemma. At first he seizes a stick and vows to break the neck of every pig in the shed, but in the midst of this second round of frenzied pig-beating, a sudden solution dawns on him: let them go. Throwing open the back door of the sty, he shepherds the pigs out in a final gesture of liberation, of "immediate and unconditional release." The powerful sound of the stampeding pigs brings Praskovya rushing into the barn where she is even further undone by the unexpected sacredness of the silence that she finds there. Admitting it is lunacy to laugh at the loss of their livelihood, Praskovya still congratulates Pavel for the "imagination" and "courage" he has used to free them. She rushes out again to fetch Pavel's wedding suit, and the curtain descends on the two paused in the open doorway, arm-in-arm, about to step back into the world of men.

The tableau ending is a favorite technique of Fugard's, and the concluding image he has chosen of two people bound to each other is one that he has previously employed. But unlike earlier tableaus of couples who are joined together by shared oppression, such as the sight of the manacled prisoners running in place which closes ***The Island,*** Pavel and Praskovya are united by love and by hope. In fact, standing in the doorway of the sty which is now as silent and as peaceful as a church, Pavel in his wedding suit and Praskovya veiled by her shawl and clutching her prayer book, the couple assume the bridal pose associated with the traditional ending of comedy.

This unambiguously affirmative ending is one sense in which ***Pigs*** is an important new dramatic enterprise for Fugard. For while the drama never denies the existence of evil and the human motivations for it, never undercuts the consequences of this evil and the suffering it imposes, it nevertheless insists that purposeful action, fueled by imagination and courage, can bring an end to oppression, whether systematically imposed or born of private demons.

To some, this assertion may seem too simplistic, too optimistic. But, as the fourth scene asserts, Fugard is unrelenting in his belief that no man is meant to endure a life of constant emotional privation and self-torture. In this sense, Fugard's psychology in this latest play is not very different from that of one of his earliest, ***The Blood Knot.*** Just as racism has engendered a kind of self-hatred in the black community, manifested by their privileging paler complexions over darker ones, so too the guilt of being a member of the tormentor class causes a kind of self-loathing among white South Africans which, unless transformed, fuels only harsher, more abusive behavior. ***Pigs*** claims that such a transformation might be possible, and it ends not with a stand-off, but with survival. For Pavel, more than anything else, survives and gives testimony to Fugard's assertion that he "doesn't believe in dead ends anymore." Ultimately, ***Pigs*** argues for a fundamental self-acceptance that gives way to a fundamental code of decency.

Obviously, Fugard's parable lends itself to readings not bound to historical circumstance. It offers insights into the dynamics of self-victimization, whatever the causes may be. But as a parable of one segment of South African society—the white South African who is committed both to dismantling apartheid and to remaining in his homeland—it adds a new voice, an authentic one, to those clamoring to decide the future of South Africa. (pp. 82-91)

Jeanne Colleran, "'A Place with the Pigs': Athol Fugard's Afrikaner Parable," in Modern Drama, *Vol. XXXIII, No. 1, March, 1990, pp. 82-92.*

Athol Fugard with Lynn Freed (interview date January 1992)

[Freed is a South African-born American novelist and writer of children's literature. In the following interview, published in the summer of 1993, she and Fugard discuss numerous topics, including his writing methods, his thoughts on living and working in the United States and England, "political correctness," and the character of opposition groups in South Africa.]

[In an author's note, Freed states that this "interview was conducted in New York City in January 1992, just prior to a new production at the Manhattan Theatre Club of Fugard's play, ***Boesman and Lena.*** Since then, Fugard's old friend and collaborator, the actress Yvonne Bryceland, has died. His new play, ***Playland,*** of which he had the first draft with him during the interview, opened at the Market Theatre in Johannesburg in July and has subsequently been produced in La Jolla in August and in Atlanta in October 1992. It had its New York premiere at the Manhattan Theatre Club in May 1993."]

. . . . .

[Freed]: I have read about you and your pens.

[Fugard]: Oh my God! I love them! They are so simple. Mind you, I'm not against things like word processors, but I think they create the illusion of facility for young writers. Young writers *think* they are writing simply because they throw paragraphs around all over the place. That's not writing. Also, you just pack up your paper and your pen. You don't have to worry about electricity.

Do you work wherever you are? Do you work here in the hotel?

I don't write. At the most, I'm able to plan. In the house I've got upstate, a place called Carmel, on the Hudson, I've spent a couple of months planning, sorting out. It's just a simple little house out in the woods. I had a shed built out in the garden because I like to work away from the house and the telephone.

If you only come for visits, why did you buy the house?

Because I earn three-quarters of my income in America. And do you know what you pay for a sublet in New York? Anyway, I'm addicted to space and nature, 'specially when I'm writing. I can step out of the room where I'm writing, literally open the door and step out and be among trees or grass or rocks.

Place is *very* important to me. There are two definitions of myself that I welcome very happily: one is South African writer, and the other is regional writer. I would *die* if I ever lost my South African roots. Creatively, I would *die.*

For a long time, I had a home next to the sea. Then I moved inland onto a bit of land, a simple house called the Ashram. And that was a great place for me, a great home for something like twenty years. And then, about five years ago, I think, there was a certain sense that I couldn't—to use the American expression *get it up any more* on the Ashram. I didn't know that at the time, but my wife, who's very insightful, said to me that she could already see me starting to feel around. It came as no surprise to her when I suddenly said I was going to renovate our holiday house in the Karroo, make it into a house in which one could live. Imaginatively, I'd already left the place that was so good for twenty years, and I had—imaginatively and emotionally—moved into the Karroo house. The Karroo is where I was born, so there's a marvelous sense of the completion of a circle. Because I've got to face it: at the age of sixty, most of my living is behind me.

It's interesting that in the two days since I've met you, you've mentioned your age several times.

Oh, ja! I'm very conscious of it because I realize that I've got to be very careful and nurturing of whatever energy

I have left. I have a lot of writing I still want to do and I can't talk about having another forty years of writing ahead of me. I think I'm into one of my last creative cycles.

What about people in your life? Do you count on them to give your working days some shape?

I'm the sort of person who would get on anybody's nerves if they had to live with me, because I'm a creature of habit and of strict control of time. The alarm clock goes off in the morning. I get up at a specific hour. And I'm at my desk by eight o'clock. I don't leave my desk until half past twelve. The morning is the most important writing period for me. There's never any writing in the afternoon. And then I write again in the evening, the *last* thing at night—after a bit of music or reading—for an hour or so.

Do you require people, company, at some point?

Don't like it at all. You see, I'm very fortunate. I've got the best of all worlds. Once the play's written, I go out into the big world to get it onto a stage. Suddenly it's like an enormous immersion in action and people and decisions and collaboration with artists and designers. And then comes the next time to write. The two and a half months that I was back in South Africa before coming for this production, I was *by myself.* I'd go for days without seeing another soul. I live in a very small little village—about fifty houses, only seven of them occupied. It's *way* off the beaten track.

Cook? Clean?

I cook for myself, clean up.

Do you like it?

Well, I was a sailor. Being a sailor teaches you about looking after yourself.

Do you have no sense, because you're so strict with your time, of time stretching out of control?

No, no. I go back to an uninterrupted four months of writing. I've got a first draft of a new play completed. And I've got to finish the play in four months. I just know that there are going to be days of devastating despair ahead of me. I know what I do to myself when I write. And especially when I come into this last period of writing. I know there are going to be periods along the way that are going to be hell. I'm going to lose confidence in myself, in the content, in the work.

Have you had experiences of not being able to write?

One horrendous experience of writer's block, and it's a *hell* unlike anything I know. I have lost loved ones. I've had the average sixty-year-old's measure of loss, pain, misery and what-have-you. But that period of writer's block stands out in terms of its spiritual torment.

Why, do you think?

I think because we invest our identities, our lives as writers. If that's not working, who the hell am I? And *why* am I? I've got no other reason for being on this extraordinary earth. That's my sense of it.

And, when you're in the middle of it, there's no future and no past.

And, I don't love myself, and, if I don't love myself, nobody else can love me. So, not even the love of someone, of a loved one, is of any value. It just adds to your torment because, how can something worthless be loved? It just makes it worse. I gave up drinking once. I gave it up. Sobering up after being an alcoholic was rough enough, but still it doesn't compare with writer's block.

How do you account for it?

I don't know.

Chemistry?

One of my plays has an oblique look at that—***The Road to Mecca.*** Miss Helen says, "They aren't coming any more. I don't know where they come from, I don't know how to make them come."

Perhaps the collaborative nature of theatre helps keep the work going when one is not blocked?

Absolutely! I doubt if I would be where I am now as writer had Yvonne Bryceland not crossed my life. I had a profoundly, an incredibly creative relationship with Yvonne. I have another creative relationship, and that's with Susan Hilferty, my designer and associate director. She has now, literally, in terms of the realization of my work, half of me. If suddenly I were by myself at this point, I don't know if I'd be able to do what I'm hoping I can do. She balances me, balances me with an energy. Susan's younger than me, but, more important, she brings with her another set of artistic disciplines. That's why we work so well together. She sees as I do.

So you have hope for peace between men and women? **Boesman and Lena** *notwithstanding?*

I think so, absolutely. People have described me as an optimist, and I am an optimist. I'm not a theoretician about human nature; I just see things happen. I have seen people change politically. And I have seen men and women sort it out. I read with fascination about the creative relationships between other men and women, men and men, women and women. One thinks of Stieglitz and O'Keefe, you know—two pretty big talents. They had a lot of problems. But neither threatened the other.

But look at someone like de Beauvoir with Sartre. The real story from her point of view is in She Came to Stay.

The ground becomes very dangerous when two people are in the same field.

That's why it's fascinating to me that you managed to keep a marriage together—

Oh well—

All those years.

Well, we never talk about work. Never. We'll make general statements at the supper table or the lunch table—"It's going well," or "It's not going well," or "It's one of those days when it's a plod." But never any specific and detailed discussions. I never know what Sheila is writing until she's finished. She never sees a play of mine until she sits in the audience.

At every opportunity, I stand up and I say to the ANC and its so-called cultural desk, "I will not accept the dictates of cultural commissars!" I reject it outright, this notion that literature must now serve the cause and be harnessed. I will not align myself with it! I refuse! You lay your hands off writers and their writing!

—Athol Fugard

You work separately?

As I say, I never work in the house any more. I always have a shed out in the garden, away from the house. And the reason for that is, simply, I'm painfully slow, pen and ink. Sheila sits down at a typewriter and the moment she puts her hands on that keyboard, it's like a machine gun. And it's the most intimidating sound I've ever heard. I mean, I used to sit paralyzed with my pen in my hand listening to the sound of somebody else talking it out. So that's why I don't write in the same space.

Do you read poetry?

I can't live without it. It's as important to me as music. I can live without other literary forms, but poetry, no.

Tell me about your feelings of displacement when you leave South Africa. It really fascinates me, the situation of artists in South Africa having to earn their money in other countries.

I don't have a problem—which a lot of friends have had and have not been able to solve—because I have never tried to make America or England home. I've watched in great distress the drying up of some wonderful poets and fellow writers from South Africa, who landed up in London. They just stopped writing. But then they had taken on exile; they weren't just visiting, or over there for a period. I don't have this problem because I'm not of this world [America]. I will never be of this world. I've never stopped thinking about South Africa, living the reality of South Africa. I go back. I write there. I think of my time in America as time away from home. I'm deeply grateful to America, and there are aspects of America that I love very, very much. But I'm going home!

What aspects do you love about America?

The physical landscape is stunning, especially out in the West. The deserts are very beautiful. I can understand how this country, in the full range of all its different types of landscape, could have produced a culture of such intense spirituality as the North American Indian.

Do you have many American friends?

Some of the best friends that have come into my life have been Americans, men and women. As a man, if you want to educate yourself in terms of how and what women are thinking, America's the place. Just being in America and being able to read as much as I have read, and listen to conversations, and actually talk to American women about their attitudes, their feelings—this has been hugely important to me. There are times when one thinks that one of the problems American women have is the permanent adolescence of their men. I mean the same is true of South Africa. It's just that I'm very conscious of it here simply because American women are demanding that men be mature.

Mature is one way of putting it.

In terms of South Africa and America, there's a nice question I'd like to ask: do you think that, having enjoyed the relative freedoms that American women have demanded and got—having enjoyed what it means to be a woman in *this* country, especially on the West Coast—do you think South Africa being what it is would make that society intolerable for you now? As a *woman,* I mean?

I have no idea how it would be to live there any more. I go back a lot. I see friends, family. I meet interesting people, men and women. But I don't know how much of my present joy there is premised on the fact that I'm leaving again.

I think one of the things about the new South Africa is that women are going to have an infinitely more creative role in it than has been the case in the past. I've met young white women, and there's no way they are going to take from their peers and from their equals the nonsense that their fathers and their uncles are handing out. And the same is true in terms of black South Africans—African, Colored, and Indian. After the Soweto riots, the school riots, and the Soweto boycotts, gender hasn't been a significant factor.

What worries me about the writing situation in South Africa, which I've encountered only peripherally, is a certain reverse requirement these days that one be politically correct.

Oh! You've immediately raised the red rag! I get so angry about that! At every opportunity, I stand up and I say to the ANC and its so-called cultural desk, "I will not accept the dictates of cultural commissars!" I reject it outright, this notion that literature must now serve the cause and be harnessed. I will not align myself with it! I refuse! You lay your hands off writers and their writing!

What about the new generation of politically correct black writers?

Awful! Awful! It's been published simply because of patronage, lionization because the writer's black or the political sentiment is correct. Even the political movements realize that.

I don't know what the correct phrase is—what should one speak of ?—the woman's revolution? The feminist revolution? But, hand in hand with the breaking down of racial barriers has got to be the breaking down of the gender barrier. It has been there as viciously in black society as it has been in white. Some of my black friends outdo my white friends in male chauvinism. But I think the people at the top of the political movements realize that that's got to take place. I think the ANC realizes that women have got to be recognized as an equal political force.

What problems, if any, do you have with America?

The rampant materialism. The way this society finally evaluates everything is in terms of the dollar. I come from a world that doesn't do that. South Africa does a lot of other terrible things, but it doesn't do that.

To me, fundamentalist America is more frightening.

That's no maybe! I mean, our Dutch Reformed Church was never as scary as these people.

The two great levellers in this country are guns and celebrity.

Isn't it unbelievable? The star system?

That *is what the American artist has to get away from. But I don't think it's confined to America any more.*

It is part of America's cultural imperialism. The culture that has gone out is the worst of America.

I have the feeling, though, that you're happier here than in England.

Yes. For two reasons. First, I'm a half bastard Afrikaner, and there's an Afrikaner's prejudice about England. Secondly—and this goes with being a bastard Afrikaner—after racial bigotry, class bigotry is next on my list of abominations. I cannot deal with that aspect of England at all. As scattered and as illusory as it is in so many areas, the attempt at democracy in this society I find genuine. I mean I can go around New York—I haven't got an extensive Armani wardrobe, ha!—and I've never had a single problem with any restaurant that I've wanted to go in to. *England!* Every *time* I make a mistake. Terrible! I can't deal with that aspect of England. I'm sure that if I went into Wales, it would be different. I remember going in to a "good tea shop" that sold teas in Chelsea, and the moment I spoke, it was obvious I came from the colonies. That woman's attitude behind that counter—because *she* had one of those voices which had cost £10,000 a year to educate—I could've upturned every table! I could've ripped her joint if I'd stayed in it too long. Whereas, in America, as I say, there's an attempt. If I were a black man, maybe—

I think you'd be as badly off in either country as a black man.

You're right. You'd be as badly off in either country. They're going to have to start their civil rights movement again. There's another long march ahead of them.

What about in South Africa? I've often had this feeling, as a Jew, when I deal with Afrikaners, that I am a newcomer there. And yet, there's also a tremendous feeling between Afrikaners and Jews.

Oh *yes!* Their destinies go back. I sort of see the Jew and the Afrikaner locked into each other in very much the same way as the black and the Afrikaner. *Not* like the black and the white English-speaking South African.

But the Jew doesn't have that sense of being dug in to that country. There's a feeling of readiness to flee that Jews tend to have in South Africa.

Whereas, the Afrikaner, as you say, has a totally rooted identity.

He has that gift and that blessing of belonging to that country in a way that a Jew does not.

But take a city like Johannesburg. The Jewish community there is as definitive in terms of the cultural life of that city as the Jewish community in New York is. Take the Jewish community out of Johannesburg and the arts will collapse. And the same in New York. They're the great patrons of the arts and produce some of the greatest artists.

And many of the South African artists have left over the years. Many of them Jews.

True, true. What seemed to me at one point in my life to be one of the real hardships of growing up in South Africa—one of the really hard prices I had to pay for being the political animal I was—was when I was cut off because I refused to leave the country on an exit permit. This was what the government was trying to get me to do. I stayed in South Africa and the government took away my passport.

It is out of that period, when I could not leave the country, that I wrote ***Boesman and Lena.*** And I regard ***Boesman and Lena,*** in fact, as the point in my writing career when I said, "Right, just think of yourself as a South African writer and your audience in South Africa. And you must make your life here. Even if, one day, you get your passport back, always think in the very first instance of yourself writing for, telling a story for, trying to talk to, fellow South Africans. Make no concessions ever to a so-called wider audience to the extent that you might water down your regionalism, try to modify your language, or avoid certain things."

So, in fact, the loss of a passport and the freedom to travel was the thing that saved me as a writer. It meant that I had to think in terms of South Africa as my audience. There was a temptation to do otherwise, because I was just starting to receive recognition overseas. It came at a point when the BBC had just televised the ***Blood Knot***—which is probably why I lost the passport. There was a lot of publicity. My plays were being done in New York, and I was receiving invitations to come overseas, and write, bring work. I'm an easily seduced animal. I think I might have been seduced away, seduced into a sort of pale existence, instead of which I was just forced to stay vividly South African. If I had started to write for a wider audience, I think I would have lost my identity and my strength. By the time they gave me back my passport, I was entrenched.

I must qualify what I say by adding that that is the way it was for me. I don't think the rules for any one writer apply to another. We are such unique animals. And this business of writing is so personal, so related to what sort of animal you are.

With the new play I am writing now, the greatest pressure on me is not that I've already got a date at the Market

Theatre. It is that the play is important to our life now, what we are trying to deal with now. That's the pressure on me. Not the bloody date. It's the need to talk to fellow South Africans. I don't think of myself as having something to say to fellow South Africans. I've never presented my writing in that way.

You said earlier that you're enraged by the cultural commissars of the ANC. What is their attitude toward you?

Oh, very angry with me! Oh, yes! Oh God, do I love it! I'm really getting on their nerves. I'm getting on their nerves, because I've really stepped out of line lately. My last big number with the cultural commissars was when I got Kathy Bates to come and do ***The Road to Mecca*** in South Africa. And without asking their permission for anything. Over my dead body! I know about other writers who've been summoned and presented with a list of things in the show that were objectionable.

Do you think this is going to get worse?

No. I think it will die, simply because it is a hangover of the worst of Russian communism, that whole huge experiment in human living. I think that men like Mandela are perceptive enough to read the lesson, but the young lions in the ANC are not. They refuse to accept that communism is a failed experiment. It's them and Cuba now, the South Africa communist party and Cuba. They're going to save the revolution.

I still don't understand this turnaround in South Africa. It seemed so impossible.

One of the things I've always objected to in terms of the overseas perceptions of South Africa was this image of the Afrikaner reality as monolithic, unyielding, unbending. In fact, the Afrikaner reality was a very organic thing, containing a lot of contradictions, paradoxes. The pressure that finally erupted was the end result of a process that goes back five or six years. If you had told me five years ago, I would have said, "You're out of your mind!" It still takes my breath away. I can't believe it!

In terms of the Afrikaner government now, would there be a danger for you in being taken up as politically correct?

I've not received any overtures. No, I've eluded a certain kind of definition so far, and I think I'll continue to do so. You see, there's nothing to their advantage in taking me up. To really score some points, or to really make an impression, they've got to take up a black writer. To take up Athol Fugard is not going to mean anything to them. They're not going to get any mileage out of that.

When do you get back to work?

I go home the end of January. I've got the draft of my play here. I carry it around. There it is. I love it! Oh! I love it!

It's in pencil.

Yes, it's in pencil.

I can see why you like to write. Your handwriting is very legible.

I love watching that pen. That's the way I avoid self-consciousness. I'm trying to change the shape of my *o* at the moment.

That's not your only copy, is it?

Ja!

Are you superstitious about making copies?

No.

But you carry this wherever you go?

No, I leave it here in the hotel. I've always had only one copy.

And you're not worried about it?

No. I don't like to think about it. I don't allow myself to think about it.

After we've had our first audience for ***Boseman and Lena*** here, I will start to return to it by giving myself a couple of hours in here every morning—not to do any writing, just to read it. Read, read, reread, reread. Read it into my system again. So that I've already returned to it by the time I come home.

Do you do a lot of work on your drafts?

Oh yes. I will end up doing three drafts. And then finally typing out a fourth and final.

Your timing, your cadences are like dancing.

I give a lot of study to structure. Music! Music is my inspiration, not other literature. Music teaches me how to move emotionally, build it up and take it down. Music teaches me how to write.

Do you play?

My father was a jazz musician, and I studied the piano for a long time. But now, no.

You don't listen while you write?

No.

How do you feel about American actors as compared with South African actors?

Oh, some of them can complicate their lives with so much nonsense. There's a wonderful story about Lawrence Olivier and Dustin Hoffman. It was during that film called *Marathon Man.* Olivier was playing a Nazi dentist who had escaped at the end of the war, and there was a scene requiring Dustin Hoffman to look particularly exhausted. Dustin Hoffman, in order to set himself up for that particular scene, apparently, went without sleep for days. And Olivier is reported to have said to him, "Have you tried just acting?" I mean, just act, you know what I mean? Just let's act!

Like writers—just write!

Just write! It's a craft! I make a play the way a carpenter makes a table. The South Africans? We're so behind the times, we *sommer* (just) act! "You can act, man! You can act! Come on, man! Get out there and pretend to be—sad! Ha! Don't really be sad, because I don't think the play's worth it, you know. Just pretend, man!"

Do you think American actors have an easier time with your plays than English actors?

Yes. The emotional life of an average South African is much closer to America than it is to England. That's why my plays get done here so often—both because American actors can do them, and because American audiences understand them. Which, to go back to an earlier question, is why I get around to feeling almost at home here on occasion. Because I'm in a similar *emotional* environment. The English make me feel so insecure.

I think that if you live away from home long enough, though, you belong nowhere any more.

Absolutely right. I could accept tomorrow, without any real complications in my life, never being able to leave South Africa again.

Ideally, if you could bring people in to South Africa as often as you liked, would you prefer to stay there?

Yes. In fact, I might have to make that decision, because travelling is a huge drain in energy. I think the time is coming when I might well have to stop visiting this country simply in order to try to keep the important thing—which is my writing—to keep that happening.

With South Africa lightening up, perhaps you'll be able to bring people out there more easily.

Oh, I would so love that! That I would really love! (pp. 296-307)

Athol Fugard and Lynn Freed, in an interview in Southwest Review, *Vol. 78, No. 3, Summer, 1993, pp. 296-307.*

FURTHER READING

Benson, Mary. "Athol Fugard and 'One Little Corner of the World'." *Yale/Theatre* 4, No. 1 (Winter 1973): 55-63.

Examines several of Fugard's plays and the dramatic theories behind them.

Cody, Gabrielle, and Schechter, Joel. "An Interview with Athol Fugard." *Theater* XIX, No. 1 (Fall-Winter 1987): 70-2.

Conversation in which Fugard discusses various aspects of writing and staging *A Place with the Pigs.* The interview was conducted in America in 1987 where Fugard was producing the play.

Cohen, Derek. "Drama and the Police State: Athol Fugard's South Africa." *Canadian Drama/L'Art Dramatique Canadien* 6, No. 1 (Spring 1980): 151-61.

Surveys Fugard's works, describing him as "the poet of pain for our times, making of the pain of his small but vital world a rich and varied truth about existence."

Collins, Michael J. "The Sabotage of Love: Athol Fugard's Recent Plays." *World Literature Today* 57, No. 3 (Summer 1983): 369-71.

Focuses on plot and characterization in *A Lesson from Aloes* and *"Master Harold". . . and the Boys,* asserting that, "while neither of the plays is perfect . . . , the faults seem small ones finally, and the plays are both inordinately effective on the stage."

Green, Robert J. "The Drama of Athol Fugard." In *Aspects of South African Literature,* edited by Christopher Heywood, pp. 163-73. London: Heinemann, 1976.

Outlines Fugard's early dramas, tracing his development from the trilogy known as *The Family* to his collaborative efforts in the early 1970s. Green pays particular attention to the influence of South African politics in Fugard's work.

Gussow, Mel. "Witness." *The New Yorker* LVIII, No. 44 (20 December 1982): 47-94.

Comprehensive biographical and critical essay which includes extensive quotes from conversations with Fugard.

Mshengu. "Political Theatre in South Africa and the Work of Athol Fugard." *Theater Research International* VII, No. 3 (Autumn 1982): 160-79.

Reassesses the commonly held opinion that Fugard is "the lone individual playwright of talent battling single-handedly in the 'forbidding environment of apartheid South Africa.'" Mshengu describes the accomplishments of black South African writers and actors, and argues that Fugard's anti-apartheid ideology is less radical than is generally imagined.

Schechter, Joel. "James Earl Jones on Fugard." *Theater* 16, No. 1 (Fall-Winter 1984): 40-2.

Interview in which Jones, an actor who frequently performs in the American productions of Fugard's plays, discusses working with the playwright.

Solomon, Alisa. "'Look at History': An Interview with Zakes Mokae." *Theater* 14, No. 1 (Winter 1982): 27-31.

Interview in which the actor discusses his long personal and professional relationship with Fugard.

Vandenbroucke, Russell. *Truths the Hand Can Touch: The Theater of Athol Fugard.* New York: Theatre Communications Group, 1985, 252 p.

Chronological critical survey of Fugard's career in the theater.

Wells, Ronald A., ed. *Writer and Region: Athol Fugard.* New York: The Anson Phelps Stokes Institute for African, Afro-American, and American Indian Affairs, 1987, 42 p.

Includes a biographical sketch, an address Fugard made at the Anson Phelps Stokes Institute's Africa Roundtable on 21 May 1984, excerpts from the discussion following his speech, and an essay on the importance of region to his works.

Additional coverage of Fugard's life and career is contained in the following sources published by Gale Research: *Contemporary Authors,* Vols. 85-88; *Contemporary Authors New Revision Series,* Vol. 32; *Contemporary Literary Criticism,* Vols. 5, 9, 14, 25, 40; *Drama Criticism,* Vol. 3; and *Major 20th-Century Writers.*

Donald Goines

1937?-1974

(Also wrote under the pseudonym Al C. Clark) American novelist.

The following entry presents an overview of Goines's life and career.

INTRODUCTION

Goines is known for grim novels which describe, in harsh, realistic terms, the lives of black drug users, prostitutes, and other outcasts and criminals in Detroit, Michigan, and other American metropolises. Although he attracted minimal critical recognition during his five-year literary career, Goines's biographer Eddie Stone noted in 1988: "[Goines] was on the cutting edge of the life he depicted in his books and saw the cancer spreading. It's a pity that not too many people took him seriously those nearly twenty years ago. As a writer, it certainly can be said that Goines didn't have great skills. But as a social observer he was light years ahead of most of the rest of us."

Goines was born in Detroit in 1937 (some sources say 1935 or 1936), where he attended Roman Catholic schools and proved a serious and cooperative student. In his mid-teens, however, Goines abruptly left school and joined the Air Force. During the Korean War, Goines was stationed in Japan, where he became a frequent drug user. Returning home in 1955 a heroin addict, Goines supported his drug habit over the next fifteen years through such illegal occupations as thief, pimp, and smuggler. He was arrested fifteen times and served seven prison terms. While in jail, he was introduced to the writings of Robert "Iceberg Slim" Beck, a pimp-turned-novelist who enjoyed substantial popularity among inmate readers. Inspired by Beck's *Trick Baby* (1967), Goines produced his first novel, *Whoreson: The Story of a Ghetto Pimp,* and solicited opinions from his fellow inmates. Goines eventually submitted *Whoreson* to Beck's publisher, California-based Holloway House. The company accepted Goines's manuscript and requested additional works.

The financial success of Goines's early novels allowed him to concentrate on writing after he left prison in 1970. Although he had resumed illegal drug use by 1971, Goines published thirteen novels over the next five years, eight in 1974 alone. In 1972 he moved to Los Angeles, California, to live closer to his publisher and the film industry, but returned to the Detroit area in 1974. He settled with his common-law wife in Highland Park, where the couple was murdered in October 1974. Police suspected that robbery was the motive behind the slayings, but there were also indications that Goines had once again become involved in drug use. The case remains unsolved.

In *Whoreson,* a semi-autobiographical tale of a pimp and his clashes with other criminals, Goines introduced the characteristic urban settings and situations of his fiction, in which weakness or error inevitably leads to violent death. Although written later, his first published novel was *Dopefiend: The Story of a Black Junkie,* in which he presented a graphic account of the drug addict's lifestyle, tracing the degeneration of two middle-class African-Americans. While relentless in describing human brutality and poverty—in one episode of the latter novel, for example, a pimp taunts a syphilitic prostitute by threatening to include her in a sex show featuring animals—these novels established Goines's reputation for accurate and unflinching portraits of black ghetto life.

In his subsequent novels Goines addressed questions related to both black and white responsibility for racism. *Black Gangster* concerns a cynical hoodlum who exploits his own people by establishing a civil rights organization as a front for prostitution and extortion, while *White Man's Justice, Black Man's Grief* relates the story of a white burglar who names a black prison inmate as the mastermind of a robbery he committed alone, thus implicating the inmate although he was in prison when the crime transpired. In 1974, Goines began publishing novels under the pseudonym Al C. Clark. Four of these works feature an ambitious militant hero, Kenyatta, a small-town hoodlum who rises to become the leader of a two-thousand-member organization. With his paramilitary gang, Kenyatta seeks to eliminate all white police officers and rid the black ghetto of drugs and prostitution. But in *Kenyatta's Last Hit*—the final work in a series that also includes *Crime Partners, Death List* and *Kenyatta's Escape*—he is killed while attempting to murder a wealthy Los Angeles financier responsible for drug traffic into the ghetto.

Goines's novels have remained profitable for Holloway House, which reprinted his entire canon after his death and has reported total sales surpassing five million copies. While critical recognition has been minimal, biographer Stone noted in 1988: "Goines has become America's Number One best selling black author. If anything, nearly a quarter of a century after the publication of his first book, Goines is more popular than ever, even more so than when he was alive."

PRINCIPAL WORKS

Dopefiend: The Story of a Black Junkie (novel) 1971
Black Gangster (novel) 1972
**Whoreson: The Story of a Ghetto Pimp* (novel) 1972
Black Girl Lost (novel) 1973
Street Players (novel) 1973
White Man's Justice, Black Man's Grief (novel) 1973
Crime Partners [as Al C. Clark] (novel) 1974
Cry Revenge! [as Al C. Clark] (novel) 1974
Daddy Cool (novel) 1974
Death List [as Al C. Clark] (novel) 1974
Eldorado Red (novel) 1974
Kenyatta's Escape [as Al C. Clark] (novel) 1974
Never Die Alone (novel) 1974
Swamp Man (novel) 1974
Inner City Hoodlum (novel) 1975
Kenyatta's Last Hit [as Al C. Clark] (novel) 1975

*This work was written in 1969.

CRITICISM

Greg Goode (essay date Fall 1984)

[*In the following excerpt, Goode surveys Goines's career as a novelist, citing him as a master of a new literary genre, the "Black experience novel."*]

Donald Goines is the foremost example of a cultural phenomenon possible no earlier than the 1970s—a successful Black author of mass market fiction written by and about Blacks. Unlike the mass market fiction of Black authors such as Samuel R. Delany and Frank Yerby, the majority of whose readers are white and are intended to be white, the books of Donald Goines are devoured by legions of Black Americans everywhere, from the inner city to American military bases abroad.

Goines's books, all paperback originals, have never been out of print since their original publication; they have sold more than five million copies and have been on option to several movie studios and independents. They are recommended reading at some urban high schools. In 1974 Goines was so prolific that his publisher asked him to adopt a pseudonym, which he did, taking the name of a friend, Al C. Clark. Primarily through Goines, his Los Angeles-based publisher Holloway House has made a name for itself in mass market publishing and has even invented a new literary genre, the "Black experience novel," of which Goines is termed the master. In spite of all this, Goines's books are largely unknown to white readers.

Goines's sixteen books, all slice-of-ghetto-life crime novels with Black characters, have ostentatious, lurid, concrete titles such as ***Swamp Man, Street Players, Death List*** and ***White Man's Justice, Black Man's Grief.*** The characters, and very often the protagonists, are whores, pimps, thieves, pushers, cardsharps, gangsters, bootleggers, numbers operators, hit men and dope addicts. With the exception of ***Swamp Man,*** the books are all set in the inner city ghettos of Goines's home city Detroit, or Watts, Harlem, or the Southwest.

Goines himself loved the ghetto street life and pursued most of these professions and activities at one time or another until his murder on October 21, 1974, and so was well qualified to write authoritatively about them.

In his short 37-year life Goines was addicted to heroin off and on for over twenty years. He was arrested fifteen times, jailed seven times, spent a total of six and a half years incarcerated, but nevertheless published sixteen books in his last five years. Like Chester Himes, Goines wrote his first novel in jail and later wrote a prison novel.

Future popular literary sociologists will find a goldmine of material in Goines. His characters exhibit patriarchal, male chauvinist values. Men are to lead, women are to follow, obey, and speak only when spoken to. The dark is the good. With a very few exceptions, the white men who appear are short, fat, ruddy-faced, middle-aged, balding, tastelessly dressed and poorly endowed sexually. White women are prizes for Black conquest. Black men are tall, strong, handsome, well dressed even if poor, and are well-equipped sexual gladiators. Black women are beautiful, especially if dark, but are subservient to the men.

The 1960s provided a fertile and formative literary climate for Black experience writers such as Goines, and his early books are fictionalized vest pocket versions of earlier well known Black memoirs and autobiographies such as *The Autobiography of Malcolm X* (1964), Claude Brown's *Manchild in the Promised Land* (1965), Melvin Van Peebles's *A Bear for the FBI* (1968), and George Jackson's *Soledad Brother* (1970). While in Jackson State Prison in 1965, Goines, who had for a long time wanted to be a writer, tried to write Westerns and, according to his friends, failed miserably. But in the same prison again five years later, he was introduced to the work of the founding father of the Black experience novel, Iceberg Slim (the pseudonym of Robert Beck), who had gained notoriety earlier from his memoirs and novels about pimps. Within just four weeks of his reading Slim's books and seeing that his own sorts of life experiences were publishable, Goines had finished ***Whoreson, The Story of a Ghetto Pimp*** (1972), a tribute to Slim's book *Trick Baby* (1967). Goines handed his ***Whoreson*** manuscript around to his fellow inmates for criticism; they suggested that he send it off to Iceberg Slim's publisher, Holloway House. In two weeks Goines had from the publisher an offer to publish and a cry for more. Four weeks later he sent them ***Dopefiend, The Story of a Black Junkie*** (1971), his second book. From then on Goines was off and running, having decided to become a professional writer.

With respect to the standards of literature, the books of Donald Goines are not considered subliterary, for they are not even considered. They are offensive to many because of the obscenity, sex, and violence, all well before their time in graphic explicitness. The titles, and, in early printings, the naive bullet-and-blood style cover art, make the books appear to be utter trash. They are poorly written for the most part, in an uneasy mix of Black English and misspelled, ungrammatical Standard English. The descriptions, transitions, plots, and narrative voice are sandpaper rough. Nevertheless the Goines *corpus* is important because it is perhaps the most sustained, realistic, multifaceted, widespread fictional picture ever created by one author of the lives, activities, and frustrations of poor urban Blacks. Goines's eye for interracial social subtleties is acute. And although he describes characters as briefly as possible, his descriptions go to the heart of the matter, so we learn a character's greatest hopes, assets, and fears, even if Goines has not told us so much as what the character is wearing. Some of Goines's passages are touching, such as the occasional portrayal he gives of family devotion, or of lovers enjoying a moment of serenity in the eye of the ghetto storm. Such scenes are well and seriously done for a writer of Goines's caliber, and demonstrate that his books are neither purely cynical stories of hate for the world of the ghetto nor action/exploitation potboilers.

Because Goines's ghettos are like zero-sum-game societies in which one man's gain must be another's loss, his characters cannot thrive or even survive without breaking the law. His books are automatically crime novels similar to the way in which *Caleb Williams* is a crime novel. The law broken is sometimes the white man's legal code, and sometimes the Ghetto Golden Rule, "what goes around comes around." Often, therefore, the sadistic pimp loses his best woman, the murderer dies, the hustler gets sent to jail, and a sort of automatic inner city justice is maintained. In other books, all the major characters die. In these books Goines seems to be expressing the hopelessness of life in the ghetto.

Goines's first several books were the most roughly written and unsentimental, but among them are his best books and those for which he will be remembered the longest. ***Whoreson, The Story of a Ghetto Pimp,*** Goines's first, is the first-person story of Whoreson Jones, the child of a Black prostitute and a white john. Abandoned by his father, having at age thirteen lost his mother to heroin addiction, Whoreson had to "come up" alone in the ghetto. The story tells of his early rise at age sixteen to a fulltime pimp, and demonstrates the ruthlessness, the abuse of friends and associates that are necessary for his survival. The book ends with Whoreson in jail, vowing to go straight and give up street life. The best example of the cold harshness of Goines's world is Whoreson's reaction to the misfortune suffered by one of his prostitutes who had gotten pregnant. When he is told by a doctor that she has had a miscarriage and is in danger of dying, Whoreson, cooler than ice, thinks,

> The last thing I wanted to do was lose a good whore. After waiting all this time for her to get streamlined, I didn't want to lose her now that she was ready for the track.

But later Whoreson gains insight into the sort of person he has become and realizes that the conditions of his immediate surroundings cause people striving for success to become brutal animals who, "faced with poverty on one side, ignorance on the other . . . exploit those who are nearest."

The book which Goines's publishers call his best is ***Dopefiend, The Story of a Black Junkie*** (1971), his second. It is the graphically vivid story of a young Black couple who sink from the respectability of the Black middle class deeper and deeper into the muck and degradation of heroin addiction. ***Dopefiend*** contains some of Goines's most repulsively memorable settings and characters. Besides recounting the insane desperation and labyrinthine rationalizations of the frantic junkie who will do anything to cop a hit to ward off the sickness, Goines describes in close-up technicolor detail the gruesome horrors of the dope house and its owner. The dope house, a 1970s version of Sax Rohmer's turn-of-the-century opium dens, is where the heroin addict buys dope, shoots up, and nods off. To read Goines's description is to imagine a bloody, pustulant cross between a pharmacy, an operating room and a torture chamber, where sick junkies frantically stab themselves with rusty, clogged needles trying to hit a track. Goines's personal ruler over this hell is Porky the dealer, to whom every possible vice and degradation is attributed. Porky, also Black, is a blubbery 380 pound bestial exploiter of female addicts, a cowardly, greedy, pitiless, perverted sadistic overseer of this vicious chamber of horrors. About the only vice not attributed to Porky is dope, for he does not use.

Other books of Goines's early period are ***Black Gangster*** (1972), ***Street Players*** (1973), and ***White Man's Justice, Black Man's Grief*** (1973). ***Black Gangster*** is the cynical account of Prince, a hustler who struggles from a young age to become number one in the ghetto. Prince exploits the rise in Black consciousness to serve his own ends by organizing a criminal gang under the guise of a revolutionary group, most of whose members are utterly fooled. While well-intentioned Blacks cry "Black is Beautiful," Prince lines his pockets with money. He feels justified, for the Blacks will revolt anyway, white man's justice is biased and means JUST US, so Prince might as well use these social phenomena to his own advantage. In ***Street Players*** (1973), Goines tells the depressing story of Earl the Black Pearl, a wealthy pimp and pusher whose world finally crashed down around him: his woman and best friend are maimed and murdered, and he loses his wealth and finally his life.

White Man's Justice, Black Man's Grief (1973) is perhaps a tribute to Chester Himes's prison novel *Cast the First Stone,* published twenty years earlier. Goines even gave his protagonist a name similar to that of Himes, that is Chester *Hines.* Goines's book is an indictment of the American criminal justice system and contains an angry preface which argues that the combination of false arrests and bail bonding is disproportionately harmful to Blacks. Chester Hines is sentenced to county jail, then to four years of prison for carrying a concealed weapon. In addition to containing sadistic, closely described scenes of jailhouse sex and violence, the book contains a final irony. Hines, still in jail, is tried for a murder committed 400 miles away on the outside by a former cellmate. The man had bungled a robbery, shot a guard, and had accused Hines of planning the job. Hines is convicted and sentenced to life imprisonment.

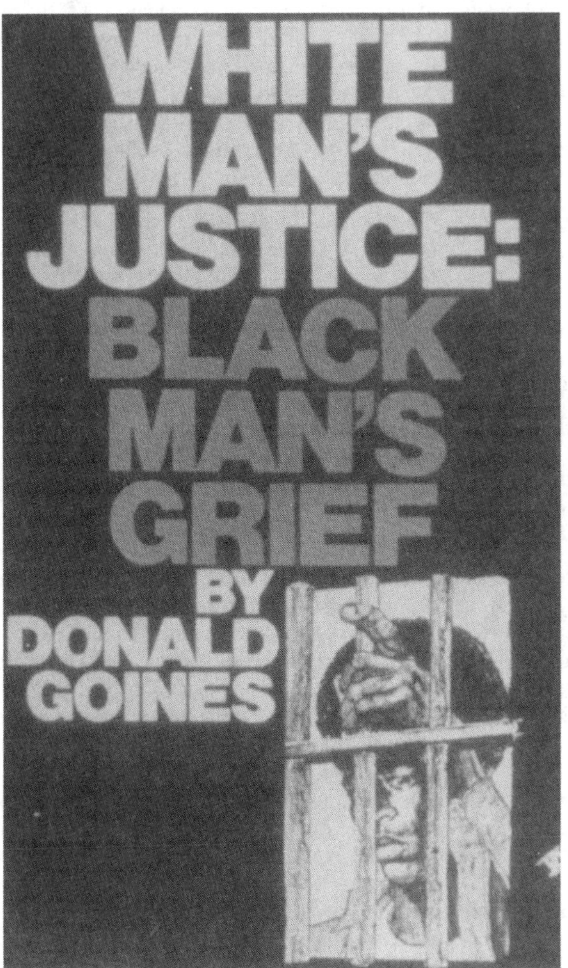

Dust cover of Goines's 1973 novel White Man's Justice, Black Man's Grief.

Such were Goines's early books, brutal, harsh, realistic and often chillingly cold. In what could be a period of development, Goines infused the next several books (with one exception) with a slight sense of freshness and hope. His writing was also improving from book to book. The one exception is ***Swamp Man*** (1974), Goines's worst book. It is set in the swamps of an unnamed southern state and is notable only for its inconsistent, muddled character motivations, and overlong scenes of sadistic sex and violence which carry no message and are not even redeemed through revenge. Other than ***Swamp Man,*** subsequent books were probably influenced by positive events in Goines's life, such as the birth of a baby girl, his only legitimate child, and his move to Los Angeles from Detroit, both of which occurred in 1972. Goines felt very tender about his baby girl and quite hopeful about his move, for he wanted to settle down into a respectable family life, kick his heroin habit, and perhaps even break into movies as a writer. His books began to display some of this tenderness, such as ***Black Girl Lost*** (1973), the relatively touching story of a girl growing up virtually alone in the ghetto from age eight, and ***Daddy Cool*** (1974), which tells of a successful hit man who is enriched but finally defeated by the strong love he feels for his daughter.

The most interesting and ambitious project of the later Goines is his creation of a Black revolutionary series hero, probably the only such hero in fiction. Just as the literary and cultural climate of the 1970s fostered Black memories and autobiographies, that of the early 1970s was suitable for a new breed of violent Black heroes who worked outside the law, and often, against it. For unlike earlier Black heroes such as Ed Lacy's Lee Hayes, Chester Himes's Coffin Ed Johnson and Grave Digger Jones, John Ball's Virgil Tibbs, and Ernest Tidyman's John Shaft, all of whom were professional detectives fighting on the side of the law, the new breed of Black heroes fought against the law most of the time. Outlaw cinema heroes such as Sweet Sweetback, Slaughter, Trouble Man, The Mack, Willie Dynamite, Black Gunn, Black Caesar, the Black Godfather, Black Samson, and Blackbelt Jones included pimps, hustlers, gangsters, outlaw private detectives, and even a revolutionary. Black pulp-fiction heroes such as B. B. Johnson's Superspade, Joseph Nazel's Black and Iceman characters, Roosevelt Mallory's Radcliffe and Joseph Rosenberger's Murder Master included renegades, vigilantes, and political fixers, but were primarily hit men working against organized crime and other corruption of inner city conditions.

Donald Goines took this extralegal trend several steps further and created a Black militant hero with an African name, Kenyatta, and a pseudonym under which he wrote Kenyatta's saga. Kenyatta's goals are to rid all American ghettos of drugs and prostitution, and to kill all white policemen, beginning in Detroit. His organization of Black militants starts with 40 members and ends up with over 2000; it branches from Detroit to Watts, as Kenyatta becomes a recognized leader. Murders, slayings, and executions in the series abound, and there is even one massacre of Blacks by police. With true collective revolutionary zeal, Kenyatta's organization kills anyone who might possibly hinder them, and will even kill Blacks, if by doing so they can kill significantly more whites.

In the four book Kenyatta series, ***Crime Partners*** (1974), ***Death List*** (1974), ***Kenyatta's Escape*** (1974), and ***Kenyatta's Last Hit*** (1975), all written under Goines's "Al C. Clark" pseudonym, Kenyatta establishes his goals, plans the robbery of a food stamp agency, buys a list of top Detroit drug dealers, and starts killing them and policemen one by one. Kenyatta keeps a training camp on the outskirts of Detroit where he trains his members in martial arts and Marxist-Muslim philosophy. When the police catch on to their Detroit activities, Kenyatta and several trusted aides hijack a plane to Algiers but crash-land in Nevada. From there Kenyatta migrates to Watts and sets up his larger organization. When he learns the identity of the Las Vegas finance tycoon who is responsible for the flow of narcotics into Watts, Kenyatta goes after him with a small army. A bloody battle ensues, the tycoon escapes in a helicopter, and Kenyatta dies, as do most of Goines's heroes.

This seems the stuff of pulps, a leap into urban fantasy fiction. In fact, however serious and ambitious Goines may have been in creating a hero to clean up the ghettos, something his hero does through organized violence because no one else does it by any means, the style of his books places them in literary limbo. They are more violent and more poorly plotted than other Black hero fiction, yet there is not enough serious or substantial philosophical treatment in them to be instructive or to warrant the action. It is even possible that Goines had mixed motives in writing this series—though Goines may have been in favor of Kenyatta's intentions, the fact that Kenyatta had to do battle in the streets against police and gangsters, and the fact that Goines killed him off might indicate that Goines thought that even organized violent means would ultimately fail.

Shortly before writing ***Kenyatta's Last Hit,*** Goines became discouraged with his Los Angeles lifestyle. He did not like the sprawling, spread-out geography of Los Angeles, which seemed to him to lack a center of action. He had not kicked his hundred dollar-a-day heroin habit. He was being bothered and harassed too much by the police. And he had not succeeded in breaking into the Hollywood film industry—in spite of some mild interest shown by a few studios, he had received no offers to write for the movies. So in autumn of 1974, Goines decided to take his common-law wife Shirley and his two young daughters (one his, one hers) and drive back to Detroit. After leaving the Southern California area, Goines stopped in Las Vegas to rest and indulge in some recreation gambling. But in Vegas he lost his entire fund of cash, some $1500, and had to call Holloway House in Los Angeles to send him money, an advance on his next book. Holloway House complied, through a contact of theirs in Vegas. But the episode was shattering to Goines, and served only to further sour his opinion of the West coast. Perhaps this helps explain why a bit later, in ***Kenyatta's Last Hit,*** Goines has Watts' main drug supplier living in Las Vegas, and why Goines set the final confrontation there, in which his series character perishes. In any case, after his gambling losses Goines finished his trip to Detroit and set up housekeeping there.

On October 21, 1974, at his Detroit home, Goines received two white "visitors" who were known to his wife Shirley, who answered their knock at the front door. According to police reports, presumably based in part on the eyewitness testimony of Goines's daughters, the two men came into the kitchen, where Shirley was popping popcorn, and shot her several times. Next they came into Goines's study and shot him over his typewriter. To this day, the crime remains unsolved. The Detroit police department does not even know the motive for the crime, though there are several theories, such as that Goines had sold some bad dope and was being "punished" for it, or that Goines, like Superfly, was planning one last score, one last caper, and was found out by his potential victims.

Goines's last book, ***Inner City Hoodlum*** (1975), was found sitting in manuscript form on a shelf in his study after his death. It is a story of vengeance wrought by a pair of teenage hoodlums on Watt's premier hustler. It represents a return of Goines's relatively more subdued stories, and lacks even the inflated, improbable sense of hope exhibited in the Kenyatta series. It is interesting to speculate on the direction Goines's writing would have taken had he lived, since he was the most prolific, popular writer of a quickly growing publisher, but unfortunately this question cannot be answered. Subsequently there have been imitators, almost all better writers than Goines. But no writer, before or since, can be compared to Goines in the breadth of criminal experience, and the prolific intensity with which he put his experience to paper. (pp. 41-8)

Greg Goode, "From 'Dopefiend' to 'Kenyatta's Last Hit': The Angry Black Crime Novels of Donald Goines," in MELUS, *Vol. 11, No. 3, Fall, 1984, pp. 41-8.*

Michael Covino (essay date 4 August 1987)

[Covino is an American poet, short story writer, and critic whose works include the short story collection The Off-Season *(1985) and the novel* The Negative *(1993). In the essay below, he provides an overview of Goines's works.]*

I read my first Donald Goines novel six or so years ago, picking it up on a friend's recommendation at the De Lauer Newsstand in downtown Oakland from the blood-and-guts-paperback crime rack alongside *The Executioner* series, *The Death Merchant* series, and *The Destroyer* series. (Goines's novels have since been moved to the store's Black section and now also turn up in bookstores devoted to black authors and subjects.) Reading it, two things struck me right away. First, the novel bore no relation to the fantasy world of the moronic white men's action novels among which it had been placed. Second, the stuff was so crazy, so unnerving, so out there on the edge that, though I recognized it as qualitatively different from the men's action genre, I couldn't quite get my bearings on it. Goines seemed to be describing situations and states of mass sociopathology as quotidian reality, the extraordinary as perfectly ordinary. It was only after I had researched and written a series of articles on Oakland's drug wars that Goines's novel started to come into focus. It was only then that I began to appreciate him for what he was: a writer of unmediated raw realism, a chronicler of the black ghetto during the precipitous decline of the 1970s.

In a series of 16 novels written between 1970 and 1974, when he was shot dead in Detroit, Goines delineated—graphically, brutally, horrifically—the life of the black American ghetto (using Detroit as his principal locale) in those years of increasing atomization, dashed hopes, and despair, following in the wake of the civil rights movement and the birth of black pride in the '60s. Goines depicts a ghetto ethic so foreign, so cold-blooded, so inhumane, that it seems to come from another world. Make no mistake. Goines's prose is not to be mentioned in the same breath as that of Richard Wright, James Baldwin, John Edgar Wideman, or even Claude Brown or Chester Himes (though like Himes's gangsters using Back to Africa schemes to steal from the poor, Goines's gangsters are capable of using a Black Panther-like front to steal from their own people [in ***Black Gangster***]). All those writers, no matter how well they dealt with black experience, appealed largely to an educated, middle-class, largely white readership. They brought news of one place to the residents of another.

Goines's novels, on the other hand, are written from ground zero. They are almost unbearable. It is not the educated voice of a writer who has, so to speak, risen above his background; rather, it is the voice of the ghetto itself. Goines's books belong to a whole different genre—a fiction about people who largely don't read, written in their language, and for that reason forever condemned to the margins (and published by a house out of the mainstream, the Los Angeles-based Holloway House, which specializes in black ghetto writers). It is for this reason that Goines's novels are perhaps most popular in American prisons—indeed, he might well be the most widely read writer there (he began writing his first novel, ***Whoreson,*** while serving time in Jackson State Penitentiary for running an illegal still).

Born in 1936, Goines was the product of the black lower-middle class. His father ran a dry-cleaing business, and Goines attended a Catholic elementary school. Yet he gravitated back toward the ghetto that his father had worked so hard to escape. Using a false ID, he joined the Air Force at age 14 and became a heroin addict while serving in Korea. He never shook the habit for any significant period of time.

Goines experienced what he wrote about: he had been a pimp, a cardsharp, a numbers runner, a still operator, a thief, an addict, et al., and he spent nearly a third of his life behind bars. His main influence was not Wright or Himes, but an older black writer popular when he was in prison, Robert Beck, "Iceberg Slim." ***Whoreson,*** a first-person narrative by a pimp who's the offspring of a black whore and a white trick, was a takeoff on Slim's *Trick Baby.*

Goines is not a stylist, not a writer of elegance and nuances. Occasionally his writing lapses into hack pornography. Yet, as in ***Dopefiend,*** he could also capture the macho defeat of a heroin addict who, in bed with his girlfriend, turns on her in blind rage when he can't arouse himself: " 'Get the fuck out of my eyesight, dopefiend ass bitch!' he yelled beside himself. 'When a bitch gets so sorry she can't even make her man get his dick hard, she ain't no use.' His anger was directed more at himself than at Terry. To cover his shame . . . " Goines goes into places few other writers have visited. And he can be gentle and subtle. There's a moment in ***Whoreson*** when a mother who turns tricks encourages her son to keep a pet cat he's found, not letting him know the real reason is so it'll guard against rats while he sleeps. And several years later, when she catches her son, now 14, with a reefer, she puts on a Billie Holiday record, then sits the boy down for a no-nonsense chat on the dangers of the harder drugs (but without ever alluding to Holiday's life).

Goines's best book is his second, ***Dopefiend.*** It opens in the apartment of Porky, a "black and horribly fat" heroin dealer "with small, red, reptilian eyes" who's thumbing through a porno mag that depicts a woman and a horse simulating intercourse. The floor of the flat, which is used as a shooting gallery, is littered with cigarette butts, bloody toilet tissues, pools of blood "from where addicts had tried to get a hit, but the works had stopped up, and they had pulled the needle out, leaving a flowing trail of blood." Porky watches one addict prepare to hit herself in the groin—the only place she can still find a vein.

The opening is such an unmitigated horror show, you wonder, "How is he going to top this? How is he going to maintain the momentum?" He does. He gives us the hysteria of a junkie, her arms and legs running with blood, who cannot find a vein to hit; a junkie idly thinking it would be nice to have a bowel movement, since he hasn't had one in 10 days, then considering borrowing his sister's douche bag to give himself an enema; the sick comedy of a pimp who stages shows with his dogs and whores, telling one woman, "If I wasn't scared of you giving my dogs the syphilis I'd have you put on a little floorshow."

There are mellow moments, too. A young black woman drives her boyfriend to the dealer's house. The woman, Terry, doesn't think he has a habit yet. Or does he?

> "Shit, Teddy, you don't need all that dope anyway."
>
> For a moment Teddy was too occupied considering the gas gauge to reply. "You got enough gas, Terry, to get to work and back," he said, "Come on, let's run to Porky's and get a little blow."

Soon enough, Terry herself acquires a habit from snorting the high-grade stuff the dealer lays on her for free every time she visits with Teddy. From there, of course, it's strictly downhill. One day her white boss, seeing her nodding and thinking she didn't get enough sleep, tells her to take the rest of the day off.

> Terry quickly got her coat and left the store before anyone else got a chance to see her. Once outside, she leaned against the building until her conscience got the best of her. What am I doing here, she asked herself. Here I am, downtown,

> nodding against the wall of one of the largest white stores in the city. . . . Two young black teenagers walked past and smiled knowingly in her direction.

The book is relentless. And Goines ends it with the chilling murder of two hotshot junkies who had dared to rip off Porky and with the horrific suicide of a pregnant junkie who, after spilling her hard-earned cap of heroin on the floor, hangs herself from a light fixture and is found "with a child's head protruding from between [her] naked legs. The head of the baby was covered with afterbirth."

The dissociated responses, the disintegration, the easy, casual violence of the milieu—it's all captured chillingly. Characters who have been with us for half a book suddenly are killed, and that's that. The novels teem with matter-of-fact violence. It's never romanticized; it's as deadpan as a police report. In ***Dopefiend,*** a lead character, Snake, is killed when, in their own house, he and two friends are stuck up by some thieves and the gun goes off accidentally. The stickup men are upset. Soon, though:

> The one who had done the shooting regained his courage. "What we goin' do about them [the two friends]? We just can't walk off and leave them."
>
> "You ain't about to get mixed up in no mass killin," another one replied as he backed toward the door.

So they leave, just like that, having killed one but deciding not to kill the other two. We all have to draw the line somewhere.

Goines's dialect can be wonderful, and funny, whether it's some guys joking about a con in federal prison assigned to the cow barn who's probably "pumpin' dick to some sorry ass cow" (***Never Die Alone***); a dying drug dealer moaning, "I done cashed the big ticket. . . . Here I thought I had Jesus in a jug, no lookin' back" (***Never Die Alone***); a dubious would-be bank robber speculating, "If we rip off that bank like you got it planned, the feds are going to be all over this motherfuckin' city before God gets the news" (***Black Gangster***); or a woman telling off a gangster: "You'd burn your mammy for her last days on earth, if you thought you could get them" (***Black Gangster***).

But the cynicism of Goines's characters finally is all-pervasive. In ***Whoreson,*** the pimp-narrator gets disturbed because he can't work his pregnant woman when she starts hemorrhaging. He takes her to a hospital, where the doctor, who thinks he's her husband, tells him:

> "She has lost the baby. Now we are trying to stop the hemorrhaging, so that we don't lose the mother, too."
>
> That rang a bell. . . . I felt the bankroll in my pocket. It was four hundred dollars short because of the hospital bill. I shouldn't have paid the damn bill so fast. If she died and I hadn't paid the bill, all I'd had to do was deny being her husband and the hell with the bill. . . . I sat down suddenly and began to pray. Please Lord, don't let that young girl die.

(In another novel, ***Street Players,*** Goines depicts a more successful pimp who checks his sick whore into a good private hospital instead of a general one, then comments to a less successful pimp, "My ladies go first class. . . . That's why I got a stable of good young whores, instead of some dopefiend bitches that shoot up all the profit." Which makes all the difference between "being a top-notch player, or just another mediocre-ass nigger out here in the streets.")

In ***Never Die Alone,*** Goines describes a drug dealer's ghetto philosophy: "He took kindness for weakness, friendship as an opportunity to take advantage of the person foolish enough to offer it." And when he falls in love he castigates himself for his weakness. In ***Eldorado Red*** a numbers operator hires a hitman to kill a witness, and the hitman contracts out to two other guys, telling them, " 'It's five grand involved if you're interested.' . . . ' 'Interested!' one of the black men replied. 'Shit!' For five grand I'd hit you, Johnnie-Bee.' The men laughed, but Johnnie-Bee knew the man spoke the truth. Five grand was a good price for a hit." While the hero of ***Black Gangster*** simply "believed kindness was the sweetest con of all." It is a bleak, utterly atomized worldview—but it is the worldview not just of Goines, not just of the characters who populate his novels, but of the real-life characters who inspired the fictions. Goines was, at least in his earlier novels, a realist.

He wrote with the speed of a junkie who has bills to pay on the hour every hour, averaging a book every four months. And then when the novels started to back up at the publishing house, he began writing another series under the pseudonym Al C. Clark—novels that marked a departure from the realism of the earlier books. In the Clark novels, which began with ***Crime Partners,*** he created Kenyatta, a black avenger who fields his own private army and battles both the police and the drug dealers, who keeps posters of Ho Chi Minh and other revolutionary men of color on his office walls, who seems a superheated amalgam of the Black Panthers and the Black Muslims. Perhaps Goines felt he had reached a dead end with the chilling realism of the early books, perhaps he was inspired by the black action movies of the early '70s, perhaps he felt the political need, the *human* need, to leave behind the cynicism and the pessimism, to posit some sort of ideal. Here too, though, the deep pessimism of the ghetto finally won out—in the last Clark novel, he has a powerful Las Vegas white crime lord kill off Kenyatta.

Goines had caught the menace of the young bloods who kill with malign indifference, the anarchism and nihilism of the ghetto streets, well before *Time, Newsweek,* and the rest of us got there in recent years with stories about the ghetto epidemic of black-on-black killings, the horrifying statistics (a white male has one chance in 186 of becoming a murder victim, a black male one in 29), the armchair analyses of social pathology. In 1985, *Newsweek* quoted Harvard political scientist Martin Kilson, who said that in the past decade and a half black intellectuals had drawn "an ethnic *cordon sanitaire*" around whole areas of the black experience. Goines, neither an intellectual nor a social protester, wrote about that quarantined area. It was the only thing he knew to write about, and he caught its menace in almost every page of his prose. Sometimes he would just state the case flat out, as in ***Black Gangster*** when an older black man is insulted by a youth: "Some instinct warned him that Donnie was searching for trouble. His whole being cried out to meet it, but a small voice in the back of his mind told him it wasn't like it used to be. The kids nowadays didn't fight anymore, they believed in killing."

Goines depicted the poverty, the random violence, the casualness about going to prison, the unemployment, the female-headed households, the birth out of wedlock, the child abuse, the pervasive drug culture, the rage, the indifference, the frustration, the cold cynicism. He depicted it all as a matter of course. His message, if he can be said to have one, perhaps lies in the very relentlessness, the magnitude, the savagery, the fury, the luminous power of his pessimism. Any life that can inspire such pessimism cries out to be changed. (pp. 48-9)

Michael Covino, "Motor City Breakdown," in The Village Voice, *Vol. XXXII, No. 31, August 4, 1987, pp. 48-9.*

Eddie Stone (essay date 1988)

[*Stone is the author of* Donald Writes No More: A Biography of Donald Goines *(1974). In the following 1988 epilogue to a reissue of that work, he assesses Goines's stature in black literature.*]

It has now been fourteen years and some days, as of this writing, since Donald Goines and Shirley Sailor were murdered in their Detroit apartment on a cool October evening (the 21st) in 1974. Think about it. Fourteen years—Richard Nixon had only recently resigned from office—and the sixteen books Goines wrote are still in print and still selling. "Each new generation discovers him," a Holloway House executive was quoted as saying in the *Detroit News* in March, 1987:

> Each generation discovers him anew. We still get fan letters from readers, a lot of them from teenagers who don't realize that he is dead. We also get at least one manuscript weekly that is an attempt to knock off Donald Goines' style and an endless stream of letters from guys who are offering to write us books "like Donald Goines only better."
>
> Holloway published several of those Goines knock offs in the three or four years after he died and some of them were written by better writers, at least technically, than Goines was. But they were *not* Goines and never were going to be and the readers knew it. Forget about that old saw that imitation is the sincerest form of flattery; it is not.

Before Goines' literary voice was silenced that night in his Detroit apartment, he'd produced sixteen books. With the exception of ***Swamp Man,*** a little sex-and-violence for the sake of sex-and-violence number that he knocked off because he was extremely hard up for money, all of Goines' books are set in the inner city ghettos of Goines' home city Detroit, or Watts, Harlem, or a never named city in the Southwest that sometimes resembles Las Vegas, where the writer spent a few weeks. (pp. 225-26)

And here, in the winter of 1988-89, all sixteen books are out in new editions and have never been out of print, and Goines has become America's Number One best-selling black author. If anything, nearly a quarter of a century after the publication of his first book, Goines is more popular than ever, even more so than when he was alive. His books are reprinted over and over and the entire package (with the exception of ***Swamp Man***) is under option for a television mini-series. "Hardly a month goes past," a Holloway House executive says, "that we don't have to rush print one of Goines' books. More and more he's become required or recommended reading at the high school and college level and where that used to happen among just a few urban inner-city high schools, now it's happening in the South as well as in some very prestigious Eastern universities."

Critics, and Goines has always had his critics, keep asking "Why?"

As in "Why on earth is he still popular? And how did he ever become popular in the first place? He wasn't really a very good writer and what he wrote would seem to have such a limited appeal to readers."

Well, yes. With the help of others, let's see if we can, in retrospect, answer some of those questions. Let's try this one from Greg Goode, writing in *Melus,* a journal of literary criticism, in the fall of 1984 [see excerpt dated 1984]:

> Donald Goines is the foremost example of a cultural phenomenon possible no earlier than the 1970s—a successful Black author of mass market fiction written by and about Blacks. Unlike the mass market fiction authors such as Samuel R. Delany and Frank Yerby, the majority of whose readers were white and are intended to be white, the books of Donald Goines are devoured by legions of Black Americans everywhere, from the inner city to American military bases abroad.

That certainly is one answer to that "why?" question but we've never believed it was the entire answer. There is probably not one entire answer. But as the years have gone on, important "mainstream" critics as well as scholars have discovered Goines and more papers have been and are being written about the writer and his work. Hardly a month goes past that Holloway House doesn't receive a request for a press kit from some author somewhere in the country where still another article is being written on Donald Goines, his books and his career.

Maybe that fails to impress you but look at it in this light: it now has been a decade since the movie studio 20th Century Fox sent out a press kit on Marilyn Monroe (that was her "home studio") or, for that matter, bothered to produce one to be sent out!

Something about the writings of Donald Goines struck a nerve; still strikes a nerve with a large audience that has been referred to by some journalists as a "cult" following.

Perhaps it was no more than his painfully raw honesty.

And perhaps that, alone, explains why Goines remains popular with young people of high school and college age, as well as with older people year after year, decade after decade.

Greg Goode of the University of Rochester expanded on one theory when he wrote:

> In his five-year literary career, Donald Goines provided perhaps the most sustained, multifaceted, realistic fictional picture ever created by one author of the lives, choices, and frustrations of underworld ghetto blacks. Almost single-handedly, Goines established the conventions and the popular momentum for a new fictional genre, which could be called "ghetto realism."

Well, perhaps. If what Goines did really did become the "ghetto realism" school of fiction, Donald Goines was just about the only writer who ever practiced it. Dozens of other black writers (and a couple of white ones), as mentioned before, tried to become "another Donald Goines." Eventually a few of them found their own voice and made a niche for themselves in the world of black street experience fiction. Still others, fine writers such as Odie Hawkins and Joe Nazel, tested the waters of "ghetto realism" and decided their calling lay elsewhere and that their writing talents could be put to, for them, better use.

And when it comes to comparing Goines, Hawkins and Nazel, we're sort of discussing oranges, apples and pears. Hawkins, in particular, writes honest realism that is sometimes painfully so. Hawkins is a much more lyrical writer but often just as gritty as Donald Goines. But he also writes from and about a broader range of experience and there is no way anyone can honestly ever refer to him as a "ghetto" writer of any sort. (pp. 226-28)

It is also true that neither Hawkins or Nazel choose to deal with the violence on a level or in the oftentimes sickeningly realistic manner in which Goines did.

And the focus on the protagonist, or main character, differs. Goines gave his characters the same illegal professions he himself had practiced. Setting almost all his books in urban ghettos where the dominant moral standard was "what goes around comes around," Goines wrote about the pecking order of the workings of ghetto criminal elements; the big fish swallowing the smaller fish. There are not a helluva lot of "self-made" men in Goines' works and those that are there mostly "self-made" it through some highly illegal activities. (p. 229)

In comparing Goines' work to that of the two most popular Holloway House writers to follow him—Hawkins and Nazel—there is an immediate and apparent difference in *who* meets a violent death and just how violent that death may be.

In Goines' ***Daddy Cool,*** for instance, the violence is relentless. The protagonist, Larry "Daddy Cool" Jackson, is, in Goines' words, "one of the deadliest killers the earth has ever spawned." He kills with a knife and does it often; his first victim is an old man who has worked as an accountant for the numbers organization and has ripped them off for $125,000. It is a contract murder for which Daddy Cool is paid $10,000.

The only warm spot in the heart of this "deadly killer" seems to be for his beautiful young and rebellious daughter, Janet. He does not harbor the same sentiments for his son, Buddy, and certainly not for his stepson, Jimmy. Nor for his wife either, for that matter. He tells us that he'd long since gotten rid of her if it wasn't for the fact that Janet needed a mother and another woman around the house. Some mother, but that sort of shading of detail never got in Goines' way of telling a story.

They all live together in an expensive home in an apparently well-to-do section of Detroit. Daddy Cool covers up his real occupation by posing as a successful dry cleaning store owner, which is run by his old and trusted friend, Earl. (Shades of Goines' own background; he grew up in a nice, middle-class area of Detroit, the son of a successful dry cleaning establishment owner.)

Ah, but in a twist that is typical of Goines ("what goes around comes around"), Daddy Cool isn't the only bad odor in this corner of middle-class paradise. Janet's good looking young man just happens to be a pimp; and a particularly odious one who is despised by Daddy Cool (who considers all pimps to be nothing more than parasites).

Janet and her father fight over her dating the pimp, Ronald, one night after she stays out way past curfew. The next morning Janet is gone, bag and baggage; brother and stepbrother having watched her run off with Ronald during the night to "go become a whore."

And where she has gone is to a fleabag hotel in a seedy part of town with Ronald. And Ronald, true to character, has her turning tricks ("just this one time so we can have some money") so quickly that one has to wonder about Janet's smarts. But, then, Janet is a typical act-on-instinct-and-think-later Goines character.

Daddy Cool sends Buddy, Jimmy and Earl out to find Janet but son (Buddy) and stepson (Jimmy) decide, somewhere along the way, to go into business for themselves, along with their sleazeball friend, Tiny. Of course the numbers house they decide to rob belongs to one of Daddy Cool's oldest and best friends. And, yes, of course his thirteen-year-old daughter just happens to have stopped by for her allowance a few minutes beforehand so that Tiny and Jimmy can brutally rape her (up against one of those old steel heat radiators!). And yes, "what goes around comes around." The father runs a numbers game, the little girl gets gang raped while her father has to watch.

And who does the numbers runner call as the instrument of his revenge? Daddy Cool, of course. Good friend, paid hit man and "one of the deadliest killers the earth has ever spawned." And he's hired to go after the two men who raped the numbers kingpin's daughter—one of whom just happens to be his own stepson he learns when he's given film of the entire episode that was taped by hidden cameras. And, in another twist that is typical of Goines, he learns that his own son was not only there but did nothing to stop the rape of the child. Daddy Cool tracks the three down, kills both Tiny and stepson Jimmy (with one of his trusty homemade knives in the back of each as they flee in panic). However, he lets son Buddy live but tells him to leave Detroit and never return.

Meanwhile the trusted friend Earl, a giant of a man, has tracked Janet and her pimp down to the sleazebag hotel where she is now turning tricks at a hot and heavy pace. Ronald has set her up as a working prostitute, Janet realizes, when he will no longer kiss her. Earl watches, realizes how far she has fallen (or how far Ronald has pushed her) and kills the pimp with his bare hands. Daddy Cool is hot on the trail and arrives about the time the police do Earl in for being a "psycho killer."

In the final confrontation between Janet and Daddy Cool at the death scene, he watches as she goes for the knife she wears in the halter between her shoulder blades (just as he wears his own). He taught her himself to reach for it, grip the hand and throw it in one fluid movement. He knows that Janet is distraught and blames himself, and that he is the target but he is "somehow pleased to see Janet close the distance between them," and thinks "she's so much like I used to be . . . " Ha! That doesn't surprise him one bit. In fact, he thinks, "she makes me proud, moving so smooth, so easy."

He goes for his knife and thinks: "Wonder if I can beat her from here? I got to do something to protect her. If she kills me straight out, she'll end up facing a first degree murder charge. Got to make my move, not to hurt her, just to save her from the law."

With knife in hand, Daddy Cool shouts: "You're wrong, Janet!"

He doesn't try to dodge Janet's knife—and hopes the police see it as self-defense for his daughter.

Instead of throwing his own knife, he grips it tighter. At the last instant he knows he would have had plenty of time to get his toss off . . .

If he had really wanted to.

The book ends with Janet crying over the body of Daddy Cool; nearby is the body of Earl. Back in the hotel is the body of lover/pimp Ronald.

No one really wins.

No one ever really wins in a Donald Goines book. (pp. 230-33)

Most of the writers who attempted to "become another Donald Goines" quickly found there was room for only one. Even today Holloway House is submitted several manuscripts each month by people who not only blatantly attempt to copy Goines' style and cover the same territory, but invariably will state that they're 'writing like Goines, only better."

Writing recently in *The Village Voice,* Michael Covino stated:

> All those (other black) writers, no matter how well they dealt with black experience, appealed largely to an educated, middle-class, largely white readership. They brought news of one place to the residents of another. Goines' novels, on the other hand, are written from ground zero. They are almost unbearable. It is not the educated voice of a writer who has, so to speak, risen above his background; rather, it is the voice of the ghetto itself.
>
> (p. 234)

Early in 1988, the motion picture *Colors* was released, starring Sean Penn and Robert Duvall, and directed by Dennis Hopper. The movie focused on drugs and gang culture and brought howls of protest, especially from the self-appointed "black leadership," some of whom accused the movie of being racist, others of promoting the drug/gang culture; still many others found various other aspects wrong with the film. The movie upset such people, so much, that a movement to boycott the film ensued.

Of course such people have never read Donald Goines. As a matter of fact some such people have demanded that Goines' books be withdrawn from school and public libraries for his use of "swear words."

Observing such antics, Joe Nazel wondered what the shouting was all about: "Those people (gang members like those in *Colors*) are out there but they are worse than anything depicted in that movie," he stated.

Yes, those people are out there. That life is out there. And it is what Goines was writing about long before anyone else wanted to think about it. He was on the cutting edge of the life he depicted in his books and saw the cancer spreading. It's a pity that not too many people took him seriously those nearly twenty years ago.

As a writer, it certainly can be said that Goines didn't have great skills. But as a social observer he was light years ahead of most of the rest of us. (pp. 236-37)

Eddie Stone, in his Donald Writes No More: A Biography of Donald Goines, *Holloway House Publishing Co., 1988, 237 p.*

Additional coverage of Goines's life and career is contained in the following sources published by Gale Research: *Authors in the News,* Vol. 1; *Black Literature Criticism; Black Writers; Contemporary Authors,* Vols. 114 [obituary], 124; and *Dictionary of Literary Biography,* Vol. 33.

For Whom the Bell Tolls

Ernest Hemingway

The following entry presents criticism on Hemingway's novel *For Whom the Bell Tolls* (1940). For further discussion of Hemingway's life and works, see *CLC*, Volumes 1, 3, 6, 8, 10, 13, 19, 30, 34, 39, 41, 44, 50, and 61.

INTRODUCTION

Drawn from Hemingway's experiences as a war correspondent and ardent supporter of the Republican cause during the Spanish Civil War, *For Whom the Bell Tolls* is considered one of the classic war narratives of the twentieth century. Critics commend Hemingway's treatment of the themes of idealism and responsibility as these are embodied in the novel's protagonist, Robert Jordan, and cite Jordan's moral journey amidst the corruption of war and his ultimate commitment to society as an apt reflection of the mood and sentiment of the American people on the eve of World War II.

The Spanish Civil War began in 1936, when Fascist forces under the leadership of General Francisco Franco and the sponsorship of Adolf Hitler's Nazi Germany began a three-year struggle with Republican troops for control of Spain. Republicans, or Loyalists, were aligned with communism and received military and financial support from the Soviet Union. Hemingway, an antifascist, began to raise money for ambulances and medicine for the beleaguered Republicans, and by 1937 he was heading the Ambulances Committee of the American Friends of Spanish Democracy. His love of Spain and frequent visits to the war-torn country as a journalist prompted him to write a drama titled *The Fifth Column,* a series of articles for the *North American Newspaper Alliance* and *Esquire,* and *The Spanish Earth,* a documentary collaboration with John Dos Passos, Archibald MacLeish, and Lillian Hellman about the struggle and spirit of the Spanish people. Hemingway had just begun *For Whom the Bell Tolls* when Spain fell to Fascist forces in March 1939.

For Whom the Bell Tolls deals with three days in the life of American professor Robert Jordan. Like Hemingway, Jordan possesses a strong love of Spain and a hatred for fascism. Volunteering to fight in the Republican army, he is sent to a guerrilla band based in the mountains near Segovia to facilitate a Republican advance by blowing up an important bridge behind Fascist lines. Jordan considers the advance ill-conceived, but continues the mission despite his misgivings and the growing realization that his initial perception of the war—altered by tales of Republican atrocities and experience with widespread cowardice and corruption—was simplistic and naive. In the vacant mountain hideout of the Republicans, he meets Maria, a young woman traumatized by her father's murder and her own rape by the Fascists. Encouraged by an old gypsy woman, Pilar, to help Maria overcome her anguish, he quickly falls in love with the young woman.

Jordan vies for leadership with the group's leader, Pablo, a man once respected and feared who now feels threatened by Jordan's growing authority and the dangerous mission. After Pilar and the guerrillas support Jordan in the conflict, the band contemplates killing Pablo, but Jordan's vacillation allows Pablo to escape with the detonators required for the assignment. Remorseful over his cowardly actions and his jealousy over Jordan's relationship with Maria, Pablo returns and resolves to help his comrades. Unaware that the anticipated Republican advance has been quelled and its mission cancelled, the guerrilla band detonates the bridge. Although mortally wounded, Jordan allows his comrades to retreat while he stays behind to delay the advancing Fascist forces.

For Whom the Bell Tolls was published in the midst of national debate in the United States over America's possible entrance into World War II, and initial critical reception of Hemingway's novel focused on his emphasis on individual responsibility to society. Some critics discussed Hemingway's intentions in the novel, interpreting the complex and contradictory treatment of Republican atrocities in

For Whom the Bell Tolls as derogatory to the cause of Republicans and sympathetic to the Fascists. Some reviewers defended Hemingway's involvement and alliance with the Republicans, but have speculated as to the extent of his belief in Communism. Hemingway's treatment of Jordan's idealism and death has been termed too romantic and unrealistic by some critics, and the dynamics of Jordan and Maria's relationship have also prompted analytical discussion. In addition, commentators have derided the antiquated and awkward language Hemingway used to approximate Spanish slang and have discussed the epic qualities of Hemingway's narrative, especially the characterization and courageous actions of Robert Jordan.

Although reviewers initially praised *For Whom the Bell Tolls* as Hemingway's best novel, the book has fallen out of favor with many critics and readers because of its romantic idealism and focus on dated historical events that have been overshadowed by such prominent milestones as World War II, the Nazi Holocaust, and the Vietnam War. Evaluating the novel's relevance for contemporary readers, commentators have concentrated on Jordan's self-analysis and resulting moral journey as a universal allegory. In this respect, according to Michael Reynolds, *For Whom the Bell Tolls* "transcends the historical context that bore it, becoming a parable rather than a paradigm. And thus, softly, across time, *For Whom the Bell Tolls* continues in muted tones to toll for us."

PRINCIPAL WORKS

Three Stories & Ten Poems (short stories and poetry) 1923
in our time (short stories) 1924; also published as *In Our Time* [revised edition], 1925
The Sun Also Rises (novel) 1926; also published as *Fiesta,* 1927
The Torrents of Spring (novel) 1926
Men without Women (short stories) 1927
A Farewell to Arms (novel) 1929
Death in the Afternoon (nonfiction) 1932
Winner Take Nothing (short stories) 1933
Green Hills of Africa (nonfiction) 1935
To Have and Have Not (novel) 1937
The Spanish Earth (commentary and film narration) 1938
The Fifth Column and the First Forty-nine Stories (drama and short stories) 1939
For Whom the Bell Tolls (novel) 1940
Across the River and Into the Trees (novel) 1950
The Old Man and the Sea (novel) 1952
The Snows of Kilimanjaro, and Other Stories (short stories) 1961
The Short Happy Life of Francis Macomber, and Other Stories (short stories) 1963
A Moveable Feast (memoir) 1964
By-Line: Ernest Hemingway: Selected Articles and Dispatches of Four Decades (nonfiction) 1968
Islands in the Stream (novel) 1970
The Nick Adams Stories (short stories) 1972
88 Poems (poetry) 1979
Ernest Hemingway: Selected Letters, 1917-1961 (correspondence) 1981
The Complete Stories of Ernest Hemingway (short stories) 1987

CRITICISM

Edmund Wilson (review date 28 October 1940)

[*Wilson, considered America's foremost man of letters in the twentieth century, wrote widely on cultural, historical, and literary matters. He is often credited with bringing an international perspective to American letters through his widely read discussions of European literature. Wilson was allied to no critical school; however, several dominant concerns serve as guiding motifs throughout his work. He invariably examined the social and historical implications of a work of literature, particularly literature's significance as "an attempt to give meaning to our experience" and its value for the improvement of humanity. Although he was not a moralist, his criticism displays a deep concern with moral values. Another constant was his discussion of a work of literature as a revelation of its author's personality. In* Axel's Castle *(1931), a seminal study of literary symbolism, Wilson wrote: "The real elements, of course, of any work of fiction are the elements of the author's personality: his imagination embodies in the images of characters, situations and scenes the fundamental conflicts of his nature." Related to this is Wilson's theory, formulated in* The Wound and the Bow *(1941), that artistic ability is a compensation for a psychological wound; thus, a literary work can only be fully understood if one undertakes an emotional profile of its author. Wilson used this approach in many essays, and it is the most-often attacked element of his thought. However, though Wilson examined the historical and psychological implications of a work of literature, he rarely did so at the expense of a discussion of its literary qualities. Perhaps Wilson's greatest contributions to American literature were his tireless promotion of writers of the 1920s, 1930s, and 1940s, and his essays introducing the best of modern literature to the general reader. In the following essay, he offers a mixed review of* For Whom the Bell Tolls.]

This new novel of Hemingway will come as a relief to those who didn't like ***Green Hills of Africa, To Have and Have Not,*** and ***The Fifth Column.*** The big game hunter, the waterside superman, the Hotel Florida Stalinist, with their constrained and fevered attitudes, have evaporated like the fantasies of alcohol. Hemingway the artist is with us again; and it is like having an old friend back.

This book is also a new departure. It is Hemingway's first attempt to compose a full-length novel, with real characters and a built-up story. On the eve of a Loyalist attack in the Spanish civil war, a young American who has enlisted on the Loyalist side goes out into country held by the

Fascists, under orders to blow up a bridge. He directs with considerable difficulty a band of peasant guerillas, spends three nights in a cave in their company, blows up the bridge on schedule, and is finally shot by the Fascists. The method is the reverse of the ordinary method in novels of contemporary history, Franz Hoellering's or André Malraux's which undertake a general survey of a revolutionary crisis, shuttling back and forth among various groups of characters. There is a little of this shuttling in ***For Whom the Bell Tolls,*** but it is all directly related to the main action: the blowing-up of the bridge. Through this episode the writer has aimed to reflect the whole course of the Spanish War, to show the tangle of elements that were engaged in it, and to exhibit the events in a larger perspective than that of the emergency of the moment.

In this he has been successful to a degree which will be surprising even to those who have believed in him most. There is in ***For Whom the Bell Tolls*** an imagination for social and political phenomena such as he has hardly given evidence of before. The vision of this kind of insight is not so highly developed as it is with a writer like Malraux, but it is here combined with other things that these political novels often lack. What Hemingway presents us with in this study of the Spanish war is not so much a social analysis as a criticism of moral qualities. The *kind* of people people are rather than their social-economic relations is what Hemingway is particularly aware of.

Thus there is here a conception of the Spanish character, very firm and based on close observation, underlying the various social types; and in approaching the role of the Communists in Spain, Hemingway's judgments are not made to fit into the categories of a political line—since he has dropped off the Stalinist melodrama of the days of 1937, a way of thinking certainly alien to his artistic nature—but seem to represent definite personal impressions. The whole picture of the Russians and their followers in Spain—which will put The New Masses to the trouble of immediately denouncing a former favorite at a time when they are already working overtime with so many other denunciations on their hands—looks absolutely authentic. You have the contrast between the exaltation of the converts and recruits of the headquarters of the International Brigade, and the luxury, the insolence and the cynicism of the headquarters of the emissaries of the Kremlin. You have the revolutionary stuffed shirt, André Marty, hero of the 1918 mutiny of the French fleet in the Black Sea, who has been magnified and corrupted in Moscow till he is no longer anything but a mischievous bureaucrat, obsessed with the idea of shooting heretics; and you have the Moscow insider Karkov, cold of head and serious of purpose while he repeats for the sake of conformity the venomous gibberings of Pravda.

You have in the center of the stage the sincere fellow traveler from the States, teacher of Spanish in a Western college; and you have, traced with realism and delicacy, the whole chronicle of his reactions to the Communists, of his relations with the Spaniards he has to work with, and of the operation upon him in Spain of the American influences he brings with him. In the end, realizing fully the military futility of his mission and balked in his effort to save the situation, by the confusion of forces at cross-purposes that are throttling the Loyalist campaign, he is to stick by his gun sustained by nothing but the memory of his grandfather's record as a soldier in the American Civil War. In view of the dramatic declamations on the note of "Look here, upon this picture, and on this!" that the Stalinists were making a year or two ago over the contrast between Dos Passos' attitude and Hemingway's in connection with the Spanish war, it is striking that the hero of ***For Whom the Bell Tolls*** should end up by cutting a figure not fundamentally so very much different from that of the hero of *The Adventures of a Young Man.*

Thus we get down out of the empyrean of Marxist political analysis, where the leaders are pulling the strings for the masses, and see the ordinary people as they come. And we see the actual layout—mile by mile and hill by hill—of the country in which they have to struggle. One of the mostly highly developed of Hemingway's senses is his geographical and strategical vision—what may be called his sense of terrain. It is no doubt from the Western frontier that he has inherited his vivid perception of every tree, every bush, every path, every contour and every stream that go to make up the lay of the land. He derives and he can communicate an excitement from the mere exploration and mastery of country that goes back to Fenimore Cooper; and he has succeeded in getting it into this new novel as he got it into his early stories. We are shown the Spanish conflict in its essential and primitive aspect of groups of imperfectly equipped and more or less groping human beings maneuvering over the surface of the earth.

The novel has certain weaknesses. A master of the concentrated short story, Hemingway is less sure in his grasp of the form of the elaborated novel. The shape of ***For Whom the Bell Tolls*** is sometimes slack and sometimes bulging. It is certainly quite a little too long. You need space to make an epic of three days; but the story seems to slow up toward the end where the reader feels it ought to move faster; and the author has not found out how to mold or to cut the interior soliloquies of his hero. Nor are the excursions outside the consciousness of the hero, whose point of view comprehends most of the book, conducted with consistent attention to the symmetry and point of the whole.

There is, furthermore, in ***For Whom the Bell Tolls*** something missing that we still look for in Hemingway. Where the semi-religious exaltation of communism has failed a writer who had once gained from it a new impetus, a vacuum is created which was not there before and which for the moment has to be filled. In Hemingway's case, there has poured in a certain amount of conventional romance. There is in ***For Whom the Bell Tolls*** a love story that is headed straight for Hollywood. The hero falls in with an appealing little girl who has been captured and raped by the Fascists, who has never loved before and who wants him to teach her love. She adores him, lives only to serve him, longs for nothing but to learn his desires so that she can do for him what he wants, talks of her identity as completely merged in his. She is as docile as the Indian wives in the early stories of Kipling; and since the dialogue of the characters speaking Spanish is rendered literally with its *thees* and *thous* and all the formalities of a Latin language, the scenes between Robert and Maria have a strange atmosphere of literary medievalism reminiscent of the era of Maurice Hewlett. Robert keeps insisting to himself on his good fortune and on the unusualness of his experience in acquiring a girl like Maria; and, for all the reviewer knows, there may be a few such cases in Spain. But the whole thing has the too-perfect felicity of a youthful erotic dream. It lacks the true desperate emotion of the love affairs in some of Hemingway's other stories. And in general, though the situation is breathless and the suspense kept up all through, the book lacks the tensity, the moral malaise, that made the early work of Hemingway troubling.

But then this early work was, as it were, lyric; and ***For Whom the Bell Tolls*** is an effort toward something else, which requires a steady hand. The hero of this new novel is no romantic Hemingway cartoon: his attitude toward his duty and the danger it involves are studied with more coolness and sobriety than in the case of perhaps any other of the author's leading juveniles. The young man is a credible young man who is shown in his relation to other people, and these other people are for the most part given credible identities, too. The author has began to externalize the elements of a complex personality in human figures that have a more complete existence than those of his previous stories.

That he should thus go back to his art, after a period of artistic demoralization, and give it a larger scope, that, in an era of general perplexity and panic, he should dramatize the events of the immediate past in terms, not of partisan journalism, but of the common human instincts that make men both fraternal and combative, is a reassuring evidence of the soundness of our intellectual life. (pp. 591-92)

Edmund Wilson, "Return of Ernest Hemingway," in The New Republic, *Vol. 103, No. 18, October 28, 1940, pp. 591-92.*

Alvah Bessie (review date 5 November 1940)

[Bessie was an American novelist, screenwriter, critic, and editor who served in the Republican Army during the Spanish Civil War. In the following review of For Whom the Bell Tolls, *he denigrates Hemingway's treatment of the war and calls his portrayal of the Spanish people superficial.]*

> No man is an *Iland,* intire of it selfe; every man is a peece of the *Continent,* a part of the *maine;* if a *Clod* bee washed away by the *Sea, Europe* is the lesse, as well as if a *Promontorie* were, as well as if a *Mannor* of thy friends or of *thine owne* were; any mans *death* diminishes me, because I am involved in *Mankinde;* And therefore never send to know for whom the *bell* tolls; It tolls for *thee.*

This is the quotation from John Donne which Ernest Hemingway sets as a rubric for [***For Whom the Bell Tolls***], and this is the touchstone by which that novel must be evaluated. Since we must assume that Donne was speaking of the universal brotherhood of man, of the interrelationship of human life and its indivisibility, we have a right to expect that Hemingway's long novel of the war in Spain will illuminate that text and not obscure it, will demonstrate the novelist's realization of the significance of that war, and find him at the peak of his achievement. For that war, which Hemingway witnessed at close hand, is being revealed with every day that passes to have been a touchstone and a turning point in human history which those who had foresight in 1936 stated it would be: "the cause of all advanced and progressive mankind."

Ernest Hemingway's relationship to that war was intimate and varied. In many senses he was as much a participant as those men he knew and loved who now are gone—Lucasz, Werner Heilbrunn, and the many anonymous dead of the glorious Twelfth International Brigade. The novelist gave freely of his substance and his spirit in the cause of Spain; he wrote and he spoke and he acted. And he commanded the admiration and respect of the men of many nationalities who fought there and who knew his name. It was during that war that he wrote a novel that represented what should have been—and what many thought was—a transition book: ***To Have and Have Not.*** It was both interesting and inevitable that that novel should have been the first work from his hand that was *not* greeted with unanimous enthusiasm by the critical fraternity of the bourgeois press. For in its pages a new note had been sounded. The old Hemingway of the postwar what-the-hell-boys and the old let's-have-another-drink was gone. A new Hemingway made his appearance, a new theme emerged. Whereas in his short stories and in two previous novels the author had exasperated his most perspicacious admirers by his inconclusive treatment of the necessity for manliness and the pervasive horror of death, a maturing artist found another subject—the problem of making a living, the necessity for human solidarity. "One man alone ain't got," whispered the dying Harry Morgan, an honest man who had found that he could not feed his wife and children by honest labor. "No man alone now." He stopped. "No matter how a man alone ain't got no bloody——ing chance."

The critics deplored this new and serious note in their pet disillusioned author, an author they had praised for being above the political arena, who dealt with eternal realities in a "lean, athletic prose." It was whispered freely among these objective gentlemen that Hemingway was slipping; he was a member of the League of American Writers; he had discovered that non-existent figment of the Reds' imagination—the Class Struggle. But many who had thought Hemingway was dead (for more valid reasons) took new hope with the appearance in his work of this wider realization of man's humanity, this deeper understanding of his struggle. Sex and death were eternal verities, but it was not until 1937 that Hemingway discovered taxes. ***To Have and Have Not*** was a vastly imperfect work; the author's satirical treatment of the human parasites who lived on luxury yachts off the Florida keys was both brittle and jejune, and his old limitations were amply manifest: the interchangeability of his conversation; his feeble understanding of female character; his inability to fully explore and *plumb* character at all. For with the rarest of exceptions few characters that Hemingway has dealt with up to date have been more than pegs on which to hang those moods and intimations of mortality which have been the author's forte, and which reveal his greatest gifts.

That those gifts are considerable no sensitive person could doubt. He has an ear for the language (in dialogue) that is unique. No human being ever talked the way Hemingway's characters talk, but every word they speak makes the reader say, "How true to life." This is a real artistic triumph. This man can create moods and crystallize certain fundamental emotions in a way few writers have ever been privileged to achieve. And it is these moods and these emotions that the reader generally remembers, not the people who live through them—the futility of the life of the expatriate, his emptiness and his frantic search for a kick; the horror of the retreat from Caporetto; the loneliness that surrounds the death in childbed of the heroine of ***A Farewell to Arms,*** the brutality of **"The Killers,"** and the frustration of **"Fifty Grand;"** the loneliness and incongruity of drunkenness, and the sense of decay that pervaded all his work up to ***To Have and Have Not,*** where the wider significance of living made a momentary appearance.

Many expected that Hemingway's experience in Spain would so inflame his heart and his talents, that his long-announced novel of that war would be both his finest achievement and "the" novel about Spain. It is not. It is his finest achievement only in the sense that he has now perfected his extraordinary technical facility and touched some moments of action with a fictional suspense that is literally unbearable. But depth of understanding there is none; breadth of conception is heartbreakingly lacking; there is no searching, no probing, no grappling with the truths of human life that is more than superficial. And an astounding thing has happened, that anyone who was even remotely concerned with what happened in Spain will find almost incredible: Hemingway has treated that war (in an essential way) exactly as he treated the first world war in ***A Farewell to Arms.*** Touched in his own flesh and spirit by the horror of that first great imperialist conflict, struck into a mood of impotent despair by its utter lack of meaning and its destruction of everything all decent human beings value, Hemingway proclaimed the futility of life and love and happiness. He killed his heroine and in a memorable evocation of utter human loneliness, his hero "walked home in the rain." The ***Farewell*** was so bitter a condemnation of imperialist war that it aroused the ire of Archibald MacLeish, who found that it had been largely responsible for destroying the new generation's faith in its misleaders.

Let us examine ***For Whom the Bell Tolls,*** and see what the author (who only recently aptly replied to MacLeish) has done with one of the greatest human facts of our century—the two and a half years during which the Spanish people held in check, with their bare hands, the forces of international fascism. His hero this time is Robert Jordan, American volunteer in Spain who is a *partizan* fighter—one of that small band of extremely courageous men who worked behind the fascist lines. Jordan is sent behind the lines again to blow up a strategic bridge—his signal for the explosion is to be the beginning of a government attack upon Segovia.

Depth of understanding there is none; breadth of conception is heartbreakingly lacking; there is no searching, no probing, no grappling with the truths of human life that is more than superficial.

—Alvah Bessie

The action takes place in three days' time. Jordan makes contact with a group of Spanish *guerilleros,* meets a Spanish girl who had been captured and raped by the fascists, falls in love with her, makes his plans to blow the bridge—a difficult enterprise in which he fully expects to lose his life. His guerrillas attack the fascist garrisons, and he blows the bridge as what is to be a futile attack gets under way—for the fascists have learned of the plans for the offensive and are prepared to meet it. In escaping, Jordan's horse is wounded, falls upon the man, and breaks his leg. He is too badly injured to be carried, and must be left behind to do what damage he can with a light machine-gun, and then to end his life.

This is a story of action, and the action is fast and furious, fused with a suspense that is magnificently handled in every incident. But this is also ***A Farewell to Arms,*** slightly in reverse. For the total implication of the novel is, again, the necessity for virility, the pervasive horror of death, the futility—nay, the impossibility of love. Given only seventy-two hours in which to live, Robert Jordan must live his life within that span. He accepts that fate, but the reader's disappointment in his fate is Hemingway's disappointment with life—for there is no tragedy here, merely pathos. Here, again, are long and fruitless and somewhat meaningless disquisitions upon the significance of death and killing (in war, in murder, in the bullring, by accident, by design). Here again is the small and personal (and the word *personal* is the key to the dilemma of Ernest Hemingway's persistent lack of growth) frustration of the individual, and here again is the author's almost pathological preoccupation with blood and mutilation and sex and death—they all go together and are part and parcel of his attitude toward life, and they are the *only* facts of life with which he has consistently dealt. I do not mean to imply that these subjects are unworthy or incapable of profound treatment, singly or together; I do mean to insist that in Hemingway's hands they have never achieved the stature of universality, perhaps because Hemingway cannot see them in perspective, cannot see them more than sentimentally.

It must be clearly stated that Hemingway's position in this novel is unequivocally on the side of the Spanish people; there can be no question of his defection from that cause. It is, however, a tragic fact that the cause of Spain does not, in any *essential* way, figure as a motivating power, a driving, emotional, passional force in this story. In the widest sense, that cause is actually *irrelevant* to the narrative. For the author is less concerned with the fate of the Spanish people, whom I am certain that he loves, than he is with the fate of his hero and his heroine, who are *himself.* They are Hemingway and Hemingway alone, in their (say rather *his,* for Jordan is the mainspring of the narrative, and the girl Maria is only lightly sketched) morbid concentration upon the meaning of *individual* death, *personal* happiness, *personal* misery, *personal* significance in living and their personal equation is not so deeply felt or understood as to achieve wide significance. For all his groping, the author of the ***Bell*** has yet to integrate his individual sensitivity to life with the sensitivity of every living human being (read the Spanish people); he has yet to expand his personality as a novelist to embrace the truths of other people, everywhere; he has yet to dive deep into the lives of others, and there to find his own.

This personal constriction has long been evident and has made inevitable other aspects of Hemingway's personality that are, to say the least, reprehensible. I refer to his persistent chauvinism, as referred to the Italian people, and to women; to the irresponsibility he has shown in publishing in Hearst's *Cosmopolitan* such a story as **"Below the Ridge,"** a story whose implications gave deadly ammunition to the enemy—Hemingway's enemy, the fascist-minded of America; to the irresponsibility he demonstrated in permitting his play, ***The Fifth Column,*** to be mutilated and distorted out of all semblance of what he originally wanted to say, to the point where it was actually a slander of the Spanish people.

There are many references in the ***Bell*** to various political aspects of the struggle in Spain. And few of these references do more than *obscure* the nature of that struggle. Robert Jordan, his American anti-fascist fighter, wonders "what the Russian stand is on the whole business." If Jordan, who is pictured as an utterly inflexible anti-fascist, did not understand what the Soviet Union felt about Spain, surely his creator did and does. And just as in his story **"Below the Ridge,"** Hemingway's sins of omission in the ***Bell*** allow the untutored reader to believe that the role of the Soviet Union in Spain was sinister and reprehensible. For certainly he must himself know—and it is his obligation to clearly state—that that role was clear and well-defined, and so honest as to command the entire respect and adherence of the Spanish people, who hung banners in their towns which read: *Viva La U.R.S.S.; Mejor Amigo del Pueblo Espanol* (Long Live the Soviet Union, Best Friend of the People of Spain!).

Now this concentration, this constriction of Hemingway's indubitable genius, to the purely personal, has resulted in a book about Spain that is not about Spain at all! It has resulted in the intensification of his idiosyncratic tendencies to the point where he, an inflexible supporter of the loyalists and an avowed admirer of the International Brigades, can conceive and execute as vicious a personal attack upon Andre Marty, the *organizer* of the International Brigades, as could be and has been delivered upon him by French fascist deputies themselves! This attack upon Marty, who is portrayed in the novel under his own name, and upon whom Hemingway exercises the presumption (both personal and artistic) of *thinking for him,* is entirely irrelevant to the narrative. To understand it at all, one would have to know, at first hand, the nature of Hemingway's personal contact with this man—a revolutionary figure of the first magnitude, organizer of the Black Sea mutiny of the French navy (an achievement that could scarcely have been conceived and executed by the criminal imbecile Hemingway portrays), a monolithic representative of the French working class, and the man who was the organizational genius and spirit of the Brigades Hemingway makes such protestation of admiring. Both as novelist and reporter Hemingway had an obligation to understand this man, whatever his personal experience with Marty, whatever his personal opinion of Marty's personality might have been. He cannot plead that his intentions in attacking Marty were good; that it was his honest conviction that Marty was a part of the incompetence, the red tape, and the outright treachery that strangled Spain, for such "facts" simply will not hold water; they are lies. And I am afraid that Hemingway will live to see his book hailed by our universal enemy *precisely because of* his attack upon Marty; I am afraid he will live to see every living and dead representative of the Abraham Lincoln Battalion attacked and slandered because of the great authority that attaches to Hemingway's name and his known connection with Spain.

Yet this man Marty is the man the author portrays as a fool, a madman, and categorically indicts as a murderer! And I wonder, when he wrote these pages, whether he considered for a moment that he was attacking him with the very terms that have been leveled at him by the French fascists who sold France down the river to Hitler. I wonder if he considered he was accusing him in the very same way and with the very same words that were used by American deserters who appeared before the Dies committee and attempted to smear the Veterans of the Lincoln Brigade, with the very words of the Hearst press which, throughout the war in Spain, characterized the Internationals as the scum of the earth, international bums, gangsters, and murderers.

This is the trap into which the individualism Hemingway's bourgeois critics so admired, has led a man who is still one of our most greatly endowed creative artists. For he has written a novel of Spain without the Spanish people, a *Hamlet* without the Dane. And he has forgotten the words he wrote earlier this year: "There are events which are so great that if a writer has participated in them his obligation is to try to write them truly rather than assume the presumption of altering them with invention." For the author of the ***Bell*** does not convince us, with this novel, that "any mans death diminishes me, because I am involved in Mankinde." He only convinces us—no matter how tenderly he may write of the love of Robert Jordan and Maria—that the imagination of his own death may yet destroy him as an artist.

It seems certain that Hemingway did not intend to write a *Cosmopolitan* love story against a background of the Spanish Civil War; yet this is what he has done. It is certain that he did not intend to slander the Spanish people or the Soviet Union; yet his method of telling the story has resulted in both. With minor exceptions, the Spanish people portrayed here are cruel, vindictive, brutalized, irresponsible. Throughout the long narrative there is evidence of much confusion: Hemingway praises the individual heroism of individual Communists, and impugns and slanders their leadership, their motives, and their attitudes. He admires the Brigades, and assails their leadership (and surely he knows enough about military affairs to realize that no soldier can fight well unless his officer commands his respect).

Already this greatly endowed writer, who on innumerable occasions has placed himself without equivocation on the side of the people against their enemies, has been readmitted by the most reactionary critics to the Valhalla of the Literary Giants. J. Donald Adams of the New York *Times* has forgiven him for writing ***To Have and Have Not;*** the defected liberal, John Chamberlain, absolves him for having (in the same novel) made "a common murderer of inferior sensibility and no moral sense whatever . . . do duty as a symbol of downtrodden humanity," cheers the fact that "If Archibald MacLeish still thinks of Hemingway as an underminer of the soldierly virtues he will have to change his mind," and becomes shrill with joy over the attack on Marty, Hemingway's "turn (ing) on the politicos of Moscow" and finally arriving at the point announced by John Dos Passos in *Adventures of a Young Man.* (This should be news to Hemingway, for Dos Passos ultimately became an avowed enemy of the republican government of Spain.) Edmund Wilson also points the Dos Passos parallel in the *New Republic,* lauds Hemingway for being more interested in "The *kind* of people . . . rather than their social-economic relations. . . . "

But this is strange company for a man like Hemingway, a man who transcended the futility created in him by the first world war, was vitalized, as a man and as an artist, by Spain; a man who won the respect and admiration of almost every International Brigade man who met him, and who gave liberally to these men of his own substance. For at the moment he is found in bad company; in the company of his enemies, and the people's enemies—clever enemies who will fawn upon him and use him, his great talents and his passion for the people's cause, to traduce and betray those talents and those people. (pp. 25-9)

Alvah Bessie, "Hemingway's 'For Whom the Bell Tolls'," in New Masses, *Vol. XXXVII, No. 7, November 5, 1940, pp. 25-9.*

Jeffrey Meyers on Hemingway's novel as allegory:

For Whom the Bell Tolls is an allegory, as well as an explanation, of the Loyalist defeat in the Spanish war. Pablo's theft of Jordan's detonators symbolizes the difficulty of fighting without adequate war materiel. Andrés' journey through enemy lines—he is "impeded by the ignorance of the anarchists. Then by the sloth of a bureaucratic fascist. Now by thy oversuspicion of a Communist"—is obstructed by the factionalism of the Left and by the dominance of political commissars over military commanders, and symbolizes the betrayal of Spain by the foreigners. Andrés' inability to convince his allies to call off the attack represents the Loyalists' failure to persuade France and England to stop the German and Italian invasion. Hemingway's allegory explains the three main reasons for the Loyalist defeat: the factionalism of the Left, the interference (at the time of the Russian Purge Trials) of political commissars, and the successful intervention of Hitler's and Mussolini's armies while the democratic countries remained passive and indifferent.

Kenneth Lynn's distorted account of Hemingway's politics in the Spanish war [found in his book, *Hemingway*]—his sneering at Hemingway's "lack of political sophistication" and "service for Stalin"—blindly ignores the fact that Hemingway was more critical of the Communists than almost anyone else on the Left. His fictional rather than propagandistic account of the Communist role in the war did not advance the cause of the Revolution. The Spanish Communist Party condemned the book as soon as it appeared, and it was not translated into Russian until 1968 (and then only in an expurgated edition, with heavy cuts in the Gaylord's chapter). But Hemingway's insight about the complexity of the Spanish tragedy, written immediately after the events it records, makes *For Whom the Bell Tolls* the greatest political novel in American literature.

Jeffrey Meyers, in his "For Whom the Bell Tolls *as Contemporary History*" *in* The Spanish Civil War in Literature, *edited by Janet Pérez and Wendell Aycock, 1990.*

Carlos Baker (essay date 1952)

[*Baker was an American educator, novelist, short story writer, and poet with an interest in the life and work of Ernest Hemingway. His* Hemingway: A Life Story *(1969) and the critical study* Hemingway: The Writer as Artist *(1952), are considered seminal works on the legendary author. In the following excerpt from the 1972 edition of the latter book, Baker examines the structure of* For Whom the Bell Tolls, *especially Hemingway's use of the epic form.*]

One displaced person in the spring of 1938 helped to dramatize for Hemingway the artist the predicament of the Spanish people. About the first of March 1939 he began to write his great novel [***For Whom the Bell Tolls***] on the predicament of the Spanish people during their Civil War. He chose as his focal point a group of Republican partisans, drawn from many parts of Spain, and living under very primitive conditions in a cave on the high forested slopes of the Sierra de Guadarramas sixty miles northwest of besieged Madrid and behind the fascist lines. The time he chose was the sixty-eight-hour period between Saturday afternoon and Tuesday noon of the last week of May 1937. He worked on the book steadily for a period of eighteen months, rewriting it every day and doing the final revisions on galley proof. When his labors were over he had written the great book about the Spanish Civil War. One could not call it a book "without politics." Yet it was important to point out that the politics had been dramatically embodied in a work of fiction whose moral values transcended political affiliations.

The driving emotion behind ***For Whom the Bell Tolls*** is

Hemingway's sense of the betrayal of the Spanish people. Not only were they "killed in vast numbers, starved out, deprived of weapons" but they were also "betrayed." Worst of all was the betrayal. In a decade of notable betrayals the events in Spain between 1936 and 1939 dwarfed the betrayals of the Abyssinians and the Czechs. The nature of the betrayal of the Spanish people was complex in the extreme. What had chiefly caused it—internal cancer or rape by international hoodlums? The intervention of foreign powers was clearly an important factor in the prolongation of the war and the ultimate fascist victory. The wanton destruction of Guernica—an excellent example of betrayal—was evidently undertaken as a test of German bombing equipment. Hemingway's ***Spanish Earth*** commentary was quite possibly correct in maintaining that the Army insurrection which opened the war could have been put down in six weeks if German and Italian aid had not been made available to Franco's professionals.

Hemingway's own perspective on the fascist-communist struggle, which had been going on sporadically throughout Europe since the close of World War I, might have indicated a kind of tragic inevitability to foreign intervention in Spain's internal troubles. Yet these troubles had been serious before the foreign powers moved in, as Hemingway had duly noted in 1933. The outbreak of the war did not suddenly make an efficient machine from a somewhat inefficient and internally divided republican bureaucracy. Nor was it likely that the native Spanish conservatives would reject the advances of their foreign allies. Any genuinely true picture of the Spanish struggle would need somehow to embody all of these considerations, and to bring them to dramatic focus in the lives of a group of people whose backgrounds and present mode of behavior would fairly represent the total betrayal of Spain.

As he worked through the complexities of his task, Hemingway was sustained by a belief he had long held to: the job of the artist is not to judge but to understand. No matter how hard it may be to believe it in our political age, there is such a thing as the artistic "neutrality" of one who puts humanity above politics and art above propaganda. What Melville said of Captain Vere, the hero of *Billy Budd,* is applicable to the artist Hemingway. "There had got to be established in him some positive convictions which . . . would abide in him essentially unmodified so long as his intelligent part remained unimpaired. . . . His settled convictions were as a dyke against those invading waters of novel opinion, social, political, or otherwise, which carried away as in a torrent no few minds in those days." Hemingway's "dyke" is a belief in the artist's obligation to truth and to art, and to humanity in its extra-political dimension.

For Whom the Bell Tolls offers many examples of the author's determination to maintain that balance without which art may degenerate into propaganda. One of the most conspicuous is Pilar's account of the massacre of the leading citizens of a town near Avila by Pablo and his mob. Pilar has the artist's observational and almost clinical interest in how each of the fascists will die. Deeper than this interest runs her sense of the humanity of the killed and the strange furious mixture of bestiality and humanity among the killers. She watches the spectacle with a cold fascination. But her humanity is revealed in the sick disgust which assails her from time to time, as it troubles some of the individuals in the mob itself. One finds explicit recognition of how far out of the line of right human action this mob-murder is. But there is also a strong implicit suggestion of the criminal neglect, the inhuman apathy which has allowed the social situation in the villages of Spain to deteriorate so far that such mob action is now the sole recourse of the underdogs. After the massacre, says Pilar, "I went back inside the room and I sat there and I did not wish to think, for that was the worst day of my life until one other day." The "other day" was the day of reckoning. It came seventy-two hours later when the Fascists took the town.

Pilar has led a hard life and is as tough as an old eagle. Yet the heart still beats for humankind even when the head coldly admits the need for violent activity against the enemy. Pilar's sentiments find many echoes among the more sympathetic characters of the novel. When they are put together, they show clearly that, unlike Picasso's "Guernica," ***For Whom the Bell Tolls*** is not a study in black and white. It is a study of the betrayal of the Spanish people—both by what lay within them and what had been thrust upon them—and it is presented with that special combination of sympathetic involvement and hardheaded detachment which is the mark of the genuine artist. One could not rightly call the novel bipartisan. Yet it is partisan in a larger way than the modern use of the term ordinarily suggests. Its partisanship is in the cause of humanity.

The artist behind his dyke of conviction must likewise be able to understand the nature of these minds which the torrent of opinion carries along in its sweep. Hemingway's grasp of the motivations which strengthened and united, but also split, the extreme leftists is well illustrated in Jordan's contrast between the two communisms of Madrid. One was symbolized in Velázquez 63, the palace which served as headquarters for the International Brigades. Here was the almost puritanical, religious-crusader's side of party feeling. It gave its adherents something like "the feeling you expected to have and did not have when you made your first communion. . . . It gave you a part in something that you could believe in wholly and completely and in which you felt an absolute brotherhood with the others who were engaged in it." The religious reference emphasizes how far this secular substitute for religion—a substitute with its own propaganda-built hagiology and its own liturgy—had been able to go in capturing the devotions of foreign idealists.

Six months of the fighting effectively dissipated such devotions for any who kept their eyes and ears open. The idealist involved was shortly aware of the other symbol—the hotel called Gaylord's where the Russian directors of the Republican movement had congregated. Gaylord's symbolized the cold, practical, hardheaded, cynical ruthlessness of the Comintern mind, completely unsentimental and in no way deceived by the propaganda which it daily originated and disseminated. A part of the struggle in

Spain lay in the attempt of the idealist to keep his devoutness whole in the face of the actualistic education he got at Gaylord's.

Another of the tensions at work under the surface of Spain's tragedy is dramatized through the boy Joaquín, one of the republican partisans on El Sordo's chancre-like hilltop. This is the conflict between the Catholic faith and the secular pseudo-religion of the communists. At eighteen, Joaquín is just old enough in 1937 to have been raised under the wing of the Church, and just young enough to have suffered irreparably when the fascists shot his parents in Valladolid. Joaquín is imbued now with party doctrine. He especially reverences La Pasionaria, the secularist Joan of Arc in Marxist Spain.

While El Sordo's men prepare their hilltop position, Joaquín admiringly quotes La Pasionaria's slogan: *Resistir y fortificar es vencer*—to hold out and to fortify is to win. The boy is obliged to endure some good-natured raillery from those of his companions to whom such propagandist watchwords are a dirty joke. Yet through the early stages of the fight on the hilltop La Pasionaria sustains him well. Then the planes come. Joaquín has not considered the vulnerability of even Pasionaria-built fortifications to attack from the air. While the drone of the fascist bombers grows in intensity, Joaquín, heavy with dread, begins to invoke La Pasionaria once again. This time her words stick in his dry throat.

Then he shifted suddenly into "Hail Mary, full of grace, the Lord is with thee; Blessed art thou among women and Blessed is the fruit of thy womb, Jesus. Holy Mary, Mother of God, pray for us sinners now and at the hour of our death. Amen, Holy Mary, Mother of God," he started, then he remembered quick as the roar came now unbearably and started an act of contrition racing in it, "Oh my God, I am heartily sorry for having offended thee who art worthy of all my love. . . . "

When the explosions of the fascist bombs roll under the boy at the very moment of his losing consciousness, he is still repeating the petitional phrase, "Now and at the hour of our death." La Pasionaria is for other times.

La Pasionaria is for bringing passionately inspired news of Marxist victories. She is the occasion for a fine travesty on sentimental propagandists like the *Izvestia* correspondent at Gaylord's hotel.

> "She was here with the news and was in such a state of radiant exultation as I have never seen. The truth of the news shone from her face. That great face . . . " says the correspondent happily. . . . "It was one of the greatest moments of the war to me when I heard the report in that great voice where pity, compassion and truth are blended. Goodness and truth shine from her as from a true saint of the people. Not for nothing is she called La Pasionaria."
>
> "Not for nothing," says the other correspondent in a dull voice. "You better write it for *Izvestia* now, before you forget that last beautiful lead."

In the welter of opposed hatreds and in the company of sentimental mystics, the artist must keep his human and moral values unimpaired. Of the native Spaniards in the book, none better exemplifies the right human norm than Anselmo, Jordan's sixty-eight-year-old guide and friend. Other members of Pablo's band show the range of political and moral attitudes across the popular front. At one extreme is the blood-thirst of Pablo, not unlike that of the moonfaced Cuban revolutionist in ***To Have and Have Not.*** Near him, though at a higher level, stands the brave, relentless, fanatical hater, Agustín, who fiercely says that he would like to swim ten leagues in a broth made from the *cojones* of all the fascists. At the opposite extreme stands, or rather lolls, the irresponsible paganism of the gypsy Rafael. But Anselmo willingly endures discomfort out of loyalty to Jordan's trust, as Rafael would obviously never do. And unlike Pablo or Augustín, Anselmo, with the wisdom of his years, still hates killing even while he admits that it is necessary.

Anselmo's important function is to serve as a yardstick of human values, as Kent does in *King Lear.* "That we should win the war and shoot nobody," he fiercely cries. "That we should govern justly and that all should participate in the benefits according as they have striven for them. And that those who have fought against us should be educated to see their error." The Republic must win and Anselmo will fight for the Republic. Yet much that he must do cuts cruelly across the absolute Christian grain of this admirable old man. With Anselmo as a norm, the tragedy of Spain shows all the darker.

Like Anselmo, Robert Jordan is capable of working for a cause without allowing its heretical errors to eat their way like acid into his deeper convictions. Knowing the inside of both Velázquez 63 and the hotel called Gaylord's, Jordan can qualify as the educated man who is in no way "sucked in." Working efficiently as a dynamiter with the Republican guerrillas, loving Spain, hating fascism, sympathizing with the people who have been and are being betrayed, Jordan still manages to be temperate without being at all tepid. His brain is neither dominated nor deceived by the propagandistic. He remains the free man, the man not taken in, the man doing the necessary job but also making the necessary mental reservations.

Jordan's soliloquy—as he listens from below to the hilltop battle in which El Sordo's partisans die—is a key passage in this connection. He reflects that he is in love with Maria, even though "there isn't supposed to be any such thing as love in a purely materialistic conception of society." Then he catches himself. Since when did he really entertain any such conception?

> "Never. And you never could have. You're not a real Marxist and you know it. You believe in Liberty, Equality, and Fraternity. You believe in Life, Liberty, and the Pursuit of Happiness. Don't ever kid yourself with too much dialectics. They are for some but they are not for you. You have to know them in order not to be a sucker. You have put many things in abeyance to win a war. If this war is lost all of those things are lost. But afterwards you can discard what you do not believe in. There is plenty you do not believe in and plenty that you do believe in."

***For Whom the Bell Tolls* offers many examples of the author's determination to maintain that balance without which art may degenerate into propaganda.**

—Carlos Baker

Robert Jordan is with, but not of, the communists. For the duration of the war he is under communist discipline because they offer "the best discipline and the soundest and sanest for the prosecution of the [Spanish] war." This is simple common sense, just as (though Robert Jordan did not live to see it) it was probably common sense for the Allies to fight side by side with the Russians in the second World War—in order to win it. But where the communist dialectic runs contrary to the older dialectics of the French and the American Revolutions, Jordan will remain as an essential nonconformist, a free man not taken in, though doing his part in the perennial attempts which free man must make if the concept of freedom is to last.

. . . . .

The structural form of ***For Whom the Bell Tolls*** has been conceived with care and executed with the utmost brilliance. The form is that of a series of concentric circles with the all-important bridge in the middle. The great concentration which Hemingway achieves is partly dependent on his skill in keeping attention focussed on the bridge while projecting the reader imaginatively far beyond that center of operations. Chapter One immediately establishes the vital strategic importance of the bridge in the coming action. Frequent allusions to the bridge keep it in view through the second chapter, and in Chapter Three Jordan goes with Anselmo to make a preliminary inspection. From that time onwards until its climactic destruction, the bridge continues to stand unforgettably as the focal point in the middle of an ever widening series of circles.

The brilliance of execution becomes apparent when the reader stands in imagination on the flooring of the bridge and looks in any direction. He will see his horizons lifting by degrees towards a circumference far beyond the Guadarrama mountains. For the guerrillas' central task, the blowing of the bridge, is only one phase of a larger operation which Hemingway once called "the greatest holding action in history." Since the battle strategy which requires the bridge to be destroyed is early made available to the reader, he has no difficulty in seeing its relation to the next circle outside, where a republican division under General Golz prepares for an attack. The general's attack, in turn, is enough to suggest the outlines of the whole civil war, while the Heinkel bombers and Fiat pursuit planes which cut across the circle—foreign shadows over the Spanish earth—extend our grasp one more circle outwards to the trans-European aspect of the struggle. The outermost ring of the circle is nothing less than the great globe itself. Once the Spanish holding operation is over, the wheel of fire will encompass the earth. The bridge, therefore—such is the structural achievement of this novel—becomes the hub on which the "future of the human race can turn." Wherever the reader moves along the circumferences of the various circles, all radial roads lead to and from this bridge.

If the reader of ***For Whom the Bell Tolls*** is hardly cramped for space, he is also free to range in time. Jordan's action, particularized though it is, has also a significance *sub specie aeternitatis.* The timelessness of the central event invites the reader to compare it with all those other small and local holding actions which are stuck like gems in the web of history and tend to assume an importance out of all proportion to their size. One civil war easily suggests another, as in Jordan's memories of his grandfather who bore arms in America's war of the rebellion. Behind that, in the long perspective, is the bridge where the republican (and anti-monarchist) "peasants" of Concord fired the shot heard round the world. On a bridge across the Tiber young Horatius delayed briefly the advance of a superior force. Still farther back is the action of Leonidas against the Persian host at the hot gates of Thermopylae. The terrain and the odds were not, after all, far different from those of Robert Jordan. There is even the prediction, comparable to Pilar's, that Leonidas will die, and there is a lone Persian cavalryman who comes, like the fascist horseman in Hemingway, to reconnoitre the mountain pass. Jordan could never complain with Eliot's Gerontion that he had not fought at "the hot gates." His bridge is at the center of the history of holding actions; and although his problem is small in scale, it is so conceived and projected as to suggest a struggle of epical dimensions.

In making such a claim for Hemingway's novel, one must reckon with his own assertion that "all bad writers are in love with the epic." Even a few gifted writers have fallen into the error of attempting too much or going about it in the wrong way. The conscious striving for an epic magnitude, as in some of Whitman's poetry and much of Wolfe's prose, may reduce the writing to rhetoric and enlarge the people to set-piece characters whose resemblance to human beings is merely coincidental. There is also the danger that the struggle for the cosmic may backslide into the comic. The grand manner too easily inflates to the grandiose; good sense may be sacrificed to size; quantity may be mistaken for quality; and what was meant to be great will become simply gross.

As a prose epic of the Spanish people, ***For Whom the Bell Tolls*** commits none of these errors. Indeed the novel is a living example of how, in modern times, the epic quality must probably be projected. The failure of certain modern practitioners of the epic manner rests perhaps primarily upon ignorance of the uses of synecdoche, the device by which a part can be made to function for the whole, and the fact to gain an emblematic power without the loss of its native particularity. Hemingway's war novel, rich as it is in symbolic extensions, is somewhere near a synecdochist's triumph.

What elements of the epic manner may be successfully adapted to modern needs? Despite the obvious gap between Spain and Ilium, the student of the epic may find part of his answer in considering the Homeric parallel. A primitive setting, simple food and wine, the care and use of weapons, the sense of imminent danger, the emphasis on masculine prowess, the presence of varying degrees of courage and cowardice, the rude barbarisms on both sides, the operation of certain religious and magical superstitions, the warrior codes—these, surely, are common ties between the two sets of protagonists. Jordan is not to be scorned as the type of Achilles, and one can recognize in Pablo the rude outlines of a debased and sulking Ajax. Pilar the gypsy, though she reads the lifeline in Jordan's palm instead of consulting the shape and color of animal entrails, makes the consciousness of the supernatural an operative factor.

Nor should the technical comparisons be overlooked. One of the most interesting of these is the intentionally heightened language. Mr. Edward Fenimore has published a valuable essay on the subject ["English and Spanish in ***For Whom the Bell Tolls,***" in *Ernest Hemingway and His Critics,* John McCaffery, ed.]. He remarks, for instance, on "the Elizabethan tone" of a number of phrases and sentences.

> That such a tone should haunt Hemingway's pages is [he goes on] inevitable. His tale has much of the epic in its breadth, in the plain fact that his characters mean more than themselves alone, the action they are engaged upon [being] unmistakably a culminating point pushed up by profound national or . . . universal forces. In the Elizabethan, the English possesses an epic language, and it is into the forms of this language that Hemingway, through the very nature of the world he is creating . . . constantly passes.

Yet, as Fenimore observes, this language is carefully tempered. A purely colloquial modern English and an English which belongs in its essence to the King James version of the Bible are brought together to mutual advantage. One example is a brief interchange between the rough-spoken Agustín and the supremely dignified Fernando—who is, incidentally, one of Hemingway's best-drawn minor characters.

> "Where the hell are you going?" Agustín asked the grave little man as he came up.
>
> "To my duty," Fernando said with dignity.
>
> "Thy duty," said Agustín mockingly. "I besmirch the milk of thy duty. . . . "

Several of Hemingway's short stories had made a similar collocation of the old and dignified with the new and crass. In **"The Gambler, The Nun, and The Radio,"** for example, the contrast is used to underscore the humor of character. Now, however, with his temperamental sensitivity to the tone of language, and an intuitive feel for what would constitute the proper blend of ancient and modern idiom in the conduct of key scenes, whether they were comic or not, Hemingway developed a language suitable to his epic purposes. The masculine vigor in the march of the narrative comes about, not alone from the author's skill in the unfolding of events but also through his responsiveness to language values.

Outside the technical aspects of language one finds an over-all seriousness of conception which, though high enough to meet even Arnold's stringent requirements, does not preclude rough humor and soldierly badinage. As a means of giving depth to his characterizations, Homer knew and used (if indeed he did not invent) the device of the flashback. As for synecdoche, Homer was very far from limiting his range of significance by carefully centering his attention on the action before Troy. All bad writers may love the epic. A few good ones, working somewhat after the fashion of Hemingway, can succeed in keeping the epic genre in a state of good health by adapting transferable elements to the needs and expectations of the modern reader.

The principle of characterization-in-depth is strong in ***For Whom the Bell Tolls***—more so than in any of Hemingway's previous work. If touch-and-go is the mark of the apprentice and the journeyman, stay-and-see may well be one of the attributes of the master. Even though the qualities which distinguished the younger writer still serve Hemingway at forty, he is now ready to move beyond them. Without, for example, sacrificing the value of *suggestion* (where the reader is required to supply his own imaginative clothing for an idea nakedly projected), Hemingway has come round to an appreciation of the value of *ingestion.* This signifies a bearing within, a willingness to put in, and to allow to operate within the substance of a piece of writing, much that formerly would have been excluded in favor of suggestion.

The result of this willingness is a notable gain in richness and depth without sacrifice of the values inherent in the principle of suggestiveness. What Hemingway allows us to know of Pilar's past, for example, enriches, activates, and deepens our sense of her vital performance in the present. The willingness, even the eagerness, to invent that past, to stay and see how it informs the present, is a mark of the transition achieved by the fully mature artist in Hemingway. The will to report has given place to the willingness to invent, though the values of the will to report have not been sacrificed in the process. There were formerly only limited vistas back through time. Now the full panoply of time past is at work in time present. This mode of operation is likewise habitual to the epic genre.

. . . . .

If ***For Whom the Bell Tolls*** is a kind of epic, it is above all a tragic epic. Like the *Iliad,* it may be seen as a study in doom. Madrid, like Troy, was fated to fall. Seventeen months of hindsight on the Spanish war helped to mature in Hemingway a feeling that the republican defeat had been virtually inevitable.

"The Spanish civil war was really lost, of course, [he wrote in 1940] when the Fascists took Irun in the late summer of 1936. But in a war you can never admit, even to yourself, that it is lost. Because when you admit it is lost you are beaten."

Hemingway's choice of the early summer of 1937 as the time of Jordan's action thus takes on special importance. He wanted a period deep enough into the war so that the possibility of republican defeat could be a meaningful psychological force. But the time must also be far enough removed from the end of the war so that some of his people could still believe in a republican victory. The struggle could not seem to be hopeless. Yet, as a study in doom, the novel must early isolate and dramatize those adverse powers and power-failures which would ultimately combine to defeat the Spanish republic.

Robert Jordan's first sight of Pablo gives him an insight into the nature of one power-failure. No republican, at the beginning of the movement, was more in command of himself or the situation than Pablo. Now the guerrilla leader is so far gone in defeatist "sadness" and moral cowardice as almost to doom in advance any undertaking in which he is to play a part.

"I don't like that sadness [Robert Jordan thought]. That sadness is bad. That's the sadness they get before they quit or before they betray. That is the sadness that comes before the sellout."

Pablo is a specific Judas, as his stealing of the detonator will later show. But he is also a recognizable symbol for the general canker of defeatism, gnawing the tissues of republican morale from within, and leading to the larger betrayal.

A second internal danger is the inefficiency of the Republican bureaucracy. A third is an aspect of the Spanish temperament. One gets the impression that a radical inefficiency stretches all the way from the higher echelons in Madrid down to the gypsy Rafael, who is so irresponsible that he runs off to shoot rabbits when he should be standing guard near Pablo's cave. The Russian General Golz, only half-believing that his attack will not be doomed to failure before it even starts, points up the larger difficulties.

> "They are never my attacks [says Golz]. I make them. But they are not mine. The artillery is not mine. I must put in for it. I have never been given what I ask for even when they have it to give. That is the least of it. There are other things. You know how those people are. It is not necessary to go into all of it. Always there is something. Always some one will interfere."

Tangled in red tape like Laocoon in serpents, Golz is not free enough to prosecute a war successfully. The Rafaels of the republican side are too free, and too irresponsible. Bureaucracy and temperament, two more internal foes of the republic, help to fix the doom.

But the most awesome symbol of doom is the air-power of the foreign enemy. All the Spaniards hate it, as they hate the foreigners for interfering in their civil war. When the fascist planes roar over the mountain hide-out, it is always in threes, like the weird sisters, or in those multiples of three with which practitioners of black magic used to conjure.

> "The three passed and then came nine more, flying much higher in the minute, pointed formations of threes and threes and threes . . . He could still hear the receding drone. . . . By now they're well beyond the pass with Castile all yellow and tawny beneath them now in the morning . . . and the shadows of the Heinkels moving over the land as the shadows of sharks pass over a sandy floor of the ocean."

When the planes return, Jordan revises his simile into something even more sinister. They have the shape but not the motion of sharks. "They move like no thing that has ever been. They move like mechanized doom." It is by three such planes that El Sordo's band will be wiped out at three o'clock of the following Monday afternoon.

Hemingway's linking of the modern bombers with the ancient magic-symbol of number three greatly enhances the emotional effectiveness of the plane-passage. The old epics and the great dramatic tragedies could employ supernatural agents in the full expectation that they would intensify the emotions of pity and terror in the spectator. The rise of naturalism, and the partial decay of superstition, denied the tragic artist direct access to one of his most evocative instruments. Yet within the shadowy subconscious, the perennial human capacity for fear and awe remained to be touched by any artist who could empower new symbols with old terrors.

The book touches the edge of the supernatural also by a considered use of premonition. The primary human agent is the gypsy Pilar, who is both a woman and a kind of witch, though a witch very naturalistically portrayed and very womanly in her witchhood. Her function in part is to sharpen the reader's foreboding and thus to deepen his sense of impending tragedy. Having watched Pablo's degeneration through fear, she is both too wise and too fond of Jordan to reveal that she has seen his coming death in the lines of his hand. (Like the Circean "witch" of ***The Sun Also Rises,*** she is a good judge of quality.) But the reader's knowledge of Jordan's coming death gives special point to the passage in which Pilar describes, with naturalistic precision, the three blended odors of the smell of death to come.

The woman-witch dialectic is marked often in the book. In this instance, the woman withholds what the witch has gloomily discovered. Her certainty that Jordan will die has motivated her in bringing the lovers together. This is done both for the therapeutic effect of a healthy love affair on Maria, and in order to give Jordan, through Maria, as much of life as three days will hold. This, one might guess, is the tender side of Pilar. But in the passage on the smell of death to come, she adopts the very tone which will arouse Jordan's doubts as to the truth of what she is saying. He doubts and he argues, and the doubting arguments divert his thoughts at least from the probability, if not from the possibility, of death. The rough railing humor of her presentation is meant to save him from a fear which might undo his resolution, or, at any rate, spoil the closing hours of his short, happy life.

This entire aspect of the novel may well remind some readers of the problem which Henry James set himself in *The Wings of the Dove*—though, as always, there is little or no overt resemblance between the two books. "The idea, reduced to its essence," said James of his own major effort, "is that of a young person conscious of a great capacity for life, but early stricken and doomed, condemned to die under short respite, while also enamoured of the world." A marked "capacity for life," a full acceptance and love of the world, is always a driving motive with the Hemingway hero. It grows even stronger as one moves with Hemingway's work through the nineteen-thirties. Yet Nick Adams has it, Jake Barnes has it, Frederick Henry has it. It is strong in Harry Morgan, though he is not very articulate in expressing what he feels. The love of life—the good life—gives special point to the dying reminiscences of that other Harry, the writer on safari in Africa. Yet the two men called Harry are stricken and doomed, condemned to die under short respite, as is Colonel Richard Cantwell, a lover of life, in ***Across the River and Into the Trees.***

There are other premonitions in ***For Whom the Bell Tolls*** than those we owe to Pilar's supersensory gifts. Jordan, as a partisan soldier, must often consider that he may die at the affair of the bridge. He is compelled to recognize the possibility of death. His life among the Guadarramas may well total three-score hours and ten—seventy hours as a substitute for seventy years. In the meteorological bad luck which brings an unseasonal snowfall, in Pablo's defection, and in the bombing of El Sordo, there is a discernible "pattern of tragedy" which he is too sensible to ignore. But he has also a special soldier's talent "not to ignore but to despise whatever bad endings there could be." From the point of view of the reader, therefore, Jordan's predicament is something like that of the torero who knows that he may be killed but despises death and enters the ring in spite of the possibility. The knowledge, derived through Pilar, that Jordan not only *may* but *will* die gives every incident in Jordan's seventy-hour span of life the special poignancy that would be felt by a spectator who knew in advance that he was watching the last fight of a torero. Through this double perspective, Hemingway gets into his novel the very "feeling of life and death" which he was seeking when he first went to watch the Spanish bullfights.

But the idea that a sane consciousness of death will give added depth and meaning to the events of life is only one of the familiar Hemingway themes in ***For Whom the Bell Tolls.*** Sparing but effective use is also made of the men-without-women, the father-and-son, and the home-versus-war themes. Jordan, for example, shows a kind of spiritual relationship to Pilar in that he can be, by turns, both tender and tough-minded. In one of his aspects, he can love human beings and allow himself to become involved with them, as in his good companionship with Anselmo or his love for Maria. At the other extreme, he must be the cold-minded and detached commander, reserving part of himself in all human relationships so that the necessary job can be done. It is in this detachment that he coldly judges his companions, estimating their relative dependability and expendability, and perfecting his battle-plan in accordance with these estimates. He cannot often expand warmly; as soldier he must contract coldly within himself. "I cannot have a woman, doing what I do," he tells Maria. "But thou art my woman now." After one of their encounters, Maria observes that he is now thinking of something else than love. "Yes," Jordan says, shortly. "My work." On another occasion, talking with Pilar, the men-without-women idea emerges very clearly. "You are a very cold boy," says Pilar. Jordan disagrees. "No," says Pilar. "In the head you are very cold." Jordan replies that he is preoccupied with his work. "But you do not like the things of life?" asks Pilar. "Yes. Very much. But not to interfere with my work." It is not now a liking for hardy masculine comradeship in hunting or fishing or skiing which motivates the Hemingway hero, but a preoccupation with the work a man must do, where women have no place and may even be in the way. The morning Jordan kills the fascist cavalryman, Maria is still beside him in the sleeping-bag. As he quickly and coldly issues orders to Anselmo and Primitivo, he is aware of Maria behind him, dressing herself under the robe. "She had no place in his life now." At the end of the book, both elements are still visible. He is the republican soldier coolly drawing a bead on the fascist Lieutenant Berrendo, and the husband covering his wife's escape.

The closing scene also rounds off the father-and-son theme which has been introduced in Jordan's soliloquies at various earlier times. Jordan's grandfather fought bravely and successfully in the American Civil War. His father, like the father of Nick Adams, died by his own hand. Jordan has long since forgiven his father for the act, but he is still as ashamed of it as he is proud of his grandfather's soldierly bravery. Now, at the end of the line, as Jordan lies nearly fainting under the ballooning pain from his fractured leg, the father-grandfather opposition once more commands his mind. Suicide would be permissible under the circumstances. But the memory of his grandfather, his true spiritual ancestor, helps him to hold onto his courage and to die in combat.

The significance of Maria, when she is seen in the light of such other heroines as Catherine Barkley, Marie Morgan, and even Dorothy Bridges, is finally symbolic. In the lonely alien region of the Guadarramas, she comes to stand as the image of "home." Most of Hemingway's women tend to take on this special symbolic meaning. Dorothy Bridges (a fairly unsympathetic portrait) is explicitly equated with nostalgia, a somewhat untrustworthy reminder of the comforts and the joys which are so rarely possible in a world besieged by the ideology of terror. Catherine Barkley and Marie Morgan, though in different ways, represent normal domesticity vanquished by war and by the economic struggle for survival. Similarly, Maria stands for the normal in the midst of a terrible abnormality. She has been subjected to all sorts of outrages by her fascist captors. The rape is an act of supreme brutality; only the true tenderness of Jordan, as Pilar well knows, can erase the psychological scars the fascists have left. The cutting of Maria's hair is a symbol of her loss of normal womanhood or girlhood, just as its growing-out indicates her gradual return to balance and health.

One might argue, of course, that the normal male-female situation in Hemingway is something like what took place in the Garden of Eden just after the eating of the fruit of the tree, but before the malediction. All these Eves are as pleasuably ductile as the Adams are hirsute and sexually vigorous. Like all travesties, such a characterization would have its element of truth. But it would tend to ignore the real tenderness with which the "good women" in Hemingway are treated. The fate of the heroines is that they are almost never at home; their virtue is that the best of them carry the home-image with them wherever they go.

A fourth well-tried theme handsomely adapted to the uses of the Spanish tragedy is that of *nada,* or nothingness militant. By placing his action among the high slopes of the Sierra de Guadarramas, a clean, well-lighted place where the weather is cold and the air clear, Hemingway has achieved a kind of idyll in the midst of war, an island (like that of Nick Adams in his afternoon grove on the way to the Big Two-Hearted River) surrounded by the sinister. It is there that Maria, raped and probably infected by fascist soldiery, is restored to health and sanity. This is a mountain fastness like Burguete in ***The Sun Also Rises,*** or like the priest's homeland of Abruzzi in ***A Farewell to Arms,*** or like the Alpine sanctuary to which Frederick and Catherine retire for their short happy life together. One sees again the lowland-versus-highland image; on the plain before Madrid the fascists are deployed, but here are high slopes, concealment, and something like the good life, a veritable island in the midst of *nada.* Still, in the words of Donne's devotion, "no man is an island." In this savage war, no mountain can serve as a permanent sanctuary. El Sordo, on his high hilltop position, finds no good life. Fascist cavalry surround it, and three fascist planes destroy it from above. Similarly, when the bridge is blown, Pablo's mountain cave becomes untenable as a refuge. The partisans plan to retreat across the war-swept lowlands to another mountain fastness in the Sierra de Gredos. But the planes of the enemy, in sinister "threes and threes and threes," can presumably come there, too. "I am tired of the mountains," says Pilar in a moment of despondency. "In mountains there are only two directions. Down and up, and down leads only to the road and the towns of the Fascists." And up, one might add, leads to the foreign bombers, assaulting even the highest and loneliest peaks.

Hemingway's sense of fascism's betrayal of the Spanish people has in fact much of the nightmare quality of Picasso's allegorical painting. The mountain-sanctuary, an essentially private symbol in Hemingway's earlier books, is now shown to be open to invasion and destruction by fascist bombers, which the artist carefully establishes as symbols of the power of evil. If one follows Picasso's pictorial allegories through the order of composition from the "Minotauromachy" through the "Sueño y Mentira de Franco" up to the "Guernica," he will see how an essentially private set of symbols is made to take on political significance. In the "Minotauromachy" of 1935, Picasso employs motifs from the bullfight to express symbolically a struggle no doubt personal to himself as artist and Spaniard. The "Guernica" of 1937, occasioned by the bombing of an open Spanish city by foreign planes, regrouped the symbols of the bull and the horse and broke the calm human figures of the *Minotauromachy* into fragments of anguish and fear. In one postwar interview, Picasso refused to identify the bull-figure of the "Guernica" with fascism, though he did give it the generic meaning of "brutality and darkness"—something like Goya's "Nada." The horse, transfixed by a spear which has fallen from above, is however for Picasso a specific symbol for the Spanish people. In somewhat the same way, the destruction of El Sordo's band on the hilltop, like the roar of Heinkel bombers above Jordan's high sanctuary, suggests the horror of brutality and darkness unleashed against a betrayed people.

Among those whom fascism will betray are the artists. Robert Jordan is not only a teacher of Spanish and a lover of Spain; he is also a writer. As an artist he is fully aware of the threat of fascist domination. If fascism were the kind of force which fed upon itself, remaining relatively limited in its dimensions, Jordan's manifest duty would belong to the development of his art—a task so huge that it takes a lifetime to accomplish. During the years of peace, Jordan wrote one book on Spain and the Spanish people. Presumably he would not be averse to doing another. But this is not the time.

In the deeper meaning of ***For Whom the Bell Tolls,*** the invasion of the high sanctuary *from above* marks a transition in the affairs of the artist. Unless the force is stopped, it can mean the death of art as it can mean the death of everything else the artist values and needs. Fascism has become militant, imperialistic, and international. The artist, devoted though he must be to the development of his art, can no more ignore it than he could ignore a storm blowing in at his study window and scattering the pages of his work in progress. His move must be to shut the window against the storm. Still it will not leave him alone. The lightning strikes his house, and it is his obvious duty to save his manuscript and put out the fire. The *blitz* is not what he asked for or what he wanted. Since it has come, he must take arms against it, and end it as soon as possible by opposing it. Then he can go back to his work, if he survives. (pp. 238-59)

Carlos Baker, in his Hemingway: The Writer as Artist, *fourth edition, Princeton University Press, 1972, 438 p.*

Jack Adler (essay date Summer 1964)

[In the following essay, Adler discusses how the secondary characters in For Whom the Bell Tolls *contribute to the themes of insubordination and courage.]*

Many of the subsidiary characters in the novels of Ernest Hemingway are not important in their own right, but there are notable exceptions in his ***For Whom the Bell Tolls.*** Pilar, Andrés, Anselmo, Maria, and particularly Pablo, though they do not occupy major positions, are given a fairly full treatment. These characters also differ from the subsidiary characters in the earlier novels in another way: they make individual responses to and provide individual illustrations of the novel's main themes, and these variant responses are contrasted with those of Jordan, the hero. I shall try to show how subsidiary characters contribute to two of the most important themes in this novel, the themes of insubordination and courage.

Jordan is aware of the difficulties which might arise in obeying orders. Circumstances may change and it may then be necessary to issue new instructions to all those concerned. If circumstances change at a crucial moment, when there is neither time nor opportunity to consult the next-in-command, it may become necessary for a subordinate to make a decision. Yet, as Jordan realizes, a subordinate seldom knows enough of the facts to be in a position to take matters into his own hands.

When Jordan finds out that there are Fascist troop movements in the Guadarramas, he concludes that the Fascists have got wind of the pending Republican attack. He decides to send a note to Golz, who is organizing the attack, suggesting that it is called off. He realizes, however, that he himself may not know enough about the nature of the attack and that Golz may have his own reasons for not wishing to call it off: "What do I know about why this attack is made? Maybe it is only a holding attack. Maybe they want to draw those troops from somewhere else. Perhaps they make it to draw those planes from the North. Maybe that is what it is about. Perhaps it is not expected to succeed. What do I know about it?"

[In his "Ernest Hemingway and the Psychology of the Lost Generation," in *The Novel and the World's Dilemma*] E. M. Burgum considers that Jordan ought to have decided on his own initiative not to blow up the bridge. He does not accept Jordan's reasons for not doing so and concludes that he lacks initiative. From this premise he argues that Jordan has no powers of analysis and this, in turn—so Burgum argues—shows that the Republican forces are anarchic. Burgum gives insufficient weight to the fact that Jordan cannot gauge the over-all situation, a fact which Jordan states very clearly. There is certainly no mysticism (Burgum claims there is) in Jordan's consideration of the complex problem of subordination:

> Should a man carry out impossible orders knowing what they lead to? . . . Yes. He should carry them out because it is only in the performing of them that they can prove to be impossible. How do you know they are impossible until you have tried them? If everyone said orders were impossible to carry out when they were received where would you be?

Jordan is obedient and expects obedience from others; for him this is the only basis on which the war can be successfully waged. He considers it right that troops running away from battle should be shot:

> Up . . . [in the Sierras] when there had been the first necessity for the enforcement of discipline he had approved and understood it. Under the shelling men had been cowards and had run. He had seen them shot and left to swell beside the road . . .
>
> It had seemed just and right and necessary that the men who ran were shot.

Burgum might have changed his mind about Jordan's lack of initiative had he taken into account the treatment of the theme of insubordination in the novel as a whole. A number of subsidiary characters are faced with similar problems, to which they respond in a variety of ways. Jordan's recommendation to call off the attack reaches Duval, an officer serving under Golz, but he too cannot take the responsibility of calling off the attack because he too realizes that he may not have enough information: "He would call the airfield directly and get the bombardment cancelled. But suppose it's just a holding attack? Suppose we were supposed to draw off all that material and those forces? Suppose that is what it is for? They never tell you it is a holding attack when you make it."

This is a case where one person's decision would directly involve a large number of others. The same problem exists, however, even when the decision does not seem to involve others; the person making the decision cannot know all the possible implications of his decision and it does not require much thought to realize that others might well be involved.

Anselmo's experience is a case in point. Jordan instructs him to observe enemy movements over the bridge and leaves him at his post for a long period of time in extreme cold. Anselmo feels that it might be in order to return to camp, but he remembers that he has been given precise instructions to wait to be relieved and he decides that he must obey these instructions. He cannot take matters into his own hands for, like Jordan and Duval when they consider having the attack called off, he is not in a position to know enough of the facts. He realizes, for instance, that Jordan might come out looking for him and might lose his way if he has not waited for him.

Jordan finds Anselmo's reaction irrational; he feels that the reasonable course of action, under the circumstances, would have been to return to camp, but this is because he, unlike Anselmo, does know all the facts relating to Anselmo's task. Anselmo's obedience makes Jordan intensely happy for, as he says elsewhere in the novel, the lack of discipline is a major weakness of the Republican forces: "He was very happy with that sudden, rare happiness that can come to anyone with a command in a revolutionary army; the happiness of finding that even one of your flanks holds."

Rafael's desertion of his post is a straightforward illustration of simple insubordination. He has no decision to make and there are no changed circumstances which call for individual action. He leaves his post in order to catch a rabbit and his absence from his post allows a Fascist horseman to enter the camp unobserved. Fortunately, Jordan intercepts the horseman and prevents him from taking the partisans by surprise.

A different situation exists when an order seems to be a foolish one because it is made by an officer who rashly miscalculates, particularly when a subordinate officer is in his presence. Berrendo is placed in such a situation and it is an extremely interesting one. This incident takes place during Sordo's last stand. The Fascists have surrounded him and his group on a hilltop, and he fires a few bursts of shot into the carcass of a dead horse in order to make the Fascists believe that he and his men have killed themselves. Mora, the Fascist commanding officer, believing that Sordo and his men have killed themselves, orders Barrendo, his next in command, to accompany him up the hillside to the spot where he thinks Sordo and his men lie dead. Berrendo refuses to obey.

Here is a case where it is judicious and correct to refuse to obey an order. The reader, knowing that Sordo and his men are alive on the hilltop, realizes that Berrendo's assessment of the situation is correct (Mora subsequently

Hemingway as war correspondent, travelling with Loyalist soldiers, Ebro River, 1938.

saunters up the hillside and is killed by Sordo). Furthermore, Berrendo is presented as a sympathetic character—he is sensitive and religious—while Mora is irritable and filled with a sense of his own importance. In this situation the subordinate officer is in possession of exactly the same set of facts as his commanding officer, and this is a case where insubordination is wise, permissible, and commendable.

It is ironical that the circumstances attending Berrendo's death should parallel those attending Mora's—both men are surprised by a concealed partisan. Berrendo may have disobeyed Mora wisely on this occasion, "but they killed you in the end. You could count on that. Stay around and they would kill you." The closing lines of the novel contain a masterly juxtaposition of two contrasted views of insubordination: Hemingway's view, which emerges from the novel as a whole, that there may be certain special cases where it is right for a man to disobey orders, and Jordan's view that a man must never refuse to obey orders and that he should even carry out impossible ones.

Hemingway presents the theme of insubordination briefly in ***A Farewell to Arms*** when Henry shoots at the two Italian sergeants who refuse to obey his orders. There are, however, no contrasted views of insubordination and the view which emerges from the novel as a whole is equivalent to Henry's view. Hemingway treats the theme of insubordination more extensively in ***For Whom the Bell Tolls*** by allowing a number of subsidiary characters to be concerned with this theme and the result is that the view which emerges from the novel as a whole is not equivalent to the hero's view. The views of the subsidiary characters differ to varying extents from Jordan's view, which is thus thrown into sharper relief. The terms and conditions of life are not as simplified in ***For Whom the Bell Tolls*** as they are in ***A Farewell to Arms.***

Another important theme in ***For Whom the Bell Tolls*** is the theme of courage. It is Jordan's ideal to be courageous, though he usually falls short of this ideal. Courageous action demands swift action with a minimum of thinking upon the event; thought inevitably blunts the edge of action.

Jordan realizes that Pablo may become a threat to the success of the venture. He considers that Pablo's first friendly act will mark his defection and on the first evening in the cave Pablo relinquishes the leadership of the group to Pilar. Jordan prepares to kill Pablo that night but fails to do so. Later he gives reasons for not having acted: he was tired, his judgment was faulty, the presence of Pablo's corpse in the cave would have been dispiriting, he is a stranger and "for a stranger to kill where he must work with the people afterwards is very bad." These reasons are based on rationalizations after the event; they are attempts to justify his failure to act and they are not the real motives which prevented him from taking action. The true reason for his failure to act is his inability to kill in cold blood: "It may be done in action . . . " He waited for Pablo to provoke him sufficiently, but he waited in vain.

Jordan experiences a conflict between reason and emotion: reason prompts him to act; emotion prevents him from acting. On the one hand, his inaction points to a falling short of the courageous action which he hopes to be able to perform; on the other hand, his restraint points to his sensitivity, for to kill Pablo at this time might appear needlessly brutal.

The second evening in the cave is similar to the first. Again Jordan is convinced that Pablo is dangerous and that he should be killed:

> "I'd like to kill him and have it over with," Robert Jordan was thinking. "I don't know what he is going to do, but it is nothing good. Day after to-morrow is the bridge and this man is bad and he constitutes a danger to the success of the whole enterprise. Come on. Let us get it over with."

Again he tries to provoke Pablo but, though Pablo makes taunting remarks, he is not sufficiently provocative to compel Jordan to act. Pablo leaves the cave, and Pilar, taking the initiative, asks the others whether they agree that Pablo should be killed. Rafael, Agustin, Andrés, Eladio, and Primitivo agree and Jordan undertakes to carry out the task: " 'I am ready to do it. Since you are all decided that it should be done, it is a service that I can do.' " When Pablo, who has overheard the plot to kill him, returns to the cave, Jordan is still anxious to kill him, but he is not prepared to provoke him. Then Jordan realizes that he cannot shoot Pablo inside the cave because the dynamite, which is being stored there, might explode. He becomes irritated: "All of this business of Pablo is something with which I should never have been saddled and it will be solved one way or another. There will be Pablo or there will be no Pablo. I care nothing about it either way."

Pablo then submits to Jordan's leadership and Jordan ought to regard this "friendly" act as a potentially dangerous one, particularly as he realizes that Pablo has overheard the plotting. However, he ignores him: he looks over his plans for the blowing up of the bridge, drifts into a reverie in which he relives certain past experiences, listens to Pilar's account of her power of intuition, and finally takes Maria with him to bed.

On this second evening, Jordan has less excuse for not acting than he had on the previous evening. On this occasion he knows that the others are in favor of the killing; by now, too, he feels more certain about Pablo's treacherous nature. He is not strictly honest in declaring that he has "been saddled" with the killing for he has volunteered to perform it. There is now less cause than there was on the first evening for his sensitivity to prevent him from taking action. His determination to act must be held in doubt.

At the close of the novel Jordan succeeds in living up to his ideal of courage. In intense pain and close to death, he manages to retain consciousness long enough to oppose the oncoming Fascist soldiers. He considers committing suicide but, by invoking the memory of his grandfather, manages to overcome the temptation to take the course which his father has taken. He thinks of his father and grandfather at a number of critical moments during a lull in the action. His father represents a man without courage; his grandfather, who fought bravely in the American Civil War, represents the courageous man. Jordan tries to model himself on his grandfather and finds a spur to courageous action by invoking his memory. His father's suicide troubles him; he is, for instance, unwilling to admit the truth of his father's death to Pilar and Maria. Rafael's song, coming as it does at the moment when Jordan fails to kill Pablo, provides an ironic comment on the powerful influence which his father's suicide exercises over him:

> I had an inheritance from my father . . .
> It was the moon and the sun
> And though I roam all over the world
> The spending of it's never done.

The novel contains a number of cowardly characters and, not surprisingly, they outlive the courageous ones. Certain acts are decidedly cowardly and we are left in no doubt about Hemingway's attitude towards them. A tank driver refuses to drive his tank through a dangerous zone and Jordan forces him to do so at pistol point. Rafael, who seeks his own safety before that of others, is one of the least sympathetic of the partisans.

Few of the characters, however, act in an altogether cowardly manner; many of them act with a qualified bravery. Indeed, it would be a superficial view which insisted on classifying actions as either completely cowardly or courageous ones. The treatment of the theme of courage in ***For Whom the Bell Tolls*** shows this moral complexity.

A wide spectrum of courageous action is shown, ranging from the superb and thoughtless courage of the silent Sordo, who is firmly attached to life yet accepts death when it comes, to the reckless, needless, and stupid bravery of Mora, which is in great part sheer bravado. Between these two extreme kinds of courage is Kashkin's, which is qualified by his fear of capture, and Andrés' which is qualified, whether in the bullring or in battle, by his fear of injury and death.

The presentation of Ricardo, one of the Fascists who is put to death by Pablo and his group, provides an instance of the unexpected and unfortunate results which bravery may produce. He is the bravest of the Fascists; he accepts his end and calls insults at those who are about to put him to death. Pilar points out that "Don Ricardo with all his bravery did a great disservice to the others. For he aroused the men in the line and where, before, they were performing a duty and with no great taste for it, now they were angry, and the difference was apparent."

The unfortunate consequences of Ricardo's bravery, which provide another illustration of the truth of the passage from Donne from which the title of the novel is taken, suggest that bravery is only one of two important qualities and that the other is consideration for others. The one is a personal quality, the other is a social one. The two qualities are often found in conflict with each other but a compromise is possible and may yield the best results. The character who possesses the two qualities in their best working proportions will act courageously when courageous action is demanded, but will also have a keen social awareness in order to be able to choose the appropriate moment for courageous action. What is most important is that he should retain his social awareness in the midst of action.

Anselmo is such a character. He is related to the priest in ***A Farewell to Arms:*** both are fond of the countryside and both love to hunt, Anselmo "more than anything." Both are opposed to war and the taking of life. But though neither of them is an intimate member of a group, the priest is permanently debarred from membership—the baiting shows how he is set apart—while Anselmo is excluded from the partisan group only because he has been appointed to serve as their courier. Anselmo is thus well placed, both formally and temperamentally, to act as a Kent. Whereas the priest, though fervently hoping that the war will soon come to an end, becomes disheartened by it, Anselmo, also wishing "that . . . [he] were in . . . [his] own house again and that this war were over" accepts his obligations and, like Kent, contends valiantly.

Anselmo points out that neither side is wholly right:

> The fascists are warm, he thought, and they are comfortable, and to-morrow night we will kill them. It is a strange thing and I do not like to think of it. I have watched them all day and they are the same men that we are. I believe that I could walk up to the mill and knock on the door and I would be welcome except that they have orders to challenge all travellers and ask to see their papers. It is only orders that come between us. Those men are not fascists . . . They should never be fighting against us and I do not like to think of the killing.

He sympathizes with the enemy soldiers but realizes that his sympathy is unavailing. When he sees the decapitated body of Sordo being carried down from the mountain, he reflects with great distaste on the task which he will have to perform on the following day. He feels that he will be able to play his part only if Jordan takes him in hand and directs his every move: "I will do exactly as the *Inglés* says and as he says to do it. But let me be close to him, O Lord, and may his instructions be exact for I do not think that I could control myself under the bombardment of the planes."

He considers it his duty to stifle the dictate of his social conscience, which "does make cowards of us all," and to take life: "Yes, man, yes . . . We have to kill them and we kill them." When the time comes to go into action, he is fearless, calm, and dignified. After firing his first shot and killing the guard, he functions smoothly and efficiently and feels excited and close to his comrades. Ironically, he is not killed by the enemy but as a direct result of Pablo's treachery. Nevertheless, his death crowns his most intense moments, during which he is acutely aware of being part of a whole: "He was one with the wire in his hand and one with the bridge, and one with the charges the *Inglés* had placed. He was one with the *Inglés* still working under the bridge and he was one with all of the battle and with the Republic."

His sensitivity, and particularly the conflict between his conscience and his duty, are features which Jordan possesses, though Anselmo's conflict is a less serious and complex one than Jordan's. (pp. 293-99)

Jack Adler, "Theme and Character in Hemingway: 'For Whom the Bell Tolls'," in University Review, *Vol. XXX, No. 4, Summer, 1964, pp. 293-99.*

Robert W. Lewis, Jr. (essay date 1965)

[In the following excerpt, originally published in 1965, Lewis explores the subjects of love and war in Hemingway's novel.]

For Whom the Bell Tolls (1940) is the last novel in what may be called Hemingway's middle, transitional period. It appeared at the end of a decade of writing which was marred by a cooling off of the critics' praise—perhaps in terms of craftsmanship a justified critical change. The Spanish novel was itself, however, highly successful and generally well received by the critics. It preceded a decade of silence; Hemingway was not to publish anything save journalistic dispatches and several introductions until ***Across the River and into the Trees*** in 1950.

Thus, though the beginning of this period is difficult to set precisely, the end of it is conveniently marked chronologically and thematically. To simplify and illustrate the marking of the periods, one might say that before the middle period Hemingway wrote ironically of Robert Cohn's devotion to W. H. Hudson's *The Purple Land* and its romantic vision. It would be hard to imagine Hemingway writing ironically about a Robert Cohn at the end of this period. In ***For Whom the Bell Tolls*** his latter-day Robert, also with a good Hebraic allusion in his last name (Jordan), has ideals and an ideal love, both of which are tested in action and proved to be sound.

That Hemingway had a conscious theme of agape in mind is indicated by the title and the epigraph. Yet the question remains whether or not the novel is a successful demonstration of that theme. Furthermore, what happens to the ideas of eros and the Tristan myth of romantic love? Has Hemingway resurrected romantic love? Restored the "necessary illusion" of love that Joseph Wood Krutch wrote of in 1929 in *The Modern Temper*? Or merely begun to go soft? One might answer each of these last questions positively, but there is a reading of the novel which transcends these questions and which sees the novel as a fairly consistent argument for a blend of eros and agape set in a mode that might be described as mythic realism, a phrase that could, after all, also describe the earlier ***The Sun Also Rises*** and ***A Farewell to Arms.***

An important difference is that of characterization. Although the Spanish novel has so-called romantic elements, the hero Robert Jordan is no Tristan—no Jake Barnes and no Lieutenant Henry. Nor is Maria a Brett Ashley or even a Catherine Barkley. Instead of the expatriates of Paris or the soldiers of World War I, Hemingway writes of Spanish guerrillas who are for the most part unlettered and unsophisticated. It is true that the love story of Jordan and Maria bears a strong resemblance to that of Lieutenant Henry and Catherine of ***A Farewell to Arms,*** but the differences at least indicate a strong shift in purpose, a conscious attempt to see love in a different way and to reinterpret its values. The difference is crystallized in the endings: not the heroine, but the hero, Robert Jordan, dies, and he dies for a reason, a cause; but Catherine Barkley of the earlier novel dies, as Lieutenant Henry believes, for no reason at all; she has simply been caught in a biological trap.

The opening of Bédier's *Tristan* ("My lords, if you would hear a high tale of love and death . . .") could preface ***For Whom the Bell Tolls,*** just as it could ***A Farewell to Arms.*** With acute ironic effect it could preface ***The Sun Also Rises*** and ***To Have and Have Not*** also; the death in the former novel is merely the death of romantic love; the love in the latter novel between Harry Morgan and his wife is singularly unromantic, in the traditional way of courtly love. But there are profound differences between Lieutenant Henry and Robert Jordan. Perhaps neither Hemingway the author nor his hero has yet understood what he is about—"All we know is that we do not know"—but they demonstrate an important shift toward agape. Their attitudes toward love will never be the same. (pp. 143-44)

The obvious material of the Spanish novel is the ancient epic material of a story of love imposed upon a story of war. It is the pattern of the *Iliad* and the *Aeneid* as well as ***A Farewell to Arms,*** and, less directly, of ***Across the River and into the Trees.*** Important differences, of course, lie in the kinds of love Homer, Virgil, and Hemingway depict. Agape and eros existed for the Greek and Roman, but romantic love was, if anything, merely an aberration of a sick mind. Nor is it likely that the earlier epic writers consciously used war as a sin or evil that diametrically opposed love as hate opposes agape. For Hemingway, the concept of love unifies the stories of war and love. The tragedy of war is not so much its death and destruction, for these are man's lot in many forms other than war. War is horrible because it is a type of complete hatred, the total, irrational negation of love. Thus civil war is the worst sort of war, for it is fought between compatriots and kinsmen who have had the opportunity to love each other. That they have turned from love and that they are most cruel and savage to each other is the bitterest of ironies.

A central dilemma for Robert Jordan is that he has come to Spain because he loves the Spanish people and their country, but he is very clearly not committed to communism or anarchism; his politics stop at a belief in liberty, equality, and fraternity. He feels he is justified in fighting against forces which seem opposed to these principles in Spain. That the fascists are being backed by non-Spanish powers (Italy and Germany) makes Jordan's decision initially simple. And his later realization that International Communism is using the Spanish people for equally materialistic ends is an unfortunate but reconcilable discovery. In the narration of the last three days of Jordan's enlistment in the cause—the period of time which the novel covers—Jordan comes to see the futility of his sacrifice, even though he heroically makes that sacrifice without tears or regret. He has, however, modified his cause. He dies *after* he has obtained the love of a woman and the respect and affection of the guerrillas, for whom he makes a final effort of will (to insure their safe escape). Without the personal love of Maria and the guerrillas, he would have died badly and futilely and bitterly.

His death, however, is not completely satisfactory. His struggle to remain conscious and to keep from destroying himself is symbolically understandable when, victorious in this struggle, he aligns the sights of his machine gun on Lieutenant Berrendo, the fascist officer who, in an earlier episode, had shown himself to be a good man. In his last act, Jordan will destroy, for the love of his friends, another soldier with virtues similar to his own. War cannot offer any satisfactory black-white, good-evil solutions. The means being destructive, the result will be destructive. The Loyalist attack which justified Jordan's blowing of the bridge and which led to his death is a debacle that was foredoomed because of treachery. The messenger who could have had the attack and the blowing of the bridge postponed is held up by the Loyalists themselves and is almost killed as a spy. (pp. 148-49)

It is significant that Jordan's eminent death is a solitary one. Whatever the justification for hate and destruction is, the man who gives himself to those forces of death will suffer isolation, loneliness, and despair. Before he volunteered for duty in Spain and for the particular assignment of blowing up the bridge, Jordan had been, it would seem, an unattached man. He has a family, of whom he thinks only briefly, but no wife. In the guerrilla's cave he finds both a wife and a family. For their safety, he resists unconsciousness and the urge to commit suicide as easy ways out. Yet he is still lonely.

Earlier, at the bridge, he had felt the loneliness of hate and destruction. "He would like to have had the squirrel with him in his pocket. He would have liked to have had anything that he could touch. He rubbed his elbows against the pine needles but it was not the same. Nobody knows how lonely you can be when you do this."

And after the bridge, the elation of action is gone.

> The anger and the emptiness and the hate that had come with the let-down after the bridge, when he had looked up from where he had lain and crouching, seen Anselmo dead, were still all through him. In him, too, was despair from the sorrow that soldiers turn to hatred in order that they may continue to be soldiers. Now it was over he was lonely, detached and unrelated and he hated every one he saw.

Jordan conquers this hatred when he remembers that he must rid himself of egotism and that then the hate will ebb. But at his sacrificial death the loneliness returns, because, whatever its merits, it is a death of hate and more destruction. The alcohol that would have helped is gone—"the flask was not there when he felt for it. Then he felt that much more alone because he knew there was not going to be even that. I guess I'd counted on that, he said"—and so Jordan must argue with himself to steel his body and mind against the pain of his broken leg (another castrative wound) and the physical and moral fear that eats at his resolution. The love of Maria makes the difference, for while she lives and loves the memory of Jordan, he had explained, some part of Jordan will be with her.

> "As long as there is one of us there is both of us. . . . What I do now I do alone. I could not do it well with thee. If thou goest then I go, too. Do you not see how it is? Whichever one there is, is both."
>
> "I will stay with thee."
>
> "Nay, rabbit. Listen. That people cannot do together. Each one must do it alone. But if thou goest then I go with thee. It is in the way that I go too. Thou wilt go now, I know. For thou art good and kind. Thou wilt go now for us both."

The function or "use" of Maria as an antidote for loneliness is known to Jordan much before his death, of course. During their second night together " . . . he felt the long light body, warm against him, comforting against him, abolishing loneliness against him, magically, by a simple touching of flanks, of shoulders and of feet, making an alliance against death with him. . . . "

In general, Pablo is a foil for Jordan, but in respect to the idea of loneliness they are much alike. Both of them turn to alcohol as a solace for their isolation that was born in them by their barbarity. In the early days of the war, Pablo says, " 'I was very barbarous. . . .

> "I am drunk on wine and and would be happy except for those people I have killed. All of them fill me with sorrow. . . . "
>
> "I would restore them all to life."
>
> "And then you would walk on the water," Pilar said.

Whiskey, Anselmo says, " '*That* is what kills the worm that haunts us.' "

When Jordan first arrives at Pablo's camp, Pilar tells the American that Pablo has " 'taken a leather wine bottle to drink alone in the woods.' " Jordan drinks wine with all the guerrillas, but he tries to save the anesthetic absinthe for himself alone. The "real" absinthe that Jordan drinks has wormwood in it and is as bitter as gall.

In his loneliness, Pablo looks for consolation in the bottom of the cup and then seeks it in conversation with his beloved horses. After the guerrillas have deposed him as their leader, he talks to his bay stallion as if the horse were a sympathetic human, as if the horse could receive and reciprocate the love Pablo cannot find with the other guerrillas and the interloper Jordan.

> "Thou my big good little pony," Pablo was saying to the horse in the dark; it was the big bay stallion he was speaking to. "Thou lovely white-faced big beauty. Thou with the big neck arching like the viaduct of my pueblo," he stopped. "But arching more and much finer." The horse was snatching grass, swinging his head sideways as he pulled, annoyed by the man and his talking. "Thou art no woman, nor a fool," Pablo told the bay horse. "Thou, oh, thou, thee, thee, my big little pony. Thou art no woman like a rock that is burning. Thou art no colt of a girl with cropped head and the movement of a foal still wet from its mother. Thou dost not insult nor lie nor not understand. Thou, oh, thee, oh my good big little pony."

But the horse is merely annoyed by Pablo. He is not human; he cannot love.

Later Pilar tells Jordan:

> "Every one needs to talk to some one," the woman said. "Before we had religion and other nonsense. Now for every one there should be some one to whom one can speak frankly, for all the valor that one could have one becomes very alone."
>
> "We are not alone. We are all together [Jordan answers]."

But Pablo hangs on the fringe of the group, mocking it and its suicidal plan to blow the bridge, but still being unable to run away from the group that he needs. Even within the cave, Pablo "sat by himself," and refused to have anything to do with Jordan's plans. He is entirely alone and even antisocial, in a profound way, when he steals Jordan's dynamite exploders and threatens to ruin the plan entirely.

Now gone from the group physically as well as spiritually, Pablo can stand the sickness and hollowness no longer. He had irretrievably thrown away the exploders, but had then found himself "too lonely." He still hates Jordan for having brought a difficult mission to his people, but he realizes " 'if we must finish we must finish together.' " Having run off, Pablo has found " 'a loneliness that cannot be borne. . . . I do not like to be alone. *Sabes?* Yesterday all day alone working for the good of all I was not lonely. But last night. *Hombre! Qué mal lo pasé!* ' "

Even the goodly Anselmo tastes the bad kind of loneliness when he spends a day by himself watching the bridge and the road. His loneliness comes from the killing he has done. When he is alone, he thinks of his violence, which he is sorry for but which he thinks was necessary because of the war. " . . . he felt so lonely that there was a hollowness in him as of hunger," a hunger that is partly assuaged when he reasons that he has at least worked hard for the Republic and "the good that we will all share later."

Thus the problem that Pablo poses: he has in the past been needlessly brutal. Now in his sorrow and remorse he is a real danger to the others in their plans to kill and destroy in order to have a good future without death and hate. Yet when the other guerrillas agree to kill Pablo, he shrewdly plays the role of an innocent, and he thinks that no one has the *cojones* to murder him. Jordan will kill him if he has to, but he does not hate Pablo. The guerrillas vacillate too long, and Pablo lives, first to betray them by stealing the exploders, second to aid them by returning to bring more guerrillas and horses, and third to guarantee their safe escape from the bridge by more brutality—he machine-guns the new guerrillas without any qualms, for his friends' lives are at stake. The bigger cause of the Republic does not matter, and Pablo does not know that "every man is a piece of the *Continent.*" " 'They were not of our band,' " he explains. The cruel wheel of fortune revolves once more. The murdered guerrillas remain in the shadows, except for one, a "good shepherd" whom Pilar knows and who feels "gravity" within him. This other good shepherd will also die futilely, and Pablo, saving his people, will again come to know their ingratitude and horror for a heinous crime committed in the name of love. [In *The Novel of Violence in America*] W. M. Frohock uses ***For Whom the Bell Tolls*** as an example of the novel of violence or, in Jean Pouillon's phrase, the novel of destiny:

> The hero finds himself in a predicament such that the only possible exit is through inflicting physical harm on some other human. In the infliction of harm he also finds the way to his own destruction. But still he accepts the way of violence because life, as he sees life, is like that: violence is man's fate.

Jordan's final sacrifice is ironically illuminated when it is compared with Pablo's sacrifice and crucifixion of the good shepherd and his band, for Jordan too will be, though unwittingly, killing a good man, Lieutenant Berrendo. Jordan is horrified by Pablo's deed and in ignorance of one aspect of his own, yet Jordan is conscious of the reasons for his need of, first, alcohol and then Maria. Both have powers to assuage the loneliness of hate. The significant difference between Pablo and Jordan is the difference of recognition. Pablo can only feel his loneliness and act, paradoxically and brutally, to remedy it. Jordan both feels and understands, and when he acts, his knowledge gives a nobility and sense of tragedy to his actions. He senses his moral dilemma, even if he does not specifically know who Lieutenant Berrendo, his final adversary, is. In the words of the Talmud, "Whosoever saves a single life is as if he had saved the whole world; whosoever destroys a single life is as if he had destroyed the whole world."

The moral predicament of a war for love is widely demonstrated in passages about the necessity of forgetting violence; reconciling the "cause" with murder; the inhuman rigidity of military orders; the brutalizing effect of war; the disillusionment of a "just" war; the necessity of lies in war; the ecstasy and purging of battle, followed by disillusionment; killing of fine people on both sides; deserting the few for the good of the many; allowing El Sordo's band to die unaided, so that the mission may be carried out; the Republican generals who hate each other and cannot believe in the people; determination of sides in the war by circumstantial facts and fate; Andrés' speeding through enemy territory but being fatally delayed by suspicion, fear, ignorance, and red tape in friendly territory; failure of Loyalist attack because of treachery; and the irony that soldiers must hate in order to live.

Certain images and episodes combine the ideas of war, hate, and death with eros, and thus they provide a link between two of the three controlling motifs of the novel: war (a kind of antilove), eros, and agape. In addition to the above-mentioned sexual allusions in Pilar's story of the Republican seizure of the village and particularly of Pablo's impotence on that night after the brutal victory, we learn that the hardened fighter Pilar had been the mistress of a bullfighter who had died of tuberculosis.

> She was with him thus five years and never was unfaithful to him, that is almost never, and then after the funeral, she took up with Pablo who led picador horses in the ring and was like all the bulls that Finito had spent his life killing. But neither bull force nor bull courage lasted, she knew now, and what did last? I last, she thought. Yes, I have lasted. But for what?

For all her loving of these two men, Pilar has never conceived. She is that rarity, a barren gypsy. Maria, too, may be a barren lover. Pilar says that when she was raped by the fascists, if she could she would have then conceived. But rape is hardly even eros; it is divorced from productivity; it is death, a form of extreme violence. While lying in his sleeping bag with Maria, Jordan kills the fascist scout:

> "Thou," she said. "I saw all."
>
> "Thou saw nothing. One man. One man from a horse. *Vete.* Get thee back."
>
> "Say that you love me."
>
> "No. Not now."
>
> "Not love me now? . . . "
>
> "One does not do that and love all in the same moment."
>
> "I want to go to hold the legs of the gun and while it speaks love thee all in the same moment."
>
> "Thou art crazy. Get thee back now."
>
> "I am not crazy," she said. "I love thee."
>
> "Then get thee back."
>
> "Good. I go. And if thou dost not love me, I love thee enough for both."

Maria's love that can combine love with death, that can unconsciously link the phallus and the machine gun, is to Jordan an insanity. She has "no place in his life now," he thinks. Perhaps he is also thinking of Pilar's morbidly fascinating description of the odor of death as being compounded of the smell of a brass porthole on a rolling ship, the smell of the mouth of an old woman who has just drunk the blood of slaughtered beasts, the smell of dead chrysanthemums, the odor of the slops and refuse of whorehouses—the "odor of love's labor lost"—and the mixed smell of dead flowers, dead earth, and the sexual doings of worn-out whores. This smell of lovemaking in such a context is no longer the smell of life, but of death. Eros corrupted is death, and Jordan fears it and will not smell Pilar's wonderful concoction.

Perhaps Jordan is also thinking of the death-through-love that was the fate of his father who was driven to suicide by a bullying wife.

In both cases the love is eros alone, and Maria feels and represents something beyond that. War is a whore— " *'Qué puta es la guerra* . . . War is a bitchery.' " Eros alone is foul, is death and the smell of death, the smell of the whorehouse. But love is not eros alone.

Eros alone is allied to anger and fear and, through its association with romantic love, it is also allied to death, paradoxical as that may be, since it is also the source of life. Perhaps the best approach to an understanding of the ambivalence of eros is through the dominant symbol of it that Hemingway uses: the horse. From the first chapter to the last, repeated references to horses focus the reader's attention upon them even when they seemingly appear as mere background shadows. It would seem more than coincidence that in ***The Fifth Column*** the names of the hero and heroine foreshadow aspects of the novel. Jordan is a bridge destroyer, and Philip Rawlings of the play sexually "destroys" Dorothy Bridges. ("Destroy" is used in this sexual sense in **"The Snows of Kilimanjaro"**, published two years before the play and also containing a bitch as heroine.) More pertinent here, though also more tenuous, is the literal meaning of Philip—"lover of horses."

When Jordan arrives at the guerrillas' camp, the first things he notices are cropped grass, signs of picketing, a horse trail, and fresh manure. Then he sees the horses in their corral. From Jordan's first arrival, the guerrillas' camp is consciously and strongly associated with these funerary and erotic symbols. The ancient use of the horse as a funerary beast is combined with his use as a symbol of maleness and virility to suggest a link with the concept of death as a desirable end to romantic love.

Pablo is a sad, isolated man, but he has some spirit and joy with his horses, of which he is very proud and loving. When he learns that Jordan too is a "man of horses," a rapport is established between them. For Pablo, stealing and capturing horses has become an end in itself; the killing of the enemy who rode the horses is almost incidental. The only glory of his life is his horses. Anselmo rebukes Pablo for his selfishness and his excessive love of his horses (a meaningful combination):

> "Thyself now since a long time. Thyself and thy horses. Until thou hadst horses thou wert with us. Now thou art another capitalist more."
>
> "That is unjust," said Pablo. "I expose the horses all the time for the cause."

They argue. " 'I am an old man who is afraid of no one,' Anselmo tells him. 'Also I am an old man without horses.' "

The burden of eros no longer troubles the old man as it does Jordan and Pablo. While Jordan tries to figure out the reliability of Pablo the horse-lover, his own thoughts wander back to the horses.

> They are awfully good horses, though, he thought, beautiful horses. I wonder what could make me feel the way those horses make Pablo feel. The old man was right. The horses made him rich and as soon as he was rich he wanted to enjoy life.

Jordan thinks of the horses as merely material possessions, but for the reader they grow in meaning. The horses are at once the wealth of and the source of danger to the little community. Yet in their corral they have no function, and Pablo is against Jordan's mission which will require the horses for an escape. Just so the differences between the loves of Jordan and Pablo: Pablo's love is unused, inactive, important, hoarded until he becomes sick of it and its loneliness. Jordan's is active, and the more it is exercised the stronger it becomes. When the guerrillas depose Pablo as their leader, he has no one to turn to but his horses—his dream of love rather than the use of it. When Pilar recounts the atrocity of the village uprising—that embodiment of hate—she remembers that the dying men " 'were screaming as horses scream in a fire.' " When Jordan watches Maria, he sees her walking "like a colt moves."

In order to escape from the darkness, the inactivity, the frustration, and the angers of their cave, the guerrillas need horses—eros. But this commodity, as Philip Rawlings called it, is hard to come by. The lack of this love is the largest obstacle to the guerrillas' success. Jordan, El Sordo, and Pilar discuss the problem, and Maria puts it in clear-cut terms.

> "I wish we had horses to ride," Maria said. "In my happiness I would like to be on a good horse and ride fast with thee riding fast beside me and we would ride faster and faster, galloping, and never pass my happiness."

Opposed to this virtue of eros are ideas and uses that indicate its limitations and dangers: the immediate fear of the guerrillas is of fascist cavalry, Pablo's politics are associated with those of horse thieves, and the horse tracks that El Sordo leaves lead to his death. "We certainly got Sordo into a fine jam with that horse business. How does it go in Spanish? *Un callejón sin salida.* A passageway with no exit." The kind of love symbolized by the horse is not enough. El Sordo's own horse is sacrificed in one last effort on the hill where his band dies. He shoots his horse "quickly, expertly, and tenderly" so that the beast will plug a gap in the defensive perimeter. But having killed the horse of love, the band will die, even though Sordo uses the horse by firing the machine gun over its back. One of the images of life that El Sordo thinks of as he awaits the fascists' attack is that "Living was a horse between your legs and a carbine under one leg and a hill and a valley and a stream . . . " (the carbine is phallic and the landscape is female). He pats his dead horse and thinks how he had carefully shot it. " 'Thou wert plenty of horse' " he says, and he knows that he will die on that hill that he once imagines as shaped like a chancre (a mark of diseased love) and once thinks of as shaped like the nippleless breast of a young girl (a mark of incomplete or immature love).

A stronger accusation is made when the cursing Agustín tries to provoke Pablo into a fight. Pablo retreats from the cave to care for his horses—he runs from hate to his idea of love, to find some consolation in their animal companionship, to avoid the struggles needed in learning to love.

> "I will be going out to see the horses."
>
> "Go and befoul them," Agustín said. "Is not that one of thy customs?"
>
> "No," Pablo said and shook his head. He was taking down his big blanket cape from the wall and he looked at Agustín. "Thou," he said, "and thy violence."

> "What do you go to do with the horses?" Agustín said.
>
> "Look to them," Pablo said.
>
> "Befoul them," Agustín said. "Horse lover."
>
> "I care for them very much," Pablo said. "Even from behind they are handsomer and have more sense than these people. Divert yourselves," he said and grinned. "Speak to them of the bridge, *Inglés*. . . .
>
> "I have thought you are a group of illusioned people," Pablo said. "Led by a woman with her brains between her thighs and a foreigner who comes to destroy you."
>
> "Get out," Pilar shouted at him. "Get out and fist yourself into the snow. Take your bad milk out of here, you horse exhausted *maricón* [sodomite]."
>
> "Thus one talks," Agustín said admiringly, but absent-mindedly. He was worried.
>
> "I go," said Pablo.

Other indications that Pablo's sickness is somehow sexual are contained in Anselmo's view of him:

> And now, he is as finished and as ended as a boar that has been altered, Anselmo thought, and, when the altering has been accomplished and the squealing is over you cast the two stones away and the boar, that is a boar no longer, goes snouting and rooting up to them and eats them.

Later when Anselmo calls Pablo's cave the Palace of Fear, Jordan jokingly corrects the name to "the cave of the lost eggs."

> "What eggs?" Fernando asked.
>
> "A joke," Robert Jordan said. "Just a joke. Not eggs, you know. The others."
>
> "But why are they lost?" Fernando asked.
>
> "I don't know," said Robert Jordan. "Take a book to tell you."

After Pablo has stolen the exploders, Jordan thinks of him as a "sod," a sodomite, just as the other guerrillas had, and he also calls him a *cabrón,* a man who consents to his wife's adultery. And finally, after Pablo returns to help Jordan and they shake hands and exchange explanations, Pilar mocks them for acting like *maricones,* homosexuals. All three terms, of course, are invectives with a figurative but not a literal truth to them.

Earlier Pilar had confided in Jordan that Pablo had a sickness for Maria, the sickness of romantic love. " 'It is another thing which destroys him. It lies on him like a sickness when he sees her.' " In turn, Pablo's views of the other characters are frequently sexually described, but for him, eros is a corruption. When he argues that Pilar is stupid, he says that she has a head of a seed bull and a heart of a whore and that she has her brains between her thighs.

Jordan and the symbolic horse have a slightly different relationship. When Jordan wakes from a night in his sleeping bag with Maria, he shoots a fascist cavalryman off his big gray gelding, the very horse on which Jordan in his turn will be injured and consequently be left to die. Though still a horse, the gelding is a maimed horse, "sick" or incomplete, as eros romanticized is and as Pablo the horse lover is; Agustín's accusation was not altogether unfounded, for actual physical contact is enjoyed by Pablo as he mounts the gelding.

> He grinned and patted the nervous horse. Robert Jordan saw him rub his leg along the horse's flank affectionately.
>
> *"Qué caballo más bonito,"* he said and patted the big gray again. *"Qué caballo más hermoso. . . ."*
>
> "See what a horse has done for him" [Pilar said].
>
> "That I should have two horses," Robert Jordan said fervently.
>
> "Danger is thy horse."
>
> "Then give me a mule," Robert Jordan grinned.

But in a moment his grin fades when Maria joins him and wants her share of love from her man. Jordan is curt with her. Now is not the time for love. But because she saw the man shot from his horse, she is strangely aroused; once more the gun becomes phallic as Maria associates death and love:

> "Thou," she said. "I saw all."
>
> "Thou saw nothing. One man. One man from a horse. . . . "
>
> "I want to go to hold the legs of the gun and while it speaks love thee all in the same moment. . . . "
>
> He looked at her and smiled through his thinking.
>
> "When you hear firing," he said, "come with the horses. Aid the Pilar with my sacks. It is possible there will be nothing. I hope so."
>
> "I go," she said. "Look what a horse Pablo rides."
>
> The big gray was moving ahead up the trail.

Later Jordan thinks, "That horse certainly did things for him." Perhaps the horse moves Pablo to action, for he steals away that night with all the horses and Jordan's dynamite exploders (his potency that he carries in sacks!), but the horses alone do not suffice for any man. He returns the next night with more guerrillas and more horses to help in the escape. Once more a man thinks he can kill other men, as Pablo plans to kill the new guerrillas, and still use their horses—their love.

This love, these horses, are, however, unreliable because some of them may panic when the fighting at the bridge begins. Even so, the two weakest members of the band, Maria and Rafael the gypsy, are assigned to hold and guard them until the fight is over. Maria does not wish to remain behind Jordan, but he tells her, " 'The horses is where thou art most useful.' " The requirement of eros alone is little, and the weak suffice to handle it; but after staying with the horses for a long time, Maria finds "they were no comfort to her. Nor was she any to them." Her love for Jordan has transcended eros and thus her nervousness among the horses as she prays for his safe return.

Jordan does return from the bridge, but he never makes good his escape. He and Maria are never to live together as man and wife, and the horse again plays a decisive role. Pablo has killed the other guerrillas—" 'They were not of our band' "—so that *his* people will have many horses. Jordan rides the big gray gelding whose former rider Jordan had shot—the boy with the Sacred Heart insignia. Jordan thinks sensually of the horse: "it was much horse between his legs and under his hands."

> He caressed the gray once with his thigh muscles, and then held him steady as they dropped down fast and sliding through the pines, telling the gray with his thighs as they dropped down what the spurs would have told him if they had been on level ground.

Like El Sordo, Jordan then tries to use a horse for his protection from the gunfire of the enemy, but the horse veers off and a tank-gun shell knocks Jordan and his gelding down. In the fall, Jordan cannot get free of the horse. Earlier Fernando had been wounded in the groin, and his wound and his giving up of his horse to the others foreshadows Jordan's fall. The horse crushes his left leg; ironically, the gelded (incomplete, undeveloped) symbol of eros administers the symbolically castrative wound. Another shot from the tank hits the horse, which then sits quietly beside him and waits to die. His "horse" wounded, the hero is only half a man; it is not worth living thus, but one can die well and help his friends escape. In effect, Jordan is a fisher-king, a sacrificial hero, just as the horse has traditionally been a sacrificial embodiment of the god of vegetation. In order to insure fecundity or life, life must be taken. Eros is killed for the sake of eros. (When the horse is identified with the cosmos, as it sometimes is, its sacrifice symbolizes the act of creation, a parallel paradox.)

Pablo looks at the big gray gelding "with true regret on his face." He feels more the loss of the horse than the loss of Jordan. But for Pablo and the rest there are still other horses, enough, in fact, to enable them to carry off their camp utensils and supplies so that life can begin again somewhere else. Eros is clearly life for them. A horse has been sacrificed, and the horses are the means to life. Jordan thinks:

> It's wonderful they've got away. . . . Look how different it would be if they were all scattered out across that hill where that gray horse is. Or if we were all cooped up here waiting for it. No. They're gone. They're away.

Then more horsemen come, but these are the enemy, Lieutenant Berrendo's cavalry.

> He saw the trooper who stopped by the gray horse and shouted to the officer who rode over to him. He watched them both looking down at the gray horse. They recognized him of course. He and his rider had been missing since the early morning of the day before.

The fascists' horses are wet and blown and have to be urged forward to meet the further death that awaits them and eros in the midst of the hate of war.

The role of the horse, the funerary animal and the eros animal, archetypically complements the conscious, overt meaning of the theme of agape. Furthermore, eros is present in much else that is implicit in the novel, in addition to the famous sleeping-bag scenes. For instance, the object of Jordan's mission is to "destroy" a bridge, an erection, over a deep gorge. The "sodomite" Pablo is at first opposed to dropping the bridge into the gorge, but after he has thrown Jordan's "exploders" into the gorge (and vicariously experienced eros with Jordan and Maria) and then returned to humanity (the guerrilla band), he agrees to help. His thoughts always turn to the last symbolically sexual activity that he remembers nostalgically as the "good time" in the past—the blowing up of the train, the destruction of the long powerful phallus spouting white clouds of hot steam, followed by the machine-gunning of the little men, the homunculi, who burst out of the exploded train. Pablo had been a great lover (before the war his trade was working with horses in the bullfights), but since the train, there had been only laziness, sloth, and failure, only living in the past glory of the last destruction, the last moment of eros that literally ended in death for so many.

Except for some connection to the idea of eros and hate, the long passage of Andrés' remembrance of his youthful bullbaiting would be tedious. As the guerrilla remembers the village *capeas,* their similarity to the act of love is apparent. The bull, eros animated and epitomized, engenders excitement, delight, and fear in the youths who bait it. Paradoxically, as with other vegetation sacrifices, the symbol of virility is killed, but only by youths who have *cojones.* Andrés had leaped on a bull, "the bull rocked and bucked under him," and he

> drove his knife again and again and again into the swelling, tossing bulge of the neck that was now spouting hot on his first as he let his weight hang on the high slope of the withers and banged and banged into the neck.

When the bull settled dead under him, the boy was both proud and ashamed, feeling empty and happy. He had proven he had *cojones:* " 'That's what it is to have a pair of *cojones.*' " Andrés, remembering, equates the war with the bullbaiting, and in spite of his courage, he is glad that his mission as a messenger has relieved him of proving his manhood once more in the blowing up of the bridge. Of course, the libido disappears in the face of great danger, although that other love, agape, can conquer fear, as it did when the guerrillas rescued Maria from the train they blew up.

Other allusions to the association of eros with hate, death, and fear range from concrete yet symbolic actions to the abstract thoughts of various characters: nearly all of the Republican *milicianas* get pregnant, because eros flourishes in wartime; hate can be "killing" and similar to sexual intercourse with a woman one does not love; the messenger Andrés frantically rides his motorcycle through another vaginal landscape; Pilar thinks of a destructive man as "a great layer of women"; when the hate-filled, foulmouthed Augustín wants to kill four fascists he pictures himself as a fearful mare in heat; and, to repeat, El Sordo imagines his last stand as on a chancre-like hill.

A special problem is the anger that Pilar feels towards the love of Jordan and Maria. Initially, Pilar acts as a procuress for Maria, but her motive is the unselfish maternal one both of finding a mate for Maria and of completing Maria's emotional cure after the shocks of her parents' murder and her rape. Pilar puts Maria on display: " 'Isn't she pretty?' she asked Robert Jordan. 'How does she seem to thee? A little thin?' " And she sends Maria to Jordan's sleeping bag for a cathartic sexual experience. Jordan says:

> "Dost thou wish?"
>
> "Yes. Everything. And if we do everything together, the other maybe never will have been."
>
> "Did you think of that?"
>
> "No. I think it in myself but Pilar told me."
>
> "She is very wise. . . . "
>
> "She said that nothing is done to oneself that one does not accept and that if I loved some one it would take it all away. I wished to die, you see."
>
> "What she said is true."

Pilar sees that her plan has worked, and at first she is happy for Maria and able to jest with Jordan about his "conquest." But then she is also reminded of her youth and of the time when she was a great lover of great men. Now she, like Pablo, is left with her memories and Pablo, the man who was made psychically impotent the night the fascists were brutally executed. Pilar is now too old, and emotions tire her. Only in her spirit, and vicariously in Maria, is she still a great lover. Thus she instructs Maria in the art of love; it is something like religious instruction, Maria says as she blushes. But it is different. Thus also Pilar must know the quality of their lovemaking, and she has a gypsy power over Maria to get her to reveal that the earth moved for her when she and Jordan made love. Jordan thinks:

> There was nothing predatory. Nor was there anything perverted about it. There was a spreading, though, as a cobra's hood spreads. He could feel this. He could feel the menace of the spreading. But the spreading was a domination, not of evil, but of searching.

If it were not for the pervading presence of a mythic dimension in the novel, this scene would be the merest sentimental claptrap. Maria admits that the earth moved. " 'Truly. It was a thing I cannot tell thee.' " Pilar warns her not to tell it to her own people (non-gypsies), for they would never believe her. It is a mystery common to the gypsies, but " 'Non-gypsies have a little luck sometimes.' " Jordan's anger and disbelief change in the face of Pilar's strength and faith:

> Nobody knows what tribes we came from nor what our tribal inheritance is nor what the mysteries were in the woods where the people lived that we came from. All we know is that we do not know. We know nothing about what happens to us in the nights. When it happens in the day though, it *is* something. Whatever happened, happened and now this woman not only has to make the girl say it when she did not want to; but she has to take it over and make it her own. She has to make it into a gypsy thing. I thought she took a beating up the hill but she was certainly dominating just now back there. If it had been evil she should have been shot. But it wasn't evil. It was only wanting to keep her hold on life. To keep it through Maria.

In Chapter 12 that kind of vicarious eros appears to be not enough for Pilar. She has been angry with Maria because she has been jealous of her, but at the same time that she envies Maria's possession of Jordan, she envies Jordan's possession of Maria. She caresses Maria, and her feeling for her is sexual, though in her own mind she denies it and says her only interest is in Maria's happiness. Like anyone else, Pilar can feel the terrible tension between her own gratifications and an intellectual or ethical commitment that includes, as a corollary reinforcement, the knowledge that free satisfaction of her desires will end as nothing but the smell of death, love's labor lost. Man is caught in something of a dilemma. To be happy, he should reject what would seem to make him happy and achieve his own happiness only through others. The remaining alternative is a longing or a perverse, never consummated approach to the object of love, that once attained immediately turns to nothingness. Pilar is a woman of intense feeling, but she is also wise and honest and strong enough to admit the truth to the somewhat bewildered Maria. Pilar does not "make perversions," but still she both loves Maria—sensually and maternally—and is jealous of her, desiring to have Jordan herself.

Pilar and Jordan allude to the bridge as a phallic banana that Pilar wishes to devour hungrily. Such talk of destruction is exciting to her, and when Pilar gets up to leave Maria and Jordan alone so that they may make love, some hint of her erotic power is detected. Jordan wants to go with her, presumably because she had looked ill before. It is then Maria's turn to defend jealously her mate from the other woman:

> "Let her go," Maria said, her head still down.
>
> "I think I should go with her."
>
> "Let her go," said Maria. "Let her go!"

Pilar is a truly noble woman who is not afraid of facing the truth of her feelings and yet is able to rise above them to an act of agape. She is no *tortillera,* she says, no Lesbian, yet she is a mother reluctantly initiating her innocent child, and at the same time she is a lover of men who sees a good man in her child's husband. She needs both loves, erotic and familial, and she is giving both of them up for the sake of Maria. Her choice, like Jordan's at the end of the novel, is inevitable, hardly a choice at all, yet both Pilar and Jordan sacrifice themselves with the least reluctance and ultimately with a kind of grandeur.

Pilar's example foreshadows Jordan's relations with Maria. At first his great happiness with Maria is, ironically, a source of bitterness to him, for he tends to value love quantitatively and he realizes that this, his first true love, cannot endure. Pilar, however, gives Maria to Jordan because she values love qualitatively. Even if Jordan were to die, Maria would have something good and enduring; while eros is repeatedly associated with destruction, agape is indestructible; a three day's experience can last forever.

In Jordan's idealistic talk with Maria in his sleeping bag, he glorifies eros in an image of union, an image corresponding to the mythic ideal of woman as life and the hero as her knower and master. The sexual joining is a type of a spiritual union; Maria takes off her "wedding shirt" and tells Jordan she will not be cold.

> "Afterwards we will be as one animal of the forest and be so close that neither one can tell that one of us is one and not the other. Can you not feel my heart be your heart?"
>
> "Yes. There is no difference."
>
> "Now, feel. I am thee and thou art me and all of one is the other. And I love thee, oh, I love thee so. Are we not truly one? Canst thou not feel it?"
>
> "Yes," he said. "It is true."
>
> "Nor any other legs, nor feet, nor of the body. . . . "
>
> "I would be thee because I love thee so. . . . "
>
> "It is better to be one and each one to be the one he is."
>
> "But we will be one now and there will never be a separate one."

One plus one equals one, but when eros combines with agape, one minus one equals one also. " 'As long as there is one of us there is both of us,' " Jordan tells Maria as he lies wounded and tries to explain why he must be left behind during the escape. " 'If thou goest then I go, too. . . . Whichever one there is, is both. . . . Thou wilt go now for us both.' "

The scenes of eros have gradually changed and have given Jordan his first true love, which in turn gives him the strength to lose his love and his life. In the first scene, Maria comes to his sleeping bag ashamed and afraid. She has been practically driven there by Pilar, and she even mistakes his pistol—that other discharger of destruction—for his phallus. Jordan's assurance that he "loves" her assuages her shame and fear, but when she tells him that she had been raped, she feels a change in his affection. Yet she is pitiful and hopeful and still spiritually innocent, and Jordan says he understands that she is.

[In his *American Fiction: 1920-1940*] Joseph Warren Beach observes that Maria is a sacrificial lamb, or virgin martyr, for humanity. Though she had been raped, she is virginal in the sense that she is the pure-hearted lover of only one man; thus her traditionally sacred name, Maria. Jordan thinks of different names for her: "Sweetheart, *chérie, prenda,* and *schatz.* He would trade them all for Maria. There was a name." Later Jordan says he loves Maria *and* her name. Maria says, " 'It is a common name.' " 'No,' he said, 'It is not common.' " Maurice Valency notes that thirteenth-century courtly poetry depicted a love so ideal that it is occasionally difficult to distinguish between Mariolatry and love poems: the Lady is almost indistinguishable from the Blessed Virgin Mary, Maria's namesake and counterpart. When Jordan kisses this deified woman, he is, naturally, "happier than he had ever been." Nevertheless, he accepts her as his woman only temporarily.

> "I love you now."
>
> "And I can be thy woman?"
>
> "I cannot have a woman doing what I do. But thou art my woman now."
>
> "If once I am, then I will keep on. Am I thy woman now?"
>
> "Yes, Maria."

Later he reiterates the isolation of his love from his other life. He likes women, and drink, very much, but only outside his work. Yet Maria, he is beginning to feel, is something special, and Pilar announces their "engagement."

The following day he wonders if perhaps the joy of the night was just another erotic dream, like the many he has had of the movie stars Jean Harlow and Greta Garbo. The dreams were always better than the real thing, and Maria was too good to be true. The dream of romance is latent in Jordan's mind, but Maria is the exception. He reaches out and touches her arm. She *is* the dream come true.

When they again love each other that afternoon, their love is so intense that the earth mystically moves "out and away from under them" and time is "absolutely still . . . having stopped." This rare phenomenon, known before only to the gypsies, is love's transcendence of time and space. Still, Jordan has a trace of romance in his blood, and though the earth moved for both of them, their views are slightly different.

> "Maria, I love thee and thou art so lovely and so wonderful and so beautiful and it does such things to me to be with thee that I feel as though I wanted to die when I am loving thee."
>
> "Oh," she said. "I die each time. Do you not die?"
>
> "No. Almost."

Maria's surrender to love is complete, Jordan's "almost." He praises Maria's body as having some magic power.

> "In a fine body there is magic. I do not know what makes it in one and not in another. But thou hast it."
>
> "For thee," she said.
>
> "Nay."
>
> "Yes. For thee and for thee always and only for thee."

Maria denies any romantic mystery in love. Only the giving of her love has created the magic. For Maria, lying on her back and looking upward to the sunlit sky, eros is "red, orange, gold-red from the sun on the closed eyes," but for Jordan, lying on her and facing the earth, eros "was a dark passage which led to nowhere. . . . always and forever to nowhere."

Accompanying the change in Jordan wrought by the special love of Maria is a "clearing of the head" which enables him to see the paradox implicit in a communistic ideal which is to be effected through war and hatred. "Continence is the foe of heresy," Jordan thinks, and eros has made him a heretic. He will still fight for the people, but he will not be bigoted, he will not use the revolutionary and patriotic clichés like "enemy of the people."

> . . . the Communists were always cracking down on Bohemianism. When you were drunk or when you committed either fornication or adultery you recognized your own personal fallibility of that so mutable substitute for the apostles' creed, the party line.

Furthermore, Jordan even begins to think of marrying Maria, a remarkable thought for a Heminway hero. But one cannot walk down the aisle with a stylization or beget children on a dream. "The real lover tends to make children, not songs . . . " Instead of seventy years, Jordan's whole allotted life span will be seventy hours. Maria is a dream and is very properly meant to be, but she is a tough-minded vision, not an Iseult. On the probability of the love story, Joseph Warren Beach [in his *American Fiction: 1920-1940*] writes that Jordan discovers the absolute importance of the love of a woman.

> This affair of Maria is highly romantic. It is a startingly effective instance of the poetic formula of shining love projected against the shadow of death. . . . However true or untrue, however plausible or implausible it may be from the historical point of view, this episode is highly symbolic in relation to the political theme and to what we may call the writer's metaphysic of emotion."

Jordan's pistol, the Tristan sword that could lie between and separate them, is placed, like the tempting Satan, behind Jordan. He will not be tempted to indulge in the sickness of romantic love.

> I am no romantic glorifier of the Spanish Woman nor did I ever think of a casual piece as anything much other than a casual piece in any country. But when I am with Maria I love her so that I feel, literally, as though I would die and I never believed in that nor thought that it could happen.

Though he is still conscious of the romantic image associating eros with death, he also associates Maria with life forces. He had been willing to sacrifice his life for the abstract Republic of Spain, but now

> he would much prefer not to die. He would abandon a hero's or a martyr's end gladly. He did not want to make a Thermopylae, nor be Horatius at any bridge, nor be the Dutch boy with his finger in that dyke. No. He would like to spend some time with Maria. That was the simplest expression of it. He would like to spend a long, long time with her.
>
> If there is not any such thing as a long time, nor the rest of your lives, nor from now on, but there is only now, why then now is the thing to praise and I am very happy with it. Now, *ahora, maintenant, heute. Now,* it has a funny sound to be a whole world and your life. *Esta noche,* tonight, *ce soir, heute abend.* Life and wife, *Vie* and *Mari.* No it didn't work out. The French turned it into husband. There was now and *frau;* but that did not prove anything either.

Jordan gropes for sweet life and finds it in Maria's love. He "marries" her:

> Two nights to love, honor, and cherish. For better and for worse. In sickness and in death. No that wasn't it. In sickness and in health. Till death do us part. In two nights.

Jordan is dramatically reminded of the contrast of life and love to death when Maria matter-of-factly asks him to teach her how to shoot his pistol (to teach her the masculine art of dealing death) so that either one could kill the other if it were necessary to avoid capture and torture. She also carries a razor blade with which to cut her throat. "You have forgotten this," he tells himself. He has forgotten about the war and hate, and if the reader has too, the relation of love and war to agape must be re-established. Like other great goddesses of religion and myth, Maria possesses simultaneously the opposites of gentleness and dread, fertility and destruction, birth and death and war. (But for a matriarchal goddess, Pilar is better suited as a type of Kali, the protective and at the same time destructive goddess.)

The passage in which the gypsy guerrilla Rafael deserts his guard post to kill two rabbits making love in the snow symbolically complements this relationship of love and war to agape. The rabbits are caught and surprised because of eros, just as Jordan and Maria were almost caught that same morning by the fascist cavalry trooper who rode by Rafael's deserted post. Rafael too was ruled by an appetite, and Jordan tells him he could be shot. Jordan forgives him, however, perhaps because he is unconsciously aware of the coincidence or parallel of the rabbits to Maria and himself. Rafael would never leave his post again; in fact, " 'Never would such an opportunity as the two hares present itself again. Not in the life of one man.' " That is to say, such a love as Maria's and Jordan's is unique and ideal.

That night, in the third lovemaking scene, Maria comes to Jordan's sleeping bag without the fear and need for "treatment" that characterized their first night. [In his *Hemingway and the Dead Gods*] John Killinger cites the sleeping bag as a womb symbol that accords "with the death instinct and the desire for reversion to the intrauterine state." Although there is no disputing the potential use of a sleeping bag for such symbolic purpose, in this context there is not enough supplementary evidence to support such a reading. The guerrilla's cave is also a warm retreat from the hardships of weather and war outside it, but, like the sleeping bag, its activities usually indicate a literal rather than a symbolic role. The guerrillas lose their safe retreat when they involve themselves in mankind by re-entering the war. Jordan has broken away from the Mother. He admires Pilar the matriarch, but he does not want her meddling with Maria. Symbolically he does not return to the protective, destructive womb of her cave, nor does he sleep there at night but rather with Maria outside, even in the snow. In this third lovemaking scene, they are "married," she wears a "wedding shirt," and they are united physically and spiritually—they become as one. This time the earth does not move for them, but neither do they romantically "die":

> ". . . it was not as this afternoon" [Maria said].
>
> "No."
>
> "But I loved it more. One does not need to die."
>
> "*Ojalá no,*" he said. "I hope not."
>
> "I did not mean that."
>
> "I know. I know what thou meanest. We mean the same."
>
> "Then why did you say that instead of what I meant?"
>
> "With a man there is a difference."
>
> "Then I am glad that we are different."
>
> "And so am I," he said. "But I understood about the dying. I only spoke thus, as a man, from habit. I feel the same as thee."
>
> "However thou art and however thou speakest is how I would have thee be."

Jordan's decision actually to marry Maria is a monumental one that invites comparison with Lieutenant Henry's decision in ***A Farewell to Arms.*** The earlier hero who breaks with society's conventions and makes his separate peace by running off with his true love is not as well motivated to desire marriage as Jordan is. Frederic Henry delays his marriage because Catherine regards it of little importance, but the rebel looks forward to it, after the embarrassing pregnancy is over, as a necessary seal of their love. Jordan has *returned* to society and compromised his ideals for the sake of a desirable goal; he does not see only in blacks and whites; he is not blinded by what Arthur Koestler calls the fallacy of the perfect cause, a disease of the mind to which young heroes are acutely susceptible. Accepting other conventions and limitations in society, Jordan can also desire marriage without the faint touch of irony that Lieutenant Henry's desire has.

Jordan will not only care for Maria in a strange way—by sleeping with her—he will also marry her. He and Augustín discuss marriage and Maria and the ways that one person cares for another. Pilar has put Maria in his care, Jordan says, and to *joder* with her all night is a lucky way to care for one so long as there is "seriousness" and responsibility in the lovemaking. Time after time Jordan repeats to Augustín his acceptance of this responsibility:

> "I care for her seriously. . . . "
>
> "I will care for her. . . . "
>
> "I care for her greatly"

He will also marry Maria as soon as he gets the chance, for the changed Hemingway hero desires the formality, the convention, and his actions have not, like Lieutenant Henry's, run counter to a certain ethical decorum. It is to the tradition of Tristan and romantic love that Jordan is a heretic: he *intends* to marry his lover. Since Frederic Henry had the same intention, the important difference must be seen to lie in Henry's inconsistency of motivation and in Hemingway's solution—Catherine must die.

The last sleeping-bag scene has, however, some Tristan-like elements. Maria is sore and in pain and does not think she will be any good for Jordan. He is disappointed, but he conceals his hurt and turns down her offer of onanism. He says, " 'We will have our necessities together. I have no necessities apart from thee.' " Besides, he cannot afford to waste on the pine needles the virility he will need the next day to perform his chivalric deeds in honor of his lady. He and Maria talk instead; they plan their future together, and Maria tells of her rape at the hands of the fascists. Jordan is angered momentarily, but he is satisfied with the kind of lovemaking that the troubadors recommended as the height of true love—warm embracing without the final act of coition: " 'Lie close against me, rabbit. I love thee as much feeling thee against me in here in the dark as I love thee making love.' " "Then they lay quiet and close together in the night, hot-aching, rigid, close together and holding her . . ."

Under the threat of his death the next day, Jordan dreams impossible dreams that he recognizes as unrealizable, and confesses a love of her that is cosmic in its scope. Maria has come to represent many things.

> "I have worked much and now I love thee and," he said it now in a complete embracing of all that would not be, "I love thee as I love all that we have fought for. I love thee as I love liberty and dignity and the rights of all men to work and not be hungry. I love thee as I love Madrid that we have defended and as I love all my comrades that have died. And many have died. Many. Many. Thou canst not think how many. But I love thee as I love what I love most in the world and I love thee more. I love thee very much, rabbit. More than I can tell thee. But I say this now to tell thee a little. I have never had a wife and now I have thee for a wife and I am happy."
>
> "We are married, now. I marry thee now. Thou art my wife."

The point that Jordan makes explicit—universalizing his love for Maria—has been made in the prior action and characterization, and the point has been made much better and more convincingly than in Jordan's speech that is rich with Lieutenant Henry's obscene abstractions. In hammering the point home, Hemingway almost destroys it, and then returns to the erotic matters at hand. Whatever the ideal of love-making for Tristan, Jordan still wishes they had spent their last night differently, and early the next morning he has his wish fulfilled when Maria awakes full of passion and clasps him to her, and they have one final time in *la gloria:*

> . . . one and one is one, is one, is one, is one, is still one, is still one, is one descendingly, is one softly, is one longingly, is one kindly, is one happily, is one in goodness, is one to cherish, is one now on earth with elbows against the cut and slept-on branches of the pine tree with the smell of the pine boughs and the night; to earth conclusively now, and with the morning of the day to come.

This last sacrifice to love will give Jordan the spirit he needs to sacrifice himself this last day. It is the culmination of his seventy-two hour education.

> "You taught me a lot, *guapa,*" he said in English.
>
> "What did you say?"
>
> "I have learned much from thee."
>
> "*Qué va,*" she said, "it is thou who art educated."
>
> Educated, he thought. I have the very smallest of beginnings of an education. The very small beginnings. If I die on this day it is a waste because I know a few things now. . . . I have been all my life in these hills since I have been here. Anselmo is my oldest friend. . . . Agustín, with his vile mouth, is my brother, and I never had a brother. Maria is my true love and my wife. I never had a true love. I never had a wife. She is also my sister, and I never had a sister, and my daughter, and I never will have a daughter. I hate to leave a thing that is so good. . . .
>
> "I find life very interesting," he said to Maria.

Hemingway suggests that his hero's education is not yet finished, but he now knows what he does not know. Nothing is left to be said, for the "nada," the absolute nothing of a Meister Eckhart, has been perceived.

The concept of agape unifies the two stories of love and war. Love is not eros alone, Jordan has learned. His love for Maria partakes of the romantic only if one limits that word to mean an ideal stylization. Maria is not meant to be "real." She is an image, a mythic woman much better than any real woman just as Jordan is an oversized hero, an epic lover and fighter.

But agape is only potential or primitive or budding between Jordan and Maria and the other characters. And thus the paradox of life: Jordan still keeps the life-giving love on the periphery of his death-dealing life. He fights and hates for love. He loses his life and his love in the only way he can find life and love. No greater love has Jordan than the love that lets him lay down his life for his friends. His noble sacrifice is, however, in some ways an avoidance of love's responsibilities. The martyr has it easy. It is the man who lives—a Santiago or even a Jake Barnes—who has it hard. Jordan lines up his sights on another Hector, Lieutenant Berrendo, and thus demonstrates the tragedy of man's fate. (pp. 153-78)

Robert W. Lewis, Jr., in his Hemingway on Love, *1965. Reprint by Haskell House Publishers Ltd., 1973, 252 p.*

Delbert E. Wylder on Robert Jordan:

Jordan's blowing up the bridge has both mythical values and a mythical basis, although, because it is a contemporary myth, it does not correspond exactly to the journeys of any popular or literary hero. One of the most important considerations in Robert Jordan's heroic journey is that it is a double one. The more obvious journey is at the physical level and is centered around the task of blowing up a bridge at a precise time through the coordinated action of an individual and a group. The less obvious journey is the moral or spiritual one, for it involves a journey within the hero, a descent into his own unconscious, and the trial involved in bringing that unconscious life into relation with the conscious life. As an exemplum, Robert Jordan's journey must also have meaning for the world at large, and must deal with man's contemporary problem—the "split" between the conscious and the unconscious. Perhaps the most obvious example of Hemingway's own recognition of the problem (other than in the remarkable story "A Clean Well-Lighted Place") is in his refusal to depict a hero in his previous novel. Even Harry Morgan's few heroic qualities become faults because he is isolated from mankind. But Robert Jordan is not isolated, and the two concurrent journeys in which he brings the conscious and the unconscious into a meaningful relation also bring him to a full acceptance of and a total involvement with mankind. He does, in a sense, through his own sacrifice, restore man to life.

Delbert E. Wylder, in his Hemingway's Heroes, *1969.*

Jackson J. Benson (essay date 1969)

[Benson is an American educator, editor, and critic. In the following essay, he assesses the defining qualities of Hemingway's protagonist, Robert Jordan.]

Illustrative of one of the changes in Hemingway's thinking that apparently took place in the ten-year interval from the writing of ***A Farewell to Arms*** to the writing of ***For Whom the Bell Tolls*** is the famous, although puzzling passage wherein Jordan declares his faith. He spells out what he is fighting for in the very abstractions that made Frederic Henry sick to his stomach:

> You're not a real Marxist and you know it. You believe in Liberty, Equality and Fraternity. You believe in Life, Liberty and the Pursuit of Happiness. Don't ever kid yourself with too much dialectics. . . . You have put many things in abeyance to win a war. If this war is lost all of those things are lost.

To the reader of the earlier Hemingway, this declaration seems weak and incongruous. Not only has Jordan used abstractions, but he uses two slogans from previous middle-class revolutions as a basis for acting in conjunction with the Communists in Spain. It could be that Hemingway just could not decide how to have Jordan make this kind of statement without using abstractions, or it could be that Hemingway is defending himself here against charges of Communist sympathy. However, a better solution is suggested by something else [Joseph Wood] Krutch says in his essay on tragedy ["The Tragic Fallacy," in *Tragedy: Plays, Theory, and Criticism,* Richard Levin, ed.]: "We accept gladly the outward defeats which it [tragedy] describes for the sake of the inward victories which it reveals. . . . However much things in the outward world may go awry, man has, nevertheless, splendors of his own and that, in a word, Love and Honor and Glory are not words but realities." The most obvious answer to the puzzle of Jordan's words, perhaps too obvious to accept (or too void of sophistication), is that this is a sincere declaration of faith. Unlike the skeptic, Frederic Henry, Jordan really believes in Liberty, Equality, and Fraternity. These are not just a slogan to him but words that represent realities; they are real to Jordan, not because they exist in immediate, tangible forms, but because he has faith in their possibility. It is such a faith that makes God real to man. And by having faith in such basic social ideals, as unaristocratic as they may be, Jordan has, in a sense, made tragedy possible.

"A tragic writer does not have to believe in God," Krutch continues, "but he must believe in man." Above all, ***For Whom the Bell Tolls*** is an expression of faith in man, and even more important, an expression of belief in man's noblest possibilities with full knowledge of the worst acts of barbarism and cruelty (as well as stupidity, selfishness, and cowardice) of which man is capable. Jordan's outward defeats, represented both by his failure to accomplish anything by the blowing up of the bridge and by his death, are completely overshadowed by the glory of his power to remain true to his faith until the end. He insists at his death that his mind remain accurate and his emotions reject cynicism. Jordan's is an inward victory of some significance.

Throughout the novel, Hemingway takes great pains to show us that Jordan is not naive or gullible, so that Jordan's faith in himself and his cause is established on firm, realistic grounds. All of Hemingway's later heroes are extremely alert and aware individuals, but Jordan is perhaps the most sharply observant of them all. From the very beginning of the novel we realize that he is a man who not only sees everything, but interprets everything properly. In the opening pages we see Jordan assessing his companion ("Robert Jordan trusted the man, Anselmo, so far, in everything except judgment. He had not yet had an opportunity to test his judgment") and his surroundings ("whoever was above had been very careful not to leave any trail"; "[He] noticed that the grass was cropped down in several places and signs that picket pins had been driven into the earth.")

In the middle of the novel, in one of the flashbacks to Jordan's early experiences in the Civil War, we learn that Jordan initially felt part of a "crusade," but after six months of fighting, his "purity of feeling" disappeared. Jordan makes friends among the politically powerful within the Republican ranks and finds himself exposed to the cynicism and maneuvering that goes on behind the propaganda veil used to maintain the faith of the naive. At Gaylord's, the Madrid hotel taken over by the Russians, Jordan learns that "the talk that he had thought of as cynicism when he had first heard it had turned out to be much too true." He finds that "Gaylord's was the place where you met famous peasant and worker Spanish commanders who had sprung to arms from the people at the start of the war without any previous military training and found that many of them spoke Russian." Jordan is by no means a dewy-eyed idealist, and that is what makes his adherence to his ideals so convincing and important. Jordan was a man who "liked to know how it really was; not how it was supposed to be." The more he fought in Spain, the more he realized that "the things he had come to know in this war were not so simple."

This last statement by Jordan appears to announce a different direction in Hemingway's thinking. Hemingway began his search for "true emotion" by observing the "simplest things" within experience, and by the time he wrote ***For Whom the Bell Tolls,*** he found that it is principle that is "simple," in the sense of being fundamental and lasting, and that it is experience, after all, which is the complicated thing. In appending his qualification "You have put many things in abeyance to win a war" to his abstract statement of belief, Jordan displays a complexity of development in his ability to deal with the world that makes the earlier protagonist, Frederic Henry, seem like a child in comparison. Like Henry, Jordan also is cynical about certain things, but this is not the full dimension of his personality. Jordan, too, is suspicious of wonderful-sounding words: "You felt that you were taking part in a crusade. That was the only word for it although it was a word that had been so worn and abused that it no longer gave its true meaning." But like the good bullfighter, and unlike Frederic Henry, Jordan is able to combine his cynicism with a devoutness that the most difficult and depressing of circumstances cannot shake. No other Hemingway protagonist, except perhaps Santiago, is so strong and tough as Robert Jordan or so truly heroic. Hemingway has made ***For Whom the Bell Tolls*** a moral laboratory; he takes a strong fabric, dips it in the strong acid of an impossibly difficult situation, and finds that the weave has held. Jordan believes; and what is more, we, the readers, believe that he believes. In short, he is the first protagonist of a Hemingway novel to be a "professional."

Jordan's devoutness, however, is not easily maintained, nor can it be and still be credible. Faith, like liberty, has the price of eternal vigilance, and for this reason ***For Whom the Bell Tolls*** can easily be seen as a novel of faith and the struggle to maintain it. Hemingway's major problem in the novel is to make this struggle both difficult and yet possible, extraordinary and yet immediate enough to touch the moral struggle faced by every reader. Some critics have maintained that there is too much internal dialogue in the novel. However, despite large segments of the novel that depart from it, Jordan's consciousness is the novel's central focus. Not to see this focus is to miss, of course, the whole point of the novel: to show *how* Jordan is able to do what he does, not just to show what he does—which, after all, would be not much more than formula heroics. Jordan's internal conflict is a highly structured one within the ethical structure which I have termed the "game context." Also, Jordan's levels of awareness and commitment are much more complex than those of previous Hemingway protagonists. Dominating Jordan's consciousness is the familiar game element in the battle to be self-honest, a battle which is a recurring motif that links together the many divergent forces, characters, and subthemes that cluster around the central external act of blowing up the bridge.

Jordan's heroic stature is in large measure achieved through his ability to transcend the many different conflicts that pull on his emotions. Under the best of conditions, Jordan's probability of success on this particular mission is extremely marginal. The reader becomes aware of the difficulty of Jordan's task at the very beginning of the novel in the flashback scene where General Golz gives him his orders. Just "how bad" the situation is becomes more and more apparent throughout the novel when we find out that Jordan is usually composed, "cold in the head," and to a certain extent gay in the face of danger. During his interview with Golz, however, he is so worried by his assignment that he is almost surly and is completely unable to respond to Golz's joking.

Through the marginal probability of the mission's success, we are made conscious of Jordan's faith as the factor which may make the difference between success and failure. In addition, a chain of being is established in the novel, starting with the large offensive at the top, moving down through the separate functions of the various units, to the function of the particular unit directed by Jordan, and resting, finally, on the accurate functioning of Jordan's mind and the soundness of his spirit. The whole weight of this pyramid-in-reverse rests on Jordan. Without his blowing up the bridge and without his blowing it up at the right time, the whole offensive (the first big Republican offensive of the war) will fail. The chain must not be broken. "Merely to blow the bridge," as Golz tells Jordan, "is a failure." Later in the novel, when a Fascist cavalry unit is in the mountains and there is the opportunity to "make a massacre," Jordan is careful to warn his men not to shoot unless they absolutely have to: "It would avail nothing. That would serve no purpose. The bridge is a part of a plan to win the war. This would be nothing. This would be an incident. A nothing."

It becomes increasingly clear that large events are crucially dependent on smaller events and that the over-all battle for Segovia is dependent on individual battles, which in turn are dependent on the internal battles fought in the minds of the key participants. General order is dependent on internal order. The importance of the individual is confirmed by glimpses given to us by the narrator of internal battles other than Jordan's, battles fought in the minds of Anselmo, Sardo, Pilar, Andres, and Maria. By employing such a structure Hemingway tries to make sure that the reader perceives that reality is an individual proposition—there is no whole except as a structure of a number of individual parts. Such a structure forces us to view the epigraph from Donne as not so much a declaration endorsing the importance of social responsibility, as a declaration endorsing the importance of the individual. "Any man's *death* diminishes *me*" because each man's battle affects every other man's welfare. The morality of the whole is the sum of the morality of the parts. There is no mankind; there are only men.

Such a view of individual responsibility is the basis of genuine Christian ethics. Although war may seem a strange setting for a demonstration of Christianity, war quite appropriately represents the inhuman forces of this world, the many pressures inherent in human existence that would seem to make it impossible for the individual to remain a responsible individual. . . . Caught up in the pattern of the whole, forced by "realistic" circumstances to kill and to destroy (representing all the demands for compromise that the world makes of every man, whether in war or not), man can still act with principle within such a framework. If we view ***For Whom the Bell Tolls*** in this way, it is possible to see the novel as a kind of "morality play." In opposition to the difficult task of maintaining principle within the worst of all circumstances are the internal emotional weaknesses, the little temptations to self-deception that would lead men astray. Principle is tested only when compromise is necessary. Human issues are never clear-cut, and from the ragged edges of experience and the complexities of emotional reactions, a "messy battle" emerges that has its larger external counterpart in the "messy" civil war which is the setting of the novel.

Faith, like liberty, has the price of eternal vigilance, and for this reason *For Whom the Bell Tolls* can easily be seen as a novel of faith and the struggle to maintain it.

—Jackson J. Benson

Hemingway is extremely careful to show that there are no real villainies in this war except those engendered by the general human frailties which make war possible. Atrocity by one side is balanced by atrocity on the other, as the tale of Pablo's massacre is balanced by the tale of Maria's rape, and the most hateful aspects of Fascism (much to the dismay of the Communist critics of the novel) are seen to be implicit in the authoritarianism, pragmatic calculation, scheming, hypocrisy, and brutal blindness of the Communist elements of the Republican side. It is as difficult to pick out the principles to be endorsed on the general political scene (and Jordan spends a great deal of time in the novel trying to clarify his precise political position) as it is to make the smaller, more detailed decisions involving principle in the individual's experience. Thus, not only is Jordan himself a man who prefers to see things as they really are as a basis for acting on principle, but reality is further added to the context in which principle must be demonstrated by making the war situation itself a non-oversimplified tissue of rights and wrongs. One of the most dramatic instances that Hemingway uses to achieve this careful emotional balance which prevents oversimplification is to have the Fascist lieutenant (whom we previously learn to admire for his humanity, maintained, like Jordan's, despite the barbarity of the duty he must perform) face Jordan at the end of the novel. Jordan is about to die to help save his friends by facing the troop of cavalry led by the Fascist lieutenant. The lieutenant, who is so much like Jordan, will be the first to die from Jordan's submachine gun.

One of the major moral conflicts in the novel is that between the duty to kill under the circumstances of war and the principle which values human life. Anselmo, whom Jordan refers to as "a Christian. Something very rare in Catholic countries," is extremely concerned about the sin of killing another human being. Early in the novel, in a discussion with Jordan, Anselmo explains that he feels that there is a great difference between animals and men, and killing men, even Fascists, is a sin. Anselmo will kill the Fascists since it must be done, "But if I live later, I will try to live in such a way, doing no harm to any one, that it will be forgiven." Since God is no longer with Anselmo ("If there were God, never would He have permitted what I have seen with my eyes"), Jordan suggests that it must be Anselmo himself who will forgive Anselmo—again leading to the individual as the moral unit emphasized in the novel.

When Anselmo does his duty by killing the guard at the other end of the bridge, he comes to help Jordan place the explosives with tears "running down . . . [his] cheeks through the gray beard stubble." Anselmo has proved himself the most reliable man among all those available to Jordan, and for this reason, Jordan chooses him for the key job of helping with the explosive. Yet it is Anselmo (in contrast to the others' impatience when Jordan repeats his orders immediately before the battle) who is concerned that Jordan repeat his orders very explicitly so that there will be no mistake and so that Anselmo will know very clearly that it is his duty to kill the guard: " 'I will do as thou orderest,' Anselmo said. 'Yes. I order it thus,' Robert Jordan said. I'm glad I remembered to make it an order, he thought. That helps him out. That takes some of the curse off. I hope it does, anyway. Some of it."

Jordan, too, is deeply concerned about killing. Not only does he mourn the death of his own friends (going into near shock at the death of Anselmo), but he mourns too the death of the enemy. When the lone cavalryman rides into camp almost up to the place where Jordan and Maria are sleeping, Jordan kills him with cool precision as a matter of necessity. But later, in going over the man's papers, he recognizes that the Fascist is no longer simply an enemy figure, but an individual human being, a boy that he has probably seen "run through the streets ahead of the bulls at the Feria in Pamplona." Ironically, the Fascist is the son of a blacksmith, a worker, as well as a member of a very religious family. It is the medal of the Sacred Heart of Jesus that was sent to the cavalryman by his sister which Jordan aimed for when shooting him—a medal that the sister insists has proved innumerable times "to have the power of stopping bullets." Jordan's reaction to the sister's and fiancée's letters is a deep sense of guilt and sorrow: "I guess I've done my good deed for today, he said to himself. I guess you have all right, he repeated." But guilt, like other destructive emotions, must be put aside for duty. "I'm sorry, if that does any good. It doesn't. . . . All right then, drop it, he said to himself."

Killing, Jordan feels, can only be justified if it is a necessity and one does not believe in killing. "If you believe in it," he tells himself, "the whole thing is wrong." On these and other matters there is a voice within Jordan that tries to keep him straight, that insists on being heard, and insists that only if these transgressions are faced honestly and not ignored can Jordan survive as a moral agent with a clear faith:

> You listen, see? Because you are doing something very serious and I have to see you understand it all the time. I have to keep you straight in your head. Because if you are not absolutely straight in your head you have no right to do the things you do for all of them are crimes and no man has a right to take another man's life unless it is to prevent something worse happening to other people. So get it straight and do not lie to yourself.

"Do not lie to yourself" is the motto embossed on the shield of Jordan's moral armor. It is a motto that at times is not easy to adhere to. Jordan finds, despite himself, that he is occasionally infected by blood lust. When Augustín has the "necessity" to kill like a "mare in heat," Jordan first thinks that it is the Spanish who have this lust for killing as an "extra sacrament," that it is part of the racial inheritance, whereas, he thinks at first, "we" do it coldly. But then once again the voice of truth interrupts him:

> And you, he thought, you have never been corrupted by it? . . . Stop making dubious literature about the Berbers and the old Iberians and admit that you have liked to kill as all who are soldiers by choice have enjoyed it at some time whether they lie about it or not. . . . Don't lie to yourself.

Throughout the novel, Jordan is able to maintain a careful emotional balance between extremes. Not only is he able to maintain his idealism while being a realist and pragmatist, but he is able to be suspicious as well as truthful, loving as well as unfeeling and calculating, and completely loyal as well as skeptical. Jordan's suspicions in the case of Pablo are, of course, quite justified, and although he is unable to prevent Pablo's making off with the detonator and caps, Jordan is usually one step ahead of the guerrilla leader, whose only virtue is his extraordinary intelligence. Jordan knows that before "the first friendly thing he does, he will have made a decision," and it is when Pablo decides to go along with the plan for the bridge that Pablo steals the materials and betrays Jordan and the guerrilla band. Jordan knows too what Pablo has in mind for the guerrillas (murdering them for their horses) that he recruited during the night after changing his mind a second time. On the other hand, Jordan is able to trust others, such as Anselmo, Pilar, and Andres, completely, not because they have proved themselves entirely trustworthy (there is not time enough for that), but because Jordan is emotionally stable enough to take the necessary risks, a stability that can arise only from a strong general faith in humanity.

Just as skepticism and trust balance each other in Jordan's personality, so also do the ability to love and the ability to act with unfeeling coldness when the occasion demands it. Of course, Jordan's most direct expression of love is that given to Maria, but his attitude toward Anselmo and Pilar must certainly be said to include a measure of love. Many readers have noted the parallel between the two rabbits that are killed by the Gypsy while they are copulating and the position of Robert and Maria as they are sleeping together in the snow. (Jordan even calls Maria "little rabbit.") A Fascist cavalryman almost rides over them before Jordan pushes Maria back into the sleeping bag and shoots the Fascist. Jordan's complete switch here from tenderness to the cold posture of an efficient killer may appear to be rather cynical: Maria "had no place in his life now." However, Maria and Robert are not rabbits; the evidence of the immediate context (Jordan's anger at Primitivo's question, "How is she in the bed?" and Jordan's promise to Augustín that he will marry Maria because he cares for her seriously, as well as the overwhelming evidence throughout the novel of Jordan's true concern, show that Maria is not just a convenient outlet for sex. If we examine the parallel with the rabbits further, we can see that one significant difference between the rabbits and the humans is that the humans are able to make a rapid transition to duty; the rabbits are dead. Principle of a sort that affects a great number of people's welfare is placed over self-satisfaction (on whatever level, sensual or romantic). Jordan's duty is primary, as we see in a fragment from a conversation that he has with Pilar:

> "You are a very cold boy." [Pilar says.]
>
> "No," he said. "I do not think so."
>
> "No. In the head you are very cold."
>
> "It is that I am very preoccupied with my work."
>
> "But you do not like the things of life?"
>
> "Yes. Very much. But not to interfere with my work."

When we consider that Jordan's work is no ordinary occupation, but the direct and courageous demonstration of his belief in social justice, his ability to rapidly shift gears from love to duty appears more selfless than callous.

Further moderation in Jordan is demonstrated in his healthy balance between skepticism and loyalty. Jordan knows of the behind-the-scenes machinations of the Communists. He shows a healthy suspicion of political slogans, examining their meanings carefully. He catches himself inadvertently falling into the use of "Enemies of the people." He decides that "that was a phrase he might omit. That was a catch phrase he would skip." He knows that the Republicans are not all pure and the Fascists not all evil: "He believed in the Republic as a form of government but the Republic would have to get rid of all of that bunch of horse thieves that brought it to the pass it was in when the rebellion started. Was there ever a people whose leaders were as truly their enemies as this one?" Jordan promises to give "absolute loyalty and as complete [a] performance" as possible during the war, but at the same time "nobody owned his mind, nor his faculties for seeing and hearing."

The "morality play" that takes place in Jordan's mind is concerned, at one time or another during the novel, with repulsing or balancing false hope, prejudice, overidealization, hatred, anger, resentment, guilt, self-righteousness, and despair. On the one side, Jordan is tempted to resent Golz's orders and what they could do to him and the people he leads; he checks himself, "That is not the way to think." On the other side, when he is tempted to be too optimistic and to think how it might be if everything concerned with the attack came off without a hitch, he reminds himself, "You must not get illusions about it now. . . . Keep your sense of proportion." On the one side, he is tempted to overgeneralize the faults he has found among the Spanish, but tells himself, "This was no way to think." On the other side, he greatly appreciates Sordo's gesture of bringing the whiskey to him and decides that this is one of the reasons he loves the Spanish, but quickly he reminds himself, "Don't go romanticizing them." When Jordan starts to think of all the things that could go wrong, he tells himself to "stop it." When he comes to admire Anselmo's respect for human life, Jordan finds it necessary to warn himself not to idealize Anselmo.

Much of the structure of Jordan's internal fight is based on a paralleling of opposing ideas, values, and courses of action. Jordan spends much of his time emphasizing the extremely moral focus in the book, making distinctions, guarding against tempting inaccuracies, and weighing the evidence of his perceptions against the demands of his faith. This pattern, which on an over-all basis can be roughly referred to as comparison and contrast in nature, is closely related to another pattern wherein the individual is implicitly compared to the group. The effect of this comparison is again to emphasize the importance of the individual.

One of the major ironies of ***For Whom the Bell Tolls*** is that all of the things we normally tend to think of, particularly in our time, in regard to the larger order (the army, the party, the country) are successfully carried out or demonstrated only by individuals. Political belief is cynical or distorted as it is reflected in the Republican camp as a whole, but it is sincere and quite well defined in the thinking of such individuals as Jordan. Armed action fails on the larger scale of the entire offensive, but succeeds in the hands of dedicated individuals such as Jordan.

The over-all picture of the Spanish Civil War presented in Hemingway's novel is a dismal one. When Golz gives Jordan his assignment to blow the bridge, Golz fatalistically predicts that something will go wrong: "Always some one will interfere" and "I have never been given what I ask for even when they have it to give." So many moral cripples within the Republican ranks are described during the course of the novel that the real question, in terms of the outcome of the war, becomes whether there are enough of the "good ones" to balance and overcome the confusion and decay caused by the cripples. Infesting the Republican cause are the horse thieves, like Pablo, who have little if any real social concern and who are antisocial parasites that have been able to take power because of the confusion of the war. Pablo's concern for the welfare only of his own band contrasts strongly throughout the novel with Jordan's willingness to submit himself entirely to the welfare of the whole, a whole that can only be conceived of in abstract terms. Pablo, on the other hand, would not fight for anything that he cannot feel directly in immediate terms, such as revenge or something he can eat or drink. In addition to Pablo, another cripple on the immediate scene is Rafael, the Gypsy, who is really more of a draft dodger than a patriot. Cripples infesting the larger scene are the general, Lister, who is a "true fanatic" and executes his troops for very little reason in order to gain discipline, the "fake soldiers" of Barcelona "who like everything about war except to fight"; and the "puffy-eyed man" who, at Karkov's party, goes into raptures over the propaganda figure, "La Pasionaria." At one point in Karkov's party, a general, disgusted at "this filthy sewing circle of gossip," declares that "one man who could keep his mouth shut could save the country if he believed he could." To top off the list of grotesques is the frightening Comrade Marty, whose vicious cleverness, à la Stalin, becomes so blind to reality that it approaches insanity.

In addition to such grotesque figures, the novel contains continual hints of mismanagement, intrigue, falsehood, and double standards. Karkov's explanation—"I have to go upstairs to see people. Upstairs people"—has an ominous sound as he takes his leave from Jordan in Gaylord's bar to go up to a meeting. Indeed, the landscape is just as dismal as Jake's postwar Paris or Frederic's Italian front in World War I, if not more so. Yet the crucial difference is that whereas the earlier Hemingway protagonists form no allegiances, or else withdraw their allegiances, Jordan finds the game worth playing despite the fact that the circumstances are not perfect. Overcoming disillusionment, his determination is made even stronger:

> Sure, Gaylord's was the place you needed to complete your education. It was there you learned how it was all really done instead of how it was supposed to be done. . . . Gaylord's was good and sound and what he needed. At the start when he had still believed all the nonsense it had come as a shock to him. But now he knew enough to accept the necessity for all the deception and *what he learned at Gaylord's only strengthened him in his belief in the things that he did hold to be true.* (italics mine)

In this statement of Jordan's the difference between the early and the later Hemingway protagonists is precisely defined. The early protagonists are amateurs, the later are professionals. The early protagonists are defensive—their only advances are tentative, their commitments outside themselves are tenuous at best. Jordan does not cut off the world because it is not perfect; its imperfection only strengthens his determination to do what little he can. Similarly, Colonel Cantwell serves well in an army full of incompetents, egomaniacs, and petty politicians; the weakness he perceives around him does not weaken his pride, his dignity, his purpose, or his faith. Similarly, too, Santiago fishes for eighty-four days without catching a fish. He goes out alone, as far out as he can, and fishes on the eighty-fifth day. He catches the biggest fish he has ever seen, watches it devoured, lost, before his eyes, bit by bit. And after the incident is all over, he makes plans with the boy to fish yet again. The human spirit, Hemingway tells us in his last story, is like the dream of a lion: A lion in itself is powerful, beautiful, sensual, dignified, as well as gay and playful. But the dream of a lion is even better. It can never be destroyed and lives in the hearts of certain men forever. The individual does count.

The individual man can become a significant moral agent even in our time, and the manner of Robert Jordan's death illustrates this as well as anything that Hemingway has written. At the end of ***For Whom the Bell Tolls,*** as Robert Jordan lies wounded, ready to die as he knows he must, forcing himself not to pass out or take the easy way by shooting himself, one is reminded of his earlier statement that "he would much prefer not to die" and that he "would abandon a hero's or a martyr's end gladly." Just as Jordan's ideals are made more meaningful by his insistence on viewing life realistically, so his death is made more meaningful by his genuine desire to live. One is also reminded of the thoughts of Sordo as he faces death on a hilltop surrounded by Fascist cavalry on the ground and aircraft overhead (thoughts that are so similar to the statement by Catherine Barkley at her death): "If one must die, he thought, and clearly one must, I can die. But I hate it." Like Sardo, who is able to face death with a certain gaiety, telling himself little jokes (earlier Jordan points out to himself that "all the best ones, when you thought it over, were gay"), Jordan through his pain is able to get off a small joke to himself before the end:

> We ought to have portable short wave transmitters. *Yes, there's a lot of things we ought to have.* I ought to carry a spare leg, too.
>
> He grinned at that sweatily because the leg, where the big nerve had been bruised by the fall, was hurting badly now.

Typically of Jordan, the battle within his spirit is fought to the very end, not just to maintain consciousness and courage, but to keep his thinking straight. One of his last injunctions to himself during the final moments is "Keep it accurate . . . Quite accurate." Having kept himself straight inside, he is ready to perform his last external, social act (an act that is symbolic in a way of the moral dilemma posed by the entire novel, since it is a necessary killing) with a dignity and skill befitting a professional: "And if you wait and hold them up even a little while or just get the officer that may make all the difference. One thing well done can make—."

"One thing well done," like Golz's statement on the telephone when he learns, after all, that the attack will probably fail (*"Nous ferons notre petit possible"*), is our modest hope. It is not much, but neither is it a whimper. Jordan dies with one of the most believable heroic flourishes of the mind and spirit in modern literature. Because he wins the game, is stern with himself to the end, he is able to do in truth all that is possible for him to do, and what he has done somehow makes faith seem possible, even in our time. Hemingway's search for "true emotion" turns out to be the search for the truth about man. Within ***For Whom the Bell Tolls*** the results of this search are presented with the deepest honesty and faith a skillful professional could employ. (pp. 153-68)

Jackson J. Benson, in his Hemingway: The

Writer's Art of Self-Defense, *University of Minnesota Press, 1969, 202 p.*

Arthur Waldhorn (essay date 1972)

[*Waldhorn is an American educator, critic, and editor. In the following excerpt, he provides an overview of* For Whom the Bell Tolls.]

In Hemingway's first three novels, each of his heroes incorporates the same theme: the isolated individual must struggle desperately to learn how to hold on in a hostile or indifferent universe. That hero appears in ***For Whom the Bell Tolls*** as Robert Jordan, but in a different place and with a different purpose. In a sense, he has been displaced, for Hemingway's focal range here extends beyond Jordan's apprenticeship and beyond the complexities of the war in which he has volunteered to serve as a guerrilla for the Spanish Loyalists. In competition for the role of hero is Spain itself. Through the people, their language, and their land, Hemingway tries to capture the spirit of an entire nation and to dramatize its tragedy. Within that tragedy—and it is here that he breaks new ground—Hemingway discerns a promise of transcendence, a unifying and sustaining spirituality that binds not only all Spaniards but all men. To reach this awareness constitutes the bulk of Robert Jordan's education; to communicate it through his thoughts and actions becomes Hemingway's purpose.

Hemingway's novel is Tolstoyan in scope but rarely in achievement. But it has many merits, and even its defects are generally interesting. Above all, it is a novel whose emotive force and integrity are never in doubt. Nor is there any question about Hemingway's instinctual commitment to the democratic spirit and his abhorrence of war, civil or other. Yet the novel falls considerably short of greatness. To some extent, Hemingway's failure in his longest, most densely populated novel is stylistic, but far more serious are his distortions of the experience he describes. Together, these technical and thematic flaws confuse and mislead the reader and, at last, diminish the novel.

Hemingway's narrative point-of-view, for example, causes difficulty. An omniscient perspective allows him a flexibility he uses on occasion to splendid advantage in the self-contained virtuoso passages: Pilar's description of killing the Fascists in her village; El Sordo's defense of the hilltop; and Andres's efforts to reach General Golz. But Jordan's is the prevailing central consciousness. Making him a college instructor of Spanish and author of a book about Spain is a plausible but not wholly persuasive ploy to erase doubts about his reliability as narrator. First of all, certain crucial episodes occur outside his ken. More important, as we shall see, he is simply too self-absorbed, too attentive to his own psychic pulse to reverberate adequately to the throbbings of those about him.

With structure, Hemingway fares better, counterpointing symbolic motifs of nature and technology that relate strands of plot, character, and setting to penetrating insights into life, love, and death. Many have noted that at the core of the novel is a single steel span of "solid flung metal grace"—the bridge, dramatic center of ***For Whom the Bell Tolls.*** The bridge, Jordan reflects, "can be the point on which the future of the human race can turn." None are untouched by their encounter with the bridge—the symbol of passage between despair and hope, betrayal and trust. All action and meaning in the novel extend from the plan to destroy the bridge and the futility of its destruction.

For the guerrillas holed up in the Guadarrama, destruction of the bridge means the end of their relatively safe refuge. Destroy the bridge, Pablo prophesies in the opening chapter, and planes will come to hunt his people like prey. But the scene has another significance too. For an instant as Pablo gazes "lovingly" at his fine horses, he stands "proud and less sad-looking." Then fear and gloom again shadow his countenance: "Here am I with horses like these. And what can I look forward to. To be hunted and to die. Nothing more." Life was not always so, not before the war, when Pablo supplied picador's horses for the bull ring. Then, the dignity of man and beast made sense. But to a twin-engined bomber or a tank, horses, hills, and men are as one, merely objects to be destroyed. Pablo is a sick, frightened man, but part of his dread and despair result from the intrusion of "mechanized doom" into the natural world. The bridge—itself a device of mechanics—now threatens the final holocaust.

Some of the tragic impulse in ***For Whom the Bell Tolls*** derives, as Allen Guttman suggests [in his " 'Mechanized Doom': Ernest Hemingway and the American View of the Spanish Civil War," in *Critiques of Four Novels*], from the sterile, repressive tyranny of machines subverting values of fertility and spontaneity identified with the earth. Certainly Hemingway images this conflict, using the bridge to link the opposing forces. If the bridge fills the middle of Hemingway's canvas, the earth frames it. At the opening and at the close, Jordan lies prone on the pine-needled forest floor. There too—and always out-of-doors—he and Maria love, and their ecstasy makes the earth move. But as always in Hemingway, nature is not entirely benign. Contradictions abound. Jordan, for example, dies as well as loves in a natural setting. And if for him the smell of nature is sweetly alive—clove and raked leaves, bacon frying and bread baking—for Pilar there is also the pungent stench of death, a compost of the breath of old women, decayed flowers, and slops swept from a brothel.

Weather too tokens (as in ***A Farewell to Arms***) oppositions in nature, though now it is snow rather than rain that mingles love and death. An unseasonal snow threatens Jordan's mission. Yet it is across the snow that he sees Maria running toward him for a night of love during which he becomes aware that their bodies make "an alliance against death." An early hint of Hemingway's effort to transcend polarities appears in Jordan's bardic response to the snowfall. At first angered and frustrated, he soon reflects that, during a snowstorm, "it always seemed, for a time, as though there were no enemies . . . it blew a white cleanness and the air was full of a driving whiteness and all things were changed and when the wind stopped there would be the stillness." More rudimentary, Pilar says, "What rotten stuff is the snow and how beautiful it looks. What an illusion is the snow."

El Sordo's fate best illustrates how nature and the machine alike ignore the poetry and the prose of human endeavor. Even as Jordan and Maria make love, El Sordo steals the horses needed to escape after the bridge is destroyed. But the horses leave prints in the snow. Jordan wakes from love to death, for he sights and must kill the Fascist scout trailing those prints. But nothing deters the cavalry, who follow hard after from tracking El Sordo to his natural fortress on a hilltop. Impregnable against land attack, the fortress crumbles and its defenders die beneath the bombs dropped from the air. Nature and technology, then, affect the form of the novel and the lives of its characters. They touch theme too, though not quite as Hemingway intends: the idealism that informs Hemingway's poetic spirit fails to alter or cancel the prosaic fatality that envelops ***For Whom the Bell Tolls.***

Hemingway's bell tolls for all men, but its deepest, most sonorous resonance honors them separately, each man alone, stranded on the island of his own lonely consciousness.

—Arthur Waldhorn

Structure, symbol, and image combine to underscore man's isolation and doom. Even the prose—more open, relaxed, and leisurely than ever before—seems to add weight to what Hemingway had written in ***A Farewell to Arms*** about how the world kills not only the gentle, the good, and the brave, but also those who are none of these—although "there will be no special hurry." The formal archaism of the dialogue (at best intermittently successful) suggests another time when life was simpler, personalized by "thee" and "thou," a time when human dignity seemed assured. But set against the quasi-Elizabethan pastoral exchanges between Jordan and Maria and the genteel, Old Testament solemnity of Anselmo and Fernando is the witty, racy, idiomatic vulgarity of Pilar, Agustin, and the others, a harsh reminder that the time is now, and that the Spanish earth is no more sacred or kind than any other, and its people no less vulnerable.

To the extent that ***For Whom the Bell Tolls*** rehearses Hemingway's familiar but always poignant sense of man's fate, the novel is relatively successful, occasionally superb. But when Hemingway tries to reconcile the struggles of lonely man with the spirit of a nation and a vision of all mankind, he drifts into a psychological smog and is soon wrapped in a philosophical mist.

Robert Jordan's politics are a striking example of this intellectual vagueness. After the war, Jordan says, he will write about his experience in Spain, "about the things he knew, truly. . . . " Before the novel ends, he has learned enough about loving and dying to tell himself in his final moments that "the world is a fine place and worth the fighting for and I hate very much to leave it." About political truth, Jordan is less certain. Bombers of both sides, for example, appear to him to be beautiful: "There's no *one* thing that's true. It's all true."

It is not that Jordan is either wholly indifferent to the political complexities of the Spanish Civil War or entirely ignorant of them. But he is hardly steeped in knowledge about a cause that has led him to leave his university and risk his life on alien soil. All of which might be surprising for a young intellectual, were he not one of Hemingway's heroes. Jordan's reading in the politics of the revolution he supports is limited to a handbook of Marxism. Most of what he knows about the inner struggles raging within the Republic he picks up from Karkov, the brilliant but cynical Russian agent. At first, Jordan had been attracted to the almost religious atmosphere prevalent at the headquarters of the International Brigade. Then Karkov drew him into the inner circle at Gaylord's, the hotel in Madrid from which coldly self-assured Russians deployed and disciplined the Loyalists. But the fine lines of distinction hold only casual interest for Jordan. Whether, as Karkov tells him, deviationists must be destroyed—Bukharinites and Trotskyites alike—is of little moment or use to him. Jordan, after all, fights neither as a member of the International Brigade nor as one of the regular Loyalist army, but as a guerrilla. All that really matters, he tells himself just before he dies, is that "I have fought for what I believed in for a year now. If we win here we will win everywhere."

Jordan's political statements suggest an inclination toward anarchism, but Hemingway avoids defining a specific position. Most of his explicit political opinions are as negative as Harry Morgan's in ***To Have and Have Not.*** Early on, he answers Maria's query about his being a Communist with, "No, I am an anti-fascist." Further along, in Chapter 13, he tells himself that he has no politics, and in Chapter 26 he reflects, "You're not a real Marxist and you know it . . . Don't ever kid yourself with too much dialectics." Occasionally, he seeds a statement with a political platitude of affirmation. He believes, he says, in "Liberty, Equality, and Fraternity" as well as in "Life, Liberty, and the Pursuit of Happiness." Or more concretely (and anarchically), he believes that "all people should be left alone and you should interfere with no one." Yet Jordan knows from experience that rarely is anyone left alone, not even generals. As General Golz tells him when they plan to blow up the bridge in support of Golz's offensive, "They are never my attacks. I make them. But they are not mine . . . Always there is something. Always some one will interfere." Nevertheless, Jordan unequivocally places himself under Communist discipline, "the soundest and sanest for the prosecution of the war."

Jordan's political stance is neither indefensible nor—despite its vagueness—incomprehensible. But one balks at Hemingway's implied suggestion that Jordan, inspired by a special vision of transcendence, has risen above the petty vulgarities of wartime politics. Contrast Jordan for a moment with another apolitical figure in another story. **"Old Man at the Bridge"**—one of Hemingway's finest—tells of an old man too exhausted to flee the rebel army advancing toward the Ebro. His sole concern is for the welfare of a cat, two goats, and four pairs of pigeons he has had to leave behind. On that Easter Sunday, the narrator says, there is nothing to do about the old man. At least, he concludes, the planes were not up that cloudy day. "That and the fact that cats know how to look after themselves was all the good luck that old man would ever have."

Only two and a half pages long, **"Old Man at the Bridge"** sounds with subdued eloquence the themes that pervade ***For Whom the Bell Tolls,*** though in the novel they are less clear, less resonant. Broken, luckless, alone, the old man symbolizes what has happened to the people of Spain. About politics he knows nothing: "I am without politics . . . I am seventy-six years old. I have come twelve kilometers now and I think now I can go no further." Yet, like the Major in **"In Another Country,"** the old man is an exemplary hero who defines his humanity by his concern for others and sustains his own dignity by quiet, uncomplaining courage. It is about such people that Hemingway writes most truly in ***For Whom the Bell Tolls,*** as he had always written about those who know or are learning the meaning of "grace under pressure." The spirit of the old man abides in Anselmo in Hemingway's novel, but it animates most of the others as well. Certainly it inspires much of what Jordan believes and what he tries too pretentiously to be.

It may well be that this kind of personal courage—the only kind Hemingway really comprehends and writes about with conviction—is too narrow, too egocentric to reflect the communal tragedy of civil war. Obviously disturbed by this possibility, Hemingway interlards his narrative with layers of noble but vague sentiment that peel off as sentimentality. He tries to write a new tragedy about mankind, but it is the old one—about the individual—that survives. In that old tragedy, the Spanish guerrillas play a more convincing role than Robert Jordan.

Betrayed by nature, machines, and by one another, the guerrillas still cling tenaciously to life and pride in self. Thrice-wounded, awaiting a hail of destruction from the sky, El Sordo accepts death without fear but (like Catherine Barkley in ***A Farewell to Arms***) hates it as a shapeless negation he cannot even body forth as an image. About living, on the other hand, El Sordo's vision is sharp, clear, concrete. Although the hill on which he must die is a "chancre," nature is still wondrous; it *is* life, for ". . . living was a field of grain blowing in the wind . . . a hawk in the sky . . . an earthen jar of water . . . a horse between your legs. . . . " Like the other guerrillas, El Sordo speaks little of politics. He fights for the Republic without question, introspection, or explanation, and he dies simply—like a bullfighter—with courage and dignity, trying to the end to kill his enemy.

El Sordo is a compendium of the virtues Hemingway admires in the Spanish personality and, by extension, in his own exemplary heroes. Most of the other guerrillas—whether gypsy or peasant—flesh out in greater detail these traits and others that amplify Jordan's conviction that there "is no finer and no worse people in the world. No kinder people and no crueler." Anselmo, for example, adds a dimension of secular sainthood. An atheist, the old man thinks in religious terms about the sin of killing a man. He kills with "a clear heart" to help the Republic, but "not with pleasure," insisting that one day all must "be cleansed from the killing or else we will never have a true and human basis for living." By no coincidence is Anselmo's counterpart a Fascist, Lieutenant Paco Berrendo, the austere young cavalryman who shoots Joaquin after the bombing raid "as quickly and as gently" as Sordo had killed his beloved horse. A devout Catholic, Berrendo loathes his blood-lusting captain, yet himself gives the order—because it is his duty—to behead the corpses of El Sordo and his men. "What a bad thing war is," he thinks as he leaves, praying. The little drama of killing by men who hate it is played to its fatal conclusion in the final paragraph of the novel, when Berrendo next appears, still "serious and grave," leading his cavalry into Jordan's gun sight.

Pablo is another matter. Yet he too is, as Jordan says, "all of them"—a compound of egotism, selfishness, and treachery. A loutish coward, he sneers at courage and seeks only survival. But as Anselmo says, Pablo "was something serious in the beginning," a leader who fought bravely and killed well. Hemingway fails to make clear whether too much killing has brutalized him, whether he is simply what Jordan calls him, a *bicho raro,* or whether both are true. He achieves a tainted dignity at the close when he returns to fight at the bridge, impelled not by commitment or by loyalty but by unendurable loneliness. Whatever his motive, he is no longer a figure of humiliation as he faces Pilar squarely for the first time in months to say, "I am ready for what the day brings." One believes him as one believes Francis Macomber, and shares Pilar's feeling that "if a man has something once, always something of it remains."

With Pilar, nothing has ever been lost. The most lavishly drawn of Hemingway's women, Pilar is abundant in body, mind, and heart. Not beautiful, she has loved often and well. Though her jealousy of Jordan and Maria occasionally finds harsh expression, her intent is never cruel. She is merely trying, as Jordan understands, to hold on to life. And living is Pilar's passion, for she has known—as mistress of the matador, Finito, and of Pablo—much of dying, and of fear and courage as well. Pablo, she reflects, "was like all the bulls that Finito had spent his life killing. But neither bull force nor bull courage lasted . . . and what did last? . . . Yes, I have lasted. But for what?"

To demonstrate how, her behavior implies, in the face of barbarism, destruction, and defeat, one retains a commitment to humanity and one's self. Politically, she too is utterly simplistic: "I am for the Republic . . . And the Republic is the bridge." Intellectually, she is at once *voyant* and clairvoyant, incisively clearheaded yet superstitious, a palmist and prophetess of doom who tries to shrug off her dark art as gypsy humbug lest she frighten Jordan, whose death she foresees. Above all, Pilar is a woman of profound sensibility. For all her barbarousness of manner and expression, she is extraordinarily sensitive to man's inhumanity and his latent decency. And she is quick to extend rough tenderness or mete harsh rebuff as each is merited. Thus, she is brusque but warm and protective toward

Maria and Joaquin, caustic and bitter to Pablo, yet forgiving when forgiveness is warranted. Nowhere is she more clearly revealed than in her dramatic narration of the massacre of the Fascists in her town. As sharp-eyed and curious as a reporter and as detached as a partisan who accepts without question that the enemy must die, she is also sickened and saddened when men become a mob. Bestiality and murder leave her "hollow and not well and . . . full of shame and a sense of wrongdoing. . . . "

Some critics look askance at Hemingway's guerrillas as inadequate representatives of those who fought and died for the Republic. One critic [Arturo Barea, in "Not Spain but Hemingway," in *Hemingway and His Critics*] writes that no village in the Sierra of Guadarrama would have accepted as Loyalist leaders "an old gypsy tart" and "a horse dealer of the bull ring." Another [Lionel Trilling, in "An American in Spain," in *Critiques of Four Novels*] suggests that El Sordo and Anselmo are less Spanish than lineal descendants of James Fenimore Cooper's noble savages. Some truth lies in each statement. But the novel is not, as we have seen, so much concerned with political verisimilitude as with capturing the spirit of a people. For Hemingway, nothing in that spirit renders incompatible Cooper's Chingachgook and the Spanish guerrilla. "All mankinde is of one Author," John Donne writes in his *Meditation,* "and is one volume."

Yet it would be futile to pretend that when the bell tolls the courage of the guerrillas, it is a resounding peal honoring the fellowship of man. Rather does it knell joylessly the doom of proud, anarchic individualism, a familiar echo in Hemingway's fiction. What cements these people is essentially their fierce pride in self ("What a people they are for pride," Pilar says). This is their collectivism. They do what they must—each in his own way—to affirm personal integrity. This is their politics, a politics of the bull ring which, not unreasonably, may be said to be no politics at all. Several of them—Pablo, Pilar, Joaquin, Andres—are people of the *corrida,* their ethics a product of its ritual. To this extent, ***For Whom the Bell Tolls*** advances but little beyond what Hemingway had said earlier in ***The Sun Also Rises, Death in the Afternoon,*** and stories like **"The Undefeated."**

Still, there is a substantial difference Hemingway intends us to feel. The bloody sands of the arena are now all of Spain, the combatants no longer man against beast but men of the same soil pitted against one another. Without choice (there is no "separate peace" in civil war), they have become, in Donne's words, "involved in mankinde." Harry Morgan's "One man alone ain't got no bloody f—ing chance" is renewed—with added dignity and point—in Donne's "No man is an Iland, intire of it selfe." It is not death the guerrillas fear so much as it is loneliness. Pablo says, "Yesterday, all day, alone *working for the good of all* I was not lonely" [italics added]. Without the bond of community and cause, loneliness is an agony, even for one so serene as Anselmo. Alone, he tortures himself about the morality of killing, but at the bridge, helping Jordan, "he was not lonely nor did he feel in any way alone. He was one with the wire in his hand and one with the bridge . . . with the *Inglés* still working under the bridge and he was one with all of the battle and with the Republic . . . he was not happy but he was neither lonely nor afraid."

In all this eloquence, Hemingway is groping toward a more comprehensive and affirmative vision of life than he had expressed in ***The Sun Also Rises*** and a clearer statement of it than he had managed in ***To Have and Have Not.*** Actually, even though a cosmic pessimism pervades ***A Farewell to Arms,*** it is imbued with the same sense of romantic idealism Hemingway strains after in ***For Whom the Bell Tolls.*** The difficulties that beset him here and his failure to resolve them are proportionately greater. The loneliness that unifies the guerrillas is, for example, poignant but too abstract to be more than half convincing. They linger in memory rather as trenchant portraits of individuals, whether as exemplars of courage and grace or of treachery and irresponsibility. That they fight as guerrillas further suggests their determination to avoid the mainstream of events determining the outcome of the war. Despite the pressures Hemingway applies, his Spaniards will not bend to his will. Although they are the logical bearers of his message about the brotherhood of man, he must at last let the burden fall—less logically and less successfully—on an outsider, Robert Jordan.

War is for Jordan, as for Nick Adams and Frederic Henry, a crucial part of his education. "It will be," he thinks,

General Enrique Lister with Hemingway near Mora de Ebro, November, 1938.

"quite an education when it's finished. You learn in this war if you listen." And what he learns, Hemingway insists, is congruent with the spiritual metamorphosis his Spanish mentors have undergone. Like them, Jordan has no fear of death. Yet, after Anselmo is killed, Jordan is "lonely, detached, and unelated," ready to indict man (Pablo) and nature (the snow) for the catastrophe. But hate wanes as he sees death the way the others must. Feeling closer to them, he rids himself of ego, "the always ridding of self you had to do in war. Where there could be no self." Above all, it is love that teaches Jordan that he, "with another person, could be everything." As he lives his final moments, Jordan not only reaffirms his faith in these thoughts—"You can do nothing for yourself but perhaps you can do something for another"—but by sending Maria away and by staying behind to stall the enemy, he translates them into action.

Jordan's farewell to war is, then, unlike Frederic Henry's, supremely idealistic. With little more insight than Frederic into his reasons for fighting and a great deal more into the bureaucratic inefficiency and personal treachery that foredoom his cause, Jordan elects to struggle on and die for what he believes in without really understanding. He bids farewell to love too without rancor; cloaking the bitterness of reality with a mystique of spiritual oneness. Urging Maria to leave, he says, "Not me but us both. The me in thee. Now you go for us both." For the first time in Hemingway's fiction, death becomes—in both love and war—a beginning rather than an ending.

Two climaxes in love with Maria (first in the heather, Chapter 13; again in Jordan's bedroll, Chapter 26) prepare Jordan for the climax of war and death he endures alone on the hill slope as the novel ends. During the first ecstasy of love, in which the earth moves for both lovers, Jordan feels time stop. From that instant, he is no longer aware of measured time or duration, only of eternal time, a continuously intense *now.* Into three days, seventy-two hours, Jordan realizes, he must compress all that a man who lives out a full three score and ten might learn of life, love, and death. If then, Jordan meditates, "there is not any such thing as a long time, nor the rest of your lives, nor from now on, but there is only now, why then now is the thing to praise and I am very happy with it." Without foregoing any of the pleasures of the flesh, Jordan achieves through his union with Maria (who, some critics have suggested, may symbolize both Spain and the Virgin) oneness as well with earth, man, and eternity. After the radiant warmth of such revelation, mortality is but a passing chill.

Some of Hemingway's most poetic writing (and overwriting) colors these passages about time and transcendence. There can be no argument about their adding a certain depth and dimension to an otherwise flaccid love affair. Concentrating on philosophical import distracts at least temporarily from recognizing that Maria is less real than Jordan's sexual fantasies about Garbo and Jean Harlow. Eternity with a creature so boundlessly and mindlessly submissive might make a lesser man long to be translated again into time. But the basic issues are neither Maria's credibility nor the baroque prose. Two other matters are. First, Hemingway's excursus on time and eternity fails to accommodate the tragedy of a nation riven by civil war. Earl Rovit argues to the contrary, suggesting that ***For Whom the Bell Tolls,*** like Whitman's "When Lilacs Last in the Dooryard Bloom'd," is a pastoral elegy that "envelops death and temporal violence in a transcendent serenity and harmony." In actual fact, the reverse is true; it is death and violence that overshadow all but a few selected moments of quietude. One might argue further that the tragedy of a man and that of a nation are not—even in the terms of John Donne's *Meditation*—truly analogous, especially when the men analogized are Abraham Lincoln and Robert Jordan.

And it is about Jordan himself that the second point must be made or, rather, extended, since it has already been stated in part. That he is an arbitrary, not an organic central character has been shown. In itself, this raises doubts about the dramatic validity of having such a character impose philosophical unity on the novel. A more serious doubt rises from Jordan's personality. He is too like Hemingway's other apprentices to effect a convincing leap from moral pragmatism to metaphysical pantheism. All the familiar traits are again in evidence: the obsessive concern with death and the equally compelling determination not to think about it. So too are the old escape routes—outdoor life, sex, food, and the "giant-killer," now an ever-present flask of absinthe. Yet Jordan thinks and worries more than Nick or Jake or Frederic, understandably so, for his world is more continuously violent than theirs, the imminence of death more constant. Jordan has also lived with death longer and, in certain respects, suffered its force more than they have. Like Nick Adams, Jordan was only a boy, seven years old, when he first saw violent death. For Nick (in **"Indian Camp"**) it was a suicide; for Jordan a lynching. "You were too young for such things," Maria says. Before he finishes school, however, Jordan must endure still another trial, his father's suicide.

Jordan has no difficulty following Pilar's advice not to speak of such things. "It is unhealthy," she says. Indeed, he mentions them only to Pilar and Maria, as if to talk about such matters with men would betray the discipline of the code. But he cannot so readily stop thinking about them, especially about his father's suicide. On the last night of Jordan's life, the image of his father as coward embarrasses and haunts him: "I understand it [the suicide], but I do not approve of it . . . You have to be awfully occupied with yourself to do a thing like that." Yet Jordan is wholly self-occupied, trying to behave otherwise, to behave like an earlier, braver ancestor. It is with his grandfather, who also fought in a civil war, that Jordan wishes he might talk at this moment, to learn from him what his father had failed to teach about courage. And in his final moments, suffering intensely the pain of his broken leg, Jordan once more renews his inward dialogue about suicide, calling again on his grandfather for strength. At last, Jordan musters the courage he seeks (putting aside even the "giant-killer"). "One thing well done can make—" is his last conscious thought. The rest is action—a glance at the sky, a touch of pine bark, and a finger on the trigger of a submachine gun.

Jordan's is an honorable death, fitting and proper for an

apprentice hero. It represents a psychological triumph over his self-doubts and fears, and a moral victory over the Fascists, who—as he knew they would—have destroyed the tactical value of his mission. In these terms, as Philip Young writes [in his *Ernest Hemingway*], "this time the hero has won." But Jordan's death fails to swell and fill the great circle of philosophical significance Hemingway circumscribes about it. For Jordan, "any man's death diminishes me" means more narrowly than Donne intended. To share selflessly the common fate of man holds for Jordan less appeal than to die as bravely as the best among men. Hemingway's bell tolls for all men, but its deepest, most sonorous resonance honors them separately, each man alone, stranded on the island of his own lonely consciousness. (pp. 163-77)

Arthur Waldhorn, in his A Reader's Guide to Ernest Hemingway, *Farrar, Straus and Giroux, 1972, 284 p.*

Praise for Hemingway's novel:

Of the novel's literary quality there can be no doubt. All the skill, experience, and technical resources at Hemingway's command went into its making. There is the dialogue, a skilful impression of the idiom and glorious cursing of Spanish speech, as strongly flavoured as onions and rough wine; the recurrent appearance of the planes as a disaster signal ("We could take thy happiness in a plane," Jordan remarks absently to Maria with unconscious ambiguity); the evocation of past content in Pilar's memories of Valencia and in Robert Jordan's odours of nostalgia, the more piercingly sweet for Pilar's foul description of the odour of death; there are the taut, subtly-varied intensities of plot, characterisation, and mood; there is Hemingway's prose, precise as ever, but moving in fuller, ampler periods; and above all there is the warm, human feeling that pervades the whole book. *For Whom the Bell Tolls* is a great novel, humane, vivid, intensely memorable.

Stewart Sanderson, in his Hemingway, *1961.*

Robert E. Gajdusek (essay date Fall 1990)

[*Gajdusek is an American educator, critic, short story writer, and poet. In his study* Hemingway's Paris *(1978), he asserted that "no American writer better understood our psychosexual dynamics and the fine and precise terms of the structuring of the sensibility/psyche." In the following essay, first presented at the Hemingway in Idaho conference in 1989, Gajdusek examines the role of Pilar's narrative in the novel.*]

Pilar's tale of the execution of the fascists in Pablo's town at the start of the revolution is one of the justly famed and celebrated passages of ***For Whom the Bell Tolls.*** It has drawn praise from numbers of critics, and some have not found the book equal to the achievement of her tale. Even critics on the far left, for whom the book was an indiscretion or an embarrassment, have praised Hemingway for the descriptive power of his prose in that section; and even Robert Jordan—to a degree a projection of Hemingway within his own work—is awed by the tale as told. Jordan, deeply moved by Pilar's description, thinks to himself:

> Pilar had made him see it in that town. If that woman could only write. He would try to write it and if he had luck and could remember it perhaps he could get it down as she told it. God, how she could tell a story. She's better than Quevedo, he thought. He never wrote the death of any Don Faustino as well as she told it. I wish I could write well enough to write that story, he thought. What we did. Not what the others did to us. He knew enough about that. He knew plenty about that behind the lines. But you had to have known the people before. You had to know what they had been in the village.

Jordan's reflections on the narrative are fascinating in and of themselves, for they well establish some of the fundamental aesthetic beliefs that were part of Hemingway's arsenal as a writer and that in part determined the composition of the tale. His commentary is intriguingly self-reflexive, for in it he stands in for the writer himself who is talking about writing the very passage he has written. Life and art come together in fascinating ways within his thoughts as he thinks of the tale that Pilar has "told" that needs to be at some future time written, that is, of course, the written story that we have already read. In this way, the future and the past are joined just as effectively as the tale has joined the fascists and the republicans in deadly struggle. Indeed, Hemingway has even answered his political critics before they have begun to assail him: the need is not to know what *we* have suffered, which we already too well know and will therefore teach us little, but rather to know what we have done to *others,* which we may not sufficiently recognize. He here simultaneously explains, as fully as he needs to, the aesthetic basis of his vision which, he anticipates, may be read as betrayal of the left. As Hemingway's protagonist Jordan argues for this self-transcendence and empathic projection into the "other," he not only defines Hemingway's own doctrine of composition, which demands in each of his major works that he cross over to the other side to explore, but he substantiates his own position at the moment, for he, as a foreigner, has crossed over from his side of the lines to be in the territory of the "other."

He also defines the writer's job as making others see what they otherwise cannot see, and suggests that a writer's craft depends upon the accuracy of his memory, the authority of his experience and also a measure of luck. He even goes on to argue that if Pilar could tell that tale, it is a tale *he* could not, for to tell it so knowingly one would have to have had knowledge of those in the village that would depend upon a knowing "before," a prior exposure to and familiarity with *them.* But we know as we hear this that Hemingway has created "them," and whatever backgrounds and histories they may be inferred as having had, and that all that Pilar knows of them is just whatever Hemingway has created to be known of them. As he goes on to pit Pilar in her tale-telling against the writing of Quevedo, he demands that we acknowledge the told tale as superior to Quevedo's art. Therefore Quevedo, existing beyond any telling in the immortality of his writing, is one of the writers Hemingway, in his writing of Pilar's tale, has taken on and has been sparring with. He, Hemingway, has outdone Quevedo.

When Jordan wishes that *he* might be able to write as well the tale that has just been told, and be the agent of getting Pilar's tale finally written, we must see that that is precisely the role Hemingway has himself already taken, and that Pilar's tale exists through and because of his writing/telling of it. Jordan's wishes are therefore singularly perverse, for the further we go in the novel, the more we see that Jordan's completion of his great work in the blowing of the bridge, and sending on those who survive the experience over the hill, into the future, carrying inside them the memory of his great achievement and his sacrifice to get it done, *and* the finishing or completion of the novel become in intricate ways ever more identical until both, the author and his creature, fuse. What remains alive at the end is what he, Jordan, and he, Hemingway, have fashioned to remain alive within those who remember what they have passed through and from where they have come. Therefore Jordan's statement, of his insufficiency to this task now, exists to suggest a yet unfulfilled ideal and a journey yet to be made, but it exists against the amazing artistry he (and we) have just seen performed.

Jordan's reflections on Pilar's narrative are fascinating in and of themselves, for they well establish some of the fundamental aesthetic beliefs that were part of Hemingway's arsenal as a writer and that in part determined the composition of the tale.

—Robert E. Gajdusek

This looking back on Pilar's tale by Jordan is really a way for all Hemingway's readers to look back towards what they have received by virtue of her telling, and to reexamine it; placing Jordan's reflection here is but to follow Hemingway's directive for reconsideration of what has been received: reaction, prepared with hindsight, has become preface to what will now be examined.

Despite the great critical attention Pilar's tale has drawn, it has not yet been adequately judged the intellectual and psychological *tour de force* that it is, for in it Hemingway has written one of his most philosophical (and also Jungian) analyses of war. Pilar's tale is an intricately fashioned, deliberate, and highly particularized study of the psychic art of revolution, in which Hemingway analyzes just what is happening on the deeper mythic and psychic levels of being as a country engages in civil war, the war that he had described in ***Green Hills of Africa*** as the "best" kind of war for a writer. There he acknowledges that he "had seen a revolution . . . and a revolution is much the best if you do not become too bigoted." The reader of ***For Whom the Bell Tolls*** is being shown a revolution by one who has seen one, and Hemingway, in the tale of the beginning of the movement and of the executions in Pablo's town, is revealing in an amazingly Jungian metaphoric structure the deeper psychic, mythic and historical significances of just such a war.

The tale itself is rather beautifully framed against the mountain journey that the three—Maria, Pilar, and Robert Jordan—are taking in order to meet with El Sordo. It begins with Pilar's imposed suggestion that they rest, as this is phrased against Robert Jordan's imperative sense they should continue. Jordan, who wanted only to stop "at the top," has been forced by Pilar to consider an alternative. He is in a hurry, but Pilar teaches him that "there is much time." Indeed, by the time the bridge is blown, he has learned that one can live a lifetime in three days, and his typically Western zeal for attainment and completion has found moderation: he has learned how to have his cake and eat it too, that the journey need not be a sacrifice to its end, that love and war can coexist, as can time and timelessness.

As they rest by a cold mountain stream and bathe their feet, Pilar educates Jordan, and each detail as she speaks in this setting Hemingway intricately describes, is in fact a preparation for the tale of the executions she will soon tell. Hemingway tells us that it was "almost as though she were lecturing." Pilar importantly insists that "the pine tree makes a forest of boredom, and that "a forest of pine trees is boredom." Arguing for the character, beauty, and individuality of deciduous or cyclical forests, and against the absoluteness of pines, she similarly argues for the plains, declaring herself tired of the mountains, where "there are only two directions. Down and up." This discussion should be significantly heard against the first sentence of the novel where the reader is first given Robert Jordan lying flat on the pine-needled floor of the forest. It will be heard again against the last words of the book as Jordan's heart is described "beating against the pine needle floor of the forest." Both the beginning and the end, his beginning and end for us, and his end for himself, are phrased against fallen pine needles, and one important learning stage on Jordan's final journey is this point of arrest on the mountainside where Pilar's disdain for the pines is opposed to her love of deciduous cycles. Jordan at last at his end will have learned how to accept the absolute *ever*green needles which, whatever their absoluteness, are nevertheless implicated in cycles and have *fallen* to be the base upon which he lies and on which he will die. But at this point in his journey, Pilar goes on to point out to him the water wagtail, a "ball" of a bird, "no good for anything. Neither to sing nor to eat," that can only bob and jerk up and down. She observes this as she unconsciously lights her cigarette from a flint and steel lighter and before she goes on to place beauty against ugliness—"would you like to be ugly, beautiful"—ugly/beautiful—she asks Maria, and then acknowledges that she herself would have made "a good man" though she is "all woman." Speaking of relations between the sexes as a sequential and repetitive male blinding and restoration of sight, controlled by the illusion of her beauty that a woman casts upon a man that will eventually be informed by the truth of ugliness, Pilar explains the cycles of male/female fascination: "then . . . another man sees you . . . and it is all to do over."

This rather long introduction to the telling of the tale of the killing of the fascists in Pablo's town is told as they have stopped half-way up the mountain and focus on the alternatives of deciduous or absolute evergreen trees, on mountains which compel ascent or descent, on the water wagtail that only goes up or down, and on the alternatives of ugliness or beauty as these relate to sight or blindness and desires for masculine or feminine identity. They talk as Pilar lights her cigarette with flint and steel. These many focused antitheses as they are skillfully linked and related by her to cycles are preparation for what follows, for the tale that Pilar now tells, however specific and historically and topically detailed, studies fascist dialectical alternatives caught in revolution, or either/or dialectics caught in a cyclical process of renewal. Such a structure is pure myth. As given, it is so pure in its many elements that even small deviations from the mythic pattern are informative variations.

The structure that Hemingway establishes for the telling of the tale, the apparatus and technique he uses, is complex. As he essentially describes a psychic battle, he interprets his terms broadly and mythically: his major pattern associates the fascists with the Apollonian and all that might be, either by Nietzsche, Jung or Neumann, associated with that, and he largely places the cyclical, the "revolutionary," with the Dionysian. Most details in Pilar's tale that are identified with the old order are distinguished by their Apollonian attributes, and most that are identified with the Republican cause are given as Dionysian attributes. These polar oppositions become in a broader perspective and another vocabulary masculine and feminine, and the struggle between them emerges partly as a solar/lunar battle in which male powers accept feminine control and the solar world yields to the lunar.

The geography and architecture of the main square in Pablo's town determines the action. The square is one, like the square in Pamplona in ***The Sun Also Rises,*** largely surrounded by arcades, and this fact in this novel, as it did in Hemingway's first, compels a basic dialectic between the area where the sun might dominate the *square* and the area under the arcades where one might, in shade and shadow, *encircle* the square. In this town the arcade covers three sides of the square; the fourth side, where there is the edge of the cliff, is still, however, in shade and shadow, being under the trees that line that edge. In ***The Sun Also Rises,*** as Jake walks towards his introduction of Brett to Romero during which he will lie to Romero thrice, he twice encircles the square. It is in that novel that the reader also notes that the entire fiesta is placed in jeopardy as (cyclical) rain comes to dominate the square, rain that drives people under the arcades, and also as mist from the sea comes to cut off the tops of the mountains. Such changes in landscape or scene are changes in powers and principles. The reader should not forget Margot Macomber (in **"The Short Happy Life of Francis Macomber"**) beginning to suffer badly from the sun as Francis, bonding with Wilson in masculine rites, begins to challenge her authority, or that Brett's power is established over Jake (in ***The Sun Also Rises***) preeminently when the night is dark and the moon and the river are high, and that it is in the dark lower wine cave that she is idolatrously enshrined as pagan goddess.

Crossing or circling the square are throughout Hemingway's work significant alternatives. Similarly, to accept the darkness or shadow beneath the romanesque arch of the arcade rather than submit to the terms of the sun in the square generally defines a retreat from Apollonian powers. Certainly, in Hemingway's aesthetics, as in any work of art, such basic oppositions are neither simplistic nor unvarying, while they yet serve to define a struggle between opposing forces.

One of the major controlling sub-metaphors of the tale is that of the corrida, a ritual death-dealing that usually takes place in a circular arena where *sol y sombra,* the dialectic of sun and shadow, oversees the action. However, *capeas* like the metaphoric one suggested in Pablo's town, do often take place in Spain in enclosed squares where the entering streets are closed or sealed off by carts and doors. Hemingway is superbly alert to the way the ring in Pablo's town is fashioned from a square, or is a squared circle, and his metaphors reflect it. If in his tale the ring and the square seem to have become one, this is also the case with *toro* and *torero.* The fascists readily seem to become, in the vocabulary of the life and death ritual of the bullfight, those who are to be slain, or representatives of the bull. This, however, is not simply the case in this tale, for Hemingway has deliberately complicated his symbolism by inverting its usual meaning—a frequent strategy in his work. Throughout Pilar's tale the fascists are associated with those values that are usually associated with the torero, and it is the revolution itself that is rather given—in this scene especially—to be associated with the dark wildness and ferocity of the bull in its attempt to destroy the insulting and goading codified forms that have provoked it to its attack. Although the drunkard among the Republicans will cry out "Qué salga el toro! Let the bull out!" establishing those in the "box" of the Ayuntamiento *as* the bulls, Don Faustino, an amateur bullfighter, who emerges like a bull from the box, is described as the torero, and is so taunted. "Don Faustino, *Matador, a sus ordenes,*" mocks one in the crowd; "Come, Don Faustino. Here is the biggest bull of all," cries another; and another, after his death, declares, "He's seen the big bull now." This deliberate confusion of toro and torero and killer and killed is a major device and part of Hemingway's intellectual and aesthetic strategy here and elsewhere in his work.

Hemingway has inverted ritual terminology for specific ends. The deliberate ambiguity Hemingway has attached to the fascists and their killers can be well seen as Hemingway describes the two lines of men that connect the Ayuntamiento and the edge of the cliff where begins "the emptiness [the nada] beyond." These lines conduct those who walk between them from linear prominence and authority high above to the chaotic darkness of death in the waters 300 feet below, and the files of men are described as standing like those who "watch the ending of a bicycle road race with just room for the cyclists to pass between, *or* as men stood to allow the passage of a holy image in a procession." The two similes are antithetical, the cyclists or the saints, and in being joined as one and the same, merge the two principles of the flesh and the spirit, the cycle and the cross, or cycles and absolutes, that Hemingway so frequently labors to fuse. Cyclists and/or saints, toro and/or torero, and square and/or circle suggest the ideal towards which the revolution unconsciously strives, a both/and existence which might replace the rigid dichotomizing either/or dialectic which the prologue called in question as it studied Pilar's ability to be a good man while being all woman, or looked at the water wagtail, a bird of the air that is also a bird of the water that, bobbing up and down, is yet a "ball" of a bird. It is no accident that the last words of the novel are "the pine needle floor of the forest," for simultaneously Jordan's heart and the pine trees themselves accept the cycles of the nondeciduous evergreen, the fallen and changing principle of unchangedness: human and vegetable life, both internal and external nature, man and landscape, rise from, attempt to transcend and yet are caught in and ultimately acknowledge the terms of their engagement.

One of the keys to Hemingway's metaphoric structure in this novel is the fountain that dominates the center of the square, and it, at the very center of the action of the tale, is the archetype of that action. The sound of "the splashing of the water in the fountain" is one of the last details of the tale as told. The fountain is described as being apparently a statue of a lion from whose mouth protrudes a brass pipe through which water pours to fall into the bowl of the fountain below, "where the women bring the waterjars to fill them." In almost unseen but elaborate detail Hemingway describes the translation of the vivifying waters, whose source is identified as the linear masculine solar lion above, through a fall into the circular bowl beneath, where they are finally described as filling the feminine vessels. This translation is of the captive waters through the line to the circle, from the male solar principle to the cyclical feminine, and it is no accident that the action duplicates the flow of movement of the soon to be "translated" victims between the lines above and down to the watery ravine beneath, just as it is no accident that the bowl should echo towards Pablo's wine bowl where he will search for his ideas or refer back towards the bowl from which Pilar seized her stirring-spoon baton of authority. What Hemingway is getting at is a theory of the restoration of absolutes through cycles, and of the masculine through the feminine, to create a both/and psychic base.

The Ayuntamiento on the square, across from the cliff edge and in which the fascists are imprisoned awaiting their execution, is described as a box, so emphasizing its association with the square. But landscape itself becomes the instrument of execution as those high above are cast out and down into the ravine far below. This overthrow of powers above, bringing them down, is the kind of therapeutic inversion that revolutions are meant to establish, to bring arrogant earth-and-life disdaining vanity down, to make that which is of the air, of the mind or the spirit, too abstract or elevated, acknowledge and accept the waters below, as life is coevally forced to accept death. The ravine therefore becomes heavily coded as the place of darkness, descent, the waters, death, and fear—it is also patently, in a Freudian sense, a feminine metaphor—and it is a clue to Hemingway's intricate structure in this novel that the action of revolution is the enforced synthesis of that which is above with that below, the sky with the waters. The blowing of the bridge, the major action at the center of this novel, in effect destroys the barrier between sky and water, air above and ravine below, and connects them, and this successful revolutionary act brings Pablo from the roadmender's hut below to join Pilar from above that these two bracing and reconciled surrogate father and mother figures may disappear over the crest of the hill at last, Maria between them. This new integration and synthesis is a psychic trinity for the future. It is important to so explore these relations between the height and the ravine, and a few of the meanings implicit in the blowing of the bridge, for the major irony of this novel—that has to do with each being part of the main, and no man being an island "intire of its self"—is that its central metaphor is the blowing and destruction of a bridge rather than the building of one. Metaphorically, it would be natural to assume that Robert Jordan, as the American who has crossed over to the other side to join others unlike himself that he may be part of their cause and share their lives, would be a bridge builder, not a bridge destroyer. It is Pilar who understands this irony, and she is the one to label his work in behalf of the common cause, as he goes on laboring below the bridge to help destroy it, masturbatory solitary and self-satisfying activity, perhaps practiced to *make* a bridge, not destroy one. And, of course, what she says is true: Hemingway's art is at once the building and destroying of a bridge.

Jordan once interrupts Pilar's tale to tell of the lynching of a Negro he had seen from the window of a house in Ohio when, at seven years of age, he had gone there to be "the boy of a pair of boy and girl" for a wedding. Maria remarks that she has never seen a Negro except in a *circus.* A black man, related to cycles, raised in the air and given to fire during a celebration of a synthesis, or wedding, is patently the exact metaphoric antithesis to polarized men thrown headlong down a ravine to waters beneath during a war. Hemingway has, in almost pure Jungian dialectical terms, illustrated in Pablo's town the psychic meaning of revolution, and in Ohio demonstrated the metaphoric meaning of patriarchal fascist control. It is exact that it should have been Jordan's mother who had pulled him away from the window, so destroying his spectatorial Apollonian disassociation.

The killing of fascists in Pablo's town is specifically described as a destructive activity that is coevally creative. It is a fertility ritual in which fertility is assured through the separation of the chaff from the wheat, through the threshing and harvesting rituals in which the act of killing with sickle and scythe, or turning or tumbling with a wooden pitchfork, is part of a death process out of which comes renewed life. The threshing of the grain, the spilling of the blood that then waters and fertilizes the otherwise barren earth, celebrate the relations between death and birth. The killing of the old king is implicit and underwrites the fertile reign of the new successor, as destruction is seen to be implicated in creation—as the birth/death imagery and rituals of ***A Farewell to Arms*** tried to show. To make this point explicit, Hemingway has one of Pablo's cohorts say, "We thresh fascists today . . . and out of the chaff comes the freedom of this pueblo." If, indeed, it is the blood of the fascists that fertilizes the earth, they are nevertheless here seen as the chaff, the part that is thrown away and that has been separated from the grain, and it is out of this that freedom comes.

As the other fascists are executed, their deaths are administered largely by the hands of peasants, men who deal with the earth, and they are killed in part by wooden instruments that relate to the crops and seasonal harvests, to fertility and its cycles: flails, herdsmen's goads, wooden pitchforks, etc. The sickles with which the priest is pursued in their very name speak of the cycles, and by their shape mythically and precisely refer to the moon and to primitive pagan fertility rites. The priest's death therefore becomes a larger victory, specifically a lunar or maternal victory, of nature religions over Christianity.

If the killings are described as a threshing, a separation of chaff and grain in a fertility ritual, in which all participate, they are also described as a feast or an eating—again, that which sustains natural process. Pilar, as the killings continue with less formality, feels she "has a bellyful," and then has a nausea "as though I had swallowed bad sea food." The smell of vomit is prevalent throughout the square, and that night, Pablo, eating, is described as "having his mouth full of young goat," suggesting the scapegoat sacrifice that has been served up to be eaten.

Hemingway throughout his work played with the cyclical though secondary meaning of "revolution" and "revolutionary." His short story **"The Revolutionist"** is a *tour de force* of such play, and in ***Green Hills,*** and ***To Have and Have Not,*** he elaborately studies the deeper ways in which revolutions are inevitably tied to cycles, and generally create them, restore them, implement them, and support them. Now, at the beginning of Pilar's tale, as she begins with the story of the attack on the barracks, cyclical forces of the movement are pitted against rectilinear and static oppositions.

The techniques and strategies of Pablo's attack and the modes of execution reveal the mythos of the encounter. The Republicans *encircle* their enemies in the barracks, cut their *lines* and *wires,* and, after having destroyed the intact *form* of the building and so having brought down much of the *roof,* execute the unwounded survivors by destroying their *heads.* The exponents of the revolution throughout the tale will either destroy or be unable to maintain linear controls. The destruction or lowering of the head—or the roof—is the means towards overthrow of their enemies, and the breaking or rupturing of intact forms their need: "Open up! Open Up! and "We're going in! We're going in!" are their cries. The four men executed at the barracks are, predictably, all *tall* men who keep tight mouths, who speak, if they do, with *dry* voices, and they are described as *mother killers.* In their deaths, the patriarchal Apollonian is overthrown: the voice of one of the *civiles* is described as "grayer than a morning *without sunrise*" (emphasis added), while the effect of Pablo's victory and destruction is to fill the air with dust that comes down over everyone as at a threshing. As the earth and passions rise, visual and mental clarity are part of the sacrifice. The officer commits suicide with his own gun and this is then taken by Pablo and turned against the other *civiles* before it is given to Pilar who then carries it with its muzzle encircled, its "long barrel stuck under the rope" about her waist. This feminine appropriation and encirclement of the male phallic linear gun is a trope that finds several variations throughout the novel as it speaks of the shift of masculine powers into feminine hands. Pablo personally executes the *civiles* with shots to the head. His act subsequently is seen as having been egoistic, and thus, for the following executions, all are formed into lines between which the victims must pass, so that all may share in the administered blows and therefore in responsibility for the deaths that follow. In this way individuality yields to commonality and integration. The killings are throughout, as they were at the barracks, described as the execution of the male principle: as one revolutionist says, "Thanks be to Christ, there are no women"; and Pilar asks, "Why should we kill their women?", suggesting that destruction is reserved for the masculine principle for male crimes.

Before the release of the first fascist from the box to the lines, water is swept in wide sweeping arcs to moisten the ground. Hemingway carefully also establishes that the land becomes truly the peasants' land when the fascists are "extinguished," by the verb suggesting the tale that is being told is one that recounts the struggle as additionally between light and darkness. As though to emblematize the meaning of the deaths that follow, Hemingway has Pilar discard her tricorner hat taken from the *guardia civil* so that it can be "destroyed." It is sailed far out into space to drop down into the ravine and river below. The destruction of the hat is an important metaphor for the assassination of masculine pride, vanity, identity, and power. It establishes the paradigm for the deaths that follow it into the ravine, even as it establishes the values that the revolution discards.

The prototypical fascist death is that of Don Federico Gonzalez. Described as a "fascist of the first order." he has been the owner of the mill and feed store, therefore proprietor/manager of the cycles and the cyclical processes of life. He is predictably tall, thin (vertical, linear), and balding (mental rather than virile), and he emerges unable to walk, "his eyes turned up to heaven . . . his hands reaching up as though they would grasp the sky." This man who has "no legs to walk," and "no command of his legs," who seems to have no lower centers to relate to the earth but instead yearns towards the spirit and the sky, "never did open his mouth." The iconography reveals a model of what is to be overthrown. The others who die are significant variations on this model—however different, they do not contradict or challenge the paradigm—like Don Ricardo, who, equally mental and earth disdaining, "trying to walk with his head up," nevertheless is overflowing at the mouth as he verbally vilifies the effeminized principle that destroys him: "I obscenity in the milk of your fathers." He shrugs off the contamination of contact: "Don't touch me."

The failed or spurious fascist ideal is represented in Don Faustino Rivera, who, despite his patriarchal credentials as the oldest son of his father, a landowner, and his tall height and sun-yellow hair, conceals behind his facade of masculine pride the coward who wanted to be an amateur bullfighter, who "went much with gypsies," and was "a great annoyer of girls." Though he "acts" brave, and looks handsome, scornful and "superb," when he sees the "emptiness beyond," the nada, he loses all his style, covers his eyes, "throwing himself down and clutching the ground and holding to the grass." In this revelation of the failed or false fascist ideal, Hemingway reveals the coordinates of the patriarchate. Don Faustino's apostasy—as he compromises his belief with superstition, his male insularity with uxoriousness, his authentic pride with poses and assumed and not genuine feeling, and then overthrows sight, verticality, belief, pride, and form—expresses the overthrown patriarchal pattern.

Having given these examples of the authentic and spurious Apollonian ideal, Hemingway provides the portrait of Don Guillermo, a man killed largely by the drunkards who are no longer able to distinguish or comprehend what they kill. Don Guillermo is carefully described as of medium height, as nearsighted, and as a "fascist, too, from the religiousness of his wife which he accepted as his own due to his love of her." Moderate in height, sight, in his masculinity, and in his faith which he moderates because of love, he finally nearsightedly rushes towards death "blindly," believing he is rushing towards his wife who calls his name. His final blindness is an important self-dethronement of the Apollonian world, as it speaks of the substitution of the woman for sight. The anomaly of Don Guillermo speaks to the two worlds that are in delicate balance within him.

Inside the box, Pablo sits with his legs hanging down, rolling a cigarette, while Cuatro Dedos sits in the Mayor's chair with his feet on the table. This inversion, where lower centers are emphasized or replace higher, is implicit in most revolutions; and the feet, legs, and cycling here speak of it. Outside the Ayuntamiento a drunkard lies on the one un-overturned table at the fascist club, his head hanging down and his mouth open. The unconscious prone man with inverted head and open mouth names what has, at this point in the revolution, replaced the vertical, keen-sighted close-mouthed capitalist proprietors, and it is this state that has metaphorically been forced upon them. Overthrown, they have had their heads destroyed and brought low and into the dust and been projected down into the dark death in the ravine. In the background on the square the destroyed lines have now become a mob that chants, "Open up! Open up! Open up!"

Pilar witnesses the death of the priest. In order to see what is going on inside the "box," she has to stand on a chair to see more and higher than the heads of others, and with her face against the bars of the window, she holds on by them. A man climbs behind her on the chair and stands with his arms around hers holding the wider bars. His breath on her neck smells like the smell of the mob, like vomit on paving stones, and as he shouts "Open up! Open up!" over her shoulder, it is "as though the mob were on my back as a devil is on your back in a dream." Meanwhile the mob itself presses forward and another man hurls himself again and again against the backs of the men before him. The image and the metaphor is an image of sodomitic rape being accomplished concomitantly with the overthrow of all order and the coeval death of the priest, or the spirit. Indeed, exactly as Pilar witnesses the fatal assault on the priest, the chair she stands on breaks and she and the drunkard mounted on her back fall to roll on the pavement among the spilled wine, vomit and the forest of legs of the mob which is all that Pilar can now see.

Hemingway has written with keen irony a study of the almost instantaneous way a revolution, even as it is being established, creates the same competitive struggle for ascendancy and power based upon sight and visual control as existed in the capitalist world it tries to replace. As Pilar and the man on her back struggle for advantage, he pushes her head down and she hits him hard in the groin: the man tries to dethrone intimidating feminine mental supremacy, and the woman tries to castrate the man. This struggle to gain advantage over another in a competitive struggle for height and sight is pointedly at the cost of the one less advantaged. Hemingway has also suggested that erectness and verticality, sight and perception are based on a relation to spirit, and that to deprive the body of the spirit is to bring it down to the underworld of legs and leavings, to roll in the dust.

Pablo's dismay at being deprived of his belief in the manliness and courage of the priest is answered by Pilar's wisdom: "I think he died very well—being deprived of all formality." She is suggesting that to destroy the forms of life leaves it without the sacramental base through and by means of which human dignity can be maintained.

In the night after the killings, Pilar awakes and looks out at the square where the lines had been that is now dominated by and filled with the moonlight. There she sees the moonlight on the trees, the darkness and the shadows, and hears "no sound but the falling of the water in the fountain." At the end of the executions, the once sun-drenched square is dissolved in darkness where amorphous and indistinguishable shapes and the sound of water falling seem to control the world. The solar (lion) principle has yielded to the lunar, the woman presides over the square, while Pablo, stuffed with goat, impotent after the day's deeds, lies unconscious, sleeping.

The mythic dynamics of Pilar's tale operate throughout the novel. One of the most poignant moments in this work is the exchange that, in a later chapter, takes place between Anselmo, Fernando, and Robert Jordan as they get ready to return to the guerilla cave.

"Back to the palace of Pablo," Jordan says to Anselmo. Anselmo alters his description, "El Palacio del Miedo. . . . The Palace of Fear," and then Jordan caps this retort with his own, "La cueva de los huevos perdidos. . . . The cave of lost eggs." Fernando, in his usual impercipience, asks, "What eggs?" and Jordan answers him, "A joke. . . .Just a joke. Not eggs, you know. The others." "But why are they lost?" Fernando asks, and Jordan replies, "I don't know. . . ." "Take a book to tell you. Ask Pilar."

The exchange is one of the few places in a Hemingway novel where the frame is broken, and deliberately broken by a character who steps beyond his role to speak for the author and the author's controlling awareness. Another similar break in a novel's fictive frame takes place in ***Across the River and Into the Trees*** and for approximately the same reasons. It is the moment when Richard Cantwell, having confronted a very similar recognition indeed, the significance of the green emeralds, which are the "eggs" of *that* novel, subsides to let the author intrude: "He was addressing no one, except, perhaps, posterity." Here, too, the lament, the pain, if not the exasperation, show—Hemingway is now beyond exasperation—and he knows well that he cannot look for contemporary recognition of his deeper structures.

Both interpolations, in ***Across the River*** and ***For Whom,*** reveal an infinite weariness in the author, the weariness of an artist whose intricately crafted structures have created no public and scant critical awareness, who labors to establish deep patterns that meet no appreciative response, hardly a glance of recognition. When Jordan, in ***For Whom,*** says, "Take a book to tell you," he knows what his creator Hemingway well knows, that the intricate and detailed pattern that the writer has carefully laid down in the novel, that studies the rivalry for power within the primal cave, the eternal battle of the sexes for phallic power or authority, and the Oedipal son/father rivalries as they relate to that battle, have been studied at a level and in such depth that no explanation or speech or essay will reveal their mystery. Hemingway would need another book like the one being written to trace the many lines and ramifications he has placed in that remarkably complex story.

On the simplest of levels, the reference to the lost eggs is, of course, to lost testicular power or male potency in the struggle for power and authority that Jordan has witnessed within the cave, a battle that has culminated in Pablo's overthrow as he has been unmanned and cowed by Pilar as she, inverting her stirring spoon, has made the baton of her cyclical function the new emblem of power in the cave. On another level, the reference goes back to Jordan's two sacks which have early been carefully coded by Hemingway to develop their testicular/egg associations, and which have been packed, we are told by Jordan, "as carefully as he had packed his collection of wild bird eggs when he was a boy." Those two male sacks were first studied by Hemingway in ***The Sun Also Rises*** when he described the driver of the stage that takes Bill and Jake up to Burguete as coming out "swinging two . . . mail [male] pouches" as they start off for their consummate male experience. Now, again in Spain, these sacks are resurrected as the containers of Jordan's potency as a dynamiter, for in them are his exploding devices, his detonators and his bundles of explosive charges, that can allow him to fulfill his mission and himself as a male.

As Jordan heads towards the mouth of the cave with a sack in each hand, Hemingway's earlier image from his first novel is revived. Jordan's "things" are now placed in the cave. Their being there can be recognized as the provocation to the scene that ensues, in which Pablo, a surrogate but cowardly father figure, will be overthrown. Jordan's "things," now in the cave after Pablo's authority there has been called in question and stripped from him, identifies Jordan's new role with respect to Pilar and introduces new plot complications. Hemingway seems to be studying the situation that exists when a son figure takes his potency through the cave mouth, and puts it in the care and under the supervision of the maternal figure at the hearth. Such metaphors are all heavily coded with the language of sexual power dynamics and rivalries. But these are only a few of the levels of the struggle that Hemingway studies. As Jordan said, for Hemingway, "Take a book to tell you."

What is important to recognize in Jordan's remark to Fernando is that he himself is only too well aware, superlatively aware, of the sexual dynamics of the power struggle that has been going on. He has been witness to much. He has seen the shift from patriarchal authority to matriarchal power and recognized his own role in that as son-usurper. He has witnessed the subsequent humiliations of Pablo, who is now identified with a flaccidity, limpness, and inert inactivity which suggest his castration. The reader is, at this point in the narrative, not yet fully aware of Jordan's own history, one in which he has effectively lost his own father, a *cow*ardly man who was cowed, like Pablo, by Jordan's *bully* of a mother; nor has Jordan yet suffered the assault on his sacks. In that attack, Pablo, as he takes away Jordan's potency, places slits on the sacks in the cave, apparently suggesting an attempt to effeminize that rival son and prevent the success of the action and task he hopes to perform. Hemingway has coevally let those readers who are aware of his self-reflexive mode in this novel see that Jordan's fulfillment of his task is simultaneously Hemingway's completion of his, and that the "father's" interference with its success is their shared problem. Jordan's remark to Fernando occurs . . . in chapter XV of the novel, yet it was exactly . . . , on page 99 in chapter X, that Pilar began to tell her remarkable tale of the execution of the fascists in Pablo's town. In order to recognize another yet more profound level of meaning behind *"la cueva de los huevos perdidos,"* that tale must be carefully examined, remembered, and related to the larger patterns of mythic struggle that the novel exists to study. (pp. 19-31)

Robert E. Gajdusek, "Pilar's Tale: The Myth and the Message," in The Hemingway Review, *Vol. X, No. 1, Fall, 1990, pp. 19-33.*

Michael Reynolds (essay date Winter 1991)

[*In the following essay, Reynolds evaluates the significance of* For Whom the Bell Tolls *for contemporary readers upon the fiftieth anniversary of its publication.*]

As ***For Whom the Bell Tolls*** eases through its 50th birthday into ripe middle age, it has already outlived its author, its war, and most of its original audience. Today the Spanish Civil War, which was once the heart's blood of this novel, has become a footnote to the violent century that bore it. Old soldiers may still argue across cafe tables, rehashing their salad days at the siege of Madrid or on the rocky slopes of Teruel, but their memories have become history, and they have become artifacts, trapped in time. So much blood has since soaked the earth, dulling our capacity for horror, that Hemingway's once great novel has reached the sticking point: it must either transcend time or become one of its footnotes, of interest to historians and graduate students but no longer part of the mainstream. Even the best-written fiction goes astray in time's good time. How could Hemingway have predicted the contemporary American reader: detached, deconstructive, postmodernist, and political only on narrow issues?

Had Hemingway been able to imagine the ideological malaise left in the wake of Korea, Vietnam, and Watergate, he still could not have written for his 1940 readers and their 1990 grandchildren with the same effect. Robert Jordan is not our contemporary, and those first readers who responded so positively to his heroism are not our emotional brothers, barely our first cousins. When the battleship *Houston* was sunk in the Coral Sea, more than a thousand Houstonians volunteered in front of the old Loew's Theatre to man the new *Houston.* Today the theatre is probably gone; maybe the bronze plaque is still on the sidewalk, but I didn't see any volunteers for Vietnam lined up there the day I faced my draft board. Having been lied to by every president during the last 50 years, the contemporary reader is closer kin to ***A Farewell to Arms'*** Frederic Henry than to Robert Jordan. Cynical, self-centered, and opportunistic, Frederic is a survivor who volunteered to participate in war but without any burning reason. For love of Spain—the land, the Republic and its people—Robert Jordan risks his life to fight fascism, to protect Maria, to wash away his father's suicide, to do his duty. There's a word to reckon with: duty. Nelson used it bluntly at Trafalgar: "England expects each man to do his duty." To Robert E. Lee, duty was the most sublime word of the English language. And as late as 1960, Hemingway's Thomas Hudson could still say that "Duty you do." In Vietnam we did the job assigned us, but few thought of it as our duty, not in the sense that Hemingway uses the word.

And yet, Robert Jordan, by the time he blows his bridge, has lost all of his innocence and most of his idealism. He is, in fact, a bit more like you and me than generalizations indicate. No one starts off cynical; none of us was born disillusioned. Each started out, if not with illusions, at least with political innocence, believing his elders, accustomed to words making sense, hoping for the political best. Then in 1940, pledging to keep us out of war, Roosevelt promised that no mother's son would die on foreign soil. And Lyndon Johnson promised no wider war in Vietnam. And Richard Nixon promised he was not a liar. And Reagan promised he would never make a deal for hostages. And George Bush promised no new taxes.

Thus, Robert Jordan's need for and loss of belief should remind us of our own needs and losses. I do not know for what ideals this generation would fight and die, but I cannot imagine them volunteering to die for another country's government. Some would go for love of slaughter, but I cannot imagine International Brigades forming to preserve the kings and kingdoms of Arabia, which, as I write these words, are being threatened by Iraq. I can imagine Americans being sent to war to keep open the flow of oil, to insure repayment of bank debts, or for any of the other money reasons that old congressmen send off the sons of others to die in foreign fields. But I cannot imagine those same young men streaming illegally into Saudi Arabia to keep a king on his throne. I cannot imagine them risking permanent blacklisting to fight for, say, black South African freedom. That is, of course, my cynicism speaking. Underneath I secretly hope for idealistic behavior, but having had it turn to mouth ash in the Tonkin Gulf I resist its temptation as well as I'm able.

Any reader born around 1936, the first year of the Spanish Civil War, has gone through more political promises made and broken than he or she can remember. This disillusionment, which has become an American rite of passage, is also part of Robert Jordan's political education. With the International Brigades, early in the war, he tells us that devotion to the Loyalist cause was like a religious experience, "the feeling you expected to have but did not have when you made your first communion." That "purity of feeling" barely lasted the first six months; survivors hardened quickly. At Gaylord's Hotel in Madrid, where Jordan was privy to gossip of the Russian insiders running the war, his innocence evaporated. "You corrupt very easily, he thought. But was it corruption or was it merely that you lost the naïveté that you started with?" In his fortunate or unfortunate fall into awareness, Robert Jordan established a paradigm for his immediate readers, many of whom would discover their political realities on the beaches of war, or in its hedgerows and jungles, or in its aftermath of deceit. It's an old lesson, maybe a universal one, a lesson we've learned by heart these last 50 years.

If Jordan's political education so resembles our own, why then is ***For Whom the Bell Tolls*** so little read, so seldom taught? Why has Hemingway become the quintessential twenties author and not the man of letters he aspired to be? Today we teach, read, and talk about his short stories (1924-36), ***The Sun Also Rises*** (1926), and ***A Farewell to Arms*** (1929). Few and strange are those of us interested in his experimental works of the thirties, fiction and nonfiction that went against the prevalent tide of tedious proletariat preaching and romantic escapes. After 1940, Hemingway published only one flawed novel, ***Across the River and Into the Trees*** (1950), and one novella. Among school children, ***The Old Man and the Sea*** (1952), because it is short, seemingly moral, and without offensive parts, has become a classic of sorts, but it is now vaguely embarrassing to many scholars. Too direct, probably. About the posthumous works, critics are divided and scholars are largely silent. ***The Garden of Eden*** was so badly edited that the present text is like reading *A Tale of Two Cities* with London left out. ***A Moveable Feast,*** a curious kind of fiction, is only marginally better in its editing. Two chapters were cut, most of the others were resequenced, and his foreword was pieced together by his editors from several different manuscripts. Which brings us back to ***The Bell,*** for if Hemingway is going to be more than a twenties period piece, this novel is his present best hope of surviving until his entire canon is reliable enough to be evaluated. That one should have to defend ***For Whom the Bell Tolls,*** make cases for its relevance, tells us two things: the novel is out of tune with these times, and it may not be the great work it once seemed, for great novels should need no apologists.

In October 1940, when the novel was first published, reviewers could not have imagined my last sentence's needing to be written. With few detractors, ***The Bell*** was a raging best seller, Hemingway's first truly mass-market novel. After his new books in the thirties sold barely in the twelve thousand copy range, he gloried in the ***The Bell***'s first printing of 210,000 copies that sold out immediately. With interest spurred on by Book-of-the-Month Club selection, Paramount purchased the film rights to the novel three days after it appeared in print; in less than six months the book sold 491,000 hardback copies. Critical consensus was euphoric: ***For Whom the Bell Tolls*** was among Hemingway's finest work. *The New York Times* called it "the best book Ernest Hemingway has written, the fullest, the deepest, the truest. It will be one of the major novels in American literature." Dorothy Parker wrote that it was "beyond all comparison, Ernest Hemingway's finest book." The *Nation* thought the book set "a new standard for Hemingway in characterization, dialogue, suspense and compassion." Clifton Fadiman in *The New Yorker* said it "touches a deeper level than any sounded in the author's other books. It expresses and releases the adult Hemingway." *Saturday Review of Literature* called it "the finest and richest novel which Mr. Hemingway has written . . . and it is probably one of the finest and richest novels of the last decade." Edmund Wilson loved the novel: "Hemingway the artist is with us again; and it is like having an old friend back." Amidst such effusive praise, only John Chamberlain, of the major reviewers, had the reserve to question whether this was Hemingway's best novel or not. We would not know, he said, "until the passions of the present epoch have subsided."

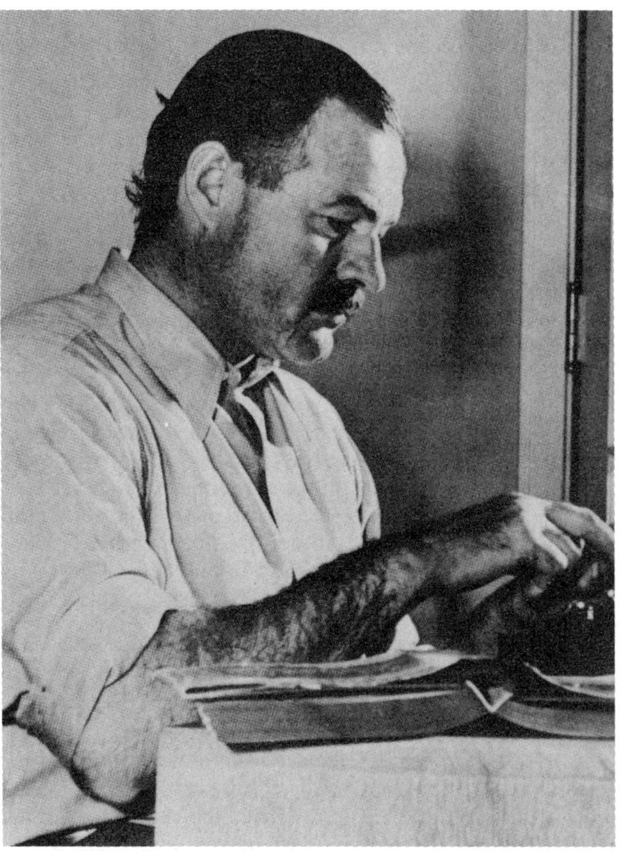

Working on For Whom the Bell Tolls, *Sun Valley, Idaho, 1939.*

Chamberlain was right. With passions not merely subsided but largely forgotten, the once burning politics of that Spanish war are lost on the reader today; it was difficult enough at the time to keep the players straight. To the American reader, unsure of the dates of his own Civil War, what happened at Burgos and Madrid four wars ago are merely blips on the ragged EKG of our times. The American reader does not particularly care who was a Fascist and who a Communist; that there were Russians and Russian-trained Spaniards running the war for the Loyalists no longer matters. That there were lies is unremarkable. That there were betrayals seems customary. That civilians were bombed at Guernica seems perfectly ordinary to an age in which the nuclear destruction of population centers is a foregone conclusion. That atrocities were committed and many died is hardly news after Auschwitz, Dresden, Stalingrad, and Hiroshima. Whatever horrors Hemingway tried to conjure in his antiwar novel, he could not fully imagine our capacity for violence. To children who grew up on World War Two, lost faith in Korea, and lost hope in Vietnam, Robert Jordan's lengthy internal debates about his politics, his motives for killing, and his hopes for a better world seem stale, flat, and profitless.

This present dearth of idealism is probably no more permanent than was its seeming demise following World War One. Everything cycles. If hula hoops and Bermuda shorts can rise from the dead, why not the capacity for idealism that characterized the 1940's reviewers and their audience? It is, however, during this lull between enthusiasms that ***For Whom the Bell Tolls*** must find new readers and wider rationale or be left stranded on the beach with other once famous but now largely unread American novels. The curious tide that brought it ashore has ebbed, and it cannot afford to wait on that same tide's return. The 1920's Melville revival refloated *Moby Dick* to its present seaworthiness; maybe postmodernism can recast ***The Bell,*** giving it a tone that rings clear for our times. This is not to imply that any novel's greatness depends upon current critical trends. Classic fiction will always prevail eventually, but critics do give teachers new handles on a novel which encourage them to take it back into the classroom. What gets taught gets talked about and becomes actively part of the cultural flow. If post-modernist interests do not restore ***The Bell,*** its time will eventually come round nonetheless. At least without the confusion of past idealism and politics, we are free to examine the novel in a far different light from that available to its first readers.

In doing so, we can broaden our scope of enquiry, widen the vista. Until recently our interests have been too narrow and too predictable. While Hemingway's invented language continues to incite his Spanish detractors and apologists, it is not a central issue, for this novel was no more written for a Spanish-speaking audience than ***A Farewell to Arms*** was written for an Italian one. The problem of Spanish slang and cursing will neither save nor silence ***The Bell;*** if besmirching the foulness of one's mother's milk is not a perfectly translated Spanish curse, American readers, upon whom ***The Bell***'s status depends, will never know or care deeply about the difference. Nor will that audience respond to historical issues: if Hemingway has maligned Andre Marty as a paranoid sadist, today's readers do not particularly care. Nor are they concerned about which characters are real, which imaginary, and which based loosely on real counterparts. Those issues are exhausted avenues, still on the street map, but no one lives there anymore.

Another main road no longer traveled, and rightly so, is the one detailing the novel's epic qualities and characteristics. Not that they are not present, and not that Hemingway did not consciously put them there, but they now are a less substantive issue than they once appeared. Books are not read because they are epics; first they must tell an interesting story. Homer wrote the *Iliad* and the *Odyssey;* Virgil wrote an epic. Hemingway once said that bad writers fall in love with the epic, implying that he never would. He also promised he would never compete with Tolstoi's *War and Peace.* Maybe he forgot, or maybe he was leaving a confusing trail of contradictions for his own amusement. The degree to which Hemingway fulfilled or failed to fulfill requirements for an epic is not an uninteresting academic debate, but neither is it an issue sufficiently central to rehabilitate the novel for most readers.

If ***For Whom the Bell Tolls*** is to become once more important to the Hemingway canon, then post-modernist readers must not so much deconstruct the novel, but reconstruct it. As modernist, Hemingway has been rightly praised for liberating the American stylist with his native voices and for reaffirming American subject matter: the loss of innocence, the American in Europe, the effects of violence, the search for values, and the definition of manhood. While these issues are less central to the contemporary agenda, it would be a mistake to assume that Hemingway does not speak, in a less obvious voice, to points dear to the post-modernist heart—gender roles, self-referencing, appropriation, multiple framing, narrative guises, and writing about writing. These elements all have their roots in the modernist period in the same way that modernist roots are deeply buried within the crannied Victorian wall. It would not be surprising, therefore, to find that ***For Whom the Bell Tolls,*** written on the transition point into the post-modernist era, contained within it the seeds of the next generation.

Take, for example, the element of appropriation. Eliot told the modernists to steal large and boldly, but few openly followed his directive. Today, in music, art, or writing, one is likely to find the artist doing a "cover," appropriating for his own use the work of some other admired artist. In freshman English we still call this plagiarism; yet Eliot plagiarized *The Waste Land* from the broken shards of his cultural inheritance, remaking them into his own work. The post-modernist artist does the same. While Hemingway never worked as boldly as Barth or Calvino, he still insisted that some writers were born only to contribute a single line to another writer. He learned that truth at Pound's knee and practiced it surreptitiously all his life. In his early vignettes, called ***In Our Time*** (1924), he appropriated the voice and stories of a British friend. His famous depiction of the retreat from Caporetto in ***A Farewell to Arms*** was taken wholesale from unacknowledged sources. In ***Islands in the Stream*** (1970) he appropriated well-known paintings of Winslow Homer and gave them to his fictional painter, Thomas Hudson. He told himself in an early unpublished note that education consisted in finding sources obscure enough that no one would recognize them when he used them. Despite his anti-intellectual public guise, Ernest Hemingway was not an uneducated man: his Cuban library held six thousand volumes, some of them obscure enough to appropriate.

In writing ***For Whom the Bell Tolls,*** Hemingway drew heavily on at least two authors: Owen Wister and T. E. Lawrence. By 1939, when he began writing his novel, Hemingway had known Wister for eleven years, having read his seminal western, *The Virginian,* as early as high school. The older writer was Hemingway's direct link to the American 19th-century old-boy tradition. Wister had been Harvard classmate and personal friend to Teddy Roosevelt, Hemingway's most obvious early role model. That *The Virginian* was dedicated to Roosevelt was not lost on Hemingway. Wister, having been encouraged in his writing by Henry James, felt he was passing the torch of tradition on to the pacemaker of the next generation when he befriended Hemingway through their mutual friend and Scribner editor, Max Perkins. As soon as one connects *The Virginian* with ***The Bell,*** both obvious and subtle appropriations appear. Jordan leaves the American West to go to a civil war, reversing the Virginian's pattern of moving West after the American Civil War. Like the Virginian, Robert Jordan is a natural leader, a horseman, a quick and deadly shot, a teller of stories, and a man facing an enormous task. Both men make decisions well under pressure and take decisive action as if they were born to it. Jordan is the hired gun, the outsider brought in to organize the local hands in a crucial task. He understands the Spanish terrain, its people and their language. Like the Virginian, Jordan bends men to his will through action and words. The Virginian has his *bete noir,* Trampas, to face over drawn guns; Jordan has his Pablo. In both novels the love interest is a strong motivating force. The Virginian teaches the New England schoolmarm to ride and shoot; she teaches him to read Dostoevsky and Shakespeare. When he is wounded and vulnerable, she defends him, saving his life. Afterward they marry: enervated East and war-weary South unite in the American West to pour grit back into the nation's chops. The parallels are not one for one with ***The Bell,*** but homage is being paid. In a role reversal, Jordan is the educated lover, a college professor; Maria is the tyro who, nonetheless, teaches Jordan to love. When he is wounded, she tries to save him, but he will not let her. In Spain there are no happy endings, no coal deposits to sell the railroad, but as Jordan lies dying on the Spanish earth, he is fortified by the memory of his courageous grandfather, Civil War veteran and Indian fighter in the West. While these parallels may not seem like appropriations in the post-modernist sense, neither are they merely allusions. Wister's novel solved a very real problem for Hemingway: how to write about the Spanish war yet isolate his protagonist from the front lines and the various historical necessities that setting entailed. Moving Jordan across the frontier into the wilderness, as Wister did in

The Virginian, gave Hemingway a freedom for invention he would have otherwise lacked. Once a man crosses the frontier, the social contract is broken and all rights and responsibilities revert to him. Wister knew it, and Hemingway remembered the lesson.

A more obvious appropriation was what Hemingway took from T. E. Lawrence's World War One adventures in the Arabian desert. In 1928, Hemingway read Robert Graves' early Lawrence biography, *Lawrence and the Arabs,* preparing himself for Lawrence's own account—*Revolt in the Desert*—which he read in 1931. Three years later Hemingway ordered the Liddell Hart book, *Colonel Lawrence;* and in 1935, he bought Lawrence's *Seven Pillars of Wisdom.* During the first two years of the Spanish Civil War, Hemingway purchased two more Lawrence biographies, and as he began writing ***For Whom the Bell Tolls,*** he bought *The Letters of T. E. Lawrence.* Suffice to say that Lawrence and his Arabs were much on Hemingway's mind during ***The Bell***'s gestative period.

Having had no firsthand experience in guerrilla warfare, Hemingway transposed what he learned from reading Lawrence's account of the desert war to Jordan in the Spanish mountains. Both characters, larger than life, are college men: Jordan teaches at the University of Montana; Lawrence was a research fellow at Oxford. Both men are fluent in local dialects, know their terrain from prewar travel, and practice the customs of the country. Both are attentive to details and are able to inspire natives to follow their outside leadership rather than that of a local leader. Both men are dynamiters: Lawrence specialized in trains, Jordan in bridges and trains. Both men, out of battlefield necessity, are forced to kill close friends. When his wounded Arab friend, Farraj, cannot be left behind to be tortured by the Turks, Lawrence kneels beside his comrade and puts a bullet through his head. Jordan faced a similar situation when his friend Kashkin was wounded by a Fascist patrol:

> "I shot him," Robert Jordan said. "He was too badly wounded and I shot him."

Both Lawrence and Jordan have divided loyalties: distrusting the politics of their superiors, they both feel more brotherhood with their guerrilla bands than with their commanding officers. In sum, Hemingway's fiction depends in large degree on his appropriations from Colonel Lawrence who, just out of sight in the novel, is nonetheless informing its action.

While Lawrence silently contributed to the casting of ***The Bell,*** Hemingway's public life played an equally strong role. Like his post-modernist kin, Hemingway, from 1930 onward, was always self-referential, continually calling attention to himself and to his earlier work. By 1940, his audience knew he had been to the Spanish war and was writing about it, for his life had become public property. If one had not read Hemingway's North American News Alliance reports from the Spanish front, he could not have escaped the author's goings and comings covered by national magazines and wire services. By 1940, Hemingway already had published a handful of short stories set at the war, written one play about it (***The Fifth Column,*** 1938), and told any number of interviewers he was at work on his Spanish war novel. All of this activity, while adding to the popular but false conception that Hemingway lived his life and then wrote about it, was a series of self-referential acts closely kin to similar activities of Ken Kesey, Norman Mailer, Joan Didion, Hunter Thompson, and numerous others writing in post-modernist time.

Even more self-referential was ***The Bell***'s basic plot: a young but experienced American volunteers for a foreign war where, while doing his duty, he falls deeply in love with an attractive woman. Hemingway used that plot in ***A Farewell to Arms,*** and he calls our attention to it in his second war novel, asking that comparisons be made. Any experienced Hemingway reader could not have gotten past the opening paragraph of ***The Bell*** without thinking of ***A Farewell to Arms*** which begins:

> In the late summer of that year we lived in a house in a village that looked across the river and the plain to the mountains. In the bed of the river there were pebbles and boulders, dry and white in the channels.

For Whom the Bell Tolls begins:

> He lay flat on the brown, pine-needled floor of the forest, his chin on his folded arms, and high overhead the wind blew in the tops of the pine trees. The mountainside sloped gently where he lay; but below it was steep and he could see the dark of the oiled road winding through the pass. There was a stream alongside the road and far down the pass he saw a mill beside the stream and the falling water of the dam, white in the summer sunlight.

The point of view has shifted from first to third, but the internal rhythms and landscape renderings are remarkably similar. Once again we are somewhere else, some place unnamed, not knowing where or why, not knowing through whose eyes we are seeing. Once more we begin in the middle of things with much left out, much to recover. Reviewers missed the point, calling ***The Bell*** a return to Hemingway's early style. Yes, it starts in the same manner, and, yes, it has a roughly similar plot, but these self-referencing devices call our attention to differences, not similarities, between the two books. It is as if Hemingway were saying to those who bemoaned his departure from his fiction of the twenties, "Sure, I can still do it if I want to, but there's more to a writer's life than his early work." There are, in fact, several Hemingways—part continuum, part discrete periods. There is no single Hemingway style, but several, and ***For Whom the Bell Tolls*** signals the transition into his late, eclectic period.

He is also transitioning into his most complex exploration of gender roles, experiments which have left his traditional readers perplexed but which should interest those post-modernists for whom gender is important. The novel's first readers saw only the love story: Jordan and Maria making the earth move out and away from them in their moment of La Gloria as Maria calls it. But there was always more to the picture. There was always Pilar. There was always the triangle: Pilar, Maria, and Jordan. It is more than Jordan's death that Pilar reads in his palm: he is the man for whom she has been preparing Maria. Pablo wanted her; the gypsy yearned for her, but Pilar, who claimed Maria for her own, gives her as a gift to Jordan in an act he neither fully understands nor questions deeply. In a rare moment, Pilar tells the two lovers,

> "Yes, he can have thee, . . . I have never wanted thee. But I am jealous. . . . I am no *tortillera* but a woman made for men. . . . I do not make perversions. I only tell you something true. Few people will ever talk to thee truly and no women. I am jealous and say it and it is there."

Tortillera is Spanish slang for lesbian, the dark side of Pilar left largely unspoken in 1940. Hemingway, who would become increasingly fascinated with such triangles, realized the androgynous side of men and women earlier than most have given him credit. In the end, with Jordan broken on the slope and waiting for his death to find him, Maria is sent away with Pilar holding her, the same Pilar who has said of herself, "I would have made a good man, but I am all woman and ugly. Yet many men have loved me and I have loved many men." Any novel that has an androgynous older woman, a rape-scarred younger woman, and an odd assortment of men working out male-identity problems ought to provoke something more than a knee-jerk response from those interested in gender studies.

Without drawing undue attention to his artistry, Hemingway has written a collection of short stories embedded in a framing novel.

—Michael Reynolds

More interesting, perhaps, than ***The Bell***'s gender issues are the complexities of its narration and its structure, both here and throughout his work much neglected aspects of Hemingway's artistry. With deceptive simplicity Hemingway was always testing the limits of narrative, extending the possibilities of how a story can be told. One of his earliest discoveries in Paris was the curious effects of skewed and shifting points of view. In ***For Whom the Bell Tolls*** he uses a curious omniscient point of view encompassing a whole range of narrative voices. When it suits his purpose, Hemingway's narrator can tell us how Anselmo suffers in the snow storm on his road watch or of Andres' difficulties taking the message to Golz. The power of that narrative voice is most felt in the gut-wrenching story of El Sordo's brave death on his lonely hilltop. When the closing chapters begin to alternate between Andres' frustrating effort to warn Golz and Jordan's effort to blow the bridge, the counterpoint works and the reader's belief is not strained. We recognize Hemingway's mastery of a traditional narrative stance.

Elsewhere in the novel, however, Hemingway twists, bends, and sometimes breaks every tacit rule for the omniscient narrator he has adopted. He can move the reader into Jordan's mind, which is an old perogative, but then, for extended periods, Jordan becomes the narrator who provides flashbacks to his earlier life and even flashforwards to fantasies of taking Maria to Madrid. Jordan's internal monologues turn into narratives, stories within stories, a device more closely associated with John Barth than Ernest Hemingway. Most of what the reader finally knows about Jordan's past he learns from these narratives, not from the omniscient author.

Interesting, you say, but not all that incredible. Look again. Look at the other narratives embedded within the larger story of Jordan's bridge: there is Rafael's story of rescuing Maria when they blew up the train; the story of Kashkin's death which is revealed over the course of the novel; the gripping story of El Sordo's hilltop fight; Maria's story of the execution of her parents and her own rape; Andres' story of his bull-baiting youth; and Jordan's story of his political education at Gaylord's in Madrid. Almost every character, including Pablo, becomes, at some point, a narrator within the larger narrative, but the most remarkable storyteller of all is Pilar. She first tells us the story of her life in Valencia with the bullfighter, Finito, and later creates its sequel—his dinner of honor turned grotesque by his horror of the bull's head on the wall. But these stories are overshadowed by her stunning account of the first day of the revolution when Pablo and the peasants executed the Fascists in the village square, beating them to death with flails in drunken, primitive rage.

Without drawing undue attention to his artistry, Hemingway has written a collection of short stories embedded in a framing novel. In fact, most of the action that makes Jordan's three-day wait to blow the bridge less tedious comes through these embedded stories. This structural experiment is a variation on Hemingway's continual investigation of narrative limits. In 1925, he embedded his terse vignettes as counterpoints between the stories of ***In Our Time.*** In 1932, he embedded several stories, both narrative and dialogic, into ***Death in the Afternoon.*** In 1937, he welded a series of Harry Morgan short stories into the novel ***To Have and Have Not.*** Inside Hemingway's last unfinished book, ***The Garden of Eden*** (1986), David Bourne writes the remarkable story of his father's elephant hunt. And in what may be Hemingway's finest if not his strangest fiction—**"The Snows of Kilimanjaro"**—he embedded at least six stories within the story of his dying writer, Harry Walden.

Written three years earlier, **"Snows"** now appears as a trying-out of ***The Bell***'s experimental structure, for almost 30 percent of the novel is stories told within the larger story, frames within frames, voices within the over-voice. And for each story the primary audience is Robert Jordan, himself a writer. He tells us that "Pilar made him see the Fascists die in that story she had told by the stream. . . . If that woman could only write. He would try to write it and if he had luck and could remember it perhaps he could get it down as she told it. God, how she could tell a story. She's better than Quevedo, . . . I wish I could write well enough to write that story." And there we are, finally, at the quintessential post-modernist moment: the story within the story being listened to by a writer who hopes one day to write the story we have just read.

Halfway through the novel, we are told that Jordan

> would write a book when he got through with this. But only about the things he knew, truly, and about what he knew. I will have to be a much better writer than I am now to handle them he thought.

For Hemingway's central character to be an author thinking he must become a better craftsman to write the story that is, in fact, being written by Hemingway cracks the realist's mirror, pushing the unsuspecting 1940's reader into post-modernist terrain where we are all cousins together. Fictions collapse into other fictions, their frames enclosed by further frames. Told at the turning point, Hemingway's ***Bell*** is the biographer's delight, a transition piece between periods, a work looking both ways, speaking beneath and between the lines directly to us, its unimaginable future readers.

But wasn't that always Hemingway's primary subject: the writer writing? Jake Barnes in ***The Sun Also Rises*** is a journalist self-consciously writing a novel; in **"Big Two-Hearted River,"** a story in which almost nothing happens except the pure prose of it, Nick Adams leaves behind him the need to write. Unwritten stories weigh heavily on the conscience of the dying writer, Harry Walden; other writing writers appear in ***To Have and Have Not, Islands in the Stream,*** and ***Garden of Eden.***

Those are the obvious occasions, but Hemingway's subject was frequently the act of authorship even when the surface story was about something else. As soon as we realize that the bullfighter, hunter, fisherman, and boxer were his metaphors for the writer and his trade, we see that his entire canon is about writing, its processes, its purpose, and the death of the artist. You can count on that with Hemingway: the artist either dies or loses so badly it amounts to the same thing. Against heavy risks and long odds, the artist, nevertheless, continues to perform: the writer on his fiction, the dynamiter at his bridge work. Driven by Hemingway's 1940 ethic, neither has a real choice: the book must be written and the bridge blown; each has become a function of the other. But each man's death diminishes mankind, as Donne's epigraph promises, and each finished work diminishes the artist's storehouse of ideas, making the cost of life and art almost unbearable. Almost, but not completely, for in the lap of death, we continue to create our art, diverse and various as its forms may be, and in the process deplete the mine from which our resources come. Each of us is his own Emersonian artist; each life a series of artistic gestures, a collection of stories. Like Hemingway, like Jordan, none of us has a choice, and all our stories are embedded within larger stories. If we make that connection, then the novel transcends the historical context that bore it, becoming a parable rather than a paradigm. And thus, softly, across time, ***The Bell*** continues in muted tones to toll for us. (pp. 1-18)

Michael Reynolds, "Ringing the Changes: Hemingway's 'Bell' Tolls Fifty," in The Virginia Quarterly Review, *Vol. 67, No. 1, Winter, 1991, pp. 1-18.*

Wolfgang E. H. Rudat (essay date Fall 1991)

[*In the following essay, Rudat discusses the influence of Milton's* Paradise Lost *(1667) on Hemingway's treatment of gender issues in* For Whom the Bell Tolls.]

When Hemingway's writing has been examined from a feminist critical stance, he has usually been stereotyped as a machismo writer, but more recently, and more leniently, he has been offered up as an artist who eventually balanced his deliberately cultivated traditional masculine personal and literary style by composing fiction which emphasized androgynous behavior. The danger in exclusively adopting one particular critical stance is that it can easily become reductive if it neglects close analysis of the text, an approach which, as Robert E. Gajdusek [in his *Hemingway and Joyce: A Study in Debt and Payment*] warned in 1984, Hemingway criticism has either got away from or never accepted as a *sine qua non:*

> Close textual reading is one of the least developed aspects of Hemingway criticism . . . the redemption of Hemingway from his legend, that *persona* that he probably fashioned partly in scorn for those who would not (not could not) read him, can only be accomplished through intense textual study. Lack of attention to the very real details of the published text keeps thousands of wonderful jokes and puns and Joycean word games from being read . . .

Close-reading Hemingway includes examining his text for possible allusive interactions with other works of literature. As I will attempt to show, in the case of ***For Whom the Bell Tolls*** Hemingway methodically uses literary allusion for the narrative function of illuminating the portrayal of Maria, who has unjustly been stereotyped as being without individual personality, as submissive, and as unimportant to the overall theme of the novel. In fact, Maria rebels against submission by taking the initiative in a scene important for our understanding of the novel, a scene which is one of the most famous and most frequently cited in Hemingway's fiction.

During the day following the consummation of the love relationship between the protagonist Robert Jordan and Maria, the gypsy woman Pilar, who had arranged the relationship, treats the young lovers to embarrassing and bitter effusions on the subject of sex. Jordan therefore suggests, "Let us all go to the camp together." He is in effect offering to give up a sexual rendezvous with Maria, a rendezvous which Pilar had just pointedly made reference to. But his suggestion draws the following rather uncooperative responses from the two women:

> Pilar nodded with her head toward Maria, who sat there her head turned away from them, saying nothing.
>
> Pilar smiled and shrugged her shoulders almost imperceptibly and said, "You know the way?"
>
> "I know it," Maria said, not raising her head.

And Pilar starts to walk in the direction of the camp. The final decision that Pilar will return to the camp alone, then, is made by Maria sitting there and saying nothing, and it is being confirmed when, after Jordan calls to Pilar, "Wait . . . It is better that we should all go together." "Maria sat there and said nothing."

While Pilar's question, "You know the way?", may give the impression of referring to geographical directions, "the way" refers to Maria's sexual approach to Jordan. The meaning of Pilar's question becomes clear when, after walking with Maria "through the heather of the mountain meadow," Jordan kisses her and asks, "Where should we go?" Jordan's question endows the scene with a goodly amount of irony because topographically Maria is not allowing Jordan to go anywhere:

> [Jordan] straightened and with his two arms around her held her so tightly that she was lifted off the ground, tight against him, and he felt her trembling and then her lips were on his throat, and then he put her down and said, "Maria, oh, my Maria."
>
> Then he said, "Where should we go?"
>
> She did not say anything but slipped her hand inside of his shirt and he felt her undoing the shirt buttons and she said, "You, too. I want to kiss, too."
>
> "No, little rabbit."
>
> "Yes. Yes. Everything as you."
>
> "Nay. That is an impossibility."
>
> "Well, then. Oh, then. Oh, then. Oh."
>
> Then there was the smell of heather crushed and the roughness of the bent stalks under her head . . .

And immediately thereafter follows the famous lovemaking scene during which they feel the earth move.

When Maria kisses Jordan on his throat we know that she has all the information on him she needs—and that she has received that information from Pilar. When the older woman initiated Maria into the gypsy-lore belief that lovemaking can lead to a rare magical experience during which the earth moves, she also must have advised her that she had noticed something strange about Jordan's throat. That there is something strange about Jordan's throat is suggested by his first reaction to Maria's presence: "Every time Robert Jordan looked at her he could feel a thickness in his throat." Kenneth S. Lynn has observed concerning the numerous throat-thickening scenes in the novel: "To get around the certainty of censorship by his editor, Hemingway substituted sensations of swelling and feeling of thickness in Jordan's throat for what happens to his member." But Lynn caught only part of Hemingway's point in what he called the author's censorship-avoiding substitute sensations. Hemingway's point is that there is something erogenous about Jordan's throat area itself, an area which also manifests the excitement of his genitalia, when Jordan's voice thickened while he was making a remark about Maria. Pilar "looked at him and shook her head. 'Ayee. Ayee,' she said, 'Are all men like that?" Pilar considers the reaction of Jordan's vocal chords in excess of the lump which she jokingly suggests "all men" must get when they are excited over a female. Pilar thinks that potentially (if I may pun on a vulgarism) Maria 'has Jordan by the throat.'

Pilar has instructed Maria, who had been gang-raped by her Fascist captors several months earlier, on how to prevent future violations during the gruesome civil war, namely, by carrying a razor blade with which she could quickly slash her own carotid artery. In light of this fact, the interpretation which offers itself is that in the battle of the sexes Maria is going for the jugular vein: Maria is trying to assert herself against the male by taking the initiative in this male-female encounter. And Maria's attack on Jordan's throat is effective: they stay right where they are, in mockery of his question, "Where should we go?" Jordan's question takes on a meaning not intended by him when she tells him the way *she* wants them to go—so that his question becomes an ironic echo of Pilar's "You know the way?" Maria does know "the way": when, in addition to having worked on his erogenous throat, she unbuttons his shirt and says, "You, too. I want to kiss, too," she is telling him that she will insist on kissing him in places where the night before he had kissed her. Since this type of kissing had increased her sexual excitement, she wants to do the same to him to increase his excitement.

This occurrence is in pointed contrast to what had happened in his sleeping bag the night before, when she had wanted to kiss him but he, rather impatiently, started the process of getting her undressed:

> " . . . I must kiss you. I must do everything."
>
> "There is no need to do anything. We are all right. But thou hast many clothes."
>
> "What should I do?"
>
> "I will help you."
>
> "Is that better?"
>
> . . . . .
>
> Now as they lay all that before had been shielded was unshielded . . .

When in his presentation of the first lovemaking scene Hemingway writes, "Now as they lay all that before had been shielded was unshielded," he is directly alluding to Milton's line in *Paradise Lost,* "Nor those mysterious parts were then concealed," in particular, and establishing a broader allusive connection with the general context of the description which Milton had given of Adam and Eve in the greatest poem about the battle of the sexes ever written in English:

> *both*
> *Not equal, as thir sex not equal sem'd:*
> For contemplation hee and valor form'd,
> For softness shee and sweet attractive Grace,
> Hee for God only, she for God in him:
> His fair large Front and Eye sublime declar'd
> Absolute rule . . .
>
> [her looks] implied

> *Subjection,* but requir'd with gentle sway,
> And by her yielded, by him best receiv'd,
> Yielded with coy *submission* . . .
> Nor those mysterious parts were then conceal'd,
> Then was not guilty shame . . .
> (*Paradise Lost,* IV, italics added)

Following the Pauline tradition that "The man is the head of the woman," Milton had presented the prelapsarian relationship as one in which Eve was in a state of "Subjection" and "submission" to Adam. Milton's Eve fell when she broke out of this God-ordained hierarchy, and Adam "complet[ed] the mortal Sin / Original" when he followed Eve's lead and relinquished his God-given superiority, which earned him this rebuke from Christ: "to her / Thou didst resign thy Manhood, and the Place / Wherein God set thee above her made of thee, / And for thee." Punning on *Adam / man,* Milton had presented our First Father's Fall as an occurrence in which he lost his adamness: Adam allowed Eve to psychologically-spiritually unman him through a gender-role reversal. In fact, Milton's language strongly suggests that Eve's rebellion against him whom God had set in the "Place . . . above her" included rebelling against the distribution of sex roles which quite literally confined her to a position of "*Sub*-jection," namely, to what today we call the missionary position. And Hemingway, in turn, is alluding to Milton in order to import from Milton's epic into his own work meanings that may not be explicit in his text. In a book chapter entitled "A Classical Epic: *For Whom the Bell Tolls,*" Gerry Brenner calls ***For Whom the Bell Tolls*** an epical novel: I submit that any attempt to judge the 'epicalness' of ***For Whom the Bell Tolls*** has to examine the novel in terms of possible intertextuality with target texts in the epics, in this particular case in *Paradise Lost.* I especially wish to argue that Hemingway's intentional allusions to Milton operate simultaneously for the purposes both of similarity and of contrast, with the interaction between similarity and contrast being very important. The most important similarity is that, just as Milton presents Eve as rebelling against the God-ordained hierarchy in which Adam/man is the woman's superior to whom she owes "Subjection." Hemingway has the namesake of the Second Eve rebel against the same Pauline hierarchy where "the man is the head of the woman."

Hemingway would deal with a subject matter similar to Milton's in ***The Garden of Eden,*** begun in 1946 and published in an edited and radically shortened version in 1986. Or let me express my point about Hemingway's subject matter a little more boldly. While in *Hemingway's Reading 1910-1940* Michael S. Reynolds lists only Books I and II of *Paradise Lost,* and while there are no references to Milton in the *Selected Letters,* to anyone familiar with the more sexually oriented parts of Milton's poem, even the shortened version of ***The Garden of Eden*** is clearly Miltonic. Not reading Book IX, in which Milton presents the Fall, and presents it specifically in sexual terms, is tantamount to not reading *Paradise Lost* at all, and Hemingway's use of *Paradise Lost* in ***The Garden of Eden*** reflects a fascination or even an obsession with Miltonic material. Few readers would call ***For Whom the Bell Tolls*** Miltonic in the same sense, but it does not require the "external" evidence produced by bibliographical and/or biographical detective-work to be able to suggest that Hemingway intentionally drew on Milton's epic. Textual evidence is persuasive enough.

Yet let me get back to ***The Garden of Eden*** for a moment. In that novel, Hemingway describes not only a gender-role reversal but quite specifically also a sex-role reversal between the Eve-figure Catherine Bourne and her husband David Bourne. Lynn summarizes this scene:

> ". . . you're my girl Catherine. Will you change and be my girl and let me take you?" [Catherine said]. He reminds her that she is Catherine, but she denies it. "No," she says, "I'm Peter. You're my wonderful Catherine. You're my beautiful Catherine. You were so good to change. Oh thank you, Catherine, so much."

When Catherine says, "I'm Peter . . . you were so good to change," she is trying to usurp from David symbolically if not literally the "Peter" alias phallus. However, what makes Catherine Bourne, whom David repeatedly refers to as "Devil," diabolical is not so much her attempt to play Adam as her desire to have the cake and eat it too; in her assumed androgyny Catherine feels omnipotent: "I'm a girl. But now I'm a boy too and I can do anything and anything and anything."

While Hemingway is not presenting Maria as diabolical, the exchange between Maria and Jordan immediately preceding the earth-moving experience—"You, too. I want to kiss, too"-"No, little rabbit"-"Yes, yes. Everything as you"—bears too much resemblance to Catherine Bourne's "I can do anything and anything and anything" not to create the impression that Maria is rebelling against what Milton had called "Subjection": rebelling if not necessarily against the missionary position, then at least against Jordan having the only say in their sex life. But then we do not really need ***The Garden of Eden*** to be able to understand the gender-role battle in ***For Whom the Bell Tolls,*** although the later novel reinforces that understanding: Hemingway's allusive transactions with Milton's lengthy espousal of the Apostle's ordinances tells us exactly what Maria is trying to do. And Maria is successful in her attempt to break out of the hierarchy where the "man is the head of the woman." Maria succeeds by being the sexual aggressor: by ignoring Jordan's repeatedly uttered plea that they accompany Pilar to the camp and initiating the sex act at a venue of her own choosing and on her own terms.

Maria is not yet the sexual aggressor during her first night with Jordan when, in order to help her overcome by means of a positive sexual experience the trauma of the rape, Pilar dispatches her to his sleeping bag. However, Maria's first-night imploration, "I must kiss you. I must do everything," bears enough resemblance to Catherine Bourne's "I can do anything and anything and anything" to suggest that Maria is already rebelling against her sex-role—rebelling for reasons which, as we will see in a moment, are from the author's stance entirely valid. Here in the sleeping bag, however, she is in a no-win situation because the neophyte has no choice but to follow what Jordan advises her is the proper protocol of sexual intercourse: "There is no need [for you] to do anything. We are all right. But thou hast many clothes." Not yet having learned about her rape, Jordan is inconsiderate to the point of making a fool of himself. He wants a quick consummation, and is concerned about nothing else at this time. Hemingway is expressing this in a splendidly comical manner when he has Jordan overrule Maria's "No. I must not [get into the sleeping robe]" by urging her, "Get in . . . And we can talk about it later": Jordan is being rather vague about the meaning of the "it" which he says they can talk about "later." The irony is that at some time "later," but significantly before he may have the consummation, she will confront him with the story of her rape, a story during whose account the lusting listener will receive an "it" that is much more than he had bargained for.

Jordan does manage to get Maria undressed before she is given a chance to talk about the rape. However, this chronology of what he 'gets' and what she 'gets' already puts her in a favorable position in terms of their gender-role conflict during their first night together. What he is in no position to know at this point is that she has a psychological need to kiss him and "do everything," a psychological need to rebel by doing that which she, the female, did not get to do during the rape when, in her own words, "things were done to [her]" and when "others did things to [her]." Learning this information after his impatient sexual approach to her makes Jordan feel as if he had joined the rapists—and in fact even as if he had become a Fascist himself in the sense that he had been trying to impose on Maria *his* "way" of having sex. Hemingway is insinuating that Jordan's awareness of having deprived her of kissing him and of "do[ing] everything" might have had a similarly enlightening effect on him—*might have* because, although during their first night together Jordan did recognize the connection between his own and the Fascists' sexual treatment of Maria, he seems to have forgotten all about that connection when she becomes sexually aggressive during their walk through the heather.

But Maria gives Jordan a lesson he will never forget. Contrary to what still appears to be the prevailing critical opinion, Maria is not what is stereotyped as, in Samuel Shaw's words, "the Hemingway woman, living to serve the physical and emotional needs of her man." Rather, Maria neutralizes, perhaps even reverses, that position of "Subjection" which at least in sexual terms she is placed in vis-á-vis Jordan during their first night together. Since Jordan presumably has overheard Pilar's "You know the way?", he realizes that the girl who the night before had not known how to kiss, not even known "where the noses would go," has been taught a few things by Pilar. And he must be puzzled by a similarity he notices between the rapid change in his sexual relationship with Maria and the relationship between the cowardly Pablo and Pilar, a relationship in which Pilar has come to wear the pants—because, as Jordan is fully aware, Pilar has earned that privilege. While Jordan may or may not fear that Maria is trying to dominate him, he must be concerned that Maria has become the sexual aggressor quite literally overnight. The night before she had practically been sent to his sleeping bag by Pilar, and been sent there for therapeutic purposes. Today, however, the decision to have sex with Jordan is Maria's own, and in one sense it is a conscious decision to defy Jordan.

Maria's decision is made in defiance of Jordan first of all in the sense that he had repeatedly pleaded that they should accompany Pilar to the camp. Second, although Maria ostensibly is deciding against Pilar and in favor of Jordan when she insists on keeping their rendezvous, she actually is making her decision in collaboration with the older woman against Jordan when she accepts the route which Pilar had mapped out for her handling of Jordan, namely, to be the sexual aggressor. In the first sleeping-bag scene he had "pulled her down" and impatiently told her to "Get in" before reassuring her that "[they] can talk about it later." Here Maria is, so to speak, turning the tables on him. After Jordan has "straightened out and with his two arms around her so tightly that she was lifted off the ground," he has total control over her insofar as she is quite literally unable to go anywhere—just as she had been the night before once he had got her into the confinement of his sleeping bag. But as soon as she has "her lips . . . on his throat," the namesake of the Second Eve has the namesake of the ever-rolling River of the Israelites pinned.

When before the assumption of their sexual relations Jordan looked at Maria, "his throat was choky and and there was a difficulty in walking": here too "there [is] a difficulty in walking"—so that he has no choice but to let her down, i.e., "put her down," as opposed to forcefully *pulling* her down the night before. Now that she has her feet on the ground and is able to walk, he has no choice but to inquire, "Where should we go?" When she starts unbuttoning his shirt, she is answering his question about their itinerary with her own version of Jordan's line, "we can talk about it later." While the text does not exactly tell us what happens, there is a strong suggestion that this time she either pulls *him* down or, with her lips on his throat, has simply caused him so much difficulty in walking that his knees buckle under him: immediately after the "Yes. Yes. Everything as you" dialogue we learn that they are lying on the ground.

In this sexual union, Hemingway is insinuating the ironic notion that Jordan has no choice but to postpone going anywhere until "later." Hemingway is parodying Milton's portrayal of Eve, a portrayal which has seemed to many to be a biased elaboration of the Genesis story, regardless of whether Milton was, consciously or unconsciously, being sexist when in the epic proposition he declared it to be the purpose of his poem to "justify the ways of God to *men*" (italics added) instead of using the more gender-neutral word *man.* Milton's epic offered splendid possibilities which the "consummate ironist" Hemingway simply could not ignore, such as the scene of Adam's and Eve's first postlapsarian lovemaking. In fact, I now wish to argue that the scene where the female leads "the way" and seduces the male, and where they perform the sex act topographically at the very spot at which Maria's "Where shall we go?"-victory over Jordan occurs, is a narratively functional allusion to the scene where Milton's Adam and Eve have sex immediately after Adam's Fall, when Adam cannot wait until they get back to the bower and they make love in a field of flowers:

> Flow'rs were the Couch,
> Pansies, and Violets, and Asphodel,
> And Hyacinth, Earth's freshest softest lap.
> There they thir fill of Love and Love's disport
> Took largely, of thir mutual guilt the Seal,
> The solace of thir sin, till dewy sleep
> Oppress'd them, wearied with thir amorous play.

After making Milton's presentation of Adam's and Eve's *prelapsarian* love life allusively operative in the first sleeping-bag scene, Hemingway is allusively appropriating Adam's and Eve's first *postlapsarian* sex act in the open-air lovemaking scene, for Jordan is tired after the lovemaking:

> he said very tiredly and from a great but friendly distance, "Hello, rabbit." And she smiled and from no distance said, "Hello, my *Inglés.*"
>
> "I'm not an *Inglés,*" he said very lazily.

The allusion to Adam's and Eve's postlapsarian coitus introduces the idea that, like Adam's and Eve's, Jordan's tiredness is a result of postcoital depression. However, there is also the allusively functional contrast that Maria is not tired at all.

Hemingway's allusive interaction with Milton explains why Maria is not tired: whereas Adam and Eve have just committed Original Sin, a mutual guilt that they seal with a sex act as a result of which they fall into a deep sleep. Maria, in a parodically oblique analogy to the Holy Virgin who was exempted from Original Sin, is presented as an Eve who in the earth-moving scene is prelapsarian insofar as she is not subject to the postcoital fatigue which Milton described so graphically. In fact, Hemingway's text itself is suggesting some sort of Mary-like exemption from Original Sin for Maria when, in response to her account of the rape, Jordan says to her, "no one has done anything to thee. Thee, they cannot touch. No one has touched thee": Maria retains the nominal sexual status of her holy namesake even after she has been gang-raped. For example, when she later puts her hands into Jordan's pockets and he says, "Thou art shameless," she delightedly agrees with him: "Yes . . . Totally." In her relationship with Jordan, Hemingway endows Maria with a kind of prelapsarian sexuality which makes her quite literally "shame-less."

Remember that Milton describes prelapsarian sexuality by stating, "Then there was no guilty shame." This passage from Book IV of *Paradise Lost* will help answer the following question: why does Hemingway explicitly present Jordan as tired after their intercourse in the heather? Hemingway's allusion to Milton's scene of Adam's and Eve's first postlapsarian sex act suggests that in this scene Jordan has become a postlapsarian Adam/man because he allowed the female to have "the way" / her way. However, this does not mean that Hemingway's character portrayal in this scene is misogynistic or male-chauvinistic: on the contrary, the allusive juxtaposition of Jordan's and Maria's to Adam's and Eve's postcoital situation introduces the idea that, unlike Jordan, the indefatigable Maria has *not* suffered a Fall.

Jordan deserves his Fall because his pride went first. At the beginning of his first night with Maria, Jordan had been guilty of male-supremacist pride when he imposed his own sexual protocol, "[his own] way" of having sex, upon her, especially in his belittling "we can talk about it later" and his patronizing "There is no need [for you to kiss or] to do anything. We are all right. But thou hast many clothes . . . I will help you [undress]." In the scene leading up to the earth-moving episode, Maria is avenging herself for his androcentric behavior the night before when, unbuttoning his shirt, she starts to undress *him*—after she has kissed him on the throat. This time she decides that there is indeed a need for her to kiss him, and she goes for his jugular. Closely relating this act to her carrying a razor blade to avoid a future rape, Maria uses Jordan vicariously to avenge herself on the Fascist rapists.

Maria tops off that revenge by kissing Jordan after the sex act and pointedly asking him, "There . . . How is that? Do I kiss thee better?" In this question she is triumphantly echoing the question she asked after undressing, possibly with the assistance he had been so eager to offer, the night before: "Is that better?" She is now asking him whether what she had just done was "better" than what she did the night before, namely, better than a woman wanting to kiss a man but inconveniencing him in the pursuit of his goal by still having her clothes on. Therefore, Maria's revenge is now complete. The male-versus-female domination struggle, which had begun with the brutal force of the Fascists, who, with one of them sitting on her head and holding her did not let her go *any*where and which had unwittingly been renewed by an inconsiderate Robert Jordan, has come to an end.

The domination struggle is over because Maria has won it. For what does it mean that during their lovemaking in the heather the narrative describes Jordan as having the following experience:

> they were both there, time having stopped and he felt the earth move out and away from under them.

Or put differently, why does Hemingway present Jordan, who is uninitiated into gypsy lore, as sharing an experience which Maria had been told in advance to expect? The answer again lies in Milton. Adam's and Eve's first postlapsarian sex act is the *seal* of their mutual guilt, with their coitus the concluding act of Original Sin. The preceding scene, then, in which Eve "gave [Adam] of that fair enticing Fruit," where the Fruit after all is a vaginal symbol, is a seduction scene. *The entire* lovemaking scene between Jordan and Maria in the heather, including their feeling the earth move, is allusively analogous to *the entire* scene where Adam completes the Original Sin. This methodically established analogy has the following implications for Hemingway's earth-moving episode. If we assume that there was an actual earthquake taking place or that Jordan and Maria merely thought there was, in either case we have the allusively functional similarity that Milton's earthquake signals a bad omen as Adam takes from Eve "that fair enticing Fruit": "Earth trembl'd from her entrails." Although it is more likely that there was no earthquake in that area as none of the other members of the guerilla group in the vicinity mentions having felt one, the ominous signs accompanying Adam's completion of the Fall will still affect our reaction to Jordan's 'Fall' in the heather.

In keeping with his writing principle of the iceberg where seven-eighths of his meaning is under water, Hemingway leaves us with an important question the answer to which we have to fathom on our own: what does it mean for our understanding of Hemingway's quasi-Miltonic epical novel that Maria has been primed by Pilar about earth-moving lovemaking but Jordan is totally uninitiated, especially in light of the associations between earth-movements and death? Maria reminds us of the Eve who, after having eaten from the Tree of Knowledge, lies to Adam in her attempt to persuade him to join her:

> were it I thought Death menac't would ensue
> This my attempt, I would sustain alone
> The worst, and not persuade thee, rather die
> Deserted, than oblige thee with a fact
> Pernicious to thy Peace . . .

An answer to the question concerning Maria withholding the information about possible earth movement during their lovemaking in the heather offers itself when we take a more thorough look at Milton's seduction scene where Eve gave Adam

> of that fair enticing Fruit
> With liberal hand: he scrupl'd not to eat
> Against his better knowledge, not deceiv'd,
> But fondly overcome with Female charm.
> Earth trembl'd from her entrails, as again
> In pangs, and Nature gave a second groan,
> Sky low'r'd, and muttering Thunder, some sad drops
> Wept at completing of the mortal Sin
> Original . . .

When Hemingway first describes Jordan's and Maria's lovemaking in the heather, then writes that Jordan "felt the earth move out and away from under them," and concludes with both of them talking about having felt the earth move, Hemingway is alluding to Milton's presentation of Adam's Fall as a sexual-seduction scene. And in his presentation of Jordan and Maria as feeling the earth move during their coitus, Hemingway is making allusively operative Milton's description of Nature's reaction to Adam's completion of the Fall: the Earth is "trembl[ing] from her entrails" again as she had been when Eve fell.

The trembling of the earth provides a key to understanding Hemingway's presentation *both* of Maria withholding information she had received as to what might happen during their next lovemaking *and* of an uninitiated Jordan indeed sharing that experience with Maria. I deliberately used the term "sharing" because it fits the Miltonic context of ideas which Hemingway is making allusively operative: Hemingway is establishing an allusive analogy between the Maria who had been primed for the earth-moving experience and the Eve who had, through her own initial perpetration of Original Sin, *already* caused earth tremors and tried her best to seduce Adam, in her own words, into "shar[ing] with [her] in bliss or woe," into sharing an act which would likewise cause the earth to tremble.

Through this allusive transaction in the earth-movement episode Hemingway first of all reinforces his portrayal of Jordan as an Adam who experiences a Fall in the Spanish heather, a 'Fall' which he earns through his first-night treatment of a Spanish namesake of the Second Eve. But through this allusive transaction Hemingway is also endowing Maria with a slightly satanic touch—something that he would expand into grand dimensions with the Eve-figure Catherine Bourne in ***The Garden of Eden.*** By this I do not mean to imply that Hemingway presents Maria as an evil and destructive woman, as he would with the Catherine whom David Bourne keeps addressing as "Devil." On the contrary, Hemingway presents Maria as instrumental in a good cause. In what can be read as a *Bildungsroman,* Maria helps Jordan change from a sexually selfish male-chauvinist, from a sexual Fascist as it were, into a considerate human being: this educational novel presents Jordan as developing from a man solely interested in immediate sexual gratification at the beginning of his first night with Maria to a man who—in the famous/infamous scene where Jordan deliberates the question, "How did Onan turn out?"—declines Maria's offer of unilateral sexual gratification at the beginning of their last night together when pain renders her incapable of coitus.

Like the Eve who had eaten from the Tree of Knowledge, the nineteen-year-old Maria is being a *femme savante* when she directs Jordan "the way" / her way, but she is not the Circean *femme fatale* whom Milton portrays in Eve. Maria is a *femme savante* in the sense that she has received privileged information from the gypsy-lore practitioner Pilar. Pilar is, if not a *Tree* of Knowledge, then a "Pilar," i.e., *Pillar,* of Knowledge for Maria: whether or not Hemingway is playing on the notion of the Philosopher's Stone, Pilar is the *pila* / fountain of knowledge for Maria. This pertains first of all to Maria's own cure from the trauma inflicted by her experience with the Fascist males: that she has indeed been cured is shown by the fact that a few hours after the "Onan"-deliberation scene the pain is gone and she is able to make love. But the idea of Maria becoming, with the help of Pilar, a *femme savante* pertains also to her ability to transform the Jordan whose treatment of her during their first night together had not been all that different from that of the quasi-onanistic Fascists: Hemingway had been conveying the notion of the Fascists' rape as an onanism of sorts when before their first lovemaking he had Maria respond to Jordan's question, "Dost thou wish?", by urging, "Yes. *Everything. Please. And if we do everything together,* the other may never have been" (italics added).

While I italicized a portion of Maria's imploration in order to illustrate the onanistic nature of what the Fascists did to Maria, I also italicized it in order to illustrate the thematic significance of the events that take place during Jordan's and Maria's last night together. During their first night, Maria had uttered the plea that "[they] do everything together" in an attempt to engage Jordan's help in overcoming the trauma. Maria had called on Jordan to serve her physical and emotional needs, thus providing to be the opposite of "the Hemingway woman, living to serve the physical and emotional needs of her man." The man whom "the psychiatrist [Pilar]" had chosen to be the sex object in this course of therapy had been rather successful. Jordan opened the door to success when he shed the androcentricism he had displayed at the beginning of their first night: during their final union, Maria is able to enjoy sex, perhaps even to the point of repeating the rare magical experience which Pilar had hoped Maria would have.

That the gypsy psychiatrist had actually been looking forward to the magical experience as the most important contributing factor in Maria's long-term recovery is suggested by the "way" which the Pillar of Knowledge prescribes for the open-air lovemaking. The Maria who had been the victim of a brutal sexual assault becomes the sexual aggressor: it is in order to obtain a cure from an ailment caused by males who had *subjected* her to their sexual domination that Maria temporarily becomes a Miltonic Eve. And her Adam is actively contributing to the progress of her cure when at the beginning of their last night Maria, because of pain which significantly she attributes to the rape, is incapable of coitus but Jordan unselfishly declines her offer of onanism: when Jordan declines her offer, he is restoring in her the faith in men which she had lost when the Fascists forced themselves upon her.

In turn, Jordan is rewarded for his cure-facilitating behavior a few hours later when Maria awakens free of pain and he is given an opportunity to prove, one more time and for the last time, his sexual adamness. Their final union on pine needles prefigures Jordan's complete integration with the Spanish Earth, an integration which he will experience while lying on pine needles during his last stand against the Fascist cavalry which is pursuing his guerilla band: "He was completely integrated now." As Earl Rovit has noted, "Maria . . . is the vessel of Jordan's complete self-realization; in his merging with her, he has achieved the immortality of becoming 'other,' of losing himself into something that is not himself."

Jordan's final union with Maria prefigures his complete self-realization because that union is the natural consequence of his having declined her onanism offer earlier, thinking to himself that he would need all the *cojones* he can muster:

> I'll keep any oversupply of that for tomorrow. I'll need all of that there is tomorrow. There are no pine needles that need that now as I will need it tomorrow. Who was it cast his seed upon the ground in the Bible? Onan. How did Onan turn out? he thought. I don't remember ever hearing anymore about Onan. He smiled in the dark.

Jordan had taken an important step toward complete integration when he realized that he could reach complete self-realization only if he gave his seed to Maria, to the "vessel" as Rovit describes Maria in a nonsexual sense—instead of wasting it in an act of onanistic narcissism.

Jordan's rejection of narcissism is the point where Hemingway establishes the ultimate allusively functional contrast between his protagonist and Milton's Adam. Jordan's final goodbye to Maria, "Thou art me too now." Thou art all there will be of me," alludes to the lines in which Adam proclaims that he will join Eve in her transgression of God's command:

> I with thee have fixt my Lot.
> Certain to undergo like doom; if Death
> Consort with thee, Death is to me is Life;
> So forcible within my heart I feel
> The Bond of Nature draw me to my own,
> My own in thee, for what thou art is mine;
> Our state cannot be sever'd, we are one,
> One flesh, to lose thee were to lose myself.

Overemphasizing the fact that Eve was created from his rib, Adam loves Eve as an extension of himself rather than as an individual. Strictly speaking, then, Adam follows Eve's destructive path not out of love for her but out of narcissism: "to lose thee were to lose myself."

Through the interaction between the alluding and alluded-to contexts, Hemingway is introducing the following meaning into his portrayal of Robert Jordan at the conclusion of his novel. While at this point in the plot of *Paradise Lost* Adam still has a chance to save himself and the entire human race after him but decides to seal his own, Eve's, and also mankind's fate and gives in to his narcissism. Jordan seals his own death sentence and stays behind in an attempt to increase Maria's chances of escaping from the Fascist cavalry. Knowing the odds against making the escape without jeopardizing the lives of the remaining members of the group, Jordan agrees when Pablo vetoes Pilar's suggestion that they free up a packhorse to carry their wounded comrade.

Unlike Milton's Adam, then, Jordan is sacrificing his life in an attempt to save, among other lives, the life of a namesake of the Second Eve who, in a curious version of the battle of the sexes, had first punished him for his androcentric behavior by cutting his adamness down to size and then actually given him an opportunity to redeem himself by declining an act of narcissism, a redemption which was sealed by their final union the next morning. I therefore disagree with Brenner's reading of the novel's conclusion: "Had Jordan truly loved Maria, he would have made some effort to escape at the end of the novel. Had he truly loved her, he would have let her remain at the pass where they could have died in a romantic finale." In his attempt to examine ***For Whom the Bell Tolls*** as a classical epic in the light of Aristotelian definitions, Brenner devoted very little space to an issue which is of a much more immediate concern in examining *any* work that might conceivably be in the epic tradition: since Virgil's *Aeneid* is an extended allusion to both Homeric epics, to the *Iliad* and the *Odyssey,* and since Milton's *Paradise Lost* is replete with allusions both to Homer and to Virgil, Hemingway's epical war novel, whose pivot is the dramatic love relationship between two people with significance-laden Biblical names, simply demands an examination of Hemingway's allusive utilization of Milton's epic.

More specifically, the conclusion of Hemingway's novel demands a still closer examination of the allusive interaction between Jordan's goodbye to Maria and Adam's announcement to Eve:

> "Stand up," [Robert Jordan] said. "Thou art me too now. Thou art all there will be of me. Stand up."

Since Milton makes it clear that Adam "eat[s] / Against his better knowledge, not deceiv'd," Adam is indeed "Certain to undergo like doom": Adam knows he will die. Jordan likewise knows that he will die, but he does to Maria precisely what Adam should have done to Eve, done for the benefit of mankind: lying moribund on the ground, Jordan sends Maria away. Jordan too is referring to an extension of himself, but in a spirit that is the diametrical opposite of narcissism: when Jordan tells Maria, "Thou art all there will be of me. Stand up," he is communicating to her, as if he were asking her to get up after a lovemaking, that she may be carrying his child—an extension of both of them.

The question of Maria possibly becoming pregnant had been discussed by Jordan and Pilar on the first morning-after when, in response to his question, "What if she has a baby?", Pilar almost cheerfully replied, "That will do no harm." The pregnancy question becomes one of the focal points of Hemingway's Spanish Civil War novel when during the dialogue which follows the onanism-refusal scene, a dialogue in which Maria talks about the murder of her heroic republican father by the Fascists, she asks Jordan: "how can the world be made better if there are no children of us who fight against the fascists?" The entire novel, then, ends with this question: did the Adamic Jordan, who had 'fallen' in a battle of the sexes and committed a *felix culpa* of sorts, succeed in a personal way of assuring that there will be people who can make this world a better place?

An analogous question concerning the future of mankind had been discussed by the couple in *Paradise Lost.* When Eve learns what effect her and Adam's sin will have on mankind, and how

> miserable it is
> To be to others cause of misery,
> Our own begott'n, and of our Loins to bring
> Into this cursed World a woeful Race. . . .

she suggests racial suicide in the form of abstinence. Adam rejects the proposal of "wilful barrenness," for such a step "savors only / . . . Reluctance against God and his just yoke / Laid on our Necks." More importantly, Adam reminds Eve of "part of our Sentence, that thy Seed shall bruise / The Serpent's head": by "childless days / Resolv'd, as thou proposest," the promised revenge against Satan and mankind's redemption through Christ would be lost.

In Milton's poem the person who proposes the wrong solution, Eve, is duly overruled by the righteous person in this dialogue, Adam. Hemingway parodies Milton's argument by reversing the roles. Maria suddenly remembers and relates to Jordan something which Pilar had told her some time ago, namely, that she might be barren:

> " . . . Perhaps you should not [marry me]. It is possible that I can never bear thee either a son or a daughter for the Pilar says that if I could it would have happened to me with the things which were done. I must tell you that. Oh, I do not know why I had forgotten that."

> "It is of no importance, rabbit," he said. *"First* it may not be true. That is for a doctor to say. *Then I would not wish to bring either a son or a daughter into this world as this world is.* And also you take all the love I have to give."

> "I would like to bear thy son and thy daughter," she told him. "And how can the world be made better if there are no children of us who fight against the fascists?" (italics added)

Through an allusively performed gender-role reversal Hemingway here is presenting *Jordan* as the analogue of Eve. Jordan is arguing—to use Eve's words—how "miserable" it would be "of [their] Loins to bring / Into this cursed World a woeful Race." However, since presumably Jordan had not done anything to prevent getting Maria pregnant before, he is merely saying this in an attempt to make the Maria who had been degraded by the Fascist rapists feel better about herself as a woman: "It is of no importance." But the Second Eve's namesake does not accept Jordan's rationalizing smooth talk, and she advances an argument which even out-Adams Milton's Adam. Since Jordan had said that "First" they needed a doctor's diagnosis and "Then" he would not wish to bring children "into this world *as this world is* [anyway]" (italics added), Maria is now in a position to counter with the argument that the present state of the world would be all the more reason for them to have children.

The Catholic Hemingway has Maria out-Milton the Protestant Milton when she proposes a way to make this world a better place. Maria, who is Catholic, proposes not a passive wait for a redemption through Christ but, instead, something that could be called Protestant activism, a 'Protestant' modification of the Catholic idea of procreation for the purpose of increasing the flock of God's children. The solution proposed by the namesake of the Second Eve is to increase the flock of children who will grow up to fight Fascism—a flock consisting of *both* genders: " 'I would like to bear thy son and thy daughter,' she told Robert Jordan." In his epical novel, then, Hemingway has allusively utilized Milton's sacred epic to suggest that a betterment of the world cannot come just from God, certainly will not come from "men" alone, but has to come from *Mankinde,* in the comprehensive sense in which that word is used in the epigraph from John Donne. (pp. 8-22)

I have attempted to show how in ***For Whom the Bell Tolls*** Hemingway illuminates his treatment of gender-issues by making Milton's treatment of such issues in *Paradise Lost* part of his novel's mode of existence. What in the process I also hope I have been able to demonstrate is that, as in his review article on "Hemingway Criticism: Getting at the Hard Questions" Jackson J. Benson has urged, "we are going to have to take Hemingway far more seriously than in the past . . . and have to consider the possibility that he was not just an innovator, but a genius." We are forced to read the novel for intricacy and compactness, which includes *allusive* intricacy and compactness—and thus come to appreciate Hemingway's writing principle of the iceberg—if we wish to really understand ***For Whom the Bell Tolls.*** (p. 22)

Wolfgang E. H. Rudat, "The Other War in 'For Whom the Bell Tolls': Maria and Miltonic Gender-Role Battles," in The Hemingway Review, *Vol. XI, No. 1, Fall, 1991, pp. 8-24.*

FURTHER READING

Bibliography

Harmon, Robert B. *Understanding Ernest Hemingway: A Study and Resource Guide.* Metuchen, N.J.: Scarecrow Press, 1977, 153 p.

Annotated bibliography containing information on different editions of *For Whom the Bell Tolls* and related criticism.

Biography

Baker, Carlos. *"For Whom the Bell Tolls."* In his *Ernest Hemingway: A Life Story,* pp. 345-51. New York: Charles Scribner's, 1969.

Describes Hemingway's involvement in the Spanish Civil War and the circumstances surrounding the writing and publication of *For Whom the Bell Tolls.*

Criticism

Adair, William. *"For Whom the Bell Tolls* and *The Magic Mountain:* Hemingway's Debt to Thomas Mann." *Twentieth Century Literature* 35, No. 4 (Winter 1989): 429-44.

Determines the influence of Mann's *The Magic Mountain* on Hemingway's novel, concluding that "the similarities between these two encyclopedic, twentieth-century epics seem too many and profound to be a matter of coincidence."

Adams, J. Donald. Review of *For Whom the Bell Tolls,* by Ernest Hemingway. *The New York Times Book Review* (28 October 1940): 1.

Asserts that *For Whom the Bell Tolls* is an improvement on Hemingway's earlier novels, "much more full-bodied in its drawing of character, visually more brilliant and incomparably richer in content."

Baker, Sheridan. "It Tolls for Thee." In his *Ernest Hemingway: An Introduction and Interpretation,* pp. 107-18. New York: Holt, Rinehart and Winston, 1967.

Provides an overview of *For Whom the Bell Tolls.*

Burgum, Edwin Berry. "Ernest Hemingway and the Psychology of the Lost Generation." In his *The Novel and the World's Dilemma,* pp. 184-204. New York: Oxford University Press, 1947.

Views Hemingway's novel as "derogatory to the cause of Spanish democracy, and therefore, by implication, sympathetic to Spanish fascism."

Cooperman, Stanley. "Hemingway's Blue-eyed Boy: Robert Jordan and 'Purging Ecstasy'." *Criticism* VIII, No. 1 (Winter 1966): 87-96.

Asserts that for Robert Jordan, "the war itself emerges as a positive value, as a means of 'purging' himself and redeeming the cowardice of his father by killing and being killed 'purely'—for no cause beyond the act of killing itself."

Hodson, Joel. "Robert Jordan Revisited: Hemingway's Debt to T. E. Lawrence." *The Hemingway Review* X, No. 2 (Spring 1991): 2-16.

Contends that *"For Whom the Bell Tolls* seems to indicate a fascination with Lawrence's military actions and the difficulties of the outsider which both Lawrence and Robert Jordan embody."

Josephs, Allen. "Hemingway and the Spanish Civil War or the Volatile Mixture of Politics and Art." In *Rewriting the Good Fight: Critical Essays on the Literature of the Spanish Civil War,* edited by Frieda S. Brown, et al., pp. 175-84. East Lansing: Michigan State University Press, 1989.

Addresses Hemingway's politics, concluding: "(1) there is no doubt which side Hemingway is against; (2) there is no doubt that he is uncomfortable about the side he is on; (3) Hemingway's reluctance about politics should never be attributed to naiveté."

Kastely, James L. "Toward a Politically Responsible Ethical Criticism: Narrative in *The Political Unconscious* and *For Whom the Bell Tolls.*" *Style* 22, No. 4 (Winter 1988): 535-58.

Alleges that part of the reason that Hemingway's novel is difficult "to place ethically and politically is a consequence of the peculiarity of its narration."

Martin, Robert A. "Hemingway's *For Whom the Bell Tolls:* Fact into Fiction." *Studies in American Fiction* 15, No. 2 (Autumn 1987): 219-25.

Maintains that "many of the characters, as well as the events and places of the novel, are based on historical fact and on the exploits of people Hemingway knew or heard of while he was covering the war."

Meyers, Jeffrey. *"For Whom the Bell Tolls* as Contemporary History." In *The Spanish Civil War in Literature,* edited by Janet Pérez and Wendell Aycock, pp. 85-107. Lubbock: Texas Tech University Press, 1990.

Discusses the political aspects of Hemingway's novel, contending that the author "not only suggests the war is lost, but also explains the reasons for the defeat."

Nakjavani, Erik. "Knowledge as Power: Robert Jordan as an Intellectual Hero." *The Hemingway Review* VII, No. 2 (Spring 1988): 131-46.

Appraises Jordan's intellectualism and perceives his death as a metaphor for the fall of the Republican forces in the Spanish Civil War.

———. "Intellectuals as Militants in Hemingway's *For Whom the Bell Tolls* and Malraux's *L'Espoir:* A Comparative Study." In *Rewriting the Good Fight: Critical Essays on the Literature of the Spanish Civil War,* edited by Frieda S. Brown, et al., pp. 199-214. East Lansing: Michigan State University Press, 1989.

Compares protagonists in both novels, concluding that Robert Jordan "appears to manifest the main characteristics of all three of the representative militant intellectuals in *L'Espoir.*"

Rudat, Wolfgang E. H. "Hemingway's Rabbit: Slips of the Tongue and Other Linguistic Games in *For Whom the Bell Tolls.*" *The Hemingway Review* X, No. 1 (Fall 1990): 34-51.

Explores Robert Jordan's use of language, concluding that "Hemingway presents his protagonist as an academician who has published a book on Spain but is inept at translating academic knowledge into practical action."

Sanderson, Stewart. "A Republican in Spain." In his *Hemingway,* pp. 89-102. Edinburgh, Scotland: Oliver and Boyd, 1961.

Furnishes a synopsis of the plot and critical commentary on Hemingway's novel.

Seaton, James. "Was Hemingway an Intellectual?" *The Hemingway Review* X, No. 1 (Fall 1990): 52-6.

Argues that in *For Whom the Bell Tolls,* Hemingway "carried on a rearguard defense, a 'holding attack,' on behalf of ideals considered obsolete among the enlightened."

Waldmeir, Joseph. "Chapter Numbering and Meaning in *For Whom the Bell Tolls.*" *The Hemingway Review* VIII, No. 2 (Spring 1989): 43-5.

Examines the similarities between Hemingway's character Pilar and Gertrude Stein.

Watson, William Braasch. "Joris Ivens and the Communists: Bringing Hemingway into the Spanish Civil War." *The Hemingway Review* X, No. 1 (Fall 1990): 2-18.

Chronicles Hemingway's participation in the Spanish Civil War, maintaining that his experience "shaped his political orientation during the war, shaped the roles he would undertake both in Spain and in the United States, and in the end shaped the manner in which he tried to extricate himself from the dilemmas his political involvement had created for him."

Whitmore, Tony. "Gaiety and Psyche: *For Whom the Bell Tolls.*" In *Hemingway: Essays of Reassessment,* edited by Frank Scafella, pp. 234-44. New York: Oxford University Press, 1991.

Surveys the humor in Hemingway's novel, determining that "although he had dealt with the theme earlier, Hemingway's fullest treatment of gaiety comes in *For Whom the Bell Tolls.*"

Wylder, Delbert E. "*For Whom the Bell Tolls:* The Mythic Hero in the Contemporary World." In his *Hemingway's Heroes,* pp. 127-64. Albuquerque: University of New Mexico Press, 1969.

Contends that Hemingway "has moved from a novel which is a condemnation of individualism to a novel which relates individualism to the group, and has created Robert Jordan as the protagonist who follows the mythical journey of the hero in a modern setting."

Young, Philip. "Death and Transfiguration." In his *Ernest Hemingway,* pp. 75-87. New York: Rinehart & Co., 1952.

Explores the defining qualities of Hemingway's novel.

Additional coverage of Hemingway's life and career is contained in the following sources published by Gale Research: *Concise Dictionary of American Literary Biography, 1917-1929; Contemporary Authors,* Vols. 77-80; *Contemporary Authors New Revision Series,* Vol. 34; *Contemporary Literary Criticism,* Vols. 1, 3, 6, 8, 10, 13, 19, 30, 34, 39, 41, 44, 50, 61; *Dictionary of Literary Biography,* Vols. 4, 9, 102; *Dictionary of Literary Biography Documentary Series,* Vol. 1; *Dictionary of Literary Biography Yearbook: 1981, 1987*; *DISCovering Authors*; *Major 20th-Century Writers*; *Short Story Criticism,* Vol. 1; and *World Literature Criticism.*

Daniel Keyes

1927-

American novelist, short story writer, and nonfiction writer.

The following entry provides an overview of Keyes's career.

INTRODUCTION

Keyes is best known for the novel *Flowers for Algernon,* a poignant story of a mentally handicapped man who temporarily acquires extraordinary intelligence. Although generally classified as a work of science fiction because of its provocative examination of the ethical dilemmas posed by scientific progress, *Flowers for Algernon* also addresses issues considered atypical for the genre, including the nature of personality, love, and self-esteem. These psychological issues are also central to Keyes's nonfiction works, which focus on abnormal behavior and the criminal mind.

Born in Brooklyn, New York, Keyes was educated at Brooklyn College. While working as a high school English teacher, he wrote the short story "Flowers for Algernon," which was published in 1959 in *The Magazine of Fantasy and Science Fiction.* After the story won a Hugo Award and was successfully adapted for television in 1961, Keyes expanded the work into a novel. Presented as a series of journal entries, *Flowers for Algernon* begins with the misspelled and simplistic prose of the protagonist, Charlie Gordon, who works as a janitor during the day and attends a school for the mentally handicapped at night. Through teachers at the school, Charlie is offered the chance to undergo a neurosurgical procedure designed to radically improve his mental capabilities. The operation, which had previously been performed on a laboratory mouse named Algernon, raises Charlie's intelligence dramatically. His writings become increasingly sophisticated as he, now classified a genius, begins to ponder the morality of the operation, the behavior of old "friends" and new colleagues, and the emotional and intellectual implications of his newly acquired reasoning abilities. Eventually, Charlie discovers a critical flaw in the scientists' calculations and, witnessing Algernon's regression, realizes that he must suffer the same end. A reviewer for the *Times Literary Supplement* observed: "Charlie's hopeless knowledge that he is destined to end in a home for the feeble-minded, a moron who knows he is a moron, is painful, and Mr. Keyes has the technical equipment to prevent us from shrugging off the pain." *Flowers for Algernon* became a bestselling novel, and the book's 1968 film adaptation, *Charly,* also achieved popular and critical success, with Cliff Robertson winning an Academy Award for his performance in the title role.

Although Keyes's subsequent writings have not attained the success of *Flowers for Algernon,* he has received high praise for his nonfiction work, where he continues to explore what he terms "the complexities of the human mind." *The Minds of Billy Milligan* concerns the first person in American judicial history to be found not guilty by reason of insanity due to multiple personalities; Milligan was a schizophrenic with twenty-four personalities, several of whom committed serious crimes. Similar in scope to *The Minds of Billy Milligan, Unveiling Claudia: A True Story of a Serial Murder* details the police investigation of Claudia Elaine Yasko, a mentally ill woman who falsely confessed to being a serial killer and was consequently never tried in a court of law.

PRINCIPAL WORKS

"Flowers for Algernon" (short story) 1959; published in journal *The Magazine of Fantasy and Science Fiction*

**Flowers for Algernon* (novel) 1966
The Touch (novel) 1968; also published as *The Contaminated Man,* 1973
The Fifth Sally (novel) 1980
The Minds of Billy Milligan (nonfiction) 1981; revised edition, 1982
Unveiling Claudia: A True Story of a Serial Murder (nonfiction) 1986

* This work has been published under several different titles, including *Charly, Flowers for Algernon: A Classic Story of a Struggle, Flowers of Algernon,* and *I.Q. 185.*

CRITICISM

Eliot Fremont-Smith (review date 7 March 1966)

[*An American editor and critic, Fremont-Smith helped launch the National Book Critics Circle Award in 1976. In the following review of* Flowers for Algernon, *he praises Keyes's deft handling of the novel's essentially predictable plot and sentimental themes.*]

Algernon is a mouse and the flowers are for his grave, which explains the innervating title of this novel but does not convey Daniel Keyes's love of problems. ***Flowers for Algernon,*** which had its origin as a much-anthologized short story (it was also a television drama and is now being made into a movie), is a technician's maze, a collection of nasty little challenges for a writer of fiction. That it works at all as a novel is proof of Mr. Keyes's deftness. And it is really quite a performance. He has taken the obvious, treated it in a most obvious fashion, and succeeded in creating a tale that is convincing, suspenseful and touching—all in modest degree, but it is enough. The obvious part is the message: We must respect life, respect one another, be kind to those less fortunate than ourselves, "Ye who are without sin," etc. To this, Mr. Keyes adds three germane (to the story) corollaries. The first is an epigraph, from Plato's *Republic,* that starts:

> Anyone who has common sense will remember that the bewilderments of the eyes are of two kinds, and arise from two causes, either from coming out of the light or from going into the light, which is true of the mind's eye quite as much as of the bodily eye; and he who remembers this when he sees anyone whose vision is perplexed and weak will not be too ready to laugh. . . .

The second and third corollaries are from the running journal of the novel's narrator, Charlie Gordon, a 36-year-old moron with an I.Q. of 68 transformed by neurosurgery into a genius with an I.Q. that is beyond measurement. Recovering from the operation, he writes in his "progriss riport" of a "skinney nerse" who said "maybe they got no rite to make me smart because if god wanted me to be smart he would have made me born that way." And later, when he is very smart indeed, he offers this hypothesis: "Intelligence without the ability to give and receive affection leads to mental and moral breakdown . . . the mind absorbed in and involved in itself as a self-centered end, to the exclusion of human relationships, can only lead to violence and pain."

All of this is expounded in a tale consisting exclusively of Charlie Gordon's written journal, which progresses from primitive literacy to eloquence as it records his mental journey "into the light." Through it we learn that he has been chosen as the first human guinea pig for an experimental operation that can transform the severely retarded into intellectual giants. Perfected by Professor Nemur and Dr. Strauss, a psychiatrist, and backed by a foundation grant, the operation has been successfully performed on animals—one animal, anyway, Algernon the mouse, who now runs mazes like crazy. But how long the effect of the operation will last the doctors and psychologists don't know, nor do they know the emotional consequences of sudden intellectual advance in a person whose intellectual and emotional responses have been those of a 6-year-old.

Charlie's progress is rapid. In a matter of weeks he is beating Algernon through the mazes, seeing pictures in the Rorschach tests, reading Dostoevsky, remembering past events—and learning that people are hypocritical, deceitful and cruel. He stumbles, of course, on love, and through some painful experiences and self-analysis he realizes that the old, retarded Charlie, maimed by his mother's desperate ambitions, is still inside him. He also realizes that the old Charlie, blind to the cruelty behind the laughter, had a modicum of happiness that is now lost. In fact, as he surpasses everyone in intelligence, his friends all turn on him in resentment: he is supposed to be the subject of an experiment, a prototype, a grateful product of scientific research; but he must, of course, be himself. What's worse, he discovers a terrible flaw in Professor Nemur's figures.

***Flowers for Algernon* is a technician's maze, a collection of nasty little challenges for a writer of fiction. That it works at all as a novel is proof of Mr. Keye's deftness. And it is really quite a performance. He has taken the obvious, treated it in a most obvious fashion, and succeeded in creating a tale that is convincing, suspenseful and touching.**

—Eliot Fremont-Smith

Now all of this is predictable, right through to the sad, inevitable end: it is a circular story with hardly a wiggle of variation. Predictable, too, are the problems of its first-person narration (credibility of misspellings, risks of repetition, pace of memory-recall, how to show Charlie convincingly a genius) and the patent incredibility of virtually everything that happens. On top of this are the dangers of sentimentality (those flowers for Algernon), pretentiousness (pseudopsychoanalytic delvings and sermonettes about the integrity of souls), too-easy humor (slapstick that can immediately undermine the delicate dignity of the book) and modesty (the circular business again: so small a conception that it may not seem to matter).

Mr. Keyes seems aware of all these problems and dangers; indeed, one senses a good deal of finger-exercising in [***Flowers for Algernon***], and reads it with considerable technical fascination. Not every trap is avoided, but the skill shown here is awesome nonetheless. One might say that Mr. Keyes runs his maze at least as well as Algernon and Charlie run theirs, which is exciting in itself. And affecting, too—how otherwise explain the tears that come to one's eyes at the novel's end?

Eliot Fremont-Smith, "The Message and the Maze," in The New York Times, *March 7, 1966, p. 25.*

The Times Literary Supplement, London (review date 21 July 1966)

[*In the review below, the critic provides a generally positive assessment of* Flowers For Algernon, *briefly stating that the work favorably compares with other major science fiction novels but lacks successfully defined minor characters.*]

Those who read [***Flowers for Algernon***] when it first appeared in America in 1959 will welcome its publication in this country, for it is a good example of that kind of science fiction which uses a persuasive hypothesis to explore emotional and moral issues. By doing more justice than is common to the complexity of the central character's responses it gives body to its speculations.

The narrator, Charlie Gordon, is a moron who allows himself to become the guinea pig for a team of neurosurgeons and psychologists who have developed a technique for increasing the intelligence of their subjects. The Algernon of the title is a mouse who has had the treatment first. The book consists of the reports written by Charlie as his intelligence changes. At first the super-Algernon is more intelligent, but slowly the man overtakes the mouse (spelling and syntax improving) and then he overhauls his mentors. All, however, is not gain. Once he thought that his workmates were laughing with him and he had good friends; he learns that they were laughing at him and he was a butt. He is able to remember his early life, too, and gropes towards a painful understanding of the life of a family which contains a moron. His emergence from silly innocence means that his emotional maturity, though it lingers behind his developing I.Q., follows, struggling. His fits of irrational annoyance grow into a measured refusal to see himself as the creation of the scientists and an assertion that he was a man before they ever got to work on him.

By the time he is more intelligent than those who have given him his intellectual powers, he also knows what is wrong with their theories; as he watches Algernon degen-

An excerpt from *Flowers for Algernon:*

March 16—I ate lunch with Burt at the collidge resterant. They got all kinds of good food and I dont have to pay for it neither. I like to sit and wach the collidge boys and girls. They fool around sometimes but mostly they talk about all kinds of things just like the bakers do at Donners bakery. Burt says its about art and polatics and riligon. I dont know what those things are about but I know religon is god. Mom use to tell me all about him and the things he done to make the werld. She said I shoud always love god and prey to him. I dont remembir how to prey to him but I think mom use to make me prey to him a lot when I was a kid that he should make me get better and not be sick. I dont remember how I was sick. I think it was about me not being smart.

Anyway Burt says if the experiment werks Ill be able to understand all those things the studints are talking about and I said do you think Ill be smart like them and he laffed and said those kids arent so smart youll pass them as if their standing still.

He interduced me to alot of the studints and some of them look at me funny like I dont belong in a collidge. I almost forgot and started to tell them I was going to be very smart soon like them but Burt intiruppted and he tolld them I was cleaning the psych department lab. Later he explained to me their mussent be any publisity. That meens its a seecrit.

I dont reely understand why I got to keep it a seecrit. Burt says its in case theirs a faleure Prof Nemur dont want everybody to laff espeshully the pepul from the Welberg foundashun who gave him the mony for the projekt. I said I dont care if pepul laff at me. Lots of pepul laff at me and their my frends and we have fun. Burt put his arm on my sholder and said its not you Nemurs worryd about. He dont want pepul to laff at him.

I dint think pepul would laff at Prof Nemur because hes a sientist in a collidge but Bert said no sientist is a grate man to his colleegs and his gradulate studints. Burt is a gradulate student and he is a majer in *psychology* like the name on the door to the lab. I dint know they had majers in collidge. I thot it was onley in the army.

Anyway I hope I get smart soon because I want to lern everything there is in the werld like the collidge boys know. All about art and politiks and god.

March 17—When I waked up this morning rite away I thot I was gone to be smart but Im not. Evry morning I think Im gone to be smart but nothing happins. Mabye the experimint dint werk. Maby I wont get smart and Ill have to go live at the Warren home. I hate the tests and I hate the amazeds and I hate Algernon.

I never new before that I was dumber than a mouse. I dont feel like riting any more progress reports. I forget things and even when I rite them in my notbook sometimes I cant reed my own riting and its very hard. Miss Kinnian says have pashents but I feel sick and tired. And I get headakes all the time. I want to go back to werk in the bakery and not rite progris *progress* reports any more.

Daniel Keyes, in his Flowers for Algernon, *Harcourt Brace Jovanovich, 1966.*

erating into a normally stupid and abnormally baffled mouse, he knows that he will follow the same path.

In its ideas, especially in its speculations about the relationship between I.Q. and maturity, this is a far more intelligent book than the vast majority of "straight" novels. Moreover, the intelligence is displayed in a treatment of subject-matter which is bound to affect us as both important and moving. Charlie's hopeless knowledge that he is destined to end in a home for the feeble-minded, a moron who knows that he is a moron, is painful, and Mr. Keyes has the technical equipment to prevent us from shrugging off the pain.

Some of the subordinate characters are less successfully created and there are passages—notably those concerned with Charlie's need for sexual love—which encourage us to turn our attention more exclusively than the author intends to the ideas as distinct from the feelings of the people. But ***Flowers for Algernon*** can stand on the shelf alongside the novels of John Wyndham and Walter M. Miller's *A Canticle for Leibowitz,* which use the mode of science fiction to ask real questions about human beings without using dummies. There are worse shelves to stand on.

"Making Up a Mind," in The Times Literary Supplement, *No. 3360, July 21, 1966, p. 629.*

Alice P. Hackett (review date 12 August 1968)

[*Below, Hackett offers a mixed review of* The Touch.]

Not even an epigraph from the Book of Job may be enough warning for the tribulations which beset the young married couple in [***The Touch***]. Barney and Karen Stark are trying desperately to become parents. As Mr. and Mrs. "Fairly Normal," or so the jacket copy describes them, they are indecisive, quarrelsome, next to humorless, vindictive in petty ways, self-pitying and down-right tiresome. But as soon as poor Barney, through a freak accident, carries home radioactive dust on his clothing, infecting himself and Karen, the story moves swiftly. Karen is at last pregnant, and thereby hangs the inescapably morbid tale. It's an all too believable could-happen insofar as the background details are concerned, but one wishes the obviously gifted author hadn't saved his one unerring jab to the heart for the very end of the novel. (pp. 46-7)

Alice P. Hackett, in a review of "The Touch," in Publishers Weekly, *Vol. 194, No. 7, August 12, 1968, pp. 46-7.*

Robert Scholes (essay date 1975)

[*Scholes is an American scholar and critic who has written extensively on modern post-realistic fiction. He has written two highly regarded analyses of contemporary critical thought,* Structuralism and Literature *(1974) and* Semiotics and Interpretation *(1982). In the following excerpt, he examines* Flowers for Algernon *as a work of science fiction, dividing its main idea into two halves: the operation to develop Charlie's intelligence—a familiar motif of science fiction—and the impermanence of the operation, which distinguishes the novel as an original and powerful work. Scholes additionally discusses attempts to promote the book to general audiences and questions the work's validity as both a novel and short story.*]

Daniel Keyes's ***Flowers for Algernon*** might be called minimal SF. It establishes only one discontinuity between its world and our own, and this discontinuity requires no appreciable reorientation of our assumptions about man, nature, or society. Yet this break with the normal lifts the whole story out of our familiar experiential situation. It is the thing which enables everything else in the novel, and it is thus crucial to the generation of this narrative and to its effect on readers. How crucial this idea is can be seen in the story's history, which, as it happens, makes an interesting fable in itself. It first appeared as a long story in *The Magazine of Fantasy and Science Fiction* in April 1959. It received a Hugo award in 1960 for the best science fiction novelette of the year. It was then reprinted in *The Best from Fantasy and Science Fiction* and in the *Fifth Annual of the Year's Best Science Fiction,* both published in 1960, and in *Best Articles and Stories* and *Literary Cavalcade* in 1961. It was made into a television drama and then rewritten to appear as a full-length novel in 1966. Then it was made into a movie and given, of course, a new title: *CHARLY* (with the R childishly reversed). In 1967 it appeared in paperback and has now been through more than thirty printings. My paperback copy, which is from the thirty-second printing (1972), has a scene from the film on the cover, with the word "CHARLY" prominently displayed, and a bundle of "rave" quotations from reviewers on the back cover. Nowhere on the cover of this book does the expression "science fiction" appear. Even the Hugo award (which is at least as reliable an indicator of quality as, say, the Pulitzer Prize for Fiction) goes unmentioned. Inside, in very fine print, the ultra-snoopy purchaser may find in the back pages some words about the author, which indicate that this work first appeared as a "magazine story" (but the name of the magazine is suppressed) and that it won a Hugo award as the "best science novelette" in 1960. Even there, the cautious editors have managed to avoid the stigmatizing expression. ***Flowers for Algernon*** has gone straight, folks; it has passed the line around the SF ghetto, and to remind us of its sordid history would be downright impolite. And it might chase away a lot of potential customers who "hate science fiction."

An interesting fable, is it not, from which a number of conclusions may be drawn. It certainly reveals something about attitudes toward SF in various quarters, and this is instructive as well as amusing. But it also reveals something about the genre itself. ***Flowers for Algernon*** could succeed in four distinct forms (novelette, TV drama, full-length film, and full-length novel) because it was based on a powerful concept which worked well in all those forms. Daniel Keyes had an exceptionally good idea for a work of fiction, and the idea is what made it originally and still makes it a work of SF. The idea is simply that an operation might be performed on a severely retarded adult male, which would enable his mind not merely to catch up with those of his peers but actually to surpass theirs. That is half of the idea. The other half, which completes and justifies this idea, is that the effects of the operation would prove impermanent, so that the story involves our watching the protagonist grow into a genius unconsciously, and then consciously but helplessly slip back toward a state of semi-literacy. When this mental voyage has come full circle, the story is over.

For many people, I suspect, the first half of this idea constitutes the domain of SF, a land of inconsequential wish-fulfillment in which the natural laws that constitute the boundaries of human life are playfully suspended. But the best writers of structural fabulation do not settle for mere imaginative play. Daniel Keyes completed the circuit of his idea, and the beauty and power of the resulting story were acknowledged by his readers at the eighteenth World Science Fiction Convention, where he was awarded the Hugo. It should be added that Keyes's execution of his idea was fully adequate to the original conception. He undertook to present the story through a journal kept by the protagonist himself, at the request of his doctor. Thus, we see the growth of Charlie Gordon's mind through the evolution of his prose style as well as in the events narrated. (Mr. Keyes, we might note, happens to be an English teacher). Charlie acquires a competence in grammar, an extensive lexicon, and a rich, vigorous syntax—and then gradually loses all these, as his mental powers fade. He also becomes an impatient, aggressive, arrogant, and unlovable man as his powers increase, inspiring envy, jealousy, and even fear in others. But as he loses his mental competence he regains the affection of those around him—an affection grounded in pity, which is, as Joseph Conrad knew, a form of contempt.

This tale is beautifully problematic. It conveys to us the deprivation involved in mental retardation as no amount of reports or exhortations could possibly do it. And it does this by the fabulative device of an apparently miraculous scientific discovery. It is fabulation that promotes speculation, and speculation that is embodied in an emotionally powerful fable. The intensity of our emotional commitment to the events of any fiction, of course, is a function of countless esthetic choices made by the author—at the level of the word, the sentence, the episode, the character, the ordering of events, and the manner of the presentation. These aspects of ***Flowers for Algernon*** cannot be dismissed without devoting much more space-time to this story than is available here. I must assert, merely, that Keyes has fleshed out his idea with great skill, and I invite those interested to investigate the text for themselves. (pp. 54-8)

I should [however] like to use this occasion to examine an aspect of this story which is typical of the genre as a whole, and of the special qualities which seem to differentiate it from other kinds of fiction. Like many works of SF, ***Flowers for Algernon*** appeared first as a story and then was "expanded" into a novel. Now all of our training in esthetics and all of our background in the critical thought of Flaubert and James, for instance, must lead us to believe that a work of verbal art consists of one set of words in one particular order. Thus, this idea of expansion seems to have more to do with packaging and merchandising than it can do with art. To some extent this must be admitted. The shapes of genres have always had something to do with the means of their communication and the needs of their audiences. But if the "same" story can appear in two different versions just to suit the exigencies of commercial publication as a magazine story and a book, then we may rightfully feel that the work must be deficient in artistic integrity. (p. 58)

Robert Scholes, "Structural Fabulation," in his Structural Fabulation: An Essay on Fiction of the Future, *University of Notre Dame Press, 1975, pp. 45-76.*

[In *Flowers for Algernon* Keyes] offers compassionate insight into the situation of the mentally retarded: how they feel, how they are treated by parents, friends, institutions.

—Mark R. Hillegas, in his "Other Worlds to Conjure," in* Saturday Review, *26 March 1966.

Barbara A. Bennon (review date 25 July 1980)

[*In the following review, Bennon provides a negative assessment of* The Fifth Sally.]

Why Keyes (***Flowers for Algernon,*** filmed as *Charly*) has written this fictional rehash of a multiple personality case is difficult to understand. Not only is there nothing new or interesting [in ***The Fifth Sally***], but Keyes indulges in formula writing and too many familiar stylistic tricks. We know we are in for a bad time straight off, when the narrator begins: "I'm the only one who knows what's been happening to us, and somebody's got to keep a record so people will understand." The narrator is Derry, one of Sally's personalities; the others are Bella, Jinx and Nola, with the usual assortment of characteristics: one shy and prim, one teasing and sexy, one foulmouthed and raucous, one angry and dangerous. Most of the personalities are ill-bred and of minimum intelligence; they speak in street lingo that further robs the narrative of any style or distinction. Keyes makes a sleazy attempt to invest his story with significance, by having the obligatory psychiatrist say that dissociative disorders are on the upswing, may perhaps even become epidemic ("the illness of our time"), but his desire to please a mass audience will not attract discriminating readers.

Barbara A. Bennon, in a review of "The Fifth Sally," in Publishers Weekly, *Vol. 218, No. 4, July 25, 1980, p. 45.*

Robert Coles (review date 15 November 1981)

[*An American psychiatrist and scholar, Coles is a leading authority on poverty and racial discrimination in the*

United States. His multivolume Children in Crisis *(1967-73) has won several awards, and he has written studies of James Agee, Elizabeth Bowen, George Eliot, William Carlos Williams, and Walker Percy, examining their works in a sociological context. In the following review of* The Minds of Billy Milligan, *he briefly chronicles the development of theories regarding multiple personalities and praises Keyes's study for its thoroughness and readability.*]

During late October of 1977 the medical school area of Ohio State University in Columbus was heavily patrolled by police. In a period of eight days, two women, one a nurse, the other an optometry student, had been kidnapped, compelled under threat of death to cash checks at various suburban banks, robbed and raped. Four days later, a third woman, an undergraduate at Ohio State, was also raped. Shortly thereafter a suspect was arrested; his fingerprints had been found on the car commandeered from one of the victims. Soon enough a kind of legal history would be made.

William Stanley Milligan, a 22-year-old high school dropout charged with extremely serious crimes, became the first person in this country's history to be declared not guilty by reason of insanity on the grounds of a psychiatric diagnosis of "multiple personality." In fact, Billy Milligan had no fewer than 24 separate personalities.

No doubt this book [***The Minds of Billy Milligan***], written by Daniel Keyes, a professor of English and the author of ***Flowers for Algernon,*** will attract a substantial readership. Such immediate predecessors as Corbett Thigpen and Hervey M. Cleckley's *Three Faces of Eve* (1957) and Flora Schreiber's *Sybil* (1973) certainly garnered an attentive response—evidence that mental life continues to possess compelling dramatic possibilities. In the 19th century the phenomenon of multiple personality was attributed to an exceptional capacity for dissociation, that is, the ability of the mind to seal off various segments of consciousness, one from the other. Some psychiatrists emphasized the trancelike aspect of the syndrome and declared it to be essentially self-hypnosis that is repeatedly utilized by particular individuals for their own obscure purposes.

A distinguished American neuro-psychiatrist, Morton Prince, devoted much study to a particular Radcliffe student, Christine Beauchamp, who demonstrated at least three different personalities in the course of treatment. Dr. Prince used hypnosis shrewdly and sensitively, thereby (he reasoned) exploring his patient's difficulties with the same mental maneuver that she had learned to use on her-

A scene from Charly *(1968), the film version of* Flowers for Algernon, *starring Claire Bloom and Cliff Robertson.*

self with such confusing and surprising consequences. His book *The Dissociation of a Personality* (1906)—an edifying instance of the careful investigation of a life, with more speculative psychological forays as to etiology kept under tight rein—is still a classic in the psychiatric literature.

But in 1911 the Swiss psychiatrist and neurologist Paul Eugen Bleuler introduced the word schizophrenia to the medical world, and that diagnostic term has increasingly become all too attractive—a catchall for many sorts of human behavioral aberrations. One recent review of the "Index Medicus" indicates a steep drop in the reported cases of multiple personality "after the diagnosis of schizophrenia 'caught on,' especially in the United States." But the issue is not merely a matter of labeling. Doctors base treatment on what they believe is happening to their patients. To be regarded as capable of self-mesmerizing behavior that results in a series of "people," each of whom is unaware of the others, is not at all the same as to be found "crazy," and consequently at the mercy of the most untreatable of mental disorders. Right or wrong, historically the term schizophrenia has carried with it an extremely negative prognosis.

As Daniel Keyes makes quite evident in ***The Minds of Billy Milligan,*** the historical tensions within the profession have yet to be resolved, and have, in fact, been given new expression in this instance. Doctors began arguing about Billy Milligan as soon as his criminal deeds brought him under sustained psychiatric scrutiny. Even as the Ohio prosecuting attorneys were quite rightfully arguing that Mr. Milligan should be jailed, a number of Ohio doctors, nurses and psychologists, not to mention experts from outside the state, were wrangling strenuously over precisely where and how such a person should be locked up. When he was found "insane," needless to say, the arguments did not by any means abate. Was he a "sociopath"—a liar, an impostor? Was he a deeply troubled man who went in and out of "states," but with whom one could gradually reason, helping him to "fuse" his many and discordant selves into one fairly intact personality? Was he a severely disturbed and dangerous "psychotic" who required careful watching, lots of medication, maybe a course or two of electric shock treatment?

Such lines of analysis obtained their own conflicting embodiments in the complex medical life of one patient. Put differently, this case of multiple personality has had to endure multiple interventions—which in sum, alas, have left Billy Milligan no better off than when he was first picked up by the police. That story, of doctors at war with one another, is an important part of the narrative Mr. Keyes gives us—to the point that one learns as much about these professional splits as about the splits in one unfortunate man's painfully eventful life.

In some respects, Billy Milligan's background may bring to mind J. D. Salinger's Glass family. Billy's father was a Jewish mimic—a nightclub entertainer whose humor, as is so often the case, covered a brooding turmoil of mind and soul. He committed suicide when Billy was a young child. Billy's mother was a Christian woman who had a propensity, it seems, for unstable men. Her second husband, a dour puritan, was capable of brutal sadism and child abuse. The sexual violence he visited upon his stepson Billy was unquestionably linked with the boy's earliest trance-like spells, which eventually became consolidated into his astonishing array of "personalities": Arthur, the English-accented self-taught scientist; Ragen Vadascovinich, the truculent karate expert who writes and speaks Serbo-Croatian; Allen, the fast-talking confidence man; Walter, a supposed Australian big-game hunter; not to mention other men, two women, several children (both boys and girls)—plus, of course, Billy.

Mr. Keyes, who spent two years with Billy Milligan and interviewed his family, friends and acquaintances, as well as some of those in the medical profession who have tried to comprehend him, tells this complicated story well. It reads like a play: Billy's "personalities" come onstage, leave to be replaced by others and then reappear.

For all the suffering and tragedy in Billy Milligan's life, he has demonstrated moments of brilliance. Several of his "personalities" are remarkably gifted. (Examples of portraits painted and drawn by the characters of Allen and Danny, a landscape done in oil by Tommy and a pencil sketch by Ragen are included in the book's picture insert.) Billy has also managed to confound an assortment of experts and, incidentally, reveal some of their inadequacies, if not blind spots. His performances on I.Q. tests, for example, range from 80 to 130.

One of Billy Milligan's psychiatrists came close to helping this fallen Humpty Dumpty put his many parts back together again. But other doctors, it can be argued, contributed mightily to yet another disastrous fall. Billy Milligan is left in a shattered condition at the end of the book. There are not, as Pirandello put it, "Six Characters in Search of an Author" but four times six, and they are all desperately trying to find for themselves one reliable, constant shelter: a mind able to tame its discordant voices and to assemble them into what the rest of us are lucky to take for granted—one particular personality. (pp. 9, 30)

Robert Coles, "Arthur, Ragen, Allen et Al.," in The New York Times Book Review, *November 15, 1981, pp. 9, 30.*

Joseph McLellan (review date 29 November 1981)

[In the following review of The Minds of Billy Milligan, *McLellan describes some of Milligan's personalities and admires Keyes's presentation of his case.]*

Negotiations for the contract to write [***The Minds of Billy Milligan***] were rather complicated—as most things in the life of Billy Milligan were complicated. To show his qualifications, Daniel Keyes sent a copy of his novel, ***Flowers for Algernon,*** to a sort of committee which examined and discussed it: "That week Allen, Arthur and Billy took turns reading the novel," Keyes reports.

"When they were finished, Billy said to Arthur, 'I think he's the one who should do the book.' " Arthur agreed, but Ragen, another member of the group, thought the book should not be written because it might reveal crimes he had committed. Allen suggested that it would be easy enough to deny anything incriminating, and Ragen was finally persuaded by the prospect that the book could make a lot of money.

This might be the account of a fairly ordinary committee meeting except for one point: Allen, Arthur, Billy and Ragen all use the same body—Billy's—which they share with 20 other persons (not, they insist, "personalities") of varied age, sex, talents, nationalities and religious beliefs. Billy Milligan is the first multiple personality to be publicly identified by his real name, extensively observed in public mental health facilities and made the subject of widely reported litigation. The reason for all this public identification is that some of the personalities are criminal; and Billy, the public personality, had to stand trial on charges of robbery, kidnapping, rape and assault with a deadly weapon—activities of which he was totally unaware.

Billy spent a good part of his life being unaware. Arthur, Ragen and the others "put him to sleep" in 1971, after he attempted to commit suicide, and he remained unaware—out of control of his own actions—until late 1977, when he woke up in jail. Arthur, the organizer and intellectual of the group (who had taught himself Arabic, among other accomplishments) had devised a strict set of rules for that six-year regency period: many of Billy's "tenants" were banished entirely because of socially undesirable qualities. Others would be allowed to hold the "spot"—the control center for public actions, communication, etc. from time to time, in situations suited to their particular abilities (which ranged from cooking, painting and playing golf to martial arts, lock-picking and the handling of explosives or electronic gadgetry). Allen, who had considerable public-relations skills and probably the best techniques for coping with day-to-day reality, would be the usual "front man" for encounters with the outside world. Arthur would make the basic decisions in non-threatening situations, but Ragen (a Yugoslav of unusual strength, agility and skill with guns and knives) would take over when there was danger. Others had highly specialized roles, usually connected to the reasons for which they had been conceived in the first place. David, for example, an 8-year-old who was the "keeper of pain, or the empath," entrusted with absorbing all the hurt and suffering of the others; or Mark, 16, sometimes called "the zombie," who would take care of monotonous labor—or just stare at the wall if he had nothing else to do; or Jason, 13, the pressure valve, who would release the others' pressure sometimes by screaming or throwing a tantrum and would absorb their bad memories, causing partial amnesia. Daniel Keyes supplies a complete, annotated list of characters at the beginning of the book—a considerable help to the reader in keeping track of who does what.

The youngest of the 24 people in Billy is Christene, a shy, pretty 3-year-old who was brought into existence in Billy's early years to provide "companionship for a lonely child." She remains 3, Arthur explains, because "It became important to have someone who knew little or nothing about what was happening. Her not knowing was an important protective device. If William had to hide something, she would come on the spot and draw or play hopscotch or cuddle the little Raggedy Ann doll . . . "

Other characters were generated to help cope with various crises of Billy's childhood, which was anything but happy. His father, a professional comedian, committed suicide; his stepfather left him (and his various alter egos) scarred with searing memories of beatings, sexual abuse, and one traumatic incident where he was threatened with burial alive.

The development of different personalities to cope with different problems is an ingenious ad hoc solution, but the various personalities in Billy did not always communicate with one another and his life became almost unmanageable. He would suffer frequent lapses of memory from periods when his own personality was not on the spot, and he would be called a liar because of memory failures or because a person who was not Billy was using Billy to speak truthfully for himself. For example, most of his personalities remained virginal long after one had had his first sexual experience. This sort of confusion and the implications that he was insane or a criminal finally led him to his suicide attempt while he was in high school and then to Arthur's establishment of the rules for what might be called the Billy Junta. Another ad hoc solution—one that worked well enough most of the time but sometimes failed abysmally during what the Billy group would call "mix-up times," when Arthur and the other leaders would lose control and others would take over.

These others were often the undesirables who were normally kept in seclusion: Philip, a petty criminal; Kevin, who dealt in drugs and masterminded a drug store robbery; April, "the bitch," whose only ambition was to kill Billy's stepfather. A special case is Adalana, a 19-year-old lesbian who suffers from loneliness and yearns for sex as a way of communicating; she is allowed to take the spot occasionally for her cooking and housekeeping skills. Billy's most serious legal problem in the book stems from three occasions when Adalana abruptly preempted the spot and began making love to women while one of the other characters was engaged in robbing them at gunpoint. The courts called it robbery, abduction and rape—adequate descriptions of what happened, but the total reality is somewhat more complex.

Complexity is, in fact, the keynote of the Billy phenomenon and equally of its treatment by Daniel Keyes. The challenge of first unearthing this story (buried in many partial and often conflicting memories) and then telling it intelligibly was a daunting one. He has carried it off brilliantly, bringing to the assignment not only a fine clarity but a special warmth, and empathy for the victim of circumstances and mental failings that made ***Flowers for Algernon*** one of the most memorable novels of the 1960s.

Like the novel, the new nonfiction work ends with a special flavor of intense anguish. The Ohio system of criminal justice was woefully inadequate to deal with a problem as unusual as that of Billy Milligan—and when he was turned over to the state's public mental health system, the results were hardly better. Billy Milligan (as Keyes tells the story—and his case is convincing) fell into the power of the wrong people repeatedly at crucial points. In the basic decision between retribution (in the name of public safety) and an attempt to rehabilitate him (in the name of common decency), the wrong choices seem to have been made again and again. At the end, after many ups and downs and some promising efforts to integrate his various selves into an effective, functioning personality, the epilogue finds Billy slowly disintegrating in a maximum-security institution for the criminally insane. He calls the place where he is now "the Dying Place," and he tells Keyes in a letter: "We, I am a freak, a misfit, a biological error. We all hate this place, but it is where we belong."

His story is an incredibly unhappy one, but at least he has found the right person to tell it.

Joseph McLellan, "Billy the Kid, Painter, Yugoslav, Cook, Lesbian, Etc.," in Book World—The Washington Post, *November 29, 1981, p. 5.*

Gregor A. Preston (review date July 1986)

[*In the excerpt below, Preston provides a positive assessment of* Unveiling Claudia: A True Story of a Serial Murder.]

Claudia Yasko, 26, confessed to a triple homicide in 1978—three of ten Ohio murders attributed to the ".22 caliber" killers. Her confession was false and she was unknown by the two men later convicted of the crimes. Yasko, an attractive but mentally ill young woman, sought out Keyes to help tell her story [in ***Unveiling Claudia: A True Story of a Serial Murder***]. For, while no one believed her capable of murder, how did she happen to know so much about the crime scene? Keyes, who wrote about a multiple-personality criminal in ***The Minds of Billy Milligan,*** spent two years unlocking Yasko's repressed memory and separating fantasy from reality. While not quite as intriguing as ***Billy Milligan,*** this is a masterfully told, absorbing story.

Gregor A. Preston, in a review of "Unveiling Claudia: A True Story of a Serial Murder," in Library Journal, *Vol. III, No. 12, July, 1986, p. 101.*

Additional coverage of Keyes's life and career is contained in the following sources published by Gale Research: *Contemporary Authors,* Vols. 17-20, rev. ed.; *Contemporary Authors New Revision Series,* Vols. 10 and 26; *DISCovering Authors;* and *Something about the Author,* Vol. 37.

Carolyn Kizer

1925-

(Full name Carolyn Ashley Kizer) American poet, translator, and editor.

The following entry provides an overview of Kizer's career through *The Nearness of You* (1986). For further information on her life and works, see *CLC,* Volumes 15 and 39.

INTRODUCTION

Kizer is best known for her mastery of both traditional and free verse forms and for her unsentimental treatment of such subjects as nature, politics, and feminism. While Kizer's early collections are noted for their penetrating satire and formal poetic structures, her later works are considered more contemplative and stylistically experimental. Underlying all of Kizer's poetry is a deep faith in humanity's ability to overcome adversity, injustice, and emotional pain. Elizabeth B. House has stated: "Kizer faces life's harshest realities without flinching. . . . Even in her treatments of unsettling topics, [she] almost invariably maintains a tone of stoic sincerity and acceptance."

Kizer was born in Spokane, Washington, and raised in Los Angeles, California. Her father was a lawyer and author, and her mother a biology professor who influenced Kizer's love of nature, a prominent theme in much of her poetry. Kizer graduated from Sarah Lawrence College in New York City in 1945 and later took graduate courses at Columbia University and the University of Washington. Her first poem appeared in the *New Yorker* in 1942 when she was seventeen. In the early 1950s Kizer participated in American poet Theodore Roethke's Washington University poetry workshop, and in 1959 she helped to found the quarterly *Poetry Northwest,* serving as its editor until 1965. Kizer, who maintains a keen interest in foreign cultures and literatures, has traveled extensively throughout Europe, Japan, China, and Pakistan, and has also translated poetry from Chinese, Japanese, and Urdu into English. A professor and guest lecturer in literature, Kizer has also served as the director of literary programs for the National Endowment for the Arts and as a United States State Department specialist in Pakistan.

In her first major work, *The Ungrateful Garden,* Kizer uses vivid and sometimes repelling imagery to examine interpersonal and philosophical questions related to nature. Eschewing romanticism, Kizer accepts the inherent inaccessibility and brutality of the natural world. In "The Great Blue Heron," for example, she presents the heron as a harbinger of death; yet, as Elizabeth B. House has noted, Kizer "never suggests that the bird is evil. As a part of nature, he merely reflects the cycle of life and death that time imposes on all living creatures." While continuing her observations of nature and human relationships, Kizer introduces her fascination with Oriental poetry in her next work, *Knock upon Silence.* This volume contains the two long works "A Month in Summer" and "Pro Femina," several translations of pieces by the eighth-century Chinese poet Tu Fu, and a poetry section entitled "Chinese Imitations." One of Kizer's best-known and most critically acclaimed poems, "Pro Femina" is a satiric work in which the poet explores the role of women artists in modern Western society, noting in particular the obstacles they face in a culture dominated by men. With *Midnight Was My Cry: New and Selected Poems,* Kizer began to favor free verse and colloquial idiom over the formal language of her previous works. In this collection, which comprises previously published and new poems, Kizer shifts her focus from nature and interpersonal relationships to social and political issues prominent during the 1960s, including desegregation, the Vietnam War, and the murder of Robert Kennedy.

Issues related to sexuality and gender roles are prominent in Kizer's recent collections, including *Yin: New Poems, Mermaids in the Basement: Poems for Women,* and *The Nearness of You.* In *Yin,* for which she won the Pulitzer

Prize in Poetry in 1985, Kizer examines such institutions as motherhood, marriage, and religion from a feminist perspective. "A Muse," for example, recounts Kizer's childhood impressions of an overly supportive mother; "Fanny," a poem frequently singled out by critics as one of the collection's best, focuses on the wife of Scottish novelist Robert Louis Stevenson as she nurses her husband through the last year of his life. *Mermaids in the Basement* similarly addresses feminist concerns, while *The Nearness of You,* considered a companion volume to *Mermaids,* explores themes of manhood and fatherhood and delineates Kizer's childhood relationship with her father.

Critical reaction to Kizer's poetry has been generally positive. While some early reviewers faulted Kizer's verse as affected and emotionally inaccessible, most critics agree that Kizer's later collections are more relaxed in tone. Several have noted, for example, that in works such as *Yin* and *Mermaids in the Basement,* Kizer tempers potentially bleak subject matter with humor and a variety of voices ranging from the wise to the affectionate. While she has been praised for her objectivity, generosity, and versatility, some critics maintain that Kizer has yet to receive the recognition she deserves.

PRINCIPAL WORKS

Poems (poetry) 1959
The Ungrateful Garden (poetry) 1961
Knock upon Silence (poetry and translations) 1965
Midnight Was My Cry: New and Selected Poems (poetry) 1971
Mermaids in the Basement: Poems for Women (poetry) 1984
Yin: New Poems (poetry) 1984
Carrying Over: Translations from Many Tongues (translations) 1985
The Nearness of You (poetry) 1986

CRITICISM

William Dickey (review date November 1961)

[*Dickey is an American poet, critic, editor, and educator. His poetry collections include* The Rainbow Grocery *(1978) and* Brief Lives *(1985). In the following review, he faults the poems in* The Ungrateful Garden *for being too academic and emotionally detached.*]

The work of Carolyn Kizer seems Alexandrian; the poems [in ***The Ungrateful Garden***] are markedly profuse in references, various of them have the writing of poetry as their subject, and they are more concerned with the manner of their expression than with the material to be expressed. Her poetry has considerable technical sophistication; it plays with French or Japanese forms, it delights in slants of sound and paradoxes. But even when colloquial phrases enter, they are enmeshed in a formal, self-conscious rhetoric, and when ingenuousness appears, we can be sure it is there at the summons of ingenuity.

Thus, though the subject of a number of the poems is passion, they themselves are not passionate; they communicate their surfaces brightly, and their interiors scarcely at all. One love poem ends:

> The world's a tinted shell borne up where waves
> embrace.
> Its thin, convolving valve will close and clasp
> This love, so blessed:
> Our sea-life, swooning as it swims, to reach
> Tentacular and cleaving arms that touch
> A milky flank, a drowned, reviving face.

I cannot convince myself that this poem is about love at all; not only its medium but its subject appears to be language. Nor can I feel, as I can with O'Gorman's poetry, that the elaborations of language are made necessary by difficulty of statement. Miss Kizer's poetry has the surface of intellect, but it is really emotion-based; her matter and her manner have become detached.

Only occasionally is this detachment healed; when that happens, it is because the autonomous activity of the language has been brought under control. **"The Great Blue Heron"** shows such control, and so does much of **"Hera, Hung from the Sky."** These poems are unified, moving, and direct; but so far they have few companions in their breakthrough. (p. 128)

William Dickey, "Revelations and Homilies," in Poetry, *Vol. XCIX, No. 2, November, 1961, pp. 124-29.*

Robert Dana (review date Fall 1964)

[*Dana is an American poet, critic, and educator. In the review below, he praises Kizer's poetry and examines what he considers the three principal themes in* The Ungrateful Garden: *"the relationship between Man and Nature, between Man and his gods, and between Man and Man."*]

In today's jumbled landscape of first books of poetry, cut by the crosswinds of style (fresh styles, old styles, and old innovation tricked out to look like new ones), one picks up Carolyn Kizer's ***The Ungrateful Garden*** with a sense of relief, saying, "It's poetry," as matter-of-factly as one might say, "That's a tree."

It would be a mistake and an injustice to label this work, to call it *Academic, Avant-garde,* or as one critic [William Dickey] *has* done, *Alexandrian.* It is none of these things, though with a little wrenching, pieces here and there might be pigeonholed. It is true Miss Kizer has occasionally borrowed a manner, a kind of syntax, an image, but when has it not been the poet's right to do so? Somewhere, Judson Jerome wrote a sage piece of advice, something like this: "Invent it, and if you can't, then beg, borrow, or steal it. But get on with the work; for if it is important at all, it is too important to let false pride stand in the way." Miss Kizer gets on with it, and what emerges is a firm, honest piece of work. Sometimes she fails, more often she succeeds, and often she overpowers with the dazzle and aptness of her images, and the poignance or savagery of her resolutions.

The Ungrateful Garden, divided into three major sections, is made up largely of poems exploring three related themes: the relationship between Man and Nature, between Man and his gods, and between Man and Man.

Of the poems supporting the first theme, the title poem and **"The Intruder"** are perhaps the richest. The first poem, in tight, rhymed, tetrameter quatrains, uses the Midas myth as the basis of its extended metaphor, and brings the myth home to us as fresh as a live bird in the hand:

> This gift, he'd thought, would gild his joys,
> Silt up the waters of his grief;
> His lawns a wilderness of noise,
> The heavy clang of leaf on leaf.

But not content with simply rendering the Midian world, Miss Kizer carries us swiftly and crisply into the still eye at the center of the universal problem of self-projection:

> Dazzled with wounds, he limped away
> To climb into his golden bed.
> Roses, roses can betray.
> "Nature is evil," Midas said.

Thus, in one of the best traditions of poetry, Miss Kizer breathes new life into an old legend.

"The Intruder" is an anti-romantic poem dealing with another aspect of the theme, Man and Nature. The central figure in the piece, a woman full of a "tender, wounding passion" for the wild and natural; for children, frogs, and flowers; indulges her tenderness in the rescue of a bat. But her trust in the purity of the Nature she has imagined is decisively and irreparably broken by a casual glimpse of Truth:

> . . . lice, pallid, yellow
> Nested within the wingpits, cosily sucked and snoozed.

In disgust and disillusion, she washes "the pity from her hands."

In the best of the other poems on this theme, **"The Worms," "A Widow in Wintertime"** (superb), **"Complex Autumnal," "The Suburbans,"** and **"A Muse of Water,"** Miss Kizer makes it clear that, in her view, while man distorts Nature, and in some cases even deforms and corrupts her ("The seagull is our bird, who eats our loot, / Adores our garbage, but can rise above it / . . . get clean away / Past bays and rivers of industrial waste, / Infected oysters, fish-bloat, belly up / In sloughs of sewage, to the open sea") he is at his best as the "ex-animal" working stubbornly through his "arbitrary disciplines":

> Most of them trivial: like covering
> The children on my way to bed, and trying
> To live well enough alone, and not to dream
> Of grappling in the snow, claws plunged in fur, . . .

The poetry of Columns and Caryatids, part two of ***The Ungrateful Garden,*** derives its thematic strength from a focus upon the gods, Greek and Christian their nature and their fate, and human attitudes toward that fate. The best of these poems is **"Persephone Pauses";** but the long, loose pieces from "A Heine Journal"—**"The Old Gods," "The Apostate,"** and **"Tying One on in Vienna"**—brings us something refreshingly energetic in the way of tone and strategy. These three poems taken together give us in English a fair approximation of Heineian tongue-in-cheek invective, and delight in the outrageous for its own sake. Take for example, Heine's voice in **"The Apostate,"**

> Ask Dr. Heine, expert practitioner and self-surgeon
> Who could carve his own carcass in public

or

> Again, for the world as it is: "where holy water
> Does double duty, washing souls and thinning tea . . ."

or this one from **"Tying One on . . . ,"**

> O those grand autumn days, when we crushed Immaculate Conception,
> And the Society of Jesus provided cheerleaders,
> Though both teams flopped down on the field to pray,
> Just before game-time. And I debated the girls from the convent
> On, "Resolved: We should have government ownership of railroads"
> And God was on my side, the affirmative.
> Though I spoke with the tongue of gargoyle and angel,
> God and I lost, because the girls of St. Mary's
> Kept their skirts over their knees, and their hands folded. . . .

But beneath the parti-colored comic surface of the pieces from the "Journal" lie the hard, fine lines of the modern dilemma, as recognizable as the black lake in a recurring dream. The old Greek pantheon has crumbled before the "windy deities" of later times, and the Christian god is an odd cross between a referee and a debate coach done in by the primness of the girls from St. Mary's; Nature itself has shed its romance, and shows itself woundingly ambivalent. The last centers of the older orders have fallen. What now remains to Man as a possible clear focus for the orientation of self?

The poet answers with the best sensibilities of the age, with Freud and Watts, with Eiseley and Roethke: Love.

For all its instability and poignance, which Miss Kizer serves up in the fullness of shock and sense of loss in **"Death of a Public Servant," "The Great Blue Heron,"** and **"To My Friend, Behind Walls";** despite its "whiskey and ripe fruit / Stale with fulfillment," there is no doubt that Love, the sexual act with all its radiating meanings, stands clearly at the center of whatever order human life has and is to have:

> I think that Yeats was right

That lust and love are one.
The body of this night
May beggar me to death,
But we are not undone
Who love with all our breath.

This stanza from **"What the Bones Know"** and the final lines from **"Afterthoughts of Donna Elvira"** state the case purely and succinctly:

Now that I see, I see
What you have known within:
Whenever we love, we win
Or else we have never been born.

One could go on enumerating Miss Kizer's virtues; stringing, like cockleburrs and wildflowers, her lines and images; quoting whole poems to illustrate her range. And it is true her poems "in the Japanese mode" are disappointing. (So are practically all such imitations doomed, by the pictorial nature of the Japanese written character and the near-stresslessness of the language.) But beyond all this making of cases for and against the work, all snippets and private tastes aside, lies the work itself. *There* is the range. *There* is the sensibility. *There* is experience developed and developing, through forms and language, into poetry.

The best way to be convinced of it is to read ***The Ungrateful Garden.*** (pp. 271-74)

Robert Dana, "Explosion on the Plains of Sleep," in Prairie Schooner, *Vol. XXXVIII, No. 3, Fall, 1964, pp. 271-74.*

Dabney Stuart (review date Winter 1966)

[*Stuart is an American poet, critic, and educator whose poetry collections include* Rockbridge Poems *(1981) and* Common Ground *(1982). In the following review, he compares* The Ungrateful Garden *to* Knock upon Silence, *noting the differences in method and subject matter between the two volumes.*]

In both ***The Ungrateful Garden*** (1961, dedicated in part to [Theodore] Roethke) and her recent volume, ***Knock Upon Silence,*** Miss Kizer is her own poet. When she needs a pattern to order the significance of certain primary discoveries she assembles it from the details of her own experience. This is best shown in **"By The Riverside"** from ***The Ungrateful Garden,*** in which she dramatizes emerging sexuality in the figure of a nude Indian wading a creek in winter, "Breaking the thin ice with his thighs," manhood "roused by the shock of ice." As the poem develops, this is associated with bestiality and Christ, and Miss Kizer's careful construction allows her to conclude the poem tersely, bringing various thematic suggestions to fulfillment in a few lines, as a composer might close a sonata:

Now I call up god-head and manhood both
As they emerged for a child by the riverside.

Such composition, in which themes and images interact and then merge into a larger perception, is typical of the poems in ***The Ungrateful Garden.***

As a whole the book reveals a similar order. There are a number of poems about women confronting the chaos of love and age. As these poems recur the response to some inevitable disaster or grief, usually expressed by a metaphor of descent—into earth, darkness, water, or hell—changes. First, the speaker resists disaster.

trying
To live well enough alone, and not to dream
Of grappling in the snow, claws plunged in fur.
("Widow in Wintertime")

Then she attempts to accept it and salvage something affirmative from loss itself.

Reminding me as I decline
That half my life is spent in light.
("Persephone Pauses")

Finally, the speaker seeks it, calling for admittance into hell.

Teach me anguish so outrageous that known pain
Will seem as trivial as an ant with one leg gone
Laboring up the mound with a dead fly. Amputate my whine.
("The Damnation")

Yet she learns from hell's citizens that what she seeks, the burning away of self, is impossible there.

Interwoven with this development are two other major concerns: the writer's need for her craft and the shape she may give life through it, and a sense (whose irony cauterizes its bitterness) of her relationship to a larger society more or less indifferent to art of any sort. **"The Suburbans"** and **"A Muse of Water"** reveal this most clearly. Here is the next to last stanza of the latter:

Rejoice when a faint music rises
Out of a brackish clump of weeds,
Out of the marsh at ocean-side,
Out of the oil-stained river's gleam,
By the long causeways and grey piers
Your civilizing lusts have made.

As these lines indicate, this poem deals unnervingly with the poet's awareness of the power and fragility of small music sounding in an environment being gradually choked of its energy by urban shapes.

I spend so much time with ***The Ungrateful Garden*** because an understanding of ***Knock Upon Silence*** depends a good deal on its relationship with Miss Kizer's first book. In ***Knock Upon Silence*** Miss Kizer turns Eastward, noticeably altering the method of her poetry, and indicating by her solidification of attitude that this change in method is not so much part of a general tendency among our poets to translate poetry from other languages, but rather a more basic desire to suit her manner to her vision.

Roughly seven-eighths of ***Knock Upon Silence*** is either imitation or translation of Chinese poetry, especially poems by Po Chü-I and Tu Fu, and Miss Kizer's work here becomes, not surprisingly, oblique and spare. For instance, this haiku from the series titled "A Month in Summer":

Lights in every room.
I turned on more!

You sat with one hand
Shading your eyes.

"Amusing our Daughters" is a poem about the death of a child, yet the poem dances softly around this fact as if it were a secret. In ***The Ungrateful Garden*** there were poems marked by strained and ornate convolutions. For example:

As our mirror selves
Slipped back to sea, unsundering, bumped gent-
ly there,
The room a bay, and we,
Afloat on lapping, gazes laving,
Glistered in its spume.
(**"Epithalamion"**)

This sort of indulgence disappears in the new book, as these lines from another poem about marriage show.

I sulk and sigh, dawdling by the window.
Later, when you hold me in your arms
It seems, for a moment, the river ceases flowing.
(**"Summer Near the River"**)

As I have said, the change from direct and sometimes turgid metaphorical statement to lean suggestiveness is part of a deeper development. The identity which has sought hell and discovered its irony has turned to the world again, seeking discipline and a kind of resignation. The forces of passion and the loss of lust in age are still present in ***Knock Upon Silence,*** but Miss Kizer considers a different response to them. She is explicit about this.

We are meant to be stripped down, to prepare
us
for something better.
(**"Singing Aloud"**)

And, at last, surely it is time to study restraint?
("A Month in Summer")

The basic concern of this collection is with studying restraint, something Tu Fu does in the poems Miss Kizer has chosen to translate here. This is a *studying,* however, not an achieved control, and I don't mean to imply that Miss Kizer has written a static book. ***Knock Upon Silence*** is dramatic in relationship to ***The Ungrateful Garden*** and within itself. Tu Fu struggles to accept his age and the minimal importance he has for his society, and part of this struggle is embodied in a desire for sensual leisure. Without a force to be restrained, there is no need for restraint. And warring with the Eastern attitudes Miss Kizer entertains is the aggressive, Western assertiveness of the three [sections in] **"Pro Femina"** which she places in the middle of the volume. There is, after all, an infinitude of silence to knock upon, and more music to be made. (pp. 97-100)

Dabney Stuart, "Weights and Measures," in Shenandoah, *Vol. XVII, No. 2, Winter, 1966, pp. 91-102.*

Helen Fowler (review date Spring 1966)

[In the following review, Fowler praises Kizer's use of traditional Chinese poetry methods in Knock upon Silence *to create modern narrative poems.]*

I must admit that until I read Carolyn Kizer's ***Knock Upon Silence*** I had not understood at all the possibilities which an intimate appreciation of the methods of Chinese poetry put at the disposal of an American poet. I had not seen how well these techniques could be used to produce a really modern narrative poem. We have been badly needing such a narrative technique for many years. Our contemporary verse has lost much of its range and power since it has not been able to find a satisfying method in which to tell a story, ever since the discrediting of the American Victorians. Carolyn Kizer shows us how this may be done, both in her translations of Tu Fu and in her adaptations from the Chinese and Japanese. Here is the first section of **"The Skein"**:

Moonlight through my gauze curtains
Turns them to nets for snaring wild birds,
Turns them into woven traps, into shrouds.
The old, restless grief keeps me awake.
I wander around, holding a scarf or shawl;
In the muffled noonlight I wander around
Folding it carefully, shaking it out again.
Everyone says my old lover is happy.
I wish they said he was coming back to me.
I hesitate here, my scarf like a skein of yarn
Binding my two hands loosely
that would reach for paper and pen.

This seems to me wholly admirable. I respond to it with all my unsatisfied desire for the narrative mode in poetry. It takes space, which this reviewer does not have at her disposal, to show how these techniques manage with superb economy a story line, character, setting, and feeling both personal and social, portraying the tone of a whole society. All I can do is to recommend Carolyn Kizer's book for careful reading, with special reference to those sections based on Oriental traditions.

When she comes to adapting that of Juvenal to her own purposes, I have certain reservations. It's not that I don't enjoy the bite of her wit. But the satirical mode, and especially the aggressively masculine method of Juvenal, seems to me to impose restrictions on her that reduce her satire to polemics. Perhaps it's because I don't see the need for the vigor which can be whipped up by polemics, to my mind a wholly meretricious source of energy. I heartily dislike its reducing vital subjects to ground-fights. I can't help but feel that such trivialization scarcely advances the role of poetry in American culture. (pp. 35-6)

Helen Fowler, "More about 'Approach' Authors," in Approach, *No. 59, Spring, 1966, pp. 30-6.*

Bruce Cutler (review date July 1966)

[In the review below, Cutler discusses Kizer's rendering and translation of Oriental literary forms in Knock upon Silence.*]*

Carolyn Kizer's new collection of poems [***Knock upon Silence***] shows the strong influence of Oriental literature, and includes a number of translations of the poems of Tu Fu as well. In or out of oriental forms, what she does well rests on a kind of virile use of language, close to the epigrammatic; but the best poems in this collection, it seems to me, have the least to do with things Oriental. One is set on the Italian island of Ischia (**"For Jan, In Bar Maria"**); and another, **"Pro Femina,"** in tone and execution is even farther removed. There is an ingenious complexity to the contrastive descriptions in Part Two:

. . . Our masks, always in peril or smearing or cracking,
In need of continuous check in the mirror or silverware,
Keep us in thrall to ourselves, concerned with our surfaces.
Look at man's uniform drabness, his impersonal envelope!
Over chicken wrists or meek shoulders, a formal, hard—fibered assurance,
The drape of the male is designed to achieve self-forgetfulness. . . .

A very significant portion of the book is given over to translations of poems by Tu Fu, and they are pleasantly enough rendered. The problems involved in turning a calligraphic work into a syllabic one are very complex, and my comments would add nothing to that which is already in print. Sufficient to say that the pleasant qualities of Tu Fu come through in these versions, as in others—a great credit to a master poet.

I cannot put Carolyn Kizer's book down without recalling Carl Jung's comments in *The Secret of the Golden Flower* some thirty years ago on the problems encountered, in the largest, philosophical sense, when any of us tries to adopt the modes and methods of classical Chinese thought without taking the greatest care that we not give up "ourselves" for that which we are not. All of us who work toward comprehending and utilizing classical Chinese and Japanese forms need to remind ourselves of this difficult truth. (pp. 269-70)

Bruce Cutler, "What We Are, and Are Not," in Poetry, *Vol. CVIII, No. 4, July, 1966, pp. 269-72.*

An excerpt from "Pro Femina"

I will speak about women of letters, for I'm in the racket.
Our biggest successes to date? Old maids to a woman.
And our saddest conspicuous failures? The married spinsters
On loan to the husbands they treated like surrogate fathers.
Think of that crew of self-pitiers, not-very-distant,
Who carried the torch for themselves and got first-degree burns.
Or the sad sonneteers, toast-and-teasdales we loved at thirteen;
Middle-aged virgins seducing the puerile anthologists
Through lust-of-the-mind; barbiturate-drenched Camilles
With continuous periods, murmuring softly on sofas
When poetry wasn't a craft but a sickly effluvium,
The air thick with incense, musk, and emotional blackmail.

I suppose they reacted from an earlier womanly modesty
When too many girls were scabs to their stricken sisterhood,
Impugning our sex to stay in good with the men,
Commencing their insecure bluster. How they must have swaggered
When women themselves endorsed their own inferiority!
Vestals, vassals and vessels, rolled into several,
They took notes in rolling syllabics, in careful journals,
Aiming to please a posterity that despises them.
But we'll always have traitors who swear that a woman surrenders
Her Supreme Function, by equating Art with aggression
And failure with Femininity. Still, it's just as unfair
To equate Art with Femininity, like a prettily-packaged commodity

When we are the custodians of the world's best-kept secret:
Merely the private lives of one-half of humanity.

Carolyn Kizer, in her Mermaids in the Basement: Poems for Women, *Copper Canyon Press, 1984.*

Richard Howard (essay date Fall 1966)

[*In the essay below, Howard focuses on Kizer's depiction of womanhood in her poetry.*]

A teacher and a friend and even a subject of Miss Kizer's, as in this pair of apochromatic *tankas:*

The stout poet tiptoes
On the lawn. Surprisingly limber
In his thick sweater
Like a middle-aged burglar.
Is the young robin injured?

A hush is on the house,
The only noise, a fern
Rustling on a vase.
On the porch, the fierce poet
Is chanting words to himself.

—Theodore Roethke once listed the charges most frequently levelled against poetry written by women: lack of range in subject matter, in emotional tone; lack of a sense of humor; spinning out; the embroidering of trivial themes; a concern with the mere surfaces of life; refusing to face up to existence; lyric or religious posturing; running between the boudoir and the altar, stamping a tiny foot against God; lapsing into a sententiousness that implies the author has reinvented integrity; carrying on excessively about Fate, about Time; lamenting the lot of the woman; caterwauling; writing the same poem about fifty times; and so on. These are scarcely the faults of a sex, of course, unless they are those faults of men which they *prefer* to see in women, as Simone de Beauvoir would say, or as Miss Kizer does say:

> Juvenal set us apart in denouncing our vices
> Which had grown, in part, from having been set
> apart . . .

No, these are the faults of selfhood itself, to oppose which is very much like being dead set against sin—they are no more than the possibilities and the problems that must be faced by any writer. Miss Kizer, whom Roethke himself acknowledged as "willing to take chances with unusual material," has approached the baleful list in the bravest way, not seeking to escape the damages but rather to incur and so transcend them. She does not fear—indeed she *wants*—to do all the things Roethke says women are blamed for, and indeed I think she does do them (though if she lacks a sense of humor, it is never when the joke is on *her*), and this makes her terribly suspect, of course—no one could be *really* womanly if so womanly as all *that.* But doing them or not, being *determined* to do them makes her a different kind of poet from the one who manages to avoid the traps of his condition, and gives her a different kind of success from the one that "in circuit lies," as Emily Dickinson put it. Carolyn Kizer has succeeded otherwise, has succeeded head on, in a most difficult exertion—she has transformed her character into fate, or shown, by the most markedly contrasting and often contesting means, that aspect of her character which *is* fate. Employing or suffering—undergoing, at any rate—all the potential disqualifications Roethke asserts to be imminent in her enterprise—"the raw material of a ritual"—Miss Kizer has made the woman of her poems a Figure rather than a Character, an emblem rather than a case, so that what we discover in reading her, or what we deserve if we have heard the poems in the right voice—one that allows if it does not itself release the Grand Gynaesic Gesture—is something larger and more luminous than life, though composed, surely, of just the details we are accustomed to reckon with in accounts of selfhood smaller than life—the accounts of prose, I mean, and smaller in that their scrutiny is more intense and deliberate than our living will ordinarily bear. In her idiophany, Carolyn Kizer has been able to raise our implicit recognition of the *via naturaliter femina* into explicit distinction; from the fatal etcetera of things in a woman's life, as well as from its unique occasions, from what I have called the household bonds as well as the heroic body:

> We who must act as handmaidens
> To our own goddess, turn too fast,
> Trip on our hems, to glimpse the muse
> Gliding below her lake or sea,
> Are left, long-staring after her,
> Narcissists by necessity;
>
> Or water-carriers of our young
> Till waters burst, and white streams flow
> Artesian, from the lifted breast:
> Cup-bearers then, to tiny gods,
> Imperious table pounders, who
> Are final arbiters of thirst.
>
> Fasten the blouse, and mount the steps
> From kitchen taps to Royal Barge,
> Assume the trident, don the crown,
> Command the Water Music now
> That men bestow on Virgin Queens;
> Or, goddessing above the waist,
>
> Appear as swan on Thames or Charles
> Where iridescent foam conceals
> The paddle-stroke beneath the glide:
> Immortal feathers preened in poems!
> Not our true, intimate nature, stained
> By labor, and the casual tide.

—from these acknowledgments worthy of a Colette, Miss Kizer has wrought a new shape of consciousness; with the admission that the prison and the desert are not within everyone's range, that the Criminal and the Adventurer, as in, say, the work of Genet and of T. E. Lawrence, do not represent forms of activity which most appeal to her as life, she has worked out of the old Austrian precept *immer fortwurschteln,* always muddle along, a kind of suburban sanctity—out of these "dull and partial couplings with ourselves . . . afraid to become our neighbors," by some brilliantly contrived and often exotic distancing effects, she has created what I like to call a *Figure,*

> . . . nailed to our domesticity
> Like Van Gogh to the wall, wild in his frame,
> Doubling in mirrors, that the sinister self
> Who moves along with us may own at last
> Her own reverses . . .

something impersonal and unaccommodating, as Antigone and Phèdre would be Figures—of that condition which the personal only hides. (pp. 109-11)

. . . . .

[Kizer's] first book, ***The Ungrateful Garden,*** published when she was in her middle thirties, is by its reach West to "the Japanese Mode" and East to Vienna and the Greek myths an ambitious reversal of the usual directions in which we venture to possess such things. "One half the individual is locality," Frost once wrote to a friend, and it was early that Miss Kizer discovered the advantages to the other half of her situation on the stiff upper lip of the Pacific: the exile that belongs to oneself, the interior exile. The "gravely gay" book is dedicated, in its three parts, to her mother, her father and her children, in fulfilment of those ritual pieties she has taken care to repossess in her own uncomfortable way:

> . . . in these austerities,
> These arbitrary disciplines of mine,
> Most of them trivial: like covering
> The children on my way to bed, and trying
> To live well enough alone, and not to dream
> Of grappling in the snow, claws plunged in fur,
> Or waken in a caterwaul of dying.

Its content, in every sense, is what the author knows already—as a child knows best, first of all:

> *Thomas Love Peacock! Thomas Love Peacock!*
> I used to croon, sitting on the pot,
> My sympathetic magic, at age three.
> These elements in balance captured me:
> Love in the middle, on his right hand a saint and
> doubter . . .

On Love's left hand, the coarse essentials: . . .
Thomas Love Peacock! Thomas Love Peacock!
The person unsung, the person ritually sung.
But that was thirty years ago; a child's loving
Of God, the body, flesh of poetry . . .

then what as a woman writer she has learned:

Perhaps not happiness, but still
A certain comfort . . .
I know, I know. I've gone before . . .

A poet to whom no one cruel or imposing listens,
Disdained by senates . . .

Our limited salvation is the word,
A bridge between our Nature and our Time.

and what as a human being she must merely endure:

Delivered at last from my thought and my things,
My net weight, my engorged heart,
So humbled that my purposes grow grass . . .

Accepting ravage as the only tribute
That men can pay to gods . . .

The book's title and a good deal of its business—the practice of poetry which reveals perfection to be impossible—is an acknowledgment that we perform our functions—bodily, creative, official—in an alienated nature:

We live on ironed land like cemeteries,
But cemeteries are a green relief:
Used-car and drive-in movie lots alike
Enaisle and regulate the gaudy junk
That runs us, in a "Park" that is no park . . .

The seagull is our bird, who eats our loot,
Adores our garbage but can rise above it—
Clean scavenger, picks clean, gets clean away!—
Past bays and rivers of industrial waste,
Infected oysters, fish-bloat, belly up
In sloughs of sewage, to the open sea . . .

as well as in an alien one: "a whole wild, lost, betrayed and secret life." To render that life, to recover at least the sense that something has been lost, Miss Kizer learned a lot from Mr. Roethke. Take worms:

pearly and purple,
curling and opal . . .
bruised as a blueberry,
bare as a rose,
vulnerable as veins,
naked as a nose . . .

But where Roethke would rush out and fling himself upon the thorns of life, ecstatic even in natural ruin, there is a sour or at least a wry centripetal impulse in Miss Kizer's witty emblems of womanhood, as shaped in the magnificent **"Columns and Caryatids"**:

the wife: "I am Lot's pillar, caught in turning,
Bellowing, resistant, burning . . .
I saw Sodom bleed, Gomorrah smoke,
Empty sockets are a joke of that final vision.
Tongueless, I taste my own salt, taste
God's chastisement and derision."
. . . God's alliance with weather
Eroding her to a spar, a general grief-shape,
A cone, then an egg no bigger than a bead.

the mother: I am God's pillar, caught in raising
My arms like thighs to brace the wall . . .
The world is a womb.
Neither I nor the foetus tire of our position.
My ear is near God, my temples to his temple.
I lift and I listen. I eat God's peace."

the lover: "I am your pillar that has fallen . . ."
Stripped of all ornament she lies,
Looted alike by conquerors and technicians;
So boys will turn from sleep and search the darkness,
Seeking the love their fathers have forgotten.
And they will dream of her who have not known her,
And ache, and ache for that lost limb forever.

And there is a bitter acceptance in her myths of identity: Persephone pausing on the sill of her downward journey, "nerves dissolving in the gleam / of night's theatrical desire"; Hera hung from the sky, "half strangled in my hair, / I dangle, drowned in fire"; Midas cut and bruised by his ungrateful garden, who

Hugged his agues, loved his lust
But damned to hell the out-of-doors.

—certainly history and human disposition, as certified by the myth, turn out tragically. The consolation, not the hope, is in natural process, the rhythm of nights and days, of breathing, of decay and rebirth:

Wreathed in our breathing,
We will exceed ourselves again:
Put out in storms, and pitch our wave on waves . . .
Get thee to a compost heap.
Renew, the self prays to decay. Renew!
And buckles on its shell to meet the day.

The shell Miss Kizer has contrived to encounter necessity with is, in her second book, ***Knock Upon Silence***—"for an answering music," as its Chinese epigraph advises—both more exotic and more capacious than the studied and tough-minded poems of ***The Ungrateful Garden.*** She has looked East and West again for personae, masks and voices that will "renew" her need, and if her wit is less explicit in reference than when she sang:

Come candidly, consort with me,
And spill our pleasure for a day . . .

it is more inclusive, it can afford, in a declension of the same refrain, the music of experience rather than that of convention:

> I am monogamous as the North Star
> But I don't want you to know it. You'd only take advantage.
> While you are as fickle as spring sunlight.
> All right, sleep! The cat means more to you than I.
> I can rouse you, but then you swagger out.
> I glimpse you from the window, striding toward the river.

Abandoning Marlowe and Heine and the careful rhymes of what it would be perversely modest to regard as her apprenticeship, let us call it her initiation, Miss Kizer here lights on Arthur Waley and on Juvenal—the received English version of classical Chinese and that most relaxed of Western metrics, the Roman hexameter. The book is deceptive, appearing to be given over altogether to literary ventriloquism, though as soon as we get beyond the titles of its four sections—"Chinese Imitations"; "A Month in Summer, after Issa's *The Year of My Life*", which revealed to Miss Kizer "the most satisfactory method of writing *Haiku*"; "from *Pro Femina*", and "Translations of Tu Fu"—we discover that the stomach Miss Kizer is speaking from is her own, and that all the masks are necessary to keep her pangs from drowning out her perceptions. The Chinese "imitations" reveal how much more personal this poet has allowed herself to become in what Colette once called the honorable if not the lively pleasure of not speaking of love:

> By the time we reach middle life, we've all been deserted and robbed.
> But flowers and grass and animals keep me warm.
> And I remind myself to become philosophic:
> We are meant to be stripped down, to prepare us for something better.

And surely it is because of the wonderful poise-in-disaster she has learned in the twenty translations from Tu Fu (A.D. 712-770), with their resignation to exile and disgrace yet their insistence on the value of nature, "randomness, Art's impulse, true disorder" and of friendship, drinking and memory, that she has made these imitations so much her own. Like Morris Graves, whom she had already praised in her first book for his Oriental capacity to make something out of unpromising materials—

> poor crockery, immortal
> on twenty sheets of paper—

Carolyn Kizer has found a voice for her woman's condition, and her human one, which allows her to bring forth only the more for all she has borrowed:

> You, my brother, are a good and violent drinker,
> Good at reciting short-line or long-line poems.
> In time we will lose all our daughters, you and I,
> Be temperate, venerable, content to stay in one place,
> Sending our messages over the mountains and waters.

As in this message to Creeley, **"Amusing Our Daughters,"** the poet gathers up all her tones, all her tempers into a hovering posture of control, a swaying form, so that such "Chinese imitations" are indeed what Coleridge said an imitation was: the mesothesis of likeness and difference. The difference is an essential to it as the likeness, for without the difference it would be Copy or Facsimile.

The volume further contains a curious record, in the form of a prose diary, of a broken love affair, or its actual breaking, punctuated by *haiku.* The prose pieces keep pulling away from the agony, seeking release in the distractions of learning:

> One of the profound consolations of reading the works
> of Japanese men of letters is their frank acknowledgment
> of neurotic sloth. Or the overwhelming impuse, when faced
> with hurt or conflict, to say in bed under the covers!

but the demanding little syllables of the *haiku* are relentless in their return to the pain:

> Alone in my house
> I can make gross noises
> Like a caught hare or stoat
> Or a woman in labor.

Why these artifices appropriated from a culture that does not belong to her? Perhaps, Miss Kizer suggests, because the only way to deal with sorrow is to find a form in which to contain it.

. . . . .

As an equipoise to this mutilated apology for a love poem, ***Knock Against Silence*** also contains Miss Kizer's public voice: fragments from a Juvenalian apology **"Pro Femina,"** dedicated to our most famous translators from Greek and Latin, Robert Fitzgerald and Rolfe Humphries. Here the critical intelligence that in the first book focused so sharply inward is allowed its most generous locus in the Situation Abroad. The independent woman, and the woman of letters are cracked open, in these looping hexameters, like so many husks, and the satiric truth threshed:

> Our masks, always in peril of smearing or cracking,
> In need of continuous check in the mirror of silverware,
> Keep us in thrall to ourselves, concerned with our surfaces . . .
> Freed in fact, not in custom, lifted from furrow and scullery,
> Not obliged, now, to be the pot for the annual chicken,
> *Have we begun to arrive in time?* With our well-known
> Respect for life because it hurts so much to come out with it;
> Disdainful of "sovereignty", "national honor" and other abstractions;
> We can say, like the ancient Chinese to successive waves of invaders,

"Relax and let us absorb you . . ." Meanwhile,
observe our creative chaos,
Flux, efflorescence, whatever you care to call it!

I would care to call it poetry, of a fruitfully damaged, unresolved and nearly inescapable order. There is, on the jacket of this new book, a photograph of the poet, a beautiful woman looking out at us in a Chinese gown, on a Consular chair—with just that combination of the Roman Matron and the Oriental Courtesan which makes up all her authority and all her indecision—"creative chaos." It is odd to find Cornelia and the Geisha together, but Carolyn Kizer proves that such manners are no more than the means by which a poetry obtains access to reality, to the realized values of a life else no more than endured or evaded:

Now, if we struggle abnormally, we may almost .
seem normal;
If we submerge our self-pity in disciplined industry;
If we stand up and be hated, and swear not to
sleep with editors;
If we regard ourselves formally, respecting our
true limitations
Without making an unseemly show of trying to
unfreeze our assets;
Keeping our heads and our pride while remaining unmarried;
And if wedded, kill guilt in its tracks when we
stack up the dishes
And defect to the typewriter. And if mothers,
believe in the luck of our children,
Whom we forbid to devour us, whom we shall
not devour,
And the luck of our husbands and lovers, who
keep free women.

(pp. 111-17)

Richard Howard, "Carolyn Kizer," in Tri-Quarterly, *No. 7, Fall, 1966, pp. 109-17.*

William H. Pritchard (review date Spring 1972)

[*Pritchard is an American educator and critic who has written numerous books on major British and American twentieth-century authors. In the following review, he offers a balanced assessment of* Midnight Was My Cry, *noting in particular Kizer's self-deprecating tone.*]

Carolyn Kizer's poems [in ***Midnight Was My Cry***] often go on for too long and there is a sense of diffuseness about her new and selected volume. But also lots of intelligence, a relaxed sense of how much she can do and a less than total infatuation with her own powers. **"Singing Aloud"** begins with the admission that:

We all have our faults. Mine is trying to write
poems.
New scenery, someone I like, anything sets me
off!
I hear my own voice going on, like a god or an
oracle,
That cello-tone, intuition. That bell-note of wisdom!

But the self-deprecation is never mawkish; she accepts the fact that when a new poem comes along "I no longer rush out to impose it on friendly colleagues," and ends up as a poet talking to the animals:

When I go to the zoo, the primates and I, in
communion,
Hoot at each other, or signal with earthy gestures.
We must move further out of town, we musical
birds and animals
Or they'll lock us up like the apes, and control
us forever.

It is easy to like and take seriously the presence behind these lines:

The moonlight on my bed keeps me awake;
Living alone now, aware of the voices of evening,
A child weeping at nightmares, the faint love-
cries of a woman,
Everything tinged by terror or nostalgia. . . .

This collection might well have included **"Pro Femina,"** a witty and effective rallying cry.

But Carolyn Kizer may be too easy to take in; she never gets really *angry* in poems, never dips into what the excited *Sunday Times* reviewer referred to (in connection with Diane Wakoski) as "the hive of her anger." (pp. 124-25)

William H. Pritchard, in a review of "Midnight Was My Cry," in The Hudson Review, *Vol. XXV, No. 1, Spring, 1972, pp. 124-26.*

Richard Howard (review date August 1972)

[*In the review below, Howard praises the poems in* Midnight Was My Cry *for being more accessible and universal than those in Kizer's previous volumes.*]

It is a dangerous interval, the one somewhere between juvenilia and senilia, when poets decide they must represent their achievement (concilia?) at the retrospective pitch, the abyss of "selection": the danger is one of sclerosis, for the trouble with getting it all together, as we say now, is getting anything, afterwards, apart. Consider Carolyn Kizer's case. To thirty-five poems from ***The Ungrateful Garden*** (1961) and to eight (less shapely, more ambitious) from ***Knock upon Silence*** (1965), both books being out of print, she has added [in ***Midnight Was My Cry***] another sixteen from the last decade, two of these poems no more than newspaper leaders (or followers), one or two others no less than autovoyeurism, the remainder as fine as anything she has done, unresolved but inescapable, learned but not knowing, fluent yet anything but easy—say, then, she has reinforced her canon by some dozen first-rate poems, observant, solicitous, lithe: where does the new emphasis thereby fall, the refinement and recognition, now, of certain shared contours, of welcomed limits? An answer is brought home to me as much by what is left out as by what is committed to the leavings: an early villanelle **"On a Line from Julian"** has given way to—or been outdistanced by—one **"On a Line from Sophocles."** And the new line is "Time, time, my friend, makes havoc everywhere"—a poetical sententia which must be earned, as it is here, by a concrescence of experience, disastrous, wide-ranging, amical. To forego the Apostate and his futile rebellion against the odds of history for the all-seeing Greek, tragic in his presentment of events but articulating so much more life in his very acknowledgment of what happens—that is the burden Miss Kizer so gracefully shoulders here. The additional poems are not fractious, merely frank in their response to hopes and horrors alike ("for women learn to be a holy show . . . but we break out of the harem of history!"), and there is no effort merely to will The Enemy out of the way by stamping a tiny foot ("You failed, I failed . . . we are true neither to life nor nature, / but perhaps to one another as we write"). Instead, the Kizer poem "wrapt in a caul of vulnerability", weds chaos and failure, welcomes pain and farce, "signalling, / self-amazed, its willingness to endure", for as the poet writes to an attempted suicide to whom she sends, with her words, white azaleas:

> . . . we live in wonder,
> Blaze in a cycle of passion and apprehension
> Though once we lay and waited for a death.

The effect, *en gros* and better still, in fine, of this selection is to dispel the dangers of its program. She has submitted her figure to her fate, has worked out of the exoticisms which once rather specialized and so limited Carolyn Kizer—this is to say, she has given up impersonating Mae West and Shanghai Lily and your all-purpose Women's Libertine for the sake and the success of a style we may recognize anywhere—in Holland, in Ohio; in dudgeon, in delight—as consistently Carolingian, fruitfully injured:

> This bronze is mortal, gaping in defeat,
> The form that wombed it split to let it be.

(pp. 302-03)

Richard Howard, "Pursuits and Followings," in Poetry, *Vol. CXX, No. 5, August, 1972, pp. 296-303.*

Kathryn Stripling Byer (review date Spring 1973)

[*In the following review, Byer praises "the skill, depth, and variety" of the poems in* Midnight Was My Cry.]

I have often heard the comment made by men and intended as a compliment, "She doesn't write like a woman." Kizer would find that no compliment. Hers, though, is clearly a woman's consciousness, and the poetry that comes out of it is strong indeed. Her third book, ***Midnight Was My Cry,*** is a collection of recent verse as well as selections from her two previous volumes. By virtue of its skill, depth, and variety, it should establish her as one of our better poets.

I suppose what impresses me most about this book is its mastery of different types of poems, from love poems to narrative poems to poems in the Oriental manner, to name a few. I especially like the latter, perhaps because they remind me of my own earlier attachment to Oriental verse. Such poems as **"Winter Song," "The Skein"** (which reminds me of Li Ch'ing Chao's verse), **"For Jan at Bar Maria," "Amusing Our Daughters,"** and **"Summer Near the River"** show how she has adapted the Oriental tradition to suit her own voice. This is the ending of **"Summer Near the River"**:

> When you return, reeking of fish and beer,
> There is salt dew in your hair. Where have you
> been?
> Your clothes weren't that wrinkled hours ago,
> when you left.
> You couldn't have loved someone else, after lov-
> ing me!
> I sulk and sigh, dawdling by the window.
> Later, when you hold me in your arms
> It seems, for a moment, the river ceases flowing.

Throughout we hear the echoes of those centuries-old Chinese voices, but up-dated, made more distinctly erotic, more frankly female.

I also like the poems about the poet's mother. They are not sentimental; nor are they examinations of neuroticism a la Plath or Sexton. In them Kizer's mother emerges as a strong, admirable woman. **"A Long Line of Doctors"** is a good example. It is a witty, brilliant poem and I am dazzled by the craftsmanship and energy of it. It begins:

> Mother, picked for jury duty, managed to get
> through
> A life of Voltaire in three volumes. Anyway, she
> knew
> Before she half-heard a word, the dentist was
> guilty.
>
> As a seminarist whose collar is his calling
> Chokes up without it, baring his naked neck,
> The little, furtive dentist is led across the deck,
> Mounts the plank, renders a nervous cough.
> Mother frowns, turns a page, flicks a fly-speck
> With her fingernail. She will push him off!

An excerpt from "Streets of Pearl and Gold"

> Art is this marveling fury of spurned love.
> Caught in this present, impatient of histories,
> Even your own, while you mourn what vanishes.
> Who endures, rootless? But our roots are strewn
> On every pavement, smashed or drowned in
> brine.
>
> Observe the world with desperate affection;
> Snatch up your brush to catch it, fix it all
> On canvases which, stacked against a wall,
> Dozen on dozen, are crumbling unseen.
> Paint out the day and you will keep the time:
>
> Exhaust fumes, and a building's trembling dust,
> Fish entrails, wino-reek, attic waste,
> The shapes below the names on billboard signs,
> And—what the bums find early—paint the dirt
> Which we all come to: paint the old dirt sleep.
>
> So stamp your canvas with the X of loss,
> Art mutilated, stained with abuse and rage.
> But mark it also as the cross of love
> Who hold this woman-flesh, touch it alive,
> As I try to keep us, here upon the page.

Carolyn Kizer, in her The Nearness of You, *Copper Canyon Press, 1986.*

And even though the poem is rather long, it never loses its momentum.

"The Great Blue Heron," which deals with her mother's death, is to me the most moving poem in the collection. After seeing a heron on the beach, the poet remembers seeing the "spectral bird" years before and running to fetch her mother, only to return and find the heron gone. She says "In the middle of my loss, I realized she knew: / My mother knew what he was." The bird becomes the symbol of loss, specifically the loss of her mother as the poet realizes that for fifteen years the bird has stood patiently in her mind,

> Waiting upon the day
> When, like gray smoke, a vapor
> Floating into the sky,
> A handful of paper ashes,
> My mother would drift away.

This is one of her most emotional poems, but its emotion is kept under firm control. Kizer is always the good craftsman.

A few poems do not measure up to the majority. **"Singing Aloud,"** for example, promises to be another good poem on the subject of writing poetry itself but is marred by an incongruous ending. And some of the poems dealing with classical mythology seem less strong than the others. But even these are marked by her insight and learning. I can only agree with John L'Heureux on the dust jacket that "she is a first-class poet." (pp. 117-18)

Kathryn Stripling Byer, in a review of "Midnight Was My Cry: New and Selected Poems," in The Georgia Review, *Vol. XXVII, No. 1, Spring, 1973, pp. 117-18.*

Patricia Hampl (review date 25 November 1984)

[*Hampl is an American poet, short story writer, and memoirist. In the following review, she discusses* Mermaids in the Basement *and* Yin: New Poems.]

"I will speak about women of letters, for I'm in the racket. / Our biggest successes to date? Old maids to a woman." These lines from the long poem **"Pro Femina"** first appeared in Carolyn Kizer's ***Knock Upon Silence*** in 1965—the year Sylvia Plath's *Ariel* was published posthumously. "Sister," Miss Kizer writes, "forget yourself a few times and see where it gets you: Up the creek, alone with your talent."

The admonition isn't addressed to Plath, but the punishment is reminiscent of her: sexual exile, loneliness, renunciation as the price of a writing life. ***Mermaids in the Basement,*** an anthology of Miss Kizer's poems for women, collected from previous books and including new poems, would benefit as a retrospective of her career, I think, if the poems were assigned dates, not simply gathered into bundles ("Mothers and Daughters," "Female Friends" and the like.) She wrote early about these feminist issues. And she didn't write safely in code; she spat it out.

For all its acuity and wit, the poem **"Pro Femina"** doesn't carry the authority of a lyrical, personal poem. Other, briefer poems are more emotionally, if less rhetorically, eloquent, including **"Thrall"** and **"Where I've Been All My Life"** (which would have made a wonderful title for the collection).

The craft for which Miss Kizer is known serves her well in **"Thrall"**; a remarkable compression allows her to review the entire disappointing history of her relationship with her father. The final lines are remorseless and steady:

> You feed him his medicine.
> You tell him you love him.
>
> You wait for his eyes to close at last
> So you may write this poem.

There are other attractive poems about family—insistent mother, silent father—and about women friends (including a respectful poem to her daughter; she says the two have "learned to moderate our hates").

She is drawn—as her versions of Chinese poems, also collected here, show—to refined patterns. But the long sequence "A Month in Summer" uses the Japanese haibun form, combining prose and poetry. This piece, about a doomed love affair, is less satisfying. Miss Kizer puts her finger on the trouble in a prose-like section that links the haiku in this Japanese form:

> Why the artifice of this haibun, which I have appropriated
> from a culture which doesn't belong to me? Perhaps to
> lose me. Perhaps because the only way to deal with
> sorrow is to find a form in which to contain it.

Perhaps. But form is not a container; it is created from a poem's materials, not for them.

Much of the pilgrimage of these poems moves from grudge to acceptance, from reiteration of griefs to the good grace of letting go. There is a great effort toward humor in these poems. But the tone is uneven; the humor, as well as the outrage, seems arch at times.

. . . . .

Yin is a collection of new poems, some of them also found in ***Mermaids in the Basement.*** But the most striking offering, a real find, is the prose memoir, **"A Muse."** This piece, about Miss Kizer's extraordinary mother, is not only a fascinating portrait, but a model of detachment and self-revelation.

Her mother, who had led a vivid intellectual life until her late marriage, settled herself into motherhood with her only child in her mid-40's as into a new, absorbing career. When her small daughter laboriously formed the letters A, R, T with a crayon, she decided this ("Her first word!") meant she was "fated to become an artist."

Miss Kizer "was entirely aware at the time that the conjunction of the letters . . . was wholly accidental." But like Sartre's account of how his family turned him into a miracle child in "The Words," the great family creation had begun.

It is a testimony to Miss Kizer's generosity of spirit that

her account of this relationship is not bitter, but astonished. The humor here is certain of its territory, and the tone modulates beautifully, arriving at a tenderness and acquiescence that are moving and memorable. If only it were longer; this is a story to read and read.

Patricia Hampl, "Women Who Say What They Mean," in The New York Times Book Review, *November 25, 1984, p. 36.*

Mark Jarman (review date Summer 1985)

[*Jarman is a Canadian short story writer, poet, educator, and critic. In the review below, he offers a mixed assessment of* Mermaids in the Basement.]

The major service Cooper Canyon Press has done us with Carolyn Kizer's new collection [***Mermaids in the Basement***], is to reprint many fine poems that were included in now out-of-print editions. So, in one book, we have her best work: her poems from the Chinese in a section entitled "Chinese Love"; "A Month in Summer," her experiment with prose and haiku to narrate a deteriorating love affair; **"Pro Femina"** now with a fourth part spoken in the voice of Robert Louis Stevenson's wife Fanny; and two other poems it would have been sad to lose, **"The Great Blue Heron"** and what I think of as her very best poem, **"For Jan, in Bar Maria."**

The most interesting addition is "Part Four: Fanny" of **"Pro Femina."** Fanny writes in her diary of the life she and R. L. S. lived in Samoa before his death. She gardens and plants, gardens and plants, obsessed with what can be grown there, what the domestic earth of the South Pacific can yield; she is in "a fever of planting" that equals and exceeds her husband's fever of dying, and this fever lasts through thirty-three seven-line stanzas. The poem is the signal contribution to a book subtitled "Poems for Women," for it reveals the feminine imagination that Samuel Butler intuited in the *Odyssey.* It pits her experience of Samoa against her husband's imagination of it (although on the whole Stevenson is rather a pale character, like Lowell's father in *Life Studies*).

In Kizer's best work a colloquial voice works against a high rhetorical pitch. This is perfectly accomplished in **"For Jan, in Bar Maria"** and in the versions from the Chinese, and allows the former to have a robustness and fellow-feeling and the latter to have a kind of sexual excitement. But when Kizer does work overtime in other poems, she overextends metaphors and overemphasizes prosody, becoming heavy-handed and melodramatic. **"The Intruder"** about how her mother, a lover of wild animals, once rescued a bat from the pet cat, only to discover that it was swarming with lice, ends,

> She swept to the kitchen. Turning on the tap,
> She washed and washed the pity from her hands.

Metaphorically, that last line follows from the poem, but the reification of pity and the meter itself are too much.

There is little of Elder Olson's judicious restraint in Kizer's formal poems, when she chooses to write them. For her, as for her fellow Northwesterner Theodore Roethke, traditional prosody is one style. And she succeeds at it best when her voice is shrewdly satirical, as in **"Pro Femina"** and in **"Fanny,"** too, a new masterpiece. (pp. 329-30)

Mark Jarman, "Generations and Contemporaries," in The Hudson Review, *Vol. XXXVIII, No. 2, Summer, 1985, pp. 327-42.*

Anthony Libby (review date 22 March 1987)

[*Libby is an American educator and critic. In the following review, he discusses Kizer's depiction of men in* The Nearness of You.]

Women writing about men: can it be as hazardous, can they be as vulnerable to the judgments of history as men writing about women have proved to be? Carolyn Kizer's new book of poems about men [***The Nearness of You***], a companion piece to her collection of poems about women, ***Mermaids in the Basement,*** shows evidence that writing about the other sex involves different struggles than writing about one's own. Despite many local triumphs, the new collection is in many ways less striking, technically and psychologically more self-conscious, for reasons it begins to announce in its first poem. **"Afternoon Happiness"** addresses the poetic problems of romantic peace and monogamous joy. It consists of verse so light as to be nearly trivial. As Ms. Kizer writes, "So how does the poem play / Without the paraphernalia of betrayal and loss?" In the 20th century, serious poetry that celebrates happy heterosexual love is very hard to achieve.

Carolyn Kizer is extremely aware of this, as she is consciously aware of the formal possibilities of poetry; her art is highly wrought, as she plays with the forms of poems and her memories of men. In both cases the play can become a distraction, but often the strategies of the poet make the right magic. She handles the problem of depicting romantic love by describing it indirectly, embedding it in the world, the cruel world in **"Season of Lovers and Assassins"** and the elegantly transformed physical world in **"Streets of Pearl and Gold."**

In some poems the conceits and the general tone of affectionate amusement with men can get in the way of engagement. But this can hardly be said of the emotional center of this collection, the deeply engaging poetry and prose meditation on the poet's father. The mixed form serves her well, as it did in the prose and haiku account of love and loss, "A Month in Summer," in the earlier collection. She introduces the father as a remote figure in **"Thrall':**

> The room is sparsely furnished:
> A chair, a table and a father . . .
> You tiptoe past as he eats his apple
> And reads. He looks up, angry.
> He has heard your asthmatic breathing.

This rather chilling figure is gradually humanized in the beautifully affectionate prose piece, primarily a letter to a friend, entitled **"My Good Father."** Here the vision of the "authoritarian and severe" paterfamilias experienced by "that stranger, his child" resolves into the grown woman's softened memory of an extraordinarily good and loving man. For his insensitivity to her as child, she writes, "I almost forgave him." "Almost" is the operative word in this portrait of the archetypal patriarch as a nice guy. The energy of the piece is generated partly by Ms. Kizer's stress on the tension between opposed characteristics in her father. But it comes perhaps even more from the duality in her own response: sentimental forgiveness works against the desire to tell it straight, not to sentimentalize. In the end the dance of opposites is resolved in love. The right to such lavish admiration is earned by the stylistic and emotional grace of the daughter as much as by the late forgiven father.

Anthony Libby, "Fathers and Daughters and Mothers and Poets," in The New York Times Book Review, *March 22, 1987, p. 23.*

Diane Wakoski (review date September 1987)

[*Wakoski is an American poet who has published numerous verse collections, including* The Lady Who Drove Me to the Airport *(1982) and* Making a Sacher Torte *(1982). In the following review of* The Nearness of You, *she dismisses the first half of the work for lacking "power," but praises the latter sections for their generous and spirited tone.*]

Carolyn Kizer's collection, ***The Nearness of You,*** reveals yet another mother-daughter-woman speaking to the world in yet another voice. How much happier Kizer would have been in medieval Provence, writing fine tightly-woven poems about her life, full of secrets, secret meanings, having no other purpose than to entertain the rich, the courtiers, the people of power. The first half of this book assaults you with her desire to write a different kind of poetry than the Whitman tradition has made possible. She, like so many of us today, longs for order, deception rather than violence, language that is polite and beautiful, that covers up rather than reveals. Her belated popularity comes in this decade when Americans are longing for the order that more formal times and customs would provide.

On the other hand, had I been the editor of ***The Nearness of You,*** I would have cut the entire first half of the book out and left it in manuscript, since compared to sections III and IV its poems seem like exercises in verse. They are well written but with no power and practically none of the flamboyant beauty and generosity Kizer has become famous for.

Sections III, "Father," and IV, "Friends," are quite another matter. They remind the reader that sometimes Pulitzer prizes go to more than good writing. They also go to poets who give something of themselves to the poetry world, who are its ambassadors of goodwill and its decent arbiters of taste. The poems in these two sections of the book remind me of the best of Robert Lowell. **"My Good Father,"** like its predecessor **"91 Revere St.,"** uses prose to dramatic and poignant effect. Kizer is the judge's daughter, as Lowell was Commander Lowell's son, and this relationship informs everything she does as well, from her love of the tight old-fashioned conventions of European poetry to her desire to be, always, sophisticatedly elegant and acceptable to the world of important fathers. And **"Thrall,"** its companion piece written in sparse (irregular—what a relief!) stanzas is a personal and beautiful variation on "Father's Bedroom," as if Lowell were there and present in her thoughts at writing. **"Reading Your Poems In Your House While You Are Away (for Richard Shelton)"** could easily have been written for many other poets.

> Remember this when you come home:
> One day, as you pause in composing,
> a phrase of mine will leap into your stanza.
> Just as, in writing this,
> I borrow the words that belong to you
> and give them back, like moonlight.

There are delicate, lovely lines for Roethke her teacher and mentor, and for the painter Morris Graves, fellow native of the Pacific Northwest. The triumph is the concluding poem in the book, **"Final Meeting,"** obviously written to James Wright, a poet who also studied with Roethke. Not only does this elegy do what all great elegies do, invoke the beauty of the person being mourned, the specialness of that person's life, this poem also gives the truest portrait of Carolyn Kizer that could be painted: her lifetime desire to be that elegant, scented, gracious and totally desirable woman her father raised her to be (as she describes going to the hospital for a last visit with Wright).

> Old friend, I dressed in my very best,
> Wore the furs I never wear,
> Hair done at Bloomingdales,
> Even a manicure; splashed on the good perfume
> . . .
> I swept in with an air
> Wrapped you in fur, censed you with my perfume.
> Jaunty and thin, with the fine eyes and pursy lips
> of one of Holbein's Unknown Gentlemen,
> You could not speak

These poems, in "Friends," resonate with Kizer's sexuality (**"Horseback"**), her love of power and the ability to use it to help others (**"To An Unknown Poet**), her pleasure in the community of artists and intellectuals which becomes the real family for her (**"Amusing Our Daughters"**). The beauty of these poems has more to do with the spirit which is demonstrated in them than with the language. Wright is probably the only student of Roethke's who had the lyric gift to carry on his voice and tradition, though all of his students from Hugo to Kizer continue to carry the burden of trying for that voice.

What this book convinces me of, finally, is that Carolyn Kizer is a poet of occasion, of person and personality. When she becomes historical or formal, when she attempts either love-lyrics or story poems, she is mediocre at best. Intelligent, knowing how to write, she can make a long narrative out of historical materials (as she did in ***Mermaids in the Basement***), but it will never convince this reader that anything in it is memorable. Nor can one believe the stance of feminism from a woman so into her furs and long gold lamé gloves. But as the ambassador of goodwill in the poetry world, as the powerful and elegant daughter of her father the judge, as the woman longing for a family of artists and intellectuals who will replace the one she lost in growing up and leaving her father—yes,

yes, yes. Believable, strong, someone who deserves to be remembered.

Diane Wakoski, "Poets of Our Time," in The Women's Review of Books, *Vol. IV, No. 12, September, 1987, p. 7.*

Alice Fulton (review date January 1988)

[*Fulton is an American poet whose works include* Dance Script with Electric Ballerina *(1983). In the excerpt below, she provides a brief overview of Kizer's career.*]

Although [Kizer's] robust appreciation of the world is akin to [Walt] Whitman's, the wit, urbanity, and classical balance of her best poems recall Pope. An irreverent, unromantic stance distinguishes her from many of her peers. Perhaps Hecht and Wilbur are most similar in style. ***Mermaids in the Basement*** collects work from three out-of-print books, along with a few new poems and translations. It's a joy to have the work of a major poet readily available; however, the number of duplications in Kizer's recent volumes make me wish for a single *Collected Poems.* Although the book is subtitled "Poems for Women," it's more important that men read these poems. Women are well acquainted with both women's and men's writing: as Annette Kolodny notes, "for survival's sake, oppressed or subdominant groups always study the nuances of meaning and gesture in those who control them." But the reverse is not true.

Kizer's early poems tend to be formal and well-crafted. They seldom make a false move. The later work is less rigorously structured; the tone is more varied, the form often analogous. Kizer was analyzing the image of women well before the second wave of feminism took hold. ***Mermaids*** begins by exploring relationships between mothers, daughters, and women friends. In one delightful narrative, the poet's mother is a juror during the trial of a dentist accused of drilling through his patient's tongue while flirting with a nurse. Kizer's mother, "with eleven good men in her pocket," reads Voltaire during the trial, knowing "before she half-heard a word, the dentist was guilty." The rift between Kizer's world view and that of her strong-willed mother adds a fine complexity. Though men poets often bespeak a rugged fly-rod camaraderie, less has been said about the bonding rites of women. It's refreshing to see women swim, sun, run, drink, dance, joke, and exchange confidences with one another as they do in these poems.

The book's centerpiece, **"Pro Femina,"** recalls Pope's "Essay on Man" in its summary of a major issue, though Kizer's topic is "the fate of women." The first three sections of **"Pro Femina"** appeared in 1965, not long after [Adrienne] Rich's groundbreaking "Snapshots of a Daughter-in-Law" (1963). Both poems regard women with a critical eye, untempered by the revisionary feminism of the seventies. Kizer notes the tactics of women scabs "Impugning our sex to stay in good with the men"; of "sleek saboteuses" who "try to be ugly by aping the ways of men / And succeed"; of "Quarterly priestesses / Who flog men for fun, and kick women to maim competition"; of "cabbageheads" who, "vague-eyed and acquiescent, worshipped God as a man"; and of those good girls who "took notes in rolling syllabics, in careful journals, / Aiming to please a posterity that despises them." The latter assessment echoes Rich's "Snapshots": "mere talent was enough for us— / glitter in fragments and rough drafts." In Kizer, however, "us" becomes "they," turning women into Others. The poem does praise women as peacemakers "Disdainful of 'sovereignty,' 'national honor.' " And it angrily recounts the price independent women have paid under patriarchy, the damned-if-you-do-or-don't quality of the choices. Of course, women accomplished more great work than either Kizer or Rich admit in these early poems. And the fourth section of **"Pro Femina,"** added in 1984, presents a female hero as corrective. "Fanny" acquaints us with the pluck, resourcefulness, adventurousness, and physical strength of the indomitable Fanny Osbourne Stevenson (wife of Robert Louis) during 1890, when she lived in Samoa. Kizer's diaristic narrative reveals details gradually. Rather than defining Fanny at the onset as wife to the famous man, the identity of "RLS" dawns slowly. "I have been planting . . . ," Stevenson writes, in a colossal understatement. Her life was a farmer's nightmare: the strawberry plants rot; horses trample the corn; the lettuce gets too much sun; rats eat the second crop of corn. After reading of her relentless physical labor, one is amazed to learn Stevenson was fifty years old and ill at the time. "I cured my five ulcers with calomel," she says. Although Louis writes every morning, Fanny has little time for her hidden journal, which someone continually finds and censors. To further complicate matters, she lives among headhunters. A tale that could easily have sunk into melodrama or martyrdom is saved by a matter-of-fact tone. "Mr. Haggard begged us to stay in town / Because he bitterly wanted women to protect," she notes. I suspect that Fanny Stevenson's actual diary is *not* a delight to read. But I am glad her fascinating life has been retrieved from a fragmentary obscurity through Kizer's art.

Kizer's work addresses one of the "main things" of twentieth-century literature: "Merely the private lives of one-half of humanity." In its size, integrity, and finesse, her canon is comparable to Elizabeth Bishop's. For these reasons, as well as for her blithe spirit and rigorous mind, Kizer deserves our esteem and readership.

—Alice Fulton

The book also contains translations of Chinese love poems, and poems based on Greek myths. **"Hera, Hung from the Sky"** shows a woman punished for ambition. Venus is **"The Dying Goddess"** since no one makes sacrifices to her anymore and "Odd cults crop up, involving midgets." In an imaginative re-telling, Semele describes her transformation into "altar, oracle, offal, canoe and oars" after seeing Zeus in his immolating blaze of glory. Section Six, a prose journal interspersed with haiku, focuses on love and self-destructiveness. The entries are sometimes insightful: "Perhaps at the extremes of happiness or unhappiness, one should take care that only inferior works of art will be contaminated by nostalgia." This cautionary tale of pain and self-exposure casts woman in the familiar role of sufferer. Reading it, I wondered why it is so hard to think of long poems by contemporary men poets on the pain, rather than the blame, of divorce.

The final section, "Where I've Been All My Life," is largely autobiographical. The former poem contains the line "Love, become feminized, tickles like a feather," "feminized" being synonymous with "weakened" or "trivialized." Such disparagement makes me feel that Kizer regards women with some ambivalence. I also was ready to dislike a poem called **"Bitch."** There's certainly no analogous term for a spiteful man. However, rather than depict the bitch as a destructive force, Kizer shows her to be a result of causes. In this poem, bitchiness is the honest anger people feel for those who misuse them. Thus, the civil woman carrying on small talk while the bitch rages within, is something of a hypocrite. Another fine poem shows a "large lady" climbing a gun emplacement in hope of damaging the weapon. After failing in her attempt, she leaves an eggshell from her lunch on the gun. Kizer captures the endearing (perhaps lifesaving) goofiness of this symbolic gesture, which embodies pacifism more effectively than the bravado of heroism. **"A Muse of Water,"** the concluding poem, builds a witty conceit in which female creativity is made to serve as reflecting pool, cofferdam, fountain, and reservoir. "And you blame streams for thinning out, / Plundered by man's insatiate want?" Kizer asks. No wonder there are "Dry wells, dead seas, and lingering drouth," or that women's creativity sank "To silent conduits underground. . . . " Once found, however, female imagination "Is water deep enough to drown." This is the ambiguous, final warning of ***Mermaids in the Basement.***

Although Kizer's new book, ***The Nearness of You,*** explores such themes as "Manhood" and "Father," it is not subtitled "Poems for Men." And the section of poems about men friends is called simply "Friends," unlike the parallel segment of ***Mermaids*** designated "Female Friends." Although the slight difference in subtitles might have been an oversight, the distinction is like the one commonly made between "women poets," who are of course female, and "poets" who are of course male. (How often does one encounter the term "man poet"?) Thus, women are singled out for difference, and men assumed as the norm.

This book, like ***Mermaids,*** is a compilation of old and recent poems. And again, I marvel at Kizer's technical skill and inventiveness. Her fondness for wordplay, puns, and extended conceits recalls seventeenth-century aesthetics: "We will be well, and well away / until our pulse and pallor tell / That we are ill, of being well." While the metaphysical strategies often work, they occasionally feel overdetermined, and the language is conventionally poetic at times: lovemaking becomes "hushed rapture" and drowning. On the other hand, a witty prologue poem describing the difficulties of writing about happy love succeeds in doing just that. And **"By the Riverside"** makes good use of puns to imply connections between a child's idea of Christ and of Indians. This poem of recollection bears a fine epigraph from a telephone directory: "Do not call from memory—all numbers have changed." Although the adult recalling a memory is not put off by an operator "Saying, 'Sor-ree, the lion is busy,' " the child would have trembled, "seeing a real lion / Trammeled in endless, golden coils of wire, / Pawing a switchboard in some mysterious / Central office, where animals ran the world. . . . " **"Streets of Pearl and Gold"** eloquently laments the demolition of America's historical buildings and suggests art as a hedge against the wrecking ball. The mutable imagery finds subtle correspondences between the X that stands for kisses, the X of destruction on condemned buildings, the hairs crossing in a gun sight, and the figurative crosses artists are to America.

Kizer is as critical of men as she was of women. She casts a canny eye at the sad lechery of a visiting poet, and a "Promising Author" is something of a male bitch. "I watched you curl your lip / As you ran down every writer in the place," she says, but by the last stanza she realizes that this "great white shark" is "Vulnerable, whiskery, afraid. . . . " Kizer's extraordinary insouciance and confidence can make one forget her compassion. She is able to capture the excessive, sentimental foolery of a happy drunk seeing the world in a mug of beer (**"Tying One on in Vienna"**), or to mourn "gentle heroes" of good conscience (**"The Death of a Public Servant"**). The latter poem addresses an ambassador who killed himself after being accused of Communism in the fifties. Here she describes the breakdown of men who wounded in name are wounded in mind:

> Or they, found wandering naked in the woods—
> Numbed from the buffets of an autumn storm,
> Soaked blissfully in its impersonal furies—
> Are wrapped and rescued after a long dark night,
> Are bustled into hospitals and baths
> While the press explains away their aberrations:
> "Needed a rest . . . and took no holidays. . . . "
> But even so, they have managed to catch their death.

"Thrall" portrays the relationship between an emotionally remote father and an outwardly obedient, inwardly rebellious daughter. The most moving exploration of paternity is occasioned by a letter from a man writing a study club paper on Kizer's father. Her reply forms an affectionate, insightful portrait, and its prose is a graceful change from the density of poetry. The poems to male friends are sometimes interesting only as literary gossip. However, two with strong moral implications are quite fine. **"The Good Author"** contrasts Malamud's advice to be "pure in spirit" with the vain posturing of a predatory male writer. **"To an Unknown Poet"** shows a scruffy, uninvited bard arriving at Kizer's door with wife and kids. Annoyed at first, she then remembers Rimbaud and the tenuous relation fame bears to genius or justice. In poems like these, Kizer is loving, smart, and as tough on herself as she is on others. Her work addresses one of the "main things" of twentieth-century literature: "Merely the private lives of one-half of humanity." In its size, integrity, and finesse, her canon is comparable to Bishop's. For these reasons, as well as for her blithe spirit and rigorous mind, Kizer deserves our esteem and readership. (pp. 372-77)

Alice Fulton, "Main Things," in Poetry, *Vol. CLI, No. 4, January, 1988, pp. 372-77.*

Dolph Corradino (review date February 1988)

[*In the review below, Corradino praises* The Nearness of You.]

Well, why can't a poet stay on the charts with a reissue of greatest hits? And, hey, just who says you can't remain a close personal friend of the Muse, and still keep an eye on your basic PR, networking and distribution channels?

These impertinent questions spring to mind from the acknowledgement page of Carolyn Kizer's new book, [***The Nearness of You***] where 9 of 38 poems have been booked before, including 4 from her Pulitzer winner ***Yin*** (1984). The title for her new collection is from a Hoagy Carmichael song, but although she is not drifting into any Hollywood or pop chart venues neither is she visiting any new neighborhoods. The new poems continue Kizer's cool and knowing observations on personal experience which often serve as the prologue for wider themes. She remains a clinician of the emotions and the little fates of daily life, and of a feminist perspective perhaps more muted in this collection, which sees the trials of the sexes in the long reach of history.

The book is arranged in four sections: Manhood, Passions, Father and Friends. Section three, one of the most riveting parts of the book, includes a prose sketch of Kizer's father, a formidable gentleman, stern and wise. These prose pieces give the reader marvelous insights into Ms. Kizer's family and her formative years. Should one feel uncomfortable with such biographical disclosures? Or chagrin that they seem to overshadow the poems? Perhaps, but for those who like their poetry in a warp and woof of known history and experience, Kizer's familial histories are illuminating.

Dolph Corradino, in a review of "The Nearness of You," in Western American Literature, *Vol. XXII, No. 4, February, 1988, p. 371.*

FURTHER READING

Stitt, Peter. "The Typical Poem." *The Kenyon Review,* n.s. VIII, No. 4 (Fall 1986): 128-33.

Discusses the structure of Kizer's poetry, offering praise for her Pulitzer Prize-winning collection *Yin.*

Additional coverage of Kizer's life and works is contained in the following sources published by Gale Research: *Contemporary Authors,* Vols. 65-68; *Contemporary Authors Autobiography Series,* Vol. 5; *Contemporary Authors New Revision Series,* Vol. 24; *Contemporary Literary Criticism,* Vols. 15, 39; and *Dictionary of Literary Biography,* Vol. 5.

Richard Llewellyn

1906-1983

(Born Richard Dafydd Vyvyan Llewellyn Lloyd) Welsh novelist, playwright, screenwriter, and journalist.

The following entry provides an overview of Llewellyn's career. For further information on Llewellyn and his works, see *CLC,* Volume 7.

INTRODUCTION

A prolific author, Llewellyn is best known for *How Green Was My Valley,* his novel about the social and political tribulations of a Welsh mining family. While dealing with diverse themes and settings, each of his works share a concern with the conflict between individual aspirations and the demands of society. Although Llewellyn's strict adherence to a realistic evocation of dialect and environment is often perceived as detracting from his novels' concision, his storytelling abilities have garnered his novels worldwide popularity.

Llewellyn was born in Wales to a hotelier and his wife. His family moved to London in 1912. He attended eight different schools in Wales and England and developed a strong interest in visual art before travelling to Italy in 1922 to work in a series of hotels. Llewellyn joined the British army in 1924 and was posted in India and Hong Kong. Returning to England in 1930 he experienced a short period of unemployment and transiency before becoming first a reporter for *Cinema Express* and later an assistant director and screenwriter. He also worked as a coal miner in South Wales in order to gather experience for his debut novel *How Green Was My Valley.* Published in 1939 to tremendous popular acclaim, the book inspired a movie version that won an Oscar from the U.S. Academy of Motion Picture Arts and Sciences in 1941. Llewellyn rejoined the army in 1940 and reported on the Nuremburg trials following the fall of Nazi Germany in World War II. In the 1960s and 1970s he lived in Africa, South America, Europe and Israel, all of which became settings for his novels. Llewellyn died in 1983.

Llewellyn is noted for his examination of the individual in society, and he often employs regional dialect and historical themes to create a realistic portrait of his characters' milieu. *How Green Was My Valley* examines the effects of industrialization and unionization on the inhabitants of a Welsh mining town. Set in the late nineteenth century, the work relates the childhood memories of Huw Morgan, the youngest of nine children. Reviewers commended Llewellyn for his accurate portrayal of life in Wales, the country's dependence on the mining industry, and the political and social consequences of unionization on Welsh society. While some critics considered Llewellyn's use of Welsh dialect to create a lyrical prose style confusing and melodramatic, others cited the characterizations of Huw and his family as evidence that Llewellyn had succeeded in depicting individuals whose hopes are tempered by the limitations of a changing society.

Although Llewellyn has authored a diverse body of work that includes plays and a quartet of spy novels, *How Green Was My Valley* remains his most successful and popular work. Critics often fault the unclear focus and meandering plot of most of his novels, especially his later works. Despite these difficulties, commentators note that Llewellyn was particularly effective in portraying individuals who seek a balance between self-interest and community values. In summarizing the significance of Llewellyn's fiction, critic Mick Felton has concluded that "most of his works end with an affirmation of the individual, although that affirmation is compromised by duties to society. . . . Llewellyn contends that a responsible, unselfish attitude to others, whether to a single person or to a country, produces a better and mutually beneficial society and adds to the ability of the individual to achieve the huge potential which Llewellyn sees in every human being."

PRINCIPAL WORKS

Poison Pen (drama) 1938
How Green Was My Valley (novel) 1939
None but the Lonely Heart (novel) 1943
Noose (drama) 1946
A Few Flowers for Shiner (novel) 1950
A Flame for Doubting Thomas (novel) 1953
The Witch of Merddyn (novel) 1954
The Flame of Hercules (novel) 1955
Mr. Hamish Gleave (novel) 1956
Chez Pavan (novel) 1958
Up, into the Singing Mountain (novel) 1960
A Man in a Mirror (novel) 1961
Down Where the Moon is Small (novel) 1966
White Horse to Banbury Cross (novel) 1970
The Night is a Child (novel) 1972
Bride of Israel, My Love (novel) 1973
A Hill of Many Dreams (novel) 1974
Green, Green My Valley Now (novel) 1975
Tell Me Now, And Again (novel) 1977
A Night of Bright Stars (novel) 1979
I Stand on a Quiet Shore (novel) 1982

CRITICISM

The Times Literary Supplement (review date 7 October 1939)

[*In this favorable appraisal of* How Green Was My Valley, *the reviewer stresses the visceral appeal of Llewellyn's writing.*]

How Green Was My Valley is a first novel and a very remarkable one—vivid, eloquent, poetical, glowing with an inner flame of emotion. One hesitates to say how good it is, not only because in freshness and truth of substance this is the type of first novel that everybody is reputed to be able to write, but also because such great gifts as Mr. Llewellyn displays have their consummation in a certain austerity of sense and feeling which he does not as yet possess. Nevertheless, it is some time since a first novel has made so deep an impression. Mr. Llewellyn gives us a rich and full story of a mining family in a South Wales valley from the late seventies or early eighties to the beginnings of the present century, a family chronicle set down in our own day by old Huw Morgan, young Huw when the valley was green, who has lived to see it grow black and to be driven away by the desolation it bred.

In the self-consciousness that has been nourished upon such transformations of scene the modern novelist's eye turns towards a sophisticated type of experience. The great Victorian novelists are eminent and dead; we have apparently no wish to see their like again. To write from the heart, to measure experience in love and sorrow, to bear witness to the nobility or the idealism of men—this is not the sort of thing a serious novelist tries to do nowadays. It is what Mr. Llewellyn does, however. His story makes a direct and powerfully sustained appeal to our emotions, and is in fact deeply and continuously moving. He is not a sentimental writer, as that expression is now understood. An older and more disciplined generation of readers was shaken by "John Halifax, Gentleman," which similarly discovered the enduring stuff of experience within the cycle of birth and love and death. The emotional facility of that book, as it happens, goes some way towards explaining our rejection of Victorian models. Mr. Llewellyn may pluck the heart-strings too insistently, but there is never a note of falsity.

Two other qualities of the novel assist in holding a reader. One is the breath of Welsh incantation in Mr. Llewellyn's flow of language, the touch of half-bardic, half-Biblical utterance. There are a few momentary lapses into the sonorous pomp or void that sometimes goes by the name of prose poetry, but otherwise the slightly exotic flavour of Mr. Llewellyn's diction seems to sharpen his powers of eloquence. Then there is the picturesque force of his lament for the lost valleys of the land of his fathers. There was a time when the slag-heaps did not spread from the mountain-side across the whole length of the valley, when the rivers ran swift and clear, when the pits were prosperous and colliers were paid in sovereigns and their wives kept open house and there was a baron of beef on the table and brandy broth fit for a king. Mr. Llewellyn's descriptions of succulent dishes, by the way, may be almost too potent for a moderately hungry person.

In this Welsh valley Gwilym Morgan and his wife Beth brought up a large family in traditional ways of conduct and belief. Not a character in the book but is lifelike and individual, though every one of these Morgans has something of Dada's conscience and his uncompromising humanity. There are episodes of high dramatic power. The boy Huw's fortitude in danger, after his mother, when she is bearing her last child, comes down from the strike meeting on the mountain and falls unconscious in the snow; the terrible justice meted out to a child-murderer when Welsh law knew neither police nor magistrate; the blinding of Dai Bando in a ghoulish bare-fist fight; Dada's death in attempting to save the pits from being flooded—these are superbly done. And the story of Huw's constancy of love for Bronwen, his brother's wife, and the study of the Reverend Mr. Gruffydd in Christian faith and worldly defeat are both extraordinarily impressive.

One cannot do justice to the book in brief space. Yet although it may seem an obstinate indulgence to persist in criticism, a final comment in necessary. Like other storytellers as richly endowed, Mr. Llewellyn has most to fear from his greatest gifts. The glamour of the heroic is too much with him; his danger is a lushness of common earth such as Mary Webb gave to the border country. For the rest the root of the novelist's matter is in him.

"Light from Wales," in The Times Literary

Supplement, *No. 1966, October 7, 1939, p. 575.*

B. E. Bettinger (review date 9 February 1940)

[*In the following review, Bettinger examines the religious and epic qualities of* How Green Was My Valley.]

[***How Green Was My Valley***] is the story of life in a Welsh mining community before Wales had become a "depressed area." With it Wales joins the procession of countries whose writers are looking backward for a way of life based on folk integrity and dignity. To find this life among his own people, Mr. Llewellyn has had to ignore several eras showing evidence of decay—the Edwardian, the pre- and post-war. The dole, he shows, did not spring from only yesterday. The origin of the rot which is destroying Welsh labor, taking the lives of its men, violating the earth and driving its most virile youth to faraway countries with strange tongues and occupations, is shown to lie in the growth of empire, which exploits the man-power and resources of weaker peoples from a distance.

The beginning of the book is the end; Huw Morgan, the community's fictional biographer, is about to leave the valley and its life. It has been a good life and it has built good men, men of character. It is as a man of character and sensibility that he faces an unknown destination—with a natural nostalgia for the good past, but the sober courage that accepts life. We see the community through Huw's eyes, first the eyes of a small child, then a young man. Here are people, apparently fresh from the hand of God, presented by their Creator with bodies made in His own image and likeness, and the gifts of nature to sustain them. They are noble gifts and they must be nobly used, with gratitude to their giver. The flesh of animals and the produce of the fields must be turned into worthy food, cloth must do justice to the sheep who provide the wool, good thought and honest labor must go into the making of homes and utensils of wood and stone. Sex is not a pastime; it is a holy gift through which man shares with God the power and joy of creation—and its responsibility. They are an independent people, who recognize no superiors but God and conscience—although they seem at times to confuse the two. Violation of their code brings terrible vengeance, meted out with stern justice, but *justice.* It is not an idyll that is revealed: tragedy—cruel and bitter tragedy—alternates with joy; hard work is their lot, but both are the fate of man and part of a whole life.

Although it is a sober and responsible people Mr. Llewellyn deals with, this is not a dour book. It is revelation of the poetry of common things and common people, written in their own idiom. Every object, every event, has its deeper meaning. About food: "Wait until it has been in the hot oven for five minutes with a cover, so that the vegetables can mix in warm comfort together and become friendly, and the mint can go about his work, and for the cress to show his cunning. . . . "

The grandiloquence of Owen's courting paean may strain credulity until one considers that speech for great moments was drawn from the only reading the villagers had—great literature, and even common life held no cheapness to corrupt language by expressing it.

> "I have known you five thousand years," said Owen. "In jewels and gold."
>
> "In jewels and gold?" said Marged. "Since when, now?"
>
> "By the brook of Hebron," said Owen. "Oh, Marged."

Comparison with another minor folk classic, *Twenty Years A-Growing,* written a few years ago by a native of the Blasket Islands, is inevitable. Both books project the freshness of people removed from the world's complexities, and of speech grown from the simple needs of their lives. Both present a deeply religious people. But the temper of the two is basically different. The Irish book has a lighter, lyric tone that is lacking in the Welsh, for all its happy satisfactions. The religious concepts are different. In the Welsh community one feared God; in the Blasket Isles He was of the intimate nature of loved things, like the birds and the sun. The God of the Green Valley was God the Father, stern though generous; the mortal father who approached him in authority—and a grand man he was—was the same, tempered by knowledge of human frailty in himself among others. The God of the Islands had a merciful Son and a protecting Mother who had been human like the natives themselves and whose names were an everyday greeting. Of the two books, ***How Green Was My Valley*** has the broader scope. It is epic, rather than lyric. More factors enter into the story—moral, industrial, social. Living their own lives, according to their own code, the times were impinging on them. The question of Marxism rises in the labor struggle, divides the young who believe in the new radicalism from the old who believe this creed involves unChristian hatred and debases man. To the literary question asked, through word and experiment, by artists of today: Can a literature of drama and general interest be developed in the proletarian field? it answers by example. Yes—if the factors which make drama—spiritual force, conviction and grandeur—characterize the actors and its events. Without these factors, the result is a mess. (pp. 349-50)

B.E. Bettinger, "A Welsh Valley," in The Commonweal, *Vol. XXXI, No. 16, February 9, 1940, pp. 349-50.*

Although it is a sober and responsible people Mr. Llewellyn deals with, *How Green Was My Valley* is not a dour book. It is revelation of the poetry of common things and common people, written in their own idiom. Every object, every event, has its deeper meaning.

—B.E. Bettinger

Clifton Fadiman (review date 10 February 1940)

[*Fadiman became one of the most prominent American literary critics during the 1930s with his insightful and often caustic book reviews for the* Nation *and the* New Yorker *magazines. In the following review, he questions the scope and structure of* How Green Was My Valley.]

A novel of Wales—the Wales of fifty years ago—called ***How Green Was My Valley,*** by a pleasantly talented newcomer, Richard Llewellyn, furnishes the occasion for more ecstasy than we have had from anyone since the début of Hedy Lamarr. A Mr. Godfrey Winn sounds off with "I think this book is the greatest modern novel I have ever read. It has made me forget everything except the magnificence of human courage." Among the things it has made Mr. Winn forget, may I suggest, are several hundred other modern novels. (Titles and authors available on request.) Messrs. Frank Swinnerton, Ralph Straus, and L. A. G. Strong also go in heavily for what Swinburne called "the noble pleasure of praising." If Mr. Llewellyn doesn't watch his step, he'll find himself as great a writer as Charles Morgan, whose press clippings will stand, I daresay, among the masterpieces of all time.

How Green Was My Valley is a quaint, "poetical" story whose main fault (to revive that good old one-line book review) is simply that its covers are too far apart. Had Mr. Llewellyn reduced his pages from five hundred to about three hundred, the result would have been a better book which would still, in all probability, have made Mr. Godfrey Winn forget everything except the magnificence of human courage. Also, the author would have brought into relief the essentially lyrical, short-breathed quality of his story. The Welsh are a greatly gifted race, one of their most notable talents being oratory, the most effective means yet devised by man for saying simple things in a long-winded manner. ***How Green Was My Valley*** is a very Welsh book, in its defects no less than in its qualities.

Huw Morgan, its hero, looking back at sixty upon his childhood and youth, tells the story of his large family, his first loves, his schooling, the development of working-class consciousness in a miners' community. The tale is conventional enough—the usual development novel—but is given considerable charm by its Welshness, the singing quality of its dialogue, its curious religiosity, half Bardic, half Chapel. All the characters are orators, a circumstance that is particularly effective in the love scenes. We poor stuttering human beings, almost all of us, speak well when we are in love, but the Welsh speak like angels.

Structurally the book is a sorry mess, consisting of a loose series of domestic scenes and rhapsodic interludes. The first hundred pages attract one by their quaintness and a Syngelike vividness, but once you have accustomed yourself to the genuine charm of Mr. Llewellyn's mannerisms, your interest tends to decrease. Some scenes stick with you, but the characters, at least for me, have wavering outlines, and the haze of memory in which Mr. Llewellyn plunges his story makes for a certain nebulosity.

The author assuredly has a more original talent than most of the newer English novelists and is a man to watch. If the London press gang do not kill his present, he may conceivably have quite a future. (pp. 65-6)

Clifton Fadiman, "The Thirties—Welsh Bards and English Reviewers," in The New Yorker, *Vol. XV, No. 52, February 10, 1940, pp. 65-7.*

Ben Ray Redman (review date 10 February 1940)

[*Redman was an American editor, journalist, translator, author, and poet. In the following review, he defends the romanticism of* How Green Was My Valley.]

This full-bodied, full-flavored novel [***How Green Was My Valley***] is romantic and frankly sentimental, but its romanticism embraces much earthly realism and its sentimentality has bone and muscle with which to make itself respected. In the singing rhythms of Welsh speech Huw Morgan tells the story of himself and his family and his coal mining village, as this tale was lived during some three decades that ended thirty-odd years ago. He speaks as a man of sixty or so, looking back upon his childhood, youth, and early manhood, and, whatever turnings the tale may take—whether they lead through scenes of beauty or ugliness or homely well-being—those Welsh rhythms always sing one nostalgic song: The old times were best, and they are gone forever. "An age of goodness I knew, and badness too, mind, but more of good than bad, I will swear. At least we knew good food, and good work, and goodness in men and women. . . . How green was my Valley, then, and the Valley of them that have gone."

There was badness, yes, but it grew only with the growing badness of new times—mounted with the heaps of slag that rose and spread like lava to blacken the green of the valleys. When Huw's father and mother were married, the slag had not yet shown itself above ground. There was steady work for all in the collieries, and the good pay was in jingling sovereigns. When the Saturday whistle went, the women put stools outside their doors and sat waiting for the men to come up the hill, and the men came and threw their wages, sovereign by sovereign, into the laps of the women.

> My mother often had forty of them, with my father and five brothers working. And up and down the street you would hear them singing and laughing and in among it all the pelting jingle of gold. A good day was Saturday, then, indeed.

The tin box on the mantelpiece was always heavy. There were a dozen hams in the kitchen, and hens in the yard. The folk of the Valley worked hard and lived well. Physically satisfied, they found spiritual satisfaction at Chapel. They walked in the fear of God, but not too fearfully; cleanliness was almost a second religion, and fair-dealing a faith. Reason for happiness in one family was enough to make all celebrate—sorrow was communal. They were glad and proud to be Welsh, and England was a foreign country far away.

Then came a time when wages were cut and a new order of things began. Huw's father, Gwilym Morgan, who was a leader in the Valley, put his trust in reasonable argument; but argument failed, and the men struck tentatively, doubtfully, without organization. They won the strike, but their wages were lower than before. That was only the beginning. Other strikes were ahead, and increasing bitterness. Davy and Owen worked hard to build the union, but they were struggling against forces that bore them down with the years. The closing of a single pit left four hundred men idle. Times grew ever blacker as the slag rose. Strangers appeared in the Valley, with the names of Marx and Hegel on their tongues—they found hearers, and a new spirit possessed the men. And to those like Huw Morgan it was a great pain to know that the brave ideas, "and the brave ones of early days, had all been forgotten in a craziness of thought that made more of the notions of foreigners than the principles of Our Fathers." The alien notions prevailed, and at last there was war in the Valley. But that came after the Morgan sons had been scattered abroad, and Gwilym himself did not live to see much of it. Fighting to the end against forces he believed to be evil, he died in the earth where he had worked so long, and his death was the crown of his living.

At the heart of this Valley history are the Morgans and those with whom their lives were most closely linked, and at the very center is Huw, through whose words past things live on. Around the growing boy the web of drama, domestic comedy, and tragedy is spun; and with his growth, and his increasing understanding of life, this web becomes increasingly complex. The strands of the tale are many and various, deftly and honestly interwoven, and each gives strength and substance to the whole. Life's poetry and prose are both embraced by a way of thinking and feeling and by a writing style that are capable of compassing both. The texture of the narrative is enriched by a wealth of detail—thought, felt, and observed. No message of the senses is too trivial to be underserving of a worthy record, and so the author has time for such things as the taste of brandy broth, the smell of tweed, and the feel of good wood when worked by sharp tools. A little passage on the art of tickling trout is no more scamped in the writing than is a longer passage on the significance of kissing or the lyric description of Huw's finding manhood with Ceinwen. Every one of the many characters who people this book crosses the threshold of reality, and, best of all, the pull of the story is like the pull of a strong tide, with the difference that we have no wish or need to resist it.

Doubtless it will be argued that the novelist has exaggerated the greenness of Huw's Valley, as he knew it as a boy and as his father knew it before him; that Huw, looking back through a sentimental mist of memory, has ignored the blackness that was already there. Nor do I doubt that statistics and documents in plenty can be mustered to support the argument. But the novel, as novel, will still stand sturdily against any such onset. Dissenting opinions will be written, too, by those critics who must be fashionable at all costs—for ***How Green Was My Valley*** lies outside the range of "significant fiction" as that range is delimited by present critical fashion. But it belongs to a line and a tradition that have outlasted more than one fashion. In the many-mansioned house of literature there is place for the Llewellyns as well as for the Steinbecks, and literature will be the poorer if there ever comes a time when there is not.

Ben Ray Redman, "'An Age of Goodness I Knew'," in The Saturday Review of Literature, *Vol. XXI, No. 16, February 10, 1940, p. 5.*

Katherine Woods (review date 11 February 1940)

[*In the following review, Woods discusses the characters of* How Green Was My Valley.]

It was a mining valley in Wales, still green and fair and sequestered half a century ago. The long street of stone houses climbed steeply from the collieries, and at noon every Saturday the women would take chairs outside the front doors and wait as their husbands and sons came laughing and singing to throw the week's wages into their starched white aprons, the sovereigns jingling as they fell. Then when the men had bathed every family would have its big Saturday dinner—such dinners as they were for Huw Morgan to look back to after fifty years! And such a home as the Morgans had—father and mother and nine children, so proud and strong and tender and gay!

Conflict? Of course. Grief? That, too; and even tragedy. Struggle, adventure, change. But how they could sing and work and hold fast to affection, the Morgans! And with what clarity and valor they looked at life, and sought justice, and thought their problems through! ***How Green Was My Valley*** is the story of the Morgans as it is remembered by Huw, the youngest son. It is a remarkably beautiful novel of Wales. And although it follows stirringly in the romantic tradition, there is the resonance of a profound and noble realism in its evocation, its intensity and reach of truth.

This was the Wales where beauty lived in a mining valley, where there was always music, and where stern piety and salty plain-speaking were no enemies to a ready laugh. There was neighborliness here for every contingency of joy or sorrow; and along with the neighborliness went a fierce self-sufficiency that could take care of its own rough justice as it could celebrate its traditions and uphold its rights. Pride there was, deep-rooted for a thousand years. And the wild loveliness of the country was so dear and familiar that its very wildness was like an intimate possession, and its remoteness and earthy richness were in the people themselves. Huw cherished the memory of the good food and the good smells of kitchen and garden, the dancing freshness of the little river before the slag heap soiled it, the daffodils scattering thick gold in the freedom of the mountain, the songs of the choirs as they filled the village street. It was all part of the valley's heritage, bound up with pride, independence, courage, love.

It was characteristic that Gwilym Morgan, that righteous man of earnest prayer, should teach young Huw to fight back with well-placed blows against all bullies. It was equally characteristic that "singing was in my father as sight is in the eye," and that one of his life's sweetest prizes was in his oldest son's triumphant command visit to Windsor, to conduct his choir before the Queen. When

Huw went to the English school it was natural, too, that he should be far ahead of his years in his classes. Just as the Welsh miner was a musical conductor in his time of leisure, so the miner's family read Boswell's Life of Johnson of an evening at home.

Hard-working they were, and their lives were simple and isolated. Primitive, either in thought or in living, they were not. And as Huw gathers the valley and its people into his memories, the sonorous music of classical English mingles naturally with the quaint and charming idiom of local speech in a beautiful and revealing simplicity. This novel's prose has an echoing magic.

The memories themselves were homely at first. There were strikes in the valley, to be sure, and Davy, "the brain of the family," looked forward sadly to worse in the time to come. But Huw likes to recall, like a colorful folk idyl, Ivor's marriage to the lovely Bronwen, who is always to be the ministering spirit of his own dreams. Then when Davy and young Gwilym disagree with their father over the labor situation there is swift crisis within the family. And the novel reaches its first high peak of dramatic event when Beth Morgan rushes through the Winter night to take up cudgels for her husband at the miners' meeting on the mountain, and she and little Huw almost lose their lives in a blizzard coming home.

Huw, housebound with rheumatic fever for several years after that, is at the heart of most of the family happenings. He sees the beginning of poor Marged's tragic love story, as he is later to be present at its end. He shares the splendid excitement when all the valley turns out, with five choirs, to welcome Ianto home from foreign wandering. He becomes pupil and friend to Mr. Gruffydd, the new preacher, who is no mere figurehead of Chapel but truth's militant saint. And when he is well again, and goes to school on the other side of the mountain, the adventures of his adolescence are suddenly flung against the dark background of the people's suffering in a five months' strike. Years later, when Huw himself is a man, ill-will and bigotry and evil gossip work disaster in his own community. And when even truth falls before error the valley's ancient justice is forgotten in the confusion of new greeds. Yet as Huw looks back on the eventful lives of the Morgans, the reader can see how within Man's own spirit truth may be still unconquered, and courage and love be as bottomless wells.

The book has no set plot, save such as is personally compassed within the Morgan family story and socially symbolized by the ever-closer encroachment of the mines' slag heap. But even its slighter episodes, like its minor personalities are vital. And from incident to incident the Morgans and their neighbors move as vigorous individuals, even though many of the characters are sketched in only a few strokes. Huw's father is the novel's chief protagonist: strong and authoritative like a patriarch of old, but with such swift laughter and brave imagination as is beyond the range of despots. And though Bronwen is generous and wise, Angharad appealing and Ceinwen aflame with youth's seductiveness, it is Huw's mother, Beth, who is the story's high-spirited heroine. As for the prizefighters, Dai Bando and Cyfartha, they may be remembered as major characters. Cheek by jowl with a robust humor, the book has its sentimental passages and attitudes, especially in the second half; but it is quite possible that these may seem more sentimental to us than they may actually have been to their own time and place.

Their own time and place—we come back to that, in this novel which brings a gift from Wales to our modern literature. The women in their tall hats, with red petticoats no brighter than their spotless kitchens and their pride; the quiet of the hills and then the sound of music on them; the green beauty of this loved valley, and the wholeness of life that it holds—this re-creation will not soon be forgotten by readers of this book. It is a nostalgic novel, pregnant with judgment upon the "progress" that can turn such a green valley into a "depressed area." But it is no mere lament for a lost paradise. It is a story of exquisite distinction and vibrant interest, clear and strong as the music under the sky. (pp. 3, 19)

Katherine Woods, "The Sound of Music on the Green Hills of Wales," in The New York Times Book Review, *February 11, 1940, pp. 3, 19.*

Rose Feld (review date 26 September 1943)

[Feld was a Romanian-born American journalist and author. In the following review, she praises Llewellyn's portrayal of the London underworld and calls None but the Lonely Heart *"a masterpiece of characterization."]*

Richard Llewellyn's first book, ***How Green Was My Valley,*** was a song that tugged at your heart with its unforgettable melody of the grandeur of humble human beings. His new novel, ***None but the Lonely Heart,*** makes equal assault upon the emotions—but with a difference. There is melody in his story of Ernie Mott, but it is a melody that stabs rather than tugs. It is a melody made up of the backwash of humanity, of the people of London streets and London dives, of poverty and the distortion of living. It is a song of the spiritual blind valley in which a little man, frightened of life and lonely, is trapped.

As a work of creative art, ***None but the Lonely Heart,*** in some respects, is greater than Llewellyn's first novel. For in this new book it is not a Welshman writing nostalgically of his homeland but a master of narrative telling a tale that has implications beyond geographical lines. The biographical notes about him report school days in Cardiff and London, jobs in coal mines, a sojourn in Italy learning the restaurant business, an interest in painting and sculpture, jobs on newspapers and in the film industry, periods of unemployment. Today he is in Africa, a captain in the Welsh Guards. What there is beneath the surface of the man, still in his thirties, that can turn the grist of ordinary experience into the essence of pure beauty lies hidden beneath these facts.

Ernie Mott is an ordinary little Cockney, but under Llewellyn's hand he becomes a symbol that makes him kin to millions. He is weak, he is petty, he is ambitious in his own limited little way; he has his moments of self-knowledge and exaltation. All he asks of life is a place in the sun, money in his pocket, posh clothes, and a beautiful girl to love.

Ernie was 19, a little bloke with pimples and shabby clothes. He lived with his mother, who owned a second-hand furniture shop on one of the poor streets of London. Ernie's father, who had "rolled up" at the Battle of Verdun, had been an artist. He had also been a drunkard and a philanderer. Ernie had never known his old man, but he liked the sense of superiority his father's work gave him, and for that reason, mainly, he had apprenticed himself to a firm of commercial artists. Being a painter gave a bloke something. The only trouble was that "never mind how hard He tried, that there crayon in His hand never done what He wanted it to, nor never did, nor He never see where He went wrong, nor how to shove it right." But life had its compensations for Ernie. There was Ma, from whom he could always wangle a bit of money; there was the Fun Fair with its music and crowds, where he was a wizard at the shooting gallery. Best of all there was Ada, the lovely "bride" who presided over the slot machines. Mainly it was Ernie's infatuation for Ada that started him on his career as a gangster.

That came after Ernie lost his job at the art studios. Only a man who has tasted the bitterness of fear and insecurity and self-pity could get into the narrow, terrified little soul of Ernie as Llewellyn does. "The big blue world, with straight lines of lights flashing away there, all shining with colored neons, and full of people, was chucking Him out of it. It, or nobody else, wanted Him. They was all against Him, the lot of them."

It was during his night of terror, of fear of facing his mother, that Ernie met Henry Twite, Lord of the Manor of Tookover. In Henry Twite, elderly Robin Hood of the fugitive and the derelict, Llewellyn creates as unique a character as has ever enlivened the pages of a book. He is fantastic in his language and his actions but he is real and heartwarming. Crime as a temporary solution to the exigencies of life he understands and condones but crime as a way of life is foul to him. Henry tried to set Ernie straight about jobs and being an artist, but Ernie had small use for the ancient bloke and his strange cronies. The important thing was to think up a story that would go down with Ma.

Just as the Mother in ***How Green Was My Valley*** was a person that clung to the reader's mind long after the book was closed, so is Ma in this book. "As far back as He could remember, Ma had never been no different. She was always in black for a start, and always wore a hat in the shop. Sometimes she wore it in the kitchen and the feathers always got caught in the gas bracket and either got burnt a bit, before she knocked the flame off, else they busted the mantle." Ma made a good living in her shop, what with one thing and another, and the neighbors liked and respected her. Even when the coppers came and arrested her for being a fence for stolen goods, Ma still was all right in the community.

That Ma should be happy at Ernie's losing his job was more than Ernie could comprehend. He didn't know that all his life she had been afraid he would take after his father. She wanted a son she could understand and love, and Ernie's confession that he was no artist destroyed the barrier that she had built up against him. Ma was going to make him a solicitor, a respectable profession, and that was okeedoke with Ernie.

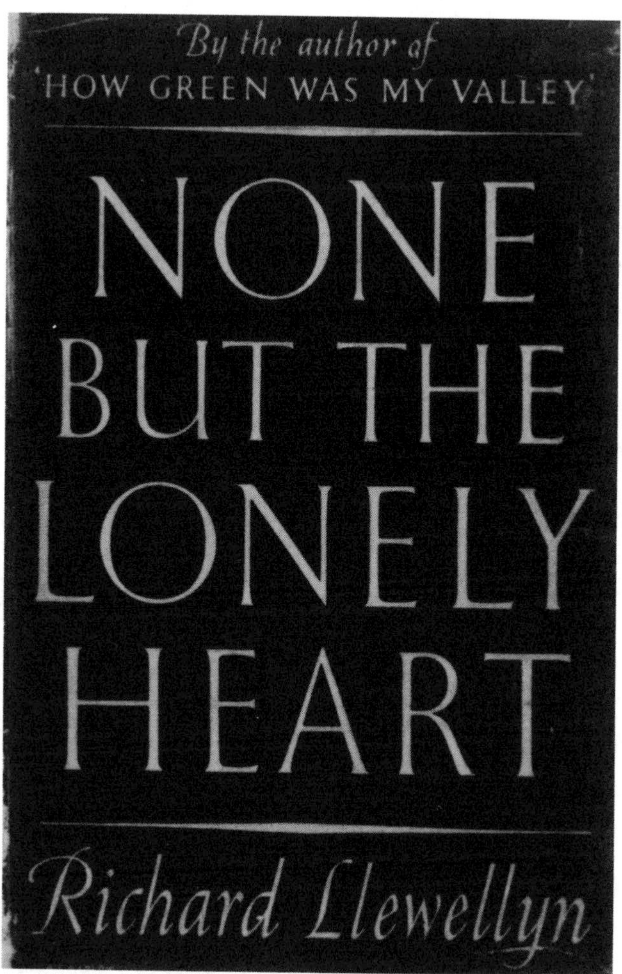

Dust jacket for Llewellyn's 1943 novel.

Perhaps the most poignant part of this remarkable book is Llewellyn's understanding of the love of the mean-spirited little Cockney for Ada. It has courage and chivalry and humility. When she confessed her unhappiness, "He wanted to put His arms around her and keep everybody out of her way, or sing her to sleep or something barmy. He never wanted her to be hurt no more. . . . He wished He could do what the blokes in the pictures always done when it comes to say it nice, but He knew if He give her any of that, it might come back on Him, specially if she see the same ones, and knew the same blokes."

It was through Ada that Ernie met Jim Mordinoy, owner of the Fun Fair and leader of London's underworld. One lesson from Jim and Ernie Mott, erstwhile artist and hanger-on, became The Smasher, who got thirty quid as his share of a thieving job. Life was simple after that, even if Ma died in jail, not knowing that Ernie was responsible for the coming of the coppers, even if Ada married the man she hated, even if he walked in constant fear of the law. Life was simple and life was lonely but Ernie Mott had found his destiny.

To say this book is a masterpiece of characterization is not enough. To say it is as richly and robustly peopled as Dickens or Hugo in their portrayals of the submerged is not enough. It is all these things plus something that is uniquely Llewellyn, something that is alive with imagination and understanding and poetry, wedded to a powerful and individual gift for story telling.

> *Rose Feld, "Richard Llewelyn's Novel of a Cockney's World," in* The New York Times Book Review, *September 26, 1943, p. 3.*

The Times Literary Supplement (review date 2 October 1943)

[*The following review derides Llewellyn's use of the Cockney dialect in* None but the Lonely Heart.]

Mr. Llewellyn's judgment is at fault in this second novel of his [***None but the Lonely Heart***]. ***How Green was My Valley*** had glowing life and colour but came a little too near to being lush to capture the highest effect of imaginative realism. Now he has gone to the other and worse extreme, and stayed there consistently through all the length of a starkly drab and excruciatingly mannered invention. This is the story of the nineteen-year-old Ernest Verdun Mott, a London slum product, pimpled and forlorn, who came to no good because life or heredity or society, or perhaps all three, offered him nothing better than the pleasures of a fun fair.

The intention is plain, and as the possessor of a social conscience Mr. Llewellyn is to be respected for it. As a novelist he has gone sadly astray. For whatever the significance of his hero's life history, it is related from beginning to end in a style of ungrammatical, slangy and violently debased speech that is a great weariness to read. Mr. Llewellyn can scarcely have realized how little opportunity the use of so poverty-stricken, so unendurably monotonous a jargon would leave him. The worst of it, too, is that he does not even pretend that Ernest Verdun Mott himself is the narrator of his fortunes; this is a third-person narrative all through. And why Ernest Verdun Mott needs to be spoken of, from the first page to the last, as He or Him, in capital letters, is a mystery. Is it the egotism of the nineteen-year-old unemployed youth that Mr. Llewellyn wants to emphasize? If so, the device is more enervating than he can have bargained for.

"The High Road done Him good to be in, with the tram lines sliding round the corner like butcher's hooks polished up special for the afternoon." "So there went a tanner down the drain hole, and what was more, she knew He was there, and never even give Him eye room." In this fashion Mr. Llewellyn tells how his hero (who, quite incredibly, wanted to be an artist) was in love with Ada, who tended a machine at a fun fair, who would have nothing to do with the passionate gangster owner of the fun fair and who was herself desperately in love with a dance band leader. He tells, too, how Ernie's mother used a second-hand miscellaneous shop as a blind for the activities of a gang of shoplifting women in the Kingsland Road and was eventually caught and died, and how Ernie was lured by the gangster fun-fair owner into lending a hand with smash-and-grab exploits. There is less point or pathos in all this than is evidently intended. Mr. Llewellyn's honesty and sympathy are never in question, but, setting aside the monotony, the tale itself never comes off.

> *"Sweet Victim," in* The Times Literary Supplement, *No. 2174, October 2, 1943, p. 473.*

The Commonweal (review date 8 October 1943)

[*In the following excerpt, the reviewer describes the milieu of* None but the Lonely Heart *and its sociological effects on the protagonist, Ernie.*]

London is the *mise en scène* [of Richard Llewellyn's ***None but the Lonely Heart***], that part of London down by the railway tracks with a gas works just down the end of the road. Ernie's back yard, which keeps getting covered with cinders, was mostly concrete. "There was circles and squares left open down the middle in a kind of pattern, and in them Ma Chalmers had planted privets and something else as never come to anything except a lot of weeds and marigolds."

Despite Ma's heroic efforts to keep the place clean and do for her nineteen-year-old son, Ernie's life is bare indeed. For five years now he has been working half-heartedly as a lithographer's apprentice. His face is always breaking out and his clothes are always soiled and frayed; he has not a boon companion to his name. The only things that keep him going are a September-mornish plaster statuette he once won at the Fun Fair and the most graphic and tantalizing thoughts of a sweater-girl named Ada, who makes change at one of the games at that Coney Islandish establishment.

Ernie first arouses, then, all the pity of a character from Graham Greene. Consider the hopelessly bleak surroundings in which he lives. His loneliness and longing for something or someone to love in his own animal-like fashion and his pathetic concentration on getting what he wants—be it only two half crowns from his thieving mother—arouse great expectations in any Greene addict. But except for a new jauntiness and self-confidence (maintained even when he is hunted by the law) when his mother passes on, Ernie never gets anywhere. To the last his conversations never get beyond a certain animal cunning which consists of saying only what he senses will get him farthest with the person from whom he wants something at the time. Only on the rarest occasions there is a moment of revulsion or courage or love.

Starting out as a mere good for nothing, Ernie embarks on a criminal career and what was merely bleakness, ugliness and poverty now descends to new depths. There is a Hugo-ish escape through a sewer with a mortal duel and rats in great prominence, while his new companions in crime have a decidedly Dickens cast about them. But the Victorian tabus on rough language are no longer present. Here and there flickers a spirit of human kindness and of brave humor in the face of destitution. Ernie's musings and some of the conversations are just the type of thing that can be found drawn or written or carved in American public washrooms.

So although it is the story of Ernie, who presents his reactions to the various sorry developments in the third person, but with capital letters as if to drive home his complete obsession with himself and his own primitive pleasurable or painful sensations, it is more of a study of environment than anything else. The effect of living in the squalid district down by the tracks, in the abandoned tenements where criminals hide out, even his exaggerated satisfaction with the tinsel and excitement of the Fun Fair, make ***None but the Lonely Heart*** a powerful indictment against a society that would permit such conditions to continue. Environment is the villain against which numerous human wills are powerless—an extreme view which has its elements of truth. As a sort of preface the author cites Robert Owen to the effect that "man is now reduced, by a total change of laws and customs, to the lowest state of mental degradation." Except for the skill and occasional emotional fire with which it is written this book is a far cry from ***How Green Was My Valley.*** And not only because Huw's innocence contrasts with Ernie's obsession with sex. The main difference is that Mr. Llewellyn's earlier best seller was a positive nostalgic evocation of a hard but beautiful way of life, while his current volume is the very opposite. (pp. 613-14)

"A New Limehouse," in The Commonweal, *Vol. XXXVIII, No. 25, October 8, 1943, pp. 613-14.*

Appreciation for Llewellyn's language:

In this book, far removed from the scene of war, there is plenty of rough stuff done up in the modern manner and in a novel that can grip and sadden the oldest sinner. As to Mr. Llewellyn's ***None but the Lonely Heart,*** I read many of the current reviews of it. No one of them gave me an adequate idea of the emotion, the passion, the urgency of this book. Never having moved in the underworld of London, I was yet seldom at a loss to interpret the extraordinary Limehouse cockney jargon in which Mr. Llewellyn clothes his stirring tale. Hardly a page is free from some expression that my sainted mother would have called "coarse," but it seems only a part of the sordid and lively scene. It is hard to believe that this Richard Llewellyn is the same young man who wrote ***How Green Was My Valley,*** that poignantly lovely tale of the Welsh coal miners. Yet perhaps we can see in the hopeless Ernie Mott's yearning for his hard-bitten but devoted mother, in his longing for Ada whose delights of the flesh he can never hope to attain, some of the same spirit that made Mr. Llewellyn's Welsh romance so full of understanding and appeal. But I can well imagine that most of the nice people who loved ***How Green Was My Valley*** will turn up their noses in disdain and even horror over the vulgar, even though human, emotions spread forth in Shakespearean lustiness of phrasing on the pages of ***None but the Lonely Heart.***

Thomas W. Lamont, in The Saturday Review, *December 11, 1943.*

Philip Toynbee (review date 6 November 1943)

[*Toynbee is an English novelist and critic. The son of historian Arnold Toynbee, he gained a considerable reputation as the author of experimental novels such as* Tea With Mrs. Goodman *(1947) and* The Garden to the Sea *(1953).* Pantaloon *(1962-68), a series of four novels-in-verse, is generally considered by critics to be Toynbee's most important work. A contributor to several prominent English periodicals, he joined the editorial staff of* The Observer, *London, in 1950. In the following mixed review of* None but the Lonely Heart, *he commends the use of dialect as justified and fitting, but concludes that aspects of Llewellyn's novel are uninspired.*]

The time when talent could languish in obscurity or die of neglect is surely long past. Spotters have taken up strategic (and competitive) positions covering the whole wide literary field, and there is now little chance for Miltons to remain inglorious. But one are, not, indeed, an obscure one, is seldom or never explored. The spotters have surveyed every yard of jungle, scrub and desert; they have snatched from the darkness many rare and curious specimens (which too often withered in the light of day), but they have neglected with assured contempt the streamlined city of the established best-sellers. In this neglect both probability and experience overwhelmingly support them. During the last fifty years creative art has so outstripped public appreciation that popular art has become almost synonymous with something retrogressive and inferior. There are striking exceptions in some fields, though few in literature. Yet it is dangerous and obscurantist to assume that a best-selling novelist can be safely disregarded. Already a subtle seismographer of educated literary opinion will have detected a faint undulation in the curves of Galsworthy and Bennett.

The publisher of Mr. Llewellyn's new book has done his best to raise the bile of any critic who holds that the price which the film rights of a book has fetched is no criterion of its quality. I was so repelled by the sales-talk which accompanied my review copy that I began to read ***None but the Lonely Heart*** with profound revulsion. Revulsion survived many pages, though it was to some extent supplanted by boredom. The first chapter of this book can hardly fail to bore or offend, but neither the offence nor the boredom are of the kind usually associated with a best-selling novel.

> Earnest Verdun Mott thought it was dead funny how a blanket over bent knees with the sun on it gets like a lot of little grey trees growing over a couple of smooth mountains, with hundreds of camp fires all along the top burning curly hairs of light. Beyond, where the sun had took a clip of his shears along the shadows, thousands of them, these little flashing white bits fell out of the dark part and rolled about in the light, just floating round, they was, turning over and over, regardless as a shower of millionaires.

It would be hard to claim that this is an enticing first paragraph, yet the whole of chapter one strictly conforms to the texture of its opening passages. In the second chapter I found that a flicker of curiosity had lightened the boredom, and after fifty pages the film-rights were forgotten.

A book written in dialect is liable to cause an initial, and in some readers an overpowering, weariness. Instead of familiar intelligible prose we are presented with a foreign language which is oral by nature. Is the attempt justified? I believe it to be not only justified, but, in a novelist of any scope, almost inevitable. One of the most important innovations of *Ulysses* was the variation of style and vocabulary corresponding to different characters and situations. To do this successfully requires laborious research—perhaps more research than Mr. Llewellyn has been prepared for. His cockney dialect is not wholly convincing; far less convincing, for example, than the conversation of Henry Green's firemen. But this book remains a courageous, and surprisingly successful, attempt to solve a perennial literary problem. With patience a reader can not only accustom himself to the idiom, but recognise that any other would have been inappropriate.

None but the Lonely Heart (a title almost ludicrously typical of the current fashion) is the story of an East End adolescent who falls, by subtle stages, into gangsterdom. The seed of his corruption is a bewildered arrogance, an undefined but irrepressible discontent with his gloomy environment. Initially, he sees himself as a great artist frustrated by lack of opportunity. His naïve ignorance of art is well described, and the final recognition of his total artistic incapacity leads very naturally to the choice of an alternative apotheosis. Crook or artist, he is determined that he will not remain as he is. And this dæmonic urge for change is finely understood. It would have been easy to make of Earnie Mott a simple *enfant du siècle,* a type-character nurtured on the culture of the cinema. To make him an aspiring artist as well is at once to add a third dimension. Though he lacks artistic talent and lacks, still more, artistic patience and devotion, Earnie retains the vision and imagination of an artist. The result is that a richly romantic element is added to a book which might otherwise have been both sordid and conventional. Through Earnie's eyes the drab story is elevated to a more vivid and at the same time a more moving plane. Funfairs, pin-table *cafés* and the *palais de danse* lose much of their habitual squalor and achieve a naïve, almost an endearing, glamour.

The book has serious weaknesses. There are long passages of interior monologue which are dull and stereotyped; there are characters whose oddity is self-conscious and displeasing. But Mr. Llewellyn has had the courage to follow a best-selling success with a book of genuine originality. If the sales can compare with those of ***How Green was my Valley,*** will it be a sign of the public's appreciation or the magic of a name?

Philip Toynbee, in a review of "None but the Lonely Heart," in The New Statesman & Nation, *Vol. XXVI, No. 663, November 6, 1943, pp. 304-05.*

James Walt (review date Autumn 1965)

[*In the following review, Walt outlines the plot and notes a defining quality of Llewellyn's novel* A Man in a Mirror.]

The mirror of Llewellyn's novel [***A Man in a Mirror***] is the delicate and troubled self-consciousness of a young African tribal leader who may soon become prime minister of an on-the-brink-of-emerging nation. Nterenke is the child of two cultures, each as wary of the other as a mongoose and a cobra. Many of the young Masais who tasted an English education rebelled against the iron conventions, the beatings, the mutilations, the incredible rigors that had shaped a perhaps uniquely self-reliant people. Other tribesmen, far from regarding the Reserve in which the white man had penned them as a prison, scorned the mysterious outside world. It became Nterenke's task to reconcile the "irreconcilables."

Llewellyn writes authoritatively of a culture which makes even the austerities of the Biblical patriachs look like self-indulgence. There is more anthropology here than the theme requires. Nevertheless, the book has the pulse-beat of a warm, living, organic creation.

James Walt, in a review of "A Man in a Mirror," in Books Abroad, *Vol. 39, No. 4, Autumn, 1965, p. 481.*

FURTHER READING

Bates, Ralph. "A Story of Wales." *The New Republic* 102, No. 7 (12 February 1940): 219-20.

Argues that the ending of *How Green Was My Valley* is not commensurate with the intensity and vitality of Llewellyn's portrayals of the Morgan family in the rest of the book.

"Elegy for South Wales." *The Christian Science Monitor* XXXII, No. 75 (24 February 1940): 11.

Praises *How Green Was My Valley* for its affectionate, vivid portrayal of turn-of-the-century Welsh mining life.

Fadiman, Clifton. Review of *None but the Lonely Heart. The New Yorker* XIX, No. 33 (2 October 1943): 82, 84.

Maintains that the "peculiar" Cockney dialect and "pathetic" protagonist of the novel are confusing and ultimately boring.

James, Trevor. Review of *How Green Was My Valley. Life and Letters To-day* 23, No. 28 (November 1939): 391-92.

Contends that Llewellyn's novel "is a good story, though as a picture of mining life, it is marred by many inaccuracies, and as a piece of prose it is spoilt by fulsomeness."

Levin, Martin. Review of *Green, Green My Valley Now. The New York Times Book Review* (14 September 1975): 42.

Positive review of the sequel to *How Green Was My Valley.*

Littell, Robert. Review of *How Green Was My Valley. The Yale Review* XXIX, No. 3 (March 1940): viii, x.

Extols the spare, visceral language in the novel.

Mair, John. Review of *How Green Was My Valley. The New Statesman and Nation* XVIII, No. 450 (7 October 1939): 494, 496.

Questions the positive critical reception of *How Green Was My Valley,* concluding that the novel "does, after all, appeal only to the emotionally discontented, while the novels that really make history must appeal to dissatisfied minds."

O'Brien, Kate. Review of *None but the Lonely Heart. The Spectator* 171, No. 6014 (1 October 1943): 320, 322.

Derides the novel as uninspired and lacking in vitality.

Salomon, Louis B. "The Hills of Home." *The Nation* 150, No. 6 (10 February 1940): 221-22.

Claims that *How Green Was My Valley* presents a balanced, satisfying portrait of Huw Morgan's life and village.

Stern, Philip Van Doren. "The Darker London." *The Saturday Review of Literature* XXVI, No. 42 (16 October 1943): 42.

Presents a mixed review of *None but the Lonely Heart,* admitting that Llewellyn is an excellent storyteller who understands well the common person.

Strong, L. A. G. "Ichabod." *The Spectator* 163, No. 5807 (13 October 1939): 524.

Praises *How Green Was My Valley,* calling it "a first-rate novel in the romantic tradition, imaginative, vigorous, musical and sure of its direction."

Additional coverage of Llewellyn's life and career is contained in the following sources published by Gale Research: *Contemporary Authors,* Vols. 53-56, 111; *Contemporary Authors New Revision Series,* Vol. 7; *Contemporary Literary Criticism,* Vol. 7; *Dictionary of Literary Biography,* Vol. 15; and *Something About the Author,* Vols. 11, 37.

Juan Rulfo

1918-1986

Mexican novelist, short story writer, screenwriter, essayist, and editor.

The following entry provides an overview of Rulfo's career. For further discussion of Rulfo's life and works, see *CLC,* Volume 8.

INTRODUCTION

One of Mexico's most important literary figures, Rulfo is best remembered for *Pedro Páramo,* a landmark work that in part represents a reaction against the traditional realism that dominated Latin American literature in the nineteenth and early twentieth centuries. Rulfo's novel is one of the earliest precursors of magic realism, a style in which fantastic occurrences are interwoven with realistic and historical events to obscure distinctions between fantasy and reality. In addition to his experiments with narrative structure, Rulfo is known for writings that emphasize death, pathos, and the history and culture of the Mexican people.

Rulfo was born in central Mexico in the small community of Apulco in the state of Jalisco. His childhood was spent in nearby San Gabriel, where he witnessed the war of the *Cristeros*—a political uprising led by the Catholic clergy against the Mexican government following the revolution of 1910. During this period Rulfo lived for a time with his grandmother, whose home was federally protected because Rulfo's mother was related by marriage to a high-ranking official in the Mexican Army. The local priest, whose residence was being used to house army troops, stored his personal library at the home of Rulfo's grandmother for safekeeping. From a young age, Rulfo read extensively from the priest's collection, which consisted mainly of adventure stories. In 1925, when Rulfo was seven years old, his father was murdered for political reasons. Two years later his mother died of heart failure, and in 1928 Rulfo was sent to an orphanage school in Guadalajara, where he remained until he was fifteen.

In 1934 Rulfo enrolled in the national university at Mexico City, intending to study law. Financial difficulties necessitated his departure, however, and he instead became an immigration agent for the next ten years. During that time Efrén Hernández, a co-worker who had published several short stories, encouraged Rulfo to write. Rulfo completed a novel but destroyed the manuscript because he was dissatisfied with the results. In 1945 his short story "La vida no es muy seria sus cosas" ("Life Is Not Very Serious about Things") was published. The same year he also collaborated with two other writers, Juan José Arreola and Antonio Alatorre, with whom he founded the literary magazine *Pan,* where two more of his stories appeared. In 1952 Rulfo received a fellowship from the Centro de Escritores Mexicanos that allowed him to finish his collection of short stories, *El llano en llamas, y otros cuentos (The Burning Plain, and Other Stories).* Following favorable critical reception, the fellowship was renewed, enabling Rulfo to complete his novel *Pedro Páramo,* published in 1955. Rulfo stated on many occasions over the next ten years that he was working on a second novel entitled "La cordillera" ("The Mountain Range") but was unhappy with its progress. Although he intended to make substantial revisions, these were never completed and the work remains unpublished. Rulfo moved to Guadalajara in 1959, where he edited history books and worked at various government-sponsored organizations. After returning to Mexico City in 1962, he was employed by the Instituto Nacional Indigenista, a federal agency that studied and attempted to alleviate the problems of Mexico's indigenous peoples. Although he also wrote several film scripts, later collected and published as *El gallo de oro y otros textos para cine,* Rulfo expressed disappointment in these efforts. In 1970 Rulfo was awarded Mexico's highest literary honor, the Premio Nacional de Letras, and he received Spain's Premio Principe de Asturias in 1983. He died in 1986.

In his novel *Pedro Páramo,* Rulfo employs a complex narrative structure that at first renders the book's plot difficult to follow. The story relates Juan Preciado's search for his father, Pedro Páramo, who had abandoned Juan's mother when Juan was an infant. As he approaches the town of Comala, Juan learns from a passerby that Pedro Páramo is dead. After Juan encounters the few residents of the nearly deserted town, Rulfo reveals that Juan and the town's inhabitants are also dead. Conversations emanating from characters' graves recollect the past—particularly Pedro Páramo's rise to power as a local political boss, known in Mexico as a *cacique;* his exploitation of the local people; and his obsessive love for his childhood friend, Susana San Juan. Because of the novel's difficult narrative structure—which makes use of flashbacks, illogical interior monologues, and a nonchronological juxtaposition of events—*Pedro Páramo* was not initially well received by critics. Rulfo, however, maintained that "life is not a sequence of events. Years can pass without anything happening and then all of a sudden a multitude of events is unleashed. Things happen to no one in a constant manner and I set out to tell a tale with the facts and deeds well distanced, breaking with time and space." Eventually the novel was recognized as a masterpiece, and its complex structure and narrative style have since been extensively analyzed. George D. Schade has called *Pedro Páramo* "a bold excursion into modern techniques of writing," and the novel has been variously discussed as a social commentary on Mexico's *caciquismo,* as a mythic journey, and as a reflection on the significance of death in Mexican culture.

Rulfo's short stories in *The Burning Plain* are set in the harsh, arid countryside of the Jalisco region where he was raised. These pieces explore the tragic lives of the region's inhabitants, who endure poverty, family discord, and crime. The title character of "Macario," for example, is an orphan raised by a neurotic foster mother. The narrative voice reflects the boy's thoughts as he sits alongside a drainpipe at night, carrying out his foster mother's instructions to kill the bullfrogs, whose croaking disturbs her sleep. "Nos han dado la tierra" ("They Have Given Us the Land") depicts the impact of the Mexican government's land reform program on four poor countrymen who are each given a parcel of land that is located too far from any source of water to be of any use. "La noche que lo dejaron solo" ("The Night They Left Him Alone") tells the story of federal troops who kill the family members of a man they are pursuing when they cannot locate him. While *The Burning Plain* has not received as much critical commentary as *Pedro Páramo,* the collection's content and, in some cases, narrative technique, have been viewed as precursors to *Pedro Páramo.* Both works share a bleak, essentially hopeless view of the lives of their characters. Luis Harss and Barbara Dohmann have written of Rulfo's characters that, "[because] of their lack of inner resource, ultimately they inspire little more than pity. And that is the danger. We are often on the verge of falling into pathos. But the attentive reader will go beyond that. There is a deeper grain running through the stories. To live, in Rulfo, is to bleed to death." Despite its similarities to *Pedro Páramo, The Burning Plains* is now recognized as an important work in its own right. Rulfo's terse, unadorned writing style in these stories reflects the parched terrain of the Jalisco region and the sterility of the lives of its inhabitants.

Critics note that Rulfo's work has influenced all subsequent Latin American literature. Although frequently categorized as a provincial writer, Rulfo transcends strictly regional concerns to embody universal themes. According to Harss and Dohmann, Rulfo's "theme is simply human sorrow in dispossession. He writes with a sharp edge, carving each word out of hard rock, like an inscription on a tombstone. Therefore his work glows with a lapidary purity. It is written in blood."

PRINCIPAL WORKS

El llano en llamas, y otros cuentos (short stories) 1953; revised edition, 1970
[*The Burning Plain, and Other Stories,* 1967]
Pedro Páramo (novel) 1955; revised edition, 1970
[*Pedro Páramo,* 1959]
Obra completa: El llano en llamas, Pedro Páramo, otros textos (novels, short stories, and essays) 1977
Antología personal (novels, short stories, and essays) 1978
El gallo de oro y otros textos para cine (screenplays) 1980

CRITICISM

George D. Schade (essay date 1967)

[*Schade is the translator of a 1967 edition of Rulfo's* El llano en llamas y otros cuentos (The Burning Plain, and Other Stories). *In the following excerpt from his introduction to that work, Schade provides an overview of the characters and themes in Rulfo's short stories.*]

Juan Rulfo is perhaps the best writer of fiction in Latin America today, and a writer to be reckoned with on a universal scale, as his fame continues to spread beyond his native Mexico. If we take soundings here and there of his reputation, in Europe—France, Germany, Spain—or in the countries of South America, we find the critical acclaim swelling constantly.

Born in the state of Jalisco, Mexico, in 1918, Rulfo published his first short stories in the provincial little magazines of Guadalajara in the 1940's. Later on he moved to Mexico City, where the two books which have brought him such celebrity were published: his collection of short stories [***El llano en llamas*** (1953)] followed by his singular short novel ***Pedro Páramo*** (1955). . . . A second novel, called *La Cordillera,* which Rulfo evidently has been working on for several years, has long been announced as forthcoming by his Mexican publishers.

Most critics of Rulfo's work have concentrated their attention on his brilliant novel ***Pedro Páramo,*** a bold excursion into modern techniques of writing; however, Rulfo achieves some of his finest moments in the short stories, where the elaboration of a single event or the introspection of a single character allows him to illuminate the meaning, often the utter despair, of a man's life.

Rulfo's world is extremely primitive and profoundly alien to us, at least in its outer aspect, though it is plagued within by the same convulsive agony and fears that strike men's hearts everywhere. The atmosphere is full of repressions and is often mute—a paralytic world seemingly beyond the orbits of time and space. Crude and perverse passions, solitude and death stand out as tangible phenomena against the opaqueness of the Indian characters' tragic lives.

The novels of the Mexican Revolution, beginning with *The Underdogs* (1916) by Mariano Azuela, which dominated the Mexican literary scene for several decades, portrayed a turbulent world where the individual all but disappeared at times. In the 1940's, with such works as Agustín Yáñez's *The Edge of the Storm,* and in the 1950's, with the novels and stories of Carlos Fuentes, Rosario Castellanos, and Juan Rulfo, this collective mask is largely stripped away. The Indians who live and die on the burning Plain in Jalisco are usually treated by Rulfo as individuals with interior lives full of anguish as well as exterior lives of struggle against hardship and abuse. Behind their innocent faces often lurk unspeakable horrors of tragedy and violence: murder, incest, adultery, all the violence of need and desire. These characters seem to live on grief and suffering without friends or love. Indeed, love is an emotion which scarcely appears in these stories, though it plays an important role in ***Pedro Páramo.***

Rulfo peels many of his characters down to the core, but some of them, like the landscape, frequently clouded over and hazy, remain blurred, imprecise, and taciturn figures. They are never seen in full face, but always in a silhouette, like the lugubrious, black-garbed crones of **"Luvina."** The one thing standing forth clear and ubiquitous is death—overpowering life—which seems to hold scant value in this world.

Rulfo has an uncanny feeling for describing the bleak landscape. In the harsh area where his characters live almost nothing stirs or moves, not even buzzards. Life seems to have come to a stop in this paralyzed region, producing a static quality in many of the stories. Macario, for instance, starts out on his rambling monologue, "I am sitting by the sewer waiting for the frogs to come out." And he is still there waiting at the end of the story.

A black, macabre humor of a very special order runs through the collection as a leitmotiv. It is most persistent in **"Anacleto Morones,"** a tale streaked with naturalistic touches: the description of the foetus, and of Pancha's mustache, the vomiting, the women streaming sweat. But the characters' suffering and unhappiness in this bizarre story of a pseudo saint's hypnotic power over ten middle-aged hags occasionally blots out the predominate acrid, humorous tone.

Unlike the novels of the Mexican Revolution and certain Indianist novels of the 1930's, Rulfo's fiction contains no preaching about social abuses, though he refers briefly to the Mexican agrarian question in several stories and sketches the wetback problem most effectively in **"El Paso del Norte."** Large social ills are commented on dispassionately only when they have bearing on the personal dramas Rulfo is unfolding.

Various techniques which have oriented contemporary fiction along new pathways are present in ***The Burning Plain.*** Some stories are one long, sustained, interior monologue (**"Macario," "We're Very Poor," "Talpa," "Remember"**). In **"Macario"** the past and present mingle chaotically, and frequently the most startling associations of ideas are juxtaposed, strung together by conjunctions which help to paralyze the action and stop the flow of time in the present. Rulfo succeeds in this excellent story in capturing the sickly atmosphere surrounding the idiot boy, who is gnawed by hunger and filled with the terror of hell, and protected, and at the same time exploited, by his Godmother and the servant girl Felipa.

Dialogues are inserted in other stories that are essentially monologues, sustained by the same person who reconstructs situations and scenes from memory (**"Luvina," "They've Given Us the Land," "Anacleto Morones"**). In **"At Daybreak"** and **"The Man"** the action takes place on several levels simultaneously. In the entire collection the pace is slow and sometimes comes to a halt, giving the static effect of eternity that has so caught the critics' attention. As one Mexican commentator aptly declares, there is a triumph of characters over plot, of persons over acts, of the author over time.

In **"Talpa"**—a classic tale of adultery in which the gripping emotion is not love or desire, but remorse—we are told the outcome of the story at the very beginning. But the suspense, rather than being destroyed by this technique, becomes sharper under Rulfo's dramatic handling. Chronology is broken effectively here, too, and time is immobilized.

A few stories are scarcely more than anecdotes, like **"The Night They Left Him Alone,"** when Feliciano managed to save himself from being hanged like his two unfortunate uncles. Rulfo unfolds this tale in all its dramatic force, pruning away superfluous material, but repeating details and reiterating phrases that give punch to the story.

Rulfo's narratives are composed with the greatest attention to dramatic effects. He knows how to begin a story with a sentence or two of the right cadence to grasp and hold the reader. Urgency, tension, conflict fill the air. For instance, the opening lines of **"No Dogs Bark"** set the tone of mystery and doom in a brief dialogue between father and son, a foreboding note swollen with uncertainty that permeates the entire story. The dramatic effect is intensified by the short, agonizing sentences of the dialogue, and the narrative's principal action between the father's words and the son's silence. Here, as in the majority of these stories, the author narrates in a few, brief pages an intense, intimate drama, terse of language, somber in color, with no exterior character description. With remarkable skill Rulfo succeeds in provoking a static impression with his throbbing, dynamic fragments of life.

The technical complexity varies from one story to another: some are relatively simple and develop chronologically, others have different points of view and shifts and shufflings in time. Flashbacks, interior monologues and dialogues with subtle undertones, and an occasional passage of impersonal reflection are employed to give the effect of simultaneity. Time fluctuates among the levels of the present and the causal past, which is vivid in the characters' memories and usually rancorous in its recollections.

The spontaneity of Rulfo's monologues and dialogues is deceptive and points to a conscientious, hard labor on his part to reach this level of stylistic polish. He writes a splendid prose of firm muscularity, its contours never sagging with long patches of commentary. The language is sparse and laconic, unflinchingly realistic, yet charged with poetic qualities. His imagery has a marked rural flavor: earth, rocks, dust, wind, moon, buzzards, coyotes. This imagery never intrudes upon the narrative; it either serves to point up what he is suggesting or else takes on an essential role in the story. In **"We're Very Poor"** the central image is the river, bringing perdition and ruin in its wake. The river's presence runs through the story, as Rulfo makes us feel its swirling, filthy waters through all our senses. We hear its lapping waves, we smell the stench it leaves as the flood subsides, we witness and shudder at the dirty tears streaming down Tacha's face "as if the river had gotten inside her."

Dominant in Rulfo's stories are the themes of vengeance and death, and the struggle and desire to live. Human nature must always and inevitably assert itself, and in these tales of Biblical power and simplicity it does so convincingly. Rulfo's characters are moved by greed, hate, lust, revenge; they are hampered by fate and beset on all sides by the problems of daily existence. Reality is unendurable but must be faced. Man is abject and lonely. He seeks communication but usually is thwarted. Several stories in the collection, for example, treat the lack of understanding between father and son with particular poignancy. In the domain of violence Rulfo is supreme, and this is all the more impressive as the tone of his writing never becomes rhetorical. It remains calm and measured, pervaded with a classical dignity.

Rulfo's work has immense literary vitality and extraordinary originality. His stories shock and grip us, and many of them make us feel that we are sharing in his characters' pathetic anxiety just to live, to stay alive (**"Tell Them Not To Kill Me," "Talpa"**). The elements of the harsh physical environment combine with the Mexican Indian's fatalism to forge almost a symbiosis of man and landscape. The parched, dry plain is overwhelming. The Indian accepts life as it is there, and his acts are almost inevitable. He is perpetually in flight, or wracked by fear, mistrust, and remorse, often losing his few cherished possessions and his peace of mind. Impotence and despair reign, and death rattles in the scorching air, the howling wind, the throttling dust of the plain. (pp. ix-xiv)

George D. Schade, in an introduction to The Burning Plain and Other Stories *by Juan Rulfo, translated by George D. Schade, University of Texas Press, 1967, pp. ix-xiv.*

Joseph Sommers (essay date 1968)

[An American critic, educator, and editor, Sommers specialized in Hispanic literature. In the following excerpt, he examines Rulfo's use of narrative structure, viewpoint, characterization, and myth and folklore in Pedro Páramo, *which, he asserts, delineates a worldview emphasizing "the tragic immutability of man's anguish."]*

[In ***Pedro Páramo,*** his novel of rural Jalisco,] Rulfo found such elements as the dynamic progression of history and the complexities of Freudian psychology to be nonessential baggage. Appropriate to his *weltanschauung,* his narrative technique shuns a sequence that might relate causality to progression in time, and his depiction of character is almost bare of interior conflicts.

Rulfo finds the key to human nature elsewhere. He approaches the opaque side of man's psyche, where the dark imponderables reside: "Why does the world press in on us from all sides, and break us into pieces, and water the ground with our blood? What have we done? Why have our souls rotted?" It is this zone, timeless and static as Greek tragedy, which in his view decides the vagaries of man's encounter with fate.

How to distill this bitter poetic vision into novelistic form? The author's choice of ingredients is a paradoxical combination of highly stylized folk language on the one hand, and, on the other, a daringly complex structure which deliberately confounds the reader in its mazelike obscurity. At moments it is scarcely prose. "He heard the weeping. That woke him up, that soft, thin sound of weeping, perhaps because it was so thin it could slip through the mazes of sleep to the place where the fears dwell." The result is a sensitive Mexican variation on the tragic immutability of man's anguish.

The nature of incident in ***Pedro Páramo*** is difficult to describe, because Rulfo fragments his narrative into tiny divisions (there are no chapters) which are more often than not unrelated to each other in time or place, and are populated by diverse characters who are rarely introduced and almost always difficult to identify. The reader must strain for connections, and is compelled to construct events and identities in order to wrest meaning from apparent disarray.

The novel begins in retrospective first person with an account by Juan Preciado of his arrival at Comala. On her deathbed his mother had urged him to seek out Pedro Páramo, the father who had abandoned them. He finds Comala an infernal ghost town—dry, seared, and empty except for a few mysterious individuals. Most, or all of these creatures—it slowly becomes clear—are in fact dead, though their memories of Juan's mother and Pedro Páramo are still vivid.

Interspersed with the boy's strange encounters are sections of remembered speech which present his mother's description of Comala. Her images of pastoral fecundity contrast with the arid lifelessness which Juan encounters. Other sections, at first inexplicable, introduce the memories of Pedro Páramo, recounted both in first-person musings and in dialogue of scenes which he recalls.

A vision of Pedro Páramo begins to emerge, but only tenuously, for identities are often in doubt. Gradually it becomes apparent that Juan is communicating with the spirits of dead people whose bodies are interred while their souls are condemned to roam the earth. Midway in the narrative, Juan tells of his own death and burial. By this time, various moments in the life of Pedro Páramo have been described from one source or another: his childhood love for Susana San Juan, his assumption of the family's debt-ridden ranch, his revenge of the gratuitous murder of his father, and his relentless ascent to power. One of Pedro's least violent methods of building an empire was marriage to Dolores Preciado (who later was Juan's mother) in order to possess her land.

The death of Pedro's illegitimate, wastrel son Miguel also figures in the narrative. Miguel is thrown from his horse during a nocturnal escapade in search of women. Earlier, he had murdered the brother of the village priest Padre Rentería, and had seduced the niece of this hesitating, guilt-ridden cleric. The latter, aware of Miguel's depredations, and of Pedro's evil grip upon the region, is rendered impotent by his own weakness.

Although these are the narrative threads of the first half, they reach the reader indirectly. The story seems to center on Juan's encounter with the unreal atmosphere of Comala—his strange meetings with living-dead characters and with a few funereal ones who appear to be alive, and the random, unexplained rememberings of Pedro Páramo, emanating from a source unidentified in time and place.

The central narrative device of the second half consists of dialogues from the tomb, between Juan and the old woman Dorotea, with whom he lies buried. It now becomes clear to a startled reader that Juan's earlier first-person remembrances were also part of this exchange between two dead characters. A further narrative medium is the series of monologues which Juan overhears from the adjacent grave, where Susana San Juan lies twisting and turning, remembering the past. As in the first half, there are also sections recounted in third person by an unknown narrator.

The diverse fragments continue to develop the fortunes of Pedro Páramo, whose epic stature as *cacique* is matched only by his obsessed love for Susana. The latter had left Comala as a child, but Pedro Páramo, throughout his rise to power, had sought news of her, keeping track of her marriage and subsequent widowhood. With characteristic ruthlessness, he invited her father to return with Susana, and then urged him off to a prearranged death. Susana, left behind, was to consummate the crowning desire of the *cacique.* Having felt genuine passion in her marriage, however, Susana rejects further participation in life, seeking refuge in madness. In this state she can take solace from remembered moments of sensual joy, withdrawing totally from Pedro's love and from Padre Rentería's pressure for remorse. Within the novel, she is the only figure whose memories include a minimal glimpse of happiness, although significantly it is happiness encased in insanity.

Simultaneous with the frustration of Pedro's lifelong desires is the advent of the Revolution, which serves secondarily to relate events to the chronology of the outside world. Through bribery and sagacious maneuvering, Pedro manages to ride the waves of the upheaval. His tactic is to ally himself with spontaneously risen bands of rebels, providing men and a minimum of help, and channeling their marauding to adjacent villages.

The ensuing death of Susana is not mourned in Comala. Indeed, the incessant bells attract the curious from miles around, and initial expressions of grief slowly give way to a riotous fiesta. Angered and embittered, Pedro Páramo swears to avenge himself by allowing the village to go to waste.

This promise he fulfills, passing the remainder of his days on his ranch, in stolid meditation by the side of the road, calling forth the memories which have appeared throughout the novel and which now take on meaning in the context of his impending death. The final scene is that of Pedro's demise at the hands of the drunken Abundio, grief-stricken at the death of his own wife. The scene is tinged with double irony, for Abundio is Pedro's illegitimate son, who in his drunken state does not even recognize his father.

This brief resumé places into orderly relationship the anecdotal substance of the novel—the story that is told. More important is the specific nature of the process—how it is communicated—for in the discussion of technique lie the clues to the literary uniqueness of ***Pedro Páramo.*** Point of view, structure, style, development of character, and a mythic substructure all combine to project special dimensions to an implicit world outlook.

Essential to Rulfo's method of narration is the perspective from which he portrays people and events in his novelistic world. The fact that we learn from the first few pages that Pedro Páramo is dead, and that Comala is some sort of ghostly village, imposes a particular color upon the entire work. Indeed, by the second half, when it becomes clear that Juan himself is in the grave, the specter of death completes its earlier, tentative invasion of life.

Death as a narrative vantage point heightens the sense of inexorability. The fate of those whose lives are recalled is viewed from a perspective which reduces the importance of anecdote and conflict, since climax and resolution are cut off in advance. Rather than being narrated as though brought to life, which is the case in most fiction, the essential contours of the story are uncovered as static, almost isolated phenomena seen from across a vast boundary in time. One could even say, seen from the timeless perspective of the afterlife. The loss of suspense which this procedure entails is compensated in the handling of structure.

A second function of narrative perspective is to create a tone of apparent objectivity, separating the author from his characters. Much of this effect is achieved by introducing a "witness" narrator, Juan Preciado, whom we follow as he gathers information about Pedro Páramo. Significantly, as Carlos Blanco Aguinaga has observed, Juan never evaluates or ponders on information, which the reader receives untouched by Juan's personal interpretation, and is forced to interpret for himself. Also there are remembered occurrences, in which various characters, such as Eduviges, Damiana, Susana, describe particular events to Juan, most frequently in language which is brief, unsubjectivized and understated. Even the monologues and memories of Pedro Páramo perform a function which is largely narrative, rather than one of subjective self-analysis.

At various moments in the novel the author returns to an already known incident, approaching it from a new angle or point of view. This process of multiple focus rounds out the reader's apprehension of the events and their impact on various characters. An excellent example is the death of Miguel Páramo. First it is recounted in the magical-folk version of Eduviges, who recalls her conversation with the dead Miguel shortly after his fatal accident. Several pages later comes a report of the funeral mass, highlighting Padre Rentería's reactions: at first, moral condemnation of the sinful deceased, then acceptance of Pedro Páramo's financial donation and reversal of his earlier refusal to bless the body. In the second half of the novel, a third-person narration describes how Pedro Páramo was notified of the death, and how he reacted with the fatalistic observation, belying a sense of his own misdeeds: "I'm beginning to pay. Better to start early. You finish sooner." Immediately following are the memories of Padre Rentería which serve to explain the priest's deep guilt. The interlocking nature of these four sections establishes their credibility, allowing the reader to piece together some of the tiles of a mosaic which at first confuses him. The emphasis is not so much on the events themselves as on the interrelationships which the multiple foci illuminate.

Thus Rulfo employs a series of techniques which endow with apparent objectivity the narrative fragments of his novel. The dispassionate "witness" narrator; the nonjudgmental tone of other characters; the reinforcing nature of versions of the same set of events—all these dispose us to accept as truthful the accounts we receive of Rulfo's Comala.

On the other hand, when placed in an order which permits synthetic interpretation, these components make up a total world which is far from clear and objective. The perspective of death, with its consequent nullification of temporal sequence and the logic of cause and effect, serves to attenuate reality and to affix a particularly subjective seal to the anguished world of ***Pedro Páramo.*** (pp. 70-6)

Rulfo discards realism entirely, seeking instead to make an overall subjective statement about the nature of man. Precisely because his goal is subjective, he resorts to the techniques of objectivity to carry the reader along.

The structure of ***Pedro Páramo*** is one of the aspects which immediately stands out as unique. Though it may make life difficult for the reader, its distinctiveness performs a vital role esthetically and conceptually within the novel.

The very first impression is perhaps related to the elemental, laconic style of the opening paragraphs, followed by the realization that all is not in traditional order in this first-person account by Juan Preciado. For one thing, on the second page, when he describes the road to Comala, another description is juxtaposed, in italics and in present tense:

> The road went up and down; *"it goes up and down depending on whether you're coming or going. If you're going away, it's uphill, but it's downhill if you're coming back."*

Half a page below, a similar passage appears, but now the voice in italics is identified as that of Juan's mother. The identification must be applied retroactively by the reader to the first fragment. This is the first taste of the interpolation of unexpected material. In this case, explanation is withheld only for one-half page, thus softening the impact.

The second, third, and fourth narrative sections concentrate, along with the first, upon the arrival of Juan in Comala, his initial impressions and his encounter with Eduviges Dyada—all initiating the reader into the novel's rarefied atmosphere. Gradually the customary foundations of time and substance are weakened: Pedro Páramo, Juan learns, is dead, although he is also termed "a living hate"; Comala is seen both as a ghost town and formerly fecund village; in its searing heat and airless atmosphere, Comala, it is suggested, is an infernal place; Eduviges, the first person Juan meets, seems to straddle the boundary between life and death, and the lodging she offers him seems strange; most important, she reveals foreknowledge of his coming, casually referring to notification by his dead mother.

This growing incomprehensibility produces in Juan a feeling of stupor and bewilderment—a sensation at least partly shared by the reader:

> I thought the woman must be crazy. Then I didn't think any thing at all. I felt like I was in a far-off world, and I just let myself be carried along. My body seemed to be floating, it was so limp, and you could have played with it as if it were a rag doll.

At this declaration of psychological weightlessness, indicating the absence of normal bases for reckoning with time and reality, the full force of structural innovation is brought to bear. The next segment changes abruptly in characters and setting, providing no clues for the reader, who, indeed, for a moment is misled. It switches to a dialogue between Pedro Páramo as a boy and his mother. Injected suddenly into this interchange are fragments of the adult Pedro Páramo's memories of boyhood, and his early love for Susana, set off only by quotation marks. And then, after three of these narrative sections in four pages, the reader is suddenly jolted back to the speech of Eduviges, in dialogue with Juan. Soon there will be more sudden shifts.

Such is the labyrinthine pattern of narrative sequence, a pattern which does not vary, except that the death of Juan occasions a clear and natural division into two parts. The second part will now be narrated from the "present" of death, as he and Dorotea lie in their adjoining graves. Although it becomes clear that Juan really had been dead while narrating the first part, the author had good reason to withhold this information.

Juan's death actually serves as a dividing line between two perspectives of narration. Here structure and the technique of withholding information are related to the vision of reality. Emphasis was placed, in the first half, on an apparently live Juan with whom the reader could identify as he encountered death, in the form of the infernal mystery of Comala. The ghostly, cadaverous face of the town was perceived by one who seemed still to live, but whose vitality was increasingly sapped by the overwhelming impact of death on his senses.

The second half—more in emphasis rather than uniformly—reverses the process, and is a mirror image of the first. From the grave, Juan and Dorotea (and through Juan, Susana) now focus on the days when Comala was alive. Once again, despite the reversal of perspective, the same pessimistic premise is clear: death predominates over life. In the first half, the presence of death contaminates existence; life is a living hell. In the second half, life contaminates death, making that condition hell also.

In this static world the only thing that alters is the backdrop. We can, in fact, discern four stages in the process by which the impact of Pedro Páramo changes the landscape. First, out of the past, is the lyric beauty described in the memories of Dolores and Susana. Then, at about the time of Miguel's death, Padre Rentería tells his priest confessor: "I've tried to raise grapes in Comala. They don't bear. Only oranges and berries. Bitter oranges and bitter berries. I've forgotten what sweet things taste like."

Years later, when social disturbances of the impending 1910 Revolution compel his return, Susana's father describes Comala:

> Some villages taste of bad luck. You can tell them by drinking a little of their stale air. It's poor and thin, like everything else that's old. This is one of those villages, Susana.
>
> Back at La Andrómeda you could at least pass the time watching things being born: the clouds, the birds, the moss. Do you remember? But there isn't anything here except that stale yellow smell wherever you go. The village is bad luck. Nothing but bad luck.

Clearly, the village is well on its way to total barrenness.

Finally, Pedro Páramo's death takes place against a physical background which corresponds to Rulfo's estimate of man's condition. The sterility which the name Páramo implies, and which is the state Pedro dictated for Comala, is also his own fate, for of his three sons none is destined to survive or to have issue who survive. Miguel's capricious death occurs within the novel. Abundio, whose wife and infant son are dead, dies after killing his father, for it is his spirit which guides Juan to Comala. And Juan, we realize at the novel's end, will arrive at some subsequent point of time (the novel's beginning), committed to a search which will result in his death but will enable him to continue to reconstruct the tragedy of Pedro Páramo.

While the two halves of the novel switch their focus, as though the narration were projected by reversed lenses, the dominant element in both is death, whether the focus be on subject or object. In the first half it is Juan the narrator-subject whose devitalization we witness, against the background of the ghostly Comala he encounters. In the second half it is Susana and Pedro Páramo, and with them Comala—the objects of narrative interest—which move inexorably toward absorption into timelessness, while the state of the narrator remains suspended.

Structure plays a multiple role in contributing to the particular literary unity upon which ***Pedro Páramo*** is based. Most obvious is the fact that sudden narrative switches in time, place, and person destroy the normal process of tracing causality in its relation to the stately procession of events in temporal sequence. Certainly the reader will reorder the diverse fragments, striving to reconstruct chronology. Nevertheless, the novel's structure, which forces him to view occurrences *initially* out of real context, shunts his search for causality elsewhere.

Thus, for example, our estimate of Pedro Páramo is first formed by events which take place after his death. We are introduced to him through Juan's visit to the Comala strangled by Pedro Páramo, who is characterized on the fourth page as "a living hate." Juxtaposed with this posthumous view are contrasting flashbacks of Pedro's past: a fragment from his childhood, adolescent memories, then the sequences involving Miguel. The result of this apparently chaotic sequence is to isolate events and character from the flow of the world about them, thus muting the traditional interplay between man and his social and historical circumstance.

Structure also contributes to a nonsequential view of time. The dominant process in ***Pedro Páramo*** is neither development nor progression, but the revelation of finality—the static, permanent qualities inherent in human existence. Events flow backward and forward, with the future and present merged into the past.

Structure similarly helps to erode the divisions between reality and irreality, divisions which for Rulfo must be blurred in order to affirm the presence of mythic and magical elements in man's psyche.

Esthetically, the mazelike form stands in contraposition to the elementality of its language. This interplay between simplicity and complexity is a distinct new quality in the Mexican novel. (pp. 76-81)

Mystery is another attribute to which structure contributes. Bewilderment of the reader is substituted for the suspense which frequently accompanies plot or character development. An example of this technique is the withholding of the name of the first person narrator, Juan Preciado, until page forty-six. If, when this fact is finally provided in passing, the reader notices it, he is then able to establish the relationship between Juan and the Dolores Preciado who had been lured into marriage by Pedro Páramo. Further, he can recall with new meaning a different version of the wedding night which had been provided earlier by Eduviges.

Jean Paul Sartre was aware of this type of procedure in Faulkner, and his comments on *Sartoris* [in "Sartoris, par William Faulkner," *Nouvelle revue française* 50, No. 293 (February 1938)] are in many ways transferable to Rulfo's novel.

> There is a formula: not to tell, to remain silent, disloyally silent—to tell *just a little*. We are told furtively (some information). . . . Furtively, in a phrase that risks passing unnoticed, and which it is hoped will pass *almost* unnoticed. After which, when we expect storms, we are shown instead just gestures, in long and minute detail. Faulkner is aware of our impatience, he counts on it. . . . From time to time, as though negligently, he unveils a consciousness for us. . . . Only what there is *within* this consciousness he doesn't tell us. It is not that he wants precisely to hide it from us: he wants us to guess it for ourselves, because guessing renders magical whatever it touches.

Closely related is the question of reader involvement. Just as in the above example, we are called upon to make connections, the essence of Rulfo's technique is to deny his own omniscience, compelling us to share his own imperfect view of reality, and to supplement it if we can. Indeed, Rulfo goes to the extreme of setting out snares which entrap us, first into confusion, then into esthetic reward if we were able to find our way.

The nature of incident in *Pedro Páramo* is difficult to describe, because Rulfo fragments his narrative into tiny divisions (there are no chapters) which are more often than not unrelated to each other in time or place, and are populated by diverse characters who are rarely introduced and almost always difficult to identify. The reader must strain for connections, and is compelled to construct events and identities in order to wrest meaning from apparent disarray.

—Joseph Sommers

The figure of Pedro Páramo is both poetic image and flesh-and-blood character in his embodiment of tragedy. Carlos Blanco Aguinaga has indicated the fundamental lines of Rulfo's character presentation [in his "Realidad y estilo de Juan Rulfo," *Revista Mexicana de Literatura* I, No. 1 (1955)]:

> Among this world of people-echoes, Pedro Páramo is the only one in whom the double dimension of character is well delineated: with his own life outwardly—individuality—and his own life of interior illusion—personality.
>
> . . . . .
>
> Through Susana San Juan, Pedro Páramo attains the double level of a complete character which the others do not have in the novel. And it is this double level, the tension created in him by two opposed human planes (exterior violence, dreamy interior lassitude) which makes of Pedro Páramo a character of tragic dimensions. All his violence and his cold exterior cruelty are no more than the vain effort to conquer the impregnable fortress of his interior dream and pain.

Blanco Aguinaga also observes that the two levels of character are isolated one from the other and do not influence each other until the end of the narrative when the *cacique* renounces his life of dynamic activity after Susana's death. Further, the contrast between interior sensitivity and exterior hostility is present as a consistent phenomenon, in the boy as well as the man. There is no significant change or evolution in Pedro Páramo.

Not only does the protagonist fail to evolve, in the traditional manner of the "round" character, his personality and individuality are discernible only in the barest, most essential terms. The scope of his interior life is limited to his love for Susana, in brief flashes which are magnified because there is no competing glimpse of other areas of his psyche, and because of their concentrated lyricism. An early passage captures the paradoxical sensitivity of an otherwise brutal man:

> I was thinking of you, Susana. In the green hills. When we flew kites in the windy season. We heard the sounds of the village down below us while we were up there, up on the hill, and the wind was tugging the string away from me. "Help me, Susana." And gentle hands grasped my hands. "Let out more string."
>
> The wind made us laugh; our glances met while the string paid out between our fingers; but it broke, softly, as if it has been struck by the wings of a bird. And up there the paper bird fell in somersaults, dragging its rag tail, until it was lost in the green of the earth.
>
> Your lips were moist, as if they had been kissing the dew.

The performance of Pedro Páramo in the world around him, conveyed in terms of its impact on others and therefore obliquely described, is also narrated in fragments which concentrate only on the highlights necessary to apprehend the full force of his destructiveness.

The result of this characterization process is a figure of giant size but still a "people echo," as Blanco Aguinaga so aptly stated. One might also describe Pedro Páramo as a silhouette—all black and white with no grey areas. His transcendental conflict is reduced to its barest essentials: violence, arrogance, and lust versus love and sensibility to beauty.

Pedro Páramo is the center of the novel, the figure who shapes and defines others. He achieves vast proportions because he incarnates the elemental nature of myth, because he is an abstraction, an essence. His tragedy can be summed up in one word—death. His dream dies, and with Susana, his love. His offspring die, and he kills Comala. So powerful that he controls the lives of all around him, he cannot make death have meaning, not even through love.

> He had thought he knew and understood her. But even if he didn't, wasn't it enough to know that she was the creature he loved best in all the world? And to know also, and this was the most important, that she would help him depart from this world illuminated by the image that erased all other memories?

That redeeming image proved inaccessible to Pedro Páramo, because there is no such image within the tragic vision of Juan Rulfo.

The forces which drive the character Pedro Páramo are independent of any social environment, transcending it. The rhythm of his life story does not correspond to conditions outside Comala, barely alluded to in historical references, for the clues to his behavior lie in more basic human traits. His brutality is made sharper by the startling beauty of his love, the very force of which, converted into hate, determines the depth of his vengeance against Comala, the degree to which the village will be submerged into a timeless inferno.

In contrast to Pedro, and serving as his foil, is the unattainable Susana. Despite their opposition, they have much in common, for both are obsessed with lyrical reveries of past love; "the impregnable fortress of [their] interior dream and pain." In Susana's case, we know nothing of the object of her distress other than sensual musings, for the crisis in her life occurs outside the novel. We can judge that her love was as unattainable as Pedro's from such fragments as these: " . . . but he felt lonely, even though I was there with him." and, a few lines later:

> "I like to bathe in the sea," I told him.
>
> But he didn't understand.
>
> And the next morning I was out on the beach again, to clean myself. To give myself up to the sea. . . .

The polarity between Pedro Páramo and Susana is shown by the ways they react to their misery. Pedro responds with violence; Susana retreats to the private hell (and joy) of madness. She becomes completely passive, while his energies burst outward against others. Susana rejects Pedro Páramo and the comfort that religion offers, while he adds the burden of her suffering on to his own. The two counterbalance each other, although Susana is scarcely more than a charcoal sketch. (pp. 82-6)

Juan Rulfo's protagonist is all bony structure and spirit. He is an abstraction, not a human being. Instead of explicit descriptions there are story fragments and scraps of conversation, and most of these issue from illusory sources . . . We are dealing now with magic.

A key aspect of Rulfo's creation is the aura of myth which invades it. Carlos Fuentes noted this quality in a recent statement [appearing in his "La nueva novela latinoamericano," *La Cultura en México,* No. 28, a supplement to *Siempre!* (29 July 1964)]: "Juan Rulfo [proceeded] to the mythification of the situations, the character types and the language of rural Mexico. . . ." Fuentes went on to discover links with Greek mythology, finding correspondences between Juan Preciado's search and the Odyssey, between Dolores Preciado and both Jocasta and Eurydice, mother and lover—suggesting that Juan Preciado embodies elements of the myths of both Oedipus and Orpheus.

Actually, a better case can be made for Fuentes' sharp perception by observing the *quality* of myth than by following vague suggestions of specific Greek tales. For within most cultures, including that of rural Mexico, are motifs of search, of an underworld, of love unrealized. As a whole, Rulfo's novel has the flavor of myth, combining the elements of many. There is the timelessness, the lack of a beginning or an end, and the negation of history, which leaves the legend suspended. Poetic images suggest symbols for the reader who wishes to search for them. Most pertinent of all, the tale is removed from the reality the reader knows to a supernatural realm where life and death have no boundaries.

Pedro Páramo's mythic aura flows organically from its source. Here a clear distinction must be made, eliminating the term "folkloric," with its literary connotations calling to mind descriptions of indigenous or regional customs and idiosyncrasies. The stress in Rulfo falls rather on folk motifs endowed with vast symbolic reference, broad enough to approach universality.

The very substance of ***Pedro Páramo*** is fashioned from the concept, current in the folk belief of rural Mexico, of "ánimas en pena"—souls in pain, condemned to roam the earth, separated from their corporeal origins. The suggestion is that Eduviges, who we later learn has long since committed suicide, is in this state of being when she serves as the vehicle by which Juan is first introduced to the present and the past of Comala. One of the few "live" persons Juan encounters tells him: " . . . the village is full of spirits, a whole throng of wandering souls that died in sin and can't find any way of getting pardon. . . . " Indeed, one of the spirits whom Juan briefly meets, Damiana, says to him: "Poor Eduviges. Then she must still be suffering."

By contrast, in the second half of the novel, it is in dialogue with the soulless body of Dorotea that Juan completes the process of bringing to light the final phases of Pedro Páramo's life. In a moving answer which establishes in her the same sense of guilt which envelops every character of whom Juan has learned, she tells him of the separation of body and soul:

> "And your soul? Where do you think it's gone?"
>
> "It must be wandering around up there on earth, like all those others, looking for people to pray for it. I think it hates me for the bad things I did, but that doesn't worry me any more. I'm rid of all the pain it used to give me. It made me feel bitter about everything . . . and it made the nights unbearable, full of terrifying thoughts. . . . When I sat down to die, it told me to get up again and keep on living, as if it still hoped for some miracle that would clean away my sins. But I wouldn't. This is the end, I told it . . . I opened my mouth so it could leave, and it left. I felt something fall into my hands. It was

> the little thread of blood that had tied it to my heart."

Such folk beliefs are so much a part of the structure and so important to Rulfo's assumptions concerning existence that they constitute the living reality of ***Pedro Páramo,*** superimposing magical elements on the "realistic" narrative process. In this sense, the unearthly Comala falls within the bounds of myth as defined by Richard Chase [in his "Notes on the Study of Myth," *Partisan Review* XIII, No. 3 (Summer 1946)]:

> Literature becomes mythical by suffusing the natural with preternatural force toward certain ends, by capturing the impersonal forces of the world and directing them toward the fulfillment of certain needs.
>
> . . . . .
>
> Myth performs the cathartic function of dramatizing the clashes and harmonies of life in a social and natural environment. But myth can be understood as the aesthetic leaven which heals or makes tolerable those deep neurotic disturbances which in primitive culture are occasioned by the clashing attitudes of magic and religion.

The dramatizing of "ánimas en pena" underlies the device by which a major section of the story is conveyed to the reader, rendering the narrative perspective of death authentic. It is made more complex by a third state of being, also a common folk motif, the animated corpse. Dorotea, in the passage quoted above, lying in the grave and, at last, free of the soul that hates her, says, "Heaven is right here where I am." Susana's corpse is not as satisfied. Her body continues to writhe as it did in life, until the coffin breaks.

A number of sub-motifs reinforce the pattern of superimposed folk-fantastic elements. In each case they contribute to the elaboration of a central theme—the blurring of the lines between life and death, with a resultant fusing of the two states. On several occasions there are passing, casual references to communication between living and dead as a normal pattern, references which fill out the context of Juan Preciado's intitally strange and mysterious encounters.

Other such magical elements are the dead horse which gallops at night in search of its dead master; the room in Eduviges' hostelry in which the screams of a hanged man continue to resound years later; the assumption that Bartolomé appeared after his murder in the form of a cat, to visit his daughter Susana.

On one level, all the above occurrences defy logic and confound rational explanation. On another, they exemplify the supernatural system of belief which, for the rural folk of Mexico, is necessary in order to reconcile otherwise insoluble phenomena. The novel's oscillation between what for the reader are reality and irreality is consonant with the mentality of its characters. This matter-of-fact treatment of magical elements enables Rulfo to absorb the myths of rural Mexico into the total picture he paints. To carry Carlos Fuentes' insight to its logical conclusion, Juan Rulfo has used the situations, the character types, and the language of rural Mexico to create the new myth of Pedro Páramo. (pp. 87-91)

Rulfo's is basically a fatalistic view of existence. The novel's structure, piecing together the shards of an already preordained tragedy, dramatizes Rulfo's cosmic pessimism with regard to man's ability to control his own fortunes, to master himself, to achieve love, or to evolve a meaningful morality. Existence, in these terms, is a closed system, cyclical in its repetition of past patterns and in its reliving of basic mythic themes. Rulfo clearly demonstrates much more affinity for Jung than for Freud.

Written in post-Revolutionary 1955, ***Pedro Páramo*** condenses extreme bitterness into its evaluation of the Revolution. Implicitly, it runs directly counter to the widely circulated versions of the past two decades of progress and reforms. The fortunes of Mexican man in the novel show no signs of progressing as the nation evolves. On the contrary, the formation of the protagonist's character antedates the Revolution, remains oblivious to it, and survives it unchanged. Within the novel, the Revolution symbolizes the futility of all history in its ineffectual consequences and its essentially barbaric nature.

Rulfo's tragic vision implies the deep inadequacy of Christianity. The weight of a burden closely akin to original sin oppresses not only Pedro Páramo, but Padre Rentería, Susana, and all the minor characters except the neutral observer Juan. But, in opposition to Christian concepts, Rulfo's characters carry this burden through life with no prospect for relief, no effective sacraments to act as countervailing forces, and no hope for redemption in another world, since life and death constitute a continuum. Heaven is beyond the reach of all. Neither religious faith nor humanistic solidarity offer any antidote to a mode of being in which man is condemned to suffer and to cause others to suffer.

There could be no more pitiful a creature than Dorotea, who tries to explain her frustrated maternal instincts in terms of sin-ridden dreams. The lyricism of Pedro's deep longing for Susana is movingly beautiful, as are the memories of Dolores Preciado of a formerly blissful pastoral life in Comala. Yet in each case, an instinct for love and an awareness of beauty are inevitably ground down by the abrasive effects of sin and guilt in the characters themselves, as well as in their fellow men. Susana's question, "And what do you think life is, if not sin?" underlies the entire conceptual fabric of the novel.

In these terms, Rulfo's world contrasts sharply with that of [Agustín] Yáñez, whose anticlericalism implied the need for reform, for new adjustments of moral norms. Rulfo projects doubts so deep as to question any foundations of belief of modern society. On an earth where life has the characteristics of hell, and beauty in effect serves as a gauge of suffering, man's fate is abject and final. (pp. 92-3)

Rulfo proceeds to disintegrate his universe—then he puts together enough pieces to form a coherent, highly personalized expression of despair. His image is magic, poetic, irrational. The novel for him is a means of expressing, in original terms, his own subjectivity. Literature becomes, in Rulfo's sense, a highly individualized art form, and the responsibility of the creative artist is to affix his own distinct seal upon the world, in an act of creation which may well be his only recourse. (p. 94)

Joseph Sommers, "Through the Window of the Grave: Juan Rulfo," in his After the Storm: Landmarks of the Modern Mexican Novel, *University of New Mexico Press, 1968, pp. 69-94.*

Luis Leal on Rulfo's fiction:

It is the combination of a native subject matter observed from a new perspective and expressed by means of up-to-date techniques that has given Rulfo an international status as an extraordinary fiction writer, in spite of the fact that his production is quite limited. And it is his sensitive, poetic vision of his own world that has elevated him to the ranks of the great interpreters of Mexican reality. His fiction has endured the test of time, and it stands as a monument to a modest, sincere, and unobtrusive writer.

Luis Leal, in his Juan Rulfo, *1983.*

Walter M. Langford (essay date 1971)

[*In the following essay, Langford provides an overview of Rulfo's career and discusses* Pedro Páramo, *which he briefly compares with Agustín Yáñez's 1947 novel* Al filo del agua (The Edge of the Storm).]

Among today's most notable Mexican writers the case of Juan Rulfo is a quite remarkable one. Born in 1918, his total published output up to 1971 consists of two slender volumes—one of short stories and the other a novel. They appeared in 1953 and 1955, respectively, yet his name and his influence are very much alive in literary circles today, both in Mexico and elsewhere. This is confirmed in these recent words [from *Los narradores ante el público,* 1st ser., 1966]: "It is pleasant to observe when one travels abroad—and, besides being pleasant, quite surprising—that on initiating a conversation on literary themes and personages with critics, fellow writers, or readers in general, they immediately ask about Juan Rulfo." It almost seems that because he is not writing, Rulfo's fame grows like a myth or a legend.

In 1970 Rulfo was awarded the Premio Nacional de Letras (National Literary Prize). When one voice was raised against giving this honor to someone whose total printed works occupy fewer than 250 pages and who has published nothing for fifteen years, critic and writer Raúl Prieto responded at once that those 250 pages or so just happen to represent a collection of short stories and a short novel superior to any other such selections produced in Mexico in the past seventy years. Mexican literary circles in general seemed to be of the definite opinion that the award was an act of deserved and just recognition.

Considering the paucity of Rulfo's production and the enduring influence of his works, perhaps no other writer has ever derived so much from so few pages. This obviously is a substantial tribute to the nature and quality of what little he has published. Yet we must come to the question of why an author of Rulfo's undeniable gifts and interest in literature has not published more. Is he just another one of the "dead-end" novelists who dot the pages of literary history in Spanish America? These writers, a most numerous breed, turn out one or perhaps two novels, sometimes excellent ones, and then are never heard from again. Their disappearance from the literary scene generally is due to the hard economic reality that they and their families must eat and that they can't expect to do it on the pittance they receive from their novels. So they turn to politics, journalism, business, or whatever and their literary career ends almost at its beginning. But this really isn't the case of Juan Rulfo.

Rulfo considers himself an active writer, and so does everyone else. The truth is that he has been working for years on another novel, always promising to publish it soon. We know the title: *La cordillera,* and the setting: the villages of Jalisco, and Rulfo can occasionally be persuaded to talk about it. He reveals that the story traces the history, from the sixteenth century to the present, of a certain family who have large landholdings, concentrating on a female character who is the last descendant. He says that he wants "to show a reality that I know and that I want others to know . . . , to show the simplicity of country people, their candor. The man of the city sees their problems as country problems. But it's the problem of the whole country" [quoted in Luis Harss and Barbara Dohmann's *Into the Mainstream,* 1967].

But *La cordillera* has not yet been published, and even if it were to appear in print as these words are being written, the implications of his hesitant attitude remain. He has simply gone on year after year, promising the book and then reworking it, followed by more promises and yet further reconsideration. When and if it does appear it may be a masterpiece to outshine ***Pedro Páramo,*** or it may be overrefined and anticlimactic. Rulfo's vacillation is evidently a case of a great psychological hang-up. Perhaps there is a subconscious fear that anything he does from now on will not match ***Pedro Páramo*** or again, his hesitancy could be an extreme manifestation of his own personality, insecure, lacking in self-confidence, unable to take a forthright decision. Whatever else it is, it is a personal tragedy and a distinct loss to the nation in the literary realm. (pp. 88-9)

[Rulfo] comes from the lowlands of the south of Jalisco, once quite important but now a dusty, dying, depressed area. This fate of his native soil dominates Rulfo's mind and inspiration. He is obsessed with death, both of the land and of the people on it. Despite having lived practically all his adult life in Mexico City, the problem and atmosphere of his part of Jalisco constitute his one literary theme. The fact that he can make this desolate land with its dead or dying people come to life so realistically and hauntingly for his readers testifies to his genius and sensitivity. It may be, however, that Rulfo's sparse output is explained in part by his strict limitation of theme, as well as by his own personality.

Rulfo at work in his Mexico City office during the 1970s.

Juan Rulfo is a shy man, unbelievably shy, an introvert, a "loner." Humble and lacking in self-assurance, he has never mixed in literary circles. He is a worrier—too concerned about too many things ever to relax. No doubt the experiences of his own early years have played a part in making him the way he is.

Rulfo's family, once apparently comfortably fixed, lost its possessions during the Revolution. He recalls moments and scenes from the days of the Cristero revolt in the late twenties. He lost his father in the first days of this struggle and his mother died only a few years later. For a time he was in an orphanage in Guadalajara, and in 1933 at the age of fifteen he went to Mexico City, where he studied accounting for a while and a little law, and then for more than ten years held a minor job in the Mexican immigration service. Following several years with Goodrich in Mexico, Rulfo worked briefly with the vast Papaloapan irrigation project near Veracruz. For a time he tried script-writing for the movies and some TV work in Guadalajara, and since 1962 has been with the Instituto Nacional Indigenista, an organization that compares in a general way with the U.S. Bureau of Indian Affairs.

Luis Harss gives us a vivid picture of Rulfo at his work with the Instituto:

> It is tiring and depressing work that keeps him constantly on the move. He disappears for days at a time on some lonely mission into the misty backlands, and returns looking haggard, as if back from a lost weekend. Every trip is an added blow to him. On off days he sits humped over his desk in his antiseptic office on an upper floor of the Institute, starting every time the phone rings anywhere in the building and reaching for the receiver next to him as if the call were always for him. He is forever under the pressures of waiting. At any moment he might jump up and vanish. . . . Visitors who catch him on the way out, suddenly unavoidable, become honored guests. He makes an endless bustle, opening doors and pulling out chairs for them, excruciatingly shy, gazing at them out of frightened eyes. Installed at his desk in his dark suit, kneading his nervous hands, looking perpetually worried and disoriented, he is like a harried village priest at the end of a long day. . . .

Yet it seems clear that Rulfo has been influenced little if at all by the several work experiences we have enumerated. Profoundly affected by his early years, he has never been able to shake the solitude he knew then, both in the orphanage and elsewhere. His inwardness and reticence seem to be characteristics of the poor country people of southern Jalisco. Of them, Rulfo himself has said: "Their vocabulary is very spare. In fact, they practically don't speak at all." The desolation and abandonment and sadness of this region left a vivid and haunting impression on his mind. It is this—and all of this—that provides the setting, the motivation, and the tone throughout Juan Rulfo's two published works.

If Rulfo has trouble in putting his thoughts on paper to suit him, he likewise is slow to begin talking. In June 1965, when he was to appear in a series of informal talks by writers about themselves, Rulfo asked that Juan José Arreola, his long-time friend, come and sit beside him to help him get started. Arreola was born in the same year and the same part of Jalisco as Rulfo and is himself one of Mexico's foremost writers, principally of the short story. With his friend nudging him on, Rulfo gradually opened up. As is usual when he does so, he ranged back into the past of his Jalisco birth ground.

This sort of thing—the history of southern Jalisco all the way back to the days of the conquistadores and of the prominent families of the area—obviously fascinates Rulfo. It is a part of his abiding preoccupation with the past. Actually, Rulfo has devoted a lot of time in an attempt to track down information on his ancestors and other families of his region. This effort has taken him to various libraries, banks, and museums in different parts of Mexico and as far north as California.

Rulfo's first novel was never published. He admits that he finally destroyed the manuscript, which was about life in Mexico City. Of this initial venture into writing and its aftermath, Rulfo tells us that it had "a somewhat rhetorical style" which he knew wasn't really the way he wanted to say things. "So," he continues, "practicing ways to free myself of all that rhetoric and bombast, I started cutting down, working with simpler characters. Of course I went over to the opposite extreme, into complete simplicity. But that was because I was using characters like the country people of Jalisco, who speak a pure brand of sixteenth-century Spanish."

Then he tried his hand at the short story. It was some ten years, at one or two stories a year, before he had enough for his one collection, titled—after one of the stories—***El llano en llamas (The Burning Plain and Other Stories),*** published in 1953. Here are fifteen of his stories, not all that he has written but most of them. Few though they are, they have been enough to give Rulfo an influence on the Mexican short story equal to what he achieved in the novel with ***Pedro Páramo.*** With regard to this collection, Luis Harss has written some rather poetic but very apt comments about Rulfo and his work:

> Rulfo is a man attuned to the primitive poetry of desert landscapes, dusty sunlit villages, seasonal droughts and floods, the humble joys of the harvest, the hard labor of poor lives lived out always close to plague and famine. His language is as frugal as his world, reduced almost to pure heartbeat. He has no message. He sings the swan song of blighted regions gangrened by age, where misery has opened wounds that burn under an eternal midday sun, where a pestilent fate has turned areas that were once rolling meadows and grasslands into fetid graves. . . . His theme is simply human sorrow in dispossession. He writes with a sharp edge, carving each word out of hard rock, like an inscription on a tombstone.

The reader is caught up in these stories of ***El llano en llamas*** and becomes an active participant, not through interiorization, density, or deliberate secretiveness . . . , but rather through the stark simplicity and directness, the somewhat astounding talent of Rulfo for relating his story in a way so faithful to the environment that the reader sees, hears, and feels everything as if he were physically present.

As an example we can cite **"Nos han dado la tierra" ["They have given us land"]**, a satire on the land-reform program of the ruling Revolutionary Party. Narrated in the first person by one of the campesinos, the story points up the fact that the distribution of land can sometimes be no more than a cruel jest. In this case four campesinos have been given a "generous" parcel of land, the only drawback being that it is all on the plain rather than down near the river where the water is to be had. As we walk across the plain with them, we experience in a vivid manner the reality they are living: the searing and unrelieved heat; the blinding glare; their parched, dehydrated state after hours of walking the plain; the desolation of the land, completely without trees or vegetation and so baked as not even to be dusty; the extreme dryness of their mouths; the sweltering frustration of it all. "So much land, for nothing," says our narrator. The starkness of everything, together with the simpleness of thought and word, magnify by contrast the cynical insistence of the agrarian administrator that they are getting preferential treatment.

In 1955, while still enjoying the recognition and popularity gained through ***El llano en llamas,*** Rulfo published ***Pedro Páramo.*** This work shot him into a foremost spot among Mexican and Spanish-American writers, a position he still retains. ***Pedro Páramo*** as a novel has evident kinship with the stories of the earlier volume. There is the same landscape, the same atmosphere, the same sparse language and overall brevity. Some of the characters could move easily from one book to the other and fit perfectly in either place. But obviously there is the difference too that here, instead of a series of stories, we have a plot revolving around the one central character, Pedro Páramo.

On first reading ***Pedro Páramo*** can be one of the most difficult and confusing works imaginable, especially if the reader has no advance knowledge about the story and its structure. A second and a third reading will bring the reward of seeing its complexity and obscurity dissolve into clarity if the reader has acquired the key for understanding. And the key is that Rulfo has done away with time. The living and the dead seem to mingle freely and dialogue casually. There is no way to tell the ones from the others. Later it appears that all the characters are dead and are talking among themselves about their days among the living. This somewhat startling discovery orients the reader perhaps more than anything else. Even so, the reading of ***Pedro Páramo*** is a challenging exercise.

This story of a local *cacique* named Pedro Páramo starts around the turn of the century and moves on through the Revolution and the Cristero revolt and beyond. When his father is murdered the young Pedro gives up being a playboy and begins to exact revenge on the village of Comala and all the area and its people. He makes himself the boss, the big landholder, the law. Nobody is spared and no method is too low if it adds to his power. To avoid paying off large debts left by his father, Pedro marries Dolores Preciado but soon his disinterest in her is such that she leaves him for good. He continues his ruthless way as lord of his estate, the "Media Luna," and ruler of the region until the Revolution comes, and then Pedro assumes that same role of opportunist that Mariano Azuela observed on all sides to his intense disgust. Like a character from an Azuela novel, Pedro Páramo professes to embrace the Revolution solely to save his own hide and his possessions.

The one thing Pedro Páramo wants and can't have is his childhood sweetheart, Susana San Juan. Her mother dies and she moves to other parts with her father. Yet Pedro remembers her, relives moments spent together, yearns for her. Clearly, she is a symbol of what he has lost: innocence, youth, love. There is also something Pedro has but can't keep. Of the several sons he has fathered, Pedro has eyes only for Miguel, who, still in his teens, has killed a man and violated many a girl. One night, riding off on his usual round of adventure, Miguel is thrown by his horse and fatally injured. Since Death knows no bribe, Pedro Páramo is helpless in the face of this blow. Other than the departure of Susana, this is the only setback he has known that can not be reversed by his money, his power, or his ruthlessness.

After many years of longing for Susana, it seems he is to get his wish. A deal is made whereby her father, now broken and in poverty, comes back to be maintained by Pedro Páramo, and Susana becomes Pedro's wife. But they don't live happily ever after. Susana, always a strange girl existing on the outer fringe of sanity, has grown worse with time and abuse by her father. Moreover, she has no love for Pedro Páramo and increasingly calls for Florencio, whom she loved in her adolescent years (before Pedro had him killed). When Susana dies, Pedro orders that the church bells be rung for three days without cessation, in his grief and frustration at losing the one prized possession he never really had. Then, angered at observing in the village a spirit of festivity while the bells are still ringing, he vows: "I will cross my arms and Comala will die of hunger." It is a threat which he carries out.

Such is the story of ***Pedro Páramo,*** though the reader will be hard pressed to string together even this broad resume the first time through. For it is not presented in a neat chronological manner, but is given to the reader a bit at a time (there are no chapters, just a series of short sections). He must pick up little items here and there and try to fit them together, taking clues from gossip, rumors, thoughts, dialogue between the living and the dead—or between the dead harking back to different moments when they were living. Rulfo describes how he came to this approach: "I imagined the character. I saw him. Then, wondering how to handle him, I logically thought of a ghost town. And, of course, the dead live outside space and time. That gave me freedom to do what I wanted with the characters. I could have them come in, then simply fade out."

The trouble is that on many occasions Rulfo makes a point of not identifying who is speaking. Gradually one becomes more adept in determining these and other unknowns, for there is always some clue if it can only be recognized. Another puzzling factor is that Rulfo, perhaps necessarily, shifts the narrative viewpoint around a good bit, which is always a little upsetting.

A summary of the first portions will give a close-up view of the unique way in which Rulfo lays out the story. In the first section we find Juan Preciado approaching the village of Comala. Juan is the narrator and tells how he promised his dying mother, Dolores, that he would find Pedro Páramo and demand redress for Pedro's neglect of her. Juan meets a muleteer named Abundio, who says he also is a son of Pedro Páramo. Abundio adds that in the village they will be glad to see someone after so many years. Juan comments that the village seems to be abandoned, and Abundio replies: "It's not that it just seems that way. That's the way it is. Nobody lives here." When Juan asks, "What about Pedro Páramo?" Abundio says: "Pedro Páramo died many years ago."

Told by the muleteer to look for Eduviges Dyada, Juan is directed by a shadowy female figure (who appears, disappears, and reappears) to a certain house, where doña Eduviges meets him and remarks, to Juan's growing mystification, that his mother, Dolores, had told her he would come on this very day. There follows a section in which a young lad (only later can we identify him as Pedro Páramo) is daydreaming about Susana. A few pages later Eduviges reveals that Abundio also is dead, and when Juan looks more closely at Eduviges herself he realizes that her face is transparent as if lacking blood, her hands are withered and wrinkled, and her eyes can't be seen.

Later, doña Eduviges hears a horse galloping in the night—although Juan hears nothing—and identifies it as the horse of Miguel Páramo, roaming restlessly in search of its master. Then she tells how Miguel met his death on a night escapade. The two pages which follow tell how young Pedro's father was murdered, although nowhere is either actually identified. The somewhat pathetic figure of the village priest, Padre Rentería, next enters the story as he resists giving the blessing and final pardon at the funeral of Miguel Páramo; after all, Miguel was thought to have killed the padre's brother and violated his niece. The padre's inner struggle is heightened by his realization that it is only through the monetary support of Pedro Páramo that he is able to eat.

Damiana Cisneros, who had been Juan's nursemaid at birth, appears at his room in Eduviges's house and asks him to come and stay at her place, adding that poor Eduviges must still be wandering the earth in penance. A series of sections then show us Pedro Páramo and his scheming administrator, Fulgor Sedano, at work, specifically in the case of planning Pedro's marriage with Dolores for the sake of erasing large debts. We also are privy to Fulgor's amazement at finding the hitherto worthless Pedro so sharp and ambitious—and grasping. Walking across the deserted town, Damiana tells Juan not to be scared if he hears echoes in Comala, for it is filled with the echoes of departed souls still wandering the earth. She herself hears them all the time. When Juan asks her if she is alive, he is suddenly completely alone in the empty street. But he continues to hear voices, all revealing bits of the Pedro Páramo story: how he seized the lands of others, how Filoteo Arechiga's job was to find young girls to sleep with Pedro, and so on.

Juan is invited into a house where a man and woman (actually brother and sister living in incestuous relationship) let him sleep the night. Juan asks if they are dead. The woman smiles, the man looks at him seriously and says he is drunk. The woman thinks he is only scared. At dawn Juan hears them talking:

> From time to time I heard the sound of the words, and I noticed the difference. Because the words I had heard until then, and only then I realized it, didn't have any sound; they didn't sound, they were felt, but without sound, like the words we hear during dreams.

If this gives Juan the notion they really are among the living, other things which are said or which occur in this long and important section merely leave him in greater doubt, confusion, and fear. The woman tells him of the crowd of spirits that roam the streets by night, and later she calls it a pure wandering of people who died without pardon and for whom there is no way of getting it. By midnight of his second night in this house, Juan Preciado feels that he has to go out into the street to find air he can breathe.

> There was no air. I had to suck in the same air that escaped from my mouth, by stopping it with my hands before it went away. I felt it going and coming, always less of it; until it became so thin that it filtered through my fingers forever.
>
> I say forever.

> I recall having seen something like foamy clouds swirling above my head and then of rinsing myself in that foam and of losing myself in all that cloudiness. It was the last thing I saw.

What appears to be logically the second half of the book (although there is no division or special indication of this in the physical format) begins at this point. From now on we have a sort of reverse focus as Juan Preciado speaks from his grave next to the old woman Dorotea, who in life was right in the middle of the whole Pedro Páramo picture. In fact, she was enlisted by Miguel Páramo to be his procuress. Susana is buried near them and they hear her thoughts and those of many others as the story of Pedro Páramo continues, piece by piece, to fill out the chronological sequence we already have presented. It even seems possible that Juan has been dead all along, in which case the first half of the book really was a case of his relating to Dorotea his arrival and stay in Comala and of his listening to the words, or thoughts, of the other souls buried near him as they recalled moments from life. Many of these are souls in anguish and, if they aren't exactly turning over in their graves, at least they are restless and squirming and remembering.

An interesting technique employed by Rulfo is that of returning several times to the same incident, but from different perspectives, so that it becomes well-rounded and the principal character of the episode assumes added dimension. The best example of this is the death of Miguel Páramo, which we see or hear discussed in four separate scenes. By the end of this we have a rather complete picture of the event and its implications in various lives.

And yet as we read—and reread—***Pedro Páramo,*** we are aware that none of the figures in the story is developed exactly as we would expect in more conventional works. Not even Pedro Páramo himself, who in the aggregate clearly dominates the story, emerges as a flesh-and-blood person we could recognize if we met him on the street. And of course it is not intended that we should. After all, Pedro is dead and we see him only in a kind of afterworld way of recreating him: hazy, vague, less than three-dimensional, compounded of certain thoughts and memories of his own, rumor and comments about him by others, and something very much like myth. It is pertinent to point out the apparent symbolism intended by Rulfo in the choice of the name Páramo. The word *páramo* means "bleak or barren land," and its aptness in this case is surely apparent.

Almost as certainly as we can affirm that the true protagonist of [Agustín Yáñez's] *Al filo del agua* is Yáñez's village, we can conclude that Rulfo intends death to be the real protagonist of ***Pedro Páramo*** in the final analysis. Death is the overriding truth and presence in the story. We recall the line from Yáñez's "Acto preparatorio" saying that in his village the people had no other ambition than to go on living until the hour of a good death arrived. Here death has prevailed—even when these people were living, we might say—and it is evident that in few cases was it a good death. In this connection it is well to recall Joseph Sommer's comment [in his *After the Storm,* 1968] that "the very substance of ***Pedro Páramo*** is fashioned from the concept, current in the folk belief of rural Mexico, of 'ánimas en pena'—souls in pain, condemned to roam the earth, separated from their corporeal origins."

While ***Pedro Páramo*** is definitely not in imitation of *Al filo del agua,* it does not seem improper to say that ***Pedro Páramo*** carries the Mexican novel a step farther down the road. Some elements in the two works are in contrast: density and length in *Al filo del agua,* relatively few details and overall brevity in ***Pedro Páramo;*** full-bodied characterization of a number of figures in the former, as compared with no well-delineated character in the latter; the rich, poetic, artistic language of Yáñez, and the extreme simplicity of the folk language of Rulfo; the tense, pressurized, guilt-conscious town portrayed by Yáñez, alongside the much more relaxed though *cacique*-dominated village of Comala. Interior monologue plays a large role in *Al filo del agua,* together with a psychological probing in depth of the subconscious. In ***Pedro Páramo*** we may say that there is inner dialogue from the grave, and although psychology is of much less importance in this work, the whole story is narrated on the plane of the subconscious.

On the other hand, these two momentous novels coincide in some aspects. Each strives—and successfully—to create artistically an image of the rural reality in the same part of Mexico in the early years of the present century. Both books demand a high degree of reader involvement, more than any other Mexican novel up to their time. In achieving this, both Yáñez and Rulfo resort to the *hermetismo buscado* or sought-after confusion which forces the reader to look for clues, analyze everything, and make connections, in the manner of a literary detective.

As I see it, the extra step which ***Pedro Páramo*** takes is Rulfo's negating of time and thereby more or less equating the natural and the supernatural, the living and the dead. He obviously is not the first writer to explore the supernatural and to give the dead a voice, but I know of no other modern novel that tells all or nearly all of its story from the grave. This is not something that is interesting merely because it is out of the ordinary. It is a daring concept, and it took unusual narrative skill to bring it off. In doing so Rulfo scores a signal success. Pedro himself is, of course, representative of a very common breed in the Mexican novel, but Rulfo's vision and treatment save him from being commonplace.

Naturally, ***Pedro Páramo*** was soon translated into various other languages (a total of seventeen up to now) and, as might be expected, the Mexican film industry was interested in the success attained by the novel. It was made into an ambitious movie in 1966, with the screen adaptation handled by Carlos Fuentes. For the exterior scenes they found a town in the state of Guanajuato which in recent years has dwindled in size from 40,000 people to barely a thousand. But in the film the story is allowed to unfold in chronological order before the eyes of Juan Preciado when he reaches Comala. This would seem to negate much of the value possessed by the novel. Apparently Rulfo felt the same way about it, for he is quoted [in *Tiempo* (19 December 1966)] as saying that they made ***Pedro Páramo*** into a sort of "western" which has no relation to the spirit of his work.

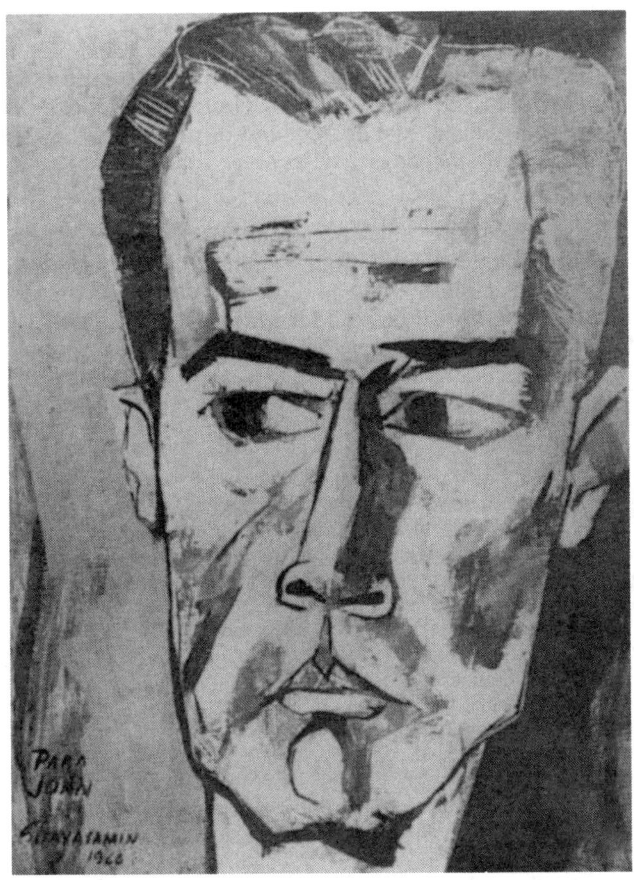

Portrait of Rulfo by Oswaldo Guayasamín.

Will we ever have more Rulfo works to enjoy and discuss? In the face of a publishing silence lasting nearly fifteen years and of the seeming psychological block which besets him, it would be easy to predict that Rulfo's significant literary output ended with the publication of ***Pedro Páramo*** in 1955. I believe, however, that he will one day release *La cordillera.* It is also known that he was working on some short narrative pieces which he promised to publish soon under the title of *Días sin floresta,* and there is mention too of another novel, called *La vena de los locos.* It is greatly to be hoped that this splendid novelist will return with other works as stimulating as ***Pedro Páramo.*** (pp. 90-101)

Walter M. Langford, "Juan Rulfo, Novelist of the Dead," in his The Mexican Novel Comes of Age, *University of Notre Dame Press, 1971, pp. 88-102.*

Lanin A. Gyurko (essay date Autumn 1972)

[*In the following essay, Gyurko examines ways in which the structure and themes of* Pedro Páramo *were prefigured by Rulfo's earlier stories, collected in* The Burning Plain, and Other Stories.]

The fictional world of the contemporary Mexican author Juan Rulfo is one of reduction and denial. Character is stripped of external appearance and splintered into existential shards; plot is inconsequential or nonexistent; action decelerates into stasis. Narrative continuity is fragmented into bits of dialogue and truncated memories. Structural disintegration reflects the physical and moral dissolution of the universe. Man is reduced to a voice and sometimes to a mere echo.

The most profound expression of Rulfo's nihilism is his first and only novel to date, ***Pedro Páramo,*** which depicts a nightmare of suffering founded upon the violent existence of a Mexican *cacique.* The somber vision of the novel is prefigured in the author's collection of short stories, ***El llano en llamas.*** Three stories in particular presage the hellworld of Comala: **"Macario," "El hombre,"** and **"Luvina."** The pathetic idiot boy Macario creates within his conscience a psychic purgatory that adumbrates the world of lost souls in ***Pedro Páramo.*** Narrative devices in **"El hombre,"** including the rupture of chronological sequence through flashbacks and premonitions, rapid alternations in point of view, and the juxtaposition of strips of interior monologue from various consciousnesses, prefigure the intricate structural techniques of the novel. The town of Luvina with its muted, stagnant life anticipates the ghost town of Comala. In both short stories and novel the frequent use of first-person narrative underscores the solipsistic nature of Rulfo's universe. Characters are unable to sustain meaningful relationships with one another; they retreat into private worlds of revery and fantasy.

In **"Macario,"** the reader is plunged into the disturbed mind of the protagonist, who is stationed near a drainpipe waiting to kill the frogs whose croaking disturbs the sleep of his godmother. Throughout the story there is no external action. Macario remains silent and inert, seemingly suspended in time. The entire drama is played out on the stage of his psyche. The object of the narrative is to evoke a mood of helplessness and fear, as the idiot sits trapped within his stricken conscience. His thinking is graphic, simplistic, and reiterative. Mental life is expressed in short spurts of thought, often devoid of logic. The result is weird and startling:

> Las ranas son verdes de todo a todo, menos en la panza. Los sapos son negros. También los ojos de mi madrina son negros.

Macario's primitive mind blends the animal with the human. The effect is to cast the shadow of grotesqueness on his exploitative grandmother, who is dehumanized by being juxtaposed with a toad. The old woman implants within the idiot's conscience the spectre of condemnation to hell for crimes he is not even sure he has committed. In order to bind Macario in a servile relationship, the godmother plays upon his superstitious simplemindedness, which blows up her threats into an obsessive vision of suffering:

> Y entonces le pedirá, a alguno de toda la hilera de santos que tiene en su cuarto, que mande a los diablos por mí, para que me lleven a rastras a la condenación eterna . . .

Like most of Rulfo's characters, Macario is conscious of the futility of his efforts to satisfy his desires. The sole figure to provide him with comfort and consolation is Felipa, the servant girl, who shares her food with him and even gives him the milk of her breast:

> Por eso quiero yo a Felipa, porque yo siempre tengo hambre y no me lleno nunca, ni aun comiéndome la comida de ella. Aunque diga uno que se llena comiendo, yo sé bien que no me lleno por más que coma todo lo que me den.

Through his insatiable consumption of food Macario attempts to alleviate not only a physical hunger but a spiritual one as well. Afflicted by a gnawing sense of guilt, he looks to the prayers of Felipa as his only means of salvation. But the relief that the memory of the girl affords him is soon replaced by a feeling of dread based on the certainty of his damnation.

Like Macario, the characters of ***Pedro Páramo*** cling to the fragile illusion of redemption. Throughout their lives the inhabitants of Comala are condemned to a purgatorial existence in a land that has been poisoned by Páramo's greed and hate. Death does not bring an end to their suffering but only an extension of it. From beyond the grave they continue to be afflicted by the tantalizing vision of a paradise from which they are forever excluded.

The inferno of Comala with its swarm of guilt-ridden consciousnesses is foreshadowed by the bizarre, ominous world of Macario, who refuses to light a torch for fear that his sins will discover him. The death-in-life anguish of the idiot boy presages the life-in-death agony of the souls in Comala. Like the bodies confined to their tombs, Macario is forced to dwell in a fixed space. His survival is constantly threatened by the stonings and beatings of the villagers, who drive him from the street into his darkened hovel. But solitude, instead of providing a refuge, only exacerbates his torment. External persecution is replaced by mental self-torture.

The idiot's life of quiet desperation, his helplessness before forces that he can neither comprehend nor subdue, and his almost total estrangement from the outside world, are intensified through the form of his narrative, a first-person direct interior monologue that focuses on the inner self. Macario struggles vainly to ward off a fate that pursues him through an assault on his conscience. Ironically, the destiny he fears so much is self-exacerbated. The idiot boy creates within himself the hell of existence that he fervently hopes to avoid. His character has become his fate. The same self-perpetuated psychic hellworld characterizes Pedro Páramo and Susana San Juan, both victims of their own obsessive fantasies. Comala, on one level a ghost town of deserted streets and abandoned houses, is, for the spirits that are doomed to haunt it, a tortured state of mind. Hell for Rulfo is not a flaming world of external punishment but an inner world of mental anguish.

As an impotent figure—a mere congeries of psychic states—Macario foreshadows the listless form of the aged Pedro Páramo, who after the death of Susana abandons his empire, worthless to him after the person for whom he has constructed it is irrevocably lost. The once aggressive and powerful *cacique* now subordinates himself entirely to the memory of Susana. Oblivious to external reality, he attempts to restore his lost love through the only mode now left to him—the psychic realm of memory and imagination. In their brooding passivity and suffering, the decrepit Páramo and the idiot Macario are one. At the end of his narrative, the thoughts of the boy circle back to the lyric memory of Felipa, just as the mind of the *cacique,* like a needle on a broken record, obsessively reiterates the theme of Susana San Juan.

In both short story and novel, time as chronological progression dissolves into temporal nullity. Just as the boundaries between the animal and the human, the concrete and the abstract, are all blurred for Macario, so also are past and present jumbled together within his defective consciousness. Events seem to occur in an extended present. Experience is presented as isolated fragments of the past, hazily recalled, free-floating within his psyche:

> Sin embargo, lo de tener la cabeza así de dura es la gran cosa. Uno da de topes contra los pilares del corredor horas enteras y la cabeza no se hace nada, aguanta sin quebrantarse. Y uno da de topes contra del suelo, primero despacito, después más recio y aquello suena como un tambor. Igual que el tambor que anda con la chirimía, cuando viene la chirimía a la función del Señor. Y entonces uno está en la iglesia, amarrado a la madrina, oyendo afuera el tum tum del tambor . . .

The associational flux of his consciousness finds a parallel in the chaotic narrative movement of ***Pedro Páramo.*** The welter of images within the idiot's monologue becomes translated in the novel into a bewildering succession of characters and incidents. Structurally, the novel is fragmented into sixty-five segments. Temporally, there is an oscillating movement, from the eternal present of the tomb to the remote and recent past of Pedro Páramo. Time, place, narrative perspective, and style are all changed abruptly and repeatedly to portray a noncausal universe. The art of Rulfo consists of a deliberate and masterful construction of a world in chaos.

In order to make the meanderings of Macario's consciousness meaningful to the reader, Rulfo unifies the dislocated images through adherence to a single point of view. Every image serves to reveal the psychic identity of the protagonist. Even though point of view in ***Pedro Páramo*** is constantly shifting, the narrative fragments are unified through the dominant presence of the *cacique.* During Páramo's life his shadow falls over the whole of Comala; after his death he lives on as an indelible memory in the psychic remnants of those whom he has victimized or who suffer guilt for having collaborated with him.

Condensation, understatement, and allusion are hallmarks of Rulfo's art. Beneath the images of Macario's narrative lie worlds of unexplained sordidness and suffering. He remarks that Felipa will soon go to heaven, but the statement is left unelaborated. He later makes a single brief reference to his parents in purgatory. The image is sufficient to conjure up a universe of hereditary sin. Likewise the narrative of Juan Preciado evokes myriad histories of unredeemed sinners like the suicide Eduviges Dyada, the incestuous couple Donis and his sister, and the procuress Dorotea.

A structural and thematic prefiguration of the novel is found in **"El hombre,"** a story of relentless pursuit and blood vengeance in which reality is portrayed in shifting panels of objective and psychic narrative. Surface action, that depicts the tracking down and slaying of Jose Alcancía by Urquidi to avenge the murder of his family, is underlaid by another pursuit—the assault of guilt and remorse upon the consciences of both hunter and hunted. **"El hombre"** is related from multiple perspectives, including the first-person direct interior monologues of Alcancía and Urquidi, third-person omniscient author portrayal of setting and surface action, and the first-person narrative of the shepherd, an author-witness whose recounting before a tribunal of the death of Alcancía completes the story. All three perspectives are united thematically through their focus on the controlling incident—the treacherous slaughter in cold blood of Urquidi's innocent family.

Although the outcome of the pursuit is foreshadowed from the beginning, dramatic tension is maintained through constant shifting in time and point of view. Time oscillates between present and past. The initial paragraph describes the flight of Alcancía away from the scene of his crime. In the second paragraph, point of view shifts to the monologue of Urquidi, also in the narrative present. But in the three ensuing paragraphs time is past. The omniscient author flashes back to concentrate on the steps of Alcancía as he approaches Urquidi's house, resolved to kill the man who has slain his brother:

> El hombre caminó . . . deteniéndose en cada horizonte para medir su fin: *"No el mío, sino el de él"*, dijo.

The monologue of Alcancía is italicized, to distinguish it from the thoughts of Urquidi. This technique and the use of the epithetic phrases "el hombre" for Alcancía and "el que lo seguía," "el que lo perseguía," and "el perseguidor" for Urquidi, are the only devices used to mark changes in point of view. Just as the name of Juan Preciado is not made known until well within his narrative, that of José Alcancía is not mentioned until halfway through the story, when he is mentally addressed by his pursuer. Urquidi's name is also revealed indirectly, through the testimony of the shepherd: "¿Dice usted que mató a toditita la familia de los Urquidi?" The points at which time shifts are not indicated by the omniscient author. The reader himself must piece together the temporal sequence from the antiphonal pattern of narrative structuring. From a focus on Alcancía as he steels himself for the murder, point of view shifts back to Urquidi who is tracking the fugitive. Time has changed once more; we are again in the narrative present. Chronological time is erased in order to present a simultaneity of experience. Details of Alcancía's grisly crime are evoked through flashbacks in the minds of both men. The slaughter of Urquidi's family is depicted not as an isolated and objectified part of the past, but as an everpresent reality within the conscience—a psychic wound incapable of healing.

Páramo's career of vengeance and exploitation is also evoked in fragments of memory divorced from time as linear progression. Within the novel, several psychic narratives are projected in isolation, without introductory explanation by the omniscient author. The narrative of Preciado is interrupted by interpolations that depict the adolescence of Pedro Páramo. Dolores Preciado's impressions of Comala are presented as involuntary memories within the monologue of Juan. As in **"El hombre,"** italics are used to distinguish the recollections of Dolores from those of her son.

In both short story and novel, depth of character is achieved through the evocation of the principal figures from multiple points of view. The omniscient author in **"El hombre"** maintains a detached viewpoint that contrasts the external roles of hunter and hunted. Initial focus on the tracks made by the clambering feet of the fugitive reduces him to the status of a hunted animal. Alcancía loses his identity; the hunter forces him to assume the role of the hunted. Causality is reversed; instead of the pursuer patterning his movements upon those of his prey, it is the victim who is inescapably bound to the will of the hunter. Alcancía himself recognizes the futility of his quest for self-preservation: "Camino y camino y no ando nada." His flight leads him into the trap that becomes his coffin.

In contrast to the objective narrative of the omniscient author is the testimony of the shepherd, who depicts the pursued man in a sympathetic light, not knowing at the time of his encounter with Alcancía that he is a murderer. The author-witness notes the emaciated appearance of the fugitive and is moved by the man's expression of concern for his family. Alcancía is also humanized through his first-person stream of consciousness narrative, that endows him with an inner dimension. Instead of a mere target of a hunter's bullet, he becomes a complex figure, with a range of feelings, from anxiety to defensive cynicism.

A similar contrast between brutality and sensitivity is found in the life of Pedro Páramo. The dichotomy in the *cacique*'s nature, like that within Alcancía, is conveyed through a variation in style, tone, and point of view. Omniscient-author narrative depicts Páramo as a ruthless despot. But interior monologue reveals an emotional sensibility of which his destructive acts and cynical speech give no inkling. The aged *cacique* recalls himself as a young boy imagining Susana or grieving over her absence:

> El aire nos hacía reír; juntaba la mirada de nuestros ojos, mientras el hilo corría entre los dedos detrás del viento, hasta que se rompía con un leve crujido como si hubiera sido trozado por las alas de algún pájaro. Y allá arriba, el pájaro de papel caía en maromas arrastrando su cola de hilacho, perdiéndose en el verdor de la tierra.

The relationship between Páramo and Susana is as tenuous as that between the kite and its string. In its flight heavenward, the kite represents the aspirations of Páramo, his striving toward the ideal. But Susana is as elusive as the fragile paper bird that slips from his grasp and is lost forever.

Within the novel psychic narrative is often suffused with a lyric quality. An intimate experience or emotion is made more intense by being converted into a poem. Through stream-of-consciousness soliloquy, Páramo's love for Susana is expressed with beauty and poignancy. In contrast to the hell of existence that he has fashioned for the inhabitants of Comala, the *cacique* creates a heaven around the memory of Susana:

> Fue la última vez que te vi. Pasaste rozando con tu cuerpo las ramas del paraíso que está en la vereda y te llevaste con tu aire sus últimas hojas. Luego desapareciste. Te dije, "¡Regresa, Susana!"

The interior monologue of the bereaved father Urquidi is also imbued with a lyric tone as he recalls the lost world of innocence and tranquillity shared by his family on the night of their murder. Alcancía arrives at precisely the moment when the family is most trusting:

> Debió llegar a eso de la una, cuando el sueño es más pesado; cuando comienzan los sueños; después del "Descansen en paz", cuando se suelta la vida en manos de la noche y cuando el cansancio del cuerpo raspa las cuerdas de la desconfianza y las rompe.

The nocturnal blessing "Descansen en paz" acquires an ironic meaning. Instead of restful sleep it becomes the prelude to violent death.

The fatalism that marks ***Pedro Páramo*** has its dark roots in Rulfo's shorter narratives. Urquidi is endowed with an uncanny ability that enables him to predict the movements of his prey. The anonymity that Alcancía seeks is categorically denied him by the pursuer, who is converted into an instrument of implacable retribution. Although the panic-stricken fugitive remains totally absorbed within the self, the thoughts of Urquidi are calmly and calculatedly directed toward his victim. With morbid meticulousness the hunter determines the exact manner in which his quarry will die, a prediction later confirmed by the shepherd. From initial reference to Alcancía in the third person, Urquidi abruptly shifts to the second person of direct address, as he imagines the fugitive present before him. The effect is to negate time by merging present and future in dramatic anticipation of the confrontation:

> Terminaré de subir por donde subió; después bajaré por donde bajó, rastreándole hasta cansarlo. Y donde yo me detenga, allí estará. Se arrodillará y me pedirá perdón. Y yo le dejaré ir un balazo en la nuca . . . Eso sucederá cuando yo te encuentre.

For the hunted man, frantically seeking an escape route while it is still day, time is measured in agonizing moments. For the avenger, time is inconsequential. The destiny of his victim is irrevocable; the exact moment of retribution is unimportant. What perturbs Urquidi is the significance of his act. He does not kill in triumph or with satisfaction, but out of necessity. He must obey the rigorous code that demands the removal of the stain on his honor. But the death of Alcancía cannot compensate him for the loss of his family or mitigate his biting feelings of inadequacy. The memory of his dead son continues to afflict his conscience. The father reproaches himself for his inability to protect his family at the hour when they most need him.

Fatalism takes many forms in Rulfo's short stories. In **"Nos han dado la tierra"** it is a political force against which the *campesinos* are powerless. Deprived of horses and rifles, their only means of defense, they are compelled to accept the wasteland that the government has given them to cultivate. In **"Es que somos muy pobres"** poverty and natural disasters like the flood that sweeps away the remnants of family livelihood make the young girl Tacha's recourse to prostitution inevitable. The genetic determinism found in **"Macario"** also is a factor in the sordid life of Urbano Gómez, the protagonist of **"Acuérdate"**: "Quizá entonces se volvió malo, o quizá ya era de nacimiento." Heredity also plays a role at the end of **"El llano en llamas,"** when El Pichón, a revolutionary turned outlaw, is finally released from prison. He confronts the girl whom he had abducted years before and who now shames him into acknowledging the paternity of her child:

> Y el muchacho se quitó el sombrero. Era igualito a mí y con algo de maldad en la mirada. Algo de eso tenía que haber sacado de su padre.

Oppressive fate weighs upon all the characters of ***Pedro Páramo.*** The impulsiveness and recalcitrance of the adolescent Pedro foreshadow his adult personality. His fate is ominously prophesied by his grandmother: "— . . . Siento que te va a ir mal, Pedro Páramo." The sins of the father are visited upon the *cacique*'s offspring. Fearful of the consequences of raising the illegitimate child who he believes carries the bad blood of the *cacique,* Rentería quickly relinquishes the infant after Páramo's surprising acknowledgment of paternity. The priest thereby forfeits the opportunity to exert a moral influence upon Miguel, and, ironically, fosters what he most hopes to avoid. Miguel later becomes the murderer of Rentería's brother and the seducer of his niece. Even the innocent Preciado cannot escape the consequences of his father's life. He becomes contaminated by the miasma of guilt and suffering that constitutes the *cacique*'s only legacy to his son. The pall of fatalism hangs over Susana as well. From childhood her life is marred by misfortune. Exploited by her father, crushed by the death of her mother, she succumbs to permanent insanity upon the loss of her husband Florencio.

Together with adverse fate, the theme of unexpiated sin resounds throughout the whole of Rulfo's fictional universe. Susana San Juan, guilty of an incestuous relationship with her father, denies the possibility of salvation. She links herself with damnation and hell: "—¿Y qué crees que es la vida, Justina, sino un pecado?"; "—Yo sólo creo en el infierno." The woman who lives incestuously with her brother in Comala perceives her body as a sea of mud. Father Rentería feels guilty for truckling to the will of Páramo and for absolving the soul of Miguel not out of Christian charity but in return for the *cacique*'s gold. The hypocritical priest later refuses absolution to the spirit of Eduviges Dyada, a suicide whose sister lacks the money to purchase her redemption. The most intense expression of guilt is found in Rulfo's short story **"Talpa."** The protagonist hastens the death of his diseased brother Tanilo in order to facilitate his illicit relationship with Natalia, Tanilo's wife. Ironically, the death serves only to drive the lovers apart. Natalia feels closer to her husband after his death than during his life. Within his guilt-stricken conscience the narrator relives the pilgrimage to Talpa, the place to which Tanilo was dragged with the promise of salvation. Like Macario, the narrator's fate has become internalized. He sits alone, isolated within a past that he cannot escape.

The fictional world of the contemporary Mexican author Juan Rulfo is one of reduction and denial. Character is stripped of external appearance and splintered into existential shards; plot is inconsequential or nonexistent; action decelerates into stasis.

—Lanin A. Gyurko

Both Alcancía and Páramo are also haunted by the memory of their crimes. The steep, tortuous path that the hunted man follows is made still more difficult by the guilt that presses down upon him like an almost palpable burden: " *'No debí matarlos a todos*—dijo el hombre—. *Al menos no a todos*'." Páramo too is troubled by the images of death, which surround him from adolescence—first that of his grandfather, then the accidental shooting of his father, and finally the myriad deaths of those upon whom he vents his desire to avenge the death of Lucas Páramo as well as his frustration over the loss of Susana. Just before the *cacique* receives notice of the death of his son Miguel, he has a premonitory vision. His conscience is flooded with the images of mangled corpses, all seeking vengeance. In the closing years of his life he is afraid not of dying but of the nightmares that continue to torment him. After the physical death of the *cacique,* his guilt-ridden conscience is externalized and perpetuated in the infernal realm of Comala.

The short story that most explicitly presages ***Pedro Páramo*** is **"Luvina."** The anonymous narrator who recounts his journey to the town and his devitalization there foreshadows the figure of Juan Preciado, who from the tomb narrates the history of his descent to Comala in search of his father. Preciado's narrative seems to be a monologue. Not until it is almost concluded does it become apparent that he is engaged in a dialogue with Dorotea, one of the unredeemed souls of Comala. The narrative situation in **"Luvina"** is similar. Although ostensibly a dialogue between a man who has left Luvina and another unidentified person soon to make the journey there, the only voice we hear is that of the narrator, whose compulsive monologue terminates only when he falls into a drunken stupor. The fate of the protagonist and most likely that of his listener as well is symbolized by that of the flying ants, which are attracted to the flame of the oil lamp that cripples them by scorching their wings.

The narrator of **"Luvina"** is drawn to the town by the same force that impels Preciado to Comala—the power of illusion. Although the former, unlike Preciado, succeeds in escaping physically from the town, he is drained of will, hope, and desire and reduced to an existential husk: "Allá viví. Allá dejé la vida. . . . " The muleteer who brings the newcomer and his family to Luvina then hastily departs "como si se alejara de algún lugar endemoniado," prefigures the mule driver Abundio who escorts Preciado down into Comala. The disorientation felt by the narrator upon being abandoned in the silent town is paralleled by the bewilderment of Preciado, who gradually loses his identity in a world of nonbeing:

> Me sentí en un mundo ajeno y me dejé arrastrar. Mi cuerpo, que parecía aflojarse, se doblaba ante todo, había soltado sus amarras y cualquiera podía jugar con él como si fuera trapo.

In the limbo realm of Luvina, the pulse of human activity is faint. Social institutions have all but vanished. The ruined church, with its dismantled altar and its stations of the cross whipped by the wind, symbolizes the spiritual desolateness of the town. The conversation between the narrator and his wife becomes a dialogue of absences: "—'¿Dónde está la fonda?'—'No hay ninguna fonda.'—'¿Y el mesón?'—'No hay ningún mesón.'" This reality of negation reaches its extreme in Comala, where Preciado knocks on a door that does not exist and is led into a furnitureless room by the spectral Eduviges.

The bleak reality of both towns is conveyed through simile, metaphor, personification, and hyperbole, figures of speech that grant a strange, poetic quality to the sites. They are removed from an earthly realm and suffused with a mythic aura. The swarm of black-robed women who glide like shadows through Luvina prefigure the eery phantoms of Comala. The mute, hermetic women who emerge from their hovels at dawn to comprise a phantasmagoric procession, are perceived by the terrified narrator as huge black bats. Preciado also is confronted by mysterious beings, like the woman who disappears "como si no existiera." Toribio Aldrete, a landowner murdered by agents of the *cacique,* is initially presented as a scream of agony perceived by Preciado. As he enters a room in Doña Eduviges' house in which Aldrete was executed years before, Juan is exposed without warning to the most terrifying moment of the victim's life—his struggling against the hangman's noose—a moment stripped of temporal limits and made eternal. The uncanny experience is only later clarified, through flashbacks developed by the omniscient author.

Even after his death, Preciado continues to dwell upon his perplexing experiences in Comala. Although the narrator of **"Luvina"** remains far away from the town, he too is mesmerized by the past. Fifteen years after his departure, he is still reliving the traumatic events of his brief stay in Luvina. The despondency that he finds there is now part of his own life. Alcohol provides only temporary relief. When the joyful shouts of the children playing nearby intrude upon his recollections, he warns them away, resenting their carefree enjoyment of life. He is oblivious to his present environment—a tranquil setting of verdant land and flowing water. His mind is riveted on the memory of the ashy gray and sterile white colors of the living cemetery that is Luvina:

> Todo el lomerío pelón, sin un árbol, sin una cosa verde para descansar los ojos; todo envuelto en el calín ceniciento. Usted verá eso: aquellos cerros apagados como si estuvieran muertos y a Luvina en el más alto, coronándolo con su blanco caserío como si fuera una corona de muerto.

Although Luvina is situated on a physical summit, the town represents a nadir of existence. The thoughts of the narrator begin affirmatively, as if he were hoping to find something of value in Luvina, but their initial promise is always negated:

> Está plagado de esa piedra gris con la que hacen la cal, pero en Luvina no hacen cal con ella ni le sacan ningún provecho. . . . la tierra de por allí es blanca y brillante como si estuviera rociada siempre por el rocío del amanecer; aunque esto es un puro decir . . .

Life is only an illusion, impossible to sustain, like the fragile poppies that bloom briefly, then shrivel into rasping husks. The wasteland of Luvina adumbrates the "páramo" or barren plain left by the *cacique* of Comala.

The same specter of fulfillment brutally undercut by a reality of living death is found in both the short story and the novel. Susana from within her grave fitfully recalls her awakening to sensual pleasure. The lyric images of a world of beauty and abundance contrast with the dampness and horror of her tomb. As a young girl, responding to the new and mysterious forces within her body, she longs to exult in the burgeoning sensuousness of nature. But her joy is restrained by the hand of death. The grotesque reality of the discolored corpse of her mother intrudes upon her erotic fantasies. The adolescent experience prefigures the tragic outcome of her marriage to Florencio. Here too the initial ecstasy of sensual desire proves ephemeral; her joy is once again truncated by death. The crone Dorotea, obsessed by a maternal desire, retreats into fantasy to escape the painful reality of her sterility. She pathetically cradles the mere illusion of a child and willingly becomes the procuress for Miguel, perhaps to compensate for her own sexless life.

In the short story, the narrator contrasts the spiritual promise of Luvina with the bleak reality he has found there: "San Juan Luvina. Me sonaba a nombre de cielo aquel nombre. Pero aquello es el purgatorio." Preciado travels to Comala with the paradisiacal image of the town acquired from Dolores, who in exile idealizes the land of her birth:

> Mi pueblo, levantado sobre la llanura. Lleno de árboles y de hojas, como una alcancía donde hemos guardado nuestros recuerdos. Sentirás que allí uno quisiera vivir para la eternidad. . . . Allí, donde el aire cambia el color de las cosas; donde se ventila la vida como si fuera un puro murmullo; como si fuera un puro murmullo de la vida . . .

Ironically, the gentle "murmullo" that for his mother is a life-giving essence is transmuted into the "murmullos"—the low moaning of souls in torment that takes Preciado's life. The fragrant smells of alfalfa and honey evoked by Dolores become for her son the rotten smell of the saponaria and the fetid odor of the urine-soaked bed belonging to the incestuous couple with whom he takes lodging. Like the protagonist of Luvina, Preciado is initially filled with optimism, in his case centered around "la esperanza que era aquel señor llamado Pedro Páramo." Both characters are brutally disillusioned.

The monotony of existence in Luvina, where the immobility of facial expression reflects the paralysis of will, is broken only occasionally—and then by violence. Although the government is distant and unconcerned about improving the welfare of the town, violators of its law are brusquely summoned and swiftly executed. Like the inhabitants of Comala, who in their passivity and willingness to collaborate with the *cacique* serve to perpetuate his power, the people of Luvina submit without resistance to the government's will. Obedience to legal authority is but a part of their subservience to the wider law of tradition, that holds an unbreakable sway over their lives:

> Los hijos se pasan la vida trabajando para los padres como ellos trabajaron para los suyos y como quién sabe cuántos atrás de ellos cumplieron con su ley . . .

The confluence of the living and the dead characterizes both towns. The inhabitants of Luvina stubbornly refuse to leave the home of their ancestors. The weight of the dead smothers their potential for life. In ***Pedro Páramo,*** the living are also locked in the memory of the dead. The existence of Susana, dominated by the memory of Florencio, is reduced to the level of feverish dreams:

> "Hemos pasado un rato muy feliz, Florencio."
> Y se volvió a hundir entre la sepultura de sus sábanas.

Her retreat into self anticipates the fate of Páramo after her death. The crippled *cacique* resembles the inert figures of the old people of Luvina, vacantly staring at the rising and falling sun, waiting only for death.

In contrast to the feeble, dehumanized inhabitants of Luvina is the bizarre animation of natural forces, the blistering sun and chilling wind. Colored a funereal black by volcanic ash, the wind looms as a demonic power:

> Se planta en Luvina prendiéndose de las cosas como si las mordiera . . . uno lo oye a mañana y tarde, hora tras hora, sin descanso . . . hasta sentirlo bullir dentro de uno como si se pusiera a remover los goznes de nuestros mismos huesos.

Although the narrator perceives the wind as a destructive force—"El acabará con ustedes"—it is fatalistically endured by the townspeople, who even emphasize its positive value. The wind acts as a buffer agent to protect them from an even greater danger—the merciless heat of the sun. Concomitant with the insidious force of the elements is the awesome power of negative psychic states. In Luvina as in Comala, joy and hope are elusive but sadness and despair are indestructible.

Rulfo's vision is characterized by a circle of futility. The monologues of his characters never lead to insight, resolution, or purgation. They cannot prevail either over adverse circumstance or over their own moral weakness. They remain circumscribed by a past that absorbs the present and precludes hope of a future. And since there is no temporal flow, and no change either in the external or psychic world, there is no possibility that their destinies can be modified.

Rulfo's nihilism is expressed through a terse, incisive style. Reality is not presented all-of-a-piece or developed in a linear sequence of thought and action because such techniques would imply a logic, order, and continuity of existence absent from his world. In his short stories, he portrays lives that are muted by despair. In ***Pedro Páramo,*** disintegration is total and irreversible. The world dissolves into chaos from which there is no redemption. (pp. 451-66)

Lanin A. Gyurko, "Rulfo's Aesthetic Nihilism: Narrative Antecedents of 'Pedro Páramo'," in Hispanic Review, *Vol. 40, No. 4, Autumn, 1972, pp. 451-66.*

Julianne Burton on Rulfo's vision of Mexico in *Pedro Páramo:*

The pessimism of Rulfo's personal vision stems from his having witnessed the progressive desolation and depopulation of his native region, the destructive aftermath of the Mexican Revolution and the Cristero wars, the lives of the impoverished peasants continually sacrificed on the altar of the rich to the hypocritical cadences of revolutionary ideology. The fruits of this bitter vision of postrevolutionary Mexico are visible in the consistently negative and pessimistic implications of Rulfo's variations on traditional mythic patterns. . . . To live in Catholic, *cacique*-dominated Mexico, Rulfo suggests, is to inhabit a hell-on-earth where the distinction between life and death is blurred, where ruthless exploitation determines social interaction, and anxiety and guilt dominate the life of the spirit; where sexuality is tained, religion corrupt, and revolutionary social change blocked and bought off. Salvation—be it sexual, spiritual, or revolutionary—is precluded by the structure of life.

Julianne Burton, in her "Sexuality and the Mythic Dimension in Juan Rulfo's 'Pedro Páramo'," in Symposium, *Fall 1974.*

Gordon Brotherston (essay date 1977)

[Brotherston is an English educator, critic, and translator who has written extensively on Latin American literature. In the following excerpt, he analyzes characterization and narrative technique in Pedro Páramo *and also explains the novel's social and political background.]*

Noises. Voices. Murmurs. Distant songs:

My girl gave me a handkerchief with a hem of weeping . . .

Falsetto. As if the people singing were women.

I saw the carts go by. The oxen moving slowly. The creaking of the stones under the wheels. The men looking as though they were still asleep.

'. . . *Early every morning the village shakes as the carts go by. They come from all around, heaped up with salt-lick, maize cobs, para grass. The wheels squeak making the windows vibrate, waking people up. It's at this time of day that the ovens are opened and it smells of newly-baked bread. And the sky may suddenly fill with thunder. The rain may fall. Spring must be near. There you will get used to the cloudbursts, my son.*'

Empty carts, grinding the silence of the streets. Vanishing on the dark road of night. And the shadows. The echo of the shadows.

I made up my mind to go back. Up above me I felt the track I had come along like an open wound in the blackness of the hills.

Then someone touched me on the shoulder.

'What are you doing here?'

'I came to look for . . . ,' and I was just about to say whom when I checked myself: 'I came to look for my father.'

'Why don't you come in?'

I went in. It was a house with half the roof fallen in. The tiles on the floor. The roof on the floor. And in the other half a man and a woman.

'Aren't you dead?' I asked them.

And the woman smiled. The man looked at me seriously.

'He's drunk,' said the man.

'He's just startled,' said the woman.

There was a paraffin stove. There was a canvas bed, and a chair with her clothes on it. Because she was naked, as God cast her into the world. And he too.

'We heard someone moaning and knocking his head against our door. And there you were. What's been happening to you?'

'So many things have happened to me that I'd most like to sleep.'

'We were already asleep.'

'Let's sleep then.'

Pedro Páramo (Mexico 1955)

The person talking is the legitimate but unacknowledged son of the man after whom this novel of Rulfo's is named: Pedro Páramo. His own name (which is not revealed straight away) is Juan Preciado and he inherits it from his mother Dolores. It is she who urges him, on her death, to go to her old village, Comala, to find his father and avenge himself and her for the bad life Pedro Páramo has made for them. Her last conversations with Juan come back to him insistently, like her memories of the village as it used to be, in italicized fragments like the one above. The contrast between that lost springtime and the atmosphere Juan encounters could not be greater, and Rulfo reiterates it liturgically.

Juan's actual entry into ghostly Comala, with its half-heard, half-anonymous 'noises, voices and murmurs' is skilfully narrated. His first words in the novel show that he is already there ('I came to Comala to look for my father'). Sure details of his arrival and of any place he came from can be only fragmentarily put together. Only vague information can be gleaned from his mother's last instructions, or from his exchange with the carter (whose name we never know) who shows him the road. The same obscurity surrounds the object of his search. Answers to his questions come piecemeal and evasively from informants who themselves have nebulous identity. For many pages we know little more than what the carter says, that Pedro Páramo is 'living rancour', ('un rencor vivo'). Only when Juan gives up his endeavour and dies 'into' the village about half-way through the book does the whole story begin to come out. Then Pedro Páramo emerges as a brutal greedy man, a cacique or local potentate who murdered repeatedly to gain more land, aided by his crooked lawyer; who abused countless women, aided by an abject procuress; who maims out of insane jealousy and betrays his closest allies without a twinge of guilt, and who possesses a Darwinian instinct for political survival during the upheavals of the Mexican Revolution. His only reason for marrying Dolores Preciado, Juan's mother, had been to acquire her large estate. The only son he recognizes, not hers and illegitimate, is one closest to him in depravation, Miguel. But he is by no means a caricature: some of the most intensely lyrical passages in the novel reveal his tenderness for the lovely Susana San Juan, who rejects him, and for his son Miguel. Rather, such love as he is shown to be capable of feeling is manically limited to the very few he favours, and whose lives he spoils as much as anyone else's. His last act is his grandest. To settle an imagined affront he decides to starve Comala to death, and does so. His enduring rancour populates the village with 'sombras', shadows in the half-light, and the shades of people only half-alive, and reduces the countryside to the arid plain (*páramo*) of his own name.

While Juan Preciado enters the novel as a more or less defined character, his identity derives from little more than his reason for going to Comala, and his mother's pervasive, lyric memory. He reports few of his thoughts beyond the repeated, and never achieved, desire 'to go back'. As he wanders from ruin to ruin through weed-covered streets his 'encounters' with others are always oblique and never full enough to reassure him even of his own continuing existence. When he thinks of going back, of recovering a notional past of his own, a hand will touch him on the shoulder, or a voice from nowhere will invite him to come in, to penetrate further. In this way he becomes absorbed by Comala, and copes as an individual ever less easily with his situation. Voices, which are echoes 'locked in the hollowness of the walls or under the stones', and which 'tread on his heels', threaten increasingly to make him no more than one of themselves, they in turn being destined to fade altogether one day. His presence becomes less substantial than the disembodied dialogues which make up most of the book and which Rulfo composes with such evident mastery.

By the time Juan Preciado enters the half-ruined house of the naked couple, he is nearing the end of his existential tether. Before long he is incorporated into their company, his last, to the extent of taking the man's place; the man is the woman's brother and soon abandons the house on an obvious pretext. Finally Juan sleeps with the woman; a suffocating encounter with unredeemed clay, and for him, ultimate knowledge. 'That woman's body made of clay, caked with clay, fell apart as if it was dissolving into a pool of mud. I felt myself swimming in the sweat which poured off her, deprived of the air you need to breathe.' He goes out into the street to find relief, but finds none: 'I had to inhale the same air that left my mouth.' Anagnorisis is complete; he has come home to expire.

> I recall having seen something like foaming clouds whirling above my head and then drenching myself in that foam and being lost in its cloud. It was the last thing I saw.

From this moment on his grammatical first person vanishes from the narrative and joins the collective unconscious. The awareness of Comala as a situation, which Juan Preciado had provided as a narrative thread, becomes the more immediate responsibility of the author, who now orchestrates the voices of the village, including Juan's, to tell less elusively the tale of the bad-man Pedro Páramo. And as we hear Juan's voice emerging from a grave next to that of Dorotea, Pedro Paramo's old procuress, with Susana San Juan lying restlessly a little further off, we are faced with the disconcerting possibility that he may have been dead all along.

Once in Comala Juan Preciado can find no escape, being drawn to an ineffectual end which no amount of will or imagination can avert. For the ghosts are stronger than he, paradoxically solider, more earthy. His very appearance makes them think he is odd, 'drunk' or 'startled'. They disregard him as a casual event, a kind of soothsayer endowed perhaps with larger awareness of their general predicament, but by that very token more vulnerable, like a certain 'prophet' from Media Luna for example, who proved unable to prophesy that the local *patrón* would do him in. The ghostly voices around him permeate his being and still him. His psychic independence and his flesh alike are sapped by his surroundings, drained to the end. His search is stopped by the stasis of the village, the dazzling immobility of the *capitana* grass on the cobbled streets, the dusty smell of decay in the woman's bed ('como de orines'), the pillow stiff with old sweat, the jagged hole in the roof against the sky. Up above he may see clouds and birds move untrammelled, though even the birds must hurry before the dark 'closes their roads' as it closes his own track in the hills. He is held by the atmosphere of Comala, in its voices, shapes and smells, without escape. The movement of time itself relentlessly solidifies into the place which confines him.

With its atmosphere of suffocation and abandonment,

Comala stands as the heritage of rural Mexicans whom Rulfo has known and spent many years of his life with. The paternal gift that is Pedro Páramo's to Juan, was first made with the arrival of Cortes and the conquistadors, who brought the title 'Don' that Páramo so insists on, and the fiery stallion ridden by his pathological son Miguel. These were the men who felled the forests and killed the birds of Mexico, purposefully to make a desert, a *páramo,* which would remind them of the eroded landscape of home; who devastated the habitat of the women they allotted themselves with the same callousness with which Pedro Páramo takes his 'fistfuls of flesh'. They have been there too long to be resented simply as intruders (as, for example, Asturias's *maiceros* and *ladinos* are), or even to be conceptualized as such. That is part of Juan's problem as the 'avenger' of his mother Dolores, one of Páramo's victims. The commingling of 'cultures' has reached the point of incest, so that as a glimpse of fresh innocence Dolores is anomalous (as she is also naive and defenceless, being only too easily exploited and appropriated with her estate). Juan's task is hopeless from the start; penetration has been too deep.

The only apparent survivors of this historical catastrophe are the Indians, who later on come down from the hills with their herbs in the rain, laughing and joking amongst themselves. The freshness around them may be reminiscent of Dolores's memories, of the spring rain and the fat maize cobs recalled in turn by Juan. But Rulfo certainly does not encourage us to associate her with them, to politicize in this way. His Indians are decidedly less accessible than Altamirano's Nicolás, or than those of the artists of the Mexican Revolution. In Diego Rivera's murals, for example, Mexican Indians are depicted as the first principle of nationhood; and Gregorio López y Fuentes's novel *El indio* (1935) proposes them as a social model. The Indians in ***Pedro Páramo*** are by definition intact, beyond reach, and therefore cannot be party to Dolores's intuitions of a lost Mexican Eden. Significantly enough, these memories of hers fade entirely from the text as soon as her son 'dies' and meets his true inheritance in Comala.

The Church, the traditional source of redemption in Mexico since the traumatic arrival of Pedro Páramo's ancestors from Spain, cannot help his descendants and victims any more than the Indians in the hills can. Centuries of abuse have killed whatever virtue that institution had, so that it is no longer in the power of a rural priest to absolve even when he wants to. The spiritual guardian of Comala, Father Renteria, has so compromised himself, so consented to the evil committed by Pedro Páramo and the depraved Miguel, that he can no longer help his flock. They have all fallen from grace and live in a Dantesque purgatory with oblivion as their only future. Indeed, as Joseph Sommers has pointed out [in his *After the Storm,* 1968], the 'very substance' of ***Pedro Páramo*** is the pagan belief of Mexican folklore in 'ánimas en pena', souls condemned and unabsolved, who wander the earth bodiless, and overcome the living. One of the most explicit passages in the novel is the upbraiding Renteria receives from the diocesan authority at Contla. The problems of 'poor villages' like Comala are presented here from the outside as nowhere else in the novel. As overt political comment, this passage exposes the rawness of Rulfo's own anger at the peasants' dependence on an authority which has cynically persisted in appeasing their worst oppressors.

As an intimate of a forlorn American hinterland which holds neither glamour nor mystery, Juan Rulfo, in his one novel and his single short-story collection ***The Burning Plain*** (***El llano en llamas,*** 1953), may well be compared to Graciliano Ramos, one of the authors of the Brazilian North East. His *Barren Lives* (*Vidas secas,* 1938) conveys a sense of utter erosion by means startlingly similar to Rulfo's. He, too, familiarizes us with the basic conditions of his region by returning to the same undeniable events from more than one point of view and by dwelling on its unavoidable truths. Colours especially acquire the same elemental intensity they do with Rulfo, even to the point of detail: 'the pure bad blue of the sky'; 'the blackness of the hills'; 'the blackness of the vultures' are phrases taken from one or other book. In both novels yellow also has an elemental function, as the baleful colour of a policeman's uniform (Ramos) and a sinister bad smell (Rulfo); and the lush green paradise of Dolores evokes the one dreamt of by Ramos's character Fabiano. But we also find a crucial and most instructive difference. For Ramos does not leave the poor man of his landscape totally without hope, sucked dry as he is by his environment and his exploiters. At the end of *Barren Lives,* Fabiano gives up and goes 'back' to the town where there is a possible forum for the kind of revolutionary change Ramos believed was necessary in Brazil. Juan Preciado is not left even with that remote hope, simply because Mexico is supposed to have had its revolution already. Indeed, the failure of successive Mexican governments to put their revolutionary programmes into practice in the countryside is for Rulfo a profounder reason for anger than the weakness of the Church.

This is shown well in his short story **'They gave us the land', ('Nos han dado tierra')** which records the thoughts and conversations of a group of peasants walking over the lot apportioned to them as a result of the government's redistribution of property. The piece of plain in question is so 'hard and eroded' as to be unploughable, a point which a delegate they meet asks them to put in writing before he disappears. The hopeless lack of understanding between the politicians, good or bad, and the rural communities of Mexico (examined again recently in Gleizer's film *The Frozen Revolution*) is the bitter source of other stories in ***The Burning Plain.*** In the novel, ***Pedro Páramo,*** Mexico's revolution could hardly be presented more disenchantedly. Even during the early heroic days Páramo, the landowner, survives its challenge without too much difficulty, turning to his own advantage the ignorance and the bloodlust of the leaders and the troops who arrive, exploiting their ill-defined and shifting loyalties. They are shown as supporters now of Villa, then of Carranza, next of the Catholic Counter-Revolutionaries, in a tautly narrated confusion reminiscent of Mariano Azuela's despairing chronicle of the decade 1910-20, *The Underdogs* (*Los de abajo,* 1915), which however does not expose why rural Mexicans behave as they do. Platoons and ideologies pass through and by Comala, too little connected with it in any way to change the atmosphere which suffocates Juan Preciado.

The body of literature about the Mexican Revolution is of course formidably large. Foreign writers like D. H. Lawrence, Graham Greene, Antonin Artaud, Malcolm Lowry have responded strongly to it, each in his own way. In Mexican literature the line stretches from Azuela's *The Underdogs,* to novels like Fuentes's *The Death of Artemio Cruz* (*La muerte de Artemio Cruz,* 1962), which registers the corruption of the revolutionary leader Cruz by ideologically hostile forces, above all those of U.S. capitalism, and to Octavio Paz's famous essay *Labyrinth of Solitude* (*El laberinto de la soledad*), which traces certain psychological patterns back to the trauma of the Conquest and to pre-Columbian times. Rulfo is apparently less ambitious than this, and indeed would not disown the epithet provincial. This is precisely the source of his strength. He stems from the dry southern part of Jalisco. But we need no map to locate Comala. He no more chronicles the peculiarities of his region, unlike Agustín Yáñez, for example (whose chronicles of revolutionary Mexico are very much 'set' in the more fertile north of the same province), than he diagnoses national problems on the grand scale of Fuentes or Paz. If we want analogues for Rulfo's achievement they would sooner be found among the novelists of 'marginal', isolated communities further afield with whom he has expressed sympathy: the French-Swiss Ramuz, the Icelander Halldor Laxness and certain Scandinavians including Onetti's early model Knut Hamsun. This firm preference of his, which contrasts as if purposefully with that of many 'mainstream' Latin American authors, has in it an implicit comment of its own which some of those authors, among them Paz, have not always found to their liking.

Rulfo is immersed in provincial Mexico to the point of ultimate recognition. He is superlatively aware of how hard it is to preserve a moral or even psychic independence in that world, of the kind which guarantees Juan Preciado's individuality at least for a time (though Juan ventures no overt comments of his own), or which those anonymous 'soothsayers' have who come to a bad end. In these circumstances, rather than enforce a strong narrative line, Rulfo relies on conversation and spoken thoughts, turns of phrase which he has learned to translate and arrange with a skill comparable to Onetti's, dialogue being a supreme test. Without recourse to dialect or regional expression, Rulfo finds a mode of speech which is local, integral with its landscape. He operates more with cadence and syntax than lexically. There is a kind of grim disheartenedness in what Juan Preciado and the inhabitants of Comala say which stems partly from their refusal to conjoin or erect structures grammatically, and partly from the withdrawal implicit in their use of the undefined 'they', impersonal and modified personal particles, and in their preferring the accusative to the nominative first person (incidentally a feature of certain Mexican Indian languages). 'I came to Comala because they told me my father lived here, a certain Pedro Páramo. My mother told me.' The resignation exuded already in these opening phrases grows steadily through the book to the point of hypnosis. The closest thing in Spanish to the speech of Comala's inhabitants are the recordings made by anthropologists among rural Mexicans (including the remarkable autobiography of a Maya Indian from Chiapas, *Juan Pérez Jolote,* published three years before ***Pedro Páramo***), familiar to Rulfo in his capacity as director of the editorial department of the National Indigenist Institute. In his novel he so orchestrates their voices that their collective effect is to render precarious any consciousness other than their own.

The degree to which Rulfo's characters persuade is well brought out in a short story which anticipated the end of ***Pedro Páramo*** in many respects. This is the story of Juvencio Nava, who has been brought in for murder committed many years before; it is called by the words he insistently repeats, **'Tell them not to kill me!' ('¡Díles que no me maten!')** and told mostly through his spoken thoughts and exchanges with his son. The atmosphere Rulfo evokes from the smell of the road ('como de orines', like Juan Preciado's last bed) and the shadows on it, is so convincingly shaped by Nava's speech that the reader comes to accept it like a code, and feels neither indulgent towards him as a doomed man, pathetic as he is, nor outraged by the murder he has committed, hideous as it was. In this way we become attuned even to the grim humour of the son after Nava's summary execution: he brings his father home, telling the corpse how odd the family will find his face, deprived by gunshots of the last vestiges of human form. Nava is made 'inhuman' and yet familiar, like Pedro Páramo himself by the time he slumps to the ground 'like a heap of stones' at the end of the novel. Bad as he is, he inspires neither revulsion nor sympathy within his world, which Rulfo makes his reader share; and the last justice

Peter Beardsell on Rulfo's short stories:

[The enduring value of Rulfo's *El llano en llamas*] lies in its depiction of universal human experience intensified and warped by the extreme local circumstances. Poverty, hardship and suffering dominate the human condition in an apparently hostile environment. It is a world of violence, cruelty, anarchy, incest, prostitution and religious hypocrisy. Thieves and murderers are found in abundance. Revenge is one recurrent theme, and guilt another. In most of these stories Rulfo fascinates us with the psychological implications of events. At times he gives an insight into a character's mind, but more frequently he creates a strange dissonance between the tone of the narrative and the nature of the events described. His first-person narrators are particularly effective in this respect when their neutrality or indifference runs counter to our own moral or emotional standpoint. Indeed our active collaboration as readers is required to compensate for Rulfo's deliberate avoidance of analysis and explanation. But we are willing collaborators, for Rulfo easily holds our interest with a masterful versatility of techniques, such as the unexpected changes of narrative standpoint, the delayed presentation of vital facts and the extensive use of foreshadowing.

Peter Beardsell, in his "Juan Rulfo: 'Pedro Páramo'," in Philip Swanson's Landmarks in Modern Latin American Fiction, *1990.*

administered on him by the drunken Don Abundio is as unhelpful as that received by Nava.

According to Rulfo the would-be reformer of this situation should move warily and has a lot to learn. In such ruins of 'living rancour' and such 'natural' vindictiveness the true and successful avenger of Dolores Preciado will be hard to find. On the other hand, whatever their interest in Latin America, anyone who reads Rulfo carefully cannot fail to recognize the quality of his witness. (pp. 71-80)

Gordon Brotherston, "Province of Dead Souls: Juan Rulfo," in his The Emergence of the Latin American Novel, *Cambridge University Press, 1977, pp. 71-80.*

Juan Rulfo (essay date 1980)

[In the excerpt below, taken from comments made to Fernando Benítez for an interview appearing in Juan Rulfo: Homenaje nacional *(1980;* Inframundo: The Mexico of Juan Rulfo, *1983), Rulfo discusses the writing process and his aims in* Pedro Parámo.]

I wrote stories trying to find a form for ***Pedro Páramo,*** which I carried in my head since 1939. The idea came to me from the hypothetical situation of a man who receives a vision of his life just before he dies. I wanted it to be a dead man who told the story. Originally only Susana San Juan was dead and from the tomb, reviewed her life. There, among the tombs, she established her relationships with the rest of the characters who also were dead. The town itself was dead. I must say that my first novel was written in sequences, but I learned that life is not a sequence of events. Years can pass without anything happening and then all of a sudden a multitude of events is unleashed. Things happen to no one in a constant manner and I set out to tell a tale with the facts and deeds well distanced, breaking with time and space. I had read a good amount of Spanish literature and discovered that the writer filled empty spaces with digressions and elucubrations. I had done the same thing before and I thought that what really counted were the facts and deeds not the interventions of the author, his essays, his manner of thinking, and I reduced myself to the facts, eliminating the essayistic. Towards that end I searched for dead characters who were not of space or time. I suppressed those ideas with which the authors could fill vacuums, and I avoided the adjective, then in fashion. It was believed that the adjective adorned the style of a writer, but it only destroyed the essential substance of the work, in other words, the noun. ***Pedro Páramo*** is an exercise in elimination. I wrote 250 pages (and rejected them) where the author once again put in his two bits. The practice of writing the short stories disciplined me, and made me see the need to disappear and to leave my characters the freedom to talk at will, which provoked, it would seem, a lack of structure. Yes, there is a structure in ***Pedro Páramo,*** but it is a structure made of silences, of hanging threads, of cut scenes, where everything occurs in a simultaneous time which is a no-time. I also pursued the goal of allowing the reader the opportunity to collaborate with the author and allowing him to fill these empty spaces. In the world of the dead, the author could not intervene.

The town where I discovered solitude, because everyone goes away as braceros, is called Tuxcacuesco, but it might be Tuxcacuesco and it could be another one. Look, before writing ***Pedro Páramo*** I had the idea, the form, the style, but I was missing the setting and perhaps unconsciously held on to the speech of those places. My language is not an exact language; the people are hermetic, they don't talk. I have returned to my town and the people talk on the benches, but if you come near, they fall silent. For them, you are a stranger and they talk of the rains, about how long the drought has lasted and you can't participate in the conversation. It is impossible. Maybe I heard their language when I was a boy, but later I forgot it, and I had to imagine how it was by intuition. I hit on a realism that doesn't exist, on a deed that never happened, on people who never existed. Some North American professors of literature have gone to Jalisco looking for a landscape, people, some faces, but the people of ***Pedro Páramo*** don't have faces and only through their words might one guess how they were, and as you might imagine, these professors found nothing. They spoke to my relatives who told them that I was a liar, that they knew of no one with such names and that none of the things that I wrote about had happened around there. It's just that the people from my province do not distinguish fiction from history. They think the novel is a transposition of facts, that it should describe the region and the people of it. Literature is fiction and thus is a lie. (pp. 15-17)

Juan Rulfo and Fernando Benìtez, in a conversation in Inframundo: The Mexico of Juan Rulfo, *translated by Frank Janney, Ediciones del Norte, 1983, pp. 13-18.*

James Torrens (essay date 10 May 1986)

[In the following excerpt, which was taken from an obituary written upon Rulfo's death, Torrens argues that Rulfo's writings are preoccupied with "old Mexico" and death.]

The old Mexico persisting under the new—this was Juan Rulfo's bittersweet theme. He brought it out so well that his death on Tuesday, Jan. 7, drew the President of the Republic to the Palacio de Bellas Artes, as the first public mourner at his bier, and occupied the newspapers and television for days. Yet Rulfo, shy and nonvocal, had always tried to dodge publicity, fearing that popular acclaim had blown his own work out of proportion. He achieved only two slim volumes, after all: a short-story collection, ***El Llano en Llamas*** (***The Plain in Flames*** [1953]) and a novel, ***Pedro Páramo*** (1955).

Rulfo excluded himself from the "intellectuals"; he was a professional writer of stories. For this, he read widely in Scandinavian and North American fiction and in the Latin American "new wave." He supported his family by government work, mostly with the National Indian Institute. This is not without its ironies since it is to the government that a peasant responds, in **"They've Given Us the Land":** "Mister Delegate, the land that you have given us is bare and hard. We don't think we can sink a plough into this quarry. Of course, we're not saying anything against the Center, only against the Plain." Hard-bitten humor, spare and exact description, the lines of suffering etched in, like a steel engraving of Landacre's.

Rulfo's characters have a sort of tough dignity, like the old man carrying his son, full of stab wounds, on his shoulders at night toward a town that they reach too late: "I'm not doing this for you. It's for your dead mother. Because, to begin with, you've caused me nothing but difficulties, trouble, pure shame" **("Don't You Hear the Dogs Barking?").**

In the long title story, **"The Plain in Flames,"** the least pleasant of Rulfo's speakers rides with a revolutionary band. They exchange fire with the Federals who are hard on their heels, hanging up on high stakes whomever they catch, as a warning. The peasant leader Pedro Zamora shows his own meanness in a bull-fighting game with the agents he captures, but he watches out sleeplessly for every one of his men. Then the peasants start burning the crops of "los ricos," the "rich" landowners: "How beautiful it looked to see the fire stepping through the pastures," catching in the corn and sugar cane, "with the smoke smelling of reed grass and honey." Eventually the raiders derail a troop train into a deep gully; sobered by the piteous massacre, they scatter into the mountains ahead of the inevitable wrath.

Rulfo's masterpiece is ***Pedro Páramo,*** which unfolds on the plains of the Media Luna. One person dominates the story, Pedro Páramo, the "cacique," or town boss, who owns almost everything (even the otherwise faithful parish priest), outwits the peasant raiders who try forcing contributions from him, attracts and exploits the women. He is "bad blood." Still, he ends up dejected and languishing for love of his childhood sweetheart, Susana San Juan, whom he watches die slowly of her remembered passion for him.

We begin ***Pedro Páramo*** seeing things through the eyes of a young man, Juan, who is fulfilling his mother's dying wish that he visit her home town, Comala. He finds the harsh white pueblo abandoned, yet people keep appearing out of nowhere; their voices take over, so that at one point the murmurs of the past craze him. For the reader, too, the story goes in multiple directions, so that only by close attention to the verb tenses and the person of the pronouns, and by piecing together the various actors, can we follow. Little by little the whole town's story comes out, but in an atmosphere as of the dead, into whose number even Juan, the visitor, is drawn.

Old Mexico's preoccupation with death—its sense both of morbidity and of continuing presences—has dictated Rulfo's way of treating the country people with whom he grew up, their illusions, dreams, passions, supernatural hopes. Out of this harsh land, despite all, beauty arises. One of the dead whispers its praise in words that explain well why his fellow citizens responded so warmly to Rulfo: "There's my village ('mi pueblo'), rising upon the plain. Full of trees and leaves, like a treasure box where we have kept our memories. There where the air changes the color of things, where life airs itself as if it were purely a murmur." (pp. 383-84)

James Torrens, "Mexico Mourns Juan Rulfo," in America, *Vol. 154, No. 18, May 10, 1986, pp. 383-84.*

FURTHER READING

Bell, Alan S. "Rulfo's *Pedro Páramo*: A Vision of Hope." *Modern Language Notes* 81, No. 2 (March 1966): 238-45.

Asserts that *Pedro Páramo* is an essentially optimistic work, stating that "the exalted death of Susana San Juan and the disintegrating image of Pedro Páramo represent forward progress in time and new hope for Mexico."

Boldy, Steven. "The Use of Ambiguity and the Death(s) of Bartolomé San Juan in Rulfo's *Pedro Páramo*." *Forum for Modern Language Studies* XIX, No. 3 (July 1983): 224-35.

Discusses ambiguity in *Pedro Páramo,* focusing on the episode in which Susana San Juan is lowered into a mine shaft by her father and set on fire.

Burton, Julianne. "Sexuality and the Mythic Dimension in Juan Rulfo's *Pedro Páramo*." *Symposium* XXVIII, No. 3 (Fall 1974): 228-47.

Examines the significance of Juan Preciado's sexual encounters in *Pedro Páramo.*

Crow, John A. "*Pedro Páramo:* A Twentieth Century 'Dance of Death'." In *Homage to Irving A. Leonard: Essays on Hispanic Art, History, and Literature,* edited by Raquel Chang-Rodriguez and Donald A. Yates, pp. 219-26. Lansing: Latin American Studies Center of Michigan State University, 1977.

Considers Rulfo's treatment of the modernist quest for spiritual renewal in a time of sterility and death in *Pedro Páramo.*

Hart, Stephen. "Juan Rulfo's *Pedro Páramo* and the Dream of the Dead Father." *Forum for Modern Language Studies* XXVI, No. 1 (January 1990): 62-74.

Offers a psychoanalytic analysis of Rulfo's novel, focusing on the Freudian theme of the mythical "search for the father."

Mac Adam, Alfred J. "Juan Rulfo: The Secular Myth." In his *Modern Latin American Narratives: The Dreams of Reason,* pp. 88-90. Chicago: University of Chicago Press, 1977.

Explores the mythical structures of *Pedro Páramo.* Mac Adam notes: "Where one might expect a liberator or renewer of society, a new king, one finds only death."

Magnarelli, Sharon. "Women, Violence, and Sacrifice in *Pedro Páramo* and *La muerte de Artemio Cruz*." *Inti* 13-14 (Spring-Fall 1981): 44-54.

Compares *Pedro Páramo* with Carlos Fuentes's *La muerte de Artemio Cruz,* asserting that in both works female characters "precisely fit the role of sacrificial victim."

Ramirez, Arthur. "Spatial Form and Cinema Techniques in Rulfo's *Pedro Páramo*." *Revista de Estudios Hispanicos* 15, No. 2 (May 1981): 233-49.

Analyzes the structure of *Pedro Páramo* and Rulfo's use of "spatial form" and juxtaposed images, asserting that the novel must be apprehended as a whole rather than as a sequence of episodes.

Rodman, Selden. "Dead but Not Gone." *The New York Times Book Review* (7 June 1959): 5, 27.

Assesses Lysander Kemp's English translation of *Pedro Páramo.*

Rodríguez-Alcalá, Hugo, and Barricelli, Jean-Pierre. "Dante and Rulfo: Beyond Time through Eternity." *Hispanic Journal* 5, No. 1 (Fall 1983): 7-27.

Compares Dante's *Inferno* with Rulfo's novel, purporting that resemblances between Hell and Comala and each author's depiction of time offer "a key to the basic meaning of *Pedro Páramo.*"

"The Living and the Dead." *The Times Literary Supplement* 3023 (5 February 1960): 86.

Reviews Lysander Kemp's translation of *Pedro Páramo,* praising Rulfo as "among the most interesting and promising young novelists whose work is available to the English-speaking world."

Additional coverage of Rulfo's life and career is contained in the following sources published by Gale Research: *Contemporary Authors,* Vols. 85-88, 118; *Contemporary Authors New Revision Series,* Vol. 26; *Contemporary Literary Criticism,* Vol. 8; *Dictionary of Literary Biography,* Vol. 113; *Hispanic Writers;* and *Major 20th-Century Writers.*

Nathalie Sarraute

1900-

(Born Nathalie Tcherniak) Russian-born French novelist, essayist, and playwright.

The following entry provides an overview of Sarraute's career. For further information on her life and works, see *CLC,* Volumes 1, 2, 4, 8, 10, and 31.

INTRODUCTION

One of France's most respected and important authors, Sarraute is often identified as one of the originators of the *nouveau roman,* or "new novel," a contemporary form of fiction whose practitioners eschew traditional plot structures, identifiable characters, metaphorical language, and other realistic conventions of the novel in favor of precise, objective observation. While Sarraute acknowledges certain affinities between her own fiction and the works of such new novelists as Alain Robbe-Grillet, Claude Mauriac, Robert Pinget, and Samuel Beckett, her novels and plays are distinguished by a fiercely independent and iconoclastic preoccupation with the interior dimensions of social intercourse. Sarraute's circumvention of such traditional novelistic devices as character and plot have been cited as contributing an existential gravity and poetic intensity to her prose that also separates her work from the more programmatic efforts of her contemporaries.

Sarraute was born in Ivanovo-Voznessensk, Russia, to Ilya Tcherniak, a chemist, and Pauline Chatounovsky Tcherniak, a writer. After her parents divorced when she was two years old, Sarraute alternately spent her childhood with her mother in Paris and with her father in Russia. As a child, Sarraute mastered French and Russian with equal fluency and learned German and English from her stepmother's mother. At age seven she wrote her first novel and offered it to a friend of her mother's, a writer who advised her to "first learn to spell, before you write a book." Sarraute became an excellent student, graduating with a degree in English from the Sorbonne. After living briefly in Oxford, England, Sarraute attended law school. In 1925 she married law student Raymond Sarraute and became a member of the Paris bar, practicing law until 1940. Over the next five decades she devoted herself to writing.

Despite her early facility with languages, Sarraute came to professional writing at the comparatively advanced age of thirty-two, when she began drafting the series of dialogic fragments that comprise her first book, *Tropismes* (*Tropisms*). Consisting of twenty-four short sketches, this work encapsulates Sarraute's essential aesthetic. According to Sarraute, tropisms—originally a scientific term referring to the natural tendency of plants to grow in the direction of heat and sunlight—are the barely perceptible "inner movements" that form the foundation of speech and gestures of quotidian conversation. While Sarraute's tropisms are more arcane and submerged than mere connotative meaning, they function similarly, as a kind of counterpoint to the surface meanings of language. The technique which Sarraute devised as a medium of expression for tropisms is "subconversation." Subconversation consists not of unspoken dialogue, but of half-formed thoughts and feelings which are conveyed to the reader impressionistically through metaphor, imagery, sound, and rhythm. In describing the psychological repression and subversion signified within subconversation, Sarraute frequently abandons physical description, character, and plot, although these elements are reconstituted in an oblique manner through dialogue.

Sarraute's subsequent novels, while somewhat more traditional in their apparent inclusion of plot and character, similarly focus on the tropistic interplay among a few characters whose personalities become concrete through commonplace utterances. In *Portrait d'un inconnu* (*Portrait of a Man Unknown*) Sarraute introduces the postmodern theme of the self-conscious author/creator, so that the inner workings of fictional technique encroach upon the domain of the "subject," thereby blurring the boundary between fiction and the novel's presumed "realism." In both *Portrait of a Man Unknown* and *Martereau* the narrator is a sensitive young man who is obsessed with unraveling the mysteries of other people's lives; though largely removed from the action of the story, his tropisms become the primary focus of the novel. Paralleling the author's struggle to create a work is the narrator's effort to construct a reality from disparate, often random pieces of information. In *Le planétarium* (*The Planetarium*), a comedy of manners that satirizes the literary world, Sarraute eliminates the narrator entirely, relying solely on fragments of dialogue and subconversation in an effort to avoid inherent subjective limitations. *Les fruits d'or* (*The Golden Fruits*), containing neither narrator, identifiable characters, nor plot, focuses on the critical and popular reception of a book of the same name. Using disembodied voices, Sarraute questions the relationship between literary merit and an author's name by chronicling the rise and fall of the book's reputation while revealing nothing of the book or the character of its critics or author.

Most critics of Sarraute's works have sought to explain her relationship to the new novelists while respecting her independence and originality. They note that her mature style was already evident in her first book, the publication of which preceded the new novelists by over a decade. In addition to the difficulty of placing Sarraute squarely within a literary school or movement, critics have been sharply divided over the intrinsic value of her works. Some commentators have maintained that Sarraute's innovations in technique are a futile attempt to move beyond the traditional novel and that nothing in her work justifies its difficulty. While they admire Sarraute's use of tropisms to take the psychological novel a step beyond the work of such writers as Fedor Dostoevski, Marcel Proust, and Virginia Woolf, many contend that the psychological elements of Sarraute's work cannot stand without an ordering of the many details of sensibility which she relates. Another common appraisal of Sarraute's work is that it has duplicated the tedium and boredom of the real world so faithfully that the books themselves are tedious. Nevertheless, her concept of the tropism and her technique of subconversation are considered major contributions to the development of the modern novel. Many concur with the opinion of Claude Mauriac: "What [Sarraute] says corresponds to what our experience has taught us, but nobody has expressed it before her."

PRINCIPAL WORKS

Tropismes (novel) 1939
 [*Tropisms,* 1967]
Portrait d'un inconnu (novel) 1948
 [*Portrait of a Man Unknown,* 1958]
Martereau (novel) 1953
 [*Martereau,* 1959]
L'ere du soupçon: Essais sur le roman (essays) 1956
 [*The Age of Suspicion: Essays on the Novel,* 1963]
Le planétarium (novel) 1959
 [*The Planetarium,* 1960]
Les fruits d'or (novel) 1963
 [*The Golden Fruits,* 1964]
Le silence, suivi de Le mensonge (drama) 1967
 [*Silence, and the Lie,* 1969]
Entre la vie et la mort (novel) 1968
 [*Between Life and Death,* 1969]
Isma, ou ce qui s'appelle rien, suivi de Le silence et Le mensonge (drama) 1970
Vous les entendez? (novel) 1972
 [*Do You Hear Them?,* 1973]
Disent les imbéciles (novel) 1976
 [*Fools Say,* 1977]
**Théâtre* (drama) 1978
 [*Collected Plays of Nathalie Sarraute,* 1980]
L'usage de la parole (sketches) 1980
 [*The Use of Speech,* 1983]
Pour un oui ou pour un non (drama) 1982
Enfance (autobiography) 1983
 [*Childhood,* 1984]
Paul Valéry et l'enfant d'éléphant; Flaubert le précurseur (essays) 1986
Tu ne t'aimes pas (novel) 1990
 [*You Don't Love Yourself,* 1990]

*This work is comprised of *Le silence, Le mensonge, Isma, C'est beau,* and *Elle est là.*

CRITICISM

Susan Sontag (essay date 1965)

[*An American essayist, critic, novelist, short story writer, editor, screenwriter, and film director, Sontag is the author of such works as* The Benefactor *(1963),* Illness as Metaphor *(1978), and* Under the Sign of Saturn *(1981). In the following essay, originally written in 1963, revised in 1965, and reprinted in 1966 in her* Against Interpretation, and Other Essays, *Sontag discusses Sarraute's contribution to the evolution of the modern novel, focusing specifically on Sarraute's essay collection* The Age of Suspicion. *A portion of this essay was included in* CLC, *Volume 4.*]

A new mode of didacticism has conquered the arts, is indeed the "modern" element in art. Its central dogma is the idea that art must evolve. Its result is the work whose main intention is to advance the history of the genre, to break ground in matters of technique. The paramilitary imagery of *avant-garde* and *arrière-garde* perfectly expresses the new didacticism. Art is the army by which human sensibility advances implacably into the future, with the aid of ever newer and more formidable techniques. This mainly negative relation of individual talent to tradition, which gives rise to the rapid and built-in obsolescence of each new item of technique, and each new use of materials, has vanquished the conception of art as giving familiar pleasure, and produced a body of work which is principally didactic and admonitory. As everyone knows by now, the point of Duchamp's "Nude Descending a Staircase" is not so much to represent anything, much less a nude, descending a staircase, as to teach a lesson on how natural forms may be broken into a series of kinetic planes. The point of the prose works of Stein and Beckett is to show how diction, punctuation, syntax, and narrative order can be recast to express continuous impersonal states of consciousness. The point of the music of Webern and Boulez is to show how, for example, the rhythmical function of silence and the structural role of tone colors can be developed.

The victory of the modern didacticism has been most complete in music and painting, where the most respected works are those which give little pleasure on first hearing and seeing (except to a small and highly trained audience) but make important advances in the technical revolutions which have taken place in these arts. Compared with music and painting, the novel, like the cinema, lags well to the rear of the battlefield. A body of "difficult" novels comparable to Abstract Expressionist painting and *musique concrète* has not overrun the territory of critically respectable fiction. On the contrary, most of the novel's few brave ventures to the front line of modernism get marooned there. After a few years they seem merely idiosyncratic, for no troops follow the brave CO and back him up. Novels which, in the order of difficulty and of merit, are comparable to the music of Gian-Carlo Menotti and the painting of Bernard Buffet, are garnished with the highest critical acclaim. The ease of access and lack of rigor that causes embarrassment in music and painting are no embarrassment in the novel, which remains intransigently *arrière-garde.*

Yet, middle-class art form or no, there is no genre in greater need of sustained reexamination and renovation. The novel is (along with opera) the archetypal art form of the 19th century, perfectly expressing that period's wholly mundane conception of reality, its lack of really ambitious spirituality, its discovery of the "interesting" (that is, of the commonplace, the inessential, the accidental, the minute, the transient), its affirmation of what E. M. Cioran calls "destiny in lower case." The novel, as all the critics who praise it never tire of reminding us and upbraiding contemporary writers who deviate, is about man-in-society; it brings alive a chunk of the world and sets its "characters" within that world. Of course, one can treat the novel as the successor to the epic and the picaresque tale. But everyone knows that this inheritance is superficial. What animates the novel is something wholly missing from these older narrative forms: the discovery of psychology, the transposition of motives into "experiences." This passion for the documentation of "experience," for facts, made the novel the most open of all art forms. Every art form works with some implicit standard of what is elevated and what is vulgar—except the novel. It could accommodate any level of language, any plot, any ideas, any information. And this, of course, was its eventual undoing as a serious art form. Sooner or later discriminating readers could no longer be expected to become interested in one more leisurely "story," in half a dozen more private lives laid open for their inspection. (They found the movies doing this, with more freedom and with more vigor.) While music and the plastic arts and poetry painfully dug themselves out of the inadequate dogmas of 19th century "realism," by a passionate commitment to the idea of progress in art and a hectic quest for new idioms and new materials, the novel has proved unable to assimilate whatever of genuine quality and spiritual ambition has been performed in its name in the 20th century. It has sunk to the level of an art form deeply, if not irrevocably, compromised by philistinism.

When one thinks of giants like Proust, Joyce, the Gide of *Lafcadio,* Kafka, the Hesse of *Steppenwolf,* Genet, or lesser but nonetheless masterly writers such as Machado de Assis, Svevo, Woolf, Stein, the early Nathanael West, Céline, Nabokov, the early Pasternak, the Djuna Barnes of *Nightwood,* Beckett (to mention only some), one thinks of writers who close off rather than inaugurate, who cannot be learned from, so much as imitated, and whom one imitates at the peril of merely repeating what they have done. One hesitates to blame or praise critics for anything that happens in an art form, whether for good or bad. Yet it is hard not to conclude that what the novel has lacked, and what it must have if it is to continue as a generally (as opposed to sporadically) serious art form, is any sustained distance from its 19th century premises. (The great flowering of literary criticism in England and America in the last thirty years, which began with the criticism of poetry and then passed on to the novel, precisely does *not* contain such a reevaluation. It is a philosophically naïve criticism, unquestioning and uncritical of the prestige of "realism.")

This coming-of-age of the novel will entail a commitment to all sorts of questionable notions, like the idea of "progress" in the arts and the defiantly aggressive ideology expressed in the metaphor of the avant-garde. It will restrict the novel's audience because it will demand accepting new pleasures—such as the pleasure of solving a problem—to be gotten from prose fiction and learning how to get them. (It may mean, for example, that we shall have to read aloud as well as with the eye, and it will certainly mean that we must expect to read a novel a number of times to understand it fully or to feel ourselves competent to judge it. We have already accepted this idea of repeated looking or hearing or reading with serious contemporary poetry, painting, sculpture, and music.) And it will make self-conscious aestheticians, didactic explorers, of all who wish seriously to practice the form. (All "modern" artists are aestheticians.) This surrender of the novel's commitment to facileness, to easy availability and the perpetuation of an outmoded aesthetic, will undoubtedly give rise to a great many boring and pretentious books; and one may well come to wish the old unself-consciousness back again. But the price must be paid. Readers must be made to see, by a new generation of critics who may well have to force this ungainly period of the novel down their throats by all sorts of seductive and partly fraudulent rhetoric, the necessity of this move. And the sooner the better.

For until we have a *continuous* serious "modern" tradition of the novel, venturesome novelists will work in a vacuum. (Whether critics will decide not to call these prose fictions novels any more doesn't matter. Nomenclature has not proved an obstacle in painting or music or poetry, although it has in sculpture, so that we now tend to drop that word in favor of words like "construction" and "assemblage.") We shall continue to have monstrous hulks, like abandoned tanks, lying about the landscape. An example, perhaps the greatest example, is *Finnegans Wake*—still largely unread and unreadable, left to the care of academic exegetes who may decipher the book for us, but cannot tell us why it should be read or what we can learn from it. That Joyce expected his readers to devote their whole lives to his book may seem an outrageous demand; but it is a logical one, considering the singularity of his work. And the fate of Joyce's last book presages the obtuse reception of a number of its less mammoth but equally plotless successors in English—the books of Stein, Beckett, and Burroughs come to mind. No wonder these stand out, as stark isolated forays, on an eerily pacified battleground.

Lately, however, the situation appears to be changing. A whole school—should I say a battalion?—of important and challenging novels is being produced in France. There are actually two waves here. The earlier was led by Maurice Blanchot, Georges Bataille, and Pierre Klossowski; most of these books were written in the 1940s and are as yet untranslated into English. Better known, and mostly translated, are a "second wave" of books written in the 1950s, by (among others) Michel Butor, Alain Robbe-Grillet, Claude Simon, and Nathalie Sarraute. All these writers—and they differ greatly from each other, in intention and achievement—have this in common: they reject the idea of the "novel" whose task is to tell a story and delineate characters according to the conventions of 19th century realism, and all they abjure is summed up in the notion of "psychology." Whether they try to transcend psychology by Heidegger's phenomenology (a powerful influence) or undercut it by behavioristic, external description, the results are at least negatively similar, and constitute the first body of work on the form of the novel which gives promise of telling us something useful about the new forms which fiction may take.

But perhaps the more valuable achievement to come out of France for the novel has been a whole body of criticism inspired by the new novelists (and, in some cases, written by them) which amounts to a most impressive attempt to think systematically about the genre. This criticism—I am thinking of essays by Maurice Blanchot, Roland Barthes, E. M. Cioran, Alain Robbe-Grillet, Nathalie Sarraute, Michel Butor, Michel Foucault, and others—is, by far, the most interesting literary criticism today. And nothing prevents novelists in the English-speaking world from drawing sustenance from the brilliant reexamination of the premises of the novel expounded by these critics, but doing work in the novel very different from that of the French novelists. The reason these essays may prove more valuable than the novels is that they propose standards that are ampler and more ambitious than anything yet achieved by any writer. (Robbe-Grillet, for example, admits that his novels are inadequate illustrations of the diagnoses and recommendations put forth in his essays.)

This is, to me, the importance of the appearance in English of ***The Age of Suspicion,*** a collection of Nathalie Sarraute's essays in which, ostensibly, the theory behind her novels is fully set forth. Whether or not one enjoys or admires Sarraute's novels (I really like only ***Portrait of a Man Unknown*** and ***The Planetarium***), whether or not she really practices what she preaches (in a crucial respect, I think she does not), the essays broach a number of criticisms of the traditional novel which seem to me a good beginning for the theoretical reconsideration long overdue on this side of the Atlantic.

Perhaps the best approach to Sarraute's polemic for an English-speaking reader would be to compare it with two other manifestoes on what the novel should be, Virginia Woolf's "Mr. Bennett and Mrs. Brown" and Mary McCarthy's "The Fact in Fiction." Sarraute scorns as "naïve" Virginia Woolf's dismissal of naturalism and objective realism, her call to the modern novelist to examine "the dark places of psychology." But Sarraute is equally hard on the position represented by Mary McCarthy's essay, which may be read as a rebuttal of Virginia Woolf, calling as it does for a return to the old novelistic virtues of setting forth a real world, giving a sense of verisimilitude, and constructing memorable characters.

Sarraute's case against realism is a convincing one. Reality is not that unequivocal; life is not that lifelike. The immediate cozy recognition that the lifelike in most novels induces is, and should be, suspect. (Truly, as Sarraute says, the genius of the age is suspicion. Or, if not its genius, at least its besetting vice.) I wholeheartedly sympathize with what she objects to in the old-fashioned novel: *Vanity Fair* and *Buddenbrooks,* when I reread them recently, however marvellous they still seemed, also made me wince. I could not stand the omnipotent author showing me that's how life is, making me compassionate and tearful; with his obstreperous irony, his confidential air of perfectly knowing his characters and leading me, the reader, to feel I knew them too. I no longer trust novels which fully satisfy my passion to understand. Sarraute is right, too, that the novel's traditional machinery for furnishing a scene, and describing and moving about characters, does not justify itself. Who really cares about the furniture of so-and-so's room, or whether he lit a cigarette or wore a dark gray suit or uncovered the typewriter after sitting down and before inserting a sheet of paper in the typewriter? Great movies have shown that the cinema can invest pure physical action—whether fleeting and small-scale like the wig-changing in *L'Avventura,* or important like the advance through the forest in *The Big Parade*—with more immediate magic than words ever can, and more economically, too.

More complex and problematic, however, is Sarraute's insistence that psychological analysis in the novel is equally obsolete and misguided. "The word 'psychology,' " Sarraute says, "is one that no present-day writer can hear spoken with regard to himself without averting his gaze and blushing." By psychology in the novel, she means Woolf, Joyce, Proust: novels which explore a substratum of hidden thoughts and feelings beneath action, the depiction of which replaces the concern with character and plot. All Joyce brought up from these depths, she remarks, was an uninterrupted flow of words. And Proust, too, failed. In the end Proust's elaborate psychological dissections recompose themselves into realistic characters, in which the practiced reader "immediately recognizes a rich man of the world in love with a kept woman, a prominent, awkward, gullible doctor, a parvenu bourgeoise or a snobbish 'great lady,' all of which will soon take their places in the vast collection of fictitious characters that people his imaginary museum."

Actually Sarraute's novels are not so unlike Joyce's (and Woolf's) as she thinks, and her rejection of psychology is far from total. What she wants herself is precisely the psychological, but (and this is the basis of her complaint against Proust) without the possibility of any conversion back into "character" and "plot." She is against psychological *dissection,* for that assumes there is a body to dissect. She is against a provisional psychology, against psychology as a new means to the old end. The use of the psychological microscope must not be intermittent, a device merely in the furthering of the plot. This means a radical recasting of the novel. Not only must the novelist not tell a story; he must not distract the reader with gross events like a murder or a great love. The more minute, the less sensational the event the better. (Thus ***Martereau*** consists of the ruminations of a nameless young man, an interior decorator, about the artistic aunt and rich businessman uncle with whom he lives, and about an older, not-so-well-off man named Martereau, concerning why and in what circumstances he feels comfortable with them, and why and when he feels he is succumbing to the force of their personalities and the objects with which they surround themselves. The aunt and uncle's project of buying a house in the country provide the only "action" of the book, and if for a time it is suspected that Martereau has defrauded the uncle in the matter of the house, you can bet that in the end all suspicions are allayed. In ***The Planetarium*** something does happen. A social-climbing young man, shamelessly trying to gain admittance to the circle of a rich, vain, and very famous woman writer, actually does manage to dispossess his doting, gullible aunt from her five-room apartment.) But Sarraute's characters do not really ever act. They scheme, they throb, they shudder—under the impact of the minutiae of daily life. These preliminaries and gropings toward action are the real subject of her novels. Since analysis is out—that is, the speaking, interpreting author is out—Sarraute's novels are logically written only in the first person, even when the interior musings use "she" and "he."

What Sarraute proposes is a novel written in continuous monologue, in which dialogue between characters is a functional extension of monologue, "real" speech a continuation of silent speech. This kind of dialogue she calls "sub-conversation." It is comparable to theatrical dialogue in that the author does not intervene or interpret, but unlike theatrical dialogue it is not broken up or assigned to clearly separable characters. (She has some particularly sharp and mocking words to say about the creaky *he said's, she replied's, so-and-so declared's* with which most novels are strewn.) Dialogue must "become vibrant and swollen with those tiny inner movements that propel and extend it." The novel must disavow the means of classical psychology—introspection—and proceed instead by immersion. It must plunge the reader "into the stream of those subterranean dramas of which Proust only had time to obtain a rapid aerial view, and concerning which he observed and reproduced nothing but the broad motionless outlines." The novel must record without comment the direct and purely sensory contact with things and persons which the "I" of the novelist experiences. Abstaining from all creating of likenesses (Sarraute hands that over to the cinema), the novel must preserve and promote "that element of indetermination, of opacity and mystery that one's own actions always have for the one who lives them."

There is something exhilarating in Sarraute's program for the novel, which insists on an unlimited respect for the complexity of human feelings and sensations. But there is, for me, a certain softness in her argument, based as it is on a diagnosis of psychology that is both excessively doctrinaire in its remedy and equivocal. A view which regards "the efforts of Henry James or Proust to take apart the delicate wheelworks of our inner mechanisms" as wielding a pick and shovel has dazzling standards of psychological refinement indeed. Who would contradict Sarraute when she characterizes the feelings as an immense mobile mass in which almost anything can be found; or when she says that no theory, least of all a cipher like psychoanalysis, can give an account of all its movements? But Sarraute is only attacking psychology in the novel on behalf of a better, closer technique of psychological description.

Her views of the complexity of feeling and sensation are one thing, her program for the novel another. True, all accounts of motivation simplify. But, admitting that, there still remain many choices available to the novelist besides seeking a more refined and microscopic way of representing motives. Certain kinds of overviews, for example—which scant the minutiae of feeling altogether—are, I am sure, at least as valid a solution to the problem Sarraute raises as the technique of dialogue and narration which she takes as the logical consequence of her critique. Character may be (as Sarraute insists) an ocean, a confluence of tides and streams and eddies, but I do not see the privileged value of immersion. Skin-diving has its place, but so has oceanic cartography, what Sarraute contemptuously dismisses as "the aerial view." Man is a creature who is designed to live on the surface; he lives in the depths—whether terrestrial, oceanic, or psychological—at his peril. I do not share her contempt for the novelist's effort to transmute the watery shapeless depths of experience into solid stuff, to impose outlines, to give fixed shape and sensuous body to the world. That it's boring to do it in the old ways goes without saying. But I cannot agree that it should not be done at all.

Sarraute invites the writer to resist the desire to amuse his contemporaries, to reform them, to instruct them, or to fight for their emancipation; and simply, without trimming or smoothing or overcoming contradictions, to present "reality" (the word is Sarraute's) as he sees it, with as great a sincerity and sharpness of vision as he is capable. I will not here dispute the question of whether the novel should amuse, reform, or instruct (why should it not, so long as it justifies itself as a work of art?) but only point out what a tendentious definition of reality she proposes. Reality, for Sarraute, means a reality that is rid of the "preconceived ideas and ready-made images that encase it." It is opposed to "the surface reality that everyone can easily see and which, for want of anything better, everyone uses." According to Sarraute, for a writer to be in contact with reality he must "attain something that is thus far unknown, which, it seems to him, he is the first to have seen."

But what is the point of this multiplication of realities? For truly, it is the plural rather than the singular that Sarraute should have used. If each writer must "bring to light this fragment of reality that is his own"—and all the whales and sharks have been catalogued; it is new species of plankton she is after—then the writer not only is a maker of fragments, but is condemned to being an exponent only of what is original in his own subjectivity. When he comes to the literary arena bearing his jar of tiny, and as yet uncatalogued, marine specimens, are we to welcome him in the name of science? (The writer as marine biologist.) Of sport? (The writer as deep-sea diver.) Why does he deserve an audience? How many fragments of reality do readers of novels need?

By invoking the notion of reality at all, Sarraute has, in fact, narrowed and compromised her argument when she need not have done so. The metaphor of the work of art as a representation of reality should be retired for a while; it has done good service throughout the history of the analysis of works of art, but now it can scarcely fail to skirt the important issues. In Sarraute's exposition, it has the unfortunate result of giving further life to the tedious alternatives of subjectivity versus objectivity, the original versus what is preconceived and ready-made. There is no reason why the novelist cannot make new arrangements and transformations of what everybody has seen, and restrict himself precisely to preconceived ideas and ready-made images.

Sarraute's allegiance to this rather vacuous notion of reality (a reality lying in the depths rather than the surface) is also responsible for the unnecessarily grim tone of some of her admonitions. Her chilly dismissal of the possibility of the writer's providing "aesthetic enjoyment" to his readers is mere rhetoric, and does serious injustice to the position she, in part, ably represents. The writer, she says, must renounce "all desire to write 'beautifully' for the pleasure of doing so, to give aesthetic enjoyment to himself or to his readers." Style is "capable of beauty only in the sense that any athlete's gesture is beautiful; the better it is adapted to its purpose, the greater the beauty." The purpose, remember, is the recording of the writer's unique apprehension of an unknown reality. But there is absolutely no reason to equate "aesthetic enjoyment," which every work of art is by definition designed to supply, with the notion of a frivolous, decorative, merely "beautiful" style. . . . It really is science, or better yet sport, that Sarraute has in mind as model for the novel. The final justification for the novelist's quest as Sarraute characterizes it—what for her frees the novel from all moral and social purposes—is that the novelist is after truth (or a fragment of it), like the scientist, and after functional exercise, like the athlete. And there is nothing, in principle, so objectionable about these models, except their meaning for her. For all the basic soundness of Sarraute's critique of the old-fashioned novel, she still has the novelist chasing after "truth" and "reality."

Sarraute's manifesto must thus be finally judged to do less justice to the position she is defending than that position deserves. A more rigorous and searching account of this position may be found in Robbe-Grillet's essays "On Several Dated Notions" and "Nature, Humanism, and Tragedy." These appeared in 1957 and 1958, respectively, while Sarraute's were published between 1950 and 1955, and collected in book form in 1956; and Robbe-Grillet has cited Sarraute in a way that might lead one to think that he is a later exponent of the same position. But Robbe-Grillet's complex criticism of the notions of tragedy and of humanism, the unremitting clarity with which he demolishes the old shibboleth of form versus content (his willingness, for example, to declare that the novel, so far as it belongs in the domain of art, has no content), the compatibility of his aesthetic with technical innovations in the novel quite different from those he has chosen, put his arguments on a far higher level than those of Sarraute. Robbe-Grillet's essays are truly radical and, if one grants but a single of his assumptions, carry one all the way to conviction. Sarraute's essays, useful as they may be to introduce the literate English-speaking public to the important critique of the traditional novel which has been launched in France, in the end hedge and compromise.

Undoubtedly, many people will feel that the prospects for the novel laid out by the French critics are rather bleak; and wish that the armies of art would go on fighting on other battlefronts and leave the novel alone. (In the same mood, some of us wish we were endowed with a good deal less of the excruciating psychological self-consciousness that is the burden of educated people in our time.) But the novel as a form of art has nothing to lose, and everything to gain, by joining the revolution that has already swept over most of the other arts. It is time that the novel became what it is not, in England and America, with rare and unrelated exceptions: a form of art which people with serious and sophisticated taste in the other arts can take seriously. (pp. 101-11)

Susan Sontag, "Nathalie Sarraute and the Novel," in her Against Interpretation, and Other Essays, *Farrar, Straus and Giroux, 1966, pp. 100-11.*

Gore Vidal (essay date 1967)

[*The author of such works as* Visit to a Small Planet *(1956),* Myra Breckenridge *(1968),* Burr *(1973), and* Lincoln *(1984), Vidal is an American novelist, short story writer, dramatist, and essayist. He is particularly*

Jérôme Lindon of Editions de Minuit (standing in front of doorway) and the New Novelists, 1959: (left to right) Alain Robbe-Grillet, Claude Simon, Claude Mauriac, Robert Pinget, Samuel Beckett, Nathalie Sarraute, and Claude Ollier.

noted for his historical novels and his iconoclastic essays. In the following excerpt from an essay on theories of the nouveau roman *which originally appeared in* Encounter *in 1967, Vidal assesses Sarraute's technical and stylistic innovations.*]

Since the Second World War, Alain Robbe-Grillet, Nathalie Sarraute, Michel Butor, Claude Simon, and Robert Pinget, among others, have attempted to change not only the form of the novel but the relationship between book and reader, and though their experiments are taken most seriously on the Continent, they are still too little known and thought about in those countries the late General de Gaulle believed to be largely populated by Anglo-Saxons. Among American commentators, only Susan Sontag in *Against Interpretation, and Other Essays,* published in 1966, has made a sustained effort to understand what the French are doing, and her occasional essays on their work are well worth reading, not only as reflections of an interesting and interested mind but also because she shares with the New Novelists (as they loosely describe themselves) a desire for the novel to become "what it is not in England and America, with rare and unrelated exceptions: a form of art which people with serious and sophisticated [*sic*] taste in the other arts can take seriously." (pp. 270-71)

The two chief theorists of the New Novel are Alain Robbe-Grillet and Nathalie Sarraute. As novelists, their works do not much resemble one another or, for that matter, conform to each other's strictures. But it is as theorists not as novelists that they shall concern us here. (p. 271)

In attacking the traditional novel, both Robbe-Grillet and Miss Sarraute are on safe ground. Miss Sarraute is particularly effective when she observes that even the least aware of the traditionalists seems "unable to escape a certain feeling of uneasiness as regards dialogue." She remarks upon the self-conscious way in which contemporary writers sprinkle their pages with "he saids" and "she replieds," and she makes gentle fun of Henry Green's hopeful comment that perhaps the novel of the future will be largely composed in dialogue since, as she quotes him, people don't write letters any more: they use the telephone.

But the dialogue novel does not appeal to her, for it brings "the novel dangerously near the domain of the theater, where it is bound to be in a position of inferiority"—on the ground that the nuances of dialogue in the theater are supplied by actors while in the novel the writer himself must provide, somehow, the sub-conversation which is the true meaning. Opposed to the dialogue novel is the one of Proustian analysis. Miss Sarraute finds much fault with this method (no meaningful depths left to plumb in the wake of Freud), but concedes that "In spite of the rather serious charges that may be brought against analysis, it is difficult to turn from it today without turning one's back on progress."

"Progress," "*New* Novel," "permanent creation of tomorrow's world," "the discovery of reality will continue only if we abandon outward forms," "general evolution of the genre" . . . again and again one is reminded in reading the manifestos of these two explorers that we are living (one might even say that we are trapped) in the age of science. Miss Sarraute particularly delights in using quasi-scientific references. She refers to her first collection of pieces as ***Tropisms.*** (According to authority, a tropism is "the turning of an organism, or part of one, in a particular direction in response to some special external stimulus.") She is also addicted to words like "larval" and "magma," and her analogies are often clinical: "Suspicion, which is by way of destroying the character and the entire outmoded mechanism that guaranteed its force, is one of the morbid reactions by which an organism defends itself and seeks another equilibrium. . . . "

Yet she does not like to be called a "laboratory novelist" any more than she likes to be called a formalist. One wonders why. For it is obvious that both she and Robbe-Grillet see themselves in white smocks working out new formulas for a new fiction. Underlying all their theories is the assumption that if scientists can break the atom with an equation, a dedicated writer ought to be able to find a new form in which to redefine the "unchanging human heart," as Bouvard might have said to Pécuchet. Since the old formulas have lost their efficacy, the novel, if it is to survive, must become something new; and so, to create that something new, they believe that writers must resort to calculated invention and bold experiment.

It is an interesting comment on the age that both Miss Sarraute and Robbe-Grillet take for granted that the highest literature has always been made by self-conscious avant-gardists. Although this was certainly true of Flaubert, whose letters show him in the laboratory, agonizing over that double genitive which nearly soured the recipe for *Madame Bovary,* and of Joyce, who spent a third of his life making a language for the night, Dostoevsky, Conrad, and Tolstoi—to name three novelists quite as great—were not much concerned with laboratory experiments. Their interest was in what Miss Sontag calls "the subject"; and though it is true they did not leave the form of the novel as they found it, their art was not the product of calculated experiments with form so much as it was the result of their ability, by virtue of what they were, to transmute the familiar and make it rare. They were men of genius unobsessed by what Goethe once referred to as "an eccentric desire for originality." Or as Saul Bellow puts it: "Genius is always, without strain, avant-garde. Its departure from tradition is not the result of caprice or of policy but of an inner necessity."

Absorbed by his subject, the genius is a natural innovator—a fact which must be maddening to the ordinary writer, who, because he is merely ambitious, is forced to approach literature from the outside, hoping by the study of a masterpiece's form and by an analysis of its content to reconstruct the principle of its composition in order that he may create either simulacra or, if he is furiously ambitious, by rearranging the component parts, something "new." This approach from the outside is of course the natural way of the critic, and it is significant that the New Novelists tend to blur the boundary between critic and novelist. "Critical preoccupation," writes Robbe-Grillet, "far from sterilizing creation, can on the contrary serve it as a driving force."

In the present age the methods of the scientist, who deals only in what can be measured, demonstrated and proved, are central. Consequently, anything as unverifiable as a novel is suspect. Or, as Miss Sarraute quotes Paul Tournier:

> There is nobody left who is willing to admit that he invents. The only thing that matters is the document, which must be precise, dated, proven, authentic. Works of the imagination are banned, because they are invented. . . . The public, in order to believe what it is told, must be convinced that it is not being "taken in." All that counts now is the "true fact."

This may explain why so many contemporary novelists feel they must apologize for effects which seem unduly extravagant or made up ("but that's the way it really happened!"). Nor is it to make a scandal to observe that most "serious" American novels are autobiographies, usually composed to pay off grudges. But then the novelist can hardly be held responsible for the society he reflects. After all, much of the world's reading consists of those weekly news magazines in which actual people are dealt with in fictional terms. It is the spirit of the age to believe that any fact, no matter how suspect, is superior to any imaginative exercise, no matter how true. The result of this attitude has been particularly harrowing in the universities, where English departments now do their best to pretend that they are every bit as fact-minded as the physical scientists (to whom the largest appropriations go). Doggedly, English teachers do research, publish learned findings, make breakthroughs in F. Scott Fitzgerald and, in their search for facts, behave as if no work of literature can be called complete until each character has been satisfactorily identified as someone who actually lived and had a history known to the author. It is no wonder that the ambitious writer is tempted to re-create the novel along what he believes to be scientific lines. (pp. 276-80)

Recently in France the matter of science and the novel was much debated. In an essay called *Nouvelle Critique ou Nouvelle Imposture,* Raymond Picard attacked the new critic Roland Barthes, who promptly defended himself on the ground that a concern with form is only natural since structure precedes creation (an insight appropriated from anthropology, a discipline recently become fashionable). Picard then returned to the attack, mocking those writers who pretend to be scientists, pointing out that they

> improperly apply to the literary domain methods which have proved fruitful elsewhere but which here lose their efficiency and rigor. . . . These critical approaches have a scientific air to them, but the resemblance is pure caricature. The new critics use science roughly as someone ignorant of electricity might use electronics.

> What they're after is its prestige: in other respects they are at opposite poles to the scientific spirit. Their statements generally sound more like oracles than useful hypotheses: categorical, unverifiable, unilluminating.

Picard is perhaps too harsh, but no one can deny that Robbe-Grillet and Nathalie Sarraute often appropriate the language of science without understanding its spirit—for instance, one can verify the law of physics which states that there is no action without reaction, but how to prove the critical assertion that things in themselves are what caused Camus' creature to kill? Yet if to revive a moribund art form writers find it helpful to pretend to be physicists, then one ought not to tease them unduly for donning so solemnly mask and rubber gloves. After all, Count Tolstoi thought he was a philosopher. But whether pseudo-scientists or original thinkers, neither Robbe-Grillet nor Miss Sarraute finds it easy to put theory into practice. As Robbe-Grillet says disarmingly: "It is easier to indicate a new form than to follow it without failure." And he must be said to fail a good deal of the time: is there anything more incantatory than the repetition of the word "*lugubre*" in *Last Year at Marienbad?* Or more visceral than the repetition of the killing of the centipede in *Jealousy?* While Miss Sarraute finds that her later essays are "far removed from the conception and composition of my first book"—which, nevertheless, she includes in the same volume as the essays, with the somewhat puzzling comment that "this first book contains *in nuce* all the raw material that I have continued to develop in my later works." (pp. 280-81)

Like Robbe-Grillet, Nathalie Sarraute regards Camus' *The Stranger* as a point of departure. She sees the book's immediate predecessors as "The promising art of the cinema" and "the wholesome simplicity of the new American novel." Incidentally, she is quite amusing when she describes just what the effect of these "wholesome" novels was upon the French during the years immediately after the war:

> By transporting the French reader into a foreign universe in which he had no foothold, [they] lulled his wariness, aroused in him the kind of credulous curiosity that travel books inspire, and gave him a delightful impression of escape into an unknown world.

It is reassuring to learn that these works were not regarded with any great seriousness by the French and that Horace McCoy was not finally the master they once hailed him. Apparently the American novel was simply a vigorous tonic for an old literature gone stale. Miss Sarraute is, however, sincerely admiring of Faulkner's ability to involve the reader in his own world. To her the most necessary thing of all is "to disposses the reader and entice him, at all costs, into the author's territory. To achieve this the device that consists in referring to the leading characters as 'I' constitutes a means." The use of the first person seems to her to be the emblem of modern art. ("Since Impressionism all pictures have been painted in the first person.") And so, just as photography drove painters away from representing nature (ending such ancient arts as that of the miniaturist and the maker of portrait busts), the cinema "garners and perfects what is left of it by the novel." The novel must now go where the camera may not follow. In this new country the reader has been aided by such modern writers as Proust and Joyce; they have so awakened his sensibilities that he is now able to respond to what is beneath the interior monologue, that "immense profusion of sensations, images, sentiments, memories, impulses, little larval actions that no inner language can convey." For her, emphasis falls upon what she calls the sub-conversation, that which is sensed and not said, the hidden counterpoint to the stated theme (obviously a very difficult thing to suggest, much less write, since "no inner language can convey it"). (pp. 285-87)

On the question of how to establish the separateness, the autonomy of things, Robbe-Grillet and Miss Sarraute part company. In contemplating her method, she ceases altogether to be "scientific." Instead she alarmingly intones a hymn to words—all words—for they "possess the qualities needed to seize upon, protect and bring out into the open those subterranean movements that are at once impatient and afraid." (Are those subterranean movements really "impatient and afraid"?) For her, words possess suppleness, freedom, iridescent richness of shading, and by their nature they are protected "from suspicion and from minute examination." (In an age of suspicion, to let words off scot-free is an act of singular trust.) Consequently, once words have entered the other person, they swell, explode, and "by virtue of this game of actions and reactions . . . they constitute a most valuable tool for the novelist." Which, as the French say, goes without saying.

But of course words are not at all what she believes they are. All words lie. Or as Professor Frank Kermode put it in *Literary Fiction and Reality:* "Words, thoughts, patterns of word and thought, are enemies of truth, if you identify that with what may be had by phenomenological reductions." Nevertheless, Miss Sarraute likes to think that subterranean movements (tropisms) can be captured by words, which might explain why her attitude toward things is so much more conventional than that of Robbe-Grillet, who writes:

> Perhaps Kafka's staircases lead *elsewhere,* but they are *there,* and we look at them step by step following the details of the banisters and the risers.

This is untrue. First, we do not look at the staircases; we look at a number of words arranged upon a page by a conscious human intelligence which would like us to consider, among a thousand other things, the fact of those staircases. Since a primary concern of the human mind is cause and effect, the reader is bound to speculate upon why those staircases have been shown him; also, since staircases are usually built to connect one man-made level with another, the mind will naturally speculate as to what those two levels are like. Only a far-gone schizophrenic (or an LSD tripper) would find entirely absorbing the description of a banister.

Perhaps the most naïve aspect of Robbe-Grillet's theory of fiction is his assumption that words can ever describe with absolute precision anything. At no point does he acknowledge that words are simply fiat for real things; by their nature, words are imprecise and layered with meanings—the signs of things, not the things themselves. Therefore, even if Robbe-Grillet's goal of achieving a total reality for the world of things was desirable, it would not be possible to do it with language, since the author (that man full of torments and passions) is bound to betray his attitude to the sequence of signs he offered us; he has an "interest" in the matter, or else he would not write. Certainly if he means to reinvent man, then he will want to find a way of defining man through human (yes, psychological) relations as well as through a catalogue of things observed and gestures coolly noted. Wanting to play God, ambition is bound to dictate the order of words, and so the subjective will prevail just as it does in the traditional novel. To follow Robbe-Grillet's theory to its logical terminus, the only sort of book which might be said to be *not* a collection of signs of absent things but the actual things themselves would be a collection of ink, paper, cardboard, glue, and typeface, to be assembled or not by the reader-spectator. If this be too heavy a joke, then the ambitious writer must devise a new language which might give the appearance of maintaining the autonomy of things, since the words, new-minted, will possess a minimum of associations of a subjective or anthropomorphic sort. No existing language will be of any use to him, unless it be that of the Trobriand Islanders: those happy people have no words for "why" or "because"; for them, things just happen. Needless to say, they do not write novels or speculate on the nature of things.

The philosophic origins of the New Novel can be found (like most things French) in Descartes, whose dualism was the reflection of a split between the subjective and the objective, between the irrational and the rational, between the physical and the metaphysical. In the last century Auguste Comte, accepting this dualism, conceived of a logical empiricism which would emphasize the "purely" objective at the expense of the subjective or metaphysical. An optimist who believed in human progress, Comte saw history as an evolution toward a better society. For him the age of religion and metaphysics ended with the French Revolution. Since that time the human race was living in what he termed "the age of science," and he was confident that the methods of the positive sciences would enrich and transform human life. At last things were coming into their own. But not until the twentieth century did the methods of science entirely overwhelm the arts of the traditional humanists. To the scientific-minded, all things, including human personality, must in time yield their secrets to orderly experiment. Meanwhile, only that which is verifiable is to be taken seriously; emotive meaning must yield to cognitive meaning. Since the opacity of human character has so far defeated all objective attempts at illumination, the New Novelists prefer, as much as possible, to replace the human with objects closely observed and simple gestures noted but not explained.

In many ways, the New Novel appears to be approaching the "pure" state of music. In fact, there are many like [Susan] Sontag who look forward to "a kind of total structuring" of the novel, analogous to music. This is an old dream of the novelist. Nearly half a century ago, Joyce wrote (in a letter to his brother), "Why should not a modern literature be as unsparing and as direct as song?" Why not indeed? And again, why? The answer to the second "why" is easy enough. In the age of science, the objective is preferred to the subjective. Since human behavior is notoriously irrational and mysterious, it can be demonstrated only in the most impressionistic and unscientific way; it yields few secrets to objective analysis. Mathematics, on the other hand, is rational and verifiable, and music is a form of mathematics. Therefore, if one were to eliminate as much as possible the human from the novel, one might, through "a kind of total structuring," come close to the state of mathematics or music. . . . (pp. 287-90)

But no matter what happens to language, the novel is not apt to be revived by electronics. The portentous theorizings of the New Novelists are of no more use to us than the self-conscious avant-gardism of those who are forever trying to figure out what the next "really serious" thing will be when it is plain that there is not going to be a next serious thing in the novel. Our lovely vulgar and most human art is at an end, if not the end. Yet that is no reason not to want to practice it, or even to read it. In any case, rather like priests who have forgotten the meaning of the prayers they chant, we shall go on for quite a long time talking of books and writing books, pretending all the while not to notice that the church is empty and the parishioners have gone elsewhere to attend other gods, perhaps in silence or with new words. (p. 294)

Gore Vidal, "French Letters: Theories of the New Novel," in his Homage to Daniel Shays: Collected Essays 1952-1972, *Random House, 1972, pp. 268-94.*

Ihab Hassan (essay date 1971)

[*An Egyptian-born American educator and critic, Hassan is the author of a number of books on critical theory and contemporary literature. He has elaborated ideas about the modern tradition of "anti-literature" in such books as* Radical Innocence: The Contemporary American Novel *(1961) and* The Literature of Silence: Henry Miller and Samuel Beckett *(1968). In the following excerpt from* The Dismemberment of Orpheus: Toward a Postmodern Literature, *originally published by Oxford Univerity Press in 1971, Hassan discusses Sarraute's role in the development of contemporary anti-literature, noting that she abandons such traditional novelistic devices as character and plot in favor of a phenomenological and linguistic examination of the foundations of reality.*]

With few exceptions—[Sartre's and Camus's] *Nausea, The Stranger,* and *The Fall,* perhaps—Existentialism tends to express radical thought in conventional literary form. Its ambitions are Promethean, didactic, or political; its judgments weigh on the language of art; and its personalities almost dominate the reader's awareness. By contrast, the literature that follows seems neutral, self-effasive. Pretending to eschew ideology, protest, and analysis, it cultivates a certain flatness—Roland Barthes calls it "*matisme complet*"—in order to avoid imposture. This literature goes by many names: anti-literature, objective novel, *écriture blanche, nouveau roman, chosisme, école du regard, école de minuit.* Germaine Brée may be right in asking for a new name to designate fictions of this type. I simply choose the generic term of "Aliterature," intended by Claude Mauriac, one of its practitioners, to suggest the power of avoidance, of self-refusal, that this movement seeks. The term will not greatly affect the authors themselves who include Nathalie Sarraute, Alain Robbe-Grillet, Michel Butor, Claude Simon, Robert Pinget, Marguerite Duras, and Jean Cayrol, among others. Obviously, so many authors are not likely to adhere strictly to a school. But their common rejection of tradition puts them in a certain relation to one another, and tempts them to explore certain possibilities of fiction.

Aliterature shares with the tradition of silence what Hegel calls the "patience and labor of the Negative," what Heidegger calls the "mystery of oblivion." It moves toward a still center, and within that toward a point yet more still. Kafka anticipates its qualities; Beckett also, and in some measure Sartre and Camus. Even the interior monologue of Edouard Dujardin's *Les Lauriers sont coupés* (1887) may suggest a remote antecedent. But Aliterature emerges mainly as the language of consciousness at its reflexive task, the creative process giving phenomenological evidence of itself. It takes from Husserl the concept of "intentionality," and adapts it to a narrator who lacks an isolate self, an identity separate from what he may recall or perceive. The nominalism of Aliterature, its concern with trivial *things,* sensations of the banal, is therefore epistemological. True knowledge resists abstraction; myth and metaphor yield to the feigned concreteness of fact; self and surface are one. But a sociological view is also thereby implied. As Lucien Goldmann shows, the active functions of capitalism in its last stages pass from men to things; the world of objects constitutes an autonomous order, a dominant structure, to which all human expression adheres. The aesthetic of Aliterature responds to this bondage of postmodern man with a small measure of freedom. Out of the given data of experience—images, perceptions, memories—new patterns are created, new *fictions.* Fictions of this kind may exercise the only freedom of a mind threatened by nominalism on the one hand and solipsism on the other. Such fictions can refer only to the internal time of consciousness, not of history or the stars; they refer to the phenomenological present, where discontinuous reality escapes from each word even as it is read or uttered. Self-reflexive, Aliterature exploits its narcissism; it dramatizes on the page, Sturrock says, "the assembly of a novel;" and in doing so reveals "the opposition or tension that exists between language and silence."

Nathalie Sarraute begins writing in that mode before it receives a name. . . . Her first book appears before the war, in 1939, an early version of ***Tropismes. Portrait d'un inconnu*** waits till 1948 for publication. The book, though it carries a famous preface by Sartre in which he speaks of the contemporary phenomenon, "lively and totally negative works that might be called anti-novels," scarcely makes a revolution. Mme. Sarraute persists; she lectures and appears on radio interviews; she writes criticism for *Les Temps modernes.* Gallimard publishes ***Martereau*** (1953). As an editor of the Editions de Minuit, Robbe-Grillet brings out a new version of ***Tropismes*** (1957). ***Le Planétarium*** appears in 1959, ***Les Fruits d'or,*** which wins the Prix International de Littérature, in 1963. By that time, critics and plain readers know of the *nouveau roman,* though few may read the genre and fewer still appreciate what they read.

Two reasons, at least, account for the uncertain resistance to the new literature. Claiming for itself new assumptions, its fails to edify or entertain, indeed to render "reality," in any way that even a modernist reader expects. But claiming also for its theory more than its practice shows, the new novel leaves room for both adverse and sympathetic critics to question its achievement. The critical statement of Mme. Sarraute, ***The Age of Suspicion,*** reflects in some measure this uneasiness.

In her treatise, Mme. Sarraute pretends to reject psychological analysis, the idea of human depths: ". . . modern man, having become a soul-less body tossed about by hostile forces, was nothing, when all was said and done, but what he appeared to be on the surface. . . . The 'tumult like unto silence' that adherents of the 'psychological' had thought they saw in his soul was nothing, after all, but silence." This is in keeping with the phenomenological doctrine of mind as a field of perceptual relations; it denies only one kind of psychology in favor of another. What Mme. Sarraute finds spurious is the convention of "character," that psychological prop on which the novel so often rests. The character of fiction, she says, has lost his ancestors, his well-filled house, his discernible manners; now he must lose his name. The novel must reckon with the suspicions of its author and reader: "For not only are they [author and reader] both wary of the character, but through him, they are wary of each other." Moreover, both have become wary of fiction itself. The facts of outrage push reality to the very limits of our dreams: in a certain sense, Kafka can go no farther than Himmler. What more can the novelist say? Perhaps he can only present surfaces, render tenuous states of consciousness, as multiple, changeful, and ambiguous as the states of matter and energy, in modern physics. "Suddenly, the reader is on the inside, exactly where the author is. . . . He is immersed and held under the surface until the end, in a substance as anonymous as blood, a magma without name or contours." In an age of mutual suspicions, Mme. Sarraute is grateful for the quality of doubt that compels the novelist to discover new modes of sensibility, and prevents him from repeating the efforts of his predecessors.

Yet her final view of literature is not altogether original: literature, she says, gives to its readers "a deeper, more complex, cleaner, truer knowledge of what they are, of their circumstances and their lives, than they can acquire alone." Mme. Sarraute does not condemn words; on the contrary, she permits them to take the central place in fiction, in absence of character, plot, or setting. Her interest in "subterranean movements that are at once impatient and afraid" brings her closer to Marcel Proust, Henry James, or Virginia Woolf than her theory allows. And her penchant for certain critical terms—"surface," "hard," "compact," "opacity"—seems at variance with her own fastidious style, refined secretly by poetic means. She sets fiction against itself, but ends with an art work as *made* in its way as a Mallarmé sonnet. Her true achievement may be a poetry of existence that evades the fond inauthenticities of older narratives. In an interview reported in *Tel quel* (Spring 1962), she says: "For me, the poetry in a work is what reveals the invisible. . . . Believing what I do about poetry, how should I not think my own works poetic? It would amount to believing that I do not reveal an atom of the invisible world."

Poetry meets fragments of a new psychology, sentiments anterior to verbal expressions—*sarrauteries* they are sometimes called—in "tropisms." Dostoyevsky, here as elsewhere, is the acknowledged master of Nathalie Sarraute. She quotes a passage from one of his stories, "A Bad Anecdote": "We know that entire arguments pass sometimes through our heads instantaneously, in the form of sort of sensations which are not translated into human language and even less into literary language." These "arguments," in the form of images or infradiscourse, suggest her own tropisms. Deriving from a Greek root, "to turn," tropisms "slip through us on the frontiers of consciousness" and present, in the collection of prose-poem-play-stories by that name, little, anonymous actions, sinister, quotidian, magical, "the secret source of our existence, in what may be called its nascent state."

Mme. Sarraute retains tropisms as the "living substance" of her subsequent works, amplified into larger dramatic actions and more complex verbal interplays. ***Portrait d'un inconnu,*** for instance, is an account of domestic deceptions, desires, despairs, couched in the language, banal and insidiously poetic, of a hypersensitive observer. This voyeur looks inward to tell a phenomenological tale of an old miser and his sickly daughter. His tale could also be his own, for he too is the son of a father, the old friend, perhaps, of the miser. Speaking in the first person, his stream of modified consciousness becomes omniscient; his internal notations transform a mundane family affair into an archetype of existence, shuttling between self and other, appearance and reality, concreteness and generality. His cracked vision dwells on fragments of public experience, bits of quotidian life, moments of language and time, subverted continuously by his inwardness. For the speaker, nothing remains ordinary, without oddness, fear, lust, pain, or cruelty; nothing remains in its place. His phrases, even his images, bring all the small solaces of the daylight world; his dislocations of that world twist and snap underneath.

And what is the motive of that speaker? His erotic interest in the daughter, his fascination with her father, his guilt toward his own, his ambivalence toward all the others—they, they, they, their whispers, their rumors—blend into his compulsion to see "the other aspect," and to find discoveries in "old forgotten things." "They" imagine a picture he paints, called "l'Hyper-sensible-nourrie-de-clichés." But his motive is deeper: he wants to rescue father and daughter from their fate as objects, heavy, opaque, created by the language of others; and deeper still: he wants to rescue himself from a worse fate as an object created by his *own* language. The Portrait of an Unknown may be that of a nameless old miser. But there is also a painting by that name, in a Dutch museum, to which the narrator returns. Its painter is as anonymous as the subject; so is the old miser; and so is the narrator. The painting itself, however, directs an "appeal" to the speaker, projects a "silent flame" that melts the chain binding him to "others." "I ask only this, that they empty me, that they deliver me," he says to a medical "specialist." We begin to see: Mme. Sarraute, a narrator, a painter, and several portraits of nameless people, within the context of a single artistic consciousness, search for mutual deliverance, separate authenticity.

The threat to authenticity comes from others, which is to say, from common parlance, words. But it also comes from death. The old man speaks of "my awakenings of a condemned man." The narrator goes farther; he senses that death weighs on language, smothers objects, and deceives men with the false euphoria of all clichés. In this novel, refrains, slogans, tropisms, serve to imply death continually, and to exorcise it in the silent prayer beneath the words. The novel ends:

> Everything will quiet down, little by little. The world will take a smooth and clear aspect, purified. . . .
>
> After death? . . . No, that too is nothing . . . Even that slightly strange air, as if petrified, that slightly inanimate look will disappear in turn . . . Everything will take care of itself . . . It will be nothing . . . Just one step more to take.

Portrait d'un inconnu can be read as a novel about an egoistic miser near death, a family romance, a satire on bourgeois society, a philosophic reflection on language and consciousness. Its central impulse, however, comes from the need of the artist to define his form and function—indeed, his life—in the process of writing, without recourse to traditional definitions of art. The result, nonetheless, appears literary, richly allusive. Certain elements—ideas, objects, feelings of a viscous, opaque, and sweetish ("douceâtre") kind—remind us of *Nausea.* Mme. Sarraute also refers to other painters and writers, making complex use of their symbols, the mask of Prince Bolkonski, for instance, in *War and Peace.* Her incantations of foreign names and places, the meaningless patter of dialogue, recall the language of Nonsense, recall sometimes the secret rhythms of Ivy Compton-Burnett, sometimes of Ionesco: "Biarritz? huh? huh? Ustarritz? Do you know what it is? Do you know? Ustarritz? He rolls his *r*'s very strongly. Biarritz? La Bidassoa? huh? huh? Chocoa?" Like Hemingway, she learns to omit, and makes her statement by exclusion; the silence on the other side of banality tells her tale. So does the sudden poetic image. In a crucial episode, the daughter steals a piece of a soap bar from her father; his mortal rage collapses in sleep; then: "The awakening is peaceful. The soap bar, on the board above the sink, shines gently in the morning sun, like rippling sand on a beach after a stormy night." Still, Mme. Sarraute cannot maintain the tension between speech and silence throughout her novel; its final section has directness, rawness of emotion, almost the character of a climax or denouement. This shift betrays a larger issue, the inherent artistic problem of the *nouveau roman:* how to convert boredom and flatulence, the dumbness of things, into literary use? Diffused, diffracted, the attention of the reader may wander about; the purely imagistic resources of language cannot always hold it in place. In some real sense, the reader is released from conventions of the past as well as from significations of the future. Perhaps this is in the nature of Aliterature, which Mme. Sarraute brilliantly demonstrates in ***The Golden Fruits,*** a novel about a novel called *The Golden Fruits* which commits itself to oblivion in the act of reading. (pp. 160-67)

Ihab Hassan, "Interlude: From Existentialism to Aliterature," in his The Dismemberment of Orpheus: Toward a Postmodern Literature, *The University of Wisconsin Press, 1982, pp. 139-76.*

Nathalie Sarraute with Germaine Brée (interview date January 1972)

[*A French-born American critic and translator, Brée has written numerous critical works on modern French literature, including* Marcel Proust and Deliverance from Time *(1955),* The French Novel from Gide to Camus *(1962), and* Gide *(1963). In the following excerpt from an interview conducted in January 1972, Sarraute discusses her theories on language and writing.*]

[*Brée*]: *Could you tell us when and how you began to write?*

[Sarraute]: Well, I always wanted to write, ever since I was small. Perhaps it was because I spent my early childhood in a literary milieu; perhaps it was because my mother and her second husband, my stepfather, were writers that I didn't dare write for awhile. I liked to do the assignments in French literature at the Sorbonne, and later on I had the impression that I had no substance of my own. It was a time when the novel seemed to be dead—at least the traditional novel. Max Jacob and Valéry were both saying so. As for me, after reading Proust and Joyce, which I did between 1922 and 1924, and then reading Virginia Woolf, I felt that it was no longer possible to write as people had done previously and so, since I couldn't find anything to write about, I didn't write. The first things which I did write were wholly spontaneous. This was between 1932 and 1933 and consisted of fragments which haven't ever been changed and which still remain in the little collection of ***Tropismes.*** I wrote these almost unconsciously just as one writes a first poem.

You call them "fragments," but they are quite perfect in a way and full of humor and a kind of human understanding. You are quite objective and yet one feels that you are not removed from your work. You describe reactions . . . you see them very clearly, but you do not arrogate to yourself the right to judge.

Yes, any such superiority seems to me absolutely inconceivable. I think that at a certain depth everyone has much the same interior movements and the same reactions, and it is not possible to show them if one has not experienced them oneself somehow, even with respect to things other than what one is writing about.

So, after this first work, what really started you on your career as a novelist? I believe that you are about to publish a novel right now, your sixth or maybe your seventh. . . .

It's the seventh, if you count ***Tropismes*** as a novel, which it really isn't. It is, rather, a collection of short texts, but because it doesn't have the slightest plot, people have considered it as my only real novel from the point of view of the *nouveau roman.* I don't totally agree with that judgment because there is no link whatsoever between the fragments and I had no thought of making them into a novel at all. But in my new novel, ***Vous les entendez,*** I wanted to show a kind of interaction between consciousnesses which are extremely close to one another to the extent that they almost fuse and communicate by a kind of continuous osmosis. It is about a father and a group of young people who are his children but who are not differentiated. What each one feels and attributes to another becomes blurred in a sort of kaleidoscopic conflict in which each becomes any one of the others at any given moment.

I was interested in creating the constant motion, the actual physical motion, involved in the novel's action, since the father goes up and down the stairs to talk, to knock at the door of the children, who are laughing on the floor above him. Everything pivots around a work of pre-Columbian art and the father's and the young people's attitudes to it. By extension, it concerns all art in general, so that there's conflict involving aesthetic feeling, aesthetic joy, fatherly love, and the threat which hangs over art in general, in the father's eyes, because of the scorn shown by the new generation.

After the young people have politely looked at the sculpture, which fascinates the adults, they go upstairs and laugh and laugh endlessly. "One hears them." The father raises his head, listens to them, and becomes exasperated. He ascribes all kinds of meanings to the laughter; he reads all sorts of movements into it.

Which the laughter may not imply?

Which it may or may not imply.

Since it may imply them, you are purposely being ambiguous?

Yes.

You let the reader work out for himself what the meaning might be. What is the connection between this novel and the one which preceded it, **Entre la vie et la mort?**

Since the publication of ***Les Fruits d'or,*** I have been preoccupied mainly with the relationship between the work of art, the environment into which it falls, and its fate in general. ***Entre la vie et la mort*** is concerned more with the author, the one who creates the work. Then in ***Vous les entendez,*** I take up again what seems essential, an attitude with respect to a work of art, namely, the aesthetic sense. After I had finished writing the book, I ran across an article in *L'Express,* I believe, or in *L'Observateur* which stated that Mao Tse-tung had said, "Art is the consolation of the gentleman," and I said to myself, "My two old men are like that," and that is how the young people see them . . . the two old men who sit there in ecstasy before the sculpture of a stone animal.

What is your point of view about this situation?

I don't really have one. I pass from one side to the other.

When you published **L'Ere du soupçon** *in 1956, a book which really counted in the new self-awareness of the novelist, you had behind you* **Tropismes, Le Portrait d'un inconnu** *and* **Martereau.** *Could you explain the relationship that existed between your practice of the novel and your reflections on it?*

When I wrote ***Tropismes,*** I was convinced that it was absolutely impossible to continue writing novels with characters and a plot; I thought I would be able to keep on indefinitely choosing movements that just barely depended on a support that itself was almost invisible and very light, a character who is a sort of shadow, but in whom what counts would be this movement, the tropism, as it was developing. Even before this book was published in 1939, I had already begun trying to find developing tropisms like the first ones, fastened to nothing and hanging in the air all by themselves, and it was extremely difficult to do. Max Jacob had written me that it was like fishing in an enormous bowl. I stayed for days on end with the line cast and there were no bites. I told myself that perhaps it would be interesting to show someone who seeks out these tropisms through two semblances, characters externally resembling traditional ones, like the miser and the old maid in ***Le Portrait d'un inconnu.*** Thus I would have a richer matter that would radiate from the same center instead of my having to look here and there for disjointed fragments with which to work. And afterwards, a character right out of the traditional novel was to appear and put a stop to all that; he was to destroy all the movements, and everything would fall back again into the norm, into the classical novel. Then, when I wrote ***Martereau,*** I knew it was going to be the continuation of ***Le Portrait d'un inconnu;*** that meant a character who has a name, a profession, an external appearance, and whose dialogues with others are written in the wholly traditional form which one uses to describe attitudes—that character would be called Martereau. He would have the reassuring appearance of a character such as we are accustomed to see but this time he would be less strong than the others and, instead of destroying them and bringing the tropisms to a halt, he, in turn, would fall to pieces by coming into contact with the others.

During that time, I lived in almost complete solitude from a literary point of view, and I thought that it would be interesting to find out why these novels didn't awaken even a slight echo since no editor had accepted ***Le Portrait d'un inconnu*** even with a preface by Sartre. With a good deal of difficulty, one was found who sold the novel for the price of the paper. After getting rid of 400 copies, I didn't have a cent, and I said to myself, "Why do I feel that I'm going in the right direction and that it is not possible to give in and write in the traditional manner?" Because I should tell you that when I tried to write the ending of ***Le Portrait d'un inconnu,*** the last scenes in which Dumontet, the character who was so conspicuous and visible, is so active, I found that it was very enjoyable and amusing to do, that it didn't bother me in the least, and that I could have continued for pages describing characters like that and plots of every sort which I could have invented very easily. I wondered why I didn't do it. The truth of the matter is that I felt that something was wrong. As a result in 1947, I wrote my first article, which had as its purpose the defense of psychology. People misunderstood me. I had not wanted to defend traditional psychology, the usual analysis of feelings, but I wanted rather to state that there was a kind of psychology in movement, an inner world in movement, which should be brought to light—that people were wrong always to oppose Dostoevsky to Kafka because Kafka himself certainly had not been able to do without the inner world of the psyche.

For me, the poetry in a work is what reveals the invisible. . . . Believing what I do about poetry, how should I not think my own works poetic? It would amount to believing that I do not reveal an atom of the invisible world.

—Nathalie Sarraute

People thought you had said exactly the opposite.

They misinterpreted the essay; given all that I owed to Proust, Joyce, and Virginia Woolf, who had already expressed very interesting ideas on the need to reform the novel, it was unthinkable that I should begin to say that these people were obsolete. I had spoken but I was probably so sure I would be understood that I wasn't clear enough. I said "some of us" but I was thinking about other writers (and not about myself), people who considered those writers as decrepit monuments for school children. And people took me to task violently and would have been right had it been true, for I would have shown extraordinary ingratitude.

Sometimes it is dangerous to be ironic.

Yes. I was also berated for something else, for having advocated a return to the analysis of feeling. I would like to insist that this was not my concern; nevertheless, I felt that the complete absence of an inner core led to a kind of sclerosis or void. I couldn't conceive of literature without the existence of that inner core. Afterwards in 1950, I wrote the second article of ***L'Ere du soupçon,*** the one which gave its title to the book, in order to show to what extent today's writer, in trying to set limits, creates various kinds of totally academic *trompe l'oeil,* and that today the character in a novel conceived by an author trying to imitate Tolstoy or Balzac could not, as I saw it, produce anything interesting. These essays came out in *Les Temps modernes,* but they didn't create the slightest stir. People asked me what I was talking about. The word "traditional" didn't mean anything to anybody. There was the novel, that's all. By dealing with *sur*-[exterior] and "subconversations," I had also tried to consider a new way of looking at dialogue. It all fell on deaf ears. It was only when the essays were reissued in book form in 1956, when probably, the situation having changed, the time was ripe, that it interested the critics and the readers much more than my other books, which had hardly been of interest to anyone. ***L'Ere du soupçon*** received rather wide acclaim.

It was at that moment that it attracted the attention of Alain Robbe-Grillet, who had himself written novels in an entirely different vein. He thought it would be interesting for us to form a group and to create something which has since been called *nouveau roman* by the critics. I believe it was Emile Henriot who used this expression when ***Tropismes,*** reedited by the Editions de Minuit, appeared or, rather, reappeared at the same time as *La Jalousie.* After that Michel Butor, who had published *L'Emploi du temps* and *Passage de Milan* with the Editions de Minuit, joined our group and so a connection was established between people who had practically nothing in common except the desire to change the forms of the novel—such changes had already been made in music and painting. Each of us had his own style and we didn't work at all in the same area.

It seems in fact that you went off in quite different directions.

One could say that Robbe-Grillet and I are almost at opposite poles.

Furthermore, Butor is far more abstract.

He is extremely far from both of us.

After **Le Planétarium,** *do you think there was a shift in your concerns? By that I mean more specifically towards the life of the author, his relationships with others, with himself, with his work?*

Certainly. The idea came to me when I was writing ***Le Planétarium;*** I had just completed a passage about Germaine Lemaire, the writer, and I thought that it would be very interesting to do something about the literary text itself. I thought of ***Les Fruits d'or.*** It would be interesting to take a book, which would become the true hero of the novel, and follow its destiny as it rises and falls and especially to examine the tropisms which its publication generates around it. And then afterwards I thought that it would be interesting to concentrate on the writer as such, not on *a* writer. I did not portray an individual writer and anyone can see that the attitudes I described could hardly belong to the same person.

This was for **Entre la vie et la mort?**

Yes.

It is a novel which moved me and made me laugh, too. I must confess that I laughed out loud when I read it and that happens rather infrequently, I think.

I'm delighted at that because I like humor in general, and I was surprised to see that the English, for instance, thought that there was no humor in my books—they have such a sense of humor, so I wondered how they could consider ***Martereau*** and ***Le Planétarium*** as humorless.

They may have read your novels too earnestly, without sufficient perspective perhaps, to see that they are extremely funny in a subtle way. But **Martereau** *and* **Le Planétarium** *are very amusing just the same. And it seems to me that in* **Entre la vie et la mort** *you settle the score with the critics. It is unusually entertaining because it subtly attacks all the myths that grow up around the writer.*

I hoped it would. Some things, for example, have always exasperated me. When something is unsuccessful and somebody tells the author so, the author invariably answers, "I did that on purpose." I wrote a whole passage about that reply, but it left people indifferent and they continued to say, "That bit is dull because I made it so on purpose."

I am convinced that you do it on purpose.

Yes. But I don't think that books influence life. Life goes on and books do not change people's attitudes.

Perhaps not right away, but don't you think that in the long run they make people more sensitive to certain issues?

I don't know.

It seems to me that they could make people sensitive, for example, to a certain "tropism" which they had not seen for what it was until then. It seems to me that your books have done that at any rate. I was saying a moment ago that I found **Entre la vie et la mort** *moving because I thought it also described a drama, the drama of the struggling writer.*

Certainly. I had wanted to show the terrible kind of ambiguity in which he works. He is constantly tossed back and forth between the need for total solitude and the need for a certain amount of understanding on the part of others, of approbation, because in order to live a book needs a reader. A writer also suffers because the materials with which he would like to work have already been, and are all the time being, covered over with clichés, a certain varnish he has to scrape away to uncover something which, at first glance, seems ugly and even repulsive.

It seemed to me that in this book there are some moments which are quite dramatic whose intensity is conveyed by a lyricism in the imagery. The richness of the imagery is sometimes ironic with respect to the consciousness of the writer. In any case, one sees a certain mystery taking shape; for example, you say there is a moment when your writer moves into the virtual, where, all at once, his work begins to grow and take on a kind of life of its own. Doubt then besets him.

Yes, yes, indeed.

Is he deluded or is the work really alive?

It is very hard to say. This is what makes writing almost agonizing. The more you polish the form and perfect it, the more it hardens, becomes frozen, and dies, so that you can count on no gain from the work you have done. It is often almost dangerous to polish the writing and the form too much. It often happens—precisely when the polishing has been intense and the form has taken on an aspect of great beauty which delights the writer when he first reads it—that when he comes back to it a few days later he sees that it is a corpse, entirely dead and meaningless. The reason is that, having lost all contact with his initial feeling, he has been carried away by the charm of language as such. Language has taken over and has necessarily sought harmony and an extremely dangerous aesthetic form; the surge, the aggressive force, and the expectation of something which is about to be born have all been lost.

Is that what you were saying a moment ago when you spoke of a sort of dual personality in the writer?

Exactly. I think that each writer, each artist in general . . . this is equally true of painters . . . has a kind of double, who, from time to time as he works, stands back and looks at his painting or rereads his text. He is both himself and someone else. He often becomes a completely merciless judge. And it is he who suddenly sees that that wasn't what he wanted and that the work is dead.

Yet there seem to be times in the novel when perhaps the writer himself is mistaken.

There are times when he can be mistaken, but when it comes to the work, it is almost imperative that he have faith in his judgment since he is the only judge.

In this development of a kind of judgment on the technique itself which is used, do you have a point of view? In a word, are your techniques conscious or do they develop as your novel grows?

They are unconscious. For instance, I noticed in my last book—and realized it only a long time after I had begun the book—that I was no longer separating dialogue from "subconversation." That came about quite naturally. I even thought that maybe I ought to have put in quotation marks, all the same, so as to show that the conversation starts right there. Then I thought it didn't really matter. When I wrote ***Le Portrait d'un inconnu,*** I hadn't even realized that it was impossible for me to give the characters names. With the exception of Dumontet, there was "he," "she," "the old man," "the daughter"; and when I was correcting the proofs, I said to myself occasionally, "Just the same, I ought to give some indication here. . . . " I don't like obscurity for its own sake. I even considered putting a name in, but I saw that it was impossible. It ruined everything because as soon as I gave a name, "Jeanne said," for instance, I found myself standing at a distance . . . I was no longer at the center. There, there are no names; there is nothing. There's a kind of anonymous substance that functions on its own. It's worked that way every time. Here, for example, there are chapters in which everything takes place purely in the realm of the imagination. These chapters happened that way without my realizing it. I kept going exactly as if I were always in the realm of the real, although I had moved out of it quite spontaneously. Sometimes I say to myself beforehand, "I ought to do some particular thing here," but it is always to give more life to the initial sensation.

And now that a new novel is about to come out, will another one follow or are you going to turn to the theater?

At present, I am finishing a play for the Stuttgart radio. It's a very funny play. It comes from the same source as ***Vous les entendez*** and will be called ***C'est beau.*** I've got about two-thirds of it done. And then, after that, I shall have to think about a book again.

A novel?

I have lots of ideas about it but still. . . .

How about your two earlier plays which are also very funny?

There are really three, ***Le Silence, Le Mensonge,*** and ***Isma.*** The last one was only given over the radio but it will be produced on stage with my next play.

Do your characters first come to you as voices when you start writing a play?

Exactly—as voices. I don't visualize any characters. And when Barrault wanted to stage ***Le Silence*** and ***Le Mensonge,*** he asked me how old the characters were and who they were. It was almost by accident that I wrote "man" or "woman." In truth I could have switched those designations or put them in the plural. I don't see them and I don't visualize the stage either. I don't see any exterior action. I just hear voices and rhythms. (pp. 138-46)

Nathalie Sarraute and Germaine Brée, in an interview, translated by Cyril Doherty, in Contemporary Literature, *Vol. XIV, No. 2, Spring, 1973, pp. 137-46.*

Barbara Wright (review date 30 July 1982)

[*In the following essay, Wright praises Sarraute's depiction of human relationships in* Pour un oui ou pour un non.]

Once again, in this brilliant, amusing little play, Nathalie Sarraute illuminates the complications and murky depths of human relationships. And once again she takes as her starting-point: words. Simple, casual, innocent words.

Her two protagonists in ***Pour un oui ou pour un non*** are given no names, they are merely Man 1 and Man 2. They are lifelong friends, but Man 1 is worried because Man 2 has recently seemed to be avoiding him, so he goes and asks him why. M 2 replies it is for no reason; or at least, for no reason that anyone would understand. M1, an extremely well-established, successful intellectual, presses him, and the more reticent M 2 finally allows himself to be drawn. The breaking point came, he says, when he too had just had a success, albeit a minor one, and he couldn't refrain from mentioning it to his old friend M 1. The latter's comment had been: "C'est bien, ça". More significantly, M 1 had pronounced these three little words in a particular fashion: "C'est biiien . . . ça". I imagine that Mme Sarraute intends us, her audience and her readers, to greet this "revelation" with the same stupefaction as that evinced by M 1. What is there in that to make such a song and dance about? Why read hidden depths into such an innocuous rejoinder? But the rest of her play convinces us of our error.

Three of Mme Sarraute's main themes are craftily exposed and graphically illustrated in this play: her conviction that almost all our relationships are not merely ambivalent but polyvalent; her equal conviction that it is rare for anything we say to be trivial or meaningless, even though words can give only the vaguest impression of what lies beneath them; and above all, her vital vendetta against the sloppy, or even evil, habit we have of only feeling safe when we have given everything a label, when we have imprisoned other people—and ourselves, too—in pigeon-holes, stereotypes, categories, catalogues.

Man 1 considers himself happy in his role as a member of the intelligentsia; Man 2 considers himself equally happy as a member of nothing, as a one-off individual who lives an unambitious life with no desire for a personal image. Man 2 despises Man 1 as a conventional creature whose life-style would stifle him if he ever tried to follow it. Man 1 despises Man 2 as a failure. The play develops from initial shadow-boxing into a bitter, ding-dong battle between their opposing points of view. M 2 saw implicit condescension in his friend's reaction to his modest success: "C'est biiien . . . ça". Whereas M 1 thought he had intended it as cordial encouragement. In just a few pages the "friends" pass through the most violently conflicting emotions: from anxious concern, to suspicion; on to regret, to sarcasm, anger, affection, jealousy, exasperation, defensiveness, pathos, apprehension, embarrassment.

All this Mme Sarraute achieves in her usual deceptively colloquial and laconic language. She is adept at conveying a profusion of layers of simultaneous meanings and emotions in a minimum of words. Cunningly, interestingly, intensely, dramatically, she presents us with a panorama of the human comedy and invites us to make up our own minds. Her words are like silicon chips: apparently insignificant, but vastly powerful. There is never any rhetoric, but her use of metaphor is of unfailing force. We are always intended to see, and we do see, not merely their poetic but their concrete imagery: a mole burrowing underneath well-kept lawns, soldiers in enemy camps, or massing on frontiers.

Mme Sarraute was asked the perhaps naïve question about her two characters in ***Pour un oui ou pour un non:*** "Lequel des deux est le plus gentil?" She replied that she had tried to be fair to them both, but she confessed that she did have her own preference. Anyone at all conversant with her work will be able to make an informed guess.

Barbara Wright, "Said and Unsaid," in The Times Literary Supplement, *No. 4139, July 30, 1982, p. 835.*

Frank Kermode (review date 25 October 1984)

[Kermode is an English critic who combines modern critical methods with traditional scholarship, particularly in his work on Shakespeare. In his critical discussions of modern literature, Kermode has embraced many of the conceptions of structuralism and phenomenology, characterizing human knowledge as either poetic or fictive—constructed by humans and affected by the perceptual and emotional limitations of human consciousness. In the following excerpt from his essay "What Nathalie Knew," he examines Sarraute's attempts to incorporate truth and psychological realism into her autobiography.]

Even if you stay away from all the books that nowadays offer you theories of it, autobiography appears to have become almost impossibly difficult to write. The old assumption that there were things back there to be remembered and set down in a reasonably coherent fashion has withered; infancy in particular has no official history, hardly even an official myth. Even in the psychoanalytic consulting room it is no longer pretended that the topics presenting themselves belong to a real past that can be recollected, rather than to the here and now; one has not so much a past as a transference.

If the word "truth" comes up at all, it has to be enclosed in quotation marks. If a narrative emerges, possessing the virtues of plausibility, causal connection, and closure, it may well provide a measure of satisfaction; but these after all are the virtues of fiction, and fiction that completely satisfies such conventional requirements can be suspected of mendacity. Memories of childhood are perhaps the most suspect of all, since they are shaped by forces that are the mortal enemies of veracity. (p. 49)

Nathalie Sarraute, now eighty-four years old, has long been preoccupied with the truth of written representations, and with psychological realism. It is forty-five years since ***Tropismes*** first appeared, and that book, with its experimental techniques for exploring such matters, is, as she herself remarks, the foundation of all she has written since. Her more abstract meditations upon them, published as ***The Age of Suspicion,*** have been available for nearly thirty years.

Tropism is a phenomenon associated with certain plants that grow, or bend, in response to the stimulus of light. Sarraute takes the stimulus to be everyday conversation; underneath it occur the private unspoken movements of reaction and response. This is the world of what she calls *sous-conversation,* "hidden beneath these utterly banal words and actions." (This account underrates the complexity of the idea; it has often been more fully expounded, and best, perhaps, in Stephen Heath's admirable book *The Nouveau Roman,* published in 1972.) What matters is not what is said, but the unspoken stir of activity beneath, the restoration of a protective banality, and then again disturbance, activity.

Novels written on this plan have no use for ordinary notions of character, which depend on a measure of conformity with stereotypes and assume the possibility of drawing firm psychological outlines. All such firmness is banished, and the character is no longer a meeting ground for author and reader, each with similar preconceived ideas; instead it is the very point at which they converge "in mutual distrust." We know too much, and can believe in the truth only of that which defies stereotype and possesses no clear outline.

The old style of character, Sarraute wrote in ***The Age of Suspicion,*** made one think of "the mushy consistency and general insipidness of overchewed food"; the new one must somehow be fluid and evasive in an entirely different way. Even Proust is not quite adequate as a model, for whenever there occurs in his work a gap between conversation and sub-conversation he intervenes to fill it with comment or explanation instead of leaving the task to the reader. The need is to develop a technique (it will of course depend almost entirely on dialogue) by means of which the reader may be plunged into the stream of sub-conversation and given the illusion of repeating its dramas "without losing that element of indetermination, of opacity and mystery that one's own actions always have for the one who lives them."

Such, for Nathalie Sarraute, is to be the manner of writing narrative in this self-reflexive, suspicious age. A writer holding these views is likely to approach the project of childhood reminiscence with caution, perhaps with trepidation. Hence the presence of the alter ego already mentioned. She is there at the beginning of [***Childhood***].

> Then you really are going to do that? "Evoke your childhood memories" . . . How these words embarrass you, you don't like them. But you have to admit that they are the only appropriate words. You want to "evoke your memories" . . . there's no getting away from it, that's what it is.
>
> —Yes, I can't help it, it tempts me, I don't know why . . .
>
> —It could be . . . mightn't it be . . . we sometimes don't realize . . . it could be that your forces are declining. . . .

Will not this attempt require her to abandon the element in which she has done her best work, work in which "everything . . . fluctuates, alters, escapes . . . evades you . . . "? Isn't she afraid that she may be handling something that "isn't trembling," that "has become fixed once and for all"? No, she replies; it's still "quivering."

As you would expect, the book quivers, trembles, and shuns whatever is fixed in advance, part of the official record. For example, a recurring theme in traditional accounts is a childhood experience of bliss, of total belonging and identity with the world.

> Eternity was manifest in the light of day, and something infinite behind everything appeared, which talked with my expectation and moved my desire. The city seemed to stand in Eden, or to be built in heaven. The streets were mine, the temple was mine, the people were mine, their clothes and gold and silver were mine, as much as their sparkling eyes and ruddy faces. The skies were mine, and so were the sun and moon and stars, and all the world was mine, and I the only spectator and enjoyer of it. . . .

So Traherne. In *The Prelude* Wordsworth faced the problem of installing a good many such moments—when he saw blessings spread around him like a sea—with a more continuous narrative of the growth of a poet's mind. And for him the relation of such moments, appareled in celestial light, with adult experience was harder to explain, especially since some "spots of time" seem memorable as much because of a mysterious charge of anguish or terror as of anything that could simply be called happiness: only a woman with a pitcher on her head, a mountain peak full of menace.

The stereotype, however, is rather the paradisiacal vision, the moment of total belonging, as when Nabokov, remembering an uncle reading, sees again his schoolroom reflected in a mirror above the man's head:

> A sense of security, of well-being, of summer warmth, pervades my memory. That robust reality makes a ghost of the present. The mirror brims with brightness; a bumblebee has entered the room and bumps against the ceiling. Everything is as it should be, nothing will ever change, nobody will ever die.

This seems straightforward, but the tense is, cautiously, the present, and the rhetoric is appropriate to that. Sarraute has to deal with an experience of this kind, and one would expect some difference of approach. She was sitting in the Luxembourg gardens and either her father or her stepmother had been reading her a fairy tale, perhaps from Hans Andersen.

> . . . I was looking at the blossom on the espaliers along the little pink brick wall, the trees in bloom, the sparkling green lawn strewn with pink and white petaled daisies, the sky, of course, was blue, and the air seemed to be gently vibrating . . . and at that moment, it happened . . . something unique . . . something that will never again happen in that way, a sensation of such violence that, even now, after so much time has elapsed, when it comes back to me, faded and partially obliterated, I feel . . . but what? what word can pin it down? not the all-encompassing word: "happiness," which is the first that comes to mind, no, not that . . . "felicity," "exaltation," are too ugly, they mustn't touch it . . . and "ecstasy" . . . at this word, everything in it recoils . . . "Joy," yes, perhaps . . . this modest, very simple little word may alight on it with no great danger . . . but it cannot gather up what fills me, brims over in me, disperses, dissolves, melts into the pink bricks, the blossom-covered espaliers, the lawn, the pink and white petals, the air vibrating with barely perceptible tremors, with waves . . . waves of life, quite simply life, what other word? . . . of life in its pure state, no lurking menace, no mixture, it suddenly attains the greatest intensity it can ever attain . . . never again that kind of intensity, for no reason, just because it is there, because I am inside it, inside the little pink wall, the flowers on the espaliers, on the trees, the lawn, the vibrating air . . . I am inside them with nothing else, nothing that does not belong to them, nothing that belongs to me.

I quote at length, partly to give some idea of the excellence of the translation, partly to illustrate the blend of positive assertion and hesitation, withdrawal, quite different from Nabokov's sturdy affirmations and very conscious of itself as a researched piece of writing. It suggests strongly enough the affinity between the unique pulsations of the recollected experience and the tremulous movement of the prose; but it remembers also that pure fiction might do just the same things. "The sky, of course, was blue," because it had to be.

We learn later that when required at school to write an essay called **"My First Sorrow,"** Nathalie invented a bit of autobiography. Writing it, she found that the words guided her choice of incident. At first she set the story in springtime, but, needing a pale sun and gold and purple foliage, switched it to autumn. Seventy years later that "of course" (*bien sûr*) recapitulates what she discovered about autobiography as a schoolgirl.

She inserts into the present narrative some reminders of what it might be like to have a "model childhood." English girls, the daughters of parsons and schoolmasters, come to teach her English and form a sharp contrast with the cosmopolitan child who already knew French and German as well as her native Russian. They were "fresh blown from their country childhoods . . . which could only have been what 'real' childhoods are, lived in insouciance, in security." Such girls were amazed and wretched in the household dominated by Sarraute's passionate and erratic stepmother, but they had happy memories. Sometimes it occurs to Sarraute that she, too, had some: for instance, her mother reading *Uncle Tom's Cabin* to her when she was sick. But counter-memories intervene; weren't there signs that her mother was all too anxious to stop reading and get away? The alter ego comments: "This is the end of the 'happy memories' which you had such scruples about . . . they conformed too closely to the model. . . . Yes . . . it didn't take long for them to regain the privilege of conforming to nothing but themselves. . . ."

There was perhaps not much danger of this childhood conforming too closely to models. The details that emerge (with an appropriate lack of definition) from Sarraute's text are of a childhood spent in Russia and Paris—a history of comfortable exile among émigrés with their revolutionary deeds behind them. The principal persons are seen with the double vision of child and adult: a mother evidently selfish and careless, and her amiable second husband; an adored father and an unpredictable and sometimes wantonly cruel stepmother (beware the Cinderella stereotype), who prefers her own child to Nathalie. It is the evidence of desertions and rejections great and small that comes before adult consciousness. And the child is also something of a foreigner; Jewish, too, though that only comes to be important much later. There are glimpses of St. Petersburg, but mostly of the streets and parks of Paris, and its schools. The story stops on the threshold of the *lycée.*

Yet all this is only a frame. The book deals mostly in discontinuous moments, hesitantly remembered and qualified. The child is represented as mother to the woman in one respect above all, her obsession with words. When her stepmother, with astonishing cruelty, tells her she has been abandoned, she does so not in French but in the relative ferocity of Russian: *Tyebya podbrossili,* with its undertones of furtive force quite absent from the French *t'a abandonnée.* And the writer maintains, against the protest of the alter ego, that she sensed "all the hidden riches" of the Russian words. Needs are converted into words; the young child, seizing dressmaker's scissors, wishes to rip the silk of a settee: *Ich werde es zerreissen,* "I'm going to slash it." Did she know German that well? No matter, "the word *zerreissen* has a hissing, ferocious sound. . . ." We may reflect that this is what the writer later wishes to do to "conversation"—to slash it so that its interior spills out (so she expresses the process in ***Les Fruits d'or***).

The book is much concerned with certain obsessions. The child makes a great nuisance of herself by literal obedience to her mother's requirement that she chew each mouthful of food until it has the consistency of soup (but which has priority, this memory or the passage quoted above from ***The Age of Suspicion***?). She is also, though quietly, concerned with cruelty and violence. Her half sister tears her teddy bear to pieces. She herself has what she calls "ideas." These are uncontrollable desires, the need to say what can only cause trouble and damage. Having decided that her mother is less beautiful than a certain doll, she is obliged to tell her so, and must then bear the guilt of being the only child that does not love its mother.

Or she is visited by the idea that her mother's skin is like a monkey's, imagining, before she communicates this news, various kind or dismissive replies her mother might be expected to make, but didn't. Having heard her mother describe her stepmother as stupid, she is bound sooner or later to let the stepmother know this. She asks the stepmother quite casually, "Do you hate me?" and again gets not the expected reply but "How can anyone hate a child?" which she doesn't find comforting as she contemplates a future in which she will qualify to be hated.

There is certainly a sense in which this kind of writing thrives on the reader's frustrations, resisting attempts to bring it into conformity with inherited notions of what such a narrative ought to be like. And yet it can't quite defeat us; it isn't strange enough for that. The intrusive voice I called the alter ego is not a wholly unfamiliar device, and is fully complicit with the voice of the narrator. It registers objections, but they are nearly always ignored so that one gets the story as it were straight, as well as complicated by gestures of ironical questioning or dissent. It puts the conventional in question but without obscuring it.

So if what we really want, in an old-fashioned way, is an autobiography that says something positive about its writer, we can have it in reasonable measure. Here is a childhood that has what might pass for a recognizable pattern. Here is a book recognizably in the familiar hand of Nathalie Sarraute. If it doesn't itself explore the biographical and psychological implications of its story, it still isn't the kind of book that can stop us from trying to do so if we wish. The author seems to be saying that she has quite enough to do in controlling the language, in insuring that the match between word and imagined or recollected event is free of falsity or, worse, banality. This really is the New Autobiography; but if you choose you can without too much difficulty treat it as quite like the older kind. (pp. 49-51)

Frank Kermode, "What Nathalie Knew," in The New York Review of Books, *Vol. XXXI, No. 16, October 25, 1984, pp. 49-51.*

John Simon (review date 10 June 1985)

[*Simon is a Yugoslavian-born American author and drama critic. His books include* Acid Test *(1963),* Private Screenings: Views of the Cinema of the Sixties *(1967), and* Ingmar Bergman Directs *(1972). In the following excerpt, Simon offers a mixed assessment of* For No Good Reason *and* Childhood.]

In Nathalie Sarraute's radio play ***For No Good Reason***

and prose memoir ***Childhood*** (jointly staged under the latter title), she has found two texts that are so far removed from the genuinely theatrical that she must have jumped for joy at the sheer unsuitableness of them and immediately put her mental pulleys to Sisyphean work.

In her volume of essays ***The Age of Suspicion,*** Mme Sarraute describes the goal of her fiction:

> the immense profusion of sensations, images, sentiments, memories, impulses, little larval actions that no inner language can convey, that jostle one another on the threshold of consciousness, gather together in compact groups and loom up all of a sudden, then immediately fall apart, combine otherwise and reappear in new forms; while unwinding inside us, like the ribbon that comes clattering from a telescriptor slot, is an uninterrupted flow of words.

On the page, this can be intellectually stimulating and psychologically satisfying; on the stage, it is as dramatic as watching motes dance in a sunbeam. The opener, ***For No Good Reason,*** concerns two good friends who gradually realize that they variously patronize, envy, and resent each other, and that even if society, called in as arbiter, can find no valid grievance, the duo can nag and excoriate each other into a perfect symbiosis of hostilities. . . . Although the piece is overlong, it does manage to generate enough emotional reverberation to keep us, if not on the edge of our seats, at least on the edge of some ideational precipice into which we stare with somewhat fatigued awe.

But ***Childhood,*** which is much longer, much more novelistic, and much more narcissistic, does not come to any sort of theatrical life. The author is represented by a reminiscing actress as the remembering self, and by a taped voice (Mme Sarraute's)—when will the avant-garde theater finally give the over-worked tape recorder a rest?—as the prodding, revising, organizing self. Call it the human being in collaboration with, and sometimes in opposition to, her auctorial consciousness. (pp. 91-2)

Essentially, we follow young Nathalie's shuttling between Russia and France, between mother and (first conjoined, then separated) father, between dwindling passive innocence and awakening awareness. We witness the birth of aggressions, doubts, shifting or crumbling loyalties, and the growth of discrimination. Psychic states and ratiocinative evolution are splendidly captured, but there is no theater in any of this: Even when they disagree, the two selves do so dialectically rather than dramatically, and since the others are subsidiary to the point of subservience to this brace of omniscient Nathalie Sarrautes in their orgy of Olympian hindsight (the author, now 85, was 80 when she wrote this), the whole thing emerges not only repetitious and overextended but also self-serving. In a book, which one negotiates at one's own speed and with self-prescribed dosage, it would be ever so much pleasanter. (pp. 92-3)

John Simon, "Not Quite Close-Shavian," in New York *Magazine, Vol. 18, No. 23, June 10, 1985, pp. 91-3.*

Jean-Paul Sartre on Sarraute:

One of the most curious features of our literary epoch is the appearance, here and there, of penetrating and entirely negative works that may be called anti-novels. . . . These curious and hard-to-classify works do not indicate weakness of the novel as a genre; all they show is that we live in a period of reflection and that the novel is reflecting on its own problems. Such is [*Portrait of a Man Unknown*] by Nathalie Sarraute: an anti-novel that reads like a detective story. . . .

Nathalie Sarraute has a horror of the tricks of the novelist, even though they may be absolutely necessary. Is he "with," "behind," or "outside" his characters? And when he is behind them, doesn't he try to make us believe that he has remained either inside or outside? Through the fiction of this soul-detective, who knocks against the shell of these "enormous beetles" from the "outside," sensing dimly the "inside" without actually touching it, Nathalie Sarraute seeks to safeguard her sincerity as a storyteller. She takes her characters neither from within nor from without, for the reason that we are, both for ourselves and for others, entirely within and without at the same time. The without is neutral ground, it is the *within* of ourselves that we should like to be for others and that others encourage us to be for ourselves. This is the realm of the *commonplace.*

Jean-Paul Sartre, in his preface to Portrait of a Man Unknown, *1958.*

Bettina Knapp (essay date Spring 1987)

[*An American educator and critic, Knapp has contributed articles on French drama to such publications as* Columbia Encyclopedia, Grolier Encyclopedia, *and* Yale French Studies. *She is the author of numerous critical studies, including* Jean Genet *(1968),* Antonin Artaud: Man of Vision *(1968),* The Prometheus Syndrome *(1979), and* Word/Image/Psyche *(1985). In the following essay, Knapp analyzes Sarraute's treatment of androgyny and the creative process in* Between Life and Death.]

Nathalie Sarraute's ***Between Life and Death*** (1968) deals with the creative process, from the uncreated work of art embedded in the *prima materia*—the great *void*—to its completion—the book. The Writer, the focus of Sarraute's attention, takes the reader through the multiple stages of his literary trajectory: the struggle involved in the transmutation of the amorphous word into the concrete glyph on the blank sheet of paper; the pain and anguish accompanying the birth of the created work, alluded to as the "thing" or the "object"; the attitude of the successful Writer, who postures and panders to his public; and the rebirth of the creative *élan* following an inner vision.

Like the ancient seer, or *Vates,* Sarraute's Writer is also a miracle worker or a magician, able to inject "life" into what has previously been "dead," or uncreated: the written word. How is such a sleight of hand accomplished? How does the course of words from the uncreated to concretion in the empirical world affect both the Writer and the reader during the happenings in ***Between Life and Death***?

Descriptions of the creative process *per se* have been undertaken by many poets and novelists, for example, Nerval, Rimbaud, Goethe, Baudelaire, Woolf, Joyce, and Gide, to mention only a few. Sarraute's approach is different. She concentrates on the word alone: the sensations, feelings, and ideations that make for its *livingness* or its *deadness.* She organizes, on a verbal, conscious level, what might be called polyphonic musical compositions, emerging from the interweaving of successive voices from the unconscious into single or double oft-repeated themes. Sarraute's images and vocal devices take on a fugal quality as they impose themselves—amplified or diminished—at various stages during the creative process, in keeping with her willed, disordered order.

The creative process, as viewed by Sarraute in ***Between Life and Death,*** transcends temporal philosophical, aesthetic, and sexual schemes. Values and demarcation lines have changed. Heretofore, the notion of giving birth—be it to an object or an infant—has almost always been linked to the Great Mother, since she is the bearer of life, nourisher and devourer, and is identified with *Eros,* the relating principle which brings things together in nature and within the psyche. Spiritual and intellectual factors—*logos*—have usually been associated in the West with the male. Sarraute's Writer, however, exists in an archetypal dimension. Although alluded to as masculine, since the masculine personal pronoun (*il*) is used to identify him, he is neither male nor female. Androgynous, he is composed of both sexes, a complex of opposites, as is the creative spirit in general. He transcends polarities and reaches beyond the empirical into eternal realms. Pierre Teilhard de Chardin's remark [in his *The Prayer of the Universe*] with regard to the creative process is applicable to Sarraute's androgynous Writer:

> Everything in the Universe is made by union and regeneration—by the coming together of elements that seek out one another, melt together two by two, and are born again in a third.

Androgyny is archetypal. It is a universal and collective image that implies "unity-totality" emerging from primordial wholeness or nothingness into the empirical world as divided entities (man and woman). Androgyny has been alluded to in the Bible (Gen.2:21), Plato's *The Banquet,* the *Rig-Veda,* the *Tao te Ching,* and alchemical and Kabbalistic tracts, etc. The notion of self-containment in the spiritually and psychologically androgynous being, if approached in a relatively objective manner, may pave the way for expanded consciousness, greater evaluation, development, and maturation. Once the potential for increase has been exhausted, however, death ensues—a return to the uncreated world of the absolute, to be followed by rebirth. Thus is the *circle* completed; thus does it pursue its course in endless gyrations. Androgyny should *not* be confused with hermaphroditism, which has always been considered "an aberration of Nature," writes Mircea Eliade [in her *Mephistopheles and the Androgyne*]; the former is "not an augmentation of anatomical organs," as found in hermaphrodites, "but symbolically, the union of the magico-religious powers belonging to both sexes."

Not only is Sarraute's Writer androgynous, he is also physically unidentifiable. In fact, he is sexless and torsoless. Outside of a few appendages (hands, fingers which gesticulate and mime every now and then), he is all *head.* As a kinetic object dramatizing his emotional experience, he is forever distorting, foreshortening, expanding, rotating, and shifting spatial and sensorial illusions. Nor does this metaform convey much feeling; love, warmth, tenderness are virtually banished in his non-relationships with others or even with himself. Interaction exists only on an intellectual and sensorial level—no other. *Thinking* is the Writer's dominant function. His rational capabilities enable him to structure and synthesize data via categories, concepts, abstractions, and generalizations. As a *sensation* type as well, he is able to perceive and adapt to external reality through his sight, hearing, touch, taste, and smell. Introverted in the extreme, his world revolves around his creative output—and later, when he becomes famous, the admiration his works elicit from his reading public. Like a hypersensitive instrument, the Writer is forever monitoring his internal environment via his mind, perceptions, and bodily sensations, which relay information concerning external situations to his inner world, and thereby affect his entire system, including his nerve endings or receptor-neurons. There is little that is human about the Writer. Like Athena, he is all intellect, all mind, all thought; he knows how to develop good tactics during moments of conflict, think clearly when challenged, and avoid personal entanglements. He uses sensation as his catalyst.

Unlike the conventional novel, Sarraute's fiction—and ***Between Life and Death*** is no exception—has no real plot. It centers around a controlled or contrived situation: in the Writer's case, the creative process. The essence of the work concerns words as individual entities or archetypal forces, as universal recurring images or patterns of behavior. One word interacts with another, affecting the Writer and his listeners or readers, and drawing energy and power to itself from other words, letters, or figures of speech. In the process, pace slackens or increases, thereby altering the meaning, weight, emphasis, substance, rhythm, sensations, and impact of clauses, sentences, paragraphs, pages. This makes for the narration's sharp, frequently brutal, dramatic effects.

Sarraute, to be sure, is not the inventor of this kinetic literary technique based on the energetic power of the word. Nor is she the first to consider words and letters tantamount to God's creation of the world or to Prometheus's creation of the human race and to his theft of fire. Both notions go far back in history, to the *Sefer Yetsirah* (*The Book of Creation*), which predates the second century A.D., and to other mystical tracts. The *Sefer Yetsirah* describes cosmic creation and ways for humanity to share in it through ten "elementary" or "primordial" numbers (defined as God's Ten Emanations or the ten expressions of His "unfolding" into matter) and the twenty-two consonants of the Hebrew alphabet. The twenty-two letters are looked upon as composing the structural elements of the universe and are, therefore, the foundation of the world. It is through the infinite combinations and phonetic divisions inherent in these "basic letters" that the "roots of all things" exist. Each letter is thought to be charged with its own energy and varies in power, meaning, sound, and image, depending on its placement in the sentence and on the page. Analogies to the three realms of creation may also be drawn by means of a written character: the human sphere, the celestial domain, and [according to Gershom Scholem in his 1941 *Major Trends in Jewish Mysticism*] "the rhythmic flow of time through the course of the year."

Just as every act of creation (animate or inanimate) occurs through combinations of letters, words, and numbers, as demonstrated in the *Sefer Yetsirah,* so, too, does Sarraute's kinetic literary technique bring the unactualized into being. Repetitions, flashbacks, reworkings of words and syntax, positional shiftings of clauses: all are used by Sarraute to create emotional experiences, and to alter pitch, pace, and orientation, thereby affecting concentration, perception, and affect.

Bringing forth the word from nothing, as Sarraute's Writer does, may be looked upon as paralleling a cosmogonic event. It arises from the Beginning, the Void, Chaos (psychologically speaking, from the deepest layers of the collective unconscious—the very source of creation and of reality); it then undergoes a transfiguration, from *Nothingness* to *Something* (or *Being*). The Kabbalists have illustrated this transformation linguistically, by means of the Hebrew words *ain,* which means "nothing," and *ani,* defined as "I." A mere rearrangement of the same letters alters the meaning of the words. Such a change implies, symbolically, the passage from "a gap of existence," or the Void (Nothingness), to existence. It is this instant of transformation, and what leads up to and follows it, that Sarraute's Writer attempts to understand and to convey.

Since some words and letters—emerging from the Writer's collective unconscious and considered the living creative matrix of "all of our unconscious and conscious functions"—are archetypal in dimension, they are endowed with substance, energy, rhythm and patterns of behavior. They are "idea force"—a certain word or letter, capable of instigating a dynamic process, which sets into motion a feeling, an imagining, or an action. Once the letter(s) or word(s) is written, or even thought or sensed, it takes on contour: becoming at once concretion and abstraction, sign and symbol, it also has the potential to develop virtualities and possibilities in time and space.

Since certain words are archetypal in ***Between Life and Death*** they may appear, disappear, and reappear, assuming not only the role of flesh-and-blood characters, but of affects as well. Suprapersonal and nonindividual, their impacts are frequently inaccessible to conscious awareness. They appear or are sensed every so often as autonomous presences or tonal emanations which hover about for a bit, only to fall back into oblivion. At times, they reappear during other sequences as formless substances, as floating opacities, or as glistening crystallizations in an everdilating word/world.

Words in Sarraute's orchestrated prose achieve a scale of nuanced timbres, intonations, and amplitudes which at times triturate, lacerate, exacerbate, striate, bombard, and sear the Writer and reader as well. Or, they may work their charms on listeners by means of velvety, mellifluous, endearing, siren-like harmonics, depending upon their connotations, their positionings in a sentence, and their juxtaposition with other words of the "tribe," as Sarraute calls them.

Cases in point are plentiful. When, for example, the Writer hears a woman at the next table in a restaurant say to her son, "Armand, if you continue, your father will prefer your sister," the power of the words he has just heard affects him deeply; they cut and dig into his flesh, insidiously and mercilessly. On another occasion, the Writer's mother unabashedly accuses him of "ruminating": of literally and figuratively chewing his words, swallowing, masticating, pulverizing, regurgitating them as he probes their origin, meaning, and effect upon him during his word-play sequences. She does not understand him—the artist in him—and for this reason is forever attempting to *normalize* him. She would like him to be just like the others. Once he has achieved fame, however, she makes a swift turnabout. She swells with pride—the pride of a Mother who gave birth to a genius. He was "predestined" to become a great writer, she now claims. The minute he was brought to her in his swaddling clothes, "J'ai *su*" ("I *knew*"), she states with authority—the way the Virgin *knew* the Annunciation or the manner in which the priests instinctively chose the child who was to be the Dalai Lama. Words in this instance are premonitory signs of some sacred event in the offing; their numinosity transcends the event.

Between Life and Death begins as the Writer attempts to convey to his audiences the stages involved in the creation of his book. Sarraute's verbal and gestural language in the opening image is arresting; it offers the reader a mirror reflection of the Writer's unconscious and conscious attitudes—a world of tropisms:

> He shakes his head, puckers his lids, his lips . . . "No, positively no, that won't do." He stretches out his arm, bends it again . . . "I tear out the page." He clenches his fist, then his arm drops, his hand relaxes . . . "I throw it away. I take another sheet. I write. On the typewriter. Always. I never write by hand. I reread . . ." His head moves from side to side. His lips are pouting . . . "No, no, and again no. I tear it out. I crumple it. I throw it away. And so, three, four, ten times I start over . . ." He puckers his lips, frowns, stretches his arm, bends it again, lets it drop, clenches his fist.

Sarraute has drawn her Writer, verbally, in a series of studied poses. But are they really studied? Or are they spontaneous? Ambiguity and mystery lie at the core of Sarraute's figurations throughout ***Between Life and Death.*** Each time she repeats the above sequence in one form or another, repositioning certain words, omitting others or adding some new ones, drama is heightened, as is the acuteness of the pantomimic sequence.

Sarraute's Writer is unforgettable as we see him nodding, frowning, rising, sitting, extending his arm, then bending and lowering it, tearing a sheet of paper out of his typewriter, clenching his fist, opening his hand, grabbing another sheet of paper, inserting it into the machine, typing, reading what he has just written, deciding it is not quite right, tearing it out again, crumpling it up, throwing it away, and so forth. There are times, he remarks in another sequence, when he reaches such a peak of frustration—so preoccupied is he with finding the specific word that will evoke the right idea/sensation—that he leaves his study in a sweat, oblivious to all outside noises or presences. Then, for no apparent reason, the very word or letter he is searching for incarnates itself in his mind's eye and he transcribes it: "on the white page and sentences form. Miracle. How do we do it? It's a great mystery."

The very *mystery behind creation* heightens the Writer's fascination with the transformatory process, from nothing to being. As he pursues his self-interrogation, even awakening at night in his continuous struggle to find the right word—that single power that will encapsulate meaning and sensation—his obsession imposes upon him a stinging torment. "Why my God, why?" he asks—as if experiencing excoriating martyrdom.

The Writer's continuous quest for *the word,* which he dredges up once he sinks into his unconscious, or which ejaculates without any apparent rhyme or reason, may be considered a kind of transformation ritual. The gestural language used by Sarraute in the opening episode (quoted above) takes on a religious flavor, accompanied as it is by specific *signs*: punctuation, figures of speech, and other literary devices. (Religion here is to be understood in its original sense, derived from the Latin, *religio,* "link"—that which unites.) In keeping with the numinosity of the opening ceremony, its formality, increased each time it is repeated during the course of the narrative, discloses an ontological need on the Writer's part to repeat symbolically the original act of Creation.

The reactualization of a cosmogonic act serves several purposes. It regenerates time for the Writer, lending the entire novel a cyclical scheme and, therefore, a mythic dimension. In such a scheme, time is reversible and the Writer can regress to his childhood, becoming linked with events that have faded out of his consciousness and that he brings back to a present reality. The repeated transformations of the opening episode also commemorate for him the primordial conflict: the passage from *Chaos* to *Cosmos,* which parallels his struggle to articulate the Word and to give substance to the amorphous. In reexperiencing childhood and bringing forth language, the Writer experiences a sense of fulfillment and joy and a *raison d'être.* The written word—indeed, the entire creative process—acts as a compensatory device for the Writer. It takes him out of his world of unbearable loneliness which is caused in part by his inability to relate to people on a human level. Later, when his readers describe his torment using the simplistic and banal term, "unadaptable," they believe they have resolved the entire unresolvable problem. Mystery for them is an open book.

Examples of the Writer's extreme sensitivity to language and to the impact of meanings, rhythms, amplitudes, sensations, and variations of form and pronunciation are given early in the book. When he was a child, the verb *faire* (with many meanings, including "make," "do," and "play a role," and "give the appearance of being") disoriented him completely. He recalls the time when he was in school and one of his teachers, noticing he was reading James Fenimore Cooper, questioned him: "Tiens vous 'faites' de l'anglais?" ["So you're 'doing' English?".] The verb is used here idiomatically and actively, as when referring to someone doing the marketing, the ironing and other chores. *Faire* is also used passively as in "Je fais une pleurésie" ("I have pleurisy") or "I am having a heart attack." The verb depicts character traits as well, such as in the description of the Writer: "Vous faites assez inadapté."

The question remains: why did the young boy feel physically and emotionally bruised—even lacerated—by *faire*'s multiple uses? Why did he sense danger ahead for him? His reactions are not as outlandish as they might at first seem. The teacher's question (and the many examples of the use of *faire* given by Sarraute) aroused heretofore unknown sensations in the highly intuitive lad. The discovery that no one word had just one definition was like stepping into quicksand. He sensed that just as *faire* had many meanings and could be used in multiple ways, depending upon the context, so varied options and courses were open to him in the life experience which was his writing. The straight and narrow path was gone; barriers had vanished, and with them the security he thought existed in the empirical domain of words. Gone was the fixity and solidity—the very foundations—of his psyche and aesthetics. Everything existed in a state of flux; anything could become something else, transform, altering its own consistency and scope.

Only as he grew older and began to write literary works were the feelings which he had sensed as a lad understood consciously. He came to experience the truth that the very idea of security in general is an illusion—in the verbal domain first of all.

Psychologically, we may say that what had formerly been *whole* or *one* had become *differentiated.* The ego was emerging from the unconscious and had to weather the life experience itself, with all of its vagaries, and tensions. The One had become Two. Choice and an unsteady course had superseded the fixed and facile way. But there is more to it than this. Like Proust's Narrator, Sarraute's Writer learns in time that he is not even *One* person, so to speak, but the sum total of all the people and events he has experienced, both passively and actively, during the course of his life. As Sarraute remarked in ***L'Ere du soupçon,*** there is no single extreme bottom or depth in anyone; everyone is endowed with "multiple depths; and these rise tier upon tier to infinity." As the multiple selves inhabiting the Writer increase in dimension and scope, so, too, do his feelings of confusion, to the point that he sometimes wonders who he is. Today we label such anxieties as identity crises.

There is, however, a positive side to the Writer's anguish. The very notion of unlimited depths existing within each being may be viewed as an enrichment; like Aristotle's *entelechia,* human potential may be considered infinite. If this is true, so, too, are the Writer's possibilities. Within him, then, exists an inexhaustible source of creativity which he has to learn to tap.

Technique is now called into play. Without discipline, innovative *élan* may be dissipated. To be able to sift the dross from the pure requires a highly tuned *thinking* function: the power to rationalize, to differentiate, to distinguish, and to evaluate the outflow of new contents emanating from the collective unconscious. The Writer's *eye,* one of the most powerful of perceptive instruments, must be turned into a tool. Inquisitive and discerning, it must be object- and subject-observer and participant—wandering about in unchartered territories within his psyche, apprehending the psyche's unknown forces, then integrating them into what will become the work of art. Such a trajectory is arduous, for during moments of intense creativity the Writer must learn to cohabit, to coexist, and to co-function with what may sometimes prove to be mephitic, insalubrious forces inhabiting him, as well as with sublime opalescent sensations—each learning to nurture the other.

Words, for the seven-year-old child, as mentioned previously, were *playthings*—toys which he set in motion or immobilized, whenever the spirit moved him. These treasures, which stimulated further verbal associations and incredible fantasy images, are presented by Sarraute in a spectacular bout of active imagination during a train trip the young boy takes with his mother.

As the train rolls through bleak and snowy countrysides, the lad turns inward, entertaining himself by pronouncing homonyms and homophones in rhythm to the sound of the turning wheels. As each archetypal word comes into consciousness, heteroclite images form, removing him increasingly from his circumscribed and referential world, and plunging him more deeply into vaster, more nebulous spheres.

Active imagination can start with a fantasy, a dream, or an impression of a hypnagogic nature. Jung preferred the word "imagination" to "fantasy," considering the latter a kind of phantasm or fleeting impression. Imagination, on the other hand, he considered to be [according to Barbara Hanna in her 1981 *Encounters with the Soul: Active Imagination*] an "active, purposeful creation." The images issuing forth into consciousness through the process of active imagination are endowed with both a life and a logic of their own. [In a 1953 edition of his *Complete Works*] Jung described active imagination as "the only way toward a direct encounter with the reality of the unconscious without the intermediary use of tests or dream interpretation."

The lad's starting point for his periods of active imagination were words which spurted forth homophonically and homonymically: "Hérault, héraut, héros, aire haut, erre haut, R. O." Words and archetypal images hurtled forth almost simultaneously, and together they made up an entire story. The child's creative and pleasurable pastime in his mind's eye was forever being interrupted by his mother, seated in the same compartment, who criticized him for "ruminating." Not for one moment did she realize that her son was exploring the magical world of imagination—a domain where wholeness exists.

For the future Writer, *active imagination* "opened negotiations" with powers and forces in the unconscious which must have answered a specific need within him. Introverted and unhappy, living with a mother who had little if any understanding of her son's real nature, he used active imagination to help him escape into a land of warmth and comfort; but it also challenged and encouraged his creative *élan.* Unlike the dream, which is experienced passively, active imagination can be directed. The lad accomplished just that. The wanted or willed words he activated released images in his mind's eye, which in turn constellated clusters of sensations and feeling tones.

A whole world of secret desires and compensatory states of being emerged. Hérault (the name of a department in France), herald, hero, an eagle's nest, a wanderer on high, R. O., were, for the lad, archetypal in dimension. They evoked white landscapes, a lavender horn, a knight followed by others riding a richly caparisoned charger, fog breaking out, dark skies lit by flickering stars. The *R* evoked a bulldog standing erect with his legs firmly set on the ground. The *O* symbolized the closed circle: "Everything closes and we start over again."

What do these images disclose about the child's needs and his personality? Does he see himself as Herald, Hero, or Wanderer? The words he uses imply aggressivity, power, and energy. He is struggling to be heard, to be understood, and to penetrate areas that will require of him a show of heroic strength. The charger that forges ahead into untraveled, snow-covered terrain will help him achieve his goal. A whole medieval atmosphere is conjured up as a spectacular battle scene unfolds before him: flags, horses, and men arrayed in brilliant tonalities, each bearing the heraldic symbol of his family or master, pursue their heated struggle. This is a violent, cruel, and electrifying *action painting* at its height.

This sequence of active imagination may also be viewed as a prefiguration of the Writer's future fight with words and his symbolical wanderings through opaque and dismally dark inner landscapes, illuminated only every now and then by scintillating stars. His projection onto a hero figure emphasizes his weakly structured ego, his inadequate or painful life experience, and his need to bring into existence what he lacks: strength, direction, and vision. Thus he removes himself from his circumscribed and individual frame of reference and plunges into the collective experience of timelessness.

The whites and purples daubed onto this same verbal canvas show the lad's feel for color and form and also inject a sense of tremulous excitement. Reminiscent in tone of some canvases by Monet, Cézanne, and Matisse, they ally the medieval to the modern in diachronic relational patterns, thereby linking, associating, and fusing past and present in a space/time continuum.

The *R,* associated with the growling bulldog, stands for strength, fortitude, willpower, attention, and feeling. This archetypal protector (the dog as man's best friend), may also be envisaged as a positive father image or the power that will prevent any harm from coming to the boy. The dog is power; but he is also caring.

The *O,* following the *R,* is a semiotic device that stands for all of the Writer's work and the various stages and variants it has undergone. It also includes the techniques and tools—abstract and concrete—used in the actual writing process: lines, spirals, dichroisms, punctuation, sensations, and literary and aesthetic devices, all communicating with each other in a circular round. Psychologically, the *O* stands for the Self: the total psyche comprising both conscious and unconscious spheres.

The train in which the lad is riding is also *sign* and *symbol.* As it speeds across the snow-covered landscape, activating his imagination, time expands and mythical time is born. The boy feels himself living in the medieval period; the charger in his imagination is festooned in colorful array, and the knight, strong and virile in his coat of mail, bears his heraldic symbols for all to see. Since the train represents the mechanistic world of objects, the boy is also part of the linear time scheme in a contemporary world, which functions scientifically, and with the accuracy of an impeccable clock. Inflexible in its order, disciplined, controlled, and punctual to the extreme, the train is unconcerned with any human factor. It is a link in a complicated communicatory network that links a variety of areas and circadian cycles. Like a human artery which carries the blood from one part of the body to another, it also functions as part of its own vast circulatory system: relocating travelers and merchandise in a continuous round. A train imposes its laws and rhythms on the human being physically and psychologically, since it determines the destinations of all those within its metal frame—both on an individual and collective basis. Another factor also comes into play with the train: its circuit must be set well ahead of time. Such a situation implies the need to define one's course, thereby relying upon discipline and order. Any changes in scheduling or programming must be anticipated beforehand and carried out with precision and care.

Psychologically, the just-discussed sequence of active imagination implies an urge on the lad's part to precipitate the destruction of anything that might impede his course toward creativity or stifle his lunge for life—for creativity. It also suggests the opposite: his dependence upon the scheduled, rational function, the urge to plan ahead, to see to it that all factors in his world are linked, associated, and part of a cohesive whole.

At this stage of his life, the would-be Writer may be said to be symbolically *charging* and fighting his mother, rebelling against her demands that he return to reality. Over and over again, she suggests that he look out of the window at the scenery. But the speed of the train and the child's agitation blot out any definable shapes. Enjoying the freedom of his fantasies and mesmerized by the cadenced rhythmic patterns issuing forth from the repeated archetypal images and the even-sounding wheels as they speed ahead on the tracks, he is endowed with a sense of continuity and contentment.

Although the woman in the train is the young boy's mother, she may also be looked upon as an *anima* figure: a negative, collective mother figure with a decidedly disturbing, provocative, and irritating bent that the Writer meets in various avatars in restaurants, at gatherings, and at lectures. As an interlocutor who never lets him rest in the serenity of his creative imaginings, she plays the role of Devil's advocate, constantly challenging him at play, and criticizing him for his laziness. She rebukes him for his futile meanderings, his overly introverted ways ("tourné en dedans, en train de ruminer"), his inability to see outside of himself, and his spasmodic span attention. When the Writer later makes a name for himself, this same self-sacrificing and overly critical mother will gloat over what she considers to be her doing. He was "predestined" to become a great Writer, she remarks, because as a child he played with words. Other *anima* figures appear at one of the Writer's lectures: a faceless listener who questions him about his creative bent. The woman identifies with him, kowtows to him, blushes fleetingly as she talks to him, then vanishes into the crowd of worshippers—into nonbeing—"un chaînon anonyme" ["an anonymous link"]. Whether mother, reader, or listener, *anima* figures highlight the Writer's hidden, shadowy, opposing, and conflicting side. The *anima* figure is that force that triggers discussion, provokes argumentation, compels analytical evaluation, and thereby increases the Writer's consciousness. It is the *anima* figure in part that invites the ego to come to terms with the polarities facing it in the differentiated realm—in the unfriendly world of contention.

At the conclusion of ***Between Life and Death*** the Writer is no longer alone. Rather he is surrounded by his word-protagonists. As an androgynous principle, he is endowed with two selves—the traditionally "feminine" creative force and the traditionally "masculine" analytic force—and from these is born the third—THE WORK OF ART! (pp. 239-51)

Bettina Knapp, "Nathalie Sarraute's 'Between Life and Death': Androgyny and the Creative Process," in Studies in Twentieth Century Literature, *Vol. II, No. 2, Spring, 1987, pp. 239-52.*

Sarah Barbour (essay date 1989)

[*In the following excerpt, Barbour offers a feminist reading of Sarraute's* Tropismes.]

Nathalie Sarraute began writing ***Tropismes*** in 1932, and the characteristics of the novels that follow from this text became guidelines for what critics 20 years later called the Nouveau Roman. What has always fascinated me about Sarraute's being called "founder/member" of this genre is that the other writers grouped with her were men, and that she has continued to remain apart from them in her statements about the novel and about its language. I attributed her differences in concern and focus from her fellow *nouveaux romanciers* to the fact that she was a woman, and found justification for this opinion in the following statements from her preface to ***L'Ere du soupcon,*** a collection of essays published in 1956 in an effort, as she said, to explain her work to the public.

> Les textes qui composaient ce premier ovrage [***Tropismes***] étaient l'expression spontanée d'impressions très vives, et leur forme était aussi spontanée et naturelle que les impressions auxquelles elles donnaient vie.

> Je me suis aperçue en travaillant que ces impressions étaient produites par certains mouvements, certaines actions intérieures sur lesquelles mon attention s'était fixée depuis longtemps. En fait, me semble-t-il, depuis mon enfance.

I read her insistence on the spontaneous and natural quality of her work as not simply an answer to critics who called the *nouveaux romanciers* "des froids expérimenteurs," but also as her claim to the *right* to express *her* view of reality as a woman, especially because she adds that she had been fascinated by the reality of tropisms since her childhood.

My introduction to Sarraute came at a time when I was identifying the silence which I was just beginning to break personally as one which had been imposed upon me as a woman by patriarchal conventions and language. Here was a French woman writer whose writing broke apart those conventions—her works decentered the narrative voice, they disrupted narrative and syntactical order, they insisted that poetry has a place in the novel, and they presented a view of reality that it seemed only a silent, marginal observer could discern. These were the qualities of writing that Hélène Cixous was making polemics in the 1970's. In a work which reviews French feminisms of that period, *Sexual/Textual Politics,* Toril Moi describes these qualities of writing as a "struggle to undermine phallogocentric logic, split open the closure of binary opposition and revel in the pleasures of open-ended textuality." When Cixous further specified, however, that the term "l'écriture féminine" was a "dangerous and stylish expression full of traps" because such naming simply reinforced the binary logic which imprisons us, I agreed intellectually, but my body did not listen—Sarraute was a woman, I was a woman, so I set about to characterize her writing as distinctly *feminine.* I realize now that I was reading Sarraute from a position that Julia Kristeva describes [in her *Kristeva Reader* (1986), edited by Toril Moi] as "second generation feminism" emerging after 1968: "Essentially interested in the specificity of female psychology and its symbolic realizations, these women seek to give a language to the intrasubjective and corporeal experiences left mute by culture in the past."

My position became confused, however, when I read of an interview with Sarraute in which she is reported to have said that "Any good writer is androgynous, he or she has to be, so as to be able to write equally about men and women." Simone de Beauvoir had accused Sarraute of ignoring her social, historical context in her work, and I knew that I could read her refusal to be labeled a woman writer as an extension of that accusation: Sarraute was denying her feminine specificity. Unfortunately, that reading would also lead me to the same end as de Beauvoir and of later feminists, to dismiss Sarraute for polemical reasons. And Cixous' refusal was still ringing through feminist criticism as well: by looking for a feminine essence in women's writing, feminists would be locking themselves into an identity which would always and only be not-Male. Sarraute's work was too significant and too poignant to me to be dismissed, and I still had to contend with the fact that I was a woman reader seeking a feminist aesthetic, even though at the time I had mistaken it for a *feminine* aesthetic.

I use these terms now in the sense that Gisela Ecker does in her edited work entitled *Feminist Aesthetics.*

> . . . [A] myth of non-alienated expression of gender and sexual identity must necessarily lie behind a utopian project like feminist politics. [. . .] Although we know that "authentic" femininity cannot ever find full social expression [because it continually leads back to polar oppositions] we have to be sure of a vague utopia, [. . .] an idea of not only what we want to be liberated *from* but also liberated *to.* [. . .] I am convinced that it is important to pursue not a "feminine" but a "feminist" aesthetics. The second demands reflecting on the first.

The disruption of the novel's conventions and the specificity of point of view which at first invited me to identify Sarraute's work as "l'écriture féminine," open onto another aspect of her work that I had experienced personally, but had not yet adequately analyzed critically, and that is the practice of reading that her work demands as it calls upon the subjectivity of the reader. Responding to that call, I had inflected her texts with my own sex(uality) and mistaken her work as primarily an expression of female experience. My reading of Sarraute had been made as a desire to be liberated *from* silence, and a closer look at Sarraute's work helped me to see what it might offer as a liberation *to* another way of reading and writing women's experience.

As I began a close textual analysis of ***Tropismes,*** and a subsequent investigation of the narrative voice as it evolves in her novels, I found that I was being invited to situate myself both inside and outside these texts. I soon realized that these two positions represented two ways of knowing, analytical knowing from outside and intuitive knowing from inside. By giving me this dual role as reader, I was being forced to recognize the traditional dichotomy which has aligned "women's writing" with intuitive ways of knowing as opposed to what has been considered standard (male) approaches to writing, analytical and rational. A closer look at these two ways of knowing as they are experienced in ***Tropismes*** reveals that a breakdown of the dichotomy occurs through the shifting alignment of the reader with the narrative voice.

The traditional means by which a narrative "I" sets up a dialogic relationship with the reader in relation to the material presented is first-person narration: I-narrator speaks to you-reader about "them" or "it." In this relationship, the reader can remain at a distance from which to judge, analyze and evaluate "their" activity. Although none of Sarraute's prose pieces in ***Tropismes*** enacts a first-person narration, the anonymity of the "characters" presented as Ils, Elles, Il, Elle, and the distance by which the narrator observes and describes "them," invite the reader into that analytical position. A few examples from the first lines of several of these prose pieces help to exemplify this positioning: "Ils semblaient sourdre de partout, éclos dans la tiédeur un peu moite de l'air, ils s'écoulaient doucement comme s'ils suintaient des murs, des arbres grillagés, des bancs, des trottoirs sales, des squares" ("Tropisme I"); "Elles baragouinaient des choses à demi exprimées, le regard perdu et comme suivant intérieurement un sentiment subtil et délicat qu'elles semblaient ne pouvoir traduire" ("Tropisme IV"); "Le matin elle sautait de son lit très tôt, courait dans l'appartement, âcre, serrée, toute chargée de cris, de gestes, de halètements de colère, de 'scènes' " ("Tropisme VI"). The language and structure of the narration, however, involve the reader in a way that disturbs the security of that analytical look at others' tropistic movement to place the reader in the flux of the movement itself.

A textual reading of the opening paragraph of "Tropisme III" offers a more specific example of this disruption.

> Ils étaient venus se loger dans des petites rues tranquilles, derrière le Panthéon, du côté de la rue Gay-Lussac ou de la rue Saint-Jacques, dans des appartements donnant sur des cours sombres, mais tout-à-fait décents et munis de confort.

ILS are shadowed by numerous, progressively qualifying indicators of place. ILS come to live "dans des petites rue tranquilles"; these streets are then positioned "derrière le Panthéon," which are vaguely "du côté de la rue Gay-Lussac ou de la rue Saint-Jacques." By the middle of the sentence, ILS have been deposited "dans des appartements," but the qualification continues. These are apartments "donnant sur des cours sombres, mais tout à fait décents et munis de confort."

The qualifying spatial indicators are central to this paragraph, and they operate like deictic indicators which are demonstrative adverbs or adjectives organizing the spatial and temporal relations in the passage and announcing some subject as "point de repère." This subject is not represented specifically in the text, but its implied position is one of an observer of the scene described. The reader is at first invited to perceive this scene with this subject outside the textual space, at the same time that the reader is being "dislocated" conceptually within that space by these indicators.

The reader is also "dislocated" semantically, in the sense that an effort to locate the meaning of two of the four adjectives in the passage by means of a referentiality to some "objective real" outside the text is thwarted. The adjective "tranquilles" modifying "rues," when it is read on a denotative level signifies "immobiles, silencieux." Its connotation implies "une idée de paix et de sécurité" (*Petit Robert*). Given the "mobility" within the paragraph which the reader has experienced conceptually, however, the word's semantic meaning is destabilized by the unidentified subject of "énonciation." The concept of tranquility is again destabilized as the reader seeks to understand the word "sombres."

This word is not left to lie in its semantic state from which the reader may derive meanings ranging from the quality of light to the disposition of the soul. The reader is immediately told by the unidentified narrator that although the courtyards are "sombres," the apartments are "tout à fait décents et munis de confort," thus qualifying the qualifier. ILS (and the reader) are at first moved from place to place by the spatial indicators, and now the reader experiences a further manipulation as the significance of the modifier "sombres" is dislocated, or re-located, to have a qualified meaning in this text.

The third-person pronoun which opens this paragraph pretends to invite the reader into the analytical position of the narrator, but the reader is quickly placed in a non-analytical position by these textual strategies. As the piece proceeds, the reader will continue to oscillate between these two positions of perception, thus re-presenting tropistic movement not simply as an activity to be observed but also as a phenomenon to be experienced.

This kind of interaction between reader and text is at work throughout the 24 prose pieces in ***Tropismes.*** In Sarraute's first novel, ***Portrait d'un inconnu,*** the use of the narrative "je" marks a more specific identification between the reader and the narrator. As the narrator seeks, through the act of narration, to impose order on the disorder of his perceptions, however, the difficulty of that activity displaces any mere description of tropistic movement. The reader experiences with the narrator a more active *disordering* which ultimately displaces narrative authority in the text and, by extension, the reader's orientation there.

The first-person narration continues in the second novel, ***Martereau,*** but here the disordering experience broadens to include other characters. Outside observers are in turn observed in the third novel, ***Planétarium,*** and the reader's experience is thus diffused as the narrative voice shifts from character to character. In the subsequent ***Les Fruits d'or,*** discourse originates in first one unidentified voice and then moves to another, conversation replaces narration and unidentified voices replace characters to the extent that the reader's identification is continually called into question. As Sarraute's work evolves, the narrator disappears for the most part, giving way to conversation and "sous-conversation." The more easily discernible line between analytical and intuitive ways of knowing seen in ***Tropismes*** fades with the diminishing role of the narrator, to create a kind of intuitive intellection or an intellectual intuition. The changing nature of the narrative voice and of the interaction between reader and text represents an exploration of the relationship between the polarities of intuition and intellect, and by extention, between the gender constructs of female and male, not in an attempt to privilege one over the other, but rather to find a way to let them play off one another.

Although Sarraute refuses the label "woman writer," she is still a woman writing, and it is Sarraute's pursuit of a style which would adequately express her personal view of reality that offers a challenge which is particularly relevant to women writing today. Sarraute's critical writings show her to be preoccupied with the novel's evolution and with fitting her own work into that evolution. Her search for a style through a reinterpretation of her predecessors (the majority of whom were male) brings to mind the definition of style that Hans Gadamer describes [in his 1975 *Truth and Method*]: style is "by no means a mere individual expression, it always refers to something fixed and objective that is binding on individual forms of expression."

For many women writers and feminist critics, literary genres, the novel's language, the idea of what constitutes a "substance romanesque," have all been presented as "fixed and objective" systems which were established at the cost of women's exclusion. Sarraute's refusal to be labeled a "woman writer" is troubling in a political sense because it reminds us that this term still signifies writing which is considered Other or "not standard" writing.

Sarraute's critical writings, however, can serve to widen our awareness of the dialectical relationship between that literary horizon and a writer's work. They also propose a belief that future writers must maintain a healthy suspicion of what is given. . . . This belief in the necessity of an evolution in literature frees new writing from an adversarial relationship with its past, just as it can free what is considered "marginal" writing from such a relationship with "established" work.

When writing that is done by women and people of color is classified as "women's writing," "Black writing," "Chicano writing," writing is then presumed to be a fixed entity, and the literary horizon to be a "rigid frontier." Sarraute has warned us to be suspicious of such notions. In her pursuit of a continually evolving form lies an investigation of reading which calls upon the subjectivity of the reader and forces us to recognize that reading and writing are enacted by socialized biological beings, as Nelly Furman writes [in the 1980 essay collection *Women and Language in Women and Society*], who "inflect these activities, consciously or not, with their sex(uality) and cultural values." Sarraute's gender unavoidably comes into play in her writing, and her particular view of reality cannot help but be a product of that fact. But by calling on the gendered subjectivity of the reader, she shifts the question from a concern with *her* gender to an investigation of our own.

Sarraute's dialogue with tradition, her constant reshaping of traditional form in order to present her own view of reality, and the form that she offers, all invite feminist critics, women and men as writers and readers to consider that writing is not simply the vehicle for the content of their experience, but more importantly, that it is the space where the form of that experience can take shape. (pp. 132-39)

Sarah Barbour, "A Feminist Reading Nathalie Sarraute's 'Tropismes'," in French Literature Series, *Vol. XVI, 1989, pp. 132-40.*

[To write], I go every morning to the same cafe: I have my table there, always the same one—when it's free—and I stay for two or two and a half hours. It is a neutral place, and no one disturbs me—there is no telephone!

—Nathalie Sarraute, in* The New York Times Book Review, *18 November 1990.

Gabriel Josipovici (review date 13 October 1989)

[*Josipovici is an English novelist, playwright, critic, and educator. His books include* The Inventory *(1968),* Words *(1971), and* The World and the Book *(1971). In the following review, he examines the dialogue and narration in* Tu ne t'aimes pas.]

Human beings, normally so sophisticated in the drawing of distinctions, after three millennia of meditation on the nature of narrative are still constrained to lump together under the heading of *novels* books as diverse as the later works of Beckett, Rosalind Belben's recent *Is Beauty Good* and the works of Nathalie Sarraute on the one hand, and books about small-town life in America in the 1950s or about the state of England—or India—today, on the other. We try to draw distinctions, perhaps between books which explore and books which mirror, or between fiction-as-truth and fiction-as-anecdote. But admirers of (as it might be) John Updike or Margaret Drabble or Salman Rushdie will call the other kind of fiction unreal, cerebral and *avant-garde* (in a pejorative sense), while admirers of Beckett and Sarraute will call the others cheap, sentimental and trite. This only shows us that in order to win adherents of one camp over to the other it is not enough to undertake an aesthetic analysis of the works in question; "literature" keeps spilling over into "life", and nothing short of a total conversion is required.

Certainly Nathalie Sarraute, that quiet, retiring Russian-born lady, now in her eighties, who for fifty years has been writing novels in French, is difficult to reconcile with anyone's image of an "avant-garde" writer—in either sense of the term. Much of the pleasure her work affords comes from its coolness, its impersonality. There is no narrative voice in her latest novel, ***Tu ne t'aimes pas.*** Lines of dialogue are laid alongside one another, introduced by dashes. These sometimes include quotations (in quotation marks) from the conversations of other people. But who is speaking to whom? In one sense the answer is simple. This must be the only first-person narrative which is in the first person plural; and, because the protagonist is made up of many voices, his or her way of speaking can only be through a dialogue between these voices. And what do "we" talk about? In the first instance about others. About those who first startle "us" by telling us that what is wrong with us is that we do not love ourselves. For "they", these others, certainly do love themselves. This is evident from the way they lay their hands on the table, for example, and look lovingly at them. Or from the way they speak about themselves: "Moi, vous savez, je suis plutôt d'une nature insouciante . . .", they say; or "Vingt ans de bonheur. . . . Eh oui . . . j'ai eu ça . . . "; or "Vous ne pouvez pas comprendre. Ce sont des choses qui ne doivent pas m'arriver!"; or "Si c'était moi, voilà ce que je ferais . . ."; or "Oui, j'ai des remords. . . . J'ai été égoiste. J'ai été lâche. . . . "

In the face of such self-love, self-confidence, "we" can only stare in amazement and bewilderment. How marvellous to be like that, to be able to do and say such things. "We" cannot even find it in ourselves to say "I", let alone regard ourselves so tenderly. We feel ourselves weak, fragmented, uncertain. It may be, as they tell us, that we do not like ourselves, that that is what is wrong with us. So we try to will ourselves to love ourselves, but it doesn't work. And when we are forced to come out with phrases like "Do you love me?", we feel like children playing games. The novel charts the anxiety caused us by the accusation that we do not love ourselves, but it ends on a kind of resolution:

> —Comme ce serait bon pour tout le monde . . . comme tout le monde y trouverait son compte si on pouvait, nous aussi, l'éprouver, cet amour de soi . . .
>
> —Si on pouvait . . .
>
> —On ne demanderait pas mieux . . .
>
> —On ne demanderait pas mieux?
>
> —Pas mieux? Vraiment?

As with so many of Yeats's poems, the ending on a question mark is a sign of anything but irresolution. "We" may not be at ease in the world or with ourselves, but we are clear, by the end, that we would not want to be like "them". And, as always in such fiction, the mode of narration is contingent upon the truths affirmed by the narrative. For "them", the self-assured ones, let there be novels which fill out, as it were, "twenty years of happiness", or "Oh yes, I feel remorse all right", or which bludgeon us into accepting their view of life, or applauding their brilliance, wit, depth and so on; for "us" on the other hand there can only be this quiet, hesitant, insistent groping, a clearing of falsehood from the air rather than any assertion of truth.

Gabriel Josipovici, "Us and Them," in The Times Literary Supplement, *No. 4515, October 13, 1989, p. 1130.*

Germaine Brée (essay date 1989)

[*In the following excerpt from an essay in* Breaking the Sequence: Women's Experimental Fiction *(1989), Brée considers the experimental nature of Sarraute's narrative techniques and speculates on the reasons for her apparent evasion of an explicitly feminist orientation.*]

> Really, universally, relations stop nowhere, and the exquisite problem of the artist is eternally but to draw, by a geometry of his own, the circle in which they will happily appear to do so. (Henry James)

When Nathalie Sarraute's name appeared among the small group of "new novelists," she was in fact already launched on what is indubitably a unique career as an "experimental" writer. In 1932 she had begun to write the first of the texts later published in a volume entitled ***Tropismes*** (1938) and she had then brought out two novels, ***Portrait d'un inconnu*** (***Portrait of a Man Unknown***) (1948), prefaced by Sartre, and ***Martereau*** (1953). The four Sarraute essays that came out in 1956 in ***L'ère du soupçon*** (***The Age of Suspicion***) had been written between 1947 and 1956, antedating the first versions of the programmatic Robbe-Grillet essays on the "new novel": "The Use of Theory" (1955), "A Future for the Novel" (1956), "On Several Obsolete Notions" (1957). Robbe-Grillet's first novel, *Les gommes* (*The Erasers*), had come out in the same year as ***Martereau*** and Butor's *Passage de Milan* a year later. If I recall these facts, it is not to claim any superiority for Sarraute, merely to point to the precedency, the independence of her work.

L'ère du soupçon is a personal meditation on the writing processes that Sarraute had been trying out for some years. Much later, in the preface to the excellent translation of ***Tropisms*** (1963) by Maria Jolas, Sarraute warned her readers against the notion that "theorizing novelists are cool calculators who began by constructing theories, which they then decided to put into practice in their books," "lab experiments" as it were; for "no literary work can be a mere illustration of a principle however convincing." ***L'ère du soupçon*** describes a process: the recognition by the reader, Nathalie Sarraute, of a well-defined problem and the effort of the writer—Nathalie Sarraute—to correct it. As reader reflecting on the traditional elements of decor (description), character analysis and presentation, social commentary and plot, she briefly and approvingly sketches some examples of innovative strategy in that realm: Dostoevski, Proust, Kafka, Camus—later Ivy Compton-Burnett and Virginia Woolf. In relation to these she defines her own project, making no claim to a break with the literary tradition but rather to her role as discoverer of further regions to be explored and integrated within a continuous literary tradition of innovation in narrative creation. Her position is clear. Novels deal with the human psyche; in new ways, these novelists explore, in fiction, the psychological substrata of human activity. This as yet little known domain, when more carefully observed, dissolves that convenient entity and vehicle for moving the reader into the world of the novel via the plot, i.e., the solid character named, provided with a social status and a fixed personality. Sarraute shows the manner in which the novelists she examined brought about the "demise" of that fictive creation as she sees it. The reason for this change? In the light of the psychological knowledge of the time, the "solid" character carries no conviction.

This is the psychological domain then, which Sarraute has chosen to investigate with its consequences for the novelist. Her problem is not simple. As she sees it, the outer relations between human beings, the "stuff" of fiction, appear as the flimsiest of surface signs. These sign-gestures—tone, silence, word—emanate from the turmoil, the fluctuations, the underlying impulses of sensation and emotion that accompany human encounters and overt communications. Unconscious in great part, they are, for her, subvocal or prevocal. The technical problem of a novelist holding this view is thus defined. And it too is a difficult one: how to introduce those silent, fleeting, nonverbal moments into the narrative, which by definition rests exclusively on language; and language, the writer's tool, is a structured system that arrests and reifies and so cannot convey the fleeting aspects of human psychological life as it is really experienced.

All Nathalie Sarraute's fictions are experiments in dealing with that problem. The problem, however, has its source in a personal insight arising out of a double experience—a subjective experience and encounters with certain of its "materializations" in literary works. These in turn triggered her need to write, to explore the implications of her point of view in regard to the fiction-making process, and the writing "strategies" required. Her point of view itself is not founded on any systematized knowledge or theory: "I am absolutely unaware of the genesis or evolution of these inner movements. I wrote my first few short texts . . . ***Tropisms*** spontaneously, without even knowing what tropisms really were nor what they represented. My impressions guided me. . . ."

Nathalie Sarraute has spoken freely of her "research" in lectures and interviews. She designated by the metaphor "tropisms" the concealed world of psychological eddies she discerned in all human encounters. The word, first introduced in plant physiology in the mid-nineteenth century, was later also applied to animals. "Tropisms" referred technically to those movements caused in organisms by mechanical reactions to outer stimuli, chemical or physical: the sun or the temperature, for instance. She thus had to de-individualize the field under scrutiny to make visible the unconscious stratum of the psyche and free it from preconceived ethical categorization or judgment. Tropisms are common to a whole group of organisms, collective phenomena: "I gave them this name because of their spontaneous, irresistible instinctive nature, similar to that of the movements made by certain living organisms under the influence of outside stimuli such as light or heat." By analogy, in Sarraute's human world, these movements are set off by the presence of "others" or objects from the world outside. Sarraute's first attempt was to communicate, translate into words, what in her terms is wordless: "Tropisms cannot be expressed by means of the written word, but only through images capable of generating sensations. . . . To discover them requires tremendous effort, concentration, attention, preparation, work." The verbal tissue of the writing is then a medium, of consequence only as it opens a way for the real adventure of the writer: communication with the reader, through words, of that which is "real" but beyond words: that is, the world of inner sensation, which the readers must be induced to recognize in themselves. The "truth" of the transcript is of the utmost importance.

Tropisms is composed of 24 short sketches, which were developed over some half dozen years. They illustrate the close connection between Sarraute's purpose and the technical experiments with narrative structures which she implements. "Tropisms," she had described as movements of attraction and repulsion, common to human organisms in contact with one another. Her sketches, consequently, narrow the field of vision, isolate apparently trivial situations and miniscule incidents of everyday city life: small groups of people, families, for instance, looking vacuously at shop windows, women gossiping in tearooms. These are anonymous, of course, described as "they"; sometimes a "she" or a "he" becomes detached, an anxious fragment of the whole; an outcast, swayed by sensations, fears, inner perturbations; separated from the reassuring collective agglomeration clad in its suffocating "miasma" of clichés.

In the first episode recalled in ***Childhood,*** Sarraute sets up the following scenario: a hotel in Switzerland, a governess sewing, a pair of scissors, a little girl Tachok watching, a couch upholstered in blue silk. The child seizes the scissors, announces her intent to rip the blue silk cover, and does it. What comes out from underneath is grey, messy, formless, strange. The scene is emblematic of the situations described in ***Tropisms:*** the ripping off of the smooth surface of the conventional attitudes, clichés, gestures. Some small shift in the mood starts the plunge into the disconcerting psychic world of some personage—a plunge not explained to the reader, but "existed." The role of the personages, as Sarraute sees it, is that of "sensitive detectors." Unsure, uneasy, they lose control over their social self, their certainties. So they reveal to the reader the frightening quagmire beneath the circumscribed reassuring patterns of the so-called real. In Sarraute's fictional world these "falls" are a source of high comedy. They lay bare the myth-making process that presides over the most quotidian relations, the "social" language that overlaps the reality with the "abominable stability of the lie," as her younger contemporary Le Clezio put it. The theme in itself could be seen as emblematic of the times.

In that frame, all the novelist's tools are called into question: point of view, character, decor, event, dialogue, relationships; the use of personal pronouns, the process of naming. The vaguely present human beings become the focus, not the activators of the microdramas developing, inwardly lived, not verbalized, not explained by some well-identified narrator, whether character or author. Sarraute, as would any good investigator, has proceeded very methodically in her successive novels, from limited situations involving closely knit family relations to more complex scenarios setting in motion coteries bound by the rhythms of habits and language codes. She evokes the attraction and repulsion that sway them, disrupting the ceremonials and word ballets under which the dangerous eddies of distrust, of suspicion, rise and fall, keeping the relations of particular individuals in perpetual mobility.

The evolution of her writing strategies, as each novel incorporates and moves beyond the last, has been thoroughly studied. It is not by chance that increasingly Sarraute raises along the way questions concerning the artist and the world of art. For it is from the psychic inner "magma" as Sarraute calls it, that the doubts arise, which destroy the immobile absolutes inscribed in a societal language out of touch with the inner hidden life of the human psyche that it seeks to stifle. The fiction writer, in fact the artist in general as Sarraute sees it, is like all human beings a mythmaker, but in a reverse process from the societal. The fiction writer unmasks the evasions, the comedies, and the truth of human life, but indirectly as it were by the narrative mode developed. In Sarraute's work the dialogue of subconversation and conversation is the means by which the unconscious struggles against the dominating social clichés are transmitted to the reader. Sarraute uses the interaction of the two languages to unmask the solid "character" and as a magnificent tool for the comical and satirical, working, as it were, of itself without the intervention of the writer. To achieve her purpose, to bring the underlying puzzled, mobile "tropisms" to life, she also experimented with time dimensions: whereas for the "outer" situations she narrows the field of vision, setting up schematically devised frames, the brief plunges into the unspoken are drawn out and balloon, extending the time- and space-frames of the incident. Paradoxically moving from outside in, from a narrow frame inward, she leads the reader to a sense of a limitless world, maintaining an aura of ambiguity without censorship, changing the expected order of presentation of the narrative. Her method is associative, not logical. But the structures adopted are not gratuitous. For according to Sarraute, their aim is to disclose certain truths. The contrast between the two spaces and their relation, the process of constant passage from one to the other, is the mimetic equivalent of a struggle inherent to human life: the social will to fix, to order and the conflicting desire to merge with the other.

The force that governs human tropisms is never named or analyzed within the fiction. It is, Sarraute says, the drive to merge with others, the desire to escape solitude. That desire is erotic in essence, but not narrowly sexual. The metaphoric language she has chosen to transcribe that upsurge is dramatized, violent, excessive; it juxtaposes with the trivial world of daily petty concerns a dangerous world of metamorphoses, aggression and destruction, a world of phantasms, of imaginary, contradictory projections. They are triggered in the mind of her personages by sudden doubt as to the apparently "real," "known," familiar distribution of roles in his or her "real" world. Here another technical problem concerning point of view arises—how to focalize, to orchestrate these inner scenarios inaccessible to all. The simplicity and indeed monotony of Sarraute's world is deceptive; it is impressive in scope and refinement.

Sarraute is well aware of the systematic codifications of the narrative mode worked out by a long line of critics and theoretical linguists. Starting from her own view of the function of the novelist in today's world, she drew from it the technical consequences and put them to work in a sequence of varied fictional situations. She took little interest in theories but consciously experimented with the narrative techniques through which the reader would perceive her world, live it, and so think it, in turn.

For the feminist critic, she proffers no genderized theory, eschews it in fact. Within the text her "sensitive detectors" can be either male or female, "he" or "she" according to their social position in an established relationship: father-daughter; father and undifferentiated children; uncle-nephew; or they can bear names: Germaine Lemaire and Alain in the relation of the revered writer and admirer. It is the tension, the relation between two emotional extremes with their undertow of questions and uncertainties that determines the tides of repulsion and attraction that give substance to the narrative, not necessarily or uniquely the sexual determination. Sarraute's originality is hers, like the space she has explored. It may seem "circumscribed" as she once admitted, but it is fully hers, and in that degree it is not only experimental, but astonishingly innovative. (pp. 269-74)

Germaine Brée, "Experimental Novels? Yes, But Perhaps "Otherwise": Nathalie Sarraute, Monique Wittig," in Breaking the Sequence: Women's Experimental Fiction, *edited by Ellen G. Friedman and Miriam Fuchs, Princeton University Press, 1989, pp. 267-83.*

Ginger Danto (review date 18 November 1990)

[*In the following review, Danto examines Sarraute's "rendering of the language of the self" in* You Don't Love Yourself.]

Like hypnotists who will their subjects into altered states in order to tap the subconscious mind, French writers of the now middle-aged *nouveau roman* wanted readers to shed conventional expectations of literature to avail themselves of a more distilled, if cryptic, narrative form. Novels without plot, characters stripped of identity, and events outside a logical continuum were the hallmarks of a literary technique that offered not so much an escape as a detour back into the labyrinth of individual thought.

That this once-radical genre has survived attests not to its legitimacy but to its importance for the novel's evolution, according to Nathalie Sarraute, the doyenne of the *nouveau roman,* who sustained her Spartan style for 30 years before the anointment of a new literary movement in the 1960's propelled her work into the discerning public eye. "I was very alone from a literary point of view and I asked myself why I could not write like the others," Mrs. Sarraute said during a recent interview in the French journal *Globe* in which she recalled a frustrated reader's suggestion: "Couldn't you put names [alongside the dialogue]. It would make it easier."

But Mrs. Sarraute did no more succumb then than she does now, a half-century later, in her latest book. ***You Don't Love Yourself,*** which has been cogently translated into English by Barbara Wright in consultation with the author, is an anonymous dialogue on the theme of self-hate, one that Mrs. Sarraute considers highly relevant to the human condition. As such, the anonymity of the novel's voices emphasizes the universality of the ideas expressed in it, echoing a majority who are largely lacking in self-love.

This premise is where Mrs. Sarraute's expedition into the conscience begins, and applying the generic lexicon of literature's who, what, when and where is as ineffectual in understanding her work as using a spatula might be to dig through rocky terrain. Indeed, it is not smooth going in this internal landscape of nuance, observation and often paranoid projection, this territory of inconclusive arguments and repressed retorts—and of ideas, endless ideas that trail off in series of dots, as elusive as the details of dreams that one attempts vainly to harness on waking. For this is Mrs. Sarraute's rendering of the language of the self, notably the self that does not love itself, whose fractured ego ebbs now into self-loathing and illusion, now into envy and regret—subjective musings possibly, but not necessarily, provoked by circumstance.

In lieu of characters, interior voices generate the book's dialogue, volleying back and forth the threads of thought that stir action or reaction in the person they inhabit. Mrs. Sarraute puts a microphone to these voices, which, like bats' cries, are not otherwise audible in life or in literature, except by the stylistic device of "he thinks," "she thinks," which is too mundane for the *nouveau roman.*

Theoretically, Mrs. Sarraute maintains that the self is actually a composite of myriad selves, something she has likened to schools of fish that appear as a unit but, on closer scrutiny, reveal dozens, even hundreds, of individuals moving in unison. Adhering to the same behavioral metaphor—that schools of fish disperse to navigate better—Mrs. Sarraute believes that similarly minded selves group to form an us, hence the intermittent use of *us* in this dialogue of *I* and *you.*

Having decomposed the character to the point of nonrecognition, wresting from this improbable autopsy only inner voices, Mrs. Sarraute allows these voices to utter guilelessly what is normally unspoken, inhibited by convention. How often are we told, "Keep that to yourself"? This is the very stuff Mrs. Sarraute airs, on behalf of those of us, or them, without self-love.

Alternately serious and sarcastic, the selves' voices discuss, commiserate with and cajole one another in a collective attempt to decipher what happens outside, in the empirical world beyond the book's covers. This is their raw material—the infinitesimal inventory of appearances—and Mrs. Sarraute documents how that information reverberates inside, setting off sequences of thought that fashion the selves' intimate, if sometimes intolerable, versions of reality.

A typical interplay of selves, contemplating the blurred realities of the factual and the perceived, goes thus:

> "You remember how he came up from behind, he put his hand on your shoulder, on our shoulder . . . and he said in a pitying, rather sorrowful tone . . . 'You know what's the trouble with you? You don't love yourself' . . . as if not loving oneself were a defect, a disease."

Filtered through such a perception, given events are magnified, so that individuals initially appear disembodied by the self's field of vision:

> "Something is coming into view . . . "
>
> "Yes, what is it?"
>
> "For the moment it's only a hand. The man it belongs to, we can't see him, he's in the shade. . . . It's only his hand there in the bright light in front of us . . . a long, rather gnarled hand with very short nails."

This passage introduces, for the sake of the book's argument, one who loves himself, an attitude the protagonist selves discern in the man's intent observation of his own hands. "And so much love in his gaze," they say, enviously concluding: "That's the way it is with people who love themselves . . . their love goes first to everything they can see that belongs to them . . . their hands, their feet, their forearms . . . and then their reflection in the mirror."

Just as vanity belongs to those who love themselves, disinterest and disgust are symptomatic of those who don't: "We don't think about it. We would never take it into our head to spread it out on the table like his. Why should we do that? Our hands are utilitarian objects, utensils limited to their function." Tired of its own belittlement, the self attempts to love itself, taking cues from the likes of the man who is enchanted with his own physique, who is elsewhere able to say "I" with the assurance of one who feels viable in the world. This is a difficult exercise for the self who is inclined to be unassertive to the point of obsequiousness, for whom even saying "I" is problematic. And while this effort cannot be called a denouement in a novel that has no conclusion, it is perhaps key to the self-examination that is the gist of the book.

For Nathalie Sarraute, nothing—or very little—of importance occurs on the surface, a philosophy she forged in her first novel, ***Tropisms,*** published in 1939, and maintained through to her 1983 autobiography, ***Childhood,*** which is written as a dialogue between the preadolescent protagonist and her double. However difficult or disturbing it may be, Mrs. Sarraute's literature is a refreshing proposition in a world keyed to the superficial, to the lengths of hemlines and the progress of beard stubble, the glittering action poses of public figures one believes, by virtue of where and with whom they are, one can know. For Mrs. Sarraute, the usual sorts of investigation—what people do, earn, invest in—are inconsequential. What matters is nuance, notion and the other often illicit elements of motives that lie below the illusory surface of bronzed or pallid, bejeweled or naked skin.

Ginger Danto, "Me, My Selves and I," in The New York Times Book Review, *November 18, 1990, p. 7.*

Gretchen Rous Besser (review date December 1990)

[*An American educator, critic, and translator, Besser is the author of* Balzac's Concept of Genius *(1969) and a contributor to the* Columbia Dictionary of Modern European Literature. *In the following review, Besser assesses the effectiveness of Sarraute's treatment of language, identity, and knowledge in* Tu ne t'aimes pas.]

As if her previous novel ***Enfance*** (1983), with its tenuous evocation of the author's carefully-edited childhood, had been an aberration in the increasingly-abstract progression of Sarraute's work, ***Tu ne t'aimes pas*** begins so to speak where ***Disent les imbéciles*** (1976) left off. The latter book fastened on the title phrase, which it then dissected and examined for its repertory of "tropistic" evocations. Disembodied voices representing a multiplicity of consciences (no names or distinguishable characters, of course) emitted judgments, provoked arguments, voiced opinions. Always at the center was the lone nonconformist who above all interests Sarraute—surrounded, harassed, badgered, misunderstood by the group.

In the present work conversation (and sub-conversation) among a variety of nameless voices represents an even more daring concept. Instead of expressing opposing views and opinions within a group of people, these entities (who call themselves "tu," "vous," "moi," and "nous") are conflicting tendencies within a single personality. Mobilized at the outset by a kind of shibboleth—"Tu ne t'aimes pas"—they (and the author) continue for the remainder of the book to analyze the type of person who loves or likes himself. "They" (Sarraute uses the first-person plural "we" to insinuate the reader directly among them) are incapable of such love.

As always, "we" for Sarraute are the weak, fearful, timid, self-conscious, uncertain, and hypersensitive, who stand in awe of and in contrast to the self-loving, self-satisfied, strong, stable, smug and solid "others." In the course of numerous fragmented sections, "we" attempt to personify, characterize, comprehend—and copy—the type of person who likes himself. Can the reader discern a gradation from the self-satisfied man relating details of his digestion, to the dominating personality who invites "us" to spend a month of vacation together (thus precipitating our anxious attempts to interest and humor our host), to the person who possesses a precise internal machine that decides infallibly between right and wrong, and ultimately to the man of utter and arbitrary power who debases the dignity of those in his grasp (he is called a great genius in the art of self-love)? These last examples suggest that self-love carried to extremes (like the suppression of ideas in ***Disent les imbéciles***) can lead to religious dogmatism and tyrannical abuse.

Questions of identity and self-image, knowledge of self and of others, the numbing power of language to falsify by codifying, group coercion and individual helplessness, the use (and abuse) of trite expressions are also touched on in Sarraute's inimitably delicate and glancing way. None of these concerns is new for Sarraute; they are repeated, reworded, refined. To capture flitting feelings and express the inexpressible, Sarraute resorts to her all-but-patented stylistic devices. She spins out strings of synonyms that encircle and encompass the meaning she seeks. When words fail, she resorts to sparse but deftly-appropriate imagery. "Happiness" (with a capital H) is like a holiday brochure touting smooth seas and sunny skies, while underlying boredom is a "grosse et grise poupée de caoutchouc." Sarraute co-opts the reader's attentive cooperation by leaving sentences unfinished, thoughts half-expressed; the reader must not only read between the lines but must also complete them. The pleasures afforded by Sarraute's latest works are primarily cerebral. Although we are all familiar by now with her injunctions against the stultifying use of character, plot, "he said" and "she said" in the modern novel, we nonetheless read fiction for delight, distraction, vicarious excitement—we crave emotional along with intellectual stimulation. When we pick up a characterless, plotless, bloodless "novel," unless it piques our interest by its ingenuity and innovation, we are liable to let it slip from our fingers. Life is too short to accept being bored. Sarraute has said she constantly mines the same small bit of territory she has appropriated as her own. By dint of persistent digging in a single confined space, is it conceivable that Sarraute has by now exhausted her mother lode? (pp. 391-92)

Gretchen Rous Besser, in a review of "Tu ne t'aimes pas," in The French Review, *Vol. LXIV, No. 2, December, 1990, pp. 391-92.*

FURTHER READING

Bibliography

Bell, Sheila M. *Nathalie Sarraute: A Bibliography.* London: Grant & Cutler, 1982, 91 p.

Standard bibliography.

Criticism

Besser, Gretchen Rous. *Nathalie Sarraute.* Boston: G. K. Hall, 1979, 192 p.

Biographical and critical overview of Sarraute's career.

Britton, Celia. "The Self and Language in the Novels of Nathalie Sarraute." *The Modern Language Review* 77, No. 3 (July 1982): 577-84.

Analyzes Sarraute's use of tropisms and subconversation to delineate the limitations of language and to propound a deterministic view of human psychology.

Cornwell, Ethel F. "Gertrude Stein: The Forerunner of Nathalie Sarraute." *The International Fiction Review* 5, No. 2 (July 1978): 91-5.

Cites stylistic and technical parallels between Stein and Sarraute, focusing on their iconoclastic tendencies to eliminate punctuation, character, and plot, and their mutual interest in subconversation as a mode of characterization.

De Julio, Maryann. "The Emergence of a Feminist Voice: Nathalie Sarraute's *Le planétarium.*" *The International Fiction Review* 15, No. 1 (Winter 1988): 37-40.

Relates Sarraute's use of a fragmented narrative voice in *Le planétarium* to the feminist theories of Julia Kristeva. De Julio concludes that while Sarraute is not engaged in a feminist project, her experimental narration articulates a feminist poetics at a deeper, imagistic level.

Fleming, John A. "The Imagery of Tropism in the Novels of Nathalie Sarraute." In *Image and Theme: Studies in Modern French Fiction,* edited by W. M. Frohock, pp. 74-98. Boston: Harvard University Press, 1969.

Discusses Sarraute's innovative use of imagery in her novels. Fleming states: "Even the most casual reader will be impressed by the fact that images are no mere decorative element in [Sarraute's] work. Nor are they used simply for thematic or symbolic purposes. They have become a complex structural device which makes possible the elimination or diminution of traditional novelistic techniques in accordance with the general tenor of her critical writings."

Greene, Robert W. "Nathalie Sarraute's *L'usage de la parole,* or Re(en)trop(iz)ing *Tropismes.*" *Novel: A Forum on Fiction* 16, No. 3 (Spring 1983): 197-214.

Focuses on the moralistic aspects of *L'usage de la parole.*

Gross, Janice Berkowitz. "Women Writing across Purposes: The Theater of Marguerite Duras and Nathalie Sarraute." *Modern Drama* XXXII, No. 1 (March 1989): 39-47.

Comparative study of the plays of Sarraute and Marguerite Duras. Gross focuses on their stylistic and technical similarities, particularly their commitment to experimentation and their rejection of convention.

Heath, Stephen. "Nathalie Sarraute." In his *The Nouveau Roman: A Study in the Practice of Writing,* pp. 44-66. London: Elek Books, 1972.

Situates Sarraute among her fellow new novelists, emphasizing the differences between her writing and that of Alain Robbe-Grillet. Heath maintains that while Sarraute is more "conventional" than Robbe-Grillet because of her emphasis on psychological realism, her experiments with language and form helped to define the *nouveau roman* at its inception.

Minogue, Valerie. "Sarraute, Auden, and the Great Tall Tailor." *The Modern Language Review* 84, No. 2 (April 1989): 331-36.

Psychoanalytical discussion of the imagery in Sarraute's *Childhood* and W. H. Auden's *A Certain World.*

Wood, Margery. "Norman Mailer and Nathalie Sarraute: A Comparison of Existential Novels." *The Minnesota Review* VI, No. 1 (1966): 67-72.

Compares the existential elements in Mailer's *An American Dream* and Sarraute's *Portrait of a Man Unknown.*

Additional coverage of Sarraute's life and career is contained in the following sources published by Gale Research: *Contemporary Authors,* Vols. 9-12, rev. ed.; *Contemporary Authors New Revision Series,* Vol. 23; *Contemporary Literary Criticism,* Vols. 1, 2, 4, 8, 10, 31; *Dictionary of Literary Biography,* Vol. 83; and *Major 20th-Century Writers.*

E. F. Schumacher

1911-1977

(Full name Ernst Friedrich Schumacher) German-born English economist, essayist, and nonfiction writer.

The following entry provides an overview of Schumacher's career.

INTRODUCTION

An unorthodox economist, E. F. Schumacher fused economic philosophy with elements of Christian and Buddhist theology to create a unique strategy for reforming the world's socioeconomic systems. He is best known for *Small Is Beautiful: Economics as if People Mattered,* a treatise that generated a minor cult following among counterculture and other activists for its philosophical attack on Western materialism and stringent call for ecological conservation. Recognizing the implications of the present course of world development, Schumacher believed that in order to build a lasting community, development must exploit neither the environment nor human laborers and must combine smaller, more efficient manufacturing units with modern technology.

Born in Bonn, Germany, Schumacher attended Bonn and Berlin Universities in Germany and Columbia University in the United States before earning his doctorate in economics from Oxford University. He emigrated to England in 1937, where he was forced to work as a farm laborer in an internment camp for three years during World War II. Schumacher became a naturalized British citizen in 1946, when he accepted a position with the British section of the Control Commission of West Germany. He was appointed to Great Britain's National Coal Board in 1950 as an economic advisor and subsequently served as its top economist, director of statistics, and head of planning until 1970. Schumacher's credentials also included the directorship of Scott Bader Company; a position as the economic advisor to Burma; a professorship at Columbia University; and a stint as the president of the Soil Association, an organization that advocates worldwide organic farming. His quest for alternative plans for sustainable development, or "alternative technology," led him in 1966 to found the Intermediate Technology Development Group, which advocated and helped implement feasible, humane, and economically sound alternative growth plans for third-world countries. Schumacher died in 1977.

Schumacher's works combine the philosophy of sustainable development with an amalgamation of Christian and Buddhist theology. *Small Is Beautiful* echoes the teachings of G. K. Chesterton and Mahatma Ghandi in Schumacher's call for an economy that emphasizes people rather than goods. In this proposed system, industry, technology, and consumption are scaled down and growth is not measured by how many goods are made, but by how they are made. Envisioning the rapid depletion of the earth's resources and continuous poverty for over two-thirds of the world's population, Schumacher argues that continuous economic growth is more destructive than productive, maintaining that expansion should be directly proportionate to human need. Noting the West's tendency to equate increased worker proficiency with materialism and consumption, Schumacher argued that worker education must instead be viewed as a means of conserving natural resources and enhancing the worker's lives and work environment.

Juxtaposing science and religion in his second work, *A Guide for the Perplexed,* Schumacher created a hierarchical map of the physical world. According to this system, self-awareness distinguishes humanity from the mineral, plant, and animal levels of being and provides a key to living in and understanding the world. Schumacher's final book, *Good Work,* is a collection of reprinted speeches in which he examined the nature and purpose of human work. These pieces relate the work ethic to the Christian emphasis on individual and communal fulfillment and the human aspiration toward perfection. Believing that large-scale technology deprives workers of meaningful labor, Schumacher concluded that work should enhance the human experience, produce goods and services, and help poor and underdeveloped countries achieve economic and social progress.

PRINCIPAL WORKS

Britain's Coal: A Study Conference Organized by the National Union of Mineworkers (report) 1960
Roots of Economic Growth (nonfiction) 1962
Clean Air and Future Energy (pamphlet) 1967
Small Is Beautiful: Economics as if People Mattered (nonfiction) 1973
Think about Land (pamphlet) 1974
Education for the Future (pamphlet) 1977
The Face of God in Contemporary Society [with J. Dominian] (pamphlet) 1977
A Guide for the Perplexed (nonfiction) 1977
Public Forum on the Future of Montana's Economy, Helena, Montana, 1977 [contributor with others] (report) 1977
The Future Is Manageable: Schumacher's Observations on Non-violent Economics and Technology with a Human Face [compiled and edited by M. M. Hoda] (nonfiction) 1978
Good Work [with Peter N. Gillingham] (nonfiction) 1979
Schumacher on Energy [edited by Geoffrey Kirk] (nonfiction) 1982

CRITICISM

Times Literary Supplement (review date 28 September 1973)

[*In the following unsigned review, the critic praises* Small Is Beautiful *as a worthwhile statement of Schumacher's philosophy, despite the fact that the essays are roughly assembled.*]

Start a pub argument about Maplin and Concorde and the Tunnel, and you'll probably find that you've polarized opinion more sharply than you ever could with an argument about Labour versus Tories. Quite suddenly, this has become one of the great divisive issues of the time. Those three great massive projects, and similar: do they represent Progress and our dynamic future; or are they just pointless white elephants, unrelated to real human needs? More generally: does "The Modern World" have a workable future before it? And if so, is it a future that anybody wants?

So we take sides, as "people of the forward stampede" or as "homecomers", to use E. F. Schumacher's useful terminology [in ***Small Is Beautiful***]; and those of us who are homecomers tend to feel rather helpless, since the politicians and the power-men and the experts all tend to be people of the forward stampede. This book goes some way towards a redressing of that imbalance. Dr Schumacher is certainly an expert, an economist of distinction, sometime economic adviser to the National Coal Board, and thus a power-man in his degree. But he has been right through economics and come out on the other side, and here he reports findings which transcend that discipline and show up its limitations. [***Small Is Beautiful***] has been carpentered together rather crudely, out of many self-contained articles and lectures, and it does not add up to a single progressively reasoned argument; but as the manifold and most vigorous statement of a homecomer's philosophy, it carries weight and deserves close attention.

Much of it goes over fairly familiar ground: the environmental crisis, the energy crisis, our folly in neglecting coal in favour of soon-to-be-gone oil, our greater folly in plunging ahead with nuclear energy without first solving the insoluble problem of wastes; the dehumanization of industrial work; the flight from the countryside, the breakdown of the cities: the negativism of the humanities as currently taught, the consequent ethical vacuum, the consequent despair; the moral squalor of any society which drives itself on by avarice, greed, envy, and a contemptuous bullying of the natural environment; the need to establish a simpler, more decentralized, more permanently viable sort of life-style and economy.

About a great many such matters, Dr Schumacher has good things to say, a proportion of them already familiar from Chesterton and Tawney and *Blueprint for Survival* and other sources, but here argued with remarkable force, well supported by hard facts and figures, and stated so apothegmatically as to tempt a reviewer to immoderate quotation.

Dr Schumacher's most distinctive contribution concerns aid to the developing world. Here, he argues very cogently that we miss the point: thinking in terms too crudely economic, we offer rich men's answers to poor men's problems; this means that our "aid" only exacerbates the disease, which is one of rural decay coupled with a cancer of unviable urbanization. The solution proposed—and in Dr Schumacher's energetic practice, not merely in this book—is "Intermediate Technology": intermediate in its capital cost per work-place, available therefore to poor societies; labour-intensive rather than capital-intensive, ordered to the multiplication of useful and decentralized employment and the recovery of human dignity rather than to mere output, sharply relevant therefore to the actual needs of real people.

Such a programme is open to an obvious political objection: the Third World—or its politicians and power-men at least—can reply that like so much else that is said about environment, it is merely a White man's patronizing plan for holding the poor Niggers down at the romantic-savage level. The actual poor won't talk like that, and it is an imprecise criticism anyway; but it was made at Stockholm in various contexts, and it will be made about this book.

A wider difficulty is that Dr Schumacher writes by implication, and, quite frankly in places, as a moralist and almost a theologian. This is fair enough, since it is certainly an ethical and religious sort of problem. But should we therefore not drop all this technical stuff about economics and environment and ecology, and get back to the simply religious preaching of a quasi-Franciscan—or perhaps Buddhist—revolution? Otherwise we shall just be fiddling around with symptoms: as long as men still worship Mammon and are determined to keep on with the life of grab, no matter how suicidally, wise and austere programmes of Dr Schumacher's kind are not going to catch many votes. He tells us of one initially capitalistic enterprise that managed to give itself a human face; but this was the result of pure altruism on the owners' part, not likely to be imitated very widely until there has been a sweeping revolution at the purely religious level. And (*salva gratia*) how probable is that?

In a sense, this book cuts its own throat: it speaks so emphatically about our need to "seek first the Kingdom" as to make its other and more particular themes—economic and ecological—seem almost irrelevant. Arguably, that lesson is the one we really need to learn: meanwhile, Dr Schumacher offers stimulation and plenty of nice knock-down arguments for the distressed homecomer, who can take comfort. Controversially at least, he appears to be on the winning side.

"A Homily for Homecomers," in The Times Literary Supplement, *No. 3734, September 28, 1973, p. 1108.*

J. C. Cooper (essay date Spring 1976)

[*Cooper, a frequent contributor to* Studies in Comparative Religion, *has written several books on Taoism and mysticism. In the following excerpt, she claims* Small Is Beautiful*'s emphasis on the spiritual, mental, and physical well-being of humankind makes it one of the most important books of our time.*]

[***Small Is Beautiful***], although based on a variety of lectures and articles, reads as a coherent whole. Despite the fact that its message is, on the surface, economic, its implications go far deeper and touch the spiritual as well as the material well-being and survival of man. The book deals with the excessively quantitative orientation of modern economics, an orientation so totally devoid of qualitative understanding that even the quality of 'orders of magnitude' ceases to be appreciated. Modern man has been nurtured on the illusion of unlimited power over nature, not regarding himself as part of that nature but as an 'outside force destined to dominate and conquer it . . . forgetting that even if he won the battle he would be on the losing side' since he is using irreplaceable capital which man has not made but simply found, treating this capital as an income item. We optimistically look to 'nature' or to science to redress the balance, but 'already there is overwhelming evidence that the great self-balancing system of nature is becoming increasingly unbalanced in particular respects and at specific points'. The further this process (or 'progress', as some like to call it) is allowed to go, the more difficult it will be to reverse it, if, indeed, the point of no return has not been passed already.

Quoting the Machiavellian—or crassly stupid—statement of Keynes that: 'We must pretend to ourselves and to everyone that fair is foul and foul is fair; for foul is useful and fair is not. Avarice and usury and precaution must be our gods for at least another hundred years', (one wonders, in parenthesis, what difference there is between this line of thought and that of any dedicated criminal) Dr. Schumacher points out that we have already enthroned Keynes' gods and 'recklessly and wilfully abandoned our great classical-Christian heritage'. To combat this soul and life-destroying philosophy the task of our generation is one 'of metaphysical reconstruction. Wisdom demands a new orientation of science and technology towards the organic, the gentle, the non-violent, the elegant and beautiful'. The more successful man becomes, the more he needs to face the problems of spiritual and moral truth. In an age of giantism and its consequent violence, 'there is a wisdom in smallness, if only on account of the small-ness and patchiness of human knowledge'. The mistakes of small communities are 'trifling in comparison with the devastations caused by gigantic groups motivated by greed and envy and the lust for power', in which, 'the future counts as nothing compared with the slightest economic gain now'. We primarily and consistently 'cultivate greed and envy and build up a vast array of totally unwarrantable wants' and the frenzy does not abate with our higher standards of living. 'Wisdom has been replaced by cleverness and although much has been written *about* wisdom it can only be *found* inside oneself following liberation from the pursuit of material ends and seeking the spiritual'.

The role of economics is examined in the affluent society in which 'economic performance, economic growth, economic expansion . . . have become the abiding interest, if not obsession, of all modern societies, with their total suppression of the qualitative in favour of the quantitative, and the timorous refusal to look into the real nature of things', finding that growth is no valid goal in itself since it may be pathological, disruptive or destructive growth, such as is demonstrated by the foot-loose rootless, (as opposed to normal mobility which obtained in earlier times) population concentrated in giant cities, with all their consequent problems of crime, alienation, stress, social breakdown, mass unemployment, escapism and ugliness, while 'vitality is drained out of the rural areas' with the consequent threat of eventual famine.

Out of other equally possible examples, Dr. Schumacher chooses Buddhism to illustrate the need for 'meta-economics' and abandoning western materialism; he writes of 'Buddhist economics' since right livelihood is a prerequisite for spiritual health united with material well-being; an outlook which regards it as essential that man must be able to develop and use his true faculties, that he must overcome ego-centricity and work for the common good, making man a craftsman instead of a mechanical slave. The goal of right living should be natural growth, simplicity and liberation from attachment to riches. From simplicity rises non-violence. Natural growth imposes limits in size, speed or violence and so 'tends to be self-balancing, self-adjusting, self-cleansing'. Technology, with its mass-production, recognises no such self-limiting principles and is 'inherently violent, ecologically damaging, self-defeating in terms of non-renewable resources, and stultifying for the human person'. (pp. 114-15)

Although the various essays are not all of the same quality, and certain inconsistencies occur, ***Small is Beautiful*** is one of the most significant books of our time and must be read by all concerned with the health of man's environment, body mind and spirit. (p. 115)

J. C. Cooper, in a review of "Small Is Beautiful," in Studies in Comparative Religion, *Vol. 10, No. 2, Spring, 1976, pp. 114-15.*

Martin Mayer (essay date Spring 1977)

[*In the following excerpt, Mayer suggests that* Small Is Beautiful *is too emotional, impractical, and vague.*]

[***Small Is Beautiful***] is a peculiar performance, some of it interesting and cogently (if rather abstractly) argued, some of it highly emotional, uninformed, and self-contradictory to the point of incoherence. Unfortunately, the latter sections seem to have drawn for the book its following.

Schumacher's serious argument is the Club of Rome thesis dequantified. The productive accomplishments of modern society, he claims, rest less upon human effort and genius than upon the temporarily easy accessibility of nonrenewable natural resources (especially energy resources). We are not living on our income and increasing our capital, as we think, but eating into the "capital" of the earth. Thus the prosperity of the advanced societies lacks "permanence" (a favorite word: "nature" has "permanence"), and the little poor countries questing for a Western European standard of living are following a Pied Piper. The mountain that will swallow them up is urbanization, a bad thing at best (no city should ever be home to more than half a million people), and for poor countries an inevitable source of unemployment, wasted labor, and wasted lives.

The nonmodernized two-thirds of the world should be seen as "two million villages" with roughly a thousand inhabitants apiece, and aid from the rich to the poor should be directed toward helping those inhabitants improve the life they can make for themselves with the available local resources. Comparative advantage is a fallacy, and trade is essentially bad. In "Buddhist economics," which Schumacher invents and admires, "production from local resources for local needs is the most rational way of economic life, while dependence on imports from afar and the consequent need to produce for export to unknown and distant peoples is highly uneconomic and justifiable only in exceptional cases and on a small scale." You do the poor no kindness when you give them the most advanced equipment. They probably won't be able to use it properly; if they do, it will be only by a slavish imitation that is the worst and most inescapable form of neocolonialism.

At the same time, the inherited technology of primitive agriculture and village industry is clearly inadequate to people's needs. The sympathetic adviser from the modernized world must therefore study the existing techniques of the village, then ask himself what improvements he would want if he were a villager, and only then apply to the problem his superior understanding of production processes. The result should be an "intermediate technology" that will enable his beneficiaries to escape from poverty without escaping from the village or its religio-cultural traditions.

A lot of this is appealing, and plausible on first sight, though not always on consideration. Schumacher notes the old saw that you help a man more if you teach him fishing than if you give him fish—and expands it to argue that you help him more if you teach him to make his own fishing tackle than if you give him the equipment. But what if he's a carpenter and would rather sell chairs for cash and buy fish? Do we really have to do without the productivity of the division of labor to practice Schumacher's "economics as if people mattered"? Worse—what if this white man's burden and his family are hungry right now? It takes time to make fishing tackle.

When Schumacher suggests that instead of sending bulldozers to build a road we teach natives about wheelbarrows and help them create the back-up shops they will need to make wheelbarrow parts, what he is really saying is that these fellows don't need that road for another generation. (He doesn't like roads anyway; they're part of the damnable modern transportation technology that makes men "footloose.") These people may not have that much time—they certainly don't think they do. For all his insistence on the need to take a dynamic view and relate the parts of the problem, Schumacher ignores entirely the impact of public health technologies that, by reducing the death rate, created a population explosion. Neither cultures nor technologies come as snap-together independent parts; we are dealing with conflicts not of technique or attitude, but of commitment.

The desire to believe Schumacher is ultimately eroded by his bad manners as a controversialist (he is forever putting into the mouths of unnamed antagonists things nobody worth arguing with would ever say, like "People talk freely about 'machines to foretell the future' "), and by an astonishing absence of specificity. ***Small Is Beautiful*** does not offer a single example of the recommended "intermediate technology" or, as its author coyly puts it, "technology with a human face." (Lord knows what that is supposed to mean, other than "good.") The book offers only one incident drawn from life, with a specific problem to solve, a specific tactic for solving it, and a specific result—and this incident, strangely, involves the creation by the National Coal Board of a reporting form that compelled the managers of local collieries to abandon unprofitable small veins of coal and concentrate their efforts on the main face.

Schumacher ventures some nice *aperçus.* My favorite is the observation that if Germany had conquered Denmark in the 1860s or if Napolean had not been forced from Belgium, we would now regard an independent Denmark or

Belgium as nonviable, and Danish or Belgian separatist movements as foolishly romantic. Mostly, though, the book is rhetoric, and when dealing with contemporary life in the rich countries it is simply hysterical. "The leading ideas of the nineteenth century . . . are themselves a bad, vicious, life-destroying type of metaphysics. We are suffering from them as from a fatal disease." "There can be little doubt that the whole of mankind is in mortal danger. . . . " " . . . the modern world . . . tumbles from crisis to crisis; on all sides there are prophecies of disaster and, indeed, visible signs of breakdown." " . . . actual people . . . find themselves oppressed by increasing frustration, alienation, insecurity, and so forth." (That "and so forth" is almost irresistible.) Still, Schumacher thinks we may be able to handle it. What we need is "a generous and magnanimous intellectual effort—the opposite of nagging, malevolent criticism." Also "an effort of the imagination and an abandonment of fear." Bushwah.

Steady-state philosophers like Schumacher get into trouble because they claim radical credentials for an intensely conservative, even reactionary, attitude. No significant ideational or technological advance may be dreamed in their philosophies; the problems they see can be solved only by turning back. Schumacher is fairly explicit about this, concluding with a call for rededication to the cardinal virtues (in Latin, too). (pp. 232-33)

Martin Mayer, "The Closet Conservatives," in The American Scholar, *Vol. 46, Spring, 1977, pp. 230, 232-33, 236-37.*

Charles Fager (essay date 6 April 1977)

[*Fager, a frequent contributor to several periodicals such as the* Boston Globe *and* Harper's, *comments on* Small Is Beautiful*'s underlying theme of Roman Catholicism and its effect on Schumacher's philosophy.*]

What does it mean that E. F. Schumacher's book ***Small Is Beautiful: Economics As If People Mattered*** has caught on so strongly, especially among people who are exploring "alternatives" of various sorts—economic, political, spiritual? Originally published in England, the volume has now sold more than a million copies worldwide. Is its best-selling status another sign of decay in the old establishment world view, and further evidence of growing efforts to transcend that world view through a new consciousness, replace it with a new life style, and outlive it in a New Age?

Well, maybe. Those who think so include people who have compiled records of intelligent and dedicated radicalism going back a decade or more. But then again, other people have seen the book as representing something very different. One of them is E. F. Schumacher himself. As he puts it with unusual bluntness, "All this lyrical stuff about entering the Aquarian Age and reaching a new level of consciousness and taking the next step in evolution is nonsense. Much of it is a sort of delusion of grandeur, the kind of thing you hear from people in the loony bin. What I'm struggling to do is to help recapture something our ancestors had. If we can just regain the consciousness the West had before the Cartesian Revolution, which I call the Second Fall of Man, then we'll be getting somewhere."

I talked with Schumacher recently when he passed through the San Francisco Bay area on a nationwide tour. While in the area he dropped in on one of his biggest local fans, California Governor Edmund G. Brown, Jr., for a private dinner, then for two days sat in on a big conference on ***Small Is Beautiful*** held by the extension department of the University of California at Davis.

Reporters thronged his press conferences, underlining his underground superstar status. During his U.S. visit he was hosted by five governors and a lieutenant governor, a passel of universities and social-change groups, and—with fine ecumenical sense—the heads of several large corporations. My conversation with him came in bits and pieces between lectures, local tours, speech preparations and fugitive efforts to catch a little sleep.

Most of his talks and the bulk of the questions he fielded had to do with the unorthodox economic proposals set forth in his book and his other writings: the idea, above all, of an "intermediate technology" appropriate in scale and cost to the needs and conditions of the people using it—neither too large nor too small. But most of his specific suggestions seemed secondary to what came through as the primary message of ***Small Is Beautiful***—a message so skillfully delivered that it has been absorbed by his audiences apparently without being noticed. What is the message? Nothing less than a passionate plea for the rediscovery of old-time Western religion—Roman Catholic religion, to be precise.

That's right: E. F. Schumacher is really an apologetical preacher, one of the rare breed whose experience has made it possible for him to employ effectively the language and concepts of economics as a medium for communicating what is essentially a sermon, a call for readers to repent, believe the gospel and reorder their lives accordingly.

Schumacher himself insists that it is this "meta-economic" foundation of his argument that is most important, rather than the specifics of, say, his attacks on nuclear power or the use of chemicals in agriculture. "Everywhere people ask," he writes in the book's final paragraph, " 'What can I actually *do*?' The answer is as simple as it is disconcerting: we can, each of us, work to put our own inner house in order."

The key word here is "inner." Skim over it, and one can easily imagine that, like some Earth Day orator, he's only saying, "Ecology begins at home," with recycling your bottles and flattening tin cans. He recommends these things, to be sure, but they aren't the point.

This "inner" part was what I wanted to talk to him about. He readily owned up to being a Catholic, a certified convert as of five years ago. This item is not mentioned in his book; in fact, one of the most frequently cited chapters, "Buddhist Economics," almost made it appear as if he were deeply involved in Eastern religions. But wasn't this chapter, I inquired, really more informed by the Catholic writings and thinkers he mentioned so frequently elsewhere in the book—the papal encyclicals, Newman, Gilson and, above all, Thomas Aquinas?

Schumacher grinned. "Of course. But if I had called the chapter 'Christian Economics,' nobody would have paid any attention!"

This is not to say that the reference to Buddhism was a sham: he is firmly convinced that the basic elements of a common religious outlook are to be found in all the world's major religions. But it was done artfully, to help get his message across. "You see, most people in the West are suffering from what I call an anti-Christian trauma," he explained, "and I don't blame them. I went through that for 20 years myself." (pp. 325-26)

"Schumacher is a contemporary voice of what I call social Catholicism," commented John Coleman, who shared a panel with the Englishman at the Davis Extension Conference. Dr. Coleman is professor of religion and society at the Jesuit School of Theology in Berkeley, and he had delivered a paper discussing some of the ethical implications of the approach. "By this I mean the stream of Catholic thought that built on Thomistic principles, as particularly reapplied in the work of Jacques Maritain. Its adherents stressed that human institutions ought to be manageable in size, respectful of the human scale, and sanely run so that they did not damage the people involved in them."

"These writers," said Coleman, "also asserted that there were institutions in society outside the government which stood between the individual and the state, and which did not derive their right to exist from the state. In other words, they stood alongside and, if necessary, over against the state. The two institutions usually cited as being of this character were the family and the church itself. Schumacher extends this approach to technology.

"The problem with social Catholicism," Coleman continued, "is that it has been mainly enunciated rather than acted upon. But in Europe, for instance, most of the Christian Democratic parties have endorsed the idea of workers' councils as part of management in corporations—a policy which Schumacher proposed in his book. And in England earlier in this century there was a group of Catholic distributists, headed by G. K. Chesterton, Hillaire Belloc and Eric Gill, who talked of decentralizing industry along lines that in spirit were very much like what you find in ***Small Is Beautiful.***"

Coleman added: "Maritain was very much opposed to the bourgeois capitalism of his time; yet he also could not accept totalitarian socialism. So his work represents among other things an effort to find a 'middle way' for Christians. In his work as well as Schumacher's you find a tension, an almost paradoxical character: they're 'conservative revolutionaries' or 'reactionary radicals,' mixing the old and the new with all the risks that involves."

Schumacher agreed with this catalogue of thinkers as sources for his own outlook. In keeping with their thought, he frequently repeated, in his talks at the Davis Extension Conference, his conviction that the first task of the people in the audience who agreed with him is "to sort out our values and our views of reality, to clear our minds."

But as he urged them then to get down to more concrete work in support of various efforts of appropriate technology research and development, their comments and questions kept skimming past this first priority to the practical pros and cons, the alleged sins of the oil companies, his attitude toward women's liberation, the possibility and desirability of violent revolution.

Schumacher did not harangue them on the point. But he confirmed for me his strong sense of the priority of what he calls "metaphysical reconstruction." "That is the first task," he said, "because without it all these various technological fixes will only add to the confusion. But nowadays, to talk openly about such issues is hardly permitted in polite society."

This comment reminded me of something else he had said often during the question periods following his lectures: "I'm not a scholar, or even a writer. I'm a practical man: I run things and get them going." It is, I suspect, part of this practicality that leads him to approach the abstract side of economics—its metaphysical and religious underpinnings—through more "practical" (that is, saleable) concepts like Intermediate Technology and Buddhist Economics. (pp. 327-28)

Charles Fager, "Small Is Beautiful, and So Is Rome," in The Christian Century, *Vol. XCIV, No. 12, April 6, 1977, pp. 325-28.*

The Economist **(review date 1 October 1977)**

[In the following review, the anonymous critic offers an unfavorable assessment of A Guide for the Perplexed.]

The late Ernst Schumacher was, and will deservedly remain to his readers, a high priest of ecology. Like other priests of this cult, he turned next to philosophy, and here is the result. When he speaks from the heart, he is deeply moving. When he regurgitates half-digested semi-truths from other writers, he is boring. When he assumes the reader is ignorant of these ideas, he is downright irritating.

[In ***A Guide for the Perplexed,*** Schumacher] starts in Leningrad with a map that shows no churches. The maps of life given to men by educators and by rational, scientific culture have gaps on them too, he says. Fair enough. Next, he argues, there are four levels of being, starting with mineral, going on to plant, then animal, and then man. Again, fair enough. Like the physicist's four forces, and the four horses of the Apocalypse, Mr Schumacher may have his set of four, and this is not his only one.

But there is a catch. In passing, Mr Schumacher adds that there is nothing in physics and chemistry to explain or describe the transition from mineral to plant. Has he not heard of experiments duplicating much of this transition with an astonishing verisimilitude? Well, he is only an economist, turned philosopher; how is he to know?

Towards the end of [***A Guide for the Perplexed***] it becomes clear, however, that he has heard of these experiments. He rejects them, along with evolution. His distaste for science verges at times almost on disgust. It is true that scientists disagree about the details of evolution, but the principle is established beyond reasonable doubt, and reasonable hypotheses can explain an astonishing range of its features.

Much of the middle of the book is concerned with the value of self-knowledge. At one point, there are no less than 10 successive quotations on the theme of the Delphic utterance, "Know thyself". These are followed by the amazing claim that the culture of self-knowledge has fallen into almost total neglect: amazing, considering the popularity of introspection, psychoanalysis, encounter groups, meditation and so on.

Mr Schumacher's own views on self-knowledge are sometimes extreme. You can, he argues, only understand in others what you have experienced yourself. Interpreted strictly, this would make communication very limited. In fact, men use analogies of their own experience to extend their communication. And to assert that St Francis talked to the animals because of his self-knowledge is going rather far.

It is always perplexing to try to reconcile the scientific world with that of poetry, feeling and the spirit. But this odd mix of over-reaction against the one and secondhand recital of the other's virtues is little help towards a synthesis. (pp. 129-30)

"Know Thyself," in The Economist, *Vol. 265, No. 6996, October 1, 1977, pp. 129-30.*

Harvey Cox (review date 2 October 1977)

[*Cox has written several books on religion in which he discusses the benefits and the drawbacks of Eastern religions for Western people. In the following review, he describes* A Guide for the Perplexed *as unconvincing and confusing, but occasionally wise.*]

[***A Guide for the Perplexed***] begins literally where [***Small Is Beautiful***] ended. It is small, only half the length of the previous one. Whether it is beautiful, however, is open to question. I found parts of it wise, much of it hard to follow, and some of it not at all convincing. ***A Guide for the Perplexed*** is a call, more like a plea, for a radical turn toward self-awareness, something about which the author believes only the great religious traditions of the world, not science, have something to teach us. The longest chapter is devoted to an extensive, though somewhat random, survey of the religious and philosophical literature endorsing self-knowledge. This is followed by descriptions of some of the contemplative practices designed to make such self-knowledge possible.

The trouble is that Schumacher violates his own best advice. He goes big. He pours on too much and therefore is not persuasive. We are led through sentences and aphorisms from Socrates, Philo Judaeus, Plotinus, the "Theologica Germanica," Paracelsus, Swami Ramdas, Azid ibn Muhammed al-Nasafi and the Tao Tê Ching. Lest the reader be dazzled by the unseemly display of erudition, Schumacher candidly mentions in a footnote in the back of the book that all of these quotations were drawn not from their original sources but from Whitall N. Perry's "A Treasury of Traditional Wisdom."

This evidence behind him, Schumacher then goes on to try to draw out the alleged similarities among such diverse texts as "The Cloud of Unknowing," the "Philokalia," the "bare awareness" of Buddhist meditation and the teachings of P. D. Ouspensky. To my surprise, he also includes a page of praise for Edgar Cayce, the late American seer, and Therese Neumann, the German peasant woman who is alleged to have lived 35 years eating nothing but the daily wine and wafer of the Eucharist.

This illustrates the most severe problem I had with the book. I kept feeling that something urgent was being said about how the reductionist logic of modern science has indeed misled us and is useless when it comes to the most perplexing questions we face. Ironically, however, the man who has taught so many of us the virtues of modesty and restraint has resorted to a kind of scattershot and overkill. Not only has he tried to do too much in one small book—repudiate scientism, reinstate the hierarchical mode of thinking, reclaim the perennial philosophy—but the firepower he has concentrated is so mixed and so massive that his original point frequently gets lost.

I hope not completely lost, however. Schumacher surely has something important to say. He knows that the really serious issues facing us today cannot be "solved" but must, as he says, "be grappled with" and that such grappling will require us to learn more than most modern people want to from the great religious traditions. He feels very strongly that the modern experiment of living without religion has failed, and without a certain kind of self-knowledge all our knowledge of the outside world will be worse than useless. So, behind the prolixity lies a truth that a very thoughtful man is trying to get through to us: In order to survive as a species, we must change in ways that will exact much more from us than we now anticipate, and if we want to survive, we had better get on with it.

Harvey Cox, "A Subtreasury of Traditional Wisdom," in The New York Times Book Review, *October 2, 1977, p. 10.*

Arthur Koestler (essay date Spring 1978)

[*A prolific British novelist and essayist, Koestler frequently writes about science and philosophy. In the following excerpt, he examines the structure of* A Guide for the Perplexed.]

The late Dr. Schumacher's "Small is beautiful" has become a catchword almost as popular as "Make love, not war." Both slogans point towards a desirable end; both can be sneered at as products of wishful thinking. This is even truer of Schumacher's posthumous opus [***A Guide for the Perplexed***], but that should not deter the reader, for (to quote the physicist J. R. Platt) "the world has now become too dangerous for anything less than Utopia."

The perplexing title of the book is taken from a once-famous treatise by Rabbi Moses ben Maimon ("Maimonides"), a Jewish philosopher who flourished towards the end of the twelfth century and tried to reconcile the Old Testament with Aristotelian philosophy. Perhaps Dr. Schumacher's motive in adopting the title was to indicate that he was aiming at a similar synthesis between modern science and Christian ethics (with a sprinkling of Buddhist thought). Be that as it may, if the title sounds somewhat presumptuous, the book itself shows no trace of it. But it is difficult to summarize its contents, for these 150 pages are themselves a condensation of a vast and refreshingly unorthodox system of ideas.

In the first chapter, "On Philosophical Maps," we are told by the author that "my map or guidebook is constructed on the recognition of four Great Truths—landmarks, as it were—which are so prominent, so all-pervading, that you can see them wherever you happen to be . . . and if you cannot recognize them, you are lost." The "four landmarks" are specified as follows:

The Great Truth about the world is that it is a hierarchical structure of at least four great Levels of Being.

The Great Truth about man's equipment wherewith to meet the world is the principle of "adequateness," *(adequatio).*

The Great Truth about man's learning relates to the "Four Fields of Knowledge."

The Great Truth about living this life, living in this world, relates to the distinction between two types of problems, "convergent" and "divergent."

The four great Levels of Being are: the mineral kingdom of lifeless matter (m); add to this the factor x which distinguishes living from inanimate matter and you get m+x, the level of plants; add to this the factor y which stands for consciousness and you get the animal m+x+y; lastly, add the faculty of self-awareness, and you get man: m+x+y+z. However, the plus signs do not signify simple increases in quantity, but the emergence of qualitatively different levels which, in their ensemble, constitute the hierarchy of being.

The successively higher Levels of Being show various "progressions" compared to the lower ones. The most striking progression is from passivity to activity, from object to subject. A stone is "wholly passive, a pure object, totally dependent on circumstances." A plant is "mainly, but not totally, passive; (it) is to a small extent a subject with its own power of doing, organizing and utilizing." At the animal level, these powers are dramatically enhanced through the appearance of consciousness and an "inner life." On the human level, "there is a subject that says 'I.' . . . To treat a person as if he or she were a mere object is a perversity, not to say a crime." On the other hand, even a human being has its inert, material aspect; and aware of this shortcoming, mankind has extrapolated the progression from object to subject to an even higher level of existence—"*a Person* above all merely human persons, in no way an object, above all circumstances and contingencies, entirely in control of everything: a *personal* God, the 'Unmoved Mover.' "

Closely related to the progression from passivity to activity are other progressions from necessity to freedom, from "outer space" to the "inner space" of mental events, and towards integration and wholeness. There is no discernible limit or ceiling for these progressions. "Self-awareness . . . is a power of unlimited potential, a power that not only makes man human but gives him the possibility, even the need to become superhuman." Personally speaking, I am skeptical about that possibility, but it is nice to hear an optimistic solo voice breaking through the chorus of Cassandras.

The second of the Four Great Truths is *adequatio,* a concept derived from the neo-Platonists; it says that the understanding of the knower must be *adequate* to the thing to be known; or in Schumacher's definition, that "nothing can be perceived without an appropriate organ of perception, and nothing can be understood without an appropriate organ of understanding."

This may sound like a tautology, but the two chapters devoted to the subject contain a valuable discussion of how to acquire and train and develop that "organ" or instrument capable of understanding reality in all its aspects, including those that are "invisible," contained in inner space; an understanding of "the truth that does not merely inform the mind but liberates the soul."

This leads to Schumacher's distinction between "science for understanding" and "science for manipulation" (the former, one might say, striving to comprehend nature, the latter to exploit nature). One wonders, however, whether such a neat division exists. Einstein certainly was motivated by the pure desire to understand, but by equating mass and energy he pointed the way to Hiroshima.

The third "Great Truth" is contained in the "four fields of knowledge." The first is self-knowledge, attained through the exploration of the individual's inner space; the second is knowledge of the other person's inner space, attained by empathy; the third is the study of the self as an objective phenomenon (in "outer space"); the fourth is the study of the outer world (including society) as an objective phenomenon.

The fourth and last "Great Truth" is that there are "convergent" problems and "divergent problems"—which seems to me an eminently useful formulation. Convergent problems arise in the exact sciences and are in principle soluble. Divergent problems are concerned with systems of values, existential questions such as determination versus freedom, and other paradoxes which cannot be solved by logical reasoning. They must be referred to higher levels in the Hierarchy of Being where "opposites cease to be opposites," and "lie down together peacefully like the lion and the lamb."

The only appropriate comment I can think of is: "So be it. Amen." (pp. 72-4)

Arthur Koestler, in a review of "A Guide for the Perplexed," in The Critic, *Chicago, Vol. 36, No. 3, Spring, 1978, pp. 72-4.*

Francis Flaherty (review date Spring 1978)

[In the following review, Flaherty contends that A

Guide for the Perplexed *is poorly written but has good ideas.*]

Until his death in Switzerland last autumn, E. F. Schumacher, Rhodes Scholar in economics and for twenty years Economics Advisor to the British National Coal Board, was one of the handful of economists openly critical of the crude materialism and simplistic psychology on which their discipline rests. He achieved international fame four years ago for his ***Small Is Beautiful: Economics as if People Mattered,*** a collection of essays whose common theme is the plea for a saner economic policy than one which measures human happiness as the number of jelly donuts consumed per capita per year. The essays are diverse, treating such disparate topics as the awful dangers of nuclear energy, the idolatry of giantism, Buddhist economics (a favorite text of California Governor Jerry Brown), and unemployment in India. But the basic contention of that book is clear: modern economics has become so myopic that it can neither discern the dire poverty of two-thirds of mankind nor foresee the imminent depletion of the earth's resources.

By the time of his death, Schumacher had emerged as a major spokesman for ecologists, altruists, and all sensible people who realize that "permanent, limitless expansion in a finite environment" is, eventually, disastrous. Schumacher's vision of doom is persuasive because he was not a visionary. Director of an organic farming association, leading Third World consultant, and key figure in the decentralization of the British coal industry, Schumacher was hardly an academic economist. He developed and applied and stumped for the concept of "appropriate technology" for underdeveloped nations; he was a prime mover behind the Scott-Bader Company, a worker-owned British chemical firm whose constitution provides that half the company's appropriated profits be donated to charity, that the salaries of the lowest and highest paid employees not exceed a one to seven ratio, and that no products be sold for war-related purposes. In his work and in his writing, Schumacher is squarely in the tradition of Aldo Leopold, John Kenneth Galbraith and Buckminster Fuller, a maverick tradition which stresses the maximization of human happiness with a minimum of consumption, rather than the reverse state of affairs which classical economics has foisted upon us.

A Guide for the Perplexed, however, is theistic, abstract, and refractory of classification. From the time of Descartes, Schumacher claims, Western man has neglected his inner life, embraced materialism, and searched for the answers to spiritual questions in the formulae of science. The methods of science, in the phrase of Karl Stern, have become the "mentality" of society. When confined to the laboratory the scientific method insures the validity of results, but when applied to the social sciences or to philosophy it is an inappropriate tool, a slide rule used to measure the dimensions of God.

Schumacher, who practiced Buddhism, argues that there are inner experiences that are quintessentially human and that are knowable solely through meditation or prayer or other spiritual exercise. Before Descartes, this spiritual quest was the greatest of human traditions. Schumacher cites scores of notables from all ages and both hemispheres; Aquinas, Paracelsus, Dante, Gandhi, Coomaraswamy and others attest to the timeless validity of the adage, "Know thyself." In dispensing with any endeavor not subject to empirical tests, Descartes bequeathed to modern man a surfeit of knowledge and a scarcity of wisdom.

From that bleak legacy, the reader can infer, arises the modern passion for possessions, the anomie of our societies, and the vapidity of much of our lives. Schumacher is an advocate of religion in its broadest sense: the belief that there is something out there (and within every human) which cannot be explained but must be experienced. Only by reviving his lost traditions can modern man solve his social ills and salve his existential wounds.

A Guide for the Perplexed has very good ideas very badly phrased. It is scattershot, full of curt dismissals of reputable disciplines, and somewhat random in its organization. A dyed-in-the-wool Cartesian will dismiss it for its inscrutable Buddhist style ("the Great Chain of Being," "the Four Fields of Knowledge"), and the sympathetic reader will not quite know what he is agreeing with. But it is true that twentieth-century men place no great premium on inner development, and it does seem unusual that the dictum "Know thyself," so valuable to our ancestors, has no currency for us because it is not susceptible to scientific articulation. Twentieth-century thinking assumes that people are interchangeable units with certain physical needs and predictable patterns of behavior—but, if there is anything that each individual knows, it is that he is unique, that his most important needs transcend the physical, and that his behavior is no more than the denouement of the teeming, energetic story of his inner life.

If twentieth-century thinking can come up with no better vision of man than that, we had better not rely on it too heavily. And time is short: "We are now far too clever to survive without wisdom," says Schumacher in his gentle but urgent way. There is probably not a thinking man or woman who has not devoutly wished that the world's destructive nuclear capability could be controlled by those for whom wisdom and inner development were the goals of life. (pp. 227-28)

Francis Flaherty, "Schumacher's Guide," in The Hudson Review, *Vol. XXXI, No. 1, Spring, 1978, pp. 227-28.*

Robert Lekachman (review date 20 May 1979)

[*Lekachman's writing reflects his belief that economic growth and social justice should be correlated. In the following review of* Good Work, *he concentrates on Schumacher's philosophy of intermediate technology.*]

The most attractive of Schumacher's concepts, particularly in developing societies, has been the idea of intermediate technology—simple machines, devices and administrative forms more powerful than hoes and less expensive than tractors, and thus far better suited to the resources of impoverished peasant cultivators and small entrepreneurs than the conventional products of the advanced technology of North America and Western Europe.

Good Work supplies examples of the approach. In Zambia, eggs were spoiling for want of inexpensive egg trays to convey them to market. Schumacher's Intermediate Technical Development Group designed trays appropriate for the limited production of Zambian poultry raisers. His associates created the "snail" in lieu of standard plows, which cost far more and operated economically on farms much larger than the six or seven acres available to African cultivators. In both rich and poor countries, Schumacher has preached the gospel of organic farming.

By no means a Luddite, Schumacher saw a place for large-scale technology. The 747 is not a project for small entrepreneurs. However, Schumacher insistently argued that small-scale brick, cement, machine-tool and lumber plants are more efficient than large, centralized installations whose products must be expensively shipped vast distances to customers who frequently cannot afford them, and, if they could, would be much better served by local products tailored to their individual requirements.

Although Schumacher served for many years as chief economic adviser to the British Coal Board, his objective extended far beyond his colleagues' conventional preoccupation with the familiar aggregates of national income. What counted for Schumacher in this posthumous volume based on lectures delivered in the last years of his life, as in his previous writings, was the quality of human experience, not the quantity of the items meaninglessly summed up in Gross National Product comparisons.

A deeply religious person, Schumacher was attracted by Gandhi during a period he spent in India, and in England he worked with Quakers, among other sympathizers. In ***Good Work,*** whose tone fluctuates between pessimism about what technology has done to deform the human spirit and optimism about the chances of personal and social renewal that have against all odds survived, he levies a severe four-count indictment of modern technology. Its gigantic scale discourages community and individual imagination. Its complexity separates the educated from the rest of the population. Its enormous cost discourages progress in poor societies. Finally, it violently assaults the natural environment.

Even in the richest communities, advanced technology drains meaning and satisfaction out of work. Yet, urges Schumacher, good work is essential to the fulfillment of the Creator's three intentions—fulfillment of our own potentialities, aid to others and aspiration to the divine. How can human beings advance toward even the first and most self-centered of these goals within the crushing context of infinitely subdivided tasks that are the common experience? Schumacher quotes Adam Smith to telling effect: "The man whose whole life is spent performing a few simple operations . . . has no occasion to exert his understanding. . . . He naturally loses, therefore, the habit of such exertion and generally becomes as stupid and ignorant as it is possible for a human creature to become."

Schumacher took comfort from signs that increasing numbers of citizens of rich societies are sufficiently unhappy to strike out for themselves in small enterprises, organic farms and local cooperatives. Schumacher, who must have been an exceptionally persuasive advocate, even reported occasional success in enlisting the good will and active cooperation of multinational corporations. When markets were too small to attract their attention, large corporations sometimes helped design small-scale machines and devices.

The message here, as in Schumacher's previous volumes, is a call, not for class or economic warfare, but for the improvement of individual behavior and activity and the transformation of industrial society into a humane residence for creative and consequently happy men and women. It is not at all difficult to comprehend Schumacher's immediate and enduring appeal. He asks us to start where we are—with ourselves and our immediate environment. Let each cultivate his own garden and by so much reduce the pollution of the universe.

However much one may doubt the possibility of checking the momentum of modern technology, it is hard to deny Schumacher's anguished warning that at present rates of consumption the world's inhabitants will soon exhaust existing stocks of non-renewable resources and in the process poison the thin layer of atmosphere within which we subsist. Schumacher could not quite bring himself to believe that the Creator intended the human race to commit suicide. For nonbelievers, the outlook is truly desperate. (pp. 12, 24)

Robert Lekachman, "Between the Hoe and Tractor," in The New York Times Book Review, *May 20, 1979, pp. 12, 24.*

John Naughton (review date 21 December 1979)

[*In the following excerpt, Naughton offers a mixed review of* Good Work.]

Essentially a collection of reprints of speeches given during a successful lecture tour of the United States, ***Good Work*** is addressed to a question with strong metaphysical connotations: what is the purpose of human work? To this [Schumacher] gives three answers: to produce goods and services which are both necessary and useful; to enable us to perfect our gifts and skills; and to serve, and collaborate with, other people in order to liberate ourselves from our inborn egocentricity.

Inevitably, any collection of speeches, if published in unedited form, is likely to be uneven. This is certainly the case with ***Good Work,*** and the fact that the book has been abysmally proof-read does not help either. On the credit side, there are three impressive chapters: a succinct summary of the events which led up to our current energy predicament; an excellent exposition of the idea on which Schumacher's main claim to fame rests—the notion of "Intermediate" or "Appropriate" technology, i e. technology adapted, not to the dictates of the Law of Diminishing Marginal Returns, but to human needs and specific social contexts; a third chapter presents some evidence, culled from practical successes in implementing intermediate technology, for the view that we do not have to remain intellectually paralyzed in the face of our global difficulties. These chapters show Schumacher at his best—marshalling the complex facts of life into a coherent and compelling order, making a sophisticated analysis look simple and "obvious".

The remaining three chapters of ***Good Work*** are less satisfactory, largely because the author's exposition and style of reasoning are not really suited to metaphysical speculation. "On Appropriate Forms of Ownership and Action" presents an unduly simplistic picture of the possibilities for alternative forms of organizational structure, and underestimates the complexity of the forces which shaped conventional structures. "Education for Good Work" sets out to identify some features of an educational process which might prepare people for meaningful work, but comes to no very obvious conclusion. "The Party's Over" starts out as a tirade against the tyranny of GNP and ends up with a biblical exhortation to purge ourselves of the slavish adulation of scientism.

The trouble with these chapters is that they promise more than they deliver. They are presented as an unpretentious, Mark Twain-type exploration of troubling questions about human priorities and aspirations, but are in fact engaging expositions of personal conclusions which are rigidly determined by their author's religious and ethical premises. No doubt this is partly a reflection of the deficiencies of the popular-lecture format. But it is also a reminder that a gift—such as Dr Schumacher possessed in abundance—for clear thinking about issues such as energy is no guarantee of success when the subject of discussion lies submerged in the murky waters of the soul.

John Naughton, "The Appropriate Alternative," in The Times Literary Supplement, *No. 4005, December 21, 1979, p. 148.*

Michael Ashley (review date March 1980)

[*In the following excerpt, Ashley reviews* Good Work *and analyzes the themes of technological determinism and cultural convergence.*]

"Small is beautiful." This proposition, the much quoted title of a previous book by the late E. F. Schumacher, remains the basic theme of his new book [***Good Work***], based on a series of lectures given in the mid-1970s, but it is incorporated within a more general philosophy of work which comes from the same stable as Marx's and particularly Mills'.

Schumacher's diagnosis of the ills of modern industrial society is self-consciously iconoclastic in intent and strongly evangelical in tone. He comes across as a wise, compassionate man, with a deeply-felt outrage at all manifestations of loss of human community and fellowship—whether produced by large-scale technology, bureaucratic and uncaring organisations, uncontrolled economic growth, autocratic management, or by the selfish pursuit of "private pecuniary gain." He presents an attractive vision of a future industrial society based on the principle of cooperative production, "organised in much smaller units with an almost infinite decentralisation of authority and responsibility." Strong on sentiment, then, but somewhat soft-centered when it comes to providing a theoretical understanding of what is wrong, where the real fault lies, and how the transition to a world of small-scale, cooperative production and work with real meaning might be effected.

At one level, this comment does him an injustice: he was not the romantic, armchair moralist he sometimes appears to be in his writings. Rather, he was an energetic and committed practical man, constantly attempting to translate his ideals into immediate reality, rather than wait for the millennium. He promoted "intermediate technology" in the Third World, introduced modest schemes of decentralisation at the National Coal Board (whose Economic Adviser he was from 1950 to 1970), and was involved in the Scott Bader Commonwealth—one of the relatively few successful examples of a cooperative productive enterprise in Britain, and one which takes seriously the "human scale" philosophy by not allowing any of its companies to grow above 400 workers.

What is Schumacher's view of modern work? "Mechanical, artificial, divorced from nature, utilising only the smallest part of man's potential capabilities, it sentences the great majority of workers to spending their working lives in a way which contains no worthy challenge, no stimulus to self-perfection. . . . " But to what should these evils be attributed? To Capitalism? Or to Industrialism? His answer is the latter, "irrespective of the social form", and he justifies his position with the aid of a decidedly crude technological determinism:

> Once a process of technological development has been set in motion it proceeds largely by its own momentum, irrespective of the intentions of its originators.

Against those on the Left who claim that the problem is the capitalist system or the profit motive, and those on the Right who blame management for failing to provide the workforce with a sense of purpose in their work and a sense of belonging within the enterprise, Schumacher insists that the technology itself is the main culprit, rather than "the system", the social form, or the super-structure, which are only "the inevitable product" of the technology:

> As I compare the societies which appear to have different "systems", the evidence seems to be overwhelming that where they employ the same technology they act very much the same and become more alike every day. Mindless work in office or factory is equally mindless under any system.

Schumacher's reification of technology is an ironic testament to the strength and insidiousness of the very processes and ideologies about which he feels so strongly and of which he is struggling to make sense. What, after all, is technology, and what are we to make of his twin theses of technological determinism and cultural convergence?

There is, certainly, a usage of the concept of technology which does involve the idea of a system, a complete "package." This incorporates not merely the interrelationship of a set of machines or production processes, "the hardware", but also what might be described as "the social software" of a particular work design, division of labour, and method of working, which appear to be inexorably linked to the nature of the hardware. But are they? Surely the way in which a machine, or interrelated set of machines, or an integrated production process is operated—in terms of the extent of the division of labour, the scope of the tasks thereby created, the nature, indeed the very existence, of supervision, the degree of discretion, control and responsibility given to the workers, and so on—is not simply given by the physical nature of the machinery. It expresses the goals and conceptions of how work "must" be organised to realise those goals of the individual or collectivity which has the right to make authoritative decisions about the organisation of production. In short, technology can be used to perform the same technical operations under very different forms of work organisation and in pursuit of very different goals. These could be, for instance, maximisation of private profit, as against use-value to the community, or a deliberate commitment to forgo some part of the technically possible level of production in order to realise other valued goals, democratically decided by the workers in the factory or by the wider community, such as providing more interesting work.

It might well be argued that assembly-line work in car manufacture—whether located in England, Russia, or, more tellingly perhaps, in a hypothetical future socialist society (organised in such a way that it avoids neo-Marxist critiques of "state capitalist" Eastern bloc societies)—is, by its very nature, incapable of providing interesting, meaningful work. Such an argument might well accept that in the truly socialist society workers may take part in a fully democratic decision-making process at factory and society level about the organisation and scale of production, and that the conditions of work, including the speed of the "track", might be more favourable than in any of today's car factories. Following Marx's critique of the fixed occupational division of labour in *The German Ideology,* or the more modest Chinese experiment in giving intellectuals a taste of manual work from time to time, workers might not even be expected to work for more than a certain period of time in such a job. But however great these improvements, assuming they are seen as such, the actual work itself would remain repetitive and uninteresting.

This seems to me an important and defensible argument, one which tends to be dismissed too easily by some advocates of this future socialist paradise. The appropriate response is to question the alleged or merely assumed "necessity" of an assembly-line production system in the first place: cars do not have to be built with this kind of technology, as Aston Martin workers know. However, it is essential to remember the intense competitive pressures of the international market for mass-produced (as opposed to limited edition, specialist and very expensive) cars. Any car company or any country operating in this market would be courting certain bankruptcy if it decided to go it alone and hand-assemble its cars in order to increase job satisfaction among the workforce—and this provides a good example of one important structural constraint under-estimated by Schumacher: the impossibility of Socialism in One Country.

Schumacher would, of course, agree wholeheartedly with the proposition that mass production of cars could be undertaken in smaller factories, with a less rigid division of labour, small work groups rather than an assembly-line, and less supervision of and more discretion allowed to the workers. What he seems to shy away from is a recognition of the conditions under which such a change could take place, namely, the transcendence of the international capitalist system of production for profit, and the cultural values which are both the product and ideological underpinning of this system, such as instrumentalism. But Schumacher does not like the language of political change, or "the system." He prefers to see the world as a morality play, in which the heroic "little people" slowly undermine the villainous world of Massive Technology from within by developing their own "human scale" technology. At some point in the future the multinational corporations quietly wither away, and industrial harmony and human fellowship break out all over: a perfect omelette made out of good intentions, and achieved without breaking a single (free-range) egg. (pp. 58-60)

Michael Ashley, "The Enrichment of Boredom: Good Work & Bad Work," in Encounter, *Vol. LIV, No. 3, March, 1980, pp. 56-62.*

Witold Rybczynski (essay date 1980)

[*In the following excerpt, Rybczynski identifies the development of Schumacher's intermediate technology theory and the impact of* Small Is Beautiful *as precursors to the alternative technology movement.*]

The question has sometimes been asked, "Intermediate between what?" Schumacher's original definition [of intermediate technology] was quite clear. He described the need of the poor in less developed societies for a technology that was "more productive than the indigenous technology but immensely cheaper than the sophisticated, highly capital-intensive technology of modern industry." In order to be successful, according to Schumacher, this technology, which he called "intermediate," should have four characteristics. First, it should create employment in the rural areas to reduce the urban migration that characterized most developing countries. Second, this technology should be labor-intensive rather than capital-intensive; that is, it should create jobs with the minimum of investment. This was aimed at reducing the high unemployment found in many less developed countries. Third, methods employed should be "simple" so as to reduce demand for skilled labor and management. Fourth, production should be, as much as possible, for local use.

The theory of intermediate technology was proposed by Schumacher at a particularly critical moment. Notwithstanding the fact that all poor countries were referred to as "developing," the unpleasant and depressing fact was—and is—that many of these countries were not developing at all. The United Nations Development Decade had been hopefully announced in 1964. The stated aim was for all the poor countries to increase their per capita income by

50 per cent (5 per cent per year). This would have still left the poor countries far behind the industrial nations, but it was considered a bare minimum of the change necessary. By the early seventies, statistics indicated that although the average growth had indeed slightly exceeded the target figure set down by the United Nations, fully two thirds of the less developed countries had experienced a growth rate that was significantly lower than 4 per cent, and in some cases they had even suffered a decline. The optimism of plans such as the Development Decade was not completely without foundation. The Marshall Plan of 1948-51 had had an extravagant effect on postwar Europe. Countries which had been bombed "back to the Stone Age," to use a phrase from a later war, revived and prospered as they had never done before. Surely, it was felt, the same could be done for the poor countries, many of which had become independent in the fifties and early sixties.

One such effort was the so-called green revolution. This term referred to the development of various high-yield crops for the tropics, chiefly rice and wheat. These were introduced into a number of less developed countries, together with modern agricultural techniques such as controlled irrigation, fertilization, and weeding. The initial results of the green revolution, greatly publicized, were almost too good to be true: wheat production in certain countries doubled, rice harvests tripled. The first countries to feel the benefits were Mexico, India, Pakistan, and the Philippines—a not inconsiderable experiment. The green revolution was the prototype for solving the problems of the developing countries with modern technology, for, though the high-yield rice and wheat were developed in the Philippines and Mexico, the green revolution was very much a Western approach, involving both the Rockefeller and Ford foundations.

It became apparent, however, that the green revolution was not a panacea; as with all development, new problems had to be faced. Particularly in the early stages, the beneficiaries of the innovative agriculture were the larger and richer farmers who could afford to invest in the required seeds, irrigation, and fertilizers. The optimistic production figures of the first phase were often the result of planting the best land first; later production tended to drop. In spite of the fact that enormous progress was made in countries like India, where food production had previously been stagnating, the green revolution was not equally successful in all countries. In many cases, after the initial burst of activity, government support for the agricultural programs dwindled; the research that was necessary to sustain a modern agriculture was not continued. It was easy to criticize the pretentiously named green revolution, and many did so, particularly those from advanced rather than less developed countries. Although some of these criticisms were no more than scholarly carping, others had validity, particularly in those cases where improved agricultural technology was adopted without significant parallel agrarian reform.

The result of partial failures such as the Development Decade or of perceived failures such as the green revolution created a climate of pessimism as regards the ability of technology to solve the pressing problems of the poor countries. Of course, the extent of this pessimism should not be exaggerated. The Soviet Union still gave a hydroelectric dam to Egypt, Canada built nuclear reactors in India, and China constructed a railway in Mozambique. Even as advanced technology was criticized, it was apparent that it remained the only way to progress, and for most less developed countries, the only desired way.

Nevertheless, when Schumacher came on the scene with the "intermediate technology" proposal, there were many who were willing to listen, first, because modern technology could obviously not solve all the problems, especially in the rural areas, as the green revolution had shown. Second, as the Development Decade had so graphically illustrated, it was unlikely that most of the less developed countries would be able to modernize in a hurry, the reconstruction of Europe notwithstanding. Thus, even when industrialization was considered to be the ultimate goal, intermediate technology was seen as a desirable technique for bridging the gap, a stepping stone to modernization.

By the early seventies the intermediate technology approach was beginning to be accepted as an adjunct to traditional theories of development. Though a certain number of small groups which lobbied for more emphasis on rural development and small-scale technology had sprung up, there was no general "movement" in this direction. Perhaps because the ideological base of intermediate technology was narrow, perhaps because it was aimed solely at the less developed countries, or perhaps because it really was seen as second best, the impact of intermediate technology, particularly on the public, was very limited.

The publication, in 1973, of ***Small Is Beautiful: A Study of Economics As If People Mattered*** propelled Schumacher into the limelight. This collection of Schumacher's lectures and essays, "carpentered together into a single book" as the London *Times* reviewer put it, became an international bestseller and was translated into fifteen languages. It bears a remarkable similarity to another bestseller, Betty Friedan's *The Feminine Mystique.* Both books are ponderous (Schumacher's, less scholarly, makes no pretense at continuity at all), yet both have served as cultural milestones. ***Small Is Beautiful*** was quoted by figures as disparate as the heir to the British throne, Prince Charles, and an heir of another sort, Governor Jerry Brown of California. If Schumacher's name was hardly to become a household word, "small is beautiful," at least, would take its place in the true popular literature of the Modern Age—the T-shirt slogan.

The success of ***Small Is Beautiful*** can probably be attributed to its most serious limitation: it did not attempt a reasoned argument but appealed directly to the emotions. Since it was a collection of essays on a variety of subjects, it gave the impression of covering a lot of ground, and even though some of the statements were contradictory (which is inevitable in a book, by a single author, that contains material spanning more than a decade), it offered simple and understandable solutions.

What was this book really about?

Small Is Beautiful was first and foremost a diatribe

against modernization: the bureaucratization and rationalization of all aspects of modern life, the depletion of nonrenewable resources, environmental decay, even the Bomb. This in itself was hardly news; there had been a series of books that had done this more comprehensively, and sometimes more convincingly, beginning with Jacques Ellul's *The Technological Society.* Schumacher took the moral and material decay of the modern world pretty much for granted (as did most of his readers, one suspects), and the appeal of his message rested on two other attributes.

Most critiques of modernization had been confined to Western technological society. Schumacher pointed out, perhaps for the first time, the link that existed between the discontents in the West and those in the less developed countries. The latter discontents can be characterized as movements toward countermodernization, most frequently evidenced by traditionalism (the Middle East) or nationalism (Africa). Demodernization and countermodernization spring from different sources; vastly oversimplified, the former could be said to be of the left, the latter of the right. Though one is a reaction against modernization and the other is fear of an alien imposition, they are both engaged in a rebellion against modernization and its effects.

The second appeal of Schumacher's book is the fact that, unlike Ellul, a French sociologist, he did offer a solution to the malaise of modernization, and, in spite of his disclaimers, it appeared to be a technological solution. A conundrum emerged from this book and became more evident in Schumacher's later writing. All of Schumacher's training and experience had made him a technocrat; perhaps a particularly sensitive technocrat, but a technocrat nevertheless. Schumacher was an economist and he tended to see the solutions to problems in economic terms. His remedies for the self-destructive tendencies of modernization consisted in looking for answers within the technocracy itself; changing the kind of decision that technocrats make; choosing, for instance, smaller instead of larger industries. For these reasons, ***Small Is Beautiful*** elicited a strong positive response from state institutions.

It is tempting to compare Ernst Friedrich Schumacher with another German economist, Karl Heinrich Marx (1818-83). The superficial similarities, though coincidental, are curious. Both came from upper-middle-class backgrounds; they were born within seventy miles of each other. They attended the same two German universities, Bonn and Berlin. They both had large families (Marx six children, Schumacher eight), both left Germany and spent the most productive part of their careers in England (where both are buried), and both wrote books on political economics. Schumacher, however, was no Marxist. It is unlikely that he was even a socialist; his endorsement of socialism in ***Small Is Beautiful*** was tentative indeed, since he recognized that most forms of socialism share the same attitude to technology as do most capitalist societies. Nevertheless, one has to conclude that Schumacher did largely share Marx's doctrine of "economic determinism." I have already pointed out that ***Small Is Beautiful*** was a collection of lectures and essays which made for uneven and sometimes inconsistent reading. It is difficult to make conclusive statements about the views it contains, since often opposing sides of an argument are supported in two different chapters. However, the impression of the book as a whole, and certainly its popular impact, was economically and technologically deterministic; that is, it assumed that the modern world was shaped less by politics, geography, and national culture than by economics and technology.

Schumacher, a complicated man, was also a complicated economist. He grew up in post-World War I Germany in the same region as did the German youth movement which originated in 1896 but continued in various forms until 1938, encompassing the sons, and later the daughters, of the middle class. This was a unique occurrence, unparalleled in the rest of Europe and not to be repeated until the "hippies" of the 1960s. The *Jugendkultur* was apolitical and pacifist and included such things as whole-food diets, exercise, and vegetarianism, all cast in a romantic criticism of bourgeois society. If the reader sees a similarity between this movement and the Californization of present-day youth culture, he is not mistaken. Eastern religion, mysticism, folk singing, communes, and free schools were all part of the German youth movement. A favorite German author of the 1920s, Herman Hesse, underwent a revival in the 1960s in the United States and Canada, if not exactly for the same reasons, at least with the same age group. It would be surprising if Schumacher were not also influenced by the ideals of the *Jugendkultur.* Much of what later went toward making Schumacher a cult figure—his organic gardening, his pacifism, even his Buddhism—were by no means a pose. Through a series of historical accidents Schumacher bridged the gap of forty years that separated the American hippies from the German *Wandervögel.* The moral, sometimes mystical, side of Schumacher attracted the American *Jugendkultur* to AT, but it did something else as well. Because it was genuine, not an affectation, it created a very real tension in Schumacher between the moralist and the economist.

Schumacher's religious development was greatly affected, by his own admission, by the visit he paid to Burma, which followed his earlier interest in mysticism and psychic research. (Rudolf Steiner, the inventor of "anthroposophy," was a big influence on German youth of the twenties and thirties, and Schumacher frequently lectured at a Steiner school in England.) In ***Small Is Beautiful*** Schumacher introduced the idea of Buddhist economics, which consisted basically of applying restraint and self-discipline to economic decision making. This was an attempt to try and resolve the dilemma between the moralist and the economist. The moralist wanted to change man, the economist wanted to change the social system. This dilemma was never satisfactorily resolved. In his last book, ***A Guide for the Perplexed,*** there are indications that Schumacher-the-economist had deferred to Schumacher-the-moralist: "Even if all the 'new' problems were solved by technological fixes, the state of futility, disorder, and corruption would remain. It existed before the present crisis became acute, and it will not go away by itself." This despairing statement, however, was made four years later; at the time that ***Small Is Beautiful*** appeared, it was still the economist who predominated. The ills of society were caused by technology, he wrote; to correct these ills it was necessary to choose a different kind of technology, a "technology with a human face."

There were very few examples in ***Small Is Beautiful*** of what this technology might be, or indeed if it *could* be—the bulk of the book dealt with what *should* be. These human-faced machines were to be "cheap enough so that they would be accessible to virtually everyone; suitable for small-scale application; and compatible with man's need for creativity." If we would only develop machines with these characteristics, Schumacher pleaded, we could have a revolution in technology which would reverse the destructive trends that threatened us all. (pp. 8-19)

There was a curious unworldliness to ***Small Is Beautiful.*** It isolated man, his natural environment, and his machines and ignored history, culture, and politics. When the latter were mentioned, they were as minor factors—"technology must be adapted to local traditions" or "political factors should also be considered." There seemed to be little appreciation that technology is the creation of man, and the latter, with his dual propensity for good and evil, is always facing a choice. His decisions are conditioned, more than is generally admitted, by his history. If there was something dislocated in this book, it may have been due in part to Schumacher himself, the perennial outsider, or to the rootlessness and lack of historical sense of the Californized youth who made up an important part of the AT [appropriate technology] movement. (p. 24)

Witold Rybczynski, "What Is Appropriate Technology?" in his Paper Heroes: A Review of Appropriate Technology, *Anchor Press, 1980, pp. 1-40.*

Additional coverage of Schumacher's life and career is contained in the following sources published by Gale Research: *Contemporary Authors,* Vols. 73-76 [obituary], 81-84; and *Contemporary Authors New Revision Series,* Vol. 34.

Gary Soto

1952-

American poet, memoirist, short story writer, essayist, and editor.

The following entry provides a general overview of Soto's career through 1992. For additional information on his life and works, see *CLC,* Volume 32.

INTRODUCTION

Soto is recognized as one of America's best Chicano writers. Incorporating his working-class background and Hispanic culture into his poetry and prose, Soto addresses such social issues as discrimination, violence, and poverty. Noting the relationship between his ethnicity, upbringing, and writing, he asserts: "I write because there is pain in my life, our family, and those living in the San Joaquin Valley. My work may appear personal, but perhaps it should remain that way. . . . I write because those I work and live among can't write. I only have to think of the black factory worker I worked with in L.A. or the toothless farm laborer I hoed beside in the fields outside Fresno . . . they're everything." Critics argue, however, that Soto's ability to exceed solely personal and local concerns has established him as a major contemporary author. Gerald Haslam asserts: "Soto is a Chicano author who is true to his heritage, but whose literary reputation transcends that fact. He is in no way dependent upon overcompensatory critics, for his voice is universal."

A third-generation Mexican American, Soto was born in Fresno, California, and raised in the San Joaquin valley where, as a child, he worked as a farm laborer. Attending Fresno City College, Soto initially majored in geography before transferring to Fresno State, now California State University, in the early 1970s. Inspired by Donald Allen and Robert Creeley's anthology *The New American Poetry, 1945-60* (1960), Soto began taking workshops with American poet Philip Levine, whose writings often depict the harsh realities of urban life. During this time Soto met several other noted authors, including Ernest Trejo and Christopher Buckley. Soto graduated magna cum laude in 1974 and earned an M.F.A. from the University of California at Irvine, publishing his first poetry collection, *The Elements of San Joaquin,* in 1977. He has since received numerous awards and fellowships: the Academy of Poets Prize in 1975, the United States Award from the International Poetry Forum in 1976, and the 1985 American Book Award from the Before Columbus Foundation for *Living up the Street: Narrative Recollections.* A finalist for the Lenore Marshall Poetry Award in 1979, Soto was also the first Chicano writer to be nominated for a Pulitzer Prize.

Much of Soto's poetry documents his upbringing and experiences as a Chicano in California's Central Valley. *The Elements of San Joaquin,* for example, focuses on Fresno in the 1950s, the agricultural community of San Joaquin, and the violence associated with barrio life; in "San Fernando Road" Soto writes of one character: "He did not think / Of the cousin / Spooning coke / Nor the woman / Opening / In her first rape." The harsh and desolate existence of farm life and the opportunities denied many Chicanos are similarly alluded to in "Field": "The wind sprays pale dirt into my mouth. . . . / Already I am becoming the valley / A soil that sprouts nothing / For any of us." Despite this ethnic consciousness, Soto has been praised for his ability to address private concerns concurrently with broader issues. For example, in *Black Hair* Soto discusses the problem of prejudice within the context of his parental responsibilities: "Daughter, though we smile with bread, / I'm troubled at not knowing what tugs the soul, / God or love, women or love, / And at how we can live in this world / With the dead itching on their racks, / A country in flames, the poor / Crouching before their banged-up bowls. / How can I tell you this? How can I show / You the men who want to hurt us all the way / To the grave." Commentators also attribute Soto's ability to avoid strict polemicization of Chicano concerns to the humor often present in his writing. For instance, in "Mexicans Begin Jogging" Soto relates the time he was mistaken for an illegal alien while working in an American tire factory: ". . . the border patrol opened / Their vans and my boss waved for us to run. / 'Over the fence, Soto,' he shouted, / And I shouted that I was an American. / 'No time for lies,' he said, and pressed / A dollar in my palm, hurrying me / Through the back door. . . . / What could I do, but yell *vivas* / To baseball, milkshakes, and those sociologists / Who would clock me / As I jog into the next century / On the power of a great, silly grin."

Soto's memories are also central to his prose collections, which Soto and his critics generally perceive as extensions of his poetry. Commenting on *Living up the Street,* Soto observed that a prose format provided him the opportunity to create "a set of narrative recollections with very little commentary. I would rather show and not tell about certain levels of poverty, of childhood; I made a conscious effort not to tell anything but just present the stories and let the reader come up with the assumptions about the book—just show not tell, which is what my poetry has been doing for years."

PRINCIPAL WORKS

The Elements of San Joaquin (poetry) 1977
The Tale of Sunlight (poetry) 1978
Father Is a Pillow Tied to a Broom (poetry) 1980
Where Sparrows Work Hard (poetry) 1981
Black Hair (poetry) 1985
Living up the Street: Narrative Recollections (memoirs) 1985
Small Faces (memoirs) 1986
Lesser Evils: Ten Quartets (memoirs and essays) 1988
Baseball in April, and Other Stories (short stories) 1990
A Summer Life (memoirs and short stories) 1990
Who Will Know Us?: New Poems (poetry) 1990
Home Course in Religion (poetry) 1991
Taking Sides (juvenilia) 1991
Neighborhood Odes (poetry) 1992
Pacific Crossing (juvenilia) 1992
The Skirt (juvenilia) 1992

CRITICISM

Alan Williamson (review date March 1980)

[*Williamson is an American critic and educator. In the following excerpt, he examines several poems in* The Tale of Sunlight, *praising Soto's descriptions of poverty and use of memory and detail.*]

[It] is a pleasure to turn to the zest for concrete experience, and for the figures of speech that often have the trick of reanimating it, so evident in the young Chicano poet Gary Soto. "The cricket that ticks / Like fire"; a chicken's "eyes / Blown deep / As targets"; "My crotch puffed / Like a lung / And holding its breath"—Soto's gift for simile is as lavish as Alfred Corn's, at the opposite end of their generation in subject matter and apparent literary affinities. Soto's ground-theme can be found near the end of **"The Street,"** the longest, and most carefully written, poem in ***The Tale of Sunlight:***

> The poor are unshuffled cards of leaves
> Reordered by wind, turned over on a wish
> To reveal their true suits.
> They never win.
>
> This means Theresa Fuentes,
> Palm reader and washerwoman,
> Stacking coins into vertebrae of silver
> Fingered dull by the cold

The "wish," as I read these lines, may be the world's, but may also be the poor man's own, as vulnerably obvious as his one good suit. (Soto's rhetoric, for all its lucidity, often has such fruitful puns and byways of implication. The silver "vertebrae," for instance, may seem an excessive visual cleverness—unless one begins to think of the money, and the magic, as "backbone" in the colloquial sense—another pitifully exposed "wish" for strength.) Soto never—or rarely—makes the mistake of arguing back to middle-class stereotypes of his people, either by producing the walking statues of the proletarian novel, or by justifying traits of negative identity such as violence. Rather, it is this aspect of entrapment and psychic exposure in the life of the poor—including, as in **"The Cantina,"** their sometimes savage sense of their own ugliness—that he stresses. Place, in his poetry, has the combination of arbitrariness and almost enviable solidity it must have for those who cannot leave it easily:

> You watch the dark become a backdrop
> To hunger, the streetlight
>
> A moon that will not pull west,
> Dragging its light under the rule of another heaven.
>
> You think of the bus
> And the dust that trailed it like a cape,
>
> The slashed mountains rung pale
> With roads that climbed through a fever of new air.
>
> **"Antigua"**

His Proustian enabling memory is a childhood sense of comradeship with yard junk—sharpened, one feels, by the foretaste of a life whose objects would always be few, outworn, ill-made.

Yet Soto also records the amazing gallantry—less toward each other than toward a feeling of community which exists only if affirmed—of those who, in a phrase he borrows from Elio Vittorini, "would hardly eat except to be seen."

He records, furthermore, a vein of consolatory fantasy which passes beyond escapism into a pure imaginative generosity toward life. I am not thinking, now, of his slightly unconvincing excursions into the world of *brujos,* but of the poem in which an uncle's gray hair is seen as a visitation of magical butterflies; or the poems in which enforced closeness to nature takes on a quality of animistic warmth, **"The Space"** or **"The Shepherd":**

> He is returning at
> The pace at which the sun untangles itself
>
> By the moon's laughter,
> The willow's desire to touch its feet.
> *There is no hurry,* toss the trees.
> *Good Wood, Good Fire,* fall the chinked coins of
> leaves.

Soto still has room to grow as a poet. The impress of the middle style shows itself in the many poems written in two-to-four-word lines; these thin, columnar pieces are often—though not always—duller than the others, and more given to easy rhetorical sighs ("it no longer / Mattered to say / The world was once blue"; "Watching . . . For . . . a miracle / To fall like rain"). There are a few pious message-poems, notably about ecology (**"The First"**). But at his frequent best, Soto may be the most exciting poet of poverty in America to emerge since James Wright and Philip Levine. (pp. 351-53)

Alan Williamson, "In a Middle Style," in Poetry, *Vol. CXXXV, No. 6, March, 1980, pp. 348-54.*

Theresa Melendez (review date Winter 1982)

[*In the following mixed assessment, Melendez compares the themes and stylistic devices in* Where Sparrows Work Hard *to those in Soto's earlier works.*]

Where Sparrows Work Hard is Gary Soto's third full-length collection of poems from the [University of Pittsburgh Press] not including the chapbook ***Father Is a Pillow Tied to a Broom*** from which nine poems are reprinted in ***Sparrows.*** In contemporary Chicano poetry, four books published by a non-Chicano press is a significant accomplishment given the emergent nature of the literature and the difficulties of access to "mainstream" publishing houses. For Soto, the significance lies in the assertion of his poetic stance, poet as observer and architect of meaning, the "chameleon poet" who has no inherent identity and no scheme of what should be. This stance takes different forms in the four works but is a constant in development.

The earlier persona of ***The Elements of San Joaquin*** (1977) is that of the isolated self, who lives in a working class world of unmitigated poverty and despair. The first section of the book is a collection of violence: rape, mental illness, death, fear and alienation brought about by the material existence of the oppressed. The violence, however, is faceless, and the poet can do nothing but watch it. In his next section, Soto gives us the landscape from which he views this world: the vegetable realm of the migrant farmworker who reaps nothing for himself except an awareness of destitution, and where even the rain and the fog are reminders of his insignificance: "there is a pain that gets up and moves, like the night attendant." The last section is another collection of memories from his childhood and his culture, character sketches of relatives and friends and *things,* trivial items, among which Soto searches for, but cannot find, meaning.

It is easy to arrive at a list of his favorite motifs: cats, slugs, chinaberries, ants, brooms, bottlecaps, shoes, filling dusty streets and cluttered rooms. These images are minute memories of seemingly indiscriminate associations laid evenly before us for our examination. And among these recalcitrant items that negate meaning by their very insignificance, we, along with the poet, find an understanding of our task: to see is to know.

Soto carries this task into his next book, ***The Tale of Sunlight*** (1978), in which his role as observer is markedly set out but with a change of tone, a new insistence. As observer, the poet, the artist, must point (a favorite word of Soto's) the way, must mark the trail of humanity's journey through the world, like the child in Soto's first poem in ***Sunlight*** who steps out and makes appear "what I lost / Years back." As the child names the things he sees, the poet rediscovers magic, a sense of unity with the natural world. In another poem, **"The Street,"** we glimpse a new note of hope: "I saw small things . . . Step slowly, as if shy, / From their kingdom of mold / Into a new light." The things he sees now promise him some respite from his isolation, "Where, if someone / Moved, I could turn, / And seeing through the years, / Call him brother. . . . "

It is in this volume also where Soto's poetic technique of creating meaning through the juxtaposition of images is set out more finely. His images exist in a taut line drawn between alternative but almost undifferentiated courses of action: rearranging and renaming a map; people clearing paths that close behind them; or contemplating time, "I turn 40. The sun / Does not turn." Voices "reach . . . and vanish," hands "fold and unfold," and a rooster stretches "to the day not there yet." These are not binary opposites which a near mediator can resolve, but instead the tension between them demonstrates the futility of discovering order in the world. Only through personal experience can the potential choices the poet *sees* achieve meaning. Soto affirms that the elements fixed by his line of vision—what the poet chooses to perceive—gain significance through his engagement of them. "It is enough, brother," he says, to be among those elements, in one of the "Manuel Zaragosa" poems, eleven short pieces developed around a fictional avuncular character who lives among the vicissitudes of life—a spouse's death, a chance encounter with friend or lover, a miraculous event—with an air of acceptance. Manuel's journey through the world, Soto's in this work, suggests a narrative of exploration and discovery, in which the real and the unreal, the trivial and the eminent, are disclosed as valid entities for contemplation.

In ***Where Sparrows Work Hard,*** the poet's voice is more personal, more intimate than that allowed in the past, and there are flashes of dark humor not seen before. The poems are also less contemplative and and ordered more through narrative. The familiar landscape of poverty and futility become mere backdrops for his characters' lackadaisical emotional fits as Soto documents their (and his) misery and powerlessness: "I see this and note / That when someone calls / No one has to go." The suppressed rage of the younger poet of ***Elements*** has become tempered into a sardonic stance, cool and distanced. Accordingly, situations that earlier might have been framed by the poet's anger—an industrial accident (**"Mission Tire Factory, 1969"**), the disparity between middle-class materialism and working class deprivation (**"TV in Black and White"**), and civil rights violation (**"Mexicans Begin Jogging"**)—are now expressed through cynical wit.

Soto's images and use of juxtaposition are just as powerful as in his other works, especially in his longer poems, such as **"Chuy,"** another character sketch. In this poem, Soto again charts the quest of "making significant," of a person seeking reprieve from non-meaning through individual affirmation. As Chuy travels through his mundane existence, he writes down abbreviated observations of his sojourn, "Light / Is only so strong," and "a street is only so long." Chuy's final act in the poem is to bury a bottle with "gifts" of himself, a bit of thread from his lapel, a lock of hair, and his name, so that future generations would know that here "Stepped Chuy, stooping / Among the ruins." It is not difficult to discern the poet's presence in this poem nor his desire for personal validation.

But in two poems, **"Sueño"** and **"Sueños,"** Soto questions his abilities and / or his needs. The first is an inversion of the *tempus fugit* theme, " 'die while you still have time.' " The persona, like dying summer, grows mute and has nothing to offer, or seems unwilling to exchange his gifts for a "totem of stacked coins," "God / For a small fee." He no longer can distinguish objective suffering from subjective despair: "is it rain or are we all weeping?" The second poem is composed of twelve imagistic scenes that conjure up muteness and oblivion: "I can no longer talk," "I can go higher, even disappear," "I am drowned, unremembered," "No one's talking."

The dilemma portrayed in the **"Chuy"** and **"Sueño"** poems, how the artist can remain meaningful in a meaningless world, is the predicament of the modern American poet. For it is in this tradition that Soto writes; "William Carlos Williams is responsible for us all," said Soto in a recent informal interview I had with him. Soto feels no allegiance to Chicano literature, as indeed a poet so intent in validating individual experience cannot. "It doesn't matter what the theme is," he says; "it is the power of the style" that draws him to particular poets. Chicano poetry with its adherence to theme, self-determination and the cry for justice, and with its collective spirit, can hold little interest for one who does not see "message" as an integral part of the poem. Soto's latest work displays the mastery of his technical craft, his images moving and sensitive, his vision acute and provoking. He is at his best in the reminiscence of childhood and in the evocation of loneliness. But having left the cultural home where his alienation was bequeathed to him by oppressive conditions, Soto loses the effectiveness of his major theme; the solitary wanderer who struck us with the pain of his insight and the immediacy of his metaphors no longer suffices. Soto continues to demonstrate the fine control of language and the skill of surprising us with flashes of images. But once delight over form turns into a questioning of content, the reader seeks sustenance; and the poet gives us a lean diet of isolation and retreat from the world. Alienation is useful only if it indicts the alienating forces and if it is transformed into a commitment to change. In itself, alienation becomes a maze with no solution, a self-defeating chore. We would hope that Gary Soto's undoubtable achievements will lead him out of that stale box known as "art for art's sake," writing as its own justification, and towards the direction of a unified art, content becoming form, as his potential so ably promises. (pp. 76-9)

Theresa Melendez, in a review of "Where Sparrows Work Hard," in MELUS, *Vol. 9, No. 4, Winter, 1982, pp. 76-9.*

In all his work, Soto establishes his acute sense of ethnicity and, simultaneously, his belief that certain emotions, values, and experiences transcend ethnic boundaries and allegiances.

—Raymund A. Paredes, in his "Review Essay: Recent Chicano Writing," in* Rocky Mountain Review of Language and Literature, *1987.

Gary Soto with Ernesto Trejo (interview date Summer 1982)

[*Trejo was a Mexican-born poet and translator. Both members of the Fresno School of Poets, Trejo and Soto became friends while attending college. In the following interview, Soto discusses his formative experiences as a poet, the writing process, and his early works.*]

[*Trejo*]: *Let me begin, Gary, by asking a very simple question. When did you first start writing poetry?*

[Soto]: I was 20 and at City College (Fresno). In fact, it seems strange how I started writing: an instructor had assigned a research paper, the kind you ended up copying from books but fucked up the grammar so it looked like yours. Well, my topic was the continental drift—the break-up of the land masses, you know. I went to the library but dreaded the idea of looking up "sources" so I just walked around doing nothing until I spotted a poetry anthology that looked interesting. It was propped up, almost staring at me, and I opened it. Up leapt Corso's "Bride of Frankenstein," and Ginsberg's "Howl," and the wonderful poem by Edward Field called "Unwanted," a quasi-Woody Allen piece about no one liking you. That poem was magic, and still is.

What anthology was this?

Donald Allen's *New American Poetry,* the one with the American flag on it.

After discovering this anthology you then started writing your own poems?

No. I was pleased with just reading poems from it. But after a couple of weeks, I thought to myself, "Hell, I can do something like that." I started writing and the first poem that I thought was a hot number was **"Little League Try-Outs."** I worked on it for a week—long, long hours of adding one word only to get rid of it later. This was followed with your basic "hobo/derelict" poem and again I thought, "Hmmm, not bad." But I caught hell when I turned them in to Levine's poetry writing class that coming Fall at Fresno State. As you know, he's a very astute reader of poetry and if you turned in bad poems he'd rub his hands together and go to town tearing them up. It was a truly humbling experience for him to go line by line pointing out your stupidity. And of course, in the whole process, he'd have the class laughing at you—or laughing with him. He's a brilliant man with a clever wit, and he wouldn't spare you if you turned in insipid and poorly wrought poetry. In fact, I remember Leonard Adame telling me the same thing, how when he turned in his first poem and sat back to hear praise, he instead heard laughter.

What did he teach you?

Craft. He taught us how to handle language with care. Or at least this perhaps was the single most important thing he shared with me. He was more or less a "nuts and bolts" man, who could point out flaws in your writing. He embraced no deep theory, no abstraction, no bullshit. Just stuff that you could apply to your poems right there and then.

Did your poems have a certain weakness that you had to overcome?

I was very sloppy in my writing, grammatically and otherwise. I mean, until then I hadn't really ever done anything with language that required exactness of detail and delivery. What I tried to do at the time was simply to write *better.*

Let's talk about your first book, **The Elements of San Joaquin.** *How did it start?*

It started piece by piece—or at least it was like that at first. I remember Levine liking a couple of poems during that first semester (Fall, 1973), and one was **"Field Poem."** This would be the first poem I'd keep for ***Elements.*** But it really started after returning from Stevens Point, Wisconsin, where I had been invited to attend an ethnic writing workshop. A strange week and a half. That was the first time I had been out of California and for me the sense of alienation was so acute that I was certain that I was not living that experience, that my life had been severed from the past . . . In a way it took a distance to look back on my home town, Fresno—the San Joaquin Valley—to love its small time beauty and shake my head at its tragic nature—racism, I mean . . . When I got back from Wisconsin I was filled with poems.

Just like that?

Just like that. I came back, unpacked the sad suitcase my mother had lent me, and started writing. . . . I wrote most of the poems at my girl friend's house—the woman that I would later marry. She lived two houses away from where my brother and I were holed up with two other friends. All of them were artists, or would-be artists. One drew monkeys—that's all. Monkeys looking left, monkeys looking right. Monkeys doing magic tricks. Wonderful guy. My brother was air-brushing—believe it or not—futuristic Fresnians with no hair. And then there was this other guy, D. L., who did some strange art work—things with dots and ashtrays and bowls that looked like elephant feet. He wanted very much to be rich. He kept talking how he was going to go to the Bank of America and ask for a loan to help out with his art work. Inside, I was laughing at his schemes. I mean, can you imagine someone carrying ashtrays into the Bank of America and approaching a loan officer. The house was nuts. . . . Anyhow, I started on the ***Elements*** that summer and wrote maybe two or three poems a week, some of which were good and others simply pieces I'd end up throwing away. I worked at a sewing table at my girl friend's—she cleared away a tiny space for me, and while she was at work I pounded away at the typewriter, a beautiful 1950 Royal.

So you returned to Fresno State and once again enrolled in Levine's class.

Yes. By the end of summer I must have had at least twenty poems, and I turned them in to him, two or three at a time. He liked most of them and, I think, was stunned by my leap from writing poems about Little League, cheerleaders and what-not, to poetry with real subjects. It pleased him very much.

You depended, then, upon his criticism to shape your poems?

Yes. Again, he was a very good reader of poetry, especially student poetry, and what he offered was genuine. You could trust what he was saying, even if it hurt. You see, no one works alone. You have to have a sounding board if you want to grow and deepen as a poet—or as an artist or musician, for that matter. The only person I know of who was lit with brilliance was Mozart. At four and a half he was already composing very complex and startling movements. He was a genius, of course, with an IQ that was out of this world. Most people I know aren't brilliant. In fact, most people I know are on the other end, average in mind and looks, and drive Volkswagens.

Did you show your poems to others at the time?

No, not really. You see, I have never really hung around other writers, people I could show my work to. The people I saw were my brother and girl friend. We never really talked anything that was literary—though I must tell you that Carolyn (the girl friend) is a good reader. She can read a poem and give me a general sense of what's wrong or good about something.

But Christopher Buckley is a reader of your poems.

That's true. But that was later at Irvine. In fact, I remember the first time he looked at a poem of mine. We were in Diane Wakowski's workshop and he was sitting across from me, raising hell about the poems we were looking at that day. And what do you know, my poem **"History"** comes up. I read the poem and of course waited for his comments. The class was kind of dull, with students who were afraid to offend. They sucked their thumbs and when they didn't say anything, big old Buckley scratched his head, unscrewed the biggest pen I had ever seen, and started off with something like, "This is not a bad poem, but . . . " and off he went, ripping up the poem, in a very verbose Orson Wells manner. I took it, though. He had fine things to say and knew he was being helpful, though at one moment I wanted to get up and break his pen across my knee. . . . Another reader of my poetry was Jon Veinberg. A Fresno boy. He and I were in Levine's class together, the one in Fall of 1973, and we were rooming together in Laguna Beach—a two bedroom apartment that overlooked the Pacific Ocean.

Sounds wonderful!

It was great. I mean, I had just come from living on ninety dollars a month to a $340.00 fellowship. The bad thing was that Jon had very little money—in fact, at one time he didn't have any. So I covered for him, bought the beer, and showed him my poems. He was a good reader, too. Not as precise as Buckley, but very helpful.

Did you by chance look at their poems?

Oh, sure. Again, no one works alone, except maybe God. If they came to me, which they did often, I'd unscrew my pen and help out.

What poets were you reading at the time?

James Wright, Merwin, Weldon Kees, Roethke . . . many, many poets. But perhaps my favorite was Pablo Neruda. Now there was a poet. He had talent, vision, sympathy for the poor and the beautiful. For years I modeled my poems after his—the linear lines of his odes and the zest of his imagery.

In an indirect way you're saying that to become a poet one must read poetry. Would you say that this is true?

Certainly. You've got to work by something. You need to base your own poems on form, texture, stanzas, rhythm, and so on. You just don't sit down and say to yourself, "Hey, I'm going to write a poem." If you do, then you write what you "imagine" is a poem and more often than not it's a kind of poem that you might write in high school—or worse, like touchy feely rock lyrics. In some ways it's like a carpenter. Because you possess a hammer doesn't mean that you can simply build a house. There are things you have to learn if you don't want the building to fall on your toes, especially if people are looking on to watch you fuck up. There are many poets banging away with their hammers and the houses are leaning this way and that way. They're going to collapse in no time. Just watch.

Are you speaking of Chicano poetry?

No, not necessarily. I'm speaking of poetry in general. Remember, excellence is difficult to come by. Not everyone who decides to write poetry will become a good poet, just as not everyone who takes up a hammer will become a decent carpenter. Or will every young person who takes up the violin play for the Cleveland Symphony. It's a matter of talent and perseverance. Guts, too. And vision. . . . Do you remember what Rilke says in *Letters to a Young Poet?* I forget just where, but he says something to the effect that you will have to work for years, many years, that instead of going out to fuck up the town, like everyone else, you, you the poet, will have to sit at your desk and write and write and write—and the scary thing is that though you will give yourself over to this strange art, there is a good possibility that what you will be doing will be all wrong, that your poetry will be second rate and collapse two weeks after your death. Talk about being humbled.

Do you think your poetry will collapse too?

Yes, I do. It's difficult to become a literary giant, like Williams or Stevens or Pound. But by no means am I going to give up. If I have a goal, it's to write well, to speak about things that are important—and human.

Would you have advice for a young poet?

Ernesto, you make me sound old, on my death bed. . . . Well, I would say to a young student poet to write when he felt and not before, and to take his work seriously, not himself. And he should strive toward some kind of excellence—whatever that might mean to him. Don't just be okay. You've got to be better than that. If you want to be mediocre, then go into pharmacy or business. Don't fool around with poetry.

Earlier I asked you about your favorite poets and you left off Luis Omar Salinas.

Yes, I forgot. He is one of my favorite poets, and I'm thinking of his wit and poetic brilliance. I mean, think of some of his wonderful lines, lines like "Someone is chasing me up my arm." Or the lines, "A Mexican worker is smiling with his money / the dirt on his face is America." I really can't think of too many poets who write better than Salinas, Chicano or otherwise.

You think he's that good?

Yes, I do. Let me risk something and say that he's writing a poetry that is as good as anything being published in the U.S. today. I said it. It's off my chest.

But he's not being received very well, critically, that is.

No, but people didn't pay Melville much mind either. I'm not saying that Salinas is as good as Melville, but I think there's truth to the fact that a lot of writers are not reckoned with, that they are overlooked in favor of writers who are easily definable. I don't think people know what to do with Salinas' poetry. To some, he may seem a bad version of Spanish or Latin American poetry. A preposterous imitator. But the fact of the matter is that his sensibilities are very much Latin American. His manners, his behavior. His personality is shaped by his Mexican heritage, by his environment, by the lushness of the reality he perceives, and this all spills over into his poetry. If you meet him, then read his poems, they are one and the same. For instance, he has a poem called "The Road of El Sueño by the Sea." Sounds exotic, doesn't it? But the truth of the matter is there *is* a road called El Sueño and it so happens that it's very close to the sea. It's in Santa Barbara, and

Omar wrote the poem while he was visiting Chris Buckley there. He has a poem called "A Bit Crazy," and it's just that: he's a bit crazy. It's not a poeticism at all.

Let's turn to your second book, **The Tale of Sunlight.** *When did you start writing this book?*

I was living with Jon Veinberg in Laguna Beach. I was actually working on two books, ***Elements*** and ***The Tale of Sunlight.*** I was writing quite a bit then, at least a poem a week, because graduate school was a cinch and because there was so much free time . . . I'd wake up in the morning, drink a couple of cups of coffee, take a look at the sea, fool around in the house for a while, and start up.

"Start up?" Sounds mechanical.

Well, I mean I would try to get going, to write a few lines. In fact, the way I work is I scratch out a prepositional phrase or two, something like "between trees" or "in the wind." Simple throat clearing, in other words. If I'd start this way and if something followed, great. If not, I'd drink another cup of coffee and wait.

Most poets are idiosyncratic about the creative process.

They're an odd bunch. Like Roethke. He'd get on his knees and pray that something would happen, like a good poem. Dylan Thomas used to eat a hearty breakfast of eggs, ham, muffins, potatoes, the kind of Denny's deluxe you might get on Sunday, and then walk off to his little studio behind his house and start writing.

And Williams wrote between seeing patients.

That's right. He wrote when he could, muse or no muse.

But let's return to **The Tale of Sunlight.** *There seems to be an obvious plan to the book. Would you agree?*

There is in a way. The book is divided into three sections and each one has its own themes and ideas. The first, as you know, concerns childhood; the second is about place and transformation; and the third is the Manuel Zaragoza poems. I find that poetry is at its best when it's not miscellany—that there is a connection between one poem and the next.

I would say to a young student poet to write when he felt and not before, and to take his work seriously, not himself. And he should strive toward some kind of excellence—whatever that might mean to him. Don't just be okay. You've got to be better than that. If you want to be mediocre, then go into pharmacy or business. Don't fool around with poetry.

—Gary Soto

But don't you believe that a poem should stand as it is?

Of course. But I also feel that there should be a link, however vague, from one poem to the next. Look at Blake's *Songs of Innocence and of Experience.* The poems connect, don't they? Look at Roethke's *Far Field,* they connect . . . But true, a poem can only stand on its own merits, and it shouldn't depend upon other poems to keep it up. You can't make excuses. If a poem is obscure, vague, utterly lost, then most likely it's a bad poem. Still, I enjoy a *book* of poems, not poems in a book.

Do you have a favorite poem in **The Tale of Sunlight**?

I do. It's **"The Street,"** the long one. To me, the writing is there, it's complex without being stupidly obscure, and the tone is haunting. But what I really enjoy about the poem is that I settled some things that were bothering me, and it had to do with remembering people from my past—childhood. What I mean is this: I grew up on a street that was slowly being torn down. I lived in a part of industrial Fresno. If I looked out my bedroom window, I saw a junkyard. If I looked across the street from the porch, I saw a printing shop. Down the street were factories: Sun Maid Raisins. Challenge Milk, Coleman's Pickles. Houses were being torn down, for reasons I never understood, and with each house, they were tearing down my past. Tearing it down so in a way I wouldn't know who I was. . . . And houses aside, people were dying around me. Like my uncle. He had cancer. He was on the couch, day after day, until he was gone. And as you know, my father died very young, a neck injury while at work. And here I am, a kid, thinking, "What is going on?" And then there were people leaving, moving to better parts of town, like my grandparents. Neighbors were leaving, too. Other family members, like aunts and uncles, were marrying or getting the hell out. Anyhow, the poem, **"The Street,"** names these people, calls them up from the past. It was a very satisfying poem to write.

There's an epigram to the poem. Could you explain it?

It's from Elio Vittornini's *Twilight of the Elephant* and the line is "Then we would hardly eat except to be seen." That was me when I was a child. There are several ways to read this line, but I'd rather not say. Let others figure it out.

Could you say a few words about the Manuel Zaragoza poems? For instance, why would you want to write persona poems?

It goes back to childhood, when we used to have people over who wore suits, hats, gold watches—relatives and friends—and they seemed to me so worldly and rich and complicated. Very Mexican in their manners, you know. Polite, kind, low-speaking. They intrigued me because we were poor and nothing like them.

Could you give an example of a family member?

My grandfather. He worked as a security guard at Sun Maid Raisins, and when dressed in his best, he was sharp. Suit, shined shoes, sunglasses. He carried himself with that old-fashioned word, "dignity." In fact, it's from such a person that I imagined Manuel Zaragoza.

From reading the poems, you seem to have enjoyed writing them.

They were effortless to do; they came from God knows

what small space in my brain. What I remember about writing them was their zaniness and magic. Very little revising with them.

What about the middle section of the book?

These poems are more or less pastoral, bucolic pieces of places that exist in reality or in what I would like to call an "invented" reality—a landscape you make up from the imagination. For instance, **"The Shepherd"** is an example of an invented reality. I know of no shepherds, but what I wanted to do was to write a poem celebrating the simple act of returning home. It's a wonderful thing to come home, to open the front door and to flop down in a chair, utterly happy that you belong there. I felt that way when I was a kid. I'd often wake up on a Saturday, dress and eat something, and take off up an alley just to look around and walk miles, many miles, only to turn around and walk home with a private feeling of happiness. This is the lyrical section of the book, each line breathing openly and freely. For the most part it's not painful, like the first section or the ***Elements.***

You appear to be a prolific poet. You've published three collections in a span of five years: **The Elements** *in 1977,* **The Tale of Sunlight** *in 1978 and* **Where the Sparrow Works Hard** *in 1981. Would you consider yourself prolific?*

Yes and no. I mean, I've been writing ten years, almost eleven, and what do I have? ***The Elements*** has some thirty-two poems, ***Sunlight*** thirty-three and ***Sparrows*** twenty-nine. What is that? Ninety-four poems? Less than a hundred poems in books. If you break it down in those terms, I suppose you wouldn't consider me prolific. But of course I've written much more, maybe three hundred poems. But I don't keep everything. I chuck the bad poems into the fireplace.

Literally?

Yeah, I've thrown away many poems.

But how do you know a poem is really bad?

Again, I show my poems around, and if a poem should come back with its face kicked in, then I warm myself by the fire.

Was there ever a time when you couldn't write. . . or write well?

Right after finishing ***The Tale of Sunlight.*** That was late 1977. I couldn't do anything worthwhile. It took me about a year to recover from that blank. I was living in Berkeley then, teaching, as they say. Slowly the ***Sparrows*** book took shape, very slowly.

Why do you suppose you had a writing block?

God knows. If I knew the answer to that I'd be living in the Berkeley hills and driving an Alfa Romeo. It just happens and you just have to ride it out. And I did, I think.

I believe you did. **Where Sparrows Work Hard** *seems like your finest collection.*

Thank you. I think it might be.

You are working on a new book, aren't you?

Better yet, I'm *completing* a new manuscript called ***Black Hair.*** It's a big book, not necessarily in bulk, but plenty of poems. At last count there are about fifty poems, maybe more.

Would you be willing to say a word or two about the book?

Not at this moment, Ernesto. I want to keep it under for awhile.

Why?

Because it's off to a publisher who may do the book in a year, year and a half, and that's a long time away. Why announce a book when it's not around? All I can say is that I enjoyed writing it. Unlike ***Sparrows,*** which was a tug and pull effort for the most part, ***Black Hair*** came easily. It started last December (1981) when I wrote eighteen poems in two weeks. A wonderful time. I couldn't stop, and good for me.

Okay, I won't press you on this manuscript. So one last question. If this manuscript **Black Hair** *is almost complete, what then?*

I'm working on a manuscript of prose. I have my fingers crossed on this one. Prose is so much different from writing poetry, at least for me. With prose you have to be so patient. With poetry, not so. I mean, you can write a poem in a day and feel satisfied, but with a novel or a book of short stories, it may take years before you feel released. But we'll see about this manuscript. Ask me in a year. (pp. 25-33)

Gary Soto and Ernesto Trejo, in an interview in Revista Chicano-Riqueña, *Vol. XI, No. 2, Summer, 1982, pp. 25-33.*

David Wojahn (review date June 1985)

[*Wojahn is an American poet, editor, and educator. In the following review, he faults the adolescent themes, journalistic descriptions, and languid poetic structures in* Black Hair.]

In his fourth collection, [***Black Hair***], Gary Soto has chosen to dwell mainly in a Never-Never Land of early adolescence. Soto's speaker seeks to perpetually view the world in the way that a streetsmart twelve-year-old would. At its best, this stance conveys some of the brooding confusions of the pubescent mind. Soto employs a diction that's lyrical and colloquial by turns:

We're in bunk beds, one brother
Talking football, another
Turning to the dreamed girl
He'd jump from a tree to die for.
Later, in the kitchen,
He tells me, Love is like snow
Or something. I listen
With a bowl at the stove, dress,
And go outside to trees dripping
Rain, a pickup idling
With its headlights on.
I look for something to do
Slowly with a stick
In the absence of love,
That Catholic skirt in a pew.

"Morning on This Street"

More often than not, however, Soto's point is merely that boys will be boys. While there is a certain charm in the way Soto memorializes pelting his teachers with spitballs, or watching a friend fall through a screen window while he dances in a frenzy to an early Rolling Stones song, such reminiscences quickly grow tiresome, and Soto does not abandon his Holden Caulfield persona when he chooses to examine the events that exist beyond the splendours of adolescence. However, by limiting his responses to a naïve aplomb, Soto enables himself to write with a freshness that is at times arresting. This is especially true of the poems in the book's second section addressed to Soto's daughter. Soto has a good time in these poems, in part because he sees himself as his daughter's child-like compatriot:

It's the Hall of Science
Where we stand before mirrors
That stretch us tall, then squeeze us
Squat as suitcases bound for Chicago.
There are rocks, the strata
Of earth, a black cut of oil far down.
There are computers, a maze of lights
And wires, steel balls bouncing
About—they could be us, if we should make
The moon one day. But you tire
In a room mixed up with stars
And it's juice and a pretzel
On a bench, with me thinking
I'm a good father.

"Saturday Under the Sky"

Yet, despite its attractive writing, ***Black Hair*** is a disappointment. Soto's first two collections, ***The Elements of San Joaquin*** (1977) and ***The Tale of Sunlight*** (1978)—written when the poet was still in his early twenties—were stunning volumes, superbly crafted, thematically urgent, and ambitious in their scope. Compared to them, ***Black Hair*** is a distinctly minor achievement. In his earlier books, Soto used the terse enjambments of the short line and the image catalogs of surrealism to powerful effect. Both in the vivid recollections of his impoverished Chicano childhood in ***The Elements of San Joaquin,*** and in the oddly mythic narratives of ***The Tale of Sunlight,*** Soto's accomplishment was impressive. In ***Black Hair,*** Soto's care for the line is rather blasé, and his abandonment of surrealist poetics for more journalistic methods of description gives his poems a much less interesting texture: he has left the almost visionary mythmaking of his earlier books for some too-familiar anecdotes of adolescence. Has Soto chosen to become a minor poet, to deny his early promise? I hope not. (pp. 171-72)

David Wojahn, in a review of "Black Hair," in Poetry, *Vol. CXLVI, No. 3, June, 1985, pp. 171-72.*

Gary Soto has become not an important Chicano poet but an important American poet.

—Tom D'Evelyn, in his "Soto's Poetry: Unpretentious Language of the Heart," **The Christian Science Monitor, *6 March 1985.***

Geoffrey Dunn (review date Summer 1986)

[*In the following review, Dunn lauds Soto's descriptions of life as a Chicano in the American Southwest in his* Living up the Street.]

In the nine years since Berkeley poet Gary Soto burst onto the American literary scene with his award-winning ***The Elements of San Joaquin,*** he has continuously culled his Mexican-American youth in Fresno, California, for poetic imagery and vision. His poems, ranging from the terse, often bitter elegies of his first book on through to the more lyrical, if less piercing, lines of last year's collection, ***Black Hair,*** capture both the pain and spirit of a people relegated to the fringes of American society.

Soto's world is one of "twisted faces behind neon lights," of "Pontiacs with scorched valves," "Catholic skirts," and "harvests that are not his." The American Dream, for Soto, is the elusive myth of the white world, a tortuous benchmark for his own faded dreams and isolation. As he solemnly declared in the title poem of his seminal work:

Already I am becoming the valley,
A soil that sprouts nothing
For any of us.

In his latest volume, ***Living Up the Street,*** Soto has changed literary forms, though he returns once again to the dusty fields and industrial alleyways of his Fresno childhood. The twenty-one autobiographical short stories (or, more accurately, vignettes) assembled here recall with amazing detail the day-to-day traumas, tragedies and occasional triumphs of growing up brown in the American Southwest.

Living Up the Street begins with Soto as a precocious, streetwise five-year-old, "polite as only Mexicans can be polite," though with a "streak of viciousness" which Soto defines simply as "being mean." His neighborhood is full of Mexican kids like himself, most of whose parents are employed in the sweltering vineyards of the San Joaquin Valley or in the dreary confines of the Sun-Maid Raisin factory.

Soto posits implicitly in these recollections that the incandescent anger of his youth was the inevitable, perhaps even rational, response to the often violent social setting into which he was thrust by birth. In a passage that is delicately charming, yet distressing as well, Soto recounts his response to being called a "dirty Mexican" by a white playmate. "I looked at my feet and was embarrassed, then mad," he writes.

I approached him slowly in spite of my brother's warnings that the kid was bigger and older. When I threw the bottle and missed, he swung his stick and my nose exploded blood for several feet. Frightened, though not crying, I ran home . . . and dabbed at my face and T-shirt,

> poked mercurochrome at the tear that bubbled,
> and then lay on the couch, swallowing blood as
> I slowly grew faint and sleepy.

In **"Father,"** the book's most poignant vignette, Soto reminisces about a warm summer's day on which he was taught by his father how to water a lawn. "Standing over me," writes Soto, "he took the hose and placed his thumb over the opening so that the water streamed out hissing and showed silver in the dusk. I tried it and the water hissed silver as I pointed the hose to a square patch of dirt that I soaked but was careful not to puddle."

The next day his father suffered a neck injury at work. Two days later he was dead:

> A week after that, Rick, Debra, and I were playing in an unfinished bedroom with a can of marbles Mother had given us. Behind the closed door we rolled the marbles so that they banged against the baseboard and jumped into the air. We separated, each to a corner, where we swept them viciously with our arms—the clatter of the marbles hitting the walls so loud that I could not hear the things in my heart.

Soto's poetic prose goes right to the core of the Chicano experience (and, in many ways, to all ethnic experiences) in the United States during the past quarter century. His continual references to the vast chasm between his own reality and the "Father Knows Best" imagery of American television brought back a truckload of memories—and anxieties—from my own Italian-Catholic childhood.

I was particularly struck by Soto's painful description of a so-called beauty contest sponsored by an after-school recreation program. The contest, according the the program director, was to determine which "little kid was the best looking." Soto, then nine, was too old for the competition, so he entered his younger brother, Jimmy.

At the contest, Soto remembers, he was "awed by the blond and fair skinned kids in good clothes. They looked beautiful, I thought, with their cheeks flushed red from the morning heat." The Mexican kids had already developed a sense of inferiority about their looks—their dark skin, their eyes, their hair—so that they were certain they would lose.

And they were right. "A little girl with curlicues" received the crown, and the inferiorities, along with the resentments, became even more imbedded. Soto, already accustomed to such defeats, responded angrily to the decision; his little brother ran away quietly to play on the swings.

Such little incidents, insignificant as they may seem from the distance of the suburbs, constitute a terrible psychological tragedy taking place daily in the ghettos, barrios, and labor camps of this country, and Soto is absolutely brilliant in placing them under the magnifying glass of his literary perceptions. While ***Living Up the Street*** may not hold up to the very best of Soto's poetry, it is certainly a formidable work by one of America's more gifted and sensitive writers.

Geoffrey Dunn, in a review of "Living up the Street: Narrative Recollections," in San Francisco Review of Books, *Summer, 1986, p. 11.*

Alicia Fields (review date January-February 1987)

[*In the review below, Fields praises Soto's emphasis on memory, poverty, and everyday life in* Small Faces.]

The emotional weather ranges from sunny with blue skies to dark and stormy in ***Small Faces,*** Gary Soto's collection of prose reminiscences. One moment he contemplates the pleasures of his everyday life, such as marriage, parenthood, friendship, and making a living without breaking his back or numbing his mind. The next moment, he is roaming the sad, mean streets of his youth in Fresno, California. It's a "past that won't lay down and die for good," Soto writes.

Poverty is a dominant subject in ***Small Faces,*** as it is in Soto's poetry. Sometimes it is grim, sometimes humorous. In the opening vignette, **"Like Mexicans,"** Soto recalls his apprehensions about marrying outside his culture. He recounts his first meeting with his future in-laws, Japanese-American farmers, who, much to his relief, prove to be as poor as his family and neighbors. They "were like Mexicans, only different."

Poverty teases and haunts Soto's memories in many forms. A new jacket "the color of day-old guacomole" made him cry when he was eleven "because it was so ugly and so big that I knew I'd have to wear it a long time." He tells about the desperately impoverished—a hitchhiking bum who was once a successful brick mason and a ragged old married couple who foraged in garbage cans and lived a life "that scared even the poor." Poverty even appears in canine form when Soto indulges in a bit of dark humor and dubs a scavenging dog on a college campus a "blood brother to bad days" because it reminds him of a childhood spent searching alleys for discards.

Soto is the author of four volumes of poetry and another book of essays and is an associate professor at the University of California at Berkeley. Despite his publishing and academic credits, he often seems tenuous and incredulous about his middle class success. In **"To Be a Man,"** he recounts his childhood fear of following in his stepfather's weary footsteps as a factory laborer. "Now I am living this other life that seems like a dream," Soto writes, and he notes that it is accompanied by a lingering nightmare about becoming a bum to avoid the grind of the assembly line.

Although ***Small Faces*** contains stories about major events in the author's life, such as the death of his father when he was young, this is primarily a book about small but telling moments. In one sense, it is literally about "small faces" because it often focuses on children—what the author was like as a child and what his daughter is like today. Although often sad, the stories about Soto's childhood are also playful and filled with a sense of wonder. In **"Animals All Around,"** he recalls sitting in a tree with his best friend and pretending to be on an African safari. Their rich, imaginative adventures lead to a desire for the real thing. The boys don't have ten cents apiece to get in to the local zoo, so they try to sneak over a fence to continue their big game hunt. "At the top we rested and scanned the trees for monkeys that might drop on us," he recalls. But it was a cross zookeeper and angry parents who presented real danger. His zoo misadventure segues into a vignette about catching his nephew in the act of stealing pennies and suspecting his daughter of being a willing accomplice. This is typical of the way Soto deftly darts back and forth in time to form meaningful connections between past and present.

Soto's remembrances are as sharply defined and appealing as bright new coins. His language is spare and simple yet vivid. For example, remembering a date in a darkened movie theatre with his wife-to-be, he notes that his hand "crawled like a dizzy crab into her hand, which she snapped up to my surprise."

If ***Small Faces*** has a flaw, it is a matter of omission. Readers may find themselves wanting to know more about Soto's wife, Carolyn, who rescued him from bachelor meals of beer and rice with raisins. Was she a student when they met? Does she work outside the home? At one point, Soto mentions purchasing rosin for her violin. Is she a professional musician? Perhaps he will tell in his next book. Whatever he chooses to share will likely be well told and well worth reading.

Alicia Fields, "Small but Telling Moments," in The Bloomsbury Review, *Vol. 7, No. 1, January-February, 1987, p. 10.*

[Soto's] memories are like photographs, frozen in time, short vignettes that capture the small moments both funny and poignant falling between the cracks of larger events. A poet, Soto has an ear for rhythm and a eye for texture.

—Claudia Logan, in a review of* A Summer Life *in* The Washington Post Book World, *9 September 1990.

Patricia de la Fuente (essay date Autumn 1987)

[*In the essay below, de la Fuente examines Soto's focus on entropy and deterioration in his poetry.*]

In discussing the relationship between entropy and art [in his 1971 *Entropy and Art: An Essay on Disorder and Order*], Rudolf Arnheim points out that "when the Second Law of Thermodynamics began to enter the public consciousness a century or so ago, it suggested an apocalyptic vision of the course of events on earth" by stating "that the entropy of the world strives towards a maximum, which amounted to saying that the energy of the universe, although constant in amount, was subject to more and more dissipation and degradation." Arnheim qualifies this definition, however, by adding that "the popular use of the notion of entropy has changed. If during the last century it served to diagnose, explain, and deplore the degradation of culture, it now provides a positive rationale for 'minimal' art and the pleasures of chaos." If Arnheim's "positive rationale" may be taken to mean a logical and therefore organized body of principles, his definition of the entropy theory as, among other things, "a first attempt to deal with global form," provides a critical basis from which to explore the philosophical framework, structural dynamics, and thematic configurations in all forms of art. Hence the title of this essay, which examines the presence of entropy in the poetry of the Californian poet Gary Soto and in particular its metaphorical function as a reflection of the structural theme.

Arnheim conceives of this structural theme dynamically, as "a pattern of forces" rather than "an arrangement of static shapes." Such forces include the anabolic, creative force, and the catabolic erosion which leads to the eventual destruction of all organized shape. From a philosophical standpoint, Soto's choice of images in developing his seemingly antagonistic themes of corrosive social pressures and a subtle yet persistent search for a viable form of individual, social and universal order is indicative of a world view in which catabolic erosion predominates.

The catabolic destruction of shape, Arnheim speculates, is one of the two fundamentally different kinds of processes which result in the increase of entropy. The other is the principle of tension reduction or of decreasing potential energy. Arnheim describes the catabolic effect as "rather a broad, catch-all category, comprising all sorts of agents and events that act in an unpredictable, disorderly fashion and have in common the fact that they all grind things to pieces." Catabolism, he suggests, occurs because "we live in a sufficiently disorderly world, in which innumerable patterns of forces constantly interfere with each other."

If we accept Arnheim's premise that a work of art, among other things, "is intended as a portrayal of a significant type of order existing elsewhere," then it seems reasonable to say that the structural theme of, in this case, a poem "derives its value—even much of its value as a stimulant—from the human condition whose particular form of order it makes visible or audible." In the poetry of Gary Soto this revelation of order is articulated through images of violence, desolation, and disintegration; i.e. through the catabolic effect.

For the purpose of this discussion, Soto's poems may be divided into two principal groups, those which portray a gradual, often painful process of disintegrating structure involving a deep personal sense of disorientation, loss and desolation, and those which depict a more violent approach to changing form through suddenly unleashed disaster or the threat of it, in particular that caused by the death of the father. Although by no means absolute, these general categories will allow the identification of a consistent philosophy in a series of poems in ***The Elements of San Joaquín***, Soto's first collection, which deal essentially with the same theme: the search for form and significance in a world which is perceived as disintegrating, degenerating and generally in the throes of catabolic forces.

Since Soto's poetic vision reveals an environment of physical and spiritual decay, it is appropriate that his recurring images are of dust, dirt, and the corrosive wind which grinds down mountains and men with equal indifference, and erodes the emotional resources that make life both bearable and meaningful. One of the most impressive examples of gradual human disintegration occurs in **"County Ward,"** a cheerless half-way house for those who are in the final stages of mental and physical dissipation. Here the catabolic force intrudes as a concrete, creeping presence of pain and cold into the world of those who have come to die in the County Ward. A distinctly threatening air accompanies its progress: "It begins in a corridor . . . It continues . . . It comes to speak in the drugged voice / That ate its tongue." Catabolism, the breaking down of tissue material, in this case human tissue, into simpler and more stable substances, is evident in the adverse effects of pain and cold:

> There is a pain that gets up and moves, like the night attendant,
> Pointing to the cough
> That rises like dust and is dust
> A month later . . .
>
> **("County Ward")**

And towards the end of the poem, the effects of this process are treated more explicitly as inmates of the Ward approach a state of entropy or equilibrium in death:

> This cold slowly deepens
> The old whose bones ring with the coming weather,
>
> . . . . .
>
> The stunned face that could be your father's—
> Deepens the gray space between each word
> That reaches to say you are alone.

It is not only the old who are relentlessly ground down by hostile forces. In **"San Fernando Road,"** a young factory worker, whose energy is drained faster than he can renew it, becomes another casualty in a mechanized system when he ceased to dream of drugs and sex and thinks instead of "his body, / His weakening body, / And dawn only hours away."

This gradual erosion of energy is most consistently revealed on the intimate, individual level, where the very essence of the human condition is undergoing a pervasive disintegration. The wind often appears as the principal agent in this process, and dust as the concrete image of the state of equilibrium or entropy towards which the catabolic tendency aspires:

> The wind sprays pale dirt into my mouth
> The small, almost invisible scars
> On my hands.
>
> . . . . .
>
> The pores in my throat and elbows
> Have taken in a seed of dirt of their own.
>
> . . . . .
>
> A fine silt, washed by sweat,
> Has settled into the lines
> On my wrists and palms.
>
> . . . . .
>
> Already I am becoming the valley
> A soil that sprouts nothing
> For any of us.
>
> **("Field")**

The gradual encroachment of dirt into the mouth and pores of the field worker, while certainly suggestive of death, may also be viewed in terms of the entropy theory as the decomposition of a complex system into a simpler form. The molecular structure of the man's body appears to be breaking down, through loss of energy, into a form which is physically and symbolically closer to his own perception of himself when he says: "Already I am becoming the valley." Thus, a man who sees his existence as unproductive, assumes the metaphorically barren identity of the "soil that sprouts nothing," a physical state which reflects his inner disorientation and sense of futility. This movement towards entropy expresses the thematic structure of the poem; it gives dramatic form and substance to the narrator's barely articulated sense of worthlessness.

This action of the wind is a central catabolic image in Soto's poetic vision and embodies the essential indifference of the environment, one of Arnheim's "innumerable patterns of forces which constantly interfere with each other." Pitted against this cosmic force, Soto's narrator reveals a critical lack of energy, a physical lassitude which mirrors a pervasive spiritual weariness. His resistance has been whittled down to a minimum: he bows before the pressures of a harsh reality:

> The wind pressing us close to the ground
>
> **("Daybreak")**
>
> The wind crossed my face, moving the dust
> And a portion of my voice a step closer to a new year
>
> **("Harvest")**
>
> . . . . .
>
> Dirt lifted in the air
> Entering my nostrils
> And eyes
> The yellow under my fingernails
>
> **("Hoeing")**
>
> . . . . .
>
> The wind picks up the breath of my armpits
> Like dust
>
> **("Wind")**

Other elements provide catabolic images of grinding down, peeling or flaking away, collapsing, falling, decaying, unraveling, drowning, and graying in Soto's poems and contribute to the overall impression of a world that is winding down. The narrator at one point somberly anticipates the coming of rain in autumn, a time of unemployment, when his

> . . . two good slacks
> Will smother under a growth of lint
> And smell of old dust
> That rises

When the closet door opens and closes
("Rain")

This scene of gradual decay, of slow, seemingly inevitable disintegration of man and his environment is echoed repeatedly. The fog, another catabolic force which appears as "a mouth nibbling everything to its origins" **("Fog")**, contributes to the narrator's deterioration and eventual disappearance:

Graying my hair that falls
And goes unfound, my fingerprints
Slowly growing a fur of dust

. . . . .

One hundred years from now
There should be no reason to believe
I lived.
("Fog")

The enervating effects of this general increase in entropy are also evident in the environment of Soto's narrator. His is a world of "smashed bus window(s)" **("Field Poem")**, where "nothing will heal / Under the rain's broken fingers" **("Daybreak")**. Here the unpicked figs become "wrinkled and flattened / Like the elbows / of an old woman" **("Summer")**, while "the fog squatted in the vineyard / Like a stray dog" **("Piedra")**. It is a disintegrating world of "smashed bottles flaking back to sand" **("Piedra")**, where an abandoned hotel hides "A jacket forever without a shadow / And cold as the darkness it lies in" **("Street")**. People here "no longer / Bothered to shrug off / The flies" **("Town")**, and "A cane refused / The weight of the hand that carved it" **("The Level at Which the Sky Began")**.

The degree of physical and spiritual deterioration in the narrator's world may be judged by a comparison with the past where the energy level was noticeably higher. The vitality in the narrator's past is particularly evident in the figure of the grandmother. It is she who kept things moving in a constructive way; she "lit the stove . . . sliced papas / Pounded chiles . . . hosed down / The walk her sons paved," and later "Unearthed her / Secret cigar box / Of bright coins. . . . counted them . . . And buried them elsewhere" **("History")**. She is putting up a fight to survive, is aggressively protective of her family and will even shoplift food from the market to feed them. Eventually, she, too, will succumb to the catabolic effect:

. . . . her insides
. . . washed of tapeworm,
Her arms swelled into knobs
Of small growths—
Her second son
Dropped from a ladder
And was dust.
("History")

This sudden death of the father signals both an emotional crisis for the narrator and the growing intrusion of destructive forces into his life. The disintegration of home and family seem to date from this event:

. . . . the moment our father slipped
From the ladder . . .
. . . . It was the moment
I came down from the tree
And into our home
Where a leash of ants
Swarmed for the rice the cupboard the stove
Carrying off what there was to carry.
("The Evening of Ants")

Years later, the physical destruction of the family home is still associated with the father's death:

It's 16 years
Since our house
Was bulldozed and my father
Stunned into a coma . . .
("Braly Street")

and the loss of energy is apparent in the images of encroaching catabolic forces that have reduced the past to rubble:

. . . the long caravan
Of my uncle's footprints
Has been paved
With dirt. Where my father
Cemented a pond
There is a cavern of red ants
. . . When I come
To where our house was,
And a sewer line tied off
Like an umbilical cord.
("Braly Street")

Although there is undoubtedly a prevalence of such images of destruction in Soto's poetry, a subtle, anabolic or constructive force also makes itself felt as a necessary counterbalance to establish, according to Arnheim, the "structural theme, which introduces and maintains tension." "The antagonistic play of forces (which) is the structural theme" established what Arnheim calls a "definitive order" when it comes to a standstill; i.e., "achieves the maximum of entropy attainable for the given system of constraints." In philosophical terms, this suggests that Soto's world view is not necessarily nihilistic, as the preponderance of negative images might indicate, but rather represents an uneven balance between an oppressively hostile environment and a personal credo of survival in such a world.

Admittedly this faint optimistic note is difficult to detect in the cacophony of a world falling to pieces around our ears. It may be heard, however, above the noise of the wind peeling "mountains, grain by grain, / To small slopes, loose dirt," and stoking "The skulls and spines of cattle / To white dust, to nothing." Caught up in this inevitable cycle of dissolution, the narrator seeks to reestablish intellectual order for himself out of physical chaos:

The wind picks up the breath of my armpits
Like dust, swirls it
Miles away
And drops it
On the ear of a rabid dog
And I take on another life.
("Wind")

This same impulse to withstand the forces of destruction and establish an inner stronghold, a reservoir of strength and resistence, is apparent in the distinction between the unresisting creatures in the fields:

> The thick caterpillars
> That shriveled
> Into rings
> And went where the wind went

and the intellectual resistance of the narrator, who sees his sweat not as evidence of a physical drain on his energy but rather as a part of "the sea / That is still within me" (**"Hoeing"**). This concept of the "sea" as a source of primitive energy enables the narrator to withstand, at least intellectually and momentarily, the fate of the shriveled caterpillars.

The idea of taking on another life, of establishing an anabolic force in the face of destructive catabolism, recurs in various subtle, often ambiguous images. The dead body of the drowned friend in **"Avocado Lake"** "moves under the dark lake," its hands are like "those of a child reaching for his mother," its fingers need to be "rubbed and kissed" as if death were not an absolute, irreversible step towards physical dissolution but rather an alternative form of existence in which the drowned man can find a compatible environment:

> His phlegm drifts beneath the surface,
> As his life did.

Perhaps the most significant of these anabolic images, however, is one which is also connected to the death of the narrator's father and thus suggests a level of order that has withstood the disintegration associated with that event. Sixteen years after his father's death, the narrator returns to **"Braly Street"** to find the almond tree gone, the uncle's footprints "paved with dirt," the pond invaded by ants, the house bulldozed. But one thing has survived intact. The narrator comes back

> To the chinaberry
> Not pulled down
> And to its rings
> My father and uncle
> Would equal, if alive.
>
> (**"Braly Street"**)

This is the same tree the narrator "came down from" the moment his father died to witness the ant "carrying off what there was to carry" from the house (**"The Evening of Ants"**). This earlier scene foreshadows the actual destruction of sixteen years later. But something has been salvaged from the past. The chinaberry has resisted demolition and the wind has momentarily ceased its catabolic effect. Violence is held at bay and a metaphorical state of truce has been achieved. To the extent that the anabolic, constructive force survives in Soto's poetic vision in the form of the narrator's personal stronghold of intellectual resistence, symbolic perhaps of the creative energy of the poet himself, total chaos is averted and, in Arnheim's words, an uneasy "state of final equilibrium, of accomplished order and maximum entropy" is reached. (pp. 111-20)

Patricia de la Fuente, "Entropy in the Poetry of Gary Soto: The Dialectics of Violence," in Discurso Literario, *Vol. 5, No. 1, Autumn, 1987, pp. 111-20.*

Patricia de la Fuente (essay date Spring 1989)

[*In the essay below, de la Fuente discusses Soto's use of time and emphasis on death in* Black Hair.]

In *Feeling and Form,* a theory of art developed from her *Philosophy in a New Key,* Susanne Langer defines the role of the poet in terms of how well he "uses discourse to create an illusion, a pure appearance, which is a non-discursive symbolic form." Central to this theory is the distinction between the "actual" and the "virtual" experience:

> The appearances of events in our actual lives are fragmentary, transient and often indefinite, like most of our experiences—like the space we move in, the time we feel passing, the human and inhuman forces that challenge us. The poet's business is to create the appearance of 'experiences,' the semblance of events lived and felt, and to organize them so they constitute a purely and completely experienced reality, a piece of 'virtual life.'

('Virtual' in this sense is used to mean 'being in essence or effect but not in fact' = an illusion of reality.) This "illusion of life" she believes, "is the primary illusion of all poetic art." And without a doubt, any illusion of life cannot be plausible without taking into consideration the concept of *Time,* which, in one form or another, dominates and dictates the actual existence of all of us.

In the poetry of Gary Soto, whose poetic consciousness often appears to be, if not obsessed, at least profoundly concerned with the effect and passage of Time, it is interesting to note that as a 'virtual' experience in the life of the narrator, Time often exists on two levels or in two mutually exclusive dimensions. In Soto's latest collection, ***Black Hair,*** in particular, this duality of experience creates that dynamic tension within the poems which is directly responsible for their success as what Langer has called pieces of "virtual life." Soto's conflicting images of Time articulate, on the purely illusory level, those events in our actual lives which are, as Langer points out, "fragmentary, transient and . . . indefinite." In many of Soto's poems, these fragmentary, transient experiences which make up the virtual world of the narrator are presented in one dimension of Time against a background of, or in juxtaposition to a second set of experiences which occur in another dimension of Time. Thus the poetic illusion seems to hinge on the intersection of two separate, though often intimately interwoven, experiential levels. The one in the foreground creates the illusion of physical mutability in the swift passing of Time, in a fleeting awareness of mortality and in a focus on the present, sensual activity of living, especially in images of eating and drinking; the impression is of a life lived in double-time, with double intensity. In the background or as a counterbalance to so much energy and vitality, Soto often imposes an experience in slow-motion, or a scene that is completely static. This illusion of simultaneous experiences, one in double-time, one in slow-motion, lends a sense urgency to the poems which heightens the primary illusion of events lived and felt, which are usually those presented in the foreground.

This superimposure or juxtaposition of time-frames occurs as a technique in Soto's poems in different degrees of intensity. In **"Black Hair,"** for example, the controlling or "lived" time in the poem is the fast-paced present of the baseball game which is being played in the foreground by men like "Hector Moreno / Quick and hard with turned muscles," whose actions are dynamic and described with food imagery, "The gloves eating balls into double plays." As a spectator, the narrator is also dynamically present in the swiftly moving foreground action—

> Waving players in and stomping my feet,
> Growing sweaty in the presence of white shirts.
> I chewed sunflower seeds. I drank water
> And bit my arm through the late innings.

—and even participates vicariously in the game itself: "In my mind I rounded the bases / With him, my face flared, my hair lifting / Beautifully." In the middle stanza, however, the static past intrudes into the momentum of the present as the narrator hovers for an instant between the two worlds:

> My black torch of hair, about to go out?
> Father was dead, his face no longer
> Hanging over the table or our sleep,

For a moment, the game is interrupted, life itself seems to be suspended as the young narrator experiences, in an instant of static self-awareness, the mutability of his own flesh, symbolized here as the black hair of youth, that "torch" which Time will inevitably dim and eventually put out. Within the poetic illusion of this fragmentary event which takes place in the narrator's mind, the presence of his dead father—whose image from another time-frame might at first seem to be an arbitrary digression in the poem—is actually essential to the articulation of the central illusion of the poem, that of directly experienced mutability (life and death). The virtual, world of the narrator thus embraces both the rushing, live time of Hector Moreno, whose gloves are described as "eating" and hence as associated with living, and the static, dead time of the father, whose passive "hanging over the table" is non-participatory in the act of living.

This technique of presenting one time-frame within another is characteristic of many of the poems in Soto's ***Black Hair*** collection and serves to create the illusion of philosophical or psychological depth to the virtual experiences detailed in the poems. For example, the virtual experiences of these poems often contain flashes of poetic reflections which Langer claims "are not essentially trains of logical reasoning . . . [but rather] create the 'semblance' of reasoning; of the seriousness, strain and progress, the sense of growing knowledge, growing clearness, conviction and acceptance—the whole experience of philosophical thinking." One such poem is **"In August"** which merges, more subtly than in **"Black Hair,"** the two levels of fast and slow time. On one level, in the vital, eating-time of the living, the narrator climbs a plum tree to pick "its dark fruit, notched and open / Where birds ate," and later joins in a ritual of eating at:

> Coleman Pickle
> Where brother, friends, tiny sister
> Were standing in barrels,
> Pickles in their hands

On another level and in another time-frame, coexisting with the first but yet removed from the realm of the activities of living and eating, lies another world, suggested in the image of the blimp, whose different nature is recognized by the narrator who, from inside the barrel, pickle in hand,

> —came up to see the blimp
> Pass quietly as a cloud,
> Its shadow dark enough to sleep
> Or dream in

In its quietness, its dark shadows, its association with sleep and dreams, the blimp becomes the embodiment of that other, static time-frame, symbolic of the ephemeral nature of the narrator's world and everything in it, here one moment

> And then gone,
> Like all I would ever know.
> Like father with hands in my hair.
> Like uncle on the porch with his arms
> And little else.

Once again, the narrator's intuitions of his own mortality hinges on his fragmentary recollection of his dead father and uncle, both "gone, / Like all [he] would ever know," both removed from the sphere of active time, of eating plums and pickles, and imprisoned in the momentary, static vision of the blimp—now "above us / And then gone." As these two time-frames intersect briefly, the narrator experiences the fleeting moment of insight:

> We watched
> It, with food in our mouths,
> All wondering, until it was above us
> And then gone,
> Like all we would ever know.

He stands with the other children, momentarily suspended in the act of living, "with food in [their] mouths," and participates briefly but vividly, through his "wondering," in that other time-frame into which his father and uncle have already passed, and into which "all [he] will ever know," and by extension all he will ever be, is in the process of passing—even in that very instant of life-sustaining, eating activity. In essence, Soto has captured, in this fleeting image of mortality, the illusion of a mutability deeply lived and felt by the narrator.

In other poems Soto uses complex variations of this same technique of intersecting time-frame to heighten the illusion of life. **"The Plum's Heart"** contains several layers of action, each in its own time-frame. First there is the obvious present time in which the narrator recounts the event of picking plums with his father; "I've climbed in trees / To eat, and climbed / Down." Then there is the implied time in which this event occurred, a living-time of eating and action for both the narrator and his father. Within this fragmentary illusion of life lived in fast-time by the narrator in his plum-picking and plum-eating past there are two quite distinct intrusions of static time. One such shift in time projects forward to glimpse the familiar brief insight into the narrator's own mortality through identification with the dead father. After recalling the vitality of the past experience through food imagery:

My hands
Opened like mouths,
The juice running
Without course down
My arms, as I stabbed

For plums . . . the narrator moves forward in time to a stark glimpse of the process of mutability, not only in his father and figuratively in the fruit, but also in himself as part of the same process of change:

I called to father
To catch—father
Who would disappear
Like fruit at the end
Of summer, from a neck
Wound some say—blood
Running like the juice
Of these arms.

The plum juice running "down" the narrator's arms in one time-frame is metaphorically fused with the father's blood running, in a shift to a static time-frame in the future "at the end of summer." This brief glimpse into the immediate future provides the narrator with the insight into his own mortality, vividly implied in the poem by a smooth shift back to the plum-picking time-frame in which the narrator identifies with the doomed-but-not-yet-dead father in the image of his blood "Running like the juice / Of these arms." This last image of blood/juice is especially successful in conveying the illusion of a deeply felt event because the ambiguity of the preposition in "Of these arms" includes both the possibility of the plum juice and the father's blood which is, biologically, also that of the narrator.

The second shift in time occurs in the first few lines of the poem in which the narrator, his mouth coloured by the fruit juice, sees himself, "mouth red / From plums that were / Once clouds in March / —rain I mean," as a connecting link in the vast process of mutability in nature. This illusion of the narrator's experience of his own mortality is heightened as he re-cognizes, from the vantage point of the future, that his father

his mouth
Already red and grinning
Like the dead on their
Rack of blackness

—was already doomed, even in the same act of eating, to take his place in that inescapable sequence of universal change just as the plums, evolving from the March rains, must disappear "at the end / Of summer."

The interplay of time-frames in this complex illusion of life might be diagrammed as follows:

1. Extended past:
clouds-rain
= plums
= red juice

2. Active-past:
father-son
plum = picking
juice-running

3. Static-past:
End-of-summer
father dead
blood-running

4. Static-present:
narrator recalls
past-times

but in doing so, we destroy the "semblance of events lived and felt . . . [that] piece of virtual life" which Langer defines as the creation of the poet. Just as music "spreads out time for our direct and complete apprehension, by letting our hearing monopolize it—organize, fill, and shape it," so a poem spreads out time for our imaginative perception. To create the illusion of a lived and felt mutability, the poet must create the illusion of change which is, Langer maintains, "not itself something represented; it is implicitly given through the contrast of different 'states,' themselves unchanging." Soto's use of contrasting states of action and meditation, of fast-time and slow-time effectively sustains the illusions of change in poems like **"Landscape in Spring,"** in which the speeding pickup, where

my brother and me
And some fat guy, are drinking from paper bags,
Our necks blackened, our hair loose in wind.

is shown against a static background of "A woman in the yard with a hose, pointed / At a tree," and a house that "is going to stay / Where it is," while the narrator and his friends go "speeding / Through the days." Ironically, the existence of these speeding characters, so apparently full of vitality and freedom, implied in the image of "drinking," and "hair loose in wind," is merely another dimension of the static time-frame of the woman in the yard. Like the "hose pointed / At a tree," they will, "if . . . pointed / To a field, cotton or beet, . . . cut it / With a hoe." These two dimensions of time or "states" of existence, at first so different, converge towards the end of the poem into similar time-frames of slow-motion and boredom: "It's all the same if you're brown / And given hours to think about the sun."

In another poem called **"The Day After,"** the converging and contrasting of the two time-frames is more dramatically realized since it entails the intersecting of two normally mutually exclusive worlds:

My brother says you came back
And were at the foot of his bed,
Green and telling him it was OK,
The darkness, the place where
You sit, waiting for this country
To turn with flames.

The narrator immediately identifies with the static existence of the dead friend:

I'm waiting
Too, . . .

I'm waiting for this day, and for you
Frank, to show yourself, green
Or any other way—to tell me
It's OK

Implicit in the narrator's recognition and acceptance of the static time-frame of the waiting, presumably dead, Frank, is a rejection of the apocalyptic nature of his own living-time, that time of impending holocaust, "The bloom of smoke and the bones / Lit under running flesh." By experiencing this semblance of world destruction in his mind through the horror imagery of radioactive bones and melting flesh, the narrator vividly lives and feels a projected future time of death and chaos, while simultaneously existing, on a psychological level, in the dark place of the dead friend where things are "OK." In other words, Soto has taken fragmentary events from actual life and conflated them into a single, intense moment of virtual life. This poem is a particularly successful example of what Langer has called the "Illusion of life":

> What makes [the latter] quite different from any actual segment of life is that the events in it are simplified, and at the same time much more fully perceived and evaluated than the jumble of happenings in any person's actual history . . . The virtual experience created out of those very adroitly jumbled impressions is a full and clear vision of social tyrannies, with all of the undertones of personal dread, reluctance, half-delusion, and emotional background to hold the assorted items together in a single illusion of life.

In terms of Langer's theory of art, therefore, Soto's often complex articulation of Time in its many psychological and physical dimensions can be seen as a creative technique for achieving that essential and primary illusion of all poetic art: the illusion of life. (pp. 100-07)

Patricia de la Fuente, "Mutability and Stasis: Images of Time in Gary Soto's 'Black Hair'," in The Americas Review, *Vol. XVII, No. 1, Spring, 1989, pp. 100-07.*

Gerald Haslam (review date May 1989)

[*Haslam is an American novelist, critic, editor, and educator. In the following review, he offers a favorable assessment of* Lesser Evils.]

Gary Soto remains one of the brightest talents of his generation. His ability to produce probing-yet-lyric poems is unquestioned, and his sketches are adding a dimension to his reputation. Most important, perhaps, Soto is a Chicano author who is true to his heritage, but whose literary reputation transcends that fact. He is in no way dependent upon over-compensatory critics, for his voice is universal.

Soto's latest prose collection, ***Lesser Evils,*** for instance, begins with a sketch entitled **"Between Points."** It talks about the realization that we are suspended between birth and death as we trudge this earth: "I'm between these two points, the first days and the last days, and I'm wondering what I should do about this." What indeed. He simply and directly reveals our existential condition, no matter what our ethnicity.

"Today I don't feel good about being where I am, aged thirty-four, and a bright childhood gone and the mad-gray years ahead of me." This writer takes nothing for granted, and he can grasp unlikely material and sail it to unlikely, sometimes startling insights.

Soto's work is also, one imagines, threatening to some, for his life has opened upon possibilities unknown to most of his family and friends in Fresno, his hometown. "As a kid I imagined a dark fate," he writes. "To marry Mexican poor, work Mexican hours, and in the end die a Mexican death."

The upward mobility that Soto exemplifies is limned by his mother in **"Piedra":** "*Mexicanos* pruning orange trees on ladders, and our mother's talk that if our grades didn't improve we would be like *those* people." In the same sketch, a young Soto climbs a hill, far above his picnicking family, the river, the world, and "Except for the wind it was quiet, and I was quiet too, with just one thought, and this thought was happiness. . . . I will have my chance."

These brief pieces are autobiographical and understated, though several feel unpolished. In **"A Short History of Sex,"** readers experience the frustration and curiosity of a virginal boy who overhears others say, " 'It feels like the inside of your mouth.' What feels like that?" Unfortunately, his hot curiosity is not well developed and the interesting essay just sort of drifts, demanding another revision, as do several others.

But that is small potatoes, since ***Lesser Evils*** is another confirmation of Gary Soto's special vision and flashing talent, and is well worth reading. (pp. 92-3)

Gerald Haslam, in a review of "Lesser Evils: Ten Quartets," in Western American Literature, *Vol. XXIV, No. 1, May, 1989, pp. 92-3.*

Alastair Reid on Soto's poetry:

Gary Soto is a Chicano who now works in English, and the consequences are twofold. First, it has given him a dual identity . . . ; second, he has brought the rhythms and wave lengths of Spanish with him into English. Miracles are expected to happen in his world, and his language is ready for them. His [*The Tale of Sunlight*] is not a collection of separate poems, but a carefully modulated whole. At one stroke he contains and articulates a linguistic duality, in a language as clear and unencumbered as running water. We should be glad to have him.

Alastair Reid, in his "The Lenore Marshall Poetry Prize," in Saturday Review, *27 October 1979.*

Julian Olivares (essay date January-June 1990)

[*An American critic, educator, and Hispanist, Olivares is the author of* The Chicano Struggle *(1984). In the following essay, he provides a thematic and stylistic examination of Soto's poetry.*]

In the poem **"Chuy"** from Gary Soto's ***Where Sparrows***

Work Hard, the speaker describes his protagonist in a cafe:

> Chuy noted
> On a napkin
> *—a street is only so long—*
> And stared outside
> Where already the day
> Had a dog drop
> Limp as a dishtowel
> And the old staggering
> On a crutch
> Of fierce heat.
> "There is meaning
> In that bus, those kids,"
> He thought,
> And turned the dime
> In his coat pocket.

Here Chuy attempts to conceive the street solely as geographic space, a conception which he affirms by writing it down. Yet this belief is false, as apt to dissolve as the tissue he writes it on. Although he may add to the dime he has and take a bus away from the spatial barrier of his street, it will remain as a psychic barrier wherein hostile cosmic and social forces confine him to an oppressive existence.

Gary Soto is the most recognized Chicano poet in the American literary mainstream. The fact that he writes exclusively in English and has published his four books of poetry in the Pitt Poetry Series has given him access to the American literary public like no other Chicano writer who relies on Chicano publishing media. Marketed for the middle-class audience which purchases his books in bookstores that do not generally include Chicano writers among their stock, Soto's poetry conveys a tone not usually found in Chicano writers who write specifically for a Chicano audience. A third-generation Mexican American, Soto is an English-dominant speaker and writer; consequently his use of English is not a matter of choice. However, if this may make his poetry at times linguistically complicitous with the object criticized, it also allows his poetry to speak "to a *you* who is part of the middle class he is attacking" [Juan Bruce-Novoa, in his 1982 *Chicano Poetry: A Response to Chaos*]. Furthermore, through markers and icons that refer to his own cultural context, Soto is not only able to express himself both as an individual and member of an ethnic group, but to simultaneously redirect the Anglo American reader so as to see, for example, an existential theme in the context of a Chicano point-of-view. A case in point is the poem **"Chuy."**

The Anglo American reader, already familiar with the themes of existential bleakness and alienation, probably experiences a defamiliarization provoked by the poem's title, **"Chuy,"** which he/she may not even be able to pronounce (CHEW-y). The Spanish name, a cultural marker, redirects this reader's attention, causing him/her to now contextualize familiar themes from the unfamiliar perspective of the Chicano. That is, in addition to the expression of modern urban themes, the protagonist's name functions as an ethnic substratum that orients the reader to encompass the position of the culturally marginated. The text, therefore, gains a different resonation than would be the case if the protagonist were named "Jimmy." In this manner, then, these universal themes are redirected and intensified by the particular, Chicano point-of-view.

For the Chicano reader, on the other hand, the protagonist's name serves as the orienting device. "Chuy," the nickname for "Jesús," is frequently used by Chicano writers as a Chicano "Everyman," frequently as symbolic of the oppressed, marginated, rebellious, poverty-stricken Chicano youth. This type of orienting device is necessary because the Chicano reader in many of Soto's poems encounters unfamiliar poetic terrain. Soto's existential despair, his cadences, frequently terse and elliptical imagery, and models stem largely from Anglo American schools, which make his poetry "strange" to various Chicano readers (and frequently disconcerting to non-Chicano readers, especially Marxist-oriented Europeans, who expect the expression of a more "ethnic" content). Soto's orienting device for the Chicano reader allows him/her to note Soto's personal vision and also to see the particular situation of the Chicano experience in the context of "universal" and "mainstream" modes of expression. Perhaps more than any other American writer, then, Gary Soto's poetry manifests the problematic of polyculturalism. For the Anglo American reader, the "strangeness" in Soto's poetry may be caused by its contextual markers, often brief but always pervasive; for the Chicano or Latino reader, the "strangeness," is often provoked by the poetry's style and form.

With regard to his personal vision, Soto often selects from his view of the streets negative signs. In the poem **"Street"** of ***The Elements of San Joaquin,*** the speaker declares: "What I want to remember is a street, / A wide street." The speaker does not explain why he wants to remember this street; he only affirms his volition to recall a certain wide street. Of the numerous associations conveyed by this manifold sign, such as the hustle and bustle of people, glittering neon signs, outdoor restaurants, glamorous shops—all connoting the positive semes of dynamic and joyful activities, Soto, in most instances, selects negative associations. And so the poem continues:

> And that it is cold:
> A small fire in the gutter, cats running
> (. . .) A short woman
> With a short cane, tapping
> Her way
> Past the tracks.
> Farther away
> An abandoned hotel

Gutters, sewers, cans and broken bottles, stray cats, the poor and feeble, the vagrants and criminals, the world of the outsider, industrial blight are the elements that Soto often selects from his streets.

Another indication of Soto's personal vision is noted in the poem **"Piedra"** (**"Stone,"** ***Elements***), in which surrealistic imagery conveys a matrix of desolation where two types of elements threaten life, the elements of nature and the elemental violence of mankind:

> When the day shut like a suitcase
> And left for the horizon
>
> When the fog squatted in the vineyard

Like a stray dog

We fished there   Later we
looked for soapstone   but found

A piece of the night rising from within us
And spreading among the cottonwoods

The dark water wrinkling
Like the mouth of an old woman whispering
  Lord

I pointed out carlights fanning past the orchard
Where the road narrows

Toward the collapsed bridge   My woman
Showed me a card of bark

The smashed bottles flaking back to sand
And farther away   near the road

Someone walking toward us—
My hand closed in my pocket

Gary Soto's poetry expresses an apocalyptic vision of the universe. As Patricia de la Fuente notes [in her "Ambiguity in the Poetry of Gary Soto," *Revista-Chicano-Riqueña* 11, No. 2 (Summer 1983)], "Recurring images of loss, disintegration, decadence, demolition, solitude, terror and death create a desolate landscape in which the voice of the narrator is that of a passive, impotent observer, helplessly caught up in the inexorable destruction of human ties." In this desolate landscape, de la Fuente perceives that "although the Christian backdrop is not conspicuously negated in Soto's poetry, it does not occupy a prominent place in his philosophical vision. Therefore, when the poet speaks of death, he usually does so in worldly, physical terms related to individual existences that have been truncated or worn down by indifferent forces."

The desolation and violence that Soto encounters in his streets also reflect his expression as a member of a group. Within the elements of chaos that Soto selects, there are ethnic markers which point to the Chicano experience where poverty, violence, desolation and disorientation are facts of *barrio* existence. Thus, while we are presented with an apparent realism in Soto's depictions of street life, what we encounter is a selection from a wide range of reality which underscores a personal subjectivity and social concern both molded by an apocalyptic vision.

In three of Soto's books—***The Elements of San Joaquin*** (1976), ***The Tale of Sunlight*** (1978), ***Where Sparrows Work Hard*** (1981)—the street appears as a major motif in much of his poetry and forms the title of three poems, one in each book. Although a street or road implies movement, literally through time and space, and allegorically as life's journey, in Soto's poetry the image of the street is also used as a structural component and unifying principle of his poetic vision. The street provides the realistic background for the speaker, his personae and the Chicano minority. Metaphorically, it represents their state of mind; and, allegorically, it depicts a human condition subjected by socio-economic and cosmic forces to an oppressive existence. Here, then, are Gary Soto's "mean streets."

The Elements of San Joaquin is framed at the beginning by **"San Fernando Road,"** near Los Angeles, and at the conclusion by **"Braly Street,"** in South Fresno. With **"San Fernando Road,"** we find the space of industry—"On this road of factories / Gray as the clouds"—and not of travel or escape. This is the **"Mission Tire Factory" (*Sparrows*)**, where Soto worked. In **"San Fernando Road"** it is the poet's alter ego, Leonard, who "was among men / Whose arms / Were bracelets / Of burns." Here Leonard "handled grinders, / Swept the dust / Of rubber / (. . .) / Scrubbed the circles / From toilets / No one flushed," and with

Young Mexicans
Went into ovens
Squint-eyed
And pulled out the pipes
Smeared black

The young Mexicans go into the ovens; realistically, this is what they do. But this laconic statement conjures up two levels of imagery. In the first, the ovens are a metaphor for a state of Hell, from which there is no escape for the blackened workers. Space here is an infernal one to which the young Mexicans are damned to suffer their socio-economic plight. They are dehumanized and reduced to the category of machines: "Shivering / Like the machinery / That went on and on." On the second level, the poem presents allegorical imagery of genocide by which the Mexicans are removed from the mainstream of societal space.

The poem's significance stands in ironic relation to its title, **"San Fernando Road."** Instead of a road to socio-economic salvation, a group of people are damned to the lowest level of society. Although they are enslaved by the "bracelets / Of burns" and trapped in "circles" of drudgery, the workers can withstand physical pain; but it is the mental pain that agonizes them: "whose families / Were a pain / They could not shake off." San Fernando, the saint and representative of religion, is of no real consolation to their strife. This road is an allegory of the workers' *via crucis* on which they are burdened by familial responsibilities and are concerned solely with survival. The street, then, does not lead to social and economic well-being, but is a sign of violence—industrial, social and, as indicated by other poems, criminal violence.

As Bruce-Novoa has demonstrated, ***The Elements of San Joaquin*** traces a journey to the poet's origin on **"Braly Street"**; it is a personal allegory of a painful peregrination that takes him through the San Joaquin Valley. Here the elements of city streets are supplanted by the elements of nature. [In Wolfgang Binder's *Partial Autobiographies, Interviews with Twenty Chicano Poets* (1985)] Soto has commented on his awareness of the forces of nature upon his return to the Valley from the Ethnic Writers Workshop in Wisconsin: "When I came back from Wisconsin, I paid very much attention to forces like the wind. I was shocked—it was the power of nature which grabbed me by the throat and said, 'Wake up, sucker!' I became very conscious of these things. They later became symbols, but they also became part of my life." Thus, in the poem **"Wind,"** we note the disintegration of the skeletal remains of cattle, wiping out all traces of their existence—and by extension those of man's: "The wind strokes / The skulls and spines of cattle / To white dust, to nothing." And in the poem **"Fog,"** in an absurd enumeration, a heavy mist consumes and envelops organic and inorganic life, becoming a metaphor for a dark vision of nothingness:

> Not all the sweaters
> Hung in closets in summer
>
> Could soak up this mist. The fog:
> A mouth nibbling everything to its origin,
> Pomegranate trees, stolen bicycles,
>
> The string of lights at a used-car lot
> A Pontiac with scorched valves (. . .)
>
> One hundred years from now
> There should be no reason to believe
> I lived.

The elements of societal oppression, however, still prevail here. This agricultural San Joaquin Valley, the United States' cornucopia, is no paradise for the Chicano field worker. The poems of this section constitute an anti-pastoral, in which the laborers are broken physically and spiritually by agribusiness. The poem **"Field,"** for example, brings together two elements of destruction. It begins with an awareness of the destructive forces of nature and concludes with the realization of the exploitation and oppression waged against Chicanos:

> The wind sprays pale dirt into my mouth
> The small, almost invisible scars
> On my hands (. . .)
>
> Already I am becoming the valley,
> A soil that sprouts nothing
> For any of us.

"Field Poem" crystallizes an image that is a metaphor of the book's fragmented vision:

> We returned to the bus
> Speaking
> In broken English, broken Spanish (. . .)
> From the smashed bus window,
> I saw the leaves of cotton plants
> Like small hands
> Waving good-bye.

There is no other Chicano poet who can achieve as condensed an expression as Soto can in depicting Mexican American life. Frequently, the references and allusions to this life are so elliptical and of such subtlety that they may not be discerned by the non-Hispanic reader. The above field workers may appear to be linguistically deficient, due to a lack of education, but their broken English and Spanish essentially refer to a bicultural experience in which the Mexican American is marginalized from American society, yet is not really Mexican, either. In whatever language they speak, they are "broken" by the working conditions imposed by the institutions of the majority society. The bucolic innocence of the valley's agricultural products is subverted by the institution, the "bus," against which the Chicano workers can only make a token reprisal by smashing its window. Through this dark vision the poet at once speaks for himself and his group,.

The personal, fragmented vision extends to images that the speaker encounters on the streets to home, which derive from the poet's preoccupation with death and corruption. In **"Sadako"** the speaker notes "Chickens gutted and noosed on poles / In the unlit butcher shops," and in **"Town"** he states: "The town smelled of tripe / pulled from an ox / and hanging." These images remind us of Pablo Neruda's "Walking Around": "Hay pájaros de azufre y horribles intestinos / colgando de las puertas de las casas que odio" ["There trussed to the doors of the houses I loath / are the sulphurous birds, in a horror of tripes"]. This impression is confirmed in an interview where Soto states that, of the poets he was reading while writing the ***Elements,*** his favorite was Neruda [Ernesto Trejo, "Interview of Gary Soto," *Revista Chicano-Riqueña* 11, No. 2 (Summer 1982)].

In the third section of ***Elements,*** the poet returns to **"Braly Street,"** an archaeological site of lost artifacts, lives and memories retained in the strata of asphalt, earth and time:

> Bottle caps and glass
> Of the '40s and '50s
> Hold their breath
> Under the black earth
> Of asphalt and are silent
> Like the dead whose mouths
> Have eaten dirt and bermuda.

This is the street of his childhood where tragedy struck; his father killed in an industrial accident and his uncle killed by cancer. The other cancer, the industrial blight, bulldozed his home, so that:

> Braly Street is now
> Tin ventilators
> On the warehouses, turning
> Our sweat
> Towards the yellowing sky;
> Acetylene welders
> Beading manifolds,
> Stinging the half-globes
> Of retinas. When I come
> To where our house was,
> I come to weeds
> And a sewer line tied off
> Like an umbilical cord;
> To the chinaberry
> Not pulled down
> And to its rings
> My father and uncle
> Would equal, if alive.

As in the image of "the circles / From toilets / No one flushed," of **"San Fernando Road,"** with this image of "a sewer line tied off / Like an umbilical cord," Soto equates life as birth into a world of waste, a circle of despair. These are images with which the poet retrieves the past and which reveal the causes of his experience of discontinuity. Unlike the chinaberry, the tree of poverty, still there, the poet has been uprooted by personal and social tragedies which are at the source of his apocalyptic vision. Nevertheless, this vital discontinuity—as we shall note later—is challenged by the continuity the poet finds in the space of literature. ***The Elements of San Joaquin,*** then, is a book enclosed by two streets, both wielding industrial violence and images of fire. The first poem expresses the oppression of a minority; the final poem expresses a highly personal vision of loss and desolation. The book ends at the source of both an individualistic and communal point of view. There is a reckoning up of one's youth and environment: desolation, oppression, crime, death, cosmic forces—all of these are the "elements" that shape a life and an outlook which becomes exorcized but not erased in its recounting.

In his books, Soto relates two aspects of Chicano life: the urban and the rural. As we have noted in ***Elements,*** the poems of the rural space—the San Joaquin Valley—are inserted between the poems of the two urban places, Los Angeles and Fresno. This is the formal arrangement of the poetry, yet this ordering corresponds to a fact of Chicano life. Juxtaposed to the rural labor fields, only a short bus trip away, the Chicano labors in factory infernos. Most of Soto's poetry deals with each of these activities separately, but there are poems in which the urban and rural environments are brought together. This juxtaposition and unification is accomplished through Soto's reconstruction of a street in South Fresno. The Chicano inhabits the outskirts of the town where the houses face the city and the factories, while their back doors open to animals and vegetable patches.

Soto has said [in his interview with Trejo] that his favorite poem from ***The Tale of Sunlight*** is **"The Street":**

> To me, the writing is there, it's complex without being stupidly obscure, and the tone is haunting. But what I really enjoy about the poem is that I settled some things that were bothering me, and it had to do with remembering people from my past—childhood. What I mean is this: I grew up on a street that was slowly being torn down. I lived in a part of industrial Fresno. If I looked out my bedroom window, I saw a junkyard. If I looked across the street from the porch, I saw a printing shop. Down the streets were factories . . . Houses were being torn down, for reasons I never understood, and with each house, they were tearing down my past. Tearing it down so in a way I wouldn't know who I was . . . And, houses aside, people were dying around me. Like my uncle. He had cancer. He was on the couch, day after day, until he was gone . . . . [My] father died very young, a neck injury while at work. And here I am, a kid, thinking, "What is going on?" And then there were people leaving, moving to better parts of town, like my grandparents. Neighbors were leaving, too. Other family members, like aunts and uncles, were marrying or getting the hell out.

"The Street" has an epigraph taken from Elio Vittornini's *Twilight of the Elephant,* "Then we would hardly eat except to be seen," which, as Soto clarifies in the same interview, describes his life as a child. The poem deploys two points of view. One is unvoiced, that of the child Molina, the poet's alter ego, who digs in the ground, oblivious to his squalid surroundings; the second is that of the child turned speaker and adult, and who sees the street, its Chicano residents and the past through the perspective of his experience, selectivity and subjectivity of imagery. All this is presented through shifting impressions, through a montage of images which are often surrealistic and absurd, but whose ungrammaticalities are resolved on the levels of death, loneliness, poverty and violence.

The poem begins with a widow who appears among her vegetables and whose realistic description is abruptly altered by an incongruous image: "Among onions and tomatoes poled waist-high, / Chiles and the broken fingers of peas / That point down." The ungrammaticality of "broken fingers of peas" is the sign of fragmentation that will characterize the poem. Boredom and futility become concrete when the widow hangs the town wash on the line:

> Waving off the chickens,
> She pins the grayness to the line, and beyond
> This line, in the same boredom
> That drips from the wash

These ideas of monotony, boredom and futility—expressed through the fabric of the town's wash—are now revealed in the faces of the old, who, awaiting death, "suck their tongues / And stare at each other's shoes."

As the child plays at digging and the sun begins to set, Julio, the retired butcher,

> Sits under the full skirt of a willow,
> Talking to the photo
> Of his first wife,
> Her face greased with a thumbprint
> And caught in a lean year.

Then the scene shifts on the street to Goyo's house: "Goyo at the window, and no uncle / Arrives on the porch." Here we have an ungrammaticality caused by an incongruity between an action—"Goyo at the window"—and a state of being, "and no uncle." We would expect, for example, "Goyo at the window, and no shirt on." However, the element of absence is not an article of clothing but a relative; and another one is missing two lines later: "No aunt comes, / Heavy-breasted, to bend over the sink / and gut a chicken."

In the poem's first section, the primary element is the absence caused by the death of a relative. On this street, there is a widow, a widower, the elderly who will soon die and be missed by their relatives, Goyo without an uncle or aunt, and in their midst a child. Absence, emphasized by the disappearance of the sun, is the cause of loneliness. Extratextually, this points to the poet, traumatized by the death of his father and uncle.

At night, on the rural fringe of the city, people of various occupations meet and share a silent space at the edge of a ditch. They smoke and watch the water flow beyond them, each person isolated in his own thoughts: "Barber or fieldhand, / Whore's brother, pickpocket's son / They come, shoeless, to the ditch."

Daybreak reveals additional elements in the street and in the poem: frustration, oppression and violence. Fleeing from his street but not from his condition, Cruz seeks alcohol and violence:

> When the morning is a tablet
> Of cold spit he cannot swallow,
>
> Cruz leaves
> For the Westside,

The neoned juke box and the warm beer
Sending up its last bubble,
For the cue stick
Swung hard against an ear, the mouth blooming.

When Cruz returns to his street and house, he stands on the porch, peering in, as if this were not his house, as if he did not want to enter: "He looks in as though this were not his / House and squints."

Somewhere, in another section of town and on a different street, there is a white woman who cannot understand the inhabitants of Soto's street. She cannot guess why somebody's uncle would steal and inflict violence:

The white woman over an electric range
Will not know the pain
That stiffens
Like a star in a second of full darkness.

Nor what makes him push
His gloved fist
In the windows that eat their echoes—
She can't even guess.

The final section of the poem declares the source of the street's troubles:

The poor are unshuffled cards of leaves
Reordered by the wind, turned on a wish
To reveal their true suits.
They never win.

Despite the outbursts of violence, which is repetitive, nothing happens on this street; there is no change. The stasis of the condition is emphasized by the poem's representational technique. This street, like all of Soto's streets, provides a gallery of images—as if visible to a stroller from the street; here, a widow, a widowed butcher, a child digging; there, the petrified elderly, Goyo and Cruz, etc., but their depiction underlines a static condition. Nothing happens but loneliness and death, the monotony of poverty and oppression. Here, on this street, the Chicano occupies the space at the juncture of the rural and urban, where each hardly provides the means to overcome his impoverished and pessimistic existence.

Returning to Soto's statement on this poem [in his interview with Trejo] he says: " **'The Street'** names these people, calls them up from the past. It was a very satisfying poem to write." What we can take this statement to mean is that the poem was satisfying because, as Soto said, it "settled some things that were bothering me"; and, although the poem's substance deals with death, poverty, oppression and disintegration, the past has been retrieved through images, and the chaos of the experience—in the particular context of a Chicano neighborhood—has been offset by the esthetic order that the poem imposes on the recounting of that experience. The discontinuity experienced in life, and which is at the heart of the poem, is transcended by the creation of the poem and by the continuity realized in the literary space.

"The Street" from ***Where Sparrows Work Hard*** deals with the speaker's own house and family, where the scenes shift among each of its members, each framed by imagery and references to dead animals:

Not far
From the cat dropped
by a .22, among
The slouched weeds
Of South Fresno,
Or the old janitor
Pasting bottle caps
Into a scrapbook,
Prieta is a five-year old
At the kitchen table
Coloring a portrait
Of God, in the blank face
Of a frying pan.

Religious relics are replaced by the relics of bottle caps whose only meaning is to fill the space of tedium. Prieta's crayon drawing absurdly juxtaposes God and a frying pan, thereby inverting the biblical passage of Jesus distributing loaves of bread among the poor. The words of God are no longer decipherable:

Where his hands
Reach out, offering
A flower hooded
in the approximate light,
There is scribbling
She tries to undo
With an eraser
And a string of spit.
It never looks right.

The poem builds up on a matrix of death, tedium and absence: an absent God, the empty frying pan of the poor. As in **"Chuy,"** the name of "Prieta" [Dark Girl] serves to contextualize the themes of existential purposelessness and poverty within the Chicano experience. By means of this frame of reference, Soto is able to express both his personal and social vision.

The poem proceeds to depict the poet's Uncle, home on leave from the military (and whose absence will come with cancer), killing time by doing push-ups. He spits at the cat, which, in the chain of violence and death, sniffs for the rat, both of which scavenge food and the remains of dead chickens. The grandmother is next depicted picking the fruit trees, but she is lassoed by the speaker's kid brother with a rope linked to death:

She is Indian,
My brother believes,
And lassoes her
To a fence
With the rope
That pulled a cow
To its death

The brother plays at cowboys, a game by which, ironically, the *mestizo* child innocently internalizes the Whites' hatred of Indians, a racial attitude implicit in the game of Cowboys and Indians. Under the guise of play, death and violence underlie the domestic scenes:

Poverty is a pair
Of boots, rain,
Twin holsters slapping
His side, and a hand
Cocked into a pistol.

The speaker then views himself as a child, himself innocently participating in a chain of violence:

I'm the child
In a chinaberry
Flicking matches
Into a jar of flies, wingless (. . .)
I shake them,
And they are a raffle
For the ants,
A small cargo
For the wind
To haul into the smeared
Ash of evening.

There appears to be no escape from poverty and a condition threatened by cosmic forces. The poem concludes with a sense of inertia, as even cars stall:

A car rattles
From the drive
And stalls in
A great sigh of steam.
I see this and note
That when someone calls
No one has to go.

One other poem from this collection and worthy of note with regard to our theme is **"Mexicans Begin Jogging."** The Border Patrol raids the Mission Tire Factory in search of illegal aliens; and Soto, who is American but Chicano and brown, has to run with the Mexicans:

. . . the border patrol opened
Their vans and my boss waved for us to run.
"Over the fence, Soto," he shouted,
And I shouted that I was American.
"No time for lies," he said, and pressed
A dollar in my palm, hurrying me
Through the back door.

So the fleeing aliens engage in an American middle-class activity: jogging. And as they jog from the industrial area through the neighborhoods of comfortable houses, Soto is aware of the paradox of his situation, both comic and pathetic:

Since I was on his time, I ran
And became the wag to a short tail of
Mexicans—
Ran past the amazed crowds that lined
The street and blurred like photographs, in rain.
I ran from that industrial road to the soft
Houses where people paled at the turn of an
autumn sky.
What could I do but yell *vivas*
To baseball, milkshakes, and those sociologists
Who would clock me
As I jog into the next century
On the power of a great, silly grin.

Here Soto and the Mexicans engage in a *race* from the Border Patrol, and in doing so transgress the border of comfortable White America whose inhabitants grow even paler at the sight of the brown *race* on their streets. Soto, in comic desperation, tries to convince them that he, too, is American by saluting America: "What could I do but yell *vivas* / To baseball, milkshakes." Nevertheless, he is an outsider on White America's streets, only of statistical concern to sociologists who will measure into the next century his degree of assimilation into the majority society. In this poem, in which the street now becomes a metaphor of the speaker's search for a place in American society, we note another problematic of polyculturalism. On the one hand he is rejected by the dominant society because he is Brown and insists on affirming his bicultural values—being "American" means casting aside one's cultural and ethnic inheritance—; and, on the other, the Mexicans know he is not one of them, an illegal alien. The thrust of Soto's poetry, then, like all of Chicano literature, is to create a cultural space which the "alienated" Chicano can call his own. The tensions which press upon both borders of this space are, paradoxically, those which threaten to sunder it, and those which help define its cultural space and production.

The street, then, serves Soto as an organizing element of his poetic material and as a poetic figure. The street is a real place in whose houses and factories people live and work; it is the metaphorical space of the lost outsider besieged by cosmic forces; it conveys an allegory of an underprivileged minority; and it is a metaphor of the poetic voice that enunciates a cultural space.

Gary Soto's poetry is unique in American literature. Unlike many meritorious Chicano and mainland Puerto Rican poets, Soto does not—and cannot—write in Spanish or mix interlingually Spanish and English. Yet, precisely because Soto writes in English, and not because he is a better poet, he—more than any U.S. Hispanic poet—can relate to the Anglo American reader the social afflictions of his minority group. By dealing with themes and utilizing a style familiar to Anglo readers, he not only can express his personal "existential" burden but is able to overcome the criticism of some of these readers that Chicano literature is not universal. Reading his street poems, for example, is an experience akin to that of reading "The Wasteland," but stripped of its "universal" classical figures and stocked with Chicano figures and cultural icons. Through his use of cultural contexts and markers, that is, by means of cultural foregrounding, he redirects the Anglo American reader to include a Chicano perspective

Cover illustration by Barry Root appearing in Soto's Baseball in April, and Other Stories.

and thrusts into their sight of universals the particular situations of Chicano society. (pp. 32-46)

Julian Olivares, "The Streets of Gary Soto," in Latin American Literary Review, *Vol. XVIII, No. 35, January-June, 1990, pp. 32-49.*

Roberto González Echevarría (review date 20 May 1990)

[*A Cuban-born American critic and educator, Echevarría is a noted Hispanist. In the following review, he asserts that* Baseball in April *is concerned with adolescence, generational conflict, and cultural change.*]

Gary Soto's sensitive and economical short stories [in ***Baseball in April, and Other Stories***] center on Mexican-American boys and girls becoming teen-agers. They are set in homogeneous lower-middle-class Hispanic neighborhoods in California. At the same time the young people are turning into adolescents, their milieu is becoming progressively Americanized, largely through the pervasive influence of the media. The overall theme of the book is thus individual and social change being provoked by strong outside forces. The boys and girls are transforming themselves awkwardly into facsimiles of adults; the world of adults is turning into an anxious copy of the Anglo world.

Mr. Soto, who was born and raised in Fresno, Calif., teaches Chicano studies and English at the University of California, Berkeley. Because he stays within the teenagers' universe in ***Baseball in April,*** he manages to convey all the social change and stress without bathos or didacticism. In fact, his stories are moving, yet humorous and entertaining. The best are also quite subtle.

In **"Two Dreamers,"** Luis, Hector's grandfather, is inspired by some advertisements to plot a real estate deal that will make him rich, so he can return to the Mexican town of Jalapa in triumph. But to make phone calls, he needs Hector as interpreter—a common situation in immigrants' homes. Hector, both skeptical and embarrassed, demurs. At the same time he is fascinated by Luis's knowledge and his memories of Mexico ("his hometown with its clip-clop of horse and donkey hooves"). As Hector grows older, the situation is reversed. With his command of English, Hector is now a probe into the future, and into the alien yet alluring world that surrounds him. The story is about this swap of roles. It is very revealing that the contrast of generations skips the father, a figure generally absent in this collection. Luis and Hector better embody the generational differences. The grandfather is unwaveringly Mexican; Hector is on his way to becoming something still undefined, but certainly not Mexican anymore.

The title story is a poignant tale about compromise and resignation. Michael and Jesse practice hard to make the Little League. At the tryout, nervously watched by other boys' fathers (obviously Anglo and middle-class), they both fail. But they join an independent team, the Hobos, run by Manuel, a fatherly man who coaches with affection and compassion. The team does not do very well, and neither do Jesse and Michael, who are not very good. The Hobos disband slowly, as the boys lose interest in baseball. April is over. What was a consuming interest is suddenly left behind, like so many other things. Life can and will go on without baseball—a somewhat melancholy lesson.

The same air of resignation prevails in other stories, like **"Barbie,"** where Veronica finally gets the doll she wants, only to have it lose its head. This story has a lurking sexual subtext that gives it a more serious and compelling tone than the others, though everything is very understated. The best by far is **"The Karate Kid,"** which has a quixotic theme. Gilbert Sanchez, who is delicate and sensitive, is overwhelmed by the movie *The Karate Kid.* He assumes the persona of his movie hero and challenges his tormentor at school, Pete the Heat, who beats him up unmercifully. Gilbert begs his mother to pay for karate classes. She gives in and he attends a school run by a Mr. Lopez, who is something of an impostor. After a few months, Gilbert feels ready for his second sally. The Heat demolishes him again before all his friends. Gilbert gives up karate gleefully for fiction—that is, for "super-hero comic books; they were more real than karate. And they didn't hurt."

Baseball in April is more than literature for teenagers. The stories give a bittersweet account of reconciliation to the givens of self and life while growing up that will be recognized as authentic by all.

Roberto González Echevarría, "Growing up North of the Border," in The New York Times Book Review, *May 20, 1990, p. 45.*

Ernesto Trejo (review date 5 August 1990)

[*In the review below, Trejo favorably assesses* A Summer Life.]

Life in [***A Summer Life***] is not always easy, but most of the time it is fun. And recalled in a prose that bristles with energy, it is never dull.

Presented as a series of "snapshots" that shed light on particulars (**"The Buddha," "The Grandfather," "The Taps," "The Shirt,"** etc.) these 39 brief essays make up a compelling biography of the author's early childhood growing up Chicano in California's Central Valley. Much like in his earlier book, ***Living Up the Street*** (1985), Soto holds the past up to memory's probing flashlight, turns it around ever so carefully, and finds in the smallest of incidents the occasion for literature. Of course, the small turns out to be not so small after all; it's life played out before our eyes.

More than with William Saroyan, another author who wrote about growing up in Fresno, we find correspondences with Follain and Gorki: It's not so much the kid having a hell of a time growing up; this is rather the work of an adult intelligence dealing with time. Always the world is out there, just about to close in on the lives of the characters who breathe in these recollections.

Soto has been, from his first book of poetry, ***The Elements of San Joaquin,*** to this ***A Summer Life,*** a writer of careful, intense attention to language. This style, described as "poetic," is simply the stuff that good writing, both poetry and prose, is made of: the direct vision of the world.

And what a vibrant world. Helping Uncle Shorty, just

back from the Korean War, collect copper from abandoned machinery in the neighborhood, the young boy, probably 4 years old, notices

> the flakes of egg shells, nails, broken bottles, bottle caps pressed into asphalt, grass along fences, sleeping cats, boards, shattered snail shells, liquid-eyed jays, pot holes, black ants, red ants, jaw-lantern insects with blue eyes, half-eaten fruit, ripped shoes, buttons, metal slugs, cracks in the earth, leather thongs, ripped magazines—everything except copper.

Though unwilling to yield its copper treasures, the world parades before the attentive eyes of this child.

The 39 short essays in this collection are built around objects, events, and persons or animals. But the subject in question usually is a point of departure or a point of arrival, a talisman holding anecdote and meditation together, an emblem of a larger meaning.

For example, in **"The Rhino,"** the author at 4 years old, after seeing a billboard with the picture of a rhinoceros in front of a tire factory, mistakenly believes that car tires are made of rhino hide. He later gathers enough courage to ask his father if this is true. Father and Uncle explain to

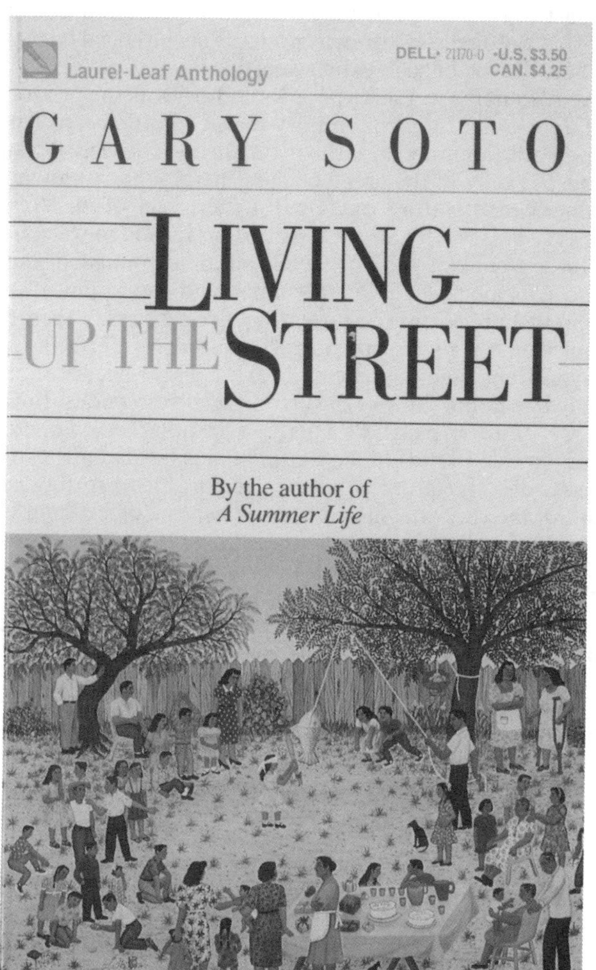

Cover of Soto's memoir collection Living Up The Street.

him that this is not so, and that "rubber drops from trees into buckets."

But in the meantime, the child has noticed, remembered and described a monumental carnage around him: We eat cows, pigs' feet, bacon (with the happy faces of pigs grinning from the wrappers), and drink goats' milk from cans and cows' milk from cartons decorated with the picture of Hopalong Cassidy, whose horse has no feet. His and his father's shoes are made from hide; Father's belt came from an alligator; Mother and her pillow, a "restrained cloud of feathers," contributed to the demise of chickens; a rabbit had to give up one of its feet for her key chain; the Molinas stir bony pigeons in pots of boiling water.

Later, Father and Uncle watch two boxers hurt each other on television. Dogs and cats lie splattered on the road. Broken pigeons are found on the grills of cars.

Something has happened here. By the end of the essay, the accumulated horror and fear, the realization that we live surrounded by death, renders the rhino a plausible sacrificial victim on the altar of our comfort and survival, the point being that if rubber could not be obtained from rubber trees or petrochemicals, we would not hesitate to slaughter rhinos (or any other animal) and turn them into tires.

However, preaching or pontificating is the last thing that the reader will find in this brilliant collection. Soto has honed down his artistry to the point where language (a slight description; a character sketch, a passing thought) conveys a vision of the world. He goes for the little particulars, the telling facts. The dull sociologist, or social psychologist, who studies the Chicano Experience will despair at Soto's way of describing what they might consider trivial, unnecessary matters instead of thoroughly examining and solving the problems of barrio existence.

Here is an excerpt from **"The Weather":**

> Wind was one thing, frost another. I walked on hard lawns and looked back, happy that my shoe prints were visible, that a dog would stop and sniff them. I followed bike tracks and got nowhere. I followed clouds as well, the heavy machinery of rain that did more than keep me inside. It made my brother and me fight a lot, made my mother sit at the table stirring black-black coffee, the worry of bills resting on a sharp elbow.

Instead of describing the child's mood and worries, Soto gives us here, as well as in the rest of the book, what is authentic literature.

The book is divided into three sections and roughly follows a chronological order. In the first section, the father plays a prominent role in the mythology of the child and the memory of the adult. In the second section, the subject is late childhood, the mood introspective, the focus on the immediate family. Finally, in the third section, we see the author entering the world of adolescence, a world larger and more bitter, as it now includes the dreaded stepfather, a character who, though briefly sketched, will linger in the reader's mind for a long time.

Events in these recollections usually happen during the long summer days. Most of the time the vision, though clouded by doubt and discovery of harsh realities, is celebratory; the child is enthralled and amazed at his own existence. In **"The Guardian Angel,"** he exclaims, "I loved my life, and loved playing and eating the same meal over and over and even the loneliness of a thirteen-year-old in jeans bursting with love."

A Summer Life as a whole is a joyous book. After reading the last page, which speaks so eloquently to anyone who pays attention to his childhood or who enjoys literature, we can identify with these words:

"The tennies lay like struck animals on the side of the road. But they are warm and soft, as they let off the steam of a full day." (pp. 1, 9)

Ernesto Trejo, "Memories of a Fresno Boyhood," in Los Angeles Times Book Review, *August 5, 1990, pp. 1, 9.*

Soto's ethnic and class consciousness constitute an essential part of his literary sensibility. His recollections, from childhood to his current position as a Berkeley professor, are punctuated by flashes of endured bigotry and his awareness that in the United States to be "Mexican" generally means to be poor.

—Raymund A. Paredes, in his "Review Essay: Recent Chicano Writing," in **Rocky Mountain Review of Language and Literature, *1987.***

Hector Torres (review date Spring 1991)

[*In the following review of* Baseball in April, A Summer Life, *and* Who Will Know Us?, *Torres provides a thematic and stylistic discussion of Soto's poetry and prose.*]

With [***Baseball in April, A Summer Life,*** and ***Who Will Know Us?***] Gary Soto displays exceptional stylistic elegance and thematic subtlety. All three are recent works and span from prose to poetry, from the short essay to the short story. The three works show a Gary Soto who is mature in his art, confident in the ability of his language to transform the everyday things of life into literary figure. The issues and questions that have concerned Soto in his previous works—the experience of cultural poverty in its broadest sense, of growing up Chicano in Fresno, of coming to sense the mysteries of everyday life in language—reappear in these three new works. As before, Soto's texts present their message not in the mode of argument but in the manner of inference on the part of the reader.

Baseball in April is a work of fiction aimed at a young readership. ***Baseball*** is the kind of work that could be used to teach high school and junior high school English classes. The characters that live through these pages are young teen and pre-teen kids who, in one way or another, are having to confront the realities of the worlds that surround them. What is engaging about this collection of short stories is how Soto bridges the gap of his own childhood experiences of growing up poor in Fresno during the 1950's and the experience of a whole new generation of young Chicanos and Chicanas now growing up around the same Fresno area. The eleven stories reach out to an audience that will recognize itself in the names—from Alfonso who feels the twinges of a first love to Maria who feels the first twinges for independence. The Spanish expressions Soto uses throughout this collection give the stories a strong sense of the social context from which they are drawn and demonstrate his ability to turn sociolinguistic detail into a literary figure with referential power. For instance, in the opening story, titled **"Broken Chain,"** Soto delights with his portrayal of Alfonso, his young protagonist, who is aware that his family eats "a lot of *frijoles,* which was okay because nothing tasted so good." Such lines remind the reader that Chicano kids need not grow up feeling ashamed about the foods they eat, and by metonymic extension, their culture. With ***Baseball in April,*** Soto succeeds, as he did with his own Chicano upbringing, in drawing out the universal flavor from the particularities of everyday life. There is no mistaking the fact that in the midst of their impetus for a universal level of appeal, the stories Soto tells are drawn from a Chicano social context. Thus, the use of such expressions like *menso, pendejo,* and *chale,* to name just a few, mark the stories as the products of a sociolinguistic community that is so little heard from and so little understood in mainstream America. This is true not only in the arena of the general literary canon of American literature but also in the arena of children's books. This is why Soto's ***Baseball in April*** is so welcome. This is a book of stories that can speak to young Chicanos and Chicanas—to their dilemmas and aspirations—and help them to affirm their everyday lives. Through their reliance on Spanish expressions, Soto's stories affirm the everyday language of home and barrio. This reviewer found only one minor fault in the use of these expressions. In the story **"Two Dreamers"** Luis is a grandfather character, immigrated to the United States in "his late twenties." He persuades his young grandson Hector, fluent in English, to call the realtor selling a home down the block from his own. Luis, wanting to know the asking price for the house, tells Hector: "Son, just ask how much. *Es no problema.*" The Spanish expression, such as he utters it and in the context in which it is uttered, is perhaps not the kind of syntax that would be used by someone who immigrated to the United States in his late twenties. In the context of the book as whole however, this minor fault is heavily outweighed by the stylistic and thematic graces of each and every story. Above all, ***Baseball in April*** represents Soto's sensitivity towards a new generation of young voices of a Fresno that keeps calling him back.

A Summer Life is a series of short narrative recollections in the same autobiographical mode as ***Living Up the Street*** (1985) and ***Lesser Evils*** (1988). Nevertheless, this work is distinct from those two; ***A Summer Life*** moves with greater stylistic elegance and richer thematic coherence. Dividing the work into three sections, Soto writes in a balanced, precise style, the themes of the work running deep in human time, in the cares of everyday life. Soto works well with the short story mode—a mode of exposition and telling he has innovated—as he uses it to convey the mysteries that inhabit everyday life. Thematically, ***A Summer Life*** plays with the metaphor of the edge of the world. That is, in many of the stories the reader finds Gary Soto, at various stages of his life, exploring the limits of his world and wondering what lies beyond those limits. In the story titled **"The Bike"** for instance, Soto recalls how he disobeyed his mother's orders not to go beyond Braly Street, part of the block on which his house was located. Thus concerning his first bike Soto writes: "Going up and down the block was one thing, but taking the first curve, out of sight of Mom and the house, was another. I was scared of riding on Sarah Street." What five-year-old Gary Soto finds when he ventures beyond the confines of his street is not only the exhilaration of freedom but also the pain of epiphany. On Sarah Street Gary learns that having someone run over your ankle with a tricycle is painful and makes it difficult to pedal your own bike, making it likely that your pants leg will be caught in the chain and cause you to fall off. "I fell to the ground, bike and all, and let the tears lather my face again," says Soto, adding, "I then dragged the bike home with the pants leg in the chain." It is a wiser Gary Soto who returns to Braly Street, resigned to the belt that awaits him at home in his mother's hand.

Similarly, in the last story, **"The River,"** Soto the mature writer recalls his seventeenth year, a time when he and a friend named Scott go to Los Angeles in search of a new life. Soto plays with the metaphor of the road as river in order to portray the strength of the desperation that carried their young lives along into the future. Gary and Scott are on the way to the home of the former's uncle, who was, Soto tell us, "[a] foundry worker." The road upon which they walk Soto describes as "a four-lane river of black asphalt hardened by junky cars and diesels." The shock of (mis)recognition reaches deep into both of them, and Soto captures that moment when he says, "We knew this place, but from where?" The mood throughout their walk is one of loneliness, as they discuss going to Viet Nam as buddies and not getting killed. As they continue to walk, they come across what at first they take to be a canal, and they are surprised to find later, after looking at a map, that it is the Los Angeles River. The Los Angeles River, filled as it was with "mangled bicycles, tires, chairs, pissy little puddles, and winos washed downstream to settle on rafts of cardboard," reminds the two wayfarers that they have uncovered no new frontier but merely have exchanged their canal in Fresno for a would-be river in Los Angeles. In the final paragraph Soto masterfully intensifies this mood as he allows the reader to see him bunking on the floor of his uncle's house and thinking about his family back on Braly Street in Fresno, about his uncle who fought in the Korean War and who had "slept on a cot on the sunporch" of his Braly Street home. "We had only the floor," Soto tells his reader. The final sentence of his story speaks about a future that is very close to the present in which the young (narrated) Soto finds himself: "We had yet to go and come back from our war and find ourselves a life other than the one we were losing." In this bleak picture of what the present and future hold for their lives, Soto shows that he had not yet dreamt of the power of language to open new frontiers. As the painter of the prosaic picture in particular and of ***A Summer Life*** in general, Soto at the same time demonstrates what happened when he did.

Stylistically, ***A Summer Life*** presents a Soto who not only displays great ease with the figures of metaphor and metonymy but also exercises a cool, well-paced control over his syntax and style. Soto's syntax is lean and precise, his style elegant and informative. In a story from section one, which he titles **"The Grandfather,"** Soto employs a topicalization transformation that lends his prose a rhythmic grace. Recalling that his grandfather believed that "A tree was money," Soto writes: "*Apricots* he got by the bagfuls from a son, who himself was wise for planting young. *Peaches* he got from a neighbor, who worked the night shift at Sun Maid Raisin." These two sentences with the topicalized nouns in italics and non-restrictive relative clauses are perfectly balanced syntactically. Semantically, with the two relative clauses Soto balances two referring expressions which function as a background discourse on all those people who worked the factories of industrial Fresno, his own father included. To unpack this political discourse is beyond the scope of this short review, but it is perhaps enough to say that Soto has gotten better at letting his background discourses carry the weight of his political views. Syntax and discourse of this kind abound in all the stories, making ***A Summer Life*** a superb work for reading in classes of Contemporary American Literature/Autobiography.

Divided into three sections, ***Who Will Know Us?*** contains a total of forty-one new poems by Gary Soto. With this new collection of poems Soto further solidifies his position as a poet of the American landscape. What Soto portrays in his poetry is a sense of what it is to be a Chicano poet who not only observes but also lives out of the daily rhythms of California America. Soto crafts each of his poems with care and precision, writing each one in a narrative syntax that balances subtlety of expression with elegance of style. That these poems aim to unfold more of what is at the core of California America is strikingly clear in a poem from section two entitled **"At the All-Night Cafe,"** with its opening clause declaring "America is at work." The description Soto offers of the busy Cafe is a quintessential American picture—a diner, a waitress, customers, controlled mayhem. Soto punctuates the celebratory mood of the poem as it closes; on the way out, one of the customers, "the appliance guy," pays for two glazed donuts, "sweating behind glass. / A moist hand grabs one, no two, / For the sweet drive three blocks home." Here the poet observes America closely and celebrates the simple things that constitute it—a day at work, a meal at a diner, the drive home, glazed donuts.

If Soto is a poet who observes and celebrates America, then he is also a poet who observes the everyday things of American life and transforms them into poetic figure. **"Evening Walk"** for instance, is a poem that focuses on a walk that the poet takes with his young daughter Mariko. Soto creates poetry from this simple event by in-fusing the narrative scene with a sense of the passing of time and the distance time can create between parent and child—the childhood of the one with the present childhood of the other. The poet observes his own daughter doing what she can to avoid being under his shadow: "She starts to skip. I walk faster, / Loud as a fool. / When I was a kid, / I lugged oranges and shared plums with Okies . . . / But she's on the run, the branch / Fluttering like a green fire / because the corner is up ahead / And an evening without me / Can't be far beyond." Soto no doubt sees himself in his daughter's desire to extend her own sphere of independence, and as such, he turns a simple evening walk into a literary figure representing the changes that time brings.

Nowhere in this collection of new poems is the concern with the inevitable passage of time more salient and poetically figured than in the title poem of the book, which appears at the end of section one. Dedicated to the late Czech poet Jaroslav Seifert, winner of the Nobel Prize for literature in 1984, **"Who Will Know Us?"** is a meditation on death. The meditation takes place on a train as the poet gazes out his window and transforms the landscape into defamiliarizing images. The occasion for the mediation stems from the fact that the poet is en route to the cemetery: "I'm on a train, rocking toward the cemetery / To visit the dead who now / Breathe through the grass, through me." The poet's subjective meditation deepens his appreciation for human time, though in the end, it is insufficient to keep him from remembering the train's rocking motion as it takes him to his destination. It is thus that the poet presents the rocking train as a metaphor for the simultaneous process of living and dying: "The train. Red coal of evil. / We are its passengers, the old and young alike. / Who will know us when we breath through the grass?" These powerful lines parallel the opening lines, quoted above. The difference in the syntax—the absence of the prepositional phrase "through me"—indicates that a slot is left open for the poet who will in the future provide the subjective space upon which another meditation on death will take place. Soto's deep awareness of the finitude of human time is concurrently an awareness of the way in which narrative repetition, in a sense, overcomes that finitude by letting the poet hold open the possibility that the meditation itself does not end. That is, even if the poet must of necessity bring his/her personal meditation to an end, the possibility is held open that the agency of the meditation—human consciousness—will in the future, again and again, take up this theme and breath through new poets.

In affirming such confidence in poetry, Soto at the same time displays a deep seated maturity in his own art. There can be little doubt that Soto is one of the most interesting Chicano writers on the landscape of American poetry and prose. He has been a chief innovator in the short essay/story genre and his poetry has been consistently of high quality. Now that he has excelled in these genres, perhaps Soto will explore his talents in the genre of the novel. (pp. 111-15)

Hector Torres, in a review of "Baseball in April," "A Summer Life," and "Who Will Know Us?" in The Americas Review, *Vol. XIX, No. 1, Spring, 1991, pp. 111-15.*

Frank Allen (review date 1 May 1991)

[*Allen is an American poet, critic, and educator. In the following, he praises the autobiographical aspects of* Home Course in Religion.]

[***Home Course in Religion***] is a spiritual autobiography of growing up Mexican American in Fresno, California in the 1960s. Author of many poetry volumes, essays, and prose memoirs, Soto documents a Catholic family's rite of passage by showing how "the blown tires that bumped along / on a filthy current" are transformed into a spiritual quest for the mysterious meanings of "the stained-glass windows / Breathing in light." These novelistic, narrative poems—about the death of his father, his stepfather's drinking, wrestling and karate, marriage and fatherhood—seek religious dimensions of a secular age: "I want very badly to know how to talk about Christ." He does so in compassionate poems that define the holy in terms of everyday life. One man's path to belief becomes a struggle to articulate how we all take a "home course in religion."

Frank Allen, in a review of "Home Course in Religion," in Library Journal, *Vol. 116, No. 8, May 1, 1991, p. 79.*

Gerald Haslam (review date August 1992)

[*In the following, Haslam positively assesses* Home Course in Religion.]

Gary Soto is perhaps the most honored individual to emerge from that creative cluster known nationally as the Fresno Poets. He is also arguably the most accomplished of Chicano poets. Ironically, one reason for both those things is that Soto's work transcends labels.

It is his triumph in this book as in his previous collections that his particular scenes are so often doorways to the universal; what the young Mexican-American boy experienced in Fresno resonates with what other youngsters experienced elsewhere.

Home Course in Religion reveals one more important aspect of Soto's success: he is unwilling to reap easy praise by repeating what he's already done well. Instead, he ranges widely over subjects, styles and even diction. The poetry collected here veers stylistically from his earlier work but continues his exploration of important themes from contemporary life.

Like many Catholic kids, Soto has lived through a sort of blank acceptance, then skepticism, then agnosticism and finally adult reconciliation:

> I miss not eating fish on Friday,
> The halved lemon squeezed a third time around,
> And our prayers, silent mutter
> To God, whom we knew, whom we trusted
> To make things right . . .
>
> (from **"Pink Hands"**)

This collection ventures to the author's high school and the social scene there: "Drinking made you popular at school, / And laughing while you drank / Made you friends. . . . " He also reveals a preoccupation of many high-school boys: " . . . Everyone was larger / in the showers, their cocks like heavy wrenches, / their hair like the scribbling of a mad child."

Soto's last collection, ***Who Will Know Us?,*** was dominated by the death of the poet's father. In this book, a new persona begins to dominate the family's life:

> I didn't like home.
> Especially in summer. But eventually I returned to watch
> My stepfather eat fried chicken on a TV tray.
> He ate for bulk, not taste,
> And every night he drank to flood the hole inside him.

The poetry of Gary Soto is marked by an oddly satisfying mix of wonder and crust. He has never succumbed to the overcompensatory praise available to writers from oppressed minorities, but has instead continued to challenge himself and his readers. As a result he is, if not a major poet, then a strong candidate to be one. Don't miss this latest revelation of his expanding vision and craft. (pp. 143-44)

Gerald Haslam, in a review of "Home Course in Religion," in Western American Literature, *Vol. XXVII, No. 2, August, 1992, pp. 143-44.*

FURTHER READING

Addiego, John. "Chicano Poetry: Five New Books." *Northwest Review* 21, No. 1 (1983): 147-58.

Praises Soto's use of characterization and voice in *Where Sparrows Work Hard.* Addiego observes that Soto's writings—which, he claims, exemplify Chicano literature—are thematically concerned with place, community, ancestry, and self.

Buckley, Christopher. Review of *Who Will Know Us?: New Poems,* by Gary Soto. *Western American Literature* XXV, No. 4 (Winter 1991): 365-67.

Positive assessment of *Who Will Know Us?,* which, Buckley asserts, is Soto's "most accomplished work to date."

Bus, Heiner. "Sophisticated Spontaneity: The Art of Life in Gary Soto's *Living up the Street.*" *The American Review* 16, Nos. 3-4 (Fall-Winter 1988): 188-97.

Thematic and stylistic analysis of *Living up the Street,* emphasizing Soto's treatment of the past.

Cheuse, Alan. "The Voice of the Chicano." *The New York Times Book Review* LXXXVI, No. 41 (11 October 1981): 15, 36-7.

Discusses Soto's place among contemporary Chicano writers.

Comerford, Lynda Brill. "For Young Adults." *Los Angeles Times Book Review* (27 May 1990): 8.

Praises Soto's prose style, use of memory and emotion, and descriptions of Chicano life in *Baseball in April.* Lauding his status as a writer of juvenile fiction, Comerford concludes: "With tremendous success, Soto transfers to prose his poetic skills of crystallizing a moment and revealing many layers of meaning through ordinary events. His sensitivity to young people's concerns and his ability to portray the world as it is perceived by children is nothing less than remarkable."

Dunn, Geoffrey. "Central Valley Boys." *San Francisco Review of Books* 16, No. 1 (Summer 1991): 38-9.

Favorable review of *Who Will Know Us?, Baseball in April,* and *A Summer Life.* Dunn places Soto in the tradition of such writers as William Saroyan, John Steinbeck, Joan Didion, and Maxine Hong Kingston, all of whom frequently set their works in California's Central Valley region.

Erben, Rudolf, and Erben, Ute. "Popular Culture, Mass Media, and the Chicano Identity in Gary Soto's *Living up the Street* and *Small Faces.*" *Melus* 17, No. 3 (Fall 1991-1992): 43-52.

Examines how television and the mass media influence Soto's perception of Chicano identity.

Romero, Rolando J. Review of *Lesser Evils: Ten Quartets,* by Gary Soto. *Hispania* 73, No. 3 (September 1990): 671-72.

Mixed assessment of *Lesser Evils.*

Torrens, James S. "U.S. Latino Writers—The Searchers." *America* 167, No. 2 (25 July 1992): 39-42.

Discusses the popularity of Chicano literature and assesses work by such Chicano writers as Soto, Cristina García, Sandra Cisneros, and Victor Hernández Cruz.

Tremblay, Bill. "Midlife Books." *American Book Review* 13, No. 3 (August-September 1991): 16, 18.

Offers a thematic analysis of *Who Will Know Us?*

Additional coverage of Soto's life and career is contained in the following sources published by Gale Research: *Authors and Artists for Young Adults,* Vol. 10; *Contemporary Authors,* Vols. 119, 125; *Contemporary Literary Criticism,* Vol. 32; *Dictionary of Literary Biography,* Vol. 82; and *Hispanic Writers.*

Christina Stead

1902-1983

(Full name Christina Ellen Stead) Australian novelist, short story writer, and screenwriter.

The following entry presents an overview of Stead's career. For further information, see *CLC,* Volumes 2, 5, 8, and 32.

INTRODUCTION

Neglected by critics for decades, Stead has been reappraised as a major twentieth-century writer whose work addresses important issues related to sociology, politics, and psychology in modern society. In graphically realistic works, she explored such diverse topics as family dysfunction, international finance, and women's struggles for personal and political identity.

Born and raised in Sydney, Australia, Stead was the daughter of naturalist David Stead. She received a teaching certificate from Teachers' College in Sydney, and subsequently worked in the Australian public schools. In 1928 Stead left Australia to live in England. While working as a grain company clerk, she met and married William Blake, an American who was a Marxist economist and writer. Through the 1930s and 1940s Blake and Stead lived in various cities in Europe and the United States, with Stead working as a bank clerk in Paris and a senior writer for Metro-Goldwyn-Mayer in Hollywood. The couple settled in England in 1953. After Blake's death in 1968, Stead returned to Australia, where she continued to write until her death in 1983.

Stead's fiction reflects her diverse personal experiences through varied settings and a wide range of subject matter. For example, *The Salzburg Tales* is a collection of short stories that revolve around a multinational group of tourists at a music festival in Salzburg, Austria. Modeled after Geoffrey Chaucer's *The Canterbury Tales* and Giovanni Boccaccio's *Decameron,* the book comprises the self-revealing tales each member of the group relates to fellow tourists. Set in post-World War I Australia, *Seven Poor Men of Sydney* is an exploration of poverty that ends in the despair and suicide of the main character. *Cotter's England* treats a very different subject in its focus on a socially and politically idealistic young English journalist who manipulates and destroys those around her. *The Man Who Loved Children,* Stead's most critically acclaimed work, takes place in and around Washington, D.C. An autobiographical family psychodrama, the novel centers on the teenaged Louisa Pollit's attempts to escape her father's obsessive interest in her sexuality and the incessant domestic battle between her father and stepmother. In the end, Louisa leaves home after her attempt to poison both parents results in the death of her stepmother.

Stead's work went generally unacknowledged until, in an afterword to a reprint edition in 1965, Randall Jarrell praised *The Man Who Loved Children* as "a better book . . . than most of the novels people call great." As interest mounted, critics reexamined Stead's entire canon, noting both the wide range and thematic unity of her subject matter. Stead's often extravagant use of language, detail, and drama is considered both an asset and a detriment to her work, leading to comparisons with the highly ornamental works of nineteenth-century novelists. Joan Lidoff has written, "Standing in sympathies between eras, her novels keep the nineteenth century's devotion to realism, its scope of social concern, texture of observed detail, interest in character. Yet her understanding . . . is informed by Marx and Freud, by a material social critique and by in-depth analysis of individual fantasy life and family relations." Despite critical neglect of her work, most commentators agree that Stead ranks as a significant twentieth century author due to her insightful probing of dark aspects of the Western psyche. Daphne Merkin remarked: "Hers is an obsession with human savagery, especially in its licit manifestations . . . which are unavoidable because they are endemic to our race."

PRINCIPAL WORKS

The Salzburg Tales (short stories) 1934
Seven Poor Men of Sydney (novel) 1935
The Beauties and Furies (novel) 1936
House of All Nations (novel) 1938
The Man Who Loved Children (novel) 1940
For Love Alone (novel) 1944
Letty Fox: Her Luck (novel) 1946
A Little Tea, A Little Chat (novel) 1948
The People with the Dogs (novel) 1952
Dark Places of the Heart (novel) 1966; published in England as *Cotter's England,* 1966
The Puzzleheaded Girl (novellas) 1967
The Little Hotel (novel) 1975
Miss Herbert (The Suburban Wife) (novel) 1976
Ocean of Story (short stories) 1985
I'm Dying Laughing (novel) 1986

CRITICISM

Charles Thomas Samuels (review date 9 September 1967)

[*Samuels was an American educator and critic. In the following review, he finds three of the novellas in* The Puzzleheaded Girl *superficial, but praises the fourth, "The Girl from the Beach," for its unsentimental portrayal of a middle-aged man's ill-fated relationship with a young woman.*]

Christina Stead's ***The Salzburg Tales*** (1934) was considered a promising debut; but by 1952, Miss Stead had fallen from favor with readers and critics, and she published nothing for 14 years. Now embarked on a second career, she is being recommended through a falsification of her first. When she recently appeared in the *Saturday Evening Post,* the editors asserted, "she has had an ardent following among critics . . . although her works have never met with popular success." In the 30's and early 40's, snob appeal aside, Christina Stead sold respectably; whereas her ardent admirers were Clifton Fadiman and *Time* magazine. More serious critics found her prolix, aimless, and showy.

Writing in *The New Republic* in 1941, Mary McCarthy judged ***The Man Who Loved Children*** "an hysterical tirade," but two years ago, when at a single whistle from Randall Jarrell, the critical community launched a bandwagon to herald the book's reappearance, Miss McCarthy's important criticisms were simply ignored. Thus the *Post* could maintain, "belated recognition" makes it certain that Christina Stead will be acknowledged "one of the best novelists of the century." Well, it won't because she isn't; though she does possess an authentic talent that can't be described through hyperbole or legends.

Stead appeals through the oddness of her characters and the relentless, uniquely resourceful dialogue through which she creates them. But the very amplitude of her portraits demands a significance she finds difficult to establish. The baby-talking egoist Sam Pollit (in ***Children***) never comes to represent colonial condescension, though Stead hints at the connection, just as Nellie Cotter, in last year's ***Dark Places of the Heart,*** never quite distills the cant of England's welfare state. Since the novellas which make up [***The Puzzleheaded Girl***] are both short and witty, they don't seem aimless; but, for the most part, they are scarcely more edifying than her novels.

"The Dianas," for example, portrays a nervous, virgin tease, who is apparently an object of satire. Juggling dates like a busy executive, Lydia satisfies none of her admirers, preferring to give her attention to the love-crossed girlfriend she torments with unwanted solicitude. Sick with waiting for her married lover's divorce, Tamara criticizes Lydia's romanticism:

> ". . . Marriage is give and take." "Oh, no, no," cried Lydia. "It must be all give, he must give. I won't give. A man must be a light to a woman and guide her whole life and she must lean on him and have nothing more to think of. . . . "
>
> ". . . You must bring something to marriage."
>
> "I bring twenty thousand dollars and a grand piano."

With such wacky confidence, Lydia decides to tackle the middle-aged professor whom her mother, another "Diana," has held dangling. Citing her admirers, Lydia begs his protection on a continental holiday—at her expense. But the poor man learns the price when Lydia insists on sleeping in a double bed, denies his advances, and advertises his alleged impotence to the hotel staff. Though Tamara ends a suicide, Lydia, who has littered Europe with wounded males, is back in America at the story's end, the bride of some special Acteon.

Lydia's machinations are amusing and her ultimate success through surrender is both ironic in itself and in contrast with Tamara's failure. But the implication that love conquers even so devious a maiden seems banal for such vivid eccentricity, while the hint that nice girls finish last is merely sarcastic. In its original magazine appearance, the story was called **"The Huntress"**; significant universality can't be achieved through a change in title.

In **"The Puzzleheaded Girl,"** universality is the obvious goal, but this story only indicates how Stead's characters resist definition. Honor Lawrence, who materializes one day at the Farmer's Utilities Corporation, is a mystery crying out to be interpreted. One of the firm's partners, Gus Debrett, thinks her innocent but tantalizing; as the story progresses, she feeds the latter impression by qualifying the former. Is her avowed superiority to trade an indictment of the firm's shady business practices or an affectation? Does she hold men off in the manner of a silly virgin, or, since she expertly obtains handouts, is she a cynical tease? Throwing herself, in turn, on the wives of two partners, Honor succeeds in stirring their marital resentments. Though she also insults clients and shirks her duties, Debrett clings to his belief that she is a holy fool.

Years later, after Debrett's marriage has collapsed and Honor has evidently disappeared, she turns up looking like a prostitute. But to Debrett's second wife, Honor, now a bigamous syphilitic hurling curses at love, represents "the ragged wayward heart of woman that doesn't want to be caught and hasn't been caught."

Unfortunately, Mrs. Debrett's exegesis evades some facts. Left out of account are Honor's social conceptions and suggestive past (despite New England manners, she is an Italian immigrant's child). Also ignored is her identification with life's general uncertainty, the "gadfly of fate." We are told that, like "the ghouls of Prague," Honor enters the forms of many women, yet Stead also insists that the girl is no fantasy figure; and, in any case, obscure realism can't be solved through intermittent allegory. Though some of the characters sport names like Honor's—Good, Zero, Magna—at least two—Debrett and Scott—resist hermeneutics. Finally, the puzzleheaded girl is too various for Stead's summation. She is also too fey; what begins by resembling "Bartleby, the Scrivener" veers fatally in the direction of *Breakfast at Tiffany's.*

A third novella, **"The Rightangled Creek,"** is even more baffling. This story begins with a self-styled socialist, potboiling his way to literary prominence, who resembles both Nellie Cotter and Sam Pollit. Suddenly, however, Davies and his family pass out of the tale, leaving their rented farm to some friends. Then a neighbor tells the Parsons of a murder committed in their farmhouse by the original owner's daughter, while Stead's "sort of ghost story" begins to concentrate on mice in the wainscoting and a particularly benign presence which never becomes visible. Flirting with the notion of making the property into an artist's retreat, the Parsons hire an architect who believes that poison ivy is harmless and rolls in a patch of it to prove his point. Effrontery kills him, the Parsons move away, and that, despite some tart jokes and a vivid depiction of nature's appeal, is that.

Though energetic and witty, all three stories have similar flaws. Dotty characters parade in such profusion that we sometimes see only a vaudeville lacking principles of inclusion more expressive than the impresario's taste and the curtain's fall. Aphorisms, excellent in themselves, becloud the plots which transpire in an atmosphere of demirealism that is frequently disorienting and sometimes incredible. Typical obsessions—with sexual warfare and bogus ideology—are evident, but they never quite achieve the status of themes. Just as we are ready to write Stead off, however, she comes along with a novella, richly ironic and admirably developed, but similar in technique to her comparative failures.

"The Girl from the Beach" convincingly realizes that comedy of senescent lust versus lethal girlishness which unites the three best tales. Half of the story, originally published in *The Paris Review* as **"George,"** depicts a Bulgarian crime-reporter, sentimental in his womanizing, theatrical in his nationalism, and ludicrous in the care of his fifty-year-old body that retains the muscle tone of a young man's. Stead has often done such charming phonies, but never with such *brio;* **"George"** deserves the Aga Khan Prize that it was awarded earlier this year.

The second half introduces a young tease like Lydia and Honor Lawrence, but it makes of her a more representative, believable figure. Living on the parental dole in Paris, Linda Hill rooms with homosexuals to save rent, fills a deep-pocketed skirt with stolen silverware to occupy her time, and passes with studied insouciance through her identity crisis. Crossing her path, George immediately succumbs. For him, mature women are "an army of aunts and mothers, midwives and charwomen"; Linda must become the fourth of his girl-wives.

In his sentimental adoration of youth, however, George ignores the wisdom of Eve. Bilking him of his possessions and money, Linda also strips away his pretensions. "I don't think he cared for me. He was always doing what he wanted to," she tosses off while preparing for the safe American marriage that Daddy has insured by taking the young man into his business. She craftily goes "in the folkways," while the flamboyant European decides to marry yet another girl from the beach. Though gayer and less adorned, Stead's story is an unsentimental, small-scaled *Lolita.*

Finally, Stead seems to exist between the extremes set by her critics. In an age when most novelists are shooting the form through a cannon, making up in technical display for loss of purpose and confidence, her mimetic zeal is invigorating despite its frequent pointlessness. Moreover, her attempts at articulating a theme are so lively and musical in themselves that one wants to test the possibility of a leitmotif throughout her work. If her new publisher can be persuaded to reissue her books in reasonably priced editions new readers may just solve the puzzle of a 65-year-old writer vigorous enough to start a second career, yet heedless enough to leave her wrinkles as visible as her wise old eyes. (pp. 30-1)

Charles Thomas Samuels, "The Puzzling Miss Stead," in The New Republic, *Vol. 157, No. 11, September 9, 1967, pp. 30-1.*

Terry Sturm (essay date 1974)

[In the following essay, Sturm argues that Stead created a new "mode of realism" in her novels by rejecting the ideological orientation of naturalism and bourgeois and socialist realisms.]

Christina Stead has always seemed a marginal figure in relation to 'mainstream' traditions and developments in English fiction of this century, a writer whose work does not fit comfortably into received categories. Paradoxically, the circumstances of her personal history as a writer, which cut directly across Australian, American and English cultural provincialisms, have contributed to this kind of isolation. Christina Stead is an expatriate Australian writer, but this fact never seems to have provided any direct imaginative basis for her art in the way in which it has for other writers, like Patrick White. She has been more uncompromising than most writers in rejecting any sustaining myth of place, the idea of a 'necessary atmosphere' for art:

> I know some people say they must get out of England in order to write, but that's just for them,

> it's a myth they've created to sustain their art, and maybe they need it. I at least don't feel restricted in England. You can write anywhere, except on a Greek prison island. There is no such thing as a necessary atmosphere.

This freedom has given her a more than usually large range of subjects. Only one of her novels—her first, ***Seven Poor Men of Sydney*** (1934)—has a wholly Australian setting. Her next two novels—***The Beauties and the Furies*** (1936) and ***House of All Nations*** (1938)—have European settings, and express her reactions to the political turbulence of Europe in the 1930s, the years immediately following her departure from Australia in 1928. During these years her political commitments intensified. The theme of economic exploitation, already dominant in the 1920s milieu of ***Seven Poor Men of Sydney,*** remains a constant preoccupation in all her novels, giving them their distinctively Marxist character. In 1935 she attended the first *International Congress of Writers for the defence of culture* held in Paris, as a member of the English delegation—which included E. M. Forster, Aldous Huxley, John Strachey, and the Australians Nettie Palmer and John Fisher—and she contributed a report on this Congress, 'The Writers Take Sides', to the English magazine *Left Review.* During this period also, she married the American political economist and novelist, William Blake, and they were in Spain at the outbreak of the Civil War.

During the Second World War Christina Stead lived in the United States, and in the twelve years 1940-1952 five more novels were published. Four of them are 'American' novels, with American settings and themes, the most impressive—and perhaps the best known of all her novels—being ***The Man Who Loved Children*** (1940), a novel 'treating of the family of an egoistic humanitarian'. However in her fifth novel, ***For Love Alone*** (1944), she returned partly to an Australian setting, drawing imaginatively on her earlier experience to present the theme of 'the quest for love of a young woman across the world'. In both of these novels economic themes retain their importance, but are more closely interwoven with issues of sex, family and social mores, the creation of a political texture for personal relationships. During the years spent in the United States, she also contributed reviews to the American Left weekly, *New Masses.* Since 1952 Christina Stead has lived in England, and the one novel she has published since then reveals yet another shift of setting and theme. ***Cotters' England*** (1967) returns to the working class focus of ***Seven Poor Men of Sydney,*** but the setting is England, and the novel's concern is with the specific character of working class experience in England.

This unusual range in the subject matter of the novels is matched by the originality of their form and style. The experimental nature of Christina Stead's writing was evident from the start of her writing career. ***The Salzburg Tales*** (1934), her first published work, has a very unusual form: it is a collection of tales and fables, many of them deriving from her interest in European folktale and romance traditions, given unity by its Salzburg setting, and by a structure based on *The Canterbury Tales* and *The Decameron,* in which a character interest is developed in the story-tellers themselves and in the narrator of the whole. ***The Salzburg Tales*** is not a novel, in any conventional sense of the word; nor is it simply a random collection of stories. ***Seven Poor Men of Sydney*** was also an extremely original work for an Australian writer in the '30s. The most significant aspect of the novel's form was its rejection of the conventions of social realism—the dominant tradition in Australian fiction at the time—in favour of a much more experimental approach. The novel has no plot, in the conventional sense, and no 'hero', no central protagonist providing a single focus for its action. Instead, it analyses the motivations and aspirations, under the pressures of poverty, of a range of characters whose lives happen to cross and recross through their shared experience of work, of political ideology, or of casual personal relationships. In this kind of structure Christina Stead is able to give her characters' experience of poverty, and their thwarted political or romantic aspirations, a personal intensity which would be impossible in the formulaic approach of socialist realism. The novel's style, also, is unconventional: it incorporates the naturalism of older modes, but transforms it into a new kind of realism that is primarily geared to the intensity of her characters' experience, rather than to a simple 'documentation' of environment.

Christina Stead's main contribution to twentieth century fiction, as a stylistic innovator, lies in her perfecting of this new mode of realism. Its major achievements are ***The Man Who Loved Children, For Love Alone,*** and her recent masterpiece ***Cotters' England.*** As a mode, it needs to be clearly distinguished from previous realisms. It breaks down the antagonisms on which bourgeois theories of realism are built, and which socialist realism, as a form, inherited: in particular, the assumption that there is an irreconcilable conflict between personal and public (or political) realms of behaviour, between reality and ideology, both in life and in art. Alain Robbe-Grillet has written very critically of socialist realism's compromise, as a form, with bourgeois realism, asking

> why socialist realism has no need of any experiment in novelistic form, why it so mistrusts any innovation in the technique of the arts, why what suits it best, as we see every day, is the most "bourgeois" expression.

His answer to these questions is that socialist realism *shares* with bourgeois realism the assumption that fiction 'illustrates' pre-formed theories or explanations of behaviour, thus depriving it of any radical exploratory possibilities.

Christina Stead writes from a very different standpoint from Robbe-Grillet. She is ideologically a very self-conscious writer, and her novels express strongly held moral and political convictions. Nevertheless the direction of Robbe-Grillet's criticism of socialist realism—the need for writers to assert the exploratory character of their art—is very relevant to the impulses behind her own approach to form.

In the interview with Jonah Raskin she insists repeatedly on the non-manipulative nature of her approach to fiction, the absence of programmatic intentions ('I write to please myself, to express my own ideas, and not those of a magazine, or a social or political group.'):

> Sometimes I start with a situation, sometimes with a personality. I never question or argue. I'm a psychological writer, and my drama is the drama of the person. The start of a story is like a love affair, exactly. It's like a stone hitting you. You can't argue with it. I wait and wait for the drama to develop. I watch the characters and the situation move and don't interfere. I'm patient. I'm lying low. I wait and wait for the drama to display itself. . . . I write a lot of *schemata,* but don't adhere to them. You can't write according to a scheme, but on the other hand you can't let the thing run away with you. The story inevitably goes its own way.

Form, in this kind of description, is a mode of respect for the freedom and individuality of her characters, a necessary condition for what Michael Wilding has described as her unique capacity for 'creative identification with her characters . . . allowing them compulsively to talk, and express themselves and their confusions, contradictions and insincerities' [Wilding, in a review of R. G. Geering's *Christina Stead* in *Australian Literary Studies,* No. 4 (1970)].

A critical terminology derived from the older categories of bourgeois realism, naturalism and socialist realism does not then, take us very close to the centre of Christina Stead's art. And in fact, critics approaching her novels from one or other of these standpoints have tended to find the novels confusing and formless. ***For Love Alone,*** for example, has been described, paradoxically, as excessively rich in unstructured detail and as a too rigidly formularized feminist tract, lushly overwritten in some sections and boringly documentary in others. From the standpoint of the assumptions of bourgeois realism, the novels' radical political preoccupations are likely to be either underemphasized, in order to present the author, safely, as a novelist of human foibles with a sharp eye for the idiosyncratic in human behaviour, or else attacked on the grounds that they politicize areas of reality which ought not properly to be regarded as political at all. A typical example of this would be what is seen as her 'intrusion' of ideology into issues of sexual relations and family life. On the other hand, from the standpoint of orthodox socialist realism she is likely to seem too individualistic a writer, and her interest in the 'psychological drama of the person' a dangerous tendency threatening to undermine the ideological 'substance' of the novels. With rare exceptions Christina Stead has never been seen as an ideologically significant writer by the Australian Left.

The formal and stylistic originality of Christina Stead's novels lies in the way they register the contours of her characters' experience from within, without manipulation, without 'tailoring reality to fit theory'. The mode of realism she has invented makes for inclusiveness and open-endedness in her novels, and an exploratory attitude towards character. It does not proceed reductively, like much politically committed fiction extracting a 'typical' reality from beneath the surface of the 'merely' personal in her characters' lives: such thinking, which implies a necessary opposition between the 'individual' and the 'typical', is quite alien to the author's literary (and political) stance. Her novels are saturated with ideology—ideologies of sex, of family, of economics and politics and culture. Ideology is part of the texture of characters' individual lives, inseparable from their experience and from the way they respond and react to events. More often than not it provides individualizing rather than typifying qualities in their behaviour, associated as much with personal feeling and fantasy, with unconscious rationalization or violent prejudice, as with a rationally formulated attitude or set of attitudes. Some of the most surprisingly realistic effects in her novels come from the way apparently idiosyncratic behaviour, and extremities of feeling, are made to appear quite logical when hidden motivations are revealed; or from the way apparently logical attitudes can suddenly reveal themselves as rationalizations of grotesque or violent obsessions. Christina Stead dramatizes ideas at points where they are not quite conscious in the minds of her characters, where they clash in confusing and often destructive ways with inarticulate aspirations and needs.

Teresa Hawkins and Jonathan Crow, in ***For Love Alone,*** are typical examples of these processes in action. The opening sections of the novel recreate the atmosphere of Sydney's urban and inner suburban life in the 1920s. The poverty and squalor of urban slums, the drabness of work rituals, the stereotyping pressures of middle class social and sexual conventions all suggest, to Teresa, an unnatural limitation of horizons, an unnecessary crippling of energies and passions which she senses beneath the surface of other people's lives and feels deeply within her own. These reactions provide the immediate impetus for her revolt against what she comes to realize is the expected pattern of her life, an 'iron circle of home and work'. She refuses to conform socially, especially to a stereotyping sexual role, impelled by an 'insensate thirst for the truth above passion, alive in their home itself, in her brothers and sister, but neglected, denied, and useless; obnoxious in school, workshop, street.' The novel explores this revolt, tracing the contours of Teresa's experience as she quests for an alternative life style, a personal fulfilment that lies outside the alienating roles Australian society imposes on her as a woman.

However the course of this revolt is by no means a straight progression, and what gives the novel its effect of intense realism is its focus on the ironies, the blind confusions and wrong turnings, and the personal suffering, which complicate Teresa's quest. At the beginning of the novel Teresa is a romantic idealist whose aspirations are essentially inarticulate; and it is precisely this inarticulateness which makes her vulnerable, initially, to the crude intellectual theorizing of Jonathan Crow and leads her to glamourize his ideas and sentimentalize his poverty. Teresa's knowledge, at the end of the novel, has been very painfully acquired; what she has had to learn, Christina Stead implies, is that idealism and generous humanitarian sentiment are not, by themselves, sufficient to sustain her personal rebellion. In particular, they are not sufficient to enable her to see through Crow's false theory of 'personal freedom', to the negations on which it is based.

The 'freedom' which Crow offers—Teresa only gradually and after prolonged personal suffering comes to realize—is in fact a blatant form of compromise with the society whose values he claims to reject. Crow's 'rebellion' takes the form of an aggressive and egotistical cynicism masked as an independent playing of the system for his own purposes; his cynicism is based on illusions, parasitic on the social structure that Teresa also rejects. He believes that all women are predatory, that the only relationships possible are those of possessor and possessed, and offers himself to Teresa's compassion as one who austerley renounces and sublimates his sexuality in order to ensure his survival in the world of predatory human nature around him. Crow's intellectual theories—his belief in a Darwinian 'survival of the fittest' universe, his racism, and his reduction of sexuality to lust and predatoriness—all contain at their core a belief in exploitation and power as the only possible basis for personal and social relationships. It is one of the major ironies of the novel that Teresa acts out, in her relationship with Crow, the oppressed woman's role she imagines she has rejected, just as Crow is an unwitting parody of the values of bourgeois society. He is its most complete victim, expressing its values with great cunning while appearing to be independent of it, and for this reason he offers the most powerful challenge to Teresa's entirely different values. In the character of Jonathan Crow, by contrast with Teresa, theory is the rationalization of behaviour which is basically egotistic and manipulative. He manipulates ideas to give an appearance of logic and intellectual respectability to impulses that are quite irrational, sado-masochistic in origin.

In ***The Man Who Loved Children*** the same psychological subtlety is brought to bear on an analysis of the stresses and tensions in an American middle class family. Here, again, the novel's form—which is quite unconventional in comparison with more orthodox realisms—is geared primarily to events and situations which have the capacity to yield insights into the emotional texture of the lives of her characters, to reveal their compulsions and needs. It is characteristic of Christina Stead's novels that one tends to remember them not in terms of neatly ordered and resolved plots or in terms of some encompassing symbolic or metaphysical scheme, but through one's recall of specific incidents and events which retain their power of immediate revelation, sparking off insights into the motivation and feelings of individual characters, and their relationships with each other. ***The Man Who Loved Children*** is extraordinarily rich in such moments: the scene in which the intolerable conflict of wills between the parents, Sam and Henny Pollit, suddenly erupts, after simmering throughout one particularly tense day, in a violent slanging match and Henny's desperate defence against Sam with a breadknife, and then subsides into a shocked and uneasy silence, 'one of those absences of hatred, aimless lulls that all long wars must have'; the scene, later in the novel, in which Sam forces the children to stand at the foot of the stairs, where they listen astonished and horrified to Henny's screams in the room above, during childbirth, while he enthusiastically lectures them on the mysteries of Nature; the scene in which Sam, puzzled and threatened by his eldest daughter Louisa's growing rebellion against the wretchedness of family life, gives her another of his well-intentioned lectures on the essential goodness of human nature and the inevitability of human Progress, while she idly fills two sheets of paper with the words '*Shut up, shut up, shut up, shut up, shut up, I can't stand your gassing, oh, what a windbag, what will shut you up, shut up, shut up.* And so *ad infinitum*'.

One could go on and on providing illustrations of the kind of realism the novel achieves, with astonishing consistency, throughout. What is more difficult to understand is how it is achieved, and why its effect is so powerful. Taken out of context such incidents—and dozens of others scattered throughout the book—might seem implausible, untypical.

Randall Jarrell, in his fine introduction to the novel, describes its imaginative source as 'an almost frightening power of remembrance', and invokes Dostoevsky to explain the distinctive character of its realism:

> Defending the reality of his own novels, he used to say that their improbable extremes were far closer to everyday reality than the immediately plausible, statistical naturalism of the books everyone calls lifelike . . .

The Man Who Loved Children is one of those very rare novels which transform our perspective, by challenging and undermining the order of priorities that we habitually assume, to distinguish between the normal and abnormal, between (in the language of aesthetics) the probable and the improbable in character and action. The capacity of the novel to involve its readers constantly in acts of surprised recognition, bringing to the surface repressed memories of painful or pleasurable childhood experiences, continually undermines the automatic adult tendency to rationalize the violent extremes of the novel as exaggerated or comic or implausible. Our sense of what Jarrell calls 'the reality of the implausible' in ***The Man Who Loved Children*** is the result of precisely this kind of disorientation of perspective, breaking down taboos surrounding the idea of the family. Christina Stead's imagination, in ***The Man Who Loved Children,*** recovers dozens of seemingly unimportant incidents from the limbo of the trivial, the forgotten or the repressed, and places them at the centre of her drama of the family. The effect is one of extraordinarily sympathetic identification with the inner workings of a family, an understanding of its real motivations, its power as a social idea, its economic basis, its hidden tensions and very private pleasures.

The family whose workings Christina Stead analyzes is the nuclear family of modern Western society. There are hints of an older, more stable and extended family structure, based on inherited wealth, on Henny's aristocratic Collyer side, but it is in the last stages of decay. Henny receives no real help or support, in her marriage, from any of her Collyer relatives, and in fact the loss of Tohoga House after the death of her father accentuates the downward spiral in her life, isolating the family in what is (for Henny) the suffocating and squalid environment of Spa House, and precipitating the final crisis of her suicide and Louisa's departures from home. The isolation of the family unit has two consequences which are central to Christina Stead's analysis. In the first place, it makes the family particularly vulnerable to external pressures, especially economic pressures. Throughout the novel attitudes to money, and lack of money, provide a constant source of friction between

Sam and Henny, and its effects are intensified, and felt throughout the family, after the shift to Spa House, as Sam blithely refuses to take any practical interest in Henny's struggles to provide bare necessities. Secondly, the isolation and concentration of the family, as a kind of nerve centre for social life as a whole, exposes internal tensions and stresses which it is increasingly unable to control. I know of no other novel which creates so powerful a sense of the centrality of experience within the family to the development of personality, of the extent to which learned behaviour, attitudes, feelings, habits and mannerisms, and language are a complex product of the family environment.

For the parents, in ***The Man Who Loved Children,*** family life is a battleground in which Sam's male egotism and Henny's survival instinct and desperate cunning compete for dominance; both characters have quite different backgrounds, temperaments, needs and attitudes; marriage intensifies these incompatibilities, setting them on a collision course from which neither character is able to escape. The children themselves are unwilling participants in these tense struggles, neutral parties to be won over to one side or the other by various kinds of moral intimidation or bribery; but they have remarkable powers of resistance and resilience. The novel is unusually free of adult preconceptions in its unpatronizing, unsentimental presentation of the Pollit children, and many of its subtler ironies are directed at the parents' misunderstanding of their children. Henny, for example, from early on in the novel, convinces herself that she ought to dislike Louisa because she is Sam's daughter, and Sam, for his part, believes that Louisa, as *his* daughter, has a special relationship with him. *Neither* understands why Louisa, as she gets older, identifies much more strongly with her stepmother than with her father. Both parents constantly underestimate the intelligence of their children, their ability to sense the moods of their parents, to see through their insincerities and hypocrisies. Nevertheless the impression gradually built up over the novel as a whole is of the negative, destructive effects of the parents' perpetual assault on the innocence and credulity of the children—the seemingly inexhaustible fund of goodwill they have towards their parents—in the claustrophobic environment of the home. It is in the daughter, Lousia, that Christina Stead analyzes most closely the scarring effect of her parents' unceasing war of attrition. As Louisa grows into adolescence, she loses the resilient capacity of the younger children to simply accept the strife between her parents as an inevitable fact of life; her innocence gives way to intense personal suffering, as she struggles to understand the meaning of the wasted energies in her parents' lives, and searches for some alternative. The novel ends, on a question mark, with her decision to leave home altogether; like Teresa Hawkins, she has become one of Christina Stead's questers.

Some recent criticism of ***The Man Who Loved Children*** has tended to approach Henny and Sam with a kind of moral balance sheet, to fix on one or the other the whole responsibility for the failure of their marriage. Such approaches have ranged from appallingly sexist objections to Henny's 'slovenliness', her failure to be a 'good wife and mother', to the more plausible argument that Sam's liberal American platitudes are the expression of a totalitarian personality. Both reactions, I think, miss the main direction of the author's sympathies, and the ways in which her unsentimental judgments of character operate.

Sam, in fact, has two personalities that are ultimately incompatible, just as he speaks in two quite different languages; the high flown proselytizing rhetoric in which he lectures the family on his pet theories and protests his moral uprightness under Henny's onslaughts and provocations, and the delightful fairytale world which he creates for the children with his Artemus Ward imitations. Christina Stead, disagreeing with interpretations of Sam as a totalitarian character, described him as a 'grown-up child', and it is precisely this quality of innocence that complicates his character—that explains much of his behaviour, though it does not of course explain away the havoc which it causes in the lives of others. There is a great deal of evidence in the novel to suggest that Sam *is* still a child, that his emotional development has been prematurely arrested. His asexuality is insisted on throughout the novel, and is obviously a key factor in his personality. He is disgusted and embarassed at any manifestation of sexuality—in Henny, and later on, in Louisa—and his theories about the higher purposes of sex, marriage and the family, which so incense Henny, are obvious rationalizations of more fundamental feelings of guilt and inadequacy. He constantly converts life into a game, and is upset and astonished when life breaks the rules—when Henny turns on him, or he loses his job. He has a child's petulance and optimism, a child's sense of being aggrieved when things go wrong, a child's astonishment that schemes he has thought up *can* go wrong, a child's desire to see the world in terms of heroes and villains. Even his egotism has much in it of the ego-centredness of a child, just as the games he perpetually plays with the children have to be games *he* has thought up, in which *he* acts the role of leader. He remains incredibly ignorant about even the most obvious reasons for Henny's—and later, Louisa's attitudes towards him. Sam brings to the relationships he forms as an adult—as a husband, a father, and in his job—a fatal combination of generous humanitarian sentiment and personal egotism. And when his childish simplicities about Reason and Progress, about forces of Light triumphant over forces of Darkness, collapse (as they must, continually, when confronted with real situations), his egotism asserts itself in blind, ruthless ways. His behaviour is most dangerous, and most unpredictable when he feels thwarted, when he is momentarily deprived of his belief in his humanitarian idealism.

Henny's situation under Sam's authoritarian household regime is an exhausting, and eventually demoralizing, struggle for survival. The desperate strategies she is forced to adopt, as she attempts to retain some measure of personal independence and dignity in the face of Sam's consuming male egotism, range from tactical retreats into silence, or into the privacy of her own room (where she is able to create an environment which is wholly her own, mysterious and fascinating to the children) to aggressive verbal counter-attacks in direct confrontations with Sam. Like Sam, Henny is defined consistently throughout the novel by her speech; and her rhetoric is the polar opposite of Sam's enthusiastic and self-justifying abstractions. It is the rhetoric of direct and passionate personal attack, imaginatively charged with physical and sensory detail. It is partly a contrived speech, aimed consciously at puncturing Sam's ego and partly an instinctive speech, born of desperation, expressing feelings rather than attitudes. Its real significances lie not so much in the content of the words, as in the rhythms, intonations and gestures with which they are spoken. The children, early in the novel, see Sam as 'household czar by divine right', and Henny as 'the czar's everlasting adversary, household anarchist by divine right'. In its more conscious aims Henny's rhetoric is the heckler's response to Sam's pompous platform oratory—an attempt to ridicule the man by flailing out at him with a mixture of catcalls, jeers, slogans, insults, insinuations, attacks on his past, his relations, his children, his friends, anyone or anything that will serve, for the moment, to knock him off his pedestal and reveal the real man beneath the smooth public pose. The effect is often very funny; it is also deadly serious, a matter of life and death to Henny.

The bitterness and frustration of the whole of Henny's married life are released into her rhetoric. It is a protest against the slavery she has had to endure as a household drudge and child-bearing machine, the squalor she is forced to live in, the ruthlessness of Sam's success ethic and the brutalities committed in its name, and the sheer ignorance of her personal needs which his incessant moralizing betrays.

Yet despite Christina Stead's obvious sympathies with Henny throughout the novel, her authorial attitude is not the same as Henny's. Henny has a marvellous capacity to cut through the pomposities of 'Big-Me' and 'the Great I Am' in a single word or phrase. But the truth, in Henny's utterances, is overlaid with much that is sheer exaggeration or prejudice (especially her class prejudices against what she thinks of as Sam's slum mentality). She is blind to qualities of Sam's character which the author herself is careful to distinguish from their overlay of egotism and sentiment, even though Sam himself cannot. Henny sees Sam's game-playing with the children as a plot against her (which is true, but not the whole truth, about Sam's relationships with the children), and she cannot separate Sam's genuine curiosity about natural history from the crude theories he imposes on it. Sam's moral puritanism, reducing everything to the single dimension of a conflict between forces of Darkness and Light, is opposed by Henny's amoralism, her tactical lies, evasions and exaggerations. It is often difficult to tell how committed Henny is to the attitudes she expresses or how aware she is of the incompatibility of many of the attitudes and assertions caught up momentarily into the flow of her rhetoric.

This analysis of the characters of Sam and Henny has emphasized what I see as the polar oppositions in their personalities. The key point Christina Stead is making, I think, is that Sam's good intentions and generous sentiment lead him into monumental self-deceptions because of the ideological bankruptcy of the liberalism on which it is based; and that Henny's gut reactions, on the other hand, which express so much of the truth about her own situation, nevertheless exist in an ideological vacuum. The two characters are caught in a deadlock from which neither can escape; the tensions in their situation can only deepen and intensify because neither possesses sufficient understanding of its fundamental causes. The novel's analysis constantly flows outwards, then, to issues of politics and ideology, exploring Engels's proposition that the modern family is 'the cellular form of civilized society, in which the nature of the oppositions and contradictions fully active in that society can be studied'. The character in whom the possibility of change rests, at the end of the novel, is Louisa, whose rejection of the family life she has experienced is feeding into a conscious search for an alternative.

Cotters' England, Christina Stead's most recent novel, is a strange, fascinating book that breaks new ground but also reveals very clear continuities with the earlier novels. It is an exploration of working class life in England, focusing on the life of one particular family in a setting which shifts between the East End of London and the northern industrial area of Newcastle and Durham. As in the earlier novels, the striking impression it creates initially has to do with the unique character of its realism, its quite unconventional way of conveying the texture of working class experience and its underlying patterns, registering its bleak economic deprivations and its complicating psychologies and aspirations in the moment by moment interaction of characters. The true centre of the novel is its analysis of character, its 'drama of the person'. But the definition of personality on which the novel is built is radically different from the conceptions of character in traditional bourgeois or socialist realism.

The novel has 'public' and 'personal' themes, but its fundamental strategy is to break down the reader's habitual tendency to see them as irreconcilable contradictions or in terms of the prior 'reality' of one over the other. ***Cotters' England*** might have had the subtitle 'why England hasn't had a revolution'; it is, almost overwhelmingly on first reading, a grim picture of apathy and stunted aspiration, and of betrayals from within the working class movement by the confusions and opportunism of many of its political leaders in the Trade Union movement, in Labour Party politics and in journalism. It is also a novel about the variety of human sexuality (especially female sexuality)—heterosexual love (within and outside marriage), lesbian love and incestuous love—a psychological analysis of the inner drives and compulsions of the characters, and of the tangle of illusions and egotisms in which they are involved. The novel's achievement, however, lies in its *complication* of what I have separated out as 'public' and 'personal' themes. Nellie Cook, the novel's main character, is never more 'personal' than when she is engaged in passionate political argument with other characters; and she is never more 'political' than when she is manipulating those who are closest to her, establishing power bases, in what she calls her 'work', in her intimate relationships with other women, with her brother Tom, with her husband George.

This effect is very much a product of quite conscious formal strategies. The novel is essentially a structure of subtle dramatic ironies, in which what characters actually do is set against what they think they are doing, in which one character's understanding of a situation is set against another's, gradually exposing their evasions, self-deceptions and exaggerations, revealing hidden or unacknowledged motivations. As in the earlier novels, there is no plot, in any conventional sense; but there is a much more clearly defined centre to the action than is usual in her novels, a greater concentration in its structure and in the writing generally. Each of the main characters—the sisters Nellie Cook and Peggy Cotter and their brother Tom—is faced with a significant change in the circumstances of their everyday lives, and the novel is an exploration of the forces which impinge on the decisions they need to make. When the novel opens Nellie Cook is living in London, as a journalist on a Left-wing newspaper, where she has involved herself in the lives of a number of working class and derelict women while her husband, a Trade Union organiser, is in Europe looking for a position that will set him up in comfort and security for the rest of his life, living parasitically on the working class he claims to represent. Early in the novel also, Nellie's brother Tom arrives in London, after the death of a woman to whom he has devoted the past eight years of his life, in a *ménage à quatre* with two other men. The third member of the family, Peggy, lives in the family home in Bridgehead, near Newcastle. She has spent a number of years in an asylum, after a disastrous love affair early in life, and now drudges resentfully in the house which Nellie and Tom had left, in their restless search for a more fulfilling life than Bridgehead's desperate poverty can offer.

In the course of the novel both parents die, and Peggy is faced with a new decision about her future. The death of Marion Ilger confronts Tom also with new decisions, and the possibility of finding some direction for his aimless, uncommitted life. But it is in the crisis Nellie faces that the novel finds its central focus. The immediate decision she faces, about whether to fight to preserve her collapsing marriage, precipitates and intensifies a conflict in her loyalties to others. The novel develops primarily as an analysis of these conflicts in Nellie's relationships, of the anxieties, needs, and beliefs which motivate her intense, destructive involvements with others. There is, then, in the novel a dramatic emphasis on character-in-action in the present—on Nellie's confused and uncertain handling of specific problems in her marriage, in her relations with other women and with Tom. But this is gradually complicated by the reader's growing awareness of Nellie's past—particularly, of her earlier life in Bridgehead—and the way it feeds into her present attitudes and feelings.

The sense of an impinging past—not only in Nellie, but in all the characters—is not given us in obtrusive documentary set-pieces, as an 'objective' history, but comes to us through the dramatic necessities of character, through their shifting states of mind and feeling. ***Cotters' England*** is a quite unconventional historical novel, its sense of history geared to the kind of realism it aims at. In the first place, Christina Stead captures a remarkable sense of history as it is simply *assumed* in the lives of her characters, referred to in casual and allusive ways; for this reason, it often comes to us, at the beginning of the novel, in fragmentary or cryptic ways—a name casually dropped, an incident alluded to. At other times it is filtered through mood and feeling, evoked in anger or bitterness or nostalgia by her characters. And eventually it emerges—in characters like Nellie and Eliza Cook (George's first wife) and Tom—as an aspect of their more conscious struggles to understand the significance of their lives, the subject of intense argument and confrontation. The historical method of the novel is very similar to its way of presenting the economic and political texture of working class life. Again, there are no set-piece descriptions and textbook analyses of economic and political conditions, no abstract moralizings. The sense of a specific environment is most powerfully conveyed, often, through the apparently casual detail of particular lives; the oppressiveness of Bridgehead, for example, evoked by the bronchitic cough which Nellie takes with her wherever she goes; or by the sense of unprecedented luxury which Tom's possession of a car arouses in Peggy, and her pleasure at being taken on a rare outing around the suburbs of Newcastle; or by the grim domestic comedy of the boiling of the chicken which Tom brings as a gift on one of his periodical visits to Bridgehead.

It is characteristic of Christina Stead's novels that one tends to remember them not in terms of neatly ordered and resolved plots or in terms of some encompassing symbolic or metaphysical scheme, but through one's recall of specific incidents and events which retain their power of immediate revelation.

—Terry Sturm

History and environment, then, suffuse the novel as part of its 'drama of the person', and not as abstractions from it. The title itself conveys the author's aim: England, in the novel, is England as it is experienced and understood by the Cotters, and the process is carried into the novel in very detailed ways. The meaning of their experience in Bridgehead, for example, is very different for Nellie and Tom and Peggy, and for George Cook and Eliza. One particularly interesting example is the novel's presentation of Nellie's involvement, shortly after leaving school and starting work in Bridgehead, in the life style and ideas of the libertarian anarchist, Jago, who established himself as a kind of cult figure among young people seeking some more stimulating and meaningful existence than Bridgehead offered. Initially, references to him are cryptic and sinister, and Nellie's reactions seem evasive and defensive. It is only gradually (in fact, not until Eliza Cook gives her account of the nature of Jago's attitudes) that we realize how potent an influence he has remained in Nellie's own life. In Jago the character of Jonathan Crow reappears, the figure of the corrupt intellectual with a seductive power over youthful or innocent minds seeking intellectual stimulus. Many of Nellie's attitudes are a mish-mash of ideas retained from her involvement with Jago: her romantic prejudices against 'theory' (especially Marxist theory) in favour of a mystique of socialism as a kind of inner inspiration of the heart, expressed in generous personal impulses of the Sam Pollit variety; her prejudices against 'the State', by which she means any political activity, as the inevitable expression of disguised personal egotisms and the lust for vengeance; her sentimental bohemianism, and her habitual labelling of Marxist intellectuals as 'philistines', despisers of culture and of the 'personal' in human relationships, concerned with merely material issues at the expense of the 'spiritual' yearnings which she sees herself as satisfying in the people she meets. 'Philistine', like the word 'middle class', is part of a vocabulary of abuse which Nellie uses quite indiscriminately to label anyone who resists the schemes of personal salvation she sets in motion.

Nellie Cook's personality is a strange mixture of elements derived from earlier characters as diverse as Henny and Sam Pollit, Jonathan Crow and Catherine Baguenault. She has Henny's extraordinary individuality and nervous energy, and her instinctive gift of vital, imaginative speech combined with Sam's exhausting loquaciousness; she has Sam's curious combination of naive innocence, blind egotism and sentimentality; and she is as predatory and destructive in her influence on others as both Sam and Jonathan Crow.

What attracts us to Nellie is our identification with her sense of desperation, and with her energies. Her life is an exhausting struggle to find an authentic identity, to establish some equilibrium between the 'perfect unions' she wishes to have with other women, with her husband, with her brother. The phrases 'perfect union' and 'incurable disease' are favourites of Nellie, and they indicate the romantic absolutes within which she tries to order her personal life: the poles of Nietzschean despair and aspiration. Christina Stead's detachment of her readers from Nellie is accomplished through a gradual exposure of the frighteningly destructive illusions to which her energies are committed. She is a character who feeds on sentimentalities without ever understanding the self-deceptions on which they are based; and they have an immediate, seductive appeal to other characters, especially when they first meet Nellie, because of the spell-binding, imaginative character of her speech (a quality which Peggy describes, with characteristic unsentimentality, as her 'sooth-saying' and 'soft talk'), and because of the surface plausibility of the ideas she dresses them up in. Nellie retains her power of conviction for others—even for those, like Eliza and Tom, who have the clearest understanding of her illusions—by her sheer, unwavering belief in *herself.*

There is a close connection between Nellie's capacity for *self*-deception and her misunderstanding of the social and political character of English working class life. Nellie sees herself as a person gifted with a quite unsentimental, realistic understanding of society, and of the forces motivating individual lives; and her life is an intense, totally involving commitment to a personal vision which she feels could transform these lives, making actual the 'perfect' relationships she wants with others. Initially, her attitudes appear plausible because they are clothed in a language appealing for self-awareness, an understanding of the 'personal' in human relationships, and an uncompromising rejection of illusions. She is fiercely antagonistic to what she sees as the abstractions of armchair socialism ('tailoring reality to fit theory'):

> All right, loves! I respect you for your principles; but when you're down in the blood and muck, you've got to feel with them that never read a bloody book in their lives and don't know the name of Robert Peebles, nor what I write, to our shame. What is the good of theory? It's not good for you, Lize; you've got the Bridgehead gray in your lungs; you need sun and air and a rest. It's good for George to climb with. Theory is to climb up into the fresh air above the working class. You can be running your extramural forums from now to kingdom come, but it's they who must fight for themselves and you too, without theory. I don't mean you Eliza love, I mean them. It makes me wonder if they're not all playing games, the men. They sit there in their swivel chairs and swop book talk and elbow each other for a seat on the council and only take an interest in an evicted family if they've got a photographer with them. Not one word of their theory can put a roof over that family's heads. There are evicted families living in halfway houses, council barracks, crying for their father, for the other half. Will ye come and say, Here's no father, but here's a good hunk of socialist theory to cheer ye up? This'll put meat in your stone broth. I don't understand you, Eliza, and you a working woman. Wage rises are got with strikes, I said to him. They've got to go out like bloody pirates with a knife between their gap teeth to get anything; and they get it and ye sit there and applaud, the self-satisfied pack of you, leading the working class on your bottoms.

Much of what Nellie says here is true, but it is mixed up with prejudices and absurd generalizations which make for an extraordinary confusion in her attitudes and judgments. Her comments are certainly true of George Cook (and they carry a lot of weight as a general indictment of British labour politics), but they are quite untrue of Robert Peebles, against whom Nellie is ostensibly directing them here. Because she rejects the need for 'theory' in such absolute terms, Nellie often commits herself to the most absurd propositions without ever realizing how absurd (and how 'theoretical') they are. The attitude to theory expressed in the long speech above, for example, leads her to present socialism as a religious mystique, in the same argument with Camilla and Eliza:

> "You can't teach socialism, Camilla; it comes to you. It comes to one, not to another; it comes by mysterious ways. It is the way; but you can't point it out to another."
>
> Eliza and Camilla burst out laughing.
>
> Nellie said solemnly, "You know if you've got it in you, that's all."

And earlier in the novel, her personal antagonism to the editor Robert Peebles as 'a man with a machete clearing a path for himself through a jungle of other egotisms and cutting down the innocent wild creatures in his path', produces a Conrad-like rejection of all political action:

> isn't any man-made law an iron hand reaching out to squeeze us poor creatures into faceless mud? Isn't any political action the same as fascism, the same as repression? You must repress someone to get your way. Isn't it a paradox, pet? Don't let your regret for human suffering turn you into a Philistine; you'd lose my respect. For your intelligence and sensitivity; for the unusual individual I thought you.

One of the major ironies unfolded in the novel, then, is Nellie's intensely personal commitment to abstract (especially, Romantic) theories of life, which she never pauses to examine because she is never aware of them as abstractions. Her mystique of socialism is one such belief; but this is simply one aspect of a much more all-embracing romantic mystique which she projects obsessively onto life, which becomes a kind of Procrustes bed for ordering and evaluating her experience. Despite her assertions to the contrary, Nellie is an incorrigible sentimentalist who romanticizes the situations of everyone she comes into contact with—especially the situations of working class and destitute women. She continually converts the lives of the women she knows into the terms and metaphors of romantic tragedy, in the Nietzschean sense, and offers her own passionate aspirations and her saving personal vision as a solution. She continually submerges the hard social and material facts of their oppression and poverty in metaphysical absolutes, in a manner reminiscent of Sam Pollit's universal conflict of Forces of Light and Darkness. In Nellie's tragedy, the tragic characters are sensitive, isolated, innocent Individuals reduced to despair by a corrupt rapacious Society, passive suffering victims of the egotisms of others (especially men—though she sees Marion Ilger as the female predator preying upon her brother Tom's innocence); and her role, as heroine, is to protect their innocence, directing its thwarted energies into the 'perfect' relationships only she can offer.

Nellie's attitude to her sister Peggy in Bridgehead is an example:

> "I feel so guilty towards the poor pitiful creature. Ah, the poor thing. The frail white camellia. It's a house of storm. I have bloody dreams; and I wake up in terror, all in a sweat, every night in a sweat, dreaming she's over the edge. The beautiful thing that she was, an early bloom, pure white, and now like a flower crushed by a rough hand, only a dark shred where there was a miracle."

The picture of Peggy which Nellie paints here is partly an attempt to assuage her own feeling of guilt at having led her younger sister astray early in life, and partly an expression of pity for the innocent victim of male brutality. (The image of the pure white flower 'crushed by a rough hand'—and many others like it which Nellie uses throughout the novel—convey an explicit sense of men as sexual aggressors and of women as naturally pure, virginal and innocent. Nellie's mystique of the feminine is yet another of the abstractions she imposes on the real facts of women's oppression.) However the actual Bridgehead scenes which recur throughout the novel present a very different Peggy from the vulnerable, fragile figment of Nellie's romantic imaginings. Peggy emerges, in fact, as the toughest and most resilient of all the Cotters, a character with a quite unsentimental determination to make the best of unpromising circumstances. Despite the appearance she gives of being completely tied down in the decaying family home, it gradually becomes clear (as Tom discovers on one of his visits to Hadrian's Grove) that she has developed a vigorous independent, secret life outside the family; and Peggy's final scene in the novel (after the death of Mrs. Cotter) in which she ruthlessly manoeuvres the ageing Uncle Sime out of the house he's lived in and paid the rent of for forty years, into an old men's home, carries an irony which would be quite lost on Nellie.

Not surprisingly, Peggy's no-nonsense, iconoclastic temperament gives us aspects of Nellie's character which none of the other characters sees in quite the same way. She sees Nellie as 'the spitting image of Pop Cotter', always, like her father, 'wanting to be the star performer':

> "I know Nellie," she said, beginning her sing-song, "I know what's going on, man. He's [George Cook] as indifferent as a block of wood and Nellie feels she's doing us a favour giving us a notion of what real life is like: not the life of ghosts in this house which we've all led and you lead too, Tom, for you're not a real man, like the others. I know ye all. Nellie always was an exhibitionist: there's nothing she won't do to be cock o' the walk. I see into ye all, man. Ye never pulled the wool over my eyes, though I had to sit back and pretend to know nothing when ye were all soothsaying."

Peggy's description of Nellie is not the whole truth about her, but what she does recognize is the element of pose Nellie has inherited from her father, and the dangerous egotism on which it is based. Its major victim (in the full sense of the word) is Caroline Wooller, whose relationship with Nellie provides one of the main actions running through the centre of the novel.

In the development of this relationship the full destructiveness of the illusions on which Nellie's romantic idealism is based is gradually revealed. When Nellie first meets her, Caroline is living alone trying to work out difficult problems in her personal situation: feeling the pressure of possessive middle class parents, she has left her husband in America and returned to England, not knowing quite what to do. She feels attracted (like Nellie earlier in her life) to the idea of establishing an independent career for herself as a journalist. Nellie, however, sentimentalizes Caroline's situation from the start, in terms which we later recognize as characteristic (as Tom accuses her, 'You have to keep thinking to yourself that there are people for whom everything is finished'). She sees Caroline as a 'beautiful soul' who in her innocence and ignorance 'believes in the world, wants the world to be beautiful', who for this reason is doomed to know only 'the tragedy of failure and the dead end on the lonely road'. The scheme of personal salvation which she sets in motion—the conversion of Caroline to her own vision of the true way—

produces a long, exhausting struggle in which Nellie's sheer determination and her ruthless manipulation of Caroline's life gradually break down her resistance. What Nellie wants to offer Caroline is 'a great friendship, the perfect communion'; but it is offered in terms which demand an exclusive, totally self-sacrificing commitment on Caroline's part:

> My great truth is freedom from illusion, from lies, deceptions, from hypocrisy, from all those shameful loves, the opium of the heart. I want them to come to me and learn, come to me; I can teach them that there is only one way, and they must find it in pain, but I can help.

Nellie's manipulation of Caroline's life is a constant attempt to cut her off from any meaningful relationships with others. She browbeats her into rejecting any possibility of going back to her husband ('That's a terrible confession . . . of weakness, inferiority, of needing the superior conquering sex'), persuades her to give up jobs, ridicules her attempts at writing, and adopts desperate stratagems to break up an incipient relationship with her brother Tom. Tom sees her as trying 'to dangle a whole human being' on 'a little twisted spider thread of sympathy':

> However fast she makes connections with real things, and real people, you cut them away one by one, and soon the whole spider web will be adrift.

Above all there is Nellie's incessant, spell-binding talk, day and night, alternately vehement and coaxing, angry and affectionate, its northern croon laced with chicks, pets and sweethearts, exhausting Caroline emotionally and physically, demanding that she Introspect and Confess—acknowledge her defeat in a world dominated by satanic male forces—and insinuating her 'two solutions' to the 'incurable disease' of life: love and death. The struggle reaches its climax in a scene in which Caroline acknowledges that the world has been torn away from her and Nellie has a fantastic Nietzschean vision of herself as a great leader:

> Nellie was incapable of saying anything, her face shining with the light of a planet. She asked in an intense low tone, controlling her excitement. "Will you die for me, Caroline? Because you understand death through me? It would be a great triumph. It would set me on my path. Your life would go along with me in me. Have you a great passion for me, Caroline? Will you do what I say? What I need is the confidence your beautiful sacrifice would give me. Then I would be the thing I am meant to be, the great leader—some saw in me. When I was a child, they saw it in me. My brother believed in me then; he knew he had nothing and I had the power. But he wandered away from me, inconstant and incredulous. But you believe. If you made the sacrifice I would look straight in the face of my destiny. Sacrifice, the blood of one dear and devoted—"

Caroline's suicide, and the events leading up to it, contain some of the most powerful writing Christina Stead has ever achieved—especially the moment in which Nellie, dressed in her brother's cast-off airman's suit and holding Caroline in a passionate embrace, physically forces her to witness, as if revealing to her the final depth of human depravity, a scene of naked orgy among the women she has invited to her home for a weekend party. Caroline's subsequent death, however, is not a submission in Nellie's terms; in fact she sees through Nellie's theories, *as* theories, and knows that she is being manipulated. Nellie's predatoriness is more insidious than this because it eats away at Caroline's personality, eroding her confidence in herself, depriving her of a sense of identity—its effects gropingly defined by Caroline in her suicide note as 'dishonour', a loss of self-respect. Images of Nellie, throughout the novel, as a kind of demonic spirit—an 'imp of Satan' or spellbinder or sorceress dabbling in the souls of others—are given a specific psychological force in a passage like the following, as Caroline walks towards her death:

> Caroline now floated along over-shadowed by the lank, hobbling stride of the woman who had taken her up, haunted her, and ruined her. She was walking away from her, but Nellie was someone she carried with her, as you carry a bad parent always with you; Nellie had got into her being, like the knowledge of drunkenness. There had been nothing in Bridgehead, Nellie said, to satisfy their youthful intellectual and moral hungers, so they had taken to drink, vice, unbridled chaotic speculation and gnawing at each other. Hunger will prey on garbage, rather than be extinguished in death. But Nellie had not called it garbage, she called it knowledge.

Nellie's appearance in Tom's airman's suit at a moment of climax in the novel emphasizes the crucial importance of her relationship with her brother; and the novel's exploration of this relationship expands on issues raised in the characters of Catherine and Michael Baguenault in ***Seven Poor Men of Sydney.*** There are curious complementary qualities in the characters of Nellie and Tom, as if each is the *alter ego* of the other, as if, at times, each is striving to compensate for what they see as the inadequacies of the other. The relationship between Nellie and Tom places at the centre of the novel the theme of sex role conditioning.

Nellie is the older sister; Tom the younger brother. Yet in much of their behaviour it seems that they are acting out roles in which Nellie plays the experienced, protective older brother while Tom plays the innocent, passive younger sister. If Nellie is, as Peggy says, 'the spitting image of Pop Cotter', Tom has always been (according to Nellie) a 'mother's boy', an only son given special treatment:

> She made him what he is, afraid of his own shadow, starting at every word, full of deceit and shamming. Aching for love, for she never had a true love, the poor body: and he learned that of her too. He was always mother's boy. She adored him, Eliza; it was pitiful. She grovelled before him, as she did before every man of her own . . . So you can see how it is that now he says, All I ask is to be let alone. I'm a man who is better alone.

The strongly 'masculine' elements in Nellie's character—her clothes, her mannerisms, her aggressive manipulativeness—are balanced by predominantly 'feminine' elements in Tom's character—his sexual passivity, which attracts the maternal affection of characters like Eliza Cook and Camilla Yates, and his narcissism. If Christina Stead is exploring, in the personality of Nellie, the implications of a male-centred romantic Nietzscheanism, Tom's personality, I think, offers its obverse side in the romantic pathology of the *femme fatale.* Tom has a curious kind of fascination to women, who are lured into relationships with him by his delicate physical beauty, his amiability and 'poetic' temperament, his appearance of being transparently simple and vulnerable—only to find, beneath the surface, an uncompromising hardness and coldness.

The closeness of the relationship between Nellie and Tom enables them to understand each other in ways that other characters (apart from Eliza Cook, and Peggy) only glimpse. Just as Tom sees most clearly into the predatory nature of Nellie's behaviour, so Nellie is the character who has clearest insight into the manipulativeness underlying Tom's facade of injured, vulnerable innocence, who insists (even when contradicted by Eliza) that he 'makes experiments with human beings', 'killing souls with his purposeful evasiveness'. Whereas Nellie's manipulativeness is aggressive and personal, demanding exclusive commitments to herself and to her private vision, Tom's manipulativeness operates in very different ways. Tom has *no* vision, no personal commitment to anything, and appears to make no demands on anyone (Nellie describes him as a 'nonresister': 'It's almost a principle with him. Life happens to me, he says.')—and he has developed a quite conscious role to preserve this illusion of freedom from deep involvement with others. Its effects, in the relationships he forms with others, are as destructive as Nellie's; he toys with the affection of others, stimulating commitments and loyalties, which he is never able or willing to reciprocate.

Tom's inability to feel sexual passion is clearly central to his fear of intense involvements with others, and its repression is associated, in his relationships with marion Ilger and with his former wife Estelle, with death and disease. Other women—like Frida, Eliza and Camilla Yates—all gradually come to realize that the attractive surface Tom offers women is a mask; as Frida says:

> "Yes, there is something funny about you. Part is very, very cold, stone cold. I keep feeling the stone cold. That's very unusual in a man. Generally, you can feel heat, like an oven."
>
> She looked to see if she had offended him. No; he was pleased. It was as if he had been waiting for those words.

The most crippling effect of Tom's game-playing, in the novel, is its contribution to Caroline's suicide. He involves Caroline in one of his detached flirtations, taunts Nellie with the possibility of his marrying Caroline, and in this way precipitates the crisis in Nellie's struggles to 'save' her. Caroline is as much a victim of Tom's game-playing as she is of Nellie's manipulation.

Tom's sexual inadequacy with other women is the result of his repression of a sexuality directed primarily at Nellie. And it is also this deep sexual attraction which underlies the conflict in Nellie's behaviour towards him—which makes her see him as both innocent and corrupt, continually appealing personally to his 'purity' and 'loyalty', the 'communion' and 'perfect understanding' they once had, while presenting him to other women as a man with 'no real heart', incapable of passion, feeding on illusions, trifling with their affections. Perhaps the strongest single motive behind her belief that women need protecting from men is her fear of being betrayed by Tom. Estelle accuses Nellie of breaking up her marriage to Tom ('I never had a husband. You made him yours early.') However Tom's greatest betrayal, for Nellie, has been his relationship—extending over eight years—with Marion Ilger; and even after her death, when Tom once again comes within Nellie's ambit, she sees Marion as a vampire still feeding on him—ironically, in ways in which she herself feeds on others. Tom's strange relationship with Marion, however, is not quite the betrayal which Nellie believes it to be; his devotion to her only develops when he finds out that she is dying, and it is not a sexual attraction so much as a sublimation of his sexuality in a developing sense of mission as a great healer (again, here, there is a counterpoint with Nellie's sense of mission as a great leader). Tom's sense of mission, obviously very tenuous even when he first meets Nellie after Marion's death, does not survive Nellie's pressures for long, and Tom remains, throughout the novel, an aimless, drifting character, weaving casually in and out of the action, caught up in Nellie's schemes and forming his own temporary, unsatisfying attachments. Above all, as in so much of Christina Stead's fiction, one remembers Tom as a voice, spinning endless tales about 'horrifying experiences'.

Tom's tale spinning 'defines' his character in a kind of counterpoint to Nellie's passionate personal speech. The anecdotes all have, at their core, a description of macabre or violent incidents, but they are told by Tom with a strange detachment and enjoyment, with an eye to the effect his own detachment from the horror might have on his listeners. And they have the same kind of spellbinding effect, initially on women, as Nellie's more personal, persuasive speech. The 'horror' stories are very much part of the game Tom plays with women—an attempt to present himself as a vulnerable innocent in a malign universe, in need of sympathy and understanding. Perhaps, also, they are his way of coping with the actual destructiveness of his own and Nellie's world. One imagines that, for Tom, Caroline's history will be passed on as yet another of the 'horrifying experiences' that had once happened to him; just as, for Nellie, Caroline's suicide will simply confirm her romantic belief in a universe hostile to its most sensitive, individual spirits.

Cotters' England is, I think, extremely pessimistic in its analysis of social and sexual alienation, in the impression it creates of energies thwarted and misdirected. Its most powerful image, in personal relationships, is the scene, in the Palace of Mirrors at the fairground, where Nellie and Tom dance together, fascinated by the images of themselves—'distortions of human beings'—which they see reflected in the mirrors around them: 'in the dusty narrow corridor, a ballroom of the strangest people, but always the same two'. The ending of the novel reveals Christina Stead's remarkable control over the difficult realism she strives for. Tom drifts out in much the same way as he drifted in; and there is a sudden narrowing of focus on one of the 'minor' characters, Mrs. McMahon, a victim of George Cook's vanity and arrogance, who provides new weight for Nellie's sense of women's oppression in a man's world. It is a measure of our identification with Nellie's struggles that we see her decision to join George Cook in Europe—to settle for marriage—as an escape and a defeat, even if only a temporary one. Shortly before she leaves, Nellie impresses Eliza with one of the most passionate and persuasive statements of her romantic credo in the novel; it is typical of Christina Stead's creative 'drama of the person' that Nellie's voice should be allowed to establish her personality, at the end of the novel, in such irreducible terms, and yet remain so 'placed' by the dramatic revelations of the novel as a whole:

> "How do I see life, Eliza? With a rosy tender veil. It's the palpitating heart of life, I must put in, with the language of love. I feel it, the rich thing like a rose. I've had terrible experiences, no one can ever know. I've had strange things happen to me, strange loves that nothing can explain, that can only be explained in their own terms, in terms of themselves. Yes, darling, I can express it all to you, it's strange, you're my only friend. We only go two by two and my brother is not as fine as you, Eliza, sweet angel," she said pausing for breath and having lost hold of the idea. She mused for a while in the dark and went on, "Loves! That is what hasn't been expressed, Eliza love, and it is hard to express: love, If I could express it, for that's the message in me, I'd be far beyond them with their rule-of-thumb explanations of the universe. What can Marxism say to a lover, or to a mother? Or what can Einstein? Aye, he can say more, for there's something wonderful and beautiful in the idea that we have an attic window only, open on the swamp of stars."

(pp. 9-34)

Terry Sturm, "Christina Stead's New Realism: 'The Man Who Loved Children' and 'Cotters's England'," in Cunning Exiles: Studies of Modern Prose Writers, *edited by Don Anderson and Stephen Knight, Angus and Robertson, Publishers, 1974, pp. 9-35.*

Rebecca West (essay date 1982)

[*West was a prominent English novelist and critic during the mid-twentieth century. Her early criticism was noted for its militantly feminist stance and its reflection of West's socialist concerns. Her first novel,* The Return of the Soldier *(1918), evidences a theme that entered into much of her later work: the psychology of the individual. West's greatest works include* The Meaning of Treason *(1947), which analyzes the motives of Britain's wartime traitors, and* Black Lamb and Grey Falcon *(1942), a record of the author's 1937 journey through Yugoslavia. In the following essay, she examines Stead's evocation of the political and literary landscapes of the 1930s in England in* For Love Alone *and France in* The Beauties and Furies.]

Several novels by Christina Stead have the value of being a good deal better than most works written by her contemporaries; and two seem to me to have a special historical value. One is ***For Love Alone*** and the other is ***The Beauties and Furies***; and they owe their distinction to the same cause. The first novel is about an Australian girl who came to England in search of the sexual equality she did not believe then existed under her native sunlit skies. It was written very soon after Christina Stead had done that very thing (in 1928, when she was twenty-six). The second novel ***The Beauties and Furies*** describes the lives of some English people in Paris, to which she moved later, but still with a fresh eye.

The dates of these books explain, I think, their peculiar vividness. The features of a landscape a writer has known continuously since childhood often fade quickly from his or her perception. The memory has so often recorded them that it gets bored and puts them at the back of the store-cupboard. (Borges, asked to suggest the origin of some pictures of a desert country, correctly guessed they were painted not by explorers but by the natives of such territory because there was not a camel in sight. This, he felt sure, meant that the painters had got their fill of camels early in life and no longer noticed them.) But London and Paris were freshly imprinted on the retina of Christina Stead's memory. Down they went on the page, colours bright, edges sharp. For the reality of these places was actually at odds with the images of them which she had formed when she was a child at home. That is what makes ***For Love Alone*** so poignant. It is a magnificent achievement. It is like a scene out of a great play: like, indeed, a very famous scene out of a very famous play. In the living-room of her Australian home her father, an elderly man of the King Lear kind, harangues his motherless children, adolescent boys and girls. He nags them until Teresa, who is nineteen, answers him with the spirit Cordelia lacked, and shows that that poor girl was in the right, for it did no good. The old man stands up half naked, and harangues his ill-dressed and frustrated daughters with a rambling speech about the glory of the male sex in general and of himself in particular, and of the pain it gives him to have daughters who are not beautiful and triumphant, though his sons are not that either. He swells up like a bullfrog with hatred of his daughters' ungracious femininity—and indeed they are not looking their best, they have no decent clothes, and are so far as they or anyone else can see, completely futureless. Regarding that, he remarks as Teresa begins to set the table for a wretched meal:

> 'I personally,' he said in a low, vibrant voice, 'cannot stand ugliness. Trees. I worship beauty,' he said throwing his limbs about in a frenzy of enthusiasm, 'and all my life I have served her, truth and beauty.'
>
> Teresa took the worn damask cloth out of the side-board drawer and set five places.

The two daughters of this monster are abundantly aware that they are going to be incarcerated with this rhetoric until they die, unless they get married, and that will not be worth doing unless their husbands have some property and intelligence. But men of property pursue brides who are attractive, well-dressed and cheerful, and the two girls are haggard and their clothes disfiguring. Still, Teresa knows she is intelligent; and though that is not an asset in the group to which she belongs, she has the feeling that somewhere things will be different. Australia had, when this book was written, quite a promising culture, but that culture had come from England. And she supposes that if she could get to England she might be respected for her brains, and even, which is of immense importance to her, be loved for it by some cultured man.

Therefore, and for no other reason, she falls in love with Jonathan Crow, a student at the local university. She falls in love with him for no other reason than that he is about to leave and go to study in England. He does in time talk vaguely of love to her, and so she follows him as soon as she can. But when she gets to London it is not as she had hoped, Greece in the days of Plato, but more like the London of Dickens (who had died sixty years before). It is a sinister and dirty place, and Jonathan now matches it. He does not care a fig about his women being intelligent; he wants them to be sexually available, and he really cares for nothing else. Fortunately in the end he explains this so clearly that she cannot miss the point. She then has the luck to meet a man who appreciates her spirit and her willpower, and is delighted to marry her and give her all she wants, even to the point of shortly afterwards encouraging her to be unfaithful to him with a young man who is oscillating between London and the Red Front in the Spanish Civil War. It is here that we get a glimpse of the past which only the strongest, most muscular writers can give. Nobody who was alive at that time and was anti-Franco can doubt that we were on the right side: on the evidence of what appeared at the time, it was certainly not right to break the peace, to accustom governments and their people to resort to bloodshed on the pretexts that were put forward. But it is very difficult to paint a picture of the people that fought on the Left or the Right as volunteers in that war. Looking back on the evenings, they were filled to the brim with controversial talk; but what was it about? It is hard to remember. One remembers only the passion. People agreed with each other. People quarrelled with each other. And people went back to the front and were killed, or returned. The words have vanished into the air. They were not the same as the words in the books and pamphlets that were written so carefully and published so neatly. No impression remains except the emotion, which now seems to have been too commonplace to be important, and seemed to convey what had to be said to pass the time on the eve of battle. This book (and portions of the writings of Rosamund Lehmann) suggests that this talk was not remembered because it was too commonplace, too vague, too much the repetition of what the speakers had recently read. The same impression is given by Christina Stead in some chapters of ***For Love Alone,*** where the warriors talk about love as if their power of precise expression had been shot away. This was quite unlike the Second World War, when many people talked and talked, with dialectic skill, out of immense stored knowledge. It was not so at the time of the Spanish Civil War, and Christina Stead proves it to us.

The Beauties and Furies is not nearly such an impressive work, but it gives a sensitive picture of France as it was in 1930, when France, having struggled out of the First World War, was approaching the Second. This was a time to which Proust's great work was still holding up a mirror that showed France as a place where the cocotte and the exhibitionist homosexual and the great writers and the great painters and musicians, and the most bogus or the most authentic aristrocrats, were all in their ways performing brilliantly. The case of Colette was as remarkable. Accomplished writer, vaudeville mimic, a manufacturer of cosmetics, wife to a bunch of highly differentiated husbands—she was typical of the grotesquerie of the age; and there was certainly nothing quite like it to be seen in England. In ***The Beauties and Furies*** Christina Stead describes how an Englishwoman, wife of a London doctor, elopes to Paris with a working-class Englishman who is a rising left-wing historian, and they both become intoxicated by the atmosphere. She becomes pregnant, the husband is sent for; there are agonies and embarrassments reduced only by the fatigue of participating in immensely protracted conversations, and as much refined by subtle conversation and good manners as if they were put through a strainer. The whole thing recalls the fiction of a forgotten but not untalented French writer, Paul Morand. It is all not the real thing, but has nevertheless some connection with reality. There is indeed a curious *trompe l'oeil* effect, due, I think, to the fact that this was not pure French that Christina Stead was looking at; these were the days of the invasion of Paris by American expatriates, seen here by a woman writing in English but who was Australian. It is a fantasy based on fragmentary impressions of a real country and fragmentary dreams of an imaginary country.

Is it then something crazy? No, not at all. It correctly records the look and feeling of France at a moment when fancy had taken over from imagination, with a beautiful sense of the effects that could be got from the bric-à-brac that was in truth lying around. For example, scattered through the pages of this work is a most accomplished account of an old lace-making business that was carrying on its commercial side in the heart of Paris. This book is not a literal transcription of the real Paris at any time; but it is a charming and, in technique, subjective picture of what several ancient historical epochs had left behind them when they had finished picnicking beside the Seine. There is even some florid fairy-taleish writing which recalls the Belgian writer, Maeterlinck (this reminds us that Anatole France also enjoyed the mystical tales of Hoffman). How exciting is the art of Christina Stead who can not only recall for us the beginning of *King Lear,* but also render a 1930 skirt dance with real gaiety. (pp. 31-3)

Rebecca West, "Christina Stead—A Tribute," in Stand Magazine, *Vol. 23, No. 4, 1982, pp. 31-3.*

Lorna Sage (essay date 1982)

[*In the essay that follows, Sage assesses* For Love Alone *as a "heroic fantasy" that features a female in the typically male role of the epic quester.*]

Christina Stead's exorbitant imagination makes demands

we have not yet come to terms with. Her idiom seems often as alien as it is impressive—a tribute to her originality and power as a writer, doubtless, but a backhanded one, since it's partly because her work was so thoroughly neglected, so unassimilated that she is hard, still, to take. With a less ambitious writer, it would matter less but in reading her now it's an abiding irony. Her passionate craftsmanship should have been part of the diet we grew up on: major writers need re-readers. There's an image in ***For Love Alone*** (1944) that anticipates the tragi-comic theme of riches gone begging—Malfi's miraculous trousseau, contributed by Miss Wetherby-Smith. It may be the apotheosis of lingerie, but it's also a desperate embarrassment, the gift of an idealist dreaming of consummation to a defeated young woman who's settled for a lot less.

Randall Jarrell, writing on ***The Man Who Loved Children*** (1940) in 1965, suggested that the failure and disappearance of that novel damaged Stead as a writer, made her build in defeat:

> When the world rejects, and then forgets, a writer's most profound and imaginative book, he may in spite of himself work in a more limited way in the books that follow it . . . The world's incomprehension has robbed it, for twenty-five years, of ***The Man Who Loved Children***; has robbed it, forever, of what could have come after ***The Man Who Loved Children.***

For Love Alone was her next book, and though Jarrell seems to me wrong about the loss of scope, he's right that a new consciousness has entered the writing. Most obviously, in the fact that ***For Love Alone*** weaves its epic ambitions into a mock-naive 'first novel' format (a young woman's entrance into the world): Christina Stead digging into her hope chest, taking stock. As a novel about beginning—beginning *again*—it's a good way into her work, complete with defiant ironies.

In the opening scene, nightmare Sam from ***The Man Who Loved Children*** has been re-christened Andrew Hawkins, and has been re-placed, along with his motherless brood, in an Australian setting, the 'Fisherman's Bay' of Stead's first novel, ***Seven Poor Men of Sydney*** (1934), the Watson's Bay of her own adolescence. These steps back towards the actual geography of her life are, however, a preface to a rich array of more or less mythic patterns. Rites of passage are the obsessive topic—'The step between being an unattached girl and getting married is so enormous, thought Teresa, how does anyone get over it? How is it done?' This banal mystery blossoms into an heroic quest. On one level it's about the doubtful project of reverse emigration—from the new world to the old—that has characterised so many 'English' writers. ('Not long ago people set foot for the colonies—the right sort of people, that is,' Doris Lessing was to write, sardonically. 'These days . . . the horizon conquerors . . . set sail or take wing for England . . . ') A further and odder layer of hints makes this passionate search into a version of the voyage of the *Beagle*: ' "If you think my life is real to me—it's only a passage," ' says Teresa, in scorn, ' " . . . To Cytherea, perhaps . . . night passage, isn't it? . . . a kind of Darwin's voyage of discovery, as the voyage to Cytherea." ' Getting married involves evolutionary researches in her own psyche, in short. Christina Stead talked of herself in a recent interview as a 'naturalist' ('I was brought up as a naturalist, and I *am* a naturalist') and ***For Love Alone*** bears out her self-description—only if you imagine cross-breeding Darwin with Venus. Teresa's voyage takes in all the old idealisms, a whole series of old-worlds-of-the-mind.

We revisit some of the timeless metaphors. Ortega y Gasset's meditations on love seem relevant: 'In loving we abandon the tranquility and permanence within ourselves and virtually migrate towards the object . . . this constant state of migration is what it is to be in love.' It's something like this primitive, restless motive that structures the narrative—much as it structures that other famously 'lost' novel of the 1940s, Elizabeth Smart's *By Grand Central Station I Sat Down and Wept* (1945). Like Elizabeth Smart, too, Stead mobilizes a mass of quotation and allusion, though her literary territory is very different—epic and romance, not metaphysical poets. Homeric echoes, for example, dominate the beginning: 'He seemed to thrust back the walls with his muscular arms; thick tufts of red hair stood out from his armpits.' This is father in a characteristically modest pose, the amorous patriarch consumed with self-love. Aunt Bea, too, is larger than life, a kind of bard who celebrates the mating customs of suburban Sydney. Her account of Malfi's trousseau (a version, surely, of the Homeric catalogue of ships?) launches the novel on its epic way. The chapter (Four) is simply titled 'She Had—':

> . . . six voile nightgowns for summer, and two ninon . . . half a dozen hand-made panties, three *crepe de Chine* and three lawn with Madeira work and hem-stitched borders . . . six dozen handkerchiefs . . . in choice arty combinations, so to speak, of navy and leaf, lilac and rust, eau-de-Nile and salmon, chaminade and ibex, Mediterranean and coral, black and chromium . . .

This bottomless bottom drawer of sensuous delights, lavished by a lonely spinster on a sullen, cynical bride, is an unbearably apt emblem of the gulf between women's sensuous imaginings and their actual lot. Aunt Bea's account of it is enough to reduce one of her listeners to taking refuge in the bathroom and banging her head on the lino. For Teresa Bea's 'miraculous descriptions of weddings and feasts long past' are a particularly galling provocation, because she is already starving on a diet of imagined plenty. Her mental inventory is a match for Malfi's treasures:

> Teresa knew all the disorderly loves of Ovid, the cruel luxury of Petronius, the exorbitance of Aretino, the meaning of the witches' Sabbaths, the experiments of Sade, the unimaginable horrors of the Inquisition, the bestiality in the Bible, the bitter jokes of Aristophanes and what the sex-psychologists had written . . . her world existed and was recognised by men. But why not by women? She found nothing in the few works of women she could find that was what they must have felt.

Women have no articulate tradition of erotic lore—their lusts are silent and impotent. 'I am certain that as I lie here now,' thinks Teresa, 'frenzied with desire and want, all women have lain for centuries, since innocent times, and never an ounce of bravado to throw off the servitude of timidity.' She imagines an academy of love, where the young learn and elaborate the languages of passion; the university she didn't attend takes on the improbable guise of a love school:

> . . . a gleaming meadow, in which beautiful youths and girls strolled, untangling intellectual and moral threads, but joyfully, poignantly, and weaving them together, into a moving, living tapestry, something into which love, the mind, the soul, and living beauties like living butterflies and early summer flower-knots were blended.

The tapestry metaphor is a glimpse of what a 'spinster' might be up to. Like Teresa's favourite but shamefully eccentric green dress 'embroidered with all kinds of things, pagodas, butterflies, geraniums' it announces her secret apprenticeship as Venus's nun, her quest for a female art of love. (These terms can be shuffled: she's also, less obviously, moved by the desire to become an artist, so that the love of art and the art of love get woven together too.)

Out of her loneliness and want Teresa generates an object—' . . . all other things were secondary to the need to leave the lonely state that galled and humiliated her as a woman and free-man. It was an accident, perhaps some early song, some tale of Britain, that made her think she could escape by sea . . . She cast about for a man to love.' A phantom candidate, perhaps at a university in Europe, has long figured on the fringes of her mind, and now materialises in Jonathan Crow, graduate and extramural guru to a fascinated bevy of frustrated women, shortly *en route* to London to take up a scholarship. Teresa, in Ortega y Gasset's useful phrase, 'migrates towards her object' in imagination, and becomes a stranger in her own life. Father, Aunt Bea, even her loved sister and her loved and hated brothers recede into shadowy distance, and the 'epic' idiom of communal rites gives way to a language of medieval romance ('some tale of Britain'). Her ordeal has truly begun.

This central section of the novel is one of Stead's most savage and sustained ironic feats—a brilliant study of the perversions of passion, and of the much nastier perversions, as it turns out, of loveless 'realism'. Jonathan Crow is eminently hateful, of course, but the important thing about him is that he exists, he survives. Indeed he knows it himself (this is the secret of many of Stead's most appalling creations) and his favourite topic is his drab, drudging career as a self-made man, a struggler from the slums with 'a knack of biological survival'. Here Stead the 'naturalist' comes into her own, setting Teresa's archaic aspirations against Crow's smug social Darwinism. We're not allowed, even for a moment, to share Teresa's vision of him. Instead he enters the novel to a ribald chorus of insults from his male university contemporaries, who understand him very well—' "Mr. Master of Arts Crow . . . back from a trip to the nearer suburbs with lectures on free love in Croydon, contraceptives in Strathfield, and sterilizing the unfit in Balmain . . . or How the Modest Man Can Ravish Women with No Cost to Himself. . . " ' The lecture he delivers to his faithful study group (men and women are 'two races with different minds'; intellectual women 'imitate men's civilisation' only to fail in their biological purpose; 'the elect of the race are going towards vanishing point') might seem ill-calculated to charm women who have sacrificed much for what education they have, least of all to charm Teresa. However, this is precisely where Crow's 'knack' comes in—he names the secret fear and shame of his audience, and without in the least compromising himself, covertly challenges *them* to make the advances: 'the restive tumultuous breed of women always did the work of passion for him.' He's irresistible to passionate auto-didacts, and, above all, to Teresa, because he calls on all the energies and desires that (ironically enough) make her heir to 'men's civilization'.

Their affair—or rather, her affair—flourishes on frustration. After several farcical and abortive encounters between her practical ignorance and his frigid expectancy, his departure for England perfects her delusion, leaves her free to play all the parts herself. As she works and starves, and saves, and reads, and writes letters, 'behaving as behaves a gallant and a brave man who passes through the ordeals of hope deferred, patience and painful longing, to win a wife', she conveniently coincides with Crow's thesis about scarecrow women, Nature's rejects. She is now dedicated to chastity, her flesh like that of a sick child, her imagination, high on fasting, decaying into visions of holy dying:

> She would make six lawn handkerchiefs with drawn thread work and Johnny's initial, on the boat. She would embroider something for him—what?—in which their history would be pathetically referred to—she would show him on a cloth, as a priest of learning in a chasuble, green, gold, and white. He could use the cloth later for his household when he had one and she might be dead. What matter if she got nothing out of it?

Not for nothing are his initials JC. Teresa's self-immolation is celebrated in a flurry of appropriated images—she is the knight in 'La Belle Dame Sans Merci', she is Death *and* the Maiden; she is (in the language now of fairy tale) the princess sewing nettle-shirts, or imprisoned thirty years in an oven.

It doesn't quite take so long. Nonetheless, the reader is made to yearn for the consummation of her folly, and her arrival in London so very exactly equipped for suicide (antipodean female dreamer as doomed species) manoeuvres one—almost—into collusion with Crow. He, after sizing her up with satisfaction, plays his part. Asked, where does she stand (he has, after all, encouraged her to join him, or hasn't he?) he answers 'You do not stand anywhere', and the words levitate out of the text as a chapter-heading, a sentence of non-existence. And she, the female Quixote, is craft adrift on a sea of 'broken and blurred images'—

> . . . the rigmarole of her buffoon Odyssey torn out of privations of which Jonathan knew nothing; this last thought she hastily put away, ashamed of all she had done, because every hour of it was only a stronger proof that she was a detestable thing, an ugly, rejected woman, distorted and lost. She was lost. It was enough to know this once.

But for a woman so expert at wanting, what is ever enough? As Teresa struggles to create her end—'I'll write about the sorrows of women . . . It will be called "The Testament of Women" . . . Or "The Seven Houses" '—we find she has found herself after all.

Her escape makes Teresa—and indeed the reader—feel like victims of a practical joke. All the ritualised self-sacrifice, so absurdly devoted to 'winning' Jonathan, has turned her into a strange, powerful woman, set her apart. Like a heroine (very like, for instance, Jane Eyre) she conjures a lover out of nowhere (absent-mindedly, dreaming like a love-adept) in the person of her American London employer, James Quick. And as if to justify her heroic fiction he's introduced in the idiom of epic:

> . . . a subtle black and white man, a prepotent, agile, clean, sweet-smelling sloven, a heady man, a sitting man, a man who loved to live by candle-light, pushed out of doors by an unspeakable greed of men . . .

And—'He loved women as equals.' The effect is shattering, and more than a little comic. Quick reduces Crow's intellectual pretensions to a succinct statement of self-interest ('The whole of organised scholarship is about promoting themselves') and his synopsis of the famous lecture about biological destinies, now written up as a 'paper', is blissfully to the point:

> Love me and the world is mine, not yours, you bastard, Bastardess. No wonder Miss Hawkins looks like Karenina after the railway accident. Crushed by a one-horse pedant . . .

And so Jonathan loses his 'knack', though (the sequence of events here gets vertiginously complicated) not before a final confrontation with Teresa, an expedition into the English countryside to an ominously George Eliotish water mill, where he nearly wills her to suicide, and she tries for the last time to salvage her old vision of her quest: ' "I wish we could live for a while a long time ago, with everyone in the century dead . . . Or to be on the high seas and go backwards and forwards, coming down with the spring floes to the Behring [sic] Sea, and back again, in winter." '

This sad, sterile prospect is banished by Quick's love, and her love for him. But it's characteristic of Stead that her creatures remain bounded (or freed, as the case may be) by the natures they've made themselves. Crow remains uncrushed by the exposure of his frigid, vicious manipulation of Teresa (' "Here I was offered a true example of masochism and also a perfect example of mythomania, and I couldn't resist it" '). Also—this is the second major shock of the 'happy ending'—Teresa in love is 'restless', vagrant, faithless. Her 'marriage' to Quick (he is already, unhappily, married) 'is the only love, but not the first and not the last', and she loves another man too, almost immediately. She is a wanderer and a spendthrift, and she spins a prodigal future out of her privations:

> . . . at present she had merely fought through that bristling black and sterile plain of misery . . . beyond was the real world, red, gold, green, white, in which the youth of the world would be passed; it was from the womb of time she was fighting her way and the first day lay before her . . . there was something on the citied plain for all of them, the thousands like thin famished fire . . .

Her 'perverse' fantasies turn out to have made her the mutant who will not merely survive, but flourish. (Crow will doubtless 'get on' too in his grubby way.)

It's a protest against 'realism', and against the acceptance of rejection. Crow's point is that he is a 'poor man' in every sense, he has accepted his poverty and glorified it as real:

> He would feel grit, see glare, all sounds would be raucous, the world hopeless and full of oppressors and haters; and everything, with thick outlines, in crude black and white, stood out like figures in a stereopticon. This vision to him was reality . . . Come down to brass tacks, the world was like that but mercifully we had to have illusions to go on living . . .

He is a Jude the Obscure gone wrong. He accepts imaginative deprivation, sensuous illiteracy (he is, we discover, actually colour-blind), and reduces nature's riches to a few shabby axioms for survival.

The novel's rejection of rejection is Stead's own statement as a writer, too. Her tapestry of echoes and allusions lays claim to an heroic inheritance. A contemporary reviewer (Desmond Hawkins in *the Listener*) noticed connections closer to home—'I can best describe ***For Love Alone*** as an Australian *Sons and Lovers* with a feminine Paul Morel'—though that seems a more tangled relationship than he implied, a *Sons and Lovers* written by Miriam's original, Jessie Chambers, perhaps, if Jessie Chambers had had genius? Lawrence certainly fascinated Stead, negatively and positively, and there are allusions to *Women in Love* in, for example, the placing of Malfi's wedding at the beginning, and the description of the way Teresa and her sister Kitty dress to attend it. At the same time, the epic echoes, the lists, the joy in language, the sheer literariness recall Joyce. Stead was, I've suggested, taking stock, as a writer who seemed to be losing out in the struggle for (literary) survival. What she came up with, in ***For Love Alone,*** was a defiantly heroic fantasy about a woman who inherits the future. (pp. 35-9)

Lorna Sage, "Inheriting the Future: 'For Love Alone'," in Stand Magazine, *Vol. 23, No. 4, 1982, pp. 34-9.*

Lorna Tracy (essay date 1982)

[*Tracy is an American short story writer and editor. In the excerpt that follows, she discusses Stead's narrative form in* The Salzburg Tales.]

The Salzburg Tales is a treasury of stories—a miscellany of types—a specimen book of all the modes of story-telling. A full range is there, embracing virtually every genre and sub-genre of the short story: sketch (both of person and of place), anecdote, jokes cunning, philosophical, and biting, legends and fairy tales and fragments, romance and folklore, horror stories, parody, burlesque myths and moralities, even serious moral tales, fables, dialogues, par-

Christina Stead on short stories:

I love *Ocean of Story,* the name of an Indian treasury of story; that is the way I think of the short story and what is part of it, the sketch, anecdote, jokes cunning, philosophical, and biting, legends and fragments. Where do they come from? Who invents them? Everyone perhaps. Who remembers them so that they pass endlessly across city life? I know some of those marvellous rememberers who pass on their daily earnings in story; and then they are forgotten to become fragments, mysterious indications. Any treasury of story is a residue of the past and a record of the day; as in Grimm, we have ancient folklore and church-inspired moralities and some tales to shiver at which are quite clearly frightening local events.

What is unique about the short story is that we all can tell one, live one, even write one down; that story is steeped in our view and emotion. The passerby who looks up and wonders why one window is lighted in a town at 3.00 in the morning and the invalid looking down who wonders why that woman comes out of the doorway so late, followed by a man more like a jailer than a lover. The short story is what everyone has and so is ever new and irrepressible.

Christina Stead in The Kenyon Review, *1968.*

ables. The book's project calls to mind thirteen-year-old Louisa Pollit's creation of a cycle in honour of a beloved teacher in which there would be 'a poem of every conceivable form and also every conceivable metre in the English language.'

The Salzburg Tales is framed, like two of its great models, *The Decameron* and *The Canterbury Tales,* within a social occasion that brings into temporary community a broad diversity of human beings. Instead of ten young aristocrats gone into the country to avoid the plague in Florence, or springtime pilgrims whiling away a journey, Stead conjures an international group of festival visitors. They are already *in situ,* in a town famous for its culture, attending open-air performances—by daylight, *Jedermann,* by evening, operas and concerts. For one week in August in the early 1930s, members of the audience and a few of the performers gather in the pleasant Capuchin woods to tell one another some forty stories under the rule of their chosen Master of Ceremonies, the Viennese Conductor. But as Ian Reid has observed, the real cohesion for such a collection of stories is not its framing device but 'the author's fascination with the manifold roots and branches of narration itself . . . , the sources and forms of fiction.'

> '. . . for the earth breeds tales and songs quicker even than weeds.'

The Salzburg Tales, to the glancing reader, may appear as informal as a moss. Inspection reveals a lacework of interlocking elements that range from philosophical problems to the mute correspondences in the depths of the human soul that only the senses can verify. Underlying the whole design is the principle of association which works as fortuitously as the ricochet of a pun. It is a form that puts out runners, sends up shoots, so that it goes by leaping—up, down, from side to side, wanting anything but a straight line. The connection between clusters of pattern at times is as thin as a single word offered in one sense, taken in another. Sometimes, as in the midst of conversation, one stops to wonder how did we get onto this subject—weren't we talking about something else altogether?

If one hasn't understood this process by the time the last story's been told one will get another chance in the Epilogue. It is late at night. The Viennese Conductor, who has served as Master of Tongues and is now tired of this chore, offers it to the Schoolboy who is watching while the Conductor and the polymath Centenarist play chess together. The latter seems hardly to be paying attention to his game. He is singing a ballad that he appears to be inventing as he goes along, something about an Arab horseman in the desert, and a city having seven gates, where the horseman's bride is imprisoned and his brother bewitched. Thus singing oblique hints in advance of his moves he threatens the Conductor's king and then his knight. On one level ***Salzburg Tales*** is a game, one that's played on a sphere instead of a plane, with precious counters of music, language, natural and artificial wilderness, cities built on stone. And nothing human is alien to it. Games—as well as the gaminess of life—figure throughout Stead's fiction. ***The Salzburg Tales*** ends with this chess game. For those familiar with ***The Man Who Loved Children*** there is an echo of it in Henny's last game of solitaire, but the awful difference is that Henny wins her cheating game for the first time and thus reaches the end of her life—for having won the game at last what is left? But the chess game in the Epilogue is never finished. The writing stops with the suggestion that the Conductor and the Centenarist will play on through the night. To prolong the game, not finish it, is the whole point of playing. Who, after all, wants a *quick* game of life, the pun notwithstanding?

The book, of course, is something more than entertaining talk and games; it is more than an analogy between the protean forms of fiction and the protean nature of life. It *is* that as well, however, and one comes to know the unique quality of each storyteller through Christina Stead's power to produce a sensuous and minutely discriminating account of the characteristics of the speaker, the place, the hour, the tale. The living essence is in the details; the art is in the selection and arrangement. One does not find value-laden exposition. Stead is far too respectful of the universe to be trapped into preaching one part of it against another. The reader, of course, remains free to draw moral conclusions.

To make such an 'ocean of story' and offer it as one's first book is to announce with a *fait accompli* that one is a writer of comprehensive ambitions. The ensuing fifty years have shown us that Stead is a force of nature, containing multitudes, constantly throwing off concentrated passages that a less endowed writer might make whole chapters of. She tosses paragraphs off as if they encumbered her unbearably—'let's be rid of this handsome, heavy thing'—and she throws some marvelous description down by the side of the road. She has always been a torrential writer and must always be plunging on. (pp. 49-50)

Reviewers in 1934 were not *over*-warm in their welcome, were, perhaps, restrained in the face of something so European written by an Australian woman. American reviewers in particular complained about 'the mannered style' and someone in *The New York Times* remarked: '[She] evidently disdains the old-fashioned rules of story-telling with their emphases on clarity and the development of suspense and climax . . . insubstantial stuff, though undeniably clever.' Here is real ignorance. The reviewer is entitled to say, 'I don't get it,' which he does say in so many patronizing words, but in addition he offers to be referee in a game of story. What he claims are 'the old-fashioned rules of story-telling' are actually as modern in relation to the antecedents of ***The Salzburg Tales*** as the prescriptions of Edgar Allan Poe ('singleness of effect,' 'moment of crisis', 'symmetry of design') codified by Brander Matthews in his immensely influential essay, 'The Philosophy of the Short Story', *Saturday Review* (London) 1884. The models for the majority of Stead's tales come from a good deal farther back, out of a centuries-long line of romancers and raconteurs in which Hawthorn and Hoffman are only late exponents.

The British press responded to ***The Salzburg Tales*** with a shade more perception. The anonymous reviewer in the *Times Literary Supplement* at least discerned in Stead 'a writer of unusual interest', while V. S. Pritchett in *The New Statesman,* though unmoved by the tales themselves, was deeply impressed by 'the intensely original commentary' that surrounds them.

Whether Stead's relation to Boccaccio and to Chaucer is as intimate as that of Sterne to Rabelais is a subject for speculation, but it is possible to argue that ***The Salzburg Tales*** is as individual a mixture of borrowed elements as *Tristram Shandy* and the result is just as much 'a wholly new thing.' In attempting to account for Stead's authority, fecundity and originality it's necessary to go back to the beginning of fiction, and here Erich Kahler's *The Inward Turn of Narrative* is helpful. Kahler traces the changes in narrative form from its beginning in the Gilgamesh Cycle to the end of the eighteenth century. The distinctive quality of the tale is the impulse to add novelty to the visible fact as dominant reality. To life that had been expressed as gesture—acts of heroism, martyrdom, reverence for the dead—the tale added something new, although in general what it added was merely a variation on traditional form. The result is 'the curious incident—preferably spiced with eroticism—meant to stimulate curiousity or excite the imagination.' As Kahler draws his line of development from *The Thousand and One Nights* through Boccaccio and company he reminds us that at the beginning of this tradition one is still very near the myth and the external formulae governing mythic elements. The first inward turn of narrative is towards the expression of the individual psyche's experiences. This first inward turn, or second stage of narrative, is one we still produce in quantities today on social occasions and Radio Four. It is pure anecdote.

Later stages contributed the moral and didactic element, principally Christian (not Christina!), which fiction soon learned to subvert, or to duck out from under altogether, leaving the story free to express meaning within itself. It was then possible to give free play to pleasure in the world and in the senses.

Is there another writer who has more prodigally spent her concentrated attention on creating animates, human or otherwise, which she then as often as not allows to disappear altogether from the text? It is a measure of how active Stead's curiosity and intelligence are, how abundant her energies.

—Lorna Tracy

Stead's particular genius, like Chaucer's, is not so much for narration as for characterization. She is a superb dramatizer, as Victor Pritchett observed. In ***The Salzburg Tales*** all the personages are presented from at least three points of view. In the Prologue they are introduced, often in groups of two or three but always as individuals, seen by the penetrating and objective eye of the author. Her observations are recorded in passages that, though brief, are full of curious detail, scientifically precise but never dry. The personages also speak with their own voices about their own lives and thus reveal themselves in all their tender subjectivity. Finally, they expose their psychological qualities through the kinds of stories they choose to tell and the manner in which they tell them. This rounded, vitally detailed and unjudgmental treatment of character, brilliantly married to the imagination, is a constant feature in Stead. She seems to be able to apply it to every sort of subject and she seems especially sensitive to whatever is bizarre, furtive, ungainly and mixed in its nature. Is there another writer who has more prodigally spent her concentrated attention on creating animates, human or otherwise, which she then as often as not allows to disappear altogether from the text? It is a measure of how active her curiosity and intelligence are, how abundant her energies. She scants nothing on earth. Nor does she cling. Once a thing is finished with out it goes. In the 1960s novella, **'The Rightangled Creek'** [one of the four novellas published under the title of ***The Puzzleheaded Girl***] she devotes herself to the delineation of a tragically deluded family that drives off in the middle of the narrative and is scarcely referred to again. The story re-inhabits itself with another set of human beings and starts over. But it starts over in only one sense, for **'The Rightangled Creek'** is as much as anything else about the character of a dell in summer, when 'the earth is breeding at every pore,' a particular and haunted bit of ground seemingly as innocent as Eden. Human beings who briefly live there are items in its fauna. The author is quite as interested in what the spider that lives under the loose plank on the bridge can see at a certain hour of the morning as anything human animates do. Like the spider, human beings disappear over night.

Here one senses another aspect of that life-view Christina

Stead developed while not asleep upon the packing crate: 'a curious feeling still with me, of terrestrial eternity . . . During millions of years, all these creatures had lived and died . . . I knew that death was necessary "for evolution to take place". But there was their frail print, they had been there.' This continual passage of individuals strained up from oceanic darkness, examined under high magnification by an artist's imagination and then returned to oblivion contributes to the characteristic 'feel' of Stead's fiction. Passages in Stead can be as elegant and formal as an atom of plankton in a drop of sea water, but she soon pours each vivid individual into a text the size of Sydney Harbour where it must get on with the odd coelacanth, the wrecks on the bottom and the water-skiers at the surface. She is Whitmanesque, yet her microcosm with its fine taxonomic distinctions, breadth of reference, and elegant lineaments also recalls that other American poet, Stead's older contemporary, Marianne Moore, first formally trained in biology. The ant on a blade of grass is 'like three drops of jet' and might have been seen so as much by the poet as by the novelist.

This feature of rapt precision 'squandered' on frail prints and vanishing individuals is to be found everywhere in ***The Salzburg Tales*** but because that book is a compendium of types such 'squandering' goes more or less unmarked. When the deaf boy in **'The Triskelion'** dies the story, which one had assumed would be his story, continues without a backward glance. One does not expect continuity of character in a collection of discrete pieces; one does expect it within the span of a single story, and one *certainly* expects it in a novel. All at once one realizes that in everything she has written Christina Stead is a breaker of literary conventions as well as a champion of tradition; her originality is deeply involved in re-animation.

'The essence of style in literature, for me,' she said in the early 1940s, 'is experiment, invention, "creative error" (Jules Romains), and change.' Stead sometimes abandons her characters so as to establish a different kind of connection from that manifest in continuity of character. Art is supposed to make sense of life while remaining more or less faithful to it. Art establishes pattern and design; life appears to dispose of pattern and design. Stead exploits the randomness of actuality and the now-conventional inadmissibility of coincidence into 'the best plots'. Hers is not the way of the Modernists nor is it quite the way of 'the nineteenth century novel' which Stead's in some respects resemble.

Stead maintains that the irrepressible will to make stories exists wherever a single human being is to be found, and that we all tell stories—or want to tell stories—to another 'in the hope of recognizing and having explained our own experience.' Genuine experience and a personal viewpoint provide the vitality of fiction. 'It isn't necessary that these stories should be artistic or follow formula or be like Chekhov or the last metropolitan fad, or anything. The virtue of the story is its reality and its meaning for any one person: that is its pungency.' Christina Stead not only admits meaning—literature's New Taboo—she admits absolute death and admits it nature's way: individual by individual with the understanding that species may continue for eons. Thus she subverts the form that carries the meaning. She undoes those neat, Poe-Matthews structures and posits another principle, a different logic altogether. It is only in fiction (and only in a certain kind of fiction) that a disregarded window washer should not return in the very last paragraph with a suggestion concerning the unknowable. Cultivated taste has been schooled by recent literary convention to reject such contingent re-appearances, to be pained to see life rush into fiction crying 'Really, universally, relations stop nowhere . . . '

Christina Stead's subtle design in ***The Salzburg Tales*** provisions the reader as comprehensively and with as many tests of his or her discrimination as ever the Redshields provided for a Poet's weekend. Everywhere in this amazing book one finds equivalents of '*The Arabian Nights* bound in oasis goat . . . the lost archives of Gortchakov bound in sharkskin.'

Let the reader choose. (pp. 51-3)

Lorna Tracy, "The Virtue of the Story: 'The Salzburg Tales'," in Stand Magazine, *Vol. 23, No. 4, 1982, pp. 48-53.*

Laurie Clancy (essay date 1983)

[*Clancy is an Australian educator, novelist, and critic. In the following essay, he examines sexuality as an economic quandary for Stead's female characters.*]

> Teresa knew all the disorderly loves of Ovid, the cruel luxury of Petronius, the exorbitance of Aretino, the meaning of the witches' Sabbaths, the experiments of Sade, the unimaginable horrors of the Inquisition, the bestiality in the Bible, the bitter jokes of Aristophanes and what the sex-psychologists had written. At each thing she read, she thought, yes, it's true, or no, it's false, and she persevered with satisfaction and joy, illuminated because her world existed and was recognized by men. But why not by women? She could find nothing in the few works of women she could find that was what they must have felt.
>
> **(*For Love Alone*)**

Ironically, it is Christina Stead herself who has to a remarkable extent redressed precisely this imbalance of which the young Teresa Hawkins complains. In two of her novels, ***The Man Who Loved Children*** and ***For Love Alone,*** she addresses herself explicitly and with a passionate absorption to the question of what it is like for a woman to undergo the experiences of adolescence and early adulthood—in the case of the latter, specifically the onset of the torments of sexual love and frustration. As I have suggested [in *Christina Stead's "The Man Who Loved Children" and "For Love Alone,"* 1980], both novels concentrate on the growth of the imagination and inner life of a young girl or woman. Collectively they offer one of the most sustained, exhaustive and intense explorations of the progress through adolescence to adulthood of a young girl, to be found anywhere in contemporary fiction.

The first chapter of ***For Love Alone*** seems consciously to pick up the theme and even narrative of the previous novel. Andrew Hawkins, it is immediately apparent, bears a striking physical resemblance to Samuel Pollit and the ideas that each expounds on the role and nature of women are almost identical. There is a further similarity in the respective relationships between the two men and their daughters, and the sense of half-smothered rebellion that the latter display. Even the similarity of names (Louisa—Teresa—Christina?) is curious.

That is not to say that Louisa and Teresa are the same person. From Chapter 2 of ***For Love Alone*** onwards Teresa quickly develops her own distinct nature; the Louisa who set out "to walk around the world" might have become something like her but there are many other people she could have become instead. Indeed, while Teresa's pride and faith in herself are as forceful as Louisa's they tend to take a less expansive, more inwardly directed form. But what links the novels is the comprehensiveness and objectivity of the author's exploration of the successive stages of young womanhood.

In ***The Man Who Loved Children,*** which deals in some detail with a ruinous marriage but is even more vitally concerned with the growing to adolescence of a complex young girl, Stead puts forward the mutual propositions of the general oppression of womanhood and the resulting formation of a kind of intuitive bond between women who would otherwise have little in common; between whom there exists even antipathy.

Totally unfitted, perhaps by nature but certainly by training and background, to run any household, let alone the kind of household that Sam wishes to arrange, Henny is clearly doomed from very early on in the novel. But if Henny is forced to retreat steadily in the war between them she leaves an heir to her rebellion in her stepdaughter Louisa. Sam, we quickly see, had not been wholly wrong in his constant suspicions of a conspiracy between the entire race of what he calls "domesticated women-animals". Despite Henny's active dislike of her stepdaughter and frequent depiction of her in animalistic images, Louisa is drawn very early towards her. Although she is of Sam's blood and not Henny's it is Henny whom she takes after temperamentally and very early in the novel there grows up between them what Christina Stead calls "an affinity of misfortune". Throughout the novel Henny hectors and berates Louisa yet the girl never exhibits resentment or regards this as unnatural. Where Sam woos the children openly, almost more like a lover than a father, Henny ignores Louisa, preferring to place her hopes in the male child Ernie, but the effect is still to draw the girl to her:

> Louisa was Henny's stepchild, as everyone knew, and no one, least of all Louie, expected Henny to love this girl as she loved her own. But though Henny's charms had perceptibly diminished, Henny's treasures, physical and mental, the sensual, familiar house life she led, her kindness in sickness, her queer tags of folk-lore, boarding-school graces, and femininity had gained on Louie . . . As for affection, Louie did not miss what she had never known. Henny, delicate and anaemic, really disliked the powerful, clumsy, healthy child, and avoided contact with her as much as she could. It happened that this solitude was exactly what Louie most craved. Like all children she expected intrusion and impertinence: she very early became grateful to her stepmother for the occasions when Henny most markedly neglected her, refused to instruct her, refused to interpret her to visitors.

Henny can never bring herself actually to like the girl and, later in the novel, the peace that descends between them does not last long: "The short entente between Louie and her stepmother was at an end". But in a way this makes the rapport between them all the more singular. Stead points to it specifically as stemming from a sense of the fellowship of subjugation of their sex, what Sam complains of as the "tyranny of tears". Where Sam fails to see his oldest daughter's apostasy, Henny senses it instantly: "Henny was one of those women who secretly sympathize with all women against all men; life was a rotten deal, with men holding all the aces. The stepmother did nothing extraordinary to bring out Louisa's sympathy, because she had left too much behind her and gone too far along her road to care about the notions of even the flesh of her own flesh, but this irresistible call of sex seemed now to hang in the air of the house". The victimized always have something in common, whatever their personal differences. This Sunday-Funday chapter ends on a note of grimly ironic hope for Henny. As Sam beats Louie and she promises "I will never forgive you", Stead tells us that "Henny, half indignant, half interested, behind the curtain, would think, 'Wait, wait, wait: only wait, you devil!' "

Henny's hope of vengeance is eventually fulfilled. As she herself steadily retreats in the war between them, and collapses finally on her first glimpse of Spa House, when, Stead tells us quite simply, "At that particular moment, Henny awoke from a sort of sullen absence and knew what was happening: her heart was breaking. That moment, it broke for good and all", so Louisa moves steadily to the forefront of the novel, her power and presence growing perceptibly as Sam tightens the screws of his repressive possessiveness. If Henny is physically and morally enfeebled, the strength of her will can still inspire her stepdaughter:

> Whenever her irritations got too deep, she mooched in to see her mother. Here, she had learned, without knowing she had learned it, was a brackish well of hate to drink from, and a great passion of gall which could run deep and still, or send up waterspouts, that could fret and boil, or seem silky as young afternoon, something that put iron in her soul and made her strong to resist the depraved healthiness and idle jollity of the Pollit clan.
>
> It was a strange affection. It could never express itself by embraces or kisses, nothing more than a rare, cool, dutiful kiss on the withering cheek of Henny. It came from their physical differences, because their paths could never meet, and from the natural outlawry of womankind.

When Henny says of Sam, "He talks about human equality, the rights of man, nothing but that. How about the rights of women, I'd like to scream at him. It's fine to be a great democrat when you've a slave to rub your boots on", the charge carries a moral authority and urgency that lifts it above the mere hysterical tirade it must have seemed to its audience, Bert Anderson. In a stark and elemental way, Christina Stead confronts us in the novel with what are for most of her female characters the basic facts of male-female relationships: the fickleness of men, a law which is quick to deprive the unfaithful woman of her children, and above all in this novel the terrible fact of pregnancy, which is regarded almost with dread by the female characters.

No novelist since Balzac has concentrated so relentlessly and exhaustively on the economic imperatives governing the structures of a society and finally even the individual lives of the citizens of that society as Christina Stead. Money is one of the most central facts in almost all her novels. It is present in the title as well as part of the theme of her first novel, is the subject of her encyclopaedic ***House of All Nations,*** plays a significant background part in both ***The Man Who Loved Children*** and (even more) in ***For Love Alone,*** where the spiritually stunting effect of poverty is graphically testified to in the person of Jonathan Crow; and is a vital concern in most of the later novels. Moreover, in several of these later novels, in which the central female characters are not idealists and strivers but rather women flailing about in a morass of sexual unfulfilment and financial impoverishment and threat, she postulates the unfashionable thesis that marriage and the financial security it can bring is an indispensable precondition of a woman's life.

If it is unfashionable, there is nothing idealized or sentimental about this view. Marriage is not, as it is in Jane Austen's novels, the natural fulfilment of love between two people, the transformation of one life into a fuller and richer, if largely unseen, one. It is rather that, given the scorn with which unmarried women are viewed in the worlds of Stead's novels, and given also the limited access that her women have to economic and educational opportunities, marriage is simply indispensable for any woman who wishes to live free from moral vilification and physical want. The few alternatives are considered, only to be dismissed out of hand.

Stead remains curiously unchanging in this belief, even as she displays the obverse side of it, the cynical manipulation of marital laws that favour women by the card-playing harpies in ***Letty Fox,*** who marry and then divorce men in order to live off the alimony they are awarded. Early in the first novel she wrote, ***Seven Poor Men of Sydney,*** Michael Bagenault accuses Mae Graham, the calculating young woman with whom he is infatuated, of marital fraud: "You're marrying an insurance policy, aren't you?". Even if it makes it clear that Mae lives in a different world from that of Stead's idealists, her reply is not unreasonable: "Why not? A woman's got to look ahead". There are really very few alternatives to what Michael sneers at as "the haven of life-long closeted connubial love" in these novels, even if that haven itself usually proves to be a delusion. When the old lady in **"The Musical Critic's Tale"** from ***The Salzburg Tales*** advises a young woman against marriage, Stead records the response without comment: "The young girl smiled incredulously".

In ***For Love Alone,*** the imperative of the marriage bond is never in question. Throughout the early pages of the novel Teresa is surrounded by countless examples of surrender to it. There is her cousin Malfi, about to be married as the novel opens to a man whom she despises, because, as we discover later, she is pregnant by someone else. Or Tina, who similarly compromises. Or Teresa's sister Kitty who takes up the appointment as housekeeper to a widower in the hope that he will marry her. Or Teresa's friend Annie, who wants to leave her mother and meet some man but does not dare. Or her Aunt Di, "the family's only elderly spinster", who feels keenly the degradation and ridiculousness of her position. Or her cousin Ellen, who has been "educated out of a husband", as her parents believe, and is trying frantically to reconcile her personal dignity and standards of propriety with the risks she needs to take and temptations she must offer as well as submit herself to, in the hope of winning one. Or Queenie, married at fifteen to a man twice her age. Or even Quick's estranged wife Marian: "She never loved me—poor woman!", ponders Quick sympathetically. "They certainly have no sort of life, to get married at the first opportunity. And then to find out the vacancy . . . ".

It is true that most of the marriages Teresa observes either do not eventuate or are unsuccessful ones, and it is true also that she herself refuses to compromise in her search for the right man as a husband for fear of not winning one at all. "I hate Bernard Shaw because he says that life is compromise. It isn't. I'll never give in". It is even true that, once married, she does not hesitate long before taking another man as lover, although not without some compunction and feelings of distress. But the significant thing is that she still does see personal fulfilment and self-justification in terms of marrying a man, and that nothing in the novel contradicts this. The same is true of most of the later novels, except perhaps for the very last scene of ***Miss Herbert.*** Work, for instance, is scarcely considered as a possible alternative and what little we see of Teresa's teaching in a school for handicapped children shows merely her dissatisfaction with it. In fact, her career as a teacher is quite explicitly made irreconcilable with marriage: "We don't want to train women", the Education Department representative tells her sternly, "who intend to marry or take up some other profession", and the girls are compelled to take a kind of vow of chastity. Marriage is the only escape from "the iron circle of the home and work".

Nor is chastity an answer. The women who stay on in the Education Department, declining marriage, are spoken of in patronizing tones at best, virgins are described as "desiccated", and throughout the novel Teresa (and at times, seemingly, the author as well) voices her opinion of chastity as being unnatural, and perhaps even the sign of some kind of sublimation that will fester and lead to corruption. Early on in the novel Teresa's brother Lance is spoken of, apparently in the authorial voice, as "chaste and impure". Later Teresa tells Jonathan Crow directly, "I hate chastity. It is torture, invented to make us suffer, and I don't know why. The people who invented it do not suffer themselves. It is for us, the young. I hate it and them, they are hypocrites". In the mistaken belief that Crow is suffering as a result of his celibacy (she does not know about his affair with the French maid) she makes this diagnosis of him to Quick: "Through purity and chastity he is becoming obscene and rotten within . . . Out of excessive innocence, belief and aspiration, out of application, chastity and decorum, he has grown into a lazy hopeless man, full of lustful but important wishes".

Teresa finally enters into a marriage in which she attains emotional security and equality though at a certain price. Christina Stead shows briefly but tellingly the limitations and delusions of the man who had been presented to us earlier almost as a female ideal of masculinity, and she outlines the web of involuntary deceit which Teresa is forced to construct. When she tries to explain the reality of the emotions she feels towards him he backs away. He wants, she soon comes to understand, "a woman's love", "the intensely passionate, ideal, romantic love of famous love affairs", just as earlier he had spoken of making her "a Stael, a Recamier, a Catherine II" And so, out of her unselfish love for him, Teresa is virtually forced into playing a part and making those compromises she had earlier shunned, concealing from him many aspects of her real self. At the same time as Stead offers a detailed and sober account of the unexpected emotional luxuriousness and profligacy of Quick's love, compared to the girl's limited expectations and previous experience, she shows Teresa also becoming necessarily a part of what the author calls bluntly "the labyrinth of concealment and loving mendacity". It is a distinctly unsentimental view of marriage and all its limitations, and the implication is that it is the male who is the weaker and who needs to be pampered and protected from reality.

There are suggestions also in Stead's treatment of the relationship between Quick and Teresa of sexual inadequacy on Quick's part. We are told of Teresa that "She did not revel in the physical pleasures of marriage, but her secret life became more intense". With the introduction of the figure of Harry Girton, however, the powerful sensuality that had characterized her early in the novel returns. "Her hunger had made her insatiable", we are told, "and she was not content, as [Quick] thought she might be, with what he told her, she was not at all satisfied with the end of physical craving; she wanted to try men". Her thoughts of Girton are strongly erotic in a way that they never are with Quick: "She dreamed of him, and presently daydreamed of him, and differently from any other man till then, it was of his body that she dreamed; its secret nakedness became robed in incomparable, ever-flowing, everborn, shadowy loves and nameless pleasures, as yet without form, but not without scent and touching the secret knowledge of the body". With him she can come "to relish the abandon of the senses".

Louie and Teresa are both Nietzschean in the faith they have in the power of their own will to overcome obstacles and achieve their desires. Teresa rejects such a lesser mortal among her friends as Annie in much the same way as Louie leaves Clare behind, as creatures who fail to follow the bent of their souls. Despite their youth, each girl experiences seizures of immense power and certainty, akin almost to mystical visions, in which they feel an absolute conviction that they will attain what they desire. In Christina Stead's later novels the qualities of ardour and idealism that Louie and Teresa were possessed of are notably absent; there is a much more hard-headed and at times even cynical awareness of the way in which social and economic necessity governs a woman's capacity to experience and receive love.

Jonathan Crow in ***For Love Alone*** had postulated a connection between female views of love and the capitalist system. In one of the first scenes in which he figures predominantly he expounds to Clare his rather threadbare theory concerning the connection between female sexuality and property. It turns out to be, in essence, an intellectual rationalization of his advocacy of sexual unrestraint. "Under a different system", he explains to her, "with free love, you could see me and I could see you". Clare, in other words, could make love to both Jonathan and her own husband. "You know what I believe", he goes on disingenuously, "that monogamy is rusty, it's tied up with the old system of property, it's simply making woman man's property. If women didn't hold themselves as something apart, think so much of their bodies as property, we wouldn't have all this flesh-tearing and grinding of teeth, don't you see?" Later he makes the same accusation to Teresa: "You must own men, husbands or sons", to which she replies imperturbably, "We have no other property".

Given the presentation of Jonathan in the novel, and especially of his treatment of women, it is impossible to believe that Stead lends any credence to these ideas. Nevertheless, the tone of the later novels is at best subdued. The eponymous heroines of ***Letty Fox: Her Luck*** and ***Miss Herbert,*** the two novels among her later work in which Christina Stead most fully explores issues relating to the nature and function of women in contemporary society, both achieve a victory of sorts at the end. Letty finally catches a rich husband (though there are suggestions that as a result he will probably be disinherited) and Miss Herbert proves her ability to make a living for herself and her two children after she is abandoned by her husband—although the sense of sexual unfulfilment in the closing incident of the novel overrides any strong affirmative impulses. In these novels, as well as in ***A Little Tea, A Little Chat,*** Teresa's tentative explorations of pre- and extra-marital relationships are transformed into matter-of-fact promiscuity. And in all three novels love and money are inextricably intermingled. Discussion of one is never far from discussion of the other.

Letty Fox opens with the young narrator having just quarrelled with her most recent lover and rushed out into the streets of New York pondering the dilemma of her life:

> In general, things were bad with me; I was in low water financially and had nothing but married men as companions . . . My twenty-fourth birthday was just gone, and I had spent two hours this same evening ruminating upon all my love affairs which had sunk ingloriously into the past, along with my shrunken and worn outfits. Most of these affairs had been promising enough. Why had they failed? (Or had I failed?)

For most of its five hundred or so pages, she tries to answer that question until, just before the end of the novel, she is proposed to rather suddenly and fortuitously by one of her former lovers and accepts. ***Letty Fox*** is the first of only two Stead novels to be written in the first person and the author reportedly created the central figure in order to show her critics that she could do a different kind of woman. She is, indeed, the polar antithesis of Teresa. Despite the apparent adventurousness of her life and uninhibitedness of her sexual behaviour, Letty is at heart a profoundly conservative and orthodox woman, something she freely and repeatedly confesses, who would like nothing better than to settle down and marry, have children and serve her family contentedly. Very early in the novel she remarks that "My supreme idea was always to get married and join organized society. I had, always, a shrinking from what was beyond the pale", and again, "At this time, I had one aim—that was to marry". To her mother, she says, "I'm absolutely determined, when I find the right man, to be the perfect wife". They are claims she makes almost incessantly throughout her story and there is no reason to doubt her sincerity. Why, then, does this intelligent, attractive and spirited young woman have so much difficulty in attaining this apparently straightforward ambition?

Meaghan Morris in her perceptive introduction to the novel would have it that it is in large part because "Free love is free only for men, who have the power to withhold emotional commitment which Letty can never do once an affair is underway". This, certainly, is Letty's own view. "I was one of those marrying women who married even her casual lovers: I had a very honest instinct", she tells us, and again with regret, "I shall never be a dangerous woman; I can make men love, but I cannot make them suffer".

There is some truth to this; but it is a very partial truth, in need of severe qualification. Morris is right to acknowledge the justice of Letty's claim that "Men don't like to think that we are just as they are. But we are much as they are". But it is one thing to protest against the double standard and even to applaud the honesty and frankness with which Letty describes her own conduct and motives and another to sentimentalize them. For all Letty's alleged vulnerability, this is after all the woman whom we first see in the novel cold-bloodedly tricking a much needier woman out of the apartment she has just acquired, who competes unscrupulously for the love of any man she wants even if like Clays Manning he is committed already to someone else, who attempts to blackmail her lover Bingham into marriage, who deceives her husband-to-be with two men before he has even had time to consummate the marriage, and who betrays her sister twice, first by seducing Gondych, the man with whom Jackie is idealistically in love, and then by informing her father about the relationship. She is genuinely ignorant of ethical values, at least as concern sexuality, and remarks of her seduction of Gondych: "I acted out of curiosity, without morality. With regard to sex, I have never been able to see where moral behaviour began; it seems to me that everyone is for himself; yet in this case, I know that I betrayed poor Jackie". It is her sole, brief homage to moral values in sexual behaviour. For most of the time she is genuinely unaware of their existence; as she says of herself: "I was wicked just as other people were wicked, not more nor less".

At one point Letty images sexuality as capital. Speaking of another of the self-styled "love careerists" she says of Phyllis that she "worked quite hard to learn to manage men without herself being got" and goes on: "Many men make money and spend it on all their passions. Some are able to keep it and have dime and nickel passions, a kind of safeguard. Some women are able to have greater and more frequent passions, it is not all dollars and cents, and this capacity is their capital when they make love their career; Pauline could love, Phyllis not". The notion of sex as a commodity is shared by most of the characters in the novel. Grandmother Morgan, for instance, advises Phyllis cynically that Montrose is attracted to her and would pay her fare abroad "for the sake of a few kisses". She adds, "But see that you give nothing for it but kisses, my girl". Throughout the novel, in fact, Phyllis is regarded as no more than a piece of valuable, yet docile, marital flesh, an attitude which she is not merely complaisant in but in which she enthusiastically collaborates. But the question is not, I think, one of the difference between the two sexes. Some men and some women can withhold emotional commitment; some cannot. The novel shows us Solander, Letty's father, as a type of the male who can form a constant relationship while endeavouring to uphold previous obligations. A man commits suicide for love in the course of the novel, and another attempts to—just as, at the other extreme, we are shown many of the love careerists, the Phyllises and the alimony chasers.

That would be perhaps all to it, except for the striking departure in the figure of Letty's idealistic sister Jackie, who seems a leftover from previous novels. Letty genuinely fails to understand her sister. Although, like most of Stead's main characters, she has some artistic aspirations or abilities, some pretensions to becoming a writer (even the least likely of them, Robert Grant, aspires to be a writer by proxy, by making his own experiences the stuff of someone else's best-seller) unlike her predecessors Letty completely discounts the imagination. In a passage in Chapter VI of the novel Letty attempts to define the relationship between reality and the imagination (or "fantasy" as she calls it) through a comparison between herself and her less worldly sister.

Although the argument is not easy to follow and the terms she employs slippery, the view that Letty is putting forward is that of the complete materialist, whose only reality is the reality of appearances, of the phenomenal. Nothing has any reality unless it has some material existence, or at least effect—most often, that means "can be translated into some material benefit". Therefore, any acts of fantasy or invention are condemned as falsifications of reality—except that it is an easily observable fact that some falsifications of reality do confer on the falsifier tangible benefits. So, the lines an actor speaks mean nothing to Letty in themselves but if they confer fame or material fortune on the speaker they must have a reality. Or, less obviously (and this is the furthest that Letty will depart from the material world), the romantic, deluded visions of herself that Letty's mother develops and fosters enable her to cope with the failure of her own life—and are therefore of some value and have a reality.

In a stark and elemental way, Christina Stead confronts us in *The Man Who Loved Children* with what are for most of her female characters the basic facts of male-female relationships: the fickleness of men, a law which is quick to deprive the unfaithful woman of her children, and above all in this novel, the terrible fact of pregnancy, which is regarded almost with dread by the female characters.

—Laurie Clancy

It is an extraordinarily strange view of the world for a would-be writer to possess, although admittedly Letty sees writing solely as a means to other ends. As Barbara Baynton found fifty years before this novel appeared, writing can be one of the few avenues through which women can throw off their cultural and social bondage. It requires nothing more than pen and paper and you can even, as some nineteenth century writers did, adopt a male pseudonym if you suspect editorial prejudice. But the interesting comparison is with the more obviously artistic, if equally unproductive, sister Jackie. Hers is almost the only voice in the novel, and the last in Stead's body of work, to speak for a conception of love that is higher than mere social convenience; and the ease with which she is swept aside in the novel by Letty's conquest of the man Jackie worships from afar suggests her relative impotence. The "Teresa" kind of woman has been moved into a subsidiary position, preparatory to disappearing from Stead's work altogether. Nevertheless, hers is the sole voice of dissent from Letty's brand of reductive, and finally deluded "realism". Writing to her sister, Jackie says: "I try to reason out (but vainly) the steps by which a girl like you came to your view of the world—sameness, a geometrical pattern, women in overalls at machines and men talking about dams and cross-country trains; no travelling, no *objets-d'art,* no beauty, no joy, no great passions. It is incomprehensible. I am obliged to say to myself, it is a mere fad". It is a question Letty is unable to comprehend, let alone answer.

Letty's sexual exploits have, of course, nothing of the viciousness, the sheer depravity of Robert Grant's exploitation of woman in ***A Little Tea, A Little Chat.*** He is the most monstrous in Stead's long line of egotistical self-deceivers, a man beside whom even Samuel Pollit seems a relative innocent. But at the same time, the very multiplicity of Letty's loves, the naive credulousness with which she enters into what, it is immediately obvious to the reader, are the most unpromising of relationships, believing that at last, this time, she has found the right man, defeats Letty's practical object as much as it does Stead's artistic one, because of its sheer tediousness and repetition. There is a shallowness about her reduction and simplification of the world to the merely visible that is as fallacious in its own way as its polar opposite, the self-deception of men like Pollit, Crow, Henri Leon (in ***House of All Nations***) and Grant.

Although Christina Stead rarely passes explicit judgments on her characters, preferring merely to allow them to reveal themselves in action and incessant conversation, there is no doubt that the later novels concern themselves mostly with love from the "realist" and especially financial point of view professed by Letty. The equation of love and money—or more specifically of women and property—is most frequently made by the egregious Grant in ***A Little Tea, A Little Chat.*** There indeed he refers repeatedly to women as "cattle" and even says contemptuously at one point, "If they can be bought and sold like cattle—cattle too are good for something". The madly confused, incoherent speech from which the quotation comes is an encapsulation of most of his prejudices, and the response of his friend Flack is a perceptive one: "Your schemes on the side are like speculation in blondes".

Constantly throughout the novel, Grant, his lovers and his friends insist that love cannot be bought; but the kind of love Grant receives is bought—except that he is so corrupt that he reneges on the deal and refuses to pay, ruining several women financially and driving at least one to suicide. Finally, he meets his match only in a sexual adventuress as corrupt and suited to the turbid world of the novel as he is. Stead tells us of Barbara Downs that she

> . . . naturally did not appear to herself as an adventuress, as Grant did not appear to himself as a lecher. Barbara, for example, believed that she was in the center of a kind of exchange of values; she was the broker. She knew a few laws, enough for her purpose, and for the rest she put nothing on paper, but her name to a marriage certificate.
>
> Her society was full of women like herself, who made connections, put people in the way of things, mentioned names, made love in the routine of business, and in return received money in cash. All that she met could be paid for and was: she was therefore only a dealer. She surely believed that everything was for sale.

With ***Miss Herbert (The Suburban Wife)*** finally, we return to a woman as superficially free and independent as Letty Fox but as similarly conservative and conventional at heart, bent for all her dutiful promiscuity on the security of the marital bond and as indignant as Mathilde Fox when she discovers the fallaciousness of what she has been taught as axiomatic. Her cry is the cry of so many of Stead's women—"why can't I keep a man?"—just as the men's answering bay is Robert Grant's "All I Want is a Woman".

She is the epitome of the conventional. She drops one *fiancé* because he is arrested in a demonstration and takes on another who, from his letters, is a compulsive careerist and the stuffiest of stuffed shirts. Her intellectual life is as shallow as her emotional. She feels it beyond her capacity or even right to question the nature of things, views with a kind of prurient wonder the prospect of a couple living together out of wedlock, admires the tolerance of England in not immediately jailing all admitted Communists and asks herself in apparently genuine terror, "Can I live in a world where the British Empire does not live?"

When she finally marries, she lives totally by rote, carrying out faithfully the obligations of the role of wife and mother as she has been taught, largely by women's magazines, to interpret them. She is literally incapable of recognizing that her perfectly constructed paradigm of the roles could differ from the living and individual actualities of a particular marriage. She ignores her husband's repeated warnings in the lecture notes he leaves exposed (it is not clear whether deliberately), rejects his suggestion of innovation in their sexual life, and even after it has long become clear to the reader that her husband has left her, clings with condescending complacency to the delusion that he will eventually get over his immature habits and return to her.

If this were all there were to her, she could hardly sustain our interest over thirty, let alone three hundred pages. But as the novel develops we begin to find her more interesting, not so much because her character changes radically as because the changing situation in which she finds herself brings out previously concealed and rather more admirable qualities in her character. The other side of the naive, shallow, politically reactionary matron is a woman who, when the crunch of poverty really comes, refuses to submit to it and fights tooth and nail for her family.

Then, at the end of the novel, comfortably settled in her mundane ways and capable even of laughing ruefully over the proposal of marriage she was almost foolish enough to accept, she meets the man her daughter is going out with, and for a devastating moment she experiences what true love might have been like, before suppressing the knowledge within herself:

> Her heart began pounding out hard and real thoughts, like pieces of metal, too; and she heard them, forceful, unanswerable: This is love and he knows it; it would be too strong for me, my life would be carried away into a whirlpool, round and round and down, in the center, lost and gone; I wouldn't want to get out of it, I would lose myself, I'd be swept away; I don't want that. I couldn't live, then all would mean nothing. I can't live like that; what of the past and future? There'd be no meaning to the world or time, but this hour and the future hours with him would break into everything, flooding everything, everything would be washed away: I couldn't stand it, I'm not strong enough, I'm too old to go in for it—
>
> . . . When she got home with Deborah, she stood for a moment at the door, pretending to fumble with the key, feeling the great joy on her: I can love him, and he loves me. Then she went in with an ordinary suburban face and ordinary suburban remarks.

Such moments of rapture are as rare in the later fiction of Christina Stead as they are numerous in ***For Love Alone.*** In the end, social necessity dictates that sexual love, at least for women, is firmly subject to questions of economy and security. It is remarkable how little mention there is in the later novels of even physical fulfilment as a cause of satisfaction in sexual relationships. (pp. 136-49)

Laurie Clancy, "The Economy of Love: Christina Stead's Women," in Who Is She? *edited by Shirley Walker, St. Martin's Press, 1983, pp. 136-49.*

Rudolf Bader (essay date Winter 1984)

[In the essay below, Bader discusses several of Stead's novels as works in the bildungsroman tradition.]

Christina Stead (1902-1983), along with Patrick White certainly the most imaginative and the most significant writer from Australia, has not been given the critical attention which is due to her. One reason is the fact that her work went beyond nationalism before a large proportion of potential readers in her home country were ready for this. As John Barnes writes in his recent obituary article ["Christina Stead (1902-1983)," *Australian Book Review,* June 1983]:

> Nationalism simply wasn't an issue for her: she didn't regard herself as an expatriate, she didn't reject her homeland, but neither did she feel any compulsion to assert an Australian identity. She was perhaps the first Australian writer to be truly cosmopolitan.

In this sense, she could almost be called the most un-Australian of all Australian novelists. But of course, she was much more: a very prolific writer (who could turn out up to 20,000 words a day); a fast writer who never re-read her books once she had written them; a writer who never had a literary career in mind, who wrote because she had something to say and not to make money; a writer who developed her own particular kind of realism, displaying an acute and imaginative vision and a corresponding style; and a writer whose novels cover a wide range of different human constellations in different societies and milieux.

Another reason for the relative neglect of her novels may be their diversity in theme, setting and tone. However, if we look for typical elements in her work, we can find some themes that establish links among some of her novels, themes that place her work in a literary context that goes beyond nationalism. Some of the connecting themes that can be found in several of her novels are the intellectual exploration of socialism, the view of woman as a man's natural companion, or [according to Dorothy Green in *Ulysses Bound,* 1973] "the faint gleam of heroism that works in obscurity." All these themes are combined and connected with others when we dare to look at some of her novels in the literary context of the *bildungsroman.*

The genre of the *bildungsroman,* as the term itself suggests, has its roots in German literature, its archetype being *Wilhelm Meisters Lehrjahre* by J. W. von Goethe; in the course of the past 180 years, however, the genre has not only established a substantial tradition in German literature, but there have also been many exponents in English. Christina Stead, who had left Australia in 1928, at the age of 26, and lived in many different countries, some of them in Europe, was influenced by a number of Europeans (as well as American) writers, such as Balzac, Maupassant, Dickens, Dostoyevsky and Nietzsche. These and her familiarity with Sigmund Freud's writings must have prepared the way to her own treatment of the *bildungsroman,* a genre with which she was certainly familiar and which she probably employed consciously.

The plot of a *bildungsroman* tells the physical and psychological events in the life of a sensitive protagonist, from his or her youth to young adulthood. In this process the young protagonist is shown as an eager apprentice of a philosophy of life. He or she wants to learn the ways and the nature of the world. The genre is therefore also called "apprenticeship novel" in English. If we look for such developments in Christina Stead's work, our attention is drawn towards her three novels ***The Man Who Loved Children*** (1940), ***For Love Alone*** (1945), and ***Letty Fox: Her Luck*** (1946). According to R. G. Geering [in *Christina Stead,* 1979],

> ***The Man Who Loved Children*** and ***For Love Alone*** . . . draw together a number of basic recurring subjects, all of which are either handled or foreshadowed in ***Seven Poor Men of Sydney***—the tensions of family life, rebellious youth, the search for love and freedom, the stirrings of artistic impulse, and the dilemmas of womankind.

The Man Who Loved Children, For Love Alone and ***Letty Fox: Her Luck*** show the development of a young girl from her early teens to womanhood in her late twenties. The three female protagonists, Louisa Pollit, Teresa Hawkins and Letty Fox, mark three stages in this development, and they all draw heavily from Christina Stead's biography. According to Christina Stead herself, sexual emancipation is the most important barrier for women artists to cross in order to have some sort of equality with men. In this way, we are given a portrait of the artist as a young woman, especially in ***For Love Alone,*** and, as Christina Stead's later great novel, ***Cotters' England*** (1966) shows, these women, victimized as young girls, can turn into tyrants themselves in later life. This interpretation rates these novels among the genre of the *künstlerroman,* a subgroup of the *bildungsroman.* But let us look at the three major stages in this development.

Christina Stead's first novel, ***Seven Poor Men of Sydney*** (1934), introduces the character of Catherine Baguenault, a young girl who does not conform to the limitations of the society in which she happens to live. She runs away from home at fifteen and tries to follow her ideals, but she ends up in a mental hospital. Christina Stead's acknowledged masterpiece, ***The Man Who Loved Children,*** brings a more fully developed character with the young teenager Louisa Pollit. Louisa is introduced on the first page of the novel as a girl of eleven-and-a-half:

> Strict and anxious when their parents were at home, Louisa when left in sole command was benevolent, liking to hear their shouts from a distance while she lay on her belly, reading, at the top of the orchard, or ambled, woolgathering, about the house.

This introduces puberty behaviour that characterizes Louisa throughout the novel. It establishes Louisa's need for a world of her own, into which she can retreat whenever the atmosphere in her family becomes too oppressive. Often we find sentences like this:

> Louie, who had spent several hours already in an uncommunicable world, woke to hear riding again the night rider in the street outside.

And so she loses herself in daydreams with increasing frequency. The need for a world of her own becomes more urgent with the knowledge that she is her father's child by his first wife, rejected by his second wife, Henny:

> Louisa was Henny's stepchild, as everyone knew, and no one, least of all Louie, expected Henny to love this girl as she loved her own.

And indeed, there are enough of Henny's children who claim motherly love. So Louisa finds herself an outsider in her own home. From this detached position she begins to scrutinize and analyse her father's second marriage. This critical attitude has been hers ever since her eleventh birthday. As she approaches her twelfth birthday, Louisa begins to understand her stepmother's plight with the sympathy of one woman for another. Louisa also begins to read poetry.

Louisa's contacts with physical objects are determined by puberty. She drops, smashes or bends everything, she spills food, cuts herself, stumbles and falls: she has become a square peg in a round hole. This gives her a general sense of uneasiness and insecurity. And it is from this situation that she begins to look back at herself as an innocent child:

> There was a picture of a sweet, gay, shy little girl with curls all over her head, in an old frame in her father's room. She could hardly believe that she, the legend of the family, whom everyone had a right to correct, had been that little girl.

And these thoughts make her look ahead: "she felt a growing, sullen power in herself which was merely darkness to the splendid sunrise that she felt certain would flash in her in a few years." She acknowledges "her unwieldiness and unhandiness in this little world," but she has an utter contempt for everyone around her. She knows she is the ugly duckling: "But when a swan she would never come sailing back into their village pond; she would be somewhere away, unheard of, on the lily-rimmed oceans of the world. This was her secret." Thus, Louisa's secrets and daydreams separate her more and more from her family as the narrative proceeds.

She demonstrates her aloofness by an act that acquires the quality of an initiation rite: she, the daughter of Sam Pollit, who loves all animals (just as he loves children), performs the unpleasant task of drowning a cat for a neighbour.

Louisa's development through puberty becomes involved more thoroughly in the plot of the novel by her father's inability to recognize this development. He still treats her as a child. This is particularly evident in the episode of their common walk, when he insults her.

Thus, Louisa reaches the point where it is not enough for her to find guidance and consolation in books. When the domestic situation becomes almost unbearable for her—almost daily rows in the family, the financial situation worsening, her father resenting her obvious aloofness as well as her bodily development at thirteen—Louisa is in need of some guiding personality. She finds such a person in her new teacher, Miss Aiden. Indeed, as her name suggests, Miss Aiden becomes a great aid for Louisa by strengthening her belief in the power of literature.

By the time Louisa is fourteen it is obvious that she lives her own life in isolation from her family. She has already discovered sensuality when her father still thinks of her as a stupid child. She starts to write poetry herself. However, even this outlet cannot save her from countless domestic conflicts, and the novel reaches its climax when Louisa tries to poison her father and stepmother by putting cyanide in their tea. Her stepmother deliberately drinks it, killing herself, and when Louisa confesses her crime to her father, he does not believe her, dismissing her confession as a neurotic lie of a girl in puberty. This is the final break, and Louisa leaves her father's home for good.

Christina Stead's next novel, ***For Love Alone,*** introduces the character of Teresa Hawkins, and Teresa begins where we lose sight of Louisa. In the course of the development that the female protagonist undergoes, there are many adversary forces, and ***For Love Alone*** starts off with the restricting force that was the dominant theme in ***The Man Who Loved Children:*** a domineering, possessive, self-centred father figure. On the first few pages of ***For Love Alone,*** we meet Teresa's father as an exact copy of Louisa's father. He uses the same sort of insulting language towards his daughter, he cannot accept the fact that she is no longer a child. In this respect there is an overlap of the two novels: Teresa has to wait for the second half of the book before she can leave her father's world. However, this is only one aspect of the whole development. There are other restrictions to be thrown off, particularly restrictions of tradition and of society. The protagonist has yet a great deal to learn about the world and about herself. And this also involves some errors.

As the title of the novel suggests, it is love in all its aspects that the protagonist has to learn about in this novel. She has to face and digest the manifestations of love in body and mind, its implications, its complications, its promises and its disappointments. The theme of love is ideal for the presentation of the development that a young girl must go through, particularly the stage between puberty, through adolescence, to young womanhood.

Because of the oppressive atmosphere at home on one hand and Teresa's romantic dreams on the other hand, it is only natural that her violent struggle for psychic survival should concentrate on love as a romantic passion, which, at first, remains a passion without experience. This is shown very clearly in the passage where she walks near the beach in the evening and hears the muffled sounds of couples making love on the beach: she cannot grasp the full meaning of those sounds and feels embarrassed. "She felt the swarm of lovers thick as locusts behind her when she turned into the beach path." Soon there are warning signals looming along the road that stretches ahead of her: misconceptions about love and marriage (for example Malfi's wedding, Aunt Bea's ideas, Teresa's experiences on her way to Harper's Ferry), suicides, madness, etc. So this adolescent seeker rejects all constraints of family and tradition in order to undertake a literal and psychological odyssey of independence. In the course of this odyssey through theoretical and practical schooling she must learn from a number of mistakes in the name of love. Her worst illusion is her relationship with Jonathan Crow, her idealizing attitude towards him. The reader senses the true nature of Crow's parasitical character long before Teresa does. On the positive side of her development, however, the reader gains confidence in her endeavours when she performs her first act of pure will power: her abortive pilgrimage to Harper's Ferry. This establishes an obvious connection with ***The Man Who Loved Children,*** where Louisa also sees a place in the country called Harper's Ferry as a blissful retreat or escape from the restrictions and destructions of family life.

There are three male partners for the adolescent Teresa: the first (Jonathan Crow) almost kills her psychically and spiritually, the second (James Quick) restores her to life, and the third (Harry Girton), although a mere passing fancy, works as a sort of retarding element and becomes a final confirmation of Teresa's independence. The end of the novel, although the reader knows that Teresa is going to marry Quick, is remarkably unromantic and mature. Teresa has achieved her aim. As Christina Stead herself has put it, Teresa's struggle has been to achieve union with a man. The word "free" in the last chapter heading, according to Christina Stead, has a different meaning from the one that feminist critics like to attribute to it. She says: "You can't live alone. Freedom is association with other people, and especially with a sexual partner, a companion, a mate."

The theme of love, then, serves as a vehicle for all the aspects of Teresa's development. Through love she learns the ways of this world, and her aim is perfection: "She did not want to be eccentric, but on the contrary, to be noble, loved, glorious, admired; perfection as far as she could be perfect." She learns about the dichotomy of "agape" and "eros," she learns about emancipation from her family and her society, she reaches liberation, self-realization, and creativity.

If ***For Love Alone*** resembles Homer's *Odyssey* in its spiritual, emotional and intellectual quest, Christina Stead's next novel, ***Letty Fox: Her Luck,*** adds a touch of the picaresque by its reliance on the importance of personal experience and by its almost cinematic development along associative but separate incidents. The new protagonist, introducing herself as a first-person narrator, is twenty-four years old, the exact age at which Teresa in ***For Love Alone*** left Sydney for Europe. Letty is unmarried at the beginning of the book, another overlap between the two. But in this novel we are in the impersonal atmosphere of New York. Letty Fox begins her rather long narrative with a question that is to dominate large sections of the book:

> My twenty-fourth birthday was just gone, and I had spent two hours this same evening ruminating upon all my love affairs which had sunk ingloriously into the past, along with my shrunken

> and worn outfits. Most of these affairs had been promising enough. Why had they failed? (Or I failed?)

So this is a young but grown-up woman who reviews some of her own actions and decisions about her adult life. Throughout the novel she tries to come to terms with her relations to other people, men and women. The main connections between ***For Love Alone*** and ***Letty Fox: Her Luck*** are the continuing explorations into the realm of love and the heroine's attempts "to get into literature." However, Letty Fox is not only interested in finding the right partner for life, but also in a process of socialization. She says: "My supreme idea was always to get married and join organized society." And indeed, it has been suggested that "this novel is much more about the process of socialization than it is about individual experience, or it is more about the relations between the self and society than about the relation between the self and its experience." Of course it is about both types of relations. This fact makes this a modern picaresque novel and a psychological novel at the same time. The former genre, as has been suggested before, appears in the loosely structured sequence of adventures, the typified character of Letty and the light-hearted, occasionally rather self-effacing sense of humour employed. The psychological dimension of the novel appears whenever Letty learns a lesson from one of her adventures with human nature. After running through numerous jobs, careers, and sexual partners, she marries her good old friend Bill van Week and settles down to a more relaxed, quiet life. She has accepted herself, although there is still a streak of irony in the final passage:

> I don't think for a moment that this is the end of everything, but I'm no tea-leaf reader. I can only tangle with situations as they come along. "On s'engage et puis on voit." Perhaps I just love life. I certainly expose myself to it; and I'm accessible to it. I don't ask myself, Will this last? It's a question of getting through life, which is quite a siege, with some self-respect. Before I was married, I had none; now, I respect not only my present position, but also all the efforts I made, in every direction, to get here. I was not always honest, but I had grit, pretty much; what else is there to it? The principal thing is, I got a start in life; and it's from now on. I have a freight, I cast off, the journey has begun.

The seafaring image at the end recalls the preamble about "Sea People" at the beginning of ***For Love Alone*** and the constant presence of the sea in ***The Man Who Loved Children*** (the *pater familias* being a marine biologist).

Although ***Letty Fox: Her Luck*** carries the protagonist on well into adult life, the three novels mentioned in this context can be seen as one long *bildungsroman.* The three stages of development are now quite obvious. And it has also become clear how the protagonists achieve their progress. In the earlier stages, that is in ***The Man Who Loved Children*** and in the first half of ***For Love Alone,*** there is still a strong need for guiding figures. The protagonists acquire knowledge through books, through advice from more advanced personalities (although there is considerable danger about the reliability of these, as the example of Jonathan Crow illustrates), and their own movements are primarily negative: away from domineering father figures, away from restricting family life, away from home even in a geographical sense, what Christina Stead has called "the impulse of a young adult to wander." This reminds us of the *wanderjahre,* the advanced stage of education in the European *bildungsroman* tradition. Later, in the second half of ***For Love Alone*** and ***Letty Fox: Her Luck,*** their learning process becomes more self-critical and more self-ironical, but also more positive, no longer away from anything, but rather towards something, towards fulfilment, towards complete freedom and happiness, towards creativity and self-respect; and this stage is also less absolute, the protagonists having become acquainted with compromise. Thus Letty Fox, who appears almost as a materialist in some of her adventures, is happy to marry a disinherited man in the end.

Christina Stead's sources, among many others, were her own experiences as a girl and as a young woman, and the whole European tradition of the *bildungsroman.* This shows that she is more than a social realist. The development of a young woman from innocence to knowledge through her own demands in the face of a society dominated by male values goes back to Henrik Ibsen's play *Et Dukkehjem* (*A Doll's House,* also known under the title *Nora*) (1879), where a light-hearted young woman learns about her true position in life by an honest analysis of a crucial situation. And Christina Stead was as familiar with this tradition as she was with the *bildungsroman* and *künstlerroman* traditions. As we have seen, her use of the *bildungsroman* has several elements of the *künstlerroman.* Her heroines have artistic aspirations. Some of their creative energy is developed at an early age. Louisa is attracted to poetry as a young teenager, and Teresa is convinced of her great destiny. This most obvious quality of the artist that we can find in them, however, is their courage to explore the true nature of human existence, psychologically and sociologically, not through the intellect alone, but through all the other spheres of the human mind as well, including emotions and the response to art.

These interpretations show that the romantic element in Christina Stead's best-known novels is as strong as the female view of the world; and yet she can be called neither a romantic nor a feminist. By employing a careful symbolism such as the one connected with names, particularly in ***For Love Alone,*** and also by destroying antiquated myths such as the ones about male superiority and family loyalty, she offers an exploration of new myths and opens the path to new fantasy.

This study has attempted to show one facet of Christina Stead's art that justifies her reputation as a truly international novelist apart from her cosmopolitan biography and the mere geographical setting of her novels and short stories. There is a danger for the critic dealing with her work, especially if the critic is bound to one particular view, such as Australian nationalism or feminism, and that is the danger of interpreting her novels too narrowly. Christina Stead may be considered an Australian writer or an international writer (whatever that may mean), but her true country is the country of the human mind or the world of international literary traditions. (pp. 31-8)

Rudolf Bader, "Christina Stead and the 'Bildungsroman'," in World Literature Written in English, *Vol. 23, No. 1, Winter, 1984, pp. 31-9.*

Bruce Holmes (essay date September 1985)

[*In the following essay, Holmes asserts that Stead successfully combines authentic characterization and a Marxist perspective in* House of All Nations.]

Published in 1938, ***House of All Nations,*** set as it is in France of the early thirties, blends fiction with history; yet though Paris and France from the immediate background, there is reference to a wider sphere, as indicated by the title and by the assortment of nationalities represented among the gallery of characters. As in much of Stead's work, a specificity of locale and situation is used as a means of commenting on universal aspects of society and behaviour. The book's title itself, ***House of All Nations,*** is an indication of this dual function.

Explaining her setting for the novel, Stead says:

> And it was right in the centre of fashionable Paris, and had many fashionable people of all nations there. The reason I called it that—that's the reason, though—it refers to something quite other.

The reference to "something quite other" is to the brothel of the same name, a happy choice of title considering the suggestion of the nexus of sexuality and money that Stead finds so pronounced in modern society. It is curious that in spite of the book's preoccupation with material concerns, there is an authorial detachment from them, a wistful inclination towards what might be called an idealized condition of which gold is an emblem. A dialectic of moral provenance is posed, dealing with the continuum represented by money (more specifically gold), at one end of which is gross cupidity, and at the other end, a certain aesthetic, even spiritual, refinement. On the one hand is "pure theft" and "titanic pickpocketing"; on the other hand we are told authorially and in lyrical vein that gold "is an absolute and in its presence the anxious heart breathes sweetly and the blood laughs and the toiling brain sheds its dew of agony." The search for fulfilment leads towards a "golden" sense of *communitas,* a refined social intercourse in a communion of people conspicuous for their ability and individuality. Henri Léon, Jules and Alphendéry show between them a rapport that is independent of different ideologies they might hold, and it is to this sort of rapport Stead accords special attractiveness and value. Ironically, such rapport, stimulated by money making, has a worthy ring to it when contrasted with the shabbiness of Raccamond (crusading under a banner of righteousness). Tied in with this are the "golden" aspirations of the socialists Jean Frère, his wife Judith, Adam Constant and Alphendéry, though there seems to be more efficacy in the social dimension of their relationship than in the ideology they espouse.

An ambiguous attitude towards materialism is shown in the fact that clichés to do with materialism are evoked in order to suggest antithetical values related to the spiritual and the aesthetic. Anticipating this treatment are Stead's references to gold in some of ***The Salzburg Tales***: there are symbolic overtones of aesthetic and spiritual wealth in **"The Gold Bride"** and the Centenarist's tale of the Rabbi finding gold in the dung heap; and in the Banker's Tale, **"The Sensitive Goldfish,"** there is a link between the aesthetic qualities of goldfish and gold itself.

Clearly there is an indictment of greed and chicanery but that is only one aspect of the novel's moral significance. Beneath this literal level is one of a more metaphorical nature suggestive of the value derived from the challenges of pursuing "gold," be it in the form of money or of altruistic achievement. This is similar to the literal and metaphorical bifurcation of moral issues in ***The Man Who Loved Children***; Louisa's action as a potential murderess has a Nietzschean ambience to it which distances her from the literalness of conventional morality.

House of All Nations was written in a short time and Stead has expressed her wish to have revised it. It does suffer from a want of pruning and revision, but at the same time it carries a feeling of spontaneity and a deft, impressionistic registering of the times. It projects the ambivalence of a detached recording of the relaxed moral tone of the 1930s, together with a celebration of vitality and an empathy with the era's excitements; the implied judgement of the capitalist system is countered by a relish for its excitements and joustings. (A similar duality is shown in Sam Pollit who from one angle is seen to be repugnant, from another, rich in vitality and individuality). The resultant dialectic is reinforced by a multifarious play on tensions and contradictions, not least of which is the contradiction between and within characters. For example, Alphendéry the socialist is ideologically opposed to the capitalist Jules; but at a less obvious level we realize there are certain affinities between them, mutual respect being one, as well as a haughty indifference they show towards the gold they aspire to.

Contradiction is expressed in a number of oppositions and paradoxes, often given aphoristic neatness and point; the effect is to confront and expose conventionality of idea. Alphendéry maintains "Decision, giving commands, shouting at people, slitting Gordian knots, is often a way of expressing mental confusion." Alphendéry, in his dilemma of split loyalty, is well suited to the expression of contradiction. He is "bound to the bank by money needs and affection for the Bertillons, as well as inertia," and he "disliked the bank much more than he admitted to himself." Plowman speaks the truth when he says to him "you don't believe in money. You believe the financial world is nothing but a carcass." But for all his aversion to money, Alphendéry is avowedly materialist. In considering Kant and Diderot he asserts that the "only philosopher for me is the one who is ostentatiously physiological." He is motivated by the Marxist's wish to benefit man by a proper application of materialism, but this paradoxically entails the expression of spiritual values, as he implies when talking to Jules: "You have to be born to love of humanity, and trained to it, the way you have to be born to money love." This and his spartan regimen suggest the austere dedication of a priest. There is, in Alphendéry's psychology, a pushing towards the spirit, rather than the material, for all his preoccupation with the latter.

Léon, in fact, values him for his "spiritual partnership" and thinks of him as an "inspired messenger" a "shilee'ach." The clerkly, gentle strain in him ("You have the courage to be kind and unassuming") is at odds with the Mammon he needs must serve, and he is led to compromise his finer intuitions. Alphendéry had worked for a rentier millionaire and now leaves the Bertillon bank to work for Léon, a strange situation for a Marxist, and in this regard very much like the situation of Baruch in ***Seven Poor Men of Sydney,*** when he accepted employment with the Baltimore millionaire. Idealism *in vacuo* usually draws the scorn of Stead and by yoking it with money she is pointing the way to how idealists should come to terms with Caesar, if only to influence him ultimately towards less material concerns. One cannot be so impractical as to dismiss materialism—one can at best provide it with a leavening of spirit.

Jules to some extent shares Alphendéry's disdain of money. We are told that he "cared not so much for money as for money-making." Furthermore, he is so consistently defined in terms of gold and lightness as to suggest something etherial, so that moral judgement of him is suspended, in spite of his often childish limitations of character. The pattern of imagery relevant to Jules, emphasizing a mercurial lightness, seems to claim for him a significance that derives from a romantic, almost transcendental, craving of the human spirit, a craving which is at variance with his fiscal machinations. Jules had been a flier in the War and is described as "a flier, a dancer—a messenger of the gods." Plowman says "he's Mercury . . . He flies through the air with the greatest of ease." He has a Gatsby aura about him, an elegance that comes of his wealth and nonchalant air, together with his distinguished war record.

Disjunction of some inner trait and the quotidian externals of personality is thus seen in both Alphendéry and Jules. It is also suggested in the conflict of ideologies in both Alphendéry's situation with the Alsatian rentier millionaire—who is a Marxist—and Léon's professed political sympathies:

> Léon's a follower of MacDonald in England, Blum in France, Louis de Brouckere in Belgium, Fritz Adler in Austria—Fritz Napthali—all the great beans of the Second International. That's your conservative for you!

Ironic inversion of complacently accepted values is part of Stead's stylistic equipment. As in ***A Little Tea, A Little Chat,*** there are numerous references to the essential goodness of wars and revolutions. Haller maintains "revolutions are necessary to purify the financial system"; Léon that "you can only make a fortune in a war"; and Alphendéry that "it pays the British capitalist class to inflate." Ironically, the stability associated with the "absolute" of gold is seen to depend on patterns of social and economic instability; looked at in another way, the flux and constancy of life have a necessary interdependence, feeding and reinforcing each other.

The stance of the author affects a worldly cynicism not unlike that of La Rochefoucauld, and this is part of the ironic treatment. Jules, in repeating "the theme of his life music," says to Léon "You and I both believe in altruism, Henri because altruism is selfishness out with a pair of field glasses and imagination." Earlier it was said of Jules that he saw in altruism "the perspicacious self-interest of cunning ambition." He is like Sam Pollit, inverted, full of charm, and given to categorical pronouncements which, unlike Sam's, preen themselves on moral inpropriety. The charm which should command loyalty is exposed as superficial when Alphendéry and William vacillate in their admiration of Jules. William's usual display of loyalty is sometimes followed by mild perfidies, as when he exclaims "Let him stay away: he does not work anyhow." And the bond between Alphendéry and Jules can be threatened by the latter when he makes such threats as "Let's fire Alphendéry . . . I don't want smart men . . . I can do the thinking." As so often happens in Stead's fiction, the threat of betrayal hovers at the edge of relationships.

For example, Jules betrays Léon's wheat scheme with his jealousy, William holds a set of keys in secrecy from Jules, and Jules, on a few occasions is disloyal to Alphendéry. For all their openness, the protagonists are not averse to using deception for their own ends (and often the deception turns out to be self-deception). William gives a paradoxical assessment of this brother's weakness and strength: "even Jules doesn't know everything I've been doing . . . And I don't know what he's been up to; that's the weakness of our strength." Not to let your left hand know what your right hand is doing is part of the bank's credo. The importance of bluff and ostentation is, clearly, crucial to the bank's success, and this shows how appearance can belie reality, a recurring motif in Stead's fiction. "There's as much difference between the image and reality as between the joy of conception and the chaos of childbed."

Clearly, throughout her novels, Stead draws ironic contrasts between illusion and reality, and this particular novel shows as illusory one of the key tenets of bourgeois society, that money is an admirable pursuit, one which bestows dignity and honour on its champions. Here the contrast is dramatized in the awesome facade to the bank which conceals all manner of nefarious activity. Jules is quite blatant in encouraging the deceit: "You must have decent people around you: a bank is a confidence trick." The Englishman, Stewart, resolves on a good display when he enjoins Constant to "get all the classics . . . I want it to look like a big-time show." Style is all important in its capacity to camouflage a threadbareness of substance, even at a national level. As Stewart, again, says:

> The people see a bank clerk wearing a top hat and a morning coat in the tube in the morning. They know he's poor but he has the dignity of the power, experience, wealth of the men who rule the nation. They know they couldn't run the nation. And so respect on respect, you keep order in the country.

The deception that goes with such style works also within the bank, as is shown by Raccamond, who, for all his percipience, is deceived by the surface appearance of the place. It is ironic, therefore, that, although loathed by the principals of the bank, he is tolerated because his "moral look and his moral feelings are an asset in his business." As for moral feelings, Alphendéry feels depressed by such deception, as if it touches on his own self-deception and guilt:

> The more Michel looked at these facades, fine furnishings, crystal panes, brass rods, chased mirrors, carved panes, and soft carpets, the more depressed he became, the more was he convinced that he had to leave the bank and find another job. This came not only from his natural penchant for simplicity but also from a constant guilty picture in his mind's eye: a ganger sweating on the permanent way and the subtitle "these stones, grilles, mahoganies came that way". It was too much: it was too good.

There is about the bank a theatricality to which he is reluctant to subscribe, although Aristide himself endorses such theatricality, maintaining that "The bank is a stage," and Jules believes "It's all in the sign. This is a stage." This gulling of people leads Marion to the conviction that "They don't care how crooked you are if you make money." There is the suggestion, indeed, that criminality can be admirable for the great mass of population, provided that it is clever and does not hurt people individually. A question is posed implicity as to roguery and its fascination: "People love thieves." One is reminded of Goebbels' cunning in exploiting Nazism's theatricality and glamour in these very times, the early thirties. It would seem no accident that Davigdor's surname is Shicklgruber, Adolf Hitler's name, and that he cultivates a theatricality, a "professional Boeotianism" so that "no one suspected him," thus providing yet another example of the way appearance can be at odds with reality.

There is a wistful yearning for something fine, even spiritual, that marked those aspirations, expressed in ***Seven Poor Men of Sydney,*** for some sort of socialist brotherhood, and in ***For Love Alone,*** for fulfilment through sexual love. In ***House of All Nations,*** the aspiration is to establish something meaningful and absolute in an aesthetic of "golden" criteria—criteria for the realization of selfhood in a community of warm, clever and vital people.

The morality of the novel is seen to be double-stranded—there is the stock disapproval of chicanery alongside an oblique approbation of such human qualities that include warmth, living at risk, courage. Such qualities, the real "gold" of the novel, are part of a moral absolute against which the amassing of money, and losing it, are shown to be mercurial fripperies, part of the flux of existence. This is integral with that fundamental dialectic at work in Stead's fiction, involving the tension between permanent value and transience.

In tracing similarities with the other novels, one notices a strong vein of familial disaffection—relationships are not what they should be, as far as bourgeois expectations are concerned. Jules, Carrière and Constant all hate their mothers. Henrietta Achitophelous loathes her parents, Francois Legris' relationship with his daughter is conspicuous for its lack of affection, and Estelle Constant prefigures the embittered Xanthippe in Henny Pollit. It is interesting that Estelle is also the name of the unhappy wife of Tom Cotter, an ineffectual dreamer like Constant. As for the foreshadowing of Henny, Estelle Constant proclaims, "I didn't know I was well off when I was a virgin: I had to get myself tangled up with a sort of martyr saint." Saintliness for Estelle and Henny, ironically, is antithetical to worthiness. Inversion of stereotyped values and patterns of behaviour is seen too in the assumption of sexual role.

This is shown in the attitudes and actions of characters like Michael, Catherine, Nellie, Tom, Miss Herbert, Alphendéry and Jules. There is an obvious closeness between the last two of these, in fact Alphendéry is referred to as the "alter ego" of Jules who, to add to the unreality, is described as having "something not entirely human" about him. In spite of the token references to wife and family, there persists in his character a puzzling neuter quality. Much the same could be said of Alphendéry who has "something feminine, compliant" about him.

I am not suggesting a homosexual link between the characters, but rather drawing attention to the fact that so many of Stead's male characters have "feminine" characteristics. Conversely, so many women characters have "male" traits—like Lucy Headlong, Nellie Cotter, Miss Herbert and Marianne Raccamond. For all the exacerbated sexuality of the novels there is a movement towards androgynous characterization which could evoke "the kind of androgynous mind which Virginia Woolf considered to be the mark of a great writer" [as Ann Summers commented in "The Self Denied: Australian Women Writers—Their Image of Woman," *Refractory Girl,* Autumn 1973]. It is likely, however, that Stead recognizes the psychological fact of shared attributes between the sexes, and repudiates stereotyped pigeonholing of sexual differences in behaviour.

Complexity is seen too in Alphendéry, as I have noted, and it is significant that he, Baruch, and Quick are all based on Stead's husband William Blake. There appears to be a consistent attempt on her part to express, reconcile and understand the contradictions in her husband's position as a communist financier, and this bolsters the impression of dialectic in the novels. A similar fascination of a dialectical kind results in the creation of characters based on the contradictory traits of her own father.

Complexity, grotesquerie and sheer unlikeableness mark many a character in ***House of All Nations*** but (as in many of Stead's novels) some of the minor ones show in a quiet way conduct of a meritorious kind—people like Mouradzian, Judith and Anna, the servant of the Hallers, who sends money to "a brother much younger than herself and sick, in Transylvania." One thinks, in this regard, of the self-sacrifice displayed by Luisa in ***The Little Hotel*** and Wang Hoe in ***The Man Who Loved Children.*** Touchstones of moral worth are never very far away from a seeming preponderance of folly and wickedness, the polarities enriching the effect of moral dialectic.

The quiet and righteous characters have Stead's endorsement, but others win her emotional engagement. To say that Stead's criteria are interwoven with élitist strands may sound perverse, considering her democratic and socialist bent, nevertheless I sense a dichotomy in her view of people. Perhaps here she was influenced by Nietzsche, for whom the will to assertion was an essentially artistocratic conception, though it is more likely she is merely expressing her own subjective predilections. On the one hand she is supportive of ordinariness because it is too often synonymous with the exploited, and on the other hand it seems that she does not tolerate fools easily, that she is by temperament drawn to people of strong personality and ability, clever, colourful people like Jules, Léon, Marpurgo, Alphendéry, Baruch and Quick. Alphendéry's contempt for the likes of Rosenkrantz and Guildenstern, and indeed Aristide, has a marked tone of authorial identification.

There is a meanness of spirit in some characters, regardless of ideological alignment; and there is an atmosphere of brotherhood and warmth that surrounds certain people of talent, like those leading the Bertillon organization with their elegance, wit and cavalier gambling. Hardworking and unimaginative dullards hardly excite Stead's admiration. It is significant that her writing sparkles when describing the ingenious rascality of people like Léon, Jules and Comba; it wilts (as it does in ***Seven Poor Men of Sydney***) when dealing with situations like the socialist meetings that are peopled by types so sincere they appear atrophied of human interest.

True, the contrapartie operations of the bank are not ethical, but what detracts from the immorality is the fact that Alphendéry and Jules hold themselves aloof from the debasement that cankers such types as Aristide, Rosenkrantz and Guildenstern. Aristide's cause may well be "just," to echo the popular title of the Athenian Aristide, but the justice is a façade to self-interest, and as such draws the scorn of the "goodies," and presumably of Stead herself.

The moral tenor of *House of All Nations* correlates pretty closely with that of France at a national level; the fiction's closeness to history is useful in pointing up a poverty of moral resource on the part of individuals and governments.

—Bruce Holmes

Part of the fascination of people like Jules, and to a lesser extent, Léon, is the way they allow spontaneity, and sometimes irrationality, to influence their actions. We are told that "wealth, like genius, is to madness near akin." And indeed there is a touch of craziness in Jules' make-up—as well as genius. Stead seems to advocate on occasion a romantic surrender to irrationality (again one is reminded of the possible influence of Nietzsche). But irrationality can be good or bad depending on its effect. Sometimes it works for Jules, sometimes not, as shown in his irrational choice to bet with Carrière. Stead effectively deploys the various associations of irrationality, both at the personal and the international level, and she evokes the psychological climate created by the breakdown in international order that led to World War II.

The story is interwoven with elements of history and larded with a strangely prescient feeling of disaster that informs the *carpe diem* feeling prevalent at the bank. As Alphendéry says "With war coming there will be immense speculation in commodities," and Jean comments on the "scandals, the alarums, the war that's coming." There is, in this book, perhaps more than in Stead's other work, a strong ideological flavour, so interwoven is the plot with historical incident. The historical allusions are more than colouring for background and enrich the moral aspect of the novel, reflecting on deficiences of individual characters, as well as deficiencies of ideology.

An air of imminent disaster, corresponding to the anticipated crash of the bank, is conveyed in the general unfolding of plot and in such authorial remarks as "The world was really crumbling: all speculators hoped to make money out of the death and decrepitude of something or other." Tied in with this are the references to Mussolini, that "confused, nineteenth century tyrant," who is depicted as vulgar and opportunistic, and to Hitler, who is referred to with feelings of distrust and mockery ("Hitler looking for votes is like a man making love to a woman").

Another instance of Stead's mixing fiction with history is her presentation of Adam Constant. Like some of the characters in the other novels, the young, revolutionary types eager to spread abroad the cause of socialism, he wants to join the Red Army "fighting for civilization in China." Such idealistic commitment is countered by cynical reference to the ethically moribund, and in this respect the turncoat behaviour of MacDonald is a favourite butt—"by God, he's almost a gentleman. They say, he's a friend of the King."

Apart from MacDonald and communist crusaders, Stead refers pointedly to a number of important leaders and events—to Chiappe, Churchill, Lloyd George, Briand, Honfleur, Dreyfus, Morgan, Hoover, Bruning, the failure of the Dawes and Credit-Anstalt banks, to mention just a few. The effect is to emphasize that the destinies of the personalities in the narrative are inextricably bound up with external, political forces, and that the unfolding of the characters' lives, in their drift to vacuity, is analogous to the contours of world history.

Ironically counterpointing the lyrical adulation of gold as an "absolute" in Chapter 17 is the setting of the novel in France, a country which chose to stay on the gold standard in the thirties while both the U.S. and England did not. In the rise and fall of fortunes the book mirrors the economic fortunes of France in the thirties; France at the beginning of the thirties was attractively stable, but a period of economic distress led to a sweeping left victory at the general elections of 1932. Moreover, condemned by the gold standard to high costs of production, France was passing into depression. In 1933 she was the most stable country in Europe but barely six months later convulsions had begun.

The wheeling and dealing, the extravangance of the financial schemes, the collapse of the bank itself in ***House of All Nations,*** these are all consonant with the easy-going ethics of the times, represented most dramatically by the météques who were allegedly the ruin of France. One is reminded particularly of the Stavisky affair whose scheme "for marketing bonds issued to compensate Hungarians resident in what was now Rumanian territory" has all the hallmarks of a scheme by Léon or Cambo. Stavisky's last coup was the issuing of millions of bonds on behalf of his Bayonne pawnshop; but the extraordinary amount of capital required for the working of his pawnshop in a small country town attracted attention in the long run. Most of the victims were insurance companies and the discovery of the fraud was postponed by the device of two sets of books. How like Raccamond's use of books to undermine the Bertillon Bank!

Governments were infected by the relaxed moral tone, and the parliamentary system as a whole seemed a little dingy. The "Republic of Pals" meant that "rigorously honest men were on good terms with fairly honest men who were on good terms with shady men who were on good terms with despicable crooks." Then there was the Oustric affair:

> The gullibility of great banks of all countries was no secret by 1930, but for the great national controller of the French money market (i.e. the Bank of France) to be caught out as a sleeping partner in a vulgar fraud which wrecked several important local banks did not increase its prestige.

So it can be seen that the moral tenor of ***House of All Nations*** correlates pretty closely with that of France at a national level; the fiction's closeness to history is useful in pointing up a poverty of moral resource on the part of individuals and governments. The externals of history thus are used to illuminate features of thematic interest, and a similar function is served by aspects of imagery which assume symbolic significance.

There are the "crystal towers of his dreams" of Jules, which are related, because of the aerial associations, to the birdmen *"luftmenschen"* metaphor that is based on the fact of his experience as a flier in the First World War, imagery which fits in neatly with the elaborate pattern of Mercury references.

The polarity of aerial and light significance is counterpointed by images that suggest grotesquerie and disorder. Chief among these is Jean Frère's garden where weeds and caterpillars are to be found in rank confusion. Instead of edenic associations we have "tangled weeds, grass, shrubs, and lumps . . . old garden shrubs gone to seed and choked in weeds and rubbish." Later the garden is described as "wild."

There is a curiously fugal pattern of paradisal intimations with the reality synonymous with weeds. Alphendéry hopes to meet people who "spoke his language." Adam too flirts with the ideal and utopian: "I still have the feeling that all communists ought to be angels and work together singing psalms." The religious associations are extended in Constant's thinking of his own fate: "He was convinced his life would be a short one. But the thought of where he was going and how he might die, as well as the soft night air, filled his lungs with an almost divine gust." The obviousness of the name "Adam" does not escape us in the description: "Adam, too, looked different, above his naked body: he looked more the frail earthly first man hearing the strains of sun music in one of William Blake's dawn pictures." The edenic picture is furthered in the suggestions of Judith's seductiveness towards Adam. But nothing comes of all this (just as nothing comes of the "golden" harvest of Henri Léon's scheme).

Adam says in the next chapter "Platitudes and vain health go together: you see it in new colonies, virgins, and humanitarians." He seems suspicious and cynical of ideas, presumably of the success of socialism when jeopardized by man's predatoriness. The notion, which unsettles Alphendéry too, is given allegorical embroidering in this scene:

> Alphendéry had been walking up and down more than half an hour when he glanced for the first time at the shrubs along the paddock track. He recoiled and his heart flopped stickily around. They were loaded with swarms of small black caterpillars, living for the most part in communal cocoons, very large, white, and flossy and through which, though imprisoned they could still be seen, moving sluggishly. This vermin had attacked a great number of green things in the neighbourhood. They ate up the leaves and covered the bare branches with their horrible black masses and their giant cocoons. They confirmed Alphendéry's worst suspicions about the country.

The adjective "communal" strengthens the implication that the plight of communism is being described.

As well, the caterpillars and weeds of Frère's garden could be seen as extensions of the grotesquerie, surfeit and disorder that characterize so many of the human relationships in the book. People may be intent on pursuing sexual fulfilment, but the result is often unhappiness. For example, Léon's womanizing, however frenzied, is consistently sad in its grossness and fatuity.

The effect of grotesquerie is focussed in the chapter called "A Stuffed Carp" where so many of the novel's thematic strands come together—useless wealth, social parasitism, and the urge to dominate, which is given bizarre sexual expression ("Some strange feminine instinct prompted Mme. Haller to feed that great mountain of flesh till his eyes popped"). The occasion is a prime example in Stead's fiction of dinners with symbolic function.

Moral dialectic is suggested in the contrast of the Hallers' mode of life with Alphendéry's, and in the contrast of the meal's fulsomeness with the countering effect of words like "laxative" and "cathartic." The satirical tone of the writing is pointed by the irony of Haller's remarks about how revolutions "are necessary to purify the financial system" and how Lenin functions as a "cathartic," for the "ruling classes in Russia had stuffed themselves to bursting on interest." Stead's technique of correspondences is similar to that of Chekhov for whom food was often equated with emotional grossness, quite frequently with moral turpitude.

A grotesque sterility is predicated on the Hallers' attitudes, a sterility that is apparently physical as well as spiritual: the childless Hallers are the "sump of a large childless family," and Haller maintains "I realized that not only was the world sterile . . . but I was sterile." Moral cleansing is a concomitant of reform, as Haller owns in hypocritical vein: "The government should force us all to do some vulgar labor, like weeding gutters, or cleaning sewers, for a month every year: it would act as a purgative for our laziness." The metaphor of a disordered body, that goes with the notion of purging, together with other references to disease, anticipates the disease imagery of later books like ***Cotters' England*** and ***The Little Hotel.*** Syphilis is mentioned at least twice: "cancer" infects the bank: and we are told that Jules' father died of cancer.

But characteristically with Stead there is wry qualification to the vision of excess and disorder, in that the Bank is seen as not wholly chaotic nor unproductive. Alphendéry speculates that Adam's book of poetry, at least, will be "produced" by the Bank. The Nietzschean sound of this is similar to Louisa's dream for self-fulfilment expressed in Nietzsche's "Out of chaos ye shall give birth a dancing star." As with Stead's fiction generally, the end of the novel anticipates beginnings. There is an emphasis on different applications of the word "new" in the last chapter, as if to suggest the possibilities of new growth and hope.

Renewal and growth, however miniscule the hope for them, are pitched against a prevalent sense of metaphorical death and decay. Underlying this is a dialectical tension provided by the opposition of fate to free will, of an external determinism to the individual's assertiveness. The Bertillon bankers are seemingly men of action, capable by dint of willpower of affecting their own destinies; and yet there is a pervasive feeling that fate is working against them. It seems strange that Jules and his cronies should not put up more of a fight against Aristide. For all their brave and hectoring rhetoric they pussy-foot in acquiescence to his demands. Of the many references to fate in the novel, Aristide is perhaps the most frequent object as if he has been designated the chief agent of change. Such identification with the forces of history has the endorsement of the handwriting expert who prophesies that Aristide will come into money, and that "you run in cycles." Jean de Guipatin says of Aristide that, "He seems fated to do this . . . There's a positive fatality in it." An authorial comment provides a telling gloss: "he was ventripotent with destiny."

Not only does Jules decide not to fight, he courts disaster in his bet with Carrière when he could have rectified the situation. In his deliberate passivity he appears tantalized by the prospect of tragedy, and in this respect illustrates the Freudian construct of the death-wish. Indeed it is said of Jules, "In such voluntary types especially, the will persistently, unconsciously, day and night, and when the body is fatigued, it works as much towards death as life."

The drift towards spiritual death, from an ideological point of view, can be seen as the logical outcome of an alienated society, according to Marx's "analysis of reification." In this Marx showed that

> already in liberal capitalist society, relations between men had lost much of their qualitative and human character and had been transformed into mere quantitative relations. Moreover, their essence as social and interpersonal relations disappeared from man's consciousness to reappear in a reified form as a property of things . . . in capitalist societies an individual is split into two or three parts: the citizen, the actor in economic or professional life, and the private individual. In each of these sectors he had different values and rules of conduct and he is not able to realize unity in his life or a harmonious development of his personality.

So many of the book's characters could be cited as illustrating these ideas, but the novel is more complicated than a mere ideological polemic directed against the external greed of mankind. The intellectual approbation Stead might give to Marxist moral precept is balanced by the heart's endorsement of people who are richly human and the tension this provides is the essential quality of ***House of All Nations.*** (pp. 266-78)

Bruce Holmes, "Character and Ideology in Christina Stead's 'House of All Nations'," in Southerly, *Vol. 45, No. 3, September, 1985, pp. 266-79.*

Pearl K. Bell (review date 8 September 1986)

[*In the excerpt below, Bell negatively reviews* Ocean of Story *and provides an overview of Stead's work.*]

Throughout her long, restless, and productive life, the reputation of the Australian novelist Christina Stead rose and sank with disheartening regularity. Before her great novel of family life, ***The Man Who Loved Children,*** was reissued in 1965, 25 years after it was originally published and soon forgotten, all nine of the books she had by then written were out of print. Even when that novel received appreciative reviews, one looked in vain for some mention of Christina Stead in the Oxford and Penguin reference tomes on English literature. The omission could not be explained by her Australian origins, since such compatriots as Patrick White and Henry Handel Richardson were given respectful attention. . . .

It may well have been that the idiosyncratic diversity of Christina Stead's fiction, the bewildering unevenness of its quality, her astonishing shifts of setting and method from one book to another, made it difficult for reviewers and readers to discern a recognizable continuity of theme, subject, and purpose in her work, as though there were several different writers inside this novelist. (p. 32)

For a number of years before her death, the thick dust of

An excerpt from *The Man Who Loved Children*

Louisa was his first adolescent, too: he was full of the mystery of female adolescence of which, in his prim boyhood, he had been ignorant. He poked and pried into her life, always with a scientific, moral purpose, stealing into her room when she was absent, noting her mottoes on the wall, *By my hope and faith, I conjure ye,*

throw not away the hero in your soul
—Nietzsche

and investigating her linen, shivering with shame when suggestive words came into her mouth. Her speech, according to his genteel ideas, was too wild, too passionate, too suggestive. He told her not to use the words "quick and the dead," because "quick" meant the unborn; and not to use the words "passionate" or "passional," which she was fond of, and not to recite certain of her favorite passages because she did not know the meaning of them; and all with a shrinking niceness, a qualmish sensibility which surprised and repelled her. His nice Louisa, brought up on sawdust excerpts from potted philosophers, intended for the holy life of science, he could see (much as he closed his eyes), was a burning star, new-torn from the smoking flesh of a mother sun, a creature of passion. This was what her years of sullenness had concealed, not a quiet and patient nature, like her mother's, but a stern, selfish, vain nature like her grandfather's, wicked Israel's angry seed.

Sam tried all the recipes. He gave her her mother's photograph to hang above her bed.

"What is a photograph to me?" asked Louie insolently, "Mother is my mother" (meaning Henny). He gave her a photograph of himself taken when he was twenty-three, just before marriage, an incredibly mild, beaming angelic face, blond as the sun, dreamy and self-doubting. He carefully went through her books, her notebooks, and scraps of paper in order to guide her, set her right: his palpitating heart could not bear to think of her coming to shipwreck on the hidden reefs of youth: and, for her sake, he went through all the literature on adolescence, becoming more horrified every day as Satan's invisible world was revealed to him, who had been a bloodless youth living on greens and tap water. Youth was one of the beasts of Revelations, the worst, and more insolent than the Sun. He writhed within himself to think that his high-souled, sober-minded Louie had to go through all that. Why? With the proper training and abstracted from all bad companions, and carefully watched, he felt, and kept in touch with pure adult minds, she would pull through without scar or blot. He would be her constant companion: they would communicate thoughts, and she would be drawn to his side.

With mental lip-licking, he followed her in her most secret moments. She had papers and all sorts of rubbish to burn (she was always "clearing up her drawers"); she would build a fire by the side of the orchard and stand by, in a dream, smelling the smoke, differentiating the odors of burnt grass, paper, rag, and printed cardboard and so on, with the intoxication of an old drug fiend, adding things to the fire to get the smell: and then he would come creeping behind her, stealing up on her to discover what she was doing, what was in the fire, and what in heaven caused this strange drifting nebula to spin.

Christina Stead, in her The Man Who Loved Children, *Holt, Rinehart and Winston, 1940.*

neglect that shrouded Christina Stead's name for so long had begun to lift. Many of her books have been in print for some time, owing in part to the indefatigable salvage work of the feminist Virago Press in England. Clearly the feminist rediscovery of forgotten women writers was an important factor in the revival of interest in her work, though she herself was brusquely dismissive of women's lib. She told an interviewer in 1973 that it was "nonsense . . . a waste of time. . . . It's totally, purely middle class." And she added, with pungent Australian forthrightness, "What put me off is throw away their bra [sic]. What would I do without a bra, I should like to know?"

Now that her unfortunate literary fate has to some extent been redressed, Stead's publisher has paid her the customary posthumous homage with ***Ocean of Story,*** a ragbag gathering of previously uncollected short stories, false starts on several novels, sketches of boardinghouse life in England and Switzerland, a brief memoir of her father, and some rather disjointed reflections on the literary life. Like many such collections, this volume adds no luster to the writer's fame. One can only wonder what purpose is served by publishing such decidedly minor and fragmentary literary remains, since there is hardly anything in ***Ocean of Story*** that enhances one's understanding or appreciation of Christina Stead's work as a whole. Particularly in her case, it seems almost perverse to put these shreds and patches between covers, for her characteristic canvas, at its best, was huge, unconfined, profuse in detail. She was a writer whose very essence was excess.

Christina Stead was constitutionally incapable of brevity, of self-restraint, of discriminative spareness of any kind. She consumed words with the prodigality of a Dostoyevskian gambler hurling every coin he has at the croupier. Individual character was the absorbing passion in everything she wrote, and she pursued its sinuous and treacherous complexities with untamable confidence and sprawling vitality. In ***The Man Who Loved Children,*** there is a typically overpowering passage in which she describes the loathing that engorges Henny Pollit, a mother driven over the edge by a house too full of children, chaos, and poverty:

> Every room was a phial of revelation to be poured out some feverish night in the secret laboratories of her decisions, full of living cancers of insults, leprosies of disillusion, abscesses of grudge, gangrene of nevermore, quintan fevers of divorce, and all the proliferating miseries, the running sores and thick scabs, for which the flesh of marriage is so heavily veiled and conventually interned.

A writer capable of such demonic torrents is only crippled by the bounds of a short story. Stead needed largeness and space for her obsessively charged language and vision, space as vast and uncontained as her native country. This was clear in the first book she published, ***The Salzburg Tales,*** at the age of 32. The writing is all brilliance and gusto, but one can feel her straining against the limitations of the form she chose, a Boccaccian chain of some 40 monologues drawn from European folklore and legend, as told by a haphazard assemblage of people who have come to Salzburg for the August festival. The tales themselves, though spun with the pyrotechnical bravura of a young virtuoso eager to show her stuff, are less interesting than the biting satiric portraits of the tellers—a pretentious Viennese conductor, a Scottish woman doctor, an Italian singer, a French journalist, and others. But only four years later, using her experiences in the Paris bank, Stead hit her stride in the first of her two major novels, ***House of All Nations*** (1938), an enormously long (almost 800 pages), savagely observed, headlong dive into the world of international finance.

Stead took the ironic title from the name of a famous Parisian brothel. In over a hundred chapters bursting with an avaricious mob of crooks, speculators, impostors, dreamers, and degenerates, she laid bare the poisonous nature of money-making on a grand scale in the Europe of the 1930s as it staggered toward economic breakdown and war. (The theme of decadent Europe sliding into the hell-hole attracted many novelists in the 1930s, among them Robert Briffault, whose panoramic *Europa* was enormously popular in its time and is now totally forgotten.) Catching her gallery of scoundrels in a tightly woven net of stock quotations, grain options, exchange rates, bookkeeping manipulations, and legal skulduggery, she constructs her monstrous edifice of greed and corruption until, when it finally collapses, we are left not only with the stench of moral disgust toward this labyrinthine world of financial swindlers but with awe at her omnivorous mastery of exactly the way it all works. Stead could not let go until the absolute rottenness had been plumbed with merciless clarity. As one rogue in the story remarks, "There's no subject so rich in ideas as Money."

But memory, as Stead demonstrated two years later (her fluency and speed were phenomenal), was even richer in literary possibility, more daunting and more fruitful than money. With the same copious, unrelenting intensity she had brought to the machinations of banking, Stead turned back to her adolescent years (transposed from Australia to Washington) in her saga of the Pollit family, awash in misery and tenderness as domestic war rages day and night within the walls of the shabby house.

The husband, Samuel Clemens Pollit, was based on Christina Stead's father, a naturalist and Fabian socialist who worked for the Australian Fisheries Service. Sam is a windbag idealist who "loves" children (with seven, he yearns for more) because he is an overgrown child himself. Full of exasperating Darwinian optimism about progress and the perfectibility of man, Sam is, like so many of Stead's autocrats of the ego, a geyser of self-satisfied cant, a chirping domestic tyrant who exploits his children under the guise of play. For Sam, the family romance is a jolly kindergarten and his bitter wife Henny the wicked witch threatening to devour them all. Coarse, mawkish, and cruel by turns, a Dickensian grotesque yet horribly believable, Sam is too complacent, too self-absorbed, too pleased with his inventive cuteness—he talks to his children in a language that is part baby talk, part Uncle Remus and Artemus Ward—to notice the extremity of his wife's despair.

Henny, as Randall Jarrell remarked in his lyrical introduction to the novel's reincarnation, is "the book's center of gravity, of tragic weight." The most haunting and fully realized of Christina Stead's many driven, unhappy women, Henny leaves an ineradicable scar in the mind. The spoiled favorite of a well-to-do father, she has become, after ten years of marriage, too many children, and never enough money, a ranting, slatternly hag worn out with drudgery and rage at the fate dealt her by her mortal enemy, her husband. Henny, Stead writes, "was beautifully, whole-heartedly vile: she asked no quarter and gave none to the foul world," and her screaming tirades ring with the stark universality of epic poetry as she gives voice to "the natural outlawry of women." Stead's novels are full of obsessive histrionic talkers, unstoppable monologuists borne on a tidal wave of words, but Henny is the most incessantly complex of them all, as heartbreaking as she is terrible. Only death can silence her.

None of the novels that Stead wrote after this profoundly original triumph of imagination and memory has anything of the turbulent life, the harrowing inexorability and fateful reality of ***The Man Who Loved Children.*** In trying to explain this, Jarrell argued that the failure of the Pollit novel, both with critics and with the reading public, led Christina Stead to "unconsciously work in a more limited way in the books that follow[ed] it." The world's incomprehension, he felt, had stunted the genius that flowered in ***The Man Who Loved Children.*** He may be right, though it is not a simple matter to know why a writer's work declines, loses some vital strength and conviction, after a great achievement.

Nonetheless, Stead was the kind of exuberantly natural writer who couldn't stop putting one word after another. She wrote eight books after 1940, nine if one counts the unpublished ***I'm Dying Laughing,*** an American novel about the McCarthy years that she worked at off and on for decades. (One chapter, "UNO 1945," is included in ***Ocean of Story,*** and while it has one of her gloriously vituperative husband-and-wife battles, and some intriguing remarks about disillusioned radicals, the piece, torn out of context, yields very little as it stands, in part because her point of view is unclear.) Though the novels that followed her finest book are now and then enlivened by her shrewd intelligence and harsh wit, by her earthy candor about sex (in a much more inhibited literary climate than our own), by her unique way of seeing and defining her characters, such novels as ***Letty Fox: Her Luck, A Little Tea, A Little Chat,*** and ***The People with the Dogs*** can be repetitious and tedious, marred by unexpectedly flaccid and mechanical prose, as though her burning way with words was beginning to run out of steam. Even the most ambitious of her later novels, ***Cotter's England*** (1966), unfathomably renamed ***Dark Places in the Heart*** in America, is too unrelievedly single-minded in its relentless portrayal of the heroine, a destructive left-wing journalist in postwar Britain. The subtle authenticities that she endowed with such life, affection, and fierce truth in ***The Man Who Loved Children*** for some reason eluded her grasp in the work that came after.

And still the question nags, and will do so as long as Christina Stead is remembered: How could that brilliant novel have fallen between the cracks when it first appeared?

Ironically, some of Stead's communist friends in New York may have been partly responsible for its neglect. Isidor Schneider, the culture commissar of *The New Masses* in the 1930s and '40s, meant to praise the book and buried it when he hailed ***The Man Who Loved Children*** as "a novelization of Engels' *Origin of the Family.*" A surer way of killing all interest in a literary work is hard to imagine. But for Schneider a novel's value lay only in its ability to raise the consciousness of the working class.

Despite her involvement in communist politics, Stead was never tempted to write such dreary sagas of revolutionary uplift as Clara Weatherwax's *Marching! Marching!* and other politically "correct" socialist realist works of the '30s. Stead was entirely too independent a spirit, always her own woman, and she remained impatient with cultural fashion to the end of her days. Yet the Marxist claim on her was incredibly persistent. As late as 1965, José Yglesias insisted in the *Nation* that the Pollit novel was primarily an attack on the bourgeois family, "that soul-destroying monster." The reason for her neglect, he wrote, was political: "It is Stead's Marxist point of view which has delayed her recognition. . . . Marxist ideas [are] inseparable from Stead's literary vision." With such friends, Stead didn't need enemies.

As for ***Ocean of Story,*** whose publication once again prompts interest in Christina Stead—forget it. Go back and read the novel that earns this remarkable writer a permanent place in the pantheon of literature. (pp. 32-4)

Pearl K. Bell, "The Woman Who Loved Words," in The New Republic, *Vol. 195, No. 10, September 8, 1986, pp. 32-4.*

Susan Sheridan (essay date 1988)

[*In the following excerpt from her book* Christina Stead, *Sheridan examines* Letty Fox: Her Luck *and* Miss Herbert (The Suburban Wife) *as portraits of their titular heroines.*]

Letty Fox: Her Luck (1946) and ***Miss Herbert (The Suburban Wife)*** (1976), although published thirty years apart, were written at about the same time in the late 1940s and early 1950s. Both novels are more readily imaged in the circlings of frustrated will and desire than in the outward flight or the onward march of the 'free woman'. Like painted portraits they guide the eye in concentric circles, and each is characterized by a rhythm of repetition rather than a strong narrative line.

The narrative, always in close-up, accumulates details without ever clarifying direction. The concluding words of each protagonist reiterate this sense of aimless movement:

> . . . but I'm no tea leaf reader. I can only tangle with situations as they come along. *On s'engage et puis on voit.* (***Letty Fox***)

> 'I kept to the rules, but the rules didn't keep me. But I hewed to the line; I cultivated my garden.' (***Miss Herbert***)

Each of these heroines emphasizes both her antiheroism and her struggle for self-respect. In this way they sign themselves as pre-eminently bourgeois figures, portraits of middle-class women (North American and English, respectively) who proudly proclaim their own ordinariness: 'just an ordinary woman' (Eleanor), a 'typical New York girl' (Letty). It is a mark of the peculiarity of Stead's ironic portraits that this claim is presented as part of their strength, their robust gift for social conformity and thus survival, even while their capacity to deny responsibility for their actions by hiding behind that same claim to ordinariness is being exposed by the narrative's ironies. Letty, claiming always to shrink from 'what was beyond the pale', is portrayed as a female adept of the sexual picaresque; Eleanor, the ladylike English rose, is observed engaging in all manner of sexual and social hypocrisies.

Yet neither novel could be satisfactorily described as a study in bad faith, for the portraitist's ironic shading moves sometimes into the sharp contrasts of satire, sometimes in the opposite direction towards straight reportage. Because of this variation, the position constructed for the reader to occupy proves unstable, and there is no easy access to either judgement or sympathetic identification of the kind one expects as a reader of realist narrative. The instability of one's position as reader is the more noticeable because both are *single* portraits, concentrating fully on the female protagonist (even more than on Teresa in ***For Love Alone***), so that other characters are known only through their report, or in relation to them.

That is to say, these single portraits are presented as self-portraits. Letty tells her story in her own words, while Eleanor's is reported from her own purblind point of view, with her own line in clichés. Each woman is made up out of her language, which is itself made up out of the discourses of contemporary capitalist popular culture—populist political rhetoric, women's magazine advice columns, and so on. But both, too, are educated women, and just as likely as Louie [in ***The Man Who Loved Children***] or Teresa to appropriate for themselves the commonplaces of European high culture. The situations in which they do so, however, render such allusions ironic, if not satirical: Letty's Napoleonic motto (*'on s'engage et puis on voit'*) sees her through some particularly fierce and sordid campaigns in the sex war, while Eleanor Herbert ('I cultivated my garden') emerges as a female Candide whose innocence is dangerous indeed. Yet the ironic presentation of these women is not entirely at their expense, for it shows them struggling to construct their own subjectivities out of the ideological materials at hand. It is a technique involving fidelity to these materials, and implying an unusual respect for the ways in which they function as structures of reality, as truths, for these social/historical subjects. Its targets are social and political rather than personal and moral.

If we read these novels to learn 'what women have felt and experienced', [as Elaine Showalter wrote in her "Towards a Feminist Poetics", in *Women Writing and Writing about Women,* edited by Mary Jacobus, 1979,] then we shall only learn again what misogynists have always maintained, that women are innately conservative—for this is how they present themselves. These somewhat disreputable protagonists seem far from providing the kind of access to female experience which has been most prized in feminist literary criticism. Neither heroines nor victims of patriarchal society, each is thoroughly a creature of her time, as she is formed by, and engages in articulating, the ideologies and institutions of her particular society. They portray women living out the realities of these ideologies, and yet each 'lives a full life, she fulfils herself in her own way'. These novels challenge directly the feminist critic's expectation of hearing the true voice of women's experience behind the clamour of competing ideologies, of seeing the true face of womanhood beneath the masks of femininity: they challenge the adequacy of sex-role theory, in effect. Stead even provides in each novel a sketch of the contrary view that we all only ever act parts, and that perhaps the quality of that self-fulfilment depends on the quality of the script chosen: Mathilde, Letty's mother, only ever shows her strength when she is reliving her days as an actress, before she became a mother; and Eleanor remembers playing the part of Lady Teazle, when a student, as the most intensely lived moment of her life.

If we read these portraits, instead, to learn how middle-class women have been culturally constructed in English and U.S. society in the first half of the twentieth century, then both ***Letty Fox*** and ***Miss Herbert*** emerge as *historical* novels of a kind that are especially interesting to feminists. Each of them is 'a complete social stereotype—the woman of the women's magazines', in the words of [Pamela Law in 'Letty Fox, Her Luck', *Southerly* 38, No. 4 (1978)], who discusses ***Letty Fox*** as a novel 'more about the processes of socialization than it is about individual experience, or . . . the relations between the self and its experience'. And if we attend closely to their claims to representativeness, we can read as well in their narratives trenchant analyses, in a kind of allegorical form, of these whole societies. Their ordinariness and representativeness are established by the accumulation of linguistic detail that precisely identifies the working of contemporary sexual, political and social ideologies. Letty and Eleanor both contribute to the public articulation and circulation of these discourses, through their work in journalism and publishing, and also live out these meanings in their personal lives. Their wasted educations, unhappy relations with men, lack of political commitment, and retreat into respectable marriage and motherhood, all appear to confirm parodically the dire predictions of those who opposed women's emancipation at the turn of the century. Yet as educated middle-class women in a male world that denies them real freedoms, their choices may be interpreted as rational ones.

The great events of economic depression, political mobilization, war and reconstruction structure the lives represented in these novels without themselves being elaborately drawn in. At one level, Letty and Eleanor can be seen as allegorical figures representing the dominant responses of their class and nationality to these events.

For Letty, the 'wide-awake New Yorker', to become socialist during her buoyant adolescence in the 1930s means to be youthful and progressive, but it has no social urgency for this indulged child of middle-class survivors for whom the Wall Street crash had meant proceeding to live on debts:

> We did not want things to remain *in statu quo* for our lifetime . . . because, actually, things had been changing since we were born, and we were enthusiastically used to it. Although our parents (my mother, I should say) worried about my *sense of security* (a cant phrase of the time), none of us had ever had that; and it was rather the struggle that made us strong.

What Letty means by 'struggle', however, is not class struggle but a 'Darwinian' notion of life that 'relates me, *Letty-Marmelade-always-in-a-jam,* to the plant in my window-box'. A few years later and no longer buoyant but fed up with her romantic encounters and ready to settle down, she complains to her idealistic sister:

> I don't want to be a real worker. Why do we have to struggle? I don't believe in the struggle of youth. Things ought to be made easy for us when we are at the height of our powers . . .

Shrewd Letty has already pointed out that 'radicalism is the opium of the middle class', and she is a sharp observer of her fellow radicals who, once the war effort was stepped up after Pearl Harbor, had all 'fallen into line with an ungraceful bump and there was no more official iconoclasm'. She cheerfully admits that:

> I had enough red blood not to like a lot of things I saw passing under the name of patriotism and the war effort, but I hadn't the guts, folly, or lunacy to go out on my own hook. I had to belong to society.

This was the 'moral bottom, which always comes with the profit-taking hour'; rather than take a stand against it, Letty resolves to get with the strength:

> My marshal's baton was once more peeping up out of my knapsack and sprouting. . . . If only I could get in touch with a great man of action, if only I could work together with men of energy and intelligence, modern men who think the way I do. I couldn't do anything with the compatible groups in which I was happy but lazy . . . ; and I couldn't do much as a stenographer, a special article-writer, or a messenger girl; and I couldn't do much, truth to tell, bringing more larval human beings into the daylight and worrying about diapers and cute little sayings and lisping geniuses for years, at least, not at my age. I felt the world was too small for me.

This is not a choice between conformity and heroic action so much as a desire to be one of the boys, for whatever they are doing will be preferable to the limited roles allocated to women. This classically feminine dilemma is exacerbated by the wartime conditions, of course, but when the war is over Letty is more than ready to marry and have her baby: 'One can't make a great stir, but one can be on the side of the angels'. Letty has a phrase for everything, no matter how sharply it might contradict her previous statements, but this is all of a piece with her vaunted pragmatism, capacity to respond to change and to survive through adaptation. This is her specifically American version of common sense, the hard-headed *laissez-faire* realism which is the legacy of nineteenth-century liberalism.

Miss Herbert's appeal to commonsense and realism is of a different hue from Letty's, but it is the sign of her conformity to a different society, in England, and to a different moment in bourgeois ideology, that of Tory conservatism. Just as Letty's narrative demonstrates the private and social conditions in which U.S. Left radicalism gained and then lost its momentum, so the presentation of Eleanor's Tory populism shows both the power of its reassuring rationality, and its constitutive force in all areas of this woman's life. She is the woman of the century, 'nothing more nor less than a representation of the home life of Britannia from the Twenties until almost the present day' [as Angela Carter commented in 'Unhappy Families', *London Review of Books,* September 16 to October 6, 1982]. She wants to be a good woman, asking nothing more than a 'plain, wholesome life', choosing a 'rational' modern marriage, a business arrangement, 'no closed world, but society, neighbours, the stream of time'. Populist discourse draws on such organic images as this, as well as recalling the classical liberal terminology of natural rights ('Society wants us to be happy, doesn't it? And it's our natural right. So why shouldn't it all chime together?').

The allegorical mode is pronounced in ***Miss Herbert*** where, for instance, her friend Linda Mack is said to belong to a 'well-to-do Whig family' and to be 'a champion of many liberal causes, of free trade, minority rights, social services, nationalization of industry'; and where Eleanor herself is connected through her family to other political alternatives, the vaguely socialist anti-imperialism represented by her father and brother and their not quite self-sufficient 'Commonwealth Farm', and an opposing moral revivalism represented by her mother's membership of the New Religious Society. The political associations of the Society are indicated by the fact that Eleanor's profascist husband is employed by it on mysterious missions all over Europe. Eleanor and he are divorced, appropriately enough, during the course of the Second World War, yet she continues in her mild but deadly way to share his views, refusing to countenance ' "bogey" talk of fascism renascent', declaring that the people in 'those camps' were only 'Communists and such fomenters of disorder and gypsies and such who are outsiders anywhere'.

During this period of the war, Eleanor is forced to confront doubt and disorder on both personal and national fronts. Her response to the war is identical to her bewilderment about the failure of her marriage:

> 'Did I marry the wrong man? . . . It's as if there's something I don't understand, but I do understand, I face all my problems squarely.' . . . 'What if we go down? If it's all been for nothing? If we've all been wrong? Can I live in a world where the British Empire does not live?'

It is said that 'she never recovered from those days, she never recovered her self-possession'. In the second half of the novel her life and, by implication, England's, go downhill all the way in aimless muddling and inefficient hard work. After the war, when she tries to earn a living by selling her literary talents on Grub Street, consumed by the passion of 'guinea fever', she ends up working for a petty political spy, feeding him information about the personal lives of her Leftist acquaintances.

She takes on the mindlessly conservative ideological role attributed to middle-class English women by political pundits of the Right and Left, and she takes it on with enthusiasm. She is a dyed-in-the-wool Tory populist, sentimentally patriotic about 'old England' but passive in the face of change. Believing that 'change comes by itself', Eleanor criticizes as 'rash rank outsiders' those who would intervene in this natural process and cause disorder, people like her father, brother and sister-in-law. They, meanwhile, contradict her claim that England is 'a perfectly free society', arguing that 'covert understandings had repressed thoughts and thoughts had dwindled and died'. The statement is as true for Eleanor as it is for the country: both suffer intellectual atrophy.

Not to mention sexual atrophy. Eleanor believes there is a clear-cut choice for a woman between passionate love and respectable marriage, but on the way to the latter she allows herself a string of aimless sexual encounters, satisfying her curiosity and testing her capacity to attract men. She justifies her actions as 'striking a blow for freedom' or, later, romanticizes her past as 'struggle and dreams and youth'. (It is interesting to see in her notes that one of the alternative titles Stead considered for this novel was 'The Lady and the Slut'.) Much later, as a divorced woman, the separation between her scattered masturbatory fantasies and sentimental friendships with men is bridged by the narcissistic relationship with Quaideson, the old man who watches her pose and never touches her. She is finally able to feel 'perfectly feminine' in the gaze of this necrophiliac admirer, posing among his collection of ancient torture instruments. In her, as Helen Yglesias wrote, 'private and social anguish mesh perfectly' ['Christina Stead, Australia's Neglected Maverick', *National Times,* 5-10 July 1976.].

Eleanor's life touches significant social and political conflicts of her times, yet events in the public sphere scarcely impinge on her consciousness. She remains calm, like a somnambulist, or, when aroused, becomes merely confused. At the same time, the story of her life comes to represent a specific response to those events, specified through the national, class and gender ideologies in which it is told. It is through the silences and the contradictions in this ideological texture that the meaning of political events and personal desires and fears can be understood.

With Letty, in contrast, everything is said, but nothing is reflected upon. The metaphor for *her* text is a visual rather than verbal one. She is, by her own admission, short-sighted and cannot see very far ahead: 'if I could only see clearer ahead, I'd make my way with a straight mind, for I can always look myself in the face and add one and one'. Here, then, the first-person narrative allows for both direct social criticism of sexual-economic hypocrisies and, through the revelation of the narrator's short-sightedness, indirect criticism of the ideologies which inform her commonsense realism.

The discourses of common sense constantly produce new forms, such as the cant phrases that Eleanor draws on (and reproduces in her own magazine stories) to regulate social and personal exchanges. Here, for instance, her rules meet some resistance, and her angry reaction finds immediate expression in a racist accusation against her German husband, Henry:

> Over and over again she had read that 'before dinner just one glass of sherry . . . is correct . . . ' She had written it herself. 'More leads to raised voices and flushed faces'. Now, mortified, in her mind accusing the immoderate habits of Continentals, she went away ('slipped away' she thought to herself) and put on the dinner; Henry should not have the second bottle of sherry.

On many occasions, her rules are resisted by some unrecognized, unacknowledged part of herself, which interrupts the constant process of editing her reactions in conformity to the ideological norms of femininity:

> . . . [T]o her confusion, indignant phrases repeated themselves in her mind while she recalled scenes which had left her sore—even though she had always been considerate, sensible, humane and 'exercised her saving sense of humour'. . . . A scene. In the original: 'Henry, what you call self-reliance and self-control, I call plain self . . . you retire into this self-sufficiency, to humiliate me. I won't be humiliated.' This mental record ran quickly through, and she edited as it ran, till it then took on its enduring form: 'Henry dear, let us just sit down awhile and thrash this thing out. . . .' Henry then ideally replied, 'I admit I am too self-sufficient . . . You have a better form of it, self-reliance. A mother is closer to the human race.' . . . But this rainbow interchange was coarsely interrupted by fierce words hurtling across her mind: 'He gets the best end of the stick and leaves me all the dirty work. He's a brute, the cold little climbing devil.'

Like Letty, too, she has a phrase for everything, and all the phrases can be traced to contemporary discourses on psychology, politics, and so on. They could, theoretically, *all* be enclosed in quotation marks. But it is more than that. Rather, the phrases make her, they *are* her reactions. Stead's writing, in all the later texts but especially in these two, repeatedly demonstrates that we are constructed by language, that language makes us rather than we it, in the sense that it gives a material existence to emotions and ideas which could not otherwise be knowable.

Letty's difference from Eleanor, which could be read as a national as well as a temperamental difference, is that she is aware that these social rules and recipes rarely work, and inevitably contradict one another. She is an expert on women's rules for knowing and controlling men, having listened since babyhood to her deserted mother's friends ('these gossips and pocket Machiavellis') offering useless advice to the luckless Mathilde. Letty's training is thorough, and she learns from a variety of sources apart from family gossip. As a schoolgirl, she learns to extract money from her father to help her 'meet the right boy' and get established:

> Every magazine in the country was on my side. They all showed a slick, amusing Powers model gouging money out of smooth Papas for clothes, motor-cars, hair-dos, and society colleges.

Stead makes it perfectly clear that realities are constructed, not given, and that their construction is a function of social institutions such as the media and the education system. She also, in Eleanor, makes it clear that, whether we allow ourselves to recognize it or not, we are never passive victims of this socialization process but rather use what we need. But it is social not moral criticism that results for, as another character puts it in ***Cotters' England,*** a hungry mind will feed on garbage if that is all there is available. One thing that makes Letty's story more enjoyable to read than Eleanor's is that her garbage is more interesting: it includes wisecracks and jokes, and its effect is mostly comic. The effect of recounting Miss Herbert's socialization as a lady tends instead to the absurd.

Sex and love are central preoccupations in both these portrait novels. Through Letty, Stead analyses the sexual economics of middle-class marriage in all its sordid detail. It is women's business in life to 'know men', and yet Letty knows that the men do what they like (despite groans of anguish from charmers like her father Solander and Uncle Philip), while the women merely survive, their professed high morality inevitably at variance with their actions, and ranged against each other in the competition for men:

> Impossible to become corrupt in this school for girls, for no one had the recipe for getting anything. Even Grandmother's recipe for getting Solander back had not yet worked, and Grandmother didn't seem to care much.

It is Grandmother who offers Mathilde the cynical fruits of her wisdom, that is, that with two small children to raise and no money of her own, she cannot afford the luxury of love. That must wait until she can pay for it: ' "When you're forty or forty-five, it'll be time to think about necking and—" her voice softened—"love—and men—and all that" '. This principle of robust submission to the conditions of life for women in a world run by men becomes Letty's guide.

Letty's picaresque tale, from her childhood onwards, is a 'veritable encyclopedia of the relations between men and women', [according to Mary Kathleen Benet in her introduction to ***Letty Fox,***] and there are few novels in English before the 1970s which have been so matter of factly frank about taboo subjects like female sexual aggression, male impotence, or the fatal combination of a woman's erotic obsession with a man who is 'a tease, a hound of love'. Unlike the sexual autobiographies of the 1970s, however, these experiences are not given the status of major narrative turning-points, measures of the heroine's approach to selfhood, but are represented in the picaresque mode as brief episodes. But, although never elaborated in detail, they are made significant as illustrating Letty's theory of the material basis of love:

> 'You know love isn't something mystic; it's a

> bloody real thing, there's nothing realer; and it grows out of all that madness at night, that growing together in the night, that thing without eyes, but with legs, that fit of convulsions, all that we had—'

A different kind of love is set against this theory in Letty's sister Jacky's passion for old men, in particular Gondych, whom she imagines as a modern Faust, herself as Marguerite. It is interesting that Stead's manuscript notes relating to this novel contain a great deal more material on this theme, and it recurs in other notes on a fable of a woman's sexual initiation and obsession. These notes also include more explicit sexual descriptions than any she published, whereas in this novel there is a dramatic separation between Jacky's apparently unfulfilled passion (much like Teresa's in ***For Love Alone***) and Letty's varied sexual encounters with men. Yet it is Letty, not her sister, who fears her own capacity for insatiable desire and for whom marriage offers safety, a rest from sexual tourism.

The second part of Letty's story, 'On My Own', is mainly concerned with her experiences of what Grandmother succinctly calls 'the tourist business', that is, free love as invented by men. What promises to be an exploratory journey into unknown and exotic country turns out to be expensive, repetitive and often painful, and after a few years Letty is more than ready to go home. Her recurrent images of herself as a ship indicate the contradictions of her position as a 'free woman'. When her freewheeling life goes well, she sees herself as a pleasure boat cruising from one port to another leaving the dullards behind on the wharf holding broken streamers. When a string of disastrous love affairs and an abortion leave her feeling depressed, she thinks that:

> the woman looking for love is like a little boat meeting waterspout after waterspout. She is tired of steering, rowing, looking for land, hanging up old shirts for sails and the rest of it. But the pirates, they are not tired at all. . . . Perhaps I would weather the troubles and begin to regard men and their passions merely as trade winds.

The world of men is her element, but she is unhappy floating aimlessly around in it. She wants a chance to fulfil her proper purpose:

> I was no hulk nor ghost-ship, but a good freighter made to carry bread and bibles around the world; I was a good, deep draught, built on dependable old-fashioned lines, no victory ship, no canal boat, and no ship of the line. But a freighter doesn't particularly care for the heaving billow; a freighter has a destination. . . .

To be good is to be useful, for this child of the New World, and so marriage and pregnancy confer on Letty the self-respect she had felt lacking. It's notable, however, that for all her talk of great men, she is not looking for a pilot, only for a freight; and in the end she believes she has found this in maternity, what she was looking for all along, 'union with something, an ideal, a lover'.

She respects, she declares, 'not only my present position, but also all the efforts I made, in every direction, to get here'. Her morality is much the same as that attributed to Moll Flanders two hundred years earlier, and it serves a similar purpose, to reveal a situation essentially unchanged since the eighteenth century. Prostitution is the inevitable by-product of a 'free' marriage market where women's economic and social vulnerability obliges them to sell themselves to the highest bidder, the 'free woman' being the one who hires herself rather than selling outright. Like Moll, Letty defends the system with a stoical realism that allows for little self-pity, even less compassion for other women, and no possibility of rebelling against it:

> I do not even see a scandal in this, for wide-awake women. In other times, society regarded us as cattle or handsome house slaves; the ability to sell ourselves any way we like is a step towards freedom; we are in just the same position as our Negro compatriots—and they would not go backwards towards their miserable past.

Letty's cheerful acceptance of capitalism's commodication of everything, and her Roosevelt-like rhetoric about taking the good with the bad and looking towards the future, require an immense capacity for self-contradiction. One is tempted to see this, as Elizabeth Perkins does [in 'Energy and Originality in Some Characters of Christina Stead', *Journal of Commonwealth Literature* 15, No. 1 (1980)], as the clue to Letty's psychology as a 'converter of facts' who constantly reconstructs reality according to her needs. Or one can read it as a clue to her times, to the fluctuations of political fashion. Yet what it also does—and this is primary in the novel as a literary fiction—is constantly to unsettle the established hierarchy of truths, weighing them all equally whether the language in which they materialize is banal or profound. It becomes impossible to extract from this levelling of discourses the kinds of moral affirmations that literary critics most frequently demand from fiction.

The problem posed by reading this text is similar to that posed by Defoe's Moll Flanders, as others have remarked—How reliable is this first-person narrator? What is the centre of value in all this flux of detail? Letty has been judged [by Angela Carter] 'a self-righteous bitch and a heartless betrayer'. Yet she can equally be regarded as managing to survive and to stay human by playing the rules of the game—and by being lucky. [In *Christina Stead,* Diana Brydon] takes her at her own description as a 'generous fool' who is instrumental in revealing social folly. Readers tend to emphasize either her iconoclasm, her refusal to 'live the way a woman ought to live according to male mythology', or to point out that 'neither does she live the way a woman ought to be able to live' [Meaghan Morris, in her introduction to the 1974 edition of ***Letty Fox***]. In this open situation, the reader's judgement of the character determines which narrative mode is identified as dominant; a satirical analysis of the rules of the game by a shrewd player, a revelation of social folly by a 'generous fool', or a comic study in female bad faith.

With Eleanor Herbert the problem of how to read the heroine is exacerbated: the option of seeing her as a social critic in her own right is not available, and she is consistently the object of the novel's satire. She arouses pity, then disgust, then a kind of shocked amusement. She is surely one of the most disconcerting heroines in fiction, and this is one of the most curious novels, with its pastiche of popular discourses and a predominant comic effect that is mordant rather than scintillating.

Yet some readers conceive her as a tragic figure in that her attempts to 'measure down' [Elizabeth Perkins] to the middle-class norm of femininity demonstrate such a waste of energy, and it has been further suggested that her refusal of passionate love is a measure of that waste—that the possibility of love provides the novel with a centre of value. This feminist reading seeks a fictional resolution of the contradictions set in play by Stead's characters in their capacity for love, even if this capacity goes unrealized. Can we, then, take Letty at her word that her life's voyage is only now beginning? Can we read Eleanor's life as a tragedy of unfulfilled passion? It is true that she is presented as an unawakened Venus, that her life is a series of shabby failures and hypocrises which appear to be the consequences of her having chosen conformity. Yet, as I have already suggested, there is little narrative encouragement to read her story as either a tragedy or a moral condemnation of the unfulfilled life, for the moral condemnation is ultimately directed at a society which could set such rules, and Eleanor is too enthusiastically part of it to be tragic.

Nevertheless there is something about the writing in the two incidents where passion enters her life which singles them out from the insistent ordinariness of the prose throughout ***Miss Herbert.*** With a sudden shift in register to language signifying passion, all that has been absent from the rest of the narrative seems to emerge, like the return of the repressed, an eruption of utopian desire and the fear of death. Eleanor's response to certain men each time shakes the foundations of her rational common sense, but each time she rejects passion, and in similar terms: it was 'a threat, like a premonition of disease' that would ruin her life, it would be like submitting to 'the hand of fate'; it was 'as if a new world came somewhere near her world and she felt its attraction and feared to be pulled away off the earth, out of life'. This cosmic, mystical language suggests that Eleanor may be read as a development of the character type Stead has one of her characters in ***The Beauties and Furies*** describe as a 'complex, subtle nature—chiefly latent, though, so that her will only appears in common rational-mystic forms known to dream doctors and psychiatrists'. That is, the mystical powers which are attributed to passion are the other side of the coin from her determinedly one-dimensional rationalism; the same might be said of the contrast between Letty's 'realism' and Jacky's idealism *vis-à-vis* love and sex.

Side by side with Eleanor's fearful responses to the man, there occurs in each incident a passage of hallucinatory images of pleasure. The first of these encounters occurs in a church, at a wedding:

> She might have been asleep hearing a dream symphony, the people and church swirled round her in a stately circle. Thoughts went through her mind that had never been part of her before: There are side booths, confessionals, I suppose, thousands of lives have been lived before me. . . . Just streaming out into what's far away. And those to come—a cataract of light! Ages and ages of people. . . .
>
> These stray ideas were as fragrant and delightful to her as patches of low-growing flowers on a forest floor. . . . A great quiet wind blowing round and round her on which the church and audience were dim paintings from past time, carried before her eyes, recollections, images and breaths of passion, like sprays of flowers. . . .

The imagery recalls Teresa's epithalamium, her vision of time floating away like a river in full flood, a vision which is only reached by breaking through the 'iron circle' of individual consciousness, and by breaking the social/moral law, even risking 'madness'. Kinetic images (swirling, streaming, blowing) suggest bodily sensation as well as violent mental and emotional activity, and this pattern recurs in the second such incident, towards the end of the novel when, as a woman of fifty, Eleanor meets her daughter's lover at the opera:

> Her heart had begun a great circular thrumming, so it felt. Round and round it gadded, making larger swoops, . . . as if she were floating, with her large body, round the great dome. Her heart began pounding out hard and real thoughts, like pieces of metal, too; and she heard them, forceful, unanswerable: This is love and he knows it; it would be too strong for me, my life would be carried away into a whirlpool, round and round and down, in the centre, lost and gone. . . . There'd be no meaning to the world or time, but this hour and the future hours with him would break into everything, flooding everything, everything would be washed away . . .

Like the church setting on the previous occasion, the music provides a structure within which both her vertiginous fear—of losing control, of chaos and death—and her intimations of pleasure can be accommodated. Might this be read as an implicit comment on the role of art?

Yet there is a more troubling question here than that of the role of passion in the novel's structure or the character's psychology, and it is a question of the codes of representation. Both these moments of passion in the novel are marked by the appearance of a further discourse, distinguishable from the cosmic and kinetic imagery quoted above. It is a sub-Lawrentian or Mills and Boon discourse on sexual attraction:

> But he had looked at her and she at him with the same intensity and knowledge that an animal has, when it looks straight into the eyes of a human, a meaningless but profound and moving look.

and again, her daughter's fiancé, meeting her:

> looked straight into Eleanor's eyes with the glance of a man who understands a woman wants him and who gives himself and means to take all, a dark look that existed long before language.

At this point we have not only to deal with this recognizable code of commodified sexual mysticism, but also with the shift to a projected masculine point of view, to the male gaze ('a man who understands . . .'). It is difficult for readers to know where we stand.

What is more, the opera is Verdi's *La Forza del Destino.* The narrative's only comment on this fact is the aside, 'for some reason Eleanor always called it *La Sforza del Destino'.* The slip is revealing, for *sforza,* effort or exertion, is the keynote of her own destiny: it is what she substitutes for this fearful submission to fate. Her namesake in the opera, Leonora, on the other hand, follows the dictates of passion and brings about the deaths of her father and brother as well as herself. If this is Western culture's story of the woman who commits herself to passion, perhaps Eleanor is right to leave it well alone. The parodic effect established by this mixture of popular sexual-mystical language and allusion to high culture's representations of tragic passion puts in question the possible status of passion as authentic, or a moral centre.

Yet these 'parallel texts' of popular and high culture are both products of a patriarchal culture, representations of a femininity which in fact serves to elicit male desire and subsequent action. They both signify male desire, and so raise the problem of how *female* desire may be signified by such cultural codes, a question addressed in the novel itself. The allusion to Verdi's Leonora recalls another story mentioned in ***Miss Herbert,*** the novel written by her father about Sabrina, the consumptive *femme fatale* who makes all the men in the village fall in love with her, and ruins them. Obviously, it flatters Eleanor's fantasy of her power to attract men, particularly as she has renounced this eroticized image of woman since her marriage and taken on its complement in patriarchal iconography, the image of the asexual and censoring mother. There are, of course, no reflections of this kind in the text—only the throw-away line: 'the story was tender, forgiving, like a man writing about his daughter'. The *femme fatale* (like Leonora) represents disorder and ultimately death for men, and if Eleanor is flattered by the story's representation of Woman, she is perhaps even more attracted by its tender tone because, as we have seen earlier, a daughter may need forgiveness from the father for being a woman at all. Eleanor's father's choice of the name Sabrina for his heroine recalls the chaste nymph in Milton's 'Comus', defender of women's 'honour' and controller of the stream of life. Such a woman might be especially pleasing to a jealous father.

Eleanor's response is to take the book over: she revises it, writing in the 'female psychology', but there is some quarrel about the latter, her father maintaining that 'every man has something feminine in him', and then she has to rewrite again to suit editors' demands for 'reader identification' and 'common coin'. Finally it is published, as *Brief Candle,* 'not much noticed but well sold'.

This aspect of the incident links it to other instances of literary satire, parody and pastiche in ***Miss Herbert.*** There is the saccharine story which Eleanor produces at her father's suggestion that she write about her own anger, 'the story of the ill-treated wife'. Its very title, 'Deb and Russ [her children] at Sunnytop Farm' recalls the classic tear-jerker, *Rebecca of Sunnybrook Farm,* just as the title of *Brief Candle* suggests popular writers of the period like Howard Spring. (And, incidentally, the title of ***Letty Fox: Her Luck*** recalls countless Victorian schoolgirl novels.) Eleanor's mother's favourite author, Elinor Glyn, provided her as a child with information about sexuality, just as the short stories in women's magazines later provide her with guides to action as well as formulas for her own writing ('How true, thought Eleanor, there is humble truth under these banalities. It had meaning for romantic women like herself. . . . She extracted the outline and rewrote the story a little'). The final third of the novel, her Grub Street period, abounds with gems such as this, from one of her reader's reports: ' . . . he has a kind of intuition of genius and we must put our foot down firmly there, or it will ruin his talent'. The object of the novel's satire expands from Eleanor herself to encompass the literary world and the commodities it produces for sale, its promiscuous mixtures of 'Verdi and Mills and Boon' and their material effects on the woman who attempts to live by it and its values.

These two novels, ***Miss Herbert*** and ***Letty Fox,*** may be read as cautionary tales for women, as answers to the liberal feminists of an earlier period who believed that emancipation into an idealized notion of the public world would at last allow women to fulfil themselves. Among twentieth-century women novelists Christina Stead is the great ironist of female experience. Her fictions not only criticize patriarchal capitalist social structures and their ideologies but also insist that women are neither immune from their corruptions nor their passive victims. Her women characters are shown to be capable of exploiting others—and of simultaneously denying that they do so. They are shown to be accomplices in the suppression of their own desires and the construction of oppressive ideologies of femininity. The utopian possibility of love as a mode of knowledge for women rather than a romantic or a picaresque tale, which emerges in ***For Love Alone,*** does not reappear in her post-war novels. In these satirical portraits, knowledge and love appear in the form of ready-made ideological constructions of reality. The theme of struggle takes the form of a struggle for 'normal' social existence, rather than creative engagement. In the final two novels to be considered here, we see something more like a life-and-death struggle for survival—there is blood on the floor, and 'love', along with 'politics', can be a murder weapon. (pp. 82-105)

Susan Sheridan, in her Christina Stead, *Harvester Wheatsheaf, 1988, 155 p.*

Hazel Rowley (essay date Winter 1990)

[*In the following essay, Rowley addresses the autobiographical dimension of* The Man Who Loved Children, *especially focusing on the influence of Stead's relationship with her father.*]

"***The Man Who Loved Children*** is a 527-page study of an egotist," wrote the American critic Clifton Fadiman, in his 1940 review of the novel. "I think Miss Stead studies him too hard and too long, but there can be no doubt that when she's through, Sam Pollit exists, just as surely and implacably as does Balzac's Père Goriot. He's repulsive, a swine, often a damned bore whose long-windedness and infinite complacency tear at your nerves till you are ready to scream at him. But that's the nub of it—you're ready to scream at him as if he were not a character in a book but a man in your living room."

Christina Stead would have agreed, quite literally, with the comment "Sam Pollit exists." She liked to say that she invented nothing—neither characters ("You can't invent people or they're puppets") nor plots. (Hers were "real plots that occur in life.") In interviews in later life she took this stance to its extreme. When asked, once, whether ***The Man Who Loved Children*** had any connection with her own childhood, she replied emphatically, "Of course, it's exactly word for word." About Sam Pollit she said, less ingenuously, "He's a picture of my father—that's no secret." Frequently, when she talked about her fictional characters, as she liked to do in interviews, she made no distinction between the character and the real-life model; she used the fictional name as a pseudonym. Sam Pollit, Jonathan Crow, and the others referred to actual people.

Christina Stead's literary credo was firmly within the naturalist tradition: she aimed to observe reality minutely, accepting everything she found. Her influence was not Flaubert or Zola so much as her father: "Even my way of writing novels comes from his scientific way of looking at things. . . . I became an observer, dispassionate and observant of any society you can think of. People. Ants. Film moguls." Characteristically, proponents of naturalism in fiction have overlooked the artifice inherent in all art. Art, after all, does not mirror the shapeless raw material of life. One of the paradoxes of naturalist fiction is that its characters are, in fact, "larger than life." Sam Pollit seems real: he is a character whom you never forget, a character seared into your memory. Yet he is a *fictional* figure, a construction, a concentrated, distilled representation of the person he is modeled on.

Sam Pollit closely resembles David Stead. And if we readers are ready to scream at Sam Pollit after a mere 527 pages, we can imagine how Christina Stead felt after twenty-six years. After she left Australia, in 1928, she never saw her father again. But she could not escape him so easily: he continued to loom large in her head. Biographical material suggests, as I will show, that her father's legacy can hardly be overestimated. David Stead filled his daughter's imaginative universe with language and story; he implanted in her a deep love of Australia, of its natural treasures and timeless space; he furnished her with his socialist vision of the world. Along with this cultural heritage, he left her, unwittingly, with deep psychological scars. There is no doubt that Christina Stead was profoundly divided in herself.

For Stead—as for Virginia Woolf—writing about her childhood eventually became a pressing need. She was thirty-six when she began ***The Man Who Loved Children*** in New York in the winter of 1938-39. For Woolf, writing *To The Lighthouse* (at age forty-four) went some way toward dispelling the parental ghosts which haunted her. In Stead's case, plunging into the past brought violent emotions to the surface. Shortly after the novel's publication, she told Thistle Harris, her father's third wife (then living with him at Watson's Bay), "not to see him [David Stead] again is one of my aims in life."

When Stead left Australia, at the age of twenty-six, she was resolutely leaving behind her father, her stepmother, and her past generally. Having arrived in the northern hemisphere, she wholeheartedly embraced new ideas, other cultures. Soon after arriving in London, she met William J. Blake, a banker of German-Jewish parentage from New York. It is revealing that whereas David Stead was prejudiced against Jews, businessmen, and the French language, abstained from alcohol, and never went to the theater or cinema, Christina Stead enthusiastically celebrated all these aspects of her new existence. During the next ten years, she lived with William Blake in London, Paris, and New York and published four books—all with minimal autobiographical content. After finishing ***House of All Nations*** in 1937 she went eighteen months without embarking on a new novel. It was, on the whole, an unhappy period. Then, suddenly, she felt herself compelled to confront what she had avoided till then: the murky material of her past.

When Christina Stead refers to the distress she experienced when writing ***The Man Who Loved Children,*** we can take it as understatement rather than hyperbole. She rarely discussed her private self. Although she had majored in psychology at Sydney Teachers' College and made no bones about being fascinated by the psychology of others, she was exceptionally reticent when it came to herself. Moreover, she was fiercely impatient with the psychoanalytic theories fashionable in the thirties and forties. The way popular jargon reduced everything to the "Oedipus complex" or a "father fixation" is thoroughly mocked in both ***The Beauties and Furies*** and ***Letty Fox.***

Perhaps Stead protested too much about psychoanalysis. From her own comments it seems that writing ***The Man Who Loved Children*** was like an intense experience of psychotherapy. And even if she disliked the Freudian vocabulary, she must have recognized in her struggle with the shadow of her father a classic Freudian scenario.

In a *Melbourne Sun* interview, at the age of seventy-five, Stead explained that the novel "demanded to be written": "I was quite solitary, although I was very happy with Bill, my husband. . . . But I was crying every two months and just couldn't stop. I didn't know it then, but it was because of my terrible experiences as a child. Then one day I wrote down everything to clarify my feelings." In a 1976 radio interview, Stead (in her characteristically digressive, circumlocutory style) recalled the writing of ***The Man Who Loved Children***: "I wrote it in the center of New York—in a rather dark apartment, overshadowed by loft buildings—high rises with factories on one floor. It was rather a dreary sort of place. They had an Italian garden, so called, downstairs, but I was rather unhappy at that moment. Nothing special, I think. Just being cooped up in all this stonework and brickwork. And I decided to get that off my chest, and that was how it was." Six months into the writing time, in July 1939, Stead wrote to Thistle Harris (and thus, surely, indirectly to her father): "The book I am writing now, ***The Man Who Loved Children,*** has a plot derived from, although not exactly mirroring, our home in the early days, not the procès-verbal, but the dramatic truth. . . . I have left it all these years, not able to touch such an autobiographical subject, but last winter I decided to get it off my chest once and for all."

It is interesting that while writing the book, Stead was quite aware—as she seems not to have been later—of the part played by artifice and invention. The novel was to be the "dramatic truth," an artistic reconstruction, not an exact record. She continued:

> It has been a grand thing for me to get this plucked out of the back of my mind. But, as David could not realise, that home was so atrociously wretched and I was so ill at ease as a result that I do not want to see Australia, except on some gilded visit, if I ever get the gilding.
>
> I'm not unforgiving—how could it be so when no-one is to blame? They just made an etching out of me, I am deep-bitten.

Almost twelve months later, with the book about to go into galley proofs, Stead told a friend that writing ***The Man Who Loved Children*** had given her "the jitters" and that she had been "too down" to write letters to Australia. It was "a snake's life," she considered, to shed one's skin as she had done. The choice of image—more evocative of her Sydney childhood than her life in urban New York—suggests that she had not shed her skin completely.

The writing and revision of ***The Man Who Loved Children*** took Stead a year and a half. The original manuscript sent to Simon and Schuster was apparently over a million words. At the behest of her publishers, Stead cut the material down, first to eight hundred pages and finally to five hundred pages. Years later she recalled: "Bill had to drag me through the last revision by the hair of my head, I couldn't bear it any more." It was a harrowing process partly because of the sheer mass of material; the "surplus material" and "surplus drama" kept getting in the way. (Autobiographical fiction was *not,* after all, just a spilling-onto-the-page of life.) The other difficulty was that the primary material from which she worked was largely her father's writing—and this, we will see, was to pose specific and complex problems.

All around her on her work table, as Christina Stead was writing the novel, were her father's writings. (Either she had taken these with her when she left Australia, or she had written to the family more recently asking for them.) As well as being a voluble talker, David Stead was a prolific and fluent writer. By 1938 he had written a number of short books, pamphlets, and articles on naturalist subjects—fishes, trees, the rabbit plague in Australia. More useful for Christina Stead's purposes were his newspaper columns and radio broadcasts for schoolchildren about his travels and the "great outdoors," for they were written in the chatty, vivacious, and instructive style David Stead used with his own children. Most important of all were the letters David Stead had written to his children when he was in Malaya for two years. Some, if not all, of these letters are extant.

To what extent did Stead actually draw on her own life in ***The Man Who Loved Children***? For reasons not relevant here, she transposed the story's location from Sydney to the Chesapeake Bay area; she changed the time frame from 1914-15 (when she herself was twelve) to the late 1930s. Certain minor details and incidents were invented or transposed. Her imagination filled in the gaps. On the whole, however, the Pollit family closely resembles the Stead family. David Stead was a self-educated man, who became a well-known naturalist. (He was included in the 1927-28 edition of *Who's Who in Australia.*) His first wife, Christina Stead's mother, died when Christina was two (in 1904). Three years later, David Stead married Ada Gibbins, youngest daughter from a large, wealthy family. Her father supplied the young couple with their house at Lydham Hill. Ada Stead had six children within ten years. The family chaos was further supplemented by the opossums, turtles, birds, and snakes kept in the garden. Ada Stead was not suited to practical household management. And she soon became disillusioned with her husband's naive idealism and high-minded rhetoric. Nor was she always patient with her dreamy and physically unprepossessing stepdaughter.

When Ada's father died insolvent in 1917, Lydham Hill had to go under the hammer, and the Stead family was obliged to move to a sprawling, ramshackle house in the harborside district of Watson's Bay. The location was idyllic for a naturalist and his children. The house, which fronted directly onto the harbor, was within a short walk of the Heads, where the harbor opened into the wild Pacific Ocean. The ocean became a vital part of their lives. David Stead was at one time a fisheries commissioner; later he was general manager of the state trawling industry. In late 1921 he went to British Malaya, to inquire into the colonial fisheries. He stayed away almost two years.

The letters David Stead wrote from Malaya provided an important primary record of his personality, and Christina Stead made good use of them. Given her talent for imaginative reconstruction, Stead was able to use her father's letters to describe Sam Pollit in Malaya, a place she herself had never seen. Chapter 6 of ***The Man Who Loved Children,*** entitled "Letters to Malaya" (rather than "Letters *from* Malaya"), contains one of David Stead's original letters, almost verbatim. In the novel it is split into two letters. This appropriation poses an interesting question. When does "naturalism" become "plagiarism"? Although modernist and postmodernist writers delight in "intertextuality," their systematic borrowings are from published, usually well-known works and therefore traceable—whereas appropriating unacknowledged, unpublished letters necessarily involves an element of usurpation. But a more interesting aspect of the incorporation of the whole of one of David Stead's letters into the novel is what it means in narrative terms. The fact that the tone and language of David Stead's letter blend in perfectly with Sam Pollit's utterances in the rest of the novel attests to the extraordinary verisimilitude of Stead's fictional re-creation of her father. What is surprising is that she scarcely needed to change her father's letter—neither the prose itself nor the content. There was no need to transform or heighten his portrait for fictional purposes. David Stead's self-dramatizations were sufficiently extravagant, delicious, and infuriating exactly as they stood. (Nor did Christina

Stead's rage toward her father incline her to distort his character.) The two "fictional" letters from Malaya reveal an almost complete convergence between the two "constructions": Sam Pollit, Christina Stead's construction, is almost identical with David Stead's own self-construction. The difference is the narrative frame: by placing her father's letter within *her* novel, Christina Stead annexed and asserted power over her father's creative product.

The letter from Sam Pollit to "Looloo-Dirl" (Louisa) is copied from a longer letter that David Stead wrote to Christina Stead from Singapore on July 5, 1922. (David Stead used to call his eldest daughter "Peg" or "Pegler"; and in his letters he addressed her, in his affectionate baby talk, as "Pedler Dirl.") In this letter David Stead describes some wall paintings depicting torture scenes which he had seen in a Chinese Buddhist temple. His lively, witty account of these indicates a genuine literary talent:

> The walls are covered with terrible pictures showing what will befall the unbeliever who flouts the gods. They are all in colors and are wonderfully "executed." And so are the poor souls in the pictures. There are two women who wouldn't do what their husbands had told them. They are tied down onto a bench and two demons are hacking off their heads. In fact one is off already and is hanging up and the other is nearly off. And the expressions on the heads! I saw one poor Chinese woman looking at the picture, and SHE looked very pale—pale ivory—so I guess HER husband would have no trouble with her for a while.

He aimed quite consciously for narrative effectiveness, rather than any personal intimacy. In the same letter, he told Christina, as one writer to another: "I started this letter for Woit [Weeta], but when I found how the story was drifting I altered it to you, Pedler; as I know you love blood-and-thunder."

If David Stead goes down in biographical history as the model for Sam Pollit, that far from attractive character, it must also be acknowledged that he created the "ocean of story" in which his eldest daughter learned to swim almost before she could walk. His letters show that Christina Stead was not the first or the only literary talent in the Stead family.

The rest of David Stead's letter to his daughter describes the debilitating tropical heat. Christina Stead also used this passage in the novel—again almost word for word. This time, though, she has Sam Pollit writing to his young admirer Gillian Roebuck—a young woman the same age as his daughter Louisa—with whom he is a bit in love. The oedipal overtones are obvious. An extract from David Stead's letter reads:

> It isn't such fun seeing anything here. You have an ever-present and all-pervading conscious and subconscious sensation that it is HOT. And then some more. You see a lovely vista of palms and wonderful trees—and it is too hot to go for a walk. You see a wonderful mountain, and it is too hot to even attempt to go even a part of the way up—apart from the dense jungle, which you would have to cut your way through. Then you see a lovely sheet of water; but it is too hot to go out on it. Because it is TOO HOT everywhere. The heat wilts you like a soft leaf—just like a pumpkin leaf goes in our place on a very hot day in Sydney. You put on nice clothes in the morning and you are full of perspiration before you have completed your little bit of dressing. You sweat at breakfast and you sweat at tiffin and you sweat at eight o'clock dinner. You cease to want to go out anywhere after dinner, because you have one paramount thought—again conscious and subconscious—"let's get clothes off."

One reason for minor changes in Christina Stead's text seems to have been to make Sam Pollit convincing as a contemporary American. Thus she altered the last sentence to "Let's strip Jack naked!"—which David Stead, who clung ferociously to his puritanical Victorian upbringing, was unlikely ever to have said.

How must Christina Stead have felt—having reproduced her father's long letter almost exactly—when Clifton Fadiman commented, in his review of ***The Man Who Loved Children,*** that the novel as a whole did not come off, but that Sam's letters from Malaya were astounding—"extraordinary writing"? Ironically (given that writing the novel was an attempt to subjugate the shadow of her father in her life), Christina Stead had not contained her father's ghost after all. He had burst out of his literary confinement. In the very domain in which she struggled to break free—her writing—he maintained his power.

Other surviving letters from David Stead—which his daughter would have found useful as primary material, even though she did not make direct use of them in the novel—project a loving but firm father, eager to develop his children's skills. A letter dated May 27, 1922 is written in the eccentric Artemus Ward language which Sam Pollit also uses. It ends: "Luv to evryboddie and all be goode. Thoes who duz thare dutie ar luvly wuns thay will get some frottie and some kurren bunz. From DadPad the Boald." (Sam Pollit calls himself Sam-the-Bold.)

Another letter is typed in purple ink, with a paragraph for each literate member of the family—except his wife, whose absence is conspicuous. If the May 27 letter is interesting because it shows the imaginative lexical system in which David Stead taught his children to romp, the (undated) purple ink letter shows that David Stead saw it as his role to teach his children the art and practice of writing. The first and longest section is for "Pegler." Among lively descriptions of Malayan boys (with whom he has "fairly fallen in love"), he tells her: "I have not read Thoreau, at least not Thoreaughly, only excerpts. I think you made a mistake *copying* out anything to get used to rapid writing. You might have spent that time writing some observations of your own. Then you would have had writing practice and great mental exercise at the same time. But never mind." He replies to fifteen-year-old Dave: "Was glad to get your letter old boy, but be a little more careful about the writing, and be sure of what you are going to write before you put your pen on the paper; then you won't have to cross out anything at all." In the brief lines he writes to "Tweet," "Huxley," and "Woit," he encourages them with their schoolwork and corrects their spelling—a practice that must surely have turned their letters from communications into exercises for a schoolmaster.

Other letters to "Pegler" reveal a hortatory, self-satisfied side to David Stead which, equally, is reproduced in the fictional Sam Pollit. In a letter from Singapore in September 1922, David Stead lectured Christina (who appears to have made lofty complains about her education) about the need to be always curious and alert. The letter is unusually badly expressed, but it is worth quoting at some length because of what it tells us about the character of the man on whom Sam Pollit was modeled.

> Pedler dear, . . . you should understand why your foolish talks against the education or the form of it that you are acquiring, and your worship of certain inerudite but polished on the surface persons, hurts me so much. You will find, certainly, later on, if not immediately, that every track that you are following is leading to some bright discovery—even if it is only a discovery in your own thoughts. To me these are the greatest discoveries of all.
>
> But coming back to your letter: It is quite true as you say that one who goes out imbued with a purpose, *sees* things. But, even he is constantly seeing more things in spots that he thought he had completely ransacked before. Wherever I go I hear the saying (to me): "Well, I've been here for donkey's years (or words to that effect) and I have never seen that." Most—nearly all—people are extraordinarily unobservant. It is the same in Australia, and it is the same everywhere in the world that I have travelled in. Is it any wonder then that I am solitary. I do all my rambles in the cities of the world exactly as I did my rambles up and down the coast and in the fastnesses of mountains and gullies in my beloved Australia—alone.

David Stead's tendency to deliver homilies which circled back to himself is even more evident in a letter from Pagi Pagi, November 1922. He was obviously exhausted and needing to spur himself on. His letter to Christina (who merely functions as a convenient "ear") takes the form of a pep talk to himself:

> So, Pedler dear, I suppose Fate sent me here after all to do something more to make the idea of justice for the helpless a living one. But I couldn't have those ideas without having built myself up in the study of social and international economics. I get on splendidly with all these villages and villagers. They say I am *good* and *just.* I am *not;* but I think they are good and must be helped and *shall* be helped, by me and by my men. . . . I am like a wet sock, but that love of right and justice—specially for the ones down under (who need help above all) which my Mother first planted in me—spurs me. I *must* do it, at all costs.

For all his "Pedler dear," David Stead's letters lack tenderness and empathy. His world was peculiarly solipsistic. His dreams for his children are revealed as mere extensions of his dreams for himself—universal abstractions rather than ambitions tailored to each individual child.

The same letter continues, in rhetoric which is strikingly messianic:

> Pegler, I love humanity and the mass more than anything else. I am inconsistent, no doubt, being human, and, being human, I have "nerves." And thinking, thinking over, doesn't help nerves much. And now I am washed out, just with my intense thinking this morning, but I felt I must tell you, because I want all you children to be Apostles of Right, Justice and Truth so that the wicked (who are merely insufficiently educated ones) shall hate, but shall respect you, and so that the great mass of the people shall know you as *their* friends.

He added, in brackets: " 'Lectured' to 60 dark girlies last night—from 6 years to 18. Splendid. We laughed and laughed. I 'jolly' nearly all these people about their color. They *do* enjoy the way I do it."

The content of David Stead's several letters from Malaya gives some insight into the various psychological binds in which Christina Stead found herself, as his eldest child. She evidently occupied a special, yet equivocal and strangely awkward place in her father's affections. He encouraged her in his schoolmasterly way, but she always felt that he did not love her enough. As an apprentice writer she wanted both to impress *her father* and to express *herself.* This, indeed, was the central bind. How could writing be a means of finding and asserting *herself,* if in this, as in all things, she was her father's "apostle"? David Stead supplied the fertile seedbed in which his daughter's talents were nurtured—and also confined. Language was first of all *his* soil, *his* medium. By writing in her own voice, she was defining herself against him.

It is interesting briefly to consider the "dramatic truth"—the novel. Louisa Pollit struggles with the same dilemma as her creator. For her father's fortieth birthday, Louisa writes a play, which she and the other children act out in front of him (echoes of Hamlet). The play, called, significantly, *The Snake Man* (traces of Louisa's naturalist father), is written not in English but in an obscure code which only the author herself (Louisa) can unravel. And in case this is not protest enough—for Sam Pollit is duly dismayed by all this—the play itself re-enacts an oedipal drama, which Louisa eventually translates for him into English. The daughter (Megara) tells her father (Anteios), "I see you are determined to steal my breath, my sun, my daylight." At the end of the play the father turns into a snake and strangles her. Megara's dying words are "Father is strangling me. Murderer!"

Christina Stead created Louisa who (in fictional terms) created Megara. The further one dives into the textual vortex, the purer the daughter's hatred is for her father. In reality, Christina Stead, the creator of them all, remained highly ambivalent.

In her old age, having mellowed toward her father, Christina Stead wrote two deeply affectionate, moving tributes to him. Unfortunately, he was no longer alive to read them.

Christina Stead's lifelong fascination with strong, energetic characters can almost certainly be traced to her father. The pattern of love-hate was one which readily reproduced itself in Stead's relationships with others. Indeed, ambivalence, I would suggest, is the essential drive behind Christina Stead's creative impulse. Sam Pollit, after all, is only one of the magnetic, overbearing figures in Stead's gallery of portraits. There is also Jules Bertillon, Jonathan Crow, Robbie Grant, Nellie Cotter, Emily Wilkes. All were based on people Christina Stead knew and—at one time or another—loved.

The indissoluble link that made Christina Stead closer to her father than his other children was their writing. Yet, paradoxically, it was one more area of profound ambivalence. When she came to write ***The Man Who Loved Children,*** the problem became acute. There were problems of rivalry; above all, there were problems of control and containment. Who, she must have asked herself, surrounded as she was by David Stead's writing, was strangling whom? Though she "captured" him in her novel, she never freed herself of her father. In the final analysis, as much as he was the man who loved children—with all the title's ironical nuance—she was the woman who loved her father. (pp. 499-510)

Hazel Rowley, "How Real Is Sam Pollit? 'Dramatic Truth' and 'Procès-Verbal' in 'The Man Who Loved Children'," in Contemporary Literature, *Vol. 31, No. 4, Winter, 1990, pp. 499-511.*

FURTHER READING

Criticism

Anderson, Don. "Christina Stead's Unforgettable Dinner-Parties." *Southerly* 39, No. 1 (March 1979): 28-45.

Asserts that meals in Stead's fiction are "dramatic microcosms in which the dominant themes and images—money, politics, sex, disease, and death, for example—are both discussed by the characters, and rendered metaphorically and analogically through the language of food."

Arac, Jonathan. "The Struggle for the Cultural Heritage: Christina Stead Refunctions Charles Dickens and Mark Twain." *Cultural Critique,* No. 2 (Winter 1985-86): 171-89.

Argues that Stead takes a revisionist stance in *The Man Who Loved Children* by employing the character Samuel Clemens Pollit as a "composite figure of Charles Dickens and Mark Twain as petty-bourgeois paterfamilias" emblematic of the failures of humanism.

Boone, Joseph A. "Of Fathers, Daughters, and Theorists of Narrative Desire: At the Crossroads of Myth and Psychoanalysis in *The Man Who Loved Children.*" *Contemporary Literature* 31, No. 4 (Winter 1990): 512-41.

Applies a psychoanalytic approach to *The Man Who Loved Children,* exploring the idea that "Sam uses his offspring to impose his identity on an external reality whose otherness, whose very externality, poses a threat to his perception of his autonomy, power, and superiority as a man and father."

Calisher, Hortense. "Stead." *The Yale Review* 76, No. 2 (Winter 1987): 169-77.

Memoir of the first meeting between Stead and Calisher.

Clancy, Laurie. *Christina Stead's "The Man Who Loved Children" and "For Love Alone."* Melbourne: Shillington House, 1981, 46 p.

Surveys major themes and characters in *The Man Who Loved Children* and *For Love Alone.*

Gardiner, Judith Kegan. *Rhys, Stead, Lessing, and the Politics of Empathy.* Bloomington: Indiana University Press, 1989, 186 p.

Includes Stead's work in a psychoanalytic-historicist discussion of "what characterizes writing by twentieth-century women."

Geering, R. G. *Christina Stead.* Melbourne: Oxford University Press, 1969, 48 p.

Overview of Stead's life, writing, and place in Australian literature.

Green, Dorothy. "Chaos, or a Dancing Star? Christina Stead's *Seven Poor Men of Sydney.*" *Meanjin Quarterly* 27, No. 2 (1968): 150-61.

Contends that *Seven Poor Men of Sydney* examines "how the species is to survive without the destruction of the individuality of its separate members."

Higgins, Susan. "Christina Stead's *For Love Alone:* A Female Odyssey?" *Southerly* 38, No. 4 (December 1978): 428-45.

Maintains that the character Teresa Hawkins's "psychological journey" is in the tradition of the epic quest.

Lidoff, Joan. "Home Is Where the Heart Is: The Fiction of Christina Stead." *Southerly* 38, No. 4 (December 1978): 363-75.

Examines setting and national identity in Stead's novels.

———. *Christina Stead.* New York: Frederick Ungar Publishing Co., 1982, 255 p.

Survey of Stead's career; includes an interview.

Nestor, Pauline. "An Impulse to Self-Expression: *The Man Who Loved Children.*" *The Critical Review* 18 (1976): 61-78.

Examines the character Louisa's development within the framework of her relationship with her father and her family.

Pybus, Rodney. "*Cotter's England:* In Appreciation." *Stand* 23, No. 4 (1982): 40-7.

Overview of *Cotter's England.*

Reid, Ian. "Form and Expectation in Christina Stead's Novellas." *The Literary Criterion* XV, Nos. 3-4 (1980): 48-58.

Addresses the ways in which Stead's novellas pose "challenges to a reader's normal expectations," particularly in their narrative structure.

Segerberg, Anita. "Getting Started: The Emergence of Christina Stead's Early Fiction." *Australian Literary Studies* 13, No. 2 (October 1987): 121-38.

Exploration of the biographical origins of Stead's fiction.

Yelin, Louise. "Fifty Years of Reading: A Reception Study of *The Man Who Loved Children.*" *Contemporary Literature* 31, No. 4 (Winter 1990): 472-98.

Traces critical reaction to and interpretation of *The Man Who Loved Children* since its publication.

Interviews

Raskin, Jonah. "Christina Stead in Washington Square." *London Magazine* 9, No. 11 (February 1970): 70-7.
Stead relates her attitude toward writing and literature.

Wetherell, Rodney. "Interview with Christina Stead." *Australian Literary Studies* 9, No. 4 (October 1980): 431-48.
Stead discusses her life, works, and political beliefs.

Additional coverage of Stead's life and career is contained in the following sources published by Gale Research: *Contemporary Authors,* Vols. 13-16 rev. ed., 109 [obituary]; *Contemporary Authors New Revision Series,* Vols. 33, 40; *Contemporary Literary Criticism,* Vols. 2, 5, 8, 32; and *Major 20th-Century Writers.*

Desmond Tutu

1931-

(Full name Desmond Mpilo Tutu) South African orator, sermonist, and essayist.

The following entry focuses on Tutu's life and works through 1992.

INTRODUCTION

Recipient of the 1984 Nobel Peace Prize, Anglican archbishop of Capetown, South Africa, and one of the world's foremost critics of his nation's apartheid government, Tutu has collected two volumes of speeches and sermons: *Crying in the Wilderness: The Struggle for Justice in South Africa* and *Hope and Suffering: Sermons and Speeches.* "Like all great preachers," wrote Joshua Hammer, "his every speech and press conference is a blaze of emotion, his every gesture a drop of oil fueling the oratorical fire. Waving his arms, punching the air like a boxer, the elfin . . . figure draws in his followers with a stream of whispers, shouts and sobs, punctuated with roars of laughter."

Since the 1970s Tutu has campaigned vigorously for the abolition of apartheid, South Africa's system of legalized segregation that allocates political power and privileges to Afrikaners—members of the white minority who preside over the country's black majority. Tutu first encountered apartheid while growing up in the western Transvaal mining town of Klerksdorp. He stated that at first the constant racial taunts of the white boys were not "thought to be out of the ordinary," but that as he got older he "began finding things eating away at [him]." Recalling one incident in which he heard his father referred to as "boy," Tutu remarked: "I knew there wasn't a great deal I could do, but it just left me churned. . . . What he must have been feeling, . . . being humiliated in the presence of his son. Apartheid has always been the same systematic racial discrimination: it takes away your human dignity and rubs it in the dust and tramples it underfoot."

In 1943 Tutu and his family moved to Johannesburg, where Tutu's father became a teacher and his mother a cook at a missionary school for the blind. While at school, Tutu was deeply moved by the dedication and service shown by staff members and by Father Trevor Huddleston, who would become his most influential mentor and friend. A leading British critic of South Africa's apartheid system, Huddleston served as the parish priest of Sophiatown, a black slum district of Johannesburg. Tutu recalled his first meeting with the priest: "I was standing with my mother one day, when this white man in a cassock walked past and doffed his big black hat to her. I couldn't believe it—a white man raising his hat to a simple black labouring woman." Following a bout with tuberculosis, Tutu resumed his education and entered the School of Medicine at Witwatersrand University, intending to become a doctor. However, he was forced to drop out of medical school because he could no longer afford the tuition fees, and he soon began training as a teacher instead. Tutu received his B.A. from the University of Johannesburg in 1954 and taught high school in Johannesburg and Krugersdorp until 1957, when he resigned in protest of government plans to introduce a state-run system of education intended for students in black districts. Limiting both the quality and extent of education, the system was generally considered to be deliberately second-rate. Inspired by the ideals of his mentor Huddleston, Tutu began theological studies with the priests of the Community of Resurrection, the Anglican order to which Huddleston belonged.

Following his ordainment as priest in 1961, Tutu worked in small Anglican parishes in England and South Africa. In 1966 he received a master's degree in theology from King's College, London, and in 1972 he accepted a position in England as associate director of the Theological Education Fund. Thoroughly enjoying his role, he traveled extensively throughout Asia and Africa and presided over the allocation of World Council of Churches scholarships. During this time, however, thoughts of South Africa and the discrimination faced by his black countrymen continually troubled Tutu. He finally returned to his homeland in 1975.

Choosing to live in his parish in Lesotho, Tutu monitored closely the feelings of his congregation and the local community. In an atmosphere of mounting racial tension, he attempted to pacify angry black youths, encouraging them to seek change through peaceful means. In 1976 he met with black activist Nhato Motlana in an effort to curb violent riots in the black township of Soweto on the outskirts of Johannesburg. He also wrote to incumbent South African Prime Minister Balthazar J. Vorster, warning him of the dangerous situation. Tutu later claimed that Vorster dismissed his letter as a ploy engineered by political opponents. On 16 June 1976 racial tension exploded into violence as black demonstrators met untempered reprisal from white security forces. Six hundred blacks were shot to death in the confrontation. The tragedy of the Soweto riots focused the world's attention on the antiapartheid struggle in South Africa. For Tutu, the increasing number of violent confrontations between blacks and security forces marked a change in his perception of his own involvement.

In 1979 Tutu voiced a major condemnation of the South African government before an international audience. In an interview for a Danish television program, he called on the government of Denmark to cease buying South African coal as a sign of support for the antiapartheid cause. The appeal subsequently moved people in other countries to consider implementing economic sanctions against South Africa. Tutu's actions were met with reprisals by the South African government. When he returned from Denmark in 1979, authorities seized his passport, a move generally seen as a warning of possible imprisonment or expulsion from the country. Tutu ignored the signal, however, and continued his antiapartheid campaign. The South African government eventually returned his passport in January 1981 but confiscated it again in April of that year. Thereafter, Tutu was allowed to travel outside South Africa only with the government's permission and special travel documents that listed his nationality as "undetermined."

During a permitted stay in the United States in 1984, Tutu received word that he was the 1984 Nobel peace laureate. Part of the Nobel citation read: "It is the committee's wish that the Peace Prize now awarded to Desmond Tutu should be regarded not only as a gesture of support to him and to the South African Council of Churches of which he is leader, but also to all individuals and groups in South Africa who, with their concern for human dignity, fraternity and democracy, incite the admiration of the world." According to *Time* magazine, "much of white South Africa reacted grumpily or indifferently to the news." Said Tutu in response: "You feel humble, you feel proud, elated and you feel sad. One of my greatest sadnesses is that there are many in this country who are not joining in celebrating something that is an honor for this country."

In 1990 the white South African government, led by President Frederik Willem de Klerk, released many of its black political prisoners, including African National Congress leader Nelson Mandela. The government also expressed its willingness to move toward the establishment of a multiracial democracy. Despite violent confrontations between black political factions that stalled negotiations in 1992 and 1993, the Afrikaner government promised that free elections would be held in April 1994. While Tutu has been a less prominent critic of apartheid since Mandela's release, he has maintained a firm Christian commitment to human rights. Following an incident between black political factions that claimed forty-two lives in June 1992, Tutu observed: "There is no situation from which God cannot extract good. Evil, death, oppression, injustice—these can never again have the last word, despite all appearances to the contrary."

Many of Tutu's orations have been collected in *Crying in the Wilderness* and *Hope and Suffering.* The latter contains Tutu's writings from 1976 to 1982. According to critic John F. Whealon, "*Hope and Suffering* illustrates well the unique dynamic that is Desmond Tutu, who is blunt, fearless, filled with faith and courage, charismatic." In *Crying in the Wilderness,* Tutu pleads for non-violent change in South Africa but warns that unless conditions improve, there will be more "blood riots" in the streets. "[Tutu] stoutly denies that he is preaching Marxism or Communism," Eugene A. Dooley observed of the work. "Instead he pleads for justice against inhuman life conditions."

PRINCIPAL WORKS

Crying in the Wilderness: The Struggle for Justice in South Africa (speeches, sermons, and interviews) 1982
Hope and Suffering: Sermons and Speeches (sermons and speeches) 1983
The Words of Desmond Tutu (quotations) 1989

CRITICISM

Eugene A. Dooley (review date November 1982)

[*In the following excerpt, Dooley summarizes Tutu's position in* Crying in the Wilderness.]

Bishop Desmond Tutu, a brilliant Anglican cleric, is easily the most influential black leader in South Africa. He is no mere demagogue, either, but rather a scholarly Church orator who has chosen the task of convincing the white people of his land that apartheid is cruel, counter-productive, anti-social and anti-Scripture. [In ***Crying in the Wilderness,*** Tutu is] devastatingly logical in showing not only that the white religious sects hypocritically misrepresent their Christian faith but also in scoring the bigoted policies of political leaders who refuse to budge from their consistent cruelty toward the black natives.

Since blacks there outnumber the white five-to-one, it stands to reason that the whites had better read the handwriting on the wall. Their powerful sun is setting, and they had better institute some cooperative efforts to establish a better social order for their land. The Roman Catholic Archbishop, Denis Hurley, O.M.I., of Durban, has been saying that for many years past, and his voice was also one "crying in the wilderness for justice" until very recently when he summoned all his auxiliaries to push for a crusade for Justice and Rights.

[***Crying in the Wilderness***], subtitled "The Struggle for Justice in South Africa," contains many of Tutu's speeches, press releases and sermons. He stoutly denies that he is preaching Marxism or Communism, though some whites are using that as a scare tactic against him. Instead he pleads for a system that will allow emerging tribes to be given a system where men will not be tossed into horrible prisons for merely asking simple rights, pleading for justice against inhuman life conditions. Some white leaders, he says, are totally unChristian in their arbitrary use of police powers. All the black wish, he says, are the abolition of the hated apartheid, along with the human right to work for better home life and family security. Whether the whites like it or not, he says that the day is surely coming when black people there will have political power, and that day can come without bloody riots if the whites are willing to sit down and negotiate. Black Africa is awakening daily, and the whites cannot deny it. The Bishop is optimistic that a peaceful solution can be reached.

Eugene A. Dooley, in a review of "Crying in the Wilderness," in Best Sellers, *Vol. 42, No. 8, November, 1982, p. 313.*

Huston Horn (review date 27 January 1985)

[In the review below, Horn assesses the strengths and weaknesses of Hope and Suffering.]

With the resolute confidence of an Old Testament psalmist, South Africa's Bishop Desmond Tutu [in ***Hope and Suffering***] raises impassioned cries against his nation's white-skinned oppressors. They may hold the blacks in thrall for now, but surely God in his time will bring apartheid crashing down. But, while his Anglican anger roils like dense smoke from the printed page, a beckoning, reconciling light shines through it. Notwithstanding the intransigent foes he faces, Tutu's gaze rarely wanders from a benign, visionary South Africa ruled together by blacks and whites. Nothing less, the bishop holds, would fit God's prescription for humanity.

To those familiar with the thought and writing of the winner of 1984's Nobel Peace Prize, this will sound like vintage Tutu, and so it is. Since most of the bishop's energy goes into spoken words denouncing the plight of South Africa's tyrannized black majority, the book before us is in fact a collection of sermons and speeches delivered by him in the early '80s and late '70s. Published first in Johannesburg in 1983, it now comes in an edition opportunely produced (and casually edited) by William B. Erdmans within weeks of the peace prize announcement. Celebrity apparently is more marketable than an enthusiasm for justice.

While a warmed-over work it may be, the bishop's preachments have contemporary relevance and ring. For one thing, so little seems to have been accomplished since Tutu took up his assault on apartheid years ago. "What have we got to show for all our talk of peaceful change? Nothing!" he told a black South African reporter just the other day. For another (and better) thing, Tutu's style is literate and readable, his ironic wit no less than his irenic wrath.

"One rule about South Africa that has the validity of a Euclidian axiom," Tutu writes, "is the one stating that on any major matter, you can be sure that most White South Africans will be ranged on one side and the majority of Black South Africans will be found on the opposite one. . . . Following the application of this rule, Blacks knew they were in trouble when their White compatriots went into transports of ecstatic delight and joy when Mr. Ronald Reagan won the 1980 U.S. Presidential elections."

Even back then, Tutu was pessimistic about Ronald Reagan's vaunted "constructive-engagement" approach to the government of South Africa, "a policy of appeasement with . . . the most vicious system since Nazism." And, after a recent White House meeting with the President, Tutu had not changed his mind. Those soothing claims that the lot of blacks in South Africa is on the rise—in sports, in the creation of international hotels and restaurants, in the removal of discriminatory signs—are without substance, Tutu writes.

"It is a charade because . . . they are mere concessions that depend on the whim of those who have political power," he says. Put simply, it is that political power that blacks must share if they are ever to have true liberty.

And, as he looks at the world about him and sees how the United States *sometimes* contends with tyranny, as it did in imposing sanctions against martial law in Poland, the bishop comes to a doleful conclusion: "The U.S. Government does not really care about Blacks. Poles are different. Poles are White."

Hope and Suffering reflects its author's strengths, but in spite of them, somehow, it is unsatisfying. Perhaps it is too recent to be history; too dated to be news. One must still scan the daily papers regularly to see, for example, if the White House ever will adopt a stern policy against apartheid; if those 119 U.S. corporations doing business in South Africa ever will exert economic pressure to effect political change for the voteless blacks; if, indeed, humane and moral stirrings ever will arise in South Africa's minority white government.

A more irritating flaw in ***Hope and Suffering*** is the editorial abandon (some items dated, some not; some items introduced by explanatory notes, some not); the book seems to have been rushed into print ere the Nobel bloom was off the bishop.

Huston Horn, in a review of "Hope and Suffer-

ing: Sermons and Speeches," in Los Angeles Times Book Review, *January 27, 1985, p. 2.*

John F. Whealon (review date 27 April 1985)

[*In the following article, Whealon offers a summary of* Hope and Suffering.]

Publicity about the writer of this book has exceeded any publisher's fondest dreams. ***Hope and Suffering*** was published in South Africa in 1983, and in Britain and the United States in 1984. Then the author, Bishop Desmond Tutu, General Secretary of the South African Council of Churches, gained international attention as winner of the 1984 Nobel Peace Prize and then again as Johannesburg's first black Anglican bishop.

This book, a compilation and editing of some of Tutu's sermons and writings from 1976 to 1982, begins with considerable biographical material. There is an authoritative foreword by Anglican Bishop Trevor Huddleston, himself a veteran of the South African racial struggle. And there is an eloquent introduction by the Rev. Buti Tlhagale, a Roman Catholic priest from Soweto. All writings in this book refer to the evil of apartheid and the yearnings for freedom of blacks in South Africa. Therefore the book's title, ***Hope and Suffering.*** The various writings are presented in four separate chapters or sections.

The first section, entitled "Introducing South Africa," describes in detail the moral evil that apartheid is: "Blacks forming 80 percent of the population were relegated to 13 percent of the land. They enjoyed none of the rights that citizens take for granted in a democracy—they had to carry passes; they were subjected to influx control measures; they lived in segregated areas little better than ghettoes; they received a segregated education with glaring disparity in annual government expenditure per capita between black and white (at present it is in the order of 1:10)."

The second section, from my viewpoint, shows Tutu at his best and strongest. The chapter "Liberation as a Biblical Theme" focuses on the biblical teachings and the theology underlying his public stance against apartheid. He was a seminary teacher, and that dimension of his life is shown here. From the Old Testament he treats at length the Exodus theme, with deliverance from oppression and journeying to the Promised Land of Freedom as applicable to the South African blacks. He talks of the Jews in exile, developing at that time the Deutero-Isaian future exodus theme and the P account of creation in Genesis. From the New Testament he shows how Matthew presents Jesus as the new Moses, the new Joshua, the liberator of peoples. And in a challenging fashion, he holds up this theological teaching on the immorality of apartheid to the Christian Government of South Africa and to the Dutch Reformed Church that gives biblical support to apartheid. Tutu is solid and updated in his biblical bases. He shows the hopeful, courageous spirit of Romans 8.

The third section, "Current Concerns," presents the bishop's personal and pointed comments on the political scene in South Africa and in the United States. Impatient for change now, he is strongly critical of any temporizing measures in the Reagan Administration and in the current South African Government. Perhaps it was the abundant acronyms, local names and references, so mystifying to this foreigner. Anyway I thought the bishop better as a theologian than as a political commentator. The final section, "The Divine Intention," contains personal religious testimony about the Will of God in the present South Africa trials. This chapter is deeply spiritual.

Hope and Suffering illustrates well the unique dynamic that is Desmond Tutu, who is blunt, fearless, filled with faith and courage, charismatic. At this critical time in his nation's history, he is the right man in the right place. Once in a comparable struggle for racial equality, the Rev. Martin Luther King Jr. served as the inspiring moral leader. May Bishop Desmond Tutu be protected and given more authority by his Nobel Prize and status as bishop. And may his dream of racial equality and freedom for his people soon come true. (pp. 349-51)

John F. Whealon, in a review of "Hope and Suffering: Sermons and Speeches," in America, *Vol. 152, No. 16, April 27, 1985, pp. 349-51.*

Patrick Jordan (review date 6 September 1985)

[*In the following, Jordan describes Tutu's theme in* Hope and Suffering *as the "abhorrent evil of the South African system."*]

Bishop Tutu has said elsewhere the church has five marks: it is one, holy, catholic, apostolic, and suffering. In this brief collection of addresses and sermons [***Hope and Suffering***], he describes the sufferings of South Africa's majority black population under apartheid. He proposes, but does not detail, a prophetic vision for societal change there, and simultaneously offers his personal example of enduring hope, one capable of sustaining the long-suffering in movements of human rights everywhere.

Desmond Tutu's theme is singular and unabashed: the abhorrent evil of the South African system. His theological method is here likewise singleminded: liberation-exodus is the lens by which to examine and weigh the apartheid situation. The bishop speaks with flowing ease and ready passion. What he has to say is not always couched in irenic terms. On occasion, he caricatures opponents, a fact not likely to engender their trust. He is firmly set as to his goals: the solution must be political. "Either there is going to be power-sharing or . . . we must give up hope of peaceful settlement in South Africa." The international community must bring economic pressure to bear on Pretoria. Finally, Tutu and his people are watching. "When we are free," he writes, "we will remember those who helped us to get free." It is that deliverance which animates Tutu. It is a hope assured, and richer than mere words. (pp. 477-78)

Patrick Jordan, in a review of "Hope and Suffering: Sermons and Speeches," in Commonweal, *Vol. CXII, No. 15, September 6, 1985, pp. 477-78.*

Tutu on black racism:

I expect that there are many [blacks who hate the white minority]. They must, you know. What do they think happens to you? You work for the white person in a salubrious suburb of Johannesburg, in a huge house that probably has only got two people in it. You have had to leave your home when it was still dark because transport is so inadequate. You go back home to your ghetto, you haven't seen your children, and by the time you get home they've probably fallen asleep. You are in your home, which is perhaps no larger than just the den of the home from which you have just come. What does that say to you? What do they think is happening to you as a human being? However, I think there is still the recurring miracle of blacks still talking to whites. There is an extraordinary fund of good will, still, despite all of what has happened here.

Desmond Tutu, in an interview in Rolling Stone, *21 November 1985.*

Bonganjalo Goba (essay date 1986)

[In the excerpt below, Goba delineates Tutu's conception of liberation theology.]

Those of us who have listened and have been taught by Archbishop Tutu, know that he is a serious biblical theologian. His theological vision is grounded in a profound faith that believes that the God of the Bible is on the side of the down-trodden, the oppressed or if you like, the wretched of the earth. This vision is reflected in his sermons, speeches and even conversations which reflect a deep spirituality whose characteristics are utter devotion and trust in God who has been revealed in Jesus Christ; and a deep concern for those who suffer and are victims of oppression. The Biblical ethos informs and shapes Archbishop Tutu's theological vision. This is a point which is misunderstood by those who think his statements and actions are motivated by political ambition.

But his theological vision is grounded in his understanding of the church. He makes the following observation about the church [in ***Hope and Suffering: Sermons and Speeches***]:

> The Church of God must produce a relevant theology which speaks to hopelessness and despondency. The Church of God must declare the Lordship of God and of Christ—that God is the Lord of History and of this world despite all appearances to the contrary, that He is God of justice and cares about oppression and exploitation, about deaths in detention, about front-end loaders, squatters' shacks, about unemployment and about power.

Archbishop Tutu's biblical vision of a God who is concerned about the plight and suffering of people moves him to be part of God's liberating mission in the South African context. We can say it is this obedience to the divine call of a God who cares so much for the wretched, that moves Archbishop Tutu to engage so forcefully in the struggle for authentic liberation. This involvement and passionate call for justice in this land is a response of obedience to God who in Jesus Christ has come to liberate the world. It is a response of faith; but one that challenges the structure of bondage in the South African apartheid society. Archbishop Tutu's moral outrage against apartheid is the product of his deep faith in a God who cares for people irrespective of who they are. Apartheid, according to Archbishop Tutu, is not simply contrary to the gospel, but it is demonic in that it breeds suffering and chaos.

It is this theological vision that influenced and inspired some of us to engage in black theological reflection within the South African context. As a special tribute to Archbishop Tutu I want to share with you some of his major theological concerns, as expressed in his sermons, speeches and lectures. In no way will I suggest that these can be arranged systematically; but I propose to give a broad outline of these theological concerns as well as reflect on them. In doing so, I am also inviting young budding black theologians to address themselves to some of these issues. I want to reflect on two of his major theological concerns, a response to the challenge he has posed to the black Christian community:

> (a) A concern to develop a biblical theology of liberation.
>
> (b) A call for the church to be a community of liberation.

Archbishop Tutu is basically a biblical theologian. By this I want to suggest that the foundations of his theological hermeneutic are grounded in the liberating message of the Bible. To illustrate this point let me quote from one of his statements [in ***Hope and Suffering***]:

> Where there is injustice, exploitation and oppression then the Bible and the God of the Bible are subversive of such a situation. Our God, unlike the pagan nature gods, is no God sanctifying the *status quo.* He is a God of surprises, uprooting the powerful and unjust to establish His Kingdom. We see it in the entire history of Israel.

Archbishop Tutu makes numerous references to the Bible as part of the development of his theological hermeneutics. Unfortunately this biblical hermeneutics thrust in his theology is not developed in the form of a theological treatise—but merely as a crucial ingredient in his theology. I want to show why this theological concern is crucial to the way we do theology in the South African context. (pp. 61-3)

There is renewed interest in the study of the Bible particularly using methods from the Social Sciences. More biblical scholars are turning to Sociology and Sociology of Knowledge in their attempt to unravel the early social world of both the Old and the New Testaments. I believe this is a very important development which hopefully will shed new insights on the significance of the Bible for theology and preaching. This will also enable us to appreciate why certain Biblical themes have attracted the attention of particularly those who engage in the theology of liberation, especially the theme of the Exodus. As the scope of this essay does not permit me to examine these new developments, I will focus my attention on one aspect, that is, viewing scripture as a liberating word and then use it as a basis for understanding the place of the Bible in black theological reflection.

One of the prevailing misconceptions about the theology of liberation is that this kind of theology is inspired purely by radical ideologies such as nationalism and Marxism, and not the Bible. We need to examine this misconception in order to put the record straight. What we must recognize is that one of the central themes of the Bible is liberation/salvation. What theology of liberation has succeeded to impress on our minds is that the God of the Bible is the God of liberation. Daniel Migliore in his book *Called to Freedom* makes the following observation:

> Liberation theology finds the centre of Scripture in its story of God's liberating activity. In the Old Testament God's saving action is focussed in the Exodus, the liberation of a people from political, cultural and religious bondage. By this event God has become known as the liberating God. "I am the Lord your God, who brought you out of the land of Egypt, out of the house of bondage" (Ex. 20:2).

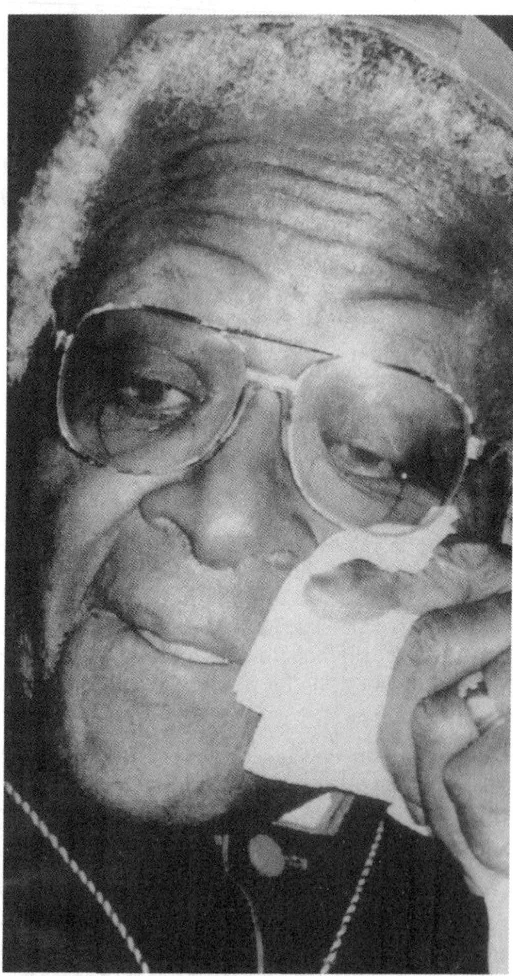

Tutu after attending a funeral for forty-two black South Africans killed in June 1992 at Boipatong.

Because of this basic theological thrust Migliore has suggested that the Bible should be interpreted (a) historically, (b) theocentrically, and (c) contextually.

Let us examine what he means by these three categories. (a) To interpret the Bible historically plays an important role in theology, or preaching for that matter, in that it compels the exegete to take seriously the particularity of God's actions. This approach enables us to appreciate the liberating acts of God in history. But more than this consideration, it enables us to appreciate the problems and the limitations of the early Christian community.

We come to understand the possibilities that remained as a challenge to that community. As Migliore states, "To interpret the Bible historically is to see in its narratives not only memories of past events but promises of new possibilities." The point which Migliore emphasizes is that in studying the past of God's liberating activity, we are challenged to understand its implications for the present. But further, this approach enables us to link our present struggle with that of the early Christian community.

I believe Archbishop Tutu, as a biblical theologian, has been very conscious of this principle in his work. He displays a very strong consciousness that the God of the Bible acts within human history. That God sides concretely with the wretched of the earth within the historical context of their struggle. For Archbishop Tutu the incarnation is a historical event that signals God's determination to liberate humanity from oppression and dehumanization. The God of the Bible acts in history to liberate humanity, this is the message of the ministry of Jesus Christ. In one of his important sermons delivered at Steve Biko's funeral he made the following statement:

> Yes, the God Jesus came to proclaim He was no neutral sitter on the fence. He took the side of the oppressed, the poor, the exploited, not because they were holier or morally better than their oppressors.
>
> No, He was on their side simply and solely because they were oppressed. Yes, this was the good news Jesus came to proclaim—that God was the liberator, the one who set free the oppressed and the poor and exploited. He set them free from all that would make them less than he wanted them to be, fully human persons as free as Jesus Christ showed Himself to be. And so all the mighty works which Jesus performed, healing the sick, opening the eyes of the blind, forgiving the sins of all sinners, were to set them free so that they could enjoy the glorious liberty of the children of God. And His followers believed He would restore the Kingdom again to Israel. He would set them free from being ruled by the Romans and give them back their political independence.

For Archbishop Tutu God is involved in the struggle of the oppressed. God takes sides within a specific historical context. This principle is important for it compels whoever reads the Bible to contextualize.

The other important point which Migliore makes is that the Bible should be interpreted theocentrically. This principle, I believe, is so central to our theological hermeneutic that without it, it becomes impossible to engage in any meaningful biblical exegesis. Migliore makes the following observation about this:

> Scripture must be interpreted theocentrically; however, the meaning of "God" is radically redefined in the biblical story of liberation.
>
> The central actor in the biblical drama is God, Scripture witnesses to the reality of God, to the purpose of God, to the kingdom of God. The content of the biblical story is God's faithfulness in acts of judgment and mercy, in the covenant with the people of Israel and in the history of Jesus. The biblical narrative has many aspects, but in the midst of the many aspects is the central theme: the mystery of the faithful God who takes up the cause of justice, freedom, and peace on behalf of the creation oppressed by sin and misery. Scripture witnesses on the promise of God even in the midst of judgment. It declares God's benevolence toward us even in the depth of our sin: "While we were yet sinners Christ died for us" (Rom. 5:8). Scripture proclaims the decisive ratification of all God's promises in the resurrection of the crucified Jesus. "For all the promises of God find their Yes in him" (II Cor. 1:20).

Reading his articles or listening to Archbishop Tutu one gets an interesting insight about how his theology is centred on the notion of God. For Archbishop Tutu God is alive and involved in the struggle of the oppressed. It is thus the God of liberation of the exodus who is the source of his prophetic piety. God is not just an idea but becomes the vision the embodiment of a real liberating presence in the world. In one of his sermons Archbishop Tutu made the following observation:

> So let us remind ourselves again and again just what kind of God our God is. He is always there. He has always been there. So don't despair. No matter how long it may take or seem to be. He is there. He hears, He cares and will act. We must not doubt that He will take our side and that He will rescue us and lead us out of bondage, out of our slavery, out of our poverty, out of our suffering. He will make us His own people to worship Him and He is almighty. Nothing will eventually stop Him.

This vision of a God who takes sides is so real for Archbishop Tutu, God is not neutral for in Jesus Christ He identifies with the poor and the oppressed. This theocentric approach, I believe, is reflected in most theologies of liberation. Liberation theologians are so conscious of this God who liberates the wretched of the earth. I believe this principle is a pivot on which our hermeneutic is based for without this profound consciousness of a God who is involved in the struggles of humanity, there would be no theology or theologies of liberation.

The other important principle that Migliore mentions in his book is that the Bible must be interpreted contextually. He makes the following observation about this:

> Scripture must be interpreted contextually; however, the context of our interpretation must be increasingly open to and inclusive of the yearnings of the whole creation to be free.
>
> The context of our interpretation of Scripture will always include and will frequently begin with our now personal awareness of captivity and yearning for freedom and new life: with our own anxiety, guilt, frustration, alienation, loneliness and despair.

I believe that Archbishop Tutu has been very faithful to this principle. For in his sermons and speeches he interprets the Bible contextually. For him the Bible is so relevant to every situation of life. The word of God addresses the South African situation. It is the word that unravels the contradictions and the evils of the political system of apartheid. Speaking about the church he makes the following statement:

> The church in South Africa must be a prophetic church which cries out 'thus saith the Lord' speaking up against injustice and violence, against oppression and exploitation, against all that dehumanizes God's children and makes them less than what God intended them to be. The Church of God in this context must show forth the features of the Lord and Master who tied a towel around His waist to wash the feet of His disciples.

This concern with the present contest of oppression and suffering is reflected in his theological vision. As he attempts to interpret the word of God contextually, he at the same time proclaims its promise for liberation in the here and now. Through Archbishop Tutu, God speaks so powerfully to the South African situation. It is this commitment that has earned Archbishop Tutu both enemies and friends.

So what we see in this brief analysis is the development of a biblical vision that addresses itself to the current political struggle of the oppressed. The Word of God addresses itself to the plight of the poor and the oppressed. It is not only the word but the word made flesh in the liberating ministry of Jesus Christ. What we see in Archbishop Tutu's theological vision is the development of an incarnational approach in which God's concern becomes alive through the commitment of those who serve God in the world today. In this, Archbishop Tutu succeeds to make the Bible relevant to the struggle of authentic human liberation. I believe Archbishop Tutu must be given credit for this, for the Bible has been silent for a very long time in our struggle for liberation within the South African context. (pp. 63-7)

Bonganjalo Goba, "A Theological Tribute to Archbishop Tutu," in Hammering Swords into Ploughshares: Essays in Honor of Archbishop Mpilo Desmond Tutu, *edited by Buti Tlhagale and Itumeleng Mosala, 1986. Reprint by Africa World Press, Inc. and William B. Eerdmans Publishing Company, 1987, pp. 61-71.*

Desmond Tutu with John Bierman (interview date 13 March 1989)

[*In the following interview, Tutu discusses political reforms in South Africa.*]

[*Bierman*]: *Are you at all impressed by the statement of Frederik de Klerk [leader of South Africa's governing National Party] that white domination must end?*

[Tutu]: Only the most gullible can continue to believe the statements this government makes that sound so grand. Nine years ago, [Foreign Minister Roelof] Pik Botha said at the UN that we are moving away from discrimination based on race, and here we are still moving away from it under a constitution that excludes 73 per cent of the population. What is that if it is not domination?

But some of the bulwarks of apartheid have fallen—the Pass Laws, the Immorality Act. Is that not progress?

You can say it is progress if you are looking for peripheral things. You mention bulwarks, but in fact the bulwark of apartheid is the Race Classification Act. Why, if you are moving away from discrimination based on race, should you have a law that says people are to be classified according to their race? And why have the Group Areas Act and the Separate Amenities Act [laws enforcing segregated living areas and services]? Why do you have education on a discriminatory basis as they still have it?

But there are indications that those acts might be repealed. If so, would that not be a major advance?

They are taking a very strange way toward the repeal of the Group Areas Act. They had intended putting out a version of the act with far more severe penalties than at present and only abandoned it because there were very strong protests. Now, how can you say we are moving away from Group Areas? I think you are too trusting of them. I have been part of the community that has been the victim of these people and I have been willing to believe them. I have been attacked by many in our community for wanting to speak with the government. I said to President [Pieter] Botha once that he could conceivably be the one white man that black people would be willing to put up a statue to, because he could actually get rid of apartheid.

Given right-wing opposition, doesn't the government have to move slowly if it is to abandon apartheid?

But you can't get rid of apartheid stealthily and work away at it bit by bit, because what happens is that you raise the hackles of your right wing, and then that scares the hell out of you, and that is what has happened. In the meantime, the blacks on the other side aren't waiting for apartheid to be made less horrendous; they want apartheid removed. And in the final analysis, the question at the heart of our issue is political power. At the moment, [the whites] are able to do whatever they like because they know that they are not accountable to us.

Isn't South Africa's agreement to get out of Namibia and allow it to become independent a sign of progress?

I don't think they would be moving out if their economy was strong. But it has been weakened [by sanctions], and they no longer feel able to cock a snook at the world. They are making a virtue of necessity. Still, never mind why they are getting out. With Namibia independent, the only item remaining for the liberation of all southern Africa will be the Republic of South Africa itself. And victory in Namibia is going to egg on opponents of apartheid to intensify their efforts.

Is that a reason for optimism?

It could, of course, have the opposite effect on the world, especially the West. The West might say, "Look here, these guys have done something; let us acknowledge that, let's not be too tough on them." And we may get a great deal of resistance to further intensification of [anti-apartheid] pressure. But, on the whole, I think the consequences of Namibian independence could be very positive. And if Namibia goes the way of Zimbabwe, showing that it is an experiment that is working, then that will be all to the good.

Despite your skepticism about the government's intentions, isn't it possible that the reform process will generate inexorable forces that will push the Nationalists into surrendering white domination?

There is something of that, to some extent. I mean, you start a process and you gain momentum. But look at the things they have done to stop momentum—the state of emergency we have had since 1986, the number of people that have been killed since 1984. The casualties are people, man. I tend to be more trusting of people than most, to believe that everyone is potentially an angel until the contrary is proven. But when you think that even children have been put into detention, sent into exile, killed, that many of our people have been in detention now for three years without charge; when you think of how they trample on our dignity, no, those inexorable forces you are talking about seem too puny.

Desmond Tutu and John Bierman, in an interview in Maclean's Magazine, *Vol. 102, No. 11, March 13, 1989, p. 22.*

Desmond Tutu with Thomas Giles and Timothy Jones (interview date June 1992)

[*In the following interview, which was conducted one day after the deaths of forty-two South Africans at Boipatong in June 1992 and later published on 5 October 1992, Tutu comments on the role of religion in promoting political activism.*]

[*Giles and Jones*]: *What role has faith played in your life, and how has it led you to the fight against apartheid?*

[Tutu]: I have come to understand that a person's worth derives not from extraneous things, such as achievement, status, or race. One's worth is intrinsic and comes from being created in the image of God. God values his own image in mankind even after the Fall.

God has also sent his Son to further underline our infinite worth. He says, "You are of such worth that I will ransom you from the clutches of the Devil—not with perishable things, such as gold and silver, but by the precious blood of my Son."

As if that were not enough, God says, "I will sanctify you by the gift of my Holy Spirit." So human beings are of worth not only because they have been created in the image of God and are offered redemption by the precious blood of our Savior, but also because they may become tabernacles of the Holy Spirit.

It is like spitting in the face of God to treat a child of God as if he or she were anything less. Injustice and oppression are not simply wrong or evil, they are positively blasphemous. And that is the passion we have. We are inspired not by political or any other kind of ideology, but by our faith. If we are followers of Jesus Christ and accept the implications of our faith, we don't have any other option than to oppose oppression, injustice, and evil.

What is the biblical basis for political activism on behalf of the oppressed?

It is the whole nature of God. He is a gracious God. And grace means he operates on behalf of those who do not deserve it, those who have no claim on him. We see that right at the beginning, in the Exodus, when he intervenes on behalf of a rabble of slaves who have done nothing to deserve his intervention.

What is true religion? In Isaiah 1, God says, "I will not accept a religion merely of outward observances. If you want to repent of all the wrong you have done, show it by doing justice—not just to anybody, but to the widow, the orphan, the alien, the most voiceless of the voiceless."

And what is the true fast? In Isaiah 58, God says, "The fast I want is not that you be bent like a reed and starve yourself, but that you loose the prisoners' chains."

When God intervenes decisively in the lives of human beings, he does not come as a disembodied spirit, he becomes a human being; this also gives us a clue as to how we should operate. For the parents of his Son, he chooses not the high and the mighty, but a village lass married to a carpenter. Jesus is not born in the home of a king, but in a stable. And very soon this child becomes a refugee. He identifies with those who are the least in any community.

There are people who think in terms of a dichotomy between the secular and the sacred. But Jesus does not say, "I am concerned only with the spiritual side of you that is your soul," but rather, "I am concerned for the whole of you. When you are hungry, I feed you. When you are sick, I heal you. When you are a sinner, I forgive your sins."

Can we take activism too far?

We can easily think we have a hotline to God and that our purely human insights have divine approval.

And activism based on religion, in and of itself, is not necessarily a good thing. It has been religious fanatics who have done some of the greatest damage in the world; many of the world's wars have been sparked or exacerbated by religion; and a great deal of the prejudice and tyranny in the world today has a religious base.

We can also be intolerant. Activism can mean dismissing those who hold a different point of view as being beyond the pale. When we identify with a good cause, we must as well have proper distance from it and maintain respect for those on the other side.

How do you balance the spiritual and the political aspects of your life?

I do not have a sense of tension between the two. I have come to learn that spirituality is absolutely essential to an authentic Christian life. That is how it was with almost all God's servants. Their encounters with God were not for their own self-aggrandizement but for the sake of others. You meet God as a burning bush in order to be sent to Pharaoh to redeem captives.

You see this pattern in the life of our Lord; you see a rhythm of disengagement and engagement. He spent whole nights in prayer, then spent himself prodigally on behalf of others. He was constantly replenishing his spiritual resources. I, too, have learned to replenish mine.

What are your personal priorities for your church and for your country?

The church has to be God's instrument for the extension of his kingdom in any setting. Even in democratic systems, those who form the government are not transformed into gods. They are mortal, and they will be tempted by the blandishments of power. At the same time, there will always be voiceless, marginalized ones who feel miles away from the corridors of power and that they count for nothing. And the church has got to be there on behalf of them. It has to vigilantly declare to those in power, "Thus saith the Lord."

It must also be an agent of reconciliation. People often evacuate that word of its meaning, making it almost a term of abuse. They think reconciliation means crying "peace, peace" where there is no peace—that it does not mean confrontation. But true reconciliation confronts people with the sinfulness of sin—political sin, personal sin, structural sin.

In our setting, reconciliation means calling those who have benefitted from apartheid to confession and penitence for the hurt they have inflicted. Then, those who have been forgiven must demonstrate the genuineness of their contrition. There must be restitution wherever possible.

We must also help people not be embittered or to seek revenge. And it is we who are to be a kind of audio-visual aid of how human society ought to be.

How is the church to do that?

The church has to model the fact that Jesus Christ is our peace—that he has in fact broken down the dividing wall. Warring factions are at war no longer. There is now neither Jew nor Greek, neither male nor female, neither slave nor free. We are one in Christ.

Together, we must work to transform our society into one that says human beings matter more than things and profits. Our society must set a high premium on sharing rather than on hoarding, on cooperating rather than competing.

What steps should Christians in the U.S. take toward racial reconciliation?

You shouldn't be overly despondent. Actually, on the whole, you have had a wonderful capacity for self-criticism. Yes, people often tried to turn a blind eye, but more and more people were aware that something was wrong—that there was a disease. And recognizing that there is a disease is an important part of the cure.

But it is also important for you to hear what the wronged—the ones who are discriminated against—actually say. We must not be the ones who say, "This is the hurt and this is the cure" as infallible know-alls. Let us hear what they identify as points of hurt and what can be done to redress that hurt.

How can we stand with our brothers and sisters in South Africa?

We depend so much on your love and prayers, and we deeply appreciate what people have done in that regard. Many of you in your churches pressured your legislators and business people to impose sanctions that worked. Those sanctions have gotten us to where we've come. One of the pressures you could continue to exert is to impress on the South African government that you look to them to do something to end the violence.

Are you hopeful as you look ahead?

I am always hopeful. A Christian is a prisoner of hope. What could have looked more hopeless than Good Friday? But then, at Easter, God says, "From this moment on, no situation is untransfigurable." There is no situation from which God cannot extract good. Evil, death, oppression, injustice—these can never again have the last word, despite all appearances to the contrary. (pp. 39-41)

Desmond Tutu, Thomas Giles, and Timothy Jones, in an interview in Christianity Today, *Vol. 36, No. 11, October 5, 1992, pp. 39-41.*

Additional coverage of Tutu's life and career is contained in the following sources published by Gale Research: *Contemporary Authors,* Vol. 125; *Black Literature Criticism,* Vol. 3; and *Black Writers.*

Orson Welles

1915-1985

(Full name George Orson Welles) American filmmaker, screenwriter, actor, playwright, and novelist.

The following entry provides an overview of Welles's career. For further information on his life and works, see *CLC,* Volume 20.

INTRODUCTION

With few objections, Welles is considered the single most important influence on modern filmmaking. His first film, *Citizen Kane,* has been cited by numerous directors as the reason they became filmmakers, and broadly within western culture the film has been raised to iconic status as the greatest film ever made due to its psychological complexity and technical innovations. The growth of *Citizen Kane*'s reputation and the presumed decline in Welles's abilities as a filmmaker have obscured full consideration of his work. However, his lesser-known films, his prodigious work in theater, radio, and television, and his numerous unreleased and unfinished films and screenplays have attracted increasing attention and further enhance his artistic stature.

Welles was born in Kenosha, Wisconsin, to Beatrice Ives Welles, a woman with artistic talents and ambitions, and Richard Head Welles, a businessman and inventor whose dynamic and dissolute lifestyle both attracted and repelled his son. His parents divorced when he was six and his mother died when he was nine. Shortly before the death of his father in 1930, Welles was placed in the care of Dr. Maurice Bernstein, his mother's physician and longtime suitor. Bernstein, who became the model for Everett Sloane's character in *Citizen Kane,* was convinced that Welles was a genius and enrolled him in the Todd School for Boys in Woodstock, Illinois, where he studied Shakespeare and directed many school plays. A trip to Ireland in 1931 brought him to the Gate Theater in Dublin and his first professional acting experience. After his return to the United States in 1933, Welles joined Katherine Cornell's respected theatrical touring company and began writing, acting in, and directing radio programs. In 1934 he wrote and directed *The Hearts of Age,* a five-minute parody of Surrealist films. His performance in Cornell's production of *Romeo and Juliet* attracted the attention of John Houseman, with whom he founded the Mercury Theater and created some of the most highly acclaimed American stage productions. His radio production *The War of the Worlds,* which created hysteria by ostensibly reporting on an actual invasion of the Earth by Martians, further gained him notoriety when many listeners took the broadcast to be real. By 1938 Welles's fame in theater and radio earned him a place on the cover of *Time* magazine.

In 1939 Welles signed an unprecedented contract with RKO Pictures that gave him complete creative control over his projects and a generous million-dollar budget limit. These concessions were unprecedented in the heyday of the studio system, even for established directors, and engendered much resentment among Welles's peers. Welles's first feature, *Citizen Kane,* premiered in 1941. His next film, *The Magnificent Ambersons,* was significantly altered by studio executives when preview audiences objected to the film's leisurely pace and downbeat themes. When the RKO leadership changed that year, Welles was fired and much of the footage shot for his next film, *It's All True*—a documentary about South American culture—was destroyed. Attempting to prove that he "could put out a movie as well as anyone else," his next two films, *Journey Into Fear* and *The Stranger,* were made cheaply and quickly. These are generally considered Welles's least interesting works. *The Lady from Shanghai* and *Macbeth* did little to improve Welles's standing with Hollywood producers. In *Shanghai* he turned what was supposed to be a routine vehicle for Rita Hayworth, his ex-wife, into a dark, complex, subtly parodic film noir that many audiences—particularly Columbia Pictures head Harry Cohn—found difficult to understand. *Macbeth* simply did not attract audiences. Between 1948 and 1958 Welles worked primarily in Europe, completing two films financed largely with money he had made acting in other films. *Othello* took Welles four years to complete and was hailed as one of the best film adaptations of Shakespeare. *Mr. Arkadin,* often regarded as a sophisticated parody of *Citizen Kane,* displays a variety of cinematic techniques that strongly influenced the films of the French New Wave.

In 1958 Welles returned to the United States to direct *Touch of Evil,* a B-movie he significantly rewrote that many critics now consider a masterpiece. His reputation as an artistic director of consistently unprofitable films was now firmly established, making *Touch of Evil* the last film Welles directed for a major Hollywood studio. Welles returned to Europe to make his last four released films: *The Trial,* based on the novel by Franz Kafka; *Chimes at Midnight,* an elegiac story based on characters and situations from a number of Shakespeare's plays and concerning the friendship between Falstaff and Prince Hal; *The Immortal Story,* an hour-long film made for French television; and *F for Fake,* a work many critics view as a profound essay on the nature of illusion and showmanship. From this time on Welles worked as an actor and narrator and exploited his celebrity status to raise money for his own films. Commentators find it difficult to explain why producers in the 1970s and 1980s, who purportedly took greater financial risks on imaginative film projects than their predecessors, were unwilling to back his work. The American Film Institute honored him with its lifetime achievement award in 1975; at the ceremony he showed excerpts from an unfinished film called *The Other Side of the Wind,* starring John Huston as an aging director attempting to complete his last film. Welles died in Los Angeles in 1985.

Citizen Kane introduced the first of Welles's powerful, anti-heroic central characters. Like Hank Quinlan in *Touch of Evil,* Gregory Arkadin in *Mr. Arkadin,* Mr. Clay in *The Immortal Story,* and, to a certain extent, Dr. Kimball Menaker in Welles's screenplay *The Big Brass Ring,* Charles Foster Kane is a charismatic yet profoundly selfish figure who searches for love but ultimately destroys himself and those closest to him. Based in part on the life of newspaper magnate William Randolph Hearst, Kane is raised by the banker to whom his mother entrusts The Colorado Lode mining fortune, rises to prominence as a newspaper tycoon and failed political candidate, and finally retires and dies a lonely man surrounded by his possessions and dreaming of his childhood, which is symbolized by a sled emblazoned with the word "Rosebud." As Noël Carroll suggests, *Citizen Kane* offers opposing thematic viewpoints. On the one hand, the film seems to propose that a person's life is understandable, that Kane's regret for his lost innocence, symbolized by Rosebud, is the explanation for his behavior, the missing piece to the puzzle of his life; on the other hand, this proposition is undercut on numerous occasions, most prominently in the fact that the film ends not with the revelation of Rosebud, but with the close-up of the "No Trespassing" sign outside Kane's mansion, suggesting that Kane's life is finally unknowable. Stylistically, *Citizen Kane* is noted for its combination of traditional "analytical" editing—in which the scene of the action is presented in ordered pieces: long shots, medium shots, and close-ups—and deep-focus cinematography, in which a shot's depth of field is great enough to allow both foreground and background action to be in focus, giving the viewer a measure of choice in what to look at. Welles used long takes with deep-focus throughout his career, but never to the extent he and cinematographer Gregg Toland employed them in *Citizen Kane.* Critics note that in *Citizen Kane* Welles drew attention to various storytelling methods. The "March of Time" newsreel, the many flashbacks, the scenes with the investigating reporter, as well as those that open and close the film, are all stylistically different and offer unique narrative perspectives. More than the editing or the cinematography, scholars point to this heterogenous narrative strategy as being the truly revolutionary aspect of *Citizen Kane:* never before had a mainstream Hollywood film directed the viewer's attention to the act of telling a story and suggested that "official" narratives like news reports are fallible, nothing more than utterances from a specific, limited point of view.

Over the years, the reputation of *Citizen Kane* has grown dramatically, and it remains the film most studied in academic film classes. In general, critics charge that Welles's films are little more than flashy gimmicks showcasing his own blustering performances. A significant minority of critics also argue that *Citizen Kane* is not the revolutionary break with tradition it is touted to be—that a careful study of film history reveals a gradual development toward the kind of filmmaking *Kane* represents. However, the vast majority of critics argue otherwise, and Welles remains a rich source for scholarly endeavor and creative inspiration.

---

*PRINCIPAL WORKS

Macbeth [based on the play by William Shakespeare] (drama) 1936
Julius Ceasar [based on the play by William Shakespeare] (drama) 1937
The War of the Worlds [with Howard Koch] (radio play) 1938
Citizen Kane [with Herman J. Mankiewicz] (screenplay) 1941
The Magnificent Ambersons (screenplay) 1942
Journey into Fear [with Joseph Cotten] (screenplay) 1943
The Lady from Shanghai (screenplay) 1946
The Stranger [with Anthony Veiller and John Huston] (screenplay) 1946
Macbeth (screenplay) 1948
Time Runs (drama) 1950
The Unthinking Lobster (drama) 1950
Othello (screenplay) 1952
Mr. Arkadin (novel) 1955

Mr. Arkadin (screenplay) 1955; also released as *Confidential Report*
Touch of Evil (screenplay) 1958
The Trial (screenplay) 1962; also released as *Le procès*
Moby Dick Rehearsed (drama) 1965
Chimes at Midnight (screenplay) 1966; also released as *Falstaff*
The Immortal Story (screenplay) 1968
F for Fake (screenplay) 1973
The Big Brass Ring [with Oja Kodar; first publication] (screenplay) 1987

*Among Welles's works are numerous unproduced screenplays and unfinished or unreleased films, including *The Hearts of Age* (1934), *It's All True* (1942), *Don Quixote* (1955), *The Merchant of Venice* (1969), *The Deep* (1970), *The Other Side of the Wind* (1972), *The Dreamers* (1978-1985), *The Cradle Will Rock* (1984), and *King Lear* (1985).

CRITICISM

Orson Welles with Juan Cobos and Miguel Rubio (interview date Autumn 1966)

[*In the following interview, Welles articulates his general approach to filmmaking and discusses* Chimes at Midnight, The Magnificent Ambersons, *and his unreleased* Don Quixote.]

[*Cobos and Rubio*]: *In* **Chimes at Midnight,** *as in all your films, you don't give much value to landscape as such. There's a rather stylised and unreal feeling about it, so that a scene like the robbery at Gadshill ends up looking a bit like a set.*

[Welles]: Oh, that's sad to hear. Really? Well, to an extent I wouldn't object to that criticism . . . to an extent. I may have to submit to the criticism, because it may be true, but I regret it if the country doesn't seem real. But it mustn't seem *perfectly* real. In other words, one of the enemies of the film is of course the simple, banal fact, the tree or rock that looks as it looks to anybody who takes a picture of his family through a camera on Sunday. So we have to be able to invest what is real, by reason of the photography, position of the lights, the conception, with a character, sometimes with a glamour, sometimes with an allure or a mystery which it doesn't have. To that extent it must be treated as a décor.

I feel that there is almost an aesthetic problem here, one which is almost never resolved in costume pictures. I don't know why I say almost: I would say never in the history of films, with the possible exception of some films of Eisenstein. Films which I don't particularly admire in themselves, but which have solved the problem that the real world outside—sky, clouds, trees and so on—doesn't seem to have anything to do with the décor. No matter how convincing the set, whether it's a real place or made out of cardboard, as soon as people in costume ride out on their horses it's suddenly banal, it's modern. You see a perfectly-made costume, actor wearing it correctly, everything is all right: he goes outside, and it's suddenly a location. You feel the trucks behind him and everything. I don't know why. In *Henry V*, for example, you see the people riding out of the castle, and suddenly they are on a golf course somewhere charging each other. You can't escape it, they have entered another world.

The only place where you don't feel this is in Westerns, and Japanese pictures which are like Westerns because they are a tradition. And it's a tradition in which the clothes, and nature and so on, have learned to live together. But I believe the problem can be solved, and I *think* I solved it to some extent in ***Othello,*** and more here. What I am trying to do is to see the outside, real world through the same eyes as the inside, fabricated one. To create a kind of unity.

The seventy minutes we have seen of your **Don Quixote** *seems to translate just that ideal world which Cervantes dreamed for his characters.*

That's the problem, isn't it? The people must live in their world. It is a fundamental problem for the film-maker, even when you are making apparently the most ordinary modern story. But particularly when you have a great figure of myth like Quixote, even like Falstaff, a silhouette against the sky of all time. These are people who have more life in them than any human being ever had. But you can't simply dress up and *be* them, you have to make a world for them.

You originally had certain ideas about the photographic look of **Chimes at Midnight,** *a kind of grading which would give the images almost the quality of an old engraving. In the first print we saw, you used this for the credit titles, which came up over the characters present at the coronation. Why did you change this?*

They weren't able to do it in the lab. It would have produced an extraordinary effect, I think, and it's my great sorrow that it hasn't been done. In fact, the film would have been lit in a completely different way if I had known that this process was likely to fail.

From reading the plays, one had the feeling that the film might have been gayer than you made it.

It's a very sad story: perhaps it should be happier, and that may be a failure on my part. But I also think that it is funnier in the English version than in Spanish. The Spanish version loses very little in the serious story, even though you can't expect a popular audience to appreciate that speech of the King on sleep unless it is an English audience. There is a density in what Shakespeare wrote that cannot be changed, and you must understand that every time you come to a speech of that kind you must fail except in English. You just have to sit still and say 'well, we lost it.' Luckily this picture only has one speech like that; but there are technical difficulties of translation for the jokes. All the same, the thing that most concerns me about the film and my own performance is that I am not as funny as I expected to be. That was part of what preoccupied me all through the shooting: the more I studied the part, the less funny he seemed to be.

Falstaff is a man defending a force—the old England—which is going down. What is difficult about Falstaff, I believe, is that he is the greatest conception of a good man, the most completely good man, in all drama. His faults are so small and he makes tremendous jokes out of little faults. But his goodness is like bread, like wine . . . And that was why I lost the comedy. The more I played it, the more I felt that I was playing Shakespeare's good, pure man.

I have played the part three times in the theatre and now in the film, and I'm not convinced that I have realised it properly yet. It's the most difficult part I ever played in my life, and there are at least three scenes in the film that I would like to do over again from my point of view as an actor. I feel he is a wit rather than a clown, and I don't think much of the few moments in the film when I am simply funny, because I don't think that he is. But I can see that there are scenes which should be much more hilarious, because I directed everything, and played everything, with a view to preparing for the last scene. The relationship between Falstaff and the Prince is not the simple, comic relationship that it is in Shakespeare's *Henry IV, Part One,* but always a preparation for the end. And as you see, the farewell is performed about four times during the movie, foreshadowed four times.

There is a wonderful moment after the play-acting at the tavern, when they are talking about Falstaff's banishment ("banish plump Jack, and banish all the world . . .") and the Prince says "I will. . . . "

That's the clearest of all those farewells. And you discover in making the film that the death of the King, and the death of Hotspur, which is the death of chivalry, and Falstaff's poverty and Falstaff's illness run all through the play. Comedy can't really dominate a film made to tell this story, which is all in dark colours. But the basic thing is the innocence. The interesting thing about this story is that the old King is a murderer, an usurper, and yet he represents the legitimate idea. So Hal is the creation of a legitimate Prince who must betray the good man in order to become a hero, a famous English hero. The terrible price of power which the Prince has to pay. In the first part of the play, the Hotspur subplot keeps the business of the triangle between the King, his son and Falstaff (who is a sort of foster father) from dominating. But in my film, which is made to tell, essentially, the story of that triangle, there are bound to be values which can't exist as it is played in the original. It's really quite a different drama.

The film has become a sort of lament for Falstaff?

Yes, that may be true. I would like to think that . . . The film was not intended as a lament for Falstaff, but for the death of Merrie England. Merrie England as a conception, a myth, which has been very real to the English-speaking world, and is to some extent expressed in other countries of the Medieval epoch: the age of chivalry, of simplicity, of Maytime and all that. It is more than Falstaff who is dying. It's the old England, dying and betrayed.

The Magnificent Ambersons *is also a lament for an epoch which has ended.*

Not so much for the epoch as for the sense of moral values which are destroyed. In the case of ***Ambersons,*** they are destroyed by the automobile, in the case of ***Chimes,*** by the interests of power, duty, responsibility, national grandeur, all this kind of thing.

All your films are stories of a failure with a death in it. . .

Almost all serious stories in the world are stories of a failure with a death in it . . . But there is more lost paradise in them than defeat. To me that's the central theme in Western culture: the lost paradise.

Along with **The Magnificent Ambersons, Chimes at Midnight** *seems to be one of the most personal of your films, perhaps because these two are the most lyrical.*

Yes, I agree. I don't know whether lyrical is the right word, but there is a more personal feeling in those films, a deeper emotion. Yes, because people think of my films as being violent and sometimes cold, but I think ***Ambersons . . .*** this picture represents more than anything else what I would like to do in films. This question of 'an Orson Welles style' is all exaggerated anyway. I don't think that my films are dominated by style. I have a strong style, or different ones, I hope, but I'm not a formalist. The great majority of critics, whether they treat me well or badly, always treat me as a formalist. And I'm not a formalist!

How do you conceive scenes? They seem to be conceived rather like poems, with a kind of musical flow.

Music. Music and poetry. It's that rather than simply visual. The visual side comes out of a method of thinking, if thinking is the word. I hate to use pompous words like 'creating', but I'm afraid you have to. With me, the visual is a solution to what the poetical and musical form dictates. I don't begin with the visual and then try to find a poetry or music and try to stick it in the picture. The picture has to follow it. And again, people tend to think that my first preoccupation is with the simple plastic effects of the cinema. But to me they all come out of an interior rhythm, which is like the shape of music or the shape of poetry. I don't go around like a collector picking up beautiful images and pasting them together.

The danger in the cinema is that you see everything, because it's a camera. So what you have to do is to manage to evoke, to incant, to raise up things which are not really there.

—Orson Welles

Is that why editing is so important to you?

It's very central. I believe in the film as a poetic medium.

Welles in Chimes at Midnight. *"I think Falstaff is like a Christmas tree decorated with vices. The tree itself is total innocence and love."*

I don't think it competes with painting, or with ballet—the visual side of films is a key to poetry. There is no picture which justifies itself, no matter how beautiful, striking, horrific, tender . . . it doesn't mean anything unless it makes poetry possible. And that suggests something, because poetry should make your hair stand up on your skin, should suggest things, evoke more than you see. The danger in the cinema is that you see everything, because it's a camera. So what you have to do is to manage to evoke, to incant, to raise up things which are not really there.

Do you think **Chimes at Midnight** *does this?*

That's what I am reaching for, what I hope is true. If it is, then I'm reaching maturity as an artist. If it isn't true, then I'm in decadence, you know? But what I am trying to discover now in films is not technical surprises or shocks, but a more complete unity of forms, of shapes. The true form, the interior, the musical form of a picture. I believe that you should be able to enjoy a picture with your eyes closed, that a blind man should be able to enjoy a movie. We all say 'the only movies are silent movies,' but they have been talking now for forty years, so we have to say something in them. And when something is said, or a sound is made, or there is music, whatever occurs must have in it—just technically, I'm not thinking of poetry now, only technically—a shape which is immediately recognisable, so that you see that the whole thing has a shape, just as the image does. And the interior conception of the author, above all, must have a single shape.

Chimes at Midnight *was originally designed to open with the assassination of Richard II and the landing of Bolingbroke in England. Why did you change this? The part of the Bolingbroke scene which was shot was full of extraordinary visual ideas—all the flags, and the future King waiting by the camp-fire, cold and hungry.*

We shot one day on the assassination, and it didn't seem to me that the scene was sufficiently clear: instead of explaining the political background, it would tend to obscure it and confuse the audience. Also, four or five days work were necessary to complete it, and I didn't want to put the producer to that expense.

The Bolingbroke scene looked very interesting . . . but that's what divides the men from the boys, the people who can really do it from the others. What a director must have is a capacity to throw out his most beautiful shots. A film is often ruined, in my opinion, by a director who can't bear to get rid of something just because it's beautiful. Do you remember the shots of the two old men, Falstaff and Shallow, walking in the snow? Fine, marvellous shots, which I took out. Now, I could have indulged myself and had all the cinema clubs in the world say 'Look! How beautiful!' But those shots would have hurt the real, internal rhythm of the picture. And when things won't be as useful to the total film as you expected, then you must be willing to abandon them immediately.

When you were filming the battle sequence you shot longish takes, then fragmented them in the cutting-room.

On the first day I tried to do very short pieces, but I found the extras didn't work as well unless they had a longer thing to do. They didn't seem to be really fighting until they had time to warm up. That's why the takes were long, since there was no way of beginning the camera later and cutting. But I knew I was only going to use very short cuts. For example, we shot with a big crane very low to the ground, moving as fast as it could be moved against the action. What I was planning to do—and did—was to intercut the shots in which the action was contrary, so that every cut seemed to be a blow, a counterblow, a blow received, a blow returned. Actually it takes a lot of time for the crane to move over and back, but everything was planned for this effect and I never intended to use more than a small section of the arc in each case.

You edit very dynamically, breaking up your long takes with constant movement. Is that because you are apprehensive about boring the public?

Because I am so easily bored, I think the public probably is. You people who love the cinema are not as easily bored by it as I am. In other words, if I had to make films only for people who *fundamentally* love the movies, then I could be longer. But I would be false in it, because I believe that the point of boredom is very easily reached. If it isn't reached this year, it will be later. It's one of the things that dates films, that makes them seem old-fashioned, when you don't have the courage to keep it moving . . . I believe that films should be able to tell a story quicker than any other medium. Instead the tendency, in the last ten years particularly, has been to get slower and slower, and for the director to indulge himself in what you call visual ideas. If we don't have speed, I think we are basically betraying the medium. But nowadays serious directors are permitted to ask the public anything they like, at any length.

I do not like verbosity; I don't like wasted time. I like concentration in every art. And although I know that I lose, that the public loses, a great deal because of the concentration, I also hope that somebody will see one thing and someone else will see another. I think you make a very thin movie if everything in it is going to be exactly clear. I don't want to criticise my contemporaries, but there are some directors who are considered very great who make one effect and only that effect. You can go back again ten times, and you will only admire exactly the same thing again. I don't think a film should be entirely evident: there should always be something else to see when you go again . . .

The last scene at Justice Shallow's house, in which Pistol brings the news of Hal's accession, was originally shot in one five-minute take. Then you intercut it with shots of the King's castle, breaking it up and losing some minutes of this scene of the old men in front of the fire.

I had a reason for that. I believe that as it is cut now, it tells the basic story better. If you are making a film in which you are not completely at the mercy of your narrative, then anything that is interesting can give itself its own length. The scene was in itself a good one, a little like a photographed scene from the theatre, and what remains now is what I thought was good about it. What was there before seemed to me to reduce the interest of the film after the big scene of the King's death. In other words, what you had was something beautiful, well-conceived perhaps by the director, admirable cinematically but not dramatically.

You sometimes do several retakes of the same scene on different days. Do you think the scenes over and decide on a retake without even seeing the rushes?

Yes. The rushes aren't important to me. I don't really shoot a 'retake' in the classic American sense of the word: a shot that has been studied by everybody and has been discovered to be wrong technically. I make a retake because *my* work wasn't good enough.

Sometimes you shoot a scene which seems perfect, and then do it over again. Is that because you think that there was something in it that didn't work after all?

Well, it wasn't perfect . . . You can only do that, though, where you are working on the same set. I never go back for a retake on a set that's finished with; that's a luxury I can't indulge in. In Cardona we didn't retake anything, because I had to finish John Gielgud's part in two weeks. I knew when he left that I would have all the work we later did with doubles. That wasn't second thoughts: I knew I would have to use doubles because I only had him for two weeks and he plays a part that runs almost as long as mine.

When you are working, there is what you call a kind of orderly disorder on the set. The way, for instance, that you sometimes jump in shooting between one scene and another.

There are several reasons for that. First of all, sometimes what seems disorderly has a perfectly logistic purpose. But in order to explain why I'm changing the scene would take ten minutes of conference. So I don't explain, and it looks as though I am being capricious. When I'm outside, the position of the sun determines everything: I'll suddenly jump from one sequence to another, even go into a sequence that wasn't planned for that day, if the light suddenly becomes right for it. The sun is the most beautiful light in the world, and the way to make it beautiful is to film it at its moment; so that means jumping. Those are the technical reasons for the orderly disorder. Then sometimes the actors aren't right on that day, you see that they need another day, another mood. The thing isn't working. Then you must change, and the change does everybody good. Sometimes, when all the lights are in one position, in order to move logically to the next scene as planned creates an enormous waste of time. And rather than lose time in moving the lights, I confuse everybody else by jumping to the next thing I know we can shoot. I think you will agree that the disorder doesn't mean that we work slowly. I think it is terribly necessary to work quickly.

Sometimes, even if things aren't going very well, you shoot in order to get that feeling of improvisation.

We are always mendicants in the movies. To a certain extent we are standing with our hands out waiting for manna from heaven. Sometimes you shoot and see if God isn't going to put something on your plate. Sometimes He does, then you grab it.

Also, as you know, I'm in some ways a perfectionist, but in many ways not at all. When I've worked with ordinary commercial directors, people whose pride it is to be technically fast and efficient, they go over things, many things, more than I do. If I were directing the scene I would say 'All right, that's it,' because I always leave some rough edges. I don't believe that a movie is made, any more than a painting is made, by painting every leaf on the tree. I will work and work for a moment in an actor's performance, or wait and wait until the light is correct. But in general I shoot sooner and am satisfied sooner. There may be an assistant director still running out, but I don't care. I go.

The great danger of filming is that 'all right . . . silence': the long pause, all those terrible formalistic gestures; then people try to pull themselves together and make a little moment that's true after it has been framed in this deathly mechanical silence. I try to keep a little of the feeling of improvisation and conversation . . . usually I have music on the set. I didn't here because of difficulties in the technical side of the organisation, the size of the picture, the costumes, the difficulties of my own part. I had to be much more severe than I usually am directing a picture. Almost always when I'm on set or on location I have music playing to try to make people think that they are not making movies—in the ordinary sense of the word.

And I don't pay attention, during shooting, to any department which may slow things up, because I have found that three departments—sound, continuity and make-up—take about an hour between them every day. And if you just don't let them talk, you've gained an hour's shooting. At the beginning I tell them: 'You are not going to enjoy this picture because you can't do your job. I'm not going to let you. So, stay, but know you are going to be a second-class citizen. You're just going to do the sound, and nobody will ever ask "Was that all right for you?" '

There was almost no make-up in the picture. I think it's *bad.* I almost never use it except to change the shape of a face or age a character. There's no make-up in ***Citizen Kane,*** except in my character. You take a poll of all the good cameramen in the world and ask them about make-up. I *promise* that you will get 98 per cent saying 'No make-up.' But they don't want to be responsible for hurting the jobs of the make-up men, so they let them go on putting on this stuff.

About your future projects. Are you going to make The Sacred Monsters?

I must wait. After the failure of Rosi's *The Moment of Truth,* the resistance of the world market to anything which has even the suggestion of a *corrida* is very strong. I will do it, but not for a couple of years. And I must find a way to conceal the bullfighting part of it so that the distributors won't be frightened. Mine is not a *corrida* picture, but the fact that people in it are following the bullfights is enough. You know the minds of people who finance pictures.

What about your 'Abraham' episode for The Bible?

'Abraham' is my script. They shot it. I wrote it. They asked me to put my name on the credits but I refused. I was originally going to direct it. They used almost exactly the script I wrote, but the end had to be changed because of the Church. I saw nothing in the story which meant that Isaac should be a willing sacrifice. So when Isaac sees his father with the knife, he runs, and the father has to chase him . . . It's a brutal, terrible scene. But it turns out that because of the theological conception that it's a prevision of the Crucifixion, it has to be a willing sacrifice. My argument to that was that even Jesu in the Garden says 'Take the cup from Me.' So I see a nine-year-old boy saying 'Take the cup from me' in his terms. But I couldn't win that argument with the censors.

You have talked about finishing **The Magnificent Ambersons** *with two more reels, using the same actors as they are today. How is that project?*

I don't know. I must find out about it, but I begin to feel depressed by all the things I have unfinished. But it would be nice to do. I talked to Joseph Cotten about it when I saw him in Rome . . . it may be possible to do . . . just two reels to make an ending which makes sense. It would be nice. Now the film has a silly ending . . . just ridiculous.

Then there is your **Don Quixote.** *Is that made so simply because you were thinking of television, or is this your particular style for that story?*

It must be simple, very simple . . . But everything about that film that was new is now old-fashioned. I have all kinds of stop action, speeded up motion and so on. They are going to say I stole it from the Nouvelle Vague, but I made it before them.

What is curious about *Don Quixote* is the dilemma Cervantes himself found with the character. You create a joke about an old provincial gentleman who goes mad on a certain kind of story and sets out to realise it. All right, that's a funny joke for a picaresque novel; but what makes it great is that whether he succeeds or fails (and he always fails), Quixote is defending the innocent, fighting evil. He may be reviving an idea which was ridiculous even when Cervantes wrote, but he ends up by not being ridiculous. That's what interests me about it. But because the picture is so delicate, it could very easily be very bad.

Just what do I add now? That is the problem. I have a purely picaresque thing, a series of sequences, and I have to make a whole picture out of it. I feel I must exploit the modern world, and then it becomes so banal. I want to present the characters with modern times, so to speak, and yet not to make the cliché of modern times.

I shouldn't sit in Spain and give an opinion about *Quixote,* but I am absolutely convinced that Cervantes conceived it as a short story: one joke and that was all. Then the two characters seized their life and led him, with a vitality that surprised him and continues to surprise us. That's the point of the film: that they have a life I can't stop as a filmmaker either. *They* lead *us.* They are not marionettes, they are curiously independent. The thing I haven't solved in my mind about Quixote—and it worries me, and I work on and on—is that I have him existing in the modern world. I understand all that; but it seems to me that I am perhaps not being true to reality, to the moral reality of the situation, because the modern world must destroy him. And yet I can't imagine him destroyed.

Has all the writing about your films, all the critical appraisal directed at them right from the beginning, ever stopped you making some film out of fear for your career?

Not the writing: no, no. I don't care about the big things they write about me. I don't live like that. What they write about me doesn't affect my life, but I know that my films have some importance for people in various parts of the world, and that what I say on films has some importance for some people, and therefore I must try to be responsible to that position. But not to the critics: I am in no danger of changing my position because somebody writes a serious thing about me. I began seriously, thinking of myself as seriously as any writer has ever taken me. More so, alas! (pp. 158-63)

Orson Welles, Juan Cobos, and Miguel Rubio, in an interview in Sight and Sound, *Vol. 35, No. 4, Autumn, 1966, pp. 158-63.*

Peter Bogdanovich on the first test screening of *The Magnificent Ambersons:*

The first preview was held March 17, at the Fox Theatre in Pomona, California. At this point the film ran a little over two hours, with three of Welles' scenes already cut. It followed *The Fleet's In,* a Dorothy Lamour musical—not exactly an audience in the mood for a movie like ***Ambersons,*** though actually, of the 125 "comment cards" collected, 53 were positive. But the 72 negative ones and the audible bad reaction is what affected the executives attending.

The cards asked, among other things, "Did you like this picture?" Here's a sampling of the answers:

No, the worst picture I ever saw.

I did not. People like to laff, not be bored to death.

Yes. Picture will not be received by the general audience because they as a whole are too darn ingorant [*sic*]. . . .

No. A horrible distorted dream . . .

Yes, I liked it but I feel that it was above the audience. I think it was very depressing and nerve-racking, but still when I think about it in retrospect, I can see its good points.

The picture was a masterpiece with perfect photography, settings and acting. It seemed too deep for the average stupid person. I was disgusted with the way some people received this picture which truly brings art to the picture industry. Each artist is deserving of a great deal of praise.

Exceedingly good picture. Photography rivaled that of superb ***Citizen Kane***. . . . Too bad audience was so unappreciative.

. . . Too many wierd [*sic*] camera shots. It should be shelved as it is a crime to take people's hard-earned money for such *artistic* trash as Mr. Welles would have us think. . . . Mr. Welles had better go back to radio, I hope.

. . . Too many shadows and the scenery was too dark.

No, it's as bad if not worse than ***Citizen Kane.***

I think it was the best picture I have ever seen.

Peter Bogdanovich and Orson Welles, in their This Is Orson Welles, *1992.*

Orson Welles with Peter Bogdanovich (interview date 1969-1972)

[*Bogdanovich is an American filmmaker and critic who was a longtime friend of Welles. He is the director of such films as* The Last Picture Show *(1971),* Paper Moon *(1973), and* Texasville *(1990). In the following excerpt from* This is Orson Welles, *he and Welles discuss* The Magnificent Ambersons *and how the studio executives "butchered" a film Welles felt was better than* Citizen Kane.]

[Welles]: ***Ambersons*** is the only picture of mine I've seen after it was finished and released.

[*Bogdanovich*]*: When?*

One evening, when they had a special showing in Paris, André Gide, who'd invited me to dinner, told me we were going to it, so I was trapped. It was most unpleasant. I would have been happier never to know and just *hear* what had been done to it. For five or six reels things weren't so bad. I thought, "Well, that isn't so bad. They didn't do too many things—only a few stupid little cuts." And then all hell broke loose. . . . It was a much better picture than ***Kane***—if they'd just left it as it was. (pp. 94-5)

How did you come to do the film of **Ambersons***?*

Well, we'd had success with it on radio; I played a recording of the show for George Schaefer [the head of RKO Pictures] and we agreed to it. Tarkington's an extraordinary writer—

He's out of fashion now.

Unjustly. He deserves to be taken much more seriously. If the movie of ***Ambersons*** has any quality, a great part of it is due to Tarkington. What doesn't come from the book is a careful imitation of his style. What was all my own was a third act which took the story into a darker, harder dimension. I can't pay enough tribute to Tarkington. The trouble is that so much of his stuff—particularly on kids—is hopelessly dated now. The kids have changed so much.

You mean the Penrod *stories.*

You just can't imagine kids like that anymore. But the stories themselves are marvelous—wildly funny.

Why isn't Twain dated, then?

Because Twain wasn't writing about children in a middle-class atmosphere. He put them into a kind of invented anarchistic world where middle-class values only exist in parody, and very much on the periphery of things—out in the wilderness, on the river and in caves, and not on Main Street under the shadow of the elms. Also, Twain is a giant, and Tarkington isn't quite that. Twain wrote more trash than Tarkington; it's only his masterpieces that last. You can't read the rest—I can't. But you can read all kinds of Tarkington with great joy. He had a great deal of grace.

That's the thing you admire most, isn't it? That and gallantry. Isn't **Ambersons** *as much a story of the end of chivalry—the end of gallantry—as* **Chimes at Midnight***?*

Peter, what interests me is the *idea* of these dated old virtues. And why they still seem to speak to us when, by all logic, they're so hopelessly irrelevant. (pp. 95-6)

The staircase seems to dominate one's memory of **Ambersons.**

Well, the heart of a pompous house was its pompous staircase. It's all that imitation-palace business. These people haven't got any royal processions to make, but they wouldn't admit it. I had great-aunts who lived in houses exactly like that one. There was one house that had a ballroom on the top floor, just like the Ambersons'.

The top floor?

The third floor, not the attic. And at some stage somebody changed it into an indoor golf course—some second husband, I guess. I remember those terrible little green felt hills built all over the old ballroom.

Tim Holt was awfully good in the film.

Extraordinary . . . One of the most interesting actors that's ever been in American movies, and he *decided* to be just a cowboy actor. Made two or three important pictures in his career, but was very careful not to follow them up—went straight back to bread-and-butter Westerns.

He lives somewhere in Oklahoma now.

Right. He was the most marvelous fellow to work with you can imagine. We ran every picture you can think of before we found him. And then we ran all kinds of six-day movies Tim had made before we were absolutely certain. It was a lucky decision.

He had a small role in Stagecoach.

And he did an awful lot of the stunts in that film, during which he claims Ford did everything possible to kill him. He loved Ford—but like somebody who's been through the wars. I used to pump him about Jack for hours.

This part in **Ambersons** *was the largest part he'd done.* And *Anne Baxter's—that was one of her first roles.*

Yes. She's Frank Lloyd Wright's granddaughter, you know.

Oh?

Yes. The old man used to visit us all the time we were shooting and made withering remarks about the sets. I kept saying, "But, Mr. Wright, we agree with you. That's the whole point." But he couldn't get over how awful it was that people ever lived in those kind of houses. Oh my God, what a marvelous old man. What an artist, and what an *actor!*

How did you come to cast Dolores Costello?

I'd thought of Mary Pickford. I talked to her a lot and she almost did it—and I'm glad she didn't, I don't think she'd have been right. Finally, we thought of Miss Costello. Brought her back from total retirement. You might have thought she'd want to watch what we were up to. In rehearsals, I mean. But she was quite unfocused. Nothing naughty—just not wanting to be an actress.

She was the daughter of the first silent male star Maurice Costello?

Yes—who worked as an extra in ***Kane.*** And she was Jack Barrymore's ex-wife, you know.

Did he make any comments to you about her?

Yes, something about "your *bizarre* ideas of casting"—something like that.

It's a heartbreaking moment when George's mother dies. You tell it by having Aunt Fanny embrace him and say, "She loved you, George," and then fade out immediately.

It's hurt by the fact that they cut out some of the scenes that preceded it.

Some of that's there.

Some of it—but arbitrary. The full version made that sharp finish much more effective.

I read a newspaper interview with Jo Cotten recently in which he said you'd been planning to shoot a new ending to **Ambersons,** *since the old one was destroyed.*

Yes, I had an outside chance to finish it again just a couple of years ago, but I couldn't swing it. The fellow who was going to buy the film for me disappeared from view. The idea was to take the actors who are still alive now—Cotten, Baxter, Moorehead, Holt—and do quite a new end to the movie, twenty years after. Maybe that way we could have got a new release and a large audience to see it for the first time.

You see, the basic intention was to portray a golden world—almost one of memory—and then show what it turns into. Having set up this dream town of the "good old days," the whole point was to show the automobile wrecking it—not only the family but the town. All this is out. What's left is only the first six reels. Then there's a kind of arbitrary bringing down the curtain by a series of clumsy, quick devices. The bad, black world was supposed to be too much for people. My whole third act is lost because of all the hysterical tinkering that went on. And it *was* hysterical. Everybody they could find was cutting it. . . .

When did you record the narration?

The night before I left for South America to begin ***It's All True.*** I went to the projection room at about four in the morning, did the whole thing, and then got on the plane and off to Rio—and the end of civilization as we know it. (pp. 113-15)

Why did you yourself suggest so many cuts from Rio?

I was trying to protect *something.* I was trapped down there. I couldn't leave, and all I kept getting were those terrible signals about this awful movie I'd made. My own chums were running, frightened—not just RKO.

And you are affected by what your friends think and feel. Were you shaken in your confidence?

Shaken. You bet. I remember even Jo Cotten writing me in South America. I had no idea, he said, now that they'd seen the whole picture *with an audience,* how terrifying and frightening that last part really was. So even those people who truly had my interests at heart felt that I'd gone too far. I didn't believe I had. And I still don't. (pp. 120-21)

Well, it seemed to me that a lot of your cuts were somewhat drastic, too.

I was bargaining. "I'll give you that if you'll leave me this." They'd got so spooked because of a bad preview, and there'd been no preview of ***Kane.*** Think what would have happened to ***Kane*** if there had been one! In Pomona on Saturday night—you can imagine what would have happened.

There were some letter-writing scenes that you wrote in South America, which Robert Wise shot. Why did you write them?

To try and cover up some of those wild cuts they were making. I didn't know Robert Wise did the shooting. That was his beginning, wasn't it? That's when he got off the pad. (p. 122)

Didn't you have a contract which said they couldn't recut **Ambersons***? As you did on* **Kane***?*

Once you're finished with something, the owners can do anything they want. You can only protect yourself by contract *during* work. Unlike the Code Napoléon, which protects the rights of the artist [in France], English and American law protects property—but the author of a work has no enforceable rights once the person who paid for it has taken delivery. (p. 124)

Your ballroom sequence must have been rehearsed for a long time.

It was a big job technically. But not as hard as you might think, because the sets were built for it. We didn't go into a set and *then* say, "Let's do these elaborate shots." We knew that this wall was going here and that wall was there—it was all planned before we started.

Probably the silliest cut I know of comes in the middle of a long sustained shot during the ball when two characters make some comment about olives, which were evidently new to America at the turn of the century.

Yes. You didn't get to see the little joke about the olives, because some lamebrain said, "What's olives got to do with it?" One of those things. They cut twenty seconds' playing time and cut into two pieces our crane shot that would have played for a whole reel without a cut. Too bad. I like digressions, don't you? Look at Gogol. Read the first few pages of *Dead Souls* again and you'll see how one mad little digression can give reverberation and density to ordinary narrative.

Perhaps the best things in your pictures are the digressions.

Maybe that's why I've suffered so much from the cutters.

Anyway, the olives cut killed your shot.

Not stone dead, maybe, but it was kind of a shame to have worked that hard: four rooms with everything rolling back—an absolute triumph of technical engineering on everybody's part.

It must have been beautiful to watch it happen.

It was. It really was. . . . (pp. 125-26)

In the novel, they sing "The Star-Spangled Banner" during the outing in the snow—which probably would get roars today. Why did you change it to "The Man Who Broke the Bank at Monte Carlo"?

That's partly to do with my father, who really *did* break the bank at Monte Carlo—or so he always claimed. Anyway, his old chums used to like to sing that song to him, so it was partly for that reason that I used it.

Where did you shoot that snow sequence?

All inside. The "ice house"—a refrigerated soundstage in downtown Los Angeles. Our snow scene in ***Kane*** was all shot on Stage 4 at RKO with cornflakes, and it worried me because you didn't see people's breath.

You obviously saw quite a few silent movies as a child, and I wondered whether the beautiful iris-out which concludes that sequence was in any way an hommage *to the silent film.*

Well . . . , we didn't know about *"hommages"* in those days, thank God. But it does seem a shame that people don't use the iris-out anymore. It's a beautiful invention. There are a lot of silent things that ought to be revived.

One could say that, since the iris-out came from the innocent days of the movies, you used it as an end to the innocent days of the people in the film.

You could say that.

Is it true that the kitchen scene between Holt and Moorehead was improvised?

In a way it was—the rhythm of it all was set. The precise words weren't.

Sounds hard to do.

It takes rehearsal. The actors have to be used to working together, and it gets to be great fun if you do it right.

Was the scene in which George and Lucy go through town in the horse and buggy originally intended to be done with rear projection?

Never.

Where on earth did you do it? It must be the longest dolly shot in the world.

Just the old RKO back lot. We didn't build anything—just everything that was standing, redressed.

It must have been half a reel, at least.

Well, they just ride along.

And the other side of the street is reflected in the windows.

Yes, we *used* the reflections instead of trying to avoid them.

I noticed in the second long street scene with Tim Holt and Anne Baxter that they pass a movie house, and one of the films playing is Jack Holt in Explosion.

An in-joke, I'm afraid—for Tim. His father was coming to visit us for lunch that day.

Actually, it's sort of an anachronism.

Of course—Jack Holt wasn't around *that* early.

Over in the corner is a poster for a Méliès film, which would have been right.

But not for Indiana.

In the scene where the Major sits in front of the fire, Richard Bennett really looked *like he was dying.*

Yes. Dear man, I loved him so. I'd been such a breathless fan of his in the theatre. He had the greatest lyric power of any actor I ever saw on the English-speaking stage.

Really?

There's no *way* of describing the beauty of that man in the theatre.

He was the father of the three Bennett girls [Barbara, Constance, and Joan]?

Yes, and he was great and famous on the stage. By that time, he was incapable of remembering even a single word of dialogue, so I spoke every line and he repeated it after me, and then we cut my voice from the sound track. . . . I'd found him out in Catalina in a little boarding house, which was, I guess, the inspiration for the boarding house at the end of my original version of ***Ambersons.*** He was living there—totally forgotten by the world—this great, great actor. And think what it meant to him at the end of his life to be brought back and to suddenly play an important role! And to have people admire and respect him, as we did—as we all did. . . . Right afterwards, he died. (pp. 126-28)

George's "last walk home" before he gets his "comeuppance"—when we see the broken-down city at the end—were there miniatures in that?

That's downtown L.A. I went and shot it, in what's now standard practice. Then it was just me walking around holding the camera. Nobody took that material very seriously in the cutting room. In those days, for a director to hold a camera was unheard-of.

What's left is very affecting.

They left in a sort of "Coming Attractions"—type montage. . . . Then, too, you know, we had the end of all the other characters—not just Tim Holt. These other people weren't incidental to the story—they were all of equal importance, as in a Chekhov play. You followed Ray Collins right to the finish of him. And Cotten and Moorehead, and—more fully—Richard Bennett. Again, what you have now is a sort of synopsized version.

Is it true that you rehearsed Agnes Moorehead so often in her scene by the boiler that she really did *become hysterical?*

Well, she became more and more *real.* I didn't put her into a state of hysterics; I don't work that way with actors.

She was quite remarkable.

Yes, but, again, it's only half of what it was because people laughed when it was previewed. Some lumpen Saturday-night audience . . . So they ran scared and clipped the scene. The whole distance would have flayed you alive—Aggie was just that good. Why she didn't get an Academy Award for that performance, I'll never know. [Moorehead did, however, win the Best Actress award from the New York Film Critics that year.]

Anybody who knows something about your work can tell you didn't direct the last shot in **Ambersons**—*it's the only one in the film where the actors are in closeup and the background's out of focus. They walk out of frame and then the background comes into focus.*

Well, that's coming back in style. And in those days, they were doing it all the time. We broke away from it. Now it's modish again. . . . Anyway, that scene was shot without my knowledge or consent.

But there are some *scenes of yours in the last two reels.*

Little bits and pieces glued together in a sort of patch-'em-up woman's-magazine sort of style. (pp. 128-30)

Did you have Agnes Moorehead in mind when you were writing the script?

There wasn't any question about it. How could there be? She'd been all those years with us—it was going to be her great part, and indeed it was, particularly in its full version. If only you'd seen how she wrapped up the whole story at the end. . . . Jo Cotten goes to see her after all those years in a cheap boarding house and there's just nothing left between them at all. Everything is over—her feelings and her world and his world; everything is buried under the parking lots and the cars. That's what it was all about—the deterioration of personality, the way people diminish with age, and particularly with impecunious old age. The end of the communication between people, as well as the end of an era. Sure, it was pretty rough going

Welles directing an early scene from The Magnificent Ambersons.

for an audience—particularly in those days. But without question it was much the best scene in the movie.

Wasn't there a Two Black Crows record playing as counterpoint in the background?

Yes, one of those famous comic turns they used to sell in the early days of gramophone records. And there were all these awful old people roosting in this sort of half old folk's home, half boarding house. They're playing cards in the background, and others are listening to that record, with the elevated clanking by. . . . I wish the film at least existed.

I liked very much the narrating of the credits at the end, and particularly your sign-off—"My name is Orson Welles."

I got a lot of hell because of that. People think it's egotistic. The truth is, I was just speaking to a public who knew me from the radio in a way they were used to hearing on our shows. In those days we had an enormous public—in the millions—who heard us every week, so it didn't seem pompous to end a movie in our radio style. (pp. 130-31)

Orson Welles and Peter Bogdanovich, in an interview in their This Is Orson Welles, *edited by Jonathan Rosenbaum, Harper Collins Publishers, 1992, pp. 94-132.*

Joseph McBride (essay date 1977)

[*McBride is an American critic, journalist, screenwriter, and actor who has written extensively on Welles's works. Welles cast him as a film critic in his still unreleased* The Other Side of the Wind. *In the following excerpt from his book* Orson Welles: Actor and Director *(1977), McBride discusses* Chimes at Midnight.]

A few years after the 1966 release of ***Chimes at Midnight*** (called ***Falstaff*** in the United States), Welles received a telegram from his friend Charlton Heston. Heston's message was that he was planning a film about Falstaff, and would Welles play the role? It was the one part, said Heston, that he had always wanted to see Welles play. Welles shook his head in amazement as he told me about the telegram; I could see that he wanted to laugh, but the laughter stuck in his throat. What can a man do after making the greatest film of his life—and hardly anyone goes to see it in his own country?

"A plague on sighing and grief," Falstaff would say. "It blows a man up like a bladder." In their girth, in their merriment, and in the melancholy lying just below the surface, Welles and Falstaff are brothers in the blood. Indeed it *was* a role Welles was meant to play. He tried it first when he was but twelve years old, in a production at the Todd School, and he tried it again when he was twenty-four, in the unsuccessful Mercury stage pageant ***Five Kings.*** When he was ripened and ready, he tackled it again in 1960, on the Belfast stage, as rehearsal for the film. On the screen, man and role became one.

"The more I studied the part, the less funny it appeared to me," Welles told Spanish interviewers after making the film in that country. "This problem preoccupied me during the entire shooting. . . . I don't think very highly of those moments in which I am only amusing. It seems to me that Falstaff is a man of wit rather than a clown. . . . He is the character in whom I believe the most, the most entirely good man in all drama. His faults are trivial and he makes the most enormous jokes from them. His goodness is like bread, like wine. That is why I lost the comic side of his character a little; the more I played him, the more I felt that I represented goodness, purity."

Chimes at Midnight has an autumnal, mournful tone, lamenting the loss of innocence in the mythical Merrie Old England when Falstaff 's former boon companion, Prince Hal (a splendid performance by Keith Baxter), swears off his reveling for the cold practice of power as King Henry V. Welles has compared ***Chimes*** to ***The Magnificent Ambersons,*** for both films are about the destruction of a happier way of life, and both are filmed in a relatively subdued, elegiac style. Sir John Falstaff, the lovable ne'er-do-well, is a seductive figure to the young prince in Hal's wild oats period, but an embarrassment when kingly responsibilities become foremost. The way of life Hal finally opts for is the Machiavellian style of his thin, sickly, corpselike father, Henry IV (John Gielgud, definitive in the role); for Falstaff and all he represents, there is nothing left but rejection and death. The last shot of the film shows Falstaff 's giant coffin being pushed up a hill in slow motion, conveying a palpable feeling of heaviness and irremediable loss.

One of the many things Welles and Falstaff have in common is their theatricality. Falstaff, like Welles, is always *on;* he is a ham, and he loves to put on a show, ordering people around and making himself the center of attention. This "directorial" attribute helps explain why Welles is so much more at ease as Falstaff than he was in his other Shakespearean roles on film—he's better at playing an extroverted manipulator like Falstaff than he is at handling more passive characters like Macbeth or Othello, who are manipulated by others.

The notion of role-playing, of theatricality as a way of dealing with life, is one of the key dramatic (and comic) conceits in Shakespeare's Falstaff plays. Hal has to choose which role he is best suited to play in life, wastrel or king, and Falstaff is the overpowering director who tries to mold Hal's character in his own image. Welles brings out these themes with particular brilliance in his staging of the great tavern scene, in which Falstaff and Hal play multiple roles in an emotionally complex psychodrama.

"Shall we have a play extempore?" Falstaff suggests with a sly wink. Conducted on a stagelike platform with serving wenches as audience, the scene resembles a kind of prankish Mercury Theatre rehearsal session. Falstaff first takes the role of King Henry IV, wearing a pot for a crown and hilariously imitating Gielgud's voice. He chastises Hal for his wanton behavior—ironically, of course—then turns the discussion to an unabashed, out-of-character defense of himself. "Him keep with—the rest banish," Falstaff 's "king" exhorts Hal. When the tables are turned, however, Hal, playing his father, quickly reveals a vicious contempt for Falstaff, calling him "an old, white-bearded Satan" in tones decidedly uncomic. Falstaff is roused to a buoyant speech in self-defense—the speech of a lifetime for Welles, full of bluster and spirit—but when he concludes, "Banish plump Jack, and banish all the world," Hal chillingly warns, "I do, I will." Here, in a flash, the ultimate fate of their relationship is made known. The "lie" of the theatre uncovers a painful truth.

May we be accursed if we forget for one second that Orson Welles alone with Griffith, one in silent days, one sound, managed to start up that marvellous little electric train in which Lumière did not believe. All of us will always owe him everything.

—Jean-Luc Godard, in* Cahiers du Cinéma *December 1963-January 1964.

Undoubtedly the single most moving scene Welles has ever acted or directed on screen is Falstaff 's rejection by Hal at the coronation ceremony. There is an almost shocking vulnerability in Welles's acting when he bursts through the solemn crowd, scandalizing everyone, and calls out, "My king! My Jove! I speak to thee, my heart!" Hal turns to face him in a menacing low angle, his carriage rigid as a statue's, and delivers the bloodcurdling denunciation, "I know thee not, old man. Fall to thy prayers. How ill white hairs become a fool and jester!" The life seems to drain out of Falstaff before us as, eyes filling and jaw quavering in helpless anguish, he watches the king walk out of his life forever. Those who consider Welles an unemotional actor will find their rebuke here. It may have taken him fifty years to achieve such nakedness and candor, but he reached it nonetheless.

Chimes at Midnight was rapturously acclaimed in France, winning Welles a special award at the Cannes Film Festival "for his contribution to world cinema." As Kenneth Tynan reported, "Jeers and whistles greeted many of the other prizes; but for this one, everybody rose—avant-garde critics and commercial producers alike—and clapped with their hands held over their heads. The ovation lasted for minutes. Welles beamed and sweated on the stage of the Festival Palace, looking like a melting iceberg and occasionally tilting forward in something that approximated a bow." This, truly, was his finest hour.

When the film came to America, however, the distributor, Peppercorn-Wormser, seemed to have little confidence in it. The powerful *New York Times* critic Bosley Crowther had panned it in a report from Cannes, and fearing another blast, the distributor opened it cautiously in Ann Arbor before letting the national critics see it. It arrived in New York with, as *Newsweek* put it, "all the advance publicity of a Federal raid on a moonshine still." Judith Crist and Pauline Kael wrote rave notices, but Crowther repeated his complaints, and the film had only minimal distribution after that. Today it pops up frequently and successfully in sophisticated revival houses, but it never had the chance to be seen by a wide public in this country. (pp. 102-06)

Joseph McBride, in his Orson Welles: Actor and Director, *Jove Publications, Inc., 1977, 159 p.*

Richard France (essay date 1977)

[*France is an American dramatist and educator. In the following excerpt from his book* The Theater of Orson Welles, *he discusses Welles's work in radio, focusing on the techniques of—and the reactions to—the famous* War of the Worlds *broadcast.*]

The first thing that impressed [John] Houseman about Orson Welles was his voice. This astounding instrument "startled not so much by its loudness but by its surprising vibration." At one of their early meetings Houseman asked Welles to audition for the leading role in *Panic.* It consisted of Welles's reading the character's suicide speech for author Archibald MacLeish. Both men were thus able to hear "that voice for the first time in its full and astonishing range."

What Houseman is describing is a stage voice. Another, more acute, observation of Welles reveals the quality that made him so unique and defines the nature of his appeal as an actor. Houseman was not as impressed with the force and brilliance of Welles's voice as he was with its charm and courtesy. To this day when one hears Welles on the television narrating a special about the great white whale or the African baobob tree, one is struck by the magnitude that his voice gives to its subject. At the end of each performance Welles will say, as he always has, simply, "This is Orson Welles." These same four words were at the heart of his success on radio. After all the oratory, Welles leaves the impression of intimacy. The magnitude of his subject is finally a personal message to the individual listener.

This intimate quality is also central to radio as an artistic form, a form that Welles at one time (notably ***The War of the Worlds*** broadcast) was able to exploit to its fullest potential. He manipulated the devices of radio to make an artistic statement in much the same way that he used the devices of the theatre. ***Citizen Kane*** was, in fact, a summa of the devices of both radio and the theatre. All media make an appeal to the senses. Welles discovered the basic formal qualities to maximize this appeal. The rhetorical content of Welles's radio programs, of his theatrical productions, and of his movies is special because it is so inextricably bound to the most heightened appeal to perceptions and sensations that each of these media can make.

Even before his first meeting with Houseman in the winter of 1934, Welles began his radio career on "The March of Time" series. The Dionne quintuplets had recently been born, and Welles was asked by the producer if he could imitate five different baby cries. (He and his wife, Virginia, marked the occasion by begging an advance from the show to splurge on a victory meal at "21"; however, they both looked so shabby that they were turned away.) Thereafter, Welles began to make weekly appearances on "The March of Time," playing such diverse characters as FDR, Haile Selassie, Hindenburg, Horace Greeley, Paul Muni, Victor Emmanuel, Hirohito, Charles Laughton, and Sir Basil Zaharoff. Within a year of his debut Welles could claim membership in that elite band of radio actors who commanded salaries second only to the highest paid movie stars.

Welles's considerable earnings as a radio actor, peaking somewhere between fifteen hundred and two thousand dollars a week, are evidence enough of his great demand with the networks. He fulfilled his many commitments by "bicycling" from one studio to another, often arriving with barely the time for a last minute run-through before going on the air. While directing the "Voodoo" ***Macbeth,*** Welles commuted back and forth between Harlem and midtown as many as three times each day to accommodate his various radio assignments.

It was Welles's voice that assured his success as a radio performer. The extent to which his creative intellect figured into his early career in radio is hard to determine. From 1935 to 1937, he appeared mostly in shows over which he exercised little if any artistic control. (The possible exceptions to this would be the four-part adaptation of *Les Miserables* that he arranged, directed, and starred in for Mutual in the summer of 1936, plus his *Hamlet* and *Macbeth,* each in two parts, for the Columbia Workshop in the fall and winter of that year.)

Despite Houseman's contention that Welles singlehandedly raised the whole level of radio acting, the decisive factor in his being awarded his own weekly program could hardly have been his considerable gifts as a performer. In fact, "the phenomenal offer" was timed to the success of the Mercury Theatre's first season. Welles could have the hour 9-10 P.M. EDST on Mondays for ten weeks beginning July 11, 1938. CBS agreed to sustain the show, which was also to be carried by the Canadian Broadcasting Corporation. The title given to it by the network was "First Person Singular," and the show called for Welles to write, direct, and appear in each episode and, as himself, introduce and narrate them.

The *New York Times* greeted the news of "First Person Singular" with the hope that Welles would bring to radio "the experimental techniques that have proved so successful in another medium." Touted as a prestige show of general appeal, the format to "First Person Singular" capitalized on the psychological study of radio that Hadley Cantril and Gordon W. Allport had written and published three years before. Cantril showed how demagogues like Huey Long and Father Coughlin had so effectively mobilized the unique qualities of this new medium. The wild oratory of the tent-show evangelist did not translate to radio, Cantril noted. Spellbinders like Coughlin and Long, realizing this, spoke quite differently. There was less bombast and more artistry to their presentations, less brute force and more cunning. Everything was directed toward the "invisible audience," toward making each listener feel welcomed to the charmed circle. A sense of involvement in these presentations was aroused.

> Friends, this is Huey Long speaking. I have some important revelations to make, but before I make them I want you to go to the phone and call up five of your friends and tell them to listen in.

Each listener is thus made a fellow conspirator, and their friendly attention for the duration of the show guaranteed. Long worked hard at doing away with formality and awe and elevating his listeners to a position of equality with even the highest officials. The way they presented themselves, their very manner and organization, was enough to assure Coughlin and Long that their audiences would likely believe them and think their simplistic and often dangerous solutions to the national ills perfectly valid. Cantril's findings showed that "a sound argument is always less important for the demagogue than are weighted words."

That is not to suggest that Welles and CBS were aware of the Cantril study; however, in an interview with Richard O'Brien of the *Times* he also spoke of the "invisible audience." Whatever his source, Welles had certainly become aware of the first principle of his medium. "Intimacy," he told O'Brien, "is one of radio's richest possessions." He then proceeded to exploit the peculiar qualities of the medium for his own purposes as fully as Coughlin and Long had for theirs. "First Person Singular" made the drama as spellbinding as Coughlin and Long's political rhetoric—using pretty much the same devices, too. The most successful of Welles's broadcasts was, of course, ***The War of the Worlds,*** which proved that the manipulation of radio techniques (in this case, the weighted words of a news event) could lend a compelling logic even to something as farfetched as an invasion from outer space.

Welles seldom paid the kind of attention to his radio program that he brought to the theatre. Thus, it is difficult to appraise—except for ***The War of the Worlds***—just how he managed to animate the formal qualities of the medium to vitalize the rhetorical content of his productions. (Houseman credits him with inventing all sorts of "ingenious and dramatic devices." A full and comparative study of Welles's radio work, while invaluable, is really outside the scope of this discussion.) It is only because of the widespread attention that the Martian broadcast received that one is able to definitively link it to Welles's characteristic work habits.

Houseman and Welles were already an established partnership at the time of the CBS offer; therefore, it was only natural that Houseman began work on the script to their first show while Welles devoted his attention to other matters. As the "creative" member of this partnership, Welles was to supervise Houseman's efforts and direct the production. The decision was made to lead off the series with *Treasure Island,* but less than a week before going on the air Welles hit upon *Dracula.* Houseman left off the earlier project and began the cutting and pasting for ***Dracula.*** The sole surviving report of this broadcast is Houseman's reference to its innovative use of music as a radio signature (Tchaikovsky's Piano Concerto in B-Flat minor) for this and all ensuing productions.

The tenth and final program under the network's original offer was ***Julius Caesar;*** however, by that time CBS had agreed to sustain it an additional thirteen weeks, and "First Person Singular" was renamed "The Mercury Theatre on the Air." Acknowledging its growing reputation as radio's foremost dramatic series, CBS moved the show from Monday to prime time (8-9 P.M.) on Sunday nights. The first presentation in this new time slot was to have been a life of Vincent Van Gogh, but this was dropped in favor of ***Jane Eyre.*** The ***Caesar*** and ***Dracula*** scripts are the only ones that Welles is known to have had any hand at all in writing. Otherwise, the first thirteen programs were entirely the work of John Houseman. Welles would discuss the tone and mood of the production with him, and Houseman would go off and write the script. The early rehearsals were directed by Welles's assistant on the show, Paul Stewart, with Welles himself attending to such things as timing and sound effects. The nucleus of these radio casts were drawn, in the main, from such Mercury Theatre regulars as Ray Collins, Eustace Wyatt, Joseph Cotton, Agnes Morehead, George Coulouris, Arthur Anderson, and "Anna Stafford," the stage name that Welles had chosen for his wife, Virginia, during their WPA days. Still, from the top of these broadcasts until Welles signed off with "Obediently yours, Orson Welles," the results, according to Houseman, were as much improvised as planned.

For their fourteenth program, ***Hell on Ice,*** Houseman and Welles engaged a writer from outside their immediate circle, Howard Koch, who had come to their attention via the Federal Theatre grapevine. Koch's play *The Lonely Man* had enjoyed a considerable success at the Blackstone Theatre in Chicago, thanks largely, he admits, to the performance of John Houston in the role of Abraham Lincoln. The play attracted the attentions of Houseman and Welles. Discussions were underway for bringing *The Lonely Man* to the Mercury Theatre when Robert Sherwood's *Abe Lincoln in Illinois* was announced by the Playwright's Company. The Koch play was dropped, but when the awesome burden of keeping up this weekly writing chore became too much for Houseman, he was again in touch with Koch. Since CBS itself was underwriting these broadcasts, all Houseman could offer in the way of a salary was seventy-five dollars per week; however, the rights to any property that Koch developed remained with him. (In the case of ***The War of the Worlds*** this has meant for Koch an equal share in the sale of some five hundred thousand record albums over the years.) One thing more: since the radio program, like his work in the theatre, was being promoted as an all-Welles effort, Koch could expect to receive no immediate publicity. Koch agreed to these conditions, and for the next five months—from ***Hell on Ice*** on October 9, 1938, to ***The Glass Key*** on March 10, 1939—he was the writer of record for "The Mercury Theatre on the Air." (Koch quit the show to accept an offer from Hollywood. His successor was Howard Teichmann, who took up the weekly writing chore for the next two years.)

Koch followed ***Hell on Ice*** with ***Seventeen, Around the World in 80 Days,*** and then ***The War of the Worlds.*** It came with a message from Welles that ***War of the Worlds*** was to be a Halloween prank and that he wanted Koch to write it in the style of a news bulletin. For all the disclaimers, including several announcements that clearly identify it as a performance, the format for ***War of the Worlds*** was identical to a special events broadcast. It was, in effect, much like shouting fire in a crowded theatre; the audience would hardly mount a careful investigation before fleeing the premises. The more careful listener to ***War of the Worlds*** must surely have realized that the very sequence of events made it logically impossible; however, the fact still remains that thousands of people truly believed that the end of the world was at hand. This was the result of Welles's manipulation of an already established and persuasive formula.

The *Daily Worker* (November 3, 1938) attributed listener reaction to the liklihood that "Americans, in their imagination, substituted Hitler for the Martians." Whether or not this is the case, radio audiences had certainly become conditioned to having their favorite shows suddenly interrupted with news of some catastrophe or other. ***The War of the Worlds*** broadcast began innocently enough with the usual announcer's introductions. Nothing was said that might have alerted people to the Halloween prank that was to follow. Welles's opening remarks were on the order of a long, rambling history of how this world has long been under scrutiny by creatures who "are to our minds as ours are to the beasts in the jungle," creatures with designs against us. This was typical science-fiction pap and could hardly have made any special mark on its audience.

Welles's remarks were followed by an announcer who further delayed the dramatic excitement by delivering a weather forecast. At this point, however, an important, if almost imperceptible change was made. The weather forecast established the present tense. Simply but brilliantly, Welles had moved the broadcast from one of casual retrospect to the immediacy of current events. He then cut to a program of dance music by Ramon Raquello and his orchestra. This final deception in fact introduced Welles's central narrative line.

His theatrical productions were geared toward capturing audience attention from the start. He confronted them with violently expressive images even as they were taking their seats. The process in ***The War of the Worlds*** was much subtler. Its first few minutes were deliberately innocuous, even boring. Welles did not want to draw in his audience until exactly the right moment—a sudden break in the music to announce the sighting of several unaccountable eruptions on Mars. The news was kept very low-key: an atmospheric disturbance on a dead planet some forty million miles away. No danger in that. The second interruption served to play down even the suspicion that there might be living intelligence on Mars. When taken together, however, these two news bulletins, breaking in as they did on a previously scheduled broadcast (i.e., Ramon Raquello and his orchestra), left the impression of being unplanned and played on the same fears and growing concerns that radio audiences had come to attach to the real thing.

Welles, as if anticipating this sort of response, hones in on the Martian invasion through a series of fast-breaking news flashes. The first reports come from a Professor Pierson (played by Welles) of the observatory at Princeton, New Jersey. The landing is finally located in Grovers Mill, a few miles away and within easy striking distance of New York City. At this point Welles restated his dance-hall theme, just in case the audience had forgotten the show's carefully established framework. As yet the various "news" reports have all been within the realm of possibility. Not until some twenty minutes into the program, with the mobilization of the New Jersey State Militia, does Welles begin to escalate the sequence of events beyond a realistic time frame. Local residents, scientists, military men, even the secretary of the interior (sounding suspiciously like FDR), are interviewed continuously; and however fantastic their observations may be, Welles presents them to his audience as actual fact.

After the address by the secretary, the announcer returned to continue the report of ever-increasing disaster. The turn of the screw: the Martians were now attempting to paralyze communications and disorganize human society. Their war machines, rising as they did on hundred-foot metal tripods, were reported to be wading across the Hudson River to invade New York and—given the stated purpose of the show (i.e., a prank)—presumably, CBS itself. At the same time, mankind was depicted as being in a state of complete panic, scattering before the Martians' death rays and poisonous smoke. Neither our bombers nor our heaviest artillery could stem their advance. The carnage ended with a lone, anonymous radio operator calling, "Isn't there anyone on the air?"

The "middle break" occurred some forty-three mintues into the broadcast, during which it was again announced that the program was a dramatization and nothing more. The concluding few minutes of ***The War of the Worlds*** dropped the "news" format altogether. Professor Pierson (Welles) speaks aloud a bit of innocuous philosophizing and has an encounter with another survivor. Whereupon Pierson takes after the Martians on foot. Through the Holland Tunnel and up the Avenue of the Americas he walks until finally he locates one of their machines seemingly abandoned in Central Park. The Martians themselves lie dead on the grass, victims of our disease bacteria. They were, as Pierson notes, "slain, after all man's defenses had failed, by the humblest thing that God in His wisdom had put upon this earth."

In his book about the effects of the Martian broadcast upon its audience, Hadley Cantril wonders how anyone with a critical ear could have failed to notice that the show's sequence of disasters simply were impossible within the time elapsed since going on the air. Obviously, the average response to ***War of the Worlds*** was not intellectual; however, aside from the sort of internal evidence that Cantril points up, there was really no way of telling that the events themselves were a hoax. Welles's most outstanding formal device in this broadcast was the "realism" implicit in news bulletins and eye-witness reports; it provided him with the ideal expressive framework for his patently "unreal" content. It also could have validated even more outrageous content had Welles been of a mind to carry his prank any further.

Taking as a given that people thought it to be a news report at all, Cantril distinguished four types of listeners to the Martian broadcast.

> 1. Those who analyzed the internal evidence of the program and concluded that it could not be true.
>
> 2. Those who checked up successfully and learned that it was a play.
>
> 3. Those who checked up unsuccessfully and continued to believe that it was a news broadcast.
>
> 4. Those who made no attempt at all to check on the authenticity of the broadcast.

It was the last two groups of people who panicked. Local police, newspapers, and radio stations across the country were deluged with phone calls of additional "sightings" or from people who were desperate to be evacuated to a "safe" zone. The *New York Daily News* reported over eleven hundred such calls within hours of the broadcast—more than they received at the time of the Hindenburg catastrophe. Over twenty families from a single block in Newark, New Jersey, fled their homes with wet towels over their faces to protect themselves against the poisonous gas of the Martian war machines. In Indianapolis, a woman ran screaming into a church: "New York has been destroyed; it's the end of the world." Services were dismissed. A Pittsburgh man returned home in the midst of the broadcast to find his wife, a bottle of poison in her hand, ranting, "I'd rather die this way than like that!" The call went out in San Francisco for able-bodied men to form a civil patrol to keep the Martians from crossing the Rockies. And Welles himself tells this story about actor John Barrymore, who, he says, was also taken in by the broadcast. Barrymore is said to have put down his drink, hastened out to his private kennels, and thrown open the gates for his dogs. "Fend for yourselves!", he declared and set them free.

There were countless other reports, many of them undoubtedly apocryphal; however, the reaction to the Martian broadcast was sufficiently deep and widespread to form the basis of Cantril's study on the role played by radio in the lives of different groups of listeners in the United States.

The War of the Worlds also gave rise to talk of censorship. The Federal Communications Commission ordered an immediate review of the broadcast. Senator Clyde L. Herring of Iowa announced that he planned to introduce a bill in the next session of Congress that would create a censorship board to which all radio programs must be submitted. But the end result, so far as Welles was concerned, was to provide his "Mercury Theatre on the Air" with enough notoriety to warrant the attentions of a sponsor—Campbell's Soup.

Normally, Welles's involvement in these broadcasts was totally last minute. In effect, he did the final polish. Koch insists that while "his work may have been brief, it was very important. He could do wonders in a few minutes." These were wonders of timing. But ***The War of the Worlds*** was an exception. From the first Welles knew that it could be a big show, and he devoted an unusual amount of attention to it. He conducted all the rehearsals himself and was meticulous in his supervision of every sound effect and musical interlude. Koch's script for the Martian broadcast was the perfect vehicle for Welles's particular aesthetic sensibilities, and with it he brought radio to a level of high dramatic intensity that is still without equal. (pp. 171-79)

Richard France, in his The Theatre of Orson Welles, *Bucknell University Press, 1977, 212 p.*

Welles, as he concluded his "War of the Worlds" broadcast:

This is Orson Welles, ladies and gentlemen, out of character to assure you that the "War of the Worlds" has no further significance than as the holiday offering it was intended to be. The Mercury Theater's own radio version of dressing up in a sheet and jumping out of a bush and saying Boo! Starting now, we couldn't soap all your windows and steal all your garden gates by tomorrow night . . . so we did the next best thing. We annihilated the world before your very ears and utterly destroyed the Columbia Broadcasting System. You will be relieved, I hope, to learn that we didn't mean it, and that both institutions are still open for business. So good-by, everybody, and remember, please, for the next day or so, the terrible lesson you learned tonight. That grinning, glowing, globular invader of your living-room is an inhabitant of the pumpkin patch, and if your doorbell rings and nobody's there, that was no Martian . . . it's Hallowe'en.

Orson Welles, in his War of the Worlds *broadcast, reprinted in* Film Culture, *No. 27, Winter 1962.*

James Naremore (essay date 1978)

[*Naremore is an American educator and critic whose book* The Magic World of Orson Welles *is recognized as one of the best studies ever written on the filmmaker. In the following excerpt from that study, Naremore discusses Welles's political beliefs and involvements in the 1930s and 40s, and analyzes the parodic style of his 1948 film* The Lady from Shanghai.]

The Mercury Theatre had grown logically out of the New Deal, and . . . all its undertakings were attempts to keep the performing arts reasonably responsive to Popular Front idealism. But whereas the Mercury had tried to remain independent of wealthy communications interests and the studio system, it was in fact tied to these things—at the mercy of reviews, sponsors, box office receipts, and Hollywood producers. Partly as a result of this dependence, it ultimately dissolved, and for Welles and his associates things were never the same again. Even as ***Kane*** was being filmed, history seemed to be working against such organizations. Here is John Houseman commenting on the period:

> Beginning with *Panic,* through my two years on the Federal Theatre and during the rise and fall of Mercury, I had become accustomed to relating my theatrical activity to the historical movements of the time. On WPA this participation had been immediate and inescapable. . . . Some of this sense of involvement was carried over into the Mercury, where it directly affected our choice of subjects and our methods of operation. Then, gradually, as the Depression receded and international events replaced domestic crises on the front pages of our newspapers, this participation became less satisfying. Germany's persecution of the Jews, the Moscow trials, the Spanish Civil War, the successive threats against Austria and Czechoslovakia culminating in the enervating suspense of Munich—these formed a mounting tide of tension to which no positive creative response was possible and to which our theatrical activity could no longer be related.

Houseman became disillusioned early, but after the fall Welles himself continued to act as a show business maverick and a social activist, even though he was now a loner rather than the dynamic center of a group activity. In the middle and late forties he directed a couple of fairly topical thrillers (***The Stranger*** and ***The Lady from Shanghai,*** the latter obtained partly because of his marriage to Rita Hayworth), and managed to produce a low-budgeted film of ***Macbeth.*** He also remained busy as an actor and radio performer. In between ***Kane*** and ***Ambersons,*** he rejoined Houseman for a celebrated stage production of ***Native Son,*** and a few years later, together with his old associate Richard Wilson, he made an abortive, badly calculated attempt to resuscitate the Mercury Theatre in New York. . . . During this time, his political activity was as lively as ever. He campaigned vigorously for FDR's fourth term, lecturing widely and appearing on platforms with Henry Wallace. In 1944, he actually stood in for Roosevelt in a debate with Thomas Dewey at the Hotel Astor. Even more interestingly, he briefly became an editorial columnist for the *New York Post*—a job which paid him fairly little, but which gave him a platform and allowed him to speak like a man with political ambitions of his own. His daily columns began immediately after FDR's inauguration, on January 22, 1945 (the birthdate, Welles observed, of Byron and D. W. Griffith), and continued until June of the same year, just before the atomic bombs ended the war. These columns are a rich source of his opinions about literature, art, and the movies, and are especially valuable as a record of his preoccupation with world affairs—a preoccupation which bears upon some of the films he would make.

"I'm convinced everybody should be interested in politics," Welles declared at the outset. "The disaster of America in the 1920s was that everybody left the practice of politics to the politicians." Even so, he approached the topic somewhat cautiously. The columns began under the title "Orson Welles's Almanac," borrowing their name and format from Welles's radio show of that season, and were at first characterized by a cheerful, homey tone. Random, chatty observations on the day's news were interspersed with playful astrological forecasts ("We are glad to report that planetary aspects today favor thoughts which can be turned into money"), household hints ("Cut stringbeans with scissors"), and notes on the books Welles had been reading. The columns also contained items about celebrities: Welles attacked Westbrook Pegler, "whom Mr. Hearst pays to seek for the truth or something," and defended Frank Sinatra against Pegler's innuendoes; he wrote an open letter to Jack Benny, who had been unable to take Eddie Anderson along on troop shows because of segregation in the army; and he spoke disparagingly of Noel Coward, whom he accused of perpetuating an anachronistic, British public school snobbery. Within a few months, however, Welles had become less discursive, more like a straightforward editorialist. His style remained fairly witty and ironic, but there was an urgency in his voice. On April 13, FDR died, and the title of the columns changed immediately to "Orson Welles Today," in keeping with a growing seriousness of purpose.

After Roosevelt's death, Welles announced to his readers that the president had written him a personal note only a few weeks before, saying that "April will be a critical month in the history of human freedom." Indeed signs of the Cold War were appearing everywhere. The battle against Germany and Japan, which Welles portrayed as the common man's struggle against fascism, was in danger of betraying its ostensible ideals; VE Day left Welles uneasy because he felt that the spirit of Hitler was only dormant, surviving through the old device of the Red scare. (Aspects of this theme were of course explored in ***The Stranger,*** the film Welles was making at the time, where he plays a Nazi criminal hiding in a New England town. Only when the criminal is discovered and killed does a real VE Day come to Harpur, Connecticut.) "We've been on the move for quite a time now," he wrote, "along a road that's taken us from North Africa . . . to Yalta. The next objective is San Francisco [and the U.N. conference]—and we'd better continue along the same road without a stop. Otherwise we'll find out to our everlasting sorrow that we didn't take the ride at all. We were taken for it."

Welles's columns provided documentary evidence, if any were needed, of his essential liberalism and his intense concern with political affairs. His chief themes were the need to perpetuate New Deal social legislation, and the necessity of translating the Allied victory over Germany into a world democracy. He argued for a fair working relationship between labor and capital, but believed government price regulations should continue after the war; he inveighed against a "certain sort of businessman" who "openly favors a certain percentage of postwar unemployment," saying that such types "don't want any percentage of government control over their affairs. They want to be free as buccaneers, free to encourage a little convenient joblessness." He supported the basic structure of American government and encouraged the two-party system, but at the time he hoped aloud that Henry Wallace would be the next president. When Truman entered the White House, Welles was cautious: "We must reconcile ourselves that the new President will, at least temporarily, do no more than consolidate the social gains of the past twelve years. . . . Harry Truman prides himself in knowing what the little fellow's thinking about. . . . Okay. But if the little fellows of America want to press forward for a better world in the century of the common man, they'll have to let our new Chief Executive know about it again, again, and again."

Though Welles repeatedly commented on domestic affairs, his chief concern from the first column to the last was American foreign policy. The San Francisco assembly was his major preoccupation, and he also attended the Pan American War and Peace conference in Mexico City, writing for several days about the meeting. (It is an interesting coincidence that in the next year ***The Lady from Shanghai*** would be filmed partly on location in San Francisco and Mexico.) At the Latin American conference, which was sponsored by Welles's old patron Nelson Rockefeller and which has been described by historians as one of the first symptoms of Cold War politics, speakers rose again and again to utter revolutionary slogans and discuss economic reform; nevertheless Welles noted a reluctance to get down to "brass tacks." He remarked on the dark history of pseudo-revolutions in these countries ("Very few of them succeeded without the help of a couple of North American companies you could name"), and was struck by the blatant ironies of the conference itself, where the U.S. "State Department millionaires" made official deals with so-called revolutionary heads of state, many of whom were also millionaires. Most of all he was troubled by divided feelings about the true progressives; he wanted the South Americans to join the war against the European fascists, but he knew that U.S. economic colonialism had made the Latin left as naturally suspicious of the States as the Irish were suspicious of England.

The difficulties Welles found at Mexico City were symptomatic of conflicts he saw everywhere, especially inside the United States. Always there had been a disparity between American ideals expressed abroad and the actual treatment of minorities at home, but toward the end of the war this disparity was becoming especially acute:

> Internationalism [Welles wrote] can't be preached in a new government level and practiced on the old states' rights basis. The inconsistencies are just too glaring. . . . Thus, an Atlantic Charter is perused by foreigners with one eye on a lynching in Arkansas. A Crimea communique is studied in reference to a Detroit race riot. A declaration at Mexico City stirs memories of a place called Sleepy Lagoon. . . . That's the connection between the hand of American friendship extended to Haile Selassie, to Farouk of Egypt, to the leader of Saudi Arabia—and the noose around a Negro's neck in Alabama.

Such inconsistencies were enough to belie the country's claim to "moral leadership" at international meetings:

> No moral position taken by us against Col. Perón has any meaning for Spanish-speaking America until we break with Gen. Franco. . . . Our attitude towards the policy of the good neighbor matches the rest of our foreign policy. But it doesn't match at all the high principles by which we would justify our leadership in the Americas. We have armed dictators, strengthened unnecessarily the political hand of high churchmen, and everywhere underrated the Democratic aspirations of the people.

The new, more liberalized economic arrangements being made for the world were also being threatened by official hypocrisies. Welles was especially concerned about the fate of the Bretton Woods proposals, which would slash interest rates and allow all countries to borrow from a world bank "without secret, war-breeding deals." The Bretton Woods idea was aimed at preventing the rise of speculators like the "match king" Krueger, who had grown rich after the first world war, but it was being opposed in this country by Senator Taft and the Republican right wing—or, as Welles put it, by "that little Wall St. camarilla who once did so very well by floating foreign loans at fat fees." Taft had wanted to substitute another plan, whereby the U.S. and Great Britain would reach an agreement on the dollar and the pound, extending credits to other countries. What they offered, Welles remarked, was "the old 'key' notion and currency gag—and behind this gaudily altruistic facade one notices that something is missing. Something called the Soviet Union." Even the British, Welles noted, were to become "junior partners in the firm, playing an emphatically minor role, and one bound to get smaller through the years." Welles shuddered at what might result:

> We are the world's greatest production plant and the largest creditor nation. Without sensible economic agreements between England and the U.S., Mr. Luce's prediction of the American century will come true, and God help us all. We'll make Germany's bid for world supremacy look like amateur night, and the inevitable retribution will be on a comparable scale.

The mounting anger one senses in Welles's comments about reactionary politics is reflected also in his remarks on current literature and the arts. For example, he wrote at length in praise of Mexico's three famous muralists, Rivera, Orozco, and Siqueiros, but of the three he much preferred Siqueiros because of his manifestly committed, revolutionary subject matter: "It would be easy to denounce Siqueiros as a blind slave, but he is doing the most adventurous and independent work in the world of art. As for his unshackled comrades, Rivera is decorating night clubs, and Orozco is depicting democracy as raddled and bedizened." Somewhat later, in a brief note on John Hersey's *A Bell for Adano* (about to be filmed by 20th Century-Fox), Welles wrote that the popularity of the book was disturbing because of the way it ministered to America's complacent moral superiority: "For those who thought Mussolini was only funny, and who never heard of Mazzini or Garibaldi, for those who like to think that America has a monopoly on the democratic faith, *A Bell for Adano,* I'm afraid, will be most reassuring." On the other hand,

Richard Wright's *Black Boy* needed more readers. White citizens who claimed to "understand the Negro" should be "tied down with banjo strings, gagged with bandannas, their eyes propped open with watermelon seeds, and made to read *Black Boy* word for word." (Coincidentally, about a year later Welles became involved in a controversy with these same white citizens. On his New York radio show in late July 1946, he charged that black army veteran Isaac Woodward had been taken from a Greyhound bus in Aiken, South Carolina, beaten by police, and blinded. The mayor of Aiken and the local Lions Club denied any knowledge of the incident and threatened to sue, but the issue was never joined.)

By June 1945, Welles was writing from San Francisco, where it was becoming increasingly apparent that the U.N. Would become a battleground of Cold War animosities. The American government was already extending official courtesies to known fascists like Nicholas Horthy of Hungary, and the conference itself was rife with backstage politics. Welles could sense a growing propaganda effort against the Russians:

> We are still building our Bulwarks against Bolshevism. The phony fear of Communism is smoke-screening the real menace of renascent Fascism. The red bogey haunts the hotel lobbies and the committee rooms. Near the cigar stand at the Fairmont, Senator Vandenburg growls sarcastically about the 'benediction of Yalta.' . . . Averell Harriman has been talking up the Polish problem to selected groups of reporters in off-the-record cocktail parties. . . . The [anti-Stalin] gossip mill works full time . . . and Rep. Clare Luce declares war on the Soviet Union by radio.

There is a fatalistic note to these lines, which appeared very close to the end of Welles's tenure as a columnist. He had begun his first column by writing about FDR's inaugural and expressing hope for the U.N., but within six months Roosevelt was dead, liberalism was on the wane, and the new international organization seemed doomed by internecine conflict.

The frenzy and unorthodox form of Welles's work from the mid 1940s to the mid 1950s may be seen as partly a response to the growth of reactionary politics in the country, and can be related not only to Welles's working conditions but to his growing dissatisfaction with American life.

—James Naremore

If I have dealt at length with such matters, it is because Welles's tendency to become involved in controversy, together with his repeated criticism of public life in 1945, has an interesting relationship to his subsequent films. I do not mean that his movies became mere vehicles for ideas, although it is true that his thrillers are filled with topical political references and moral arguments. I mean rather that the mood and style of his later projects were indirectly affected by his alienation from the movie colony and society at large; that the frenzy and unorthodox form of his work for the next ten years may be seen as partly a response to the growth of reactionary politics in the country, and can be related not only to Welles's working conditions but to his growing dissatisfaction with American life.

The continuity between Welles's politics and his situation in Hollywood is fairly easy to detect if one simply considers the few remarks about movies in his columns. "I love movies," he says at one point. "But don't get me wrong. I hate Hollywood." Clearly it had become impossible for him to continue working as an independent, and his sense of dislocation from the industry had coincided with a rise of conservatism in the nation. Welles pointed out that the same money-men who were undermining a liberal foreign policy and arguing for an "acceptable" rate of unemployment were also consolidating their hold on the entertainment business; very soon, he suggested, they would control television communications: "Receiving sets in New York are so adjusted that you can get only ten television broadcasting studios instead of being able to dial anything you want. . . . It's a neat trick, but it shouldn't fool anybody." As for the movies, they had long been dominated by a handful of big operators, in roughly the same way as legitimate theatre had been dominated in the years before the Depression. "I think Jack Warner makes the best movies in town," Welles declared. "But the views of Jack and Harry Warner towards distribution are a good deal less liberal than those expressed in their product. . . . Jack claims that one of his theatres will play one of my pictures as quickly and cheerfully as it will give the time to one of his. I say that's spinach, and I say to hell with it anyway."

Welles had comparatively few observations about the industry product, but on the few occasions when he did turn to specific films, he heaped scorn on Hollywood's establishment. Several times he voiced support for "little" films, and twice used space in the column to recommend William Castle's *When Strangers Marry.* (Within a year Castle himself became Welles's associate producer on ***The Lady from Shanghai.***) Welles liked the film because it had the gritty, unpretentious virtues of an intelligent "B" production, making it a perfect foil to the middlebrow sanctimoniousness of Hollywood's award-winning movies:

> Did you ever hear of a "B" picture getting one of the prizes or even a nomination? *The Informer* doesn't count as a "B" in spite of its low budget because its director was famous and successful and well-paid. A real "B" is produced for half the money and is twice as hard to make worthy of attention. . . .
>
> Gold statuettes for score and photography aren't enough. The movie industry is the only big business I know of which spends no money on real research. A valid Academy of Motion Picture Arts and Sciences would be a laboratory for experiment, a studio—by which I do not mean a

> factory building for the manufacture of a product—but a place removed from the commercial standard and reserved for study, for honest creative effort.

Of course Welles's notion of an Academy "removed from the commercial standard" was somewhat naïve, because unless one contemplated revolution, such an Academy would always be influenced at long distance by commerce. Just as the Mercury could not long remain an independent theatre, free of both government dictates and the pressures of a "free" market, so a research unit funded by Hollywood would inevitably face compromises; nevertheless Welles continued to imagine an ideal setting for the performing arts, a place uninhibited by capitalists or commissars.

Welles's suspicion of these twin evils is apparent in his discussion of Eisenstein's *Ivan the Terrible* (part one), which he and Rita Hayworth had seen in May 1945 at the United Nations theatre in San Francisco. He devoted two entire columns to the film, developing a fascinating comparison between it and 20th Century-Fox's *Woodrow Wilson,* which had also recently opened in San Francisco. Here were two major productions by the two postwar Leviathans; both claimed to be portraits of historical figures and both had specific political implications. "The man in the Kremlin," Welles wrote, "is remembered for a certain ruthlessness of action and the man in the White House for a certain chilliness of personality. Eisenstein and Zanuck try to show how their heroes got that way, surrounding them respectively with scheming politicians and scheming courtiers. The Boyars, it seems, did it to the Tsar, and the Republican Senators did it to the President." There were of course certain important differences between the two subjects. Because Eisenstein was dealing with a remote historical period, his unorthodox historical interpretations were easier to accept, whereas Zanuck had problems with even the most discreet adjustments of the facts. In both cases, however, Welles felt the heroes were sentimentalized: "Maybe Ivan and Wilson were good family men, but the scenes to this effect are curiously lacking in significance." Zanuck had attempted to make Wilson a hail-fellow, "but when his impersonator harmonizes 'Down by the Old Mill Stream' we are not persuaded. . . . And as for Ivan, he is still 'The Terrible' no matter how many times in a movie he slaps his friends on the back and chucks his wife under the chin."

Welles implied that both films were propagandistic, suffused with establishment patriotism. The real interest and superiority of *Ivan* as against the American work lay not in its interpretation of history or in its implicit ideology, but in its extravagant, stylized approach to cinema, an approach the Russian audience had apparently been willing to accept:

> Critics and audiences in the English-speaking world, accustomed as they are to the pallid stylelessness of the "realistic" school, are likely to be impatient, even moved to giggles by the antics of Ivan and his friends. This is because the arts and artists of our theatre have been so busy for so long now teaching the public to reject anything larger than life unless it be stated in the special language of glamor and charm that I'm afraid many good citizens who read the comic strips with utmost solemnity will laugh out loud at Eisenstein's best moments. Our culture has conditioned us to take Dick Tracy with a straight face. But nothing prepared us for *Ivan the Terrible.*

Welles must have had his own practice in mind as he wrote those lines. From infancy he had been fascinated with Shakespeare, with the European tradition of grand opera, and with the theatrical grandiloquence of large-scale magic shows; the bizarre imagery and deliberately anti-naturalistic acting in the Eisenstein film spoke to his own tastes, but they were doubly attractive because they ran against the grain of studio cinema, giving full expression to the director's personality. Welles praised the Russian film for its "courageously radical stylization," noting how sharply it differed from American movies: "The Wilson picture, of course, has its own stylization and its own conventions. But these are Hollywood habits, not the conscious creation of Director Henry King." In other words, the American film was conservative, built out of a narrow visual and literary code from which the director was not expected to deviate. The Eisenstein film was liberating, allowing the director to make stylistic choices free of a culturally predetermined idea as to what constituted truth to nature.

Both traditions, Welles recognized, had their own peculiar strengths and weaknesses:

> When the American movie-maker becomes aware of a discrepancy between his film and the appearance of life, he corrects the difference in favor of "realism." This search for the direct and literal produces some of our best effects. The Russians go out for the effect itself—and when they find what they're after—they manage moments of an exclamatory and resonant beauty on the level of eloquence to which our school cannot aspire. When the Russian method fails it is funny; it falls flat on its bottom, and we laugh. When Hollywood fails, it falls flat, the result is merely dull, and we yawn.

Welles did not want to choose between these approaches. "We have much to learn from each other," he said, and the learning process, as he saw it, extended especially to matters of technique. Even the medium-distance, long-take photography which Welles had helped popularize (and had justified in the name of "realism") made an interesting contrast with the Russian montage school: "Because of the inferiority of Russian film stock, lenses, and other equipment, the camera must assert itself by what it selects, and by the manner of selection." The less obtrusive Hollywood camera, Welles said, "has a merchant's eye," and devotes itself to "star-hogging close-ups," or to "lovingly evaluating texture, the screen being filled as a window is dressed in a swank department store."

Hence, just as Welles's politics were progressive and liberal, seeking a middle ground between the White House and the Kremlin, so his aesthetics attempted to find a happy synthesis of two cultures. Where his own work was concerned, he had tried from the beginning to combine what he calls "moments of exclamatory and resonant beauty on the level of eloquence" with the dominant tradition of psychological realism. In both ***Kane*** and ***Ambersons,*** for example, he had chosen subjects which had many precedents in the tradition of "well-made" Hollywood films. What was relatively different about Welles was not his subject matter nor even his sophistication, but the degree to which he had brought unorthodox style and autobiography to the fore. In this respect, he had attempted to import something "larger than life" into the mainstream of American movies, a force to countervail what he called the "pallid stylelessness" of studio realism.

Looked at today, the artificial conventions of American movies in the forties are quite apparent, but Welles was correct to say that these films were striving for the "direct and literal." In costume films or in expressionist genres such as the thriller, there was indeed a degree of license, a "special language of glamor and charm," but the tendency of the industry as a whole was toward aesthetic minimalism. Anglo-Saxon critics helped perpetuate this tendency, because they grumbled (as they do today) when they encountered anything unrestrained: it was precisely this quality that made certain reviewers unhappy with ***Kane,*** and that caused Welles's detractors to portray him as a ham; certainly he took greater risks than most with convention, and when his work failed, it failed on the side of histrionics and silliness, never on the side of dullness. Nevertheless Welles's strengths came from the same sources as his weaknesses—namely what he had called, in speaking of Eisenstein, a "courageously radical stylization," which in his case meant a willingness to challenge not only the habits of the studio system but the limits of popular taste.

Given Welles's position in Hollywood in the mid-forties, however, it would seem his romantic struggle against the studios should have come to an end. After his contract with RKO terminated, he worked infrequently, always in the sort of genre projects which might theoretically have put restraints on his style; even when he ventured into Shakespeare, it was under severe limitations of time and budget under a boss whose biggest star was Roy Rogers. And yet, by staying within genres or B-budgets, Welles managed to retain more individuality than if he had been allowed into the more culturally ambitious, expensive productions. At the level of filmed biographies or adaptations of big novels, Hollywood was controlled entirely by middlebrow producers, devoted entirely to the same conservative "tradition of quality" that Truffaut once attacked so vigorously in France. Conversely, the degree of convention in the standard Hollywood melodrama sometimes worked in the director's favor; producers took less personal interest in the texture of the film so long as the basic plot ingredients were satisfied. Thus the Hollywood movie of this period was at its most exciting when it operated under obvious constraints of money or content, at a moderately low level of respectability. Its meaning lay not in the manifest content of the script, which was usually based on potboiler novels or magazine stories, but in the almost libidinal warfare between a good director's style and the pressures of convention.

I say "libidinal" partly because the Freudian model of id vs. superego provides a good analogue to the system, and partly because the most interesting aspects of Hollywood movies in the high forties and fifties tended to be sexual. The fetishistic, overheated romanticism of the *film noir* became one of the few sources of rebellious energy in the movies, although admittedly it was a fairly timid rebellion. Welles, of course, was especially suited to work in this vein, bringing to it an intelligence and integrity of purpose that kept his films from becoming, like so many others, merely lurid.

And despite the fact that he was seldom able to choose his own topics, he managed to keep his ethical and political themes virtually intact; even the familiar character types recur, sometimes adapted to fit the requirements for "glamor and charm." When he worked at all now, his films became more radically stylized than ever, as if the limitations in subject matter and budget had to be overcome by an utter strangeness of *mise-en-scène.* From ***The Lady from Shanghai*** through ***Touch of Evil*** Welles's style became more bizarre and circus-like; his films during this period reflect some of the chaos and uncertainty of his own career, becoming increasingly satiric, charged with self-conscious manipulation of popular sexual stereotypes and visual references to that most private of all Hollywood individualists, von Sternberg. In one sense, therefore, these films were as "personal" as any of his others; and as one might expect, producers and audiences became increasingly unsympathetic. (pp. 111-23)

By many standards ***The Lady from Shanghai*** is more unorthodox than Welles's previous work, but its strangeness did not result from an early, deliberate plan. The idea for the film originated when Welles entered into an agreement with Columbia Pictures to help save the foundering Mercury production of ***Around the World.*** This latter show had been initiated by Welles and Mike Todd, and was a fairly expensive musical extravaganza featuring old-time movies, a magic show, and a "slide for life" down a rope from the theatre balcony. When Todd withdrew from the partnership early on, Welles enlisted the help of Richard Wilson and continued as producer/director, feeling a certain obligation to Cole Porter, whom he had persuaded to write the score. (Welles later recalled wryly that Porter, who was born with twenty million, who made another twenty million from his music, and who then married a woman worth fifty million, never contributed money for the production.) With the shakiest financial backing, ***Around the World*** opened in the dog-days of August in New York, just when wartime gas rationing had been lifted and everyone had left town to escape the heat. The show received mixed reviews and was plagued by one financial disaster after another; ultimately Welles persuaded Harry Cohn [the head of Columbia Pictures] to advance him money for doing a movie, in the hope that he could keep the play running until audiences returned in September. His original plan was to film a thriller on a low budget, entirely in the streets of New York, at the same time that ***Around the World*** was continuing its run. The film would be done in the manner of Castle's *When Strangers Marry,* using no big stars or studio paraphernalia. Almost immediately, however, ***Around the World***

Welles as detective Hank Quinlan in Touch of Evil. *"We're trying to strap you to the electric chair, boy."*

plunged deeper into debt and was closed. Welles found himself back in Hollywood, where his plans for an offbeat potboiler were transformed into a big-budget vehicle for Rita Hayworth.

The resulting film (originally titled *Take This Woman* and then *Black Irish*) tells the story of how Michael O'Hara (Welles), a naïve vagabond, is seduced by the moneyed glamor of Elsa Bannister (Hayworth), allowing himself to become a gigolo and then a duped accomplice in murder. First O'Hara takes a job as captain of Arthur Bannister's yacht on a cruise to San Francisco, and is then persuaded by Bannister's mad law partner, Grisby, to participate in a supposedly phony murder scheme. Grisby claims that he wants to collect money from his own faked demise and then hide out on a South Sea Island, where he can be safe from the atomic bomb. As O'Hara commits himself to this deceitful group, the film becomes increasingly farcical and demonic; from the fantastic love scene with Rita Hayworth in the San Francisco aquarium until the magic mirror maze at the conclusion, the world around O'Hara turns utterly lunatic, with no release until he walks out of an amusement park Crazy House across a pier in morning light. The complex but conventional plot machinations are delivered through hallucinatory visuals, the whole movie becoming a satiric dreamwork or magic show based upon a standard thriller. (This method was natural to Welles, but it was suggested by the repeated references to dreams in Sherwood King's *If I Die Before I Wake,* the novel which was his source; it also has some interesting parallels with Robert Siodmak's less brilliant but highly expressionistic film, *Phantom Lady.*)

In *The Lady From Shanghai,* the real locales of Acapulco and San Francisco are inter-cut with retakes containing obvious studio settings or process screens, and the student can actually make a game of distinguishing shots that are authentically Wellesian from the ones that are deliberate kitsch.

—James Naremore

The movie was substantially re-edited after the second preview and long held from release, becoming a victim of Columbia's desperate attempt to "save" a story Harry Cohn said he could not understand . . . The cutting was turned over to Viola Lawrence, a friend of Cohn's but an enemy of Welles's, and a musical score was added without the director's approval. (Welles later complained, in a letter to the studio, that the music used for Rita Hayworth's dive into a lagoon resembled "a Disney picture when Pluto falls into the pool.") Like ***The Stranger*** the film is a patchwork, but it is far more energetic and dazzling, its very confusions a part of its fascination. The acting ranges from Welles's phony and inconsistent interpretation of an Irish sailor fallen among the right-wing American rich, to the sublimely grotesque performances of Everett Sloane and Glenn Anders, a pair of unscrupulous lawyers who are scorpions personified. The dialogue oscillates between the bathetic ("Give my love to the sunrise"), the tautological ("One who follows his nature will keep his original nature in the end"), and the downright opaque ("I want you to live as long as possible before you die"); but this goofiness remains somehow in keeping with the general atmosphere of comic delirium. Everywhere the movie is filled with bizarre visual dissonances, Welles's imagery coexisting with scenes or sequences that serve to mock Hollywood. Again and again a brilliant moment will be interrupted with gauzy closeups or over-the-shoulder editing, awkwardly composed and badly acted. The real locales of Acapulco and San Francisco are inter-cut with retakes containing obvious studio settings or process screens, and the student can actually make a game of distinguishing shots that are authentically Wellesian from the ones that are deliberate kitsch. It is a game worth playing, partly because the radical shifts of style in this film take on meaningful implications.

A logical place to begin is with Welles's habit of animating the environment, using it to express the emotions of his players or to comment on their behavior . . . Welles will seldom do one thing on the screen when he can do three or four. Typically he gives as much information as possible, playing off the most subtle exchanges between characters against two or more levels of action. Even the kitchen dinner scene in ***The Magnificent Ambersons*** is not so restrained as is commonly supposed: the camera barely moves, but Tim Holt wolfs down strawberry shortcake, a Gothic storm rattles outside the windows of the big kitchen, and the actors keep stepping on one another's lines. Welles depends heavily on this multiplication of artistic stimuli, so that he not only expresses psychology through the settings but gives us the feeling of many actions, visual and aural, occurring simultaneously. It is this richness, this seven-layer-cake profusion, that most distinguishes his work in Hollywood.

The Lady from Shanghai offers many examples of such density, the most obvious being the mirror-maze sequence, which is also the grandest example of Welles's delight in movie illusionism. The gun battle among the mirrors functions beautifully within the plot, compactly expressing the ruthless ambition and the self-destructive mania which has been evoked verbally in the hero's account of hungry sharks; indeed it is such a brilliant moment that it almost transcends its fictional content, turning Rita Hayworth into a series of insubstantial images which symbolize the gaudy unreality and fascination of movie stars. More to the point, however, is the way the sequence shows Welles's love of baroque dynamics; it produces an infinite depth of field and more information than we can absorb in a single viewing.

Not satisfied with the simple phenomenon of reflections in mirrors, Welles complicates the spectacle with a split screen: for example, we see two images of Arthur Bannister (Sloane) and his cane at either side of the frame, in between them two gigantic pictures of Elsa's blonde head. In another shot, two Bannisters are superimposed over Elsa's eyeball. Toward the climax, Bannister lurches to the left and produces three images of himself; the camera then pans and three more Bannisters approach from the opposite direction, the two converging groups separated by a single image of Elsa holding a gun; Bannister now takes out his own pistol, and as he points it his "real" hand enters the foreground from offscreen right. All this time the actors are delivering crucial speeches which are intended to unravel the mystery plot—in fact so much happens so rapidly that only a lengthy analysis can lead to a full understanding of the sequence. (pp. 125-28)

[The] sequence has been designed to create a montage of conflicts between Everett Sloane and Rita Hayworth. If the ugly, crippled male is reflected many times in a single shot, the unreal sex goddess will usually be seen alone; if both characters are multiplied, one will be larger than the other. Each image has the disturbing quality of abstract expressionism or surrealist art, and yet each is motivated by the plot and the psychology of the characters . . . Bannister tells Elsa that in killing her he will be killing himself, and the hallucinatory image is perfectly expressive of the way the mind can become a hall of mirrors, a distorted, paranoid vision.

The audience does not have to make this sort of analysis in order to appreciate the power of the images, but most viewers feel they have to "meet the film at least half way," as Herman G. Weinberg once said, in an effort to assimilate all the information. Thus, one of the pervasive qualities of this sequence and of Welles's movies in general is *wit,* which means not only a sense of humor but what the *OED* defines as an appeal to the mental faculties, especially to "memory and attention." Of course the typical studio film does not have much to do with wit; its chief desiderata are clarity and simplicity, and that is perhaps one reason why the scenes in ***The Lady from Shanghai*** waver between a complex satire of manners and a familiar Hollywood gloss.

Keeping to his original intention, Welles shot parts of the film on location, following a practice that was becoming increasingly popular just after the war. Even the interiors, including the sailor's hiring hall, the pierside cafe, the dusty, oppressive courtroom, and the Chinatown theatre, have a harsh surface realism overlaid with a busy, expressive shooting style. In the finished movie, however, many individual shots undercut Welles's expressionism; we catch only occasional glimpses of a startling *mise-en-scène,* usually shot in a real locale. What one recalls most vividly, aside from the trick effects in the Crazy House, are the huge closeups of the four principals: Sloane and Anders are photographed with a mercilessly sharp lens, the camera highlighting every pockmark and bead of sweat on their faces; Welles and Hayworth, on the other hand, become gigantic, romantically blurred movie stars—as fantastic and disturbing in their own way as the ugly characters, so that a glamorous studio portrait photography contributes to the film's aura of surrealism.

In fact, Welles seems to have been quite willing to make studio closeups which disrupt his elaborate blocking of the actors and his fine sense of movement within a frame. Consider, for example, the scene where Grisby calls O'Hara aside to offer a "proposition," and the two men stroll along a hillside above Acapulco Bay. The long shots filmed on location are held on the screen only briefly, but they suggest a conception that is nearly as impressive as the party scene in ***Ambersons*** or the elaborate track at the beginning of ***Touch of Evil.*** As Grisby and O'Hara climb the hillside, the whole social structure of Acapulco passes them by, from the impoverished peasants at the bottom of the hill to the American tourists and their Latin retinue at the top. The atmosphere at the bottom is dirty, crowded, and hot, but at the parapet above a sea breeze is blowing and Acapulco sparkles in the sun like a "bright, guilty world."

Welles apparently planned this episode as a series of elaborately choreographed traveling shots that express O'Hara's state of mind while at the same time showing the effects of Yankee capital. As usual, he employs a wide-angle lens, which gives the movement of the camera and actors a dramatic sweep, and he fills the screen with several layers of action; the camera spirals up the hill, picking up additional people moving past at different angles, creating a busy, swirling effect. Most of these location scenes are cut on an actor's movement in order to preserve the flow of action and dialogue; Welles tries to evoke a subtly dizzying sensation, which culminates in the final shot—a high-angle, fish-eye view of Grisby and O'Hara standing over the sea. When Grisby steps out of the screen, O'Hara seems to be hanging vertiginously in midair, his image twisted out of shape by the camera to a degree few Hollywood films of the period had attempted.

In the completed film, however, the episode has been substantially revised. Charles Higham has suggested that some of the Acapulco scenes were filmed so clumsily that they "would not cut." It is difficult to believe a sequence so painstakingly blocked as this one could have suffered from an editing problem, but in any case studio shots have been introduced, consisting chiefly of closeups of Welles and Glenn Anders. The lighting in these shots does not match Charles Lawton's strikingly naturalistic photography, and when the closeups are inserted all the restless movement ceases; the two actors are shown as big, static heads, isolated against an artificial backdrop.

A similar intrusion can be seen in the courtroom sequence, which remains one of the funniest in the film. The defendant, O'Hara, who by this time has been made the fall-guy for the villains, is supposed to be completely ignored by everybody; in fact Welles purposely keeps the camera off himself, shooting from a bewildering variety of angles and thus contributing to the maelstrom of activity. The camera leaps back and forth from harshly lit closeups to equally harsh wide-angle views of the room, showing Bannister, the "world's greatest criminal lawyer," parading before the jury on crutches or the audience breaking into spasms. Dialogue overlaps, a juror sneezes, the judge cracks jokes, and nearly everybody deliberately overacts. Now and then, however, the sequence is interrupted by shots of Welles and Rita Hayworth, done in a style which is utterly conventional and radically different from the surrounding imagery. Perhaps someone at the studio felt the trial would make no sense without "reactions" from the protagonists; whatever the cause, the movie seems to have been made by two different hands, or by a director who, out of weariness, contempt, or sheer practical jokery, chose to deface his own work.

I raise the possibility of Welles's contempt because certain defects in the film could have been repaired by any competent technician. For example, after the cataclysm in the mirror maze we are given a shot of Everett Sloane fallen to the floor, curled up, and dying, viewed through jagged edges of glass at the corners of the frame. As Elsa dashes from the room, the camera pans and the "glass" moves with it. The shards in the extreme foreground are revealed as a painting on the front of the camera, and the decision to use a panning movement is clearly a director's error. On the other hand, there is no way of knowing what opportunities Welles had for retakes, and it is obvious that the studio interfered with his more ambitious efforts. Some of his characteristic long takes have been cut to pieces, including the carriage ride through Central Park which opens the film. The long takes that do remain are especially witty moments, indications of what Welles might have accomplished elsewhere. The scene in Grisby's office, for instance, is filmed with a moving camera which snakes around the room, now and then catching O'Hara's bewilderment or Grisby's leer. Later, a complicated and extremely funny shot shows O'Hara learning that he has been framed for a murder: he drives up in Grisby's car, climbs out, and is met by the zaniest swarm of policemen since Keaton's *Cops.* In a lightning succession heightened by the continuity of the shot, the police discover a murder weapon and a signed confession: Officer Peters reads the confession aloud, Arthur Bannister limps into the picture, Grisby's corpse is wheeled under O'Hara's nose, and Elsa drives up in her convertible. The only cut is here at the end, where we are given a soft-focus closeup of Hayworth, surely intended as a parody of the *femme fatale* (as the earlier shot of her pinned to the deck of a yacht is a parody of cheesecake).

But these interesting moments might have become mere curiosities if the film itself did not retain a certain integrity of purpose. What is surprising about ***The Lady from Shanghai*** is the degree to which it remains thematically unified, despite the confusing plot turns and the many revisions it appears to have gone through during production. Even as it stands, it is based on some interesting formal ideas. O'Hara's voyage as captain of the Bannister yacht takes him around the continent, beginning with a shot of the New York harbor and ending at San Francisco Bay, as if he were a tourist taking a panoramic view of U.S. corruption. As William Johnson has pointed out, the whole adventure is filled with images of the sea. The lady of the title is of course a shanghaier of sailors, a Sternbergian Circe who lures an Irish Ulysses onto the rocks with her wet swimsuit, or who sings an incredibly bad song which turns O'Hara into a zombie. Again and again Welles combines images of madness with images of water—even the long take in Grisby's office is played off against South Sea islands music coming from a radio.

Furthermore, there is a sense in which all of Columbia's tampering with the film has not been as disruptive as, say, RKO's revisions of ***Ambersons.*** The reason is that ***The Lady from Shanghai*** is characterized by a sort of inspired silliness, a grotesquely comic stylization that has moved beyond expressionism toward absurdity. (In one of his best exit lines, Glenn Anders steps close to the camera and whines, "Silly, isn't it?" He then moves out of the frame, leaving Welles sitting there looking as bewildered as usual.) The performances are deliberately exaggerated, so that the sinister moments keep verging on farce—an effect similar to the motel scenes in ***Touch of Evil*** and K.'s interviews in ***The Trial.*** Hence the vulgarity of the movie-star imagery only adds to the feeling of satire; for example, the many bad closeups of Rita Hayworth, which seem to have been forced on Welles, often serve as a comment on Hollywood's synthetic sexuality. Welles has added to this feeling by dyeing her hair a fluorescent blonde and dressing her in near parodies of calendar-girl fashion, such as her little yachtsman's suit with white shorts, clog heels, and officer's cap. He poses her rather like a figure in an advertisement—a smiling woman in a bathing suit, reclining on a rock, her toes nicely pointed and the wind blowing her hair. He deliberately cuts from her awful siren song to a "Glosso Lusto" hair-treatment commercial, or he views her through Grisby's telescope, suddenly lowering the glass and confronting the audience with a full closeup of

Grisby himself, who is sweating and leering voyeuristically back at the camera.

These touches are not out of keeping with the mood of the film as a whole. In fact, one could argue that Welles's career during this period had begun to move more and more away from realism to fantasy, from consciousness to subconsciousness, from ports to Crazy Houses. His style, with its fantastic distortions, its complex play of light and shadow, its many levels of activity, had always been suited to the depiction of corruption and madness. But ***The Lady from Shanghai,*** probably out of sheer necessity, combines the extremes of this style with the extremes of Hollywood convention; in the process it becomes one of Welles's most hyperkinetic films, and his most misanthropic treatment of American life. In a sense it is a dream about typical movie dreams, and can almost be read as an allegory about Welles's adventures in Hollywood, showing his simultaneous fascination with and nausea over the movie industry. Hiding behind a phony Irish brogue instead of the putty nose he would later adopt, Welles enters the film as a wanderer from another country (the very country from which he entered the American theatre), and finds himself in a world of shark-eat-shark individualism. In such a world, which is ruled by what a shipmate calls an "edge," the good characters are powerless; at best they philosophize while the bad destroy each other.

This doomed world is of course basic to the *film noir,* and to most other pictures by Welles; the only difference is that he has cast himself as a naïve idealist instead of a tyrant, a vaguely working-class Jed Leland instead of a Kane. To some extent he is purveying the same left-wing, macho romanticism which characterizes all movies derived from *The Maltese Falcon;* thus his villains are deformed and effeminate men with an unscrupulous woman, and his hero is a proletarian who is trying to write a novel. (Welles was in fact a major contributor to the misogynistic tone of forties melodrama. In this film, made while his marriage to Hayworth was ending, he gives a rather bitter farewell to his wife and portrays her as a woman "kept" by rich businessmen. Later he suggested *Monsieur Verdoux* to Chaplin [who directed the film and played its title character, a murderer of wealthy women], and after ***The Lady from Shanghai*** he turned to Lady Macbeth.) In many other ways, however, Welles has not been content with the mildly alienated fantasies of the tough-guy mystery, and Columbia's revisions have not disguised his intentions. The ostensible hero of this film claims that he is not a hero, presenting himself instead as a confused and likeable fellow who has fallen into a situation over which he has no control. But just as Welles rarely treats his villains without a certain compassion, so his idealists are meant to evoke an ambiguous response. From the beginning O'Hara knows that Bannister is the "world's greatest criminal," and he blithely comments that Elsa comes from the wickedest cities in the world. He recognizes the evil around him quite easily, and the only way to explain his behavior is to say that he is either more foolish or more complicated than we expect him to be. In the introductory voice-over, he says he is "foolish," and adds, "If I'd been in my right mind . . . But once I'd seen her I was not in my right mind for some time." This early comment on insanity prepares us for the distorted style of the movie, and for Michael's voyage to the Crazy House at the conclusion. At the same time, it gives a casual hint of the irrational temptations that underlie the consciousness of the progressive, presumably rational "Hero."

O'Hara is supposed to have murdered a man in the Spanish Civil War, and in the hiring hall the shipmate remarks that "Black Irish O'Hara" can "hurt a guy" when he's angry (we see him do this later, in the funny but terrifying courtroom brawl). Grisby, Iago-like, taunts O'Hara and seems to look right into his past: "I'm very interested in murders," Grisby says. "How'd you do it? No, let me guess. . . . You did it with your *hands,* didn't you?" O'Hara looks dazed, openly conveying the guilt he can barely conceal throughout the film; in fact one suspects that his occasionally whimsical or baffled attitude comes from a reluctance to acknowledge the full extent of his temptations. When he walks the moonlit streets of Acapulco with Elsa, he passes down a long stone corridor lined with open doorways showing the hovels of the poor. When he walks with Grisby above Acapulco Bay, he glances at a peasant woman hanging out clothes, and then at a lady tourist followed by a gigolo who is saying, "Of *course* you pay me." These events are not lost on O'Hara, who remarks that the brightness of the bay can't hide hunger and guilt. The guilt, however, is perhaps as much his own as the Bannisters'.

On the surface, ***The Lady from Shanghai*** is the story of a contest between Elsa and Arthur, whose reflections we see in the apocalyptic finale. At a deeper level, however, it concerns O'Hara's highly sexual temptation with the bright, rich world—an "exchange of guilt" formula that had interested Welles from the time he arrived in Hollywood to adapt *Heart of Darkness.* Although he was essentially a humane man, Welles was always aware of the perils of humanism (to say nothing of the perils of California); thus O'Hara descends into a nightmare, coming out of it all resolving to grow older, wiser, and perhaps less complacent. The story has been a comedy, a satiric fantasy, and something of a cautionary tale. For all its imperfections, it manages to retain many of the qualities of Welles's best work. (pp. 128-36)

James Naremore, in his The Magic World of Orson Welles, *1978. Reprint by Southern Methodist University Press, 1989, 310 p.*

Beverle Houston (essay date Summer 1982)

[Houston was an American critic and educator who wrote extensively on film and film theory. In the following essay, she discusses the protagonists in Welles's films and examines how their desire for love and acceptance brings about destruction.]

In a scene of snowfall before a small house, Charles Foster Kane is cast out of his family by his newly rich mother. As generations of moviewatchers are well aware, it is to this snow scene that he returns upon his death as the text itself returns to the "No Trespassing" sign. In ***Magnificent Ambersons,*** on the other hand, family and friends spend years trying unsuccessfully to dislodge Georgie

Welles with Rita Hayworth at the end of The Lady From Shanghai.

Minafer from the family mansion and the bosom of his mother. When the infant is finally forced out, he breaks both his legs. In the same film, Lucy Morgan is forced by Georgie's refusal to enter the world of men and money to return to her father and a lifetime of celibacy. Mary Longstreet in ***The Stranger*** is forced into a similar return.

Both ***Citizen Kane*** and ***Magnificent Ambersons*** reveal a central male figure who is extremely powerful in certain ways, who can charm, force or frighten others into doing what he wants. But the desire for control is haunted by everything that evades it. The opening of ***Citizen Kane,*** with its decayed golf course and terraces, its moss-covered gothic magnificence, reveals to us two aspects of this pattern: both the overreaching ambition and its failure—a grand life, now in ruins. Even at the height of their powers, these men are revealed to be helpless in certain realms of life, unable finally to live out their desires. Focusing on ***Citizen Kane, Magnificent Ambersons,*** and ***The Stranger*** as family-centered narratives set in the United States, with substantial reference to ***Touch of Evil, Immortal Story,*** and ***Chimes at Midnight*** for close parallels of theme and/or narrative strategies, and with passing glances at a number of other Welles films, this essay will examine the ways in which the boundless fear, anger, and desire of these figures power both narrative and image in these films.

In my own years of obsession with the Welles films, I have come to call this central figure of desire and contradiction the Power Baby, the eating, sucking, foetus-like creature who, as the lawyer at the center of ***The Trial,*** can be found baby-faced, lying swaddled in his bed and tended by his nurse; who in ***Touch of Evil*** sucks candy and cigars in a face smoothed into featurelessness by fat as he redefines murder and justice according to desire; who in his bland and arrogant innocence brings everybody down in ***Lady from Shanghai;*** who, in the framed face of Picasso, slyly signals his power as visual magician and seducer and who is himself tricked in ***F for Fake;*** but who must die for the sake of the social order in ***Chimes at Midnight*** and who dies again for his last effort of power and control in ***Immortal Story;*** and who, to my great delight, is figured forth explicitly in ***Macbeth*** where, in a Wellesian addition to Shakespeare, the weird sisters at the beginning of the film reach into the cauldron, scoop out a handful of their primordial woman's muck, shape it into a baby, and crown it with the pointy golden crown of fairy tales.

Who are these infant kings who return to early scenes,

whose narratives are deflected, and whose situations are finally reversed? What do they have, and what lack? How are they both more and less than they wish to be, sometimes never reaching, but more often losing their once-great powers in the world of men and money? And what is the pattern of possibilities for their women, who are so often denied or forced into returns, whose fates are so extreme, yet so limited?

The mother of Charles Foster Kane becomes rich and powerful in a moment of transformation. She uses this power to reject Charles utterly. He is ripped untimely from a scene where he could reach whatever combination of love, fear, acceptance, and rejection that might come from the child's living out the drama of sex and power with his parents. The untimeliness of this change is suggested perfectly by the exaggeration of size relations in the Christmas shot where Charles, with his unwanted new sled, gazes up defiantly at a huge Thatcher, the money monster, on that most familial of holidays, the one based on the birth of a perfect son into a perfect family.

In the name of what does Charles's mother commit this horribly wrenching act, for which she is so eager that she has had her son's trunk packed for a week? It is true that the father moves as if to strike Charles when he pushes Thatcher. And it is true that he says: "What that kid needs is a good thrashing," moving Mrs. Kane to reply: "That's what you think, is it Jim . . . that's why he's going to be brought up where you can't get at him." Apparently Mrs. Kane thinks he is "the wrong father" for little Charles. Yet we have little evidence that the father has ever harmed or frightened the child. As the four talk outside the cabin, Charles moves eagerly toward his father's arms; the mother must stop him by calling his name sharply. Thus it is one of the film's most powerful and puzzling images when, at the moment of her insistence, Mrs. Kane slowly turns her head to the side as the camera dwells on her enigmatic look. Is it one of confidence for having freed her son from a struggle he couldn't win? Or one of cruel pleasure in having triumphed over father and son for their very maleness? Is she the terrible mother of myth and nightmare? Joseph McBride suggests: "It is simply that the accident which made the Kanes suddenly rich has its own fateful logic—Charles must 'get ahead.' What gives the brief leave-taking scene its mystery and poignancy is precisely this feeling of pre-determination." It must be emphasized, however, that the logic is not that of fate but of money and social class. Insisting that "this isn't the place for you to grow up in," the newly empowered mother pursues her son's "advantages" by removing him from an impoverished rural environment. She turns her son over to an agency—the bank—that she believes will protect and promote him better than the family. Yet we cannot fully escape the hint of a revenge and must accept the overdetermination of this genuinely ambiguous moment.

The role of the father needs to be understood in a different way as well. It is not his cruelty that is most significant. The fact that Fred Graves, the defaulting boarder who knew both Mr. and Mrs. Kane, left the fortune exclusively to Mrs. Kane, somehow brings Charlie's paternity into question. Did Graves leave it all to Mrs. Kane because he found the father wanting in some way—weak and whining, dependent on his wife, perhaps? Or is it Graves himself, in his unpredictable act of generosity, who is the right ("real") father? Even though we are made sympathetic with Mr. Kane—"I don't hold with signing my boy away. . . . Anyone'd think I hadn't been a good husband. . . . " (Why doesn't he say, "Good *father?*")—still other negative qualities are revealed. He first tries to get little Charles to believe that his forced migration from country/family to city/bank is going to be a wonderful adventure: "That's the train with all the lights. . . . You're going to see Chicago and New York. . . . " But when Charles refuses to be fooled, the father threatens to thrash him. Thus even this "wrong father" has two faces: he who promises deceitfully, who promises pleasure where there is abandonment, and he who later threatens violence. For the boy, the father becomes the promise of worldly experience and the threat of danger, both exaggerated. Longing to cling to the beloved but mysteriously rejecting mother, unable to trust the weak and deceitful father, the boy Charles reacts with rage as his life is captured in this frozen moment.

And what of Georgie Minafer, who got out, not too early, but too late? Within the basic reversal, there are a number of similarities, particularly concerning the father. In this film, money also brings about the constitution of the "wrong" family. The agency of business is this time substituted, not for the family as a whole, but for the emotional participation of the father through Isabel Amberson's choice of husband. She marries Wilbur Minafer, a "steady young businessman," instead of Eugene Morgan, "a man who any woman would like a thousand times better." Though the local women opine that Isabel's "pretty sensible for such a showy girl," they prophesy correctly the return of the passions denied by Isabel's choice: "They'll have the worst spoiled lot of children this town will ever see. It'll all go to her children and she'll ruin them." An only child receiving the full adoration of a mother who married for dollars and sense, so puny he nearly dies as an infant, young Georgie also has a father who is virtually absent. Later, when the father dies, the voice-over narrator tells us: "Wilbur Minafer. A quiet man. The town will hardly know he's gone." And Georgie hardly knew he was there. But this time the young man with the wrong father, with *no* father to love and hate on a regular basis, has not been sent away by the mother. Instead, we find that Georgie lives fully in a mutual state of uncontested love with the mother, secure inside a warm, dark house and a rich and fabled family. No reason to get a job or a profession. No reason ever to leave this nest of complete dependence and desire.

The theme of the wrong or displaced father is explicit in ***Immortal Story*** as well, where the primacy of money (over friendship rather than passion this time) once caused old Mr. Clay to drive away his partner, the father of Virginie. When he brings her back to her father's house (which Clay now occupies) to play out her role in his fable of seduction, he functions as a cruel "wrong father" over whom she is able to triumph. Throughout the Welles canon, fathers and mothers are doubled and tripled, offering, through displacement, the multiplications and contradictions of identity and representation. ***Falstaff*** (***Chimes at Midnight***) offers one of the richest and most fluid exercises in doubling and multiplicity of father/identity. Very early in the film we are presented with Falstaff as an old man who is at the same time an innocent, the one who has been shaped by the "son" he is supposed to have corrupted. As he tells us: "Before I knew thee, Hal, I knew nothing." Later on, Falstaff puts a pot on his head and plays the role of Hal's other father, the king, chastising the boy for his bad friends and wastrel's life. Then they change roles and Hal plays his own father, the king. All the way through the film, Hal's knowledge of his impending power as future king has run concurrent with his boyish playfulness and has made all his jokes and insults to Falstaff painfully cruel, as they now are in this exchange of roles. This cruelty is, of course, prophetic of his final assumption of a fixed identity as king, which entails the rejection of Falstaff after Hal has become his own father in earnest.

The main trajectory of the plot of ***Citizen Kane, Magnificent Ambersons,*** and ***The Stranger*** turns in on itself in the pattern of a return. The child/man, unable to continue his movement toward social participation and "maturity," falls back into a childhood situation, and the woman in ***The Stranger*** is forced into a similar return. In ***Citizen Kane,*** Charlie instantly defies his substitute father and the more or less innocent energy of this rebellion carries him well into young manhood. He travels, starts to run a newspaper, behaves like an aggressive young man in the world. This phase reaches a kind of peak in his "Declaration of Principles," where he lays down the law of the sons against the corrupt fathers of the money agencies (as Thatcher had earlier laid down the law of the "Trust" to his mother), his rebellious liberalism creating a link between the youthful and the poor. But he is not content to let the words and actions of the newspaper speak for themselves. He insists on foregrounding the enunciation, as it were, revealing himself as "author" of the newspaper, unmediated by an editorial persona. This authorial gesture is merely one of the ways that young Charles reveals his huge ambition. This boy, thrown out of many elegant schools, sees himself as becoming "champion of the people." His actions reveal the exaggerated picture he has of himself and his powers, which will later be revealed in the huge poster of himself at the rally, as he sets out to win everybody's love.

Love on a personal level reveals both his overarching aspirations *and* his limitations. The announcement of his engagement is read in a room full of statuary he has been sending to the office—"the loot of the world"—gifts given to no one, and never enough to fill the huge empty spaces that he and the others in his life will occupy as they grow older. In his bride to be, he has acquired another high element of culture—the president's niece. But like Isabel Amberson's, Charlie's attention is only briefly engaged by his new mate. McBride suggests that Charles has a need for affection that Emily "could not gratify," but I suggest that it is Kane who will not "gratify," turning from relations within his family to activities in which he need function only as a source of verbal or financial power, where he is never called upon to act as husband/lover/personal father. (In ***Immortal Story,*** Mr. Clay tells us that he has always avoided all personal relations and human emotions, which can "dissolve your bones.")

One night, his uncharged marriage a boring failure, his vaunting political ambitions uncertain, Charles decides to make a return to the place where his mother's goods, and his own truncated development, lie in storage. But instead, he is splashed by mud and because of this accident, the return is delayed. He comments to Susan on this deflection: "I was on my way to the Western Manhattan Warehouse—in search of my childhood."

Georgie Minafer's dream-like intimacy with his mother (as signalled by the long, slow takes and dark depth of field) is suddenly threatened by a second father (the "right father?") Eugene Morgan, who has made a return of his own. Morgan has come back to the town of his romantic defeat to try again with the soon-to-be-widowed Isabel, bringing with him a daughter (the mother is never mentioned) and a number of transformations that will be devastating for Georgie, who clings to his fixed identity as an Amberson. Trying to resist Eugene in the world of men, Georgie is ineffectual because of such misconceptions. He overestimates the power of his family identity to guarantee his superiority (or, indeed, his survival). He is wrong when he tries to ridicule Gene's invention of the automobile, and wrong again when he tries to enlist his father against the usurper by absurdly accusing him of wanting to borrow money. But he is not wrong with his mother. Oh, no. With Isabel, practically all he has to say is: "You're my mother," and she agrees to call it off with Eugene, despite his plea not to allow their romance to be ruined by "the history of your own perfect motherhood."

As in ***Citizen Kane,*** it is a sudden and unexpected change of fortune—this time a loss—that finally breaks up the family. Georgie is faced with an entirely new situation. He is alone and must support himself. His mother has died of a nameless wasting disease, having been devoured by Georgie's ravening orality. (All these Power Babies eat and eat.) Furthermore, his Aunt Fanny, who has been a kind of shadowy mother double, loving instead of being loved, seeking instead of evading, who has lived only to yearn after Eugene and to feed Georgie, is now completely dependent upon him. As he goes out in the world, one prospective employer notes that he has become "the most practical young man," but only very, very briefly. Praying at his mother's empty bed, the new Georgie begs forgiveness from the Father of Fathers, but no fathers hear, for in the next cut, Georgie has an accident. An automobile knocks him down and breaks both his legs.

Let us recall here that Kane's son was killed in an automobile accident (which also claimed his wife) and that maiming of the legs is common in the Welles canon. Recall the extreme limp and double canes of Arthur Bannister in ***Lady from Shanghai,*** the greatly reduced mobility of Mr. Clay in ***Immortal Story,*** and perhaps most complex, the bullet in the leg that Quinlan took for his friend Pete Menzies in ***Touch of Evil.*** And if the leg wound can be taken as suggesting deflected or impeded sexuality, then we must note the role of Quinlan's cane in bringing about his downfall.

Georgie has always known where the danger lay. The first night he meets Eugene and Lucy, he denigrates the automobile and wishes her father would "forget about it." Later he scorns it as useless and, prophetically in more ways than one, says it should never have been invented. Georgie's insistent and perverse dismissal of this most powerful agent of transformation is, of course, thoughtless and superficial at the rational level; he appears foolish and self-defeating, moving his Uncle Jack to remark on how strange it is to woo a woman by insulting her father. But Georgie is reacting to the car as symbol of Gene's phallic power to take away the mother love on which Georgie sustains himself so voraciously and on which, as an untried emotional infant, he believes his life depends. While others enter into mature speculation about how the automobile will change the world—Eugene himself is most confident that it will: "There are no times but new times," he says—Georgie is terrified for his life. In his identity as a new man of the future, Eugene has benefitted from an exchange of power with the Ambersons; their great fortune is gone, their living space (the home, the woman's place) is taken away, while Eugene's fortunes rise, his factories and power transformers consuming the Amberson space and returning it as a city. To move from rural safety to urban danger, Georgie Minafer need only leave the house. In his own life and in the society at large, Georgie's world of women has given way to a world of men. This shift in economy threatens him at the deepest level. Georgie has begun to fear that he will soon take his "last walk," as the narrator puts it. In the reversal implied by his *seeking* a "dangerous job," Georgie signals us that his fear is becoming unbearably acute.

As the automobile accident fulfills Georgie's prophetic panic, he is returned to the state of complete dependency that marked his place in the family of origin. But this time, it is a strangely smiling Eugene Morgan upon whom he must depend. Worse than Georgie's worst fears, this outcome brings, not the death that might even be wished for, but a bitter substitute for the ecstatic plentitude of mother love. For Eugene, his rival/double, it constitutes a triumph.

As the new money and usurping father brought terror and helplessness to Georgie Minafer, they bring rage and isolation to Charles Foster Kane. Once a dirty accident has deflected him from his return and brought him together with Susan, their relationship takes a strange turn. Kane almost seems to act out the role of her mother. Susan's youth is established—"Pretty old. I'll be twenty-two in August"—and we learn that her mother had operatic aspirations for her small, untrue voice. Immediately after this revelation, we see several of the film's few conventional, romantic close-ups as Susan declares sweetly: "You know what mothers are like," and Kane answers dreamily: "Yes, I know." The mention of the mother is linked with the sign values of shallow depth, key and back lighting, and slightly soft focus, signalling Romance even more strongly than the early scene with Emily, and suggesting that Susan has tapped into Kane's deepest desires—perhaps a fantasy of a mother staying with a child, watching over it and nurturing it, causing it to grow and flourish. Susan's reaction to this impossible program is another matter, to be spoken of later.

The meeting with Boss Jim Gettys, the other key encounter of Kane's life, turns upon the role of yet another father in the family and in culture. As his mother and Mr. Thatcher seemed to be in cahoots long ago against the little boy whose weak and unreliable father did nothing to help him, now another Mrs. Kane and another usurping father move to dislodge him once again from a place where he is perhaps living out *all* the roles of his frozen moment, but according to a new script of his archaic desires.

With inadequate experience of father and family to mediate between his infant rage and the world of signification, Kane has imagined his rival Gettys as a monster and put that monstrous image into the public realm—newspaper pictures of Gettys "in a convict suit with stripes—so his children could see. . . . Or his mother." Now Gettys must wipe out the representational power of these images. To do so, he must discredit Kane completely. Thus Gettys as powerful and successful father and son punishes Kane, not for his transgression with Susan, which stands in for the move against the father and which might have stayed a childish secret forever, but for his unbridled excess in attacking Gettys so viciously in the newspaper. Even so, Gettys is formidable but not cruel, urging Kane to do his duty and avoid family disaster by withdrawing from the race. Finally, when Kane can do nothing but scream his child-like defiance, Gettys's words are those of the elder instructing the younger: "You need more than one lesson, and you're gonna get more than one lesson." Like Georgie's, Kane's comeuppance has swept over him suddenly in a wild moment.

The image of Kane screaming down his impotent rage from the top of the steps suggests an attempt to reverse the size relations of the Christmas shot with Thatcher, and evokes similar images in a number of Welles's other films, most notably where his Macbeth, having destroyed a number of families, including that of the Kingdom itself, finally stands alone on the high wall, seeming to find a perverse ecstasy in his impotent defiance of Macduff, the outraged father (himself "untimely ripped") who has come to bring him down. In ***The Stranger,*** Charles Rankin, exposed as the Nazi Franz Kindler, screams down his defiance of Mr. Wilson, the Nazi-hunter/father figure, from the top of a clock tower.

Kane's destruction of the bedroom after Susan leaves is perhaps the most famous scene of rage in American film. Kane had tried to insert himself into the culture as a "celebrity" through public office—a space somewhere between that of a commodity and a well known friend or family member. To the child of banks, being elected is perhaps like being loved. But his excess of anger cost him that public affirmation. Now the saving fantasy with Susan has failed, bringing on the wild rage. As he picks up the glass ball, Kane completes the return begun on that night when he started for the warehouse. We have already seen Kane in the newsreel with useless legs, swaddled in white like an old baby. The narrative will now offer no more events involving Kane before death causes him to release his frozen scene of trauma. After he passes through the hall of mirrors, the camera holds on the empty reflector; his identity is erased by its repetition. As Beaudry says: "An infinite mirror would no longer be a mirror." With his smooth head, pouting lips, and single tear, Kane is almost foetus-like, back in a primordial isolation before language, before family, before self.

As Susan walks away from Kane (and from her doll, seen in the extreme foreground as they quarrel, and seen again next to Kane's sled among the final images—he longed for his; she didn't long for hers) she also walks away from the return forced upon her by Kane. As indicated by her attempt at suicide, she doesn't wish to continue as the child, living out her mother's fantasy or Charles's desire. Perhaps punished by her "alcoholism" for her aggressiveness in leaving Kane, certainly childishly imprudent in having spent all the money, Susan's real return has been to her position within another social class. But she is surviving, capable of working, playing, and feeling deep sympathy. Lucy Morgan in ***Magnificent Ambersons*** is also forced into a return, but a far more regressive one, and certainly of a different style. Georgie wouldn't enter the world of men and money, and Lucy certainly couldn't join him in the closed world of mother love. Therefore, as she tells him, "Because we couldn't play together like good children, we shouldn't play at all." In an idyllic out-of-doors scene, paralleling the one in which Morgan tried to convince Isabel to marry him, Lucy describes her situation to her father in the story of Ven Do Nah. This Indian was hated by all his tribe, so they drove him away. But they couldn't find a replacement they liked better. "They couldn't help it." So Lucy declares her intention to stay in the garden with her father for the rest of her life: "I don't want anything but you."

In several of Welles's films, a daughter, having made the wrong sexual choice, must return to the father. Perhaps the success of the fathers represents a displacement of the Power Baby's desired return, a metonymy in which the intensely longed-for power is muted as it moves into the quiet certainty and control of imagined patriarchal authority (yet another move in the representation of the diffuse subject). The most extreme version of the daughter's situation is developed in ***The Stranger.*** Mary Longstreet has chosen as her sexual partner, not a dependent infant, not a half-baked crook like the daughter (of a white slaver) in ***Mr. Arkadin,*** but the worst possible enemy of everyone in the whole world—a NAZI! And how could this perfectly nice girl make this bizarre choice, which even her brother can't believe: "Gee, Mr. Wilson, you must be wrong. Mary wouldn't fall in love with that kind of a man." But Nazi-hunting father doubles like Mr. Wilson are not wrong. "That's the way it is," he later says, because "people can't help who they fall in love with." For "people," of course, read "women." (Remember Lucy and Ven Do Nah?)

This odd choice (and the presence of a Nazi in this New England town in the first place) can perhaps be understood by recognizing Kindler as representing difference, not only because he is a German, but in another way, because he is so closely associated with Mary. She is isolated in her connection with him. Only she has chosen him; only she supports him. In a strange way, he represents her insofar as she is one who makes a sexual choice. He is Mary's difference. For fathers, and for small town America, this difference must be contained. In this deeply conservative film, Kindler's/Mary's difference must bring about his own downfall and her return. But his difference will also be recuperated. His exotic European hobby of fixing clocks will reinvigorate rural American tradition and law, as represented by the old town clock with its scenes of justice and revenge.

Wilson neatly describes the trajectory of the film: "Mary must be shown what kind of man she married, even though she'll resist hearing anything bad about Charles." And despite this resistance, they are sure that her "subconscious" is their "ally," that deep inside her she has a strong "will to truth." This resource of unconscious health will, of course, lead her to relinquish her own willful difference and allow herself to be returned to her father. Thus family (again with no mother) and town will return to their original situation. A triumph of personal and social stasis.

Touch of Evil offers a more ambiguous answer to the question: can the continued presence of woman-as-difference be tolerated? One of the strangest features of this film is the often comical forced separation of Suzie and Vargas which results from the pervasive contradiction between power and impotence, the search for and denial of sexual difference in Quinlan's character. Quinlan's regression to murder and other acts of vengeance was apparently triggered by the transgression of his young wife (with a sailor, as in ***Immortal Story*** and ***Lady from Shanghai***). He now seeks to rewrite his own history by preventing Vargas (the double of his younger, potent self) from taking the risks of coupling. Having become a candy eater whose memory of sexuality draws him into Tanya's place, Quinlan now tries to hold on to his conservative power, which effaces sexual difference in his second partnership—with Pete Menzies—in his racism, and in his excessive acts of fixing the fate of all transgressors (they are all "guilty as hell"). We must remember that the entire action of the film was triggered by the murder of a father by his daughter's Mexican lover—from the point of view of the father, so to speak, surely a wrong choice and indication of the dangers of difference. Thus Suzie, the often absurd woman-as-sexual-difference is drugged, and possibly raped (though even this sexuality is denied; she is lifted off the bed at the peak of the orgy scene, thus substantially altering the logistics of rape) and almost killed for expressing desire in the way she looks and acts. Throughout the film, she is pressured by both her husband and Quinlan's people to give up the promise of sexuality and return across the border to the US, to "safety," to the known, the predictable, the place of before-her-sexuality—the place, ostensibly, of her father. Mexico itself, like Vargas the Mexican, represents the exercise of difference, which is constantly exploding and making trouble. In the end, it is only partially controlled. When Suzie is finally reunited with Vargas in the car, his first moves toward her are not sexual, but like those of a child who needs to lean on his mother's breast. Yet the fact of the reconciliation itself implies that the conservative force of return has been resisted to some extent. Difference has been allowed some play.

In ***The Stranger,*** the control of the woman is far more complete. The dangers of active female sexuality and choice-making take on the resonance of a national and cultural disaster. Mary's father is a New England Supreme Court Justice named Adam, and her brother is named Noah. To defy them is to endanger all that's best in American culture and in the Bible as well. To prevent this, to bring the daughter back into the fold, the two fathers, Justice Longstreet and Detective Wilson, are willing to take extreme risks—with Mary's life, that is. They decide that Kindler's attempt to kill her will be the best "evidence" to convince her of whom she has really married, so they decide to use her as bait. Wilson: "Naturally, we'll try to prevent murder being done. . . . He may kill her. You're shocked at my coldbloodedness. That's quite natural. You're the father. . . . " Thus the fathers are split so that one can be conventionally horrified at the lengths to which the other is willing to go to bring her back into line. Then, since no other proof against Kindler exists, the gathering of evidence becomes a matter of watching Mary. Wilson: "From now on, we must know every move that Mrs. Rankin makes." Fathers, brother and servant combine to watch and control her, but even so, she eludes them, rushing off through the graveyard to kill or be killed on the clock tower. In the end, at the top of the tower, the Nazi gets his comeuppance, brought about by the fathers, but executed by a female avenging angel just as deadly as the daughter in ***Touch of Evil.*** Kindler is impaled on the sword of the clockwork angel, screaming in pain during this dreadful parody of an embrace. Kindler deserves it, of course, at the rational plot level. But the point is that in these films, the aroused woman, the sign of difference as danger, evoking the threat of lack (inadequacy?), is not often so genteel as Lucy in ***Magnificent Ambersons.*** It is usually a struggle to force her into passivity and return, and often a lethal one.

The conservativism revealed in some of these narratives is often contradicted in the films' means of expression, which is also marked by a kind of excess. It is, of course, well known that in the Welles films, the conventions of classical cinema are either abandoned or exaggerated to fascinating extremes. The discreetly moving or subjective camera, the illusion of three-dimensionality through depth of field, become the bizarre angles, sweeping crane shots, and dwarfing depth and scale that mark several of these texts. Even expressionistic features are taken further as light and shadow become patches of saturated darkness and blinding brightness. ***Citizen Kane*** particularly is marked by the excitement of what Julia Kristeva calls "an excess of visual traces useless for the sheer identification of objects." In the projection room sequence, where light is used, not to illuminate, but as having sign value in itself, and in other sequences like the travelling shot up the facade and through the sign of Susan's night club, and the shot up to the stagehand "critics" at the Opera House, these visual excesses and special effects convey a pleasure taken at the point of enunciation, an exuberance in the aggressive wielding of the language of film. Like Charles with his "Declaration of Principles," this enunciation declares itself boldly.

Later on, as Kane receives his "more than one lesson," the power of youth to transform aggressiveness into exuberance seems diminished and the tone changes. In relation to the negative narrative changes that they mark in scenes like the party with the dancing girls or Susan's suicide attempt, the wide angle lens and extreme camera positions now seem to invite reading as signals of distress, an enunciative energy somehow grown perverse. Sometimes, as in the eerie, empty space of Jed Leland's hospital, visual work and characterization would suggest that seeing has now become the mutual recognition of grotesquery. The long, slow-moving, sinuous takes in ***Magnificent Ambersons,*** particularly in the party sequence, suggest, not freedom of choice in processing a simulacrum of reality, but enunciative awareness of the hopelessly desirable dream of seamless flow and oneness in the world of the mother. This movement is prefigured in the flowing overhead shots of Kane's fragmented plenitude at the end of ***Kane,*** and would have been even more pronounced in its seemingly endless withholding of expected cuts in the party sequence had the film been released as Welles intended, with reel-length shots during this portion of the film.

The excess of these images also raises the question of "evidence," which is central to a number of Welles films and which becomes dominant in all the foregrounded systems of ***F for Fake.*** In the projection room sequence of ***Kane,*** for instance, light is the elusive stuff of which delusive biography is made, no more reliable than the various embedded tales of unfulfilled desire (Leland's, Susan's, Bernstein's—remember the girl in white on the ferry boat?) that make up the film's narrative. Excessive light and shadow actually deny access to images as representations, and raise the question of how they can be used as evidence, and evidence of what, setting the act of seeing over against the structuring absence of knowledge or explanation. In ***The Stranger,*** though Wilson offers Mary filmed images of the concentration camps as evidence of her husband's evil, he does not let them stand on their own. Instead, he places himself in the image or projects the images onto himself, making his body and the field of his features into the evidence, as if asserting: "Even if the images are functional representations, trust and believe *me.* I who speak am the greater authority." ***The Stranger*** is one of Welles's more visually and narratively conventional films. As its "realism" is less distressed, so the power of the law is not undermined. Wilson's authority as enunciator of diegetic truth is allowed to remain, at the partial cost of Welles's authority and presence as the film's enunciator. We observe a similar substitution of bodies (Hastler's and K's) for the "pin-screen" images of the "Law" fable where Hastler is trying to convince K of its immutability in ***The Trial.*** As Mary's body was to be watched for the invocation of evidence in ***The Stranger,*** so Virginie's sexual act will become the "final evidence" of Clay's guilt in ***The Immortal Story.*** And Pete Menzies's wiretapped body becomes the site of aural evidence in ***Touch of Evil,*** the reliability of so-called "concrete" evidence having been disposed of in the planting of the dynamite and in the history of Quinlan's entire career of manipulating "evidence."

The authority of the enunciation, the aggressiveness of the intention, is substituted for the trustworthiness of the evidence itself (perhaps suggestive of the particular way in which Welles has loved to use make-up as clearly enunciated, nonrealistic masking throughout his career, combining the contradictory qualities of an identity always recognized and a disguise insisted upon with equal clarity).

The figure of the Power Baby condenses certain irreconcilable contradictions and diffusions that we have been examining in plot, character, and visual development. These can be represented through various discourses about the subversion of the unified subject. The Power Baby's constitution in doubleness is exaggerated by the failure of the family experience to mitigate the father-related excess and rage on the one hand, and the mother-related helpless dependency on the other. The family's failure, in turn, is often seen as produced, not only by the woman's ability to confound the issue of paternity in a number of different ways, but also by the changing patterns of money and urbanization at different points in American history, by the ideologies that say banks are better than families for promoting children, that move Isabel to choose Wilbur Minafer, that conflate law and vengeance in border towns.

As we learn from the voice-over narrator at the beginning of ***Magnificent Ambersons,*** this ideology uses fashion, money, and media to create the only possible categories of identity into which the sexed subject must be forced. It also conflates female sexuality and lethal threats by posing difference as danger or disruption that is sometimes fully contained, sometimes a little too powerful for conservative strategies, and sometimes ironically (***Immortal Story***) or fully (***F for Fake***) triumphant.

George Orson Welles, age 5.

In each Power Baby, we have found an imagined social self with aspirations to greatness and total love that can only be dreams, founded in misrecognitions of both self and the social world. These mistakes are perfectly expressed in ***Immortal Story*** where the clerk, Levinsky, tells us that Mr. Clay wants "to demonstrate his omnipotence—to do the thing which cannot be done." And within the "I" together with this overreaching social self, one and the same and yet another, is a wildly flailing infant (we see him destroy Susan's room) fixed in incomprehension, terror, and rage, who returns to undo all social work and to reduce the organism to blank helplessness: the Wellesian "I" as the extremes of power and powerlessness.

The various stories of the Power Baby can also be seen as the refusal of the subject to be constituted in continuous narrative. Both Charles and Georgie are presented through versions of the *Bildung* structure that typically would move the subject from childhood through young manhood to "maturity." This form carries the conventional assumption of the infant born in powerlessness, a tabula rasa who gains experience and knowledge that become integrated into the increasing wisdom and power of the mature self. Thus in the insistence on the return to earlier scenes and conditions, these narratives deny this trajectory, using the *Bildung* narrative no less ironically than that of the retrospective biography.

For himself, his family, and his women, the Power Baby refuses the myth of personal harmony. Sometimes struggling for conservation and stasis, sometimes, as in ***F for Fake,*** flaunting multiplicity and difference, Welles the enunciator asserts the primacy of the individual without the comfort of the unified self. (pp. 2-12)

Beverle Houston, "Power and Dis-Integration in the Films of Orson Welles," in Film Quarterly, *Vol. XXXV, No. 4, Summer, 1982, pp. 2-12.*

Susan McCloskey (essay date Winter 1985)

[*McCloskey is an American educator who has written extensively on the major English dramatists. In the following excerpt from her essay "Shakespeare, Orson Welles, and the 'Voodoo'* Macbeth,*" she examines how Welles's 1936 stage production of* Macbeth *transformed Shakespeare's tragedy into a melodrama on the nature of evil.*]

Shortly after the discovery of Duncan's murder, daybreak scatters pale light over the castle's tower, battlements, and gateway. The courtiers have withdrawn confusedly to their chambers, Malcolm has fled, and Macbeth, alone in the courtyard, sits on the dead king's throne.

The castle gates swing slowly open. A grotesquely distorted figure appears, followed by another such figure, then another, and another. As Macbeth looks on, appalled and fascinated, these cripples drag their limbless, sightless, or diseased bodies across the courtyard toward the throne.

Macbeth's body tenses as the cripples approach. His alarm grows when voices from a great distance hail him as king. Suddenly, those voices are near at hand, on the battlements directly above the throne. Three voodoo priestesses huddle together there, chanting to the pounding of invisible drums. The pale dawn sky turns an angry red, the drums beat more insistently, the women's voices grow louder, and the cripples draw closer to the throne.

Far above the throne, on the roof of the tower, Hecate appears, arms outstretched, his black-cloaked figure silhouetted against the red sky. At the sound of his voice, the cripples stop moving and the priestesses cease their chant. In the stillness, Hecate looks down at Macbeth and curses him. On the last word of the curse, the drums sound once, then are silent, and the sky fades to black.

At the Lafayette Theatre in Harlem on 14 April 1936, the house lights came up at this point, closing the first act of what came to be known as the "Voodoo" ***Macbeth.*** Several months earlier, a newcomer to the New York stage, Orson Welles, had been invited to direct a classic play for the Federal Theatre's Negro Theatre Project. He chose *Macbeth* after his wife, Virginia Nicholson, suggested a production set in Haiti, with the witches as voodoo priestesses. Turning this idea into theatrical reality, Welles made theatrical history. The "Voodoo" ***Macbeth*** was the first black professional production of Shakespeare, an important critical and commercial success for the Federal Theatre, and an appropriately dazzling debut for its twenty-year-old director. It was also a respectful and irreverent, occasionally clumsy and frequently brilliant adaptation of Shakespeare's play.

Welles's remaking of *Macbeth,* and what that remaking reveals about the original play, are my subjects here. The scene I've described above, for instance, is typical of the production, and illustrates Welles's methods and aims as an adapter. It is one of the many episodes he created by borrowing and rearranging lines from other scenes. Its flamboyant theatricality indicates how he turned into an occasion for spectacle the intensely private drama that Shakespeare enacted in Macbeth's mind. He filled scene after scene with startling images and sounds, bringing to the entire production the kind of theatrical display that Shakespeare had reserved for the witches' scenes. He also stressed the original play's affinities with melodrama—the witches and their malevolence, the increasingly clear discrimination of goodness from evil, the way certain scenes, such as Lady Macduff's murder, drive toward a single, intense emotional effect. He invented the melodrama he did not find, turning Shakespeare's tragedy of a man divided against himself into the story of a good man victimized by evil forces. By the time he presented the results of his work to his first audience at the Lafayette, Welles had reduced by half the length of Shakespeare's script, redefined the play's world, enlarged the witches' roles, revised Shakespeare's characterizations, and altered *Macbeth*'s meanings. In other words, as the title page of the working script quite accurately declared, this was a production of "*Macbeth* by William Shakespeare, Negro Version, Conceived, Arranged, Staged by Orson Welles."

Some of Welles's changes in Shakespeare's text indicate that the idea of *Macbeth* set in Haiti was easier to conceive than to realize. Shakespeare presented Welles with problems more severe than an occasional reference to Saint Colme's Inch or the Western Isles. For in all his plays he located his characters not only in a particular place, but in a particular culture. The business of telling us where his characters are was quickly dispatched: "This is Illyria, lady," or "Well, this is the forest of Arden." And so was the work of establishing the situation: as they keep watch on Elsinore's ramparts, Horatio, Barnardo, and Marcellus reconstruct the recent history of Denmark. But long after Shakespeare had situated his characters in space and circumstance, the work of rendering their worlds continued. And because Welles wanted to change one of those worlds, he discovered the sturdy material of which it was made.

That Shakespeare neither possessed nor required elaborate stage sets and a wardrobe of period costumes is well known. At the Globe, a production of *Macbeth* would have looked very much like a production of *Lear* or even *Twelfth Night:* all three plays would have been performed by roughly the same company of actors, dressed in the clothing of their own day, appearing on the same platform, under the same heavens, and in front of the same architectural facade. To distinguish Scotland from ancient Britain or Illyria, Shakespeare had to rely on the suggestive as well as the descriptive powers of his language, and on his audience's powers of inference. He fashioned his worlds, that is, not only *in* but *between* and *behind* his characters' lines. Their words imply the beliefs, assumptions, values, and attitudes from which the audience derives its sense of a cultural context. Gestures and actions, ranging from a bow at greeting through the sharing of a meal to the performance of ceremonies, similarly reveal the protocols, customs, and traditions of the societies represented onstage. When Welles came to move *Macbeth*'s characters from feudal Scotland to nineteenth-century Haiti, then, he rediscovered afresh what he may already have known: nothing is harder to suppress in a text than an unspoken assumption, an implicit framework of values, or a character's taking for granted a particular social order, political structure, or system of belief.

The bleeding sergeant's report to Duncan in Act I, scene ii of *Macbeth* illustrates Welles's problem. Had Shakespeare used the scene to communicate only details of the plot—that Macbeth has defeated the traitor Macdonwald, that he and Banquo have combined their strength against Norway's invading army—Welles could simply have substituted Haitian names, titles, and places for Scottish ones. But Shakespeare was not so obliging. By the time the sergeant is carried offstage at line 44, the style of his speech, its explicit and implicit content, the manner of his speaking, the response he generates, and a few scripted details of performance have cooperated to locate the men onstage in a medieval, hierarchical, Christian world, where martial valor is valued and treason despised, and where an aging but still powerful king presides. We come to know all this in a matter of seconds by means both obvious and subtle. Duncan's retinue, for instance, signals his power; the presence of his adult son determines his age. References to rank and titles—"sergeant," "king," "captain," "lord," "gentleman"—indicate the kingdom's political and military hierarchies. The sergeant's formal diction is appropriate to a subordinate addressing his superior. What he describes prompts him to astonishing eloquence, and so testifies to what he most esteems and condemns: on the one hand, bravery and loyalty; on the other, treason. Most significantly, the sergeant's values are shared by others. His auditors understand his allusion to Golgotha. His vivid image of Macbeth unseaming Macdonwald "from the nave to th' chops" prompts Duncan to exclaim: "O valiant cousin! Worthy gentleman!" (I.ii.22, 24). The bleeding sergeant, in short, is no mere bearer of tidings. Shakespeare used his brief scene to sketch the contours of the play's world.

By weaving a particular conception of Scotland so intricately into the warp and woof of the sergeant's language and action, Shakespeare left Welles little choice but to cut the scene entirely. The world it assumes could not be made consonant with a nineteenth-century West Indian world, where former French colonials battled against supernatural powers, not invading armies. And the bleeding sergeant's scene is merely the first of many in which Scotland comes to represent the ideals Macbeth destroys. Because Duncan initially embodies those ideals, Welles had to minimize his importance by reducing or canceling his scenes. In place of the third-act banquet imaging Scotland's collapse, Welles offered a gala coronation ball, at which men and women in evening dress danced to Josef Lanner waltzes while butlers moved among them, distributing drinks from silver trays. He also canceled from the later acts most of the passages in which Scotland's distress becomes a reiterated theme. No anonymous lord yearned for the Scotland where men might once again "give to [their] tables meat, sleep to [their] nights" (III.vi.34); Macduff did not grieve for the land where "Each new morn / New widows howl, new orphans cry" (IV.iii.4-5). And when Welles's Macbeth, like Shakespeare's, considered the "honor, love, obedience, troops of friends" he "must not look to have" (V.iii.25-26), the lines lost much of their force, for Welles's Macbeth had not inhabited a world where such things were prized.

Clearly, Welles calculated Scotland's loss against what he gained by transporting the play to Haiti. His largest gain was the chance to turn *Macbeth* into a theatrical tour de force. He filled the great vacancy where Scotland had been by making costumes, stage sets, sound effects, and lighting do the work of Shakespeare's world-making words. And he made no apology for the substitution. Everything about his production was big, startling, almost impossibly lavish, and loud. *Macbeth* in 1606 had required at most a company of fourteen actors; Welles employed a cast and crew of 137. His actors appeared in Nat Karson's elegant adaptations of Directoire clothing, a visual reminder of Haiti's colonial affiliation with Napoleon's empire. According to one reviewer, Macduff's "satin-striped red and white breeches," Macbeth's "military costumes of canary yellow and emerald green," the women's dresses of "salmon pink and purple" gave the production "a hot richness." Outsized epaulettes decorated the shoulders of the men's close-fitting coats; Macbeth's soldiers strode about the stage in stove-pipe hats that must have measured nearly two feet from brim to crown. Karson also designed for the proscenium stage a castle set, complete with tower, battlements, staircases, and a massive central gateway. During the scenes in the jungle, this set was concealed behind backdrops; on one of them, luxuriant vegetation coiled into the shape of a recumbent human skeleton. The production pulsed with the sounds of voodoo drums and chantings, thunder, wails, bells, and the report of pistol fire. Banquo's ghost became a huge mask looming in the castle gateway. Abe Feder lit the cauldron scene with strobes. And when the script called for Birnam Wood to move against Dunsinane, Welles contented himself with no sorry wisps of evergreen: instead, a jungle rose over the castle's battlements, burgeoned through the gateway, and filled the stage in the play's final scene.

Haiti offered Welles more, however, than the opportunity for spectacle on a grand scale. The new setting solved the practical problem of presenting black actors as medieval Scots. Haiti's geography also aided Welles's melodramatic rendering of the play, providing him with the enclosed space and vivid contrasts on which melodrama relies. He made the island a prison from which escape was impossible; Malcolm's and Macduff's quest for safety carried them not to an English haven, but to a barren stretch of Haitian seacoast. Similarly, Haiti's history of colonial rebellion and civil war warranted Welles's presentation of a world divided against itself, defined by the contrast between the jungle and the Francophile court. At once primitive and sophisticated, vibrant and doomed, the expression of tribal nightmare and elegant fantasy, Welles's Haiti was also the place where witchcraft, in the form of voodoo, was widely supposed to be practiced. The setting that began as a novel idea ended by solving the most persistent difficulty in staging *Macbeth:* the problem of the witches.

Macbeth's stage history testifies to the ingeniousness of Welles's solution. Producers from Davenant's time to our own day have met the problem either by making the witches inoffensive to the audience's daylight sense, or by making them so fantastic that the offense is welcome. Welles's choice of a setting already associated with the practice of black magic enabled him to authenticate his witches without resort to Halloween costumes or subliminal effects. As Brooks Atkinson observed in his review, Welles avoided the "disenchantment" that the witches' scenes so often effect, with "the grimaces of the hags and the garish make-believe of the flaming cauldron":

> But ship the witches down into the rank and fever-stricken jungles of Haiti, dress them in fantastic costumes, crowd the stage with mad and gabbling throngs of evil worshipers, beat the voodoo drums, raise the voices until the jungle echoes, stuff a gleaming naked witch doctor into the cauldron, hold up Negro masks in the baleful light—and there you have a witches' scene that

> is logical and stunning and a triumph of theatre art.

Indeed, so completely was Welles's idea within the pale of probability that he was able to hire a troupe of African drummers, led by a genuine witch doctor named Abdul. When they arrived for rehearsals, they promptly requested five black goats for a ritual sacrifice; they later put a hex on a critic who panned the production.

The witches justified Welles's choice of Haiti, however, only after he had radically altered Shakespeare's text. For Shakespeare's witches were not, as Welles wished them to be, *the* defining feature of the play's world. In the original text, they appear in only four scenes (three, if one excludes the suspect III.v). Minor characters, such as Ross and Lennox, appear more frequently, and between them speak more than the witches' 184 lines. Welles dealt with this problem initially by exacerbating it: he cut all but two lines from the witches' first scene (I.i); he used only ten of the thirty-seven lines they speak before Macbeth's entrance in I.iii; and he reduced the cauldron scene by well over one-third. III.v alone survived with only minor cuts, although Welles scattered pieces of it throughout his version.

What Welles sacrificed in the lines, however, he recovered by theatrical means, and moved the witches from *Macbeth*'s periphery to his production's very center. Hecate, the three witches, and their fellow voodoo celebrants—forty-three in all—dominated the Lafayette's stage as the curtain rose, and held it through and after the first scene's meeting with Macbeth. The entire group reassembled for the cauldron scene. Welles also brought them onstage as silent witnesses to scenes from which Shakespeare had excluded them, such as Banquo's murder and the sleepwalking scene. Occasionally, their silence was broken by demonic cackling, or by the chanting of lines picked up from Shakespeare's third scene. When they appeared on the ramparts after Duncan's murder, for instance, they chanted "Weary sev'nnights, nine times nine, / Shall he dwindle, peak, and pine," as they watched Macbeth slumped on the throne beneath them (I.iii.22-23). Even when they were offstage, the sounds of their drums and chants could be heard from the wings. By such means, Welles introduced the witches into all but two of his production's eight scenes. They were absent (and silent) only during the slaughter of the Macduffs, and through Malcolm's and Macduff's interview.

Hecate provided Welles with his principal means to highlight the witches' importance. In his production, Hecate was nearly as central to the action as Macbeth—a change accomplished largely through line-reassignments. The part was played not by a woman, but by Eric Burroughs, the single member of the company who had received training as a classical actor. Bare-chested, his hair in dreadlocks, and a twelve-foot-long bullwhip in hand, he appeared to mark each stage of Macbeth's descent into hell: at the first meeting, after Duncan's murder, after the coronation ball, during the cauldron scene, and at the end of the play with the production's final line, "Peace, the charm's wound up!" (I.iii.37). Hecate appeared too in less expected contexts, speaking other characters' lines with chilling effect. He took on, for instance, the role of the Third Murderer. Later, he goaded Macbeth to the slaughter of the Macduffs (" . . . give to th' edge o' th' sword / His wife, his babes . . . " [IV.i.151-52]). And as Malcolm's troops moved against Macbeth, Hecate joined them, advising the soldiers to hew down the boughs of Birnam Wood.

By making the witches figure so prominently in the action, Welles solved the second problem that Shakespeare's text had presented to him. For Shakespeare's witches not only appear infrequently, but exercise severely constrained powers—far too constrained for Welles, who wished to present them as irresistible forces. In Shakespeare's play, they work their mischief through their powers of suggestion. Hecate herself regards them as mere specialists in malicious mischief, who need her aid to carry out the "great business" of Macbeth's destruction (III.v.22). But because Welles's witches were present at or near the crucial moments in the play, and in almost continuous contact with Macbeth, they seemed enormously powerful. Banquo's murder alone required their resort to force. Otherwise, their very numbers were daunting, and the mere sound of their drums and chants sufficed to make Macbeth do their bidding.

By redefining the witches' roles, Welles achieved the convincing physical embodiment of evil on which his production's melodramatic design depended. His witches occupied the dark side of Haiti's Manichaean world, gathering to themselves the power against which the court had no defense. Indeed, they treated Macbeth's destruction as an almost incidental skirmish in their campaign to wrest control of the island. As soon as Macbeth came under their spell, they began to move from the jungle into the palace. After Duncan's assassination, they appeared on the battlements. After Banquo's ghost disrupted the ball, Hecate came through the castle's gateway to lead Macbeth to the witches. By Welles's last act, the witches had penetrated as far as Lady Macbeth's chamber, to attend her in her madness. In the last scene, they huddled beside Macbeth and Macduff as they fought, greeting each thrust and parry of the swords with delighted squeals and shrieks. Having begun the play by casting a spell over Macbeth alone, they closed it by enthralling the entire court. The pattern of their steady encroachment, the relentless extension of their influence, redefined the shape of the play's action, and transformed *Macbeth* from a tragedy of character into a melodrama of supernatural imperialism. (pp. 406-12)

The changes Welles made in *Macbeth*'s world, witches, and human characters inevitably transformed the play's meanings. Familiar descriptions of what *Macbeth* is "about" apply only remotely to Welles's version. What he presented on the Lafayette's stage dealt neither with Macbeth's ambition, nor with his failed efforts to extinguish his conscience, nor with his imagination's atrophy. Welles was not interested in issues of fate or nihilism, in the irrevocable connection between act and consequence, or in Macbeth's futile efforts to realize the future in the present. Concerned instead with the nature of evil, Welles adapted *Macbeth* to focus on that issue alone, through the experience of a man seduced and destroyed by supernatural forces.

The consequences of this single, simplified focus can best be seen in Welles's handling of Shakespeare's Act IV, scene iii, Malcolm's long interview with Macduff. In the original play's design, the scene's thematic significance is hard to overestimate; Shakespeare did no less than to summarize and then revise *Macbeth*'s political, spiritual, and moral concerns. Malcolm begins the scene with the equivocations and concealed purposes that previous acts have made familiar. In testing Macduff, he proposes a desperate model of political recovery, the exchange of a bad ruler for a worse. His anatomy of corrupt kingship at once indicts Macbeth and implies a positive standard, which Malcolm later defines in his catalogue of the "king-becoming graces" (IV.iii.91). By the time he has driven Macduff to his "noble passion" and ended his self-slandering, Malcolm has promised to Scotland a virtuous king and a new political order (IV.iii.114). The scene's second segment, in which we hear of King Edward's gifts of healing and prophecy, elaborates the ideal of kingship in spiritual terms, restoring once again the standard Macbeth has violated. The last segment, focusing on Macduff 's response to the news of his family's slaughter, enacts in the private sphere a partial recovery of order. Resisting Malcolm's incitements to revenge, Macduff first feels the pain of his loss before committing himself to action. His slow adjustment to his loss emphasizes the scene's dominant characteristic: its sheer duration. Here in an English garden, speech, understanding, the renewal of hope, the accommodation of deep grief *take time*. In Scotland, by contrast, where Macbeth has so feverishly tried to "jump the life to come" (I.vii.7), time itself has been disrupted—a disorder imaged with special force in Macbeth's refusal to allow his enemies' children to grow to adulthood.

Welles's version did not and could not enact this scene's restoration of public and private, temporal and spiritual order. His earlier scenes had not introduced such matters for eventual resolution. The scene's focus on men in the act of *speaking* offered small opportunity for theatrical fireworks. Welles cut half the lines, retaining only those that enabled him to get on with the business of the plot. The scene drove swiftly to Malcolm's and Macduff 's understanding, without pausing to specify its terms. The episode with the English Doctor was cut entirely, because Welles earlier ascribed King Edward's powers to Duncan. Macduff heard Ross's calamitous news, and committed himself to avenging his family's slaughter without passing through the stage of self-recrimination (even though Welles's Macduff had ample warrant for self-reproach). The editing erased the distinctions of setting, content, and pace that Shakespeare had drawn between this scene and all the others in the play. Welles's scene made plain that Macbeth's tyranny was about to be opposed; Shakespeare's, by contrast, told us why, how, and most importantly, by what it would be replaced.

In all his transactions with Shakespeare's text, Welles ventured a great deal in the hope of great returns. Sometimes his hopes were justified. What he lost by changing the play's world or by elaborating the witches' roles, he regained in spectacle and excitement. His opening-night audience at the Lafayette rose to its feet and cheered when the cast took its bows. Sometimes, however, as in the scene between Malcolm and Macduff, Welles's gamble failed to pay off. What he lost in his characters' diminished interest or through his narrowing of the original play's scope, he could never fully recover.

Conventional wisdom tells us, though, that winning or losing matters less than how Welles played the game. He adapted Shakespeare with evident gusto, rising to *Macbeth*'s challenges, taking the measure of Shakespeare's art. Before he could turn Scotland into an exotic West Indian island, he had to decipher Shakespeare's ways of world-making and then devise a strategy of his own. Before multiplying Shakespeare's three Weird Sisters into a phalanx of voodoo worshipers, he had to chart and then adjust the original play's dynamics. Only by examining Shakespeare's characterizations of morally responsible men and women could he recast them as victims of witchcraft. Only by coming to terms with Shakespeare's meanings could he reshape them to his very different design. On the one hand, then, Welles's adaptation sends us back to the original with renewed appreciation. The problems he encountered point to the unity of *Macbeth*'s conception, the interconnectedness of its world and its action, its characters and its meaning, its individual scenes and the harmonies of the whole. Welles's successes, on the other hand, suggest the *Macbeth* that might have been had Shakespeare commanded the resources of a modern theatre. Indeed, the "Voodoo" ***Macbeth*** makes one wonder, almost as if under the influence of a spell, what kind of theatre artist Shakespeare would have been had he also been Orson Welles. (pp. 414-16)

Susan McCloskey, "Shakespeare, Orson Welles, and the 'Voodoo' 'Macbeth'," in Shakespeare Quarterly, *Vol. 36, No. 4, Winter, 1985, pp. 406-16.*

Welles on William Randolph Hearst:

I met him once in an elevator in San Francisco, on the opening night of *Citizen Kane* there. I introduced myself. This strange dinosaur, he had ice-cold blue eyes and a very high, eunuchoid voice. I just said that I had some good tickets for the opening of *Citizen Kane*. Would he like to come? He didn't answer and I got off the elevator thinking, as I still do, that if he'd been Charles Foster Kane he would have taken the tickets and gone.

Welles, in an interview with Leslie Megahey, in The Listener, *20 May 1982.*

Robert L. Carringer (essay date 1985)

[Carringer is an American professor of literature and film. In addition to The Making of "Citizen Kane," *he has written* "The Magnificent Ambersons": A Reconstruction, *which includes a version of Welles's original screenplay. In the following excerpt from the former*

work, Carringer details the development of the Citizen Kane *screenplay and the controversy surrounding its authorship.*]

Welles's first step toward the realization of ***Citizen Kane*** was to seek the assistance of a screenwriting professional. Fortunately, help was near at hand. Writing talent had always been in short supply in the Mercury [Theater] operation because of the inexorable demands of the weekly radio shows. When Welles moved to Hollywood, it happened that a veteran screenwriter, Herman J. Mankiewicz, was recuperating from an automobile accident and between jobs. Mankiewicz was signed to write scripts for the Mercury's "Campbell Playhouse" radio program. When the opportunity to work on a screenplay for the Mercury presented itself, Mankiewicz was still available, and he took on this additional assignment as well.

Mankiewicz was an expatriate from Broadway who had been writing for films for almost fifteen years. He had anticipated a trend in 1926 when, as an aspiring young writer, critic, and playwright, he had answered Hollywood's call. Unlike others who took seasonal contracts and used their lucrative screenwriting salaries to support what they regarded as their real work back East, Mankiewicz stayed on and worked almost exclusively in films until his death in 1953. In the early years, he mainly wrote intertitles for silent films. After sound came in, he did his best work in comedy. His credits include select specimens of sophisticated dialogue comedy (*Laughter, Royal Family of Broadway, Dinner at Eight*) and of the anarchic farce associated especially with the Marx Brothers (*Monkey Business, Horse Feathers*) and W. C. Fields (*Million Dollar Legs*). In his film work, Mankiewicz was never known as a distance runner; in all the examples just cited, he received either screenplay co-credit or some special form of billing, such as associate producer. In contrast, writers like Ben Hecht and Samson Raphaelson were getting sole or top screenwriting billing on their best comedy scripts. Mankiewicz hit his peak in 1934 and 1935, when he received sole screenwriter credit on four films at MGM—*The Show-off* (with Spencer Tracy), *Stamboul Quest* (with Myrna Loy and George Brent), *After Office Hours* (with Clark Gable), and *Escapade* (with Luise Rainer, who was making her American debut). After that, his output fell dramatically. Between 1935 and the time when he was assigned to ***Citizen Kane,*** he received screenplay credit on only two films. Not that this state of affairs was really disadvantageous to Welles. He lacked the patience that original story construction requires. He preferred to start with a rough diamond and do just the cutting and polishing himself. Besides, a more secure and better-established writer would almost certainly insist on prerogatives. As things stood, Mankiewicz was hardly in a position to make demands.

Whether Welles or Mankiewicz came up with the idea for a send-up of William Randolph Hearst is a matter of dispute. Welles claims he did. The Mankiewicz partisans—chiefly Pauline Kael (and through her Mankiewicz's widow Sara) and John Houseman—say it was the other way around. Kael maintains that Mankiewicz had been toying with the idea for years. She reports the testimony of a former Mankiewicz baby-sitter that she took dictation

Welles with Herman J. Mankiewicz—co-authors of the Citizen Kane *screenplay. Mankiewicz's other credits include writing the intertitles for some of Josef von Sternberg's silent films, producing some of the Marx Brothers movies, and the* Pride of the Yankees *screenplay.*

from Mankiewicz on a flashback screenplay involving Hearst even before he went to Hollywood. Houseman, who had broken with Welles and the Mercury by this time, writes in his memoirs that Welles sought him out in New York and pleaded with him to come back and help with a screenplay idea that, Welles said, had been proposed by Mankiewicz. The conversation is said to have taken place at "21" shortly after the first of the year in 1940. But in an affidavit taken at the time of the film's release, Mercury assistant Richard Baer swore that the original idea was first broached by Welles at the "21" luncheon and that Welles and Houseman, who agreed to sign on, approached Mankiewicz about it back in California. We will probably never know for sure, but in any case Welles had at last found a subject with the right combination of monumentality, timeliness, and audacity. Lampooning Hearst was nothing new; he had been at the center of controversy for his entire public life. But in the 1930s it became commonplace to question or even attack the older ideal of America and the system of values that Hearst represented. (Even FDR spoke out against the possessors of "self-serving wealth," such as Hearst, branding them enemies of the republic and obstacles to social reform.) Nor was the tabloid angle on Hearst's personal life as original a stroke as it has been made out to be. In his 1939 novel *After Many a Summer Dies the Swan,* Aldous Huxley had been far nastier in his insinuations about Hearst and Marion Davies than anything in the ***Citizen***

Kane scripts. What was new was to take on Hearst from within Hollywood, where he had enormous influence and power to retaliate and was almost universally feared.

For obvious reasons, the project needed to be kept as quiet as possible. Consequently, it was decided that Mankiewicz would do his work away from Hollywood. There was another motive for this, too: Mankiewicz had a drinking problem (the main cause of his career decline). Houseman would go along to provide assistance but also to keep Mankiewicz out of trouble and on course. Mankiewicz went on the RKO payroll on February 19, 1940. He was to receive $1,000 a week, with a bonus of $5,000 on delivery of the script. During the last week in February or the first week in March, he and Houseman, together with a secretary, Rita Alexander, went into seclusion at a guest ranch in the desert at Victorville, California, several hours' drive from Hollywood. There, during March, April, and early May, 1940, the first installments of the ***Citizen Kane*** script were written. First and second drafts were completed during this period. Alexander took them down from Mankiewicz's dictation; Houseman served as editor. In his lengthy account of the Victorville interlude, Houseman gives the impression that Mankiewicz started out with a clean slate and that virtually everything in the Victorville drafts is Mankiewicz's original invention. Kael made the same assumption. In arguing the case for Mankiewicz's authorship, she placed a great deal of emphasis on prior activities that were circumstantially parallel—for instance, that he had written unproduced screenplays based on Aimee Semple McPherson and John Dillinger that employed the device of multiple narration. For his part, Welles says he had lengthy discussions with Mankiewicz about the story before Mankiewicz left for Victorville. (He concludes that Mankiewicz never admitted this to Houseman or anyone else involved.) Welles gave [director and critic Peter] Bogdanovich some examples of story incidents in the script he said originated with him. By looking into Welles's past for evidence, as Kael did into Mankiewicz's, we come up with other possibilities that would seem to substantiate his claim. For instance, the unmade *Smiler With the Knife* would also have been an attack on a controversial contemporary figure. In fact, in Welles's script, the Howard Hughes figure would have been introduced to an audience in the film by means of a "March of Time" newsreel feature. There is another set of tantalizing parallels: A 1936 "March of Time" radio broadcast included an obituary of munitions tycoon Sir Basil Zaharoff, with invented dramatic episodes. In the opening scene, secretaries are burning Zaharoff's papers in the immense fireplace in the great hall of his chateau—the secret records (the narrator tells us) of a lifetime's involvement in wars, plots, revolutions, and assassinations. Other scenes present witnesses who testify to Zaharoff's ruthlessness. Finally, Zaharoff himself appears—an old man nearing death, alone except for servants in the gigantic palace in Monte Carlo that he had acquired for his longtime mistress. His dying wish is to be wheeled out "in the sun by that rosebush." Welles played Zaharoff.

In mid April, after six weeks of work, Mankiewicz and Houseman sent down a first rough draft. More than 250 pages long, *American,* as it was called, was what rough drafts usually are—excessive in content and lacking in focus. But nevertheless it provided what was most needed at this stage: a firm story structure on which to build.

American is the biography of a publishing tycoon and public figure told in retrospect after his death by the persons who had known him best. A similar plot premise had been used in *The Power and the Glory* (1933), directed by William K. Howard from a script by Preston Sturges, in which Spencer Tracy portrayed a controversial railroad magnate who was revered by a faithful few but detested by the many. One of the main weaknesses of that film is the cumbrousness of its flashback structure. To compensate for this tendency of multiple flashback plots, Mankiewicz came up with an ingeniously simple plot device—a mysterious deathbed utterance that is presumed to be the key to everything. Rosebud is a rather shameless piece of melodramatic gimmickry, but it is arguably a more effective narrative device than Welles's original idea of making the object of mystery something literary, such as a line from a Romantic poem. (Welles has always ceded the Rosebud gimmick to Mankiewicz.)

Equally as important as Rosebud is the cast of supporting characters, a gallery of stereotypes, admittedly, but an interesting and very serviceable variety: parents of humble origin from the West, a Wall Street tycoon, a pragmatic business manager, a stuffy first wife of enormous social standing, a somewhat dandified closest friend, and a shopgirl mistress.

About two-thirds of the way through *American,* there is a large story gap—probably an indication that the draft sent down at someone's insistence was incomplete. The missing portion would come to include all of Kane's early relationship with Susan—their meeting, the love nest, their marriage, her singing career. But after the gap, *American* resumes with another firm plot situation, the elderly Kane withdrawn with Susan to Xanadu, and it concludes with the identification of the rosebud clue for the audience.

Structurally, *American* has roughly the narrative order that the final ***Kane*** shooting script will have, and some of the material (especially in the first third) will remain substantially the same. But there are also some serious problems. To begin with, considerable paring is needed. Many scenes are undeveloped, superfluous, or merely dull. Among the most expendable material in *American* are scenes of Thatcher visiting Kane at his Renaissance palace in Rome on his twenty-fifth birthday to discuss the future management of Kane's interest; of Kane's honeymoon with Emily in the remote Wisconsin woods, with an army of chefs and servants in attendance (Kane's yacht, which had to be shipped up piece by piece and reassembled, is anchored in a small lake nearby); of a subplot involving Kane and the president, an oil scandal, and an inflammatory editorial that leads to an assassination attempt; of a chance meeting between Kane and his father at the theater one evening, the latter in the company of a "young tart" who turns out to be his new wife; of Kane's discovery of an affair between Susan and a young lover at Xanadu (Kane has him killed); and of the funeral of Kane's son (he was shot when he and other members of a fascist movement staged a raid on an armory in Washington). For another thing, much of the material in *American* lacks convincing dramatic motivation. Several key events are still early in gestation. Since most of the Susan material has not been written, there is no love nest to expose, and Kane's crooked opponents conspire to steal the election from him. Leland goes to Chicago not because of the election but because of an affront to his integrity as drama critic: a new policy, apparently instituted with Kane's blessing, to guarantee favorable notices to producers for their shows in exchange for advertising considerations. When Susan sings in Chicago, Leland passes out at his typewriter before finishing the review, but instead of having Kane finish it for him (an inspired touch), a box is run on the theatrical page saying the review will be a day late (the way it really happened to Mankiewicz once when he was a second-stringer on the *New York Times*). There are also internal inconsistencies. For instance, Emily is still alive in 1940, but she refuses to be interviewed; yet her part of the story appears at the appropriate place anyway, without a narrator. By far the most serious dramatic problem in *American* is its portrait of Kane. Mankiewicz drew a good deal of his material directly from Hearst without really assimilating it to dramatic need. There is a large amount of Hearst material in ***Citizen Kane***—for instance, his scandalmongering, his ideological inconsistencies, San Simeon, the vast collections of everything under the sun, the awkwardness of his May-December romance with Marion Davies, even some of his memorable lines—but this is nothing approaching what is in the Mankiewicz script. *American* is by and large a literal reworking of specific incidents and details from Hearst's life. Much of it Mankiewicz knew on his own. As a former newspaper reporter, he had the professional's familiarity with all the great legends of journalism's most colorful era. As a privileged visitor to San Simeon, Mankiewicz would have observed firsthand such things as Marion Davies's tippling, her passion for jigsaw puzzles, Hearst's fondness for arranging elaborate picnic outings, and so on.

But it is clear that Mankiewicz also borrowed from published accounts of Hearst. He always denied it, claiming all his information was firsthand, but coincidences between *American* and Ferdinand Lundberg's *Imperial Hearst* are hard to explain. Lundberg reports that Hearst's father acquired the *San Francisco Examiner* in 1880 for a bad debt of $100,000—precisely the amount Thatcher is offered for the *Enquirer* (thus spelled in *American*) after he acquires it in a foreclosure proceeding. Lundberg describes Hearst's phenomenal success in his first years in newspaper publishing and offers as a landmark the fact that by 1889 the *Examiner* had reached a Sunday circulation of 62,000. In *American,* when the *Enquirer*'s circulation reaches the 62,000 figure, Kane has it painted on a huge sign outside his rival's window. Lundberg reports that Hearst actually won his 1905 campaign for mayor of New York City:

> *Hearst won the election.* He was the victor by several thousand votes, it has since been established, but the Tammany bruisers, heeding their instructions from Murphy, went berserk. Hearst's campaign people were assaulted and ballot boxes were stolen from the Hearst wards and dumped into the East River.

Identical details appear in dramatized form in *American.* . . . (pp. 16-23)

To have played the material in *American* as written would have involved some serious problems of copyright infringement. Strictly from a legal standpoint, *American* would be unusable without massive revision. The problem also has a dramatic side. Hearst was too free and easy a source of information for an unsteady writer like Mankiewicz. Most of *American* is quite simply *à clef* plotting with only the barest effort at characterization. Kane himself at this stage is more an unfocused composite than a character portrait, a stand-in mouthing dialogue manufactured for some imaginary Hearst. In this sense, Hearst is one of the principal obstacles to the script's further development. Before any real progress with the characterization could be made, the ties to his life had to be cut. That process began immediately after *American* and continued to the end of scripting. A lot of Hearst material survives in the film, but it is far less than was there at the beginning. (Lundberg eventually brought suit anyway.) One reason why Welles could later maintain so confidently that Kane was not Hearst may be that he had eliminated so much of Mankiewicz's Hearst material from the script that he imagined he had somehow eliminated Hearst in the process.

On April 28, less than two weeks after *American,* forty-four pages of revisions emanated from Victorville. Three very important changes appear in these pages. A decision has been made about the part of the story Emily might have told—most of it is to be assigned to Leland—and the framing segments with Bernstein and Leland have been rewritten to reflect this change. The stolen election has been abandoned; now Kane actually loses. The cause is presented in two important new scenes—one in which Emily insists Kane pay a certain call with her after the Madison Square Garden rally and its sequel, the encounter in Kane and Susan's love nest.

On or about May 9, Mankiewicz and Houseman completed their work at Victorville and returned to Hollywood with a second draft. Mankiewicz immediately went off to MGM on another assignment. Though he attempted to keep up with the revisions in the following weeks, he ceased to be a guiding hand in the ***Citizen Kane*** scripting process at this point. For this reason, it is important to look at the second draft carefully.

The most striking changes in the second draft involve Kane himself. Large chunks of material obviously based on Hearst have been removed. The stolen election is one example. Another involves Kane's educational history—how he was thrown out of college on account of a prank. Only one scene showing Kane with his publishing rivals remains. *American* had several tiresomely repetitive scenes intended to illustrate the libertine aspect of Kane's nature—Kane and Leland accompanied by women of questionable character at an expensive restaurant, Rector's, at the theater, and so on. This material has been considerably reduced in the second draft. The business of Susan's lover has also disappeared. Interesting scenes for

Kane have been added—for instance, when Kane finds Leland passed out at his typewriter, he finishes the review himself, and when Susan leaves him, he smashes up her room. Other new scenes are not so fortunate—one, for instance, involving the burial of Kane's son in the chapel at Xanadu. Kane is overcome with grief. As he stares at the row of crypts, he begins to prattle about his mother, who also is buried there. He recalls how she loved poetry and begins to read the verse inscription on the wall.

Some individual narratives have been restructured, but the effect is more to bring out problems in the original material than to provide solutions. When what would have been Emily's story is shifted to Leland, one result is that he is now responsible for a disproportionate share of major episodes in Kane's life—the human side of Kane's early years as a crusading publisher, the entire story of Kane's marriage and its deterioration and breakup, Leland's growing disillusionment with Kane's compromise of his values, and their final break over the opera review. But there is an even more serious problem. Leland's narration is now loaded with dramatic crises—not only the two that were originally his, the shady promotional scheme and the opera debut, but three of Emily's—the assassination attempt, Susan, and the lost election. The difficulty stems from the nature of *American,* which is essentially a string of discrete events lifted from a colorful biography. Once the necessary process of rearranging begins, the dramatic unmanageability of such material becomes apparent. One of the main problems that subsequent revisions will face is how to deal with a large surplus of crisis moments.

A related difficulty appears in the new version of Bernstein's story. Several episodes are newly assigned to him, including Thatcher's angry encounter with Kane in the *Enquirer* office, the first installment of the opera review incident with Leland passed out at his typewriter (Leland later tells the sequel of Kane's finishing the review), scenes of Bernstein as an uncomfortable social guest at Xanadu, and the divestiture sequence in which Thatcher and company take control of Kane's newspapers. Apparently, the writers are considering whether a narrator ought to have firsthand knowledge of what he relates. If the answer is yes, serious structural imbalances will be created elsewhere (there are now no scenes between Thatcher and the adult Kane), and the pacing of events will be seriously disrupted (as when a dramatic tour de force like the opera review is broken up and shared between two narrators). Even partial fidelity to such a principle would create difficult problems for other parts of the story (Kane's intimate life with Emily, for instance). Eventually, it is sacrificed to the general principle that we ought to see a developing chronological view of Kane's life.

Elimination of redundant material, the addition of several new scenes between Kane and Susan, the inspired touch of the opera review, and the improvement of many passages of dialogue are among the main accomplishments of the second draft. But numerous difficulties still remain, especially with the portrait of Kane, and on balance the second draft might most justly be characterized as a much-improved rough draft.

Amalia Kent reworked the May 9 script into accepted continuity form, as she had done with the scripts for *Heart of Darkness* and *The Smiler With the Knife.* Copies were sent to Schaefer in New York, whose assent was needed to proceed, and to department heads so that planning could begin. Kent then prepared a breakdown script. This document contains only the scene designations and their physical descriptions. It allows the architectural values of a script to be separated from its literary values and formally stated for the purposes of budgeting the production. Once such information went into wider circulation, special precaution was needed to keep the secret under wraps. An informal conspiracy of silence began to be resolutely observed by all those immediately involved. Although it was obvious they were dealing with Hearst, no one spoke of this or acknowledged it unless it was strictly necessary in the course of work. There is one good reason why the silence worked so well despite the number of people involved: There were horror stories of how things that happened on sets somehow got back to Hearst and how even an unintentional offense could cost someone a career. . . . (pp. 23-6)

Revisions on the Mankiewicz script resumed with great intensity after Welles returned to Hollywood [from a sales meeting with RKO executives in New York] on June 1. During the first two weeks of June alone, around 140 pages were revised—more than half of the total script. When the budget estimate based on the Mankiewicz script came out in mid June, the working script with changes in progress was consolidated and identified as a new draft, the third. Altogether, more than 170 pages in this script had been added or revised since Welles had taken over the script in mid May.

The new draft eliminates around 75 pages of the Victorville scenes. Some had been intended to enhance character—Kane and Leland at Rector's with their girls, for instance. Others had been intended to foreshadow—scenes of Kane and Susan in Chicago for her opera debut, for instance, give privileged glimpses into their private relationship. Others were merely redundant—Kane and family and a group of politicians gathered to announce his entry into politics, Bernstein's appearances at Xanadu, and (perhaps the most outrageous episode in *American*) the appearance of Kane Senior and his young wife. The most dramatic changes made by Welles involved the collapsing of lengthy expository sequences played as straight dramatic interchanges into snappy and arresting montages. The circulation buildup, which originally had been played in encounters between rivals and in expository discussions between Kane and his associates, is now given in a montage: the composing room, the Declaration of Principles on a front page, a wagon with a sign "Enquirer: Circulation 26,000," various shots of the paper being delivered, a new number (62,000) being painted on the wall of a building, and Kane, Bernstein, and Leland looking at a *Chronicle* window display that includes a photograph of the rival paper's staff and a sign with its circulation figures. The scenes showing how Kane checkmated Thatcher and his cronies with pilfered documents have been eliminated, to be replaced by a three-and-a-half-page montage (expanded from a suggestion in *American*) of the *Enquirer*'s growing impact on the American scene in the

1890s. This montage ends with a close-up of Kane's passport (it reads: "Occupation—Journalist"), which provides a bridge to the scene of Kane's departure for Europe on a Cunard liner. The assassination material has been condensed in much the same fashion. The scenes showing how Kane's home life suffers as he becomes more deeply involved in the oil scandal story are eliminated. After Kane's encounter with the president, a rapid montage showing cartoon and editorial attacks on the president ends with a close-up of the word *TREASON,* then the assassination itself—a hand firing a gun, hands and uniformed arms struggling with the first hand, the White House in the background, a ticker tape spelling out the news.

The Welles revisions address two of the most glaring dramatic problems in the Victorville material, though still not conclusively. The first involves Emily. While it is possible to eliminate her as a narrator, she is still a necessary presence and force in Kane's life. The story of their marriage has to be accounted for, even if not by her. The Victorville script recognized this by retaining a series of conventional expository scenes chronologically depicting the disintegration of the marriage. Welles threw out the first of these scenes—the couple on their honeymoon—and substituted a much brisker treatment: two brief glimpses of their courtship. In the first, Kane introduces himself to Emily on board a ship bound for Europe and brashly declares his intentions; in the second, a short time later, they are making wedding plans. Welles eliminated a domestic scene that showed Kane doting over his young son but obviously preoccupied with his work and substantially revised a turgid scene after the assassination when Emily makes known her true feelings toward Kane. It is clear that Welles was dissatisfied with the Victorville treatment. In each successive draft of the script, he rewrites the material heavily, until he arrives at a totally appropriate way of playing it—the breakfast table montage.

The second problem involves the surplus of crises in the Leland narration. Most of this section has been rewritten as a kind of extended inquisitorial, in which Leland confronts Kane with the main issues and calls on him for an accounting—his complicity in the assassination attempt, the promotional scheme, his unfairness to Emily, his irresponsibility to others in general. That most of the result is either unfathomable or incoherent is hardly surprising. Welles is simply having Leland do with Kane the same thing *he* was doing with Kane. We do not move very far toward a solution to the problem of crises at this stage. But as a starting point in the necessary process of transforming Kane from Mankiewicz's cardboard portrait into the complex and enigmatic figure we see in the film, this set of revisions has significance well beyond their actual achievement.

Finally, some new material of special interest is added. Georgie, madame of a high-class brothel, makes her first appearance in the story. The party that Kane gives for his staff eventually adjourns to Georgie's Place. On the day of the assassination attempt, Kane is at Georgie's when one of his editors calls with the news. Whether these additions enhance the story or not, Welles himself was very keen on them. The first one remained in the script despite Hays Office objections to it, and although the scenes do not appear in the finished film, they were actually shot. A more durable addition is the lengthy direction that we are to see Susan's debut a second time, from her point of view—unquestionably one of the most inspired touches in the film.

On June 14, the preliminary budget estimate based on the Victorville script was ready. It showed a total picture cost of $1,082,798—more than twice the amount specified in Welles's contract as the limit above which special approval was required. It waved another red flag as well: A million dollars was a kind of magic number at RKO. Department heads worked under a standing rule of thumb never to exceed that amount except in the most extraordinary circumstances. In a similar situation, *Heart of Darkness* had been abandoned. Inconceivable as it now seems, the same thing could have happened to ***Citizen Kane*** even at this late stage. From June 14 to July 2, when the matter was finally resolved, the film was not actually shut down, but its future was definitely in doubt. During that period, the estimate was reduced by more than $300,000. Budgetary realities led to sweeping changes in all areas of the film's production. . . . Insofar as the scripting is concerned, there were two major consequences: the need for immediate and drastic reductions and the reenlistment of Mankiewicz (because Welles now had to take charge of the overall problem) to assist in accomplishing them.

Welles's initial response was that the changes he had made in the Victorville material had almost surely brought down the cost already. A new draft incorporating all changes was prepared. Before submitting it, he eliminated the sequences set in Rome. Not only did this remove several costly sets from the budget, but it was also a sound decision for the story. The Rome sequences gave us our first view of the adult Kane at a very wrong moment dramatically, where he was living it up in Europe as a young man who had yet to take on any important responsibility. Instead of advancing the story, the Rome sequences tended to slow it down. With this material removed, Kane could now be introduced with one of those sudden and stunning, impulsive strokes that were to become his trademark—just a single sharp line in a letter: "I think it would be fun to run a newspaper." The new draft was the fourth. Called Final (the usual name for the draft first mimeographed), it is the first on which the title ***Citizen Kane*** appears. It was ready from the stenographic service on June 18. The prognosis of the production estimators was gloomy—"any cuts so far made will not effect major savings," and it is still "fifty to sixty pages longer than the longest script we have ever shot in this studio."

On June 18, Mankiewicz went back on the payroll. He stayed on until July 27, around the time a regular shooting schedule began. During this period, three new drafts of the script were mimeographed. Up until this point, it has been possible to be relatively precise about who wrote what. After June 18, the identification process becomes much more difficult. The problem is not so much that Welles and Mankiewicz are both involved at the same time but rather the unusual production circumstances. Welles was preoccupied with other things now, so we can be sure it was Mankiewicz who was literally making the changes in the script. But to what degree was he determining or even influencing them? During the first week after Mankiewicz's return, the script was reduced by more than twenty-five pages. . . . Welles, art director Perry Ferguson, and [cinematographer] Gregg Toland jointly managed the budgetary crisis. Did the changes mainly involve adjusting the script to decisions that they had already made? Meanwhile, rehearsals began. To circumvent a rule against uncompensated rehearsing, the cast assembled each day at the Mankiewicz home. How many of the changes came about in rehearsal, with Mankiewicz serving in effect as a transcribing secretary? The records themselves do not provide the answers, but it seems clear that Mankiewicz's creative role was considerably diminished by this time.

The Revised Final draft, the fifth in all, is dated June 24. There are four principal changes, each one entailing an appreciable reduction in playing time or set costs. A long discussion between Leland and Emily after the election disaster is eliminated. In two other places, the action is telescoped: The early romance of Kane and Emily is now dealt with in a single shot—a closeup of a diamond ring on a hand, from which the camera pulls back to reveal the lovers kissing; the deterioration of the marriage is presented in a single scene; and the dockside scene of Kane's departure for Europe is removed, which eliminates the need for another set.

By July 2, severe cutting in all categories had made possible a revised estimate of $737,740. At this point, Schaefer gave final approval to proceed. One week later, a new draft, the sixth, the Second Revised Final, was ready for the Hays Office. It was fourteen pages shorter than the preceding draft, almost entirely as a result of one fundamental change—the removal of the assassination attempt on the president and its long, talky aftermath. The account of Kane's first meeting with Susan, originally a part of her narration, has been moved to Leland's story to replace the assassination material. In this position, their meeting is followed by the political campaign; now there is only one political crisis to be dealt with. Two of the film's most important conceptions also appear for the first time in this draft. One resolves the problem posed by Kane's first marriage, which has been reduced to the celebrated breakfast table montage: "NOTE: The following scenes cover a period of nine years—and played in the same set with only changes in lighting, special effects outside the window, and wardrobe." The second provides what may be the film's most striking, and is certainly one of its most resonant, images. The previous draft called for an unidentified scene "still being written" after Kane leaves Susan's smashed-up room; it appears in the new draft as the instruction to walk down the corridor between facing mirrors.

The seventh draft, the Third Revised Final—the shooting script—is dated July 16. It contains two very important structural changes. In the preceding draft, the newspaper party had been played in two separate segments—the first half in Bernstein's story, the second in Leland's—and Kane's European trip and engagement had been placed in between. The original justification for this was that the second part of the sequence centered on Leland's objections to Kane's behavior over Cuba. The incident of the opera review was to be broken up in the same way—Leland is found passed out at his typewriter in Bernstein's story; Kane is seen finishing the review in a continuation many pages later—so that each narrator reported only what he could have known firsthand. In the new draft, both sequences are rewritten to be played continuously. This decision smoothes out some rough edges, and it was to have an enormous impact on the effect of these scenes in the film.

Although Welles denies it, the conclusion seems inescapable that he originally intended to take sole credit for the ***Citizen Kane*** script. The principal evidence is in letters written by Arnold Weissberger, New York attorney for Welles and the Mercury Theatre, to Welles and RKO in September and October 1940. The precedent for such an action had been established on the radio shows. The contractual agreements in radio were similar to those with RKO—Welles, on behalf of the Mercury, signed the primary contract with the sponsor. Writers were engaged under subsidiary contracts with the Mercury, and they assigned all claims of authorship to the corporation. In this way, a legal basis was created for Welles to claim script authorship regardless of the nature or extent of his actual contribution to the writing. He freely asserted the privilege: On the great majority of the radio broadcasts, either Welles was given sole writing credit on the air or no credit was given. Only rarely was another writer mentioned in this connection, and seldom if ever was the writer a member of the regular Mercury Theatre writing staff.

Mankiewicz's contract for work on the ***Citizen Kane*** script was with the Mercury Theatre, not with RKO. It contained the standard waiver of rights of authorship:

> All material composed, submitted, added or interpolated by you under this employment agreement, and all results and proceeds of all services rendered or to be rendered by you under this employment agreement, are now and shall forever be the property of Mercury Productions, Inc., who, for this purpose, shall be deemed the author and creator thereof, you having acted entirely as its employee.

Apparently Welles believed that this agreement gave him unqualified right to decide the ***Citizen Kane*** scripting credit as he saw fit, as he had done in radio. In Hollywood, however, writers had been able to secure certain countervailing privileges. By industry custom, authorship and screen credit were treated as separate issues. Though a screenwriter signed away all claim to ownership of his work, he could still assert a right to public acknowledgment of his authorship of it. A set of guidelines had been worked out to ensure that those who deserved screen credit got it, and these guidelines were subscribed to by all the major studios. In certain circumstances, a writer who felt unjustly treated could submit his case to arbitration. There were unusual complications surrounding ***Citizen Kane,*** but the force of accepted practice was strongly in Mankiewicz's favor.

Mankiewicz received his last paycheck on August 3, bringing his total pay for work on ***Citizen Kane*** to $22,833.35. A letter from Weissberger to Welles on September 6 reveals the course of action they intended to pursue in regard to credits. Weissberger says he has learned that Mankiewicz will probably try to make trouble over the matter of screen credit. He does not want to go into details in writing; an intermediary who is returning to Hollywood soon will explain. He quotes the authorship waiver in Mankiewicz's contract and concludes from it that Mankiewicz has no claim to any credit whatever. He is looking into the situation further, and in the meantime Welles should say nothing. When the time comes, he can confront Mankiewicz with his contract. (Weissberger also explains that he has just learned of possible complications with the Screen Writers' Guild. This and his interpretation of the authorship waiver both indicate how thoroughly unfamiliar he was with the inner workings of Hollywood.) On September 17, the Mercury office drew up a preliminary billing sheet on ***Citizen Kane*** for review by RKO's legal department. The column for the writer credit contains this curious notation: "It has not been determined if there is to be a credit given for story or screenplay." This probably indicates that they were following Weissberger's instructions to keep quiet pending further advice. Another possibility is that they were preparing a fallback position in case Weissberger's preliminary opinion failed to hold up: to omit the writer credit altogether, as was sometimes done on the radio scripts. (Better no credit at all than to share credit—that way at least no attention would be drawn.) If so, they were not aware that such a course would have been equally problematic: A request for waiver of screenplay credit would come under a process of review similar to that for credit assignment.

On October 1, Weissberger raised the credits issue in a letter to RKO's West Coast legal department. He begins by repeating his contention that "Mercury's legal right to deny credit can be established." He acknowledges, however, that Mankiewicz may have recourse within the industry, and he asks for details on how similar complaints have been handled in the past. He is particularly concerned, he says, about whether the matter is likely to result in arbitration proceedings and "unpleasant publicity." The reply was guarded but clear in its implications: There are no agreements currently in effect under which Mankiewicz could force an arbitration. A new agreement with the Screen Writers' Guild containing a provision for arbitration has just been executed and will soon go into effect. Since Mercury is not a signatory to this agreement, it is not contractually bound to observe it. Nevertheless, RKO would not want to use this technicality to take advantage of the situation. And, to confirm Weissberger's suspicion, yes, disputes over writer credits generate a lot of publicity.

If Mankiewicz originally had some kind of understanding with Welles on the credits, the course of events can only have made him have second thoughts. As ***Citizen Kane*** moved along in production, rumors began to leak out that the early footage was sensational. It appeared that what some had predicted might turn out to be true—***Citizen Kane*** would be a high point in everyone's career. Mankiewicz began to complain openly. With the general feeling for Welles in Hollywood what it was, support was not hard to line up. In a short time, Mankiewicz was able to build a full-scale word-of-mouth campaign in his behalf. On October 3, *Hollywood Reporter* rated his prospects high: "The writer credit won't be solo for Welles, if Herman Mankiewicz can keep talking." Faced with a combined threat of public exposure and further ostracism from the industry, Welles relented. In a gesture reminiscent of Kane, he put Mankiewicz's name first. The proposed credit read:

ORIGINAL SCREENPLAY
Herman J. Mankiewicz
Orson Welles

When this proposal was submitted to the Screen Writers' Guild for review, an ironic reversal occurred. The Guild pointed out that the credit proposed violated a provision in the writer-producer agreement that a producer could not take screenplay credit "unless he does the screen play writing entirely without the collaboration of any other writer." At this point, Mankiewicz joined Welles in an appeal, whereupon the Guild disclaimed jurisdiction because of the nature of the original contract between Welles and Mankiewicz, and the co-credit was allowed to stand.

Mankiewicz also received a form of public satisfaction. On Academy Awards night, Welles suffered humiliation as ***Citizen Kane*** lost in category after category and finally won only a shared Oscar for screenwriting. However, that was Mankiewicz's last moment in the limelight. After a temporary upsurge following ***Citizen Kane,*** his career trailed off again. Welles eventually got vindication of his own. By the time ***Citizen Kane*** was revived in the 1950s, Mankiewicz's name had been forgotten, along with the dispute over screen credit. Not that the details would have been of much interest: Directors were the prevailing critical interest, and films were being considered strictly as directors' creations. As a result, everyone but Welles was shut out of a share of the newfound glory for ***Citizen Kane.*** It was against this background that Pauline Kael undertook to rehabilitate Mankiewicz's reputation.

He could not have wished for a more sympathetic biographer. "Raising Kane" is a colorful biography of Mankiewicz as a Dickensian character—a goodhearted loser, undisciplined and always in some kind of hot water, but with a wit that serves as his saving grace. (Consoling his hosts just after he had thrown up on their formal dinner table, he assured them that the white wine had come up with the fish.) It is also a classic piece of journalistic exposé. Kael brought two principal charges: that Welles conspired to deprive Mankiewicz of screen credit and that Mankiewicz wrote the entire script. The second charge made the first seem all the more heinous. Her principal evidence was heresay testimony from witnesses and participants who were openly sympathetic to Mankiewicz. The first charge seems to be true. Concerning the second, Kael wrote:

> Welles probably made suggestions in his early conversations with Mankiewicz, and since he received copies of the work weekly while it was in progress at Victorville, he may have given advice by phone or letter. Later, he almost certainly

> made suggestions for cuts that helped Mankiewicz hammer the script into tighter form, and he is known to have made a few changes on the set. But Mrs. Alexander, who took the dictation from Mankiewicz, from the first paragraph to the last, and then, when the first draft was completed and they all went back to Los Angeles, did the secretarial work at Mankiewicz's house on the rewriting and the cuts, and who then handled the script at the studio until after the film was shot, says that Welles didn't write (or dictate) one line of the shooting script of ***Citizen Kane.***

This, as we now know, is a flagrant misrepresentation.

Welles attempted a point-by-point rebuttal of Kael in his interviews with Peter Bogdanovich. He also made a brief direct reply in a letter to the editor of the London *Times.*

> The initial ideas for this film and its basic structure were the result of direct collaboration between us; after this we separated and there were two screenplays: one written by Mr. Mankiewicz, in Victorville, and the other, in Beverly Hills, by myself. . . . The final version of the screenplay . . . was drawn from both sources.

Concerning Kael's treatment of the arbitration matter with the Screen Writers' Guild, Welles claims that Mankiewicz's motive was not to guarantee himself co-credit. "Quite the opposite. What he wanted was sole credit." Both Welles's contentions have a degree of factual basis, but each requires careful qualification. There *were* two separate drafts going for a time, as we have seen, but this was *after* Victorville; Mankiewicz's Victorville script was the foundation for all subsequent development. At one point, the arbitration matter did involve a question of sole screenplay credit for Mankiewicz, as we have also seen, but this came along very late, rather than being the issue all along, as Welles implies.

Welles had given a much more accurate summation in his testimony in the Lundberg copyright infringement case. In response to a question about the authorship of a specific scene, he said that it "was written in its first and second draftings exclusively by my colleague Mr. Mankiewicz. I worked on the third draft and participated all along in conversations concerning the structure of the scenes." To summarize: Mankiewicz (with assistance from Houseman and with input from Welles) wrote the first two drafts. His principal contributions were the story frame, a cast of characters, various individual scenes, and a good share of the dialogue. Certain parts were already in close to final form in the Victorville script, in particular the beginning and end, the newsreel, the projection room sequence, the first visit to Susan, and Colorado. Welles added the narrative brilliance—the visual and verbal wit, the stylistic fluidity, and such stunningly original strokes as the newspaper montages and the breakfast table sequence. He also transformed Kane from a cardboard fictionalization of Hearst into a figure of mystery and epic magnificence. ***Citizen Kane*** is the only major Welles film on which the writing credit is shared. Not coincidentally, it is also the Welles film that has the strongest story, the most fully realized characters, and the most carefully sculpted dialogue. Mankiewicz made the difference. While his efforts may seem plodding next to Welles's flashy touches of genius, they are of fundamental importance nonetheless. (pp. 26-35)

> *Robert L. Carringer, "Scripting," in his* The Making of "Citizen Kane," *University of California Press, 1985, pp. 16-35.*

Michael Anderegg (essay date Spring 1987)

[*Anderegg is an American educator and critic who has written extensively on film. In the following essay on* Chimes at Midnight, *he examines the revisions Welles made to Shakespeare's history plays.*]

Chimes at Midnight has come to be recognized, over the last decade or so, both as one of the most intelligent and imaginative of films adapted from Shakespeare and as one of Orson Welles's finest achievements, a film at least equal in energy and brilliance to ***Citizen Kane*** and ***The Magnificent Ambersons.*** The chorus of praise occasionally includes a few sour notes, however; as so often with Welles's post ***Citizen Kane*** films, various qualifications temper even highly enthusiastic assessments. Criticism tends to center on the sound track and on the uncertain relationship between sound and image: the recording is technically faulty, Shakespeare's words are frequently unintelligible (Welles's Falstaff, in particular, is difficult to understand much of the time), several sequences are poorly synchronized, and, disconcertingly, a number of the minor actors have been dubbed by Welles himself—all signs that inadequate financing forced artistic compromise. Additionally, critics find fault with Welles for the film's haphazard continuity and for a general inattention to detail, especially in the casting and playing of the secondary roles. In short, ***Chimes at Midnight*** is often discussed in terms that remind us of Shakespeare's Sir John Falstaff himself: attractive, vibrant, large, complex, but, withal, so deeply flawed as to negate many of its virtues.

In this essay, I would like to place both the unquestioned successes and the supposed defects of ***Chimes at Midnight*** within the context of what I take to be the film's governing strategy: the rewriting of Shakespeare's text, a rewriting that includes an attempted erasure of writing, a critique of rhetoric, an undermining of language itself. Taking up what is undeniably present in Shakespeare—no writer shows more awareness of the dangerous seductiveness of words—Welles carries the questioning of language much further than Shakespeare, whose primary resource was language, ever could. ***Chimes at Midnight*** centers squarely on a conflict between rhetoric and history, on the one hand, and the immediacy of a pre-linguistic, pre-lapsarian, timeless physical world, on the other. This conflict comes to us primarily through the actions and character of Falstaff, as we might expect, but it informs as well the texture and style of each moment of Welles's film. With remarkable boldness, Welles has made a Shakespearean film in which poetry itself seems to undergo a rigorous devaluation.

To a certain extent, of course, Welles had to rewrite Shakespeare as part of the process of adaptation: no

Shakespearian film reproduces Shakespeare's text in its entirety (nor, for that matter, do most stage productions). But Welles's editorial decisions nevertheless aim at a particular end and have a specific focus. He compresses and reshapes his source material at will, reducing it to a bare minimum of words. Drawing primarily on *Henry IV,* Parts I and II, adding a few lines from *Richard II, Henry V,* and *The Merry Wives of Windsor,* Welles gives Shakespeare's story of a prince's coming of age a single plot line and a new emphasis. Critics have often noted that *Henry IV,* Part II, in many ways recapitulates, albeit in a different key, the structure and theme of Part I: Shakespeare presents two scenes of reconciliation between Hal and his father, two military engagements (Shrewsbury and Galtree Forest), two moments when Hal realizes his destiny, and so forth. Welles, while doing away with much of this repetition, shifts scenes and parts of scenes around at his convenience, placing Falstaff's recruitment of soldiers in Part II, for example, before Part I's battle of Shrewsbury. Although Welles's refashioning of Shakespeare's text(s) has a number of consequences, the primary effect is to shift the thematic emphasis away from Hal and towards Falstaff, or, to put it another way, away from history and towards satire.

The critique of history in ***Chimes at Midnight*** completes a process already begun by Shakespeare, but Welles's attack is harsher, his conclusion far less optimistic. "History," for the purposes of my argument, includes the whole world of kings and politics, of war and chivalry, as well as the language, the rhetoric, which is that world's chief expressive medium. Shakespeare's Henriad comprehends a set of binary oppositions—Court / Tavern, Honor / Dishonor, Hotspur / Falstaff, Henry IV / Falstaff, Time / Timelessness, Word / Being, Serious / Non-serious—where either the first term is the privileged one or where both terms have been suspended in an uneasy equilibrium, leaving to Hal the task of determining which to choose, or if indeed a choice has to be made at all. In Welles's film, these paired alternatives are unbalanced, diminished, reversed, or exploded. Shakespeare's Hal has always already made the choice, though he appears to be choosing all the time. For Welles's Hal, the choice poses genuine and insoluble problems. The various embodiments of "positive" values, what I have simply termed "History," have little exemplary force in ***Chimes at Midnight,*** tending at times to degenerate, at the level of language, into the incoherent babbling of poseurs, cynics, and fools. At the same time, any attempt to abolish language, to ignore the power of words, leads inevitably to destruction. Here, Falstaff stands as the cautionary figure, and his desire to abolish language and put sheer physicality in its place becomes the tragic fulcrum upon which Welles's film turns.

Welles's strategy for undermining history and rhetoric only begins with the process of adaptation. His tactics are primarily stylistic. History and (verbal) rhetoric are constantly displaced, replaced by Welles's nervous, erratic, decentered, unstable visual and aural style, a flow of images and sounds that thoroughly dismantle Shakespeare's text, peeling away layers of strategically placed and carefully joined verbal and thematic checks against disintegration. In this context, the supposed problems with the sound track become less a matter of technical flaws (though flaws there are, as Welles has publicly lamented), and more a question of Welles's intentions and methods. In some shots, for example, the actors deliver their lines as they, or the camera, or both, are in rapid motion. Or a character will make an important speech from the depth of an extreme long shot, depriving us of lip movement and facial expression, both important cues for the understanding of unfamiliar language and syntax. Furthermore, Welles constructs jarring editing patterns that easily distract from the spoken word. At several points, even what Welles has structured to resemble continuity editing turns into something unexpected. A simple reverse shot, for example, may involve illogical changes in time and / or space. These and other stylistic idiosyncrasies help to explain why we can follow the sound track of ***Chimes at Midnight*** more easily if we keep our eyes closed. In effect, Welles generates a constant tension between what we see and what we hear, a tension that points to the ambiguous status of language in its relation to action.

Welles further exhibits his ambivalence towards rhetoric in his handling of soliloquies. In his previous Shakespearian films, Welles had already suggested some discomfort with filmed soliloquies, resorting to a variety of voice-over techniques in ***Macbeth,*** and in ***Othello*** having some of his actors deliver soliloquies and speeches with their backs to the camera. In ***Chimes,*** Welles virtually does away with soliloquies as such by not allowing anyone to speak directly to the camera or to be truly alone: Hal's revelation (in Shakespeare, to the audience only) that his madcap humor is primarily for show ("I know you all") is spoken in Falstaff's presence; Falstaff delivers both his catechism on honor and his later dissertation on the virtues of sherris-sack directly to Hal. Even King Henry is not allowed a true soliloquy. His famous meditation on sleep, to choose a notable instance, though filmed in a single, uninterrupted take and in close-up, becomes an address to his courtiers; he is not, as he is in the play, alone. All soliloquies have thus become, at least implicitly, attempts at conversation, at communication within the diegetic universe, and not, as soliloquies can be, privileged moments where language provides a more or less unmediated access to thought.

We can see Welles's strategy ideally realized at that moment when Hotspur—whose bath has been interrupted by the pressing demands of history—cries "That roan shall be my throne" and simultaneously drops the towel in which he has draped himself and turns away from the camera, revealing his bare behind. Hotspur's towel falls in the midst of a highly rhetorical gesture, a wide sweep of the arm that serves as punctuation for his words. Welles comically undermines Hotspur's rhetoric, lays bare his linguistic bravado, and ridicules his historical pretensions, his (partly unconscious) desire for the English throne. Hotspur's words have already been mocked throughout this scene by the trumpeters who echo his belligerent posings with elaborate, comic fanfares. The trumpets say as much as he does, and are equally meaningful as rational statement. Hotspur's dropped towel suggests an additional meaning as well, one contiguous with that just described: for a moment, Hotspur reveals the physical he tries to deny or push aside in the semi-playful, semi-serious exchange with his wife, Kate, that follows this scene. The dropped towel signifies the return of the repressed, cancelling Hotspur's attempt to replace sensuality with rhetoric (war, history, etc.), to deny the body by asserting the word.

In what is perhaps the most remarkable sequence in ***Chimes at Midnight,*** the battle of Shrewsbury, Welles presents us with another kind of history—a history stripped of all rhetoric, denuded of language, and at the same time supremely eloquent. Here, the rhetorical dismemberment of the body politic, the scenes of accusation and counter-accusation between the royal party and the highborn conspirators, becomes displaced and mocked by the literal dismemberment of the body physical. Welles's style forcefully underlines the brutal, unheroic character of hand-to-hand combat in a nervously edited mosaic of varied shots, some photographed with a handheld camera, some filmed with wide-angle lenses, some in slow motion, some speeded up, some shots static and others that employ swish pans or other kinds of rapid movement, together with a complex, many-layered sound track of shouts and screams, of the clash of sword against sword, armor against armor, of grunts and cries and cracking bones. Welles conjures up Armageddon, a nightmare vision of destruction which points up the futility of this or any other war. By the end, both armies have become one huge, awkward, disintegrating war machine, a grotesque robot whose power source slowly begins to fail and finally comes to a frozen halt. Verbal rhetoric—language itself—seems, for the moment, both irrelevant and obscene.

In this context, the highly verbal King Henry IV, the only character in the film whose words and speeches are allowed their full Shakespearean weight and style, stands in ironic counterpoint to the carnage of Shrewsbury. As John Gielgud plays him, and as Welles directs his scenes, King Henry is reduced to a nearly disembodied voice. The most "poetic" and rhetorical figure in Welles's film, he is also the most ethereal. Cold, pinched, ascetic, photographed sitting on or standing near his throne set on a high stone platform, his face illuminated by a harsh, white light, he is an isolated, distant figure of overbearing but brittle authority. As Falstaff seems to be all flesh, Henry seems all words. But even the king's voice fails him: he can neither govern his son with it nor tame the rebels, who refuse to credit his verbal promises. Henry's highly rhetorical manner, meant to gloss over his insecurities and fears, finally serves to reveal them. His voice becomes an object of parody: at various points in the film, Hotspur, Hal, and Falstaff all imitate Gielgud's immediately recognizable vocal characteristics. The "beauty" of Henry's speech only serves to place in an even harsher light his asceticism, coldness, and largely self-imposed isolation; a supreme poseur, he cannot see beyond his role. Although never really alone, Henry seems to speak only to himself.

King Henry's dependence on words becomes ideally focused in a scene Welles has totally refashioned from Shakespeare. After the battle of Shrewsbury, Falstaff takes credit for killing Hotspur, spinning another one of his outrageous lies for Hal's benefit. Welles gives the scene a special emphasis by having King Henry present as Falstaff tells his tale. The king, for once, says nothing, and Hal, too, is silent, but their faces tell a clear enough story. Earlier, Hal had told his father that he would redeem himself for his bad behavior "on Percy's head / And in the closing of some glorious day, / Be bold to tell you that I am your son, . . ." Now is the moment when this prophecy should come true, when the moving rhetoric should be realized in action. But Hal fails to make good on his promise. Unwilling to expose Falstaff, he refuses to say the words his father so much wants to hear, and the moment slips by. The silence, emphasized by a series of static closeups, takes on precise thematic significance. We can tell, from Henry's expression, that he knows very well who killed Hotspur, but the knowledge, without the words, is not enough. We see, too, the conflict within Hal. And, finally, we can read in Falstaff's face his understanding of what the other two are thinking. For all three as well as for us, silence acquires a rhetorical force ordinarily reserved to speech.

If the world of kings overvalues words, the tavern world fatally undervalues them. In the tavern world, which for my purposes includes the Justice Shallow scenes, words are acknowledged to mean very little. Falstaff's notorious lies, and the ease with which everyone sees through them, are symptomatic, but many of his cohorts share his linguistic deviance. Shallow constantly reminisces about the old days, but "every third word" he speaks, according to Falstaff, is "a lie." Falstaff's hanger-on, Ancient Pistol, is perhaps the most unintelligible character in the film. In Shakespeare, he is already rhetorically tedious; his primary function is to cast in ironic light, through highflown speeches and outrageous behavior, the chivalric code. But in a world where rhetoric and history are so constantly and thoroughly brought into question, Welles takes the extreme course of reducing Pistol to little more than noise. Against Pistol's meaningless bombast, we have Silence's inability to say anything at all. Welles afflicts him with a stutter so severe that he cannot complete his sentences. Shallow must speak for him, must become in effect his voice (a nice joke in a film where so many characters are clearly dubbed). Words are interchangeable, attach themselves to no one in particular, have no individual meaning. Speech, in short, appears to be as debased through undervaluing in the tavern world as it is debased through overvaluing in the court world.

The difficulty of penetrating language, of determining the truth and weight of words, of reading history, comes to be, in especial, Falstaff's dilemma. Falstaff distrusts words; in a sense, he himself has nothing to say, certainly nothing with which to answer King Henry, who is all speech, all words, the very incarnation of logos. Falstaff's own words are frequently unintelligible, or nearly so, because he wants to deny the efficacy of language. (Welles the actor here exaggerates his post-***Citizen Kane*** tendency to downplay the orotund and avuncular qualities of his vocal delivery by deliberately "throwing away" words and lines and even entire speeches.) But, though words may be questioned, subverted, and parodied, they cannot be abolished. Falstaff's refusal to credit words at all leads to his undoing. Even Hal's words—especially Hal's words—

mean little to Falstaff, though Hal is at great pains throughout to make his motives clear. Welles's presentation of Hal, an attractive, appealing prince as played by Keith Baxter, runs counter to some modern, especially theatrical, views of the Henriad which condemn Hal as a cold, hypocritical careerist who cynically uses Falstaff for his own ends. Instead, Welles deliberately distorts Shakespeare's text at several points in order to stress Hal's straightforwardness. I've already noted that Hal's revealing "I know you all" meditation is no longer a soliloquy in the film; it is delivered in Falstaff's hearing, the second half of it spoken directly to him. Similarly, when Hal, speaking as his father at the end of the famous play scene, tells Falstaff that he will indeed banish him ("I do; I will"), he gives the words a moving, elegiac tone that render their meaning unmistakable to anyone not as bent on self-deception as Falstaff is.

Against language, Falstaff posits being, presence, physicality. We are made aware, throughout Welles's film, of Falstaff as sheer physical mass. His huge figure—sometimes just his face alone—often dominates the frame. Although he enters the film in the depth of an extreme long shot, a small, round object on the horizon, he gradually moves toward the camera until his head alone fills over three-fourths of the image, leaving what remains to his companion, Shallow. In the play scene, two men and a boy must help Falstaff onto his makeshift "throne." Before the battle of Shrewsbury, his followers valiantly attempt to raise him to his saddle with block and tackle, only to drop his armor-encased body to the ground. At the Boar's Head tavern, stairways and corridors seem too narrow for his passage. The point is made most strikingly in the Gadshill episode, where Falstaff's monk's robe transforms him into a huge white tent which sharply contrasts with the thin, black trees that surround him. Falstaff's girth is, of course, a running joke in Shakespeare, but Welles goes out of his way to elaborate on the theme; he seems intent on suggesting the extent to which Falstaff's world is physical, corporeal, of the flesh. Falstaff's relationships are expressed in predominently tactile ways, his rotund figure giving others, especially Hal and Doll Tearsheet, something to grasp, to hold on to, or—in Doll's case—to climb on.

Although Welles has said that, for him, Falstaff was "the greatest conception of a good man, the most completely good man, in all drama," ***Chimes at Midnight*** presents a far more ambivalent portrait of Falstaff than these words suggest. We cannot doubt that Welles sympathizes, both as director and as actor, with Falstaff's desire to bypass language and thereby gain access to an unmediated reality. At the same time, we know, and Welles knows, that in a fallen world, such a desire is folly. And we know as well that, like many Wellesian heroes, Falstaff longs for an Edenic world only because he has long since forfeited it. Welles's Falstaff is far from the jolly knight seen in various theatrical interpretations of the role. Rather, he seems more the corrupt, gross "misleader of youth" that Hal and others claim he is. Some readers have seen two Falstaffs emerging from the two parts of *Henry IV,* the second considerably less pleasant than the first. But whether the Falstaff of Part II is really a different character from the Falstaff of Part I, or whether he evolves naturally in the course of the two plays, Welles chose to combine both Falstaffs in his performance. Welles's Falstaff is, in Beverle Houston's felicitous phrase, a "Power Baby," an "eating, sucking, foetus-like creature" whose benignity is an illusion. Pre-linguistic, he is forever locked in the imaginary world of infancy. Like Kane, like Arkadin, like Quinlan, like Clay, Falstaff is fundamentally, irredeemably corrupt. A larger-than-life figure flawed by hubris, he tragically collaborates in his own destruction.

Falstaff's defeat has a specifically linguistic dimension: Hal's rejection of him is a rhetorical act, the new king of England's maiden speech, the son's entrance into the symbolic world of his father. (By staging this scene in the midst of the coronation ceremony, Welles puts the emphasis as much on Hal's humiliation as on Falstaff's.) Falstaff's response to Hal's elaborate, majestic, and witty rebuke is nonverbal: we must read it in Welles's expression. What we see are emotions in conflict: awe, perhaps pride (this is *his* king, after all), and a wistfulness not unmixed with cunning (is he already thinking of a "starting hole," a way out?). The dominant emotion, however, is disbelief: Hal's words cannot be meaningful, they are rhetoric only; Falstaff sees through and beyond them. Shakespeare's Falstaff, we feel, indulges himself in sheer bravado when he tells Shallow "This that you heard was but a color . . . I shall be sent for soon at night." For Welles's Falstaff, these words suggest not bravado so much as a deeply felt hope, a nearly desperate attempt to render words meaningless. But Hal not only means what he says, he now has the power to turn words into deeds, and his words and deeds kill Falstaff.

In keeping with his method throughout the film, Welles strips even Falstaff's death of easy sentiment. Mistress Quickly's description of Falstaff's last moments functions as a piece of information for a clearly unmoved Poins; spoken with Falstaff already in his coffin, her words lack the immediacy they have in Shakespeare's *Henry V.* Welles barely prepares us for this crucial finale: one moment Falstaff is alive, if crushed; the next moment he is dead. No illness, no tears, no bedside scene as in Laurence Olivier's film of *Henry V.* Only a final irony: words continue to fail Falstaff, even after death. In a complete departure from Shakespeare's text, Welles concludes his film with the image of Falstaff's coffin passing away in the distance while on the sound track Ralph Richardson recites a passage from Holinshed's *Chronicles of England, Scotland, and Ireland,* a passage in praise of King Henry V, who, we are told, "was so humane withal that he left no offense unpunished or friendship unrewarded." Whatever we may think of the truth or justice of Holinshed's words, one irony, at least, is certain: in ***Chimes at Midnight,*** a film that thoroughly reveals the hollowness of kings and their fine words, language and history stubbornly abide when all else is gone. (pp. 18-23)

Michael Anderegg, "'Every Third Word a Lie': Rhetoric and History in Orson Welles's 'Chimes at Midnight'," in Film Quarterly, *Vol. XL, No. 3, Spring, 1987, pp. 18-24.*

An excerpt from F. Scott Fitzgerald's short story *"Pat Hobby and Orson Welles"*:

"Who's this Welles?" Pat asked of Louie, the studio bookie. "Every time I pick up a paper they got about this Welles."

"You know, he's that beard," explained Louie.

"Sure, I know he's that beard, you couldn't miss that. But what credits's he got? What's he done to draw one hundred and fifty grand a picture?"

What indeed? Had he, like Pat, been in Hollywood over twenty years? Did he have credits that would knock your eye out, extending up to—well, up to five years ago when Pat's credits had begun to be few and far between?

"Listen—they don't last long," said Louie consolingly, "We've seen 'em come and we've seen 'em go. Hey, Pat?"

F. Scott Fitzgerald, in his "Pat Hobby and Orson Welles," in The Pat Hobby Stories, *1962.*

William G. Simon (essay date 1989)

[*Simon is chair of the department of Cinema Studies at New York University. In 1988 he organized a retrospective and scholarly conference on the many facets of Welles's career. In the following essay, he assesses the current state of Welles scholarship.*]

Orson Welles is one of the best known and most critically acclaimed of American film directors. The English-language bibliography on Welles includes at least ten books of critical analysis and two full-scale biographies. His historic role as director of ***Citizen Kane*** is attested to in virtually every text in film history and aesthetics. Others of his films hold privileged places in almost any canon of film classics. Welles shares with Charlie Chaplin and Alfred Hitchcock the status of being the only filmmakers of the classical period who are as well known to the general public as they are to film enthusiasts and specialists.

The extensive attention accorded to the life and work of a single director like Welles would suggest that his artistic and cultural output has been analyzed exhaustively and that little remains to be said on the subject of Orson Welles. Yet, this is hardly the case. Paradoxically, for all his fame (and notoriety) and for all the critical attention paid to his films, Welles remains one of the least understood of major directors. (p. 5)

Two major factors help to explain the inadequacy of Welles criticism. Firstly, large areas of his productivity remain virtually ignored and unknown. The existent critical literature deals almost exclusively with Welles's films and neglects equally fertile areas of his radio and theater work. Only one rather unsatisfying book exists on his theater work. No extended writings have been published on his radio work. While virtually all of the books on Welles's films acknowledge the importance which his theater and radio work has toward a full appreciation of his films, none has attempted to develop the absolutely central issue of the complex intertextual relations among his works in his three primary media. In addition, hardly anyone is even aware that Welles worked extensively in television. And while the catalogues of work in some books at least list his theater and radio productions in America, the very important work done in Europe after 1949 seldom merits a mention.

Even in relation to Welles's films, there remain severe gaps in our understanding. Little analytic work has been devoted to the never completed film projects, some of which (e.g., ***It's All True, Don Quixote***) are of crucial importance to a comprehensive understanding of Welles's artistic personality. Critics seem to have consigned these works to the slag-heap of archival memory even though the essays [by Robert Stam, Susan Ryan, and Catherine Benamon] on ***It's All True*** . . . prove to what extent that work is a crucial missing link in understanding Welles's cultural interests, not to mention the contours of his career. Are there other missing links? The footage of ***Don Quixote*** certainly suggests there are. The recent publication (by Jonathan Rosenbaum) of the fascinating screenplay, ***The Big Brass Ring,*** further suggests the advisability of searching out each last piece of Wellesiana. In addition to this lack of attention to the never completed projects, it should be noted that very minimal critical literature exists on some of Welles's most difficult but absolutely central films, such as ***Mr. Arkadin*** and ***F for Fake.*** The utter neglect to which so much of Welles's productivity has been relegated suggests that there remains a major task of critical recuperation to be performed in relation to Welles's career.

Beyond this proclivity for Welles criticism to restrict its purview to a few chosen masterpieces at the expense of so much that is equally interesting, a second factor helps to explain the inadequacy of Welles criticism and justifies a renewal of it. Most of the extended work on Welles was published between the late 1960s and late 1970s under the banner of classical auteurism. It thrives on the virtues and limitations of that approach to understanding films and in the best and last instance of that critical practice—James Naremore's *The Magic World of Orson Welles*—very likely exhausts its options.

Since this period, a barrage of innovative critical methodologies has animated the field of cinema studies. Developments in such areas as narratology, historiography, intertextuality, cultural studies, and discourse theory, have proposed new ways to structure and formulate our understanding of films and other cultural products.

While a critique of the very notion of the author has been central to the development of many of these new methodologies, I would argue that these methodologies can also be utilized in very productive ways to illuminate a large body of works whose unifying principle is that they were directed by a particular individual, in this instance, Orson Welles. The new methods and a concern for a specific director are not necessarily mutually exclusive; there are significant ways in which they can interact dynamically. Clearly, advances in the area of narratology can lead both to new ways of comprehending the structure of an individual film and to ways of relating that film to the entire history of narrative. Grasping the specific industrial and financial situation and conditions under which a film was made obviously contributes significantly to our understanding of it. Comprehending the complex of cultural, political, and social discourses in which an individual work intertextually participates can only add to our perception of its multiple significations and resonances. Submitting the works of an individual filmmaker to the grid of these new methods will surely sharply qualify our sense of the works as the product of a unique individual's genius. At the same time, the process has the potential to greatly expand our understanding of the complex relations that animate any work of cultural production and contribute to its systems of signification.

I would argue that almost none of the recent work on Welles has taken advantage of the newer critical options. Perhaps only Robert Carringer's *The Making of Citizen Kane,* with its attention to exhaustive primary research and its insistence on the collaborative process within the studio mode of production, borders on recent historiographic methods and offers a fresh perspective on the production of that film. The two recent biographies of Welles by Charles Higham [*Orson Welles: The Rise and Fall of an American Genius*] and Barbara Leaming [*Orson Welles*], represent the opposite of the new methodologies; they wallow in vulgar and sensationalist myth-making (or counter-myth-making) and abdicate the enterprise of serious critical thinking. Recently, however, there have been a few valuable critical essays on Welles's work, and the publication of the scripts of ***Touch of Evil*** and ***Chimes at Midnight,*** with strong supporting materials, fleshes out the bibliographies on those films.

However, I contend that the time is ripe for a renewal of critical thinking on Welles. A commitment both to understanding his works in all media in all their intertextual implications and to applying the new critical perspectives that can illuminate these works will, I think, lead to a substantial re-evaluation of his career and, most importantly, to the creation of new critical formulations through which to grasp the meaning and significance of his production.

To suggest the value of such a critical re-examination, I shall briefly consider a few of the issues that bear upon that crucial phase of Welles's career—from the mid-1930s through the early 1940s. Welles was situated in the fertile cross-current of several of the most innovative and important social and cultural discursive practices of this period, and his work, including the films, cannot be understood fully without accounting for his total immersion in those practices. As one of the foremost directors in the Federal Theatre Project, and then in his and John Houseman's Mercury Theatre, he was a vital participant in a historically unique experiment in American theater. As a leading theater director, he was caught up in the complex conjunction of Popular Front and New Deal culture that characterized the second half of the 1930s and was chiefly responsible for several of the period's most important theatrical productions. As an equally prominent director of and performer in radio drama, he was a leading contributor to the development of radio's "Golden Age." His broadcast, **"The War of the Worlds,"** is acknowledged by virtually all commentators as one of the two or three most important confirmations of radio's power and significance during the period in which it was America's most important public medium. And, to repeat, Welles's first films, ***Citizen Kane, The Magnificent Ambersons,*** and the ***It's All True*** project, are best understood when viewed as extensions of his theater and radio work in the 1930s.

Among the leading motifs of Welles's work in the 30s and early 40s is one that especially relates it to certain tendencies in American culture during this period. This is the notion of documentary expression, identified by many cultural historians as a central practice to be found in politics, the social sciences, and the arts. William Stott, for example, argues [in his *Documentary Expression and Thirties America*] that

> a documentary motive was at work throughout the culture of the time: in the rhetoric of the New Deal and the WPA arts projects, in painting, dance, fiction and theatre; in the new media of radio and picture magazines; in popular thought, education, and advertising.

Stott claims that the documentary impulse was essentially a response to the Great Depression; politicians, writers, and photographers, among others, used documentary techniques to provide evidence of the devastating economic and social conditions of this period. Out of this concern with social problems grew an all-embracing impulse to document what Stott and others call "American stuff," the impression and feel of the country, most especially as it was discovered in its popular culture. This populist emphasis was esepcially evident in the four Federal Arts Projects of the WPA, both in the content that they dealt with and in their modes of address to a large popular audience. Both Stott and Richard H. Pells (in *Radical Visions and American Dreams*) follow Warren Susman in his ground-breaking essay, "The Culture of the Thirties" [in *Culture as History*], in specifying the camera (both still and motion) and radio as the two privileged media for realizing the documentary impulse. The camera and the radio redefined the threshold of directness and spontaneity in conveying information to the mass audience of the 1930s. Providing the audience with the texture and experience of American life—both past and present—as forcefully as possible, became the central goal of the documentary imagination. Indeed, the practice was pervasive in American culture of the 30s. It can be observed in FDR's fireside chats; in the Federal Writers Project's guides; in the photographic essays of *Fortune* and *Life* magazines; in the dramas of the Living Newspapers; in Aaron Copland's music; in Martha Graham's dances; in the novels of John Steinbeck and John Dos Passos; in newsreels; in documentary books and films; and in on-the-spot radio newscasts.

Orson Welles participated actively and extensively in the documentary forms of this period. One of his first acting jobs in New York City was on the *March of Time* radio show. A product of the Luce publishing empire, the *March of Time* was a pioneering format in presenting news on the radio and, as such, was a very popular show. The weekly program reconstructed important new stories, using a portentous omniscient narrator alternating with dramatizations of events featuring actors playing the likes of Hitler, Mussolini, presidents, and kings. While clearly a very simulated form of documentary from a contemporary perspective, its method of presenting the news seems to have been a sufficiently innovative experience to persuade its contemporaneous audience of its authenticity. In any case, the *March of Time* was not only a very popular show in the mid-1930s, it was also very influential for its use of a narrator or commentator and for the ways in which it mixed narration, dramatization, music, and sound effects. For Welles, it can be seen as a fitting introduction to a very popular form of the public media, one which combined the documentary impulse and fictional recreation in an original way.

As a second piece of evidence concerning Welles's involvement with the documentary imagination, we should note that he played the role of the Announcer in Archibald MacLeish's original radio drama, *The Fall of the City* (1937). During this period Welles's career crossed paths many times with MacLeish, the so-called poet laureate of the New Deal. Welles had already played the role of an ageing magnate in MacLeish's play *Panic* in 1935. MacLeish's *The Fall of the City* was structured around the role of the Announcer, who gives a kind of play-by-play description of and commentary on the events of this anti-Fascist allegory. Adapting the device from radio newscasting, MacLeish felt it to be especially appropriate for radio drama because it created the effects associated with live news reports. Interestingly, both Stott and Pells, in discussing the documentary impulse during the 30s, give a great deal of attention to the role of the reporter / narrator / commentator and the function of direct narration and description in conveying information directly to the audience. In *The Fall of the City,* the description of events by the Announcer is undermined by the play's other major strategy, its reliance on a repertory of devices such as poetic verse and choral interludes adapted from Greek tragedy. The mix of the archaic and the modern lead to an oddly heteroglot work, which ultimately betrays its documentary aspiration. For Welles, however, playing the role of the Announcer could easily have been a most productive lesson in documentary strategies.

The radio adaptation of his theatrical production of Shakespeare's *Julius Caesar* provides another instructive lesson in Welles's involvement with documentary. Welles's theater production of *Caesar* was, of course, based on a process of topicalization. Welles set the play in contemporary dress with explicit allusions to Fascist and Nazi iconography in costume, gesture, and lighting (e.g., the famous Nuremberg lights effect). In its critique of Fascism and Nazism, the production was totally consistent with Popular Front ideology, as was a great deal of the Mercury Theatre's institutional practices (e.g., manifestoes in the *Daily Worker,* group ticket prices for unions and political groups, consultation with Communist Party intellectuals over the interpretation of *Danton's Death*). Because of its topicalization, the *Caesar* production can really be understood as Shakespeare in the form of a Living Newspaper, that most innovative wing of the Federal Theatre Project, which adapted documentary techniques (e.g., the use of a narrator, statistical information, the reading of news reports) to dramatic structures to represent up-to-the-minute economic and social ills. The function of Welles's topicalization of *Caesar* was to make it play as vividly as a news bulletin. Indeed, a publicity campaign was developed for the production in newspaper form: headlines, such as "Brutus-Cassius Stab Caesar," "Augur Warned J.C.," "Assassinated by Political Enemies on Floor of Senate Chamber," and "Fear Antonius Oration Might Incite Rabble," accompanied mock news stories and photos of the production.

For his radio adaptation of the play, Welles hit upon a strategy to further heighten the documentary thrust of the theatrical production. He hired H. V. Kaltenborn, who only a few months earlier had caused a sensation through his live radio reporting of the Munich crisis—a major "first" in direct, live broadcasting of the news. In Welles's program, Kaltenborn read excerpts from Plutarch as bridge passages in Shakespeare's play. The language of Plutarch, of course, worked against the spontaneity of the effect. But the idea of incorporating Kaltenborn into the production, given his association with the live broadcasting of political crises, is symptomatic of Welles's interest in documentary expression, an interest he was to satisfy less than two months later with the **"War of the Worlds"** broadcast.

The key to that broadcast was, of course, its transposition of the H. G. Wells story into the format of the live, on-the-spot coverage of a developing news story. First, unconfirmed news bulletins interrupted on-going shows. Then, interviews, on-the-spot description, and direct reports were used to "represent" the story's action. Even in its dullest moments in the last third or so of the show, direct description by an eye-witness was used to portray the devastation brought about by the Martian invaders.

As Stott and Pells both point out in their discussion of the broadcast, it was completely structured according to the documentary rhetoric that had developed in live broadcasting of news events only in the preceding few years. Phrases such as "We now take you to . . ." and "We return you now to the studio" were, at most, a year or two old in 1938 and were associated with crisis reporting. Stott claims that "the spontaneity of radio remotes in the Thirties encouraged audience participation." The goal was "to make the listener believe he was there." Surely, the panic caused by the **"War of the Worlds"** broadcast was, above all, a proof of radio's ability to create just such an effect. Significant portions of the audience, swayed by the new rhetoric of crisis reporting, believed that what they heard was really happening. In contrast to *The Fall of the City* and *Julius Caesar,* in which the announcer / narrator's role was distanced by the archaic language he was given to speak, the "live reporting" in **"The War of the Worlds"** sufficiently approximated the real thing for members of the audience to be taken in by the news format itself. In totally indulging his documentary imagination, Welles inadvertently created one of the strongest commentaries on its power.

Citizen Kane, The Magnificent Ambersons, and the ***It's All True*** project all reflect the documentary impulse, though in radically different modalities. Again, according to Susman, Stott, Pells, and others, the desire to capture the fabric of American life lay at the heart of the documentary impulse during the 30s. It is useful to remember that the original working title of ***Kane*** was *American*, a totalizing concept symptomatic of Welles and [co-script writer Herman] Mankiewicz's grand ambition to capture a comprehensive picture of American experience. ***Ambersons*** is best appreciated as an attempt at a large-scale sociohistorical exploration of the transition from genteel to industrial society around the turn of the century. And ***It's All True*** in its original scenario was to use four different episodes, each explicitly documentary in conception, to portray the variety of American life and culture.

Beyond this very general concern for the description of American society and culture, ***Citizen Kane*** demonstrates an additional aspect of the impact of documentary media during the 30s. Stott argues that the advent of radio news reporting put traditional newspaper journalism in a negative light. He claims that the American public distrusted the print media because, among other things, they believed journalism served partisan business interests. Resenting the newspapers' widespread opposition to FDR and impressed by the immediacy and directness of radio newscasting, the public stated its preference for radio journalism. Stott quotes Paul Lazarsfeld's 1940 study, *Radio and Printed Page,* to the effect that "radio was preferred to the press as a source of news," especially "by people of lower income, by women, and by those in rural areas."

Citizen Kane can clearly be seen as a product of this discourse. Given Welles's intimate involvement with the developing medium of radio, indeed, given the degree to which he had foregrounded the power of radio journalism through the **"War of the Worlds"** broadcast, the critique of newspaper journalism in ***Kane*** can be seen as a complementary gesture. A vital force in radio, Welles turned to the equally dynamic medium of motion pictures to criticize the ageing medium of the press. The conjoining of the critique of newspaper journalism with the critique of the magnate, a staple of 30s radical thought and art, suggests the degree to which ***Citizen Kane*** is a direct product of the decade's discursive practices.

In addition, of course, ***Kane*** also deals with one of the most contemporaneous of documentary formats, the newsreel. Replicating the verbal and visual rhetoric of the *March of Time* newsreel in precise detail, the film also places it in dialogue with the reminiscences of characters who knew Charles Foster Kane intimately. The dialogue between the modern news medium's representation of the character and the personal memories has the function of putting the newsreel's representation in quotes. Its truth value is challenged by the competing versions of Kane's life. Its status as a highly manipulated ideological formulation is exposed. As with the **"War of the Worlds"** broadcast, a very contemporary product of the media is reflected upon.

In the foregoing discussion, I have attempted to demonstrate just a few of the insights to be gained from an intertextual approach to Welles's work in radio, theater, and film and from an attempt to grasp the relations of his work to existing social and cultural discourses of the 30s. This discussion could go much further. In terms of the notion of documentary imagination, it is important to emphasize that with ***It's All True,*** Welles turned from fictional filmmaking to an explicitly documentary format. This impulse was continued in two very interesting and largely unknown radio series in 1942, *Hello Americans* and *Ceiling Unlimited,* which combined documentary and fictional procedures in complex ways that anticipated the reflexive treatment of such issues in ***F for Fake*** in 1973.

The discussion could turn to issues other than documentary expression. We could deal with formal issues and detail the ways in which the uses of sound in the radio shows are continued into the films or consider how the lighting techniques and the choreography of physical movement of the theater work extended into the films. We must insist that the documentary impulse is only one of several motifs which animate Welles's output. Potentially contradictory impulses such as expressionist aesthetics, an involvement with the New York City avant garde of the 30s (especially evident in some of the theater productions), and a reverence for old-fashioned oral story telling are as central to Welles's work as documentary expression. His method is perhaps best understood as the placing into dialogue of diverse discursive modes. We could extend the cultural analysis to an argument about the classical Welles career question. In so doing we might conclude that Welles's great productivity between 1935 and 1942 is most interestingly explained in terms of his extraordinary temperamental affinity with New Deal and Popular Front culture. From such a vantage point, it is also possible that the complex nature of the rest of his career is best understood through his post-war disaffection with American culture and politics and his status as an expatriate rather than through the notion of fear of completion.

Welles on his life as a movie maker:

Do you regret staying in movies?

I think I made essentially a mistake, but it's a mistake I can't regret because it's like saying that I shouldn't have stayed married to that woman and I did because I love her. I would have been more successful if I hadn't been married to her. I would have been more successful if I'd left movies immediately, stayed in the theatre, gone into politics, written—anything. I've wasted the great part of my life looking for money and trying to get along, trying to make my work from this terribly expensive paintbox which is a movie. And I've spent too much energy on things that have nothing to do with making a movie. It's about two per cent moviemaking and 98 per cent hustling. It's no way to spend a life.

Do you feel that's going to go on?

Oh, I'm going to go on being faithful to my girl, I love her. I fell so much in love with making movies that the theatre lost everything for me, you know. I'm just in love with making movies.

Welles, in an interview with Leslie Megahey, in The Listener, *20 May 1982.*

These concerns constitute projects for further elucidation in the critical re-evaluation of Welles's work. (pp. 5-10)

William G. Simon, "Orson Welles: An Introduction," in Persistence of Vision, *No. 7, 1989, pp. 5-11.*

Noël Carroll (essay date 1989)

[*Carroll is a professor of philosophy and theater at Cornell University and has written extensively on film theory. In the following essay, he examines two major interpretations of* Citizen Kane.]

Citizen Kane is a film that has engendered a classic conflict of interpretation. That is, there are at present two leading views of its thematic point, and these two views appear, on the surface, to be incompatible. These two interpretations can be called the enigma interpretation, on the one hand, and the Rosebud interpretation, on the other. Each interpretation is quite simple, and, I shall argue, their simplicity is important to the function they *actually* play in ***Citizen Kane.*** The enigma interpretation says that ***Citizen Kane*** illustrates the point that the nature of a person is ultimately a mystery; a person is all things to all persons, and, correspondingly, a multiplicity of selves. The Rosebud interpretation says that Kane's personality is finally explicable by some such notions as those of "lost childhood" or "lost innocence." I hasten to add that many commentators may, strangely enough, fail to see that these interpretations of ***Citizen Kane*** are incompatible. But they obviously are: if human life is inexplicable in the way the enigma interpretation says, then a life like Kane's cannot be explained in terms of a clue like Rosebud. Or, alternatively, if Rosebud yields a convincing explanation of Kane's life, then Kane's life, and, by extension, human life in general is not inevitably inexplicable, i.e., not unavoidably enigmatic.

A recent defense of the enigma view, one that is aware of its incompatibility with the Rosebud view, can be found in Ian Jarvie's *Philosophy of the Film.* He writes:

> The newsreel narrator suggested that Kane was all things to all men; to the right he was a communist; to the left a fascist; a man of the people who consorted with the rich and powerful; a foe of corruption who was himself corrupted by power; an amiable man with a stubborn and ruthless devotion to his own views. The successive stories embroider on this dual aspect of Kane; depending on who is talking he can be seen either way; his best friend finds him corrupted by egotism; his business manager sees him as a creative and dynamic boss; his guardian as a dangerous and headstrong ne'er do well; his valet sees him as a man with feet of clay.

Jarvie goes on to hypothesize that these disparities indicate that "***Citizen Kane*** is to be read as a critique of the naive theory of human identity, namely that there are clues to it which can be deciphered and so make sense of much of what a person does. . . ." Jarvie pushes the enigma approach so far as to suspect that the film is explicitly anti-Freudian; he says:

> One could then read the film as a criticism and repudiation of the very idea that there are deep childhood and sexual clues to a person. That rummaging round in people's memories of Kane does not turn up some vital clue to what makes him tick. That he eludes the best efforts of an investigative reporter. That a person is an enigma. The only real clue they have, "Rosebud," is nothing more than a sled, which is perhaps a random memory on a dying man's lips.

This view, minus Jarvie's putative perception of the rejection of psychoanalysis, is quite familiar. Borges writes: "We understand at the end that the fragments do not have a hidden unity: the unhappy Foster Kane is a shadow, a mere chaos of appearances." Borges, then, invokes the metaphor of a labyrinth, presumably one with no center.

Of course, the biggest problem with the enigma view is what to do with the final appearance of Rosebud. After the mystery of human life is intoned for the last time, the mystery appears to be cleared up. One way to try to get rid of the incongruity is to insult it, as Welles did by calling Rosebud "dollarbook Freud," and saying it was [co-scriptwriter] Herman Mankiewicz's fault anyway. Jarvie's response is more civil but equally dismissive:

> It [Rosebud] seems at the centre of things but it is actually irrelevant. This makes for a better defense of ***Kane.*** The alleged mystery of what makes Kane tick may be merely a McGuffin, a plot device to enable us to follow this reporter back into various people's memories. The interaction of the people on screen, the events that happen to them, become the point of the movie, and the hunt for the McGuffin slips into the background: then, in the incinerator scene, it is rounded off neatly, but *cynically* (emphasis added). For we see the smoke pouring out of Xanadu's chimneys, scattering this albeit meaningless clue to the winds.

In this quotation, we see that Jarvie, more than any previous commentator, is aware that the Rosebud finale seems logically to contradict the enigma interpretation. Jarvie tries to remove the contradiction by making Rosebud a matter of irony or cynicism. However, there is very little to support this interpretation. Admittedly, the ending is tricked out with Gothic conventions. But this cannot be interpreted as irony or cynicism. For these conventions are evident throughout the film; if they are to be recognized as ironic in the last instance, they would have to be ironic in earlier instances, which would make virtually any interpretation of the film, including an enigma interpretation, unintelligible. Clearly, Jarvie's main defense of this reading of the last scene is that it gives us the most satisfying interpretation of the film. But that is to defend the enigma interpretation as the best interpretation by saying it is the best interpretation. The attribution of cynicism or irony to the last sequence is not motivated by the film and it seems little more than an *ad hoc* attempt to save the theory in the face of contravening evidence.

Of course, if one takes the final apparition of the sled seriously, one is apt to have a very different view of the theme of the film. The sled becomes the emblem for a loss. By whispering "Rosebud," André Bazin [in his *Orson Welles*]

During the mid-1940s, Welles himself considered running for the Senate from his home state of Wisconsin. "I didn't. . .And that's how come there was a McCarthy." Joseph McCarthy, who went on to form the House Un-American Activities Committee, would have been his opponent.

surmises "Kane admits before dying that there is no profit in gaining the whole world if one has lost one's own childhood."

One difficulty with this line of interpretation is that, insofar as we know almost nothing about Kane's childhood or his enduring reactions to being uprooted, Rosebud might be thought to function as an explanatory placebo. In fact, the Rosebud interpretation runs the risk of being embarrassing. The idea of childhood nostalgia is about as vapid as you can get, while the Rosebud device verges on hokum. The latter criticism is, indeed, the basis on which commentators, like Parker Tyler [in his *The Hollywood Hallucination*], deride the film. So a liability of the Rosebud interpretation is that, however accurate, it has the net effect of making ***Citizen Kane*** sound pretty dumb. Thus, a critic who favors the Rosebud interpretation is likely to accompany it with a defense of the intellectual credentials of this way of explaining Kane's behavior. James Naremore provides this service when he argues that:

> Some of the psychoanalytic ideas in ***Kane*** might have come straight out of a textbook. According to Freudian terminology, Kane can be typed as a regressive, anal-sadistic personality. His lumpen-bourgeois family is composed of a weak, untrustworthy father and a loving, albeit puritanical mother; he is taken away from this family at a pre-pubescent stage and reared by a bank; as an adult he "returns" to what Freud describes as a pre-genital form of sexuality in which "not the genital component-instincts, but the *sadistic* and *anal* are the most prominent." Thus, throughout his adult life Kane is partly a sadist who wants to obtain power over others, and partly an anal type, who obsessively collects zoo animals and museum pieces. His childhood . . . seems far from idyllic; nevertheless, it is a childhood toward which he has been compulsively drawn.

Both the enigma interpretation and the Rosebud interpretation are well supported by the dialogue, the narrative structure, and the visual elaboration of the film. The basis for the enigma interpretation is amply set out in the "News on the March" sequence. Rhetorically, this sequence is structured in terms of oppositions and catalogues. The oppositions invoked run the gamut of logical types from oxymorons and binary reversals to what are meant to appear as contradictions. Kane is described as a communist, a fascist, and an American; he starts one war and opposes another; he speaks for millions and is hated by millions; few private lives were more public; he supports and denounces public figures, often supporting and then denouncing the same person; Kane made history, but then he became history; and, of course, in short order, we see a man who loves public attention and who preens for the camera become a recluse who shuns cameras. Many of these oppositions are not very deep; they are rather the artifacts of a catchy journalistic style. Nevertheless, this introduces Kane to us as "a mass of contradictions"—in the argot of newsspeak—or a bundle of opposites. Kane, in other words, is not presented as a coherent identity so much as a collision of contrasting figures.

The catalogues in the newsreel also articulate this sense of opposition both verbally and visually. These breathless catalogues stress heterogeneity. Introduced to Xanadu and its holdings, what principle of taste could accommodate that jumble of styles; the best the commentator can do is to call it a *collection of everything*. Similarly, when we learn of the extent of Kane's businesses, the meaning of the word "conglomerate" strikes home; Kane owns newspapers, radio stations, forests, paper mills, factories, mines, apartment houses, grocery stores (why grocery stores?), and ocean liners (why not?). What seems to hold this list together is a simple principle of acquisition rather than a coherent plan; his holdings are an analogue for Kane himself—a collection of activities rather than the stuff of a coherent project.

These interrelated themes—of the multiplicity and heterogeneity of Kane—recur throughout the film. Kane tells Thatcher that he is speaking to two persons—ones indeed with contradictory purposes; the idea that Kane is more than one person is also supported metaphorically in the imagery. Not only do a multiplicity of photographic images of Kane proliferate throughout the film, but Kane speaks before a giant image of himself at the political rally. And, summing up the multiplicity theme, as Kane leaves his wife's room and passes the mirrors at the end of the valet's story, at least six images of Kane are on the screen, and an infinity of others is suggested.

At the level of action, Kane's behavior is often contradictory in a way that on the face of it, at least, indicates that it issues from a divided self. He finishes Leland's review in a manner that is *at odds* with his own interests, *but then* he fires Leland, *but then* he sends Leland a check for $25,000. And, of course, as Jarvie points out above, the narrative device of the interview advances the notion of a multiplicity of selves in the sense that Kane's identity *may seem* relative to whomever is telling the story.

Throughout the film, the heterogeneity of Kane's collections continues as an objective correlative of Kane's personhood. The scenes in Xanadu's living room mix classic, medieval, and baroque artworks. And there are the massive, high-angle shots of crated artifacts that, to my mind, recall the piles of the fragmentary, unassembled pieces of Susan's puzzles—which puzzles, of course, are proffered, quite explicitly, as the visual equivalent to the narrative investigation. The reporter, Thompson, prompted by the appearance of one of Susan's puzzles, equates his investigation with it, calling Rosebud a piece in such a puzzle and going on to say that it cannot explain a man's life. Kane's life, in other words, remains a mystery, a puzzle, an enigma—a congeries of fragmentary parts that do not finally cohere.

Nevertheless, the Rosebud interpretation is *also* extensively grounded in the film. To see this, however, more has to be said about what this interpretation involves. The film offers a portrait of Kane, one in which he is shown to have great difficulty sustaining what might be thought of as reciprocal love relations. His relation to the underclasses, of whom he is a self-appointed champion, is paternalist, and his relation to his second wife is domineering and patriarchal. Kane's view of love, as he explicitly admits, is that love is something to be had on one's own terms. Kane does not adjust his affections to the purposes, rights, and desires of his love objects; he does not, or he does not easily, brook, so to speak, negative feedback from these love objects. When they fail to bend to his fantasies, his responses are rage and / or retreat. Confronted by reversals of expectation, he becomes reclusive. He hides away with his collection of art objects and his zoo.

Interestingly, the art objects he seems fondest of accumulating are statues—"people" who can't talk back to him—while his animals are completely under his control; indeed, the first specimens of these that we see are his monkeys, exactly the sorts of creatures Leland predicts Kane will lord it over after the love of the people fails him.

This behavior, which the film presents as self-destructive, also has a ready explanation. Kane has been separated from his family at an early age. That separation, of course, is one in which the sled called Rosebud is an important accessory; it cannot be satisfactorily replaced by the fancier sled, the Crusader, which Thatcher offers Kane in an ensuing shot. So, though we are unaware of its name, the Rosebud sled figures in Kane's separation from his family, most importantly in his separation from his mother. And, significantly, Kane utters "Rosebud" for the second time in the film, when he picks up the glassy snowscape after Susan—with whom he fell in love during a discussion about mothers—has left him.

This second separation—which is recounted twice—closes the investigation which itself was initiated by Thatcher's recounting of the original separation of Kane from his family, with which the second separation seems to be identified as a tragic replay. The saliently posed theme of separation, which organizes the central plot structure in the film and which is emblematized by Rosebud, in turn, can be worked into an eminently plausible explanation of Kane's behavior. Specifically, separated from a family—that is, from an at least structurally congenial context where the potential for developing a capacity for reciprocal love relations has a running start—Kane is emotionally disadvantaged in a profound way. And that disadvantage is the root of his self-destructiveness—of his inability to act within the bounds of reciprocity. In short, deprived of a certain form of family life, Kane apparently has trouble with love, specifically in terms of reciprocity.

Of course, much of this interpretation is available on the surface of the film. Basically, I have arrived at it by paraphrasing what Leland and Susan say of Kane while interpolating some quasi-technical, though not arcane, notions such as reciprocity and separation. Both Leland and Susan Alexander return to the issue of love several times, emphasizing Kane's inability to love, especially in terms of the way in which Kane confuses love relations with those of ownership and monetary exchange. Leland says Kane did everything for love but that this failed because Kane could only love himself (and, he adds as a perspicuous afterthought, his mother). Susan complains that Kane is essentially domineering—a point underscored by at least two particularly stunning, low-angle shots during her interview—and, in the course of the argument in the tent, where the tune "It Can't be Love" suggestively blares in the background, Susan charges that Kane confuses loving with buying (an especially poignant accusation since one infers that Kane is doing unto others as the bank did unto him).

The accounts that Leland and Susan offer of Kane are pivotal to any audience understanding of Kane's behavior because they are the only attempts at explaining Kane that are found in the film. That they dovetail is important as well as the fact that they are not contradicted by anything else that is said of Kane.

The latter observation undoubtedly sounds as though it flies in the face of received wisdom about the film; for it is commonplace to note that the various interviews stake out different views of Kane. However, it is crucial to note that these differences really have to do with varying evaluations or assessments of Kane's character. The interviews do not conflict on factual matters. ***Citizen Kane*** is not, as David Bordwell points out [in his "The Dual Cinematic Tradition in *Citizen Kane,*" in *The Classic Cinema,* ed. Stanley Solomon] like *Rashomon;* the descriptions, as opposed to the character evaluations, are internally consistent.

That each narrator has an opinion of Kane does not appear to affect his or her reporting; Thatcher hates Kane, but his picture of the young editor is of as ebullient a figure as Bernstein's. Similarly, what Leland and Susan say by way of summary descriptions of Kane's problems with love and reciprocity fit with everything else that is presented, and, insofar as they represent the only, as well as an unchallenged, explanation of Kane, they have *prima facie* authority as a statement of certain general facts of Kane's life.

The sequence which does the most work in connecting these general facts about Kane's life with the theme of separation is the first scene in Susan's apartment, where, as already noted, we see for the second time, in an insert shot, the glassy snowscape (which earlier occasions the word Rosebud) on Susan's vanity table. Kane talks of the death of his mother, his search for his youth, their mutual loneliness, and his trip to a warehouse, where, one infers, the sled awaits. Susan also speaks of her mother and her mother's operatic ambitions for her.

This affects Kane audibly, and one feels that it is at that moment that Susan's operatic career is born. The psychological structure, here, seems to be that Kane attempts to recover the loss of his relation to his mother by reinstating a mothering relation with Susan, one in which he will carry out the project that Susan's mother—against Susan's better judgment—elected for Susan. Their relation, then, begins under the aegis of a fantasy that denies the existence of Susan's goals and rights, but which is concocted as a way for Kane to recover his own psychic debits. That is, the lack of reciprocity in Kane's relation to Susan is a causal consequence of Kane's separation from his family. Kane's failure is an attempt to re-establish a family, which is something he is bound to botch since he was torn from his own family.

Expanded in this way, the Rosebud explanation does a nice job of explaining a great deal of the film. It illuminates why Kane attempts to find love by taking command, and it renders intelligible the reasons his projects autodestruct. It also suggests a psychic rationale for the theme of acquisition so vividly underscored in the photography. For in amassing these collections of statues and animals, Kane creates a world of beings that he can control, a world of love on his terms.

The Rosebud interpretation of Kane's behavior is not directly stated; but the various elements that comprise it are set forth saliently, and the audience is prompted to put the pieces together with the apparition of the sled. This inference is not hard to come by—though it is aesthetically gratifying to do so—not only because it is a rather simple explanation, but, more importantly, because it is a commonplace, or what might be called folk-psychological, explanation. This is not said to disparage it. This sort of explanation is perfectly adequate and acceptable; it rests on the acceptance that there is a generalization, of some marked probability, of a connection between separation and the inability to form reciprocal love relations. That there is such a generalization and since there are not other rival explanations of Kane's behavior, makes the Rosebud explanation preeminently sound. And, since the correlation between separation and the inability to love is also generally endorsed in our culture, audiences are likely to fill in the Rosebud interpretation when they see the sled.

But again, the Rosebud interpretation contradicts the enigma interpretation, which is not only well grounded in the film, but which is also rather simple and accessible, and which rests, as well, on a cultural cliché. So which one is the correct interpretation of the film? They can't both be true since they contradict each other.

The problem here may be simply that we are beginning with the presupposition that the point of the film is to offer an interpretation of Kane's behavior. An alternative interpretation of the *film*—in contradistinction to an interpretation of *Charles Foster Kane*—might be that the film is about staging a conflict of interpretations about Kane's life in particular and lives in general. Here, of course, I do not have in mind a conflict between the perspectives of Thompson's various informants; for, as I attempted to argue above, there is no real disagreement at the level of description and explanation there. Rather, the film advances two readily accessible, though incompatible, interpretations of Kane's life.

What remains of primary importance in this respect is that these interpretations are, for the most part, in the film; the enigma interpretation belongs to Thompson and, perhaps by extension, to the media. The Rosebud interpretation, in full, does not belong to any character, although most of it is put in place by Leland who, at least, has a glimmering of the importance of Kane's mother, as does Kane himself to some degree. Or, perhaps it would be better to assign the Rosebud interpretation to the ever-probing camera. In any case, like the enigma interpretation voiced by Thompson, the former is an interpretation of Kane's life that is to be found in the film.

There is no need, however, to think that the interpretation of the film must be an interpretation of Kane's life. The film, that is, may contain interpretations of Kane's life without it being necessary to identify the film with either of those interpretations. Instead, the film may be about setting the life interpretations it contains in opposition.

Another way to get at this point is to note that the output of a film interpretation need not always be a statement of what a film *means*. We might also interpret a film in terms of what it *does*. In this light, I am trying to dispel the pressure of deciding between the enigma and the Rosebud interpretations of ***Citizen Kane*** by suggesting that an interpretation of this film does not reduce to a decision about its meaning (vis-a-vis the meaning of Kane's life). Instead, we should interpret the film as an attempt—similar in purpose to many philosophical dialogues—to animate a debate. Specifically, it is designed rhetorically to draw the audience into a consideration of the conflicting claims of two commonplace views about human lives. That is, ***Citizen Kane*** is structured in such a way as to afford the opportunity for the general audience to interrogate prevailing cultural views of the nature of human life by setting them forth in competition.

This is not to say the film holds that there is no possible interpretation of a human life—that would effectively be a way of re-instituting the enigma view. Rather, the film leaves it to the audience to determine whether lives like Kane's can be explained or whether they are enigmatic. That is, the film invites further reflection, discussion, and re-viewing, rather than closing the topic unambiguously. And, as well, in considering the conflict of the common conceptions of life the film projects, the viewer comes to reflect upon those conceptions as they figure in life as well as art. Indeed, I think that where a viewer feels pulled toward one of these views over the other, it will be in virtue of reflecting on lives in general.

Of course, maintaining that there are two determinate, though incompatible, interpretations of Kane's life in the film does not imply that the film is an open text, redolent with an infinite play of meanings. The film is structured around two intricately motivated interpretations which, however inconsistent, are both thoroughly grounded in the dialogue, narrative, and visual elements of the film. And although the film has two interpretations of *Kane's life,* the *film* can be characterized in terms of one interpretation which attributes to it a unified purpose.

The primary virtue of treating the film in this way is that it explains why two obviously contradictory views of Kane's life are so forcefully posed in such close proximity. It also accounts for the way in which the film is so carefully structured in support of each of the prevailing interpretations of Kane's life. Moreover, this view of ***Citizen Kane*** seems to me more in accordance with our intuition of its singular importance than would tying the film to either of the alternative themes we have discussed. For, surely, activating the tensions between two standing cultural conceptions is more aesthetically engaging than opting for one in favor of the other.

I have often stressed that the two leading interpretations of Kane's life—the enigma interpretation and the Rosebud interpretation—are simple as well as culturally well entrenched. This is appropriate for the role they play in the dialogical structure of the film [in an endnote, Carroll adds: "As I indicated earlier, I see the philosophical dialogue as a model for ***Citizen Kane,*** and it is in that sense that I attribute a 'dialogical' structure to the film. I realize that the term 'dialogical' is also presently employed by followers of Bakhtin. Since their use of the term would appear to require a much more radical play of meaning than I argue is relevant to ***Citizen Kane,*** my usage should not be confused with theirs"]. For if I am right, the point of the film is to involve the movie audience in a conflict of views about life. And in order to be functional in this respect, the views must be relatively simple, somewhat commonplace, and near or on the surface of the work. That is, they have to be accessible. Recondite or complex views of life would lack the salience required for a movie audience to pick up and enter into the debate. And, indeed, a well-structured debate is obviously more accessible to a movie audience than would be an infinite play of signification. Thus, one advantage of postulating an interpretation of ***Citizen Kane*** as a staging of commonplace views of life for the movie audience is that it shows how it is possible for the film to remain so popular for movie audiences. At the same time, maintaining that the debate remains open indicates one reason that it may be pleasurable to re-view and to re-engage the film again and again.

Furthermore, what I have called a dialogical interpretation of ***Citizen Kane*** also has the asset of fitting together with and expanding upon some of the best observations of the film's style that we have—viz., those of André Bazin. As is well known, Bazin believed that elements of the visual style of ***Citizen Kane*** made possible a distinctive level of audience participation. Through shots where the action is articulated on multiple planes, Bazin observed, the viewer might be said to discover dramatic meanings on her own and notice telling details as she actively scans the image. Not all or even the majority of the shots in ***Citizen Kane*** are of this sort, though many important ones are—enough, in fact, that this type of shooting influences the overall feel of the film significantly. Of course, the multiplanar shots that Bazin thought encouraged audience participation were not unstructured. Rather they had a structure that facilitated and rewarded the spectator's active search for significance.

Similarly, what I have identified as the dialogical structure of the film's narrative also makes possible a level of audience participation with the film—this time, however, by articulating, in a manner of speaking, multiple planes in the film's conceptual space. There is no guarantee that every spectator will be sensitive to this play of interpretation and engage it, just as there is no guarantee that every spectator will see everything there is to see and to reflect upon in the film's visual space. Nevertheless, the structural modifications are there, and they allow, rather than mandate, a level of, albeit limited, audience participation of a sort rare in Hollywood filmmaking.

One difficulty, of course, in attempting to align our interpretation with Bazin's approach is that Bazin, as mentioned earlier, explicitly advocates the Rosebud interpretation of the film rather than a dialogical interpretation. In this regard, I am forced to say that Bazin did not take advantage of the best interpretation that was available to him. For surely the notion that ***Citizen Kane*** has a dialogical structure accords best with his intuition that what is important about Welles is the issue of choice for the spectator. It is true that Bazin generally speaks of choice in terms of camera style; but he is also aware, as his remarks about Stroheim indicate, that the camera style is part of an overall narrative approach. So in advocating a dialogical interpretation of the film, one abides by the spirit rather than the letter of Bazin's writings. Moreover, in pinpointing the overall significance of ***Citizen Kane*** in virtue of these expanded opportunities for audience participation, one is in a position to situate the importance of the film for the cultural politics of the Thirties and Forties in a way that has been hitherto overlooked.

In order to appreciate the cultural significance of ***Citizen Kane,*** it is useful to recall Clement Greenberg's extremely influential 1939 article entitled "Avant-Garde and Kitsch." It is a meditation, a professedly Marxist one, about the direction art should take in modern mass society. This article might be regarded as a clarion call for postwar fine art and its cinematic fellow-travelers. Effectively, Greenberg argues, the rise of mass society has sundered the traditional foundations of art. Industrial society produces a demand for highly consumable art, easy art, art that does not engage reflection, but which counterfeits the patina of the great artistic achievements of the past. This is kitsch. Kitsch is the hallmark of fascist and Stalinist art. Likewise, a magazine like *The New Yorker* is kitsch as is any art that is designed to elicit the "spectator's unreflective enjoyment." It is art that demands no effort. Though Greenberg does not discuss film, I would surmise that Hollywood movies, such as John Ford's films of the Thirties, would be preeminently kitsch. Moreover, the upshot of this article would appear to be that any attempt at addressing a mass audience—and, in consequence, any attempt to make a mass movie entertainment—will result in kitsch.

In opposition to kitsch, Greenberg recommends avant-garde art because it has detached itself from industrial society at large, and because, in concentrating on problems internal to art, it will preserve the great accomplishments of Western culture through dark times. Avant-garde art, by definition, enjoins reflection, effort, and participation from the spectator. It is difficult. It depends on the spectator adding something to it as a result of reflection, thereby enshrining the high premium the Kantian tradition puts on the play of perception and cognition. And, obviously, Greenberg maintains, in a gesture of immense significance for the direction art and (avant-garde) film art will take, that ambitious art must be detached from mass society in order to secure this sort of reflection on the audience's part. The choices are: kitsch versus the avant garde, mass consumption art versus isolationist aesthetics, and unreflectiveness versus audience participation. Furthermore, the way in which Greenberg has stacked the deck makes it look as though any attempt to engage a mass audience by means of movies will be illegitimate from the perspective of genuine art.

But in this context, of course, a film like ***Citizen Kane*** rep-

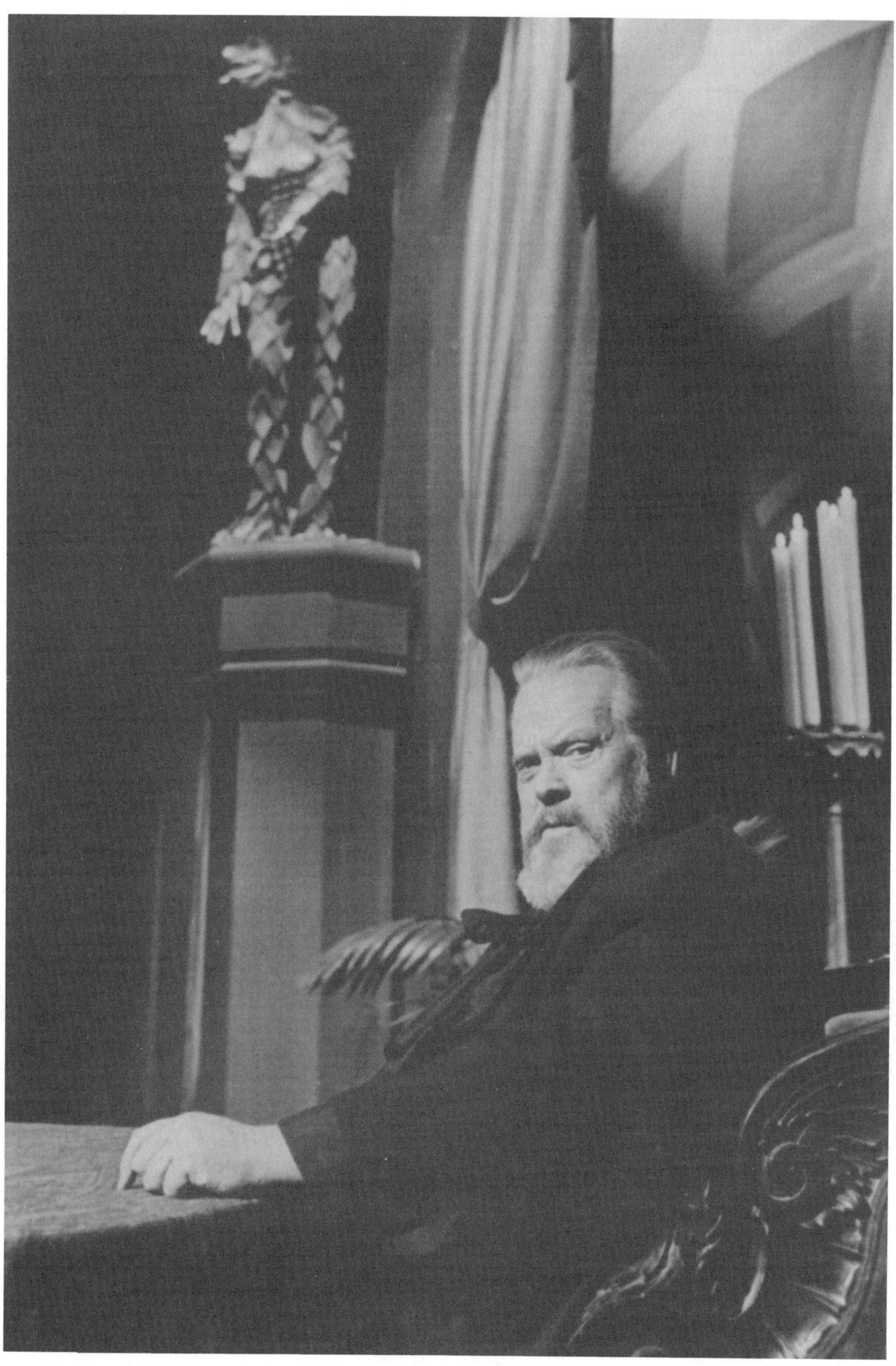

resents the possibility of a middle road. Its dialogical and visual structures—including the montage structures that Bazin often (but not always) ignores—propose a way of coming to terms with mass culture that is neither kitsch nor avant garde. ***Citizen Kane*** is a mass popular entertainment which sustains the availability of participant spectatorship. It suggests a way in which mass art can accommodate the strictures of traditional art while also welcoming mass audience participation. It is not kitsch but rather satirizes Hollywood's penchant for kitsch by way of magnifying Charles Foster Kane's colossal bad taste. As Michael Denning has argued, the project of the Mercury theater was to bring art to the people. In ***Citizen Kane*** that commitment is connected to encouraging participant spectatorship—putatively one of the highest values of traditional art—in a mass format not divorced from questions about life. ***Citizen Kane*** is a rare example of a mass popular entertainment that is also art in the *demanding* or *honorific* sense that it abets reflection. With respect to what I submit is Greenberg's still influential but by now clearly unsatisfactory dilemma—either kitsch or the avant garde—***Citizen Kane*** proposes a third way, a way that encourages rather than discourages the ambitious artist to attempt to make movies for the general public.

[In an endnote, Carroll concludes:

"Douglas Gomery and Paul Arthur were somewhat puzzled by the concluding sections of this paper and demanded to know explicitly what its connection was to the earlier discussions of the enigma and Rosebud interpretations of the film. As I see it, if *either* the Rosebud or enigma interpretation of the film is correct, then the film would turn out to be kitsch according to Greenberg's conception of it. If, however, the film is dialogical, then it promotes the kind of participatory spectatorship that Greenberg regards to be the hallmark of genuine art. Thus, if the film is structured in the way that is advanced in the earlier parts of this paper, it is an example of mass art that is a candidate for consideration as genuine art, at least by Greenberg's lights.

This, of course, entails that movies can be authentic art, again under Greenberg's conception, and that the attempt to stimulate mass audiences by means of a mass medium is not automatically kitsch. And, this, in turn, suggests a way in which the elitism and / or hermeticism of Greenberg and subsequent avant-gardists is not inevitable, even on their own terms. One can, that is, make mass popular films, for example in the manner of ***Citizen Kane,*** for general audiences in, so to say, good aesthetic conscience. The significance of this for cultural politics should be obvious: there is no deep conceptual pressure, of the sort Greenberg suggests, for art to sever its relations with the general audience. Avant-garde isolationism is not the only alternative, even within the somewhat special, traditionally derived, theoretical framework that Greenberg invokes. That is, happily, a good aesthetic conscience *can be* compatible with a good political one."] (pp. 51-60)

Noël Carroll, "Interpreting 'Citizen Kane'," in Persistence of Vision, *No. 7, 1989, pp. 51-62.*

FURTHER READING

Bibliography

Wood, Bret. *Orson Welles: A Bio-Bibliography.* Westport, Conn.: Greenwood Press, 1990, 364 p.

The most comprehensive bibliography of primary and secondary sources available, including sections on Welles's credits in theater, radio, and film, as well as a discography, a chronology, and a biographical sketch.

Biography

Higham, Charles. *Orson Welles: The Rise and Fall of an American Genius.* New York: St. Martin's Press, 1985, 373 p.

Extensively researched and generally negative study that articulates Higham's theory that Welles left numerous projects unfinished because he had a psychological "fear of completion."

Leaming, Barbara. *Orson Welles: A Biography.* New York: Penguin, 1985, 700 p.

Detailed and highly complimentary biography.

Criticism

Bazin, André. *Orson Welles: A Critical View.* Translated by Jonathan Rosenbaum. New York: Harper & Row, 1978, 138 p.

Celebrated study by a leading French film critic that includes a foreword by François Truffaut and a profile by Jean Cocteau.

Carringer, Robert L. *"The Magnificent Ambersons": A Reconstruction.* Berkeley: University of California Press, 1993, 307 p.

Reconstruction of Welles's original screenplay for *The Magnificent Ambersons.* The book also includes Carringer's essay "Oedipus in Indianapolis," which argues that the disastrous outcome of the *Ambersons* project was due primarily to Welles's emotional discomfort with the erotic component of the story's mother-son relationship.

Comito, Terry, ed. *"Touch of Evil": Orson Welles, Director.* New Brunswick, N.J.: Rutgers University Press, 1985, 280 p.

Includes the continuity script for *Touch of Evil* and reprints commentary on the film by François Truffaut, Charlton Heston, Stephen Heath, and others.

Heath, Stephen. "Film and System: Terms of Analysis, Parts I and II." *Screen* 16, Nos. 1, 2 (Spring-Summer 1975): 7-77, 91-113.

Analysis of *Touch of Evil* that attempts to describe the psychoanalytic and ideological aspects common to all classic narrative films.

Howard, James. *The Complete Films of Orson Welles.* New York: Carol Publishing Group, 1991, 255 p.

Illustrated study of Welles's work as an actor and director.

Kalinak, Kathryn. "The Text of Music: A Study of *The Mag-*

nificent Ambersons." *Cinema Journal* 27, No. 4 (Summer 1988): 45-63.

Discusses Welles's collaboration with composer Bernard Herrmann and analyzes the importance of the musical score to the film's narrative. Kalinak quotes Herrmann: "Orson is the only one with any musical, cultural background. All the other directors I worked with haven't had the temerity to tell me anything about music."

Lyons, Bridget Gellert, ed. *"Chimes at Midnight": Orson Welles, Director.* New Brunswick, N.J.: Rutgers University Press, 1988, 340 p.

Includes the continuity script for *Chimes at Midnight* and reprints commentaries on the film by Dudley Andrew, C. L. Barber, Pauline Kael, and others.

McBride, Joseph. "Welles before *Kane.*" *Film Quarterly* XXIII, No. 3 (Spring 1970): 19-22.

Describes and assesses *The Hearts of Age,* a four-minute silent film Welles made at age nineteen.

———. "The Other Side of Orson Welles." *American Film* 1, No. 9 (July-August 1976): 14-20.

Discusses the production and themes of *The Other Side of the Wind,* in which the author was cast as "a film critic named Mr. Pister. 'The high priest of the cinema,' Welles sarcastically dubbed the character."

Persistence of Vision: Special Issue on Orson Welles, No. 7 (1989): 5-179.

Includes essays by such noted film scholars as Douglas Gomery, Robert Sklar, Robert Stam, Susan Ryan, and Catherine Benamou and a catalog of Welles's work in radio, theater, and film.

Sarris, Andrew. *"Kane:* For and Against." *Sight and Sound* 1 n.s., No. 6 (October 1991): 21-3.

States that the film "was neither the beginning of anything, nor the end of anything, but more a glorious middle. The moment someone tells me that *Citizen Kane* is the only good American film, I immediately realize they do not fully understand even *Citizen Kane* itself."

Sartre, Jean-Paul. *"Citizen Kane."* Translated by Dana Polan. *Post Script* 7, No. 1 (Fall 1987): 60-5.

Disparages *Citizen Kane* as elitist, "cut off from the masses," and self-consciously artistic.

Simon, William G. "Welles: Bakhtin: Parody." *Quarterly Review of Film and Video* 12, Nos. 1, 2 (1990): 23-8.

Applies Mikhail Bakhtin's theory of parody to *Mr. Arkadin,* a film Simon argues highlights the essential challenges posed by all of Welles's works.

Stainton, Audrey. *"Don Quixote:* Orson Welles' Secret." *Sight and Sound* 57, No. 4 (Autumn 1988): 252-60.

Discusses the making of Welles's *Don Quixote.* The author of this essay was Welles's secretary for part of the film's production.

Telotte, J. P. "Narration, Desire, and *The Lady from Shanghai.*" In his *Voices in the Dark: The Narrative Patterns of "Film Noir",* pp. 57-73. Urbana: University of Illinois Press, 1989.

Analyzes the "voice-over/flashback" technique used in *The Lady from Shanghai* and concludes that, like *Citizen Kane,* the film "hints at a similar succession of narratives, a constant round of efforts at getting the story right, and with only forgetfulness or death—both dissolutions of narrative—as a foreseeable goal."

Truffaut, François. "Orson Welles." In his *The Films in My Life,* pp. 278-91. Translated by Leonard Mayhew. New York: Simon and Schuster, 1978.

Discusses *Citizen Kane, Mr. Arkadin,* and *Touch of Evil.*

Vidal, Gore. "Remembering Orson Welles." *The New York Review of Books* XXXVI, No. 9 (1 June 1989): 12-16.

Anecdotal reminiscence of Vidal's friendship with Welles and positive review of Welles's screenplay, *The Big Brass Ring.*

Additional coverage of Welles's life and career is contained in the following sources published by Gale Research: *Contemporary Authors,* Vols. 93-96, 117 [obituary] and *Contemporary Literary Criticism,* Vol. 20.

□ Contemporary Literary Criticism

Indexes

Literary Criticism Series
Cumulative Author Index
Cumulative Nationality Index

How to Use This Index

The main references

Calvino, Italo
1923-1985.....CLC 5, 8, 11, 22, 33, 39, 73; SSC 3

list all author entries in the following Gale Literary Criticism series:

CLC = *Contemporary Literary Criticism*
CLR = *Children's Literature Review*
CMLC = *Classical and Medieval Literature Criticism*
DC = *Drama Criticism*
LC = *Literature Criticism from 1400 to 1800*
NCLC = *Nineteenth-Century Literature Criticism*
PC = *Poetry Criticism*
SSC = *Short Story Criticism*
TCLC = *Twentieth-Century Literary Criticism*

The cross-references

See also CANR 23; CA 85-88; obituary CA 116

list all author entries in the following Gale biographical and literary sources:

AAYA = *Authors & Artists for Young Adults*
AITN = *Authors in the News*
BLC = *Black Literature Criticism*
BW = *Black Writers*
CA = *Contemporary Authors*
CAAS = *Contemporary Authors Autobiography Series*
CABS = *Contemporary Authors Bibliographical Series*
CANR = *Contemporary Authors New Revision Series*
CAP = *Contemporary Authors Permanent Series*
CDALB = *Concise Dictionary of American Literary Biography*
CDBLB = *Concise Dictionary of British Literary Biography*
DA = *DISCovering Authors*
DLB = *Dictionary of Literary Biography*
DLBD = *Dictionary of Literary Biography Documentary Series*
DLBY = *Dictionary of Literary Biography Yearbook*
HLC = *Hispanic Literature Criticism*
HW = *Hispanic Writers*
JRDA = *Junior DISCovering Authors*
MAICYA = *Major Authors and Illustrators for Children and Young Adults*
MTCW = *Major 20th-Century Writers*
SAAS = *Something about the Author Autobiography Series*
SATA = *Something about the Author*
WLC = *World Literature Criticism, 1500 to the Present*
YABC = *Yesterday's Authors of Books for Children*

Literary Criticism Series
Cumulative Author Index

A.
See Arnold, Matthew

A. E. .... **TCLC 3, 10**
See also Russell, George William
See also DLB 19

A. M.
See Megged, Aharon

A. R. P-C
See Galsworthy, John

Abasiyanik, Sait Faik 1906-1954
See Sait Faik
See also CA 123

Abbey, Edward 1927-1989 ...... **CLC 36, 59**
See also CA 45-48; 128; CANR 2, 41

Abbott, Lee K(ittredge) 1947- ...... **CLC 48**
See also CA 124; DLB 130

Abe, Kobo 1924-1993 .... **CLC 8, 22, 53**
See also CA 65-68; 140; CANR 24; MTCW

Abelard, Peter c. 1079-c. 1142 ... **CMLC 11**
See also DLB 115

Abell, Kjeld 1901-1961 .... **CLC 15**
See also CA 111

Abish, Walter 1931- .... **CLC 22**
See also CA 101; CANR 37; DLB 130

Abrahams, Peter (Henry) 1919- ..... **CLC 4**
See also BW; CA 57-60; CANR 26; DLB 117; MTCW

Abrams, M(eyer) H(oward) 1912- ... **CLC 24**
See also CA 57-60; CANR 13, 33; DLB 67

Abse, Dannie 1923- .... **CLC 7, 29**
See also CA 53-56; CAAS 1; CANR 4; DLB 27

Achebe, (Albert) Chinua(lumogu)
1930- ..... **CLC 1, 3, 5, 7, 11, 26, 51, 75**
See also BLC 1; BW; CA 1-4R; CANR 6, 26; CLR 20; DA; DLB 117; MAICYA; MTCW; SATA 38, 40; WLC

Acker, Kathy 1948- .... **CLC 45**
See also CA 117; 122

Ackroyd, Peter 1949- .... **CLC 34, 52**
See also CA 123; 127

Acorn, Milton 1923- .... **CLC 15**
See also CA 103; DLB 53

Adamov, Arthur 1908-1970 ...... **CLC 4, 25**
See also CA 17-18; 25-28R; CAP 2; MTCW

Adams, Alice (Boyd) 1926- ... **CLC 6, 13, 46**
See also CA 81-84; CANR 26; DLBY 86; MTCW

Adams, Douglas (Noel) 1952- ... **CLC 27, 60**
See also AAYA 4; BEST 89:3; CA 106; CANR 34; DLBY 83; JRDA

Adams, Francis 1862-1893 .... **NCLC 33**

Adams, Henry (Brooks)
1838-1918 .... **TCLC 4, 52**
See also CA 104; 133; DA; DLB 12, 47

Adams, Richard (George)
1920- .... **CLC 4, 5, 18**
See also AITN 1, 2; CA 49-52; CANR 3, 35; CLR 20; JRDA; MAICYA; MTCW; SATA 7, 69

Adamson, Joy(-Friederike Victoria)
1910-1980 .... **CLC 17**
See also CA 69-72; 93-96; CANR 22; MTCW; SATA 11, 22

Adcock, Fleur 1934- .... **CLC 41**
See also CA 25-28R; CANR 11, 34; DLB 40

Addams, Charles (Samuel)
1912-1988 .... **CLC 30**
See also CA 61-64; 126; CANR 12

Addison, Joseph 1672-1719 .... **LC 18**
See also CDBLB 1660-1789; DLB 101

Adler, C(arole) S(chwerdtfeger)
1932- .... **CLC 35**
See also AAYA 4; CA 89-92; CANR 19, 40; JRDA; MAICYA; SAAS 15; SATA 26, 63

Adler, Renata 1938- .... **CLC 8, 31**
See also CA 49-52; CANR 5, 22; MTCW

Ady, Endre 1877-1919 .... **TCLC 11**
See also CA 107

Aeschylus 525B.C.-456B.C. .... **CMLC 11**
See also DA

Afton, Effie
See Harper, Frances Ellen Watkins

Agapida, Fray Antonio
See Irving, Washington

Agee, James (Rufus)
1909-1955 .... **TCLC 1, 19**
See also AITN 1; CA 108; CDALB 1941-1968; DLB 2, 26

A Gentlewoman in New England
See Bradstreet, Anne

A Gentlewoman in Those Parts
See Bradstreet, Anne

Aghill, Gordon
See Silverberg, Robert

Agnon, S(hmuel) Y(osef Halevi)
1888-1970 .... **CLC 4, 8, 14**
See also CA 17-18; 25-28R; CAP 2; MTCW

Aherne, Owen
See Cassill, R(onald) V(erlin)

Ai 1947- .... **CLC 4, 14, 69**
See also CA 85-88; CAAS 13; DLB 120

Aickman, Robert (Fordyce)
1914-1981 .... **CLC 57**
See also CA 5-8R; CANR 3

Aiken, Conrad (Potter)
1889-1973 ... **CLC 1, 3, 5, 10, 52; SSC 9**
See also CA 5-8R; 45-48; CANR 4; CDALB 1929-1941; DLB 9, 45, 102; MTCW; SATA 3, 30

Aiken, Joan (Delano) 1924- .... **CLC 35**
See also AAYA 1; CA 9-12R; CANR 4, 23, 34; CLR 1, 19; JRDA; MAICYA; MTCW; SAAS 1; SATA 2, 30, 73

Ainsworth, William Harrison
1805-1882 .... **NCLC 13**
See also DLB 21; SATA 24

Aitmatov, Chingiz (Torekulovich)
1928- .... **CLC 71**
See also CA 103; CANR 38; MTCW; SATA 56

Akers, Floyd
See Baum, L(yman) Frank

Akhmadulina, Bella Akhatovna
1937- .... **CLC 53**
See also CA 65-68

Akhmatova, Anna
1888-1966 .... **CLC 11, 25, 64; PC 2**
See also CA 19-20; 25-28R; CANR 35; CAP 1; MTCW

Aksakov, Sergei Timofeyvich
1791-1859 .... **NCLC 2**

Aksenov, Vassily .... **CLC 22**
See also Aksyonov, Vassily (Pavlovich)

Aksyonov, Vassily (Pavlovich)
1932- .... **CLC 37**
See also Aksenov, Vassily
See also CA 53-56; CANR 12

Akutagawa Ryunosuke
1892-1927 .... **TCLC 16**
See also CA 117

Alain 1868-1951 .... **TCLC 41**

Alain-Fournier .... **TCLC 6**
See also Fournier, Henri Alban
See also DLB 65

Alarcon, Pedro Antonio de
1833-1891 .... **NCLC 1**

Alas (y Urena), Leopoldo (Enrique Garcia)
1852-1901 .... **TCLC 29**
See also CA 113; 131; HW

Albee, Edward (Franklin III)
1928- ... **CLC 1, 2, 3, 5, 9, 11, 13, 25, 53**
See also AITN 1; CA 5-8R; CABS 3; CANR 8; CDALB 1941-1968; DA; DLB 7; MTCW; WLC

Alberti, Rafael 1902- .... **CLC 7**
See also CA 85-88; DLB 108

Alcala-Galiano, Juan Valera y
See Valera y Alcala-Galiano, Juan

Alcott, Amos Bronson 1799-1888 .. **NCLC 1**
See also DLB 1

Alcott, Louisa May 1832-1888 .... **NCLC 6**
See also CDALB 1865-1917; CLR 1; DA; DLB 1, 42, 79; JRDA; MAICYA; WLC; YABC 1

Aldanov, M. A.
See Aldanov, Mark (Alexandrovich)

Anthony, Piers 1934- . . . . **CLC 35**
See also CA 21-24R; CANR 28; DLB 8; MTCW

Antoine, Marc
See Proust, (Valentin-Louis-George-Eugene-) Marcel

Antoninus, Brother
See Everson, William (Oliver)

Antonioni, Michelangelo 1912- . . . . . **CLC 20**
See also CA 73-76

Antschel, Paul 1920-1970. . . . . . . **CLC 10, 19**
See also Celan, Paul
See also CA 85-88; CANR 33; MTCW

Anwar, Chairil 1922-1949 . . . . **TCLC 22**
See also CA 121

Apollinaire, Guillaume . . **TCLC 3, 8, 51; PC 7**
See also Kostrowitzki, Wilhelm Apollinaris de

Appelfeld, Aharon 1932- . . . . **CLC 23, 47**
See also CA 112; 133

Apple, Max (Isaac) 1941-. . . . . **CLC 9, 33**
See also CA 81-84; CANR 19; DLB 130

Appleman, Philip (Dean) 1926- . . . . . **CLC 51**
See also CA 13-16R; CAAS 18; CANR 6, 29

Appleton, Lawrence
See Lovecraft, H(oward) P(hillips)

Apteryx
See Eliot, T(homas) S(tearns)

Apuleius, (Lucius Madaurensis)
125(?)-175(?) . . . . **CMLC 1**

Aquin, Hubert 1929-1977. . . . . **CLC 15**
See also CA 105; DLB 53

Aragon, Louis 1897-1982. . . . . **CLC 3, 22**
See also CA 69-72; 108; CANR 28; DLB 72; MTCW

Arany, Janos 1817-1882. . . . . **NCLC 34**

Arbuthnot, John 1667-1735 . . . . **LC 1**
See also DLB 101

Archer, Herbert Winslow
See Mencken, H(enry) L(ouis)

Archer, Jeffrey (Howard) 1940- . . . . **CLC 28**
See also BEST 89:3; CA 77-80; CANR 22

Archer, Jules 1915- . . . . **CLC 12**
See also CA 9-12R; CANR 6; SAAS 5; SATA 4

Archer, Lee
See Ellison, Harlan

Arden, John 1930- . . . . **CLC 6, 13, 15**
See also CA 13-16R; CAAS 4; CANR 31; DLB 13; MTCW

Arenas, Reinaldo 1943-1990 . . . . **CLC 41**
See also CA 124; 128; 133; HW

Arendt, Hannah 1906-1975 . . . . **CLC 66**
See also CA 17-20R; 61-64; CANR 26; MTCW

Aretino, Pietro 1492-1556 . . . . **LC 12**

Arghezi, Tudor 1880-1967 . . . . **CLC 80**
See also Theodorescu, Ion N.

Arguedas, Jose Maria
1911-1969 . . . . **CLC 10, 18**
See also CA 89-92; DLB 113; HW

Argueta, Manlio 1936- . . . . **CLC 31**
See also CA 131; HW

Ariosto, Ludovico 1474-1533. . . . . **LC 6**

Aristides
See Epstein, Joseph

Aristophanes
450B.C.-385B.C. . . . . **CMLC 4; DC 2**
See also DA

Arlt, Roberto (Godofredo Christophersen)
1900-1942 . . . . **TCLC 29**
See also CA 123; 131; HW

Armah, Ayi Kwei 1939- . . . . **CLC 5, 33**
See also BLC 1; BW; CA 61-64; CANR 21; DLB 117; MTCW

Armatrading, Joan 1950- . . . . **CLC 17**
See also CA 114

Arnette, Robert
See Silverberg, Robert

Arnim, Achim von (Ludwig Joachim von Arnim) 1781-1831 . . . . **NCLC 5**
See also DLB 90

Arnim, Bettina von 1785-1859. . . . **NCLC 38**
See also DLB 90

Arnold, Matthew
1822-1888 . . . . **NCLC 6, 29; PC 5**
See also CDBLB 1832-1890; DA; DLB 32, 57; WLC

Arnold, Thomas 1795-1842 . . . . . . **NCLC 18**
See also DLB 55

Arnow, Harriette (Louisa) Simpson
1908-1986 . . . . **CLC 2, 7, 18**
See also CA 9-12R; 118; CANR 14; DLB 6; MTCW; SATA 42, 47

Arp, Hans
See Arp, Jean

Arp, Jean 1887-1966. . . . . **CLC 5**
See also CA 81-84; 25-28R; CANR 42

Arrabal
See Arrabal, Fernando

Arrabal, Fernando 1932- . . . **CLC 2, 9, 18, 58**
See also CA 9-12R; CANR 15

Arrick, Fran. . . . . **CLC 30**

Artaud, Antonin 1896-1948 . . . . . **TCLC 3, 36**
See also CA 104

Arthur, Ruth M(abel) 1905-1979. . . . **CLC 12**
See also CA 9-12R; 85-88; CANR 4; SATA 7, 26

Artsybashev, Mikhail (Petrovich)
1878-1927 . . . . **TCLC 31**

Arundel, Honor (Morfydd)
1919-1973 . . . . **CLC 17**
See also CA 21-22; 41-44R; CAP 2; SATA 4, 24

Asch, Sholem 1880-1957 . . . . **TCLC 3**
See also CA 105

Ash, Shalom
See Asch, Sholem

Ashbery, John (Lawrence)
1927- . . . . . . **CLC 2, 3, 4, 6, 9, 13, 15, 25, 41, 77**
See also CA 5-8R; CANR 9, 37; DLB 5; DLBY 81; MTCW

Ashdown, Clifford
See Freeman, R(ichard) Austin

Ashe, Gordon
See Creasey, John

Ashton-Warner, Sylvia (Constance)
1908-1984 . . . . **CLC 19**
See also CA 69-72; 112; CANR 29; MTCW

Asimov, Isaac
1920-1992 . . . . . . **CLC 1, 3, 9, 19, 26, 76**
See also BEST 90:2; CA 1-4R; 137; CANR 2, 19, 36; CLR 12; DLB 8; DLBY 92; JRDA; MAICYA; MTCW; SATA 1, 26, 74

Astley, Thea (Beatrice May)
1925- . . . . **CLC 41**
See also CA 65-68; CANR 11, 43

Aston, James
See White, T(erence) H(anbury)

Asturias, Miguel Angel
1899-1974 . . . . **CLC 3, 8, 13**
See also CA 25-28; 49-52; CANR 32; CAP 2; DLB 113; HW; MTCW

Atares, Carlos Saura
See Saura (Atares), Carlos

Atheling, William
See Pound, Ezra (Weston Loomis)

Atheling, William, Jr.
See Blish, James (Benjamin)

Atherton, Gertrude (Franklin Horn)
1857-1948 . . . . **TCLC 2**
See also CA 104; DLB 9, 78

Atherton, Lucius
See Masters, Edgar Lee

Atkins, Jack
See Harris, Mark

Atticus
See Fleming, Ian (Lancaster)

Atwood, Margaret (Eleanor)
1939- . . . . . **CLC 2, 3, 4, 8, 13, 15, 25, 44; SSC 2**
See also BEST 89:2; CA 49-52; CANR 3, 24, 33; DA; DLB 53; MTCW; SATA 50; WLC

Aubigny, Pierre d'
See Mencken, H(enry) L(ouis)

Aubin, Penelope 1685-1731(?). . . . . **LC 9**
See also DLB 39

Auchincloss, Louis (Stanton)
1917- . . . . **CLC 4, 6, 9, 18, 45**
See also CA 1-4R; CANR 6, 29; DLB 2; DLBY 80; MTCW

Auden, W(ystan) H(ugh)
1907-1973 . . . . . . **CLC 1, 2, 3, 4, 6, 9, 11, 14, 43; PC 1**
See also CA 9-12R; 45-48; CANR 5; CDBLB 1914-1945; DA; DLB 10, 20; MTCW; WLC

Audiberti, Jacques 1900-1965 . . . . . . **CLC 38**
See also CA 25-28R

Auel, Jean M(arie) 1936- . . . . **CLC 31**
See also AAYA 7; BEST 90:4; CA 103; CANR 21

Auerbach, Erich 1892-1957 . . . . **TCLC 43**
See also CA 118

Augier, Emile 1820-1889 . . . . **NCLC 31**

August, John
See De Voto, Bernard (Augustine)

Baron, David
See Pinter, Harold

Baron Corvo
See Rolfe, Frederick (William Serafino Austin Lewis Mary)

Barondess, Sue K(aufman) 1926-1977 .... **CLC 8**
See also Kaufman, Sue
See also CA 1-4R; 69-72; CANR 1

Baron de Teive
See Pessoa, Fernando (Antonio Nogueira)

Barres, Maurice 1862-1923 .... **TCLC 47**
See also DLB 123

Barreto, Afonso Henrique de Lima
See Lima Barreto, Afonso Henrique de

Barrett, (Roger) Syd 1946- .... **CLC 35**
See also Pink Floyd

Barrett, William (Christopher) 1913-1992 .... **CLC 27**
See also CA 13-16R; 139; CANR 11

Barrie, J(ames) M(atthew) 1860-1937 .... **TCLC 2**
See also CA 104; 136; CDBLB 1890-1914; CLR 16; DLB 10; MAICYA; YABC 1

Barrington, Michael
See Moorcock, Michael (John)

Barrol, Grady
See Bograd, Larry

Barry, Mike
See Malzberg, Barry N(athaniel)

Barry, Philip 1896-1949.......... **TCLC 11**
See also CA 109; DLB 7

Bart, Andre Schwarz
See Schwarz-Bart, Andre

Barth, John (Simmons) 1930- ...... **CLC 1, 2, 3, 5, 7, 9, 10, 14, 27, 51; SSC 10**
See also AITN 1, 2; CA 1-4R; CABS 1; CANR 5, 23; DLB 2; MTCW

Barthelme, Donald 1931-1989 ...... **CLC 1, 2, 3, 5, 6, 8, 13, 23, 46, 59; SSC 2**
See also CA 21-24R; 129; CANR 20; DLB 2; DLBY 80, 89; MTCW; SATA 7, 62

Barthelme, Frederick 1943-........ **CLC 36**
See also CA 114; 122; DLBY 85

Barthes, Roland (Gerard) 1915-1980 .... **CLC 24**
See also CA 130; 97-100; MTCW

Barzun, Jacques (Martin) 1907- .... **CLC 51**
See also CA 61-64; CANR 22

Bashevis, Isaac
See Singer, Isaac Bashevis

Bashkirtseff, Marie 1859-1884 ... **NCLC 27**

Basho
See Matsuo Basho

Bass, Kingsley B., Jr.
See Bullins, Ed

Bass, Rick 1958-................. **CLC 79**
See also CA 126

Bassani, Giorgio 1916-............. **CLC 9**
See also CA 65-68; CANR 33; DLB 128; MTCW

Bastos, Augusto (Antonio) Roa
See Roa Bastos, Augusto (Antonio)

Bataille, Georges 1897-1962 .... **CLC 29**
See also CA 101; 89-92

Bates, H(erbert) E(rnest) 1905-1974 .... **CLC 46; SSC 10**
See also CA 93-96; 45-48; CANR 34; MTCW

Bauchart
See Camus, Albert

Baudelaire, Charles 1821-1867 .... **NCLC 6, 29; PC 1**
See also DA; WLC

Baudrillard, Jean 1929-........... **CLC 60**

Baum, L(yman) Frank 1856-1919 ... **TCLC 7**
See also CA 108; 133; CLR 15; DLB 22; JRDA; MAICYA; MTCW; SATA 18

Baum, Louis F.
See Baum, L(yman) Frank

Baumbach, Jonathan 1933- ...... **CLC 6, 23**
See also CA 13-16R; CAAS 5; CANR 12; DLBY 80; MTCW

Bausch, Richard (Carl) 1945- ...... **CLC 51**
See also CA 101; CAAS 14; CANR 43; DLB 130

Baxter, Charles 1947-.......... **CLC 45, 78**
See also CA 57-60; CANR 40; DLB 130

Baxter, George Owen
See Faust, Frederick (Schiller)

Baxter, James K(eir) 1926-1972 .... **CLC 14**
See also CA 77-80

Baxter, John
See Hunt, E(verette) Howard, Jr.

Bayer, Sylvia
See Glassco, John

Beagle, Peter S(oyer) 1939-......... **CLC 7**
See also CA 9-12R; CANR 4; DLBY 80; SATA 60

Bean, Normal
See Burroughs, Edgar Rice

Beard, Charles A(ustin) 1874-1948 .... **TCLC 15**
See also CA 115; DLB 17; SATA 18

Beardsley, Aubrey 1872-1898 ..... **NCLC 6**

Beattie, Ann 1947- .... **CLC 8, 13, 18, 40, 63; SSC 11**
See also BEST 90:2; CA 81-84; DLBY 82; MTCW

Beattie, James 1735-1803 .... **NCLC 25**
See also DLB 109

Beauchamp, Kathleen Mansfield 1888-1923
See Mansfield, Katherine
See also CA 104; 134; DA

Beauvoir, Simone (Lucie Ernestine Marie Bertrand) de 1908-1986 .... **CLC 1, 2, 4, 8, 14, 31, 44, 50, 71**
See also CA 9-12R; 118; CANR 28; DA; DLB 72; DLBY 86; MTCW; WLC

Becker, Jurek 1937-............ **CLC 7, 19**
See also CA 85-88; DLB 75

Becker, Walter 1950-............. **CLC 26**

Beckett, Samuel (Barclay) 1906-1989 ...... **CLC 1, 2, 3, 4, 6, 9, 10, 11, 14, 18, 29, 57, 59**
See also CA 5-8R; 130; CANR 33; CDBLB 1945-1960; DA; DLB 13, 15; DLBY 90; MTCW; WLC

Beckford, William 1760-1844 .... **NCLC 16**
See also DLB 39

Beckman, Gunnel 1910-........... **CLC 26**
See also CA 33-36R; CANR 15; CLR 25; MAICYA; SAAS 9; SATA 6

Becque, Henri 1837-1899......... **NCLC 3**

Beddoes, Thomas Lovell 1803-1849 .... **NCLC 3**
See also DLB 96

Bedford, Donald F.
See Fearing, Kenneth (Flexner)

Beecher, Catharine Esther 1800-1878 .... **NCLC 30**
See also DLB 1

Beecher, John 1904-1980........... **CLC 6**
See also AITN 1; CA 5-8R; 105; CANR 8

Beer, Johann 1655-1700............. **LC 5**

Beer, Patricia 1924-.............. **CLC 58**
See also CA 61-64; CANR 13; DLB 40

Beerbohm, Henry Maximilian 1872-1956 .... **TCLC 1, 24**
See also CA 104; DLB 34, 100

Begiebing, Robert J(ohn) 1946-..... **CLC 70**
See also CA 122; CANR 40

Behan, Brendan 1923-1964 .... **CLC 1, 8, 11, 15, 79**
See also CA 73-76; CANR 33; CDBLB 1945-1960; DLB 13; MTCW

Behn, Aphra 1640(?)-1689 .... **LC 1**
See also DA; DLB 39, 80, 131; WLC

Behrman, S(amuel) N(athaniel) 1893-1973 .... **CLC 40**
See also CA 13-16; 45-48; CAP 1; DLB 7, 44

Belasco, David 1853-1931 .... **TCLC 3**
See also CA 104; DLB 7

Belcheva, Elisaveta 1893- .... **CLC 10**

Beldone, Phil "Cheech"
See Ellison, Harlan

Beleno
See Azuela, Mariano

Belinski, Vissarion Grigoryevich 1811-1848 .... **NCLC 5**

Belitt, Ben 1911-................. **CLC 22**
See also CA 13-16R; CAAS 4; CANR 7; DLB 5

Bell, James Madison 1826-1902 ... **TCLC 43**
See also BLC 1; BW; CA 122; 124; DLB 50

Bell, Madison (Smartt) 1957- ...... **CLC 41**
See also CA 111; CANR 28

Bell, Marvin (Hartley) 1937-..... **CLC 8, 31**
See also CA 21-24R; CAAS 14; DLB 5; MTCW

Bell, W. L. D.
See Mencken, H(enry) L(ouis)

Bellamy, Atwood C.
See Mencken, H(enry) L(ouis)

Bellamy, Edward 1850-1898 ...... **NCLC 4**
See also DLB 12

Bellin, Edward J.
See Kuttner, Henry

Belloc, (Joseph) Hilaire (Pierre)
1870-1953 .... **TCLC 7, 18**
See also CA 106; DLB 19, 100; YABC 1

Belloc, Joseph Peter Rene Hilaire
See Belloc, (Joseph) Hilaire (Pierre)

Belloc, Joseph Pierre Hilaire
See Belloc, (Joseph) Hilaire (Pierre)

Belloc, M. A.
See Lowndes, Marie Adelaide (Belloc)

Bellow, Saul
1915- ...... **CLC 1, 2, 3, 6, 8, 10, 13, 15, 25, 33, 34, 63, 79**
See also AITN 2; BEST 89:3; CA 5-8R; CABS 1; CANR 29; CDALB 1941-1968; DA; DLB 2, 28; DLBD 3; DLBY 82; MTCW; WLC

Belser, Reimond Karel Maria de
1929- .... **CLC 14**

Bely, Andrey .... **TCLC 7**
See also Bugayev, Boris Nikolayevich

Benary, Margot
See Benary-Isbert, Margot

Benary-Isbert, Margot 1889-1979... **CLC 12**
See also CA 5-8R; 89-92; CANR 4; CLR 12; MAICYA; SATA 2, 21

Benavente (y Martinez), Jacinto
1866-1954 .... **TCLC 3**
See also CA 106; 131; HW; MTCW

Benchley, Peter (Bradford)
1940- .... **CLC 4, 8**
See also AITN 2; CA 17-20R; CANR 12, 35; MTCW; SATA 3

Benchley, Robert (Charles)
1889-1945 .... **TCLC 1**
See also CA 105; DLB 11

Benedikt, Michael 1935- .... **CLC 4, 14**
See also CA 13-16R; CANR 7; DLB 5

Benet, Juan 1927-................ **CLC 28**

Benet, Stephen Vincent
1898-1943 .... **TCLC 7; SSC 10**
See also CA 104; DLB 4, 48, 102; YABC 1

Benet, William Rose 1886-1950 ... **TCLC 28**
See also CA 118; DLB 45

Benford, Gregory (Albert) 1941-.... **CLC 52**
See also CA 69-72; CANR 12, 24; DLBY 82

Bengtsson, Frans (Gunnar)
1894-1954 .... **TCLC 48**

Benjamin, David
See Slavitt, David R(ytman)

Benjamin, Lois
See Gould, Lois

Benjamin, Walter 1892-1940...... **TCLC 39**

Benn, Gottfried 1886-1956......... **TCLC 3**
See also CA 106; DLB 56

Bennett, Alan 1934- .... **CLC 45, 77**
See also CA 103; CANR 35; MTCW

Bennett, (Enoch) Arnold
1867-1931 .... **TCLC 5, 20**
See also CA 106; CDBLB 1890-1914; DLB 10, 34, 98

Bennett, Elizabeth
See Mitchell, Margaret (Munnerlyn)

Bennett, George Harold 1930-
See Bennett, Hal
See also BW; CA 97-100

Bennett, Hal .... **CLC 5**
See also Bennett, George Harold
See also DLB 33

Bennett, Jay 1912-................ **CLC 35**
See also AAYA 10; CA 69-72; CANR 11, 42; JRDA; SAAS 4; SATA 27, 41

Bennett, Louise (Simone) 1919-..... **CLC 28**
See also BLC 1; DLB 117

Benson, E(dward) F(rederic)
1867-1940 .... **TCLC 27**
See also CA 114

Benson, Jackson J. 1930-.......... **CLC 34**
See also CA 25-28R; DLB 111

Benson, Sally 1900-1972 .... **CLC 17**
See also CA 19-20; 37-40R; CAP 1; SATA 1, 27, 35

Benson, Stella 1892-1933......... **TCLC 17**
See also CA 117; DLB 36

Bentham, Jeremy 1748-1832 ..... **NCLC 38**
See also DLB 107

Bentley, E(dmund) C(lerihew)
1875-1956 .... **TCLC 12**
See also CA 108; DLB 70

Bentley, Eric (Russell) 1916-....... **CLC 24**
See also CA 5-8R; CANR 6

Beranger, Pierre Jean de
1780-1857 .... **NCLC 34**

Berger, Colonel
See Malraux, (Georges-)Andre

Berger, John (Peter) 1926- ...... **CLC 2, 19**
See also CA 81-84; DLB 14

Berger, Melvin H. 1927- .... **CLC 12**
See also CA 5-8R; CANR 4; CLR 32; SAAS 2; SATA 5

Berger, Thomas (Louis)
1924- .... **CLC 3, 5, 8, 11, 18, 38**
See also CA 1-4R; CANR 5, 28; DLB 2; DLBY 80; MTCW

Bergman, (Ernst) Ingmar
1918- .... **CLC 16, 72**
See also CA 81-84; CANR 33

Bergson, Henri 1859-1941 .... **TCLC 32**

Bergstein, Eleanor 1938- .... **CLC 4**
See also CA 53-56; CANR 5

Berkoff, Steven 1937-............. **CLC 56**
See also CA 104

Bermant, Chaim (Icyk) 1929- ...... **CLC 40**
See also CA 57-60; CANR 6, 31

Bern, Victoria
See Fisher, M(ary) F(rances) K(ennedy)

Bernanos, (Paul Louis) Georges
1888-1948 .... **TCLC 3**
See also CA 104; 130; DLB 72

Bernard, April 1956- .... **CLC 59**
See also CA 131

Bernhard, Thomas
1931-1989 .... **CLC 3, 32, 61**
See also CA 85-88; 127; CANR 32; DLB 85, 124; MTCW

Berrigan, Daniel 1921-............. **CLC 4**
See also CA 33-36R; CAAS 1; CANR 11, 43; DLB 5

Berrigan, Edmund Joseph Michael, Jr.
1934-1983
See Berrigan, Ted
See also CA 61-64; 110; CANR 14

Berrigan, Ted..................... **CLC 37**
See also Berrigan, Edmund Joseph Michael, Jr.
See also DLB 5

Berry, Charles Edward Anderson 1931-
See Berry, Chuck
See also CA 115

Berry, Chuck..................... **CLC 17**
See also Berry, Charles Edward Anderson

Berry, Jonas
See Ashbery, John (Lawrence)

Berry, Wendell (Erdman)
1934- .... **CLC 4, 6, 8, 27, 46**
See also AITN 1; CA 73-76; DLB 5, 6

Berryman, John
1914-1972 ...... **CLC 1, 2, 3, 4, 6, 8, 10, 13, 25, 62**
See also CA 13-16; 33-36R; CABS 2; CANR 35; CAP 1; CDALB 1941-1968; DLB 48; MTCW

Bertolucci, Bernardo 1940- .... **CLC 16**
See also CA 106

Bertrand, Aloysius 1807-1841 .... **NCLC 31**

Bertran de Born c. 1140-1215 ..... **CMLC 5**

Besant, Annie (Wood) 1847-1933 ... **TCLC 9**
See also CA 105

Bessie, Alvah 1904-1985........... **CLC 23**
See also CA 5-8R; 116; CANR 2; DLB 26

Bethlen, T. D.
See Silverberg, Robert

Beti, Mongo...................... **CLC 27**
See also Biyidi, Alexandre
See also BLC 1

Betjeman, John
1906-1984 .... **CLC 2, 6, 10, 34, 43**
See also CA 9-12R; 112; CANR 33; CDBLB 1945-1960; DLB 20; DLBY 84; MTCW

Bettelheim, Bruno 1903-1990 ...... **CLC 79**
See also CA 81-84; 131; CANR 23; MTCW

Betti, Ugo 1892-1953 .... **TCLC 5**
See also CA 104

Betts, Doris (Waugh) 1932-.... **CLC 3, 6, 28**
See also CA 13-16R; CANR 9; DLBY 82

Bevan, Alistair
See Roberts, Keith (John Kingston)

Beynon, John
See Harris, John (Wyndham Parkes Lucas) Beynon

Bialik, Chaim Nachman
1873-1934 .... **TCLC 25**

Bickerstaff, Isaac
See Swift, Jonathan

Bidart, Frank 1939- . . . . **CLC 33**
See also CA 140

Bienek, Horst 1930- . . . . **CLC 7, 11**
See also CA 73-76; DLB 75

Bierce, Ambrose (Gwinett) 1842-1914(?) . . . . . **TCLC 1, 7, 44; SSC 9**
See also CA 104; 139; CDALB 1865-1917; DA; DLB 11, 12, 23, 71, 74; WLC

Billings, Josh
See Shaw, Henry Wheeler

Billington, Rachel 1942- . . . . **CLC 43**
See also AITN 2; CA 33-36R

Binyon, T(imothy) J(ohn) 1936- . . . . **CLC 34**
See also CA 111; CANR 28

Bioy Casares, Adolfo 1914- . . . . **CLC 4, 8, 13**
See also CA 29-32R; CANR 19, 43; DLB 113; HW; MTCW

Bird, C.
See Ellison, Harlan

Bird, Cordwainer
See Ellison, Harlan

Bird, Robert Montgomery 1806-1854 . . . . **NCLC 1**

Birney, (Alfred) Earle 1904- . . . . **CLC 1, 4, 6, 11**
See also CA 1-4R; CANR 5, 20; DLB 88; MTCW

Bishop, Elizabeth 1911-1979 . . . . . . **CLC 1, 4, 9, 13, 15, 32; PC 3**
See also CA 5-8R; 89-92; CABS 2; CANR 26; CDALB 1968-1988; DA; DLB 5; MTCW; SATA 24

Bishop, John 1935- . . . . **CLC 10**
See also CA 105

Bissett, Bill 1939- . . . . **CLC 18**
See also CA 69-72; CANR 15; DLB 53; MTCW

Bitov, Andrei (Georgievich) 1937- . . . **CLC 57**
See also CA 142

Biyidi, Alexandre 1932-
See Beti, Mongo
See also BW; CA 114; 124; MTCW

Bjarme, Brynjolf
See Ibsen, Henrik (Johan)

Bjornson, Bjornstjerne (Martinius) 1832-1910 . . . . **TCLC 7, 37**
See also CA 104

Black, Robert
See Holdstock, Robert P.

Blackburn, Paul 1926-1971 . . . . . . **CLC 9, 43**
See also CA 81-84; 33-36R; CANR 34; DLB 16; DLBY 81

Black Elk 1863-1950 . . . . **TCLC 33**

Black Hobart
See Sanders, (James) Ed(ward)

Blacklin, Malcolm
See Chambers, Aidan

Blackmore, R(ichard) D(oddridge) 1825-1900 . . . . **TCLC 27**
See also CA 120; DLB 18

Blackmur, R(ichard) P(almer) 1904-1965 . . . . **CLC 2, 24**
See also CA 11-12; 25-28R; CAP 1; DLB 63

Black Tarantula, The
See Acker, Kathy

Blackwood, Algernon (Henry) 1869-1951 . . . . **TCLC 5**
See also CA 105

Blackwood, Caroline 1931- . . . . **CLC 6, 9**
See also CA 85-88; CANR 32; DLB 14; MTCW

Blade, Alexander
See Hamilton, Edmond; Silverberg, Robert

Blaga, Lucian 1895-1961 . . . . **CLC 75**

Blair, Eric (Arthur) 1903-1950
See Orwell, George
See also CA 104; 132; DA; MTCW; SATA 29

Blais, Marie-Claire 1939- . . . . **CLC 2, 4, 6, 13, 22**
See also CA 21-24R; CAAS 4; CANR 38; DLB 53; MTCW

Blaise, Clark 1940- . . . . **CLC 29**
See also AITN 2; CA 53-56; CAAS 3; CANR 5; DLB 53

Blake, Nicholas
See Day Lewis, C(ecil)
See also DLB 77

Blake, William 1757-1827 . . . . **NCLC 13**
See also CDBLB 1789-1832; DA; DLB 93; MAICYA; SATA 30; WLC

Blasco Ibanez, Vicente 1867-1928 . . . . **TCLC 12**
See also CA 110; 131; HW; MTCW

Blatty, William Peter 1928- . . . . **CLC 2**
See also CA 5-8R; CANR 9

Bleeck, Oliver
See Thomas, Ross (Elmore)

Blessing, Lee 1949- . . . . **CLC 54**

Blish, James (Benjamin) 1921-1975 . . . . **CLC 14**
See also CA 1-4R; 57-60; CANR 3; DLB 8; MTCW; SATA 66

Bliss, Reginald
See Wells, H(erbert) G(eorge)

Blixen, Karen (Christentze Dinesen) 1885-1962
See Dinesen, Isak
See also CA 25-28; CANR 22; CAP 2; MTCW; SATA 44

Bloch, Robert (Albert) 1917- . . . . **CLC 33**
See also CA 5-8R; CANR 5; DLB 44; SATA 12

Blok, Alexander (Alexandrovich) 1880-1921 . . . . **TCLC 5**
See also CA 104

Blom, Jan
See Breytenbach, Breyten

Bloom, Harold 1930- . . . . **CLC 24**
See also CA 13-16R; CANR 39; DLB 67

Bloomfield, Aurelius
See Bourne, Randolph S(illiman)

Blount, Roy (Alton), Jr. 1941- . . . . . **CLC 38**
See also CA 53-56; CANR 10, 28; MTCW

Bloy, Leon 1846-1917. . . . . **TCLC 22**
See also CA 121; DLB 123

Blume, Judy (Sussman) 1938- . . . **CLC 12, 30**
See also AAYA 3; CA 29-32R; CANR 13, 37; CLR 2, 15; DLB 52; JRDA; MAICYA; MTCW; SATA 2, 31

Blunden, Edmund (Charles) 1896-1974 . . . . **CLC 2, 56**
See also CA 17-18; 45-48; CAP 2; DLB 20, 100; MTCW

Bly, Robert (Elwood) 1926- . . . . **CLC 1, 2, 5, 10, 15, 38**
See also CA 5-8R; CANR 41; DLB 5; MTCW

Bobette
See Simenon, Georges (Jacques Christian)

Boccaccio, Giovanni 1313-1375
See also SSC 10

Bochco, Steven 1943- . . . . **CLC 35**
See also CA 124; 138

Bodenheim, Maxwell 1892-1954 . . . **TCLC 44**
See also CA 110; DLB 9, 45

Bodker, Cecil 1927- . . . . **CLC 21**
See also CA 73-76; CANR 13; CLR 23; MAICYA; SATA 14

Boell, Heinrich (Theodor) 1917-1985
See Boll, Heinrich (Theodor)
See also CA 21-24R; 116; CANR 24; DA; DLB 69; DLBY 85; MTCW

Boerne, Alfred
See Doeblin, Alfred

Bogan, Louise 1897-1970. . . . . **CLC 4, 39, 46**
See also CA 73-76; 25-28R; CANR 33; DLB 45; MTCW

Bogarde, Dirk . . . . **CLC 19**
See also Van Den Bogarde, Derek Jules Gaspard Ulric Niven
See also DLB 14

Bogosian, Eric 1953- . . . . **CLC 45**
See also CA 138

Bograd, Larry 1953- . . . . **CLC 35**
See also CA 93-96; SATA 33

Boiardo, Matteo Maria 1441-1494 . . . . **LC 6**

Boileau-Despreaux, Nicolas 1636-1711 . . . . **LC 3**

Boland, Eavan 1944- . . . . **CLC 40, 67**
See also DLB 40

Boll, Heinrich (Theodor) 1917-1985 . . . . **CLC 2, 3, 6, 9, 11, 15, 27, 39, 72**
See also Boell, Heinrich (Theodor)
See also DLB 69; DLBY 85; WLC

Bolt, Lee
See Faust, Frederick (Schiller)

Bolt, Robert (Oxton) 1924- . . . . **CLC 14**
See also CA 17-20R; CANR 35; DLB 13; MTCW

Bomkauf
See Kaufman, Bob (Garnell)

Bonaventura. **NCLC 35**
See also DLB 90

Bond, Edward 1934- . . . . **CLC 4, 6, 13, 23**
See also CA 25-28R; CANR 38; DLB 13; MTCW

Breton, Andre 1896-1966 . . . **CLC 2, 9, 15, 54**
See also CA 19-20; 25-28R; CANR 40; CAP 2; DLB 65; MTCW

Breytenbach, Breyten 1939(?)- . . **CLC 23, 37**
See also CA 113; 129

Bridgers, Sue Ellen 1942- . . . . **CLC 26**
See also AAYA 8; CA 65-68; CANR 11, 36; CLR 18; DLB 52; JRDA; MAICYA; SAAS 1; SATA 22

Bridges, Robert (Seymour)
1844-1930 . . . . **TCLC 1**
See also CA 104; CDBLB 1890-1914; DLB 19, 98

Bridie, James . . . . **TCLC 3**
See also Mavor, Osborne Henry
See also DLB 10

Brin, David 1950- . . . . **CLC 34**
See also CA 102; CANR 24; SATA 65

Brink, Andre (Philippus)
1935- . . . . **CLC 18, 36**
See also CA 104; CANR 39; MTCW

Brinsmead, H(esba) F(ay) 1922- . . . . **CLC 21**
See also CA 21-24R; CANR 10; MAICYA; SAAS 5; SATA 18

Brittain, Vera (Mary)
1893(?)-1970 . . . . **CLC 23**
See also CA 13-16; 25-28R; CAP 1; MTCW

Broch, Hermann 1886-1951 . . . . **TCLC 20**
See also CA 117; DLB 85, 124

Brock, Rose
See Hansen, Joseph

Brodkey, Harold 1930-. . . . . **CLC 56**
See also CA 111; DLB 130

Brodsky, Iosif Alexandrovich 1940-
See Brodsky, Joseph
See also AITN 1; CA 41-44R; CANR 37; MTCW

Brodsky, Joseph . . . . **CLC 4, 6, 13, 36, 50**
See also Brodsky, Iosif Alexandrovich

Brodsky, Michael Mark 1948- . . . . . **CLC 19**
See also CA 102; CANR 18, 41

Bromell, Henry 1947-. . . . . **CLC 5**
See also CA 53-56; CANR 9

Bromfield, Louis (Brucker)
1896-1956 . . . . **TCLC 11**
See also CA 107; DLB 4, 9, 86

Broner, E(sther) M(asserman)
1930- . . . . **CLC 19**
See also CA 17-20R; CANR 8, 25; DLB 28

Bronk, William 1918-. . . . . **CLC 10**
See also CA 89-92; CANR 23

Bronstein, Lev Davidovich
See Trotsky, Leon

Bronte, Anne 1820-1849. . . . . **NCLC 4**
See also DLB 21

Bronte, Charlotte
1816-1855 . . . . **NCLC 3, 8, 33**
See also CDBLB 1832-1890; DA; DLB 21; WLC

Bronte, (Jane) Emily
1818-1848 . . . . **NCLC 16, 35**
See also CDBLB 1832-1890; DA; DLB 21, 32; WLC

Brooke, Frances 1724-1789 . . . . **LC 6**
See also DLB 39, 99

Brooke, Henry 1703(?)-1783 . . . . **LC 1**
See also DLB 39

Brooke, Rupert (Chawner)
1887-1915 . . . . **TCLC 2, 7**
See also CA 104; 132; CDBLB 1914-1945; DA; DLB 19; MTCW; WLC

Brooke-Haven, P.
See Wodehouse, P(elham) G(renville)

Brooke-Rose, Christine 1926- . . . . . . **CLC 40**
See also CA 13-16R; DLB 14

Brookner, Anita 1928- . . . . . . **CLC 32, 34, 51**
See also CA 114; 120; CANR 37; DLBY 87; MTCW

Brooks, Cleanth 1906- . . . . **CLC 24**
See also CA 17-20R; CANR 33, 35; DLB 63; MTCW

Brooks, George
See Baum, L(yman) Frank

Brooks, Gwendolyn
1917- . . . . . . **CLC 1, 2, 4, 5, 15, 49; PC 7**
See also AITN 1; BLC 1; BW; CA 1-4R; CANR 1, 27; CDALB 1941-1968; CLR 27; DA; DLB 5, 76; MTCW; SATA 6; WLC

Brooks, Mel. . . . . **CLC 12**
See also Kaminsky, Melvin
See also DLB 26

Brooks, Peter 1938- . . . . **CLC 34**
See also CA 45-48; CANR 1

Brooks, Van Wyck 1886-1963. . . . . . **CLC 29**
See also CA 1-4R; CANR 6; DLB 45, 63, 103

Brophy, Brigid (Antonia)
1929- . . . . **CLC 6, 11, 29**
See also CA 5-8R; CAAS 4; CANR 25; DLB 14; MTCW

Brosman, Catharine Savage 1934-. . . . **CLC 9**
See also CA 61-64; CANR 21

Brother Antoninus
See Everson, William (Oliver)

Broughton, T(homas) Alan 1936- . . . **CLC 19**
See also CA 45-48; CANR 2, 23

Broumas, Olga 1949- . . . . **CLC 10, 73**
See also CA 85-88; CANR 20

Brown, Charles Brockden
1771-1810 . . . . **NCLC 22**
See also CDALB 1640-1865; DLB 37, 59, 73

Brown, Christy 1932-1981 . . . . **CLC 63**
See also CA 105; 104; DLB 14

Brown, Claude 1937- . . . . **CLC 30**
See also AAYA 7; BLC 1; BW; CA 73-76

Brown, Dee (Alexander) 1908- . . **CLC 18, 47**
See also CA 13-16R; CAAS 6; CANR 11; DLBY 80; MTCW; SATA 5

Brown, George
See Wertmueller, Lina

Brown, George Douglas
1869-1902 . . . . **TCLC 28**

Brown, George Mackay 1921-. . . . **CLC 5, 48**
See also CA 21-24R; CAAS 6; CANR 12, 37; DLB 14, 27; MTCW; SATA 35

Brown, (William) Larry 1951-. . . . . . **CLC 73**
See also CA 130; 134

Brown, Moses
See Barrett, William (Christopher)

Brown, Rita Mae 1944- . . . . . **CLC 18, 43, 79**
See also CA 45-48; CANR 2, 11, 35; MTCW

Brown, Roderick (Langmere) Haig-
See Haig-Brown, Roderick (Langmere)

Brown, Rosellen 1939- . . . . **CLC 32**
See also CA 77-80; CAAS 10; CANR 14

Brown, Sterling Allen
1901-1989 . . . . **CLC 1, 23, 59**
See also BLC 1; BW; CA 85-88; 127; CANR 26; DLB 48, 51, 63; MTCW

Brown, Will
See Ainsworth, William Harrison

Brown, William Wells
1813-1884 . . . . **NCLC 2; DC 1**
See also BLC 1; DLB 3, 50

Browne, (Clyde) Jackson 1948(?)-. . . **CLC 21**
See also CA 120

Browning, Elizabeth Barrett
1806-1861 . . . . **NCLC 1, 16; PC 6**
See also CDBLB 1832-1890; DA; DLB 32; WLC

Browning, Robert
1812-1889 . . . . **NCLC 19; PC 2**
See also CDBLB 1832-1890; DA; DLB 32; YABC 1

Browning, Tod 1882-1962 . . . . **CLC 16**
See also CA 141; 117

Bruccoli, Matthew J(oseph) 1931- . . **CLC 34**
See also CA 9-12R; CANR 7; DLB 103

Bruce, Lenny . . . . **CLC 21**
See also Schneider, Leonard Alfred

Bruin, John
See Brutus, Dennis

Brulls, Christian
See Simenon, Georges (Jacques Christian)

Brunner, John (Kilian Houston)
1934- . . . . **CLC 8, 10**
See also CA 1-4R; CAAS 8; CANR 2, 37; MTCW

Brutus, Dennis 1924- . . . . **CLC 43**
See also BLC 1; BW; CA 49-52; CAAS 14; CANR 2, 27, 42; DLB 117

Bryan, C(ourtlandt) D(ixon) B(arnes)
1936- . . . . **CLC 29**
See also CA 73-76; CANR 13

Bryan, Michael
See Moore, Brian

Bryant, William Cullen
1794-1878 . . . . **NCLC 6**
See also CDALB 1640-1865; DA; DLB 3, 43, 59

Bryusov, Valery Yakovlevich
1873-1924 . . . . **TCLC 10**
See also CA 107

Buchan, John 1875-1940 . . . . **TCLC 41**
See also CA 108; DLB 34, 70; YABC 2

Buchanan, George 1506-1582 . . . . **LC 4**

Buchheim, Lothar-Guenther 1918- . . . **CLC 6**
See also CA 85-88

Buchner, (Karl) Georg
1813-1837 . . . . **NCLC 26**

Chomette, Rene Lucien 1898-1981 .. **CLC 20**
See also Clair, Rene
See also CA 103

Chopin, Kate .... **TCLC 5, 14; SSC 8**
See also Chopin, Katherine
See also CDALB 1865-1917; DA; DLB 12, 78

Chopin, Katherine 1851-1904
See Chopin, Kate
See also CA 104; 122

Chretien de Troyes
c. 12th cent. - .... **CMLC 10**

Christie
See Ichikawa, Kon

Christie, Agatha (Mary Clarissa)
1890-1976 ...... **CLC 1, 6, 8, 12, 39, 48**
See also AAYA 9; AITN 1, 2; CA 17-20R; 61-64; CANR 10, 37; CDBLB 1914-1945; DLB 13, 77; MTCW; SATA 36

Christie, (Ann) Philippa
See Pearce, Philippa
See also CA 5-8R; CANR 4

Christine de Pizan 1365(?)-1431(?) .... **LC 9**

Chubb, Elmer
See Masters, Edgar Lee

Chulkov, Mikhail Dmitrievich
1743-1792 .... **LC 2**

Churchill, Caryl 1938- .... **CLC 31, 55**
See also CA 102; CANR 22; DLB 13; MTCW

Churchill, Charles 1731-1764......... **LC 3**
See also DLB 109

Chute, Carolyn 1947- .... **CLC 39**
See also CA 123

Ciardi, John (Anthony)
1916-1986 .... **CLC 10, 40, 44**
See also CA 5-8R; 118; CAAS 2; CANR 5, 33; CLR 19; DLB 5; DLBY 86; MAICYA; MTCW; SATA 1, 46, 65

Cicero, Marcus Tullius
106B.C.-43B.C. .... **CMLC 3**

Cimino, Michael 1943- .... **CLC 16**
See also CA 105

Cioran, E(mil) M. 1911- .... **CLC 64**
See also CA 25-28R

Cisneros, Sandra 1954- .... **CLC 69**
See also AAYA 9; CA 131; DLB 122; HW

Clair, Rene .... **CLC 20**
See also Chomette, Rene Lucien

Clampitt, Amy 1920- .... **CLC 32**
See also CA 110; CANR 29; DLB 105

Clancy, Thomas L., Jr. 1947-
See Clancy, Tom
See also CA 125; 131; MTCW

Clancy, Tom .... **CLC 45**
See also Clancy, Thomas L., Jr.
See also AAYA 9; BEST 89:1, 90:1

Clare, John 1793-1864 .... **NCLC 9**
See also DLB 55, 96

Clarin
See Alas (y Urena), Leopoldo (Enrique Garcia)

Clark, Al C.
See Goines, Donald

Clark, (Robert) Brian 1932- .... **CLC 29**
See also CA 41-44R

Clark, Eleanor 1913- .... **CLC 5, 19**
See also CA 9-12R; CANR 41; DLB 6

Clark, J. P.
See Clark, John Pepper
See also DLB 117

Clark, John Pepper 1935- .... **CLC 38**
See also Clark, J. P.
See also BLC 1; BW; CA 65-68; CANR 16

Clark, M. R.
See Clark, Mavis Thorpe

Clark, Mavis Thorpe 1909- .... **CLC 12**
See also CA 57-60; CANR 8, 37; CLR 30; MAICYA; SAAS 5; SATA 8, 74

Clark, Walter Van Tilburg
1909-1971 .... **CLC 28**
See also CA 9-12R; 33-36R; DLB 9; SATA 8

Clarke, Arthur C(harles)
1917- ...... **CLC 1, 4, 13, 18, 35; SSC 3**
See also AAYA 4; CA 1-4R; CANR 2, 28; JRDA; MAICYA; MTCW; SATA 13, 70

Clarke, Austin 1896-1974. .... **CLC 6, 9**
See also CA 29-32; 49-52; CAP 2; DLB 10, 20

Clarke, Austin C(hesterfield)
1934- .... **CLC 8, 53**
See also BLC 1; BW; CA 25-28R; CAAS 16; CANR 14, 32; DLB 53, 125

Clarke, Gillian 1937- .... **CLC 61**
See also CA 106; DLB 40

Clarke, Marcus (Andrew Hislop)
1846-1881 .... **NCLC 19**

Clarke, Shirley 1925- .... **CLC 16**

Clash, The .... **CLC 30**
See also Headon, (Nicky) Topper; Jones, Mick; Simonon, Paul; Strummer, Joe

Claudel, Paul (Louis Charles Marie)
1868-1955 .... **TCLC 2, 10**
See also CA 104

Clavell, James (duMaresq)
1925- .... **CLC 6, 25**
See also CA 25-28R; CANR 26; MTCW

Cleaver, (Leroy) Eldridge 1935- .... **CLC 30**
See also BLC 1; BW; CA 21-24R; CANR 16

Cleese, John (Marwood) 1939- ..... **CLC 21**
See also Monty Python
See also CA 112; 116; CANR 35; MTCW

Cleishbotham, Jebediah
See Scott, Walter

Cleland, John 1710-1789 .... **LC 2**
See also DLB 39

Clemens, Samuel Langhorne 1835-1910
See Twain, Mark
See also CA 104; 135; CDALB 1865-1917; DA; DLB 11, 12, 23, 64, 74; JRDA; MAICYA; YABC 2

Cleophil
See Congreve, William

Clerihew, E.
See Bentley, E(dmund) C(lerihew)

Clerk, N. W.
See Lewis, C(live) S(taples)

Cliff, Jimmy .... **CLC 21**
See also Chambers, James

Clifton, (Thelma) Lucille
1936- .... **CLC 19, 66**
See also BLC 1; BW; CA 49-52; CANR 2, 24, 42; CLR 5; DLB 5, 41; MAICYA; MTCW; SATA 20, 69

Clinton, Dirk
See Silverberg, Robert

Clough, Arthur Hugh 1819-1861 .. **NCLC 27**
See also DLB 32

Clutha, Janet Paterson Frame 1924-
See Frame, Janet
See also CA 1-4R; CANR 2, 36; MTCW

Clyne, Terence
See Blatty, William Peter

Cobalt, Martin
See Mayne, William (James Carter)

Coburn, D(onald) L(ee) 1938- ...... **CLC 10**
See also CA 89-92

Cocteau, Jean (Maurice Eugene Clement)
1889-1963 .... **CLC 1, 8, 15, 16, 43**
See also CA 25-28; CANR 40; CAP 2; DA; DLB 65; MTCW; WLC

Codrescu, Andrei 1946- .... **CLC 46**
See also CA 33-36R; CANR 13, 34

Coe, Max
See Bourne, Randolph S(illiman)

Coe, Tucker
See Westlake, Donald E(dwin)

Coetzee, J(ohn) M(ichael)
1940- .... **CLC 23, 33, 66**
See also CA 77-80; CANR 41; MTCW

Coffey, Brian
See Koontz, Dean R(ay)

Cohen, Arthur A(llen)
1928-1986 .... **CLC 7, 31**
See also CA 1-4R; 120; CANR 1, 17, 42; DLB 28

Cohen, Leonard (Norman)
1934- .... **CLC 3, 38**
See also CA 21-24R; CANR 14; DLB 53; MTCW

Cohen, Matt 1942- .... **CLC 19**
See also CA 61-64; CAAS 18; CANR 40; DLB 53

Cohen-Solal, Annie 19(?)- .... **CLC 50**

Colegate, Isabel 1931- .... **CLC 36**
See also CA 17-20R; CANR 8, 22; DLB 14; MTCW

Coleman, Emmett
See Reed, Ishmael

Coleridge, Samuel Taylor
1772-1834 .... **NCLC 9**
See also CDBLB 1789-1832; DA; DLB 93, 107; WLC

Coleridge, Sara 1802-1852 .... **NCLC 31**

Coles, Don 1928- .... **CLC 46**
See also CA 115; CANR 38

Colette, (Sidonie-Gabrielle)
1873-1954 ...... **TCLC 1, 5, 16; SSC 10**
See also CA 104; 131; DLB 65; MTCW

Collett, (Jacobine) Camilla (Wergeland)
1813-1895 .... **NCLC 22**

Collier, Christopher 1930- . . . . **CLC 30**
See also CA 33-36R; CANR 13, 33; JRDA; MAICYA; SATA 16, 70

Collier, James L(incoln) 1928- . . . . . **CLC 30**
See also CA 9-12R; CANR 4, 33; JRDA; MAICYA; SATA 8, 70

Collier, Jeremy 1650-1726 . . . . **LC 6**

Collins, Hunt
See Hunter, Evan

Collins, Linda 1931- . . . . **CLC 44**
See also CA 125

Collins, (William) Wilkie
1824-1889 . . . . **NCLC 1, 18**
See also CDBLB 1832-1890; DLB 18, 70

Collins, William 1721-1759 . . . . **LC 4**
See also DLB 109

Colman, George
See Glassco, John

Colt, Winchester Remington
See Hubbard, L(afayette) Ron(ald)

Colter, Cyrus 1910- . . . . **CLC 58**
See also BW; CA 65-68; CANR 10; DLB 33

Colton, James
See Hansen, Joseph

Colum, Padraic 1881-1972 . . . . **CLC 28**
See also CA 73-76; 33-36R; CANR 35; MAICYA; MTCW; SATA 15

Colvin, James
See Moorcock, Michael (John)

Colwin, Laurie (E.)
1944-1992 . . . . **CLC 5, 13, 23**
See also CA 89-92; 139; CANR 20; DLBY 80; MTCW

Comfort, Alex(ander) 1920- . . . . **CLC 7**
See also CA 1-4R; CANR 1

Comfort, Montgomery
See Campbell, (John) Ramsey

Compton-Burnett, I(vy)
1884(?)-1969 . . . . . . **CLC 1, 3, 10, 15, 34**
See also CA 1-4R; 25-28R; CANR 4; DLB 36; MTCW

Comstock, Anthony 1844-1915 . . . . **TCLC 13**
See also CA 110

Conan Doyle, Arthur
See Doyle, Arthur Conan

Conde, Maryse . . . . **CLC 52**
See also Boucolon, Maryse

Condon, Richard (Thomas)
1915- . . . . **CLC 4, 6, 8, 10, 45**
See also BEST 90:3; CA 1-4R; CAAS 1; CANR 2, 23; MTCW

Congreve, William
1670-1729 . . . . **LC 5, 21; DC 2**
See also CDBLB 1660-1789; DA; DLB 39, 84; WLC

Connell, Evan S(helby), Jr.
1924- . . . . **CLC 4, 6, 45**
See also AAYA 7; CA 1-4R; CAAS 2; CANR 2, 39; DLB 2; DLBY 81; MTCW

Connelly, Marc(us Cook)
1890-1980 . . . . **CLC 7**
See also CA 85-88; 102; CANR 30; DLB 7; DLBY 80; SATA 25

Connor, Ralph . . . . **TCLC 31**
See also Gordon, Charles William
See also DLB 92

Conrad, Joseph
1857-1924 . . . . **TCLC 1, 6, 13, 25, 43; SSC 9**
See also CA 104; 131; CDBLB 1890-1914; DA; DLB 10, 34, 98; MTCW; SATA 27; WLC

Conrad, Robert Arnold
See Hart, Moss

Conroy, Pat 1945- . . . . **CLC 30, 74**
See also AAYA 8; AITN 1; CA 85-88; CANR 24; DLB 6; MTCW

Constant (de Rebecque), (Henri) Benjamin
1767-1830 . . . . **NCLC 6**
See also DLB 119

Conybeare, Charles Augustus
See Eliot, T(homas) S(tearns)

Cook, Michael 1933- . . . . **CLC 58**
See also CA 93-96; DLB 53

Cook, Robin 1940- . . . . **CLC 14**
See also BEST 90:2; CA 108; 111; CANR 41

Cook, Roy
See Silverberg, Robert

Cooke, Elizabeth 1948- . . . . **CLC 55**
See also CA 129

Cooke, John Esten 1830-1886 . . . . . **NCLC 5**
See also DLB 3

Cooke, John Estes
See Baum, L(yman) Frank

Cooke, M. E.
See Creasey, John

Cooke, Margaret
See Creasey, John

Cooney, Ray . . . . **CLC 62**

Cooper, Henry St. John
See Creasey, John

Cooper, J. California . . . . **CLC 56**
See also BW; CA 125

Cooper, James Fenimore
1789-1851 . . . . **NCLC 1, 27**
See also CDALB 1640-1865; DLB 3; SATA 19

Coover, Robert (Lowell)
1932- . . . . **CLC 3, 7, 15, 32, 46**
See also CA 45-48; CANR 3, 37; DLB 2; DLBY 81; MTCW

Copeland, Stewart (Armstrong)
1952- . . . . **CLC 26**
See also Police, The

Coppard, A(lfred) E(dgar)
1878-1957 . . . . **TCLC 5**
See also CA 114; YABC 1

Coppee, Francois 1842-1908 . . . . . . **TCLC 25**

Coppola, Francis Ford 1939- . . . . **CLC 16**
See also CA 77-80; CANR 40; DLB 44

Corcoran, Barbara 1911- . . . . **CLC 17**
See also CA 21-24R; CAAS 2; CANR 11, 28; DLB 52; JRDA; SATA 3

Cordelier, Maurice
See Giraudoux, (Hippolyte) Jean

Corelli, Marie 1855-1924 . . . . **TCLC 51**
See also Mackay, Mary
See also DLB 34

Corman, Cid . . . . **CLC 9**
See also Corman, Sidney
See also CAAS 2; DLB 5

Corman, Sidney 1924-
See Corman, Cid
See also CA 85-88

Cormier, Robert (Edmund)
1925- . . . . **CLC 12, 30**
See also AAYA 3; CA 1-4R; CANR 5, 23; CDALB 1968-1988; CLR 12; DA; DLB 52; JRDA; MAICYA; MTCW; SATA 10, 45

Corn, Alfred 1943- . . . . **CLC 33**
See also CA 104; DLB 120; DLBY 80

Cornwell, David (John Moore)
1931- . . . . **CLC 9, 15**
See also le Carre, John
See also CA 5-8R; CANR 13, 33; MTCW

Corrigan, Kevin . . . . **CLC 55**

Corso, (Nunzio) Gregory 1930- . . . **CLC 1, 11**
See also CA 5-8R; CANR 41; DLB 5, 16; MTCW

Cortazar, Julio
1914-1984 . . . . . . **CLC 2, 3, 5, 10, 13, 15, 33, 34; SSC 7**
See also CA 21-24R; CANR 12, 32; DLB 113; HW; MTCW

Corwin, Cecil
See Kornbluth, C(yril) M.

Cosic, Dobrica 1921- . . . . **CLC 14**
See also CA 122; 138

Costain, Thomas B(ertram)
1885-1965 . . . . **CLC 30**
See also CA 5-8R; 25-28R; DLB 9

Costantini, Humberto
1924(?)-1987 . . . . **CLC 49**
See also CA 131; 122; HW

Costello, Elvis 1955- . . . . **CLC 21**

Cotter, Joseph S. Sr.
See Cotter, Joseph Seamon Sr.

Cotter, Joseph Seamon Sr.
1861-1949 . . . . **TCLC 28**
See also BLC 1; BW; CA 124; DLB 50

Coulton, James
See Hansen, Joseph

Couperus, Louis (Marie Anne)
1863-1923 . . . . **TCLC 15**
See also CA 115

Court, Wesli
See Turco, Lewis (Putnam)

Courtenay, Bryce 1933- . . . . **CLC 59**
See also CA 138

Courtney, Robert
See Ellison, Harlan

Cousteau, Jacques-Yves 1910- . . . . . . **CLC 30**
See also CA 65-68; CANR 15; MTCW; SATA 38

Coward, Noel (Peirce)
1899-1973 . . . . **CLC 1, 9, 29, 51**
See also AITN 1; CA 17-18; 41-44R; CANR 35; CAP 2; CDBLB 1914-1945; DLB 10; MTCW

Cowley, Malcolm 1898-1989 . . . . **CLC 39**
See also CA 5-8R; 128; CANR 3; DLB 4, 48; DLBY 81, 89; MTCW

Cowper, William 1731-1800. . . . . . . **NCLC 8**
See also DLB 104, 109

Cox, William Trevor 1928- . . . **CLC 9, 14, 71**
See also Trevor, William
See also CA 9-12R; CANR 4, 37; DLB 14; MTCW

Cozzens, James Gould
1903-1978 . . . . **CLC 1, 4, 11**
See also CA 9-12R; 81-84; CANR 19; CDALB 1941-1968; DLB 9; DLBD 2; DLBY 84; MTCW

Crabbe, George 1754-1832. . . . . . . **NCLC 26**
See also DLB 93

Craig, A. A.
See Anderson, Poul (William)

Craik, Dinah Maria (Mulock)
1826-1887 . . . . **NCLC 38**
See also DLB 35; MAICYA; SATA 34

Cram, Ralph Adams 1863-1942. . . . **TCLC 45**

Crane, (Harold) Hart
1899-1932 . . . . **TCLC 2, 5; PC 3**
See also CA 104; 127; CDALB 1917-1929; DA; DLB 4, 48; MTCW; WLC

Crane, R(onald) S(almon)
1886-1967 . . . . **CLC 27**
See also CA 85-88; DLB 63

Crane, Stephen (Townley)
1871-1900 . . . . . **TCLC 11, 17, 32; SSC 7**
See also CA 109; 140; CDALB 1865-1917; DA; DLB 12, 54, 78; WLC; YABC 2

Crase, Douglas 1944- . . . . **CLC 58**
See also CA 106

Crashaw, Richard 1612(?)-1649. . . . . . **LC 24**
See also DLB 126

Craven, Margaret 1901-1980. . . . . . . **CLC 17**
See also CA 103

Crawford, F(rancis) Marion
1854-1909 . . . . **TCLC 10**
See also CA 107; DLB 71

Crawford, Isabella Valancy
1850-1887 . . . . **NCLC 12**
See also DLB 92

Crayon, Geoffrey
See Irving, Washington

Creasey, John 1908-1973 . . . . **CLC 11**
See also CA 5-8R; 41-44R; CANR 8; DLB 77; MTCW

Crebillon, Claude Prosper Jolyot de (fils)
1707-1777 . . . . **LC 1**

Credo
See Creasey, John

Creeley, Robert (White)
1926- . . . . . **CLC 1, 2, 4, 8, 11, 15, 36, 78**
See also CA 1-4R; CAAS 10; CANR 23, 43; DLB 5, 16; MTCW

Crews, Harry (Eugene)
1935- . . . . **CLC 6, 23, 49**
See also AITN 1; CA 25-28R; CANR 20; DLB 6; MTCW

Crichton, (John) Michael
1942- . . . . **CLC 2, 6, 54**
See also AAYA 10; AITN 2; CA 25-28R; CANR 13, 40; DLBY 81; JRDA; MTCW; SATA 9

Crispin, Edmund . . . . **CLC 22**
See also Montgomery, (Robert) Bruce
See also DLB 87

Cristofer, Michael 1945(?)- . . . . **CLC 28**
See also CA 110; DLB 7

Croce, Benedetto 1866-1952 . . . . . . **TCLC 37**
See also CA 120

Crockett, David 1786-1836 . . . . **NCLC 8**
See also DLB 3, 11

Crockett, Davy
See Crockett, David

Croker, John Wilson 1780-1857 . . **NCLC 10**
See also DLB 110

Crommelynck, Fernand 1885-1970 . . **CLC 75**
See also CA 89-92

Cronin, A(rchibald) J(oseph)
1896-1981 . . . . **CLC 32**
See also CA 1-4R; 102; CANR 5; SATA 25, 47

Cross, Amanda
See Heilbrun, Carolyn G(old)

Crothers, Rachel 1878(?)-1958. . . . . **TCLC 19**
See also CA 113; DLB 7

Croves, Hal
See Traven, B.

Crowfield, Christopher
See Stowe, Harriet (Elizabeth) Beecher

Crowley, Aleister. . . . . **TCLC 7**
See also Crowley, Edward Alexander

Crowley, Edward Alexander 1875-1947
See Crowley, Aleister
See also CA 104

Crowley, John 1942-. . . . . **CLC 57**
See also CA 61-64; CANR 43; DLBY 82; SATA 65

Crud
See Crumb, R(obert)

Crumarums
See Crumb, R(obert)

Crumb, R(obert) 1943-. . . . . **CLC 17**
See also CA 106

Crumbum
See Crumb, R(obert)

Crumski
See Crumb, R(obert)

Crum the Bum
See Crumb, R(obert)

Crunk
See Crumb, R(obert)

Crustt
See Crumb, R(obert)

Cryer, Gretchen (Kiger) 1935-. . . . . . **CLC 21**
See also CA 114; 123

Csath, Geza 1887-1919. . . . . **TCLC 13**
See also CA 111

Cudlip, David 1933- . . . . **CLC 34**

Cullen, Countee 1903-1946 . . . . . **TCLC 4, 37**
See also BLC 1; BW; CA 108; 124; CDALB 1917-1929; DA; DLB 4, 48, 51; MTCW; SATA 18

Cum, R.
See Crumb, R(obert)

Cummings, Bruce F(rederick) 1889-1919
See Barbellion, W. N. P.
See also CA 123

Cummings, E(dward) E(stlin)
1894-1962 . . . . . . **CLC 1, 3, 8, 12, 15, 68; PC 5**
See also CA 73-76; CANR 31; CDALB 1929-1941; DA; DLB 4, 48; MTCW; WLC 2

Cunha, Euclides (Rodrigues Pimenta) da
1866-1909 . . . . **TCLC 24**
See also CA 123

Cunningham, E. V.
See Fast, Howard (Melvin)

Cunningham, J(ames) V(incent)
1911-1985 . . . . **CLC 3, 31**
See also CA 1-4R; 115; CANR 1; DLB 5

Cunningham, Julia (Woolfolk)
1916- . . . . **CLC 12**
See also CA 9-12R; CANR 4, 19, 36; JRDA; MAICYA; SAAS 2; SATA 1, 26

Cunningham, Michael 1952- . . . . **CLC 34**
See also CA 136

Cunninghame Graham, R(obert) B(ontine)
1852-1936 . . . . **TCLC 19**
See also Graham, R(obert) B(ontine) Cunninghame
See also CA 119; DLB 98

Currie, Ellen 19(?)-. . . . . **CLC 44**

Curtin, Philip
See Lowndes, Marie Adelaide (Belloc)

Curtis, Price
See Ellison, Harlan

Cutrate, Joe
See Spiegelman, Art

Czaczkes, Shmuel Yosef
See Agnon, S(hmuel) Y(osef Halevi)

D. P.
See Wells, H(erbert) G(eorge)

Dabrowska, Maria (Szumska)
1889-1965 . . . . **CLC 15**
See also CA 106

Dabydeen, David 1955- . . . . **CLC 34**
See also BW; CA 125

Dacey, Philip 1939- . . . . **CLC 51**
See also CA 37-40R; CAAS 17; CANR 14, 32; DLB 105

Dagerman, Stig (Halvard)
1923-1954 . . . . **TCLC 17**
See also CA 117

Dahl, Roald 1916-1990. . . . . **CLC 1, 6, 18, 79**
See also CA 1-4R; 133; CANR 6, 32, 37; CLR 1, 7; JRDA; MAICYA; MTCW; SATA 1, 26, 73; SATA-Obit 65

Dahlberg, Edward 1900-1977. . . **CLC 1, 7, 14**
See also CA 9-12R; 69-72; CANR 31; DLB 48; MTCW

Dale, Colin. . . . . **TCLC 18**
See also Lawrence, T(homas) E(dward)

de Lisser, H. G.
See De Lisser, Herbert George
See also DLB 117

De Lisser, Herbert George 1878-1944 .... **TCLC 12**
See also de Lisser, H. G.
See also CA 109

Deloria, Vine (Victor), Jr. 1933-.... **CLC 21**
See also CA 53-56; CANR 5, 20; MTCW; SATA 21

Del Vecchio, John M(ichael) 1947- .... **CLC 29**
See also CA 110; DLBD 9

de Man, Paul (Adolph Michel) 1919-1983 .... **CLC 55**
See also CA 128; 111; DLB 67; MTCW

De Marinis, Rick 1934-........... **CLC 54**
See also CA 57-60; CANR 9, 25

Demby, William 1922-............ **CLC 53**
See also BLC 1; BW; CA 81-84; DLB 33

Demijohn, Thom
See Disch, Thomas M(ichael)

de Montherlant, Henry (Milon)
See Montherlant, Henry (Milon) de

de Natale, Francine
See Malzberg, Barry N(athaniel)

Denby, Edwin (Orr) 1903-1983..... **CLC 48**
See also CA 138; 110

Denis, Julio
See Cortazar, Julio

Denmark, Harrison
See Zelazny, Roger (Joseph)

Dennis, John 1658-1734............ **LC 11**
See also DLB 101

Dennis, Nigel (Forbes) 1912-1989.... **CLC 8**
See also CA 25-28R; 129; DLB 13, 15; MTCW

De Palma, Brian (Russell) 1940-.... **CLC 20**
See also CA 109

De Quincey, Thomas 1785-1859 ... **NCLC 4**
See also CDBLB 1789-1832; DLB 110

Deren, Eleanora 1908(?)-1961
See Deren, Maya
See also CA 111

Deren, Maya .... **CLC 16**
See also Deren, Eleanora

Derleth, August (William) 1909-1971 .... **CLC 31**
See also CA 1-4R; 29-32R; CANR 4; DLB 9; SATA 5

de Routisie, Albert
See Aragon, Louis

Derrida, Jacques 1930-........... **CLC 24**
See also CA 124; 127

Derry Down Derry
See Lear, Edward

Dersonnes, Jacques
See Simenon, Georges (Jacques Christian)

Desai, Anita 1937-............ **CLC 19, 37**
See also CA 81-84; CANR 33; MTCW; SATA 63

de Saint-Luc, Jean
See Glassco, John

de Saint Roman, Arnaud
See Aragon, Louis

Descartes, Rene 1596-1650 .... **LC 20**

De Sica, Vittorio 1901(?)-1974 ..... **CLC 20**
See also CA 117

Desnos, Robert 1900-1945........ **TCLC 22**
See also CA 121

Destouches, Louis-Ferdinand 1894-1961 .... **CLC 9, 15**
See also Celine, Louis-Ferdinand
See also CA 85-88; CANR 28; MTCW

Deutsch, Babette 1895-1982 .... **CLC 18**
See also CA 1-4R; 108; CANR 4; DLB 45; SATA 1, 33

Devenant, William 1606-1649 .... **LC 13**

Devkota, Laxmiprasad 1909-1959 .... **TCLC 23**
See also CA 123

De Voto, Bernard (Augustine) 1897-1955 .... **TCLC 29**
See also CA 113; DLB 9

De Vries, Peter 1910-1993 .... **CLC 1, 2, 3, 7, 10, 28, 46**
See also CA 17-20R; 142; CANR 41; DLB 6; DLBY 82; MTCW

Dexter, Martin
See Faust, Frederick (Schiller)

Dexter, Pete 1943-............ **CLC 34, 55**
See also BEST 89:2; CA 127; 131; MTCW

Diamano, Silmang
See Senghor, Leopold Sedar

Diamond, Neil 1941- .... **CLC 30**
See also CA 108

di Bassetto, Corno
See Shaw, George Bernard

Dick, Philip K(indred) 1928-1982 .... **CLC 10, 30, 72**
See also CA 49-52; 106; CANR 2, 16; DLB 8; MTCW

Dickens, Charles (John Huffam) 1812-1870 .... **NCLC 3, 8, 18, 26**
See also CDBLB 1832-1890; DA; DLB 21, 55, 70; JRDA; MAICYA; SATA 15

Dickey, James (Lafayette) 1923- .... **CLC 1, 2, 4, 7, 10, 15, 47**
See also AITN 1, 2; CA 9-12R; CABS 2; CANR 10; CDALB 1968-1988; DLB 5; DLBD 7; DLBY 82; MTCW

Dickey, William 1928-.......... **CLC 3, 28**
See also CA 9-12R; CANR 24; DLB 5

Dickinson, Charles 1951-.......... **CLC 49**
See also CA 128

Dickinson, Emily (Elizabeth) 1830-1886 .... **NCLC 21; PC 1**
See also CDALB 1865-1917; DA; DLB 1; SATA 29; WLC

Dickinson, Peter (Malcolm) 1927- .... **CLC 12, 35**
See also AAYA 9; CA 41-44R; CANR 31; CLR 29; DLB 87; JRDA; MAICYA; SATA 5, 62

Dickson, Carr
See Carr, John Dickson

Dickson, Carter
See Carr, John Dickson

Didion, Joan 1934-..... **CLC 1, 3, 8, 14, 32**
See also AITN 1; CA 5-8R; CANR 14; CDALB 1968-1988; DLB 2; DLBY 81, 86; MTCW

Dietrich, Robert
See Hunt, E(verette) Howard, Jr.

Dillard, Annie 1945-............ **CLC 9, 60**
See also AAYA 6; CA 49-52; CANR 3, 43; DLBY 80; MTCW; SATA 10

Dillard, R(ichard) H(enry) W(ilde) 1937- .... **CLC 5**
See also CA 21-24R; CAAS 7; CANR 10; DLB 5

Dillon, Eilis 1920-................ **CLC 17**
See also CA 9-12R; CAAS 3; CANR 4, 38; CLR 26; MAICYA; SATA 2, 74

Dimont, Penelope
See Mortimer, Penelope (Ruth)

Dinesen, Isak .... **CLC 10, 29; SSC 7**
See also Blixen, Karen (Christentze Dinesen)

Ding Ling .... **CLC 68**
See also Chiang Pin-chin

Disch, Thomas M(ichael) 1940-... **CLC 7, 36**
See also CA 21-24R; CAAS 4; CANR 17, 36; CLR 18; DLB 8; MAICYA; MTCW; SAAS 15; SATA 54

Disch, Tom
See Disch, Thomas M(ichael)

d'Isly, Georges
See Simenon, Georges (Jacques Christian)

Disraeli, Benjamin 1804-1881 .. **NCLC 2, 39**
See also DLB 21, 55

Ditcum, Steve
See Crumb, R(obert)

Dixon, Paige
See Corcoran, Barbara

Dixon, Stephen 1936-............. **CLC 52**
See also CA 89-92; CANR 17, 40; DLB 130

Doblin, Alfred .... **TCLC 13**
See also Doeblin, Alfred

Dobrolyubov, Nikolai Alexandrovich 1836-1861 .... **NCLC 5**

Dobyns, Stephen 1941-............ **CLC 37**
See also CA 45-48; CANR 2, 18

Doctorow, E(dgar) L(aurence) 1931- ..... **CLC 6, 11, 15, 18, 37, 44, 65**
See also AITN 2; BEST 89:3; CA 45-48; CANR 2, 33; CDALB 1968-1988; DLB 2, 28; DLBY 80; MTCW

Dodgson, Charles Lutwidge 1832-1898
See Carroll, Lewis
See also CLR 2; DA; MAICYA; YABC 2

Dodson, Owen (Vincent) 1914-1983 .... **CLC 79**
See also BLC 1; BW; CA 65-68; 110; CANR 24; DLB 76

Doeblin, Alfred 1878-1957........ **TCLC 13**
See also Doblin, Alfred
See also CA 110; 141; DLB 66

Doerr, Harriet 1910- .... **CLC 34**
See also CA 117; 122

Domecq, H(onorio) Bustos
See Bioy Casares, Adolfo; Borges, Jorge Luis

du Maurier, Daphne 1907-1989 .... **CLC 6, 11, 59**
See also CA 5-8R; 128; CANR 6; MTCW; SATA 27, 60

Dunbar, Paul Laurence 1872-1906 .... **TCLC 2, 12; PC 5; SSC 8**
See also BLC 1; BW; CA 104; 124; CDALB 1865-1917; DA; DLB 50, 54, 78; SATA 34; WLC

Dunbar, William 1460(?)-1530(?) .... **LC 20**

Duncan, Lois 1934-.............. **CLC 26**
See also AAYA 4; CA 1-4R; CANR 2, 23, 36; CLR 29; JRDA; MAICYA; SAAS 2; SATA 1, 36, 75

Duncan, Robert (Edward) 1919-1988 .... **CLC 1, 2, 4, 7, 15, 41, 55; PC 2**
See also CA 9-12R; 124; CANR 28; DLB 5, 16; MTCW

Dunlap, William 1766-1839 .... **NCLC 2**
See also DLB 30, 37, 59

Dunn, Douglas (Eaglesham) 1942- .... **CLC 6, 40**
See also CA 45-48; CANR 2, 33; DLB 40; MTCW

Dunn, Katherine (Karen) 1945-..... **CLC 71**
See also CA 33-36R

Dunn, Stephen 1939- .... **CLC 36**
See also CA 33-36R; CANR 12; DLB 105

Dunne, Finley Peter 1867-1936.... **TCLC 28**
See also CA 108; DLB 11, 23

Dunne, John Gregory 1932-........ **CLC 28**
See also CA 25-28R; CANR 14; DLBY 80

Dunsany, Edward John Moreton Drax Plunkett 1878-1957
See Dunsany, Lord; Lord Dunsany
See also CA 104; DLB 10

Dunsany, Lord.................... **TCLC 2**
See also Dunsany, Edward John Moreton Drax Plunkett
See also DLB 77

du Perry, Jean
See Simenon, Georges (Jacques Christian)

Durang, Christopher (Ferdinand) 1949- .... **CLC 27, 38**
See also CA 105

Duras, Marguerite 1914- ...... **CLC 3, 6, 11, 20, 34, 40, 68**
See also CA 25-28R; DLB 83; MTCW

Durban, (Rosa) Pam 1947-......... **CLC 39**
See also CA 123

Durcan, Paul 1944-............ **CLC 43, 70**
See also CA 134

Durrell, Lawrence (George) 1912-1990 .... **CLC 1, 4, 6, 8, 13, 27, 41**
See also CA 9-12R; 132; CANR 40; CDBLB 1945-1960; DLB 15, 27; DLBY 90; MTCW

Durrenmatt, Friedrich .... **CLC 1, 4, 8, 11, 15, 43**
See also Duerrenmatt, Friedrich
See also DLB 69, 124

Dutt, Toru 1856-1877........... **NCLC 29**

Dwight, Timothy 1752-1817...... **NCLC 13**
See also DLB 37

Dworkin, Andrea 1946-........... **CLC 43**
See also CA 77-80; CANR 16, 39; MTCW

Dwyer, Deanna
See Koontz, Dean R(ay)

Dwyer, K. R.
See Koontz, Dean R(ay)

Dylan, Bob 1941- ...... **CLC 3, 4, 6, 12, 77**
See also CA 41-44R; DLB 16

Eagleton, Terence (Francis) 1943-
See Eagleton, Terry
See also CA 57-60; CANR 7, 23; MTCW

Eagleton, Terry .... **CLC 63**
See also Eagleton, Terence (Francis)

Early, Jack
See Scoppettone, Sandra

East, Michael
See West, Morris L(anglo)

Eastaway, Edward
See Thomas, (Philip) Edward

Eastlake, William (Derry) 1917-..... **CLC 8**
See also CA 5-8R; CAAS 1; CANR 5; DLB 6

Eberhart, Richard (Ghormley) 1904- .... **CLC 3, 11, 19, 56**
See also CA 1-4R; CANR 2; CDALB 1941-1968; DLB 48; MTCW

Eberstadt, Fernanda 1960-......... **CLC 39**
See also CA 136

Echegaray (y Eizaguirre), Jose (Maria Waldo) 1832-1916 .... **TCLC 4**
See also CA 104; CANR 32; HW; MTCW

Echeverria, (Jose) Esteban (Antonino) 1805-1851 .... **NCLC 18**

Echo
See Proust, (Valentin-Louis-George-Eugene-) Marcel

Eckert, Allan W. 1931- .... **CLC 17**
See also CA 13-16R; CANR 14; SATA 27, 29

Eckhart, Meister 1260(?)-1328(?) .. **CMLC 9**
See also DLB 115

Eckmar, F. R.
See de Hartog, Jan

Eco, Umberto 1932-........... **CLC 28, 60**
See also BEST 90:1; CA 77-80; CANR 12, 33; MTCW

Eddison, E(ric) R(ucker) 1882-1945 .... **TCLC 15**
See also CA 109

Edel, (Joseph) Leon 1907-...... **CLC 29, 34**
See also CA 1-4R; CANR 1, 22; DLB 103

Eden, Emily 1797-1869 .... **NCLC 10**

Edgar, David 1948-............... **CLC 42**
See also CA 57-60; CANR 12; DLB 13; MTCW

Edgerton, Clyde (Carlyle) 1944- .... **CLC 39**
See also CA 118; 134

Edgeworth, Maria 1767-1849...... **NCLC 1**
See also DLB 116; SATA 21

Edmonds, Paul
See Kuttner, Henry

Edmonds, Walter D(umaux) 1903- .. **CLC 35**
See also CA 5-8R; CANR 2; DLB 9; MAICYA; SAAS 4; SATA 1, 27

Edmondson, Wallace
See Ellison, Harlan

Edson, Russell.................... **CLC 13**
See also CA 33-36R

Edwards, G(erald) B(asil) 1899-1976 .... **CLC 25**
See also CA 110

Edwards, Gus 1939-.............. **CLC 43**
See also CA 108

Edwards, Jonathan 1703-1758........ **LC 7**
See also DA; DLB 24

Efron, Marina Ivanovna Tsvetaeva
See Tsvetaeva (Efron), Marina (Ivanovna)

Ehle, John (Marsden, Jr.) 1925-.... **CLC 27**
See also CA 9-12R

Ehrenbourg, Ilya (Grigoryevich)
See Ehrenburg, Ilya (Grigoryevich)

Ehrenburg, Ilya (Grigoryevich) 1891-1967 .... **CLC 18, 34, 62**
See also CA 102; 25-28R

Ehrenburg, Ilyo (Grigoryevich)
See Ehrenburg, Ilya (Grigoryevich)

Eich, Guenter 1907-1972 .... **CLC 15**
See also CA 111; 93-96; DLB 69, 124

Eichendorff, Joseph Freiherr von 1788-1857 .... **NCLC 8**
See also DLB 90

Eigner, Larry...................... **CLC 9**
See also Eigner, Laurence (Joel)
See also DLB 5

Eigner, Laurence (Joel) 1927-
See Eigner, Larry
See also CA 9-12R; CANR 6

Eiseley, Loren Corey 1907-1977..... **CLC 7**
See also AAYA 5; CA 1-4R; 73-76; CANR 6

Eisenstadt, Jill 1963-............. **CLC 50**
See also CA 140

Eisner, Simon
See Kornbluth, C(yril) M.

Ekeloef, (Bengt) Gunnar 1907-1968 .... **CLC 27**
See also Ekelof, (Bengt) Gunnar
See also CA 123; 25-28R

Ekelof, (Bengt) Gunnar............. **CLC 27**
See also Ekeloef, (Bengt) Gunnar

Ekwensi, C. O. D.
See Ekwensi, Cyprian (Odiatu Duaka)

Ekwensi, Cyprian (Odiatu Duaka) 1921- .... **CLC 4**
See also BLC 1; BW; CA 29-32R; CANR 18, 42; DLB 117; MTCW; SATA 66

Elaine.......................... **TCLC 18**
See also Leverson, Ada

El Crummo
See Crumb, R(obert)

Elia
See Lamb, Charles

Eliade, Mircea 1907-1986 .... **CLC 19**
See also CA 65-68; 119; CANR 30; MTCW

Eliot, A. D.
See Jewett, (Theodora) Sarah Orne

Eliot, Alice
See Jewett, (Theodora) Sarah Orne

Eliot, Dan
See Silverberg, Robert

Eliot, George 1819-1880 .... **NCLC 4, 13, 23, 41**
See also CDBLB 1832-1890; DA; DLB 21, 35, 55; WLC

Eliot, John 1604-1690 .... **LC 5**
See also DLB 24

Eliot, T(homas) S(tearns) 1888-1965 ..... **CLC 1, 2, 3, 6, 9, 10, 13, 15, 24, 34, 41, 55, 57; PC 5**
See also CA 5-8R; 25-28R; CANR 41; CDALB 1929-1941; DA; DLB 7, 10, 45, 63; DLBY 88; MTCW; WLC 2

Elizabeth 1866-1941 .... **TCLC 41**

Elkin, Stanley L(awrence) 1930- ... **CLC 4, 6, 9, 14, 27, 51; SSC 12**
See also CA 9-12R; CANR 8; DLB 2, 28; DLBY 80; MTCW

Elledge, Scott .... **CLC 34**

Elliott, Don
See Silverberg, Robert

Elliott, George P(aul) 1918-1980..... **CLC 2**
See also CA 1-4R; 97-100; CANR 2

Elliott, Janice 1931-.............. **CLC 47**
See also CA 13-16R; CANR 8, 29; DLB 14

Elliott, Sumner Locke 1917-1991 ... **CLC 38**
See also CA 5-8R; 134; CANR 2, 21

Elliott, William
See Bradbury, Ray (Douglas)

Ellis, A. E. .... **CLC 7**

Ellis, Alice Thomas .... **CLC 40**
See also Haycraft, Anna

Ellis, Bret Easton 1964-........ **CLC 39, 71**
See also AAYA 2; CA 118; 123

Ellis, (Henry) Havelock 1859-1939 .... **TCLC 14**
See also CA 109

Ellis, Landon
See Ellison, Harlan

Ellis, Trey 1962-................. **CLC 55**

Ellison, Harlan 1934-........ **CLC 1, 13, 42**
See also CA 5-8R; CANR 5; DLB 8; MTCW

Ellison, Ralph (Waldo) 1914- .... **CLC 1, 3, 11, 54**
See also BLC 1; BW; CA 9-12R; CANR 24; CDALB 1941-1968; DA; DLB 2, 76; MTCW; WLC

Ellmann, Lucy (Elizabeth) 1956-.... **CLC 61**
See also CA 128

Ellmann, Richard (David) 1918-1987 .... **CLC 50**
See also BEST 89:2; CA 1-4R; 122; CANR 2, 28; DLB 103; DLBY 87; MTCW

Elman, Richard 1934-............. **CLC 19**
See also CA 17-20R; CAAS 3

Elron
See Hubbard, L(afayette) Ron(ald)

Eluard, Paul .... **TCLC 7, 41**
See also Grindel, Eugene

Elyot, Sir Thomas 1490(?)-1546 ..... **LC 11**

Elytis, Odysseus 1911-......... **CLC 15, 49**
See also CA 102; MTCW

Emecheta, (Florence Onye) Buchi 1944- .... **CLC 14, 48**
See also BLC 2; BW; CA 81-84; CANR 27; DLB 117; MTCW; SATA 66

Emerson, Ralph Waldo 1803-1882 .... **NCLC 1, 38**
See also CDALB 1640-1865; DA; DLB 1, 59, 73; WLC

Eminescu, Mihail 1850-1889..... **NCLC 33**

Empson, William 1906-1984 .... **CLC 3, 8, 19, 33, 34**
See also CA 17-20R; 112; CANR 31; DLB 20; MTCW

Enchi Fumiko (Ueda) 1905-1986.... **CLC 31**
See also CA 129; 121

Ende, Michael (Andreas Helmuth) 1929- .... **CLC 31**
See also CA 118; 124; CANR 36; CLR 14; DLB 75; MAICYA; SATA 42, 61

Endo, Shusaku 1923-..... **CLC 7, 14, 19, 54**
See also CA 29-32R; CANR 21; MTCW

Engel, Marian 1933-1985.......... **CLC 36**
See also CA 25-28R; CANR 12; DLB 53

Engelhardt, Frederick
See Hubbard, L(afayette) Ron(ald)

Enright, D(ennis) J(oseph) 1920- .... **CLC 4, 8, 31**
See also CA 1-4R; CANR 1, 42; DLB 27; SATA 25

Enzensberger, Hans Magnus 1929- .... **CLC 43**
See also CA 116; 119

Ephron, Nora 1941-........... **CLC 17, 31**
See also AITN 2; CA 65-68; CANR 12, 39

Epsilon
See Betjeman, John

Epstein, Daniel Mark 1948- .... **CLC 7**
See also CA 49-52; CANR 2

Epstein, Jacob 1956- .... **CLC 19**
See also CA 114

Epstein, Joseph 1937-............. **CLC 39**
See also CA 112; 119

Epstein, Leslie 1938- .... **CLC 27**
See also CA 73-76; CAAS 12; CANR 23

Equiano, Olaudah 1745(?)-1797...... **LC 16**
See also BLC 2; DLB 37, 50

Erasmus, Desiderius 1469(?)-1536.... **LC 16**

Erdman, Paul E(mil) 1932- .... **CLC 25**
See also AITN 1; CA 61-64; CANR 13, 43

Erdrich, Louise 1954-.......... **CLC 39, 54**
See also AAYA 10; BEST 89:1; CA 114; CANR 41; MTCW

Erenburg, Ilya (Grigoryevich)
See Ehrenburg, Ilya (Grigoryevich)

Erickson, Stephen Michael 1950-
See Erickson, Steve
See also CA 129

Erickson, Steve .... **CLC 64**
See also Erickson, Stephen Michael

Ericson, Walter
See Fast, Howard (Melvin)

Eriksson, Buntel
See Bergman, (Ernst) Ingmar

Eschenbach, Wolfram von
See Wolfram von Eschenbach

Eseki, Bruno
See Mphahlele, Ezekiel

Esenin, Sergei (Alexandrovich) 1895-1925 .... **TCLC 4**
See also CA 104

Eshleman, Clayton 1935-........... **CLC 7**
See also CA 33-36R; CAAS 6; DLB 5

Espriella, Don Manuel Alvarez
See Southey, Robert

Espriu, Salvador 1913-1985......... **CLC 9**
See also CA 115; DLB 134

Espronceda, Jose de 1808-1842... **NCLC 39**

Esse, James
See Stephens, James

Esterbrook, Tom
See Hubbard, L(afayette) Ron(ald)

Estleman, Loren D. 1952-......... **CLC 48**
See also CA 85-88; CANR 27; MTCW

Evan, Evin
See Faust, Frederick (Schiller)

Evans, Evan
See Faust, Frederick (Schiller)

Evans, Marian
See Eliot, George

Evans, Mary Ann
See Eliot, George

Evarts, Esther
See Benson, Sally

Everett, Percival
See Everett, Percival L.

Everett, Percival L. 1956-......... **CLC 57**
See also CA 129

Everson, R(onald) G(ilmour) 1903- .... **CLC 27**
See also CA 17-20R; DLB 88

Everson, William (Oliver) 1912- .... **CLC 1, 5, 14**
See also CA 9-12R; CANR 20; DLB 5, 16; MTCW

Evtushenko, Evgenii Aleksandrovich
See Yevtushenko, Yevgeny (Alexandrovich)

Ewart, Gavin (Buchanan) 1916- .... **CLC 13, 46**
See also CA 89-92; CANR 17; DLB 40; MTCW

Ewers, Hanns Heinz 1871-1943 ... **TCLC 12**
See also CA 109

Ewing, Frederick R.
See Sturgeon, Theodore (Hamilton)

Exley, Frederick (Earl) 1929-1992 .... **CLC 6, 11**
See also AITN 2; CA 81-84; 138; DLBY 81

Eynhardt, Guillermo
See Quiroga, Horacio (Sylvestre)

Ezekiel, Nissim 1924-............. **CLC 61**
See also CA 61-64

Ezekiel, Tish O'Dowd 1943-....... **CLC 34**
See also CA 129

Fagen, Donald 1948-.............. **CLC 26**

Fainzilberg, Ilya Arnoldovich 1897-1937
See Ilf, Ilya
See also CA 120

Fair, Ronald L. 1932-............. **CLC 18**
See also BW; CA 69-72; CANR 25; DLB 33

Fairbairns, Zoe (Ann) 1948- .... **CLC 32**
See also CA 103; CANR 21

Falco, Gian
See Papini, Giovanni

Falconer, James
See Kirkup, James

Falconer, Kenneth
See Kornbluth, C(yril) M.

Falkland, Samuel
See Heijermans, Herman

Fallaci, Oriana 1930-............. **CLC 11**
See also CA 77-80; CANR 15; MTCW

Faludy, George 1913-............. **CLC 42**
See also CA 21-24R

Faludy, Gyoergy
See Faludy, George

Fanon, Frantz 1925-1961.......... **CLC 74**
See also BLC 2; BW; CA 116; 89-92

Fanshawe, Ann .... **LC 11**

Fante, John (Thomas) 1911-1983 ... **CLC 60**
See also CA 69-72; 109; CANR 23; DLB 130; DLBY 83

Farah, Nuruddin 1945-............ **CLC 53**
See also BLC 2; CA 106; DLB 125

Fargue, Leon-Paul 1876(?)-1947 ... **TCLC 11**
See also CA 109

Farigoule, Louis
See Romains, Jules

Farina, Richard 1936(?)-1966 .... **CLC 9**
See also CA 81-84; 25-28R

Farley, Walter (Lorimer)
1915-1989 .... **CLC 17**
See also CA 17-20R; CANR 8, 29; DLB 22; JRDA; MAICYA; SATA 2, 43

Farmer, Philip Jose 1918-....... **CLC 1, 19**
See also CA 1-4R; CANR 4, 35; DLB 8; MTCW

Farquhar, George 1677-1707........ **LC 21**
See also DLB 84

Farrell, J(ames) G(ordon)
1935-1979 .... **CLC 6**
See also CA 73-76; 89-92; CANR 36; DLB 14; MTCW

Farrell, James T(homas)
1904-1979 .... **CLC 1, 4, 8, 11, 66**
See also CA 5-8R; 89-92; CANR 9; DLB 4, 9, 86; DLBD 2; MTCW

Farren, Richard J.
See Betjeman, John

Farren, Richard M.
See Betjeman, John

Fassbinder, Rainer Werner
1946-1982 .... **CLC 20**
See also CA 93-96; 106; CANR 31

Fast, Howard (Melvin) 1914- ...... **CLC 23**
See also CA 1-4R; CAAS 18; CANR 1, 33; DLB 9; SATA 7

Faulcon, Robert
See Holdstock, Robert P.

Faulkner, William (Cuthbert)
1897-1962 ..... **CLC 1, 3, 6, 8, 9, 11, 14, 18, 28, 52, 68; SSC 1**
See also AAYA 7; CA 81-84; CANR 33; CDALB 1929-1941; DA; DLB 9, 11, 44, 102; DLBD 2; DLBY 86; MTCW; WLC

Fauset, Jessie Redmon
1884(?)-1961 .... **CLC 19, 54**
See also BLC 2; BW; CA 109; DLB 51

Faust, Frederick (Schiller)
1892-1944(?) .... **TCLC 49**
See also CA 108

Faust, Irvin 1924-................. **CLC 8**
See also CA 33-36R; CANR 28; DLB 2, 28; DLBY 80

Fawkes, Guy
See Benchley, Robert (Charles)

Fearing, Kenneth (Flexner)
1902-1961 .... **CLC 51**
See also CA 93-96; DLB 9

Fecamps, Elise
See Creasey, John

Federman, Raymond 1928- ...... **CLC 6, 47**
See also CA 17-20R; CAAS 8; CANR 10, 43; DLBY 80

Federspiel, J(uerg) F. 1931-........ **CLC 42**

Feiffer, Jules (Ralph) 1929-.... **CLC 2, 8, 64**
See also AAYA 3; CA 17-20R; CANR 30; DLB 7, 44; MTCW; SATA 8, 61

Feige, Hermann Albert Otto Maximilian
See Traven, B.

Fei-Kan, Li
See Li Fei-kan

Feinberg, David B. 1956-.......... **CLC 59**
See also CA 135

Feinstein, Elaine 1930-............ **CLC 36**
See also CA 69-72; CAAS 1; CANR 31; DLB 14, 40; MTCW

Feldman, Irving (Mordecai) 1928-.... **CLC 7**
See also CA 1-4R; CANR 1

Fellini, Federico 1920-............ **CLC 16**
See also CA 65-68; CANR 33

Felsen, Henry Gregor 1916- .... **CLC 17**
See also CA 1-4R; CANR 1; SAAS 2; SATA 1

Fenton, James Martin 1949-....... **CLC 32**
See also CA 102; DLB 40

Ferber, Edna 1887-1968........... **CLC 18**
See also AITN 1; CA 5-8R; 25-28R; DLB 9, 28, 86; MTCW; SATA 7

Ferguson, Helen
See Kavan, Anna

Ferguson, Samuel 1810-1886..... **NCLC 33**
See also DLB 32

Ferling, Lawrence
See Ferlinghetti, Lawrence (Monsanto)

Ferlinghetti, Lawrence (Monsanto)
1919(?)-........ **CLC 2, 6, 10, 27; PC 1**
See also CA 5-8R; CANR 3, 41; CDALB 1941-1968; DLB 5, 16; MTCW

Fernandez, Vicente Garcia Huidobro
See Huidobro Fernandez, Vicente Garcia

Ferrer, Gabriel (Francisco Victor) Miro
See Miro (Ferrer), Gabriel (Francisco Victor)

Ferrier, Susan (Edmonstone)
1782-1854 .... **NCLC 8**
See also DLB 116

Ferrigno, Robert 1948(?)-.......... **CLC 65**
See also CA 140

Feuchtwanger, Lion 1884-1958 ..... **TCLC 3**
See also CA 104; DLB 66

Feydeau, Georges (Leon Jules Marie)
1862-1921 .... **TCLC 22**
See also CA 113

Ficino, Marsilio 1433-1499 .... **LC 12**

Fiedeler, Hans
See Doeblin, Alfred

Fiedler, Leslie A(aron)
1917- .... **CLC 4, 13, 24**
See also CA 9-12R; CANR 7; DLB 28, 67; MTCW

Field, Andrew 1938-.............. **CLC 44**
See also CA 97-100; CANR 25

Field, Eugene 1850-1895 .... **NCLC 3**
See also DLB 23, 42; MAICYA; SATA 16

Field, Gans T.
See Wellman, Manly Wade

Field, Michael .... **TCLC 43**

Field, Peter
See Hobson, Laura Z(ametkin)

Fielding, Henry 1707-1754 .... **LC 1**
See also CDBLB 1660-1789; DA; DLB 39, 84, 101; WLC

Fielding, Sarah 1710-1768 .... **LC 1**
See also DLB 39

Fierstein, Harvey (Forbes) 1954- ... **CLC 33**
See also CA 123; 129

Figes, Eva 1932-................. **CLC 31**
See also CA 53-56; CANR 4; DLB 14

Finch, Robert (Duer Claydon)
1900- .... **CLC 18**
See also CA 57-60; CANR 9, 24; DLB 88

Findley, Timothy 1930- .... **CLC 27**
See also CA 25-28R; CANR 12, 42; DLB 53

Fink, William
See Mencken, H(enry) L(ouis)

Firbank, Louis 1942-
See Reed, Lou
See also CA 117

Firbank, (Arthur Annesley) Ronald
1886-1926 .... **TCLC 1**
See also CA 104; DLB 36

Fisher, M(ary) F(rances) K(ennedy)
1908-1992 .... **CLC 76**
See also CA 77-80; 138

Fisher, Roy 1930-................ **CLC 25**
See also CA 81-84; CAAS 10; CANR 16; DLB 40

Fisher, Rudolph 1897-1934 .... **TCLC 11**
See also BLC 2; BW; CA 107; 124; DLB 51, 102

Fisher, Vardis (Alvero) 1895-1968.... **CLC 7**
See also CA 5-8R; 25-28R; DLB 9

Fiske, Tarleton
See Bloch, Robert (Albert)

Fitch, Clarke
See Sinclair, Upton (Beall)

Fitch, John IV
See Cormier, Robert (Edmund)

Fitgerald, Penelope 1916- .... **CLC 61**

Fitzgerald, Captain Hugh
See Baum, L(yman) Frank

FitzGerald, Edward 1809-1883 .... **NCLC 9**
See also DLB 32

Fitzgerald, F(rancis) Scott (Key)
1896-1940 .... **TCLC 1, 6, 14, 28; SSC 6**
See also AITN 1; CA 110; 123; CDALB 1917-1929; DA; DLB 4, 9, 86; DLBD 1; DLBY 81; MTCW; WLC

Fitzgerald, Penelope 1916-...... **CLC 19, 51**
See also CA 85-88; CAAS 10; DLB 14

Fitzgerald, Robert (Stuart)
1910-1985 .... **CLC 39**
See also CA 1-4R; 114; CANR 1; DLBY 80

FitzGerald, Robert D(avid)
1902-1987 .... **CLC 19**
See also CA 17-20R

Fitzgerald, Zelda (Sayre)
1900-1948 .... **TCLC 52**
See also CA 117; 126; DLBY 84

Flanagan, Thomas (James Bonner)
1923- .... **CLC 25, 52**
See also CA 108; DLBY 80; MTCW

Flaubert, Gustave
1821-1880 ..... **NCLC 2, 10, 19; SSC 11**
See also DA; DLB 119; WLC

Flecker, (Herman) James Elroy
1884-1915 .... **TCLC 43**
See also CA 109; DLB 10, 19

Fleming, Ian (Lancaster)
1908-1964 .... **CLC 3, 30**
See also CA 5-8R; CDBLB 1945-1960; DLB 87; MTCW; SATA 9

Fleming, Thomas (James) 1927- .... **CLC 37**
See also CA 5-8R; CANR 10; SATA 8

Fletcher, John Gould 1886-1950... **TCLC 35**
See also CA 107; DLB 4, 45

Fleur, Paul
See Pohl, Frederik

Flooglebuckle, Al
See Spiegelman, Art

Flying Officer X
See Bates, H(erbert) E(rnest)

Fo, Dario 1926-.................. **CLC 32**
See also CA 116; 128; MTCW

Fogarty, Jonathan Titulescu Esq.
See Farrell, James T(homas)

Folke, Will
See Bloch, Robert (Albert)

Follett, Ken(neth Martin) 1949- .... **CLC 18**
See also AAYA 6; BEST 89:4; CA 81-84; CANR 13, 33; DLB 87; DLBY 81; MTCW

Fontane, Theodor 1819-1898 ..... **NCLC 26**
See also DLB 129

Foote, Horton 1916-.............. **CLC 51**
See also CA 73-76; CANR 34; DLB 26

Foote, Shelby 1916-.............. **CLC 75**
See also CA 5-8R; CANR 3; DLB 2, 17

Forbes, Esther 1891-1967.......... **CLC 12**
See also CA 13-14; 25-28R; CAP 1; CLR 27; DLB 22; JRDA; MAICYA; SATA 2

Forche, Carolyn (Louise) 1950-..... **CLC 25**
See also CA 109; 117; DLB 5

Ford, Elbur
See Hibbert, Eleanor Alice Burford

Ford, Ford Madox
1873-1939 .... **TCLC 1, 15, 39**
See also CA 104; 132; CDBLB 1914-1945; DLB 34, 98; MTCW

Ford, John 1895-1973............. **CLC 16**
See also CA 45-48

Ford, Richard 1944-.............. **CLC 46**
See also CA 69-72; CANR 11

Ford, Webster
See Masters, Edgar Lee

Foreman, Richard 1937-........... **CLC 50**
See also CA 65-68; CANR 32

Forester, C(ecil) S(cott)
1899-1966 .... **CLC 35**
See also CA 73-76; 25-28R; SATA 13

Forez
See Mauriac, Francois (Charles)

Forman, James Douglas 1932-...... **CLC 21**
See also CA 9-12R; CANR 4, 19, 42; JRDA; MAICYA; SATA 8, 70

Fornes, Maria Irene 1930-...... **CLC 39, 61**
See also CA 25-28R; CANR 28; DLB 7; HW; MTCW

Forrest, Leon 1937- .... **CLC 4**
See also BW; CA 89-92; CAAS 7; CANR 25; DLB 33

Forster, E(dward) M(organ)
1879-1970 ..... **CLC 1, 2, 3, 4, 9, 10, 13, 15, 22, 45, 77**
See also AAYA 2; CA 13-14; 25-28R; CAP 1; CDBLB 1914-1945; DA; DLB 34, 98; DLBD 10; MTCW; SATA 57; WLC

Forster, John 1812-1876 .... **NCLC 11**

Forsyth, Frederick 1938-...... **CLC 2, 5, 36**
See also BEST 89:4; CA 85-88; CANR 38; DLB 87; MTCW

Forten, Charlotte L. .... **TCLC 16**
See also Grimke, Charlotte L(ottie) Forten
See also BLC 2; DLB 50

Foscolo, Ugo 1778-1827.......... **NCLC 8**

Fosse, Bob .... **CLC 20**
See also Fosse, Robert Louis

Fosse, Robert Louis 1927-1987
See Fosse, Bob
See also CA 110; 123

Foster, Stephen Collins
1826-1864 .... **NCLC 26**

Foucault, Michel
1926-1984 .... **CLC 31, 34, 69**
See also CA 105; 113; CANR 34; MTCW

Fouque, Friedrich (Heinrich Karl) de la Motte
1777-1843 .... **NCLC 2**
See also DLB 90

Fournier, Henri Alban 1886-1914
See Alain-Fournier
See also CA 104

Fournier, Pierre 1916-............. **CLC 11**
See also Gascar, Pierre
See also CA 89-92; CANR 16, 40

Fowles, John
1926- .... **CLC 1, 2, 3, 4, 6, 9, 10, 15, 33**
See also CA 5-8R; CANR 25; CDBLB 1960 to Present; DLB 14; MTCW; SATA 22

Fox, Paula 1923-................ **CLC 2, 8**
See also AAYA 3; CA 73-76; CANR 20, 36; CLR 1; DLB 52; JRDA; MAICYA; MTCW; SATA 17, 60

Fox, William Price (Jr.) 1926- ..... **CLC 22**
See also CA 17-20R; CANR 11; DLB 2; DLBY 81

Foxe, John 1516(?)-1587 .... **LC 14**

Frame, Janet .... **CLC 2, 3, 6, 22, 66**
See also Clutha, Janet Paterson Frame

France, Anatole .... **TCLC 9**
See also Thibault, Jacques Anatole Francois
See also DLB 123

Francis, Claude 19(?)- .... **CLC 50**

Francis, Dick 1920- .... **CLC 2, 22, 42**
See also AAYA 5; BEST 89:3; CA 5-8R; CANR 9, 42; CDBLB 1960 to Present; DLB 87; MTCW

Francis, Robert (Churchill)
1901-1987 .... **CLC 15**
See also CA 1-4R; 123; CANR 1

Frank, Anne(lies Marie)
1929-1945 .... **TCLC 17**
See also CA 113; 133; DA; MTCW; SATA 42; WLC

Frank, Elizabeth 1945-............ **CLC 39**
See also CA 121; 126

Franklin, Benjamin
See Hasek, Jaroslav (Matej Frantisek)

Franklin, (Stella Maraia Sarah) Miles
1879-1954 .... **TCLC 7**
See also CA 104

Fraser, Antonia (Pakenham)
1932- .... **CLC 32**
See also CA 85-88; MTCW; SATA 32

Fraser, George MacDonald 1925-.... **CLC 7**
See also CA 45-48; CANR 2

Fraser, Sylvia 1935-.............. **CLC 64**
See also CA 45-48; CANR 1, 16

Frayn, Michael 1933-...... **CLC 3, 7, 31, 47**
See also CA 5-8R; CANR 30; DLB 13, 14; MTCW

Fraze, Candida (Merrill) 1945- ..... **CLC 50**
See also CA 126

Frazer, J(ames) G(eorge)
1854-1941 .... **TCLC 32**
See also CA 118

Frazer, Robert Caine
See Creasey, John

Frazer, Sir James George
See Frazer, J(ames) G(eorge)

Frazier, Ian 1951-................ **CLC 46**
See also CA 130

Frederic, Harold 1856-1898...... **NCLC 10**
See also DLB 12, 23

Frederick, John
See Faust, Frederick (Schiller)

Frederick the Great 1712-1786...... **LC 14**

Fredro, Aleksander 1793-1876..... **NCLC 8**

Freeling, Nicolas 1927-........... **CLC 38**
See also CA 49-52; CAAS 12; CANR 1, 17; DLB 87

Freeman, Douglas Southall
1886-1953.................. **TCLC 11**
See also CA 109; DLB 17

Freeman, Judith 1946-............ **CLC 55**

Freeman, Mary Eleanor Wilkins
1852-1930............ **TCLC 9; SSC 1**
See also CA 106; DLB 12, 78

Freeman, R(ichard) Austin
1862-1943.................. **TCLC 21**
See also CA 113; DLB 70

French, Marilyn 1929-...... **CLC 10, 18, 60**
See also CA 69-72; CANR 3, 31; MTCW

French, Paul
See Asimov, Isaac

Freneau, Philip Morin 1752-1832.. **NCLC 1**
See also DLB 37, 43

Freud, Sigmund 1856-1939....... **TCLC 52**
See also CA 115; 133; MTCW

Friedan, Betty (Naomi) 1921-...... **CLC 74**
See also CA 65-68; CANR 18; MTCW

Friedman, B(ernard) H(arper)
1926-......................... **CLC 7**
See also CA 1-4R; CANR 3

Friedman, Bruce Jay 1930-.... **CLC 3, 5, 56**
See also CA 9-12R; CANR 25; DLB 2, 28

Friel, Brian 1929-........... **CLC 5, 42, 59**
See also CA 21-24R; CANR 33; DLB 13; MTCW

Friis-Baastad, Babbis Ellinor
1921-1970................... **CLC 12**
See also CA 17-20R; 134; SATA 7

Frisch, Max (Rudolf)
1911-1991..... **CLC 3, 9, 14, 18, 32, 44**
See also CA 85-88; 134; CANR 32; DLB 69, 124; MTCW

Fromentin, Eugene (Samuel Auguste)
1820-1876................. **NCLC 10**
See also DLB 123

Frost, Frederick
See Faust, Frederick (Schiller)

Frost, Robert (Lee)
1874-1963.... **CLC 1, 3, 4, 9, 10, 13, 15, 26, 34, 44; PC 1**
See also CA 89-92; CANR 33; CDALB 1917-1929; DA; DLB 54; DLBD 7; MTCW; SATA 14; WLC

Froy, Herald
See Waterhouse, Keith (Spencer)

Fry, Christopher 1907-....... **CLC 2, 10, 14**
See also CA 17-20R; CANR 9, 30; DLB 13; MTCW; SATA 66

Frye, (Herman) Northrop
1912-1991................ **CLC 24, 70**
See also CA 5-8R; 133; CANR 8, 37; DLB 67, 68; MTCW

Fuchs, Daniel 1909-1993........ **CLC 8, 22**
See also CA 81-84; 142; CAAS 5; CANR 40; DLB 9, 26, 28

Fuchs, Daniel 1934-.............. **CLC 34**
See also CA 37-40R; CANR 14

Fuentes, Carlos
1928-...... **CLC 3, 8, 10, 13, 22, 41, 60**
See also AAYA 4; AITN 2; CA 69-72; CANR 10, 32; DA; DLB 113; HW; MTCW; WLC

Fuentes, Gregorio Lopez y
See Lopez y Fuentes, Gregorio

Fugard, (Harold) Athol
1932-.... **CLC 5, 9, 14, 25, 40, 80; DC 3**
See also CA 85-88; CANR 32; MTCW

Fugard, Sheila 1932-............. **CLC 48**
See also CA 125

Fuller, Charles (H., Jr.)
1939-................. **CLC 25; DC 1**
See also BLC 2; BW; CA 108; 112; DLB 38; MTCW

Fuller, John (Leopold) 1937-....... **CLC 62**
See also CA 21-24R; CANR 9; DLB 40

Fuller, Margaret................. **NCLC 5**
See also Ossoli, Sarah Margaret (Fuller marchesa d')

Fuller, Roy (Broadbent)
1912-1991................. **CLC 4, 28**
See also CA 5-8R; 135; CAAS 10; DLB 15, 20

Fulton, Alice 1952-............... **CLC 52**
See also CA 116

Furphy, Joseph 1843-1912........ **TCLC 25**

Fussell, Paul 1924-............... **CLC 74**
See also BEST 90:1; CA 17-20R; CANR 8, 21, 35; MTCW

Futabatei, Shimei 1864-1909...... **TCLC 44**

Futrelle, Jacques 1875-1912...... **TCLC 19**
See also CA 113

G. B. S.
See Shaw, George Bernard

Gaboriau, Emile 1835-1873...... **NCLC 14**

Gadda, Carlo Emilio 1893-1973.... **CLC 11**
See also CA 89-92

Gaddis, William
1922-........ **CLC 1, 3, 6, 8, 10, 19, 43**
See also CA 17-20R; CANR 21; DLB 2; MTCW

Gaines, Ernest J(ames)
1933-.................. **CLC 3, 11, 18**
See also AITN 1; BLC 2; BW; CA 9-12R; CANR 6, 24, 42; CDALB 1968-1988; DLB 2, 33; DLBY 80; MTCW

Gaitskill, Mary 1954-............. **CLC 69**
See also CA 128

Galdos, Benito Perez
See Perez Galdos, Benito

Gale, Zona 1874-1938............ **TCLC 7**
See also CA 105; DLB 9, 78

Galeano, Eduardo (Hughes) 1940-... **CLC 72**
See also CA 29-32R; CANR 13, 32; HW

Galiano, Juan Valera y Alcala
See Valera y Alcala-Galiano, Juan

Gallagher, Tess 1943-.......... **CLC 18, 63**
See also CA 106; DLB 120

Gallant, Mavis
1922-........... **CLC 7, 18, 38; SSC 5**
See also CA 69-72; CANR 29; DLB 53; MTCW

Gallant, Roy A(rthur) 1924-....... **CLC 17**
See also CA 5-8R; CANR 4, 29; CLR 30; MAICYA; SATA 4, 68

Gallico, Paul (William) 1897-1976... **CLC 2**
See also AITN 1; CA 5-8R; 69-72; CANR 23; DLB 9; MAICYA; SATA 13

Gallup, Ralph
See Whitemore, Hugh (John)

Galsworthy, John 1867-1933.... **TCLC 1, 45**
See also CA 104; 141; CDBLB 1890-1914; DA; DLB 10, 34, 98; WLC 2

Galt, John 1779-1839............ **NCLC 1**
See also DLB 99, 116

Galvin, James 1951-.............. **CLC 38**
See also CA 108; CANR 26

Gamboa, Federico 1864-1939...... **TCLC 36**

Gann, Ernest Kellogg 1910-1991.... **CLC 23**
See also AITN 1; CA 1-4R; 136; CANR 1

Garcia, Cristina 1958-............ **CLC 76**
See also CA 141

Garcia Lorca, Federico
1898-1936.. **TCLC 1, 7, 49; DC 2; PC 3**
See also Lorca, Federico Garcia
See also CA 104; 131; DA; DLB 108; HW; MTCW; WLC

Garcia Marquez, Gabriel (Jose)
1928-.... **CLC 2, 3, 8, 10, 15, 27, 47, 55; SSC 8**
See also Marquez, Gabriel (Jose) Garcia
See also AAYA 3; BEST 89:1, 90:4; CA 33-36R; CANR 10, 28; DA; DLB 113; HW; MTCW; WLC

Gard, Janice
See Latham, Jean Lee

Gard, Roger Martin du
See Martin du Gard, Roger

Gardam, Jane 1928-.............. **CLC 43**
See also CA 49-52; CANR 2, 18, 33; CLR 12; DLB 14; MAICYA; MTCW; SAAS 9; SATA 28, 39

Gardner, Herb.................... **CLC 44**

Gardner, John (Champlin), Jr.
1933-1982..... **CLC 2, 3, 5, 7, 8, 10, 18, 28, 34; SSC 7**
See also AITN 1; CA 65-68; 107; CANR 33; DLB 2; DLBY 82; MTCW; SATA 31, 40

Gardner, John (Edmund) 1926-..... **CLC 30**
See also CA 103; CANR 15; MTCW

Gardner, Noel
See Kuttner, Henry

Gardons, S. S.
See Snodgrass, W(illiam) D(e Witt)

Garfield, Leon 1921-............. **CLC 12**
See also AAYA 8; CA 17-20R; CANR 38, 41; CLR 21; JRDA; MAICYA; SATA 1, 32

Glasscock, Amnesia
See Steinbeck, John (Ernst)

Glasser, Ronald J. 1940(?)- . . . . **CLC 37**

Glassman, Joyce
See Johnson, Joyce

Glendinning, Victoria 1937- . . . . **CLC 50**
See also CA 120; 127

Glissant, Edouard 1928- . . . . **CLC 10, 68**

Gloag, Julian 1930- . . . . **CLC 40**
See also AITN 1; CA 65-68; CANR 10

Gluck, Louise (Elisabeth)
1943- . . . . **CLC 7, 22, 44**
See also Glueck, Louise
See also CA 33-36R; CANR 40; DLB 5

Glueck, Louise . . . . **CLC 7, 22**
See also Gluck, Louise (Elisabeth)
See also DLB 5

Gobineau, Joseph Arthur (Comte) de
1816-1882 . . . . **NCLC 17**
See also DLB 123

Godard, Jean-Luc 1930- . . . . **CLC 20**
See also CA 93-96

Godden, (Margaret) Rumer 1907- . . . **CLC 53**
See also AAYA 6; CA 5-8R; CANR 4, 27, 36; CLR 20; MAICYA; SAAS 12; SATA 3, 36

Godoy Alcayaga, Lucila 1889-1957
See Mistral, Gabriela
See also CA 104; 131; HW; MTCW

Godwin, Gail (Kathleen)
1937- . . . . **CLC 5, 8, 22, 31, 69**
See also CA 29-32R; CANR 15, 43; DLB 6; MTCW

Godwin, William 1756-1836 . . . . . . **NCLC 14**
See also CDBLB 1789-1832; DLB 39, 104

Goethe, Johann Wolfgang von
1749-1832 . . . . **NCLC 4, 22, 34; PC 5**
See also DA; DLB 94; WLC 3

Gogarty, Oliver St. John
1878-1957 . . . . **TCLC 15**
See also CA 109; DLB 15, 19

Gogol, Nikolai (Vasilyevich)
1809-1852 . . . . . . **NCLC 5, 15, 31; DC 1; SSC 4**
See also DA; WLC

Goines, Donald 1937(?)-1974 . . . . **CLC 80**
See also AITN 1; BLC 2; BW; CA 124; 114; DLB 33

Gold, Herbert 1924- . . . . **CLC 4, 7, 14, 42**
See also CA 9-12R; CANR 17; DLB 2; DLBY 81

Goldbarth, Albert 1948- . . . . **CLC 5, 38**
See also CA 53-56; CANR 6, 40; DLB 120

Goldberg, Anatol 1910-1982 . . . . **CLC 34**
See also CA 131; 117

Goldemberg, Isaac 1945- . . . . **CLC 52**
See also CA 69-72; CAAS 12; CANR 11, 32; HW

Golden Silver
See Storm, Hyemeyohsts

Golding, William G(erald)
1911-1993 . . . . **CLC 1, 2, 3, 8, 10, 17, 27, 58**
See also AAYA 5; CA 5-8R; 141; CANR 13, 33; CDBLB 1945-1960; DA; DLB 15, 100; MTCW; WLC

Goldman, Emma 1869-1940 . . . . **TCLC 13**
See also CA 110

Goldman, Francisco 1955- . . . . **CLC 76**

Goldman, William (W.) 1931- . . . . **CLC 1, 48**
See also CA 9-12R; CANR 29; DLB 44

Goldmann, Lucien 1913-1970 . . . . . . **CLC 24**
See also CA 25-28; CAP 2

Goldoni, Carlo 1707-1793 . . . . **LC 4**

Goldsberry, Steven 1949- . . . . **CLC 34**
See also CA 131

Goldsmith, Oliver 1728-1774 . . . . **LC 2**
See also CDBLB 1660-1789; DA; DLB 39, 89, 104, 109; SATA 26; WLC

Goldsmith, Peter
See Priestley, J(ohn) B(oynton)

Gombrowicz, Witold
1904-1969 . . . . **CLC 4, 7, 11, 49**
See also CA 19-20; 25-28R; CAP 2

Gomez de la Serna, Ramon
1888-1963 . . . . **CLC 9**
See also CA 116; HW

Goncharov, Ivan Alexandrovich
1812-1891 . . . . **NCLC 1**

Goncourt, Edmond (Louis Antoine Huot) de
1822-1896 . . . . **NCLC 7**
See also DLB 123

Goncourt, Jules (Alfred Huot) de
1830-1870 . . . . **NCLC 7**
See also DLB 123

Gontier, Fernande 19(?)- . . . . **CLC 50**

Goodman, Paul 1911-1972 . . . . **CLC 1, 2, 4, 7**
See also CA 19-20; 37-40R; CANR 34; CAP 2; DLB 130; MTCW

Gordimer, Nadine
1923- . . . . **CLC 3, 5, 7, 10, 18, 33, 51, 70**
See also CA 5-8R; CANR 3, 28; DA; MTCW

Gordon, Adam Lindsay
1833-1870 . . . . **NCLC 21**

Gordon, Caroline
1895-1981 . . . . **CLC 6, 13, 29**
See also CA 11-12; 103; CANR 36; CAP 1; DLB 4, 9, 102; DLBY 81; MTCW

Gordon, Charles William 1860-1937
See Connor, Ralph
See also CA 109

Gordon, Mary (Catherine)
1949- . . . . **CLC 13, 22**
See also CA 102; DLB 6; DLBY 81; MTCW

Gordon, Sol 1923- . . . . **CLC 26**
See also CA 53-56; CANR 4; SATA 11

Gordone, Charles 1925- . . . . **CLC 1, 4**
See also BW; CA 93-96; DLB 7; MTCW

Gorenko, Anna Andreevna
See Akhmatova, Anna

Gorky, Maxim . . . . **TCLC 8**
See also Peshkov, Alexei Maximovich
See also WLC

Goryan, Sirak
See Saroyan, William

Gosse, Edmund (William)
1849-1928 . . . . **TCLC 28**
See also CA 117; DLB 57

Gotlieb, Phyllis Fay (Bloom)
1926- . . . . **CLC 18**
See also CA 13-16R; CANR 7; DLB 88

Gottesman, S. D.
See Kornbluth, C(yril) M.; Pohl, Frederik

Gottfried von Strassburg
fl. c. 1210- . . . . **CMLC 10**

Gottschalk, Laura Riding
See Jackson, Laura (Riding)

Gould, Lois . . . . **CLC 4, 10**
See also CA 77-80; CANR 29; MTCW

Gourmont, Remy de 1858-1915 . . . . **TCLC 17**
See also CA 109

Govier, Katherine 1948- . . . . **CLC 51**
See also CA 101; CANR 18, 40

Goyen, (Charles) William
1915-1983 . . . . **CLC 5, 8, 14, 40**
See also AITN 2; CA 5-8R; 110; CANR 6; DLB 2; DLBY 83

Goytisolo, Juan 1931- . . . . **CLC 5, 10, 23**
See also CA 85-88; CANR 32; HW; MTCW

Gozzi, (Conte) Carlo 1720-1806 . . **NCLC 23**

Grabbe, Christian Dietrich
1801-1836 . . . . **NCLC 2**
See also DLB 133

Grace, Patricia 1937- . . . . **CLC 56**

Gracian y Morales, Baltasar
1601-1658 . . . . **LC 15**

Gracq, Julien . . . . **CLC 11, 48**
See also Poirier, Louis
See also DLB 83

Grade, Chaim 1910-1982 . . . . **CLC 10**
See also CA 93-96; 107

Graduate of Oxford, A
See Ruskin, John

Graham, John
See Phillips, David Graham

Graham, Jorie 1951- . . . . **CLC 48**
See also CA 111; DLB 120

Graham, R(obert) B(ontine) Cunninghame
See Cunninghame Graham, R(obert) B(ontine)
See also DLB 98

Graham, Robert
See Haldeman, Joe (William)

Graham, Tom
See Lewis, (Harry) Sinclair

Graham, W(illiam) S(ydney)
1918-1986 . . . . **CLC 29**
See also CA 73-76; 118; DLB 20

Graham, Winston (Mawdsley)
1910- . . . . **CLC 23**
See also CA 49-52; CANR 2, 22; DLB 77

Grant, Skeeter
See Spiegelman, Art

Guillen (y Batista), Nicolas (Cristobal) 1902-1989 . . . . **CLC 48, 79**
See also BLC 2; BW; CA 116; 125; 129; HW

Guillevic, (Eugene) 1907- . . . . **CLC 33**
See also CA 93-96

Guillois
See Desnos, Robert

Guiney, Louise Imogen 1861-1920 . . . . **TCLC 41**
See also DLB 54

Guiraldes, Ricardo (Guillermo) 1886-1927 . . . . **TCLC 39**
See also CA 131; HW; MTCW

Gunn, Bill . . . . **CLC 5**
See also Gunn, William Harrison
See also DLB 38

Gunn, Thom(son William) 1929- . . . . **CLC 3, 6, 18, 32**
See also CA 17-20R; CANR 9, 33; CDBLB 1960 to Present; DLB 27; MTCW

Gunn, William Harrison 1934(?)-1989
See Gunn, Bill
See also AITN 1; BW; CA 13-16R; 128; CANR 12, 25

Gunnars, Kristjana 1948- . . . . **CLC 69**
See also CA 113; DLB 60

Gurganus, Allan 1947- . . . . **CLC 70**
See also BEST 90:1; CA 135

Gurney, A(lbert) R(amsdell), Jr. 1930- . . . . **CLC 32, 50, 54**
See also CA 77-80; CANR 32

Gurney, Ivor (Bertie) 1890-1937 . . . **TCLC 33**

Gurney, Peter
See Gurney, A(lbert) R(amsdell), Jr.

Gustafson, Ralph (Barker) 1909- . . . . **CLC 36**
See also CA 21-24R; CANR 8; DLB 88

Gut, Gom
See Simenon, Georges (Jacques Christian)

Guthrie, A(lfred) B(ertram), Jr. 1901-1991 . . . . **CLC 23**
See also CA 57-60; 134; CANR 24; DLB 6; SATA 62; SATA-Obit 67

Guthrie, Isobel
See Grieve, C(hristopher) M(urray)

Guthrie, Woodrow Wilson 1912-1967
See Guthrie, Woody
See also CA 113; 93-96

Guthrie, Woody . . . . **CLC 35**
See also Guthrie, Woodrow Wilson

Guy, Rosa (Cuthbert) 1928- . . . . **CLC 26**
See also AAYA 4; BW; CA 17-20R; CANR 14, 34; CLR 13; DLB 33; JRDA; MAICYA; SATA 14, 62

Gwendolyn
See Bennett, (Enoch) Arnold

H. D. . . . . **CLC 3, 8, 14, 31, 34, 73; PC 5**
See also Doolittle, Hilda

Haavikko, Paavo Juhani 1931- . . . . **CLC 18, 34**
See also CA 106

Habbema, Koos
See Heijermans, Herman

Hacker, Marilyn 1942- . . . . **CLC 5, 9, 23, 72**
See also CA 77-80; DLB 120

Haggard, H(enry) Rider 1856-1925 . . . . **TCLC 11**
See also CA 108; DLB 70; SATA 16

Haig, Fenil
See Ford, Ford Madox

Haig-Brown, Roderick (Langmere) 1908-1976 . . . . **CLC 21**
See also CA 5-8R; 69-72; CANR 4, 38; CLR 31; DLB 88; MAICYA; SATA 12

Hailey, Arthur 1920- . . . . **CLC 5**
See also AITN 2; BEST 90:3; CA 1-4R; CANR 2, 36; DLB 88; DLBY 82; MTCW

Hailey, Elizabeth Forsythe 1938- . . . **CLC 40**
See also CA 93-96; CAAS 1; CANR 15

Haines, John (Meade) 1924- . . . . **CLC 58**
See also CA 17-20R; CANR 13, 34; DLB 5

Haldeman, Joe (William) 1943- . . . . . **CLC 61**
See also CA 53-56; CANR 6; DLB 8

Haley, Alex(ander Murray Palmer) 1921-1992 . . . . **CLC 8, 12, 76**
See also BLC 2; BW; CA 77-80; 136; DA; DLB 38; MTCW

Haliburton, Thomas Chandler 1796-1865 . . . . **NCLC 15**
See also DLB 11, 99

Hall, Donald (Andrew, Jr.) 1928- . . . . **CLC 1, 13, 37, 59**
See also CA 5-8R; CAAS 7; CANR 2; DLB 5; SATA 23

Hall, Frederic Sauser
See Sauser-Hall, Frederic

Hall, James
See Kuttner, Henry

Hall, James Norman 1887-1951 . . . **TCLC 23**
See also CA 123; SATA 21

Hall, (Marguerite) Radclyffe 1886(?)-1943 . . . . **TCLC 12**
See also CA 110

Hall, Rodney 1935- . . . . **CLC 51**
See also CA 109

Halliday, Michael
See Creasey, John

Halpern, Daniel 1945- . . . . **CLC 14**
See also CA 33-36R

Hamburger, Michael (Peter Leopold) 1924- . . . . **CLC 5, 14**
See also CA 5-8R; CAAS 4; CANR 2; DLB 27

Hamill, Pete 1935- . . . . **CLC 10**
See also CA 25-28R; CANR 18

Hamilton, Clive
See Lewis, C(live) S(taples)

Hamilton, Edmond 1904-1977 . . . . **CLC 1**
See also CA 1-4R; CANR 3; DLB 8

Hamilton, Eugene (Jacob) Lee
See Lee-Hamilton, Eugene (Jacob)

Hamilton, Franklin
See Silverberg, Robert

Hamilton, Gail
See Corcoran, Barbara

Hamilton, Mollie
See Kaye, M(ary) M(argaret)

Hamilton, (Anthony Walter) Patrick 1904-1962 . . . . **CLC 51**
See also CA 113; DLB 10

Hamilton, Virginia 1936- . . . . **CLC 26**
See also AAYA 2; BW; CA 25-28R; CANR 20, 37; CLR 1, 11; DLB 33, 52; JRDA; MAICYA; MTCW; SATA 4, 56

Hammett, (Samuel) Dashiell 1894-1961 . . . . **CLC 3, 5, 10, 19, 47**
See also AITN 1; CA 81-84; CANR 42; CDALB 1929-1941; DLBD 6; MTCW

Hammon, Jupiter 1711(?)-1800(?) . . **NCLC 5**
See also BLC 2; DLB 31, 50

Hammond, Keith
See Kuttner, Henry

Hamner, Earl (Henry), Jr. 1923- . . . **CLC 12**
See also AITN 2; CA 73-76; DLB 6

Hampton, Christopher (James) 1946- . . . . **CLC 4**
See also CA 25-28R; DLB 13; MTCW

Hamsun, Knut . . . . **TCLC 2, 14, 49**
See also Pedersen, Knut

Handke, Peter 1942- . . **CLC 5, 8, 10, 15, 38**
See also CA 77-80; CANR 33; DLB 85, 124; MTCW

Hanley, James 1901-1985 . . . **CLC 3, 5, 8, 13**
See also CA 73-76; 117; CANR 36; MTCW

Hannah, Barry 1942- . . . . **CLC 23, 38**
See also CA 108; 110; CANR 43; DLB 6; MTCW

Hannon, Ezra
See Hunter, Evan

Hansberry, Lorraine (Vivian) 1930-1965 . . . . **CLC 17, 62; DC 2**
See also BLC 2; BW; CA 109; 25-28R; CABS 3; CDALB 1941-1968; DA; DLB 7, 38; MTCW

Hansen, Joseph 1923- . . . . **CLC 38**
See also CA 29-32R; CAAS 17; CANR 16

Hansen, Martin A. 1909-1955 . . . . . **TCLC 32**

Hanson, Kenneth O(stlin) 1922- . . . . **CLC 13**
See also CA 53-56; CANR 7

Hardwick, Elizabeth 1916- . . . . **CLC 13**
See also CA 5-8R; CANR 3, 32; DLB 6; MTCW

Hardy, Thomas 1840-1928 . . . . . . **TCLC 4, 10, 18, 32, 48; SSC 2**
See also CA 104; 123; CDBLB 1890-1914; DA; DLB 18, 19; MTCW; WLC

Hare, David 1947- . . . . **CLC 29, 58**
See also CA 97-100; CANR 39; DLB 13; MTCW

Harford, Henry
See Hudson, W(illiam) H(enry)

Hargrave, Leonie
See Disch, Thomas M(ichael)

Harlan, Louis R(udolph) 1922- . . . . . **CLC 34**
See also CA 21-24R; CANR 25

Harling, Robert 1951(?)- . . . . **CLC 53**

Harmon, William (Ruth) 1938- . . . . . **CLC 38**
See also CA 33-36R; CANR 14, 32, 35; SATA 65

Harper, F. E. W.
See Harper, Frances Ellen Watkins

Harper, Frances E. W.
See Harper, Frances Ellen Watkins

Harper, Frances E. Watkins
See Harper, Frances Ellen Watkins

Harper, Frances Ellen
See Harper, Frances Ellen Watkins

Harper, Frances Ellen Watkins 1825-1911 .... **TCLC 14**
See also BLC 2; BW; CA 111; 125; DLB 50

Harper, Michael S(teven) 1938- .. **CLC 7, 22**
See also BW; CA 33-36R; CANR 24; DLB 41

Harper, Mrs. F. E. W.
See Harper, Frances Ellen Watkins

Harris, Christie (Lucy) Irwin 1907- .... **CLC 12**
See also CA 5-8R; CANR 6; DLB 88; JRDA; MAICYA; SAAS 10; SATA 6, 74

Harris, Frank 1856(?)-1931 .... **TCLC 24**
See also CA 109

Harris, George Washington 1814-1869 .... **NCLC 23**
See also DLB 3, 11

Harris, Joel Chandler 1848-1908 ... **TCLC 2**
See also CA 104; 137; DLB 11, 23, 42, 78, 91; MAICYA; YABC 1

Harris, John (Wyndham Parkes Lucas) Beynon 1903-1969 .... **CLC 19**
See also CA 102; 89-92

Harris, MacDonald
See Heiney, Donald (William)

Harris, Mark 1922- .... **CLC 19**
See also CA 5-8R; CAAS 3; CANR 2; DLB 2; DLBY 80

Harris, (Theodore) Wilson 1921-.... **CLC 25**
See also BW; CA 65-68; CAAS 16; CANR 11, 27; DLB 117; MTCW

Harrison, Elizabeth Cavanna 1909-
See Cavanna, Betty
See also CA 9-12R; CANR 6, 27

Harrison, Harry (Max) 1925-...... **CLC 42**
See also CA 1-4R; CANR 5, 21; DLB 8; SATA 4

Harrison, James (Thomas) 1937- .... **CLC 6, 14, 33, 66**
See also CA 13-16R; CANR 8; DLBY 82

Harrison, Kathryn 1961- .... **CLC 70**

Harrison, Tony 1937-............. **CLC 43**
See also CA 65-68; DLB 40; MTCW

Harriss, Will(ard Irvin) 1922-...... **CLC 34**
See also CA 111

Harson, Sley
See Ellison, Harlan

Hart, Ellis
See Ellison, Harlan

Hart, Josephine 1942(?)- .... **CLC 70**
See also CA 138

Hart, Moss 1904-1961 .... **CLC 66**
See also CA 109; 89-92; DLB 7

Harte, (Francis) Bret(t) 1836(?)-1902 .... **TCLC 1, 25; SSC 8**
See also CA 104; 140; CDALB 1865-1917; DA; DLB 12, 64, 74, 79; SATA 26; WLC

Hartley, L(eslie) P(oles) 1895-1972 .... **CLC 2, 22**
See also CA 45-48; 37-40R; CANR 33; DLB 15; MTCW

Hartman, Geoffrey H. 1929-....... **CLC 27**
See also CA 117; 125; DLB 67

Haruf, Kent 19(?)- .... **CLC 34**

Harwood, Ronald 1934-........... **CLC 32**
See also CA 1-4R; CANR 4; DLB 13

Hasek, Jaroslav (Matej Frantisek) 1883-1923 .... **TCLC 4**
See also CA 104; 129; MTCW

Hass, Robert 1941-............ **CLC 18, 39**
See also CA 111; CANR 30; DLB 105

Hastings, Hudson
See Kuttner, Henry

Hastings, Selina.................. **CLC 44**

Hatteras, Amelia
See Mencken, H(enry) L(ouis)

Hatteras, Owen.................. **TCLC 18**
See also Mencken, H(enry) L(ouis); Nathan, George Jean

Hauptmann, Gerhart (Johann Robert) 1862-1946 .... **TCLC 4**
See also CA 104; DLB 66, 118

Havel, Vaclav 1936-........ **CLC 25, 58, 65**
See also CA 104; CANR 36; MTCW

Haviaras, Stratis.................. **CLC 33**
See also Chaviaras, Strates

Hawes, Stephen 1475(?)-1523(?) ..... **LC 17**

Hawkes, John (Clendennin Burne, Jr.) 1925- ...... **CLC 1, 2, 3, 4, 7, 9, 14, 15, 27, 49**
See also CA 1-4R; CANR 2; DLB 2, 7; DLBY 80; MTCW

Hawking, S. W.
See Hawking, Stephen W(illiam)

Hawking, Stephen W(illiam) 1942- .... **CLC 63**
See also BEST 89:1; CA 126; 129

Hawthorne, Julian 1846-1934 ..... **TCLC 25**

Hawthorne, Nathaniel 1804-1864 .... **NCLC 39; SSC 3**
See also CDALB 1640-1865; DA; DLB 1, 74; WLC; YABC 2

Haxton, Josephine Ayres 1921- .... **CLC 73**
See also CA 115; CANR 41

Hayaseca y Eizaguirre, Jorge
See Echegaray (y Eizaguirre), Jose (Maria Waldo)

Hayashi Fumiko 1904-1951....... **TCLC 27**

Haycraft, Anna
See Ellis, Alice Thomas
See also CA 122

Hayden, Robert E(arl) 1913-1980 ...... **CLC 5, 9, 14, 37; PC 6**
See also BLC 2; BW; CA 69-72; 97-100; CABS 2; CANR 24; CDALB 1941-1968; DA; DLB 5, 76; MTCW; SATA 19, 26

Hayford, J(oseph) E(phraim) Casely
See Casely-Hayford, J(oseph) E(phraim)

Hayman, Ronald 1932-............ **CLC 44**
See also CA 25-28R; CANR 18

Haywood, Eliza (Fowler) 1693(?)-1756 .... **LC 1**

Hazlitt, William 1778-1830...... **NCLC 29**
See also DLB 110

Hazzard, Shirley 1931- .... **CLC 18**
See also CA 9-12R; CANR 4; DLBY 82; MTCW

Head, Bessie 1937-1986........ **CLC 25, 67**
See also BLC 2; BW; CA 29-32R; 119; CANR 25; DLB 117; MTCW

Headon, (Nicky) Topper 1956(?)- ... **CLC 30**
See also Clash, The

Heaney, Seamus (Justin) 1939- .... **CLC 5, 7, 14, 25, 37, 74**
See also CA 85-88; CANR 25; CDBLB 1960 to Present; DLB 40; MTCW

Hearn, (Patricio) Lafcadio (Tessima Carlos) 1850-1904 .... **TCLC 9**
See also CA 105; DLB 12, 78

Hearne, Vicki 1946-.............. **CLC 56**
See also CA 139

Hearon, Shelby 1931-............. **CLC 63**
See also AITN 2; CA 25-28R; CANR 18

Heat-Moon, William Least.......... **CLC 29**
See also Trogdon, William (Lewis)
See also AAYA 9

Hebert, Anne 1916- .... **CLC 4, 13, 29**
See also CA 85-88; DLB 68; MTCW

Hecht, Anthony (Evan) 1923- .... **CLC 8, 13, 19**
See also CA 9-12R; CANR 6; DLB 5

Hecht, Ben 1894-1964 .... **CLC 8**
See also CA 85-88; DLB 7, 9, 25, 26, 28, 86

Hedayat, Sadeq 1903-1951........ **TCLC 21**
See also CA 120

Heidegger, Martin 1889-1976 ...... **CLC 24**
See also CA 81-84; 65-68; CANR 34; MTCW

Heidenstam, (Carl Gustaf) Verner von 1859-1940 .... **TCLC 5**
See also CA 104

Heifner, Jack 1946-.............. **CLC 11**
See also CA 105

Heijermans, Herman 1864-1924 ... **TCLC 24**
See also CA 123

Heilbrun, Carolyn G(old) 1926-..... **CLC 25**
See also CA 45-48; CANR 1, 28

Heine, Heinrich 1797-1856 .... **NCLC 4**
See also DLB 90

Heinemann, Larry (Curtiss) 1944- .. **CLC 50**
See also CA 110; CANR 31; DLBD 9

Heiney, Donald (William) 1921-1993 .... **CLC 9**
See also CA 1-4R; 142; CANR 3

Heinlein, Robert A(nson) 1907-1988 ...... **CLC 1, 3, 8, 14, 26, 55**
See also CA 1-4R; 125; CANR 1, 20; DLB 8; JRDA; MAICYA; MTCW; SATA 9, 56, 69

Helforth, John
See Doolittle, Hilda

Hellenhofferu, Vojtech Kapristian z
See Hasek, Jaroslav (Matej Frantisek)

Heller, Joseph
1923- . . . . **CLC 1, 3, 5, 8, 11, 36, 63**
See also AITN 1; CA 5-8R; CABS 1; CANR 8, 42; DA; DLB 2, 28; DLBY 80; MTCW; WLC

Hellman, Lillian (Florence)
1906-1984 . . . . . . **CLC 2, 4, 8, 14, 18, 34, 44, 52; DC 1**
See also AITN 1, 2; CA 13-16R; 112; CANR 33; DLB 7; DLBY 84; MTCW

Helprin, Mark 1947- . . . . . **CLC 7, 10, 22, 32**
See also CA 81-84; DLBY 85; MTCW

Helyar, Jane Penelope Josephine 1933-
See Poole, Josephine
See also CA 21-24R; CANR 10, 26

Hemans, Felicia 1793-1835 . . . . . . **NCLC 29**
See also DLB 96

Hemingway, Ernest (Miller)
1899-1961 . . . . **CLC 1, 3, 6, 8, 10, 13, 19, 30, 34, 39, 41, 44, 50, 61, 80; SSC 1**
See also CA 77-80; CANR 34; CDALB 1917-1929; DA; DLB 4, 9, 102; DLBD 1; DLBY 81, 87; MTCW; WLC

Hempel, Amy 1951- . . . . **CLC 39**
See also CA 118; 137

Henderson, F. C.
See Mencken, H(enry) L(ouis)

Henderson, Sylvia
See Ashton-Warner, Sylvia (Constance)

Henley, Beth . . . . **CLC 23**
See also Henley, Elizabeth Becker
See also CABS 3; DLBY 86

Henley, Elizabeth Becker 1952-
See Henley, Beth
See also CA 107; CANR 32; MTCW

Henley, William Ernest
1849-1903 . . . . **TCLC 8**
See also CA 105; DLB 19

Hennissart, Martha
See Lathen, Emma
See also CA 85-88

Henry, O. . . . . **TCLC 1, 19; SSC 5**
See also Porter, William Sydney
See also WLC

Henryson, Robert 1430(?)-1506(?). . . . **LC 20**

Henry VIII 1491-1547. . . . . **LC 10**

Henschke, Alfred
See Klabund

Hentoff, Nat(han Irving) 1925- . . . . . **CLC 26**
See also AAYA 4; CA 1-4R; CAAS 6; CANR 5, 25; CLR 1; JRDA; MAICYA; SATA 27, 42, 69

Heppenstall, (John) Rayner
1911-1981 . . . . **CLC 10**
See also CA 1-4R; 103; CANR 29

Herbert, Frank (Patrick)
1920-1986 . . . . **CLC 12, 23, 35, 44**
See also CA 53-56; 118; CANR 5, 43; DLB 8; MTCW; SATA 9, 37, 47

Herbert, George 1593-1633 . . . . **LC 24; PC 4**
See also CDBLB Before 1660; DLB 126

Herbert, Zbigniew 1924- . . . . **CLC 9, 43**
See also CA 89-92; CANR 36; MTCW

Herbst, Josephine (Frey)
1897-1969 . . . . **CLC 34**
See also CA 5-8R; 25-28R; DLB 9

Hergesheimer, Joseph
1880-1954 . . . . **TCLC 11**
See also CA 109; DLB 102, 9

Herlihy, James Leo 1927- . . . . **CLC 6**
See also CA 1-4R; CANR 2

Hermogenes fl. c. 175- . . . . **CMLC 6**

Hernandez, Jose 1834-1886. . . . . . **NCLC 17**

Herrick, Robert 1591-1674 . . . . **LC 13**
See also DA; DLB 126

Herring, Guilles
See Somerville, Edith

Herriot, James 1916- . . . . **CLC 12**
See also Wight, James Alfred
See also AAYA 1; CANR 40

Herrmann, Dorothy 1941- . . . . **CLC 44**
See also CA 107

Herrmann, Taffy
See Herrmann, Dorothy

Hersey, John (Richard)
1914-1993 . . . . **CLC 1, 2, 7, 9, 40**
See also CA 17-20R; 140; CANR 33; DLB 6; MTCW; SATA 25

Herzen, Aleksandr Ivanovich
1812-1870 . . . . **NCLC 10**

Herzl, Theodor 1860-1904 . . . . **TCLC 36**

Herzog, Werner 1942- . . . . **CLC 16**
See also CA 89-92

Hesiod c. 8th cent. B.C.- . . . . **CMLC 5**

Hesse, Hermann
1877-1962 . . . . **CLC 1, 2, 3, 6, 11, 17, 25, 69; SSC 9**
See also CA 17-18; CAP 2; DA; DLB 66; MTCW; SATA 50; WLC

Hewes, Cady
See De Voto, Bernard (Augustine)

Heyen, William 1940- . . . . **CLC 13, 18**
See also CA 33-36R; CAAS 9; DLB 5

Heyerdahl, Thor 1914- . . . . **CLC 26**
See also CA 5-8R; CANR 5, 22; MTCW; SATA 2, 52

Heym, Georg (Theodor Franz Arthur)
1887-1912 . . . . **TCLC 9**
See also CA 106

Heym, Stefan 1913- . . . . **CLC 41**
See also CA 9-12R; CANR 4; DLB 69

Heyse, Paul (Johann Ludwig von)
1830-1914 . . . . **TCLC 8**
See also CA 104; DLB 129

Hibbert, Eleanor Alice Burford
1906-1993 . . . . **CLC 7**
See also BEST 90:4; CA 17-20R; 140; CANR 9, 28; SATA 2; SATA-Obit 74

Higgins, George V(incent)
1939- . . . . **CLC 4, 7, 10, 18**
See also CA 77-80; CAAS 5; CANR 17; DLB 2; DLBY 81; MTCW

Higginson, Thomas Wentworth
1823-1911 . . . . **TCLC 36**
See also DLB 1, 64

Highet, Helen
See MacInnes, Helen (Clark)

Highsmith, (Mary) Patricia
1921- . . . . **CLC 2, 4, 14, 42**
See also CA 1-4R; CANR 1, 20; MTCW

Highwater, Jamake (Mamake)
1942(?)- . . . . **CLC 12**
See also AAYA 7; CA 65-68; CAAS 7; CANR 10, 34; CLR 17; DLB 52; DLBY 85; JRDA; MAICYA; SATA 30, 32, 69

Hijuelos, Oscar 1951- . . . . **CLC 65**
See also BEST 90:1; CA 123; HW

Hikmet, Nazim 1902(?)-1963. . . . . . . **CLC 40**
See also CA 141; 93-96

Hildesheimer, Wolfgang
1916-1991 . . . . **CLC 49**
See also CA 101; 135; DLB 69, 124

Hill, Geoffrey (William)
1932- . . . . **CLC 5, 8, 18, 45**
See also CA 81-84; CANR 21; CDBLB 1960 to Present; DLB 40; MTCW

Hill, George Roy 1921- . . . . **CLC 26**
See also CA 110; 122

Hill, John
See Koontz, Dean R(ay)

Hill, Susan (Elizabeth) 1942- . . . . **CLC 4**
See also CA 33-36R; CANR 29; DLB 14; MTCW

Hillerman, Tony 1925- . . . . **CLC 62**
See also AAYA 6; BEST 89:1; CA 29-32R; CANR 21, 42; SATA 6

Hillesum, Etty 1914-1943 . . . . **TCLC 49**
See also CA 137

Hilliard, Noel (Harvey) 1929- . . . . . . **CLC 15**
See also CA 9-12R; CANR 7

Hillis, Rick 1956- . . . . **CLC 66**
See also CA 134

Hilton, James 1900-1954 . . . . **TCLC 21**
See also CA 108; DLB 34, 77; SATA 34

Himes, Chester (Bomar)
1909-1984 . . . . **CLC 2, 4, 7, 18, 58**
See also BLC 2; BW; CA 25-28R; 114; CANR 22; DLB 2, 76; MTCW

Hinde, Thomas . . . . **CLC 6, 11**
See also Chitty, Thomas Willes

Hindin, Nathan
See Bloch, Robert (Albert)

Hine, (William) Daryl 1936- . . . . **CLC 15**
See also CA 1-4R; CAAS 15; CANR 1, 20; DLB 60

Hinkson, Katharine Tynan
See Tynan, Katharine

Hinton, S(usan) E(loise) 1950- . . . . . **CLC 30**
See also AAYA 2; CA 81-84; CANR 32; CLR 3, 23; DA; JRDA; MAICYA; MTCW; SATA 19, 58

Hippius, Zinaida . . . . **TCLC 9**
See also Gippius, Zinaida (Nikolayevna)

Hiraoka, Kimitake 1925-1970
See Mishima, Yukio
See also CA 97-100; 29-32R; MTCW

Howe, Fanny 1940- . . . . **CLC 47**
See also CA 117; SATA 52

Howe, Julia Ward 1819-1910 . . . . . **TCLC 21**
See also CA 117; DLB 1

Howe, Susan 1937- . . . . **CLC 72**
See also DLB 120

Howe, Tina 1937- . . . . **CLC 48**
See also CA 109

Howell, James 1594(?)-1666 . . . . **LC 13**

Howells, W. D.
See Howells, William Dean

Howells, William D.
See Howells, William Dean

Howells, William Dean
1837-1920 . . . . **TCLC 41, 7, 17**
See also CA 104; 134; CDALB 1865-1917; DLB 12, 64, 74, 79

Howes, Barbara 1914- . . . . **CLC 15**
See also CA 9-12R; CAAS 3; SATA 5

Hrabal, Bohumil 1914- . . . . **CLC 13, 67**
See also CA 106; CAAS 12

Hsun, Lu . . . . **TCLC 3**
See also Shu-Jen, Chou

Hubbard, L(afayette) Ron(ald)
1911-1986 . . . . **CLC 43**
See also CA 77-80; 118; CANR 22

Huch, Ricarda (Octavia)
1864-1947 . . . . **TCLC 13**
See also CA 111; DLB 66

Huddle, David 1942- . . . . **CLC 49**
See also CA 57-60; DLB 130

Hudson, Jeffrey
See Crichton, (John) Michael

Hudson, W(illiam) H(enry)
1841-1922 . . . . **TCLC 29**
See also CA 115; DLB 98; SATA 35

Hueffer, Ford Madox
See Ford, Ford Madox

Hughart, Barry 1934- . . . . **CLC 39**
See also CA 137

Hughes, Colin
See Creasey, John

Hughes, David (John) 1930- . . . . **CLC 48**
See also CA 116; 129; DLB 14

Hughes, (James) Langston
1902-1967 . . . . . **CLC 1, 5, 10, 15, 35, 44; DC 3; PC 1; SSC 6**
See also BLC 2; BW; CA 1-4R; 25-28R; CANR 1, 34; CDALB 1929-1941; CLR 17; DA; DLB 4, 7, 48, 51, 86; JRDA; MAICYA; MTCW; SATA 4, 33; WLC

Hughes, Richard (Arthur Warren)
1900-1976 . . . . **CLC 1, 11**
See also CA 5-8R; 65-68; CANR 4; DLB 15; MTCW; SATA 8, 25

Hughes, Ted
1930- . . . . **CLC 2, 4, 9, 14, 37; PC 7**
See also CA 1-4R; CANR 1, 33; CLR 3; DLB 40; MAICYA; MTCW; SATA 27, 49

Hugo, Richard F(ranklin)
1923-1982 . . . . **CLC 6, 18, 32**
See also CA 49-52; 108; CANR 3; DLB 5

Hugo, Victor (Marie)
1802-1885 . . . . **NCLC 3, 10, 21**
See also DA; DLB 119; SATA 47; WLC

Huidobro, Vicente
See Huidobro Fernandez, Vicente Garcia

Huidobro Fernandez, Vicente Garcia
1893-1948 . . . . **TCLC 31**
See also CA 131; HW

Hulme, Keri 1947- . . . . **CLC 39**
See also CA 125

Hulme, T(homas) E(rnest)
1883-1917 . . . . **TCLC 21**
See also CA 117; DLB 19

Hume, David 1711-1776 . . . . **LC 7**
See also DLB 104

Humphrey, William 1924- . . . . **CLC 45**
See also CA 77-80; DLB 6

Humphreys, Emyr Owen 1919- . . . . . **CLC 47**
See also CA 5-8R; CANR 3, 24; DLB 15

Humphreys, Josephine 1945- . . . . **CLC 34, 57**
See also CA 121; 127

Hungerford, Pixie
See Brinsmead, H(esba) F(ay)

Hunt, E(verette) Howard, Jr.
1918- . . . . **CLC 3**
See also AITN 1; CA 45-48; CANR 2

Hunt, Kyle
See Creasey, John

Hunt, (James Henry) Leigh
1784-1859 . . . . **NCLC 1**

Hunt, Marsha 1946- . . . . **CLC 70**

Hunter, E. Waldo
See Sturgeon, Theodore (Hamilton)

Hunter, Evan 1926- . . . . **CLC 11, 31**
See also CA 5-8R; CANR 5, 38; DLBY 82; MTCW; SATA 25

Hunter, Kristin (Eggleston) 1931- . . . **CLC 35**
See also AITN 1; BW; CA 13-16R; CANR 13; CLR 3; DLB 33; MAICYA; SAAS 10; SATA 12

Hunter, Mollie 1922- . . . . **CLC 21**
See also McIlwraith, Maureen Mollie Hunter
See also CANR 37; CLR 25; JRDA; MAICYA; SAAS 7; SATA 54

Hunter, Robert (?)-1734 . . . . **LC 7**

Hurston, Zora Neale
1903-1960 . . . . **CLC 7, 30, 61; SSC 4**
See also BLC 2; BW; CA 85-88; DA; DLB 51, 86; MTCW

Huston, John (Marcellus)
1906-1987 . . . . **CLC 20**
See also CA 73-76; 123; CANR 34; DLB 26

Hustvedt, Siri 1955- . . . . **CLC 76**
See also CA 137

Hutten, Ulrich von 1488-1523 . . . . **LC 16**

Huxley, Aldous (Leonard)
1894-1963 . . . . . **CLC 1, 3, 4, 5, 8, 11, 18, 35, 79**
See also CA 85-88; CDBLB 1914-1945; DA; DLB 36, 100; MTCW; SATA 63; WLC

Huysmans, Charles Marie Georges
1848-1907
See Huysmans, Joris-Karl
See also CA 104

Huysmans, Joris-Karl . . . . **TCLC 7**
See also Huysmans, Charles Marie Georges
See also DLB 123

Hwang, David Henry 1957- . . . . **CLC 55**
See also CA 127; 132

Hyde, Anthony 1946- . . . . **CLC 42**
See also CA 136

Hyde, Margaret O(ldroyd) 1917- . . . **CLC 21**
See also CA 1-4R; CANR 1, 36; CLR 23; JRDA; MAICYA; SAAS 8; SATA 1, 42

Hynes, James 1956(?)- . . . . **CLC 65**

Ian, Janis 1951- . . . . **CLC 21**
See also CA 105

Ibanez, Vicente Blasco
See Blasco Ibanez, Vicente

Ibarguengoitia, Jorge 1928-1983 . . . . **CLC 37**
See also CA 124; 113; HW

Ibsen, Henrik (Johan)
1828-1906 . . . . **TCLC 2, 8, 16, 37, 52; DC 2**
See also CA 104; 141; DA; WLC

Ibuse Masuji 1898-1993 . . . . **CLC 22**
See also CA 127; 141

Ichikawa, Kon 1915- . . . . **CLC 20**
See also CA 121

Idle, Eric 1943- . . . . **CLC 21**
See also Monty Python
See also CA 116; CANR 35

Ignatow, David 1914- . . . . . . **CLC 4, 7, 14, 40**
See also CA 9-12R; CAAS 3; CANR 31; DLB 5

Ihimaera, Witi 1944- . . . . **CLC 46**
See also CA 77-80

Ilf, Ilya . . . . **TCLC 21**
See also Fainzilberg, Ilya Arnoldovich

Immermann, Karl (Lebrecht)
1796-1840 . . . . **NCLC 4**
See also DLB 133

Inclan, Ramon (Maria) del Valle
See Valle-Inclan, Ramon (Maria) del

Infante, G(uillermo) Cabrera
See Cabrera Infante, G(uillermo)

Ingalls, Rachel (Holmes) 1940- . . . . . **CLC 42**
See also CA 123; 127

Ingamells, Rex 1913-1955 . . . . **TCLC 35**

Inge, William Motter
1913-1973 . . . . **CLC 1, 8, 19**
See also CA 9-12R; CDALB 1941-1968; DLB 7; MTCW

Ingelow, Jean 1820-1897 . . . . **NCLC 39**
See also DLB 35; SATA 33

Ingram, Willis J.
See Harris, Mark

Innaurato, Albert (F.) 1948(?)- . . **CLC 21, 60**
See also CA 115; 122

Innes, Michael
See Stewart, J(ohn) I(nnes) M(ackintosh)

Johnson, Benj. F. of Boo
See Riley, James Whitcomb

Johnson, Benjamin F. of Boo
See Riley, James Whitcomb

Johnson, Charles (Richard) 1948- .... **CLC 7, 51, 65**
See also BLC 2; BW; CA 116; CAAS 18; CANR 42; DLB 33

Johnson, Denis 1949- .... **CLC 52**
See also CA 117; 121; DLB 120

Johnson, Diane 1934- .... **CLC 5, 13, 48**
See also CA 41-44R; CANR 17, 40; DLBY 80; MTCW

Johnson, Eyvind (Olof Verner) 1900-1976 .... **CLC 14**
See also CA 73-76; 69-72; CANR 34

Johnson, J. R.
See James, C(yril) L(ionel) R(obert)

Johnson, James Weldon 1871-1938 .... **TCLC 3, 19**
See also BLC 2; BW; CA 104; 125; CDALB 1917-1929; CLR 32; DLB 51; MTCW; SATA 31

Johnson, Joyce 1935- .... **CLC 58**
See also CA 125; 129

Johnson, Lionel (Pigot) 1867-1902 .... **TCLC 19**
See also CA 117; DLB 19

Johnson, Mel
See Malzberg, Barry N(athaniel)

Johnson, Pamela Hansford 1912-1981 .... **CLC 1, 7, 27**
See also CA 1-4R; 104; CANR 2, 28; DLB 15; MTCW

Johnson, Samuel 1709-1784 .... **LC 15**
See also CDBLB 1660-1789; DA; DLB 39, 95, 104; WLC

Johnson, Uwe 1934-1984 .... **CLC 5, 10, 15, 40**
See also CA 1-4R; 112; CANR 1, 39; DLB 75; MTCW

Johnston, George (Benson) 1913- ... **CLC 51**
See also CA 1-4R; CANR 5, 20; DLB 88

Johnston, Jennifer 1930- .... **CLC 7**
See also CA 85-88; DLB 14

Jolley, (Monica) Elizabeth 1923- ... **CLC 46**
See also CA 127; CAAS 13

Jones, Arthur Llewellyn 1863-1947
See Machen, Arthur
See also CA 104

Jones, D(ouglas) G(ordon) 1929- .... **CLC 10**
See also CA 29-32R; CANR 13; DLB 53

Jones, David (Michael) 1895-1974 .... **CLC 2, 4, 7, 13, 42**
See also CA 9-12R; 53-56; CANR 28; CDBLB 1945-1960; DLB 20, 100; MTCW

Jones, David Robert 1947-
See Bowie, David
See also CA 103

Jones, Diana Wynne 1934- .... **CLC 26**
See also CA 49-52; CANR 4, 26; CLR 23; JRDA; MAICYA; SAAS 7; SATA 9, 70

Jones, Edward P. 1950- .... **CLC 76**
See also CA 142

Jones, Gayl 1949- .... **CLC 6, 9**
See also BLC 2; BW; CA 77-80; CANR 27; DLB 33; MTCW

Jones, James 1921-1977 .... **CLC 1, 3, 10, 39**
See also AITN 1, 2; CA 1-4R; 69-72; CANR 6; DLB 2; MTCW

Jones, John J.
See Lovecraft, H(oward) P(hillips)

Jones, LeRoi .... **CLC 1, 2, 3, 5, 10, 14**
See also Baraka, Amiri

Jones, Louis B. .... **CLC 65**
See also CA 141

Jones, Madison (Percy, Jr.) 1925- ... **CLC 4**
See also CA 13-16R; CAAS 11; CANR 7

Jones, Mervyn 1922- .... **CLC 10, 52**
See also CA 45-48; CAAS 5; CANR 1; MTCW

Jones, Mick 1956(?)- .... **CLC 30**
See also Clash, The

Jones, Nettie (Pearl) 1941- .... **CLC 34**
See also CA 137

Jones, Preston 1936-1979 .... **CLC 10**
See also CA 73-76; 89-92; DLB 7

Jones, Robert F(rancis) 1934- .... **CLC 7**
See also CA 49-52; CANR 2

Jones, Rod 1953- .... **CLC 50**
See also CA 128

Jones, Terence Graham Parry 1942- .... **CLC 21**
See also Jones, Terry; Monty Python
See also CA 112; 116; CANR 35; SATA 51

Jones, Terry
See Jones, Terence Graham Parry
See also SATA 67

Jong, Erica 1942- .... **CLC 4, 6, 8, 18**
See also AITN 1; BEST 90:2; CA 73-76; CANR 26; DLB 2, 5, 28; MTCW

Jonson, Ben(jamin) 1572(?)-1637 ...... **LC 6**
See also CDBLB Before 1660; DA; DLB 62, 121; WLC

Jordan, June 1936- .... **CLC 5, 11, 23**
See also AAYA 2; BW; CA 33-36R; CANR 25; CLR 10; DLB 38; MAICYA; MTCW; SATA 4

Jordan, Pat(rick M.) 1941- .... **CLC 37**
See also CA 33-36R

Jorgensen, Ivar
See Ellison, Harlan

Jorgenson, Ivar
See Silverberg, Robert

Josipovici, Gabriel 1940- .... **CLC 6, 43**
See also CA 37-40R; CAAS 8; DLB 14

Joubert, Joseph 1754-1824 .... **NCLC 9**

Jouve, Pierre Jean 1887-1976 ...... **CLC 47**
See also CA 65-68

Joyce, James (Augustine Aloysius) 1882-1941 .... **TCLC 3, 8, 16, 35; SSC 3**
See also CA 104; 126; CDBLB 1914-1945; DA; DLB 10, 19, 36; MTCW; WLC

Jozsef, Attila 1905-1937 .... **TCLC 22**
See also CA 116

Juana Ines de la Cruz 1651(?)-1695 ... **LC 5**

Judd, Cyril
See Kornbluth, C(yril) M.; Pohl, Frederik

Julian of Norwich 1342(?)-1416(?) .... **LC 6**

Just, Ward (Swift) 1935- .... **CLC 4, 27**
See also CA 25-28R; CANR 32

Justice, Donald (Rodney) 1925- .. **CLC 6, 19**
See also CA 5-8R; CANR 26; DLBY 83

Juvenal c. 55-c. 127 .... **CMLC 8**

Juvenis
See Bourne, Randolph S(illiman)

Kacew, Romain 1914-1980
See Gary, Romain
See also CA 108; 102

Kadare, Ismail 1936- .... **CLC 52**

Kadohata, Cynthia .... **CLC 59**
See also CA 140

Kafka, Franz 1883-1924 .... **TCLC 2, 6, 13, 29, 47; SSC 5**
See also CA 105; 126; DA; DLB 81; MTCW; WLC

Kahn, Roger 1927- .... **CLC 30**
See also CA 25-28R; SATA 37

Kain, Saul
See Sassoon, Siegfried (Lorraine)

Kaiser, Georg 1878-1945 .... **TCLC 9**
See also CA 106; DLB 124

Kaletski, Alexander 1946- .... **CLC 39**
See also CA 118

Kalidasa fl. c. 400- .... **CMLC 9**

Kallman, Chester (Simon) 1921-1975 .... **CLC 2**
See also CA 45-48; 53-56; CANR 3

Kaminsky, Melvin 1926-
See Brooks, Mel
See also CA 65-68; CANR 16

Kaminsky, Stuart M(elvin) 1934- ... **CLC 59**
See also CA 73-76; CANR 29

Kane, Paul
See Simon, Paul

Kane, Wilson
See Bloch, Robert (Albert)

Kanin, Garson 1912- .... **CLC 22**
See also AITN 1; CA 5-8R; CANR 7; DLB 7

Kaniuk, Yoram 1930- .... **CLC 19**
See also CA 134

Kant, Immanuel 1724-1804 ...... **NCLC 27**
See also DLB 94

Kantor, MacKinlay 1904-1977 ...... **CLC 7**
See also CA 61-64; 73-76; DLB 9, 102

Kaplan, David Michael 1946- ...... **CLC 50**

Kaplan, James 1951- .... **CLC 59**
See also CA 135

Karageorge, Michael
See Anderson, Poul (William)

Karamzin, Nikolai Mikhailovich 1766-1826 .... **NCLC 3**

Karapanou, Margarita 1946- .... **CLC 13**
See also CA 101

Karinthy, Frigyes 1887-1938 ...... **TCLC 47**

Karl, Frederick R(obert) 1927- ..... **CLC 34**
See also CA 5-8R; CANR 3

King, Francis (Henry) 1923- ..... **CLC 8, 53**
See also CA 1-4R; CANR 1, 33; DLB 15; MTCW

King, Stephen (Edwin) 1947- .... **CLC 12, 26, 37, 61**
See also AAYA 1; BEST 90:1; CA 61-64; CANR 1, 30; DLBY 80; JRDA; MTCW; SATA 9, 55

King, Steve
See King, Stephen (Edwin)

Kingman, Lee .... **CLC 17**
See also Natti, (Mary) Lee
See also SAAS 3; SATA 1, 67

Kingsley, Charles 1819-1875 ..... **NCLC 35**
See also DLB 21, 32; YABC 2

Kingsley, Sidney 1906- .... **CLC 44**
See also CA 85-88; DLB 7

Kingsolver, Barbara 1955- .... **CLC 55**
See also CA 129; 134

Kingston, Maxine (Ting Ting) Hong 1940- .... **CLC 12, 19, 58**
See also AAYA 8; CA 69-72; CANR 13, 38; DLBY 80; MTCW; SATA 53

Kinnell, Galway 1927- .... **CLC 1, 2, 3, 5, 13, 29**
See also CA 9-12R; CANR 10, 34; DLB 5; DLBY 87; MTCW

Kinsella, Thomas 1928- .... **CLC 4, 19**
See also CA 17-20R; CANR 15; DLB 27; MTCW

Kinsella, W(illiam) P(atrick) 1935- .... **CLC 27, 43**
See also AAYA 7; CA 97-100; CAAS 7; CANR 21, 35; MTCW

Kipling, (Joseph) Rudyard 1865-1936 .... **TCLC 8, 17; PC 3; SSC 5**
See also CA 105; 120; CANR 33; CDBLB 1890-1914; DA; DLB 19, 34; MAICYA; MTCW; WLC; YABC 2

Kirkup, James 1918- .... **CLC 1**
See also CA 1-4R; CAAS 4; CANR 2; DLB 27; SATA 12

Kirkwood, James 1930(?)-1989 ...... **CLC 9**
See also AITN 2; CA 1-4R; 128; CANR 6, 40

Kis, Danilo 1935-1989 .... **CLC 57**
See also CA 109; 118; 129; MTCW

Kivi, Aleksis 1834-1872 .... **NCLC 30**

Kizer, Carolyn (Ashley) 1925- .... **CLC 15, 39, 80**
See also CA 65-68; CAAS 5; CANR 24; DLB 5

Klabund 1890-1928 .... **TCLC 44**
See also DLB 66

Klappert, Peter 1942- .... **CLC 57**
See also CA 33-36R; DLB 5

Klein, A(braham) M(oses) 1909-1972 .... **CLC 19**
See also CA 101; 37-40R; DLB 68

Klein, Norma 1938-1989 .... **CLC 30**
See also AAYA 2; CA 41-44R; 128; CANR 15, 37; CLR 2, 19; JRDA; MAICYA; SAAS 1; SATA 7, 57

Klein, T(heodore) E(ibon) D(onald) 1947- .... **CLC 34**
See also CA 119

Kleist, Heinrich von 1777-1811 .... **NCLC 2**
See also DLB 90

Klima, Ivan 1931- .... **CLC 56**
See also CA 25-28R; CANR 17

Klimentov, Andrei Platonovich 1899-1951
See Platonov, Andrei
See also CA 108

Klinger, Friedrich Maximilian von 1752-1831 .... **NCLC 1**
See also DLB 94

Klopstock, Friedrich Gottlieb 1724-1803 .... **NCLC 11**
See also DLB 97

Knebel, Fletcher 1911-1993 .... **CLC 14**
See also AITN 1; CA 1-4R; 140; CAAS 3; CANR 1, 36; SATA 36; SATA-Obit 75

Knickerbocker, Diedrich
See Irving, Washington

Knight, Etheridge 1931-1991 .... **CLC 40**
See also BLC 2; BW; CA 21-24R; 133; CANR 23; DLB 41

Knight, Sarah Kemble 1666-1727 ..... **LC 7**
See also DLB 24

Knowles, John 1926- ...... **CLC 1, 4, 10, 26**
See also AAYA 10; CA 17-20R; CANR 40; CDALB 1968-1988; DA; DLB 6; MTCW; SATA 8

Knox, Calvin M.
See Silverberg, Robert

Knye, Cassandra
See Disch, Thomas M(ichael)

Koch, C(hristopher) J(ohn) 1932- ... **CLC 42**
See also CA 127

Koch, Christopher
See Koch, C(hristopher) J(ohn)

Koch, Kenneth 1925- .... **CLC 5, 8, 44**
See also CA 1-4R; CANR 6, 36; DLB 5; SATA 65

Kochanowski, Jan 1530-1584 .... **LC 10**

Kock, Charles Paul de 1794-1871 .... **NCLC 16**

Koda Shigeyuki 1867-1947
See Rohan, Koda
See also CA 121

Koestler, Arthur 1905-1983 .... **CLC 1, 3, 6, 8, 15, 33**
See also CA 1-4R; 109; CANR 1, 33; CDBLB 1945-1960; DLBY 83; MTCW

Kogawa, Joy Nozomi 1935- .... **CLC 78**
See also CA 101; CANR 19

Kohout, Pavel 1928- .... **CLC 13**
See also CA 45-48; CANR 3

Koizumi, Yakumo
See Hearn, (Patricio) Lafcadio (Tessima Carlos)

Kolmar, Gertrud 1894-1943 .... **TCLC 40**

Konrad, George
See Konrad, Gyoergy

Konrad, Gyoergy 1933- ...... **CLC 4, 10, 73**
See also CA 85-88

Konwicki, Tadeusz 1926- ..... **CLC 8, 28, 54**
See also CA 101; CAAS 9; CANR 39; MTCW

Koontz, Dean R(ay) 1945- .... **CLC 78**
See also AAYA 9; BEST 89:3, 90:2; CA 108; CANR 19, 36; MTCW

Kopit, Arthur (Lee) 1937- .... **CLC 1, 18, 33**
See also AITN 1; CA 81-84; CABS 3; DLB 7; MTCW

Kops, Bernard 1926- .... **CLC 4**
See also CA 5-8R; DLB 13

Kornbluth, C(yril) M. 1923-1958 .... **TCLC 8**
See also CA 105; DLB 8

Korolenko, V. G.
See Korolenko, Vladimir Galaktionovich

Korolenko, Vladimir
See Korolenko, Vladimir Galaktionovich

Korolenko, Vladimir G.
See Korolenko, Vladimir Galaktionovich

Korolenko, Vladimir Galaktionovich 1853-1921 .... **TCLC 22**
See also CA 121

Kosinski, Jerzy (Nikodem) 1933-1991 .... **CLC 1, 2, 3, 6, 10, 15, 53, 70**
See also CA 17-20R; 134; CANR 9; DLB 2; DLBY 82; MTCW

Kostelanetz, Richard (Cory) 1940- .. **CLC 28**
See also CA 13-16R; CAAS 8; CANR 38

Kostrowitzki, Wilhelm Apollinaris de 1880-1918
See Apollinaire, Guillaume
See also CA 104

Kotlowitz, Robert 1924- .... **CLC 4**
See also CA 33-36R; CANR 36

Kotzebue, August (Friedrich Ferdinand) von 1761-1819 .... **NCLC 25**
See also DLB 94

Kotzwinkle, William 1938- ... **CLC 5, 14, 35**
See also CA 45-48; CANR 3; CLR 6; MAICYA; SATA 24, 70

Kozol, Jonathan 1936- .... **CLC 17**
See also CA 61-64; CANR 16

Kozoll, Michael 1940(?)- .... **CLC 35**

Kramer, Kathryn 19(?)- .... **CLC 34**

Kramer, Larry 1935- .... **CLC 42**
See also CA 124; 126

Krasicki, Ignacy 1735-1801 .... **NCLC 8**

Krasinski, Zygmunt 1812-1859 .... **NCLC 4**

Kraus, Karl 1874-1936 .... **TCLC 5**
See also CA 104; DLB 118

Kreve (Mickevicius), Vincas 1882-1954 .... **TCLC 27**

Kristeva, Julia 1941- .... **CLC 77**

Kristofferson, Kris 1936- .... **CLC 26**
See also CA 104

Krizanc, John 1956- .... **CLC 57**

Krleza, Miroslav 1893-1981 .... **CLC 8**
See also CA 97-100; 105

Kroetsch, Robert 1927- ...... **CLC 5, 23, 57**
See also CA 17-20R; CANR 8, 38; DLB 53; MTCW

Kroetz, Franz
See Kroetz, Franz Xaver

Kroetz, Franz Xaver 1946- . . . . **CLC 41**
See also CA 130

Kroker, Arthur 1945- . . . . **CLC 77**

Kropotkin, Peter (Aleksieevich)
1842-1921 . . . . **TCLC 36**
See also CA 119

Krotkov, Yuri 1917- . . . . **CLC 19**
See also CA 102

Krumb
See Crumb, R(obert)

Krumgold, Joseph (Quincy)
1908-1980 . . . . **CLC 12**
See also CA 9-12R; 101; CANR 7; MAICYA; SATA 1, 23, 48

Krumwitz
See Crumb, R(obert)

Krutch, Joseph Wood 1893-1970. . . . **CLC 24**
See also CA 1-4R; 25-28R; CANR 4; DLB 63

Krutzch, Gus
See Eliot, T(homas) S(tearns)

Krylov, Ivan Andreevich
1768(?)-1844 . . . . **NCLC 1**

Kubin, Alfred 1877-1959 . . . . **TCLC 23**
See also CA 112; DLB 81

Kubrick, Stanley 1928-. . . . . **CLC 16**
See also CA 81-84; CANR 33; DLB 26

Kumin, Maxine (Winokur)
1925- . . . . **CLC 5, 13, 28**
See also AITN 2; CA 1-4R; CAAS 8; CANR 1, 21; DLB 5; MTCW; SATA 12

Kundera, Milan
1929- . . . . **CLC 4, 9, 19, 32, 68**
See also AAYA 2; CA 85-88; CANR 19; MTCW

Kunitz, Stanley (Jasspon)
1905- . . . . **CLC 6, 11, 14**
See also CA 41-44R; CANR 26; DLB 48; MTCW

Kunze, Reiner 1933-. . . . . **CLC 10**
See also CA 93-96; DLB 75

Kuprin, Aleksandr Ivanovich
1870-1938 . . . . **TCLC 5**
See also CA 104

Kureishi, Hanif 1954(?)-. . . . . **CLC 64**
See also CA 139

Kurosawa, Akira 1910-. . . . . **CLC 16**
See also CA 101

Kuttner, Henry 1915-1958. . . . . **TCLC 10**
See also CA 107; DLB 8

Kuzma, Greg 1944-. . . . . **CLC 7**
See also CA 33-36R

Kuzmin, Mikhail 1872(?)-1936 . . . . **TCLC 40**

Kyd, Thomas 1558-1594. . . . . . . **LC 22; DC 3**
See also DLB 62

Kyprianos, Iossif
See Samarakis, Antonis

La Bruyere, Jean de 1645-1696. . . . . . **LC 17**

Lacan, Jacques (Marie Emile)
1901-1981 . . . . **CLC 75**
See also CA 121; 104

Laclos, Pierre Ambroise Francois Choderlos de 1741-1803 . . . . **NCLC 4**

La Colere, Francois
See Aragon, Louis

Lacolere, Francois
See Aragon, Louis

La Deshabilleuse
See Simenon, Georges (Jacques Christian)

Lady Gregory
See Gregory, Isabella Augusta (Persse)

Lady of Quality, A
See Bagnold, Enid

La Fayette, Marie (Madelaine Pioche de la Vergne Comtes 1634-1693. . . . . . . **LC 2**

Lafayette, Rene
See Hubbard, L(afayette) Ron(ald)

Laforgue, Jules 1860-1887. . . . . **NCLC 5**

Lagerkvist, Paer (Fabian)
1891-1974 . . . . **CLC 7, 10, 13, 54**
See also Lagerkvist, Par
See also CA 85-88; 49-52; MTCW

Lagerkvist, Par
See Lagerkvist, Paer (Fabian)
See also SSC 12

Lagerloef, Selma (Ottiliana Lovisa)
1858-1940 . . . . **TCLC 4, 36**
See also Lagerlof, Selma (Ottiliana Lovisa)
See also CA 108; CLR 7; SATA 15

Lagerlof, Selma (Ottiliana Lovisa)
See Lagerloef, Selma (Ottiliana Lovisa)
See also CLR 7; SATA 15

La Guma, (Justin) Alex(ander)
1925-1985 . . . . **CLC 19**
See also BW; CA 49-52; 118; CANR 25; DLB 117; MTCW

Laidlaw, A. K.
See Grieve, C(hristopher) M(urray)

Lainez, Manuel Mujica
See Mujica Lainez, Manuel
See also HW

Lamartine, Alphonse (Marie Louis Prat) de
1790-1869 . . . . **NCLC 11**

Lamb, Charles 1775-1834. . . . . **NCLC 10**
See also CDBLB 1789-1832; DA; DLB 93, 107; SATA 17; WLC

Lamb, Lady Caroline 1785-1828 . . **NCLC 38**
See also DLB 116

Lamming, George (William)
1927- . . . . **CLC 2, 4, 66**
See also BLC 2; BW; CA 85-88; CANR 26; DLB 125; MTCW

L'Amour, Louis (Dearborn)
1908-1988 . . . . **CLC 25, 55**
See also AITN 2; BEST 89:2; CA 1-4R; 125; CANR 3, 25, 40; DLBY 80; MTCW

Lampedusa, Giuseppe (Tomasi) di . . . **TCLC 13**
See also Tomasi di Lampedusa, Giuseppe

Lampman, Archibald 1861-1899 . . **NCLC 25**
See also DLB 92

Lancaster, Bruce 1896-1963. . . . . **CLC 36**
See also CA 9-10; CAP 1; SATA 9

Landau, Mark Alexandrovich
See Aldanov, Mark (Alexandrovich)

Landau-Aldanov, Mark Alexandrovich
See Aldanov, Mark (Alexandrovich)

Landis, John 1950-. . . . . **CLC 26**
See also CA 112; 122

Landolfi, Tommaso 1908-1979. . . **CLC 11, 49**
See also CA 127; 117

Landon, Letitia Elizabeth
1802-1838 . . . . **NCLC 15**
See also DLB 96

Landor, Walter Savage
1775-1864 . . . . **NCLC 14**
See also DLB 93, 107

Landwirth, Heinz 1927-
See Lind, Jakov
See also CA 9-12R; CANR 7

Lane, Patrick 1939- . . . . **CLC 25**
See also CA 97-100; DLB 53

Lang, Andrew 1844-1912 . . . . **TCLC 16**
See also CA 114; 137; DLB 98; MAICYA; SATA 16

Lang, Fritz 1890-1976 . . . . **CLC 20**
See also CA 77-80; 69-72; CANR 30

Lange, John
See Crichton, (John) Michael

Langer, Elinor 1939- . . . . **CLC 34**
See also CA 121

Langland, William 1330(?)-1400(?) . . . **LC 19**
See also DA

Langstaff, Launcelot
See Irving, Washington

Lanier, Sidney 1842-1881 . . . . **NCLC 6**
See also DLB 64; MAICYA; SATA 18

Lanyer, Aemilia 1569-1645 . . . . **LC 10**

Lao Tzu . . . . **CMLC 7**

Lapine, James (Elliot) 1949- . . . . **CLC 39**
See also CA 123; 130

Larbaud, Valery (Nicolas)
1881-1957 . . . . **TCLC 9**
See also CA 106

Lardner, Ring
See Lardner, Ring(gold) W(ilmer)

Lardner, Ring W., Jr.
See Lardner, Ring(gold) W(ilmer)

Lardner, Ring(gold) W(ilmer)
1885-1933 . . . . **TCLC 2, 14**
See also CA 104; 131; CDALB 1917-1929; DLB 11, 25, 86; MTCW

Laredo, Betty
See Codrescu, Andrei

Larkin, Maia
See Wojciechowska, Maia (Teresa)

Larkin, Philip (Arthur)
1922-1985 . . . . **CLC 3, 5, 8, 9, 13, 18, 33, 39, 64**
See also CA 5-8R; 117; CANR 24; CDBLB 1960 to Present; DLB 27; MTCW

Larra (y Sanchez de Castro), Mariano Jose de
1809-1837 . . . . **NCLC 17**

Larsen, Eric 1941- . . . . **CLC 55**
See also CA 132

Larsen, Nella 1891-1964 . . . . **CLC 37**
See also BLC 2; BW; CA 125; DLB 51

Larson, Charles R(aymond) 1938-... **CLC 31**
See also CA 53-56; CANR 4

Latham, Jean Lee 1902-........... **CLC 12**
See also AITN 1; CA 5-8R; CANR 7; MAICYA; SATA 2, 68

Latham, Mavis
See Clark, Mavis Thorpe

Lathen, Emma..................... **CLC 2**
See also Hennissart, Martha; Latsis, Mary J(ane)

Lathrop, Francis
See Leiber, Fritz (Reuter, Jr.)

Latsis, Mary J(ane)
See Lathen, Emma
See also CA 85-88

Lattimore, Richmond (Alexander) 1906-1984 .... **CLC 3**
See also CA 1-4R; 112; CANR 1

Laughlin, James 1914-............ **CLC 49**
See also CA 21-24R; CANR 9; DLB 48

Laurence, (Jean) Margaret (Wemyss) 1926-1987 .. **CLC 3, 6, 13, 50, 62; SSC 7**
See also CA 5-8R; 121; CANR 33; DLB 53; MTCW; SATA 50

Laurent, Antoine 1952- .... **CLC 50**

Lauscher, Hermann
See Hesse, Hermann

Lautreamont, Comte de 1846-1870 .... **NCLC 12**

Laverty, Donald
See Blish, James (Benjamin)

Lavin, Mary 1912-...... **CLC 4, 18; SSC 4**
See also CA 9-12R; CANR 33; DLB 15; MTCW

Lavond, Paul Dennis
See Kornbluth, C(yril) M.; Pohl, Frederik

Lawler, Raymond Evenor 1922-.... **CLC 58**
See also CA 103

Lawrence, D(avid) H(erbert Richards) 1885-1930 .... **TCLC 2, 9, 16, 33, 48; SSC 4**
See also CA 104; 121; CDBLB 1914-1945; DA; DLB 10, 19, 36, 98; MTCW; WLC

Lawrence, T(homas) E(dward) 1888-1935 .... **TCLC 18**
See also Dale, Colin
See also CA 115

Lawrence of Arabia
See Lawrence, T(homas) E(dward)

Lawson, Henry (Archibald Hertzberg) 1867-1922 .... **TCLC 27**
See also CA 120

Lawton, Dennis
See Faust, Frederick (Schiller)

Laxness, Halldor.................. **CLC 25**
See also Gudjonsson, Halldor Kiljan

Layamon fl. c. 1200-............ **CMLC 10**

Laye, Camara 1928-1980........ **CLC 4, 38**
See also BLC 2; BW; CA 85-88; 97-100; CANR 25; MTCW

Layton, Irving (Peter) 1912-..... **CLC 2, 15**
See also CA 1-4R; CANR 2, 33, 43; DLB 88; MTCW

Lazarus, Emma 1849-1887........ **NCLC 8**

Lazarus, Felix
See Cable, George Washington

Lazarus, Henry
See Slavitt, David R(ytman)

Lea, Joan
See Neufeld, John (Arthur)

Leacock, Stephen (Butler) 1869-1944 .... **TCLC 2**
See also CA 104; 141; DLB 92

Lear, Edward 1812-1888 .... **NCLC 3**
See also CLR 1; DLB 32; MAICYA; SATA 18

Lear, Norman (Milton) 1922-...... **CLC 12**
See also CA 73-76

Leavis, F(rank) R(aymond) 1895-1978 .... **CLC 24**
See also CA 21-24R; 77-80; MTCW

Leavitt, David 1961-.............. **CLC 34**
See also CA 116; 122; DLB 130

Leblanc, Maurice (Marie Emile) 1864-1941 .... **TCLC 49**
See also CA 110

Lebowitz, Fran(ces Ann) 1951(?)-.................. **CLC 11, 36**
See also CA 81-84; CANR 14; MTCW

le Carre, John .... **CLC 3, 5, 9, 15, 28**
See also Cornwell, David (John Moore)
See also BEST 89:4; CDBLB 1960 to Present; DLB 87

Le Clezio, J(ean) M(arie) G(ustave) 1940- .... **CLC 31**
See also CA 116; 128; DLB 83

Leconte de Lisle, Charles-Marie-Rene 1818-1894 .... **NCLC 29**

Le Coq, Monsieur
See Simenon, Georges (Jacques Christian)

Leduc, Violette 1907-1972......... **CLC 22**
See also CA 13-14; 33-36R; CAP 1

Ledwidge, Francis 1887(?)-1917 ... **TCLC 23**
See also CA 123; DLB 20

Lee, Andrea 1953- .... **CLC 36**
See also BLC 2; BW; CA 125

Lee, Andrew
See Auchincloss, Louis (Stanton)

Lee, Don L........................ **CLC 2**
See also Madhubuti, Haki R.

Lee, George W(ashington) 1894-1976 .... **CLC 52**
See also BLC 2; BW; CA 125; DLB 51

Lee, (Nelle) Harper 1926-...... **CLC 12, 60**
See also CA 13-16R; CDALB 1941-1968; DA; DLB 6; MTCW; SATA 11; WLC

Lee, Julian
See Latham, Jean Lee

Lee, Larry
See Lee, Lawrence

Lee, Lawrence 1941-1990.......... **CLC 34**
See also CA 131; CANR 43

Lee, Manfred B(ennington) 1905-1971 .... **CLC 11**
See also Queen, Ellery
See also CA 1-4R; 29-32R; CANR 2

Lee, Stan 1922-.................. **CLC 17**
See also AAYA 5; CA 108; 111

Lee, Tanith 1947-................ **CLC 46**
See also CA 37-40R; SATA 8

Lee, Vernon...................... **TCLC 5**
See also Paget, Violet
See also DLB 57

Lee, William
See Burroughs, William S(eward)

Lee, Willy
See Burroughs, William S(eward)

Lee-Hamilton, Eugene (Jacob) 1845-1907 .... **TCLC 22**
See also CA 117

Leet, Judith 1935- .... **CLC 11**

Le Fanu, Joseph Sheridan 1814-1873 .... **NCLC 9**
See also DLB 21, 70

Leffland, Ella 1931- .... **CLC 19**
See also CA 29-32R; CANR 35; DLBY 84; SATA 65

Leger, Alexis
See Leger, (Marie-Rene Auguste) Alexis Saint-Leger

Leger, (Marie-Rene Auguste) Alexis Saint-Leger 1887-1975........ **CLC 11**
See also Perse, St.-John
See also CA 13-16R; 61-64; CANR 43; MTCW

Leger, Saintleger
See Leger, (Marie-Rene Auguste) Alexis Saint-Leger

Le Guin, Ursula K(roeber) 1929- .... **CLC 8, 13, 22, 45, 71; SSC 12**
See also AAYA 9; AITN 1; CA 21-24R; CANR 9, 32; CDALB 1968-1988; CLR 3, 28; DLB 8, 52; JRDA; MAICYA; MTCW; SATA 4, 52

Lehmann, Rosamond (Nina) 1901-1990 .... **CLC 5**
See also CA 77-80; 131; CANR 8; DLB 15

Leiber, Fritz (Reuter, Jr.) 1910-1992 .... **CLC 25**
See also CA 45-48; 139; CANR 2, 40; DLB 8; MTCW; SATA 45; SATA-Obit 73

Leimbach, Martha 1963-
See Leimbach, Marti
See also CA 130

Leimbach, Marti.................. **CLC 65**
See also Leimbach, Martha

Leino, Eino .... **TCLC 24**
See also Loennbohm, Armas Eino Leopold

Leiris, Michel (Julien) 1901-1990... **CLC 61**
See also CA 119; 128; 132

Leithauser, Brad 1953-............ **CLC 27**
See also CA 107; CANR 27; DLB 120

Lelchuk, Alan 1938-............... **CLC 5**
See also CA 45-48; CANR 1

Lem, Stanislaw 1921-........ **CLC 8, 15, 40**
See also CA 105; CAAS 1; CANR 32; MTCW

Lemann, Nancy 1956-............. **CLC 39**
See also CA 118; 136

Lemonnier, (Antoine Louis) Camille 1844-1913 .... **TCLC 22**
See also CA 121

Lively, Penelope (Margaret) 1933- .... **CLC 32, 50**
See also CA 41-44R; CANR 29; CLR 7; DLB 14; JRDA; MAICYA; MTCW; SATA 7, 60

Livesay, Dorothy (Kathleen) 1909- .... **CLC 4, 15, 79**
See also AITN 2; CA 25-28R; CAAS 8; CANR 36; DLB 68; MTCW

Livy c. 59B.C.-c. 17 .... **CMLC 11**

Lizardi, Jose Joaquin Fernandez de 1776-1827 .... **NCLC 30**

Llewellyn, Richard
See also Llewellyn Lloyd, Richard Dafydd Vivian
See also DLB 15

Llewellyn (Lloyd), Richard (Dafydd Vivian) 1906-1983 .... **CLC 7, 80**
See also Llewellyn, Richard
See also CA 53-56; 111; CANR 7; SATA 11, 37

Llosa, (Jorge) Mario (Pedro) Vargas
See Vargas Llosa, (Jorge) Mario (Pedro)

Lloyd Webber, Andrew 1948-
See Webber, Andrew Lloyd
See also AAYA 1; CA 116; SATA 56

Llull, Ramon c. 1235-c. 1316 .... **CMLC 12**

Locke, Alain (Le Roy) 1886-1954 .... **TCLC 43**
See also BW; CA 106; 124; DLB 51

Locke, John 1632-1704 .... **LC 7**
See also DLB 101

Locke-Elliott, Sumner
See Elliott, Sumner Locke

Lockhart, John Gibson 1794-1854 .... **NCLC 6**
See also DLB 110, 116

Lodge, David (John) 1935- .... **CLC 36**
See also BEST 90:1; CA 17-20R; CANR 19; DLB 14; MTCW

Loennbohm, Armas Eino Leopold 1878-1926
See Leino, Eino
See also CA 123

Loewinsohn, Ron(ald William) 1937- .... **CLC 52**
See also CA 25-28R

Logan, Jake
See Smith, Martin Cruz

Logan, John (Burton) 1923-1987 .... **CLC 5**
See also CA 77-80; 124; DLB 5

Lo Kuan-chung 1330(?)-1400(?) .... **LC 12**

Lombard, Nap
See Johnson, Pamela Hansford

London, Jack .... **TCLC 9, 15, 39; SSC 4**
See also London, John Griffith
See also AITN 2; CDALB 1865-1917; DLB 8, 12, 78; SATA 18; WLC

London, John Griffith 1876-1916
See London, Jack
See also CA 110; 119; DA; JRDA; MAICYA; MTCW

Long, Emmett
See Leonard, Elmore (John, Jr.)

Longbaugh, Harry
See Goldman, William (W.)

Longfellow, Henry Wadsworth 1807-1882 .... **NCLC 2**
See also CDALB 1640-1865; DA; DLB 1, 59; SATA 19

Longley, Michael 1939- .... **CLC 29**
See also CA 102; DLB 40

Longus fl. c. 2nd cent. - .... **CMLC 7**

Longway, A. Hugh
See Lang, Andrew

Lopate, Phillip 1943- .... **CLC 29**
See also CA 97-100; DLBY 80

Lopez Portillo (y Pacheco), Jose 1920- .... **CLC 46**
See also CA 129; HW

Lopez y Fuentes, Gregorio 1897(?)-1966 .... **CLC 32**
See also CA 131; HW

Lorca, Federico Garcia 1898-1936
See Garcia Lorca, Federico

Lord, Bette Bao 1938- .... **CLC 23**
See also BEST 90:3; CA 107; CANR 41; SATA 58

Lord Auch
See Bataille, Georges

Lord Byron
See Byron, George Gordon (Noel)

Lord Dunsany .... **TCLC 2**
See also Dunsany, Edward John Moreton Drax Plunkett

Lorde, Audre (Geraldine) 1934-1992 .... **CLC 18, 71**
See also BLC 2; BW; CA 25-28R; 142; CANR 16, 26; DLB 41; MTCW

Lord Jeffrey
See Jeffrey, Francis

Lorenzo, Heberto Padilla
See Padilla (Lorenzo), Heberto

Loris
See Hofmannsthal, Hugo von

Loti, Pierre .... **TCLC 11**
See also Viaud, (Louis Marie) Julien
See also DLB 123

Louie, David Wong 1954- .... **CLC 70**
See also CA 139

Louis, Father M.
See Merton, Thomas

Lovecraft, H(oward) P(hillips) 1890-1937 .... **TCLC 4, 22; SSC 3**
See also CA 104; 133; MTCW

Lovelace, Earl 1935- .... **CLC 51**
See also CA 77-80; CANR 41; DLB 125; MTCW

Lovelace, Richard 1618-1657 .... **LC 24**
See also DLB 131

Lowell, Amy 1874-1925 .... **TCLC 1, 8**
See also CA 104; DLB 54

Lowell, James Russell 1819-1891 .. **NCLC 2**
See also CDALB 1640-1865; DLB 1, 11, 64, 79

Lowell, Robert (Traill Spence, Jr.) 1917-1977 ... **CLC 1, 2, 3, 4, 5, 8, 9, 11, 15, 37; PC 3**
See also CA 9-12R; 73-76; CABS 2; CANR 26; DA; DLB 5; MTCW; WLC

Lowndes, Marie Adelaide (Belloc) 1868-1947 .... **TCLC 12**
See also CA 107; DLB 70

Lowry, (Clarence) Malcolm 1909-1957 .... **TCLC 6, 40**
See also CA 105; 131; CDBLB 1945-1960; DLB 15; MTCW

Lowry, Mina Gertrude 1882-1966
See Loy, Mina
See also CA 113

Loxsmith, John
See Brunner, John (Kilian Houston)

Loy, Mina .... **CLC 28**
See also Lowry, Mina Gertrude
See also DLB 4, 54

Loyson-Bridet
See Schwob, (Mayer Andre) Marcel

Lucas, Craig 1951- .... **CLC 64**
See also CA 137

Lucas, George 1944- .... **CLC 16**
See also AAYA 1; CA 77-80; CANR 30; SATA 56

Lucas, Hans
See Godard, Jean-Luc

Lucas, Victoria
See Plath, Sylvia

Ludlam, Charles 1943-1987 .... **CLC 46, 50**
See also CA 85-88; 122

Ludlum, Robert 1927- .... **CLC 22, 43**
See also AAYA 10; BEST 89:1, 90:3; CA 33-36R; CANR 25, 41; DLBY 82; MTCW

Ludwig, Ken .... **CLC 60**

Ludwig, Otto 1813-1865 .... **NCLC 4**
See also DLB 129

Lugones, Leopoldo 1874-1938 .... **TCLC 15**
See also CA 116; 131; HW

Lu Hsun 1881-1936 .... **TCLC 3**

Lukacs, George .... **CLC 24**
See also Lukacs, Gyorgy (Szegeny von)

Lukacs, Gyorgy (Szegeny von) 1885-1971
See Lukacs, George
See also CA 101; 29-32R

Luke, Peter (Ambrose Cyprian) 1919- .... **CLC 38**
See also CA 81-84; DLB 13

Lunar, Dennis
See Mungo, Raymond

Lurie, Alison 1926- .... **CLC 4, 5, 18, 39**
See also CA 1-4R; CANR 2, 17; DLB 2; MTCW; SATA 46

Lustig, Arnost 1926- .... **CLC 56**
See also AAYA 3; CA 69-72; SATA 56

Luther, Martin 1483-1546 .... **LC 9**

Luzi, Mario 1914- .... **CLC 13**
See also CA 61-64; CANR 9; DLB 128

Lynch, B. Suarez
See Bioy Casares, Adolfo; Borges, Jorge Luis

Lynch, David (K.) 1946- .... **CLC 66**
See also CA 124; 129

Lynch, James
See Andreyev, Leonid (Nikolaevich)

Lynch Davis, B.
See Bioy Casares, Adolfo; Borges, Jorge Luis

Lyndsay, SirDavid 1490-1555 . . . . **LC 20**

Lynn, Kenneth S(chuyler) 1923- . . . . **CLC 50**
See also CA 1-4R; CANR 3, 27

Lynx
See West, Rebecca

Lyons, Marcus
See Blish, James (Benjamin)

Lyre, Pinchbeck
See Sassoon, Siegfried (Lorraine)

Lytle, Andrew (Nelson) 1902- . . . . . . **CLC 22**
See also CA 9-12R; DLB 6

Lyttelton, George 1709-1773 . . . . **LC 10**

Maas, Peter 1929- . . . . **CLC 29**
See also CA 93-96

Macaulay, Rose 1881-1958 . . . . . **TCLC 7, 44**
See also CA 104; DLB 36

Macaulay, Thomas Babington
1800-1859 . . . . **NCLC 42**
See also CDBLB 1832-1890; DLB 32, 55

MacBeth, George (Mann)
1932-1992 . . . . **CLC 2, 5, 9**
See also CA 25-28R; 136; DLB 40; MTCW; SATA 4; SATA-Obit 70

MacCaig, Norman (Alexander)
1910- . . . . **CLC 36**
See also CA 9-12R; CANR 3, 34; DLB 27

MacCarthy, (Sir Charles Otto) Desmond
1877-1952 . . . . **TCLC 36**

MacDiarmid, Hugh . . . . . **CLC 2, 4, 11, 19, 63**
See also Grieve, C(hristopher) M(urray)
See also CDBLB 1945-1960; DLB 20

MacDonald, Anson
See Heinlein, Robert A(nson)

Macdonald, Cynthia 1928- . . . . . . **CLC 13, 19**
See also CA 49-52; CANR 4; DLB 105

MacDonald, George 1824-1905 . . . . . **TCLC 9**
See also CA 106; 137; DLB 18; MAICYA; SATA 33

Macdonald, John
See Millar, Kenneth

MacDonald, John D(ann)
1916-1986 . . . . **CLC 3, 27, 44**
See also CA 1-4R; 121; CANR 1, 19; DLB 8; DLBY 86; MTCW

Macdonald, John Ross
See Millar, Kenneth

Macdonald, Ross . . . . . **CLC 1, 2, 3, 14, 34, 41**
See also Millar, Kenneth
See also DLBD 6

MacDougal, John
See Blish, James (Benjamin)

MacEwen, Gwendolyn (Margaret)
1941-1987 . . . . **CLC 13, 55**
See also CA 9-12R; 124; CANR 7, 22; DLB 53; SATA 50, 55

Machado (y Ruiz), Antonio
1875-1939 . . . . **TCLC 3**
See also CA 104; DLB 108

Machado de Assis, Joaquim Maria
1839-1908 . . . . **TCLC 10**
See also BLC 2; CA 107

Machen, Arthur . . . . **TCLC 4**
See also Jones, Arthur Llewellyn
See also DLB 36

Machiavelli, Niccolo 1469-1527 . . . . . . **LC 8**
See also DA

MacInnes, Colin 1914-1976 . . . . . . **CLC 4, 23**
See also CA 69-72; 65-68; CANR 21; DLB 14; MTCW

MacInnes, Helen (Clark)
1907-1985 . . . . **CLC 27, 39**
See also CA 1-4R; 117; CANR 1, 28; DLB 87; MTCW; SATA 22, 44

Mackay, Mary 1855-1924
See Corelli, Marie
See also CA 118

Mackenzie, Compton (Edward Montague)
1883-1972 . . . . **CLC 18**
See also CA 21-22; 37-40R; CAP 2; DLB 34, 100

Mackenzie, Henry 1745-1831 . . . . **NCLC 41**
See also DLB 39

Mackintosh, Elizabeth 1896(?)-1952
See Tey, Josephine
See also CA 110

MacLaren, James
See Grieve, C(hristopher) M(urray)

Mac Laverty, Bernard 1942- . . . . **CLC 31**
See also CA 116; 118; CANR 43

MacLean, Alistair (Stuart)
1922-1987 . . . . **CLC 3, 13, 50, 63**
See also CA 57-60; 121; CANR 28; MTCW; SATA 23, 50

Maclean, Norman (Fitzroy) 1902-1990
See also CA 102; 132; SSC 13

MacLeish, Archibald
1892-1982 . . . . **CLC 3, 8, 14, 68**
See also CA 9-12R; 106; CANR 33; DLB 4, 7, 45; DLBY 82; MTCW

MacLennan, (John) Hugh
1907-1990 . . . . **CLC 2, 14**
See also CA 5-8R; 142; CANR 33; DLB 68; MTCW

MacLeod, Alistair 1936- . . . . **CLC 56**
See also CA 123; DLB 60

MacNeice, (Frederick) Louis
1907-1963 . . . . **CLC 1, 4, 10, 53**
See also CA 85-88; DLB 10, 20; MTCW

MacNeill, Dand
See Fraser, George MacDonald

Macpherson, (Jean) Jay 1931- . . . . . . **CLC 14**
See also CA 5-8R; DLB 53

MacShane, Frank 1927- . . . . **CLC 39**
See also CA 9-12R; CANR 3, 33; DLB 111

Macumber, Mari
See Sandoz, Mari(e Susette)

Madach, Imre 1823-1864 . . . . **NCLC 19**

Madden, (Jerry) David 1933- . . . . **CLC 5, 15**
See also CA 1-4R; CAAS 3; CANR 4; DLB 6; MTCW

Maddern, Al(an)
See Ellison, Harlan

Madhubuti, Haki R.
1942- . . . . **CLC 6, 73; PC 5**
See also Lee, Don L.
See also BLC 2; BW; CA 73-76; CANR 24; DLB 5, 41; DLBD 8

Madow, Pauline (Reichberg) . . . . **CLC 1**
See also CA 9-12R

Maepenn, Hugh
See Kuttner, Henry

Maepenn, K. H.
See Kuttner, Henry

Maeterlinck, Maurice 1862-1949 . . . **TCLC 3**
See also CA 104; 136; SATA 66

Maginn, William 1794-1842 . . . . **NCLC 8**
See also DLB 110

Mahapatra, Jayanta 1928- . . . . **CLC 33**
See also CA 73-76; CAAS 9; CANR 15, 33

Mahfouz, Naguib (Abdel Aziz Al-Sabilgi)
1911(?)-
See Mahfuz, Najib
See also BEST 89:2; CA 128; MTCW

Mahfuz, Najib . . . . **CLC 52, 55**
See also Mahfouz, Naguib (Abdel Aziz Al-Sabilgi)
See also DLBY 88

Mahon, Derek 1941- . . . . **CLC 27**
See also CA 113; 128; DLB 40

Mailer, Norman
1923- . . . . . . **CLC 1, 2, 3, 4, 5, 8, 11, 14, 28, 39, 74**
See also AITN 2; CA 9-12R; CABS 1; CANR 28; CDALB 1968-1988; DA; DLB 2, 16, 28; DLBD 3; DLBY 80, 83; MTCW

Maillet, Antonine 1929- . . . . **CLC 54**
See also CA 115; 120; DLB 60

Mais, Roger 1905-1955 . . . . **TCLC 8**
See also BW; CA 105; 124; DLB 125; MTCW

Maitland, Sara (Louise) 1950- . . . . . . **CLC 49**
See also CA 69-72; CANR 13

Major, Clarence 1936- . . . . **CLC 3, 19, 48**
See also BLC 2; BW; CA 21-24R; CAAS 6; CANR 13, 25; DLB 33

Major, Kevin (Gerald) 1949- . . . . **CLC 26**
See also CA 97-100; CANR 21, 38; CLR 11; DLB 60; JRDA; MAICYA; SATA 32

Maki, James
See Ozu, Yasujiro

Malabaila, Damiano
See Levi, Primo

Malamud, Bernard
1914-1986 . . . . . . **CLC 1, 2, 3, 5, 8, 9, 11, 18, 27, 44, 78**
See also CA 5-8R; 118; CABS 1; CANR 28; CDALB 1941-1968; DA; DLB 2, 28; DLBY 80, 86; MTCW; WLC

Malcolm, Dan
See Silverberg, Robert

Malherbe, Francois de 1555-1628 . . . . . **LC 5**

Mallarme, Stephane
1842-1898 . . . . **NCLC 4, 41; PC 4**

Mallet-Joris, Francoise 1930- . . . . . . **CLC 11**
See also CA 65-68; CANR 17; DLB 83

Malley, Ern
See McAuley, James Phillip

Mallowan, Agatha Christie
See Christie, Agatha (Mary Clarissa)

Maloff, Saul 1922- . . . . **CLC 5**
See also CA 33-36R

Malone, Louis
See MacNeice, (Frederick) Louis

Malone, Michael (Christopher)
1942- . . . . **CLC 43**
See also CA 77-80; CANR 14, 32

Malory, (Sir) Thomas
1410(?)-1471(?) . . . . **LC 11**
See also CDBLB Before 1660; DA; SATA 33, 59

Malouf, (George Joseph) David
1934- . . . . **CLC 28**
See also CA 124

Malraux, (Georges-)Andre
1901-1976 . . . . . . **CLC 1, 4, 9, 13, 15, 57**
See also CA 21-22; 69-72; CANR 34; CAP 2; DLB 72; MTCW

Malzberg, Barry N(athaniel) 1939-. . . **CLC 7**
See also CA 61-64; CAAS 4; CANR 16; DLB 8

Mamet, David (Alan)
1947- . . . . **CLC 9, 15, 34, 46**
See also AAYA 3; CA 81-84; CABS 3; CANR 15, 41; DLB 7; MTCW

Mamoulian, Rouben (Zachary)
1897-1987 . . . . **CLC 16**
See also CA 25-28R; 124

Mandelstam, Osip (Emilievich)
1891(?)-1938(?) . . . . **TCLC 2, 6**
See also CA 104

Mander, (Mary) Jane 1877-1949. . . **TCLC 31**

Mandiargues, Andre Pieyre de. . . . . . . **CLC 41**
See also Pieyre de Mandiargues, Andre
See also DLB 83

Mandrake, Ethel Belle
See Thurman, Wallace (Henry)

Mangan, James Clarence
1803-1849 . . . . **NCLC 27**

Maniere, J.-E.
See Giraudoux, (Hippolyte) Jean

Manley, (Mary) Delariviere
1672(?)-1724 . . . . **LC 1**
See also DLB 39, 80

Mann, Abel
See Creasey, John

Mann, (Luiz) Heinrich 1871-1950. . . **TCLC 9**
See also CA 106; DLB 66

Mann, (Paul) Thomas
1875-1955 . . . . **TCLC 2, 8, 14, 21, 35, 44; SSC 5**
See also CA 104; 128; DA; DLB 66; MTCW; WLC

Manning, David
See Faust, Frederick (Schiller)

Manning, Frederic 1887(?)-1935 . . . **TCLC 25**
See also CA 124

Manning, Olivia 1915-1980 . . . . . . **CLC 5, 19**
See also CA 5-8R; 101; CANR 29; MTCW

Mano, D. Keith 1942- . . . . **CLC 2, 10**
See also CA 25-28R; CAAS 6; CANR 26; DLB 6

Mansfield, Katherine. . . **TCLC 2, 8, 39; SSC 9**
See also Beauchamp, Kathleen Mansfield
See also WLC

Manso, Peter 1940- . . . . **CLC 39**
See also CA 29-32R

Mantecon, Juan Jimenez
See Jimenez (Mantecon), Juan Ramon

Manton, Peter
See Creasey, John

Man Without a Spleen, A
See Chekhov, Anton (Pavlovich)

Manzoni, Alessandro 1785-1873 . . **NCLC 29**

Mapu, Abraham (ben Jekutiel)
1808-1867 . . . . **NCLC 18**

Mara, Sally
See Queneau, Raymond

Marat, Jean Paul 1743-1793 . . . . **LC 10**

Marcel, Gabriel Honore
1889-1973 . . . . **CLC 15**
See also CA 102; 45-48; MTCW

Marchbanks, Samuel
See Davies, (William) Robertson

Marchi, Giacomo
See Bassani, Giorgio

Margulies, Donald. . . . . **CLC 76**

Marie de France c. 12th cent. -. . . . **CMLC 8**

Marie de l'Incarnation 1599-1672. . . . **LC 10**

Mariner, Scott
See Pohl, Frederik

Marinetti, Filippo Tommaso
1876-1944 . . . . **TCLC 10**
See also CA 107; DLB 114

Marivaux, Pierre Carlet de Chamblain de
1688-1763 . . . . **LC 4**

Markandaya, Kamala . . . . **CLC 8, 38**
See also Taylor, Kamala (Purnaiya)

Markfield, Wallace 1926-. . . . . **CLC 8**
See also CA 69-72; CAAS 3; DLB 2, 28

Markham, Edwin 1852-1940 . . . . . . **TCLC 47**
See also DLB 54

Markham, Robert
See Amis, Kingsley (William)

Marks, J
See Highwater, Jamake (Mamake)

Marks-Highwater, J
See Highwater, Jamake (Mamake)

Markson, David M(errill) 1927- . . . . **CLC 67**
See also CA 49-52; CANR 1

Marley, Bob. . . . . **CLC 17**
See also Marley, Robert Nesta

Marley, Robert Nesta 1945-1981
See Marley, Bob
See also CA 107; 103

Marlowe, Christopher
1564-1593 . . . . **LC 22; DC 1**
See also CDBLB Before 1660; DA; DLB 62; WLC

Marmontel, Jean-Francois
1723-1799 . . . . **LC 2**

Marquand, John P(hillips)
1893-1960 . . . . **CLC 2, 10**
See also CA 85-88; DLB 9, 102

Marquez, Gabriel (Jose) Garcia. . . . . . **CLC 68**
See also Garcia Marquez, Gabriel (Jose)

Marquis, Don(ald Robert Perry)
1878-1937 . . . . **TCLC 7**
See also CA 104; DLB 11, 25

Marric, J. J.
See Creasey, John

Marrow, Bernard
See Moore, Brian

Marryat, Frederick 1792-1848 . . . . **NCLC 3**
See also DLB 21

Marsden, James
See Creasey, John

Marsh, (Edith) Ngaio
1899-1982 . . . . **CLC 7, 53**
See also CA 9-12R; CANR 6; DLB 77; MTCW

Marshall, Garry 1934- . . . . **CLC 17**
See also AAYA 3; CA 111; SATA 60

Marshall, Paule 1929- . . **CLC 27, 72; SSC 3**
See also BLC 3; BW; CA 77-80; CANR 25; DLB 33; MTCW

Marsten, Richard
See Hunter, Evan

Martha, Henry
See Harris, Mark

Martin, Ken
See Hubbard, L(afayette) Ron(ald)

Martin, Richard
See Creasey, John

Martin, Steve 1945- . . . . **CLC 30**
See also CA 97-100; CANR 30; MTCW

Martin, Violet Florence
1862-1915 . . . . **TCLC 51**

Martin, Webber
See Silverberg, Robert

Martindale, Patrick Victor
See White, Patrick (Victor Martindale)

Martin du Gard, Roger
1881-1958 . . . . **TCLC 24**
See also CA 118; DLB 65

Martineau, Harriet 1802-1876. . . . **NCLC 26**
See also DLB 21, 55; YABC 2

Martines, Julia
See O'Faolain, Julia

Martinez, Jacinto Benavente y
See Benavente (y Martinez), Jacinto

Martinez Ruiz, Jose 1873-1967
See Azorin; Ruiz, Jose Martinez
See also CA 93-96; HW

Martinez Sierra, Gregorio
1881-1947 . . . . **TCLC 6**
See also CA 115

Martinez Sierra, Maria (de la O'LeJarraga)
1874-1974 . . . . **TCLC 6**
See also CA 115

Martinsen, Martin
See Follett, Ken(neth Martin)

Martinson, Harry (Edmund)
1904-1978 . . . . **CLC 14**
See also CA 77-80; CANR 34

Marut, Ret
See Traven, B.

Marut, Robert
See Traven, B.

Marvell, Andrew 1621-1678 .... **LC 4**
See also CDBLB 1660-1789; DA; DLB 131; WLC

Marx, Karl (Heinrich)
1818-1883 .... **NCLC 17**
See also DLB 129

Masaoka Shiki .... **TCLC 18**
See also Masaoka Tsunenori

Masaoka Tsunenori 1867-1902
See Masaoka Shiki
See also CA 117

Masefield, John (Edward)
1878-1967 .... **CLC 11, 47**
See also CA 19-20; 25-28R; CANR 33; CAP 2; CDBLB 1890-1914; DLB 10; MTCW; SATA 19

Maso, Carole 19(?)- .... **CLC 44**

Mason, Bobbie Ann
1940- .... **CLC 28, 43; SSC 4**
See also AAYA 5; CA 53-56; CANR 11, 31; DLBY 87; MTCW

Mason, Ernst
See Pohl, Frederik

Mason, Lee W.
See Malzberg, Barry N(athaniel)

Mason, Nick 1945- .... **CLC 35**
See also Pink Floyd

Mason, Tally
See Derleth, August (William)

Mass, William
See Gibson, William

Masters, Edgar Lee
1868-1950 .... **TCLC 2, 25; PC 1**
See also CA 104; 133; CDALB 1865-1917; DA; DLB 54; MTCW

Masters, Hilary 1928- .... **CLC 48**
See also CA 25-28R; CANR 13

Mastrosimone, William 19(?)- ...... **CLC 36**

Mathe, Albert
See Camus, Albert

Matheson, Richard Burton 1926- ... **CLC 37**
See also CA 97-100; DLB 8, 44

Mathews, Harry 1930- .... **CLC 6, 52**
See also CA 21-24R; CAAS 6; CANR 18, 40

Mathias, Roland (Glyn) 1915- ...... **CLC 45**
See also CA 97-100; CANR 19, 41; DLB 27

Matsuo Basho 1644-1694 .... **PC 3**

Mattheson, Rodney
See Creasey, John

Matthews, Greg 1949- .... **CLC 45**
See also CA 135

Matthews, William 1942- .... **CLC 40**
See also CA 29-32R; CAAS 18; CANR 12; DLB 5

Matthias, John (Edward) 1941- ...... **CLC 9**
See also CA 33-36R

Matthiessen, Peter
1927- .... **CLC 5, 7, 11, 32, 64**
See also AAYA 6; BEST 90:4; CA 9-12R; CANR 21; DLB 6; MTCW; SATA 27

Maturin, Charles Robert
1780(?)-1824 .... **NCLC 6**

Matute (Ausejo), Ana Maria
1925- .... **CLC 11**
See also CA 89-92; MTCW

Maugham, W. S.
See Maugham, W(illiam) Somerset

Maugham, W(illiam) Somerset
1874-1965 .... **CLC 1, 11, 15, 67; SSC 8**
See also CA 5-8R; 25-28R; CANR 40; CDBLB 1914-1945; DA; DLB 10, 36, 77, 100; MTCW; SATA 54; WLC

Maugham, William Somerset
See Maugham, W(illiam) Somerset

Maupassant, (Henri Rene Albert) Guy de
1850-1893 .... **NCLC 1, 42; SSC 1**
See also DA; DLB 123; WLC

Maurhut, Richard
See Traven, B.

Mauriac, Claude 1914- .... **CLC 9**
See also CA 89-92; DLB 83

Mauriac, Francois (Charles)
1885-1970 .... **CLC 4, 9, 56**
See also CA 25-28; CAP 2; DLB 65; MTCW

Mavor, Osborne Henry 1888-1951
See Bridie, James
See also CA 104

Maxwell, William (Keepers, Jr.)
1908- .... **CLC 19**
See also CA 93-96; DLBY 80

May, Elaine 1932- .... **CLC 16**
See also CA 124; 142; DLB 44

Mayakovski, Vladimir (Vladimirovich)
1893-1930 .... **TCLC 4, 18**
See also CA 104

Mayhew, Henry 1812-1887 ...... **NCLC 31**
See also DLB 18, 55

Maynard, Joyce 1953- .... **CLC 23**
See also CA 111; 129

Mayne, William (James Carter)
1928- .... **CLC 12**
See also CA 9-12R; CANR 37; CLR 25; JRDA; MAICYA; SAAS 11; SATA 6, 68

Mayo, Jim
See L'Amour, Louis (Dearborn)

Maysles, Albert 1926- .... **CLC 16**
See also CA 29-32R

Maysles, David 1932- .... **CLC 16**

Mazer, Norma Fox 1931- .... **CLC 26**
See also AAYA 5; CA 69-72; CANR 12, 32; CLR 23; JRDA; MAICYA; SAAS 1; SATA 24, 67

Mazzini, Guiseppe 1805-1872 .... **NCLC 34**

McAuley, James Phillip
1917-1976 .... **CLC 45**
See also CA 97-100

McBain, Ed
See Hunter, Evan

McBrien, William Augustine
1930- .... **CLC 44**
See also CA 107

McCaffrey, Anne (Inez) 1926- ...... **CLC 17**
See also AAYA 6; AITN 2; BEST 89:2; CA 25-28R; CANR 15, 35; DLB 8; JRDA; MAICYA; MTCW; SAAS 11; SATA 8, 70

McCann, Arthur
See Campbell, John W(ood, Jr.)

McCann, Edson
See Pohl, Frederik

McCarthy, Cormac, Jr. .... **CLC 4, 57**
See also McCarthy, Charles, Jr.
See also DLB 6

McCarthy, Mary (Therese)
1912-1989 ... **CLC 1, 3, 5, 14, 24, 39, 59**
See also CA 5-8R; 129; CANR 16; DLB 2; DLBY 81; MTCW

McCartney, (James) Paul
1942- .... **CLC 12, 35**

McCauley, Stephen (D.) 1955- ..... **CLC 50**
See also CA 141

McClure, Michael (Thomas)
1932- .... **CLC 6, 10**
See also CA 21-24R; CANR 17; DLB 16

McCorkle, Jill (Collins) 1958- ...... **CLC 51**
See also CA 121; DLBY 87

McCourt, James 1941- .... **CLC 5**
See also CA 57-60

McCoy, Horace (Stanley)
1897-1955 .... **TCLC 28**
See also CA 108; DLB 9

McCrae, John 1872-1918 .... **TCLC 12**
See also CA 109; DLB 92

McCreigh, James
See Pohl, Frederik

McCullers, (Lula) Carson (Smith)
1917-1967 .. **CLC 1, 4, 10, 12, 48; SSC 9**
See also CA 5-8R; 25-28R; CABS 1, 3; CANR 18; CDALB 1941-1968; DA; DLB 2, 7; MTCW; SATA 27; WLC

McCulloch, John Tyler
See Burroughs, Edgar Rice

McCullough, Colleen 1938(?)- ...... **CLC 27**
See also CA 81-84; CANR 17; MTCW

McElroy, Joseph 1930- .... **CLC 5, 47**
See also CA 17-20R

McEwan, Ian (Russell) 1948- ... **CLC 13, 66**
See also BEST 90:4; CA 61-64; CANR 14, 41; DLB 14; MTCW

McFadden, David 1940- .... **CLC 48**
See also CA 104; DLB 60

McFarland, Dennis 1950- .... **CLC 65**

McGahern, John 1934- .... **CLC 5, 9, 48**
See also CA 17-20R; CANR 29; DLB 14; MTCW

McGinley, Patrick (Anthony)
1937- .... **CLC 41**
See also CA 120; 127

McGinley, Phyllis 1905-1978 ...... **CLC 14**
See also CA 9-12R; 77-80; CANR 19; DLB 11, 48; SATA 2, 24, 44

McGinniss, Joe 1942-............. **CLC 32**
See also AITN 2; BEST 89:2; CA 25-28R; CANR 26

McGivern, Maureen Daly
See Daly, Maureen

McGrath, Patrick 1950-........... **CLC 55**
See also CA 136

McGrath, Thomas (Matthew)
1916-1990 .... **CLC 28, 59**
See also CA 9-12R; 132; CANR 6, 33; MTCW; SATA 41; SATA-Obit 66

McGuane, Thomas (Francis III)
1939- .... **CLC 3, 7, 18, 45**
See also AITN 2; CA 49-52; CANR 5, 24; DLB 2; DLBY 80; MTCW

McGuckian, Medbh 1950-......... **CLC 48**
See also DLB 40

McHale, Tom 1942(?)-1982....... **CLC 3, 5**
See also AITN 1; CA 77-80; 106

McIlvanney, William 1936-........ **CLC 42**
See also CA 25-28R; DLB 14

McIlwraith, Maureen Mollie Hunter
See Hunter, Mollie
See also SATA 2

McInerney, Jay 1955- .... **CLC 34**
See also CA 116; 123

McIntyre, Vonda N(eel) 1948- ..... **CLC 18**
See also CA 81-84; CANR 17, 34; MTCW

McKay, Claude .... **TCLC 7, 41; PC 2**
See also McKay, Festus Claudius
See also BLC 3; DLB 4, 45, 51, 117

McKay, Festus Claudius 1889-1948
See McKay, Claude
See also BW; CA 104; 124; DA; MTCW; WLC

McKuen, Rod 1933-............. **CLC 1, 3**
See also AITN 1; CA 41-44R; CANR 40

McLoughlin, R. B.
See Mencken, H(enry) L(ouis)

McLuhan, (Herbert) Marshall
1911-1980 .... **CLC 37**
See also CA 9-12R; 102; CANR 12, 34; DLB 88; MTCW

McMillan, Terry (L.) 1951-..... **CLC 50, 61**
See also CA 140

McMurtry, Larry (Jeff)
1936- .... **CLC 2, 3, 7, 11, 27, 44**
See also AITN 2; BEST 89:2; CA 5-8R; CANR 19, 43; CDALB 1968-1988; DLB 2; DLBY 80, 87; MTCW

McNally, Terrence 1939-...... **CLC 4, 7, 41**
See also CA 45-48; CANR 2; DLB 7

McNamer, Deirdre 1950-.......... **CLC 70**

McNeile, Herman Cyril 1888-1937
See Sapper
See also DLB 77

McPhee, John (Angus) 1931- ...... **CLC 36**
See also BEST 90:1; CA 65-68; CANR 20; MTCW

McPherson, James Alan
1943- .... **CLC 19, 77**
See also BW; CA 25-28R; CAAS 17; CANR 24; DLB 38; MTCW

McPherson, William (Alexander)
1933- .... **CLC 34**
See also CA 69-72; CANR 28

McSweeney, Kerry .... **CLC 34**

Mead, Margaret 1901-1978........ **CLC 37**
See also AITN 1; CA 1-4R; 81-84; CANR 4; MTCW; SATA 20

Meaker, Marijane (Agnes) 1927-
See Kerr, M. E.
See also CA 107; CANR 37; JRDA; MAICYA; MTCW; SATA 20, 61

Medoff, Mark (Howard) 1940- ... **CLC 6, 23**
See also AITN 1; CA 53-56; CANR 5; DLB 7

Meged, Aharon
See Megged, Aharon

Meged, Aron
See Megged, Aharon

Megged, Aharon 1920-............. **CLC 9**
See also CA 49-52; CAAS 13; CANR 1

Mehta, Ved (Parkash) 1934-....... **CLC 37**
See also CA 1-4R; CANR 2, 23; MTCW

Melanter
See Blackmore, R(ichard) D(oddridge)

Melikow, Loris
See Hofmannsthal, Hugo von

Melmoth, Sebastian
See Wilde, Oscar (Fingal O'Flahertie Wills)

Meltzer, Milton 1915-............ **CLC 26**
See also AAYA 8; CA 13-16R; CANR 38; CLR 13; DLB 61; JRDA; MAICYA; SAAS 1; SATA 1, 50

Melville, Herman
1819-1891 ...... **NCLC 3, 12, 29; SSC 1**
See also CDALB 1640-1865; DA; DLB 3, 74; SATA 59; WLC

Menander
c. 342B.C.-c. 292B.C.... **CMLC 9; DC 3**

Mencken, H(enry) L(ouis)
1880-1956 .... **TCLC 13**
See also CA 105; 125; CDALB 1917-1929; DLB 11, 29, 63; MTCW

Mercer, David 1928-1980........... **CLC 5**
See also CA 9-12R; 102; CANR 23; DLB 13; MTCW

Merchant, Paul
See Ellison, Harlan

Meredith, George 1828-1909... **TCLC 17, 43**
See also CA 117; CDBLB 1832-1890; DLB 18, 35, 57

Meredith, William (Morris)
1919- .... **CLC 4, 13, 22, 55**
See also CA 9-12R; CAAS 14; CANR 6, 40; DLB 5

Merezhkovsky, Dmitry Sergeyevich
1865-1941 .... **TCLC 29**

Merimee, Prosper
1803-1870 .... **NCLC 6; SSC 7**
See also DLB 119

Merkin, Daphne 1954-............ **CLC 44**
See also CA 123

Merlin, Arthur
See Blish, James (Benjamin)

Merrill, James (Ingram)
1926- .... **CLC 2, 3, 6, 8, 13, 18, 34**
See also CA 13-16R; CANR 10; DLB 5; DLBY 85; MTCW

Merriman, Alex
See Silverberg, Robert

Merritt, E. B.
See Waddington, Miriam

Merton, Thomas
1915-1968 .... **CLC 1, 3, 11, 34**
See also CA 5-8R; 25-28R; CANR 22; DLB 48; DLBY 81; MTCW

Merwin, W(illiam) S(tanley)
1927- ...... **CLC 1, 2, 3, 5, 8, 13, 18, 45**
See also CA 13-16R; CANR 15; DLB 5; MTCW

Metcalf, John 1938-.............. **CLC 37**
See also CA 113; DLB 60

Metcalf, Suzanne
See Baum, L(yman) Frank

Mew, Charlotte (Mary)
1870-1928 .... **TCLC 8**
See also CA 105; DLB 19

Mewshaw, Michael 1943-........... **CLC 9**
See also CA 53-56; CANR 7; DLBY 80

Meyer, June
See Jordan, June

Meyer, Lynn
See Slavitt, David R(ytman)

Meyer-Meyrink, Gustav 1868-1932
See Meyrink, Gustav
See also CA 117

Meyers, Jeffrey 1939- .... **CLC 39**
See also CA 73-76; DLB 111

Meynell, Alice (Christina Gertrude Thompson)
1847-1922 .... **TCLC 6**
See also CA 104; DLB 19, 98

Meyrink, Gustav .... **TCLC 21**
See also Meyer-Meyrink, Gustav
See also DLB 81

Michaels, Leonard 1933-........ **CLC 6, 25**
See also CA 61-64; CANR 21; DLB 130; MTCW

Michaux, Henri 1899-1984 ...... **CLC 8, 19**
See also CA 85-88; 114

Michelangelo 1475-1564............ **LC 12**

Michelet, Jules 1798-1874....... **NCLC 31**

Michener, James A(lbert)
1907(?)- .... **CLC 1, 5, 11, 29, 60**
See also AITN 1; BEST 90:1; CA 5-8R; CANR 21; DLB 6; MTCW

Mickiewicz, Adam 1798-1855 ..... **NCLC 3**

Middleton, Christopher 1926- ...... **CLC 13**
See also CA 13-16R; CANR 29; DLB 40

Middleton, Stanley 1919-........ **CLC 7, 38**
See also CA 25-28R; CANR 21; DLB 14

Migueis, Jose Rodrigues 1901- ..... **CLC 10**

Mikszath, Kalman 1847-1910 ..... **TCLC 31**

Miles, Josephine
1911-1985 .... **CLC 1, 2, 14, 34, 39**
See also CA 1-4R; 116; CANR 2; DLB 48

Militant
See Sandburg, Carl (August)

Mill, John Stuart 1806-1873 ..... **NCLC 11**
See also CDBLB 1832-1890; DLB 55

Millar, Kenneth 1915-1983 .... **CLC 14**
See also Macdonald, Ross
See also CA 9-12R; 110; CANR 16; DLB 2; DLBD 6; DLBY 83; MTCW

Millay, E. Vincent
See Millay, Edna St. Vincent

Millay, Edna St. Vincent
1892-1950 .... **TCLC 4, 49; PC 6**
See also CA 104; 130; CDALB 1917-1929; DA; DLB 45; MTCW

Miller, Arthur
1915- .... **CLC 1, 2, 6, 10, 15, 26, 47, 78; DC 1**
See also AITN 1; CA 1-4R; CABS 3; CANR 2, 30; CDALB 1941-1968; DA; DLB 7; MTCW; WLC

Miller, Henry (Valentine)
1891-1980 .... **CLC 1, 2, 4, 9, 14, 43**
See also CA 9-12R; 97-100; CANR 33; CDALB 1929-1941; DA; DLB 4, 9; DLBY 80; MTCW; WLC

Miller, Jason 1939(?)- .... **CLC 2**
See also AITN 1; CA 73-76; DLB 7

Miller, Sue 1943- .... **CLC 44**
See also BEST 90:3; CA 139

Miller, Walter M(ichael, Jr.)
1923- .... **CLC 4, 30**
See also CA 85-88; DLB 8

Millett, Kate 1934- .... **CLC 67**
See also AITN 1; CA 73-76; CANR 32; MTCW

Millhauser, Steven 1943- .... **CLC 21, 54**
See also CA 110; 111; DLB 2

Millin, Sarah Gertrude 1889-1968 .. **CLC 49**
See also CA 102; 93-96

Milne, A(lan) A(lexander)
1882-1956 .... **TCLC 6**
See also CA 104; 133; CLR 1, 26; DLB 10, 77, 100; MAICYA; MTCW; YABC 1

Milner, Ron(ald) 1938- .... **CLC 56**
See also AITN 1; BLC 3; BW; CA 73-76; CANR 24; DLB 38; MTCW

Milosz, Czeslaw
1911- .... **CLC 5, 11, 22, 31, 56**
See also CA 81-84; CANR 23; MTCW

Milton, John 1608-1674 .... **LC 9**
See also CDBLB 1660-1789; DA; DLB 131; WLC

Minehaha, Cornelius
See Wedekind, (Benjamin) Frank(lin)

Miner, Valerie 1947- .... **CLC 40**
See also CA 97-100

Minimo, Duca
See D'Annunzio, Gabriele

Minot, Susan 1956- .... **CLC 44**
See also CA 134

Minus, Ed 1938- .... **CLC 39**

Miranda, Javier
See Bioy Casares, Adolfo

Miro (Ferrer), Gabriel (Francisco Victor)
1879-1930 .... **TCLC 5**
See also CA 104

Mishima, Yukio
.... **CLC 2, 4, 6, 9, 27; DC 1; SSC 4**
See also Hiraoka, Kimitake

Mistral, Frederic 1830-1914 ...... **TCLC 51**
See also CA 122

Mistral, Gabriela .... **TCLC 2**
See also Godoy Alcayaga, Lucila

Mistry, Rohinton 1952- .... **CLC 71**
See also CA 141

Mitchell, Clyde
See Ellison, Harlan; Silverberg, Robert

Mitchell, James Leslie 1901-1935
See Gibbon, Lewis Grassic
See also CA 104; DLB 15

Mitchell, Joni 1943- .... **CLC 12**
See also CA 112

Mitchell, Margaret (Munnerlyn)
1900-1949 .... **TCLC 11**
See also CA 109; 125; DLB 9; MTCW

Mitchell, Peggy
See Mitchell, Margaret (Munnerlyn)

Mitchell, S(ilas) Weir 1829-1914 .. **TCLC 36**

Mitchell, W(illiam) O(rmond)
1914- .... **CLC 25**
See also CA 77-80; CANR 15, 43; DLB 88

Mitford, Mary Russell 1787-1855 .. **NCLC 4**
See also DLB 110, 116

Mitford, Nancy 1904-1973 .... **CLC 44**
See also CA 9-12R

Miyamoto, Yuriko 1899-1951 ..... **TCLC 37**

Mo, Timothy (Peter) 1950(?)- ...... **CLC 46**
See also CA 117; MTCW

Modarressi, Taghi (M.) 1931- ...... **CLC 44**
See also CA 121; 134

Modiano, Patrick (Jean) 1945- ..... **CLC 18**
See also CA 85-88; CANR 17, 40; DLB 83

Moerck, Paal
See Roelvaag, O(le) E(dvart)

Mofolo, Thomas (Mokopu)
1875(?)-1948 .... **TCLC 22**
See also BLC 3; CA 121

Mohr, Nicholasa 1935- .... **CLC 12**
See also AAYA 8; CA 49-52; CANR 1, 32; CLR 22; HW; JRDA; SAAS 8; SATA 8

Mojtabai, A(nn) G(race)
1938- .... **CLC 5, 9, 15, 29**
See also CA 85-88

Moliere 1622-1673 .... **LC 10**
See also DA; WLC

Molin, Charles
See Mayne, William (James Carter)

Molnar, Ferenc 1878-1952 .... **TCLC 20**
See also CA 109

Momaday, N(avarre) Scott
1934- .... **CLC 2, 19**
See also CA 25-28R; CANR 14, 34; DA; MTCW; SATA 30, 48

Monroe, Harriet 1860-1936 .... **TCLC 12**
See also CA 109; DLB 54, 91

Monroe, Lyle
See Heinlein, Robert A(nson)

Montagu, Elizabeth 1917- .... **NCLC 7**
See also CA 9-12R

Montagu, Mary (Pierrepont) Wortley
1689-1762 .... **LC 9**
See also DLB 95, 101

Montagu, W. H.
See Coleridge, Samuel Taylor

Montague, John (Patrick)
1929- .... **CLC 13, 46**
See also CA 9-12R; CANR 9; DLB 40; MTCW

Montaigne, Michel (Eyquem) de
1533-1592 .... **LC 8**
See also DA; WLC

Montale, Eugenio 1896-1981 ... **CLC 7, 9, 18**
See also CA 17-20R; 104; CANR 30; DLB 114; MTCW

Montesquieu, Charles-Louis de Secondat
1689-1755 .... **LC 7**

Montgomery, (Robert) Bruce 1921-1978
See Crispin, Edmund
See also CA 104

Montgomery, L(ucy) M(aud)
1874-1942 .... **TCLC 51**
See also CA 108; 137; CLR 8; DLB 92; JRDA; MAICYA; YABC 1

Montgomery, Marion H., Jr. 1925- .. **CLC 7**
See also AITN 1; CA 1-4R; CANR 3; DLB 6

Montgomery, Max
See Davenport, Guy (Mattison, Jr.)

Montherlant, Henry (Milon) de
1896-1972 .... **CLC 8, 19**
See also CA 85-88; 37-40R; DLB 72; MTCW

Monty Python .... **CLC 21**
See also Chapman, Graham; Cleese, John (Marwood); Gilliam, Terry (Vance); Idle, Eric; Jones, Terence Graham Parry; Palin, Michael (Edward)
See also AAYA 7

Moodie, Susanna (Strickland)
1803-1885 .... **NCLC 14**
See also DLB 99

Mooney, Edward 1951- .... **CLC 25**
See also CA 130

Mooney, Ted
See Mooney, Edward

Moorcock, Michael (John)
1939- .... **CLC 5, 27, 58**
See also CA 45-48; CAAS 5; CANR 2, 17, 38; DLB 14; MTCW

Moore, Brian
1921- .... **CLC 1, 3, 5, 7, 8, 19, 32**
See also CA 1-4R; CANR 1, 25, 42; MTCW

Moore, Edward
See Muir, Edwin

Moore, George Augustus
1852-1933 .... **TCLC 7**
See also CA 104; DLB 10, 18, 57

Moore, Lorrie .... **CLC 39, 45, 68**
See also Moore, Marie Lorena

Moore, Marianne (Craig)
1887-1972 .... **CLC 1, 2, 4, 8, 10, 13, 19, 47; PC 4**
See also CA 1-4R; 33-36R; CANR 3; CDALB 1929-1941; DA; DLB 45; DLBD 7; MTCW; SATA 20

Moore, Marie Lorena 1957-
See Moore, Lorrie
See also CA 116; CANR 39

Moore, Thomas 1779-1852........ **NCLC 6**
See also DLB 96

Morand, Paul 1888-1976.......... **CLC 41**
See also CA 69-72; DLB 65

Morante, Elsa 1918-1985........ **CLC 8, 47**
See also CA 85-88; 117; CANR 35; MTCW

Moravia, Alberto....... **CLC 2, 7, 11, 27, 46**
See also Pincherle, Alberto

More, Hannah 1745-1833 .... **NCLC 27**
See also DLB 107, 109, 116

More, Henry 1614-1687............. **LC 9**
See also DLB 126

More, Sir Thomas 1478-1535 .... **LC 10**

Moreas, Jean.................... **TCLC 18**
See also Papadiamantopoulos, Johannes

Morgan, Berry 1919-.............. **CLC 6**
See also CA 49-52; DLB 6

Morgan, Claire
See Highsmith, (Mary) Patricia

Morgan, Edwin (George) 1920-..... **CLC 31**
See also CA 5-8R; CANR 3, 43; DLB 27

Morgan, (George) Frederick
1922-....................... **CLC 23**
See also CA 17-20R; CANR 21

Morgan, Harriet
See Mencken, H(enry) L(ouis)

Morgan, Jane
See Cooper, James Fenimore

Morgan, Janet 1945- .... **CLC 39**
See also CA 65-68

Morgan, Lady 1776(?)-1859...... **NCLC 29**
See also DLB 116

Morgan, Robin 1941-.............. **CLC 2**
See also CA 69-72; CANR 29; MTCW

Morgan, Scott
See Kuttner, Henry

Morgan, Seth 1949(?)-1990 .... **CLC 65**
See also CA 132

Morgenstern, Christian
1871-1914 .... **TCLC 8**
See also CA 105

Morgenstern, S.
See Goldman, William (W.)

Moricz, Zsigmond 1879-1942 ..... **TCLC 33**

Morike, Eduard (Friedrich)
1804-1875 .... **NCLC 10**
See also DLB 133

Mori Ogai .... **TCLC 14**
See also Mori Rintaro

Mori Rintaro 1862-1922
See Mori Ogai
See also CA 110

Moritz, Karl Philipp 1756-1793 ...... **LC 2**
See also DLB 94

Morland, Peter Henry
See Faust, Frederick (Schiller)

Morren, Theophil
See Hofmannsthal, Hugo von

Morris, Bill 1952-................ **CLC 76**

Morris, Julian
See West, Morris L(anglo)

Morris, Steveland Judkins 1950(?)-
See Wonder, Stevie
See also CA 111

Morris, William 1834-1896 .... **NCLC 4**
See also CDBLB 1832-1890; DLB 18, 35, 57

Morris, Wright 1910-... **CLC 1, 3, 7, 18, 37**
See also CA 9-12R; CANR 21; DLB 2; DLBY 81; MTCW

Morrison, Chloe Anthony Wofford
See Morrison, Toni

Morrison, James Douglas 1943-1971
See Morrison, Jim
See also CA 73-76; CANR 40

Morrison, Jim.................... **CLC 17**
See also Morrison, James Douglas

Morrison, Toni 1931-..... **CLC 4, 10, 22, 55**
See also AAYA 1; BLC 3; BW; CA 29-32R; CANR 27, 42; CDALB 1968-1988; DA; DLB 6, 33; DLBY 81; MTCW; SATA 57

Morrison, Van 1945- .... **CLC 21**
See also CA 116

Mortimer, John (Clifford)
1923- .... **CLC 28, 43**
See also CA 13-16R; CANR 21; CDBLB 1960 to Present; DLB 13; MTCW

Mortimer, Penelope (Ruth) 1918-.... **CLC 5**
See also CA 57-60

Morton, Anthony
See Creasey, John

Mosher, Howard Frank 1943-...... **CLC 62**
See also CA 139

Mosley, Nicholas 1923-........ **CLC 43, 70**
See also CA 69-72; CANR 41; DLB 14

Moss, Howard
1922-1987 .... **CLC 7, 14, 45, 50**
See also CA 1-4R; 123; CANR 1; DLB 5

Mossgiel, Rab
See Burns, Robert

Motion, Andrew 1952-............ **CLC 47**
See also DLB 40

Motley, Willard (Francis)
1912-1965 .... **CLC 18**
See also BW; CA 117; 106; DLB 76

Mott, Michael (Charles Alston)
1930- .... **CLC 15, 34**
See also CA 5-8R; CAAS 7; CANR 7, 29

Mowat, Farley (McGill) 1921- ..... **CLC 26**
See also AAYA 1; CA 1-4R; CANR 4, 24, 42; CLR 20; DLB 68; JRDA; MAICYA; MTCW; SATA 3, 55

Moyers, Bill 1934-............... **CLC 74**
See also AITN 2; CA 61-64; CANR 31

Mphahlele, Es'kia
See Mphahlele, Ezekiel
See also DLB 125

Mphahlele, Ezekiel 1919-.......... **CLC 25**
See also Mphahlele, Es'kia
See also BLC 3; BW; CA 81-84; CANR 26

Mqhayi, S(amuel) E(dward) K(rune Loliwe)
1875-1945 .... **TCLC 25**
See also BLC 3

Mr. Martin
See Burroughs, William S(eward)

Mrozek, Slawomir 1930-........ **CLC 3, 13**
See also CA 13-16R; CAAS 10; CANR 29; MTCW

Mrs. Belloc-Lowndes
See Lowndes, Marie Adelaide (Belloc)

Mtwa, Percy (?)-................. **CLC 47**

Mueller, Lisel 1924-........... **CLC 13, 51**
See also CA 93-96; DLB 105

Muir, Edwin 1887-1959 .... **TCLC 2**
See also CA 104; DLB 20, 100

Muir, John 1838-1914 .... **TCLC 28**

Mujica Lainez, Manuel
1910-1984 .... **CLC 31**
See also Lainez, Manuel Mujica
See also CA 81-84; 112; CANR 32; HW

Mukherjee, Bharati 1940-......... **CLC 53**
See also BEST 89:2; CA 107; DLB 60; MTCW

Muldoon, Paul 1951-.......... **CLC 32, 72**
See also CA 113; 129; DLB 40

Mulisch, Harry 1927-............. **CLC 42**
See also CA 9-12R; CANR 6, 26

Mull, Martin 1943-............... **CLC 17**
See also CA 105

Mulock, Dinah Maria
See Craik, Dinah Maria (Mulock)

Munford, Robert 1737(?)-1783 .... **LC 5**
See also DLB 31

Mungo, Raymond 1946-........... **CLC 72**
See also CA 49-52; CANR 2

Munro, Alice
1931- .... **CLC 6, 10, 19, 50; SSC 3**
See also AITN 2; CA 33-36R; CANR 33; DLB 53; MTCW; SATA 29

Munro, H(ector) H(ugh) 1870-1916
See Saki
See also CA 104; 130; CDBLB 1890-1914; DA; DLB 34; MTCW; WLC

Murasaki, Lady.................. **CMLC 1**

Murdoch, (Jean) Iris
1919- ...... **CLC 1, 2, 3, 4, 6, 8, 11, 15, 22, 31, 51**
See also CA 13-16R; CANR 8, 43; CDBLB 1960 to Present; DLB 14; MTCW

Murphy, Richard 1927-........... **CLC 41**
See also CA 29-32R; DLB 40

Murphy, Sylvia 1937-............. **CLC 34**
See also CA 121

Murphy, Thomas (Bernard) 1935-... **CLC 51**
See also CA 101

Murray, Albert L. 1916- .... **CLC 73**
See also BW; CA 49-52; CANR 26; DLB 38

Murray, Les(lie) A(llan) 1938- ..... **CLC 40**
See also CA 21-24R; CANR 11, 27

Murry, J. Middleton
See Murry, John Middleton

Murry, John Middleton
1889-1957 .... **TCLC 16**
See also CA 118

Musgrave, Susan 1951- .... **CLC 13, 54**
See also CA 69-72

Norris, Frank
See Norris, Benjamin Franklin, Jr.
See also CDALB 1865-1917; DLB 12, 71

Norris, Leslie 1921- . . . . **CLC 14**
See also CA 11-12; CANR 14; CAP 1; DLB 27

North, Andrew
See Norton, Andre

North, Anthony
See Koontz, Dean R(ay)

North, Captain George
See Stevenson, Robert Louis (Balfour)

North, Milou
See Erdrich, Louise

Northrup, B. A.
See Hubbard, L(afayette) Ron(ald)

North Staffs
See Hulme, T(homas) E(rnest)

Norton, Alice Mary
See Norton, Andre
See also MAICYA; SATA 1, 43

Norton, Andre 1912- . . . . **CLC 12**
See also Norton, Alice Mary
See also CA 1-4R; CANR 2, 31; DLB 8, 52; JRDA; MTCW

Norway, Nevil Shute 1899-1960
See Shute, Nevil
See also CA 102; 93-96

Norwid, Cyprian Kamil
1821-1883 . . . . **NCLC 17**

Nosille, Nabrah
See Ellison, Harlan

Nossack, Hans Erich 1901-1978 . . . . . **CLC 6**
See also CA 93-96; 85-88; DLB 69

Nosu, Chuji
See Ozu, Yasujiro

Nova, Craig 1945- . . . . **CLC 7, 31**
See also CA 45-48; CANR 2

Novak, Joseph
See Kosinski, Jerzy (Nikodem)

Novalis 1772-1801 . . . . **NCLC 13**
See also DLB 90

Nowlan, Alden (Albert) 1933-1983 . . **CLC 15**
See also CA 9-12R; CANR 5; DLB 53

Noyes, Alfred 1880-1958 . . . . **TCLC 7**
See also CA 104; DLB 20

Nunn, Kem 19(?)- . . . . **CLC 34**

Nye, Robert 1939- . . . . **CLC 13, 42**
See also CA 33-36R; CANR 29; DLB 14; MTCW; SATA 6

Nyro, Laura 1947- . . . . **CLC 17**

Oates, Joyce Carol
1938- . . . . . . **CLC 1, 2, 3, 6, 9, 11, 15, 19, 33, 52; SSC 6**
See also AITN 1; BEST 89:2; CA 5-8R; CANR 25; CDALB 1968-1988; DA; DLB 2, 5, 130; DLBY 81; MTCW; WLC

O'Brien, E. G.
See Clarke, Arthur C(harles)

O'Brien, Edna
1936- . . . **CLC 3, 5, 8, 13, 36, 65; SSC 10**
See also CA 1-4R; CANR 6, 41; CDBLB 1960 to Present; DLB 14; MTCW

O'Brien, Fitz-James 1828-1862. . . **NCLC 21**
See also DLB 74

O'Brien, Flann. . . . . **CLC 1, 4, 5, 7, 10, 47**
See also O Nuallain, Brian

O'Brien, Richard 1942- . . . . **CLC 17**
See also CA 124

O'Brien, Tim 1946-. . . . . **CLC 7, 19, 40**
See also CA 85-88; CANR 40; DLBD 9; DLBY 80

Obstfelder, Sigbjoern 1866-1900. . . **TCLC 23**
See also CA 123

O'Casey, Sean
1880-1964 . . . . **CLC 1, 5, 9, 11, 15**
See also CA 89-92; CDBLB 1914-1945; DLB 10; MTCW

O'Cathasaigh, Sean
See O'Casey, Sean

Ochs, Phil 1940-1976. . . . . **CLC 17**
See also CA 65-68

O'Connor, Edwin (Greene)
1918-1968 . . . . **CLC 14**
See also CA 93-96; 25-28R

O'Connor, (Mary) Flannery
1925-1964 . . . . **CLC 1, 2, 3, 6, 10, 13, 15, 21, 66; SSC 1**
See also AAYA 7; CA 1-4R; CANR 3, 41; CDALB 1941-1968; DA; DLB 2; DLBY 80; MTCW; WLC

O'Connor, Frank. . . . . **CLC 23; SSC 5**
See also O'Donovan, Michael John

O'Dell, Scott 1898-1989. . . . . **CLC 30**
See also AAYA 3; CA 61-64; 129; CANR 12, 30; CLR 1, 16; DLB 52; JRDA; MAICYA; SATA 12, 60

Odets, Clifford 1906-1963 . . . . **CLC 2, 28**
See also CA 85-88; DLB 7, 26; MTCW

O'Doherty, Brian 1934- . . . . **CLC 76**
See also CA 105

O'Donnell, K. M.
See Malzberg, Barry N(athaniel)

O'Donnell, Lawrence
See Kuttner, Henry

O'Donovan, Michael John
1903-1966 . . . . **CLC 14**
See also O'Connor, Frank
See also CA 93-96

Oe, Kenzaburo 1935- . . . . **CLC 10, 36**
See also CA 97-100; CANR 36; MTCW

O'Faolain, Julia 1932- . . . . **CLC 6, 19, 47**
See also CA 81-84; CAAS 2; CANR 12; DLB 14; MTCW

O'Faolain, Sean
1900-1991 . . . . **CLC 1, 7, 14, 32, 70; SSC 13**
See also CA 61-64; 134; CANR 12; DLB 15; MTCW

O'Flaherty, Liam
1896-1984 . . . . **CLC 5, 34; SSC 6**
See also CA 101; 113; CANR 35; DLB 36; DLBY 84; MTCW

Ogilvy, Gavin
See Barrie, J(ames) M(atthew)

O'Grady, Standish James
1846-1928 . . . . **TCLC 5**
See also CA 104

O'Grady, Timothy 1951- . . . . **CLC 59**
See also CA 138

O'Hara, Frank
1926-1966 . . . . **CLC 2, 5, 13, 78**
See also CA 9-12R; 25-28R; CANR 33; DLB 5, 16; MTCW

O'Hara, John (Henry)
1905-1970 . . . . **CLC 1, 2, 3, 6, 11, 42**
See also CA 5-8R; 25-28R; CANR 31; CDALB 1929-1941; DLB 9, 86; DLBD 2; MTCW

O Hehir, Diana 1922- . . . . **CLC 41**
See also CA 93-96

Okigbo, Christopher (Ifenayichukwu)
1932-1967 . . . . **CLC 25; PC 7**
See also BLC 3; BW; CA 77-80; DLB 125; MTCW

Olds, Sharon 1942-. . . . . **CLC 32, 39**
See also CA 101; CANR 18, 41; DLB 120

Oldstyle, Jonathan
See Irving, Washington

Olesha, Yuri (Karlovich)
1899-1960 . . . . **CLC 8**
See also CA 85-88

Oliphant, Margaret (Oliphant Wilson)
1828-1897 . . . . **NCLC 11**
See also DLB 18

Oliver, Mary 1935-. . . . . **CLC 19, 34**
See also CA 21-24R; CANR 9; DLB 5

Olivier, Laurence (Kerr)
1907-1989 . . . . **CLC 20**
See also CA 111; 129

Olsen, Tillie 1913- . . . . . **CLC 4, 13; SSC 11**
See also CA 1-4R; CANR 1, 43; DA; DLB 28; DLBY 80; MTCW

Olson, Charles (John)
1910-1970 . . . . . **CLC 1, 2, 5, 6, 9, 11, 29**
See also CA 13-16; 25-28R; CABS 2; CANR 35; CAP 1; DLB 5, 16; MTCW

Olson, Toby 1937- . . . . **CLC 28**
See also CA 65-68; CANR 9, 31

Olyesha, Yuri
See Olesha, Yuri (Karlovich)

Ondaatje, (Philip) Michael
1943- . . . . **CLC 14, 29, 51, 76**
See also CA 77-80; CANR 42; DLB 60

Oneal, Elizabeth 1934-
See Oneal, Zibby
See also CA 106; CANR 28; MAICYA; SATA 30

Oneal, Zibby . . . . **CLC 30**
See also Oneal, Elizabeth
See also AAYA 5; CLR 13; JRDA

O'Neill, Eugene (Gladstone)
1888-1953 . . . . **TCLC 1, 6, 27, 49**
See also AITN 1; CA 110; 132; CDALB 1929-1941; DA; DLB 7; MTCW; WLC

Onetti, Juan Carlos 1909- . . . . **CLC 7, 10**
See also CA 85-88; CANR 32; DLB 113; HW; MTCW

O Nuallain, Brian 1911-1966
See O'Brien, Flann
See also CA 21-22; 25-28R; CAP 2

Oppen, George 1908-1984 .... **CLC 7, 13, 34**
See also CA 13-16R; 113; CANR 8; DLB 5

Oppenheim, E(dward) Phillips
1866-1946 .... **TCLC 45**
See also CA 111; DLB 70

Orlovitz, Gil 1918-1973 .... **CLC 22**
See also CA 77-80; 45-48; DLB 2, 5

Orris
See Ingelow, Jean

Ortega y Gasset, Jose 1883-1955 ... **TCLC 9**
See also CA 106; 130; HW; MTCW

Ortiz, Simon J(oseph) 1941- .... **CLC 45**
See also CA 134; DLB 120

Orton, Joe .... **CLC 4, 13, 43; DC 3**
See also Orton, John Kingsley
See also CDBLB 1960 to Present; DLB 13

Orton, John Kingsley 1933-1967
See Orton, Joe
See also CA 85-88; CANR 35; MTCW

Orwell, George .... **TCLC 2, 6, 15, 31, 51**
See also Blair, Eric (Arthur)
See also CDBLB 1945-1960; DLB 15, 98; WLC

Osborne, David
See Silverberg, Robert

Osborne, George
See Silverberg, Robert

Osborne, John (James)
1929- .... **CLC 1, 2, 5, 11, 45**
See also CA 13-16R; CANR 21; CDBLB 1945-1960; DA; DLB 13; MTCW; WLC

Osborne, Lawrence 1958- .... **CLC 50**

Oshima, Nagisa 1932- .... **CLC 20**
See also CA 116; 121

Oskison, John M(ilton)
1874-1947 .... **TCLC 35**

Ossoli, Sarah Margaret (Fuller marchesa d')
1810-1850
See Fuller, Margaret
See also SATA 25

Ostrovsky, Alexander
1823-1886 .... **NCLC 30**

Otero, Blas de 1916-1979.......... **CLC 11**
See also CA 89-92; DLB 134

Otto, Whitney 1955-.............. **CLC 70**
See also CA 140

Ouida .... **TCLC 43**
See also De La Ramee, (Marie) Louise
See also DLB 18

Ousmane, Sembene 1923- .... **CLC 66**
See also BLC 3; BW; CA 117; 125; MTCW

Ovid 43B.C.-18th cent. (?)... **CMLC 7; PC 2**

Owen, Hugh
See Faust, Frederick (Schiller)

Owen, Wilfred (Edward Salter)
1893-1918 .... **TCLC 5, 27**
See also CA 104; 141; CDBLB 1914-1945; DA; DLB 20; WLC

Owens, Rochelle 1936-............. **CLC 8**
See also CA 17-20R; CAAS 2; CANR 39

Oz, Amos 1939- ... **CLC 5, 8, 11, 27, 33, 54**
See also CA 53-56; CANR 27; MTCW

Ozick, Cynthia 1928-...... **CLC 3, 7, 28, 62**
See also BEST 90:1; CA 17-20R; CANR 23; DLB 28; DLBY 82; MTCW

Ozu, Yasujiro 1903-1963 .... **CLC 16**
See also CA 112

Pacheco, C.
See Pessoa, Fernando (Antonio Nogueira)

Pa Chin
See Li Fei-kan

Pack, Robert 1929-............... **CLC 13**
See also CA 1-4R; CANR 3; DLB 5

Padgett, Lewis
See Kuttner, Henry

Padilla (Lorenzo), Heberto 1932- ... **CLC 38**
See also AITN 1; CA 123; 131; HW

Page, Jimmy 1944-............... **CLC 12**

Page, Louise 1955-............... **CLC 40**
See also CA 140

Page, P(atricia) K(athleen)
1916- .... **CLC 7, 18**
See also CA 53-56; CANR 4, 22; DLB 68; MTCW

Paget, Violet 1856-1935
See Lee, Vernon
See also CA 104

Paget-Lowe, Henry
See Lovecraft, H(oward) P(hillips)

Paglia, Camille (Anna) 1947-....... **CLC 68**
See also CA 140

Paige, Richard
See Koontz, Dean R(ay)

Pakenham, Antonia
See Fraser, Antonia (Pakenham)

Palamas, Kostes 1859-1943 .... **TCLC 5**
See also CA 105

Palazzeschi, Aldo 1885-1974....... **CLC 11**
See also CA 89-92; 53-56; DLB 114

Paley, Grace 1922-.... **CLC 4, 6, 37; SSC 8**
See also CA 25-28R; CANR 13; DLB 28; MTCW

Palin, Michael (Edward) 1943-..... **CLC 21**
See also Monty Python
See also CA 107; CANR 35; SATA 67

Palliser, Charles 1947-............ **CLC 65**
See also CA 136

Palma, Ricardo 1833-1919........ **TCLC 29**

Pancake, Breece Dexter 1952-1979
See Pancake, Breece D'J
See also CA 123; 109

Pancake, Breece D'J............... **CLC 29**
See also Pancake, Breece Dexter
See also DLB 130

Panko, Rudy
See Gogol, Nikolai (Vasilyevich)

Papadiamantis, Alexandros
1851-1911 .... **TCLC 29**

Papadiamantopoulos, Johannes 1856-1910
See Moreas, Jean
See also CA 117

Papini, Giovanni 1881-1956....... **TCLC 22**
See also CA 121

Paracelsus 1493-1541.............. **LC 14**

Parasol, Peter
See Stevens, Wallace

Parfenie, Maria
See Codrescu, Andrei

Parini, Jay (Lee) 1948- .... **CLC 54**
See also CA 97-100; CAAS 16; CANR 32

Park, Jordan
See Kornbluth, C(yril) M.; Pohl, Frederik

Parker, Bert
See Ellison, Harlan

Parker, Dorothy (Rothschild)
1893-1967 .... **CLC 15, 68; SSC 2**
See also CA 19-20; 25-28R; CAP 2; DLB 11, 45, 86; MTCW

Parker, Robert B(rown) 1932-...... **CLC 27**
See also BEST 89:4; CA 49-52; CANR 1, 26; MTCW

Parkes, Lucas
See Harris, John (Wyndham Parkes Lucas) Beynon

Parkin, Frank 1940-.............. **CLC 43**

Parkman, Francis, Jr.
1823-1893 .... **NCLC 12**
See also DLB 1, 30

Parks, Gordon (Alexander Buchanan)
1912- .... **CLC 1, 16**
See also AITN 2; BLC 3; BW; CA 41-44R; CANR 26; DLB 33; SATA 8

Parnell, Thomas 1679-1718 .... **LC 3**
See also DLB 94

Parra, Nicanor 1914-.............. **CLC 2**
See also CA 85-88; CANR 32; HW; MTCW

Parrish, Mary Frances
See Fisher, M(ary) F(rances) K(ennedy)

Parson
See Coleridge, Samuel Taylor

Parson Lot
See Kingsley, Charles

Partridge, Anthony
See Oppenheim, E(dward) Phillips

Pascoli, Giovanni 1855-1912 ...... **TCLC 45**

Pasolini, Pier Paolo
1922-1975 .... **CLC 20, 37**
See also CA 93-96; 61-64; DLB 128; MTCW

Pasquini
See Silone, Ignazio

Pastan, Linda (Olenik) 1932- ...... **CLC 27**
See also CA 61-64; CANR 18, 40; DLB 5

Pasternak, Boris (Leonidovich)
1890-1960 ..... **CLC 7, 10, 18, 63; PC 6**
See also CA 127; 116; DA; MTCW; WLC

Patchen, Kenneth 1911-1972... **CLC 1, 2, 18**
See also CA 1-4R; 33-36R; CANR 3, 35; DLB 16, 48; MTCW

Pater, Walter (Horatio)
1839-1894 .... **NCLC 7**
See also CDBLB 1832-1890; DLB 57

Paterson, A(ndrew) B(arton)
1864-1941 .... **TCLC 32**

Paterson, Katherine (Womeldorf) 1932- .... **CLC 12, 30**
See also AAYA 1; CA 21-24R; CANR 28; CLR 7; DLB 52; JRDA; MAICYA; MTCW; SATA 13, 53

Patmore, Coventry Kersey Dighton 1823-1896 .... **NCLC 9**
See also DLB 35, 98

Paton, Alan (Stewart) 1903-1988 .... **CLC 4, 10, 25, 55**
See also CA 13-16; 125; CANR 22; CAP 1; DA; MTCW; SATA 11, 56; WLC

Paton Walsh, Gillian 1937-
See Walsh, Jill Paton
See also CANR 38; JRDA; MAICYA; SAAS 3; SATA 4, 72

Paulding, James Kirke 1778-1860.. **NCLC 2**
See also DLB 3, 59, 74

Paulin, Thomas Neilson 1949-
See Paulin, Tom
See also CA 123; 128

Paulin, Tom .... **CLC 37**
See also Paulin, Thomas Neilson
See also DLB 40

Paustovsky, Konstantin (Georgievich) 1892-1968 .... **CLC 40**
See also CA 93-96; 25-28R

Pavese, Cesare 1908-1950 .... **TCLC 3**
See also CA 104; DLB 128

Pavic, Milorad 1929- .... **CLC 60**
See also CA 136

Payne, Alan
See Jakes, John (William)

Paz, Gil
See Lugones, Leopoldo

Paz, Octavio 1914- .... **CLC 3, 4, 6, 10, 19, 51, 65; PC 1**
See also CA 73-76; CANR 32; DA; DLBY 90; HW; MTCW; WLC

Peacock, Molly 1947- .... **CLC 60**
See also CA 103; DLB 120

Peacock, Thomas Love 1785-1866 .... **NCLC 22**
See also DLB 96, 116

Peake, Mervyn 1911-1968 .... **CLC 7, 54**
See also CA 5-8R; 25-28R; CANR 3; DLB 15; MTCW; SATA 23

Pearce, Philippa .... **CLC 21**
See also Christie, (Ann) Philippa
See also CLR 9; MAICYA; SATA 1, 67

Pearl, Eric
See Elman, Richard

Pearson, T(homas) R(eid) 1956- .... **CLC 39**
See also CA 120; 130

Peck, John 1941- .... **CLC 3**
See also CA 49-52; CANR 3

Peck, Richard (Wayne) 1934- .... **CLC 21**
See also AAYA 1; CA 85-88; CANR 19, 38; JRDA; MAICYA; SAAS 2; SATA 18, 55

Peck, Robert Newton 1928- .... **CLC 17**
See also AAYA 3; CA 81-84; CANR 31; DA; JRDA; MAICYA; SAAS 1; SATA 21, 62

Peckinpah, (David) Sam(uel) 1925-1984 .... **CLC 20**
See also CA 109; 114

Pedersen, Knut 1859-1952
See Hamsun, Knut
See also CA 104; 119; MTCW

Peeslake, Gaffer
See Durrell, Lawrence (George)

Peguy, Charles Pierre 1873-1914 .... **TCLC 10**
See also CA 107

Pena, Ramon del Valle y
See Valle-Inclan, Ramon (Maria) del

Pendennis, Arthur Esquir
See Thackeray, William Makepeace

Pepys, Samuel 1633-1703 .... **LC 11**
See also CDBLB 1660-1789; DA; DLB 101; WLC

Percy, Walker 1916-1990 .... **CLC 2, 3, 6, 8, 14, 18, 47, 65**
See also CA 1-4R; 131; CANR 1, 23; DLB 2; DLBY 80, 90; MTCW

Perec, Georges 1936-1982 .... **CLC 56**
See also CA 141; DLB 83

Pereda (y Sanchez de Porrua), Jose Maria de 1833-1906 .... **TCLC 16**
See also CA 117

Pereda y Porrua, Jose Maria de
See Pereda (y Sanchez de Porrua), Jose Maria de

Peregoy, George Weems
See Mencken, H(enry) L(ouis)

Perelman, S(idney) J(oseph) 1904-1979 .... **CLC 3, 5, 9, 15, 23, 44, 49**
See also AITN 1, 2; CA 73-76; 89-92; CANR 18; DLB 11, 44; MTCW

Peret, Benjamin 1899-1959 .... **TCLC 20**
See also CA 117

Peretz, Isaac Loeb 1851(?)-1915... **TCLC 16**
See also CA 109

Peretz, Yitzkhok Leibush
See Peretz, Isaac Loeb

Perez Galdos, Benito 1843-1920... **TCLC 27**
See also CA 125; HW

Perrault, Charles 1628-1703 .... **LC 2**
See also MAICYA; SATA 25

Perry, Brighton
See Sherwood, Robert E(mmet)

Perse, St.-John .... **CLC 4, 11, 46**
See also Leger, (Marie-Rene Auguste) Alexis Saint-Leger

Peseenz, Tulio F.
See Lopez y Fuentes, Gregorio

Pesetsky, Bette 1932- .... **CLC 28**
See also CA 133; DLB 130

Peshkov, Alexei Maximovich 1868-1936
See Gorky, Maxim
See also CA 105; 141; DA

Pessoa, Fernando (Antonio Nogueira) 1888-1935 .... **TCLC 27**
See also CA 125

Peterkin, Julia Mood 1880-1961.... **CLC 31**
See also CA 102; DLB 9

Peters, Joan K. 1945- .... **CLC 39**

Peters, Robert L(ouis) 1924- .... **CLC 7**
See also CA 13-16R; CAAS 8; DLB 105

Petofi, Sandor 1823-1849 .... **NCLC 21**

Petrakis, Harry Mark 1923- .... **CLC 3**
See also CA 9-12R; CANR 4, 30

Petrov, Evgeny .... **TCLC 21**
See also Kataev, Evgeny Petrovich

Petry, Ann (Lane) 1908- .... **CLC 1, 7, 18**
See also BW; CA 5-8R; CAAS 6; CANR 4; CLR 12; DLB 76; JRDA; MAICYA; MTCW; SATA 5

Petursson, Halligrimur 1614-1674 .... **LC 8**

Philipson, Morris H. 1926- .... **CLC 53**
See also CA 1-4R; CANR 4

Phillips, David Graham 1867-1911 .... **TCLC 44**
See also CA 108; DLB 9, 12

Phillips, Jack
See Sandburg, Carl (August)

Phillips, Jayne Anne 1952- .... **CLC 15, 33**
See also CA 101; CANR 24; DLBY 80; MTCW

Phillips, Richard
See Dick, Philip K(indred)

Phillips, Robert (Schaeffer) 1938-... **CLC 28**
See also CA 17-20R; CAAS 13; CANR 8; DLB 105

Phillips, Ward
See Lovecraft, H(oward) P(hillips)

Piccolo, Lucio 1901-1969 .... **CLC 13**
See also CA 97-100; DLB 114

Pickthall, Marjorie L(owry) C(hristie) 1883-1922 .... **TCLC 21**
See also CA 107; DLB 92

Pico della Mirandola, Giovanni 1463-1494 .... **LC 15**

Piercy, Marge 1936- .... **CLC 3, 6, 14, 18, 27, 62**
See also CA 21-24R; CAAS 1; CANR 13, 43; DLB 120; MTCW

Piers, Robert
See Anthony, Piers

Pieyre de Mandiargues, Andre 1909-1991
See Mandiargues, Andre Pieyre de
See also CA 103; 136; CANR 22

Pilnyak, Boris .... **TCLC 23**
See also Vogau, Boris Andreyevich

Pincherle, Alberto 1907-1990 ... **CLC 11, 18**
See also Moravia, Alberto
See also CA 25-28R; 132; CANR 33; MTCW

Pinckney, Darryl 1953- .... **CLC 76**

Pindar 518B.C.-446B.C. .... **CMLC 12**

Pineda, Cecile 1942- .... **CLC 39**
See also CA 118

Pinero, Arthur Wing 1855-1934 ... **TCLC 32**
See also CA 110; DLB 10

Pinero, Miguel (Antonio Gomez) 1946-1988 .... **CLC 4, 55**
See also CA 61-64; 125; CANR 29; HW

Pinget, Robert 1919- .... **CLC 7, 13, 37**
See also CA 85-88; DLB 83

Price, Richard 1949- . . . . **CLC 6, 12**
See also CA 49-52; CANR 3; DLBY 81

Prichard, Katharine Susannah 1883-1969 . . . . **CLC 46**
See also CA 11-12; CANR 33; CAP 1; MTCW; SATA 66

Priestley, J(ohn) B(oynton) 1894-1984 . . . . **CLC 2, 5, 9, 34**
See also CA 9-12R; 113; CANR 33; CDBLB 1914-1945; DLB 10, 34, 77, 100; DLBY 84; MTCW

Prince 1958(?)- . . . . **CLC 35**

Prince, F(rank) T(empleton) 1912- . . **CLC 22**
See also CA 101; CANR 43; DLB 20

Prince Kropotkin
See Kropotkin, Peter (Aleksieevich)

Prior, Matthew 1664-1721 . . . . **LC 4**
See also DLB 95

Pritchard, William H(arrison) 1932- . . . . **CLC 34**
See also CA 65-68; CANR 23; DLB 111

Pritchett, V(ictor) S(awdon) 1900- . . . . **CLC 5, 13, 15, 41**
See also CA 61-64; CANR 31; DLB 15; MTCW

Private 19022
See Manning, Frederic

Probst, Mark 1925- . . . . **CLC 59**
See also CA 130

Prokosch, Frederic 1908-1989 . . . . **CLC 4, 48**
See also CA 73-76; 128; DLB 48

Prophet, The
See Dreiser, Theodore (Herman Albert)

Prose, Francine 1947- . . . . **CLC 45**
See also CA 109; 112

Proudhon
See Cunha, Euclides (Rodrigues Pimenta) da

Proust, (Valentin-Louis-George-Eugene-) Marcel 1871-1922 . . . . **TCLC 7, 13, 33**
See also CA 104; 120; DA; DLB 65; MTCW; WLC

Prowler, Harley
See Masters, Edgar Lee

Prus, Boleslaw . . . . **TCLC 48**
See also Glowacki, Aleksander

Pryor, Richard (Franklin Lenox Thomas) 1940- . . . . **CLC 26**
See also CA 122

Przybyszewski, Stanislaw 1868-1927 . . . . **TCLC 36**
See also DLB 66

Pteleon
See Grieve, C(hristopher) M(urray)

Puckett, Lute
See Masters, Edgar Lee

Puig, Manuel 1932-1990 . . . . **CLC 3, 5, 10, 28, 65**
See also CA 45-48; CANR 2, 32; DLB 113; HW; MTCW

Purdy, A(lfred Wellington) 1918- . . . . **CLC 3, 6, 14, 50**
See also CA 81-84; CANR 42

Purdy, Al
See Purdy, A(lfred Wellington)
See also CAAS 17; DLB 88

Purdy, James (Amos) 1923- . . . . **CLC 2, 4, 10, 28, 52**
See also CA 33-36R; CAAS 1; CANR 19; DLB 2; MTCW

Pure, Simon
See Swinnerton, Frank Arthur

Pushkin, Alexander (Sergeyevich) 1799-1837 . . . . **NCLC 3, 27**
See also DA; SATA 61; WLC

P'u Sung-ling 1640-1715 . . . . **LC 3**

Putnam, Arthur Lee
See Alger, Horatio, Jr.

Puzo, Mario 1920- . . . . **CLC 1, 2, 6, 36**
See also CA 65-68; CANR 4, 42; DLB 6; MTCW

Pym, Barbara (Mary Crampton) 1913-1980 . . . . **CLC 13, 19, 37**
See also CA 13-14; 97-100; CANR 13, 34; CAP 1; DLB 14; DLBY 87; MTCW

Pynchon, Thomas (Ruggles, Jr.) 1937- . . **CLC 2, 3, 6, 9, 11, 18, 33, 62, 72**
See also BEST 90:2; CA 17-20R; CANR 22; DA; DLB 2; MTCW; WLC

Qian Zhongshu
See Ch'ien Chung-shu

Qroll
See Dagerman, Stig (Halvard)

Quarrington, Paul (Lewis) 1953- . . . . **CLC 65**
See also CA 129

Quasimodo, Salvatore 1901-1968 . . . **CLC 10**
See also CA 13-16; 25-28R; CAP 1; DLB 114; MTCW

Queen, Ellery . . . . **CLC 3, 11**
See also Dannay, Frederic; Davidson, Avram; Lee, Manfred B(ennington); Sturgeon, Theodore (Hamilton); Vance, John Holbrook

Queen, Ellery, Jr.
See Dannay, Frederic; Lee, Manfred B(ennington)

Queneau, Raymond 1903-1976 . . . . **CLC 2, 5, 10, 42**
See also CA 77-80; 69-72; CANR 32; DLB 72; MTCW

Quevedo, Francisco de 1580-1645 . . . . **LC 23**

Quin, Ann (Marie) 1936-1973 . . . . **CLC 6**
See also CA 9-12R; 45-48; DLB 14

Quinn, Martin
See Smith, Martin Cruz

Quinn, Simon
See Smith, Martin Cruz

Quiroga, Horacio (Sylvestre) 1878-1937 . . . . **TCLC 20**
See also CA 117; 131; HW; MTCW

Quoirez, Francoise 1935- . . . . **CLC 9**
See also Sagan, Francoise
See also CA 49-52; CANR 6, 39; MTCW

Raabe, Wilhelm 1831-1910 . . . . **TCLC 45**
See also DLB 129

Rabe, David (William) 1940- . . . **CLC 4, 8, 33**
See also CA 85-88; CABS 3; DLB 7

Rabelais, Francois 1483-1553 . . . . **LC 5**
See also DA; WLC

Rabinovitch, Sholem 1859-1916
See Aleichem, Sholom
See also CA 104

Radcliffe, Ann (Ward) 1764-1823 . . **NCLC 6**
See also DLB 39

Radiguet, Raymond 1903-1923 . . . . **TCLC 29**
See also DLB 65

Radnoti, Miklos 1909-1944 . . . . **TCLC 16**
See also CA 118

Rado, James 1939- . . . . **CLC 17**
See also CA 105

Radvanyi, Netty 1900-1983
See Seghers, Anna
See also CA 85-88; 110

Raeburn, John (Hay) 1941- . . . . **CLC 34**
See also CA 57-60

Ragni, Gerome 1942-1991 . . . . **CLC 17**
See also CA 105; 134

Rahv, Philip . . . . **CLC 24**
See also Greenberg, Ivan

Raine, Craig 1944- . . . . **CLC 32**
See also CA 108; CANR 29; DLB 40

Raine, Kathleen (Jessie) 1908- . . . **CLC 7, 45**
See also CA 85-88; DLB 20; MTCW

Rainis, Janis 1865-1929 . . . . **TCLC 29**

Rakosi, Carl . . . . **CLC 47**
See also Rawley, Callman
See also CAAS 5

Raleigh, Richard
See Lovecraft, H(oward) P(hillips)

Rallentando, H. P.
See Sayers, Dorothy L(eigh)

Ramal, Walter
See de la Mare, Walter (John)

Ramon, Juan
See Jimenez (Mantecon), Juan Ramon

Ramos, Graciliano 1892-1953 . . . . . **TCLC 32**

Rampersad, Arnold 1941- . . . . **CLC 44**
See also CA 127; 133; DLB 111

Rampling, Anne
See Rice, Anne

Ramuz, Charles-Ferdinand 1878-1947 . . . . **TCLC 33**

Rand, Ayn 1905-1982 . . . . . **CLC 3, 30, 44, 79**
See also AAYA 10; CA 13-16R; 105; CANR 27; DA; MTCW; WLC

Randall, Dudley (Felker) 1914- . . . . . . **CLC 1**
See also BLC 3; BW; CA 25-28R; CANR 23; DLB 41

Randall, Robert
See Silverberg, Robert

Ranger, Ken
See Creasey, John

Ransom, John Crowe 1888-1974 . . . . **CLC 2, 4, 5, 11, 24**
See also CA 5-8R; 49-52; CANR 6, 34; DLB 45, 63; MTCW

Rao, Raja 1909- . . . . **CLC 25, 56**
See also CA 73-76; MTCW

Raphael, Frederic (Michael) 1931- .... **CLC 2, 14**
See also CA 1-4R; CANR 1; DLB 14

Ratcliffe, James P.
See Mencken, H(enry) L(ouis)

Rathbone, Julian 1935- .... **CLC 41**
See also CA 101; CANR 34

Rattigan, Terence (Mervyn) 1911-1977 .... **CLC 7**
See also CA 85-88; 73-76; CDBLB 1945-1960; DLB 13; MTCW

Ratushinskaya, Irina 1954- .... **CLC 54**
See also CA 129

Raven, Simon (Arthur Noel) 1927- .... **CLC 14**
See also CA 81-84

Rawley, Callman 1903-
See Rakosi, Carl
See also CA 21-24R; CANR 12, 32

Rawlings, Marjorie Kinnan 1896-1953 .... **TCLC 4**
See also CA 104; 137; DLB 9, 22, 102; JRDA; MAICYA; YABC 1

Ray, Satyajit 1921-1992........ **CLC 16, 76**
See also CA 114; 137

Read, Herbert Edward 1893-1968.... **CLC 4**
See also CA 85-88; 25-28R; DLB 20

Read, Piers Paul 1941- ...... **CLC 4, 10, 25**
See also CA 21-24R; CANR 38; DLB 14; SATA 21

Reade, Charles 1814-1884 .... **NCLC 2**
See also DLB 21

Reade, Hamish
See Gray, Simon (James Holliday)

Reading, Peter 1946- .... **CLC 47**
See also CA 103; DLB 40

Reaney, James 1926- .... **CLC 13**
See also CA 41-44R; CAAS 15; CANR 42; DLB 68; SATA 43

Rebreanu, Liviu 1885-1944 .... **TCLC 28**

Rechy, John (Francisco) 1934- .... **CLC 1, 7, 14, 18**
See also CA 5-8R; CAAS 4; CANR 6, 32; DLB 122; DLBY 82; HW

Redcam, Tom 1870-1933 .... **TCLC 25**

Reddin, Keith..................... **CLC 67**

Redgrove, Peter (William) 1932- .... **CLC 6, 41**
See also CA 1-4R; CANR 3, 39; DLB 40

Redmon, Anne.................... **CLC 22**
See also Nightingale, Anne Redmon
See also DLBY 86

Reed, Eliot
See Ambler, Eric

Reed, Ishmael 1938- .... **CLC 2, 3, 5, 6, 13, 32, 60**
See also BLC 3; BW; CA 21-24R; CANR 25; DLB 2, 5, 33; DLBD 8; MTCW

Reed, John (Silas) 1887-1920 ...... **TCLC 9**
See also CA 106

Reed, Lou........................ **CLC 21**
See also Firbank, Louis

Reeve, Clara 1729-1807 .... **NCLC 19**
See also DLB 39

Reid, Christopher (John) 1949-..... **CLC 33**
See also CA 140; DLB 40

Reid, Desmond
See Moorcock, Michael (John)

Reid Banks, Lynne 1929-
See Banks, Lynne Reid
See also CA 1-4R; CANR 6, 22, 38; CLR 24; JRDA; MAICYA; SATA 22, 75

Reilly, William K.
See Creasey, John

Reiner, Max
See Caldwell, (Janet Miriam) Taylor (Holland)

Reis, Ricardo
See Pessoa, Fernando (Antonio Nogueira)

Remarque, Erich Maria 1898-1970 .... **CLC 21**
See also CA 77-80; 29-32R; DA; DLB 56; MTCW

Remizov, A.
See Remizov, Aleksei (Mikhailovich)

Remizov, A. M.
See Remizov, Aleksei (Mikhailovich)

Remizov, Aleksei (Mikhailovich) 1877-1957 .... **TCLC 27**
See also CA 125; 133

Renan, Joseph Ernest 1823-1892 .... **NCLC 26**

Renard, Jules 1864-1910 .... **TCLC 17**
See also CA 117

Renault, Mary............... **CLC 3, 11, 17**
See also Challans, Mary
See also DLBY 83

Rendell, Ruth (Barbara) 1930- .. **CLC 28, 48**
See also Vine, Barbara
See also CA 109; CANR 32; DLB 87; MTCW

Renoir, Jean 1894-1979 .... **CLC 20**
See also CA 129; 85-88

Resnais, Alain 1922-.............. **CLC 16**

Reverdy, Pierre 1889-1960 .... **CLC 53**
See also CA 97-100; 89-92

Rexroth, Kenneth 1905-1982 ...... **CLC 1, 2, 6, 11, 22, 49**
See also CA 5-8R; 107; CANR 14, 34; CDALB 1941-1968; DLB 16, 48; DLBY 82; MTCW

Reyes, Alfonso 1889-1959 .... **TCLC 33**
See also CA 131; HW

Reyes y Basoalto, Ricardo Eliecer Neftali
See Neruda, Pablo

Reymont, Wladyslaw (Stanislaw) 1868(?)-1925 .... **TCLC 5**
See also CA 104

Reynolds, Jonathan 1942- .... **CLC 6, 38**
See also CA 65-68; CANR 28

Reynolds, Joshua 1723-1792 .... **LC 15**
See also DLB 104

Reynolds, Michael Shane 1937- .... **CLC 44**
See also CA 65-68; CANR 9

Reznikoff, Charles 1894-1976 .... **CLC 9**
See also CA 33-36; 61-64; CAP 2; DLB 28, 45

Rezzori (d'Arezzo), Gregor von 1914- .... **CLC 25**
See also CA 122; 136

Rhine, Richard
See Silverstein, Alvin

R'hoone
See Balzac, Honore de

Rhys, Jean 1890(?)-1979 .... **CLC 2, 4, 6, 14, 19, 51**
See also CA 25-28R; 85-88; CANR 35; CDBLB 1945-1960; DLB 36, 117; MTCW

Ribeiro, Darcy 1922- .... **CLC 34**
See also CA 33-36R

Ribeiro, Joao Ubaldo (Osorio Pimentel) 1941- .... **CLC 10, 67**
See also CA 81-84

Ribman, Ronald (Burt) 1932- .... **CLC 7**
See also CA 21-24R

Ricci, Nino 1959- .... **CLC 70**
See also CA 137

Rice, Anne 1941- .... **CLC 41**
See also AAYA 9; BEST 89:2; CA 65-68; CANR 12, 36

Rice, Elmer (Leopold) 1892-1967 .... **CLC 7, 49**
See also CA 21-22; 25-28R; CAP 2; DLB 4, 7; MTCW

Rice, Tim 1944- .... **CLC 21**
See also CA 103

Rich, Adrienne (Cecile) 1929- .... **CLC 3, 6, 7, 11, 18, 36, 73, 76; PC 5**
See also CA 9-12R; CANR 20; DLB 5, 67; MTCW

Rich, Barbara
See Graves, Robert (von Ranke)

Rich, Robert
See Trumbo, Dalton

Richards, David Adams 1950-...... **CLC 59**
See also CA 93-96; DLB 53

Richards, I(vor) A(rmstrong) 1893-1979 .... **CLC 14, 24**
See also CA 41-44R; 89-92; CANR 34; DLB 27

Richardson, Anne
See Roiphe, Anne Richardson

Richardson, Dorothy Miller 1873-1957 .... **TCLC 3**
See also CA 104; DLB 36

Richardson, Ethel Florence (Lindesay) 1870-1946
See Richardson, Henry Handel
See also CA 105

Richardson, Henry Handel.......... **TCLC 4**
See also Richardson, Ethel Florence (Lindesay)

Richardson, Samuel 1689-1761 .... **LC 1**
See also CDBLB 1660-1789; DA; DLB 39; WLC

Rosenthal, M(acha) L(ouis) 1917- . . . **CLC 28**
See also CA 1-4R; CAAS 6; CANR 4; DLB 5; SATA 59

Ross, Barnaby
See Dannay, Frederic

Ross, Bernard L.
See Follett, Ken(neth Martin)

Ross, J. H.
See Lawrence, T(homas) E(dward)

Ross, Martin
See Martin, Violet Florence

Ross, (James) Sinclair 1908- . . . . **CLC 13**
See also CA 73-76; DLB 88

Rossetti, Christina (Georgina)
1830-1894 . . . . **NCLC 2; PC 7**
See also DA; DLB 35; MAICYA; SATA 20; WLC

Rossetti, Dante Gabriel
1828-1882 . . . . **NCLC 4**
See also CDBLB 1832-1890; DA; DLB 35; WLC

Rossner, Judith (Perelman)
1935- . . . . **CLC 6, 9, 29**
See also AITN 2; BEST 90:3; CA 17-20R; CANR 18; DLB 6; MTCW

Rostand, Edmond (Eugene Alexis)
1868-1918 . . . . **TCLC 6, 37**
See also CA 104; 126; DA; MTCW

Roth, Henry 1906- . . . . **CLC 2, 6, 11**
See also CA 11-12; CANR 38; CAP 1; DLB 28; MTCW

Roth, Joseph 1894-1939 . . . . **TCLC 33**
See also DLB 85

Roth, Philip (Milton)
1933- . . . . . . **CLC 1, 2, 3, 4, 6, 9, 15, 22, 31, 47, 66**
See also BEST 90:3; CA 1-4R; CANR 1, 22, 36; CDALB 1968-1988; DA; DLB 2, 28; DLBY 82; MTCW; WLC

Rothenberg, Jerome 1931- . . . . **CLC 6, 57**
See also CA 45-48; CANR 1; DLB 5

Roumain, Jacques (Jean Baptiste)
1907-1944 . . . . **TCLC 19**
See also BLC 3; BW; CA 117; 125

Rourke, Constance (Mayfield)
1885-1941 . . . . **TCLC 12**
See also CA 107; YABC 1

Rousseau, Jean-Baptiste 1671-1741 . . . **LC 9**

Rousseau, Jean-Jacques 1712-1778 . . . **LC 14**
See also DA; WLC

Roussel, Raymond 1877-1933 . . . . . **TCLC 20**
See also CA 117

Rovit, Earl (Herbert) 1927- . . . . **CLC 7**
See also CA 5-8R; CANR 12

Rowe, Nicholas 1674-1718 . . . . **LC 8**
See also DLB 84

Rowley, Ames Dorrance
See Lovecraft, H(oward) P(hillips)

Rowson, Susanna Haswell
1762(?)-1824 . . . . **NCLC 5**
See also DLB 37

Roy, Gabrielle 1909-1983 . . . . **CLC 10, 14**
See also CA 53-56; 110; CANR 5; DLB 68; MTCW

Rozewicz, Tadeusz 1921- . . . . **CLC 9, 23**
See also CA 108; CANR 36; MTCW

Ruark, Gibbons 1941- . . . . **CLC 3**
See also CA 33-36R; CANR 14, 31; DLB 120

Rubens, Bernice (Ruth) 1923- . . . **CLC 19, 31**
See also CA 25-28R; CANR 33; DLB 14; MTCW

Rudkin, (James) David 1936- . . . . . . **CLC 14**
See also CA 89-92; DLB 13

Rudnik, Raphael 1933- . . . . **CLC 7**
See also CA 29-32R

Ruffian, M.
See Hasek, Jaroslav (Matej Frantisek)

Ruiz, Jose Martinez . . . . **CLC 11**
See also Martinez Ruiz, Jose

Rukeyser, Muriel
1913-1980 . . . . **CLC 6, 10, 15, 27**
See also CA 5-8R; 93-96; CANR 26; DLB 48; MTCW; SATA 22

Rule, Jane (Vance) 1931- . . . . **CLC 27**
See also CA 25-28R; CAAS 18; CANR 12; DLB 60

Rulfo, Juan 1918-1986 . . . . **CLC 8, 80**
See also CA 85-88; 118; CANR 26; DLB 113; HW; MTCW

Runeberg, Johan 1804-1877 . . . . . . **NCLC 41**

Runyon, (Alfred) Damon
1884(?)-1946 . . . . **TCLC 10**
See also CA 107; DLB 11, 86

Rush, Norman 1933- . . . . **CLC 44**
See also CA 121; 126

Rushdie, (Ahmed) Salman
1947- . . . . **CLC 23, 31, 55**
See also BEST 89:3; CA 108; 111; CANR 33; MTCW

Rushforth, Peter (Scott) 1945- . . . . . **CLC 19**
See also CA 101

Ruskin, John 1819-1900 . . . . **TCLC 20**
See also CA 114; 129; CDBLB 1832-1890; DLB 55; SATA 24

Russ, Joanna 1937- . . . . **CLC 15**
See also CA 25-28R; CANR 11, 31; DLB 8; MTCW

Russell, George William 1867-1935
See A. E.
See also CA 104; CDBLB 1890-1914

Russell, (Henry) Ken(neth Alfred)
1927- . . . . **CLC 16**
See also CA 105

Russell, Willy 1947- . . . . **CLC 60**

Rutherford, Mark . . . . **TCLC 25**
See also White, William Hale
See also DLB 18

Ruyslinck, Ward
See Belser, Reimond Karel Maria de

Ryan, Cornelius (John) 1920-1974 . . . **CLC 7**
See also CA 69-72; 53-56; CANR 38

Ryan, Michael 1946- . . . . **CLC 65**
See also CA 49-52; DLBY 82

Rybakov, Anatoli (Naumovich)
1911- . . . . **CLC 23, 53**
See also CA 126; 135

Ryder, Jonathan
See Ludlum, Robert

Ryga, George 1932-1987 . . . . **CLC 14**
See also CA 101; 124; CANR 43; DLB 60

S. S.
See Sassoon, Siegfried (Lorraine)

Saba, Umberto 1883-1957 . . . . **TCLC 33**
See also DLB 114

Sabatini, Rafael 1875-1950 . . . . **TCLC 47**

Sabato, Ernesto (R.) 1911- . . . . . . **CLC 10, 23**
See also CA 97-100; CANR 32; HW; MTCW

Sacastru, Martin
See Bioy Casares, Adolfo

Sacher-Masoch, Leopold von
1836(?)-1895 . . . . **NCLC 31**

Sachs, Marilyn (Stickle) 1927- . . . . . **CLC 35**
See also AAYA 2; CA 17-20R; CANR 13; CLR 2; JRDA; MAICYA; SAAS 2; SATA 3, 68

Sachs, Nelly 1891-1970 . . . . **CLC 14**
See also CA 17-18; 25-28R; CAP 2

Sackler, Howard (Oliver)
1929-1982 . . . . **CLC 14**
See also CA 61-64; 108; CANR 30; DLB 7

Sacks, Oliver (Wolf) 1933- . . . . **CLC 67**
See also CA 53-56; CANR 28; MTCW

Sade, Donatien Alphonse Francois Comte
1740-1814 . . . . **NCLC 3**

Sadoff, Ira 1945- . . . . **CLC 9**
See also CA 53-56; CANR 5, 21; DLB 120

Saetone
See Camus, Albert

Safire, William 1929- . . . . **CLC 10**
See also CA 17-20R; CANR 31

Sagan, Carl (Edward) 1934- . . . . **CLC 30**
See also AAYA 2; CA 25-28R; CANR 11, 36; MTCW; SATA 58

Sagan, Francoise . . . . **CLC 3, 6, 9, 17, 36**
See also Quoirez, Francoise
See also DLB 83

Sahgal, Nayantara (Pandit) 1927- . . . **CLC 41**
See also CA 9-12R; CANR 11

Saint, H(arry) F. 1941- . . . . **CLC 50**
See also CA 127

St. Aubin de Teran, Lisa 1953-
See Teran, Lisa St. Aubin de
See also CA 118; 126

Sainte-Beuve, Charles Augustin
1804-1869 . . . . **NCLC 5**

Saint-Exupery, Antoine (Jean Baptiste Marie Roger) de 1900-1944 . . . . **TCLC 2**
See also CA 108; 132; CLR 10; DLB 72; MAICYA; MTCW; SATA 20; WLC

St. John, David
See Hunt, E(verette) Howard, Jr.

Saint-John Perse
See Leger, (Marie-Rene Auguste) Alexis Saint-Leger

Saintsbury, George (Edward Bateman)
1845-1933 . . . . **TCLC 31**
See also DLB 57

Sait Faik . . . . **TCLC 23**
See also Abasiyanik, Sait Faik

Saki .... **TCLC 3; SSC 12**
See also Munro, H(ector) H(ugh)

Salama, Hannu 1936-............. **CLC 18**

Salamanca, J(ack) R(ichard)
1922-..................... **CLC 4, 15**
See also CA 25-28R

Sale, J. Kirkpatrick
See Sale, Kirkpatrick

Sale, Kirkpatrick 1937-........... **CLC 68**
See also CA 13-16R; CANR 10

Salinas (y Serrano), Pedro
1891(?)-1951 .... **TCLC 17**
See also CA 117; DLB 134

Salinger, J(erome) D(avid)
1919-.... **CLC 1, 3, 8, 12, 55, 56; SSC 2**
See also AAYA 2; CA 5-8R; CANR 39; CDALB 1941-1968; CLR 18; DA; DLB 2, 102; MAICYA; MTCW; SATA 67; WLC

Salisbury, John
See Caute, David

Salter, James 1925-......... **CLC 7, 52, 59**
See also CA 73-76; DLB 130

Saltus, Edgar (Everton)
1855-1921 .... **TCLC 8**
See also CA 105

Saltykov, Mikhail Evgrafovich
1826-1889 .... **NCLC 16**

Samarakis, Antonis 1919-.......... **CLC 5**
See also CA 25-28R; CAAS 16; CANR 36

Sanchez, Florencio 1875-1910..... **TCLC 37**
See also HW

Sanchez, Luis Rafael 1936-........ **CLC 23**
See also CA 128; HW

Sanchez, Sonia 1934-.............. **CLC 5**
See also BLC 3; BW; CA 33-36R; CANR 24; CLR 18; DLB 41; DLBD 8; MAICYA; MTCW; SATA 22

Sand, George 1804-1876....... **NCLC 2, 42**
See also DA; DLB 119; WLC

Sandburg, Carl (August)
1878-1967 ... **CLC 1, 4, 10, 15, 35; PC 2**
See also CA 5-8R; 25-28R; CANR 35; CDALB 1865-1917; DA; DLB 17, 54; MAICYA; MTCW; SATA 8; WLC

Sandburg, Charles
See Sandburg, Carl (August)

Sandburg, Charles A.
See Sandburg, Carl (August)

Sanders, (James) Ed(ward) 1939- ... **CLC 53**
See also CA 13-16R; CANR 13; DLB 16

Sanders, Lawrence 1920-.......... **CLC 41**
See also BEST 89:4; CA 81-84; CANR 33; MTCW

Sanders, Noah
See Blount, Roy (Alton), Jr.

Sanders, Winston P.
See Anderson, Poul (William)

Sandoz, Mari(e Susette)
1896-1966 .... **CLC 28**
See also CA 1-4R; 25-28R; CANR 17; DLB 9; MTCW; SATA 5

Saner, Reg(inald Anthony) 1931- .... **CLC 9**
See also CA 65-68

Sannazaro, Jacopo 1456(?)-1530...... **LC 8**

Sansom, William 1912-1976....... **CLC 2, 6**
See also CA 5-8R; 65-68; CANR 42; MTCW

Santayana, George 1863-1952..... **TCLC 40**
See also CA 115; DLB 54, 71

Santiago, Danny .... **CLC 33**
See also James, Daniel (Lewis); James, Daniel (Lewis)
See also DLB 122

Santmyer, Helen Hooven
1895-1986 .... **CLC 33**
See also CA 1-4R; 118; CANR 15, 33; DLBY 84; MTCW

Santos, Bienvenido N(uqui) 1911-... **CLC 22**
See also CA 101; CANR 19

Sapper .... **TCLC 44**
See also McNeile, Herman Cyril

Sappho fl. 6th cent. B.C.-.... **CMLC 3; PC 5**

Sarduy, Severo 1937-1993.......... **CLC 6**
See also CA 89-92; 142; DLB 113; HW

Sargeson, Frank 1903-1982........ **CLC 31**
See also CA 25-28R; 106; CANR 38

Sarmiento, Felix Ruben Garcia
See Dario, Ruben

Saroyan, William
1908-1981 ..... **CLC 1, 8, 10, 29, 34, 56**
See also CA 5-8R; 103; CANR 30; DA; DLB 7, 9, 86; DLBY 81; MTCW; SATA 23, 24; WLC

Sarraute, Nathalie
1900-........ **CLC 1, 2, 4, 8, 10, 31, 80**
See also CA 9-12R; CANR 23; DLB 83; MTCW

Sarton, (Eleanor) May
1912-.................. **CLC 4, 14, 49**
See also CA 1-4R; CANR 1, 34; DLB 48; DLBY 81; MTCW; SATA 36

Sartre, Jean-Paul
1905-1980 .... **CLC 1, 4, 7, 9, 13, 18, 24, 44, 50, 52; DC 3**
See also CA 9-12R; 97-100; CANR 21; DA; DLB 72; MTCW; WLC

Sassoon, Siegfried (Lorraine)
1886-1967 .... **CLC 36**
See also CA 104; 25-28R; CANR 36; DLB 20; MTCW

Satterfield, Charles
See Pohl, Frederik

Saul, John (W. III) 1942- .... **CLC 46**
See also AAYA 10; BEST 90:4; CA 81-84; CANR 16, 40

Saunders, Caleb
See Heinlein, Robert A(nson)

Saura (Atares), Carlos 1932-....... **CLC 20**
See also CA 114; 131; HW

Sauser-Hall, Frederic 1887-1961.... **CLC 18**
See also CA 102; 93-96; CANR 36; MTCW

Saussure, Ferdinand de
1857-1913 .... **TCLC 49**

Savage, Catharine
See Brosman, Catharine Savage

Savage, Thomas 1915-............ **CLC 40**
See also CA 126; 132; CAAS 15

Savan, Glenn .... **CLC 50**

Saven, Glenn 19(?)- .... **CLC 50**

Sayers, Dorothy L(eigh)
1893-1957 .... **TCLC 2, 15**
See also CA 104; 119; CDBLB 1914-1945; DLB 10, 36, 77, 100; MTCW

Sayers, Valerie 1952-............. **CLC 50**
See also CA 134

Sayles, John (Thomas)
1950-.................. **CLC 7, 10, 14**
See also CA 57-60; CANR 41; DLB 44

Scammell, Michael .... **CLC 34**

Scannell, Vernon 1922- .... **CLC 49**
See also CA 5-8R; CANR 8, 24; DLB 27; SATA 59

Scarlett, Susan
See Streatfeild, (Mary) Noel

Schaeffer, Susan Fromberg
1941-.................. **CLC 6, 11, 22**
See also CA 49-52; CANR 18; DLB 28; MTCW; SATA 22

Schary, Jill
See Robinson, Jill

Schell, Jonathan 1943-............ **CLC 35**
See also CA 73-76; CANR 12

Schelling, Friedrich Wilhelm Joseph von
1775-1854 .... **NCLC 30**
See also DLB 90

Scherer, Jean-Marie Maurice 1920-
See Rohmer, Eric
See also CA 110

Schevill, James (Erwin) 1920-....... **CLC 7**
See also CA 5-8R; CAAS 12

Schiller, Friedrich 1759-1805 .... **NCLC 39**
See also DLB 94

Schisgal, Murray (Joseph) 1926-..... **CLC 6**
See also CA 21-24R

Schlee, Ann 1934-................ **CLC 35**
See also CA 101; CANR 29; SATA 36, 44

Schlegel, August Wilhelm von
1767-1845 .... **NCLC 15**
See also DLB 94

Schlegel, Johann Elias (von)
1719(?)-1749 .... **LC 5**

Schmidt, Arno (Otto) 1914-1979.... **CLC 56**
See also CA 128; 109; DLB 69

Schmitz, Aron Hector 1861-1928
See Svevo, Italo
See also CA 104; 122; MTCW

Schnackenberg, Gjertrud 1953-..... **CLC 40**
See also CA 116; DLB 120

Schneider, Leonard Alfred 1925-1966
See Bruce, Lenny
See also CA 89-92

Schnitzler, Arthur 1862-1931 ...... **TCLC 4**
See also CA 104; DLB 81, 118

Schor, Sandra (M.) 1932(?)-1990 ... **CLC 65**
See also CA 132

Schorer, Mark 1908-1977 .... **CLC 9**
See also CA 5-8R; 73-76; CANR 7; DLB 103

Schrader, Paul (Joseph) 1946-...... **CLC 26**
See also CA 37-40R; CANR 41; DLB 44

Schreiner, Olive (Emilie Albertina) 1855-1920 .... **TCLC 9**
See also CA 105; DLB 18

Schulberg, Budd (Wilson) 1914- .... **CLC 7, 48**
See also CA 25-28R; CANR 19; DLB 6, 26, 28; DLBY 81

Schulz, Bruno 1892-1942 .... **TCLC 5, 51; SSC 13**
See also CA 115; 123

Schulz, Charles M(onroe) 1922- .... **CLC 12**
See also CA 9-12R; CANR 6; SATA 10

Schumacher, Ernst Friedrich 1911-1977 .... **CLC 80**
See also CA 81-84; 73-76; CANR 34

Schuyler, James Marcus 1923-1991 .... **CLC 5, 23**
See also CA 101; 134; DLB 5

Schwartz, Delmore (David) 1913-1966 .... **CLC 2, 4, 10, 45**
See also CA 17-18; 25-28R; CANR 35; CAP 2; DLB 28, 48; MTCW

Schwartz, Ernst
See Ozu, Yasujiro

Schwartz, John Burnham 1965- .... **CLC 59**
See also CA 132

Schwartz, Lynne Sharon 1939- ..... **CLC 31**
See also CA 103

Schwartz, Muriel A.
See Eliot, T(homas) S(tearns)

Schwarz-Bart, Andre 1928- .... **CLC 2, 4**
See also CA 89-92

Schwarz-Bart, Simone 1938- .... **CLC 7**
See also CA 97-100

Schwob, (Mayer Andre) Marcel 1867-1905 .... **TCLC 20**
See also CA 117; DLB 123

Sciascia, Leonardo 1921-1989 .... **CLC 8, 9, 41**
See also CA 85-88; 130; CANR 35; MTCW

Scoppettone, Sandra 1936- .... **CLC 26**
See also CA 5-8R; CANR 41; SATA 9

Scorsese, Martin 1942- .... **CLC 20**
See also CA 110; 114

Scotland, Jay
See Jakes, John (William)

Scott, Duncan Campbell 1862-1947 .... **TCLC 6**
See also CA 104; DLB 92

Scott, Evelyn 1893-1963 .... **CLC 43**
See also CA 104; 112; DLB 9, 48

Scott, F(rancis) R(eginald) 1899-1985 .... **CLC 22**
See also CA 101; 114; DLB 88

Scott, Frank
See Scott, F(rancis) R(eginald)

Scott, Joanna 1960- .... **CLC 50**
See also CA 126

Scott, Paul (Mark) 1920-1978 .... **CLC 9, 60**
See also CA 81-84; 77-80; CANR 33; DLB 14; MTCW

Scott, Walter 1771-1832 .... **NCLC 15**
See also CDBLB 1789-1832; DA; DLB 93, 107, 116; WLC; YABC 2

Scribe, (Augustin) Eugene 1791-1861 .... **NCLC 16**

Scrum, R.
See Crumb, R(obert)

Scudery, Madeleine de 1607-1701 ..... **LC 2**

Scum
See Crumb, R(obert)

Scumbag, Little Bobby
See Crumb, R(obert)

Seabrook, John
See Hubbard, L(afayette) Ron(ald)

Sealy, I. Allan 1951- .... **CLC 55**

Search, Alexander
See Pessoa, Fernando (Antonio Nogueira)

Sebastian, Lee
See Silverberg, Robert

Sebastian Owl
See Thompson, Hunter S(tockton)

Sebestyen, Ouida 1924- .... **CLC 30**
See also AAYA 8; CA 107; CANR 40; CLR 17; JRDA; MAICYA; SAAS 10; SATA 39

Secundus, H. Scriblerus
See Fielding, Henry

Sedges, John
See Buck, Pearl S(ydenstricker)

Sedgwick, Catharine Maria 1789-1867 .... **NCLC 19**
See also DLB 1, 74

Seelye, John 1931- .... **CLC 7**

Seferiades, Giorgos Stylianou 1900-1971
See Seferis, George
See also CA 5-8R; 33-36R; CANR 5, 36; MTCW

Seferis, George .... **CLC 5, 11**
See also Seferiades, Giorgos Stylianou

Segal, Erich (Wolf) 1937- .... **CLC 3, 10**
See also BEST 89:1; CA 25-28R; CANR 20, 36; DLBY 86; MTCW

Seger, Bob 1945- .... **CLC 35**

Seghers, Anna .... **CLC 7**
See also Radvanyi, Netty
See also DLB 69

Seidel, Frederick (Lewis) 1936- ..... **CLC 18**
See also CA 13-16R; CANR 8; DLBY 84

Seifert, Jaroslav 1901-1986 ..... **CLC 34, 44**
See also CA 127; MTCW

Sei Shonagon c. 966-1017(?) ...... **CMLC 6**

Selby, Hubert, Jr. 1928- ..... **CLC 1, 2, 4, 8**
See also CA 13-16R; CANR 33; DLB 2

Selzer, Richard 1928- .... **CLC 74**
See also CA 65-68; CANR 14

Sembene, Ousmane
See Ousmane, Sembene

Senancour, Etienne Pivert de 1770-1846 .... **NCLC 16**
See also DLB 119

Sender, Ramon (Jose) 1902-1982 .... **CLC 8**
See also CA 5-8R; 105; CANR 8; HW; MTCW

Seneca, Lucius Annaeus 4B.C.-65 .... **CMLC 6**

Senghor, Leopold Sedar 1906- ...... **CLC 54**
See also BLC 3; BW; CA 116; 125; MTCW

Serling, (Edward) Rod(man) 1924-1975 .... **CLC 30**
See also AITN 1; CA 65-68; 57-60; DLB 26

Serna, Ramon Gomez de la
See Gomez de la Serna, Ramon

Serpieres
See Guillevic, (Eugene)

Service, Robert
See Service, Robert W(illiam)
See also DLB 92

Service, Robert W(illiam) 1874(?)-1958 .... **TCLC 15**
See also Service, Robert
See also CA 115; 140; DA; SATA 20; WLC

Seth, Vikram 1952- .... **CLC 43**
See also CA 121; 127; DLB 120

Seton, Cynthia Propper 1926-1982 .... **CLC 27**
See also CA 5-8R; 108; CANR 7

Seton, Ernest (Evan) Thompson 1860-1946 .... **TCLC 31**
See also CA 109; DLB 92; JRDA; SATA 18

Seton-Thompson, Ernest
See Seton, Ernest (Evan) Thompson

Settle, Mary Lee 1918- .... **CLC 19, 61**
See also CA 89-92; CAAS 1; DLB 6

Seuphor, Michel
See Arp, Jean

Sevigne, Marie (de Rabutin-Chantal) Marquise de 1626-1696 .... **LC 11**

Sexton, Anne (Harvey) 1928-1974 .... **CLC 2, 4, 6, 8, 10, 15, 53; PC 2**
See also CA 1-4R; 53-56; CABS 2; CANR 3, 36; CDALB 1941-1968; DA; DLB 5; MTCW; SATA 10; WLC

Shaara, Michael (Joseph Jr.) 1929-1988 .... **CLC 15**
See also AITN 1; CA 102; DLBY 83

Shackleton, C. C.
See Aldiss, Brian W(ilson)

Shacochis, Bob .... **CLC 39**
See also Shacochis, Robert G.

Shacochis, Robert G. 1951-
See Shacochis, Bob
See also CA 119; 124

Shaffer, Anthony (Joshua) 1926- .... **CLC 19**
See also CA 110; 116; DLB 13

Shaffer, Peter (Levin) 1926- .... **CLC 5, 14, 18, 37, 60**
See also CA 25-28R; CANR 25; CDBLB 1960 to Present; DLB 13; MTCW

Shakey, Bernard
See Young, Neil

Shalamov, Varlam (Tikhonovich) 1907(?)-1982 .... **CLC 18**
See also CA 129; 105

Shamlu, Ahmad 1925- .... **CLC 10**

Shammas, Anton 1951- .... **CLC 55**

Shange, Ntozake
1948- . . . . **CLC 8, 25, 38, 74; DC 3**
See also AAYA 9; BLC 3; BW; CA 85-88; CABS 3; CANR 27; DLB 38; MTCW

Shanley, John Patrick 1950- . . . . **CLC 75**
See also CA 128; 133

Shapcott, Thomas William 1935- . . . **CLC 38**
See also CA 69-72

Shapiro, Jane . . . . **CLC 76**

Shapiro, Karl (Jay) 1913- . . **CLC 4, 8, 15, 53**
See also CA 1-4R; CAAS 6; CANR 1, 36; DLB 48; MTCW

Sharp, William 1855-1905 . . . . **TCLC 39**

Sharpe, Thomas Ridley 1928-
See Sharpe, Tom
See also CA 114; 122

Sharpe, Tom . . . . **CLC 36**
See also Sharpe, Thomas Ridley
See also DLB 14

Shaw, Bernard . . . . **TCLC 45**
See also Shaw, George Bernard

Shaw, G. Bernard
See Shaw, George Bernard

Shaw, George Bernard
1856-1950 . . . . **TCLC 3, 9, 21**
See also Shaw, Bernard
See also CA 104; 128; CDBLB 1914-1945; DA; DLB 10, 57; MTCW; WLC

Shaw, Henry Wheeler
1818-1885 . . . . **NCLC 15**
See also DLB 11

Shaw, Irwin 1913-1984. . . . . . . **CLC 7, 23, 34**
See also AITN 1; CA 13-16R; 112; CANR 21; CDALB 1941-1968; DLB 6, 102; DLBY 84; MTCW

Shaw, Robert 1927-1978 . . . . **CLC 5**
See also AITN 1; CA 1-4R; 81-84; CANR 4; DLB 13, 14

Shaw, T. E.
See Lawrence, T(homas) E(dward)

Shawn, Wallace 1943- . . . . **CLC 41**
See also CA 112

Sheed, Wilfrid (John Joseph)
1930- . . . . **CLC 2, 4, 10, 53**
See also CA 65-68; CANR 30; DLB 6; MTCW

Sheldon, Alice Hastings Bradley
1915(?)-1987
See Tiptree, James, Jr.
See also CA 108; 122; CANR 34; MTCW

Sheldon, John
See Bloch, Robert (Albert)

Shelley, Mary Wollstonecraft (Godwin)
1797-1851 . . . . **NCLC 14**
See also CDBLB 1789-1832; DA; DLB 110, 116; SATA 29; WLC

Shelley, Percy Bysshe
1792-1822 . . . . **NCLC 18**
See also CDBLB 1789-1832; DA; DLB 96, 110; WLC

Shepard, Jim 1956- . . . . **CLC 36**
See also CA 137

Shepard, Lucius 1947- . . . . **CLC 34**
See also CA 128; 141

Shepard, Sam
1943- . . . . **CLC 4, 6, 17, 34, 41, 44**
See also AAYA 1; CA 69-72; CABS 3; CANR 22; DLB 7; MTCW

Shepherd, Michael
See Ludlum, Robert

Sherburne, Zoa (Morin) 1912- . . . . . . **CLC 30**
See also CA 1-4R; CANR 3, 37; MAICYA; SATA 3

Sheridan, Frances 1724-1766. . . . . **LC 7**
See also DLB 39, 84

Sheridan, Richard Brinsley
1751-1816 . . . . **NCLC 5; DC 1**
See also CDBLB 1660-1789; DA; DLB 89; WLC

Sherman, Jonathan Marc . . . . **CLC 55**

Sherman, Martin 1941(?)- . . . . **CLC 19**
See also CA 116; 123

Sherwin, Judith Johnson 1936- . . . **CLC 7, 15**
See also CA 25-28R; CANR 34

Sherwood, Robert E(mmet)
1896-1955 . . . . **TCLC 3**
See also CA 104; DLB 7, 26

Shiel, M(atthew) P(hipps)
1865-1947 . . . . **TCLC 8**
See also CA 106

Shiga, Naoya 1883-1971. . . . . **CLC 33**
See also CA 101; 33-36R

Shimazaki Haruki 1872-1943
See Shimazaki Toson
See also CA 105; 134

Shimazaki Toson . . . . **TCLC 5**
See also Shimazaki Haruki

Sholokhov, Mikhail (Aleksandrovich)
1905-1984 . . . . **CLC 7, 15**
See also CA 101; 112; MTCW; SATA 36

Shone, Patric
See Hanley, James

Shreve, Susan Richards 1939- . . . . . . **CLC 23**
See also CA 49-52; CAAS 5; CANR 5, 38; MAICYA; SATA 41, 46

Shue, Larry 1946-1985. . . . . **CLC 52**
See also CA 117

Shu-Jen, Chou 1881-1936
See Hsun, Lu
See also CA 104

Shulman, Alix Kates 1932- . . . . . . **CLC 2, 10**
See also CA 29-32R; CANR 43; SATA 7

Shuster, Joe 1914- . . . . **CLC 21**

Shute, Nevil . . . . **CLC 30**
See also Norway, Nevil Shute

Shuttle, Penelope (Diane) 1947- . . . . . **CLC 7**
See also CA 93-96; CANR 39; DLB 14, 40

Sidney, Mary 1561-1621 . . . . **LC 19**

Sidney, Sir Philip 1554-1586. . . . . **LC 19**
See also CDBLB Before 1660; DA

Siegel, Jerome 1914- . . . . **CLC 21**
See also CA 116

Siegel, Jerry
See Siegel, Jerome

Sienkiewicz, Henryk (Adam Alexander Pius)
1846-1916 . . . . **TCLC 3**
See also CA 104; 134

Sierra, Gregorio Martinez
See Martinez Sierra, Gregorio

Sierra, Maria (de la O'LeJarraga) Martinez
See Martinez Sierra, Maria (de la O'LeJarraga)

Sigal, Clancy 1926-. . . . . **CLC 7**
See also CA 1-4R

Sigourney, Lydia Howard (Huntley)
1791-1865 . . . . **NCLC 21**
See also DLB 1, 42, 73

Siguenza y Gongora, Carlos de
1645-1700 . . . . **LC 8**

Sigurjonsson, Johann 1880-1919. . . **TCLC 27**

Sikelianos, Angelos 1884-1951 . . . . **TCLC 39**

Silkin, Jon 1930- . . . . **CLC 2, 6, 43**
See also CA 5-8R; CAAS 5; DLB 27

Silko, Leslie Marmon 1948- . . . . **CLC 23, 74**
See also CA 115; 122; DA

Sillanpaa, Frans Eemil 1888-1964. . . **CLC 19**
See also CA 129; 93-96; MTCW

Sillitoe, Alan
1928- . . . . **CLC 1, 3, 6, 10, 19, 57**
See also AITN 1; CA 9-12R; CAAS 2; CANR 8, 26; CDBLB 1960 to Present; DLB 14; MTCW; SATA 61

Silone, Ignazio 1900-1978 . . . . **CLC 4**
See also CA 25-28; 81-84; CANR 34; CAP 2; MTCW

Silver, Joan Micklin 1935- . . . . **CLC 20**
See also CA 114; 121

Silver, Nicholas
See Faust, Frederick (Schiller)

Silverberg, Robert 1935- . . . . **CLC 7**
See also CA 1-4R; CAAS 3; CANR 1, 20, 36; DLB 8; MAICYA; MTCW; SATA 13

Silverstein, Alvin 1933- . . . . **CLC 17**
See also CA 49-52; CANR 2; CLR 25; JRDA; MAICYA; SATA 8, 69

Silverstein, Virginia B(arbara Opshelor)
1937- . . . . **CLC 17**
See also CA 49-52; CANR 2; CLR 25; JRDA; MAICYA; SATA 8, 69

Sim, Georges
See Simenon, Georges (Jacques Christian)

Simak, Clifford D(onald)
1904-1988 . . . . **CLC 1, 55**
See also CA 1-4R; 125; CANR 1, 35; DLB 8; MTCW; SATA 56

Simenon, Georges (Jacques Christian)
1903-1989 . . . . **CLC 1, 2, 3, 8, 18, 47**
See also CA 85-88; 129; CANR 35; DLB 72; DLBY 89; MTCW

Simic, Charles 1938- . . . **CLC 6, 9, 22, 49, 68**
See also CA 29-32R; CAAS 4; CANR 12, 33; DLB 105

Simmons, Charles (Paul) 1924- . . . . . **CLC 57**
See also CA 89-92

Simmons, Dan 1948-. . . . . **CLC 44**
See also CA 138

Simmons, James (Stewart Alexander)
1933- . . . . **CLC 43**
See also CA 105; DLB 40

Simms, William Gilmore 1806-1870 .... **NCLC 3**
See also DLB 3, 30, 59, 73

Simon, Carly 1945-............... **CLC 26**
See also CA 105

Simon, Claude 1913-....... **CLC 4, 9, 15, 39**
See also CA 89-92; CANR 33; DLB 83; MTCW

Simon, (Marvin) Neil 1927- .... **CLC 6, 11, 31, 39, 70**
See also AITN 1; CA 21-24R; CANR 26; DLB 7; MTCW

Simon, Paul 1942(?)- .... **CLC 17**
See also CA 116

Simonon, Paul 1956(?)- .... **CLC 30**
See also Clash, The

Simpson, Harriette
See Arnow, Harriette (Louisa) Simpson

Simpson, Louis (Aston Marantz) 1923- .... **CLC 4, 7, 9, 32**
See also CA 1-4R; CAAS 4; CANR 1; DLB 5; MTCW

Simpson, Mona (Elizabeth) 1957-... **CLC 44**
See also CA 122; 135

Simpson, N(orman) F(rederick) 1919- .... **CLC 29**
See also CA 13-16R; DLB 13

Sinclair, Andrew (Annandale) 1935- .... **CLC 2, 14**
See also CA 9-12R; CAAS 5; CANR 14, 38; DLB 14; MTCW

Sinclair, Emil
See Hesse, Hermann

Sinclair, Iain 1943-............... **CLC 76**
See also CA 132

Sinclair, Iain MacGregor
See Sinclair, Iain

Sinclair, Mary Amelia St. Clair 1865(?)-1946
See Sinclair, May
See also CA 104

Sinclair, May.................. **TCLC 3, 11**
See also Sinclair, Mary Amelia St. Clair
See also DLB 36

Sinclair, Upton (Beall) 1878-1968 .... **CLC 1, 11, 15, 63**
See also CA 5-8R; 25-28R; CANR 7; CDALB 1929-1941; DA; DLB 9; MTCW; SATA 9; WLC

Singer, Isaac
See Singer, Isaac Bashevis

Singer, Isaac Bashevis 1904-1991 .... **CLC 1, 3, 6, 9, 11, 15, 23, 38, 69; SSC 3**
See also AITN 1, 2; CA 1-4R; 134; CANR 1, 39; CDALB 1941-1968; CLR 1; DA; DLB 6, 28, 52; DLBY 91; JRDA; MAICYA; MTCW; SATA 3, 27; SATA-Obit 68; WLC

Singer, Israel Joshua 1893-1944... **TCLC 33**

Singh, Khushwant 1915-........... **CLC 11**
See also CA 9-12R; CAAS 9; CANR 6

Sinjohn, John
See Galsworthy, John

Sinyavsky, Andrei (Donatevich) 1925- .... **CLC 8**
See also CA 85-88

Sirin, V.
See Nabokov, Vladimir (Vladimirovich)

Sissman, L(ouis) E(dward) 1928-1976 .... **CLC 9, 18**
See also CA 21-24R; 65-68; CANR 13; DLB 5

Sisson, C(harles) H(ubert) 1914-..... **CLC 8**
See also CA 1-4R; CAAS 3; CANR 3; DLB 27

Sitwell, Dame Edith 1887-1964 .... **CLC 2, 9, 67; PC 3**
See also CA 9-12R; CANR 35; CDBLB 1945-1960; DLB 20; MTCW

Sjoewall, Maj 1935-............... **CLC 7**
See also CA 65-68

Sjowall, Maj
See Sjoewall, Maj

Skelton, Robin 1925-............. **CLC 13**
See also AITN 2; CA 5-8R; CAAS 5; CANR 28; DLB 27, 53

Skolimowski, Jerzy 1938- .... **CLC 20**
See also CA 128

Skram, Amalie (Bertha) 1847-1905 .... **TCLC 25**

Skvorecky, Josef (Vaclav) 1924- .... **CLC 15, 39, 69**
See also CA 61-64; CAAS 1; CANR 10, 34; MTCW

Slade, Bernard................. **CLC 11, 46**
See also Newbound, Bernard Slade
See also CAAS 9; DLB 53

Slaughter, Carolyn 1946-.......... **CLC 56**
See also CA 85-88

Slaughter, Frank G(ill) 1908- ...... **CLC 29**
See also AITN 2; CA 5-8R; CANR 5

Slavitt, David R(ytman) 1935-.... **CLC 5, 14**
See also CA 21-24R; CAAS 3; CANR 41; DLB 5, 6

Slesinger, Tess 1905-1945 .... **TCLC 10**
See also CA 107; DLB 102

Slessor, Kenneth 1901-1971........ **CLC 14**
See also CA 102; 89-92

Slowacki, Juliusz 1809-1849 ..... **NCLC 15**

Smart, Christopher 1722-1771........ **LC 3**
See also DLB 109

Smart, Elizabeth 1913-1986........ **CLC 54**
See also CA 81-84; 118; DLB 88

Smiley, Jane (Graves) 1949- .... **CLC 53, 76**
See also CA 104; CANR 30

Smith, A(rthur) J(ames) M(arshall) 1902-1980 .... **CLC 15**
See also CA 1-4R; 102; CANR 4; DLB 88

Smith, Betty (Wehner) 1896-1972... **CLC 19**
See also CA 5-8R; 33-36R; DLBY 82; SATA 6

Smith, Charlotte (Turner) 1749-1806 .... **NCLC 23**
See also DLB 39, 109

Smith, Clark Ashton 1893-1961 .... **CLC 43**

Smith, Dave................... **CLC 22, 42**
See also Smith, David (Jeddie)
See also CAAS 7; DLB 5

Smith, David (Jeddie) 1942-
See Smith, Dave
See also CA 49-52; CANR 1

Smith, Florence Margaret 1902-1971 .... **CLC 8**
See also Smith, Stevie
See also CA 17-18; 29-32R; CANR 35; CAP 2; MTCW

Smith, Iain Crichton 1928- .... **CLC 64**
See also CA 21-24R; DLB 40

Smith, John 1580(?)-1631 .... **LC 9**

Smith, Johnston
See Crane, Stephen (Townley)

Smith, Lee 1944-.............. **CLC 25, 73**
See also CA 114; 119; DLBY 83

Smith, Martin
See Smith, Martin Cruz

Smith, Martin Cruz 1942-......... **CLC 25**
See also BEST 89:4; CA 85-88; CANR 6, 23, 43

Smith, Mary-Ann Tirone 1944-..... **CLC 39**
See also CA 118; 136

Smith, Patti 1946- .... **CLC 12**
See also CA 93-96

Smith, Pauline (Urmson) 1882-1959 .... **TCLC 25**

Smith, Rosamond
See Oates, Joyce Carol

Smith, Sheila Kaye
See Kaye-Smith, Sheila

Smith, Stevie.............. **CLC 3, 8, 25, 44**
See also Smith, Florence Margaret
See also DLB 20

Smith, Wilbur A(ddison) 1933-..... **CLC 33**
See also CA 13-16R; CANR 7; MTCW

Smith, William Jay 1918- .... **CLC 6**
See also CA 5-8R; DLB 5; MAICYA; SATA 2, 68

Smith, Woodrow Wilson
See Kuttner, Henry

Smolenskin, Peretz 1842-1885.... **NCLC 30**

Smollett, Tobias (George) 1721-1771 .. **LC 2**
See also CDBLB 1660-1789; DLB 39, 104

Snodgrass, W(illiam) D(e Witt) 1926- .... **CLC 2, 6, 10, 18, 68**
See also CA 1-4R; CANR 6, 36; DLB 5; MTCW

Snow, C(harles) P(ercy) 1905-1980 .... **CLC 1, 4, 6, 9, 13, 19**
See also CA 5-8R; 101; CANR 28; CDBLB 1945-1960; DLB 15, 77; MTCW

Snow, Frances Compton
See Adams, Henry (Brooks)

Snyder, Gary (Sherman) 1930- .... **CLC 1, 2, 5, 9, 32**
See also CA 17-20R; CANR 30; DLB 5, 16

Snyder, Zilpha Keatley 1927-...... **CLC 17**
See also CA 9-12R; CANR 38; CLR 31; JRDA; MAICYA; SAAS 2; SATA 1, 28, 75

Soares, Bernardo
See Pessoa, Fernando (Antonio Nogueira)

Sobh, A.
See Shamlu, Ahmad

Sobol, Joshua . . . . **CLC 60**

Soderberg, Hjalmar 1869-1941 . . . . **TCLC 39**

Sodergran, Edith (Irene)
See Soedergran, Edith (Irene)

Soedergran, Edith (Irene)
1892-1923 . . . . **TCLC 31**

Softly, Edgar
See Lovecraft, H(oward) P(hillips)

Softly, Edward
See Lovecraft, H(oward) P(hillips)

Sokolov, Raymond 1941- . . . . **CLC 7**
See also CA 85-88

Solo, Jay
See Ellison, Harlan

Sologub, Fyodor . . . . **TCLC 9**
See also Teternikov, Fyodor Kuzmich

Solomons, Ikey Esquir
See Thackeray, William Makepeace

Solomos, Dionysios 1798-1857 . . . **NCLC 15**

Solwoska, Mara
See French, Marilyn

Solzhenitsyn, Aleksandr I(sayevich)
1918- . . . . . . **CLC 1, 2, 4, 7, 9, 10, 18, 26, 34, 78**
See also AITN 1; CA 69-72; CANR 40; DA; MTCW; WLC

Somers, Jane
See Lessing, Doris (May)

Somerville, Edith 1858-1949 . . . . . . **TCLC 51**

Somerville & Ross
See Martin, Violet Florence; Somerville, Edith

Sommer, Scott 1951- . . . . **CLC 25**
See also CA 106

Sondheim, Stephen (Joshua)
1930- . . . . **CLC 30, 39**
See also CA 103

Sontag, Susan 1933- . . . **CLC 1, 2, 10, 13, 31**
See also CA 17-20R; CANR 25; DLB 2, 67; MTCW

Sophocles
496(?)B.C.-406(?)B.C. . . . **CMLC 2; DC 1**
See also DA

Sorel, Julia
See Drexler, Rosalyn

Sorrentino, Gilbert
1929- . . . . **CLC 3, 7, 14, 22, 40**
See also CA 77-80; CANR 14, 33; DLB 5; DLBY 80

Soto, Gary 1952-. . . . . **CLC 32, 80**
See also AAYA 10; CA 119; 125; DLB 82; HW; JRDA

Soupault, Philippe 1897-1990 . . . . . . **CLC 68**
See also CA 116; 131

Souster, (Holmes) Raymond
1921- . . . . **CLC 5, 14**
See also CA 13-16R; CAAS 14; CANR 13, 29; DLB 88; SATA 63

Southern, Terry 1926- . . . . **CLC 7**
See also CA 1-4R; CANR 1; DLB 2

Southey, Robert 1774-1843 . . . . **NCLC 8**
See also DLB 93, 107; SATA 54

Southworth, Emma Dorothy Eliza Nevitte
1819-1899 . . . . **NCLC 26**

Souza, Ernest
See Scott, Evelyn

Soyinka, Wole
1934- . . . . **CLC 3, 5, 14, 36, 44; DC 2**
See also BLC 3; BW; CA 13-16R; CANR 27, 39; DA; DLB 125; MTCW; WLC

Spackman, W(illiam) M(ode)
1905-1990 . . . . **CLC 46**
See also CA 81-84; 132

Spacks, Barry 1931-. . . . . **CLC 14**
See also CA 29-32R; CANR 33; DLB 105

Spanidou, Irini 1946- . . . . **CLC 44**

Spark, Muriel (Sarah)
1918- . . . . **CLC 2, 3, 5, 8, 13, 18, 40; SSC 10**
See also CA 5-8R; CANR 12, 36; CDBLB 1945-1960; DLB 15; MTCW

Spaulding, Douglas
See Bradbury, Ray (Douglas)

Spaulding, Leonard
See Bradbury, Ray (Douglas)

Spence, J. A. D.
See Eliot, T(homas) S(tearns)

Spencer, Elizabeth 1921- . . . . **CLC 22**
See also CA 13-16R; CANR 32; DLB 6; MTCW; SATA 14

Spencer, Leonard G.
See Silverberg, Robert

Spencer, Scott 1945-. . . . . **CLC 30**
See also CA 113; DLBY 86

Spender, Stephen (Harold)
1909- . . . . **CLC 1, 2, 5, 10, 41**
See also CA 9-12R; CANR 31; CDBLB 1945-1960; DLB 20; MTCW

Spengler, Oswald (Arnold Gottfried)
1880-1936 . . . . **TCLC 25**
See also CA 118

Spenser, Edmund 1552(?)-1599 . . . . **LC 5**
See also CDBLB Before 1660; DA; WLC

Spicer, Jack 1925-1965 . . . . . . **CLC 8, 18, 72**
See also CA 85-88; DLB 5, 16

Spiegelman, Art 1948- . . . . **CLC 76**
See also AAYA 10; CA 125; CANR 41

Spielberg, Peter 1929- . . . . **CLC 6**
See also CA 5-8R; CANR 4; DLBY 81

Spielberg, Steven 1947- . . . . **CLC 20**
See also AAYA 8; CA 77-80; CANR 32; SATA 32

Spillane, Frank Morrison 1918-
See Spillane, Mickey
See also CA 25-28R; CANR 28; MTCW; SATA 66

Spillane, Mickey . . . . **CLC 3, 13**
See also Spillane, Frank Morrison

Spinoza, Benedictus de 1632-1677 . . . . **LC 9**

Spinrad, Norman (Richard) 1940- . . . **CLC 46**
See also CA 37-40R; CANR 20; DLB 8

Spitteler, Carl (Friedrich Georg)
1845-1924 . . . . **TCLC 12**
See also CA 109; DLB 129

Spivack, Kathleen (Romola Drucker)
1938- . . . . **CLC 6**
See also CA 49-52

Spoto, Donald 1941-. . . . . **CLC 39**
See also CA 65-68; CANR 11

Springsteen, Bruce (F.) 1949- . . . . . . **CLC 17**
See also CA 111

Spurling, Hilary 1940-. . . . . **CLC 34**
See also CA 104; CANR 25

Squires, (James) Radcliffe
1917-1993 . . . . **CLC 51**
See also CA 1-4R; 140; CANR 6, 21

Srivastava, Dhanpat Rai 1880(?)-1936
See Premchand
See also CA 118

Stacy, Donald
See Pohl, Frederik

Stael, Germaine de
See Stael-Holstein, Anne Louise Germaine Necker Baronn
See also DLB 119

Stael-Holstein, Anne Louise Germaine Necker Baronn 1766-1817 . . . . **NCLC 3**
See also Stael, Germaine de

Stafford, Jean 1915-1979 . . . **CLC 4, 7, 19, 68**
See also CA 1-4R; 85-88; CANR 3; DLB 2; MTCW; SATA 22

Stafford, William (Edgar)
1914-1993 . . . . **CLC 4, 7, 29**
See also CA 5-8R; 142; CAAS 3; CANR 5, 22; DLB 5

Staines, Trevor
See Brunner, John (Kilian Houston)

Stairs, Gordon
See Austin, Mary (Hunter)

Stannard, Martin 1947- . . . . **CLC 44**
See also CA 142

Stanton, Maura 1946- . . . . **CLC 9**
See also CA 89-92; CANR 15; DLB 120

Stanton, Schuyler
See Baum, L(yman) Frank

Stapledon, (William) Olaf
1886-1950 . . . . **TCLC 22**
See also CA 111; DLB 15

Starbuck, George (Edwin) 1931- . . . . **CLC 53**
See also CA 21-24R; CANR 23

Stark, Richard
See Westlake, Donald E(dwin)

Staunton, Schuyler
See Baum, L(yman) Frank

Stead, Christina (Ellen)
1902-1983 . . . . **CLC 2, 5, 8, 32, 80**
See also CA 13-16R; 109; CANR 33, 40; MTCW

Stead, William Thomas
1849-1912 . . . . **TCLC 48**

Steele, Richard 1672-1729 . . . . **LC 18**
See also CDBLB 1660-1789; DLB 84, 101

Steele, Timothy (Reid) 1948-. . . . . . . **CLC 45**
See also CA 93-96; CANR 16; DLB 120

Steffens, (Joseph) Lincoln 1866-1936 . . . . **TCLC 20**
See also CA 117

Stegner, Wallace (Earle) 1909-1993 . . . . **CLC 9, 49**
See also AITN 1; BEST 90:3; CA 1-4R; 141; CAAS 9; CANR 1, 21; DLB 9; MTCW

Stein, Gertrude 1874-1946 . . . . **TCLC 1, 6, 28, 48**
See also CA 104; 132; CDALB 1917-1929; DA; DLB 4, 54, 86; MTCW; WLC

Steinbeck, John (Ernst) 1902-1968 . . . . . . **CLC 1, 5, 9, 13, 21, 34, 45, 75; SSC 11**
See also CA 1-4R; 25-28R; CANR 1, 35; CDALB 1929-1941; DA; DLB 7, 9; DLBD 2; MTCW; SATA 9; WLC

Steinem, Gloria 1934-. . . . . **CLC 63**
See also CA 53-56; CANR 28; MTCW

Steiner, George 1929-. . . . . **CLC 24**
See also CA 73-76; CANR 31; DLB 67; MTCW; SATA 62

Steiner, K. Leslie
See Delany, Samuel R(ay, Jr.)

Steiner, Rudolf 1861-1925 . . . . **TCLC 13**
See also CA 107

Stendhal 1783-1842. . . . . **NCLC 23**
See also DA; DLB 119; WLC

Stephen, Leslie 1832-1904 . . . . **TCLC 23**
See also CA 123; DLB 57

Stephen, Sir Leslie
See Stephen, Leslie

Stephen, Virginia
See Woolf, (Adeline) Virginia

Stephens, James 1882(?)-1950 . . . . . . **TCLC 4**
See also CA 104; DLB 19

Stephens, Reed
See Donaldson, Stephen R.

Steptoe, Lydia
See Barnes, Djuna

Sterchi, Beat 1949-. . . . . **CLC 65**

Sterling, Brett
See Bradbury, Ray (Douglas); Hamilton, Edmond

Sterling, Bruce 1954-. . . . . **CLC 72**
See also CA 119

Sterling, George 1869-1926 . . . . **TCLC 20**
See also CA 117; DLB 54

Stern, Gerald 1925- . . . . **CLC 40**
See also CA 81-84; CANR 28; DLB 105

Stern, Richard (Gustave) 1928-. . . **CLC 4, 39**
See also CA 1-4R; CANR 1, 25; DLBY 87

Sternberg, Josef von 1894-1969. . . . . **CLC 20**
See also CA 81-84

Sterne, Laurence 1713-1768. . . . . **LC 2**
See also CDBLB 1660-1789; DA; DLB 39; WLC

Sternheim, (William Adolf) Carl 1878-1942 . . . . **TCLC 8**
See also CA 105; DLB 56, 118

Stevens, Mark 1951- . . . . **CLC 34**
See also CA 122

Stevens, Wallace 1879-1955 . . . . **TCLC 3, 12, 45; PC 6**
See also CA 104; 124; CDALB 1929-1941; DA; DLB 54; MTCW; WLC

Stevenson, Anne (Katharine) 1933- . . . . **CLC 7, 33**
See also CA 17-20R; CAAS 9; CANR 9, 33; DLB 40; MTCW

Stevenson, Robert Louis (Balfour) 1850-1894 . . . . **NCLC 5, 14; SSC 11**
See also CDBLB 1890-1914; CLR 10, 11; DA; DLB 18, 57; JRDA; MAICYA; WLC; YABC 2

Stewart, J(ohn) I(nnes) M(ackintosh) 1906- . . . . **CLC 7, 14, 32**
See also CA 85-88; CAAS 3; MTCW

Stewart, Mary (Florence Elinor) 1916- . . . . **CLC 7, 35**
See also CA 1-4R; CANR 1; SATA 12

Stewart, Mary Rainbow
See Stewart, Mary (Florence Elinor)

Stifter, Adalbert 1805-1868 . . . . . . **NCLC 41**
See also DLB 133

Still, James 1906-. . . . . **CLC 49**
See also CA 65-68; CAAS 17; CANR 10, 26; DLB 9; SATA 29

Sting
See Sumner, Gordon Matthew

Stirling, Arthur
See Sinclair, Upton (Beall)

Stitt, Milan 1941-. . . . . **CLC 29**
See also CA 69-72

Stockton, Francis Richard 1834-1902
See Stockton, Frank R.
See also CA 108; 137; MAICYA; SATA 44

Stockton, Frank R. . . . . **TCLC 47**
See also Stockton, Francis Richard
See also DLB 42, 74; SATA 32

Stoddard, Charles
See Kuttner, Henry

Stoker, Abraham 1847-1912
See Stoker, Bram
See also CA 105; DA; SATA 29

Stoker, Bram . . . . **TCLC 8**
See also Stoker, Abraham
See also CDBLB 1890-1914; DLB 36, 70; WLC

Stolz, Mary (Slattery) 1920- . . . . **CLC 12**
See also AAYA 8; AITN 1; CA 5-8R; CANR 13, 41; JRDA; MAICYA; SAAS 3; SATA 10, 71

Stone, Irving 1903-1989 . . . . **CLC 7**
See also AITN 1; CA 1-4R; 129; CAAS 3; CANR 1, 23; MTCW; SATA 3; SATA-Obit 64

Stone, Oliver 1946-. . . . . **CLC 73**
See also CA 110

Stone, Robert (Anthony) 1937- . . . . **CLC 5, 23, 42**
See also CA 85-88; CANR 23; MTCW

Stone, Zachary
See Follett, Ken(neth Martin)

Stoppard, Tom 1937- . . . **CLC 1, 3, 4, 5, 8, 15, 29, 34, 63**
See also CA 81-84; CANR 39; CDBLB 1960 to Present; DA; DLB 13; DLBY 85; MTCW; WLC

Storey, David (Malcolm) 1933- . . . . **CLC 2, 4, 5, 8**
See also CA 81-84; CANR 36; DLB 13, 14; MTCW

Storm, Hyemeyohsts 1935- . . . . **CLC 3**
See also CA 81-84

Storm, (Hans) Theodor (Woldsen) 1817-1888 . . . . **NCLC 1**

Storni, Alfonsina 1892-1938 . . . . **TCLC 5**
See also CA 104; 131; HW

Stout, Rex (Todhunter) 1886-1975 . . . **CLC 3**
See also AITN 2; CA 61-64

Stow, (Julian) Randolph 1935- . . **CLC 23, 48**
See also CA 13-16R; CANR 33; MTCW

Stowe, Harriet (Elizabeth) Beecher 1811-1896 . . . . **NCLC 3**
See also CDALB 1865-1917; DA; DLB 1, 12, 42, 74; JRDA; MAICYA; WLC; YABC 1

Strachey, (Giles) Lytton 1880-1932 . . . . **TCLC 12**
See also CA 110; DLBD 10

Strand, Mark 1934- . . . . . . **CLC 6, 18, 41, 71**
See also CA 21-24R; CANR 40; DLB 5; SATA 41

Straub, Peter (Francis) 1943- . . . . . . **CLC 28**
See also BEST 89:1; CA 85-88; CANR 28; DLBY 84; MTCW

Strauss, Botho 1944- . . . . **CLC 22**
See also DLB 124

Streatfeild, (Mary) Noel 1895(?)-1986 . . . . **CLC 21**
See also CA 81-84; 120; CANR 31; CLR 17; MAICYA; SATA 20, 48

Stribling, T(homas) S(igismund) 1881-1965 . . . . **CLC 23**
See also CA 107; DLB 9

Strindberg, (Johan) August 1849-1912 . . . . **TCLC 1, 8, 21, 47**
See also CA 104; 135; DA; WLC

Stringer, Arthur 1874-1950 . . . . **TCLC 37**
See also DLB 92

Stringer, David
See Roberts, Keith (John Kingston)

Strugatskii, Arkadii (Natanovich) 1925-1991 . . . . **CLC 27**
See also CA 106; 135

Strugatskii, Boris (Natanovich) 1933- . . . . **CLC 27**
See also CA 106

Strummer, Joe 1953(?)- . . . . **CLC 30**
See also Clash, The

Stuart, Don A.
See Campbell, John W(ood, Jr.)

Stuart, Ian
See MacLean, Alistair (Stuart)

Stuart, Jesse (Hilton) 1906-1984 . . . . **CLC 1, 8, 11, 14, 34**
See also CA 5-8R; 112; CANR 31; DLB 9, 48, 102; DLBY 84; SATA 2, 36

Sturgeon, Theodore (Hamilton) 1918-1985 .... **CLC 22, 39**
See also Queen, Ellery
See also CA 81-84; 116; CANR 32; DLB 8; DLBY 85; MTCW

Sturges, Preston 1898-1959 .... **TCLC 48**
See also CA 114; DLB 26

Styron, William 1925- .... **CLC 1, 3, 5, 11, 15, 60**
See also BEST 90:4; CA 5-8R; CANR 6, 33; CDALB 1968-1988; DLB 2; DLBY 80; MTCW

Suarez Lynch, B.
See Borges, Jorge Luis

Suarez Lynch, B.
See Bioy Casares, Adolfo; Borges, Jorge Luis

Su Chien 1884-1918
See Su Man-shu
See also CA 123

Sudermann, Hermann 1857-1928 .. **TCLC 15**
See also CA 107; DLB 118

Sue, Eugene 1804-1857 .... **NCLC 1**
See also DLB 119

Sueskind, Patrick 1949- .... **CLC 44**

Sukenick, Ronald 1932- ..... **CLC 3, 4, 6, 48**
See also CA 25-28R; CAAS 8; CANR 32; DLBY 81

Suknaski, Andrew 1942- .... **CLC 19**
See also CA 101; DLB 53

Sullivan, Vernon
See Vian, Boris

Sully Prudhomme 1839-1907 ...... **TCLC 31**

Su Man-shu .... **TCLC 24**
See also Su Chien

Summerforest, Ivy B.
See Kirkup, James

Summers, Andrew James 1942- ..... **CLC 26**
See also Police, The

Summers, Andy
See Summers, Andrew James

Summers, Hollis (Spurgeon, Jr.) 1916- .... **CLC 10**
See also CA 5-8R; CANR 3; DLB 6

Summers, (Alphonsus Joseph-Mary Augustus) Montague 1880-1948 .... **TCLC 16**
See also CA 118

Sumner, Gordon Matthew 1951- .... **CLC 26**
See also Police, The

Surtees, Robert Smith 1803-1864 .... **NCLC 14**
See also DLB 21

Susann, Jacqueline 1921-1974 .... **CLC 3**
See also AITN 1; CA 65-68; 53-56; MTCW

Suskind, Patrick
See Sueskind, Patrick

Sutcliff, Rosemary 1920-1992 ...... **CLC 26**
See also AAYA 10; CA 5-8R; 139; CANR 37; CLR 1; JRDA; MAICYA; SATA 6, 44; SATA-Obit 73

Sutro, Alfred 1863-1933 .... **TCLC 6**
See also CA 105; DLB 10

Sutton, Henry
See Slavitt, David R(ytman)

Svevo, Italo .... **TCLC 2, 35**
See also Schmitz, Aron Hector

Swados, Elizabeth 1951- .... **CLC 12**
See also CA 97-100

Swados, Harvey 1920-1972 .... **CLC 5**
See also CA 5-8R; 37-40R; CANR 6; DLB 2

Swan, Gladys 1934- .... **CLC 69**
See also CA 101; CANR 17, 39

Swarthout, Glendon (Fred) 1918-1992 .... **CLC 35**
See also CA 1-4R; 139; CANR 1; SATA 26

Sweet, Sarah C.
See Jewett, (Theodora) Sarah Orne

Swenson, May 1919-1989 ..... **CLC 4, 14, 61**
See also CA 5-8R; 130; CANR 36; DA; DLB 5; MTCW; SATA 15

Swift, Augustus
See Lovecraft, H(oward) P(hillips)

Swift, Graham 1949- .... **CLC 41**
See also CA 117; 122

Swift, Jonathan 1667-1745 .... **LC 1**
See also CDBLB 1660-1789; DA; DLB 39, 95, 101; SATA 19; WLC

Swinburne, Algernon Charles 1837-1909 .... **TCLC 8, 36**
See also CA 105; 140; CDBLB 1832-1890; DA; DLB 35, 57; WLC

Swinfen, Ann .... **CLC 34**

Swinnerton, Frank Arthur 1884-1982 .... **CLC 31**
See also CA 108; DLB 34

Swithen, John
See King, Stephen (Edwin)

Sylvia
See Ashton-Warner, Sylvia (Constance)

Symmes, Robert Edward
See Duncan, Robert (Edward)

Symonds, John Addington 1840-1893 .... **NCLC 34**
See also DLB 57

Symons, Arthur 1865-1945 .... **TCLC 11**
See also CA 107; DLB 19, 57

Symons, Julian (Gustave) 1912- .... **CLC 2, 14, 32**
See also CA 49-52; CAAS 3; CANR 3, 33; DLB 87; DLBY 92; MTCW

Synge, (Edmund) J(ohn) M(illington) 1871-1909 .... **TCLC 6, 37; DC 2**
See also CA 104; 141; CDBLB 1890-1914; DLB 10, 19

Syruc, J.
See Milosz, Czeslaw

Szirtes, George 1948- .... **CLC 46**
See also CA 109; CANR 27

Tabori, George 1914- .... **CLC 19**
See also CA 49-52; CANR 4

Tagore, Rabindranath 1861-1941 .... **TCLC 3**
See also CA 104; 120; MTCW

Taine, Hippolyte Adolphe 1828-1893 .... **NCLC 15**

Talese, Gay 1932- .... **CLC 37**
See also AITN 1; CA 1-4R; CANR 9; MTCW

Tallent, Elizabeth (Ann) 1954- ..... **CLC 45**
See also CA 117; DLB 130

Tally, Ted 1952- .... **CLC 42**
See also CA 120; 124

Tamayo y Baus, Manuel 1829-1898 .... **NCLC 1**

Tammsaare, A(nton) H(ansen) 1878-1940 .... **TCLC 27**

Tan, Amy 1952- .... **CLC 59**
See also AAYA 9; BEST 89:3; CA 136; SATA 75

Tandem, Felix
See Spitteler, Carl (Friedrich Georg)

Tanizaki, Jun'ichiro 1886-1965 .... **CLC 8, 14, 28**
See also CA 93-96; 25-28R

Tanner, William
See Amis, Kingsley (William)

Tao Lao
See Storni, Alfonsina

Tarassoff, Lev
See Troyat, Henri

Tarbell, Ida M(inerva) 1857-1944 .... **TCLC 40**
See also CA 122; DLB 47

Tarkington, (Newton) Booth 1869-1946 .... **TCLC 9**
See also CA 110; DLB 9, 102; SATA 17

Tarkovsky, Andrei (Arsenyevich) 1932-1986 .... **CLC 75**
See also CA 127

Tartt, Donna 1964(?)- .... **CLC 76**
See also CA 142

Tasso, Torquato 1544-1595 .... **LC 5**

Tate, (John Orley) Allen 1899-1979 .... **CLC 2, 4, 6, 9, 11, 14, 24**
See also CA 5-8R; 85-88; CANR 32; DLB 4, 45, 63; MTCW

Tate, Ellalice
See Hibbert, Eleanor Alice Burford

Tate, James (Vincent) 1943- ... **CLC 2, 6, 25**
See also CA 21-24R; CANR 29; DLB 5

Tavel, Ronald 1940- .... **CLC 6**
See also CA 21-24R; CANR 33

Taylor, Cecil Philip 1929-1981 ..... **CLC 27**
See also CA 25-28R; 105

Taylor, Edward 1642(?)-1729 .... **LC 11**
See also DA; DLB 24

Taylor, Eleanor Ross 1920- .... **CLC 5**
See also CA 81-84

Taylor, Elizabeth 1912-1975 ... **CLC 2, 4, 29**
See also CA 13-16R; CANR 9; MTCW; SATA 13

Taylor, Henry (Splawn) 1942- ...... **CLC 44**
See also CA 33-36R; CAAS 7; CANR 31; DLB 5

Taylor, Kamala (Purnaiya) 1924-
See Markandaya, Kamala
See also CA 77-80

Taylor, Mildred D. .... **CLC 21**
See also AAYA 10; BW; CA 85-88; CANR 25; CLR 9; DLB 52; JRDA; MAICYA; SAAS 5; SATA 15, 70

Tolson, Melvin B(eaunorus) 1898(?)-1966 . . . . **CLC 36**
See also BLC 3; BW; CA 124; 89-92; DLB 48, 76

Tolstoi, Aleksei Nikolaevich
See Tolstoy, Alexey Nikolaevich

Tolstoy, Alexey Nikolaevich 1882-1945 . . . . **TCLC 18**
See also CA 107

Tolstoy, Count Leo
See Tolstoy, Leo (Nikolaevich)

Tolstoy, Leo (Nikolaevich) 1828-1910 . . . . . . **TCLC 4, 11, 17, 28, 44; SSC 9**
See also CA 104; 123; DA; SATA 26; WLC

Tomasi di Lampedusa, Giuseppe 1896-1957
See Lampedusa, Giuseppe (Tomasi) di
See also CA 111

Tomlin, Lily . . . . **CLC 17**
See also Tomlin, Mary Jean

Tomlin, Mary Jean 1939(?)-
See Tomlin, Lily
See also CA 117

Tomlinson, (Alfred) Charles 1927- . . . . **CLC 2, 4, 6, 13, 45**
See also CA 5-8R; CANR 33; DLB 40

Tonson, Jacob
See Bennett, (Enoch) Arnold

Toole, John Kennedy 1937-1969 . . . . **CLC 19, 64**
See also CA 104; DLBY 81

Toomer, Jean 1894-1967 . . . . . . **CLC 1, 4, 13, 22; PC 7; SSC 1**
See also BLC 3; BW; CA 85-88; CDALB 1917-1929; DLB 45, 51; MTCW

Torley, Luke
See Blish, James (Benjamin)

Tornimparte, Alessandra
See Ginzburg, Natalia

Torre, Raoul della
See Mencken, H(enry) L(ouis)

Torrey, E(dwin) Fuller 1937- . . . . **CLC 34**
See also CA 119

Torsvan, Ben Traven
See Traven, B.

Torsvan, Benno Traven
See Traven, B.

Torsvan, Berick Traven
See Traven, B.

Torsvan, Berwick Traven
See Traven, B.

Torsvan, Bruno Traven
See Traven, B.

Torsvan, Traven
See Traven, B.

Tournier, Michel (Edouard) 1924- . . . . **CLC 6, 23, 36**
See also CA 49-52; CANR 3, 36; DLB 83; MTCW; SATA 23

Tournimparte, Alessandra
See Ginzburg, Natalia

Towers, Ivar
See Kornbluth, C(yril) M.

Townsend, Sue 1946- . . . . **CLC 61**
See also CA 119; 127; MTCW; SATA 48, 55

Townshend, Peter (Dennis Blandford) 1945- . . . . **CLC 17, 42**
See also CA 107

Tozzi, Federigo 1883-1920. . . . . **TCLC 31**

Traill, Catharine Parr 1802-1899 . . . . **NCLC 31**
See also DLB 99

Trakl, Georg 1887-1914 . . . . **TCLC 5**
See also CA 104

Transtroemer, Tomas (Goesta) 1931- . . . . **CLC 52, 65**
See also CA 117; 129; CAAS 17

Transtromer, Tomas Gosta
See Transtroemer, Tomas (Goesta)

Traven, B. (?)-1969 . . . . **CLC 8, 11**
See also CA 19-20; 25-28R; CAP 2; DLB 9, 56; MTCW

Treitel, Jonathan 1959- . . . . **CLC 70**

Tremain, Rose 1943-. . . . . **CLC 42**
See also CA 97-100; DLB 14

Tremblay, Michel 1942-. . . . . **CLC 29**
See also CA 116; 128; DLB 60; MTCW

Trevanian (a pseudonym) 1930(?)-. . . **CLC 29**
See also CA 108

Trevor, Glen
See Hilton, James

Trevor, William 1928- . . . . **CLC 7, 9, 14, 25, 71**
See also Cox, William Trevor
See also DLB 14

Trifonov, Yuri (Valentinovich) 1925-1981 . . . . **CLC 45**
See also CA 126; 103; MTCW

Trilling, Lionel 1905-1975 . . . . **CLC 9, 11, 24**
See also CA 9-12R; 61-64; CANR 10; DLB 28, 63; MTCW

Trimball, W. H.
See Mencken, H(enry) L(ouis)

Tristan
See Gomez de la Serna, Ramon

Tristram
See Housman, A(lfred) E(dward)

Trogdon, William (Lewis) 1939-
See Heat-Moon, William Least
See also CA 115; 119

Trollope, Anthony 1815-1882 . . **NCLC 6, 33**
See also CDBLB 1832-1890; DA; DLB 21, 57; SATA 22; WLC

Trollope, Frances 1779-1863 . . . . . **NCLC 30**
See also DLB 21

Trotsky, Leon 1879-1940. . . . . **TCLC 22**
See also CA 118

Trotter (Cockburn), Catharine 1679-1749 . . . . **LC 8**
See also DLB 84

Trout, Kilgore
See Farmer, Philip Jose

Trow, George W. S. 1943- . . . . **CLC 52**
See also CA 126

Troyat, Henri 1911- . . . . **CLC 23**
See also CA 45-48; CANR 2, 33; MTCW

Trudeau, G(arretson) B(eekman) 1948-
See Trudeau, Garry B.
See also CA 81-84; CANR 31; SATA 35

Trudeau, Garry B. . . . . **CLC 12**
See also Trudeau, G(arretson) B(eekman)
See also AAYA 10; AITN 2

Truffaut, Francois 1932-1984. . . . . . . **CLC 20**
See also CA 81-84; 113; CANR 34

Trumbo, Dalton 1905-1976 . . . . **CLC 19**
See also CA 21-24R; 69-72; CANR 10; DLB 26

Trumbull, John 1750-1831 . . . . **NCLC 30**
See also DLB 31

Trundlett, Helen B.
See Eliot, T(homas) S(tearns)

Tryon, Thomas 1926-1991 . . . . **CLC 3, 11**
See also AITN 1; CA 29-32R; 135; CANR 32; MTCW

Tryon, Tom
See Tryon, Thomas

Ts'ao Hsueh-ch'in 1715(?)-1763. . . . . . . **LC 1**

Tsushima, Shuji 1909-1948
See Dazai, Osamu
See also CA 107

Tsvetaeva (Efron), Marina (Ivanovna) 1892-1941 . . . . **TCLC 7, 35**
See also CA 104; 128; MTCW

Tuck, Lily 1938- . . . . **CLC 70**
See also CA 139

Tunis, John R(oberts) 1889-1975 . . . **CLC 12**
See also CA 61-64; DLB 22; JRDA; MAICYA; SATA 30, 37

Tuohy, Frank . . . . **CLC 37**
See also Tuohy, John Francis
See also DLB 14

Tuohy, John Francis 1925-
See Tuohy, Frank
See also CA 5-8R; CANR 3

Turco, Lewis (Putnam) 1934- . . . **CLC 11, 63**
See also CA 13-16R; CANR 24; DLBY 84

Turgenev, Ivan 1818-1883 . . . . **NCLC 21; SSC 7**
See also DA; WLC

Turner, Frederick 1943- . . . . **CLC 48**
See also CA 73-76; CAAS 10; CANR 12, 30; DLB 40

Tusan, Stan 1936- . . . . **CLC 22**
See also CA 105

Tutu, Desmond M(pilo) 1931- . . . . . . **CLC 80**
See also BLC 3; BW; CA 125

Tutuola, Amos 1920- . . . . **CLC 5, 14, 29**
See also BLC 3; BW; CA 9-12R; CANR 27; DLB 125; MTCW

Twain, Mark . . . . **TCLC 6, 12, 19, 36, 48; SSC 6**
See also Clemens, Samuel Langhorne
See also DLB 11, 12, 23, 64, 74; WLC

Tyler, Anne 1941- . . . . **CLC 7, 11, 18, 28, 44, 59**
See also BEST 89:1; CA 9-12R; CANR 11, 33; DLB 6; DLBY 82; MTCW; SATA 7

Tyler, Royall 1757-1826. . . . . **NCLC 3**
See also DLB 37

Vidal, Gore 1925- ..... **CLC 2, 4, 6, 8, 10, 22, 33, 72**
See also AITN 1; BEST 90:2; CA 5-8R; CANR 13; DLB 6; MTCW

Viereck, Peter (Robert Edwin) 1916- .... **CLC 4**
See also CA 1-4R; CANR 1; DLB 5

Vigny, Alfred (Victor) de 1797-1863 .... **NCLC 7**
See also DLB 119

Vilakazi, Benedict Wallet 1906-1947 .... **TCLC 37**

Villiers de l'Isle Adam, Jean Marie Mathias Philippe Auguste Comte 1838-1889 .... **NCLC 3**
See also DLB 123

Vincent, Gabrielle a pseudonym ...... **CLC 13**
See also CA 126; CLR 13; MAICYA; SATA 61

Vinci, Leonardo da 1452-1519 .... **LC 12**

Vine, Barbara .... **CLC 50**
See also Rendell, Ruth (Barbara)
See also BEST 90:4

Vinge, Joan D(ennison) 1948- ...... **CLC 30**
See also CA 93-96; SATA 36

Violis, G.
See Simenon, Georges (Jacques Christian)

Visconti, Luchino 1906-1976 .... **CLC 16**
See also CA 81-84; 65-68; CANR 39

Vittorini, Elio 1908-1966 ...... **CLC 6, 9, 14**
See also CA 133; 25-28R

Vizinczey, Stephen 1933- .... **CLC 40**
See also CA 128

Vliet, R(ussell) G(ordon) 1929-1984 .... **CLC 22**
See also CA 37-40R; 112; CANR 18

Vogau, Boris Andreyevich 1894-1937(?)
See Pilnyak, Boris
See also CA 123

Vogel, Paula A(nne) 1951- .... **CLC 76**
See also CA 108

Voight, Ellen Bryant 1943- .... **CLC 54**
See also CA 69-72; CANR 11, 29; DLB 120

Voigt, Cynthia 1942- .... **CLC 30**
See also AAYA 3; CA 106; CANR 18, 37, 40; CLR 13; JRDA; MAICYA; SATA 33, 48

Voinovich, Vladimir (Nikolaevich) 1932- .... **CLC 10, 49**
See also CA 81-84; CAAS 12; CANR 33; MTCW

Voltaire 1694-1778 .... **LC 14; SSC 12**
See also DA; WLC

von Daeniken, Erich 1935- .... **CLC 30**
See also von Daniken, Erich
See also AITN 1; CA 37-40R; CANR 17

von Daniken, Erich .... **CLC 30**
See also von Daeniken, Erich

von Heidenstam, (Carl Gustaf) Verner
See Heidenstam, (Carl Gustaf) Verner von

von Heyse, Paul (Johann Ludwig)
See Heyse, Paul (Johann Ludwig von)

von Hofmannsthal, Hugo
See Hofmannsthal, Hugo von

von Horvath, Odon
See Horvath, Oedoen von

von Horvath, Oedoen
See Horvath, Oedoen von

von Liliencron, (Friedrich Adolf Axel) Detlev
See Liliencron, (Friedrich Adolf Axel) Detlev von

Vonnegut, Kurt, Jr. 1922- ...... **CLC 1, 2, 3, 4, 5, 8, 12, 22, 40, 60; SSC 8**
See also AAYA 6; AITN 1; BEST 90:4; CA 1-4R; CANR 1, 25; CDALB 1968-1988; DA; DLB 2, 8; DLBD 3; DLBY 80; MTCW; WLC

Von Rachen, Kurt
See Hubbard, L(afayette) Ron(ald)

von Rezzori (d'Arezzo), Gregor
See Rezzori (d'Arezzo), Gregor von

von Sternberg, Josef
See Sternberg, Josef von

Vorster, Gordon 1924- .... **CLC 34**
See also CA 133

Vosce, Trudie
See Ozick, Cynthia

Voznesensky, Andrei (Andreievich) 1933- .... **CLC 1, 15, 57**
See also CA 89-92; CANR 37; MTCW

Waddington, Miriam 1917- .... **CLC 28**
See also CA 21-24R; CANR 12, 30; DLB 68

Wagman, Fredrica 1937- .... **CLC 7**
See also CA 97-100

Wagner, Richard 1813-1883 .... **NCLC 9**
See also DLB 129

Wagner-Martin, Linda 1936- .... **CLC 50**

Wagoner, David (Russell) 1926- .... **CLC 3, 5, 15**
See also CA 1-4R; CAAS 3; CANR 2; DLB 5; SATA 14

Wah, Fred(erick James) 1939- ...... **CLC 44**
See also CA 107; 141; DLB 60

Wahloo, Per 1926-1975 .... **CLC 7**
See also CA 61-64

Wahloo, Peter
See Wahloo, Per

Wain, John (Barrington) 1925- .... **CLC 2, 11, 15, 46**
See also CA 5-8R; CAAS 4; CANR 23; CDBLB 1960 to Present; DLB 15, 27; MTCW

Wajda, Andrzej 1926- .... **CLC 16**
See also CA 102

Wakefield, Dan 1932- .... **CLC 7**
See also CA 21-24R; CAAS 7

Wakoski, Diane 1937- .... **CLC 2, 4, 7, 9, 11, 40**
See also CA 13-16R; CAAS 1; CANR 9; DLB 5

Wakoski-Sherbell, Diane
See Wakoski, Diane

Walcott, Derek (Alton) 1930- .... **CLC 2, 4, 9, 14, 25, 42, 67, 76**
See also BLC 3; BW; CA 89-92; CANR 26; DLB 117; DLBY 81; MTCW

Waldman, Anne 1945- .... **CLC 7**
See also CA 37-40R; CAAS 17; CANR 34; DLB 16

Waldo, E. Hunter
See Sturgeon, Theodore (Hamilton)

Waldo, Edward Hamilton
See Sturgeon, Theodore (Hamilton)

Walker, Alice (Malsenior) 1944- .... **CLC 5, 6, 9, 19, 27, 46, 58; SSC 5**
See also AAYA 3; BEST 89:4; BLC 3; BW; CA 37-40R; CANR 9, 27; CDALB 1968-1988; DA; DLB 6, 33; MTCW; SATA 31

Walker, David Harry 1911-1992 .... **CLC 14**
See also CA 1-4R; 137; CANR 1; SATA 8; SATA-Obit 71

Walker, Edward Joseph 1934-
See Walker, Ted
See also CA 21-24R; CANR 12, 28

Walker, George F. 1947- .... **CLC 44, 61**
See also CA 103; CANR 21, 43; DLB 60

Walker, Joseph A. 1935- .... **CLC 19**
See also BW; CA 89-92; CANR 26; DLB 38

Walker, Margaret (Abigail) 1915- .... **CLC 1, 6**
See also BLC 3; BW; CA 73-76; CANR 26; DLB 76; MTCW

Walker, Ted .... **CLC 13**
See also Walker, Edward Joseph
See also DLB 40

Wallace, David Foster 1962- .... **CLC 50**
See also CA 132

Wallace, Dexter
See Masters, Edgar Lee

Wallace, Irving 1916-1990 .... **CLC 7, 13**
See also AITN 1; CA 1-4R; 132; CAAS 1; CANR 1, 27; MTCW

Wallant, Edward Lewis 1926-1962 .... **CLC 5, 10**
See also CA 1-4R; CANR 22; DLB 2, 28; MTCW

Walpole, Horace 1717-1797 .... **LC 2**
See also DLB 39, 104

Walpole, Hugh (Seymour) 1884-1941 .... **TCLC 5**
See also CA 104; DLB 34

Walser, Martin 1927- .... **CLC 27**
See also CA 57-60; CANR 8; DLB 75, 124

Walser, Robert 1878-1956 .... **TCLC 18**
See also CA 118; DLB 66

Walsh, Jill Paton .... **CLC 35**
See also Paton Walsh, Gillian
See also CLR 2; SAAS 3

Walter, Villiam Christian
See Andersen, Hans Christian

Wambaugh, Joseph (Aloysius, Jr.) 1937- .... **CLC 3, 18**
See also AITN 1; BEST 89:3; CA 33-36R; CANR 42; DLB 6; DLBY 83; MTCW

Ward, Arthur Henry Sarsfield 1883-1959
See Rohmer, Sax
See also CA 108

Wescott, Glenway 1901-1987....... **CLC 13**
See also CA 13-16R; 121; CANR 23; DLB 4, 9, 102

Wesker, Arnold 1932-........ **CLC 3, 5, 42**
See also CA 1-4R; CAAS 7; CANR 1, 33; CDBLB 1960 to Present; DLB 13; MTCW

Wesley, Richard (Errol) 1945-....... **CLC 7**
See also BW; CA 57-60; CANR 27; DLB 38

Wessel, Johan Herman 1742-1785 .... **LC 7**

West, Anthony (Panther)
1914-1987 .... **CLC 50**
See also CA 45-48; 124; CANR 3, 19; DLB 15

West, C. P.
See Wodehouse, P(elham) G(renville)

West, (Mary) Jessamyn
1902-1984 .... **CLC 7, 17**
See also CA 9-12R; 112; CANR 27; DLB 6; DLBY 84; MTCW; SATA 37

West, Morris L(anglo) 1916-..... **CLC 6, 33**
See also CA 5-8R; CANR 24; MTCW

West, Nathanael
1903-1940 .... **TCLC 1, 14, 44**
See also CA 104; 125; CDALB 1929-1941; DLB 4, 9, 28; MTCW

West, Owen
See Koontz, Dean R(ay)

West, Paul 1930- .... **CLC 7, 14**
See also CA 13-16R; CAAS 7; CANR 22; DLB 14

West, Rebecca 1892-1983 .. **CLC 7, 9, 31, 50**
See also CA 5-8R; 109; CANR 19; DLB 36; DLBY 83; MTCW

Westall, Robert (Atkinson)
1929-1993 .... **CLC 17**
See also CA 69-72; 141; CANR 18; CLR 13; JRDA; MAICYA; SAAS 2; SATA 23, 69; SATA-Obit 75

Westlake, Donald E(dwin)
1933- .... **CLC 7, 33**
See also CA 17-20R; CAAS 13; CANR 16

Westmacott, Mary
See Christie, Agatha (Mary Clarissa)

Weston, Allen
See Norton, Andre

Wetcheek, J. L.
See Feuchtwanger, Lion

Wetering, Janwillem van de
See van de Wetering, Janwillem

Wetherell, Elizabeth
See Warner, Susan (Bogert)

Whalen, Philip 1923- .... **CLC 6, 29**
See also CA 9-12R; CANR 5, 39; DLB 16

Wharton, Edith (Newbold Jones)
1862-1937 .... **TCLC 3, 9, 27; SSC 6**
See also CA 104; 132; CDALB 1865-1917; DA; DLB 4, 9, 12, 78; MTCW; WLC

Wharton, James
See Mencken, H(enry) L(ouis)

Wharton, William (a pseudonym)
.... **CLC 18, 37**
See also CA 93-96; DLBY 80

Wheatley (Peters), Phillis
1754(?)-1784 .... **LC 3; PC 3**
See also BLC 3; CDALB 1640-1865; DA; DLB 31, 50; WLC

Wheelock, John Hall 1886-1978 .... **CLC 14**
See also CA 13-16R; 77-80; CANR 14; DLB 45

White, E(lwyn) B(rooks)
1899-1985 .... **CLC 10, 34, 39**
See also AITN 2; CA 13-16R; 116; CANR 16, 37; CLR 1, 21; DLB 11, 22; MAICYA; MTCW; SATA 2, 29, 44

White, Edmund (Valentine III)
1940- .... **CLC 27**
See also AAYA 7; CA 45-48; CANR 3, 19, 36; MTCW

White, Patrick (Victor Martindale)
1912-1990 .. **CLC 3, 4, 5, 7, 9, 18, 65, 69**
See also CA 81-84; 132; CANR 43; MTCW

White, Phyllis Dorothy James 1920-
See James, P. D.
See also CA 21-24R; CANR 17, 43; MTCW

White, T(erence) H(anbury)
1906-1964 .... **CLC 30**
See also CA 73-76; CANR 37; JRDA; MAICYA; SATA 12

White, Terence de Vere 1912-...... **CLC 49**
See also CA 49-52; CANR 3

White, Walter F(rancis)
1893-1955 .... **TCLC 15**
See also White, Walter
See also CA 115; 124; DLB 51

White, William Hale 1831-1913
See Rutherford, Mark
See also CA 121

Whitehead, E(dward) A(nthony)
1933- .... **CLC 5**
See also CA 65-68

Whitemore, Hugh (John) 1936-..... **CLC 37**
See also CA 132

Whitman, Sarah Helen (Power)
1803-1878 .... **NCLC 19**
See also DLB 1

Whitman, Walt(er)
1819-1892 .... **NCLC 4, 31; PC 3**
See also CDALB 1640-1865; DA; DLB 3, 64; SATA 20; WLC

Whitney, Phyllis A(yame) 1903-.... **CLC 42**
See also AITN 2; BEST 90:3; CA 1-4R; CANR 3, 25, 38; JRDA; MAICYA; SATA 1, 30

Whittemore, (Edward) Reed (Jr.)
1919- .... **CLC 4**
See also CA 9-12R; CAAS 8; CANR 4; DLB 5

Whittier, John Greenleaf
1807-1892 .... **NCLC 8**
See also CDALB 1640-1865; DLB 1

Whittlebot, Hernia
See Coward, Noel (Peirce)

Wicker, Thomas Grey 1926-
See Wicker, Tom
See also CA 65-68; CANR 21

Wicker, Tom .... **CLC 7**
See also Wicker, Thomas Grey

Wideman, John Edgar
1941- .... **CLC 5, 34, 36, 67**
See also BLC 3; BW; CA 85-88; CANR 14, 42; DLB 33

Wiebe, Rudy (Henry) 1934-... **CLC 6, 11, 14**
See also CA 37-40R; CANR 42; DLB 60

Wieland, Christoph Martin
1733-1813 .... **NCLC 17**
See also DLB 97

Wieners, John 1934-............... **CLC 7**
See also CA 13-16R; DLB 16

Wiesel, Elie(zer) 1928-..... **CLC 3, 5, 11, 37**
See also AAYA 7; AITN 1; CA 5-8R; CAAS 4; CANR 8, 40; DA; DLB 83; DLBY 87; MTCW; SATA 56

Wiggins, Marianne 1947-.......... **CLC 57**
See also BEST 89:3; CA 130

Wight, James Alfred 1916-
See Herriot, James
See also CA 77-80; SATA 44, 55

Wilbur, Richard (Purdy)
1921- .... **CLC 3, 6, 9, 14, 53**
See also CA 1-4R; CABS 2; CANR 2, 29; DA; DLB 5; MTCW; SATA 9

Wild, Peter 1940-................ **CLC 14**
See also CA 37-40R; DLB 5

Wilde, Oscar (Fingal O'Flahertie Wills)
1854(?)-1900 .... **TCLC 1, 8, 23, 41; SSC 11**
See also CA 104; 119; CDBLB 1890-1914; DA; DLB 10, 19, 34, 57; SATA 24; WLC

Wilder, Billy .... **CLC 20**
See also Wilder, Samuel
See also DLB 26

Wilder, Samuel 1906-
See Wilder, Billy
See also CA 89-92

Wilder, Thornton (Niven)
1897-1975 ...... **CLC 1, 5, 6, 10, 15, 35; DC 1**
See also AITN 2; CA 13-16R; 61-64; CANR 40; DA; DLB 4, 7, 9; MTCW; WLC

Wilding, Michael 1942-........... **CLC 73**
See also CA 104; CANR 24

Wiley, Richard 1944-............. **CLC 44**
See also CA 121; 129

Wilhelm, Kate .... **CLC 7**
See also Wilhelm, Katie Gertrude
See also CAAS 5; DLB 8

Wilhelm, Katie Gertrude 1928-
See Wilhelm, Kate
See also CA 37-40R; CANR 17, 36; MTCW

Wilkins, Mary
See Freeman, Mary Eleanor Wilkins

Willard, Nancy 1936-........... **CLC 7, 37**
See also CA 89-92; CANR 10, 39; CLR 5; DLB 5, 52; MAICYA; MTCW; SATA 30, 37, 71

Williams, C(harles) K(enneth)
1936- .... **CLC 33, 56**
See also CA 37-40R; DLB 5

Williams, Charles
See Collier, James L(incoln)

Williams, Charles (Walter Stansby) 1886-1945 .... **TCLC 1, 11**
See also CA 104; DLB 100

Williams, (George) Emlyn 1905-1987 .... **CLC 15**
See also CA 104; 123; CANR 36; DLB 10, 77; MTCW

Williams, Hugo 1942-............. **CLC 42**
See also CA 17-20R; DLB 40

Williams, J. Walker
See Wodehouse, P(elham) G(renville)

Williams, John A(lfred) 1925-.... **CLC 5, 13**
See also BLC 3; BW; CA 53-56; CAAS 3; CANR 6, 26; DLB 2, 33

Williams, Jonathan (Chamberlain) 1929- .... **CLC 13**
See also CA 9-12R; CAAS 12; CANR 8; DLB 5

Williams, Joy 1944-.............. **CLC 31**
See also CA 41-44R; CANR 22

Williams, Norman 1952- .... **CLC 39**
See also CA 118

Williams, Tennessee 1911-1983 ..... **CLC 1, 2, 5, 7, 8, 11, 15, 19, 30, 39, 45, 71**
See also AITN 1, 2; CA 5-8R; 108; CABS 3; CANR 31; CDALB 1941-1968; DA; DLB 7; DLBD 4; DLBY 83; MTCW; WLC

Williams, Thomas (Alonzo) 1926-1990 .... **CLC 14**
See also CA 1-4R; 132; CANR 2

Williams, William C.
See Williams, William Carlos

Williams, William Carlos 1883-1963 .... **CLC 1, 2, 5, 9, 13, 22, 42, 67; PC 7**
See also CA 89-92; CANR 34; CDALB 1917-1929; DA; DLB 4, 16, 54, 86; MTCW

Williamson, David (Keith) 1942-.... **CLC 56**
See also CA 103; CANR 41

Williamson, Jack.................. **CLC 29**
See also Williamson, John Stewart
See also CAAS 8; DLB 8

Williamson, John Stewart 1908-
See Williamson, Jack
See also CA 17-20R; CANR 23

Willie, Frederick
See Lovecraft, H(oward) P(hillips)

Willingham, Calder (Baynard, Jr.) 1922- .... **CLC 5, 51**
See also CA 5-8R; CANR 3; DLB 2, 44; MTCW

Willis, Charles
See Clarke, Arthur C(harles)

Willy
See Colette, (Sidonie-Gabrielle)

Willy, Colette
See Colette, (Sidonie-Gabrielle)

Wilson, A(ndrew) N(orman) 1950- .. **CLC 33**
See also CA 112; 122; DLB 14

Wilson, Angus (Frank Johnstone) 1913-1991 .... **CLC 2, 3, 5, 25, 34**
See also CA 5-8R; 134; CANR 21; DLB 15; MTCW

Wilson, August 1945- .... **CLC 39, 50, 63; DC 2**
See also BLC 3; BW; CA 115; 122; CANR 42; DA; MTCW

Wilson, Brian 1942-.............. **CLC 12**

Wilson, Colin 1931- .... **CLC 3, 14**
See also CA 1-4R; CAAS 5; CANR 1, 22, 33; DLB 14; MTCW

Wilson, Dirk
See Pohl, Frederik

Wilson, Edmund 1895-1972 .... **CLC 1, 2, 3, 8, 24**
See also CA 1-4R; 37-40R; CANR 1; DLB 63; MTCW

Wilson, Ethel Davis (Bryant) 1888(?)-1980 .... **CLC 13**
See also CA 102; DLB 68; MTCW

Wilson, John 1785-1854.......... **NCLC 5**

Wilson, John (Anthony) Burgess 1917- .... **CLC 8, 10, 13**
See also Burgess, Anthony
See also CA 1-4R; CANR 2; MTCW

Wilson, Lanford 1937-....... **CLC 7, 14, 36**
See also CA 17-20R; CABS 3; DLB 7

Wilson, Robert M. 1944-......... **CLC 7, 9**
See also CA 49-52; CANR 2, 41; MTCW

Wilson, Robert McLiam 1964- ..... **CLC 59**
See also CA 132

Wilson, Sloan 1920-.............. **CLC 32**
See also CA 1-4R; CANR 1

Wilson, Snoo 1948-............... **CLC 33**
See also CA 69-72

Wilson, William S(mith) 1932- ..... **CLC 49**
See also CA 81-84

Winchilsea, Anne (Kingsmill) Finch Counte 1661-1720 .... **LC 3**

Windham, Basil
See Wodehouse, P(elham) G(renville)

Wingrove, David (John) 1954-...... **CLC 68**
See also CA 133

Winters, Janet Lewis .... **CLC 41**
See also Lewis, Janet
See also DLBY 87

Winters, (Arthur) Yvor 1900-1968 .... **CLC 4, 8, 32**
See also CA 11-12; 25-28R; CAP 1; DLB 48; MTCW

Winterson, Jeanette 1959-......... **CLC 64**
See also CA 136

Wiseman, Frederick 1930-......... **CLC 20**

Wister, Owen 1860-1938 .... **TCLC 21**
See also CA 108; DLB 9, 78; SATA 62

Witkacy
See Witkiewicz, Stanislaw Ignacy

Witkiewicz, Stanislaw Ignacy 1885-1939 .... **TCLC 8**
See also CA 105

Wittig, Monique 1935(?)-.......... **CLC 22**
See also CA 116; 135; DLB 83

Wittlin, Jozef 1896-1976 .... **CLC 25**
See also CA 49-52; 65-68; CANR 3

Wodehouse, P(elham) G(renville) 1881-1975 ... **CLC 1, 2, 5, 10, 22; SSC 2**
See also AITN 2; CA 45-48; 57-60; CANR 3, 33; CDBLB 1914-1945; DLB 34; MTCW; SATA 22

Woiwode, L.
See Woiwode, Larry (Alfred)

Woiwode, Larry (Alfred) 1941-... **CLC 6, 10**
See also CA 73-76; CANR 16; DLB 6

Wojciechowska, Maia (Teresa) 1927- .... **CLC 26**
See also AAYA 8; CA 9-12R; CANR 4, 41; CLR 1; JRDA; MAICYA; SAAS 1; SATA 1, 28

Wolf, Christa 1929- .... **CLC 14, 29, 58**
See also CA 85-88; DLB 75; MTCW

Wolfe, Gene (Rodman) 1931-....... **CLC 25**
See also CA 57-60; CAAS 9; CANR 6, 32; DLB 8

Wolfe, George C. 1954-........... **CLC 49**

Wolfe, Thomas (Clayton) 1900-1938 .... **TCLC 4, 13, 29**
See also CA 104; 132; CDALB 1929-1941; DA; DLB 9, 102; DLBD 2; DLBY 85; MTCW; WLC

Wolfe, Thomas Kennerly, Jr. 1931-
See Wolfe, Tom
See also CA 13-16R; CANR 9, 33; MTCW

Wolfe, Tom .... **CLC 1, 2, 9, 15, 35, 51**
See also Wolfe, Thomas Kennerly, Jr.
See also AAYA 8; AITN 2; BEST 89:1

Wolff, Geoffrey (Ansell) 1937- ..... **CLC 41**
See also CA 29-32R; CANR 29, 43

Wolff, Sonia
See Levitin, Sonia (Wolff)

Wolff, Tobias (Jonathan Ansell) 1945- .... **CLC 39, 64**
See also BEST 90:2; CA 114; 117; DLB 130

Wolfram von Eschenbach c. 1170-c. 1220 .... **CMLC 5**

Wolitzer, Hilma 1930-............. **CLC 17**
See also CA 65-68; CANR 18, 40; SATA 31

Wollstonecraft, Mary 1759-1797...... **LC 5**
See also CDBLB 1789-1832; DLB 39, 104

Wonder, Stevie .... **CLC 12**
See also Morris, Steveland Judkins

Wong, Jade Snow 1922-........... **CLC 17**
See also CA 109

Woodcott, Keith
See Brunner, John (Kilian Houston)

Woodruff, Robert W.
See Mencken, H(enry) L(ouis)

Woolf, (Adeline) Virginia 1882-1941 .... **TCLC 1, 5, 20, 43; SSC 7**
See also CA 104; 130; CDBLB 1914-1945; DA; DLB 36, 100; DLBD 10; MTCW; WLC

Woollcott, Alexander (Humphreys) 1887-1943 .... **TCLC 5**
See also CA 105; DLB 29

Woolrich, Cornell 1903-1968....... **CLC 77**
See also Hopley-Woolrich, Cornell George

Wordsworth, Dorothy
1771-1855 .... **NCLC 25**
See also DLB 107

Wordsworth, William
1770-1850 .... **NCLC 12, 38; PC 4**
See also CDBLB 1789-1832; DA; DLB 93, 107; WLC

Wouk, Herman 1915- .... **CLC 1, 9, 38**
See also CA 5-8R; CANR 6, 33; DLBY 82; MTCW

Wright, Charles (Penzel, Jr.)
1935- .... **CLC 6, 13, 28**
See also CA 29-32R; CAAS 7; CANR 23, 36; DLBY 82; MTCW

Wright, Charles Stevenson 1932- ... **CLC 49**
See also BLC 3; BW; CA 9-12R; CANR 26; DLB 33

Wright, Jack R.
See Harris, Mark

Wright, James (Arlington)
1927-1980 .... **CLC 3, 5, 10, 28**
See also AITN 2; CA 49-52; 97-100; CANR 4, 34; DLB 5; MTCW

Wright, Judith (Arandell)
1915- .... **CLC 11, 53**
See also CA 13-16R; CANR 31; MTCW; SATA 14

Wright, L(aurali) R. 1939- .... **CLC 44**
See also CA 138

Wright, Richard (Nathaniel)
1908-1960 .... **CLC 1, 3, 4, 9, 14, 21, 48, 74; SSC 2**
See also AAYA 5; BLC 3; BW; CA 108; CDALB 1929-1941; DA; DLB 76, 102; DLBD 2; MTCW; WLC

Wright, Richard B(ruce) 1937- ...... **CLC 6**
See also CA 85-88; DLB 53

Wright, Rick 1945- .... **CLC 35**
See also Pink Floyd

Wright, Rowland
See Wells, Carolyn

Wright, Stephen 1946- .... **CLC 33**

Wright, Willard Huntington 1888-1939
See Van Dine, S. S.
See also CA 115

Wright, William 1930- .... **CLC 44**
See also CA 53-56; CANR 7, 23

Wu Ch'eng-en 1500(?)-1582(?) .... **LC 7**

Wu Ching-tzu 1701-1754 .... **LC 2**

Wurlitzer, Rudolph 1938(?)- ... **CLC 2, 4, 15**
See also CA 85-88

Wycherley, William 1641-1715 .... **LC 8, 21**
See also CDBLB 1660-1789; DLB 80

Wylie, Elinor (Morton Hoyt)
1885-1928 .... **TCLC 8**
See also CA 105; DLB 9, 45

Wylie, Philip (Gordon) 1902-1971... **CLC 43**
See also CA 21-22; 33-36R; CAP 2; DLB 9

Wyndham, John
See Harris, John (Wyndham Parkes Lucas) Beynon

Wyss, Johann David Von
1743-1818 .... **NCLC 10**
See also JRDA; MAICYA; SATA 27, 29

Yakumo Koizumi
See Hearn, (Patricio) Lafcadio (Tessima Carlos)

Yanez, Jose Donoso
See Donoso (Yanez), Jose

Yanovsky, Basile S.
See Yanovsky, V(assily) S(emenovich)

Yanovsky, V(assily) S(emenovich)
1906-1989 .... **CLC 2, 18**
See also CA 97-100; 129

Yates, Richard 1926-1992 ..... **CLC 7, 8, 23**
See also CA 5-8R; 139; CANR 10, 43; DLB 2; DLBY 81, 92

Yeats, W. B.
See Yeats, William Butler

Yeats, William Butler
1865-1939 .... **TCLC 1, 11, 18, 31**
See also CA 104; 127; CDBLB 1890-1914; DA; DLB 10, 19, 98; MTCW; WLC

Yehoshua, A(braham) B.
1936- .... **CLC 13, 31**
See also CA 33-36R; CANR 43

Yep, Laurence Michael 1948- ...... **CLC 35**
See also AAYA 5; CA 49-52; CANR 1; CLR 3, 17; DLB 52; JRDA; MAICYA; SATA 7, 69

Yerby, Frank G(arvin)
1916-1991 .... **CLC 1, 7, 22**
See also BLC 3; BW; CA 9-12R; 136; CANR 16; DLB 76; MTCW

Yesenin, Sergei Alexandrovich
See Esenin, Sergei (Alexandrovich)

Yevtushenko, Yevgeny (Alexandrovich)
1933- .... **CLC 1, 3, 13, 26, 51**
See also CA 81-84; CANR 33; MTCW

Yezierska, Anzia 1885(?)-1970 ..... **CLC 46**
See also CA 126; 89-92; DLB 28; MTCW

Yglesias, Helen 1915- .... **CLC 7, 22**
See also CA 37-40R; CANR 15; MTCW

Yokomitsu Riichi 1898-1947 ...... **TCLC 47**

Yonge, Charlotte (Mary)
1823-1901 .... **TCLC 48**
See also CA 109; DLB 18; SATA 17

York, Jeremy
See Creasey, John

York, Simon
See Heinlein, Robert A(nson)

Yorke, Henry Vincent 1905-1974 ... **CLC 13**
See also Green, Henry
See also CA 85-88; 49-52

Young, Al(bert James) 1939- .... **CLC 19**
See also BLC 3; BW; CA 29-32R; CANR 26; DLB 33

Young, Andrew (John) 1885-1971 .... **CLC 5**
See also CA 5-8R; CANR 7, 29

Young, Collier
See Bloch, Robert (Albert)

Young, Edward 1683-1765 .... **LC 3**
See also DLB 95

Young, Neil 1945- .... **CLC 17**
See also CA 110

Yourcenar, Marguerite
1903-1987 .... **CLC 19, 38, 50**
See also CA 69-72; CANR 23; DLB 72; DLBY 88; MTCW

Yurick, Sol 1925- .... **CLC 6**
See also CA 13-16R; CANR 25

Zabolotskii, Nikolai Alekseevich
1903-1958 .... **TCLC 52**
See also CA 116

Zamiatin, Yevgenii
See Zamyatin, Evgeny Ivanovich

Zamyatin, Evgeny Ivanovich
1884-1937 .... **TCLC 8, 37**
See also CA 105

Zangwill, Israel 1864-1926 .... **TCLC 16**
See also CA 109; DLB 10

Zappa, Francis Vincent, Jr. 1940-
See Zappa, Frank
See also CA 108

Zappa, Frank .... **CLC 17**
See also Zappa, Francis Vincent, Jr.

Zaturenska, Marya 1902-1982.... **CLC 6, 11**
See also CA 13-16R; 105; CANR 22

Zelazny, Roger (Joseph) 1937- ..... **CLC 21**
See also AAYA 7; CA 21-24R; CANR 26; DLB 8; MTCW; SATA 39, 57

Zhdanov, Andrei A(lexandrovich)
1896-1948 .... **TCLC 18**
See also CA 117

Zhukovsky, Vasily 1783-1852 .... **NCLC 35**

Ziegenhagen, Eric .... **CLC 55**

Zimmer, Jill Schary
See Robinson, Jill

Zimmerman, Robert
See Dylan, Bob

Zindel, Paul 1936- .... **CLC 6, 26**
See also AAYA 2; CA 73-76; CANR 31; CLR 3; DA; DLB 7, 52; JRDA; MAICYA; MTCW; SATA 16, 58

Zinov'Ev, A. A.
See Zinoviev, Alexander (Aleksandrovich)

Zinoviev, Alexander (Aleksandrovich)
1922- .... **CLC 19**
See also CA 116; 133; CAAS 10

Zoilus
See Lovecraft, H(oward) P(hillips)

Zola, Emile (Edouard Charles Antoine)
1840-1902 .... **TCLC 1, 6, 21, 41**
See also CA 104; 138; DA; DLB 123; WLC

Zoline, Pamela 1941- .... **CLC 62**

Zorrilla y Moral, Jose 1817-1893.. **NCLC 6**

Zoshchenko, Mikhail (Mikhailovich)
1895-1958 .... **TCLC 15**
See also CA 115

Zuckmayer, Carl 1896-1977 .... **CLC 18**
See also CA 69-72; DLB 56, 124

Zuk, Georges
See Skelton, Robin

Zukofsky, Louis
1904-1978 .... **CLC 1, 2, 4, 7, 11, 18**
See also CA 9-12R; 77-80; CANR 39; DLB 5; MTCW

Zweig, Paul 1935-1984 .... **CLC 34, 42**
See also CA 85-88; 113

CLC Cumulative Nationality Index